THE ROAD TO MAASTRICHT

UNIVERSITY OF
BRADFORD

D1556649

The Road to Maastricht

Negotiating Economic and Monetary Union

KENNETH DYSON

and

KEVIN FEATHERSTONE

OXFORD

UNIVERSITY PRESS

OXFORD

UNIVERSITY PRESS

Great Clarendon Street, Oxford OX2 6DP

Oxford University Press is a department of the University of Oxford.
It furthers the University's objective of excellence in research, scholarship,
and education by publishing worldwide in

Oxford New York

Athens Auckland Bangkok Bogotá Buenos Aires Calcutta
Cape Town Chennai Dar es Salaam Delhi Florence Hong Kong Istanbul
Karachi Kuala Lumpur Madrid Melbourne Mexico City Mumbai
Nairobi Paris São Paulo Singapore Taipei Tokyo Toronto Warsaw

with associated companies in Berlin Ibadan

Oxford is a registered trade mark of Oxford University Press
in the UK and in certain other countries

Published in the United States
by Oxford University Press Inc., New York

© Kenneth Dyson and Kevin Featherstone 1999

The moral rights of the authors have been asserted

Database right Oxford University Press (maker)

First published 1999

All rights reserved. No part of this publication may be reproduced,
stored in a retrieval system, or transmitted, in any form or by any means,
without the prior permission in writing of Oxford University Press,
or as expressly permitted by law, or under terms agreed with the appropriate
reprographics rights organizations. Enquiries concerning reproduction
outside the scope of the above should be sent to the Rights Department,
Oxford University Press, at the address above

You must not circulate this book in any other binding or cover
and you must impose this same condition on any acquirer

British Library Cataloguing in Publication Data

Data available

Library of Congress Cataloging in Publication Data
Dyson, Kenneth H. F.
The road to Maastricht: negotiating Economic and Monetary Union /
Kenneth Dyson and Kevin Featherstone.
Includes bibliographical references and index.
1. Economic and Monetary Union.   2. Monetary unions—European
Union countries.   3. Monetary policy—European Union countries.
I. Featherstone, Kevin.   II. Title.
HG925.D97 1999   332.4'566'094—dc21   99-25739

ISBN 0-19-828077-7
ISBN 0-19-829638-X (pbk.)

1 3 5 7 9 10 8 6 4 2

Typeset by Hope Services (Abingdon) Ltd.
Printed in Great Britain
on acid-free paper by
Biddles Ltd.,
Guildford and King's Lynn

To
Ann, Charles, and Thomas,
and Nina, Christopher, and Emily

Preface

This book is a study of an important turning-point in the politics and policies of postwar Europe. Since the mid-1980s the process of European integration has assumed more significance than ever before in the economic and political life of the Continent. In 1985 the European Community launched its single market programme, with the objective of liberalizing its internal trade including capital movements. Seven years later, at Maastricht in the Netherlands, the EC went much further and agreed the Treaty on European Union. The new Union (EU) was to have a 'Common Foreign and Security Policy' and co-operation in matters of Justice and Home Affairs. But the most radical and historic shift contained in the Treaty was the establishment of an Economic and Monetary Union. With these new elements the integration process was set to challenge the traditions of Europe's nation-states like never before in the postwar period.

EMU was the single most important strand of what was seen as the 'relaunch' of European integration in the 1980s and 1990s. At Maastricht the EC member states agreed, subject to two 'opt-outs', a timetable for replacing existing national currencies like the D-Mark, French franc, and Italian lira with a single European currency. There was to be a single monetary policy, managed by a European Central Bank (ECB) that was independent from national governments. It would, in consequence, possess considerable power over the economic fate of the Continent. In order to qualify for entry EC states had to show that they could abide by a set of tough fiscal disciplines represented by the 'no bail-out' provision and the convergence criteria.

EMU had far-reaching implications for the nature of the newly emerging European polity. Politically, it challenged assumptions about national sovereignty and identity. It was bolder, riskier, and more controversial than the single European market programme of 1985. In the context of an institutional structure for EMU that emphasized technocracy rather than democracy, fundamental concerns about accountability, transparency, and legitimacy were raised. The governance structure of EMU was based on a contrast between the centralization of monetary policy in the hands of central bankers at the EC level and the maintenance of responsibility for fiscal policy with national governments. This institutional imbalance was matched by an ambiguity about the role to be played by economic policy. The co-ordination provided for in economic policy was relatively weak, whilst what was meant by 'economic policy' was left undefined. At the same time, the 'convergence criteria', which were to be used to select which states could start the final transition to a single currency, imposed a straitjacket on the domestic policies of aspirant states. This straitjacket soon provoked fears that EMU might threaten traditional assumptions about welfare state provision, undermine social cohesion, and narrow the scope for domestic political choice. The prospect arose of alienated electorates who might be tempted to extremist politics, especially on the Right. Externally, the prospect of the single currency stimulated, albeit belatedly, a new debate about how the EMU system should be accommodated at the international level, not least within the International Monetary Fund and the Group of Seven. A single currency represented a radical shift in the external relations of the EU, threatening the long-term position of the US dollar and complicating the process of enlargement to include other European states within the EU. In short, the Maastricht Treaty provisions on EMU had profound political, economic, social and diplomatic implications.

The central aim of this book is to write a contemporary history of the negotiation of the EMU provisions of the Maastricht Treaty and to explain how, and why, the EC came to agree the project in 1991. It argues that the answers to these questions are to be found in a wide range of factors and in a long-term perspective. The intellectual challenge was to write a theoretically informed history that would seek to explain the nature of these negotiations, their origins, and their outcome.

The intellectual starting-point was the stress on the 'prestructuring' of the EMU negotiations contained in Dyson's *Elusive Union* (1994). EMU negotiators operated within a complex configuration of structural forces, of which their knowledge was limited and partial, and over which their control was imperfect. Here structure referred not just to the role of institutions in setting the parameters of choice but also to such factors as inherited beliefs and memories, policy legacies, and the structure of international monetary power. But, important as it was, structure failed to provide an adequate theory for examining the internal dynamics of the EMU negotiations. Hence the intellectual journey began with an attempt to refine our questions and the way in which we sought to answer them. Our starting-point for exploring the internal dynamics was the dimension of strategic interaction in the negotiations. We focused on their 'game-like' nature, notably the interplay of power and interest. This interplay was usefully addressed in theories that explored the way in which negotiators used the interactivity of domestic and EC levels ('two-level' bargaining games) and sought to shift conceptions of optimal outcomes by redefining the context of negotiations ('nested' games). The value of these theoretical approaches was clear. They helped us to understand how a politically acceptable EMU agreement was negotiated that reconciled vital domestic and European interests of political leaders. We were alerted to the role of transnational linkages, to such tactics as 'binding one's hands' in the negotiations, and to the effect of negotiators being involved in a whole series of policy games. Given the extreme complexity of the EMU negotiations—one participant referred to playing a thirteen-dimensional game of chess—we abandoned the attempt to formally model the negotiations as a game. More original to the study was the attempt to model the strategic choices available to negotiators and identify the conditions under which particular choices tended to be preferred. This model is elaborated in Chapter 1 and informs the later narrative.

But, as the research progressed, we became aware of a gap in our understanding. The internal dynamics of the EMU negotiations also had an important cognitive dimension. They were not just about a politically acceptable agreement but also about creating a viable and sustainable EMU. Beliefs and knowledge were vital in informing how interests were defined, especially normative beliefs about economic policy and 'historical memories'. They also shaped what negotiators saw as the minimum conditions for a 'workable' EMU in the form of causal beliefs about how monetary unions function. Hence beliefs, memories, and the transmission of knowledge into the negotiating process came to play a more central role, alongside power and interest. They drew our attention to other theoretical approaches in helping to explain agreement: to 'policy entrepreneurship', to discourse theory, to 'frame reflection' by participants, and to the possible role of 'epistemic communities' and of 'advocacy coalitions'. We were alerted, in particular, to the role of individuals in agenda-setting, in promoting ideas and in investing EMU with symbolism, to the process of learning, to the role of communities of expert professionals, and to the struggle between contesting sets of ideas held by different coalitions.

This theoretical Odyssey had the advantage of sensitizing us to aspects of the EMU negotiations that we might otherwise have missed. Equally, it made us more acutely aware of the risk of pursuing theory at the expense of forcing complex reality into a straitjacket. We eschewed the option of theoretical parsimony for an approach that remained indebted to theory but not driven by it. The main contribution of the book was clear to us. It was to break new empirical ground in our understanding of how EMU negotiations were conducted. Hence we have provided a theory chapter at the beginning. Readers are at liberty to ignore this chapter and pass on to the empirical meat of the main chapters. But the more intellectually inquisitive will, we hope, read Chapter 1 with profit. What they will see is that we found inspiration in contingency models rather than causal models. This study explores the interaction of prestructuring (including institutional factors) with knowledge and strategy as the core elements of the EMU negotiating process. This approach has potentially a wider value as a contribution to our general understanding of how EC negotiations are conducted.

The limitations of traditional causal models became evident to us in another way. As we looked closely at the EMU negotiations, we began to see that they had a life of their own. They were composed of flesh-and-blood people, whose motives were very complex and preferences by no means fixed, whose likes, aversions, ambitions, and manners played an important part in the dynamics of the process. The EMU negotiations had their own process of development, their own particular rhythm and shape, specific to the subject-matter and the precise historical context. In response, we sought to provide an historically rooted understanding of them.

We were also forced to reflect again on the relationship of structure and agency in our study. This reflection led us to try to weave structure into the narrative and draw out the complex interactivity of the motives of EMU negotiators as agents and structure. In exploring that interactivity we tried to identify in what ways agency mattered. Political leaders played vital roles as *animateurs* and *ingénieurs* of the negotiating process, as more or less skilled strategists, as more or less skilled craftsmen using the materials provided to them in the form of inherited beliefs and historical memories. In these senses Helmut Kohl and François Mitterrand mattered. But to capture this aspect of the negotiating process it was important to go beyond the more formalistic understanding of causal theories.

There were major implications for how we did the research. We were conscious of playing the role of detectives, hunting down leads and connections, and establishing motives and opportunities for action. Such research is laborious and demanding. It involves a creative process of reconstructing what happened in a manner that is faithful to the historical record. In short, the research that we were undertaking meant cultivating an imaginative but firmly grounded understanding. In this way we sought to reveal some insights, however limited, into how the EMU negotiations were 'lived' by illuminating something of the experiences of those involved. We hoped to provide some sense of what life was like on the inside. In this exercise traditional causal models offered little guidance. The key was to immerse ourselves in the material.

A central objective of the research was to generate material about the EMU negotiations that might otherwise be lost. We were, above all, concerned to recapture the experiences of those involved by the method of a large-scale, intensive elite interview programme. Altogether, over 280 lengthy interviews were conducted (see Appendix for details). They were relatively unstructured in form and crucial to capture more qualitative aspects of the negotiations. They were also strictly confidential. Over 50 each took place in Britain, France, Germany, Italy, and the EC institutions. This kind of research method is associated with various difficulties: interviewees may, for instance, have faulty memories or be selective in imparting information in a way that favours themselves. There is a risk that aspects of our account are coloured by the judgements and prejudices of those interviewed, leading to one-sided value judgements. We cannot claim that we have found a foolproof mechanism for safeguarding ourselves and the reader. But, in addition to exercising our own critical judgement, we confronted our interviewees with these problems. We engaged in further dialogue with them where we felt that they needed to be addressed. Also, we checked very carefully for consistencies and conflicts in evidence. More importantly, we cross-referred to written documentation, biographies, press communiqués, other comments by the interviewees (e.g. in press reports), private papers, and to minutes of the IGC (Intergovernmental Conference) on EMU.

The empirical value of the research was reinforced by the kindness of certain negotiators and advisers in making their private papers and a full copy of a set of minutes of the IGC in 1991 available to us. This material was not just helpful for comparison with interview notes but also opened up a picture of how negotiators interacted with each other. The availability of IGC minutes was not a resource that we had expected to have available. We remain enormously grateful for this access. At the same time there remained some areas where we had to rely on the less rigorous method of cross-checking interview notes, notably in relation to Franco-German bilaterals and to important one-to-one encounters.

It is only proper that we should draw attention to the work's unavoidable weaknesses as history. It is written from a close perspective and without access to many key archival sources. Memories of key participants have still to be published and will contain new revelations and fresh insights and perspectives that have been denied to us. Later writers will have an obvious advantage over us. Our work's great strength—salvaging the experiences of those involved, which might otherwise be lost—is offset by the problems of overreliance on interview research. It is also weaker than Dyson's *Elusive Union* on the wider international and deeper historical aspects of the EMU negotiations.

This book looks at the EMU negotiations 'from below' rather than 'from above'. It focuses on the important details of negotiating positions taken up by, and domestic political processes within, key EC states, of how these positions emerged, and how their governments approached the EMU negotiations. What we have here is the 'micro-history' of a decisively important European negotiation. The book is fundamentally an exercise in cross-national comparison, focusing on the four key EC states and their relations with the EC Commission. The strength of this focus on 'making EMU from below' is that it draws out the vital domestic or national preconditions for negotiating EMU, in particular the beliefs and understandings, strategies and tactics, and institutional settings affecting choices. It highlights the extent to which the EMU agreement was a by-product of unilateral actions taken within EC states, notably in France in 1982–3. EMU's future still remains fundamentally a question of what EC governments choose to do in the context of intensive and interrelated 'two-level' games in which the political challenge is to reconcile domestic and European interests when those governments continue to have a great deal of freedom to act unilaterally.

The perspective of 'making EMU from below' means that the title of the book must be taken as shorthand for a far more complex process. In fact, as will become clear, there were many different roads to Maastricht, some made difficult by diversions and blockages, others cross-cutting at different points. For this reason the story is by no means easy to tell. What held the negotiations on EMU together was the political will to integrate on the part of the prospective members and to use deadlines for this purpose. Given the difficulties of history, ideology, and political interests involved, what was achieved at Maastricht represented an extraordinary political achievement. It was an image of a Europe far removed from the images of *blocage* and sclerosis that had been so prevalent in the early 1980s. Here we unpack the notion of 'political will' into its constituent political processes, identifying the motives for attaching such high value to a common endeavour and in particular the motives of German negotiators as the local hegemon. In doing so, we were influenced by the economist Norman Mintz (1970: 33):

It has often been argued that the conditions under which monetary integration might reasonably be expected to succeed are very restrictive. In fact, these conditions appear no more restrictive than the conditions for the establishment of a successful common market. The major, and perhaps only, real condition for the institution of either is the political will to integrate on the part of prospective members.

The national case studies form the heart of this book. They are empirically based narratives and assume little prior knowledge of the social sciences. These chapters reveal how the EMU negotiations developed a dynamism of their own by examining the strategic moves of the players, the learning experiences that informed their discussions, and their choice of institutional routes. The motives of players are studied in depth in the context of the structural factors shaping their behaviour. Chapter 1 provides an appropriate conceptual framework for analysing the EMU negotiations. Here discussion draws on a wide range of relevant literature concerned with bargaining, public policy, institutional settings, and international political economy. Chapter 16 extends the focus from the national to the European level in order to assess the role and impact of the EC Commission, and of its President Jacques Delors in particular. The role and impact of the two EC presidencies—the Luxembourg and the Dutch—are taken up in Chapter 17, in the context of identifying the different patterns of coalition activity displayed in the IGC. This concluding chapter includes a wider reflection on themes and issues raised by the EMU negotiations.

The empirical investigation of the EMU negotiations is important in several ways. It offers an explanation of a process of treaty negotiation that was important in its own right, given the impact of EMU on the European landscape. Also, it illustrates the relevance of different types of explanation to the EMU outcome. In particular, it shows that the IGC was an arena not only for intensive bargaining but also for a shared process of policy learning and reflection. Additionally, the book sheds light on the policy content of the EMU agreement. It outlines the risks and problems attached to the implementation of EMU as a result of the ambiguities, imbalance, and incompleteness of the deal struck in 1991. These risks are of importance not only to those living and working in the EU but also to the outside world. The EU is the world's largest trading bloc, and the establishment of the single currency raises a variety of questions about the impact of the euro on the evolving international monetary system. Monetary policy may seem opaque and technical, shrouded in its own carefully cultivated mystique. But with EMU it is now of huge political importance for the whole future of European integration and international economic co-operation.

The research on which this book draws could not possibly have been undertaken without the generous support of the Economic and Social Research

Council. Their research grant (R000 23 4793) enabled us to undertake detailed fieldwork in Britain, France, Germany, Italy, and the EC institutions. Particular thanks are due to the research officer on this project, Dr George Michalopoulos. He was enormously helpful in hunting down materials and contacts and setting up and supporting us in interviews. Helena Larkin, Amanda Machin, and Margaret Haldane provided efficient secretarial help, showing great patience in serving two busy academics. Our gratitude is also due to Dimitris Papadimitriou who managed the key technical aspects of constructing the final manuscript; Liviana Ferrari who helped with translations; and Grace Hudson for her library advice and support. There were many others who offered us help and encouragement. It is impossible to thank interviewees for the time that they have given us and their obvious interest in our research. They are listed in the Appendix. We have done all that we can to respect the confidentiality of their interviews with us. Many have also commented in detail on draft chapters, sometimes arranging meetings to go through them with us, and have earned an extra debt of gratitude. We would, however, like to single out academic colleagues who have commented so kindly on first drafts, notably Professor Simon Bulmer, Dr. Alastair Cole, Professor Stephen George, Dr Marco Guiliani, Dr Claudio Radaelli, Professor Helen Wallace, and Lord Wallace of Saltaire. Others who were not interviewed but to whom we are indebted for commenting on first drafts included Philip Stephens of the *Financial Times* and Jean-Louis Bianco, former secretary-general of the Elysée. A further debt is owed to Bill Jones with whom we worked in the Brook Lapping production for BBC2 on the history of the single currency, broadcast in March 1998. He was enormously helpful in sharing information with us. Last, but by no means least, a special debt is owed to our wives, Ann and Nina, and to our children, who have put up with our long absences.

Kenneth Dyson
Kevin Featherstone

Department of European Studies
University of Bradford, October 1998

Contents

List of Abbreviations

ANAS	National Roadways Agency
AUME	Association for the Monetary Union of Europe
BdB	Bundesverband Deutscher Banken (Federation of German Banks)
BDI	Bundesverband der Deutschen Industrie (Federation of German Industry)
BIEC	British Invisible Exports Council
BIS	Bank for International Settlements
CAP	Common Agricultural Policy
CBI	Confederation of British Industry
CCBG	Committee of Central Bank Governors
CDS	Centre des Democrates Sociaux
CDU	Christian Democratic Union
CEPII	Centre d'Études Prospectives et d'Informations Internationales
CEPR	Centre for Economic Policy Research
CER	Centro Europa Ricerche
CERES	Centre d'Études, de Recherches et d'Éducation Socialistes
CFSP	Common Foreign and Security Policy
CGIL	Confederazione Generale Italiana del Lavoro
CISL	Confederazione Italiana dei Sindacati dei Lavoratori
CNPF	Confédération Nationale du Patronat Français
COREPER	Committee of Permanent Representatives
CSCE	Conference on Security and Co-operation in Europe
CSU	Christian Social Union
DC	Democrazia Cristiana
DG	Directorate-General (European Commission)
DIHT	Deutscher Industrie- und Handelstag
D-Mark	Deutschmark
DTI	Department of Trade and Industry
EC	European Community
ECB	European Central Bank
ECOFIN	Council of Ministers comprising ministers of economics and finance
ECSC	European Coal and Steel Community
ECU	European Currency Unit
EDC	European Defence Community
EEC	European Economic Community
EFTA	European Free Trade Association
EMCF	European Monetary Co-operation Fund

EMI	European Monetary Institute
EMS	European Monetary System
EMU	Economic and Monetary Union
ENA	École National d'Administration
ENI	National Hydrocarbons Agency (Italy)
EP	European Parliament
EPU	European Political Union
ERF	European Reserve Fund
ERM	exchange-rate mechanism
ESCB	European System of Central Banks
ESCS	European Coal and Steel Community
EU	European Union
EUA	European Unit of Account
FCO	Foreign and Commonwealth Office
FDP	Free Democratic Party
FT	*Financial Times*
G5	Group of Five
G7	Group of Seven
G10	Group of Ten
GATT	General Agreement on Tariffs and Trade
GDP	gross domestic product
GDR	German Democratic Republic
IGC	Intergovernmental Conference
IMF	International Monetary Fund
INPS	Istituto Nazionale di Previdenza Sociale
INSEAD	Institut Européen de l'Administration des Affaires
INSEE	Institut National de la Statistique et des Études Économiques
IoD	Institute of Directors
IRI	Istituto per la Ricostruzione Industriale
IRS	Istituto per la Ricerca Sociale
MCAs	monetary compensation amounts
MP	Member of Parliament
MRP	Mouvement Republicain Populaire
NATO	North Artlantic Treaty Organization
OFCE	Observatoire Français de Conjonctures Économiques
OPD	Ministerial Committee on Defence and Overseas Policy
OPD(E)	Ministerial Subcommittee on European Questions
PCF	French Community Party
PCI	Italian Community Party
PLI	Italian Liberal Party
PM	Prime Minister
PRI	Partito Repubblicano Italiano (Italian Republican Party)
PSBR	public sector borrowing requirement
PSDI	Italian Social Democratic Party

PSI	Italian Socialist Party
QMV	qualified majority voting
RPR	Rassemblement pour la République
SGCI	Secrétariat Général du Comité Interministeriel
SMEs	small and medium-sized enterprises
SPD	German Social Democratic Party
TEU	Treaty on European Union
TUC	Trades Union Congress
UDF	Union pour la Démocratie Française
UIC	Ufficio Italiano dei Cambi (Italian Exchange Office)
UIL	Unione Italiana del Lavoro
UKRep	UK Permanent Representation (Brussels)

Introduction: An Historical Overview

In order that the reader can make better sense of the narrative in the national case studies, it is useful to begin with a brief historical overview that sets the complexity and powerful momentum of the EMU negotiations between 1988 and 1991 in context. The route by which EMU was placed on the EC's agenda in 1988 was long and tortuous. It was also characterized by the primacy of political discourse about EMU over discourse about the balance between its economic benefits and costs. The economic case remained inconclusive (Cohen 1998: 84). But far more central were the political issues. EMU offered two main political gains. It was seen—especially by German negotiators—as indispensable to the promotion of the political unification of Europe, bringing with it a more secure framework for enduring peace and prosperity amongst states whose populations had suffered in two barbarous wars in the twentieth century. It also provided—notably in the minds of French negotiators—an opportunity to rebalance international monetary power by reducing dependency on the US dollar and promoting a new international monetary architecture. For these gains French and German negotiators, though less clearly the British, were prepared to sacrifice the symbols and benefits traditionally associated with state autonomy. This process of sacrifice was further assisted by the new 'geography' of money as financial market competition undermined the value of the historical claims of national governments to be able to manage their currencies effectively and insulate their nations from international constraints (Cohen 1998).

The Prehistory of the Maastricht Negotiations

The starting-point can be identified in the 1960s. Interest in EMU was stimulated by the mounting tensions in the Bretton Woods system of fixed exchange rates amongst the world's advanced economies and the consequent threat from this instability to the newly negotiated Common Agricultural Policy (CAP) of the EC. These developments, combined with a widely shared hostility to American power in Europe, stimulated the French initiative to seek a 'European' solution at the Hague EC summit in December 1969. Crucially, the period 1968–9 brought home vividly to French policy-makers the scale and implications of German monetary power in Europe for the first time. The growing instability of the international monetary system and the imbalance of monetary power highlighted stark policy choices.

Subsequent to the new political direction given in The Hague, the Werner Report of 1970 detailed a programme by which the EC might achieve EMU based on an approach by stages and involving 'parallelism' between developments in economic policy co-ordination and monetary policy co-ordination and progress towards political union. The main practical outcome was a new system (the 'Snake') for limiting fluctuations in exchange rates between EC currencies. But, with the collapse of the Bretton Woods system, the 'Snake' was launched into a highly unstable international environment. The British government of Edward Heath soon removed the pound from the 'Snake', and other EC governments (the French twice) followed this lead, creating an unstable climate in which further progress towards EMU was impossible (Tsoukalis 1977).

From the outset it had been clear that progress on EMU depended on close Franco-German collaboration. With Valéry Giscard d'Estaing as French President and Helmut Schmidt as Chancellor from 1974 the personal chemistry was in place to tackle the inadequacies of the 'Snake'. The opportunity was provided in 1977–8 by the collapsing US dollar and the shared Franco-German interest in shielding Europe from its effects. In 1979 the European Monetary System (EMS) was launched with the objective of creating a zone of monetary stability in Europe. Its launch was made more difficult because of the second oil crisis, and the EMS in its originally intended form was never fully implemented (Ludlow 1982; Dyson 1994). Nevertheless, unlike with the 'Snake', the French stayed on the inside—President François Mitterrand's decision to do so in March 1983 was critical to the whole future story. But, till 1990, the British chose to remain outside: in the EMS, but out of the exchange rate mechanism (ERM). The management of the ERM by the EC Monetary Committee and the Committee of EC Central Bank Governors was to provide transnational fora in which new ideas about the importance of 'sound' money and public finances could be disseminated and take root.

A new consensus about 'sound' money and public finances evolved as crises in the 1970s and early 1980s revealed the practical limitations of the established Keynesian consensus as a means of solving the problems, especially of inflation, facing European policy-makers. These crises—for instance in France in 1982–3—created an opportunity for new ideas to enter the policy process, favouring disinflation, budgetary discipline, and currency stability and stressing the vital importance of credibility of policies within the financial markets. With these ideas came a new centrality for the German Bundesbank as a policy model and more generally for EC central bankers. The context for EMU in the 1980s, and the difference from the 1970s, was in the intellectual self-confidence of EC central bankers and a process of voluntary emulation of the German model. The core of a new Europe-wide 'stability culture' was beginning to form.

Relaunching EMU

By the late 1980s the existing EMS was enjoying much success in promoting convergence. Inflation levels were falling; a stable set of currency exchange rates emerging. The EMS was functioning as an external discipline on domestic fiscal and monetary policies. At the same time tensions were surfacing, especially from France and Italy whose policy-makers objected to the dominance of the D-Mark as the standard setter and the asymmetrical distribution of responsibilities to take corrective action (favouring again the Germans). Moreover, the prospect of freedom of movement of capital as part of the EC single market programme threatened to undermine the stability of the EMS system (Padoa-Schioppa *et al.* 1987).

Against this background a new debate about the future of the EMS opened at the start of 1988. Edouard Balladur, French Finance Minister, and his Italian counterpart Giuliano Amato, issued memoranda criticizing the constraints and asymmetry of the current EMS and proposing reform. Crucially, these were followed by a personal memorandum from Hans-Dietrich Genscher, German Foreign Minister, bypassing normal channels and proposing an ECB. Though Gerhard Stoltenberg as German Finance Minister sought to counter Genscher with a statement of the traditional German view that monetary union must follow a long process of economic convergence, the political lead given by Genscher was vital. It was also facilitated by the fact that Germany held the EC Presidency in early 1988.

Following Genscher's initiative, Jacques Delors as EC President and Chancellor Helmut Kohl worked closely together to prepare an agreement to move ahead on EMU at the Hanover European Council in June 1988. President Mitterrand rallied to the idea. The Hanover meeting created the ad hoc Delors Committee to study how EMU could be achieved. This mandate cleverly diverted negotiations away from whether EMU was desirable to give it a more technical content and legitimation. In this respect the Committee's composition was also intriguing. It combined a majority comprising all the EC central bankers (to provide technical legitimation) and the most assertive Commission President in decades as chair (to ensure political direction). Kohl's astute strategy was to 'bind in' the central bankers and thereby strengthen the credibility of the project. Unlike Mrs Thatcher's strategy—which was to rely on the central bankers to block EMU—it had the merit of working.

The Delors Report of April 1989 set out a blueprint by which EMU would be implemented in three stages. No dates were set at this stage. But in its basic design much of the Report later found its way into the Maastricht Treaty. Significantly, the Report was signed by all the EC central bank governors. The Delors Report had placed EMU firmly on the agenda of the EC as a viable proposition.

Despite this success the progress towards the detailed negotiations was neither simple nor straightforward. The main problem was Britain. The

Conservative government was engulfed by an internal ministerial crisis over the issue of sterling's entry into the ERM (Thompson 1993). This internal crisis distracted attention away from EMU. Sterling did not enter the ERM till October 1990, in the process losing credibility as a partner in negotiations about EMU. On the bigger question of EMU Mrs Thatcher expressed strong opposition. Both she and her Chancellor, Nigel Lawson, argued repeatedly that talk of a single currency was far too premature. It would not happen in their lifetime. Yet Robin Leigh-Pemberton, Governor of the Bank of England, signed the Delors Report, much to the annoyance of Mrs Thatcher.

The Delors Report was to create a momentum behind EMU that the British found difficult to stop or divert. Two separate counter-proposals emanated from London in 1989–90, the first for competing currencies and the second for a new parallel currency (the 'hard' ECU). They received negligible support from elsewhere in the EC. But both proposals distracted domestic attention in Whitehall. The British misjudged the political support for EMU amongst their EC partners.

In part due to British sensitivities the EC proceeded cautiously on EMU after the Delors Report. At Madrid in June 1989 the European Council agreed in principle to an intergovernmental conference (IGC) to determine the treaty changes necessary to realize EMU. But no date was set for the IGC, only for stage 1. Under the subsequent French Presidency a committee chaired by Elizabeth Guigou endeavoured to prepare the ground for an IGC by drawing up a set of questions for it to consider. Even so, just after Madrid expectations were of a long-drawn-out process stretching well into the 1990s once the single market programme had been finished at the end of 1992.

The stimulus to speed up the EMU negotiations came from unforeseen political developments: the collapse of communism in the East and the process of German unification after November 1989. These developments provoked a new concern amongst Germany's neighbours about a subsequent rebalancing of power in Europe, to Germany's benefit and at French cost. Hence, especially from Paris, there was strong pressure on Bonn to reaffirm its commitment to European unification by naming an early date for the IGC on EMU and for its completion so that German unification and European unification could move in parallel. At the Strasbourg European Council in December 1989 a date for the IGC was agreed, one year ahead. By its next meeting in Dublin in June 1990 the European Council had agreed that a second IGC on political union should be called in parallel to that on EMU. The establishment of both IGCs was a means to bind Germany to the EC.

The Detailed Negotiations Begin

The Italian Presidency in the second half of 1990 acted to prepare both IGCs and to settle disputes about their organizational structure. Negotiations opened in Rome on 9 December 1990, but began in earnest under the Luxembourg and

Dutch Presidencies of 1991. They took place in a distinct institutional setting. The IGC on EMU met at different levels: on eleven occasions as a ministerial IGC, but twice as regularly at the level of officials ('Permanent Representatives'). Alongside the IGC negotiations, three 'informal' meetings of ECOFIN (ministers of finance) were important fora for the progress of the negotiations. The Dutch Presidency also instituted a third technical level to agree texts, involving central bank and finance ministry officials. In addition, the IGC asked the Committee of EC Central Bank Governors to make various technical submissions; its papers on the statutes of the ECB and of the European Monetary Institute (EMI) determined much of the final content.

Amongst the complex constellation of bilaterals surrounding the IGC sessions the Franco-German bilaterals took on a central importance in helping to narrow gaps in the IGC. In 1991 they included the two main Franco-German summits, the two Franco-German Economic Council meetings, and six top-secret bilaterals of French and German negotiators. The Franco-German negotiating relationship represented an inner dynamic within the wider EMU negotiations and was widely seen by others as the indispensable basis for success.

Various delegations to the IGC submitted papers. Draft treaties on EMU were presented by the EC Commission (10 December 1990), the French (28 January 1991), and the Germans (26 February). The Spanish presented a more limited text (25 September 1990); whilst the British tabled an updated version of its 'hard' ECU plan (8 January 1991). The two Presidencies were obliged to present composite draft treaties to signal the progress made in the IGC. The Luxembourg text (18 June) proved much more consensual than the various submissions of the Dutch (29 August, 24 September, 28 October, 8 November). In fighting their own corner very vigorously, the Dutch upset many of their partners, especially the French. On the transition to stage 3 they were seen as trying too hard to accommodate the British and in the process failing to make EMU irreversible.

The EMU negotiations were concluded at the European Council in Maastricht on 9–10 December 1991: though the final version of the Treaty was not signed until the following February to allow time for some 'polishing-up' of the text. Following delays in the ratification process at the national level (especially sparked by the 'no' vote in the first Danish referendum), the Treaty on European Union came into effect on 1 November 1993.

The Nature and Significance of the Maastricht Agreement

The importance of the Maastricht agreement can only be properly gauged by consideration of what followed it. Many of the problems of implementation stemmed, to a significant degree, from the ambiguities and unanswered questions bequeathed by the IGC negotiations.

The Maastricht European Council represented a high point of optimism about the future of the European integration process. However, the euphoria of Maastricht was soon undermined by the problems of ratifying what had been agreed. This delay shook market confidence that EMU would go ahead and succeed. The first shock came in May 1992 when a referendum in Denmark voted against ratification by a wafer-thin majority. This political shock coincided with economic shocks to reduce confidence in current currency rates within the ERM. These other shocks came from the compound effects of emerging economic recession with punitively high interest rates imposed by the Bundesbank to counter the inflationary implications of German unification. The result was mounting economic and political strains on the British, Italian, and French currencies in particular.

Two bouts of intense currency speculation threatened the core achievement of European monetary co-operation, the ERM, and put in serious question whether EMU could be realized in the manner outlined in Maastricht. In the first, in September 1992, the British and Italian currencies were forced out of the ERM, and the French franc only managed to cling on by its fingertips. Faced by a tight domestic referendum campaign on Maastricht the French sought to discourage negotiation about an ERM realignment. In the absence of planned realignment speculative pressures mounted. Only a demonstration of close Franco-German collaboration to save the franc deterred speculators. In the second bout of speculation in July/August 1993 the ERM all but fell apart. On 2 August 1993, following failure of the French and Germans to co-ordinate their positions, the fluctuation band for ERM currencies was increased from 2.25 per cent to 15 per cent.

Meanwhile, between these two ERM crises the ratification of the Maastricht Treaty had become increasingly problematic. In France the referendum of September 1992 produced only a very small majority in favour; in Britain Conservative members of parliament were proving increasingly Eurosceptic after the 1992 election and especially after the pound's humiliating ejection from the ERM; whilst in Germany a legal challenge to the Treaty was launched, albeit ultimately unsuccessfully.

The Maastricht Treaty on EMU had incorporated a complex compromise over how and when stage 3 might begin. The initial positions adopted by the various governments had been very divergent. France and Italy had wanted to set a clear, binding timetable and to prevent the exercise of national veto in order to ensure irreversibility of stage 3. Germany and the Netherlands sought to ensure that stage 3 would only begin when the conditions were in place to ensure a 'stability community'. These conditions involved precise, numeric indicators of convergence. Convergence was defined in terms of monetary and financial stability, of nominal rather than 'real' indicators. The final Treaty attempted to combine both a precise timetable with a set of convergence tests.

The timetable allowed two possible start dates for stage 3 (Article 109j and the protocol on the convergence criteria). If sufficient convergence were achieved, the heads of state and government could, before the end of 1996, set a date for stage 3. Failing this, stage 3 would begin on 1 January 1999. With respect to the latter date, the heads of state and government had to decide before 1 July 1998—acting by qualified majority—which member states fulfilled the convergence criteria and were therefore eligible to enter stage 3.

After the failure to begin stage 3 in 1997, the convergence criteria were to determine *who* entered stage 3 rather than *when* it was to begin. There had been much conflict in the IGC over whether the convergence criteria should be laid down in the Treaty or in an attached protocol. Incorporation in the Treaty would make them very difficult to change or ignore. In the event, the criteria appeared in both locations. Articles 104c and 109j elaborated the criteria, whilst a protocol defined them more closely. Four tests were set down, requiring participants in stage 3 to have:

- a stable inflation rate (within 1.5 per cent of the three best performing states in the EU);
- a low government deficit (equivalent to no more than 3 per cent of GDP) and a low debt level (below 60 per cent of GDP);
- no devaluation of their currency in the ERM for the previous two years;
- stable interest rates (within 2 per cent of the three best performing states).

After the ERM crises of 1992–3 these tests appeared more and more restrictive as national economies fell into recession. The exchange-rate criterion also required states to respect the 'normal' fluctuation margins of the ERM without severe tensions for the previous two years. An issue arose, especially in relation to Britain, about whether this provision necessitated ERM membership for this period.

Stage 2 began as scheduled on 1 January 1994, and the new EMI set to work to prepare stage 3. The complex formula by which the EU could decide on stage 3 in 1996 was not used in the absence of the required degree of convergence and also in the knowledge that more time was needed to complete the complex preparations in a careful manner that would ensure success.

The End-Game

In the period until 1997 the signs were that very few states were meeting all of the tests. The prospect was for stage 3 to start on a very exclusive basis, leaving a number of key states marginalized. Hence the problem of the relationship between 'ins' and 'outs' assumed a salience that it had not had during the IGC; notably there was a need to negotiate a new ERM. The two biggest problems were Belgium and Italy. Both had huge levels of government debt, accumulated from the past, and some twice the level provided for in the Maastricht Treaty. Italian political leaders became obsessed with gaining entry to stage 3. Difficult domestic reforms were introduced to try to tackle fiscal problems. Pension reform in 1995 proved highly controversial, challenging long-established benefits. Then in November 1996 the centre-left government of Romano Prodi introduced a one-off levy on incomes to help ease the fiscal position. Similar belt-tightening was introduced in Belgium.

In fact, the problems of meeting the convergence criteria also went deeper to the heart of the Franco-German relationship at the centre of EMU. In 1997 both France and Germany looked likely to have government deficits above 3 per cent of GDP in a context in which the German Finance Minister Theo Waigel spoke of 3 per cent meaning 3.0. In France, stubbornly high unemployment appeared to be the cost of a political commitment to meet the convergence tests, injecting a deflationary bias to both fiscal and monetary policies. For several months in 1995 the newly elected French President Jacques Chirac seemed ambiguous on EMU, speaking of the priority to healing social divisions. But in October he opted to pursue the logic of EMU. The scale of the strikes and demonstrations in December that followed the planned social security cuts of the government of Alain Juppé came as a shock. Their main features were retained, but the government remained extremely unpopular and lost the May 1997 elections to a new centre-left government, headed by Lionel Jospin. The new government came to power with new conditions for stage 3, including a strengthening of the political direction of EMU and a broad stage 3 including Italy and Spain. There were allegations that the Juppé and Jospin governments had sought to 'massage' the fiscal position by tricks.

The German government also found itself faced with similar problems and allegations as it desperately sought to meet the criteria set in 1991, though there were no massive strikes and demonstrations of the kind seen in France. Kohl's decision of April 1997 to stand again in 1998 as Chancellor candidate was strongly influenced by his fears that the implementation of stage 3 could be derailed and his conclusion that consistency of leadership was required. The high point of embarrassment came in May 1997 when Waigel sought to press the Bundesbank to bring forward the revaluation of gold stocks in order to defray government debt. Equally seriously for the credibility of Germany as the end-game approached, ambitious plans for taxation, economic policy, and social policy reforms fell victim to a reform 'blockade' by the opposition in Bonn. Germany appeared a less persuasive 'teacher' on fiscal and monetary virtues than when the French and German government were displaying more reformist vigour. Its negotiating power in 1997–8 no longer appeared to match its power in the period 1988–91.

Already in 1995 Waigel had sought to reassure a German public that was deeply sceptical about losing the D-Mark by proposing a stability pact that would clarify the Treaty obligation on member states to avoid excessive government deficits in stage 3. The objective was to be sound budgetary positions close to balance or in surplus. Governments were to deal with normal cyclical fluctuations whilst keeping within the reference value of 3 per cent of GDP. Difficult issues arose about the definition of normal and exceptional situations for fiscal policy, the nature of sanctions, the degree of discretion in their exercise, and the implications for mechanisms of surveillance of budgetary positions and economic policies. These were eventually resolved by two resolutions of the European Council on the Stability and Growth Pact in Amsterdam in June 1997 and by two Council regulations of July 1997.

Led in part by domestic pressures, Bonn and Paris adopted different positions on the issue of which states should join stage 3. Waigel poured scorn on the prospects of Italy being ready. In contrast, Jospin insisted that France would not enter stage 3 without Italy. By doing so he assuaged those of his supporters who feared that France was being tied to a narrow German-led zone. Once it became clear that stage 3 would involve a large grouping including Belgium and Italy, Waigel again sought to appease German public opinion by calling at the March 1998 ECOFIN in York for a declaration on stability designed to accelerate debt reduction and further tighten budget discipline. Waigel was preoccupied with reassuring Germans that the single currency would be at least as stable as the D-Mark. The German preoccupation with 3.0 per cent seemed to many theological and artificial. No theory supported such a precise figure which could in principle be adapted in the light of fiscal and economic trends. This figure and the public debt figure functioned not as immutable economic truths but had ultimately a political foundation.

EMU was divisive in another respect. Some states were likely to decide to stay outside stage 3, at least at the start, for political reasons—notably Britain. The British government was required to notify its partners whether it wished to participate or to exercise the 'opt-out' secured at Maastricht by the end of 1997. Whilst the Major government was in power, British attitudes appeared to harden against the EU. The 'Eurosceptics' in the Conservative Party gained increasing sway over the government and sought to close down the option of joining stage 3. Even so, the presence of Michael Heseltine as Deputy Prime Minister and of Kenneth Clarke as Chancellor of the Exchequer, helped to hold the line in favour of a 'wait-and-see' policy. The election of a new government under Tony Blair in May 1997 heralded a 'new start' in Britain's relations with the EU. Even so, on 27 October 1997 Gordon Brown as Chancellor announced that Britain was not ready for EMU and would exercise its 'opt-out' until the time was right. A set of tests for entry were spelt out. The Labour government appeared to be repeating the pattern of the 1950s, preferring to 'wait and see'. Economically, it believed that it had little option. Britain's economic cycle was out of kilter with that of most of its European partners. Early entry threatened to be economically destabilizing and politically risky. But politically Britain now had a government that wanted to say 'yes' to stage 3.

Ironically, the point of decision about which states should enter stage 3 was scheduled during the British EU Presidency of early 1998. By then the political climate in the EU had been transformed from that of the previous year, in part by the great efforts made by states to qualify (and the desire to reward them) and in part by signs of economic expansion. The impetus was for an inclusive rather than exclusive approach. Almost all who wanted to join were allowed to do so.

A flexible interpretation of the Maastricht convergence criteria served the interests of a majority of governments, which wished to avoid being seen as using EMU to divide the EU. Moreover, Chancellor Kohl in particular, but also Prodi in Rome, had invested much of their political reputation in realizing entry into stage 3.

A special European Council in Brussels on 2 May 1998 agreed that eleven of the fifteen member states could join stage 3 on 1 January 1999. Only Britain, Denmark, Greece, and Sweden stood apart. Of these, Greece was the most enthusiastic to join, but the least ready to do so. The ECB board was also appointed to operate the single monetary policy and oversee the transition to the single currency on the terms agreed in 1995. From 1 January 1999 the exchange rates were to be locked, with national currencies becoming denominations of the new euro and thereby ending foreign-exchange market dealings in the constituent currencies. Euro notes and coins were to appear after 1 January 2002. After a short interim period of a few months, the euro was to replace the national currencies. The Brussels meeting was, however, overshadowed by a conflict precipitated by President Chirac about the appointment of the President of the ECB. Wim Duisenberg, President of the EMI, was favoured by fourteen of the EU states and backed strongly by the Bundesbank. Chirac proposed a French candidate, the Governor of the Banque de France— Jean-Claude Trichet. A fudged and shabby deal emerged: Duisenberg was to begin his eight-year term but retire after four years and be replaced by Trichet.

Of particular interest and importance was the party political composition of the EU states on the launch of stage 3 compared to that in 1991. Social-democratic-led governments formed the large majority, with in September 1998 a substantial majority for the new Social Democratic/Green government of Gerhard Schröder in Germany. The idea of economic policy co-ordination to pursue growth and employment—of the kind pushed unsuccessfully by Delors in his 1993 White Paper on Competitiveness, Growth, and Employment—was put back on the EU agenda. Oskar Lafontaine as the new German Finance Minister was more receptive to this idea than Waigel had been. In this refashioned political context the Jospin government had new opportunities to pursue its interest in strengthening the economic policy pole of EMU by turning the Euro-11 Council into a newly significant player alongside the ECB. The institutional architecture of EMU was still in the making on the launch of stage 3.

Conclusion

This brief historical overview has illuminated some of the complexity of the way in which an agreement on EMU was forged at Maastricht. It has also shown how the Maastricht Treaty left gaps that had to be addressed later and rested on economic and political assumptions that had to be re-examined in the light of later difficulties and developments. But, up till 1998, the underlying consensus on 'sound' money and public finances remained in place, structuring, informing, and legitimizing the particular form that the discourse on EMU took. By the time of the launch of stage 3 two developments raised doubts about this consensus: the international financial crisis emanating from east Asia, Russia, and Latin America; and the new ascendancy of social democratic governments in the EU. The financial crisis raised doubts about the wisdom of reliance on 'infallible' markets as arbiters of policy; whilst new social democratic governments were likely to be more disposed to take advantage of perceived failures within markets to pursue a more robust international and European economic policy co-ordination and to re-regulate markets. For these reasons there was a new potential for the tide to turn away from EC central bankers.

1
Making Sense of the EMU Negotiations

How can we explain how the EC reached its historic agreement on EMU at Maastricht in 1991? What occurred appears as a complex drama, with many actors in different scenes following an only partially connected script. Much of the drama is a source of confusion, distraction, and obscurity rather than of clarification. The starting-point is to define what the focus is. Here we intend to get 'inside' the negotiations, to present a 'micro-history' of how they originated and progressed. What follows is a history 'from below', based on four large case studies.[1] In the language of the social sciences, the book follows an 'actor-centred' approach. It concentrates on the individual negotiators driving (and resisting) the process: their beliefs, motives, strategies, and tactics. The book seeks to analyse and compare how they defined and performed their roles and show how this activity helps us to understand how EMU emerged and was successfully negotiated.

In focusing on the actors, we are not ignoring the big picture. The negotiators were not free agents but rather were subjected to various constraints and conditioning influences which structured their roles. They were affected by reigning ideas of 'sound' finances and money which helped to structure, inform, and legitimize their discourse and empowered some negotiators—notably central bankers—rather than others—like trade unions (Marcussen 1998). Their outlooks were shaped by the institutions in which they operated, by the informal rules governing their behaviour, and in particular by transnational fora like the EC Monetary Committee, the Committee of EC Central Bank Governors, and the management of the European Monetary System (EMS). In effect, ideas of 'sound' finances and money had become institutionalized at the European level. They were also bound up in the changing geography of money, involving the deterritorialization of currencies and a market-driven competition between them with the huge growth in cross-border use of currencies (Cohen 1998). In the process the role of currency policy had been transformed: from the territorial control of money to strategic interaction of EC states with more powerful market actors; from authoritative action (symbolized by capital controls) to a concern with credibility and reputation (symbolized by 'sound' policies). Hence, EMU negotiators did not start with a clean sheet in devising their positions. They operated in a new structure of power in the hands of privileged private agents

---

[1] In this sense it differs from Milward (1984).

(generated by market competition) and of dominant ideas (about 'sound' finances and money), a context that led them to reflect on whether the traditional state-based system of monetary governance was any longer appropriate.

The 'macro-history' of the structural forces leading to the EMU agreement is given lengthy treatment in Dyson's *Elusive Union* (1994). But with this volume we stress the role of EMU negotiators as agents of change and analyse their motives. The assumption is that agency mattered. This book seeks to show that the reflection, learning, and strategic calculation of the EMU negotiators were crucial constitutive elements of the negotiating process. EMU negotiators sought, and were able, to influence the context in which they negotiated. There are relatively few 'inside' histories available of negotiations in the European Union. We hope that, in drawing attention to the importance of variables endogenous to the negotiating process, this book will help to fill this gap.

This first chapter provides the framework for the later historical case studies. It places what is an historical study in the context of the social sciences. Drawing on concepts and insights generated in contemporary political science, policy studies, and International Relations, it identifies a set of questions on which the subsequent national case studies will be based. Different approaches are evaluated, each drawing out different aspects of the terrain whilst also overlapping in their coverage. Emphasis is placed on unpacking the two main dimensions of the EMU negotiations—cognitive and strategic. The core argument is that, though the EMU negotiations were prestructured, these two dimensions were vital components of the process. In stressing the interpenetration of the cognitive and strategic dimensions we have rejected the temptation to view the history of the EMU negotiations through a single lens. We do not accept that it can be understood—and the question that we are addressing answered—by reference to any individual causal theory. Such an approach risks forcing reality into a straitjacket. The multi-dimensional nature of the EMU negotiations requires the combination of different perspectives to reveal its full complexity.

EMU Negotiations as a 'Core Executive' Activity

More precisely, the object of our interest has been how EMU was put back on the EC's agenda; the role of political leaders as craftsmen or artists of beliefs and memories; the kinds of strategic choices that they made; and how the negotiations were handled and developed in different institutional venues (the phenomenon of 'venue-hopping' by negotiators). Most notably, these venues included the Delors Committee, the Guigou Group, the EC Monetary Committee, the Committee of EC Central Bank Governors, the Intergovernmental Conference on EMU, the EC Presidencies, and the various European Councils between 1988 and 1991, and a complex set of formal and informal bilaterals, particularly Franco-German bilaterals. Though this institutional setting looks complex, we soon discovered that we were dealing with a small, intimate, and isolated set of actors in the 'core executive' territory (Rhodes and Dunleavy 1995: 12).[2]

Sectoral interests were very much excluded from the EMU negotiations. Employer organizations, trade unions, and industrial and banking associations were not incorporated in the process, either at national or EC levels. This exclusion derived from certain key attributes of EMU as a policy sector:

- the construction ('framing') of EMU as at heart a monetary problem, and the corresponding downplaying of its fiscal and structural policy dimensions as epiphenomena;
- the definition of decisions about the future of currencies as 'high politics' and therefore intrinsically a matter for states (showing how policy content drove process);
- the traditional mystique surrounding monetary policy, the sense that it was an arcane area for the exercise of central bank professionalism, a mystique that was sustained by central bankers;
- the difficulty that sectoral bodies—employers, trade unions, and industrial associations—had in specifying the likely consequences of EMU for their members. This difficulty derived from uncertainty about the likely complex effects of the transition process and of interest rates and exchange rates under EMU. The distributional effects remained too unclear for sectoral interests to be able to specify their interests in an unambiguous manner. This uncertainty created a political role for experts in helping to specify these interests.

Against this background sectoral bodies eschewed a strategy of mobilizing their members to exert influence on the EMU negotiations. The general judgement was that central banks could be relied on to define and protect basic macroeconomic interests and that, in any case, a strategy of sectoral mobilization might prove divisive for memberships. In consequence, EMU negotiators were insulated from public pressure and demands for public accountability. Space was opened for their own ideas and interpretations to shape the process and outcomes.

Hence the study of the EMU negotiations did not involve tracing and characterizing 'policy networks' that bound together state executives and sectoral interests in relationships of mutual dependency. Preparation of EMU bargaining positions and the management of the negotiations were confined to the centres of political authority at the very heart of the machinery of the state (and of the EC Commission). They involved a web of relationships surrounding prime ministers (and notably the President in the French case), their advisers, cabinets, cabinet committees, finance ministries, ministerial bilaterals, interdepartmental working groups, central banks, and Jacques Delors, his personal cabinet, and selected members of DG2 of the EC Commission. In the case of each of these structures only a very tiny group of politicians and officials were active players.

---

[2] In this respect the approach of the book differs from Kaltenthaler (1998b). He stresses the high number of state decision-makers and the constraining effect of societal organizations.

EMU negotiations were, in other words, a 'core executive' activity. They rested on the interplay and efficacy of these various mechanisms of co-ordination, at domestic and at EC levels. They revealed a subterranean, strongly bureaucratic process of competition for control of 'core executive' territory: for instance, between finance and foreign ministries; between prime ministers and ministers; or between Delors and the EC Monetary Committee. One of the more subtle aspects of EMU negotiations was 'turf-fighting' about who would have primacy in co-ordination and in gaining the ear of political leaders. Hence the EMU negotiations were a realm of cliques and intrigues, of ministerial and bureaucratic politics at the highest level, of manoeuvring to ensure that particular issues were assigned to specific institutional venues in order to shape their outcome in certain ways.

Conceptualizing the EMU Negotiations: Structural, Strategic, and Cognitive Dimensions

Analysing EMU as a negotiating process offered a formidable intellectual challenge. As the research progressed, we were confronted with the problem of the scale of its complexity as an interplay of power, interests, knowledge, and institutions. It seemed clear that each of these aspects was embedded in pre-existing structures, following tracks already laid down, for instance by sets of beliefs and by international financial markets. In his book *Elusive Union* Dyson emphasized the 'prestructuring' of EMU bargaining. This prestructuring privileged the power of some actors (notably the German Bundesbank) over others. It also helped to explain the role of unintended consequences in negotiations; the unplanned nature of the bargaining game; and the games' degree of autonomy of the moves of individual players (Dyson 1994).

Insight into the prestructuring of EMU negotiations sensitized us from the outset to a limitation of elite interviews as a research method. Interviewees were often not conscious of what had been happening in the larger negotiating context in which they had been operating. These cognitive limitations of actors were also accompanied by their strategic limitations. Forces at work were not just outside their area of knowledge; they were also often beyond their control. Hence the EMU negotiating process as a whole could not be seen from the standpoint of the individual actor's experience alone. A key task of the social scientist is to unravel and characterize the figuration of the larger negotiation process of which individual actors, like the Bundesbank or the EC Commission President, are only a part.

But *Elusive Union* was also at pains to distinguish between the prestructuring of EMU negotiations and the role of factors endogenous to the bargaining process. It drew out the complex dialectical relationship of structure and agency. Quite simply, agency matters (Bhaskar 1979; Giddens 1984; Wendt 1987). Structure offers opportunities to actors as well as constraints; actors are capable of thinking strategically and using structural conditions as means to transform the policy reality in which they operate; their calculated actions have direct effects on the structural context within which they operate; and, not least, the way in which they 'frame' issues draws attention to the importance of policy beliefs, argument, evidence, and learning in shaping the direction in which bargaining evolves as well as substantive outcomes. Borrowing from Bhaskar, the actor in the EMU negotiating process is like 'a sculptor at work, fashioning a product out of the material and with the tools available to him' (Bhaskar 1979: 43). In short, the motives and self-understandings of actors, their strategic calculations, tactical sophistication, and cognitive processes, are all vital to comprehending the EMU negotiations.

In this book we delve more deeply into the EMU negotiating process, to offer an insider account of how bargaining positions evolved, why certain kinds of proposals were made and how, and why specific deals were struck. Whilst continuing to stress the interactivity of structure and agency, we focus on drawing out *the role of factors endogenous to the EMU negotiating process* in effecting policy change. The narrative of this volume is held together by a focus on these factors and the questions to which they give rise.

- Political leaders as *animateurs*, *ingénieurs*, and as strategists of negotiations. As *animateurs* they mobilize enthusiasm and galvanize the negotiating process into action, finding means of putting policy experts to work in a framework of their own choosing. As *ingénieurs* they oil the wheels of negotiation and 'engineer' contextual changes to which negotiators have to respond. More generally as strategists they seek to define the major strategic choices, seize the initiative at decisive points in the EMU negotiations, and use external constraints or domestic opposition to enhance their power over negotiations.
- The use of the 'nesting' of EMU in other higher-order or related policy games to alter perceptions of optimal payoffs from negotiations. A major example was the use of German unification to reshape EMU negotiations, or earlier of the spillover effects from the single European market and the EMS. The context of other games in which negotiators are involved can be employed to redefine an optimal outcome in relation to EMU.
- The activation of 'transgovernmental' and 'cross-level' linkages to other negotiators. These linkages serve to create better conditions for co-operative bargaining on one's own terms. The opportunities for this kind of behaviour are enhanced by the EC's institutional structures and working methods, as well as by the Franco-German relationship. They can privilege cross-national linkages over intragovernmental linkages as means of maximizing influence.
- The use of EMU as an external discipline and force for domestic modernization and policy change, as in Italy, or of domestic opposition and political weakness to enhance external power over EMU negotiations by 'binding hands', as in the case of Chancellor Kohl.
- The role of individual 'policy entrepreneurs' as agenda-setters and promoters of ideas. They seek to match EMU to 'windows of opportunity' opened

by political events and policy developments and to 'soften up' leaders to accept and sponsor EMU.

• The importance of the 'probing' of inherited policy beliefs about EMU, and reflection on the meaning of EMU, by those interacting within the bargaining process. Inquiry opens up the prospect of 'reframing' of the issues in the light of flaws in strategy exposed by experience and hence leading on to redefinition of the interests at stake and a restructuring of policy arguments.

• The design of institutional venues—like the Delors Committee and the IGC—and the choice of venues—like the EC Monetary Committee—in order to shape how EMU issues are defined and negotiated.

• Persuasion through appropriate 'signalling' action designed to show partners that one is a serious negotiating partner (by for instance using the appropriate economic policy discourse) or to clarify the conditions in which an EMU deal could be struck.

• The formulation of an appropriate discourse to legitimate EMU, endowing it with symbolic value, for instance by linking it to powerful historical memories.

Some order can be given to these factors by grouping them within the different conceptualizations of the EMU negotiating process that evolved as our research progressed. Just as we had earlier become aware of the limitations of conceptualizing EMU as prestructured, so our interviewing cast doubt on the adequacy of traditional preoccupations with characterization of negotiations as a strategic process. Crucially, a cognitive process was also at work. These two conceptualizations of bargaining as strategic and as cognitive overlapped significantly in the practice of EMU negotiations, and interacted with each other. At the same time they remain logically distinct. One is not simply a sub-set or component of the other 'higher-order' concept; nor are they completely identical.

1. The conceptualization of *negotiation as strategy* allocates primacy to the tough-minded championing of vital interests that are exogenous givens, provided by history and geography. It focuses on the phenomenon of bureaucratic politics as players contend for the control over the territory of negotiations and seek to expand their competence. Strategy stresses the process of 'horse-trading' about relative gains and losses, the plotting of sequences of moves and counter-moves amongst players, and skills in seizing the initiative in relation to decisive points in the negotiations. Negotiators are pictured as preoccupied with retaining their freedom of manoeuvre to shape negotiating outcomes on their terms and at their pace. Strategy does, of course, have a cognitive aspect. It depends on knowledge about other players and their likely moves and counter-moves. Its definitions of interest are also cognitively informed. But strategy retains its own preoccupations and character. It highlights the problem of negotiating a politically acceptable outcome, at home and abroad.

2. The conceptualization of *negotiation as cognition* allocates primacy to the role of beliefs in constructing interests and defining policy positions, and to the transmission of ideas and knowledge into the negotiating process. Negotiators

are pictured as confronted by acute uncertainty about how EMU can be made to work, about where their best interests lie, and about their potential allies. This uncertainty creates an opportunity for experts to define the negotiating problems, clarify the interests at stake, and transform the negotiations into a learning process. They provide the basic ideas that shape the negotiations and shape the forms of discourse employed. What gave this aspect of the EMU negotiations its distinct character was the preoccupation with putting in place a technically viable EMU. This preoccupation endowed the EMU negotiations with an element of policy learning.

Unquestionably, much behaviour in EMU negotiations is to be explained in terms of strategy. Actors were motivated by definitions of vital interests at stake, which—as far as the negotiations were concerned—were exogenous givens. Ideas served as tools or instruments in the struggle for power (Goldstein and Keohane 1993; Jacobsen 1995). Negotiators operated with calculations of relative gains and losses from EMU and sought to deploy and co-ordinate statecraft for the attainment of political aims—in a more or less sophisticated and effective way (Liddell Hart 1968; Paret 1985). They oriented their behaviour to the likely moves of other players both domestically and within the EC. The negotiating problem was always about the political acceptability of any EMU outcome. Its solution required 'horse-trading' amongst interests, and part of that 'horse-trading' was a competition of bureaucratic interests about retaining and expanding competence over policy.

At the same time the negotiating problem was also about specifying the technical conditions for a viable EMU, for an EMU that would function without causing unacceptable economic and political damage to the EC and its member states. Hence the EMU negotiations took on the character of a cognitive process as well as a strategic process. In part at least, definitions of interest were shaped or constituted by ideas, and negotiating behaviour was norm-driven (Risse *et al.* forthcoming; Finnemore and Sikkink forthcoming). A complex of converging and contrasting beliefs was secreted at the heart of the negotiations, raising the question of the explanatory power of different theories about the role of knowledge and ideas (Radaelli 1995).

But the interplay of ideas and interests in the EMU negotiations was too intimate and complex to separate out beliefs as the determining causal factor. Strategy had its own dynamics. Hence the question of how best to model EMU negotiations was answered by preferring a contingency model to a causal model.[3] This contingency model stressed the internal 'connectedness' between the pre-structuring of EMU negotiations and the strategic and cognitive dimensions of the process. In short, a single independent variable could not explain so complex a field of interactive forces as the EMU negotiation process or its outcome. The EMU negotiating process is to be understood as prestructured; as strategic; and as cognitive. These elements of the negotiating process need to be 'unpacked'.

---

[3] For a similar argument see Radaelli (1997).

EMU as a Prestructured Negotiating Process

It is tempting to quote the famous observation by Bismarck: 'Politics is to perceive God's footsteps through world history, then jump out trying to catch a corner of his mantle.' Most politicians and central bankers are inclined to believe that they make history but the opposite is nearer the truth. They perform history but they do not create it.

(Hoffmeyer 1992: 31).

The structural basis of power within the EMU negotiating process, and its origins, are dealt with exhaustively in Dyson's *Elusive Union*. Here it is only necessary to summarize the main exogenous factors bearing down on and constraining that process and to highlight their key effects. The main point is that EMU negotiators were operating in an already-structured world. This prestructuring took the forms of historical inheritance; of institutional rules and policy styles; of the D-Mark as the 'anchor' currency of the ERM; of global financial markets; and of the state of economic and monetary policy knowledge and reigning economic policy ideas.

The EMU negotiations did not originate in a vacuum or *ab initio*. They also enjoyed an autonomy in relation to the individual actor's own moves. The overall course of the negotiations was not in the power of any one player—whether Delors, Kohl, or the President of the Bundesbank. Previous moves by certain actors limited and constrained not only the moves of others but also their own later moves—as exemplified by the case of the Delors Committee (Elias 1978: 94–6). We are, in short, dealing with a negotiating process in which unintended consequences resulted from intentional actions. This characteristic derived from the way in which actors found themselves bonded together in a process about which they were imperfectly informed and whose overall course defied their individual control. The unplanned course of the EMU negotiations repeatedly influenced the moves of each individual player.

Historical Inheritance: Received Ideas about Vital Interests

Past experience, embodied in institutional and personal memories, was a powerful conditioning factor in EMU negotiation. Most influential were memories of the previous failed attempt to realize EMU in the wake of the Werner Report of 1970; specific national events and experiences; and the role that European unification, and the idea of Franco-German reconciliation, played in inherited definitions of vital national interests.

Memories of Werner The failure to implement the Werner Report had bequeathed, as a general legacy, the view that EMU would be a difficult, uncertain, and protracted task. For German negotiators like Hans Tietmeyer, who had been directly involved in the Werner Group's work, the lessons were twofold: that establishing the prerequisite of economic convergence for a viable monetary union would be a long-term, very practical affair; and that, until French negotiators were prepared to put in place European political union, EMU would not be able to proceed.[4] Monetary union would be the final 'coronation' of a process of economic and political union. Such an interpretation was supported by the way in which in the nineteenth century a German monetary union had been formed: first, an economic union, then a political union, and finally a monetary union. French and EC Commission negotiators interpreted the Werner Report differently, seeing the core problem as German reluctance. It illustrated that EMU would be a long-term process. But the application of the traditional 'Community method' to EMU offered a route ahead.[5] EMU needed to be tackled by a series of successive actions, by a 'nibbling' process of putting in place new devices, like a parallel currency and a European Monetary Fund. Along with a timetable to force action such devices would enable progress to be sustained. This spirit of caution pervaded debate about EMU amongst EC economic and monetary policy officials as late as 1988–9. Indeed, as we shall see, both German 'fundamentalists' and French and EC 'minimalists' on EMU were taken by surprise and forced to reconsider their arguments and proposals.

Specific National Traditions and Experiences   National traditions and experiences prestructured EMU bargaining positions in a powerful way. For German negotiators the postwar ordo-liberal economic tradition was a key source of reference. It stressed price stability as the key economic public good that the state must guarantee. This guarantee depended on an independent central bank. Ordo-liberalism also underlined the state's role in providing a framework of market competition for the economy. These core principles were rooted in German economic and political experience in the 1920s and 1930s. German EMU negotiators saw it as their basic responsibility to ensure that they were reproduced at the EC level. No less importantly, ordo-liberal economists stressed the historical and cultural context of economic and monetary policies. This approach led to a deep scepticism about the potential to negotiate a viable and mutually acceptable EMU with French negotiators moulded by a *dirigiste* tradition (Nicholls 1994).

By contrast, British and French negotiators were moulded by political traditions that stressed the primacy of politics over economic and monetary policy. Albeit overlaid by a mounting recognition of the postwar costs of inflation, memories of interwar unemployment—and its political association with the power of bankers—tempered the political will to pursue central bank independence, not least on the part of French Socialist politicians like President François Mitterrand and Pierre Bérégovoy. Perhaps more fundamentally, constitutional traditions framed how actors responded to EMU issues. The British tradition of the sovereignty of Parliament and the French republican tradition of the sovereign people affected perceptions of the legitimation of EMU. For British nego-

---

[4] Spelt out in a speech by Hans Tietmeyer, 'Relationship between Economic and Monetary Union', 1972.

[5] A theoretician of the Community method applied to EMU was Padoa-Schioppa (1994).

tiators like Thatcher, Lawson, Major, and Lamont there was a deep problem of squaring with constitutional tradition the transfer of monetary policy sovereignty to an ECB and accepting EC rules on fiscal policy and sanctions (Lawson 1992; Thatcher 1995). The French republican tradition was a more flexible formula for sovereignty than the tradition of the sovereignty of Parliament and could be sustained by incorporating 'gouvernement économique' in an EMU accord. But, in terms of French constitutional ideas, an independent central bank was more problematic. Bérégovoy, Michel Rocard, Edith Cresson, and Mitterrand never lost their inner reservations about this aspect of the EMU negotiations (Aeschimann and Riché 1996).

The Role of European Unification in Conceptions of National Interest   Equally crucial in prestructuring EMU negotiations were inherited conceptions of vital national interests and the role of European unification within those conceptions. In the German case the first Chancellor, Konrad Adenauer, had been instrumental in fashioning a definition of the vital interests of the new Federal Republic that, with modifications, formed the continuing bases of foreign policy. Indeed, Kohl saw himself as the political heir of Adenauer. Those vital interests were defined as security and prosperity in a framework of freedom and as best realized via the embedding of Germany in a process of European union constructed by working closely with France. Quite simply, the tandem of European union and Franco-German reconciliation was in Germany's vital interest. For German Foreign Ministry negotiators the question of whether and when European unification was in Germany's vital interest did not arise. European unification and Franco-German reconciliation were judged to be, prima facie, in Germany's vital interest.

British negotiators inherited a very different conception of the relation of European unification to vital interests. Escaping German occupation and emerging as a victor from the Second World War, British policy-makers were less disposed to see European unification as the prime basis of their country's security. Also, possessed of the trappings of a world power and an imperial past, British negotiators were inclined to see the EC as one of several fora, rather than the central forum, through which her vital interests could be pursued. And, in the pursuit of vital interests, the 'special relationship' with the USA assumed a particular importance. Hence fora that involved the USA, like NATO, the IMF, and the GATT, were prioritized. Since the 1940s British politicians had been committed to an intergovernmental conception of European union that made the EC, with its supranational elements, an uncomfortable institutional arrangement. European co-operation was a pragmatic and utilitarian business, limited to those areas compatible with a definition of vital interests that emphasized international free trade and security via the USA's role in Europe.

To a far greater extent French negotiators saw in the EC a prime vehicle for the pursuit of vital interests. With memories of the scars of the First World War, of the humiliating defeat of 1940, and of being peripheral to wartime and postwar American power, they were preoccupied with German and American power and the actual and potential dependency of France. France's vital interest was defined as finding a set of European arrangements that would form an escape from this dependency and provide both security and prosperity. Hence French negotiators inherited a set of ideas that made them disposed to conclude that, in principle, the process of European union was compatible with vital interests and that Franco-German reconciliation must be central to this process. Indeed, in the eyes of French technocrats, the EC could serve as an external discipline forcing overdue domestic policy reforms on France. This theme of *vincolo esterno* was even more clear in the Italian case, where the ERM and EMU could be seen as instruments of economic and political modernization. Not least, European unification offered Italy an opportunity to play a role at the heart of Europe.

Hence, from the outset, the EMU negotiating process was embedded in the historical context of the Franco-German relationship and its key role in both countries' established definition of vital interests. The political history of its rebirth in 1987–8 and of its negotiation is secreted in that relationship, not least in the impact that German unification had in sharpening and giving new urgency to these definitions of vital interest and in inspiring an *animateur* role by Kohl and Mitterrand.

Institutional Structures and Policy Style

The actors who negotiated EMU were part of a complex and evolving set of decision rules, styles, and codes of behaviour at the EC level which endowed their interactions with a quality not apparent in other international institutions.[6] In the case of the EMU negotiations this quality had less to do with the supranational elements of the EC's institutional design. Neither the EC Commission nor the European Parliament played the key role in this sector that was available to them in other sectors. In particular, the EC Monetary Committee and the Committee of EC Central Bank Governors sought to keep the Commission at a distance. This practice encouraged the Commission to prefer to resolve EMU issues in other venues, notably the European Council and in conjunction with the Presidency of the Council. But, at the same time, the EC remained in an overall sense *sui generis*. Negotiating EMU in its institutional context was very different from negotiating international monetary co-operation in the IMF or G7.

Iterative Bargaining and the Norm of Consensus Far more influential than the supranational principle at the sectoral level of EMU was the sheer intensity of intergovernmental interaction and the fact that the EC's institutional structures depended on a sharing of power and a practice of consensus-building. A small group of finance ministry and central bank officials developed relations of close personal intimacy as they revolved between ECOFIN, EC Monetary

---

[6] On the 'new' institutionalism as applied to the EC see Bulmer (1994: 351–80).

Committee, Committee of Central Bank Governors, IGC, G7, G10, IMF, and OECD; whilst French and German officials came together additionally for the regular bilateral summits, for biannual Franco-German Economic Council meetings, for personal bilaterals, and for the Franco-German bilaterals that paralleled the IGC in 1991.

This dense institutional nexus meant that optimizing behaviour was not focused on EMU as a 'one-off' bargain or on getting all one could on a single EMU issue. EMU bargaining was ongoing and iterative, across a range of issues and extending over time. Hence optimizing behaviour involved retaining and, where possible, building one's credit. It meant attending to one's reputation as a trustworthy, reliable, and honest negotiator who respected the constraints operating on others and sought to play a constructive role in finding mutually acceptable solutions (Axelrod 1984). Against this operating code, the British Chancellor of the Exchequer, Norman Lamont, was judged a failure and liability, not least by his own Whitehall officials. Above all, EC norms included a sensitivity to the way in which individual bargaining was 'nested' inside 'higher-order' games or in related games. On this basis robust EMU negotiators like Horst Köhler and Hans Tietmeyer were prepared to concede that the policy interests consequent on German unification required certain German concessions.

And, not least, effective bargaining in EC venues required a sensitivity to the requirements of consensus-building. It was important to be part of a process of seeking constructive solutions to problems, solutions that would take account of each other's needs and difficulties so that a final outcome could be acceptable to all. This style of bargaining was deeply ingrained in the work of the EC Monetary Committee and the Committee of Central Bank Governors; it influenced ECOFIN and the European Council; and it was part and parcel of the working ethos of the IGC on EMU and of Franco-German bilaterals.

The European Council and ECOFIN   At the political apex the European Council brought together the EC heads of state and government and their foreign ministers into a forum that could exert political leadership or act as a court of last appeal in cases of unresolved conflicts. As early as 1969 the Hague summit had launched the process leading to the Werner Group study of how to realize EMU; the 1972 Paris summit endorsed EMU as a political goal; whilst the Brussels Council of 1979 had adopted the European Monetary System (EMS), with provision for a stage 2. Thereafter, EMU's resurfacing on the agenda, or reform of the EMS (often code for EMU), could always be legitimated as unfinished political business rather than as a radical new departure. But, above all, before the Maastricht Treaty, the European Council provided a political venue to consider EMS/EMU issues at a distance from finance ministers and central bankers. This institutional factor was to be crucial in facilitating the relaunch of EMU at the Hanover Council in 1988, in setting the date for the IGC on EMU at the Strasbourg Council in 1989, and in agreeing an ambitious communiqué on EMU at the Rome 1 Council in 1990.

At the sectoral level the responsible institutional structures were the Council meeting of economic and finance ministers (ECOFIN), the EC Monetary Committee and the Committee of EC Central Bank Governors. Finance ministry and central bank officials were at all times concerned to insulate EMU negotiations within these structures. Hence the way in which EMU issues were framed and acted on in this context was designed to block out those issues which were most politically sensitive, notably the fiscal union and political union components of EMU. By pushing as much as possible of the EMU negotiations into the EC Monetary Committee and the Committee of EC Central Bank Governors the agenda was focused on the monetary and financial aspects. And, given that senior central bankers formed half of the membership of the EC Monetary Committee, there was an institutional privileging of EC central bankers in the EMU negotiations that was to crucially affect the outcome at Maastricht (Dyson *et al.* 1995).

The Evolving Rules of the ERM   What was also to shape the EMU negotiations was the experience of managing the Exchange Rate Mechanism (ERM) from 1979 onwards. Just as its crises kept EMU off the agenda in the early 1980s, so by the end of that decade the apparent willingness of its partners to accept the discipline of the 'hard' ERM signalled an evolution of rules and codes of behaviour that was consistent with taking EMU more seriously. The original purpose of the ERM as a 'zone of monetary stability in Europe' was being fleshed out as EC governments resorted to use of their parities with the D-Mark as an external discipline and means of 'borrowing' credibility. The result was an emerging climate of confidence about negotiating an EMU deal amongst the actors involved in the EC Monetary Committee and the Committee of EC Central Bank Governors. In short, by 1987–8 the rules of the ERM game had evolved to induce a greater sense of shared ownership of, and mutual responsibility for, a policy project whose value was strongly endorsed.

The Regulatory Style of EMU Bargaining   Perhaps most fundamentally of all, the scope and the nature of the EMU negotiations were constrained by one fundamental fact: that the EC had very modest resources at its disposal. There was no real opportunity, as for instance in the German and US federal systems, to develop and operate an autonomous EC fiscal policy for the purposes of stabilization and/or redistribution within EMU. Given the small size of the EC budget, the only way for the EC to put EMU in place was to focus on the 'rules-based' approach favoured in monetary and financial policy: rules on excessive deficits, 'nominal' economic convergence and no 'bail-outs' for government, and developing monetary policy instruments to achieve price stability. Hence the in-built regulatory policy style of the EC pervaded the EMU negotiations (Majone 1993). It threw the burden of work on developing EMU onto the EC Monetary Committee and the Committee of EC Central Bank Governors. Here, rather than in Delors's office or in DG2 of the EC Commission, were the resources of technical expertise that were required to develop the EC-level policy instruments for EMU. The ascendancy of central bankers' ideas was mainly due to the absence of a viable alternative at the EC level, in particular an EC fiscal authority. The EMU deal hammered out for Maastricht was, in consequence, based on a limited repertoire of policy instruments and a very problematic capacity for co-ordination of monetary-policy decisions with fiscal and structural policies.

EMU Bargaining as Inquiry Most importantly to the argument of this chapter, the institutional structuring that underpinned EMU bargaining enabled negotiators to engage in inquiry and reflection. This cognitive dimension was facilitated in the following ways:

- intensive iterative bargaining at the sectoral level gave status to norms of mutual trust and co-operative problem-solving over 'win–lose' bargaining;
- the institutional environment, with its strong technical infrastructure, was conducive to trading the lessons of success and failure from policy practice, in short to a learning process;
- though the EC Commission had its own interests to advance (notably retaining its right of initiative on the economic aspect of EMU), it also played a role in mediating negotiation. It helped in getting negotiators to focus on joint gains, in stressing the educative role of negotiations, and in encouraging negotiators to see EMU issues and their interests in a new light.[7]

Domestic Institutional Arrangements EMU negotiations were also embedded in, and shaped by, the different institutional arrangements at the national level, notably:

- the way in which constitutional principles and practices influenced how 'core executive' politics was played (for instance, the role of Presidential power in French EMU policy or of the relationship between the Chancellor and departmental principles in Germany);
- the degree of independence of the domestic central banks, privileging the role of the Bundesbank over that of the Banque de France (Goodman 1992);
- the internal organization and operating norms of finance ministries, in particular whether they encouraged a strong European engagement.

Differences of constitutional, statutory, or organizational detail could prove important in giving a very different structure to debate on EMU. They are spelt out in the individual case studies.

The D-Mark as the Anchor Currency: The Hegemony of German Monetary Ideas

Since its inception the ERM's 'anchor' had been provided by the D-Mark, and Germany has served as both standard setter and broker in European monetary co-operation (Kaelberer 1996: 51). As the only EC currency never to have been

---

[7] On mediated negotiation see Susskind and Cruikshank (1987).

devalued, it had an unrivalled credibility and reputation as a 'hard' currency in the financial markets. Hence, in order to maintain their parities with the D-Mark, the domestic monetary policies of other ERM members had to be at least as virtuous as that of Germany. The result was an asymmetry in the functioning of the ERM, the burdens of adjustment having to be borne disproportionately by countries other than Germany. This factor induced a climate of complaint about the ERM as a 'D-Mark zone'. Criticism focused on the Bundesbank which was attacked, notably by the French and the Italians, for putting German before European interests.

Paradoxically, this track record of practical policy success also made the Bundesbank an ideational model for other EC central banks who envied its independence of government, its strong public profile in Germany, and its performance in achieving sustained price stability and a strong currency. There was, in consequence, a process of emulation of Germany as a policy model for locking in low inflation, an objective that had eluded others after the first oil crisis of 1973. This objective took on a more urgent form from 1979 onwards as other EC states struggled with the problems of managing the ERM in the context of the second oil crisis. Hence in the EMU negotiations the Bundesbank possessed both a practical power and a moral authority denied to any other actor, based in part on structural power but also reflecting a choice made by other EC states to treat Germany as a policy model.[8] This factor more than any other helped to ensure that the role model for EMU was central bank independence, Bundesbank-style. The shared beliefs that emerged among EC central bankers, and the practical arrangements put in place for EMU, reflected the underlying power of the Bundesbank. This power took the form of the hegemony of German monetary policy ideas, but a hegemony that owed much to a voluntarist process of policy emulation elsewhere (Dyson 1994: chapter 9; McNamara 1998: 25–9). The process of inquiry and reflection on the requirements of a viable EMU was constrained by this deeper reality.

Globalization and Deregulation of Financial Markets

With the globalization, deregulation, and huge increase of scale of financial markets since the 1970s the context of operation of EC economic and monetary policies altered radically. In particular, rising capital mobility had profound implications for the distribution of political power and the exercise of state power. The main beneficiaries of globalization and deregulation were the owners and managers of financial assets and multinational firms with internationally diversified assets. As the main players in global financial markets, they accumulated new power to act as tough disciplinarians on inflationary tendencies. Globalization constrained governments to prioritize price stability, to pursue

---

[8] For a strong statement of the German hegemony thesis see Markovits and Reich (1997). For a more qualified view see Marcussen (1998: 164–7).

policies based on the requirement of gaining the confidence of the markets, and to focus on market-based measures of performance, notably yield curves. As closer to these volatile markets, and possessed of the expertise to 'handle' them, central bankers acquired a new legitimacy. They could claim that the best route to policy credibility was to endow central banks with political independence and to give them the lead role in designing EMU. In short, globalization and deregulation were decisive to the emergence of a consensus about 'sound' money and finances as the context of the EMU negotiations and to an ideational leadership role for central bankers. It supported, as we shall see later in the chapter, the powerful role of a community of expert professionals (an 'epistemic community') in giving coherence at the level of ideas to the EMU negotiations and facilitating agreement. But it also constrained the political terms of that agreement around a framework of 'sound' money ideas.

The combination of freedom of capital movement as part of the EC single market programme with a commitment to stable exchange rates within the ERM raised a fundamental question about compatibility of goals. Were both these goals compatible with retention of national responsibility for monetary policy? Or did they require EMU? By 1987 Tommaso Pado-Schioppa and Jacques Delors were articulating the problem of the 'inconsistent triangle': the single market, stable exchange rates, and national monetary policies could not be reconciled in the long run (Padoa-Schioppa *et al.* 1987). At a minimum it was clear that new measures of co-ordination of EC monetary policies and a strengthening of reserve borrowing facilities were needed, as agreed at Basle and Nyborg in September 1987. But their significance was minor in relation to the awesome power of the financial markets, as the ERM crises of 1992 and 1993 revealed.

Common exposure to the harsh disciplines of the global financial markets was important in another sense to facilitating an EMU agreement. It induced a process of economic convergence amongst the EC states. This convergence focused around lower inflation, budget deficits, public debt, and long-term interest rates. They were recognized to be the precondition for stable exchange rates within the ERM and for a successful transition to EMU. In short, the requirements of economic-policy success in a world of global, deregulated financial markets conditioned the substance of EMU negotiations. The process of inquiry into the nature of a technically viable EMU was focused on identifying the conditions compatible with the dynamics of these markets.

More fundamentally still, the idea of globalization—like that of German hegemony in monetary policy—took on a cast of objectivity. It became taken for granted as an 'obvious' characteristic of the environment in which EMU negotiators had to operate. In important respects ideas of globalization and hegemony served to reduce negotiators' perceptions of their room for strategic manoeuvre.

Policy Beliefs and Knowledge

EMU negotiators also inherited a structure of political discourse (Majone 1989) that was important not only to the way in which they framed reality, defined their interests, and perceived pay-offs but also in providing the preconditions for negotiation. This structure of discourse can be analysed on two levels: the global and the sector-specific. EMU can be seen as bound up in a process of global restructuring based on politically ascendant economic ideas of 'sound' money and 'sound' public finances. Robert Cox traces this process back to the period 1968–75. The collapse of the Bretton Woods system signalled the collapse of the attempt to strike a balance between a liberal world market and the domestic responsibilities of states. Thereafter, states became effectively accountable to a *nébuleuse* characterized as the global economy. Their vocabulary became obsessed with inflation and competitiveness, with supply-side measures to promote employment, and with embracing rules for fiscal and monetary policy (Cox 1987, 1994). In this context budget deficits, public debt, and trade union power were defined as problems to be tackled. Political power too was redefined. It was seen as shifting to those states that converted themselves into agencies for adjusting national policies and practices to the exigencies of the global economy. The ideology of globalization that took shape influenced the terms in which EMU was debated, circumscribing what was thought and done. It privileged a discourse of 'sound' money and finances that looked to create a 'market society' on a global basis (Gill and Law 1989). Only those who took part in this discourse had much prospect of being taken seriously.

At the sector-specific level, there were three types of discourse:

- two contending 'advocacy coalitions', discernible in relation to the policy problem of the appropriate relationship between economic convergence and monetary union;
- an emerging 'epistemic community', discernible in relation to the policy problem of the appropriate model for monetary union;
- a loosely structured 'garbage can' of beliefs, discernible in relation to debate about the appropriate relationship between EMU and political union and about the basis of legitimation of EMU.

These underlying political discourses provided the knowledge and beliefs in terms of which policy arguments were developed and the activity of persuasion conducted. The beliefs were both causal and normative, offering different pictures of the way in which EC economies functioned and of the kind of values that were appropriate to their efficient and effective functioning. They also encapsulated political ideas, notably about the appropriate institutional arrangements for Europe. It is important to note with respect to the EMU negotiations that it was shaped by a multi-dimensional discourse. A traditional, divisive 'advocacy coalition' was overlaid by the integrative effects of a new, emerging 'epistemic community' and, at the macro level, by an emerging neo-liberal consensus linked to an ideology of globalization. At the same time this structuring of debate was offset by a 'garbage-can' aspect.

'Economist' and 'Monetarist' Advocacy Coalitions for EMU as Traditional Impediments to EMU Negotiations   One key aspect of the EMU negotiations was the presence of two 'advocacy coalitions' (Sabatier and Jenkins-Smith 1993). These coalitions frame issues in different ways and contend in an adversarial way for control of policy. Each coalition was glued together by shared beliefs, knowledge, and interests. In the literature advocacy coalitions are pictured as better capable of adapting to new evidence on the margins than of altering the central ground of their beliefs and interests. The presence of these two advocacy coalitions gave an adversarial character to the Werner Group negotiations of 1970, to the EMS negotiations of 1978, to the debate about stage 2 of the EMS in 1982 and to the debate about reform of the EMS and EMU from 1987–8. Essentially, they offered different solutions to the problem of the proper relationship between economic convergence and monetary union.

The traditionally dominant coalition was strongly represented by the German, Danish, Dutch, and British governments, and by their central banks particularly. Its basic argument for an 'economist' approach to EMU stressed that monetary union must be the end result of a long process of economic convergence amongst EC economies, following the freeing and opening of markets and, not least, complete liberalization of capital movements (Stoltenberg 1988). EC economies had first to demonstrate in a practical manner that they formed an economic area that functioned in a unified way, that could absorb systemic and 'single-country' shocks, and that was dedicated to the same economic policy values (in particular, the primacy of price stability). A monetary union could not be based on compromises. Theoretically, it drew its inspiration from various sources: from the idea of 'optimum' currency areas as the basis of organizing monetary unions; from the notion that the appropriate basis for European monetary co-operation was that, first, each member state must 'put its own house in order' (a key metaphor for the primacy to be given to developing an 'internal constraint'); and from the view that economic activity was embodied in a cultural, historically conditioned matrix, not readily susceptible to major change. Institutionally, the 'economist' approach had two main themes:

- that, before the final move to a monetary union, responsibility for the conduct of monetary policy must rest solely at the national level (the principle of the 'indivisibility' of monetary policy);
- that a 'two-speed' or even 'variable geometry' monetary Europe was likely, given that some states were likely to converge more quickly than others.

Members of this advocacy coalition tended to unite around belief in the primacy of fiscal and structural policies over steps to a monetary union.

The other advocacy coalition—the 'monetarist' approach—was traditionally led by the French, Italian, and Belgian governments and had the support of the EC Commission. Whilst never dominant, it was influential in the negotiation of the EMS in 1978: when Chancellor Helmut Schmidt was attracted to this view in a way not representative of traditional German positions. The 'monetarist' approach argued that by creating a new monetary institution the EC could force a process of economic convergence by changing market behaviour. It would lead rather than follow (Bini-Smaghi *et al.* 1994). This argument was consistent with the traditional 'Community method' approach to European integration, which stressed the role of elite socialization into new EC institutional structures as the most appropriate method for building Europe. Theoretically, the 'monetarist' coalition developed its arguments around the belief in using an external discipline (the Italian *vincolo esterno*) as a means of promoting both domestic policy reform and external credibility (by borrowing credibility from others). Institutionally, its advocates sought to establish a common monetary institution at an early stage in the transition process to EMU, whether a European Monetary Fund to intervene in the foreign-exchange markets in a concerted way or a European Central Bank which would learn how to use monetary policy instruments. This advocacy coalition had also a greater confidence that a large number of states could progress together to the final stage of EMU.

An 'Epistemic Community' as Facilitator of an EMU Agreement   The adversarial relations between two contrasting coalitions on the issue of economic convergence and monetary union had traditionally militated against a constructive negotiation of EMU. On the other hand, a restructuring of argument was facilitated by the emergence of an 'epistemic community'. The term 'epistemic community' refers to 'a network of professionals with recognized expertise and competence in a particular domain and an authoritative claim to policy-relevant knowledge within that domain or issue-area' (Haas 1992). Such a community, based on shared beliefs of experts, can influence the outcomes of negotiations, not least by making co-operation possible. In the case of EMU the institutional epicentre for the development of an epistemic community was the Committee of EC Central Bank Governors and included related monetary economists. Its existence was discernible by 1987–8 and was based on the harsh experience of central bankers in dealing with inflation after the oil crisis and the problems of managing the ERM in the context of more powerful global financial markets. Not least, the learning process was made possible by French responses to the ERM crises of 1982–3 and 1987.

This emerging epistemic community rested on a shared belief in the virtues of 'sound' finances and money, specifically:

- a normative belief in the primacy of price stability;
- a causal belief in the importance of 'borrowing' credibility to lower the costs of disinflation—by tying one's currency, and hence the conduct of one's economic and monetary policies, to an 'anchor' currency, defined as the hardest available (i.e. the least expected to devalue);
- an acceptance that, if EMU negotiations were to be seriously conducted, EMU must be a joint policy project based on the German model of mone-

tary policy, in particular an independent ECB with a mandate restricted to price stability.

These exogenous normative and causal beliefs drove and expedited EMU negotiations for three reasons. First, the EC central bankers acquired a pivotal leadership role in the EMU bargaining process: as members of the Delors Committee; as members of the EC Monetary Committee and, of course, the Committee of Central Bank Governors; and within Franco-German bilaterals. By these means the epistemic community had direct access to power. Through these mechanisms they were able to acquire a role of ideational leadership. Secondly, the epistemic community was able to implant its policy knowledge effectively because of the prevailing uncertainty at political levels about how a viable EMU was to be realized and the absence of a mainstream political view on this question. In this context the German model was available as the most persuasive source of ideas. Thirdly, the underlying beliefs and policy proposals of the epistemic community were adapted to the underlying political reality of the EMU negotiation process: namely, the hegemonic power of Germany over EC monetary-policy ideas. Its beliefs and proposals represented a way of reducing German reservations about getting involved in EMU negotiations. For these three reasons the policy knowledge of this epistemic community was effectively diffused as a basis for co-operative EMU negotiations.

EMU and Political Union: Negotiation as a 'Garbage Can'   The issue of the relationship between EMU and political union proved far more intractably controversial in the EMU negotiations. Its resolution was deferred to the sheduled 'Maastricht II' negotiations. It was to resurface in 1996–7 over the French proposal for a stability council in stage 3 of EMU as an instrument for co-ordination of fiscal and structural policies of member states and for considering the appropriate 'policy mix' within EMU.

At first glance, some structure seemed to be given to the debate about legitimation of EMU by two advocacy coalitions. The French government, backed by Belgium and by the EC Commission, developed the idea of a *gouvernement économique* at the EC level to stress that ultimately the economic and monetary-policy technocrats must be subordinated to political leadership and that political leadership needed to retain discretion over policy, for instance exchange rates. This policy proposal was rooted in the belief system of the French republican tradition. The principle of the sovereignty of the people was hostile to the idea of depoliticized decision-making, represented by an independent ECB. Conversely, reflecting a very different historical experience, of the trauma of hyperinflation, the German government gave primacy to the depoliticization of monetary policy in the form of an independent ECB. Responsibility for 'safeguarding the currency' was too serious a matter to be entrusted to the short-termism of the political process. Hence, *gouvernement économique* was regarded with great distrust, the Germans preferring a rule-based approach to fiscal policy co-ordination at the EC level. Primacy was to be given to a 'community of stability' (*Stabilitätsgemeinschaft*). In effect, two powerful 'stories' confronted each other in the EMU negotiating process. One stressed the danger from faceless and irresponsible technocrats; the other from the fecklessness of politicians.

In practice, these incipient advocacy coalitions offered only a minimal structure to the discourse about EMU and political union. Their glue was normative beliefs about legitimacy derived in particular from the contrasting national political experiences of France and Germany. But these normative beliefs did not necessarily resonate so strongly and vividly in other member states. More seriously, these structures of discourse were not held together by shared causal beliefs. Once it came to the 'technology' of the relationship between EMU and political union the process of bargaining was better characterized by the metaphor of a 'garbage can' (Kingdon 1984).

Following this literature, bargaining about the relationship between EMU and political union appears as extremely messy, fluid, and unpredictable. Key negotiators operated with ill-defined and inconsistent preferences about what should be the appropriate relationship between EMU and political union, most notably in Germany.

- For some, like Hans-Dietrich Genscher, the German Foreign Minister, Chancellor Kohl, and President Mitterrand, EMU was essentially an instrument for creating political union, which was the great historic prize.
- For others, like Hans Tietmeyer, political union was a prerequisite of EMU (the 'coronation' theory of EMU).
- There were different understandings of what political union involved. Did it require a co-ordinated economic strategy at the EC level (with binding rules and sanctions) or fiscal federalism, with the EC having its own taxation and spending powers? What kind of supportive political structures were necessary? A new authority for the European Parliament over a much expanded EC budget, or a concentration of authority in the Council, or a strengthening of the European Commission? Did EMU require a European foreign and security policy, a European police, and a European army as expressions and instruments of political solidarity?
- Other actors, notably in the German Finance Ministry, wanted EMU to be a 'stand-alone' project. It should be judged on its own technical merits, rather than polluted in its operation by introducing extraneous political elements into the negotiations.

Overall, the relationship between structures of discourse and EMU bargaining was complex and variegated. At two levels actors found themselves embedded in knowledge structures that conditioned policy arguments: the 'economist' and 'monetarist' advocacy coalitions on the issue of convergence and monetary union; and an emergent epistemic community on monetary policy. There were also incipient advocacy coalitions based around the French idea of *gouvernement économique* and the German idea of a *Stabilitätsgemeinschaft*. When it comes to explaining why an EMU deal was possible, the emergence of a monetary policy epistemic community illustrates the importance of shared beliefs and knowledge as a basis for co-operative bargaining about monetary policy. More problematic, because of the more adversarial nature of debate, was the forging of agreement around the issues of convergence and legitimation. Here, as we shall see later, the key to change was the willingness of the French negotiators (and of others like the Italians) to reflect critically on their own beliefs and to change them, at least in part, in the light of experience in the 1980s. More seriously, the issue of EMU and political union illustrated a failure of reflection and inquiry to resolve intractable policy controversies. On this issue there was no clear authoritative source of policy expertise, unlike in relation to the issue of monetary policy. Its absence reflected the fact that there was an unclear body of evidence and no set of shared criteria against which to assess contending arguments and develop proposals.

This survey of the structural conditions in which actors operated illustrates the multiplicity and complexity of those conditions. It follows that a single unitary structural explanation for how EMU bargaining was conducted and its substantive outcome cannot be found. There were clearly discernible threads: for instance, German hegemony over monetary policy, the conditioning effects of EC institutional structures, the global financial markets. But one structural condition often acted to blunt the effects of others: for instance, German monetary-policy hegemony was qualified by the way in which the EC institutional rules and styles required a sharing of power. More seriously still, structural conditions provided more than simply the parameters of actor choice. They also offered the materials and tools that actors could use either to reproduce or to transform those structural conditions. Thus EMU could be viewed as a process of reproducing the structural power of the German monetary-policy model at the EC level; of transforming that power by Europeanizing it; or of transforming the power relationship between EC member states and the global financial markets. Structure remains vitally important. But—as this book emphasizes—how actors respond to and use structure is crucial to understanding how an EMU deal was possible and what form it took.

EMU Negotiations as a Strategic Process: Power and Interests

We have focused on the context of policy reflection, learning, and strategy: the historical, institutional, economic, and cognitive factors which prestructured EMU negotiations and helped constitute the practices and behaviour of negotiators. It is now time to identify and analyse the substantive *strategic choices* available to EMU negotiators and the key skills and techniques employed to maximize strategic effectiveness. Study of the EMU negotiations illuminates the role of political leaders as *animateurs*, *ingénieurs*, and strategists. It also throws into relief interaction with officials in devising and implementing tactical game plans: for instance, how to manage European Council, ECOFIN, IGC, or bilateral meetings or how to sell a particular proposal, like the hard ECU plan or a fixed date for stage 3. Co-ordination of tactics was the speciality of pre-negotiation meetings, for instance, of the Wicks Group in London, of the Grosche Group in Bonn, and Delors's EMU group in Brussels. With strategy and tactics we are in the realm of cold deliberation of interests, shrewd assessment of possibilities, artful presentational management, and, above all, the seeking out of influence.

The seeking out of influence constituted an important factor in shaping how actors related to ideas in the negotiating process. Espousal of 'sound' money ideas was by no means always inspired by conviction, even in the case of EC central bankers (Hoffmeyer 1993: 83; Marcussen 1998: 180; Andersen 1994: 11, 205). It was a matter of adopting them in order to be taken seriously in negotiations and to gain influence within them rather than being relegated to the sidelines. The process of taking on board the reigning consensus was shaped by the search for a central leading role in EMU negotiations. Negotiators believed that they ought to appear to believe in these ideas.

EMU as Tactics

Tactics were, above all, about the management of one's direct contacts with other EMU negotiators. They involved such questions as:

- Who should clear what, with whom, when? An example was provided by the organization of a series of visits by senior Bank of England and Treasury officials to EC capitals to sell the 'hard ECU' plan in summer/autumn 1990.
- Who should front particular proposals, when, and how? These questions were addressed in, for instance, the informal 'pre-meetings' of Bundesbank and Danish and Dutch central bank officials before meetings of the Delors Committee.
- Scripting contributions. For this purpose, for instance, Bank of England officials provided detailed briefing for their Governor before meetings of the Delors Committee.
- The management of seating arrangements at the negotiating table. An example was Pöhl's rearrangement of the table for the Committee of EC Central Bank Governors in 1990 to place the newly arrived Tietmeyer some distance behind him rather than at his side. Similarly, the French Foreign Minister Roland Dumas appeared alongside Bérégovoy at the opening meeting of the IGC on EMU in Rome in December 1990.
- The use of 'non-meetings' during coffee breaks, lunches, or dinners. An important role was played by EC Monetary Committee lunches and dinners before meetings of the Committee of EC Central Bank Governors in Basle.

Though they overlap and interact in the process of negotiations, certain broad distinctions can be made between strategy and tactics. Strategy is about using negotiations for political purposes; tactics is about the how of deploying specific people and arguments in the immediate vision of other negotiators (Paret 1986). Strategy involves the skills of intellect and study, the gift of cold deliberation and judicious analysis in an atmosphere of calm reflection. Tactics rest on experience and intuition in handling encounters: a feel for what will and will not work in specific contexts and for when a deal can be struck; skill at reading the faces of adversaries, at deducing their innermost feelings from facial gestures, body posture, or tone of voice; and the quality of emotional and intellectual engagement that one brings to specific encounters. In any reconstruction of negotiations strategy is easier to capture than the complex subtleties and intricate details of tactical manoeuvres. Tactics is that part of negotiations which is basically 'off the record', the realm of presentation management conducted in face-to-face encounters.

A key tactical element in the EMU negotiations was *divide and rule*. This classic Machiavellian tactic appealed to negotiators when they recognized that they were faced with more powerful opponents. It involved the devising of bargaining positions with the objective of dividing these opponents and thereby weakening their strength in the negotiations. Divide and rule was identified by Mitterrand as the tactic being pursued by the new Major government in 1991. By lobbying hard in Paris for the 'hard' ECU the British government was seen as attempting to drive a wedge between the French and German governments on EMU. Bérégovoy's flirtation with the 'hard' ECU in January 1991 was rapidly squashed by Mitterrand. Conversely, by stressing his intent to be at the 'heart of Europe', his more amenable and open style than his predecessor, and his difficulties with his own party, Major was able to persuade Kohl to avoid embarrassing him by pressing for any substantial decisions on the IGC negotiations to be taken at the Luxembourg Council in June 1991. In this way Major retained his freedom of manoeuvre right up to the end of the negotiations. Other examples of divide and rule were provided by British backing for an intergovernmental conception of the political union negotiations, playing off the French against the Dutch and Germans; and by the Anglo-Italian defence policy proposals to counter Franco-German proposals. Major's great successes in the EMU negotiations can be attributed to this sort of tactical skill rather than to wider-ranging strategic skill.

Divide and rule did bear some fruit for British negotiators in 1991. But it faced severe constraints as a useful tactic in the EC and was not widely employed. First, the EC is a very 'information-rich' environment. The transparency of divide and rule in this context is counterproductive. Mitterrand was continually warning the Germans and the Dutch Presidency to avoid making too many concessions to Major in the IGCs. The Dutch proposal for an 'opt-in' for all to stage 3, which was warmly welcomed by Major, was rapidly shot down by concerted Franco-German opposition. This example draws attention to the second constraint on divide and rule as a tactic. It offended against the basic norm of Franco-German relations: that these two countries would work together to produce joint proposals to drive forward European integration. The degree of success enjoyed by divide and rule under Major owed most to the temporary political capital gained by being the successor of Thatcher. By 1992 that capital was almost used up. Within EC negotiations divide and rule was more likely to erode than help build political capital.

Another example of divide and rule was provided by the way in which French and Italian negotiators dealt with German power. They attempted to play off the Federal Chancellor's Office against the German Finance Ministry and the Bundesbank and to enlist the support of Genscher as Foreign Minister to strengthen Kohl's resolve. This strategy was pursued by Umberto Vattani in negotiating the Rome 1 communiqué on EMU, by concentrating on Joachim Bitterlich in the Federal Chancellor's Office. It was also used by the French after the publication of the German Draft Treaty on EMU in February 1991, with the aim of enlisting the Federal Chancellor's Office against what they saw as Germany's infringement of the spirit, if not the substance, of the Rome 1 communiqué. Kohl's response to this strategy was to point to the political realities of coalition politics in Bonn and direct these critics to the Finance Minister. He responded in this way to French attacks on the Finance Minister's withdrawal of the withholding tax in April 1989 and on the German Draft Treaty on EMU.

The Qualities of the Strategist

The hallmark of the political *animateur*, *ingénieur*, and strategist is a refusal to submit to the pressures created by the rush of events and an unremitting search for those elements in the *rebus sic stantibus* that are compatible with vital national interests. As *animateur* the political leader uses personal authority (charisma) and sheer individual will-power to mobilize and galvanize support for, or opposition to, EMU, at home and abroad. Delors, Kohl, Mitterrand, and Thatcher each exemplified these qualities, at least at the level of close colleagues. They were individuals possessed of an instinct for power, who enjoyed possessing it, who exuded self-confidence, and whose will was robust. They also had the qualities of the *ingénieur*, managing the context and the process of negotiation so as to shape and control their pace and outcomes.

As strategists, the object of political leaders is to enhance, retrieve, or retain their freedom of action over the negotiating process and its outcomes, not least by limiting that of others. As we shall see in greater detail, this object took different forms in the case of the EMU negotiations. Thus, French strategic thinking focused on escape from the asymmetrical functioning of the ERM by sharing power with the Bundesbank. German thinking identified the gains from extending the German model of monetary stability to Europe. Italian and French technocrats saw in EMU a means of imposing overdue domestic policy reforms. On the other hand, Mrs Thatcher stressed retention of her freedom to set interest rates as her objective.

Political leaders required two qualities to be effective EMU strategists. First, they had to be able to provide a vision of EMU. Kohl and Mitterrand did so, notably attending to its historical legitimation. This *strategic vision* was based on a powerful emotional engagement that derived from its roots in their personal biographies, in particular their memories of the way in which world war had affected their own lives. It was intellectually located in their reading of history and the common lesson that they drew: that enduring peace depended on eliminating symbols of nationalism from Europe. Secondly, to be effective strategists political leaders also had to possess a sufficient *mastery of EMU issues* to critically challenge the ideas of technicians. Being an effective strategist implied knowledge about EMU. In this respect Andreotti, Kohl, and Mitterrand were very imperfect strategists. The difficult strategic trick was to be capable of imposing political direction on the technicians of economic and monetary policy, whilst at the same time ensuring that a technically sound, viable EMU strategy was put in place.

Initiative, Surprise, and Decisive Points in the EMU Negotiations

Above all, the effective strategist had to have a third quality, besides vision and technical mastery of issues. The political leader had to possess the ability to mobilize attention to, and hurl intellectual arguments against, the decisive points in EMU negotiations. Strategy is bound up with the idea of a co-ordinated, bold, and offensive approach, ensuring that the initiative is not lost to others. Retaining the initiative and the factor of surprise are essential if a negotiator is to impose his or her will on others. In particular, it is important to try to ensure that others negotiate around one's own proposals—as the Bundesbank did in the Delors Committee and later over the negotiation of the draft statute of the ECB. There is strategic value in an early tabling of proposals, a skill traditionally cultivated by French negotiators, central to the working method of the EC Commission and emulated by the Bundesbank over EMU.

Skill in EMU negotiations involved the identification of the key decisive points, both in the spectrum of issues and in time, on which the strategist had to mobilize attention and energy in order to be effective in realizing objectives. Winning on these points was crucial because they determined the future course and outcome of the overall negotiations. In this way the effective negotiator could dislocate the strategy of others. These decisive points were located on the two dimensions of EMU negotiations—the spatial dimension and the temporal dimension. Strategists have to position themselves in the context of the temporal and spatial ordering of negotiations, deciding when to raise issues and when to go for decision and in what relationship to other issues. Thus during the IGC, German Finance Ministry negotiators had to consider what was the appropriate relationship between agreeing a date for stage 2 and determination of the entry conditions for, and content of, that stage. Which came first? The way in which IGC agenda items were sequenced over time shaped the scope to make linkages and involved difficult calculations of when to concede and when to stand firm. These time–space relations at the heart of EMU strategy were also apparent in the question of which issues to handle in non-IGC venues before the IGC began: for instance, excessive deficit and sanctions issues in the EC Monetary Committee, and the ECB statute in the Committee of Central Bank Governors.

As we shall see, for German negotiators the decisive point in the EMU negotiations was the content of stage 3. It was a point that they gained in the Delors Committee. For the British the decisive point became the content of the transitional stage. In developing the 'hard ECU' plan Sir Michael Butler and Paul Richards tried to focus the mind of the British government on the weak point of the Delors Report and seize it as an opportunity to influence the negotiating outcome. For the Italians the decisive point was using their EC Presidency of 1990 to gain agreement on an ambitious European Council communiqué (Rome 1) to provide guidance to, and prestructure the outcomes of, the IGC. The histories of the Delors Committee and of the 'hard ECU' plan provide examples of British strategic failure, notably in terms of timing: a case of too little, too late. French negotiators were, by contrast, much more effective at mobilizing and co-ordinating action against the decisive point of vulnerability in German policy on Europe. They focused on the conflict between the Bundesbank's resistance to European monetary co-ordination and the federal government's commitment to realizing European union. On this point French negotiators were prepared to seize the initiative and be bold. Similarly, French, Italian, and Commission diplomacy identified the insertion of fixed dates for stage 3 as the pressing issue that could only finally be resolved in the context of the European Council in Maastricht at the very end of the negotiations.

Political Leaders as Animateurs, Ingénieurs, and Strategists

Strategy for EMU can be defined as the calculated deployment and co-ordination of political, diplomatic, and economic instruments for the attainment of political aims. These aims were in turn derived from a shrewd and realistic assessment of vital interests. Strategy involves the establishment of these aims; identification of the economic and political prerequisites for their advancement (so that one is sensitized to 'windows of policy opportunity'); clarification of the economic and political requirements for their implementation (like progress with economic convergence or political union); measurement of performance against these requirements; analysis of the capabilities of one's own state and of other member states; prediction of the likely moves of other actors; and charting of a coherent pattern of priorities and a rational course of action. Such a broad and demanding definition makes apparent the enormous difficulties facing political leaders in general in making and implementing strategic choices on EMU. At the core of these difficulties was the correct weighing of attendant economic and political risks. Faced with such risks political leaders were generally prone to hesitate before providing policy direction on EMU negotiations firm enough to be carried out.

A key question is how much EMU strategy was provided by political leadership, and how much of it fell within the domain of central bank and finance ministry officials. Who in practice was responsible for the delineation of EMU strategy and for the process by which strategy was translated into tactical action? Clearly, given that they were ultimately responsible for vital national interests, political leaders were sensitive to the need to exercise overall control over EMU strategy, spelling out key objectives and bottom lines for negotiators. At the same time in every case they were aware of the risks from excessive meddling in operational details, both in terms of the technical credibility of the final EMU bargain and in terms of managing relations with EC finance ministers and central bankers. The way in which this balance was struck varied in detail, depending on the characters, personalities, and career backgrounds of political leaders, on the nature of their domestic political systems and the institutional character of the EC—and, most of all, on the prestige and effectiveness of central bankers, their knowledge of and proximity to the financial markets and the mystique surrounding monetary policy.

Political leaders like Kohl and Mitterrand were unquestionably prepared to act as *animateurs* and to provide strategic vision on EMU. But, given the prestige of central bankers, the arcane mysteries of central banking and their own non-economic and non-commercial backgrounds, they were cautious about attempting to provide political leadership on the detail of EMU issues. Here they lacked the knowledge to provide effective leadership on strategy. They were essentially content to leave to central bankers and finance ministry officials the task of supplying the ideas and techniques with which to build EMU. Kohl and Mitterrand were *animateurs de la victoire*, impressing their will-power on EMU negotiators, rather than leaders who put a distinctive stamp on the substance of EMU issues. Thatcher was the great *animateur de la défiance*, intent on mastering her own economic-policy establishment and relying on her economic adviser, Alan Walters, to flesh out her strategic approach to the ERM and EMU. Her combativeness exerted a price, given that she was forced by circumstances to work alongside the French and Germans. In the end their strategies defeated her. John Major was, by contrast, no *animateur*, either of *victoire* or of *défiance*. He could not even translate his greater experience of economic and monetary policy, as a former Chancellor of the Exchequer, into influence on the substantive outcomes of the EMU negotiations. On the whole, political leaders were on safer ground in seeking to control the pace and organization of the negotiating process, in short acting as the *ingénieurs* of agreement.

EMU as Strategic Choice

Faced with the question of how to conduct EMU negotiations, political leaders were confronted by the need to make strategic choices. In making those choices their object was to maximize their freedom of manoeuvre. The question was which to exclude and which to prioritize in designing an operational EMU strategy. Crucial to this choice was an awareness of the operating norms of the EC and an analysis of one's resources, of the relative capabilities of oneself and of others, and of the likely moves of those others. Basically, EMU negotiators had six main strategic options.

1. *Direct Threat* This strategic choice involved the resort to deterrence. It took two main forms in the EMU negotiations: the threat of wielding the national veto to block progress on EMU (considered by Thatcher in 1988–9); and the counter-threat of exclusion of a 'problem' state or states from the treaty-making process (suggested by Mitterrand in 1989 as a solution to the British problem with EMU). French political leaders had on occasion flirted with the idea of direct threat against Germany: for instance, Mitterrand's consideration of French exit from the ERM in March 1983 as a means of enhancing his freedom of action.

But the use of such threats faced great practical constraints within EC negotiations, given the realities of the distribution of power within the EC and the implications for subsequent influence in other policy areas where support was being sought. Direct threat was only credible given ample resources to put it into effect, if faced with states with less power, and if the potential future costs did not exceed the immediate gains. Hence, as a strategic choice, it did not play a central role in the EMU negotiations. Indeed, by the Luxembourg Council of June 1991 EC heads of state and government were agreed on the principles of 'no veto' and 'no exclusion' as bases for an EMU agreement.

2. *Sustained, Indirect Pressure* This strategic choice was attractive to negotiators when they faced severe limitations on their freedom of action. They lacked the resources to make direct threat credible, and they lacked the moral authority or coercive power to impose their own model of EMU. In this situation they could use sustained political, diplomatic, and economic pressure either to seek progress on EMU or to delay it. This pressure was backed up by the prospect that, if concessions were not forthcoming, negotiators might be forced to resort to direct threat. Indirect pressure involved a heavy reliance on putting one's counterparts under psychological pressure.

This strategic choice was generally attractive to non-German actors. They recognized that they did not have the resources to mount a direct threat to German hegemony over monetary policy. Its consequences might backfire on them. A beleaguered and isolated Germany would be a danger to European security. Delors and his cabinet persistently sought to mobilize the French government to sustain diplomatic pressure on Germany over EMU. In particular, French governments were attracted to this kind of strategy. During the French *cohabitation* of 1986–8 the Elysée (via Dumas) and Jacques Chirac in the Matignon and Edouard Balladur as Finance Minister employed this strategy *vis-à-vis* Germany, especially after the January 1987 ERM crisis. This pressure took the form of the argument that the 'asymmetry' in the functioning of the ERM (with currencies under pressure having to bear the burden of economic adjustment) was economically and politically unsustainable, backed by references to the wider political and economic costs for European union from a collapse of the ERM. Hence reform of the ERM (in the direction of EMU) had to be embraced. Otherwise, progress with other projects for European union, linked to Germany's vital interests (like security and defence co-operation), could be jeopardized. Similarly, in 1990–1 the Elysée put sustained pressure on Kohl to base the EMU agreement on the principle of irreversibility.

From the perspective of blocking or delaying EMU the British government was also attracted to sustained indirect pressure as a strategic choice. In this case the emphasis was on playing up the high economic and political risks associated with the EMU project, with the aim of spreading doubt and uncertainty. A variant of this strategic choice was resort to a protracted 'war of words' against EMU. This approach was attractive when the British negotiators recognized that their resources were too limited to make direct threat a viable option (i.e. the veto); as it became clear that they were likely to have to negotiate on the terms defined by the Delors Report; and as they recognized that EMU was a 'far-off' project so that they could afford to 'play long'. This strategy focused on identifying the weak points in the Delors approach to EMU and waging patient assault against them. The intellectual armoury for this war of words took the form of the Alan Walters' critique of the fundamental fault in the ERM; of a stress on the scale of loss of national sovereignty (especially over fiscal policy) required for a viable monetary union (witness Nigel Lawson's Chatham House speech of 25 January 1989: Lawson 1992: 909–10); and of the degree of economic convergence required (a stress on incorporating real convergence criteria like unemployment).

3. *'Salami-slicing'* This strategic choice was suitable when negotiators possessed limited resources to deploy and were content or prepared to move slowly towards the ultimate goal of EMU. In that case one could treat EMU negotiations as a 'nibbling' or iterative process, a series of successive, opportunistic actions designed to erode German monetary power.

The Bundesbank recognized 'salami-slicing' as the main strategic choice being employed by the EC Commission, particularly Delors, and by the French government. It was evident in the Commission proposals of March 1982 for a stage 2 of the EMS; in the proposals of November 1985 to the IGC preparing the Single European Act; and in the French proposal of November 1987 for a Franco-German Economic Council to be written into the body of the revised Elysée Treaty of 1988. An accumulation of concessions would present the Bundesbank with EMU as a *fait accompli*.

'Salami-slicing' could also be used against the Delors approach to EMU as sketched out in the Delors Report of April 1989. In a variant of this strategic choice, the British government was attracted by the notion of striking a single blow at the weakest point of the Delors approach: the vagueness of provisions about the transition process from stage 1 to stage 3. Hence in November 1989 the British government officially unveiled its 'competing currency' plan, followed in 1990 by the 'hard ECU' plan. The blows were in fact misplaced and mistimed: for EC central bank governors had already rejected a parallel currency in the Delors Report. That rejection was a strong, decisive point of the

Delors approach that they robustly and successfully defended. In short, the British government's flirtation with a 'single salami-slice' against the Delors approach to EMU had very poor prospects of success (as most British negotiators recognized).

4. *'Binding In' Opposition*   This strategic choice was attractive when one was faced with a powerful potential adversary, when equipped with a measure of authority over the potential adversary, but when direct threat and indirect pressure were likely to prove counterproductive.

The most important example of its use was provided by Chancellor Kohl's handling of the Bundesbank. Once the German Presidency of the EC had agreed to use the Hanover Council of June 1988 to establish a committee to study how EMU could be established, the Chancellor's Office evolved a strategy of co-opting the EC central bankers into this exercise, whilst ensuring that a measure of political direction was provided. The fear was that a report from a 'committee of wise men' would be savaged from the sidelines by central bankers, and not least the Bundesbank. Hence the Delors Committee was a formula to 'bind in' EC central bankers and neutralize their criticisms.

This strategy was used by Bonn during the IGC negotiations. The Bundesbank was involved at all points in the preparation and management of German bargaining positions: with Schlüter in the Grosche Group in Bonn, Wolfgang Rieke in the IGC backbench team, and Hans Tietmeyer in the secret Franco-German bilaterals. The intention of the German Finance Ministry was to ensure that the Bundesbank was co-opted in a detailed manner into the negotiations, thereby depriving it of later room for manoeuvre to act as critic of the final treaty.

Similarly, Major's approach to the IGC negotiations involved 'binding in' Eurosceptics by ensuring cabinet solidarity. The presence of Lamont as Chancellor of the Exchequer was in this respect a useful means of appeasing this powerful element in the Conservative Party. The fall of Mrs Thatcher in 1990 had been an object lesson on the need to engineer unity in the party on Europe.

5. *Acting as Honest Broker*   This strategic choice was attractive when negotiators were faced by a dilemma and when they wanted to minimize potential loss of political credit and thereby secure future influence. It could also operate as a cover for pursuing more self-serving ends: in short, be less honest than it at first looked.

Perhaps the best example was provided by officials in the British Treasury, Foreign and Commonwealth Office, Bank of England, and UK Permanent Representation in Brussels. They were confronted by the problem of negotiating in the IGC on the basis of two strategic objectives, defined by the Prime Minister and the Chancellor of the Exchequer: to enter a reserve on participation on stage 3 (the principle of 'no compulsion', accepted by May–June 1991), thereby maintaining future freedom of choice about EMU; and to play a constructive role in the IGC negotiations, working to facilitate an agreement. In the IGC British officials worked assiduously to offset the costs to political influence from taking up this position of reserve by seeking out a role as honest broker.

They were also sensitive to the negotiating leverage that such an approach might give them. This approach was, of course, legitimated by the support of the new Prime Minister, John Major, for constructive engagement. But it also had a life of its own in Whitehall, where officials were sensitive to the importance of rebuilding political credit after the direct threat / 'war of words' / 'salami-slicing' of Thatcher's approach to EMU. Indeed, an honest-broker role fitted well into a traditional Whitehall culture that was consensus-seeking. In negotiations on the Basle and Nyborg agreements and more generally over ERM realignments, before Britain entered the ERM, this honest-broker role was evident. However, it proved more difficult to play in the IGC, not least with Lamont as Chancellor.

The honest-broker role was not confined to British negotiators. French negotiators approached the IGC seeing an opportunity to act as mediators between the Dutch and Germans (with whom they identified themselves) and the Belgians, Italians, and others (whom they wished to be seen to help). They sought out a role as managers of the dilemma between strict convergence and ensuring that all progressed together towards stage 3. This dilemma was handled by a combination of tough convergence criteria and discretion about the trend of public debt. By playing honest broker the French government sought to maximize political credit.

6. *Getting Agreement on a Member State's Own Model for EMU*   This strategic option was appropriate when a member state's resources of economic and monetary power and prestige were clearly superior to those of other negotiators and where its negotiators had the most to lose domestically from an EMU agreement. In particular, others were disposed to emulate the member state's own practices because of superior performance.

At the outset of the Delors Committee's work the Bundesbank made the strategic choice to focus on getting agreement on stage 3 on its own terms rather than letting negotiations focus on different options for earlier stages. The latter approach would enable the French and the Commission to engage in 'salami-slicing' by putting in place intermediary institutions and policies (e.g. an EMF). By initially gaining agreement on what stage 3 should look like (notably an independent ECB with a mandate to pursue price stability) the rest of the negotiations would be provided with a set of criteria by means of which one could better fight off 'salami-slicing'. In this respect the Delors Committee negotiations represented a vital initial success for the Bundesbank in the EMU negotiations.

It was notable that neither the French nor the Commission developed their own model of stage 3 during the deliberations of the Delors Committee. Separately, Jacques de Larosière (for France) and Delors came round early to the view that their proposals on this issue would not carry conviction and credibility. The subsequent attempt of French negotiators to graft the concept of *gouvernement économique* onto stage 3 had only very limited success. British negotiators did, of course, endeavour to develop their own model for EMU: initially the competitive currency plan of Lawson and later the 'hard' ECU plan.

These plans were an attempt to develop powerful counter-proposals based on Britain's power and prestige as an international financial centre. But they failed for three reasons: in not addressing stage 3 they signalled a lack of enthusiasm, at best, and a diversionary tactic, at worst; their market credibility was not matched by monetary-policy credibility; and, not least, their timing was wrong—the initiative was already lost.

This analysis of the six strategic choices available to EMU negotiators yields three conclusions. First, no one strategic choice was suitable for all negotiators, and choices—for instance, of British negotiators—varied over time as well as over space. Negotiators had to reflect on their options against a background of differences in resources of power and prestige and against the constraints imposed by the EC and by various domestic factors. Secondly, there were some clear patterns in strategic choices. Kohl's careful prosecution of the strategy of 'binding in' the Bundesbank was absolutely crucial to the overall effectiveness of the EMU negotiations. Equally decisive for the outcome was the fact that only German negotiators could make effective use of the strategy of getting agreement on their own model for EMU. The reasons were twofold: only the D-Mark had the prestige of being the ERM's anchor currency, consequent on the superior performance of German policies; and the Germans clearly had to make the biggest domestic sacrifice for EMU in giving up the EC's most stable currency. Hence it did not make sensible strategy for others to challenge the fundamental German negotiating position: that the new single currency must be at least as stable as the D-Mark. Finally, direct threat lacked basic credibility. Threat of veto invited counter-threat of exclusion. In the context of the EC's complex, iterative, and 'nested' games it was generally perceived as too high cost a strategy.

One should not lose sight of a further pattern in strategic behaviour that was ultimately crucial to the EMU negotiations. There was a marked preference for sustained indirect diplomatic pressure on German negotiators, notably from the French and from Delors. French negotiators evinced a mastery of the arts of indirect persuasion, its practice enveloped in the carefully nurtured symbolic discourse of President Mitterrand. EMU was an object lesson in the practice of the arts of indirect pressure. The sophisticated employment of psychological pressure was accompanied by darker hints of the potential for ERM breakdown, or enforced exit of the French franc from the ERM, to extract action from the person who would, in the final analysis, have to be the policy leader on EMU— the German Chancellor. Perhaps the most striking conclusion of all is that, the further the ERM developed as a D-Mark zone, the more was indirect pressure used to drive forward progress towards EMU.

EMU as a 'Two-Level' Bargaining Game

An important source of the creative opportunities open to the negotiator derived from the fact that EMU had the attributes of a 'two-level' bargaining game (Putnam 1988: 427–60; Evans *et al.* 1993; Moravcsik 1994). Negotiators had to simultaneously satisfy and reconcile interests on two levels: domestic and EC. The game's parameters were set by the size of domestic 'win-sets': that is, the range of preferences within which EMU bargaining positions could be constructed, concessions made, and a final agreement ratified domestically. These 'win-sets' might be broad or narrow, endowing negotiators with a greater or lesser freedom of manoeuvre. In this respect the starting positions of EMU negotiators were different in Germany and Britain (narrow 'win-sets') from France and Italy (broad). Negotiators were able to extract strategic value from these differences of context by adopting one of two types of strategic behaviour:

- *'binding hands'* in EMU negotiations. Here negotiators stress domestic ratification difficulties (narrow 'win-sets'), seeking to transform domestic political weakness into enhanced external bargaining strength;
- *'cutting slack'*. In this case negotiators employ broad domestic political support for EMU to empower economic and monetary technocrats to push through an agenda of domestic policy reform (using EMU as external discipline).

'Binding hands' was a key aspect of the strategic behaviour of British and German EMU negotiators; the first stressed the divisions within the governing Conservative Party, the second the need to carry the support of the powerful Bundesbank. 'Cutting slack' was a more recognizable component of French and Italian strategy. EMU served the purpose of internal empowerment of technocrats to effect 'overdue' policy change.

The 'two-level' bargaining game draws attention to another feature of strategic behaviour: the way in which EMU negotiators sought to manipulate each others' domestic 'win-set' in order to make an agreement possible on more favourable terms. In the EMU negotiations this behaviour took two forms:

- the use of *'transgovernmental' linkages*. Negotiators sought out the support of potentially like-minded politicians and officials inside one or more other member-state governments. This 'linkage politics' was most striking between negotiators in Paris and Bonn: witness the intimate alliance-building between Dumas and Genscher as French and German Foreign Ministers or between Elysée officials—like Elisabeth Guigou, Hubert Védrine, and Jacques Attali—and Federal Chancellor's Office officials—notably Horst Teltschik, Joachim Bitterlich, and Johannes Ludewig;
- the use of *'cross-level' linkages*. Here negotiators sought to appeal directly to the domestic audiences of other negotiators. An example was Karl-Otto Pöhl's use of a key speech in Paris in January 1990 to spell out the Bundesbank's preconditions for a successful EMU negotiation, in particular French acceptance of central bank independence.

In addition, how EMU negotiators played 'two-level' bargaining games was determined by their personal preferences about leadership styles. They opted for one of three basic styles:

- a 'hawk-like' style. Political leadership on EMU reflected the mind-set of the 'conviction' politician, with consequent risk of isolation in EMU negotiations. An instance was Mrs Thatcher;
- an 'agent' style. Political leadership on EMU was driven by domestic political divisions on the issue and the preference for seeking out a median bargaining position in that context. An instance was Major's choice of combining a reserve on stage 3 with a constructive bargaining position.
- a 'dove-like' style. Political leadership on EMU was based on a mutual concern of negotiators to ensure that each others' domestic standing was not jeopardized by an EMU agreement. Negotiators sought to expand each other's 'win-set'. An instance was provided by Kohl and Mitterrand's handling of Franco-German relations over EMU.

Appropriate leadership style was often an issue of contest. Thus within the Bundesbank Helmut Schlesinger represented a 'hawk-like' style; officials on the international side like Wolfgang Rieke and Peter-Wilhelm Schlüter favoured a 'dove-like' style; whilst, as president, Pöhl resorted to an 'agent' style. In fact, the coexistence of different leadership styles within the same institution could provide negotiating advantage. In the case of the German Finance Ministry the sometimes 'hawk-like' style of Horst Köhler as State Secretary sat alongside the 'dove-like' style of Günther Grosche. These styles complemented each other.

This picture of the strategic dimensions and dynamics of EMU negotiations moves away from their characterization in terms of preferences as simply exogenous 'givens' to negotiators. Preferences are shown to be a dynamic element in negotiations, being redefined and modified by political leaders as they think and act strategically. A notable example was provided by the French government's acceptance of an independent ECB for stage 3, driven by President Mitterrand's strategic analysis of the EMU negotiations. Another important element of strategic dynamics—the process of reformulating one's assessment of optimal outcomes—is captured by the model of EMU negotiations as a 'nested' game.

EMU as a 'Nested' Game

How political leaders behaved strategically over EMU was conditioned by the basic fact that they were playing other games in different arenas. The EMU negotiating game was 'nested' in a wider context, opening up opportunities for political leaders to redefine optimal payoffs. In Tsebelis's words:

contextual factors [the situation in other arenas or bargaining games] influence the payoffs of the actors in one arena, leading to the choice of different strategies; therefore the outcomes of the game are different when contextual factors are taken into account . . . An optimal alternative in one arena (or game) will not necessarily be optimal with respect to the entire network of arenas in which the actor is involved. (Tsebelis 1990: 9)

The EMU negotiation was a 'nested' game in two senses:

- 'nested' inside a network of related games. Two such games were of importance in conditioning perceptions and shaping bargaining opportunities: the successes and problems within the management of the ERM; and the implementation of the single European market programme, notably the agreement of the EC directive on freedom of movement of capital in June 1988;
- 'nested' inside 'higher-order' games: in particular, the strengthening of the Franco-German relationship and the ambition to forge European political union. Crucially, from 1989 onwards, EMU became 'nested' within the 'higher-order' game of German unification, altering perceptions of its significance and value and the way in which its costs and benefits were debated.

Developments within these related and 'higher-order' games opened up opportunities for political leaders to redefine what constituted appropriate strategy and optimal outcomes in EMU negotiations by acting to alter their context. For Kohl in 1991 the achievement of an EMU agreement at Maastricht was at least as important an outcome as the consistency of the precise terms of that agreement with German bargaining positions. It was about securing a newly unified Germany by binding it into the EC and solidifying its relationship to France. For that reason Kohl's most fundamental negotiating position at Maastricht was that EMU had to be 'irreversible'. A clear timetable for EMU had not been part of German positions at the onset of the IGC negotiations.

The way in which the EMU negotiations involved the 'politics of playing nested games' was illustrated by the attempts of French and Italian negotiators to nest German unification in the EMU game in the winter 1989–90. In essence, they sought to establish the conditionality of German unification on an acceleration of progress with EMU. Such a linkage was pressed by Mitterrand on Kohl at their bilateral on 15 February 1990. This linkage was successfully resisted by both Kohl and Genscher. Their formula for linkage took the alternative form of nesting EMU in German unification.

Of crucial importance to the EMU negotiations was the domestic politics of playing nested games. This book traces how differences in EMU strategy at the national level were strongly conditioned by the domestic 'nested' games in which they were embedded. Negotiators faced their own particular constellations of domestic games: electoral games, games of intra-party and coalition party management, games of fiscal policy and structural policy reform, and games of monetary-policy management. Each left its distinctive imprint on the way in which EMU strategy was designed and implemented and on perceptions of optimal outcomes.

EMU Negotiations as a Cognitive Process: Ideas and Knowledge

In game theory and the literature on negotiations there is a recognition that negotiations have a cognitive dimension. But this recognition mainly takes the form of identifying the importance of knowledge with respect to two aspects of the negotiating process: knowledge about the 'rules of the game', procedural and substantive; and knowledge about the attributes and likely moves of other players. These aspects of the EMU negotiations were clearly of great importance. The effectiveness of EMU strategy depended on its being based on an accurate and adequate working knowledge of how the EC worked; and on networking well with the other players so that one had a sure sense of their resolve, of when deals could be struck, and with whom. These kinds of knowledge were the basis of the influence acquired by diplomats like Pierre de Boissieu in the French Foreign Ministry and John Kerr as British Permanent Representative in Brussels. They provided strategic and tactical intelligence. But such knowledge was concerned with the management of 'strategic uncertainty', with intelligence about other players and about the operating rules of negotiations.[9] Though crucial, it was not the only knowledge on which EMU negotiations depended.

In trying to make progress towards agreement, negotiators had to come to grips with each other's background policy 'paradigms': that is, with the way in which differing underlying sets of beliefs, both normative and causal, conditioned EMU bargaining positions. These beliefs operated at different levels and were typically poorly understood by other negotiators. At the deepest level were 'meta-cultural' beliefs (Schoen and Rein 1994: 33–4). Three sets of such beliefs shaped EMU bargaining positions:

- beliefs dealing with the basic principles of legitimacy informing the design and functioning of institutional arrangements. Perhaps the sharpest contrast was between the French republican tradition, which legitimated the political direction of economic power, and a German belief in the need to 'bind Leviathan';
- basic economic policy beliefs. Different normative and causal beliefs were secreted in British market liberalism (especially a belief in the value of an evolutionary, consumer-driven approach to EMU), in the complex set of conservative liberal, social Catholic, and social Radical beliefs in the French case, and in German 'ordo-liberalism';
- beliefs about Europe and about how one's nation related to Europe. These beliefs varied from the different varieties of British and French 'intergovernmentalism' to German and Italian federalist ideas.

These 'meta-cultural' beliefs were the most difficult to reconcile in EMU negotiations and had a habit of resurfacing and generating later controversies. It can be argued that they were the least well integrated in the EMU agreement in Maastricht.

Institutional beliefs (or philosophies) and policy beliefs represented levels that were more amenable to reconciliation. Bodies like central banks, finance min-

---

[9] For this criticism see Iida (1993). But this article fails to come to grips adequately with the cognitive dimension of negotiations.

istries, and the EC Commission had their own sets of beliefs, operating procedures, and styles of argument that informed their positions on EMU. Thus, for instance, whilst the Federal Economics Ministry and the Federal Finance Ministry in Bonn shared certain 'meta-cultural' beliefs about Europe and about the economy, each had a distinctive outlook in EMU negotiations. Institutional identities helped shape how different negotiators saw EMU. But, crucially, EMU negotiators were not simply captives of 'meta-cultural' and institutional beliefs. They were also caught up in the specific policy beliefs that had evolved to deal with EMU as a distinctive set of policy issues. These policy beliefs were more amenable to reconciliation in the dynamics of negotiation, in large part because they were more grounded in evidence and hence more susceptible to a shared learning process.

The Role of Beliefs

Why were beliefs so important in EMU negotiations? Their importance was increased by the uncertainty about the basic macroeconomic and microeconomic functioning of EMU and its likely economic effects. In such a situation of uncertainty negotiators could not treat interests as clearly specified givens but were forced to reflect on them. Beliefs played a vital role as 'road maps' directing interests along a particular track and, to vary the metaphor, as 'lenses', focusing interests on particular policy choices (Odell 1982; Goldstein 1993; Goldstein and Keohane 1993; Cram 1997; McNamara 1998). Beliefs were crucial to understanding how actors came to perceive EMU problems, define vital interests in a certain way, and make particular strategic choices. They influenced what EMU negotiators saw (and failed to see) and how they interpreted what they saw. Hence by identifying and spelling out these beliefs in our case studies we endeavour to understand how EMU negotiators came to define vital interests in certain ways, to focus on particular problems, and to perceive those problems as more or less amenable, more or less intractable, to negotiated solutions. It is also possible to understand why some actors are empowered, others disempowered.

A cognitive approach focusing on the role of beliefs in EMU negotiations is useful in two respects. First, it underlines the power and longevity of preconceptions in the face of evidence and the consequent role of misperception in EMU negotiations. One danger in EMU negotiations was for negotiators to become trapped within their own policy beliefs: to see the actions of others through the lens of domestic political ideas and traditions, conditioning the information that one selected and ignored. Another danger was for negotiators to overestimate their own importance as a source of ideas and influence and as a target for others' influence. To the extent that negotiators were prone to fall prey to such dangers, they became victims of intelligence failures (Jervis 1976). The challenge in the EMU negotiations was to ensure that information about the motives and will of other negotiators was clear, accurate, adequate, carefully interpreted, timely, and not screened out as uncomfortable. This challenge proved most hard to meet in the context of Mrs Thatcher's government. Examples were provided by her government's handling of the Delors Committee and preparations for both the Madrid (1989) and the Rome 1 (1990) European Councils. The defence of established policy could all too easily screen out uncomfortable evidence, with actors becoming captives of their own stereotypes. The case of Mrs Thatcher shows how the firmly held beliefs of a political leader conditioned the quality of intelligence about EMU. It reveals also how they affected the use of, and influence of, particular kinds of policy experts. Where such beliefs took on a pronouncedly ideological character, they impaired participation in the reflection and 'probing' within EMU negotiations (Lindblom 1990).

Secondly, a cognitive approach draws attention to the scope for negotiators to engage in the 'reframing' of EMU problems and issues within the negotiating process. It would be a mistake to see EMU negotiators as simply imprisoned within inherited beliefs. In fact, they were faced by political demands to unblock seemingly intractable controversies over EMU in order to finalize an 'historic' agreement, and by the requirement that any EMU agreement must be technically viable. In consequence, EMU negotiators were under great pressure to resort to inquiry or 'probing' within the negotiating process—as during the Delors Committee (Lindblom 1990; Schoen and Rein 1994). Crucially, the effectiveness of this method of negotiation depended on keeping the intervention of political leaders to a minimum. The scale of policy controversies involved, combined with the nature of the political demands and technical requirements on them, affected the whole approach to the EMU negotiations. There was a strong incentive for EMU negotiators to conceptualize interests, values, and preferences not as the unmovable foundations of their positions but as shaped and corrected *within* an interactive process of inquiry. In short, the EMU negotiations depended on—and to an extent revealed—a willingness to reflect on the way in which issues were framed and the search for means to 'reframe' those issues so that policy controversies could be bridged.

EMU Negotiations as the Probing and Restructuring of Arguments

EMU bargaining had to deal with 'analytic uncertainty' as well as 'strategic uncertainty'. The capacity to design an effective EMU strategy and to strike an EMU agreement depended on more than its political acceptability and 'saleability'. It had to be based on reliable knowledge about what constituted the technical preconditions for a viable EMU and for putting together an impressive and persuasive case for a negotiator's proposals. This knowledge depended on EMU negotiators entering into an activity of inquiry and discourse which went beyond simply discovering the interests and preferences of political leaders by reading their minds. They were involved in a creative activity of designing a viable EMU, probing their own as well as others' beliefs. In short, EMU negotiations had a component of reflection and learning by practitioners *within* the process (Lindblom 1990; Schoen and Rein 1994). It relied little on inputs from academic economists but occurred as part of the social interaction engendered by the negotiating process.

This activity of probing or inquiry was impeded by the fact that EMU negotiators started with different beliefs about how monetary unions were best established and made to function and about how economies actually functioned. As we saw earlier, these beliefs—normative and causal—took the form of different background beliefs, which reflected contrasting cultural and intellectual traditions—like Anglo-Saxon market liberalism and German 'Ordo-liberalism'. In order to make negotiated outcomes possible, EMU negotiators had to come to grips with the beliefs which underpinned each other's negotiating positions. These beliefs—and the intractable policy controversies to which they gave rise—impeded the activity of probing or inquiry.

Despite this constraint EMU negotiators were able to be creative. This creativity took the form of 'frame reflection' and policy learning as negotiators identified means to construct bridges between different belief systems and engaged in a restructuring of policy arguments about EMU (Schoen and Rein 1994). Various factors encouraged this activity within the EMU negotiations.

- The richness of information and mutual trust engendered by the intense interactions that were generated by the institutional 'density' of the EMU negotiating process. That process incorporated the EC Monetary Committee, the Committee of EC Central Bank Governors, ECOFIN, Franco-German bilaterals, and meetings in other international venues. It also included the special institutional venues created for the EMU negotiations: the Delors Committee, the Guigou Group, the IGC, and the special Franco-German bilaterals. The impact of these venues was to make it possible for negotiators to focus on the opportunities for mutual gains from co-operation: to foster a climate of 'win-win' rather than 'win-lose' in EMU negotiations.
- The powerful stimulus to make something happen that came from EC political leaders, notably Kohl, Mitterrand, and Delors. They stimulated a focus on sorting out the problems of the technical viability of EMU by defining it as an historic task whose completion must be made irreversible in order to secure the political unification of Europe. EMU negotiators had to 'solve' the problem defined in these terms by their political leaders.
- Elements of overlap between different belief systems. In particular, the new ascendancy of domestic concepts of *grands équilibres, rigueur,* and *franc stable* in French policy discourse after 1982–3 made it easier to find common ground with German negotiators. Continuity in this French discourse and the personal credibility and duration of office of Jean-Claude Trichet (Director of the Trésor), de Larosière (Governor of the Banque de France) and Bérégovoy (Finance Minister), each an exponent of this discourse, were crucial in supporting a sustained process of inquiry and 'frame reflection'.

- The contextual changes represented by globalization of financial markets, EC capital liberalization, the 'hard' ERM, and the ERM as a D-Mark zone fostered new reflection on reform of the ERM, which in turn reopened inquiry on EMU. They also supported the emergence of a consensus around 'sound' money ideas that underpinned the EMU negotiations.

The processes of probing the conditions for a viable EMU and restructuring of arguments to facilitate an EMU agreement depended on certain negotiating skills: creative skills of 'frame reflection'; skills in 'signalling' to others the negotiator's earnestness in seeking agreement; skills in the arts of formulating an appropriate discourse and symbolic politics; skills in choosing and designing institutional arenas or venues for negotiation; and skills as an 'ideas advocate' or policy entrepreneur.

The context of the EMU negotiations was, as we have seen, conducive to 'frame reflection' and policy learning. Negotiators reflected on, and learnt about, the requirements of an EMU bargain as they negotiated. In the process they became prepared to 'reframe' how they perceived EMU problems and policy issues. This activity of probing policy beliefs—of inquiry—took various forms in the EMU negotiations (Schoen and Rein 1994: chapter 7).

- Faced with strong political pressure to produce an EMU agreement to a timetable, negotiators had a rational interest in reducing miscommunication and intelligence failures. Reliable communication depended on skill in being able to empathize with another negotiator, thereby gaining insight into how he or she framed the policy issues. This requirement for a successful negotiation was highlighted in March 1991 when it became clear just how wide was the gulf between the French and German draft treaties on EMU and how different were interpretations of the Rome 1 communiqué on EMU. The six top-secret Franco-German bilaterals on EMU between April and November 1991 were devoted to constructing a more reliable communication by overcoming mutual blindness about each other's basic beliefs. By such means negotiators were able to reflect on the beliefs held by their counterparts and be better sensitized to the nexus of legitimate values in conflict.
- Faced with deep German reluctance to enter into EMU negotiations, and the tenacity of German beliefs about the terms on which such negotiations were practical, French negotiators, and Delors as President of the EC Commission, had a rational interest in reflecting on the way in which their own actions might have helped to entrench these German views. In short, they were led to consider how their own policy beliefs had helped to create the constraints that impeded EMU negotiations. This insight into their own responsibility for the stalemate on EMU was by no means an easy one to arrive at. But it was a precondition for reframing arguments about EMU so that conditions were more conducive to a negotiated agreement.
- Faced with sharp criticism of the Bundesbank's actions, particularly from Paris, German negotiators were forced to consider whether there were flaws

in the design of the ERM. They identified a rational interest in making sense of these criticisms so that these flaws could be corrected. Evidence of design flaws in the ERM, manifested in 1987, induced German negotiators to try to understand better the minds of the critics and to reflect on how some consistency might be created between French and German beliefs. Similarly, French negotiators were encouraged to reflect on flaws in their own approach to economic policy as their policy beliefs, and the beliefs of others, were tested against economic outcomes. This reflection produced an accentuation of particular elements within French economic policy beliefs (*franc stable*, *grands équilibres*, and *rigueur*) that were compatible with evidence of the superiority of Germany as a model of economic success. Convergence around the notion of stability was critical to the restructuring of policy argument about EMU in 1987–8.

The creative activity of probing and inquiry in order to put in place bridges across different belief systems gave a strongly pragmatic quality to the EMU negotiations. Under political direction to produce an EMU agreement, negotiators learnt to:

- acquire skills as translators between belief systems so that meanings could be understood (whilst not necessarily becoming converted to the other's beliefs);
- discover and use elements common to different beliefs;
- seek out consensual, logically independent criteria for evaluating beliefs and choosing amongst them. For instance, EMU negotiators identified the criterion of economic stability as the basis for such an evaluation, along with the criteria of no exclusion, no compulsion, and no veto to govern entry into stage 3.

But it should be noted, and stressed, that the pragmatic adjustments written into the Maastricht Treaty mitigated rather than eliminated underlying policy controversies. Sharp differences were concealed rather than tackled: for instance, about the legitimation of EMU (French *gouvernement économique* versus German *Stabilitätsgemeinschaft*); or about the meaning and interpretation of provisions on convergence (how strictly criteria were to be interpreted). Those controversies had the potential to resurface, as they did over the stability pact and stability council in 1995–7. 'Frame reflection' was not necessarily the same thing as the abandonment of original 'frames'. For EMU to be finally viable a further sustained effort at 'frame reflection' and policy learning about the substance of stage 3 was to be required after the Treaty had been signed.

EMU Negotiations as 'Signalling' Behaviour

'Signalling' skills are a vital component of 'frame reflection', policy learning and the restructuring of policy argument (Banks 1991; Iida 1993). They take several forms, notably:

- actions designed to persuade others to accept certain preconditions for EMU negotiations (giving reasons why others should shift towards a negotiator's own beliefs);
- actions designed to convince others that the negotiator is in earnest about seeking an EMU agreement (for instance, countering suspicions that a hidden motive is to sabotage negotiations)
- the use by negotiators of certain actions to persuade their counterparts that it is possible to conclude an EMU agreement with them. These actions are designed to demonstrate that the gap between their beliefs about EMU was being bridged and that they were talking a common language.

The first two types of 'signalling' were characteristic of the most powerful players in the EMU negotiations—the German Finance Ministry and the Bundesbank. From the surfacing of the issue of stage 2 of the EMS in March 1982 onwards they consistently spelt out the terms for entering into EMU bargaining, notably full economic convergence, clarity about the content of the final stage, and no challenge to the principle of central bank independence. Once the EMU negotiations had begun, they had to confront the second issue. In Franco-German relations the process of German signalling about the seriousness of their intent to achieve EMU followed a different time-scale at different levels. As early as the Franco-German bilateral meetings of 26th August 1986 in Heidelberg and 27 October 1986 in Frankfurt, Kohl clarified to Mitterrand his intent to move on EMU. But it was as late as August 1989, at the Franco-German Economic Council meeting by the Tegernsee, that the French Finance Minister Bérégovoy became convinced, by Pöhl, that the Bundesbank was serious about EMU. Indeed, in German–Italian relations some Italian officials remained unconvinced about German intentions till the Milan bilateral in October 1991, believing that German demands for tough convergence criteria were a smoke-screen for sabotaging the EMU negotiations. The second type of signalling was evident in Major's programme of visits to EC capitals in 1991. He was signalling a new style of constructive engagement: that a deal on EMU and other IGC matters could be struck with the British.

The third type of signalling was crucial for those states that had to persuade the German government to engage in EMU negotiations. Most notably of all, the restructuring of the argument between the two 'advocacy coalitions' on economic convergence and monetary union was made possible by sustained signals from the French government from 1982–3 onwards about the seriousness of their commitment to financial and monetary stability. The adoption of the 'competitive disinflation' policy and the appointment of de Larosière as governor of the Banque de France reassured German negotiators and provided an incentive for them to believe that economic convergence could be more rapid and sustained than had been assumed. French negotiators began to take policy actions consistent with the 'coronation' theory by setting their own house in order. Traditional German zealots for the 'coronation theory' were also put on the defensive by the speed with which freedom of EC capital movement was agreed in June 1988. It signalled a preparedness to pursue economic convergence. In asking Mitterrand for French agreement to this directive Kohl was asking for a signal from the French government that would enable him to push a relaunch of EMU at the Hanover European Council.

Similarly, faced by worries about the worsening budgetary situation in Italy, the Italian Finance Minister Guido Carli signalled at an IGC ministerial meeting in June 1991 that his government would submit a convergence programme for scrutiny in ECOFIN. This move was designed to counter Dutch criticism of budget laxity, to reassure German negotiators, and to maintain the credibility of Italian negotiators in arguing for flexible rules on convergence.

Delors and Kohl were also sensitive to the importance of signalling in the appointment of the committee to study EMU at Hanover. The presence of the EC central bank governors was a signal that they placed their trust in the reliability of the governors to produce a sound, effective design for EMU. Equally, the presence of Delors as chair signalled an intent to give a political direction to the process. Implicit in this strategy for EMU was a signal of Delors's preparedness to restructure his policy arguments on EMU. That restructuring was reflected in his acceptance of an independent ECB and in his de-emphasizing of fiscal federalism as a requirement for EMU.

At the same time one should not exaggerate the capacity of EMU negotiators to control the process of signalling or view signalling solely as a device for 'reframing' EMU. The lack of coherence and consistency in signalling from Paris, and from Brussels, could make German negotiators uneasy: as, for instance, when Bérégovoy or Edith Cresson attacked the principle of central bank independence in 1988–9, or when in presenting its Draft EMU Treaty of 1991 the French government used the concept of *gouvernement économique* to signal its commitment to the political direction of EMU. Doubts about the seriousness of French commitment to the principles of monetary stability were never removed from the minds of many in Bonn and Frankfurt. Signalling did not necessarily contribute to 'reframing'. It could be used to demonstrate an enduring commitment to a traditional belief (cf. French Socialist belief in the political direction of economic policy)—or one's confusion about 'reframing'. In this respect Mrs Thatcher's signalling was very consistent in rejecting the idea of pragmatic accommodation between different basic beliefs.

EMU Negotiations as the Art of Persuasion: The Role of Symbolic Politics

Arguments about EMU policy could only rarely be resolved by 'hard' economic science. In the absence of determinate evidence from economic and monetary technicians, negotiating skill depended on working through persuasion. Hence rhetorical skills were a vital element in getting others to reflect on their beliefs and to promote policy learning (Majone 1989). As with signalling, they could of course be deployed to hinder as well as expedite progress on EMU. But the key point is that the EMU negotiations were never strictly technocratic, based on the rule of experts. This statement does not, however, imply that the negotiating process satisfactorily opened up debate about the principles that should inform EMU and how it might be realized in institutional terms.

Effective negotiation depended on constructing a language to deploy for persuasive purposes: to hold together domestic support; and to win friends and allies amongst other negotiators. Faced by intractable policy controversies about EMU, political leaders could respond in four ways.

- Attempt to make progress by employing code words or phrases to hide one's real intent and to lure others into making concessions. Thus the term 'asymmetry' was used by Balladur and Chirac in 1986–8 as code for tackling the problem of the power of the Bundesbank. Delors referred to 'reform of the ERM' in the period 1986–7 as code for EMU. In this period he avoided referring to an ECB by name.
- Seek to manufacture unifying symbols which transcend policy controversies. For instance, by redefining EMU as a matter of war or peace in Europe, Mitterrand sought to neutralize criticism of concessions from within the Socialist Party, gain support in the political centre, and identify common ground with German political leaders. Kohl sought to bridge the controversies engendered by German unification in 1989–90 by employing the metaphor of German unification and European unification as two sides of the same coin (Edelmann 1964).
- Create or exploit ambiguity. Thus Major sought to hold together the warring factions within the British Conservative Party by a formula of 'wait-and-see' on entry into stage 3.
- Sharpen the rhetorical force with which a negotiator's beliefs are promoted, particularly in the way that the agenda is set out. Mrs Thatcher pursued this confrontational model of discourse, notably in her Bruges speech of 1989, with its emphasis on voluntary co-operation amongst sovereign states.

The first and third of these modes of discourse involved a concern with historical legitimation, whether of support for, or opposition to, EMU. This discourse was heavy with symbolism: for instance, Mitterrand's use of the Charlemagne myth, from 1987 onwards, to stress the shared historic roots on which Franco-German reconciliation and European unity were being built. By contrast, the language of ambiguity was more utilitarian and pragmatic. It carried the long-term risk of cultivating an image of indecisive leadership.

Rhetoric with a high content of symbolic politics was used to vest the mundane aspects of EMU negotiations with a deeper significance. For political leaders like Kohl, Mitterrand, and Thatcher it was central to their attempt to create and manipulate the climate of opinion within which EMU negotiations were conducted. This clothing of EMU in symbolic language took two particular forms.

- Constructing powerful 'causal stories'. They served to name key features of the ERM and EMU (like 'discipline'), to allocate blame for problems (to the 'asymmetry' of the ERM, for instance, or to the failure of member states to 'put their own houses in order'), and to make particular recommendations compelling (Stone 1989).

- Employing vivid metaphors to alter the way in which EMU was perceived. Thus German Finance Minister Gerhard Stoltenberg used the metaphor of 'coronation' to describe monetary union's place in EMU; Kohl employed the metaphor of the two-sided coin to draw attention to the symbiotic relationship of EMU and German unification.

The symbolic politics with which the EMU negotiations were invested had a number of functions.

- To evoke powerful emotional engagement. This could be achieved by reassuring others about the historical role of EMU (for Delors, for instance, a matter of survival or decline for Europe) or by associating oneself with warding off the threat of EMU (for Mrs Thatcher, a matter of protecting sovereignty and national identity against a centralizing and bureaucratic Europe).
- To dramatize an image of leadership competence, wisdom, and authority. EMU became symbolic for Mrs Thatcher's 'conviction politics', for Mitterrand's sense of history, and for Delors's mastery of the EC Commission and of EC agenda-setting.
- To create a rhetorical environment favourable to placing EMU on the agenda and moving monetary policy from the periphery to the core of the EC agenda. This shift was achieved by Delors and others vesting the Single European Act of 1985 and the single European market programme with symbolic importance as legitimation for putting EMU at the top of the agenda. In turn, the single market and EMU opened up the opportunity for Delors to fit them into the broader rhetoric of protecting 'the European model of society' and 'organizing Europe's space'.

In short, EMU negotiations involved activities of persuasion and convincing, using the resources of language to structure and restructure how problems were defined, and seeking out psychological advantage.

EMU Negotiations as the Choice and Design of Institutional Venues and Procedures

A critical focus of EMU negotiations was the question of *how* issues should be handled. Negotiators were conscious that they could shape which issues were handled, and who could shape outcomes, by their choice and design of the institutional venues and procedures in which they would be negotiated (Baumgartner and Jones 1991). Negotiations about institutional venues and procedures became central because they provided ways of framing or reframing the way in which EMU issues were debated. Institutional venues carried with them certain types of belief, argument, and styles of action. By choosing and designing these venues one could privilege one form of discourse about EMU over another. Hence 'venue-hopping' played an important part in the EMU negotiations.

The use of institutional venues to structure policy argument was evident at various stages of the EMU negotiations. First, the choice and design of the Delors Committee in May–June 1988 involved Kohl, Delors, and Mitterrand in shaping the parameters in which the EMU debate would proceed. The Committee met two objectives: first, to co-opt the central bank governors and thereby legitimate EMU and neutralize potential criticism from this powerful quarter; and, secondly, by appointing Delors as chair and a group of other non-central bankers, to provide political direction to the process. Neither the French Finance Ministry nor the Bundesbank welcomed this procedure and would have preferred a different venue. After the Madrid Council had endorsed the Delors Report, the French Presidency established the Guigou Group, composed of foreign ministry as well as finance ministry officials, to prepare the questions for the future IGC on EMU, again a venue designed to sustain political momentum.

Conversely, finance ministry officials responded to the Delors Report and the Guigou Group by seeking to get issues for the future IGC handled in the EC Monetary Committee, notably excessive deficits and sanctions. In a similar way central bankers took up the draft statute for the ECB in the Committee of Central Bank Governors in 1990. The intent was to generate as many policy solutions as possible away from the more politicized framework of an IGC. These institutional venues were a guarantee that EMU would be conceived as a 'technical' problem rather than as a 'political problem'. They facilitated negotiations based on inquiry into the requirements of a viable EMU.

During the Italian EC Presidency Delors, the Elysée, and the Italians sought to achieve a tight co-ordination between the IGCs on EMU and on political union with the aim of neutralizing the power of financial and monetary-policy technocrats over EMU issues. They failed in this objective of giving a leading role to foreign ministry officials. Even then, the presence of foreign ministry officials alongside finance ministry officials in the IGC on EMU induced the Luxembourg and Dutch Presidencies to push work into the EC Monetary Committee and the Committee of Central Bank Governors and, under the Dutch Presidency, to a technical working group of the IGC in which only finance ministry and central bank officials were active. This pattern of distancing and neutralizing foreign ministry officials was replicated in the preparation of EMU negotiating positions at the national level.

Conflict about the choice and design of institutional venues and procedures revealed an underlying bureaucratic politics (Allison 1971) at work within the EMU negotiations. Negotiators were keen to defend their territorial control over policy and to carve out a role as 'gatekeepers', controlling access to the negotiations. This behaviour pattern was most pronounced amongst finance ministries and central banks. 'Bureaucratic turf-fighting' was in turn reinforced by coalition politics. Thus Wim Kok, the Dutch Socialist Finance Minister, kept his Christian

Democrat Prime Minister Ruud Lubbers at arm's length; Theo Waigel as German Finance Minister sought to keep out Genscher. It was also reinforced by personal rivalries: for instance, between Bérégovoy and Dumas in the French government. At the EC level it was evident in the strained relations between the EC Monetary Committee and the EC Commission during the EMU negotiations.

EMU Agenda-Setting: Policy Entrepreneurs as Promoters of Ideas

The dynamics of agenda-setting are only fully captured once one takes on board the role of individuals as energizers of policy change and advocates of ideas. The negotiation of EMU revealed the key role of policy entrepreneurs—whether ministers or officials—in bringing new ideas to bear on the development of policy (Kingdon 1984; Goldstein 1993; Ikenberry 1993). Policy entrepreneurs are not usually or necessarily policy experts who originate policy ideas. They have a self-interest in seeking out opportunities to promote new ideas, initiatives, and alliances which attract attention. That self-interest may be only loosely coupled to the promotion of a particular policy belief. An additional factor at work is calculation of benefit to their own personal status, reputation, career interest, or place in the history books from making use of the idea. In short, policy entrepreneurs energize an idea by translating it for their own or somebody else's use, ensuring that it does not remain on the shelf (Czarniawska and Joerges 1996: 23).

The key contributions of the policy entrepreneur within EMU negotiations were twofold: to spot the appropriate short-run conditions in which to bring forward particular policy proposals to best effect; and to utilize her or his knowledge of procedures and networks for that purpose. This skill involved matching policy ideas to two dimensions of change: identification of a policy problem whose solution had become pressing; and a set of political events which were presented as a favourable opportunity to innovate. Policy entrepreneurs acted as a transmitter of knowledge in EMU negotiations. Their expertise was that of a broker between a policy idea and 'windows of negotiating opportunity'. They performed the function of 'coupling solutions to problems, problems to political forces, and political forces to proposals' (Czarniawska and Joerges 1996: 214).

Policy entrepreneurs emerged at various times and locations in the EMU negotiating process, being sometimes successful and often failing. Notable examples included:

- Tommaso Padoa-Schioppa over stage 2 of the EMS in 1982;
- Edouard Balladur on reform of the EMS in 1987–8;
- Valéry Giscard d'Estaing and Helmut Schmidt in pushing the idea of an ECB in 1988 and of fixed dates for stage 3 in November–December 1991;
- Hans-Dietrich Genscher in the relaunch of EMU during the German Presidency of 1988;
- Kohl with Delors in the design of the committee to study EMU, agreed at the Hanover Council in June 1988;

- Sir Michael Butler in the launch of the British 'hard ECU' plan in 1990;
- the efforts of Whitehall officials in November–December 1990—led by Nigel Wicks—to relaunch the 'hard ECU' plan in draft treaty form, adding provisions relating to the transition and content of a stage 3;
- Umberto Vattani, with Padoa-Schioppa, in getting an ambitious mandate for the IGC on EMU agreed at the Rome 1 European Council in October 1990;
- Graham Bishop in promoting at the EC level the idea of strengthening financial-market discipline as a solution to the problem of excessive deficits, rather than using convergence criteria as a solution;
- Padoa-Schioppa in the final formula for fixing the date for stage 3 at Maastricht.

But it can be argued that it is not the transmission of an idea or proposal into the negotiations that is important so much as the individual who takes it up and allows it to develop beyond a certain position after which it cannot be stopped—or, conversely, takes it off the table. Here we encounter the role of the policy sponsor. The difference between the fate of Butler's and Bishop's proposals in Whitehall was that Butler found a sponsor in Eddie George in the Bank of England: Bishop did not. If Genscher was the entrepreneur for an ECB, Kohl took on the role of sponsor. Entrepreneurship does not get far without sponsorship.

Conclusions

This chapter has tried to address a basic question—how is the process of EMU negotiations to be conceptualized? In clarifying our conceptualization of the EMU negotiations we have established a set of basic points that provide a reference for the empirically based chapters that follow.

- Though EMU negotiations were prestructured in complex ways, *agency mattered*. The EMU negotiating process was characterized by a dialectic of agency and structure.
- Accordingly, it is important to identify the key endogenous variables at work within the EMU negotiating process and not presume that explanations can be found in exogenous variables.
- These endogenous variables can be classified under two broad conceptualizations of the EMU negotiations—as a strategic process and as a cognitive process, including managing institutional venues.
- These conceptualizations are distinct but overlap and interact in the practice of EMU bargaining.
- There is a reciprocal, but non-deterministic, relationship between ideas and interests. Interests are shaped by ideas, and ideas are used to promote interests.

Perhaps most fundamentally of all, we have seen how the EMU negotiations were the story of two overlapping types of activity:

- strategic calculation based on the spelling out of vital interests at stake and attention to the attributes of other players and their likely moves so that a politically acceptable EMU deal could be struck that would reconcile EC and domestic levels and take other negotiating games into consideration;
- 'behind the curtain'—a process of inquiry into the technical requirements of a viable EMU which involved reflection on the cogency of existing policy beliefs and which had the potential to lead on to a redefinition of interests and evolution of positions.

There was, in effect, a complex dialectic at work. Original definitions of strategic interests (typically discovered by officials in EMU negotiations tapping the minds of political leaders) were reshaped by the cognitive process of probing beliefs *within* the bargaining process. In the context of interaction within that process, EMU issues were 'reframed', always with difficulty, and strategic choices reconsidered. But the parameters of negotiation by probing varied across national contexts, the activity of probing being more impaired in the British than the French, German, Italian, or EC Commission contexts. This impairment had its roots in the more ideological basis of 'conviction politics' associated with Mrs Thatcher. It did not, however, prevent Whitehall officials from seeking out every opportunity to shift definitions of interest in a direction more consistent with working out a viable EMU agreement.

Of particular importance to what follows is that this chapter provides us with a framework of questions to pursue in relation to the roles of the British, French, German, and Italian governments and of the EC Commission in the EMU negotiations.

- What role did political leaders play as *animateurs*, *ingénieurs*, and strategists?
- What kinds of strategic choices did they make, and why?
- How did those leaders play the politics of 'nested games', and with what effect?
- What form did 'transgovernmental' and 'cross-level' linkages take, and what role did they play?
- How did EMU negotiators seek to empower themselves to act?
- What role was played by 'frame reflection' within the negotiating process?
- How did negotiators signal their intentions and interpret these signals?
- How important was the design and use of institutional venues for shaping EMU bargaining?
- How did political leaders employ rhetoric and symbolic politics in the EMU negotiations, and with what effect?
- What role was played by policy entrepreneurs in setting the EMU agenda, and how?

These questions are addressed in the empirical chapters that follow.

2

EMU, the Mitterrand Presidency, and French Political Tradition

> Il n'est pas de force au monde, ni de force philosophique, religieuse, d'État, d'argent, de capital, à l'égard de laquelle je ne sois tout à fait libre. Et si j'avais un orgueil à tirer de ma vie, ce serait celui-là.
>
> François Mitterrand

François Mitterrand's contribution to the EMU negotiations leading up to the Maastricht Council was to be immense. His contribution was, first and foremost, strategic. It involved using the substantial resources of his Presidential Office to act as *animateur* on EMU. In this role Mitterrand sought to encourage and enthuse his negotiators, to ensure that he remained their central point of reference, and to do so by placing his views and actions in an historic vision of the interests of the French state. Mitterrand was vital in giving sustained political direction to French negotiating positions, situating them at the interface of international and domestic pressures. His strategic insight and skills were exemplified in other ways: in an unremitting search to master the technicians of economic and monetary policy in the French Finance Ministry, especially the Trésor, a task in which he was aided and abetted by Roland Dumas and Elisabeth Guigou; and in a preoccupation with seizing and retaining the initiative so that he remained the master of the EMU negotiating process, at home and abroad. But, above all, Mitterrand focused on attempting to square his domestic political stakes in European and in economic and monetary policies with his view of EMU as essentially about an historic step in rebalancing international and European monetary power in France's favour. It was a game played out on two levels. This view of EMU—and problem of squaring domestic with international and European interests—set him in a line of continuity with the thinking of Charles de Gaulle, Georges Pompidou, and Valéry Giscard d'Estaing. It reflected the related themes of using EMU to challenge the dominance of the US dollar by establishing a common European position on international monetary reform and of tackling the problem of German monetary power by Europeanizing that power. In pursuing these strategic objectives Mitterrand was situating his Presidential leadership in a cross-party consensus.

Woven into Mitterrand's broad historical and international conception of EMU was his own particular brand of Florentine statesmanship. The label 'Florentine' summed up his reputation for intrigue, for sophisticated political manoeuvring, and for allowing schemes to develop around him (Lacouture

1998). Mitterrand was a cerebral, aloof, and enigmatic figure, carefully observing others, patiently calculating his advantage, and displaying a studied indifference, and often withering contempt, in his personal dealings. It was a reputation that he had earned during his participation as cabinet minister in thirteen governments during the Fourth Republic when his career had been fired by the (failed) ambition to become Prime Minister. Mitterrand's razor-sharp strategic intelligence, honed during these years, was now clothed in, finessed under, and hidden beneath, the mantle of statesmanship conferred by Presidential office after 1981.

But he was far from being simply a tactical schemer and mere opportunist. To the Presidential office Mitterrand also brought a particular personal dignity and style, the bearing of a man of culture who was addicted to the importance of symbols and protecting the fundamental values of the French nation. This statesmanlike quality, allied to his genuine convictions about European unification, was his second great contribution to EMU. EMU was not embraced as a policy of the French Left, for which Mitterrand had acted as spokesman since the 1960s, and especially after the Epinay congress of the new Socialist Party in 1971. It was a project that engaged the status, power, and prestige of France, his role as the person entrusted to watch over the greatness of France. Mitterrand imbued EMU with 'un sens de l'Etat'. It was the expression of 'la France unie', the slogan on which he fought the 1988 Presidential election. By then, on the eve of the Hanover Council in June 1988, at which EMU was relaunched, Mitterrand was the dignified and wise 71-year-old statesman just entering his second seven-year term as President. EMU became bound up in his cultivation of an image as an historic European statesman and as a man uniquely representative of the French people.

In relation to EMU, Presidential office gave Mitterrand the capability to act as supreme arbiter, drawing its political direction into the 'reserved domain' of the Presidency with respect to EC affairs. His profound attachment to the French republican tradition added another ingredient—a belief in 'volonté politique', the role of political will in shaping and guiding events consistent with the interests of the nation. This combination of republican tradition with the ethos of a Presidential office inspired by General Charles de Gaulle lent an heroic style to his conception of leadership (Hayward 1983: 11–20). In his management of the ERM crises of 1983 and of 1992 Mitterrand was preoccupied with showing that politics could triumph over markets, that the fundamental values of the French nation—with which he identified himself—could resist the corrupting force of money. EMU was essentially about the triumph of political will.

To his office Mitterrand also brought personal qualities which defined the way in which he handled EMU. His years in the wartime French Resistance and in the political wilderness between 1958 and 1981 had nurtured qualities of rugged and defiant individualism and the courage of a man who saw himself as solitary and dependent on his own resources and acumen. Mitterrand played his cards very close to his chest on EMU as on so many issues, notably on such questions as dates and linkage to other issues like harmonization of taxation on income from savings. If he placed unqualified trust in anyone, it was in his Foreign Minister and long-standing personal adviser Roland Dumas. In the history of Mitterrand's involvement in the French negotiations on EMU Dumas played the pivotal role as the agent of the President's will.

The Role of Inherited Beliefs and Historical Memories

However heroic his conception of his office and his view on his freedom as an historical actor, Mitterrand was profoundly conditioned by a deeper underlying structure of beliefs and set of historical memories. He had a freedom of manoeuvre in determining how he would locate himself within the complexities of French political tradition and in how he reassembled and combined beliefs and memories in fresh syntheses appropriate to the political context of EMU. But Mitterrand was essentially a political craftsman, dealing with the material of beliefs and memories at hand and using them after 1983 to reinvent himself as a European statesman, with an eye both on re-election and on the history books. These beliefs and memories conditioned the way in which he considered policy options with respect to EMU, the direction in which EMU policy was developed, and the way in which EMU was legitimated. Mitterrand manoeuvred within and across the different beliefs and memories that made up the French tradition, shifting emphasis but always sought out a distinctive profile.

In particular, a set of powerful historical memories shaped how Mitterrand constructed French policy on EMU: notably, 'the spirit of 1789', the sense of a special French role in Europe as the home of values of democratic legitimacy; the intention of escaping from the association of the Left in 1924 and 1936 with financial irresponsibility; and the lessons of the humiliation of France at the hands of Germany in 1870–1 and 1940, namely that French power was best safeguarded by working closely with Germany as the 'motor' of European unification. Above all, EMU was defined in terms of Franco-German reconciliation. It was a means of ensuring that there would never again be war between these two peoples. Each of these memories in its own way conditioned the character of French bargaining positions on EMU. They gave meaning to French demands for a strong 'political pole' in EMU; to the Left's preoccupation with the *franc stable* as a means of establishing a reputation for financial respectability; and to the ambition for French leadership of *construction européenne*. Ultimately Mitterrand's creative political role was framed and conditioned by this structure of historical memories and underlying beliefs.

These beliefs and historical memories were part of an inheritance that Mitterrand shared with his political colleagues and with his administration. They provided a shared domestic discourse on EMU and gave a distinctiveness to the French contribution to the negotiations. At the same time, beneath that unity were secreted complex tensions and manoeuvrings inspired by personal

ambitions and rivalries and a bureaucratic politics within the French core executive. Seen from the outside, from the perspective of negotiators in Brussels,
London, or Bonn, positions on EMU in Paris could seem complex, elusive, and
even Byzantine. But it was not easy to discern rival 'camps' or coalitions, defined
by different beliefs and contending for control of EMU. At times contending
coalitions about economic policy were evident in Paris: notably, during the
Giscard Presidency (1974–81) between those who wished to prioritize economic
stabilization (led by Valéry Giscard d'Estaing) and those who favoured economic expansion (led by Jacques Chirac, the Gaullist leader); under Mitterrand
in 1982–3 over the question of whether France should stay in the ERM; and,
after the negotiation of the Maastricht Treaty, between the advocates of the
'franc fort' and proponents of 'une autre politique'. In the face of recession in
France there was a tendency for economic and monetary policy positions to
polarize into two camps: those who saw in Europe an essential external force for
discipline and modernization; and those, on the Left and on the Right, who
wished to retrieve a greater freedom of manoeuvre for economic expansion. But
this polarization did not occur during the Maastricht negotiations, which took
place against a background of economic expansion and of a 'permissive' domestic consensus about 'European construction' (construction européenne). The
Maastricht negotiations on EMU engendered an impressive unity of French
negotiating positions, which was facilitated by a structure of shared beliefs.

This chapter situates Mitterrand's contribution to EMU within a sketch of the
main underlying beliefs that gave coherence, direction, and legitimacy to French
bargaining positions on EMU. It goes on to identify the main traditions of economic policy belief and their implications for EMU. These beliefs are in turn
related to the main institutional structures of the French state, notably the
Inspectorate of Finance (Inspection des Finances), the Trésor, and the Foreign
Ministry. In particular, it is argued that the striking unity of French bargaining
positions derived from a common acknowledgement that France's vital interest
in EMU was defined by the problem of German monetary power in Europe and
the larger problem of rebalancing international monetary power to limit the
impact of US dollar fluctuations. Central to the definition of French negotiating
objectives were two problems: the irresponsible use of US monetary power; and
the power of the 'overmighty' D-Mark and of its guardian, the Bundesbank,
which was making monetary policy for Europe by reference solely to German
economic interests. EMU was about recreating scope for French leadership by
sharing power at the European level, harnessing Germany's economic strengths
to European objectives. It was also about opening up new opportunities for
French leadership in international monetary reform, in particular to challenge
the power of the US dollar. This external, exchange-rate dimension of EMU was
critical in French negotiating objectives. These shared beliefs provided a powerful inspiration once Mitterrand threw the weight of his Presidential power
behind them. As we shall see, they were by no means new. Indeed, much of their
weight derived from their status as traditional beliefs.

At the same time the complex underlying structure of inherited policy beliefs left fertile ground for tensions and conflicts to breed. Crucially, the legitimation of EMU remained a difficult problem for French negotiators. This problem was anticipated during the Maastricht negotiations, not least in French emphasis on a strong 'political pole' to engage in dialogue with, and balance, the 'monetary pole' of EMU represented by an independent European Central Bank and its monetary 'technocrats'. The acute seriousness of the problem of legitimation was to be underlined later, particularly with the narrow margin of victory for the 'yes' vote in the Maastricht referendum of September 1992 and with the social and political crisis of December 1995. There was a deep-seated tension, unresolved in the Maastricht negotiations, between legitimating EMU as the central agenda item in *construction européenne*—which was fairly uncontentious—and legitimating the kinds of decisions that were made in its name and the process by which those decisions were made. EMU was also a matter of consistency with the values of the republican state. Designing it, for strategic reasons, on German terms created a problem of cognitive dissonance between the French republican tradition and *construction européenne* that was to reverberate through the 1990s.

Scope for tension and conflict was also implicit in the lack of a single, ascendant, and uncontested economic policy belief around which EMU negotiating positions could be constructed. Unlike in Germany there was a set of different economic policy traditions, a situation manifested by the gyrations in economic practice during the period 1968–83. This situation generated an external perception, especially in Bonn and Frankfurt, that French bargaining positions were not to be relied on, for instance in relation to the primacy of economic stability. In fact, this perception was more accurate in relation to the political level than the administrative level. The Trésor in the French Finance Ministry was, as we shall see, united around a set of core policy beliefs that were 'conservative liberal' in the French tradition. The ascendancy of this directorate (*direction*) was a reliable signal that such values as budgetary discipline (*rigueur*), the stability of the franc (a *franc stable*), and respect for external constraints would guide policy on EMU. But, as the early period of the Mitterrand Presidency most clearly illustrated, *dirigiste* ideas, social Catholicism, and social Radicalism competed for political attention in Paris. Each in its own way was more inspired by Keynesianism and uncomfortable with 'purist' German economic policy prescriptions. Pierre Mendès France was the principal ghost of the Left at the EMU feast, sounding a note of caution and reserve to which—as will become clear later—Pierre Bérégovoy, the Finance Minister, was most acutely sensitive.

Within this complex field of ideological forces individual French politicians and officials mapped out and redrew their particular positions on EMU, shaped by their specific social and cultural backgrounds, by the nature of their career patterns, and by their personal outlooks and ambitions. In effect, each constructed his or her own story of EMU out of the available ideas. Thus, though Giscard d'Estaing and Jacques Rueff were part of the same 'conservative-liberal' economic policy tradition, their views on EMU in the 1960s were by no means identical. But, within the French administration, this individualism of inter-pretation was disciplined, not anarchic. It was subordinated to a deference to the authority of the presidency as the supreme incarnation of the values of the republic. Professionally, Trésor and Foreign Ministry officials were dedicated to service of the state ('*servir L'État*'). As Article 20 of the Constitution of 1958 reminded them, they were 'at the disposal' of the government. Ultimately, the process of arbitration (*arbitrage*) in relation to EMU centred on the President and privileged his advisers in the Elysée. Presidential leadership by Mitterrand can lay claim to be the dominant characteristic of French negotiation of EMU. The President provided the essential discipline for the French government to prepare coherent and effective bargaining positions. But it should be noted that Presidential arbitration was set within a framework of competing economic pol-icy beliefs relating to the purpose and design of EMU. The ultimate uncertainty related to the way in which one individual—the President—would choose amongst ideas competing for his attention. This characteristic of the French state was most visible during the period 13–23 March 1983 when the President wavered between remaining in the ERM, and accepting the domestic implica-tions of its disciplines, and exiting the ERM in favour of a different policy ('*une autre politique*'). In the long run this fundamental choice determined whether EMU was a viable strategic option for Mitterrand. It was a defining moment in the whole story of EMU.

The Tradition of the Republican State and EMU

French beliefs about EMU were framed by the implications of the tradition of the republican state for economic and monetary policies. This tradition was in effect a rich store of historical memories into which French politicians and officials were socialized and on which they could draw to inspire policy towards EMU and to reflect on the requirements of its legitimation. Its legacy was com-plex but vital in endowing French bargaining positions with a distinct character. What united French negotiators like Pierre de Boissieu (of the Foreign Ministry) and Jean-Claude Trichet (of the Trésor) during the Maastricht negotiations was a very strong sense of the sovereign nation and of the state as the repository of the values of the nation.

Fundamental to the republican state was the primacy attached to the sover-eign nation as the source of legitimacy. This tradition legitimated a centraliza-tion of power in relation to the exercise of economic and monetary power and the political direction of policy. The task of the state was to ensure the unity of public power in the service of the nation. In strengthening the President and the Prime Minister's power over the executive the Constitution of the Fifth Republic—inspired by General Charles de Gaulle—provided a set of institu-tional structures to ensure that this task was more effectively performed. Article

5 entrusts the President with ensuring that 'the constitution is respected', upholding 'the continuity of the state', and guaranteeing national independence, in effect legitimating a degree of independence of the executive from Parliament. The political and executive strength of the President was reinforced by the 1962 constitutional amendment introducing direct election. Thereafter, French Presidents could legitimately claim to speak for the French nation, to incorporate its long-term interests, and to represent the *grandeur* of France. Article 21 charges the Prime Minister with directing 'the activities of the government'. The outcome was a strengthened capacity for executive leadership, at least as long as the President and Prime Minister came from the same majority. This emphasis on the unity of public power in the service of the nation found its expression in the convention that EC policy fell within the Presidential 'reserved domain'. It was also reflected in the strengthened role of the central co-ordinating mechanism for EC policy, provided by the *Secrétariat Général du Comité Interministériel* (SGCI). Such centralization and capacity for co-ordination provided a different, less open, and pluralistic context for the Maastricht negotiations on EMU from that to be found in Germany.

These mechanisms and practices of executive leadership were seen as indispensable to the 'one and indivisible' republic. As we shall see later, this notion had important implications for the way in which Fifth Republic politicians pictured the design of EMU. Ultimately, the guidelines of economic policy and exchange-rate policy must remain with elected politicians. EMU required a strong 'political pole' to balance the 'monetary pole', a *'gouvernement économique'*. The domestic constitutional source for this republican belief was Article 20, which empowers the government to 'decide on and conduct national policy'. This provision acted as a constitutional impediment to making the Banque de France independent. As the Constitutional Council pointed out in 1993, domestic ratification of the Maastricht Treaty was a precondition for granting independence to the central bank. French politicians and officials had an instinctive preference for speaking of the 'autonomy' of the central bank (Prate 1987). In the classic Trésor formulation, a clear understanding of the autonomy of the Banque de France depended on remembering that there was no other source of authority than the government. The government was at liberty to create a body charged with professional advice and with whom it could engage in dialogue; it might find an 'autonomous' central bank a convenient means for shifting blame for unpopular policies. But, finally, government had the responsibility for policy. The Banque de France was, in the view of a former director of the Trésor Jean-Yves Haberer, best seen as one of several bodies, alongside the *Caisse des dépôts et consignations* and *Crédit foncier*, which formed part of the *'circuit du Trésor'* (Haberer 1973: 38). Characteristic was the careful attention given to the wording of the law of 1973 on the Banque de France by the Finance Minister Valéry Giscard d'Estaing. It was charged with the task of 'looking after' (*veiller sur*) money and credit 'in the framework of the economic and financial policy of the nation'.

With a Socialist President after 1981 and Socialist governments between 1981 and 1986 and then again after 1988, the prospects for a sympathetic view towards central bank independence seemed particularly poor. The French Left carried a store of historical memories, drawn from the experience in government of the 'Cartel des gauches' in 1924 and of the Popular Front in 1936. The Banque de France was reformed in 1936 to tackle the problem of the power of the 'two hundred families' which were associated with the general assembly of the Banque. Fear of the 'mur d'argent' (wall of money) continued to haunt the Left. Hence suspicion of the Banque de France ran deep. The Left felt that it had had a particular historical mission to defend the values of the republic: to ensure that the Banque de France was the 'Banque des Français'. The Banque de France had a different part in French political mythologies from the part played by the Bundesbank in German mythologies underpinning the Maastricht negotiations. In consequence, central bank independence—for both the ECB and the Banque de France—posed difficult intellectual problems for French negotiators. On this point the price of agreement on EMU with Germany was a major concession of principle.

An important element of the republican legacy was the notion of a 'politique volontariste'. The task of government was to impose its will on markets, not to abdicate in the face of those with economic and monetary power. This focus on 'will' was most obvious amongst 'dirigistes' who were to be found on the Right and the Left, including some Gaullists. But the notion of 'l'autorité de l'État', resting on the nation, had a wider resonance in French political culture. It was shared by politicians from such diverse political backgrounds as Chirac and Mitterrand, Edouard Balladur and Bérégovoy. The nation was important and to be respected when government spoke on its behalf. This high valuation of political will was accompanied by a preference for discretion over rules in the conduct of economic and monetary policies. Ultimately, the nation was the source of political values; government had to express, balance, and reconcile those values. It needed to be vested with the power to act on behalf of the nation. Rules were ultimately a matter for political determination. Hence in approaching the Maastricht negotiations French conceptions of the appropriate balance between discretion and rules differed from German conceptions. French politicians like Mitterrand and his Finance Minister Bérégovoy were determined to ensure the primacy of the political level over technocrats.

In another sense too the republican tradition shaped French conceptions about the design of EMU differently from German conceptions. For French negotiators a framework of democratic accountability and control and of transparency were seen as indispensable to the legitimation of EMU. Consistent with the form that the republic had taken under the Fifth Republic, Mitterrand and Bérégovoy focused on strengthening the role of the European Council and of ECOFIN in ensuring that monetary policy of an ECB was balanced with other aspects of the 'policy mix', fiscal and structural. For the Elysée and for the Foreign Ministry (the Quai d'Orsay) the big issue was the role of the European

Council both in controlling the terms of the launch of stage 3 and in setting economic policy guidelines and exchange-rate policy.

The values of the republican tradition—liberty, equality, and fraternity—shaped and constrained French attitudes towards the EMU negotiations in a further way. Fraternity legitimated a whole discourse of solidarity which was influential across the political spectrum and which, in policy terms, was represented by the importance attached to 'social protection'. The minimum wage, labour-market regulation, generous social benefits, and the role of firms in financing social provision were not simply or solely justified as 'socialist'. They were seen as representing the values of the republic. Hence, during the relaunch of EMU, Mitterrand was preoccupied with 'social' Europe. Bérégovoy was particularly exercised by the issue of fiscal harmonization. He, colleagues in the Socialist Party, and his officials sought to counter a problem of tax evasion once freedom of capital movement in the EC was established. The consequence would be fiscal inequity: the tax burden would shift from capital to labour. But the issue of the compatibility of inherited levels of social protection with the requirements of adjustment to EMU (when the exchange rate was finally lost as an adjustment mechanism) was deferred rather than faced up to in the course of the negotiations. Wage and labour-market flexibility and the social costs imposed on businesses were successfully kept off the Maastricht Treaty agenda, only to force their way onto the agenda as the deadline for stage 3 crept nearer in the 1990s.

In the final analysis, the republican tradition endowed the French state with a 'Janus-like' character in relation to economic and monetary policies. One face was represented by the 'one and indivisible' republic, prizing its unity of action, its will and resolution in the face of markets, its capacity for 'heroic' leadership. It was represented by Raymond Poincaré in the 1920s; and by de Gaulle between 1958 and 1969. The other face was more hesitant and timid, sensitive to the potential for social unrest, and prone to concede to sectional pressures. Following the Liberation in 1944, French politicians, including de Gaulle as head of the provisional government, drew back from a policy of budgetary *rigueur*, wage controls, and monetary stability, advocated by Mendès France, in favour of René Pleven's 'policy of trust' in state promotion of economic growth (Kuisel 1981: 128). Historical memories of the legacy of the savage deflation pursued between 1933 and 1936, particularly by the government of Pierre Laval in 1935, underpinned this rejection of priority to monetary stability, along with fear of the strength of the French Communist Party. The risks of social unrest were dramatically underlined by the general strike and protests of May 1968 which brought the Fifth Republic to its knees. Once again, the promotion of economic growth was identified as the panacea for social unrest. From 1969 President Pompidou pursued this strategy, followed by Chirac as Prime Minister (1974–6) under President Giscard d'Estaing. Memories of 1968 deterred French governments in the 1970s, especially Chirac, from pursuing a policy of economic stabilization at the expense of two exits from the 'Snake'. Even Raymond Barre, who as a non-Gaullist Prime Minister between 1976 and 1981 was committed to economic stabilization, hesitated to tighten policy in the face of potential worker militancy and the risk of losses in Assembly and local elections. As leader of the Gaullist party, the RPR (*Rassemblement pour la République*), Chirac continued to oppose stability measures through the Presidency of Giscard d'Estaing. Hence May 1968 and Laval in 1935 were associated in French historical memories with the social and political risks attendant on deflation. Monetary stability had nothing like the historical and symbolic importance as a unifying element behind French attitudes to EMU that it had for Germans. Far more important was the political defence of the republic, a belief that introduced an element of equivocation into the promotion of monetary stability.

The republican tradition helped to shape the mainstream elite view of European integration in general and EMU in particular. The EMU negotiations were about managing *construction européenne* to serve the interests of the French nation: which meant, fundamentally, to secure for its elected leaders scope for the political direction of European economic and monetary policies. Failure to anchor these democratic values in EMU opened up the threat that domestic politicians would use the republican tradition to reject an EMU based on conceding sovereignty to monetary 'technocrats' and 'foreign domination'. This theme was already in place by the Maastricht referendum campaign in the summer of 1992: the Maastricht Treaty as 'the anti-1789', flouting the fundamental principle of inalienable national sovereignty.

French Leadership of Europe: The Primacy to *Construction Européenne*

Greater clarity was given to French negotiating positions on EMU by the ambition to unify Europe around a primacy to Franco-German reconciliation than by any other factor. It was ultimately the decisive factor at work. Its importance derived from the energetic attention and primacy that President Mitterrand gave to *construction européenne*, particularly in his second *septennat* from May 1988 onwards. But its roots went deep into the beliefs that had evolved in the period 1944–50 about French policy towards Europe. The background to those beliefs was provided by the humiliation of German occupation, the catastrophic defeat of 1940, the ravaging of France by the 1914–18 war, and French defeat at the hands of Prussia in 1870–1. The powerful historical factor was the equation of French humiliation and suffering with German power. Hence the prime postwar question for French diplomacy was: what was to be done about German power? By 1950 the French Foreign Minister Robert Schuman had clarified the answer: German power was to be neutralized by harnessing it to the construction of a united Europe, via a sharing of power in common European institutions. To ensure the defence of French interests in this process of European unification it was essential that France assume the role of leadership in the building of Europe and harness Franco-German reconciliation for that purpose.

With the Elysée Treaty of 1963 President de Gaulle provided a different, more direct kind of answer. The form that this answer took reflected de Gaulle's complex attitudes of fascination by, fear of, and admiration for, Germany. These attitudes were informed by his years as a prisoner of war there and his memories of the interwar period (de Gaulle 1971). As Germany was the central problem for French security, the Franco-German relationship had to be established on a new, privileged, and organized footing. For Gaullists Franco-German partnership and reconciliation took on a value in its own right as an alternative to a Europe organized on the supranational terms favoured by Schuman and Monnet. In de Gaulle's words: 'Europe is France and Germany! The others are the extras' (Giesbert 1993: 280). Though he could on occasion resort to the language of a possible 'union' some day between the two peoples, his approach was fundamentally based on a realist view of French interests in Europe.

In contrast, President Mitterrand was keen to differentiate his approach to Germany. The value of this privileged relationship was grounded in its role as the 'motor' for building a unified Europe and in its evocation of shared cultural roots in the Empire of Charlemagne. He was to construct a historical mythology around the Franco-German relationship, harnessing it to their special role in, and responsibility for, negotiating EMU. Mitterrand was happier to situate himself historically as a successor to Schuman than to de Gaulle and as one of the earliest converts in the late 1940s to the cause of European unification.

Though *construction européenne* provided a unifying belief inspiring and legitimating EMU, it rested on contrasting rationales. The first rationale has maintained a hold within the Quai d'Orsay since 1944: the belief that *construction européenne* was about 'controlling' Germany in France's national interest. This belief exemplified a tradition of political realism that could be traced back to Richelieu's policy towards Germany and that found echoes in the thinking of de Gaulle. During the 1950s Foreign Ministry officials like Hervé Alphand, head of the economic department, and Maurice Couve de Murville, head of the political department, had worked to strengthen the 'control' element in French European policy. In particular, for them European integration had an instrumental purpose. It should serve the domestic needs of modernizing French industry so that France could more effectively compete with Germany. The alternative—the pursuit of the German path of trade liberalization—would prematurely expose French weaknesses. Consistent with this view, Olivier Wormser and other Quai d'Orsay officials wanted to make agreement on a customs union as part of the Treaty of Rome conditional on prior harmonization of tax, social security, wage and working conditions provisions. Jean-Marc Boegner, French Permanent Representative from 1961 to 1972, fitted into this Gaullist tradition of risk avoidance. His presence in Brussels at the time of the consideration of the Werner Report on EMU in 1970–1 symbolized an enduring French scepticism about the scope for parallel progress towards political union alongside monetary union. President Mitterrand was careful to distance himself from this conception of European integration, preferring to downplay the theme of 'seizing' power from Germany by means of a monetary union. But, especially within the French Foreign Ministry, the 'control' element was never far from the surface when considering the problem of German monetary power within the EMS.

A different rationale for European integration was ascendant in the French Finance Ministry and in the Planning Commission. Trade liberalization by means of European integration was seen by their officials as a preferred instrument for 'controlled' modernization of the French economy: for improving productivity levels by exposure to the discipline of competition. The customs union, the single market, the ERM, and, then, EMU were means of breaking domestic political, economic, and industrial deadlock by relying on external discipline. In this way Finance Ministry officials provided themselves with new opportunities to force overdue domestic economic changes. By 1989–90 EMU was viewed as an attractive means of institutionalizing the strategy of 'competitive disinflation'. European unification was grafted onto a traditional preoccupation with the value of 'external constraints' within the Trésor. It rested in turn on a particular conception of the nature of French society: as ignoring objective realities and excessively inward-looking and isolationist.

Though Mitterrand was by no means indifferent to the 'control' and 'discipline' rationales for EMU, his central preoccupation as President was with providing an historical and moral legitimation. Its first full statement came with his speech in the Aachen City Hall on 20 October 1987. In these symbolic surroundings Mitterrand focused on the common roots of France and Germany in the Carolingian Empire and on Charlemagne as a model for reuniting the two peoples. Mitterrand was concerned to draw out, and build on, the virtues of both and to stress partnership in building Europe together rather than any element of 'control'. This very long-term historical and visionary rationale recalled de Gaulle's positive reaction in March 1950 to Adenauer's suggestion of Franco-German union, when the General had pointed to the historic occasions when French and Germans had worked together. But in Mitterrand there was a stronger element of moralism and emotionalism in his conception of Europe. EMU was about sharing power on a basis of equality and about putting in place the final building block for political union. For Mitterrand EMU was pre-eminently about an architecture that would provide security and peace for Europe.

For French politicians with the historical and cultural sensitivities of Mitterrand, French leadership of Europe had a further moral dimension which drew its inspiration from their attachment to the republican tradition. They had imbibed an optimistic conception of a special French civilizing role in the world. French language, literature, and art embodied an ideal of universal man, building a new type of community in which people would be ruled by reason, principle, and altruism. Mitterrand's conception of French leadership in Europe was, in part at least, generous and idealistic. French language and culture had a contribution to make to European unification that matched the economic contribution which Germany could make. But the French role extended beyond building a 'Europe of culture'. It involved taking the lead in creating a 'Europe of solidarity' and a 'Europe of citizens'. *Construction européenne* was about creating a model of society (*un espace social européen*) that would represent a contrasting model to those of the USA and South-East Asia. Mitterrand believed in embedding EMU within a 'social' Europe that recognized the rights and dignity of workers and tackled the problem of social exclusion. EMU was not just about peace and security. It was also about building a Europe dedicated to social justice. It was in this sense that his statement of 1980 that 'L'Europe sera socialiste ou ne se fera pas' had an enduring meaning for him (Mitterrand 1980).

Mitterrand's visionary approach to Europe as a European 'of the heart' was important because, as President, he was able to use it to drive EMU. But it was by no means widely shared, either at the political level or in the Foreign and Finance Ministries. Officials like de Boissieu and Trichet had evolved as 'conviction' Europeans, but their conviction stemmed from a realistic view of French national interests. For them, as for Pompidou, European unification was in origin a diplomatic necessity for France, a matter 'of the head' rather than 'of the heart'. The alternative to French leadership of *construction européenne* was a 'German Europe': Europe as a 'D-Mark' zone. An '*écu* zone'[1] was the preferred alternative. Mitterrand presented himself as a 'European of the first hour', less cautious and inhibited than de Gaulle or Pompidou, particularly in his willingness to embrace political union. At the same time these differences of approach were subordinated to a deeper consensus enshrined in Napoléon I's phrase: 'Each state practises the politics of its geography'. Within the French elite the fact that Germany was France's most powerful neighbour conditioned policy towards EMU. There was widespread agreement that French security and prosperity depended on sharing economic and monetary power at the European level with Germany.

Institutionally, the focus of French European policy was provided by two structures: the Economic Co-operation Service (*Service de coopération économique*) of the Foreign Ministry; and the SGCI. Charged with the co-ordination of French negotiating positions in Brussels, and traditionally attached to the Prime Minister, the SGCI was in practice of little importance in relation to EMU. Despite the fact that it had a privileged position within the staffing of the SGCI, the Finance Ministry was adept at keeping the SGCI away from the process of preparing its negotiating positions in Brussels. Its basic arguments were that

[1] French negotiators preferred to use the term '*écu*' rather than ECU. Because of its historical association with a French coinage under the *ancien régime*, it acquired a symbolic importance in associating France with the new European currency. The ECU (European Currency Unit) was, by contrast, a technical term for a 'basket' currency composed of fixed proportions of different Community currencies. In this book French usage of '*écu*' during the EMU negotiations is respected. Giscard was first to seek to seize political capital from promoting the *écu* as the common currency.

ECOFIN was a special structure serviced by the EC Monetary Committee rather than the Committee of Permanent Representatives (COREPER) and that monetary matters were uniquely sensitive within EC affairs. Secretary-Generals of the SGCI gained weight in relation to EMU not from this function but when they combined it with being an adviser to the President. They were important as 'men' of the President: notably, Jean-René Bernard (1969–74) and Elisabeth Guigou (1985–90). Bernard and Guigou gained a weight and authority over EMU that had more to do with their proximity to the President than their function as Secretary-General of the SGCI. Presidents Pompidou and Mitterrand saw EMU as too important to be entrusted to their Prime Ministers. Hence their approach to EMU negotiations involved circumventing the SGCI.

Far more important in relation to EMU was the Economic Co-operation Service which was attached to the Quai d'Orsay's directorate for economic and financial affairs (direction des affaires économiques et financières). It provided a network of EC diplomats who moved between the Service, the SGCI, the Permanent Representation in Brussels, and the French embassies in member states (Lequesne 1993: 78–80). Several of its members were to play a key role in the EMU negotiations: Jean-Claude Paye, as head of the SGCI, during the EMS negotiations in 1978; Luc de La Barre de Nanteuil, Permanent Representative at the time of the IGC on the Single European Act in 1985, was its former head; Jean-Michel Casa, who dealt with EMU in the cabinet of Roland Dumas, had served at the French Permanent Representation in Brussels; Jean Vidal, Permanent Representative from June 1989 to May 1992; and, most importantly of all, Pierre de Boissieu. De Boissieu had been head of the cabinet of EC Commission Vice-President François-Xavier Ortoli from 1978 to 1984 (when the EMS was negotiated), head of the Economic Co-operation Service from 1985 to 1989, and was then director for economic and financial affairs in the Foreign Ministry from 1989 to 1993. He was a key player in the Maastricht negotiations, particularly in relating EMU to the wider strategic and institutional aspects of French policy. De Boissieu and Trichet, director of the Trésor, operated in close co-ordination before and during the IGC negotiations of 1991, with de Boissieu as Dumas's personal representative in the IGC on political union and placed alongside Trichet in the IGC on EMU. De Boissieu came to incarnate the Foreign Ministry view on EMU.

The *Franc Stable*: The Trésor and the Finance Inspectorate

As we have seen, during the interwar and postwar periods French politicians of the Right as well as Left had a record of being prepared to buy domestic social peace at the expense of devaluation and inflation. There was an influential strand of opinion that favoured sustaining economic expansion by means of a competitive real exchange rate and low interest rates, especially for domestic social and political reasons. It was accompanied by a suspicion of the way in which fixed-exchange-rate systems—like Bretton Woods—could confer economic advantage on the dominant currency. Even so, the virtues of the *franc stable* continued to enjoy broad public support in France, creating a tradition that cut across party and institutional boundaries. In international monetary diplomacy French negotiators were the most consistent advocates of fixed nominal exchange rates and the most sustained critics of floating exchange rates. An influential policy belief emerged associating both devaluation and a floating franc with poor financial management, inflation, and a weak currency and the discouragement of international trade and investment.[2]

This tradition was exemplified in French leadership of the 'Gold Bloc' in the 1930s, well after other leading states had abandoned the gold standard; in French advocacy of gold as the basis for a more secure international monetary co-operation in the 1960s; in the search of French diplomats for a European mechanism to prevent exchange-rate volatility after the breakdown of the Bretton Woods system; and in the embrace of the EMS in 1978 and of EMU in the late 1980s. The objective was to mobilize international solidarity behind a more disciplined framework for national policies. French negotiators were disposed to blame the inadequacies of the international monetary system, and later of the 'asymmetric' EMS, for the problems of the French franc rather than to focus on domestic causes. Again in contrast to Germany, there was a widely held view that monetary stability was determined by the quality of international, and European, co-operation. German negotiators argued that monetary stability had first to be built at home.

The *franc stable* had deep roots in French culture and politics. Finance ministers who had successfully put in place policies to secure a *franc stable* enjoyed the most enduring positive reputations: like Poincaré between 1926 and 1928 and Antoine Pinay at the inception of the Fifth Republic. On returning to power in 1958, de Gaulle had been quick to appreciate the value of a *franc stable* and had given firm backing to Pinay (Guillaume 1984). His objective was clear: 'I shall give to France a model franc whose parity will not change just as long as I am there . . .' (de Gaulle 1970). Hence de Gaulle backed the stabilization plan of 1963 against his Prime Minister Pompidou. He located French political and economic weakness in the specific psychology of the French which rebelled against the discipline necessary to fight inflation (Peyrefitte 1994: chapter 14). However problematic the imposition of budgetary *rigueur* and wage discipline in France, French politicians like de Gaulle were quick to recognize that the *franc stable* was the precondition for reconciling and realizing the twin objectives of international prestige and power and of domestic discipline and order. The *franc stable* was recognized as the essential precondition for international and European monetary co-operation and for arguing the French case for monetary reform. More problematic was the question—which divided de Gaulle and Pompidou in 1963—of whether the battle against inflation was an inherently

---

[2] This belief is analysed in the collection of essays in *Du franc Poincaré à l'écu* (1993).

valued instrument for this essentially political purpose or whether the real issue was international competitiveness, in which case the economic performance of other states might justify a more relaxed stance on inflation.

The political weakness of the French state at home and abroad during the 1930s and during the Fourth Republic (1946–58) was attributed by Gaullists to policies that had sacrificed the strength of the franc. Hence the birth of the Fifth Republic was associated with a renewed emphasis on the relationship between monetary power and diplomacy. This relationship was symbolized by the influence of Couve de Murville, an Inspector of Finance, as Foreign Minister (1958–68) and the influence of another Inspector, Jacques Rueff (an earlier mentor of Couve). Both were ardent prophets of gold as a monetary discipline and alternative to the US dollar. Symptomatic of this new policy emphasis was that the inspiration for the stabilization plan of 1963 derived not from Giscard d'Estaing at the Finance Ministry but from Couve de Murville at the Quai d'Orsay and his director of economic and financial affairs, Wormser, from Jean-Maxime Lévêque in the Elysée and, in the background, from Rueff (Saint-Geours 1979: 109–10). From 1965, the Banque de France began to convert its reserves away from dollars to gold. De Gaulle's rather grand view of the merits of gold was summed up in the Council of Ministers on 28 March 1968: gold '. . . alone has the character of immutability, impartiality and universality' (Sedillot 1979: 253). At his press conference of 4 February 1965 he had spoken of gold 'which has no nationality, which is eternally and universally accepted'.

In fact, the *franc stable* could be interpreted as a French tradition that had been disrupted in the interwar and postwar periods. During the nineteenth century the franc had been one of the most stable international currencies, sustained by French attitudes that had been shaped by negative experiences with paper money during the *ancien régime* and the French Revolution. This distrust derived in part from negative experiences with the introduction of paper money during these periods, notably John Law's disastrous experiment in the eighteenth century. It also reflected the values of traditional Catholic and provincial culture: more comfortable with saving than credit, valuing producers over merchants, hostile to financial speculation as a corrupter of values, and preferring that money should have a solid, fixed basis, for instance in gold (Hirsch 1969; Kindleberger 1970, 1984; Sedillot 1989). Both de Gaulle and Mitterrand derived from traditional Catholic milieux, from which they derived a respect for, but also a critical distance from, monetary values. They shared in particular an aversion to foreign-exchange markets and to the idea that the external value of the franc should be determined by market forces (Peyrefitte 1994: chapters 12–15; Stasse 1994). The best insurance against these risks was a trade surplus. Hence the pursuit of a trade surplus took on a special place in the hierarchy of French economic values. It was the precondition for a *franc stable*.

A set of political arguments sustained belief in the *franc stable*. First, there was the argument that France was a nation of small savers—of peasants and shopkeepers—who looked to the state to defend the value of their savings. This argument appealed to the Left as well as the Right. By being seen as 'unsound' with money the Left was forfeiting the support of its natural constituency. Hence Mitterrand's first Socialist Prime Minister, Pierre Mauroy, was determined that his government would break the association between the Left and 'unsound' money, a legacy of the 'cartel of the Left' in 1924 and of the Popular Front of 1936 (Favier and Martin-Roland 1990: 431–2). As Finance Minister, Bérégovoy tried to break this link by claiming that he was the first Finance Minister of the Fifth Republic not to have devalued the franc. The *franc stable* was seen as sensible electoral politics. In his determination to make the Left respectable, Bérégovoy was prepared to tolerate the label the 'Pinay of the Left'. More positively, he sought to associate himself with the figure of Mendès France, the 'man of the Left' most identified with the theme of *rigueur* and for whom he had worked.

The second political argument for the *franc stable* derived from the belief in a French leadership role in *construction européenne* and within the international monetary system. The capacity of French negotiators to play that role effectively in fora like the EC, the IMF, and G7 was seen as undermined by a weak franc. This argument applied with particular force to two key relations—with the USA and with Germany—in which French bargaining positions were motivated by a desire to place constraints on the behaviour of hegemonic powers (Jeanneney 1994). In the absence of a sound currency it was, to say the least, difficult for French negotiators to effectively criticize 'irresponsible' US economic policy management or to credibly present proposals for reform of the international monetary system. In the case of Germany, which prided itself on the strength of the D-Mark, a relationship of mutual trust and genuine partnership was difficult to build if the French were seen as lax in their basic principles of economic management. This foreign policy dimension of the *franc stable* was underlined by the man who as Prime Minister between 1976 and 1981 had presided over a major effort at disinflation, Raymond Barre: 'France had to be able to play an eminent role in the EC and in international affairs. She could not fulfil it without an economy able to sustain competition and without a solid and stable currency.'[3]

The third political rationale for the *franc stable* was provided by historical memory. The interwar period was remembered as a period of 'beggar-my-neighbour' exchange-rate policies that were seen as contributing to deteriorating international relations, monetary instability, and mounting unemployment and as setting the context for the Second World War (Develle 1988). The lesson was that co-operation over exchange rates was indispensable to a prosperous, well-functioning international economic system. From this point of view there was widespread political endorsement of the EMS in 1979 and of the G7 Louvre Agreement in 1987. This kind of historical argument impressed politicians of the generation of Mitterrand, Bérégovoy, and Dumas. *Construction européenne* was

---

[3] Interview with François Furet in *Le Débat*: September 1983: 21.

about avoiding the kinds of conditions that had operated in Europe in the 1930s. Hence the *franc stable* was seen as an indispensable aspect of European unification.

What was also striking was the degree of support for the *franc stable* from French academic economists. There was a widespread view that the exchange rate was not a 'normal' price; that it was special in that its effects were pervasive. In this particular respect French academic economists were uncomfortable with Milton Friedman's version of monetarism. The exchange rate had long been seen as an indispensable macroeconomic discipline for ensuring competitiveness and a strong external trade position. Also, the *franc stable* was viewed as suited to the specific product structure of French exports. On the whole, French firms seemed more sensitive to exchange-rate fluctuations than German. Some quality export sectors, like aerospace and luxury goods, could act as 'price-makers'. But in general French trade was concentrated in 'middle-market' products, like agriculture and mechanical engineering, where there was strong two-way trade with Germany. There was an economic case for arguing that their basic need was for exchange-rate stability (Freudenberg and Unal-Kesenci 1994). On the other hand, the small and medium-sized enterprise sector was always more likely to seek relief from competition by means of devaluation. This political pressure could surface within the employers' main organization, the *patronat* (the *Confédération Nationale du Patronat Français*), and within the Gaullist RPR. But academic economists were broadly agreed in favouring the *franc stable* as an external force to correct the weaknesses within French capitalism, notably amongst small and medium-sized enterprises (SMEs) (Albert 1991).

Finally, French economists were influenced from the 1970s to embrace the cause of the *franc stable* with a new vigour by the exigencies of the international political economy after the collapse of the Bretton Woods system, the oil-price crisis, and the changing specialization within international trade. This re-evaluation of the *franc stable* in the context of the changing terms of trade was reflected in the 'Barre Plan' of September 1976. In addition to taking on monetarist ideas of using money supply to control inflation, Barre as the new Prime Minister and Finance Minister saw in a *franc stable* a means of identifying and reinforcing the most productive and competitive sectors of the French economy. The model was Japan rather than Germany; high French investment rates before the oil crisis persuaded French economists that France could readily adjust to a new form of international specialization that would support a *franc stable*. But this confidence was to prove misplaced. Barre's policy proved increasingly unpopular and its effects were registered in sectors, like coal, steel, and textiles, close to the Socialist Party. Consequently, a Socialist President and an Assembly with a large Socialist majority were returned in 1981, committed to an alternative Keynesian policy of economic 'relaunch'. In 1981–2 economic policy objectives focused on growth, employment creation, and measures of redistribution. The consequences were accelerating inflation, rapid growth of the budget deficit (with major problems of funding it), a deteriorating balance of payments, and two devaluations within the ERM. Notably, the two main economists in the Matignon (the Prime Minister's Office)—Henri Guillaume and Jean Peyrelevade—played a major role in mobilizing support within the administration for a return to *rigueur*. The crucial turning-point of June 1982 involved a new priority of fighting inflation. The next stage was the Presidential decision of March 1983 to devalue for a third time but to stay in the ERM. This harsh experience, followed by Presidential priority to the ERM, emboldened economists to return to the arguments that had been developing during the Barre period. For French economists slow and disrupted learning of the virtues of the *franc stable* had been a costly lesson in terms of time lost in adapting to a new, fast-changing framework of international specialization.

Despite this underlying consensus about the *franc stable* after 1982–3 there was scope for continuing dispute about how such a policy should operate and what were the limits of its acceptability. On the whole, during the Socialist period, academic economists stressed the importance of putting in place the preconditions for a *franc stable*, in particular measures to strengthen the 'real' economy. This theme was developed in the Finance Ministry by the member of Jacques Delors's cabinet responsible for macroeconomics, Jérôme Vignon. Vignon brought together work on improving French competitiveness being undertaken by economists in the forecasting directorate (*Direction du prévision*) of the Finance Ministry (notably by Jacques Mistral and Jacques Régniez), by INSEE (*Institut national de la statistique et des études économiques*, in particular Gilles Oudin), by the Planning Commission (André Gauron), and by CEPII (*Centre d'Études Prospectives et d'Informations Internationales*, especially the work of Michel Aglietta). This work focused on investment in new technologies, changes in wages policy, labour-market flexibility, and measures to promote corporate profitability as means of making a *franc stable* sustainable. By these means France could be provided with a medium-term strategy within the framework of the ERM without being forced into repeated devaluations (Régniez 1995: 603–10). The key was to put in place a policy that would bear down systematically on the rate of inflation and thereby enable France to be competitive *vis-à-vis* Germany.

Later, in the context of the aftermath of German unification, the theme of preconditions for a *franc stable* was to be taken up again. This time French economists focused on interest rates and on the excessive slowness of the *franc stable* policy in tackling the problem of unemployment. High interest rates as a means of maintaining the franc/D-Mark parity were seen as too high a price to pay in the context of domestic recession. By 1991 Bérégovoy was being alerted to the risk of generalized deflation, 1930s-style, by former trusted officials, like Jean-Charles Naouri (his director of cabinet 1984–6) and Claude Rubinowicz (a former cabinet member) (Aeschimann and Riché 1996: 120–5). In October 1991 Bérégovoy boldly cut French interest rates below German rates but, as the Governor of the Banque de France Jacques de Larosière had warned him, was soon forced to reverse the move in order to protect the *franc stable*. The theme of economic costs of the *franc stable*, especially in unemployment, was taken up by the economist Jean-Paul Fitoussi, President of the OFCE (*Observatoire français des conjonctures économiques*) (Fitoussi *et al.* 1992).

This pragmatic, more conditional perspective of economists was less strongly represented in the Trésor, the Foreign Ministry, and the Elyseé. There the social and political rationales were inseparably bound up with, and increasingly driving, the economic. It was another (by then former) member of Delors's cabinet as Finance Minister, Jean-Baptiste de Foucault, who in 1986 coined the term 'competitive disinflation' (*désinflation compétitive*) (*Le Monde*: 8 April 1986). The economic rationale for the *franc stable* was presented as a virtuous alternative to the vicious circle of inflation–crisis–devaluation; 'zero inflation' combined with 'modernization' would ensure a more competitive French industry. But the socio-cultural and political dimensions of the 'competitive disinflation' strategy were now given new emphasis. The socio-cultural rationale derived from the proposition that French society had a tendency to ignore objective constraints and to take refuge in isolationist views which, as globalization spread, were less viable. 'Competitive disinflation' involved a pedagogic role for politicians. Policy must force individuals, employers, and trade unions to confront realities. Above all, the political rationale was designed to evoke a political consensus behind the strategy. Monetary credibility was a prime requirement if the French state was to be able to enhance its international bargaining power, both within G7 about international monetary reform and within the EC on reform of the EMS. *Construction européenne* could not hope to succeed without 'competitive disinflation' as a flanking measure. By sustained pursuit of 'competitive disinflation' France would eventually be able to share in the 'anchor' currency role of Germany. In this way the balance of bargaining power over EC monetary-policy co-ordination could be altered.

This strategy of 'competitive disinflation', with its intertwined political, socio-cultural, and economic rationales, was taken up by the Finance Ministry after 1986. Its internal sponsors were initially Trichet and later Hervé Hannoun as director of Bérégovoy's cabinet from January 1989. In the form that it was developed there it went beyond the arguments of academic economists to stress the role of the *franc stable* as an instrument for forcing structural change on the French economy. The franc/D-Mark parity was treated as fixed, no longer as 'stable but adjustable'. In this sense it became the '*franc fort*' policy. By means of the strategy of 'competitive disinflation' the Finance Ministry was adapting to the political primacy of *construction européenne* under President Mitterrand. In the process the inspiration lost its roots in economic analysis.

Once in command of a strategy that was politically endorsed, the Trésor invested it with political status, intellectual weight, and influence and guaranteed intense loyalty to its prescriptions. It was a directorate with a status second to none in the French administration and with access, via the Finance Inspectorate, to a network to ensure circulation of its key ideas. Above all, the

Trésor possessed an intellectual confidence in its special role as the 'brains trust' for French economic and monetary policies. It sought out influence for its ideas, in which great pride was invested. EMU was the story of trying to sell French ideas to others. The Trésor's influence derived from its special access to the Finance Minister. The normal practice is for his director of cabinet and cabinet member for financial and monetary affairs to be drawn from the Trésor. In addition, the director of the Trésor accompanies the minister to international organizations, thereby acquiring a close intimacy. The Trésor also has a wide influence over appointments across the public and private sectors (Mamou 1988). Its officials invested 'competitive disinflation' with a 'sense of the state', with a Cartesian logic and intellectual elegance, and—via the Finance Inspectorate—with a communications network that gave it status, weight, and influence. During the negotiations of EMU there was no serious rival to 'competitive disinflation', though by 1991 the strains of living with the effects of German unification were beginning to tell. 'Competitive disinflation' was the ideological basis on which the Finance Ministry constructed its bargaining positions. It furnished the Trésor with a renewed intellectual self-confidence after the eclipsing of its role in 1981–3. But, crucially, this intellectual ascendancy depended on political determination that 'competitive disinflation' was in the best interests of France. Ultimately, the Trésor's and Finance Inspectorate's loyalty was defined by their mission of 'servir l'État'.

The Finance Inspectorate was in effect an efficient network for communicating the substance and implications of 'competitive disinflation' across the public and private sectors. Its members could also be drawn on for advice by Trésor officials—like Jean-Baptiste de Foucault. This Inspectorate was one of the key *grands corps* of the French state, and its members traditionally an important element in the Trésor. Its members were to be found in top Trésor and Finance Ministry cabinet posts: notably Jean-Claude Trichet, Hervé Hannoun, Guillaume Hannezo, and François Villeroy de Galhau. They were also well represented in cabinets in other French ministries, in the Elysée, in the SGCI, in the EC Commission and other international organizations, in the leading French banks and representative and regulatory bodies in banking, in the specialized credit institutions (like the *Caisse des dépôts et consignations* and the *Crédit National*), in the Banque de France, and in many important industrial groups. Thus Pascal Lamy was head of Delors's cabinet in Brussels; Thierry Bert, a Deputy Secretary-General of the SGCI; Jacques de Larosière (a former director of the Trésor and managing director of the IMF) Governor of the Banque de France, and Philippe Lagayette a Deputy Governor

But the unity and power of the Finance Inspectorate is easily exaggerated. There was by no means an intellectual uniformity within the Finance Inspectorate, for instance between Michel Rocard and de Larosière on central bank independence. Its members were sometimes divided in party political affiliations, notably with Giscard d'Estaing a leading figure in the UDF, Rocard in the Socialist Party, and Alain Juppé in the RPR. On the other hand, many

Finance Inspectors—like Larre and de Larosière—stressed their neutrality as servants of the national interest. More importantly, Finance Inspectors played tenaciously the particular roles accorded to them. Also, the Inspectorate by no means dominated all the key Trésor posts dealing with the EMS and EMU. Various prominent officials were drawn from outside the Inspectorate, including Michel Camdessus, Daniel Lebègue, Denis Samuel-Lajeunesse, Pierre Duquesne, Ariane Obolensky, Christian Noyer, Anne Le Lorier, Marc-Antoine Autheman, and Sylvain de Forges. But there was a unifying element of respect for Trésor values at work: notably for the *franc stable* and *rigueur*. Hence the Trésor could count on a defence of its positions from across the public–private divide: and, not least, that the economists of the main banks would fall into line behind its positions, particularly on EMU.

Rebalancing Power in the International Monetary System: The Search for Economic Independence from the USA and the Problem of Asymmetry

As we have seen, the *franc stable* involved a preoccupation with the external aspects of monetary policy and a keen sense of the intimate relationship between money and diplomacy. From the 1960s onwards EMU was associated with two notions: of a concerted European approach to external monetary policy to end dependency on the USA and the US dollar as the pivotal international currency; and of strengthened French influence on reform of the international monetary system to base it on a neutral (i.e. 'non-dollar') standard.[4] Underpinning French attitudes was the search for an alternative to the international monetary 'disorder' that began to preoccupy policy from 1965 and for a means of moderating American monetary 'imperialism'. De Gaulle and Couve de Murville—influenced by Rueff—had identified the solution as a return to gold. But Giscard d'Estaing, the more pro-European-minded Finance Minister (1962–6 and 1969–74), favoured EMU as the means to greater economic independence from the USA and to rebalance international monetary power between Europe (where France had more scope to play a leadership role) and the USA (and later Japan). This view was, in the long run, to be far more influential. It gave a distinctive character to French negotiating positions on EMU—a preoccupation with gaining influence over the EC's external exchange rate *vis-à-vis* the US dollar (and later the yen) and with the idea of developing a European 'monetary personality'.

The collapse of the Bretton Woods system and the oil crisis reinforced the preoccupation of Giscard with establishing a new international economic order to work in favour of greater monetary stability. Once elected President in 1974, Giscard sought to reassert French leadership behind this objective by putting it

---

[4] This theme is emphasized in Howarth (1998).

on the agenda of the first G5 meeting, convened at Rambouillet in November 1975. In the same vein President Mitterrand used the Versailles G7 summit of June 1982 to gain agreement on 'the necessity for collective action to stabilize currencies'. He also secured the inclusion of a call for a high-level international monetary conference in the communiqué of the Williamsburg G7 summit in May 1983. Against this background, the Plaza communiqué of September 1985 and the Louvre Accord of February 1987 were interpreted as successes, albeit belated, for French diplomacy. At last, there was a commitment within G7 to stabilize currency markets. By 1985 the Trésor had picked up the idea of 'target zones' as a tougher discipline than the American proposal for 'reference ranges'.

But it was in Europe that Giscard saw the best opportunity to construct a 'zone of monetary stability' and develop a distinct European 'monetary personality' that could negotiate on a basis of equality with the USA. The creation and, from the French perspective, unhappy experience of the 'Snake' as an EC exchange-rate system in the 1970s focused French thinking on the danger that European monetary unification could replicate the problems of the Bretton Woods system. The same kinds of arguments that had been used against Bretton Woods resurfaced in relation to the 'Snake'. Just as the Bretton Woods system had endowed the USA with too much power, so Germany assumed the leadership role in emerging European monetary arrangements. With the Fourcade Plan of September 1974 French negotiators turned their attention to the problem of asymmetry in the functioning of the 'Snake', from which France had had to exit in January. The asymmetry argument united French economists, officials, and politicians behind a notion of fairness in assigning responsibility for intervention to support an exchange-rate system. French criticisms of the 'Snake', and later of the EMS—notably in the Balladur Memorandum of January 1988—focused on basing the system on a neutral pivot defined in terms of a Community average (the European Unit of Account, later the European Currency Unit). Once a country reached its margin against this average, it would be required to intervene—whether its currency was strong or weak. This proposal meant in effect redistributing the obligations entailed in exchange-rate management: increasing the costs of Germany in supporting parities (in the form of liquidity creation) and reducing those faced by France (consequent on depletion of its reserves).

There was broad underlying and consistent agreement that French negotiating positions on EMU should prioritize the problem of asymmetry. In relation to the international monetary system the answer was a strengthened European 'monetary personality' consequent on EMU. But, first, in Europe the problem of asymmetry had to be ended once and for all by putting EMU in place. In that way France could regain some influence over monetary policy both in Europe and globally. EMU was always a 'three-level' game for French negotiators, involving the simultaneous strengthening of domestic policy, European policy, and global interests. Those interests were defined in terms of greater French influence and power; new scope for political leadership of economic and monetary policy, consistent with the republican tradition; and the opportunity to use Europe as an instrument of discipline and modernization at home. In short, a set of beliefs converged to endow French negotiating positions with a firm domestic consensus.

Domestic Economic-Policy Traditions and EMU

Despite this impressive underlying consensus French negotiating positions lacked the support of a single authoritative economic-policy tradition equivalent to German 'ordo-liberalism'. There was a dominant tradition of 'conservative liberalism', represented by the Trésor and the Banque de France, as well as within academic economics, and ascendant in the Quai d'Orsay's directorate for economic and financial affairs. But it did not remain unchallenged. Chirac's economic policies as French Prime Minister between 1974 and 1976 and the Socialist economic 'relaunch' of 1981–2 illustrated its limits. 'Conservative liberalism' lacked the basis in a broad political consensus enjoyed by 'ordo-liberalism'. The republican tradition, with its legitimation of dissent, provided a powerful constraint on an austere liberalism. There were also other economic-policy traditions offering alternative prescriptions for EMU. But, on the other hand, before 1981 Keynesianism was already being discredited, and the re-emphasis on the importance of money in economic management had reinvigorated conservative liberalism. The failure of the economic 'relaunch' provided a powerful learning experience for French elites and underlined this intellectual trend. The main lesson was that French elites were faced with a radically new environment: of globalization of financial markets and of the EMS. Both combined to constrain French elites to accord a new valuation to fostering a 'stability culture' in France. Only in that way could constraint be turned into opportunity. This process of political reflection after 1983 privileged 'conservative liberalism', which was reformulated to take account of this new context of constraint (the EMS and the *franc stable*) and opportunity (*construction européenne* and EMU). It also led to a reformulation of social Radicalism. In the process the tradition of *étatisme* was squeezed out of the mainstream of EMU policy formulation. In this section these main traditions are reviewed in relation to EMU, and the influence of professional economists is assessed.[5]

Conservative Liberalism

The traditional fragmentation and electoral weakness of conservative liberalism at the level of French party politics can lead the observer to seriously underestimate its significance at the level of policy belief within the highest levels of the French state. Politically, its major representatives have been Léon Say, a frequent

---

[5] For a typology of French traditions see Hazareesingh (1994).

Finance Minister during the Third Republic; Poincaré, Georges Bonnet, and Paul Reynaud in the interwar period; and, in the postwar period, Pinay, Maurice Petsche, Barre, and—most importantly—Giscard d'Estaing. Giscard's Republican Party (a key component of the UDF) provided the main party political base for conservative liberalism. His Presidency (1974–81), especially when (1976–81) Barre was simultaneously Prime Minister and Finance Minister, represented the high point of its party political profile.

But the real source of the power and influence of conservative liberalism came from its grip on the Trésor, the Banque de France, the Finance Inspectorate, the Foreign Ministry, and academic economics. Many of its key ideas were developed within the context of the Trésor and Inspectorate, for instance by Rueff between the 1930s and the 1960s; later by Jean-Yves Haberer and Michel Pebereau; and then by Trichet and Hannoun. The long-standing domination of conservative liberalism in academic economics can be traced back to Michel Chevalier (economic adviser to Napoléon III) and Leroy-Beaulieu in the nineteenth century; to René Stourm in the early twentieth century; and to Clement Colson and Louis Germain-Martin in the interwar period. In the postwar period the economists Jean Fourastié, Barre, Edouard Malinvaud, and Christian de Boissieu worked within this tradition. Their teaching and writing, allied to that by Rueff, Charles Rist, and Pebereau, ensured that conservative liberalism retained its position as the orthodoxy of the *École Libre des Sciences Politiques* (reformed in 1945 into the *Institut d'Études Politiques*), in which the overwhelming majority of the administrative elite was trained, and of the Paris Law Faculty. Generations of senior officials imbibed its precepts: Giscard himself; three economic advisers to de Gaulle—Roger Goetze (who was influential as the architect of the 'Pinay–Rueff' Plan of 1958), Jean-Maxime Lévêque (who was influential on the 1963 stabilization plan), and Jean-Marcel Jeanneney (who was influential in persuading de Gaulle not to devalue the franc in 1968); Pebereau (a senior Trésor official before the Socialist period); de Larosière; Haberer, and many others. Malinvaud was particularly influential as director of the forecasting directorate in the Finance Ministry and then (1974–87) as head of INSEE.

With respect to the EMS and EMU, conservative liberalism provided the dominant discourse within the Trésor. Its chief hallmarks were a resistance to Keynesian economic ideas, reflecting especially the legacy of Rueff, and a scepticism about national economic planning (Rueff 1972). Both were rejected as involving the use of the state for reflation. Trésor discourse focused on fiscal '*rigueur*', safeguarding the '*grands équilibres*' (equilibrium in the balance of payments and balance in the budget and between consumption and savings), and the virtues of disinflation. A competitive economy depended on promoting restructuring by exposing actors to the rigours of the market (*assainissement*). The policy preference was for reliance on external constraints to induce economic realism: to trust in the '*force des choses*'. In this respect the *franc stable* was the bedrock of conservative liberalism. Devaluation might be unavoidable in certain circumstances, but the objective of policy was to prevent it. The *franc stable* was indispensable to creating a social order based on a respect for savings and for monetary stability. Hence conservative liberalism saw in the EMS and EMU instruments for securing monetary order and stability by importing fiscal and wage discipline. The pro-Europeanism of Trésor officials derived to a great extent from this belief in Europe as a force for discipline and modernization.

Another theme of conservative liberalism was the emphasis on the virtue of a measure of 'autonomy' in economic and monetary policies so that the values of technical experience and expertise were safeguarded. Though ultimately the political level must decide the policy of the nation, it was important to institutionalize constructive dialogue. This view governed conceptions of the relationship between the Trésor and the Banque de France. It also suggested that Trésor ideas and arguments should be respected by governments. Such respect was better guaranteed when the political level recognized external constraints, in particular by institutionalizing the *franc stable* and disinflation. For that reason the EMS and EMU were valued by conservative liberals as a device for providing both the Trésor and the Banque with a secure relative autonomy.

There was at the same time potential for tension and conflict within conservative liberalism. Banque de France governors and officials tended to be more uncompromising in their advocacy of balanced budgets, notably Wilfrid Baumgartner's tough-minded role as 'guardian of the currency' against Fourth Republic governments. This attitude reflected their greater distance from politics than Trésor officials. They were also more disposed to argue for the independence of the Banque from the Trésor than were Trésor officials. In other words, institutional loyalties and self-interests were important to how conservative liberalism was interpreted. In 1973 Wormser pressed Giscard for more independence; in 1986 Michel Camdessus sought to get Balladur to deliver on the RPR campaign promise to make the Banque independent; whilst by 1988 de Larosière saw in EMU a means to establish the principle of central bank independence in France. But they did not find the Trésor receptive.

A further source of conflict derived from the strains between the conservative and liberal strands of the tradition. It was the combination of these two strands that gave this tradition its distinctive character and its internal tensions. The conservative strand's preoccupation with order was symbolized in the regime of controls that grew up in the postwar period: price controls, exchange controls, and, in particular, the complex administrative system of credit controls (*encadrement du crédit*). They were seen as instruments for containing inflationary pressures and sustaining a *franc stable* without recourse to punitive interest rates or tight money supply. For this reason many Trésor officials and Inspectors were sceptical and worried about the implications of the '*ultra*-liberal' deregulated financial markets of the 1980s (Haberer 1990: 27–36). But the tradition's other strand supported the idea of liberalizing financial markets, including freedom of movement of capital (which was an objective of Rueff). Given that the state had to borrow, it had an interest in reducing the costs of borrowing by supporting the growth of strong and flexible financial markets. It also had an interest in promoting Paris as an international financial centre, able to compete with London and Frankfurt. This case was taken up by Rubinowicz and Naouri in the cabinet of Bérégovoy in 1984. These arguments persuaded a Socialist Finance Minister to embrace a programme of radical financial-market reform, including the creation of a futures market and the objective of freedom of capital movement. Within three years the system of credit controls had been eliminated. The *franc stable* policy depended by 1987 on the policy instrument of interest-rate changes.

In short, during the 1980s globalization and the discipline of the ERM had forced a major shift in the centre of gravity of the conservative-liberal tradition. Its liberalism had been accentuated by the implications of financial-market reform. Global financial markets were embraced as an added domestic discipline, allowing officials like Trichet and Hannoun to claim that there was no serious alternative to competitive disinflation. Credibility in the global financial markets became the litmus test of economic and monetary policy: its indicator the reduction (and eventual elimination) of the interest-rate premium that France had to pay above German rates to attract capital. By the time that EMU came back onto the EC agenda in 1988 this intellectual and policy shift was clearly in place within the Trésor and the Banque de France.

Social Catholicism

Social Catholicism emerged as a popular reformist ideology in the postwar period, dedicated to marrying Catholic social teaching to the values of the republic and, above all, to promoting a spirit of national and European reconciliation. Its early party political vehicle was the *Mouvement Républicain Populaire* (MRP). The MRP provided five Prime Ministers of the Fourth Republic and some of the most prominent pro-European politicians: notably Schuman, who served as Finance Minister, Foreign Minister, and Prime Minister, and Pierre Pflimlin. Its smaller successor, the *Centre des Démocrates Sociaux* (CDS), formed part of the UDF. The policy influence of the CDS within the RPR/UDF was in fact out of proportion to its relative size, particularly in relation to European policy. A pro-European stance is a requirement for RPR/UDF policy in order to keep the CDS on board, all the more so with impending elections. This factor helps explain why Balladur and Chirac sought out an EMU initiative just before the 1988 Presidential election and why they drew back from supporting the 'no' campaign in the Maastricht referendum of September 1992. During the EMS and EMU negotiations the support of the CDS was to be important in keeping the opposition centre-right parties lined up behind the policies of the Mitterrand Presidency.

The other source of influence of social Catholicism derived from its cross-party appeal within the centre ground of French politics. Its precepts influenced Jacques Chaban-Delmas in the Gaullist party and Jacques Delors and Michel

Rocard in the Socialist Party. Chaban-Delmas was Prime Minister during the negotiations about the Werner Plan for EMU. Under his premiership after 1969 two members of his cabinet—Delors and Simon Nora—evolved the reformist 'new society' programme. During this period Delors developed his interest in structural reform, particularly of wage bargaining and labour-market policy, designed to encourage dialogue. Delors remained closely plugged into a social Catholic network. As Finance Minister between 1981 and 1984 he gathered round him in his cabinet figures like de Foucault and Vignon who were firmly in this tradition.

Social Catholicism had a striking influence within the Finance Ministry and the Planning Commission. Its early postwar impact in the Finance Ministry could be attributed to François Bloch-Lainé, director of the Trésor from 1946 to 1953; and later to René Larre, director of the Trésor from 1967–71 during the period of the Werner negotiations and formerly director of cabinet under Pflimlin. In the Planning Commission Pierre Massé's ethical conception of planning and of the need to locate economic policies in a wider framework of social ideas was also influential. It was close to the outlook of many of those close to Delors (who worked for a period in the Planning Commission). De Foucault and Vignon were keen to situate economic policy measures in a wider social, cultural, and political framework which emphasized the themes of economic justice and co-operation. This strain of thinking fitted into Bloch-Lainé's earlier vision of an *économie concertée* and Massé's stress on the principle of *concertation*. Economic policy had to be based on co-operation and dialogue. During the EMU negotiations officials like François Villeroy de Galhau and Sylvain Lemoyne de Forges represented this enduring social Catholic influence within the Trésor.

With respect to the EMS and EMU, social Catholicism was more disposed to an interventionist approach than conservative liberalism. Its early postwar support for a positive role for the state was expressed in an enthusiasm for Keynesian ideas, which were gradually absorbed within the Finance Inspectorate by 1952. Social Catholics like Bloch-Lainé played an important role in this process of conversion to Keynesianism, along with social Radicals like Gruson, Paul Delouvrier, and Gabriel Ardant (Margairaz 1990). Keynesian demand management was seen as an instrument to ameliorate potentially dangerous social tensions by a policy of expansion. It also meant that the Trésor could be transformed into an agent of modernization by acting as 'a banker for the economy' (though in the 1960s Bloch-Lainé, Delors, and others went further in wishing to centralize powers in government away from the Trésor to break the grip of its fiscal conservatism). With the eclipse of Keynesianism and of economic planning in the 1970s, social Catholics turned to two themes: the need to establish an appropriate 'policy mix' in economic and monetary-policy management; and, within that policy mix, the importance of structural policy to promote economic adjustment and modernization. During the EMU negotiations these themes were encapsulated in the notion of establishing a

gouvernement économique within the EC: of a dialogue about the most appropriate policy mix at the European level. Implicit in this notion was a more activist
conception of a strong political 'pole'.

In relation to the EMS and EMU, social Catholicism's pro-Europeanism had
a different basis from conservative liberalism. These policy projects were seen
as endowed with an ethical basis. They were about organizing co-operation,
broadening intellectual horizons and intellectual sympathies, and engaging
interest through dialogue. In essence, the ideas that had formed the intellectual
basis of the work of the Planning Commission were transferred to the EC level.
There was a faith in the capacity of institution-building to alter the way in which
people thought about economic and monetary problems in Europe. There
might be differences of view amongst social Catholics about which EC institution was best able and suited to organize co-operation behind EMU: the EC
Commission (Delors's view) or ECOFIN (the Trésor view). But what united
them was a faith in co-operation and dialogue as the best means for tackling
practical economic and monetary problems in an EMU. Social Catholics differed
from social Radicals in being 'Europeans of the heart'. For them European
unification was sufficiently important for significant concessions of national
interest to be made in the interests of furthering the process.

Social Radicalism

The ideas of progressive Radicalism overlapped with social Catholicism, notably
in the importance ascribed to solidarity. What united them was a more optimistic view of France and the French than was contained in conservative liberalism, whose starting-point was a fear of the social unrest and political turmoil
associated with the republican tradition. Their main points of difference derived
from the secularism of social Radicalism, which saw itself as more deeply rooted
in the republican tradition; from the unequivocal commitment of social
Radicalism to alliance-building with the Left (the principle that there are no enemies on the Left); and from a different attitude to Europe. Above all, from the
1930s onwards social Radicalism was dominated by the figure of Mendès
France. Though he died in 1982, Mendès-France was to leave a powerful legacy
to the French Socialist government (Margairaz 1989).

At no time was social Radicalism the ascendant tradition within the Trésor or
elsewhere in the French administration. But it had powerful contacts and sympathizers there. Within the Finance Ministry and the Finance Inspectorate they
included Simon Nora; Gruson (who headed the service for economic and financial studies, later the forecasting division, in which Rocard worked); Ardant; and
Paul Delouvrier. Along with Georges Boris, who had been Léon Blum's director of cabinet as Finance Minister in 1938, they were the main proselytizers for
Keynesianism. Their common link was to Mendès France who had also served
under Blum in 1938. The attraction of Mendès France derived from the absolute
primacy that he gave to economic requirements and to the way in which he, and

his collaborators Boris and Ardant, challenged the orthodoxy of conservative liberals like Rueff.

But the real strength of social Radicalism came from the powerful political links and influence of Mendès France, within the Radical left (where he inherited the mantle of Edouard Daladier), occasionally to Gaullists (notably Chaban-Delmas), but crucially to Socialists like Gaston Defferre, Mitterrand (who served in his government of 1954) and Rocard.[6] Bérégovoy, who had worked with him in the 1960s, carried Mendès France as a role model with him to the Finance Ministry in 1984. When it came to economic policy, no figure on the French Left did more to define the character of 'the party of movement' in French political life as opposed to 'the party of limits' (the conservative liberals). Social Radicalism was committed to the idea of renovation of French society by means of active political leadership. Consistent with this model Bérégovoy sought to surround himself with 'Young Turks' in 1984: figures like Jean-Charles Naouri (his director of cabinet) and Claude Rubinowicz. His political inclination was to distrust the Trésor; to identify a few key modernizers within the techno-structure; and to take the lead in forcing through change with their help.

With respect to the EMS and EMU, the legacy of social Radicalism was more complex than those of conservative liberalism and social Catholicism. It induced a greater equivocation. As defined by Mendès France, social Radicalism had an austere side; it favoured *rigueur*, symbolized by his resignation from de Gaulle's provisional government in 1945 over this issue. In this respect social Radicalism was a force for order, prioritizing stabilization (Mendès France had praised Poincaré's policy of 1926). Those influenced by this tradition—including Bérégovoy—had, correspondingly, doubts about the sustainability and wisdom of the economic relaunch of the new Socialist government in 1981. But they were inclined to see the ERM as a potentially dangerous constraint on the freedom of a French government to pursue an economically equitable stabilization policy. Social Radicalism insisted on the subordination of currency policy to the larger political requirements of economic expansion and fiscal justice. This perspective suggested exit from the ERM in 1983, albeit temporarily, the position argued by Bérégovoy as Social Affairs Minister; and, later, a priority to reduction of interest rates, a preoccupation of Bérégovoy after 1988. The theme of 'fiscal ethics' was to colour Bérégovoy's approach to EMU in 1988–9. He argued strongly for EC harmonization of taxes on income from savings as a precondition for the introduction of freedom of movement of capital. Otherwise, the shift of savings to low-tax countries would generate fiscal injustice as more of the tax burden would fall on wage earners. This position was classically *mendèsiste*. Just as economic policy should contribute to the creation of a 'social Republic' in the tradition of Jean Jaurès, so EMU should be embedded in a 'social Europe'. Though Mitterrand overruled Bérégovoy on this particular point in 1988, he fully accepted the general argument about EMU and 'social Europe'.

---

[6] On the 'Mendès system' see Lacouture (1984: chapter 14).

In this respect the EMU policy of the French socialist government owed an important intellectual debt to social Radicalism.

A particular problem for Bérégovoy was that Mendès France's social Radicalism had to be reconsidered in the context of the huge changes represented by globalization of financial markets in the 1980s and by the ERM. Mendès France had derived from Keynesianism a legitimation for state intervention in the direction of production and exchange, above all in the name of efficiency and justice. But, once Mitterrand had taken the decision to remain within the ERM, and the powerful constraint of global financial markets was recognized, how was a realistic economic policy to be constructed on the social Radical foundations of *rigueur*, efficiency, and justice? This question was central for Bérégovoy. With his cabinet under Naouri the answer was found in the *mendèsiste* notion of allying the Left with heroic leadership in the battle against inflation and the pursuit of the imperatives of economic efficiency and modernization. In this way the *franc stable* was legitimated and a radical programme of financial market reform put into operation. Financial market reform was to serve the objectives of economic modernization and of reducing the costs of servicing the public debt by lowering interest rates. Mendès France had stressed that economic policy must assimilate the techniques and dynamism of capitalism in order to reform it (Margairaz 1983). It was a case of opposing the 'liberalism of the Left' to the 'conservatism' of the bourgeoisie. Hence he had been a firm opponent of monopoly power.

The attitudes of Bérégovoy and other *mendèsistes* to the EMS and EMU were embedded in a more cautious attitude to *construction européenne* that was associated with social Radicalism. Though in principle pro-European, they were 'Europeans of the head' rather than of the heart. Their caution derived from two concerns: first, as pronounced Anglophiles, admiring Britain's parliamentary tradition and social democratic tradition, their vision of Europe incorporated a necessary role for Britain; and, secondly, European policy commitments had to be consistent with the requirements of a 'social Republic'. For such reasons Mendès France had voted against the Treaty of Rome. The test for European policies was that they be 'just' and 'useful'. The ERM and EMU were, from this point of view, viewed with reservation.

Étatisme

No other French tradition of economic policy can claim the illustrious history of *étatisme*. It can be traced back to the *ancien régime*, particularly to Louis XIV's minister Jean Baptiste Colbert, and to *Bonapartisme*. The teaching of future officials in the Ecole Polytechnique and in the other technical *grandes écoles* perpetuated its values. In the postwar period *étatisme* developed an association with the figure of de Gaulle and his close associate Michel Debré. Debré was the influential architect of the Ecole Nationale d'Administration—ENA—in 1946 and of the constitution of the Fifth Republic, and Prime Minister and Finance

Minister during the 1960s. *Étatisme*'s ethos was maintained in centre-right politics by figures like Philippe Séguin (RPR), who was later to denounce EMU as 'the social Munich', as an abdication before the financial markets and the power of the Bundesbank. Within the Socialist Party it influenced the thinking within Jean-Pierre Chevènement's CERES faction (*Centre d'Études, de Recherches et d'Éducation Socialistes*). Chevènement advocated France's exit from the ERM in March 1983 and opposed the Maastricht Treaty as the 'denationalization of the monetary power' and the 'dismantlement' of the republican state. *Étatisme* had a strong appeal to Gaullists who wished to subordinate policy to the theme of the grandeur and independence of France. It was also attractive to those Socialists whose intellectual roots (unlike those of social Radicals like Mendès France) rested in Marxism; a strong state was required to transform capitalism through public ownership, national economic planning, and redistribution. In his bid for the Presidency Mitterrand had embodied the idea of a rupture with capitalism into the party programme of the Socialist Party, though his own intellectual roots were closer to social Radicalism.

In the early period of the Mitterrand Presidency the Foreign Trade Minister (Michel Jobert, a former Foreign Minister of President Pompidou), the Transport Minister (the Communist Charles Fiterman), and the Research and Industry Minister (Chevènement) were ranged in the ERM-exit camp. Their rhetoric was peppered with the metaphor of economic warfare: France was in a battle for world market share; the state's task to mobilize national resources for this purpose. But *étatisme*'s importance as an economic policy belief depended on Mitterrand's judgement of the value of the alliance with the Communist Party (PCF) and of placating CERES. With Chevènement's resignation and the withdrawal of the PCF ministers, *étatisme* was in full retreat by 1984. Thereafter, the new Socialist government of Laurent Fabius sought to unite around 'modernization'. Socialism's association with *étatisme* gave way to a model inspired by Mendès France: of a Left committed to attacking the privileges of a conservative capitalism in the name of the 'imperatives of economic effectiveness' and to bringing down inflation. In alliance with reformist elements in the techno-structure, Bérégovoy as Finance Minister and Fabius as Prime Minister pursued an agenda of *mendèsisme*: of reforming capitalism by heroic leadership.

Within the administration the influence of *étatisme* was very selective. It had been discredited in the postwar Trésor and the Finance Inspectorate by association with figures like Yves Bouthillier, who had gone on to play a role in the Vichy regime. As we have seen, the ideological ethos of the Trésor and Inspectorate was a complex blend of conservative liberalism and social Catholicism. On the other hand, *étatisme* had more solid roots in the technical corps, like the corps of mining engineers and the corps of construction engineers, and through them in the industry-related ministries, like foreign trade, industry, and transport. During the EMU negotiations there was a strong attempt, led by the Prime Minister, Edith Cresson, herself a former industry minister, to get industrial policy written into the new treaty. This agenda reflected a strongly interventionist outlook within the French industry-related ministries.

With respect to the EMS and EMU, *étatisme* induced scepticism and hostility. These attitudes followed from a profound distrust of markets and the wish to control them in the interests of the unity and power of the state. The state must be in a position to impose its will on markets and those, like central bankers, who operate in these markets. The objective to be served by the exercise of state power could be conceived differently within this tradition: whether the grandeur of France or the requirements of social justice. But the implication was the same. Devaluation was an appropriate instrument of policy: to be used to strengthen the state as an independently premeditated act, as by de Gaulle in 1958 or Pompidou in 1969, or to strengthen social solidarity. The EMS and EMU constrained the freedom of manoeuvre of the French state to achieve its most important objectives. *Étatisme* also conditioned attitudes to the EMS and EMU in a deeper sense. Given that the state's role was to promote national interests, European integration could not aspire to be more than a voluntary process of intergovernmental co-operation, tightly controlled and delimited. Involvement in the ERM could be no more than purely calculative, with the exit option always available; the EMS was not seen as part of a transition to EMU; and EMU was unacceptable as the surrender of national sovereignty in an area of core importance to the state.

But, as we saw above, the policy prescriptions of *étatisme* were rejected in March 1983 by the Mitterrand Presidency. In the process the PCF and CERES were marginalized. Instead, Mitterrand opted to organize economic and monetary policy around his belief in *construction européenne*. That choice left him to manoeuvre between three economic policy traditions: conservative liberalism, social Catholicism, and social Radicalism. Each had its representatives within the French administration, with conservative liberalism dominating within the Trésor and the Banque de France; whilst amongst his political colleagues social Catholicism and social Radicalism were the main competing strands of belief. Mitterrand was not identified with any one of these economic policy beliefs. Indeed, he had no real intellectual interest in professional debates about the technicalities of economic and monetary policy. His conception of economic and monetary policy was fundamentally political and historical. In 1983 Mitterrand opted for a model of a France that was actively engaged in the processes of change at work in the global economy and Europe. The task of political leadership was, in his view, to direct and organize this process, above all by creating a strong 'social Europe' as a counterweight to American economic power. For Mitterrand the *étatiste* alternative was unacceptable: an isolated, introverted, and sullen France that could not be at ease with itself or the world. The choice for the ERM and for EMU was seen as the basic precondition for a wider French leadership role in the management of the global economy.[7]

[7] See Mitterrand's final new-year press conference on 6 January 1995. Details in Aeschimann and Riché (1996: 170–3).

The Influence of Professional Economists on EMU

Overall, a striking feature of French economic debate was a deep suspicion of markets and of money, reflecting the inheritance of Catholicism, of *étatisme*, and of the centralizing tradition of the republic. This inheritance marked the nature of the approach of the Socialist government to EMU in the 1980s. There was a marked strain of inwardness, even introversion, in the debate. This tendency went along with the marginal position of professional economists in the economic policy process. Even conservative liberalism, which had retained a respect for the importance of money, failed to generate influential monetary economists. People like Rueff—and in social Radicalism like Mendès France and Ardant—had not been professional economists, but first and foremost lawyers with an economics training. Noticeably, those categorized as professional economists—like Barre—were often better known for their textbook writing than for path-breaking research at the frontiers of economics or for playing a leading role in international scholarship. The latter roles would have meant a greater exposure of economic debate to Anglo-American, more market-oriented ideas. Essentially academic economics research constituted an international knowledge structure whose axis was Anglo-American. Its weakness in France symbolized and was symptomatic of an introverted economic policy debate.

Till the early 1980s there was in effect a monopoly of economic policy advice in France. The Trésor guarded its role as the 'brains trust', mediating economic policy knowledge to the political realm. At any one time within the Trésor only five to six officials would typically be working on European economic and monetary issues. They had only very basic economics training. The main counterweight was provided by the forecasting division within the Finance Ministry. This division had in turn close links to the economists at INSEE and in the Planning Commission. As Prime Minister, Barre was important in breaking up this monopoly. In 1981 he established the OFCE to act as an independent source of applied policy expertise, alongside new research institutes attached to the employers' organization (CNPF) and the trade unions. Also, in the 1980s the French banks began to build up their economic research departments under, for instance, Jean-Michel Charpin at the BNP and Jean-Paul Betbeze at Crédit Lyonnais. Consequently, a new body of professional economists with some public stature began to emerge: like Fitoussi at OFCE and Patrick Artus at the Caisse des dépôts. Along with Aglietta and Jean Pisani-Ferry at CEPII, Charles Wyplosz at the INSEAD business school, and Jacques Melitz at INSEE, they sought to open up French economic debate to Anglo-American ideas, particularly to a more market-oriented approach. Their main impact was long term and contextual: in fostering a new sense of realism in economic policy debate, particularly a recognition of the limitations on what the French state could do. This underlying message fitted in with what French politicians had learnt painfully between 1981 and 1983. It also lent support to a pro-EMU position.

Professional economists played an influential role in specifying the conditions for a *franc stable* policy within the ERM, grounding their views in research on exchange rates and economic competitiveness. They also elaborated the requirements of credibility for economic and monetary policies within the 'hard' ERM. But, when it came to overall policy design and the policy details derived from that design, the impact of professional economists was blunted. Though basically pro-EMU, they harboured severe reservations about official policy with respect to the franc. Economists at OFCE were critical of the high costs in employment and output and the excessively long-term nature of competitive disinflation strategy. Wyplocz and others criticized the subordination of economic policy to political purposes, especially following German unification (preferring a D-Mark revaluation). OFCE attacked the inadequate provisions for fiscal policy co-ordination in the Maastricht Treaty. It also expressed its concerns about too long a transition period to EMU, arguing for a significant strengthening of stage 2. These reservations, particularly about there being too 'hard' a currency policy, had no practical impact. What is more, Trésor officials used private channels to warn professional economists of the dangers to the public interest in such arguments being pursued too boldly. Trésor officials were determined to control the overall design of economic policy strategy as well as to defend that strategy from detailed criticisms. Within such a context there was not the scope to develop the influential independent 'think tanks' characteristic of the USA and Britain. The basic rationale of competitive disinflation strategy and of EMU was worked out by Inspectors of Finance whose economic training was no more than basic.

Despite this continuing sense of marginalization and exclusion, professional economists grew in confidence and stature during the 1980s. Increasingly troubled about their room for manoeuvre in economic policy, French governments were more disposed than before to turn to them for ideas and advice. Hence their opportunities for influence were greater. That influence was most pronounced in a background and long-term sense: in underlining the limitations of the state in economic and monetary policies; it was also most apparent in the legitimation of policy strategies already in place.[8] But it did not take the form of designing ERM and EMU policies. In this respect a very small group of Trésor officials retained its grip on the levers of domestic power over EMU policy. For this reason Fitoussi, president of the OFCE, referred to *'le débat interdit'* on the ERM and EMU (Fitoussi 1995).

---

[8] An example was provided by the report of the working party of the Planning Commission set up under Pisani-Ferry, *A French Perspective on EMU*, February 1993. Trésor officials were keen to blunt its criticisms of official policy and to use it as an endorsement of their positions.

Conclusions

Though all of the beliefs that are outlined and analysed in this chapter shaped French negotiating positions, they were by no means equally important in informing French motives in pursuing EMU. Neither *construction européenne* nor Franco-German reconciliation required a primacy for EMU. The same can be said of the *franc stable*; it could have been achieved by other means. They were vital as preconditions, making it easier both to slot EMU into a wider set of beliefs about French diplomatic interests and economic policy beliefs—thereby legitimating it at home—and to persuade EC partners that France was both serious and reliable as a negotiator on EMU. Much the same applies to the republican state tradition. It set important limitations on French attitudes to EMU, in particular through a deep-seated concern about forfeiting the nation's control over economic and monetary power and about accepting conditions for EMU imposed by the Germans. This tradition shaped how French politicians and administrators responded to EMU. But it did not explain why it was embraced.

Far more important as a motive were considerations of international and European monetary power. There was a cross-party recognition—shared within the administration—that it was in France's vital interest to shield its economy from the negative effects of irresponsible US and German monetary policies, with the focus shifting to the problem of German monetary power during the 1970s and 1980s. Crucially, EMU offered France the opportunity to re-establish influence over monetary policy by Europeanizing it. That European platform could then be used both to shift economic objectives and the use of monetary policy instruments in a manner more compatible with French interests and to achieve international monetary reform. France could then hope to dislodge the role of the US dollar. Mitterrand was able to capitalize on this inheritance of ideas.

Mitterrand's sense of his own freedom of manoeuvre on EMU derived from his highly developed strategic skills: his refusal to become entrapped within the received ideas and wisdom of the 'technostructure' of the French state; his determination to retain the initiative and control the decisive points in the EMU negotiations; and his intent to act as *animateur*, inspiring his negotiators by an historic vision of French interests in Europe and in Franco-German reconciliation. The President's preoccupation was with the political direction of the EMU negotiations, particularly the putting in place of a timetable that would bind future negotiators to make sustained progress and prevent them slipping back into a conservative and cautious approach that would undermine progress towards the final goal of a single currency. He sought mastery of the process.

But when it came to the substantive technical content of the EMU negotiations Mitterrand's role was modest, in fact negligible. He had no taste for economic and monetary policy debates, being more comfortable with the discourse of diplomacy, defence, and security. He might have echoed de Gaulle's

words to Jean-Marcel Jeanneney during the currency crisis of November 1968:
'When it comes to military matters I know my generals, when it comes to foreign affairs I know my ambassadors, but in economic matters I can see that I
don't really know whom to trust.' Mitterrand was most at home situating EMU
in historical discussions about *construction européenne*, reconciliation with
Germany, and ensuring no future war in Europe; about its wider international
dimensions (especially in relation to US monetary power); about the republican
tradition; and about the *franc stable*. In this medium he was the masterful craftsman, happy with the materials with which he was working. Beyond that role
Mitterrand was the mistrustful, watchful observer of a process of negotiation,
of whose technical content he had little understanding.

That content was essentially in the hands of France's elite of financial administrators, whose power was reasserted in 1983. Within that elite there were
those of a social Radical and social Catholic persuasion. But the ascendant ideas
were conservative liberal. In this respect Giscard d'Estaing and Barre (who had
also taught economics to many of these officials) were the two political ghosts
at the EMU feast: for they had staked out a prior claim to ownership of this project, had helped shape inherited French ideas about EMU, and invited comparison between their own economic policy competence and the lack of technical
grasp of Mitterrand in this field. The next chapter deals with the impact of their
inheritance.

3

The Political Problem of Reconciling Domestic and International Interests in EMU: The Legacy of Barre, Giscard d'Estaing, and Pompidou

On the evening of 6 December 1991 Valéry Giscard d'Estaing was received at the Elyseé Palace by President Mitterrand as part of his consultations before the Maastricht Council meeting. During their conversation the depth of the former President's commitment to European unification was impressive: he stressed the importance of keeping the word 'federal' in the new Treaty and of reinforcing the powers of the European Parliament. But closest of all to Giscard's heart was the need to fix a final date for the transition to EMU. Consistent with the views of the Giscard–Schmidt Committee for the Monetary Union of Europe, he argued for a 1997 deadline. The meeting evoked a sense of nostalgia and of irony. Just before the Bremen Council in July 1978 President Giscard d'Estaing had invited Mitterrand as leader of the Socialist opposition to the Elyseé to seek his views on what the President hoped would be 'a new Bretton Woods for Europe' (the future EMS). Just as Mitterrand had given his support then, so in 1991 Giscard d'Estaing reciprocated in his capacity as president of the UDF (*Union pour la démocratie française*). The element of irony derived from the fact that Mitterrand was finalizing negotiations on a policy project—EMU—to which Giscard d'Estaing, the epitome of the conservative liberal, had devoted his political career, as Finance Minister, President, and, from 1986, leading figure in the Committee for the Monetary Union of Europe.

As we shall see below, almost all of the key elements of the French bargaining position on EMU at Maastricht had been developed before 1981 under Giscard d'Estaing's leadership and with a major contribution from Raymond Barre. Giscard d'Estaing and Barre could claim to be more than just the main figures in the prehistory of French policy on EMU. They had led the process of defining the core elements of that policy. The Socialist governments under Mitterrand reinvented and repackaged that policy, injecting elements of social Catholicism and social Radicalism into the way in which it was defined. But the underlying corpus of policy ideas and negotiating positions revealed a striking continuity from the Giscard years. It was hardly surprising that on 6 December 1991 Mitterrand and Giscard d'Estaing found it so easy to agree on EMU.

This chapter examines how French negotiating positions on EMU evolved from the 1960s onwards, especially after 1968; explores the impacts of the domestic and the European and international political problems facing Georges Pompidou, Giscard d'Estaing, and Barre on the way in which those positions evolved; shows the acute difficulties that Pompidou and Giscard faced in trying to square domestic with European and international interests and pressures; and identifies the EMU legacy inherited by Mitterrand in 1981. It demonstrates how the French Trésor was reluctant to seize the initiative in defining the intellectual content of EMU during the Werner negotiations of 1970. Barre and the EC Commission staked out the technical, detailed positions defended by Bernard Clappier in the Werner Group. In this respect Clappier behaved with a good deal more independence *vis-à-vis* his national government than his German counterpart Schöllhorn. It was not until 1974, and then again in 1978, during the Giscard Presidency, that the Trésor developed distinctive French positions on EMU. The trigger was not Werner but the demise of the Bretton Woods system and, above all, the gradual recognition of the intractable difficulties in resurrecting it or an equivalent. At the same time, President Pompidou was more closely involved in defining basic negotiating positions after the Hague summit than Chancellor Willy Brandt. His legacy was apparent in the way that, in the 1980s, Edouard Balladur and Jacques Chirac were to conceive of EMU and in the wider influence of an intergovernmentalist conception of EMU.

EMU and Gold in the 1960s

By the early 1960s French Finance Ministry and Banque de France officials had several motives for reflecting on the desirability of EMU. First, they shared the Belgian economist Robert Triffin's negative evaluation of the functioning of the Bretton Woods system, in particular his focus on the inherent contradictions of its gold–dollar standard (Triffin 1960). Finance Ministry officials were alerted by Triffin to a central and deepening problem of the Bretton Woods system: the convertibility and credibility problem consequent on the mismatch between the volume of US dollars in foreign hands and the quantity of US gold reserves held at Fort Knox. In fact, Finance Ministry (and Foreign Ministry) officials had been deeply uncomfortable with the Bretton Woods system since its inception, when they had felt that French ideas about international monetary reform had not been taken seriously. Hence Triffin's criticisms fell on receptive ears in Paris. During the 1960s French official opinion polarized between two views on reform: those advocating the return to gold and a policy of hoarding gold as an insurance and bargaining resource to diminish US power in Europe (Rueff, Couve de Murville, and de Gaulle); and those seeing the solution in developing an EEC 'monetary personality' and a common or parallel currency, together with the creation of a new 'composite reserve unit' to replace the dollar (led by Giscard d'Estaing). For Giscard and his officials the main attraction of EMU was the creation of a currency to rival the US dollar and the pound sterling and to ensure a discipline on national economic and monetary policies. EMU reconciled French interests at home and abroad.[1]

An additional motive was that, by the early 1960s, French officials were concerned that the new Common Agricultural Policy (CAP), from which France gained in relative terms, could be undermined by currency instability triggered by US irresponsibility and unilateral parity changes by EC member states (Tsoukalis 1993: 59). In Paris the idea began to circulate of a functional logic linking monetary union to French national interest in safeguarding one of the key French gains from the Treaty of Rome. Partly in order to flank and secure what was perceived as a vital national interest in the CAP, in February–March 1964 Giscard and his director of external finances, André de Lattre, developed a proposal for a common EC currency.

This proposal was linked to a third motive. At the meeting between de Gaulle and Chancellor Erhard in February 1964 the French Prime Minister Georges Pompidou returned to a French interest in ensuring a level playing-field in the new common market by recommending joint action to co-ordinate tax, financial, and social policies (Hentschel 1996: 654–5). Two weeks later Giscard circulated his proposal for a common EC currency, if possible beginning with a Franco-German monetary union, and justifying this by reference to what he understood to be the shared thinking of de Gaulle and Pompidou. The proposal encountered the immediate opposition of the German Economics Ministry and of Erhard, who suspected anti-American motives, an intent to extend French *planification* to Europe, and a risk of splitting the EC. The Franco-German summit of February 1964 and its immediate aftermath played an important role in persuading de Gaulle that, with the Atlanticist Erhard as Chancellor, there were no serious political prospects for this line of action. He was in any case more attracted by strengthening the franc as a symbol of French sovereignty and an instrument of national independence.

A further aspect was the close relations between French Finance Ministry officials and DG2 in developing ideas about how to take forward European integration. By 1962 Robert Marjolin, French EC Commissioner for economic and financial affairs, was trying to set new ambitious goals for the EC, in the process bringing EMU onto the political agenda. Already, influenced by Triffin and by Pierre Uri, Finance Ministry officials were considering the idea of a European Reserve Fund as a first step to the creation of an ECB and a common currency. The EC Commission's proposal for a common currency was welcomed by Giscard in January 1965. He saw in it a means to acquire an independent non-Gaullist political profile within the centre-right by differentiating himself on Europe. But this political link to the EC Commission had no resonance at the Elysée, where de Gaulle dismissed it as that 'portentous, stateless, technocratic

---

[1] More generally on the US dollar problem and reform of the international monetary system see Ungerer (1997: chapter 7).

irresponsible assembly' (Touchard 1978: 218). He had no interest in its proposals on EMU and was driven only by his notion of the EC as a grouping in which 'France has the honour and duty of being the centre and leader' (Touchard 1978: 113).

The political opportunity and momentum for reflection on EMU derived above all from the presence of Giscard d'Estaing, leader of the Independent Republican group, as Finance Minister from January 1962 to January 1966. He was appointed because of his formidable intellectual reputation as a technician of economic policy and because of the confidence that he commanded within the French economic and financial elite. Despite these qualities Giscard remained a figure who inspired neither affection nor trust. He was widely seen as cold, aloof, and too challenging in manner. Gaullists distrusted him as 'not one of us', as a man with his own political ambitions, viewing projects like EMU through the lens of his individual political reputation. Giscard quickly emerged as the most consistent long-term advocate of a common currency. This advocacy was part of his strategy of carving out a pro-European political profile distinct from the larger Gaullist party with its preoccupation with national sovereignty. In this Giscard was assisted by two key figures: Jean-Pierre Fourcade, later to be Giscard's Finance Minister and the author of the Fourcade Plan of 1974, who was then in his cabinet; and André de Lattre, who later, as Deputy Governor of the Banque de France, was to work closely with Bernard Clappier during the period of the Werner Group.

Till January 1966, when he was replaced by Michel Debré, Giscard offered a political shield behind which ideas about the content of EMU could surface in the private domain of his cabinet in the Finance Ministry. Giscard favoured giving priority to fixed exchange rates between EC states and a common currency. But de Gaulle and Foreign Minister Couve de Murville ensured that he was denied any opportunity to pursue these ideas within the government—though Pompidou showed more sympathy. Giscard's political limitations were all too apparent. Despite Giscard's private support, the French government reacted negatively to the EC Commission's Action Programme for the Second Stage of 1962 with its call for fixed exchange rates by 1970 and a common currency. Then, at his press conference in February 1965, de Gaulle endorsed the ideas of Rueff and Couve de Murville rather than those of Giscard and inaugurated a period of French isolation in debate about international monetary reform. The French government opted for a policy of hoarding gold rather than for EMU.

Pompidou, the Hague Summit, and the Werner Report: The Turning-Point of 1968

Whilst out of office from 1966 Giscard's conviction that EMU offered the solution to French problems, and that the return to gold was an irrelevance, hardened. This shift was part of a broad political strategy of distancing himself and his new Independent Republican Party from the Gaullists, especially on Europe (Abadie and Corcolette 1997: 152–5). In 1968 he campaigned publicly on behalf of his Independent Republican Party for a common EC currency in opposition to the hard-line Gaullist Finance Minister Debré, who rejected it as incompatible with French national sovereignty (Debré 1972). By this time Giscard's arguments were gaining a new resonance as a consequence of international developments.

1968 was a turning-point. March saw the creation of a two-tier gold market, involving an effective end to convertibility of the US dollar and hence its credible role as anchor of the Bretton Woods system. The events of May, with general strikes and riots, led to a major relaxation of domestic efforts to bear down on inflation in the form of generous wage awards (the Grenelle Accords) (Prate 1978: 246). November witnessed a major speculative attack on the French franc, suggesting the failure of Gaullist policies as pursued since 1965 to tackle the problem of French weakness relative to the USA. More strikingly, as a sign of later developments that were to be crucial for EMU, asymmetry between French and German economic power began to manifest itself in a new and clearer way during and after the emergency G10 meeting in Bonn. Political events and policy developments were, in short, opening a new opportunity to reappraise the relationship between France's international and European interests and EMU.

Giscard's return to the Finance Ministry under the newly elected President Georges Pompidou in June 1969 was a positive signal for EMU. He was especially alert to the argument for an external discipline to constrain domestic economic policy and disposed to seek that discipline in Europe. He was also aware that French sensitivity to growing Germany economic power—symbolized by the strength of the D-Mark—offered a new opportunity to argue the case for EMU. At the same time Pompidou distrusted Giscard, who had been equivocal about backing him in the 1969 Presidential election, and only offered him the Finance Ministry post after Antoine Pinay had refused it. Many Gaullists disliked Giscard, blaming his opposition to the referendum on reform of the Senate and of local government for the departure of de Gaulle (Muron 1994: 264–7). In consequence. Pompidou treated him with caution, preferring to work with his Foreign Minister Maurice Schumann on EC issues, including the Hague summit and its aftermath. Hence Giscard had no real scope to emerge as the policy entrepreneur on EMU in Paris.

More important were the political motives of Pompidou. He was more relaxed on European integration than de Gaulle. Pompidou was prepared to use European rhetoric and resort to EC initiatives in the service of what he saw as France's interest in remaining the ideological motive force behind the construction of a Europe to safeguard the national independence of its members (L'Express: 4 September 1967: 9). In 1969 a higher profile EC role was a means of addressing a domestic political problem: the need to broaden the basis of his political support to the centre-left by bringing the old MRP into his government.

He had to find a means of compensating for the loss of the personal support on the Left that de Gaulle had been able to attract. The implication was a shift to a stronger pro-European policy. But, as a Gaullist, Pompidou had a much more limited conception of EMU. He shared Gaullist aversion to the idea of ceding economic policy powers to Europe and to institution-building at the EC level. EMU was about improving consultation and co-ordination on economic and monetary policies, above all in order to gain greater influence over Germany. It was not about surrendering sovereignty to new supranational institutions.

Giscard was inhibited by the legacy of the 1969 Presidential election from inciting the Gaullists by taking too high a profile on EMU. In this context the intellectual initiative on EMU derived from Raymond Barre, the EC Commissioner responsible for economic and financial affairs, rather than from Giscard. Barre had the political advantage of being seen as a non-partisan appointment by de Gaulle and as a man who had been listened to by de Gaulle in November 1968. He was also a widely respected university economist. Pompidou was especially attracted by Barre's pragmatic, step-by-step approach to EMU. Barre's concerns were to insulate Europe from the effects of the collapsing US dollar and to draw economic lessons from the French crisis of May 1968. These concerns had been addressed in the Barre Memorandum of February 1969. He had sought to strengthen convergence and restore currency stability to the EC by closer co-ordination of economic policies and by new monetary support and financial assistance mechanisms (Dyson 1994: 72). Giscard backed Barre by removing French reservations on submitting France's economic policies for EC scrutiny and endorsing closer co-ordination of short-term economic policies in an ECOFIN decision of 17 July 1969. Barre was also pressing for the narrowing and eventual elimination of fluctuation margins between EC currencies in 1968–9, in short for strengthening monetary co-operation. This proposal was seen as a means of helping to prepare a common EC position if a US devaluation led to the collapse of the Bretton Woods system and a move to floating exchange rates. But, Gaullist that he was, Pompidou was much less interested in thinking about a parallel or single European currency than either Barre or Giscard.

When it came to the launch of EMU, Barre was a decisive influence in Paris. Following in the wake of such an heroic and historic figure as de Gaulle, Pompidou's priority was to take the initiative to call the Hague summit and to use it to establish his own credentials as a European statesman. Barre was important in providing him with the economic arguments for identifying EMU as his key project with which to inject a new political drive into the EC—as a means to 'deepen' the EC whilst it was being 'widened' to accommodate Britain and others. A signal of the priority to EMU was the appointment of Jean-René Bernard, an Inspector of Finance, as simultaneously Pompidou's EC adviser in the Elyseé and head of the SGCI. Pompidou relied heavily on Bernard, especially in relation to the preparations for the Hague summit and the Paris summit of 1972. Both in turn depended on Barre for the intellectual ideas that informed their approach to EMU. An additional factor was that Pompidou was less convinced than de Gaulle and Debré about the return to gold as a means of meeting the French objective of reform of the international monetary system. Hence the new President was prepared to accept Barre's arguments about prioritizing EMU and found himself on common ground with Giscard. There was also a sense that French officials had already captured the intellectual high ground on EMU with Marjolin's Action Programme of 1962 and now the Barre Memorandum. Accordingly, the Elysée felt that it had an opportunity to seize the initiative in this area of 'deepening' the EC.

A vitally important part of the rationale for adopting EMU was the lesson of the monetary crisis of 1968. There was a new sense of pressure and urgency in Paris, a sense that de Gaulle's approach had been shown to have failed. The imbalance between French and German economic power was seen as a more acute and threatening problem requiring new forms of action to protect vital French interests. This sense was sharpened by the pressures on the French franc subsequent to the domestic political crisis of May 1968 and the bitter recriminations between French and German negotiators surrounding the G10 meeting in Bonn in November 1968. In Bonn the French Finance Minister, François-Xavier Ortoli, had been lectured by Karl Schiller, the German Economics Minister, and eventually agreed to devalue the franc (by 11 per cent) subject to agreement from his government (James 1996: 193–7). Ortoli had experienced a humiliating rejection of French pressures for a D-Mark revaluation. To make matters worse, the German Finance Minister, Franz-Josef Strauss, had made a devaluation of the French franc public at the final press conference; whilst *Bildzeitung* had added insult to injury with the headline 'Germany Is Number One Again'. Subsequently, advised by Barre and Jean-Marcel Jeanneney, de Gaulle had resisted German and wider international pressure to devalue and resorted instead to tough exchange and credit controls. For de Gaulle the critical consideration was the political costs, both domestic and international, of a devaluation. French resentment at this use of German economic power at the G10 meeting rekindled domestic interest in EMU as a means to 'bind in' German power and to counter the irresponsible use of US economic power. For Pompidou in 1969 the reality of German economic and monetary power was harsher than it had been for de Gaulle in 1958. De Gaulle did not endorse an EMU initiative. But Gaullists like Pompidou could justify their advocacy of EMU by reference to de Gaulle's principal argument for European unification: that it was a means of escaping from dependency on US power and of containing German power. In short, a means could be found of reconciling Gaullism and EMU.

Pompidou shared Barre's and Giscard's views on the lessons of this Franco-German crisis: that France must seek to escape from its international isolation. The escape route involved persuading Europe to define its common interest in international monetary reform and consolidate its strength by reference to shared frustration with US irresponsibility in managing the Bretton Woods system. An EMU initiative was justified by the demonstrable need to bind German monetary power into a stronger European framework that could negotiate on terms of equality with the USA. The need to do so was underlined by the aftermath of Pompidou's devaluation of the French franc in August 1969. It was followed by a period of floating of the D-Mark. French officials were incensed by this German unilateralism and its implications for the CAP, a vital French interest. On this basis of shared views, and despite other differences, Barre, Giscard, and Pompidou could co-operate on EMU.

But Pompidou's conception of EMU was made distinctive by his own beliefs about Europe and his clinical, geopolitical analysis of Franco-German relations and Europe. He saw EMU as pre-eminently a political project: a means to 'deepen' the EC whilst simultaneously 'widening' it to embrace southern Europe and Britain. In this way Europe could be 'rebalanced'—by both EMU and 'widening'—to serve French interests and contain Germany. He differed from Barre, Giscard, and de Gaulle in his conceptions of Europe and the Franco-German relationship. For Barre and Giscard European unification was eminently desirable, a matter of the heart as well as of the head. In Pompidou's characteristically cerebral view European unification was a necessity for France, imposed by its history and geography. What Pompidou shared with de Gaulle was a hostility to supranational institutions like the EC Commission. For Barre, Giscard, and de Gaulle the Franco-German relationship was again desirable and vested with emotional significance. For Pompidou, however, it was again a necessity. Fear and suspicion of Germany were leitmotifs of the Pompidou presidency (Abadie and Corcolette 1994: 336–40). They led to his obsession with making France as economically powerful as Germany. They also lay at the root of his unhappiness with 'being alone' with Germany and his wanting Britain on board. This fear was given an added dimension by Pompidou's worry about the *Ostpolitik* of the new German Chancellor Brandt. He considered the possibility that this initiative to seek reconciliation with eastern neighbours might lead Germany to drift towards the East. In Pompidou's view, EMU would provide a firmer political anchor to the West in this context of political change in Bonn.

Pompidou came very carefully prepared to the Hague summit of 1–2 December, having clarified in advance the key elements of the French conception of EMU: priority to a European Reserve Fund (ERF) as a means of achieving concerted action in relation to the US dollar; the attainment of a united Community negotiating position in international monetary reform; and the need for a precise timetable of stages for realizing EMU. In doing so, he went well beyond the traditional Gaullist position associated with Debré and Couve de Murville. But, equally, reflecting his own Gaullist antipathy to supranationalism and ideas of a federal Europe, Pompidou departed in one respect from Giscard's and Barre's position. At The Hague, and later, he remained deliberately non-committal on the specific relationship between strengthening monetary co-operation and improved co-ordination of EC economic policies, an issue that was seen as vital by the Germans (and by Giscard). In this respect the final summit communiqué was by no means a clear victory for Pompidou. Consistent with German views, it gave priority to the 'harmonization' of economic policies and saw the ERF as emerging at the end of the transition to EMU. Nevertheless, Pompidou and Giscard—supported by Barre—had succeeded in shifting the domestic centre of gravity on EMU and in putting EMU on the EC agenda.

The summit's main outcome—a mandate to ECOFIN to draw up a plan for the creation of an EMU—suited Giscard admirably. With ECOFIN as the epicentre he seemed to be in a stronger position to influence EMU negotiations than he had been before the summit. But in fact Pompidou sought, via his Foreign Minister Schumann, to set clear parameters for the EMU negotiations (Roussel 1994: 340–2). He confirmed a set of basic French positions: that it would take at least twelve years to realize EMU through a succession of stages; that 'at no price' was the European Commission or the European Parliament to emerge strengthened by EMU, only the Council being a beneficiary; that the institutional structures of EMU must be examined 'by a magnifying glass' to ensure that France ceded nothing in this area; that the emerging EC monetary authority was to remain under the control of the Council; and that rhetorical and illusionary references to political union were to be kept out of texts. Very tight Gaullist constraints were being placed on French negotiators. Other than exit from the government Giscard had little choice but to live with the political realities of life under a newly elected Gaullist President. Pompidou's negotiating principles offered no scope for French negotiators to develop proposals on what EMU might look like in its final form. What was being sought was greater German flexibility in the form of short-term concessions, notably on an improved support mechanism for the franc.

From a French perspective the key feature of the group of experts set up under Pierre Werner in March 1970 to elaborate a plan for achieving EMU by stages was the presence of Bernard Clappier, in his capacity as chair of the EC Monetary Committee. Clappier was First Deputy Governor of the Banque de France; a member of the Finance Inspectorate; a man close to Finance Ministry thinking, having been its director of external economic relations from 1951 to 1963; and personally close to Giscard. Not least, Clappier had impeccable European credentials, having served as director of the cabinet of Robert Schuman between 1948 and 1950. Giscard was later to promote him to Governor in 1974 and to rely on him as his personal representative during the preparation of proposals for the EMS in 1978. The link to the Trésor was provided by Jean-Michel Bloch-Lainé as Clappier's deputy. The presence of Larre as director of the Trésor ensured a pro-European attitude.

Though aware of Pompidou's negotiating instructions, Clappier proved in practice to be very independent-minded. He was more influenced by the ideas of Barre—and the proposals of the Belgian and Luxembourg governments— than by any ideas emanating independently from the French Trésor or the

Banque de France.[2] In any case, the main preoccupation of the Trésor and the Banque de France was with international monetary stability and reform. Their intellectual engagement in EMU was much weaker than that of the German Economics Ministry. Indeed, they were soon able to persuade Pompidou that the problems of the franc's relations with the US dollar dwarfed the problems relating to the D-Mark. In this respect the Werner Group was a political rather than an intellectual milestone in France. Trésor caution was reinforced by three factors: an internal tension induced by the legacy of Debré's hostility to EMU within the Finance Ministry; emerging political problems for Pompidou over EMU within the Gaullist majority during 1970; and the overshadowing of the Werner Report and its implementation by the urgent need to achieve joint European action at the international level. The negotiation of the Smithsonian Agreement of December 1971, based on prior agreement with the Germans, took precedence for the Trésor. The Trésor's intellectual conversion to EMU was not completed until after the collapse of the Bretton Woods system. A first sign came in September 1971, one month after President Richard Nixon had ended the convertibility of US dollars into gold. Pompidou advocated the creation of an executive organ attached to the Committee of EC Central Bank Governors to manage the monetary reserves of the EC. Thereafter, Trésor officials took up the theme of securing France's key trading relations in Europe by stable and preferably fixed exchange rates.

Despite this lack of significant independent intellectual engagement, Giscard took a close personal interest in guarding his personal ministerial prerogatives and trying to keep Pompidou's support for the work of the Werner Group. The Banque de France was in reality able to carve out some role, helped by the fact that de Lattre, the Second Deputy Governor, had earlier worked on EMU under Giscard. Another factor was that a considerable amount of work, for instance on narrowing intra-EC margins of fluctuations and on an ERF, was delegated to the Ansiaux Group of central bank experts in Basle. In consequence, Marcel Theron as director-general for foreign services at the Banque de France gained an influential position on this issue. However, on the ERF and the narrowing of fluctuation margins, intellectual leadership derived from the National Bank of Belgium rather than the Banque de France.

The Werner Report went a long way to satisfy Barre's and Giscard's objectives.[3] There was an agreement to realize EMU by stages, with stage 1 to begin on 1 January 1971 and to cover three years. But the French idea of a precise timetable was rejected in favour of flexibility to respond to circumstances and of concentrating on the first stage. On another issue Barre and Giscard were more satisfied. The notion of the independence of the Community system of central banks was qualified. The 'centre for economic policy' at the EC level would also be furnished with effective powers of decision, and both institutions were

---

[2] For details of these plans see Willgerodt et al. (1972).
[3] On the negotiations see Werner (1991).

required to work together for the realization of the same objectives. But, before the report was published, it was clear that, on this point of parallelism between progress in economic and monetary fields, Giscard would have domestic political problems. The principle of parallelism in the report did in fact reflect Giscard's personal position. The 'monetarist' approach, with which the French became associated during the negotiations, reflected a means of accommodating Gaullist reservations about loss of national economic policy power. In the Gaullist conception, and especially in the Foreign Ministry and the French Permanent Representation in Brussels, the 'control' element of EMU in relation to German monetary power was ascendant. It was clear to Giscard at an early stage that Gaullists were not prepared to countenance the loss of fiscal sovereignty. On this point French negotiating positions diverged from Giscard's own view of the requirements for an effective EMU. He regarded the Werner Report as at least sound on this issue. EMU and political union were, to Giscard, inseparable. In Pompidou's view, they were to be kept apart.

The main French success was in gaining agreement that, from the start of stage 1, the EC central banks would limit *de facto* the margins of fluctuation between their currencies. The objective, strongly endorsed in Paris, was concerted action in relation to the US dollar. This proposal led on directly to the EC 'Snake' mechanism, launched—after delay—in April 1972. The Werner Report recommended that concerted action in relation to the dollar could be completed by interventions in EC currrencies, first at the limit of the margins and later, of importance to the French, within the margins. Giscard had given particular importance to the proposal for an ERF. This proposal was kept alive in the 'European Fund for Monetary Co-operation', which—with sufficient progress towards economic convergence and the reduction of margins—could be established in stage 1. It would gradually become an organ of management of reserves at the EC level. Overall, Giscard felt that French negotiators had retained the intellectual initiative, despite hard and difficult bargaining with the Germans. He was contented when, in February 1971, ECOFIN accepted the Werner Report, along with a commitment to establish EMU within a decade.

But neither Barre nor Giscard had much ground for optimism. Giscard had problems on two fronts. First, there were mounting and serious domestic political problems. By June 1970 Pompidou was already speaking of EMU as a very long-term project and underlining further his unwillingness to enter into discussions about institutional reforms. On publication of the Werner Report in October Gaullist politicians and President Pompidou were quick to reprimand Clappier for signing. Most ominously of all for Gaullists, the Werner Report had tied EMU to 'the progressive development of political cooperation', seeing it as 'a leaven for the development of political union which, in the long run, it will be unable to do without' (Werner Report 1970, Conclusions B). Since the early 1960s Giscard had recognized this connection and welcomed it. When, at his press conference in January 1971, the President called for a 'European confederation', with a 'European government', or later referred to a 'European Union', notably at the Paris summit of October 1972, he had in mind a structure that was essentially intergovernmental and designed to protect the French state against loss of authority.

The harsh reality was that as early as November 1970 Giscard had to contend with political difficulties in Paris, with the result that at the ECOFIN in December 1970 he found himself embarrassingly isolated. Pompidou was cautious and silent in the face of hostile reactions to the Werner Report within his Gaullist party, led by Debré. It was agreed in the Council of Ministers to concentrate only on stage 1, thereby avoiding difficulties about transfers of power and institutional reform. Pompidou reacted by downplaying the need for institutional reforms to support EMU, whilst his Foreign Minister Maurice Schumann spelt out a litany of reservations. The final ECOFIN agreement on 9 February 1971 (finally confirmed by ECOFIN on 22 March) on the Werner Report required a preliminary bilateral summit between Pompidou and Chancellor Brandt on 25–6 January 1970. Here the full scale of Gaullist objections became evident. The result of French unwillingness to spell out clear steps to create the 'centre of decision for economic policy' was equivocation on the German side about the automaticity of stage 2. In consequence, the Germans sought a safeguard clause, guaranteeing reversibility, at the March 1971 ECOFIN.

Gaullist criticisms focused on the need to remove parallelism between economic policy and monetary policy integration; to weaken the commitment to economic policy co-ordination; to put the objective of stability in perspective; and to set aside institutional reforms. The strongest public indictment of the Werner Report came from Michel Debré (*Le Monde*: 26 February 1971). He situated EMU in the context of Gaullism's essential concern with France's independence and the status of its national currency: 'The currency is first and foremost the hallmark of political authority'. With reference to a European currency Debré argued:

This would mean that Europe was one nation and that everything had been decided. This is not our approach. In contrast, we are in favour of concerted action and co-operation in order to avoid excessive changes of the exchange rates. As much as the latter aspect seems to us to be a realistic one, the first approach is currently a pipedream.

The most authoritative statement from within the Left came from Mendès France on 6 February 1971. In a speech dedicated to EMU he criticized the approach of the Werner Report as too narrowly conceived, as too technical an exercise, and too focused on 'monetarist' measures like the narrowing of fluctuation bands and the creation of a European Monetary Co-operation Fund (Mendès France 1989: 475–80). In place of a 'better administered co-operation' Mendès France called for a more broadly based and ambitious political approach. Interestingly, he endorsed the German 'coronation' theory, arguing that history taught that successful monetary unions came at the end of a process of political union. Basic to Mendès France's position was the argument that

EMU must be part of a process of political union on a wide range of fronts including fiscal, industrial, research, social, vocational training, regional development, and wage bargaining policies. For him the key problem facing the Werner Report was the lack of political will to support a European monetary union by creating a supranational political authority. Though Mendès France was not articulating an official view within the French Left, it was an influential message in the direction of caution.

Giscard's second set of problems related to the mounting problems of the US dollar and the unilateral decisions of the Germans and Dutch to float their currencies in May 1971. Trésor officials were distracted from the business of implementing Werner by these problems. It was not till after the Smithsonian Agreement had been hammered out in December 1971 that the 'Snake' could be launched (Ungerer 1997: chapter 11). Its rationale was enhanced for the French by the fact that the Smithsonian Agreement tripled the margin of fluctuation *vis-à-vis* the US dollar. The need to reduce intra-EC margins, not least to safeguard the CAP, was now more pressing. Hence the 'Snake-in-the-tunnel' appealed to the Trésor.

Subsequent to the Smithsonian Agreement, at the ECOFIN in March 1972, Giscard sought to relaunch EMU, including the commitment to fixed exchange rates and to establishment of the European Monetary Co-operation Fund (EMCF). The 'Snake' began operation in April 1972 (limiting margins to 2.25 per cent), and the EMCF in April 1973. But Giscard's problems in implementing the Werner Plan mounted: the oil crisis sharply aggravated French inflationary pressures and balance of payment problems; the D-Mark was revalued in June, September, and November 1973, putting France in the 'weak' currency camp; the EMCF was set up with only very limited technical functions (French negotiators had argued against a pooling of reserves as too supranational); and the prospects for stage 2 in 1974 receded from view, despite the declaration of intent at the Paris summit in October 1972. The biggest blow was the exit of the French franc from the 'Snake' in January 1974, a decision taken against German advice. Pompidou was determined to accommodate inflationary pressures rather than resist them. His mind was fixated on avoiding a repeat of May 1968 and on learning the lessons of the poor performance of the Gaullist party in the Assembly election of March 1973. Hence Pompidou and his Prime Minister, Pierre Messmer, opted for an economic policy to stimulate growth and protect employment (Pompidou 1974: 153–4). By 1974 Giscard, like Barre, was all too well aware that divergence of economic policy ideas between France and Germany had effectively condemned the Werner Plan to failure.

The distinctiveness of Giscard's approach was evident in his attempt to retrieve the initiative on economic policy convergence after the Werner Report ran into difficulties by proposing to the French Council of Ministers that the French government should commit itself to present balanced budgets, preferably budgets in surplus. His objective was to bind the fiscal hands of French governments to the pursuit of economic stability. In this way it would be possible to restore German confidence in French seriousness about EMU. But this initiative was undermined by Pompidou's fears of locking himself into a budgetary strategy that could induce social and political unrest and by the oil-price shock.

The Fourcade Plan and Reform of the 'Snake': The Giscard Presidency

Against this economic and political background, Giscard's opportunities to make progress on EMU as part of the wider political unification of Europe during his Presidency seemed very limited. His weakness following his extremely narrow victory against Mitterrand in the Presidential election of May 1974 (by a margin of 1 per cent) was compounded by political dependence on the much larger Gaullist Party for his Assembly majority. Giscard's political strategy was to appoint a Gaullist Prime Minister, Jacques Chirac, and then surround him with enemies. Chirac, who shared Pompidou's earlier fear of a repeat of the events of May 1968, was unwilling to take responsibility for tough measures to tackle the effects of the oil crisis. Giscard's agenda was, by contrast, to revitalize EMU as the top priority in European unification and to pursue domestic economic stabilization (Giscard d'Estaing 1977: 115–16). These objectives were, in his view, interdependent and their pursuit essential and urgent if France was to address its economic and political weaknesses at home and abroad and if European political union was to be achieved before the end of his period of office (Abadie and Corcolette 1997: 334). But in pursuing these objectives Giscard was persistently constrained by his domestic political vulnerability— not least by fear of voter backlash in the March 1976 local elections and the March 1978 National Assembly elections.

Giscard's ambitions to put in place an external discipline and to chart a new European course after sixteen years of Gaullist presidencies were signalled by his appointment of his long-standing collaborator Fourcade as Finance Minister and of Clappier, a personal friend, to replace Wormser as Governor of the Banque de France. His determination to exercise Presidential authority in the economic and monetary domain, his own field of expertise and experience, sowed the seeds for a potential clash with Chirac. Fourcade and Chirac were to be scarcely on speaking terms. Giscard's priority to giving a new dynamic to Franco-German relations was also signalled by the appointment of the French Ambassador in Bonn, Jean Sauvagnargues, as Foreign Minister. His priority was a return to the 'Snake'. He shared the Finance Ministry and Banque de France view that France should return to a reformed and strengthened 'Snake', rid of the deficiencies that had been revealed by the franc's exit just four months before in January 1974. Politically, it was important that these deficiencies (rather than Giscard's own policy as Finance Minister) were blamed for the French exit.

But the new government lacked the personal chemistry, as well as the electoral confidence, to make progress on EMU. Giscard was a cold, aloof, fundamentally cerebral figure. Though he could command respect for his grasp of techical briefs, he was more likely to inspire dislike of his arrogance and petulance. He induced anxiety, fear, and insecurity rather than inspired by personal warmth and affection. Hence Giscard lacked the personal qualities to be a successful *animateur* on EMU. Also, sharing power with the more powerful Gaullist Party, Giscard was preoccupied throughout his Presidency with domestic electoral and political threats to his position. Hence he appeared to other EC negotiators as a man with feet of clay, stronger on European rhetoric than delivery. Chirac's political opportunism accentuated his worst features in this respect. Giscard was constantly alert to the threat of being outflanked by Chirac's populism, which worsened once he resigned in 1976. He was in consequence at the end of the day cautious in delivering on EMU rather than its great *animateur* as President.

Giscard's strongest resource in negotiating on EMU was his close personal relationship with the German Chancellor Helmut Schmidt. They had met for the first time in the 1950s as members of the Monnet Action Committee for the United States of Europe and worked together as finance ministers since 1972. This relationship was fundamentally one of mutual respect for each other's technical competence on matters of international and European economic policy. The element of *complicité* between them had, however, less to do with personal warmth and affection than with a marriage of hearts and minds on European economic and monetary questions. It also rested on Schmidt's willingness to accept that the effective functioning of the Franco-German relationship rested on Giscard being allowed to '*proposer et mener le jeu*' (Abadie and Corcolette 1997: 332).

The Fourcade Plan, submitted to ECOFIN in September 1974, was the most important French proposal on European monetary reform before the Balladur Memorandum of 1988. It represented an attempt to reflect on the lessons of trying to implement the Werner Report; to identify the problems of the 'Snake' that needed to be addressed before France returned (explicitly making a linkage here); to create a convincing account of why the French franc had exited from the 'Snake'; to reduce the economic costs of future participation to France; and to regain the political initiative for the new President in relation to EMU in time for the Paris summit of December 1974. The Plan developed French thinking around the problem of asymmetry, the same problem that was to be taken up later by Balladur. Others involved in this exercise were de Larosière as the new director of the Trésor; Haberer as the senior Trésor official responsible for international affairs; and Jean-Michel Bloch-Lainé as deputy director for international affairs. There were important threads of continuity between the Fourcade Plan and later developments. Haberer was to be director of the Trésor when the EMS was negotiated in 1978–9; de Larosière, Governor of the Banque de France at the time of the Basle–Nyborg negotiations and of the Delors Committee. When the substance of these later negotiations is examined in relation to the Fourcade Plan, it is striking how little was new.

Fourcade focused on four key proposals: larger short- and medium-term credit facilities to support the 'Snake'; more use of intramarginal interventions; a joint dollar policy; and the use of the European Unit of Account (EUA)— renamed the ECU in 1978—as the pivot of a revised exchange-rate system. The radical element was the role envisaged for the EUA (in effect a basket of EC currencies) as the pivot in place of the grid of bilateral parities on which the 'Snake' was based. It paralleled French proposals for reform of the international monetary system, in this case replacing the US dollar with a basket of currencies as the pivot. This proposal was the first French attempt to solve the problem of asymmetry in a European context. In this sense it prefigured French positions in the EMS negotiations and in the Balladur Memorandum of 1988. With the EUA as pivot the burden of responsibility for intervention would be assigned more fairly; a country would be obliged to intervene when its currency reached its margin against a Community average, whether that currency was strong or weak.

The Fourcade Plan ran, predictably, into strong German and Dutch resistance but, more surprising for the French, failed to enlist the active support of weak currency states like Britain and Italy which were reluctant to embrace tougher exchange-rate discipline in the face of severe domestic inflationary pressures. The disappointment for Giscard was reflected at the Paris summit in December 1974; in the communiqué only one sentence was devoted to EMU, reaffirming past commitments. The Trésor and the Banque de France resisted a return of the franc to the 'Snake' as premature, particularly given Chirac's commitment to economic expansion in his impending budget. They argued that it would be unsustainable. But Giscard was determined to use his Presidency to assert his European ambitions and in May 1975—against the objections of the Finance Ministry and the Banque de France—announced the franc's impending re-entry (Goodman 1992: 118). This announcement was accompanied by a new presentation of the Fourcade Plan to ECOFIN. Though its main proposals were again rejected, limited changes were made to the operating procedures of the 'Snake' (notably expanded short-term credit facilities), providing helpful political cover for the franc's re-entry in July. Notably, reflecting Giscard's views, at the September 1975 ECOFIN, Fourcade raised the wider issue of economic policy convergence, particularly in fiscal policy.

A 'New Bretton Woods for Europe': Giscard, the EMS, and EMU

The incompatibility between Giscard and Chirac came to a head in 1976. Preoccupied by the prospect of Socialist victory in the March 1976 local elections, Chirac had persuaded Giscard—though not Fourcade—that, on domestic political grounds, priority had to be given to growth and employment. The price of the *relance Chirac* in September 1975 was high for Giscard. Domestic economic stabilization and EMU were sacrificed (Loriaux 1991: 201). After disappointing local election results, the French franc left the 'Snake' for a second time in the face of mounting pressure from the foreign-exchange markets, consequent on the incompatibility between France's external commitments and internal expansionary policies. Chirac then resigned in order to concentrate on building up control of the Gaullist Party ready for the next Presidential election when he intended to replace Giscard. EMU was caught up in this underlying domestic political competition within the French Right, and Giscard was left weakened by the franc's exit from the 'Snake'.

Giscard attempted to regain the domestic political initiative on economic stabilization and EMU by appointing Raymond Barre as Prime Minister in August 1976. Before his appointment Barre had already sought to embolden Giscard to give new purpose to stabilization, arguing that inflation constituted the most severe threat to growth and employment and blaming the *relance Chirac* for France's exit from the 'Snake' (Amouroux 1986: 263–4). Giscard appointed the first non-Gaullist Prime Minister of the Fifth Republic; an acknowledged and widely respected economic specialist in the conservative liberal tradition, who took on the roles of both Prime Minister and Finance Minister; and a pro-European who had served as EC Commissioner for economic and financial affairs during the period of the Werner negotiations. In his plan of 22 September 1976 Barre focused on domestic stabilization and international competitiveness: on using the exchange rate as an external discipline, especially targeting the D-Mark; on a balanced budget; on wage moderation; and on control of the money supply. The underlying purpose was to emulate the German model (Albert 1985: 164–5). To confirm the sense of a new political direction the party composition of the government was rebalanced at the expense of the Gaullists.

In this changed domestic context Giscard identified new room for manoeuvre. He determined to impress on Chancellor Schmidt the case for new steps towards EMU. This initiative was grounded on Giscard's political ambition of recovering French leadership in Europe by aligning the French economy on German standards of performance. He saw that France's political strength abroad, and his own at home, were dependent on establishing strong non-inflationary economic growth. Germany was Giscard's fundamental point of reference (Giscard d'Estaing 1981: 34). With the support of the pro-European Barre, and confident of a new start in economic stabilization, he sought to capitalize externally on this new domestic political credibility. In February 1977 Giscard used a bilateral with Schmidt to impress on the German Chancellor the case for revitalizing EMU in the framework of Franco-German relations. He stressed the changed political context in Paris and convergence in economic policy ideas as well as the economic case for ensuring that exchange-rate instability did not negatively affect trade and investment flows within the EC. He also pressed EMU on the new EC Commission President, Roy Jenkins, in the form of something different from, and more ambitious than, the 'Snake'(Giscard d'Estaing 1988: 136). Barre's own determination to give a new political momentum on EMU was signalled by the appointment of Jean-Claude Paye from the

Quai d'Orsay as Head of the SGCI in 1977, the first non-Finance Ministry official in this post. Once EMU came back onto the agenda in 1978, Paye was to play an important co-ordinating role in Paris. Giscard's case for a new initiative on EMU was further helped by external economic development in the form of the sharp fall in the US dollar during 1977. This development was a source of mounting concern to Schmidt and opened up a new opportunity for Giscard (Giscard d'Estaing 1988: 136–7).

But in practice Giscard's room for manoeuvre on EMU remained limited by domestic political and economic weakness. His dependence on Gaullist support continued. In an effort to relax this political constraint, and ward off a strong challenge from the Left under Mitterrand, Giscard had to wait on, and plan for, the March 1978 Assembly elections. Their outcome was seen as critical for a new French EMU initiative. Hence he chose to bide his time. The Left's victories in the local elections of March 1977 were a bad omen. Giscard's relative weakness was also underlined by the fact that France had exited the 'Snake' twice. The result was an attitude of caution, of only giving serious consideration to joining a different mechanism, and of not advertising a bold view of what EMU might finally look like for fear of sparking a political row within the febrile centre-right majority. The approach was one of gradualism and indirection to accommodate domestic sensitivities on EMU and not hand political weapons to opponents. In addition, there was no sign of a closing of the wide gap between French and German economic performance. Giscard and Barre were agreed that a narrowing of that gap was a fundamental requirement for effective French political leadership of *construction européenne*. The top priority was to emulate German success by stabilizing the French economy. But Barre's efforts at domestic stabilization ran into severe political opposition from the Left and from within the Right. It was clear to Giscard and Barre that an effective stabilization policy depended on a strengthening of the UDF in the March 1978 elections.

Though these weaknesses inhibited and distracted Giscard from playing a stronger agenda-setting role on EMU in 1977 and early 1978, his positive pro-European and pro-stability policy signals were crucial in emboldening Schmidt to seize the initiative in February 1978 to form a 'European monetary bloc'. The turning-point for Giscard was the result of the March 1978 Assembly elections. Advances for his UDF meant a greater independence from the RPR, a strengthened domestic political basis for stabilization policy and for a pro-European policy, and a more confident Giscard, at least for a period. The Franco-German summit at Rambouillet in April 1978 reflected this new confidence. It underlined the new spirit of Franco-German co-operation on EMU, with both leaders planning the impending Copenhagen Council.

At Copenhagen Giscard's confident intellectual mastery of the EMU brief was evident. He focused on EMU in its global economic context as an instrument for reversing Europe's poor economic performance. There Giscard and Schmidt agreed to set up the Clappier–Schulmann group to prepare proposals for the Bremen Council in July, with Clappier operating not in his capacity as Governor of the Banque de France but as the personal representative of Giscard. Giscard was determined to take an active role in agreeing French bargaining positions, working closely with Clappier, whilst Paye ensured Barre's close involvement. The French representatives in the EC Monetary Committee (Haberer as director of the Trésor and Renaud de La Génière as a Deputy Governor of the Banque de France) were initially kept at arm's length.

Giscard and Clappier returned to the ideas in the Fourcade Plan. Their fundamental objective was to create a genuinely new monetary system for Europe, what Giscard had referred to at Copenhagen as a 'new Bretton Woods for Europe'. This system was to have two main components. First, the EUA was to be the centre of the new system, both as an embryonic reserve currency and as the basis of the intervention system. In negotiations with Schulmann, Clappier underlined the basic antipathy of the French towards the 'Snake'; Giscard reinforced this message at his meeting with Schmidt on 23 June. The French would not be rejoining the 'Snake' in its present form. Hence its reform was a prerequisite for making progress with EMU. The principle of symmetry in intervention obligations between strong and weak currencies was central to the French position. Secondly, Clappier sought a more active role for the EMCF, which was to become the European Monetary Fund and the cornerstone of the EMU process. He envisaged that it would issue EUAs. Though Schulmann remained cautious about these French ideas, Schmidt gave them broad support at the Bremen Council in July. By July Giscard could feel confident. He had the backing of Schmidt and, notably, of Chirac and Mitterrand, whom he had consulted prior to the Bremen Council.

But after July the tide at EC level ran against Giscard. In contrast to the situation during the Werner negotiations, the French were more ambitious than the Germans in the Economics Ministry and the Bundesbank. They pressed hard on the EUA as pivot; for an 'indicator of divergence' (a Belgian idea); for strengthened financial support mechanisms; and for an approach by stages, with a clear date for a stage 2 (Ludlow 1982: 230–7). Once the details of the reform package went to the EC Monetary Committee and the Committee of EC Central Bank Governors, the stout resistance of the Germans and the Dutch was evident. Schmidt began to signal his domestic political problems with the Bundesbank. By the time of the Franco-German meeting at Aachen on 14–15 September Giscard was making concessions on the EUA as the pivot in recognition of the technical difficulties of such a system. Its usefulness as an 'indicator of divergence' was accepted. But intervention was to be based on the parity grid system, meaning an asymmetric system. The one commitment that was retained was to create an EMF, modelled on the IMF. But here too the French were to be forced to make last-minute concessions. The Bundesbank argued that such a development involved creating a new EC institution and therefore a process of treaty amendment. Such a process would mean a lengthy and more complex process of agreement and ratification which went beyond the time-frame set by the heads of state and government. Agreement emerged on the idea of deferring the EMF for a further two years but setting in motion the other elements of the new monetary system immediately.

More ominously still, from October 1978 onwards the political atmosphere in Paris deteriorated. Already Barre's stabilization policy was under severe attack from within the Gaullist RPR (Lauber 1983: 114). Domestic dissensions over Europe were reopened. The impending direct elections to the European Parliament aggravated Gaullist criticisms, notably of its powers; whilst the complaints of the agricultural lobby focused on the unfair advantaging of German farmers from the CAP. The high point was to be reached on the day after the Brussels Council, 6 December, when Chirac resorted to a newly aggressive style. In the so-called *appel de Cochin* he berated Giscard and his UDF as *'le partie de l'étranger'*, ready to sell out French national interests This escalating domestic conflict did not focus primarily on the EMS, though there were Gaullist and PCF criticisms of the subordination of French economic interests to Germany (*Le Monde Diplomatique*: 18 November 1978). They were joined by Wormser, the former Governor of the Banque de France, who had been dismissed by Giscard in 1974 and who expressed reservations about the EMS negotiations. Chirac's distancing of himself from what Giscard had negotiated in Brussels was made clear in *Le Monde* on 15 December: 'The ECU sounds perhaps like something from the lips of Saint-Louis, but its reality strongly resembles the D-Mark and the monetary discipline accepted is more German than European'. The mounting criticism of European policy administered a political shock to the Elysée.

This changing domestic political background induced Giscard to shift his tactical position in the run-up to the Brussels Council. He determined on a hard-line approach to placate domestic criticism. Also, by stressing the severity of his domestic problems, Giscard sought to reduce German resistance to French demands. In Brussels Giscard focused his attacks on the CAP (seeking dismantlement of the monetary compensation amounts, MCAs) and on the question of additional financial assistance via the European Regional Fund to Ireland and Italy to ease their participation in the ERM. This position eventually took the form of a veto on the commencement of the start of the ERM, which was delayed for three months by the French. Owing to the situation in Paris, the ERM was born late and in a spirit of acrimony rather than goodwill.

At the same time this hard-line position of the Gaullists failed to help Giscard wring further concessions on the ERM at the Brussels Council. Giscard pressed the issues of strengthening credit mechanisms and of toughening up the 'presumption of intervention' when a currency crosses its 'threshold of divergence'. His chief objective was to give practical expression to the agreement that 'a European Currency Unit (ECU) will be at the centre of the EMS'. As the 'threshold of divergence' was calculated in relation to the ECU basket formula, its strengthening was designed to ensure symmetry in intervention obligations. But Schmidt refused to be budged on this issue.

With French participation in the ERM, Giscard and Barre had attained their objective of putting in place an external discipline to support domestic stabilization. In the face of the second oil price shock in 1979–80 they were determined to avoid the mistakes of Pompidou and Chirac in accommodating inflationary pressures. For the two years before the Presidential election they avoided a French devaluation within the ERM. But there were huge domestic costs, with strident criticisms from the Right as well as the Left. Neither Chirac nor Mitterrand made the ERM an issue before or during the 1981 Presidential election campaign. In this respect they stayed within a consensus on the *franc stable*. On the other hand, primacy to economic stabilization was a key issue. Here Giscard and Barre found themselves increasingly isolated. Their logic—that French political leadership of *construction européenne* depended on embracing the ERM, that the ERM was an essential external discipline, and that there had to be consistency between external commitments and ambitions and internal policies—was to be rejected, temporarily, in May 1981.

Conclusions

This historical survey underlines how French motives for pursuing EMU, and the difficulties involved, were to be understood in terms of the political problems confronting French Presidents rather than in terms of any technical rationale. These problems took two interacting forms: the 'high' politics of France's relations with the USA and Germany in the monetary field and the way that these were redefined in the wake of international developments and events; and the 'low' politics of domestic electoral and party games, in which Presidents were playing for very high stakes. Squaring these two sets of problems was to prove intractably difficult for Pompidou in the face of Gaullist resistance to loss of economic sovereignty. Giscard was to be domestically bound on EMU, despite his greater enthusiasm. He was, not least, vulnerable to criticism that he was too ready to accept German conditions for EMU, in the process sacrificing French interests. It could be expected that a newly elected President Mitterrand too would be trapped within the terms of the Left's difficulties on Europe. In this historical context Mitterrand's political achievement becomes clear. He led French policy and politics into a position in which the domestic and the international and European aspects of EMU could at last be squared. That achievement was made possible by his skills as a manager of the various tendencies within the French Socialist Party.

Whatever Mitterrand's achievement, when looked at from the vantage point of the 1990s, the Giscard/Barre period of 1976–81 can lay claim to being a major turning-point with respect to EMU. Giscard and Barre were important in seeing that Franco-German reconciliation would never in itself be a powerful enough motor to achieve EMU. An appropriate economic policy infrastructure had to be provided for that purpose to be realized. Domestic economic stabilization and the pursuit of economic convergence with Germany were, for the first time, clearly and firmly linked to the active pursuit of EMU. EMU was provided with a domestic economic policy rationale. In 1969–70, by contrast, Pompidou's EMU initiative had a political rationale grounded in French international interests but without a convincing economic underpinning. For the first time French negotiators began to be serious partners for German politicians, like Chancellor Schmidt, who were keen to promote EMU. Giscard's and Barre's key contribution to EMU was in narrowing the gap between French and German objectives. Their domestic economic policy initiatives (coupled with their ambition for European union) were the indispensable basis for Schmidt's initiative on the EMS in 1978. With the EMS Giscard and Barre had secured an economic policy engine to power the motor of Franco-German reconciliation in the direction of EMU. That contribution is not to be underestimated. They had also evolved a strategy of indirection in pursuing EMU. It was recognized that Schmidt had to make the political running in launching EMU. The French role was to cajole and coax that initiative.

The EMS agreement fell short of French objectives in the sense that the ERM was not radically different from the 'Snake'. But Giscard had succeeded in binding Germany into an agreement that contained ambitions, in particular to create the EMF and to develop the role of the new ECU as a reserve currency and a means of settlement. The agreement's flexibility was both its weakness and its strength: weakness in that it had not bound the Bundesbank to Treaty obligations; strength in that it opened up opportunities for development and for French negotiators to shift their attentions to reform of the EMS as the means to achieve EMU. In that respect Giscard had shaped the EMU agenda of the incoming Socialist government. No less importantly, Giscard had bound France to the objective of creating 'a zone of monetary stability in Europe'. This European objective was designed to have domestic policy implications: to bind French governments to the pursuit of stabilization policy. This binding was to force the Socialist government to make a painful choice in March 1983 between priority to *construction européenne* and priority to domestic economic expansion.

Giscard's and Barre's impact on French negotiating positions on EMU was even longer term. The development of French policy towards EMU from 1962 onwards was marked by them as the leading and most consistent policy entrepreneurs on behalf of EMU. Along with his closest colleagues (Barre, Clappier, Fourcade, and Lattre), Giscard actively led the process of defining the substance of EMU policy positions and of seeking out 'windows of opportunity' to put it on the agenda. The high points of that influence were in 1969–70, especially for Barre, and between 1976 and 1981. But the political opportunities for Giscard to pursue EMU were, on the whole, severely restricted, especially by Gaullist concerns about supranationalism and, notably in the aftermath of May 1968, their political difficulties in sustaining a policy of economic stabilization. His weakness was evident in 1962–6 when he was overshadowed by de Gaulle, Debré, and Couve de Murville; in the equivocal support from Pompidou for the

Werner plan in 1970–1; in his political difficulties as President with Chirac; and in the mounting electoral threat from the Left in the late 1970s. What was politically striking was the narrow domestic centrist–UDF power base for an EMU based on economic stability. There was broad support within French political culture for measures to correct the trade balance and to restore competitiveness. But this did not readily translate into acceptance of austerity measures designed to achieve a low-inflation economy German-style.

What was most striking and distinctive was Giscard's and Barre's recognition of the importance of convergence of economic policy ideas and performance. They were not simple 'monetarists' or 'institutionalists' when it came to EMU. Instead, Barre and Giscard sought parallelism in economic convergence and monetary union. The 'monetarist' approach more closely reflected Gaullist political fears about loss of sovereignty over macroeconomic policy. It also reflected a stronger 'control' element in relation to EMU: the argument that EMU was about seizing monetary power from the Bundesbank. Giscard was distant from Gaullist ideas but forced by domestic political factors to take them into account, particularly in 1970–1. He adapted to them as the only means of retaining domestic political momentum on EMU, not out of intellectual conviction.

Despite these constraints, what came across most revealingly was Giscard's and Barre's longer-term intellectual ascendancy over EMU. They presided actively over the process of giving definition to French policy positions: the primacy to a joint US dollar policy; to a strengthened united voice over international monetary reform by creating a European monetary 'identity' or 'personality'; to establishing the principle of symmetry in intervention obligations and avoiding the creation of a D-Mark zone; to the creation of an EMF with stronger support mechanisms to defend the franc from speculative attacks; to realizing EMU in stages and according to a clear timetable; to the importance of co-ordination of economic policies; to building EMU on the foundation of a commitment to economic stabilization; to the importance of EMU as an institutionalization of external discipline in the form of stable and preferably fixed EC-wide parities; and to a common currency (the single currency did not figure in French thinking till 1987–8). These French policy positions were not associated with a single policy entrepreneur in Paris. EMU involved a gradual accretion of ideas within the French elite of financial administrators. The result was a formidable edifice of shared understandings.

This particular definition of French policy positions on EMU was situated under a broad umbrella of consensus: notably about the rebalancing of international and European monetary power, about French leadership of *construction européenne* and Franco-German reconciliation, and about the *franc stable*. But Barre and Giscard also gave French EMU policy positions the particular hallmarks of the conservative-liberal economic tradition. Intellectually ascendant on EMU, they operated within a distinct tradition and associated it with that tradition. Giscard was also firmly embedded within the institutional milieu of the Finance Inspectorate. This context gave him access to enormous resources of influence and gave an added authority to his views on EMU.

Against this historical and intellectual background Socialist politicians like Mitterrand and Bérégovoy were bound to have difficulties with EMU. They could relate to it at one level. As the last chapter showed, EMU appealed to certain core values around which there was a substantial consensus, notably rebalancing international and European monetary power and Franco-German reconciliation. This deeper consensus made it possible for Chirac and Mitterrand to support Giscard during the EMS negotiations. Later, they made it possible for Chirac and Giscard to support Mitterrand before the Maastricht Council. But at another level Mitterrand and Bérégovoy had reservations about EMU as an excessively technocratic project. It lacked the 'social' dimension that they looked for in economic and in European policy. The intellectual challenge for Mitterrand was to relate EMU to the centre-left intellectual traditions in which he had been reared as a politician: especially, social Radicalism and social Catholicism. Mitterrand was intellectually ill at ease with the Trésor and the Banque de France. Unlike Giscard he did not share their type of elite socialization or their endorsement of conservative liberalism. Mitterrand's intellectual examples were Mendès France and Schuman. But neither Mendès France nor Schuman (nor their advisers and collaborators) had given much attention to EMU.

The difficulty for Mitterrand was to be how to escape from the intellectual embrace of EMU by Giscard and Barre, all the more difficult a problem because that grip was institutionalized within the Trésor and the Finance Inspectorate. The handling of the EMU negotiations under the Mitterrand Presidency was in substantial part the story of how Socialist intellectual suspicions were overcome. Bérégovoy was acutely aware that negotiations about the design of EMU went to the very heart of the question of the nature of the republican state. It was to prove much easier for French Socialist politicians to agree about the priority to EMU as an agenda item for the EC than about what sorts of concessions on the design of EMU and the conditions of its operation were acceptable to gain an agreement. The core question was just how far they should go in conceding aspects of the republican tradition, in particular the political control of economic and monetary policies. In this perspective no issue was to be more problematic than conceding to the conditions imposed by the Germans—like central bank independence and strict convergence—as the price for EMU. For those like Mitterrand and Bérégovoy, whose loyalty was to the 'social' republic, this aspect was to prove more difficult than for conservative liberals like Giscard and Barre.

Once EMU resurfaced in the late 1980s, there was an interesting difference between political and technical levels in the role of historical memory of the Pompidou and Giscard periods. Few officials had much of a memory on which to draw, most—like Trichet—having begun their careers after the Werner period. Jacques de Larosière was a significant exception; whilst Pierre de

Boissieu in the Foreign Ministry was sensitive to Pompidou's very clinical geostrategic view of EMU as a 'necessity' for France. But historical memory played a bigger role amongst politicians. Balladur and Chirac looked back to the way in which their political mentor Georges Pompidou had sought to situate EMU in a Gaullist and geopolitical frame of reference, rooted in suspicion of German power and the need to 'rebalance' European and international monetary power. Pomidou's important legacy was his frustrated attempt to find a way of accommodating Gaullists to EMU by conceiving it in terms of an inter-governmental model of Europe. As Europeans 'of the heart', Barre and Giscard incarnated different historical memories. They were a formidable background presence for Socialist politicians who had been out of national power for this whole period.

4

Challenging the 'D-Mark Zone': Agenda-Setting on EMU and the Strategy of Indirection under Mitterrand, 1981-1989

On 1 December 1988, at his own request, the Governor of the Banque de France, Jacques de Larosière, met for one hour with President Mitterrand in the Elysée Palace. The ostensible purpose of this strictly private meeting was to report on progress in the Delors Committee, the committee established at the previous European Council meeting in Hanover to study how EMU might be realized. De Larosière, who was acting in a 'personal capacity' as a member of this committee, justified the meeting by pointing out that work in the Delors Committee was about to reach a critical stage. Clarification of French positions was crucial. But he was there to persuade rather than to seek instructions. De Larosière's real purposes were twofold: to convince Mitterrand that—on strategic and tactical grounds—certain preconditions must be accepted if he was to have any prospect of securing an EMU agreement; and to provide himself with the highest-level political cover against his exposure to Finance Ministry criticisms.

The requirements as outlined by the Governor of the Banque de France were, in effect, a restatement of the French conservative-liberal economic tradition in the framework of facilitating a deal with Germany on EMU. According to de Larosière, EMU had to be based on the principle that monetary policy was founded on the pursuit of price stability: and, in order to achieve price stability within EMU, the principle of central bank independence had to be accepted by the French government. Crucially, the principle of central bank independence would have to apply to national central banks—including the Banque de France—as a precondition. It would be impossible for the ECB to function on behalf of price stability if its member governors were having to negotiate endlessly with their governments. De Larosière's message to Mitterrand was clear: unless the French government is prepared to endorse these preconditions, it is pointless to engage in EMU negotiations.

De Larosière's argument was by no means new to Mitterrand. It had been put to him earlier by Kohl. And it remained unwelcome. The idea of an independent Banque de France offended his political sensitivities as a republican and a socialist. His intellectual disposition was to oppose it, then and later. But that disposition did not surface in his meeting with de Larosière. As a disciplined strategist

Mitterrand could readily recognize that acceptance of the principle of central bank independence was necessary for the sake of *construction européenne*. But strategy was not the only consideration. It was not just a case of adapting to dependency on Germany in EMU negotiations. Mitterrand was faced by a cognitive problem in attempting to resist central bank independence. If he were to reject this principle, he would have to be able to offer a practical alternative site for the exercise of monetary power. A role for the EC Commission was absolutely unacceptable, whilst neither the European Council nor ECOFIN could be expected to play a serious role in monetary policy, except in an area like exchange rates. Hence the principle of central bank independence seemed built into the idea of EMU. In short, once EMU had been endorsed, Mitterrand found that, irrespective of strategic calculations about doing a deal with Germany, he lacked a practical alternative to the approach advocated on 1 December 1988 by de Larosière. In not questioning that approach, he gave the green light to de Larosière to hammer out a deal in the Delors Committee that would shock the Finance Ministry and its minister, Pierre Bérégovoy.

This brief meeting symbolized the complex nature of the interaction between Presidential leadership and the 'technostructure' of the French state in the development of French policy towards EMU. It illustrates the conditioning influence of Mitterrand's belief in *construction européenne*, and just how important this cognitive dimension was in shaping negotiating positions and in 'animating' French positions. It also shows how the strategic and tactical requirements of *construction européenne* were used by parts of the French 'techostructure' to empower themselves to pursue their own agendas for domestic institutional and policy reforms. Adoption and pursuit of EMU involved a shift in the domestic balance of power, in particular in the centre of gravity of economic policy ideas.

The next two chapters explore the role of Presidential leadership on EMU; the interactivity of international, European, and domestic factors in shaping the political character of that leadership; and the significance of the Finance Ministry and of the Banque de France in developing positions on EMU. Particular stress is placed on the character of, and rationale behind, the strategic choices made by French negotiators; on the complex relationship between domestic party political and geopolitical interests in informing French negotiating positions; and on the shaping influence of bureaucratic politics within the core executive. This chapter focuses on the vital French role in agenda-setting on EMU in the phase up to German unification: on explaining why, when, and how Mitterrand, his ministers, and officials sought to place EMU once again at the heart of the preoccupations of the EC.

Mitterrand's Beliefs about Europe and Strategy for EMU

Neither on entering office nor later did Mitterrand have a clear vision of what a politically unified Europe might look like. He was not interested in institutional issues or in debates about an 'intergovernmental' Europe or a 'supranational' Europe or in working out a federalist design. His approach to *construction européenne* combined a stress on functionalism as the basis of the Community method with pragmatism. In this way he came later to see a linkage between the single European market, EMU, and political union, in that order. EMU was the priority after the single market. Mitterrand's underlying pragmatism derived from a view of European unification as an inherently extremely difficult exercise confronted by enormous practical obstacles. This historical viewpoint led him to the political conclusion that European statesmanship was a matter of seeking out opportunities to move the process forward, wherever they might be found, and, not least, of keeping up the momentum (Cohen 1998: 148–50). There were at the same time certain unifying themes. One theme was a dislike of the technocracy characteristic of the EC Commission, leading to a certain critical distance from Delors. Another was Mitterrand's stress on situating EMU in a strong social dimension at the EC level (Cohen 1998: 151–2). Mitterrand's pragmatism was most clear over political union in 1990–1. Though keen on these negotiations, he was cautious about what could be achieved. Externally, there was a risk that EMU might founder as a consequence of pushing the British and some others too far and too fast on this front. But, more importantly, Mitterrand was conscious of the domestic political risks in offering too clear a target that could be used by the nationalist elements in the French Right to mobilize public opinion against Europe.

Mitterrand had already taken up a position on EMU. As early as his candidature in the French Presidential election campaign of 1965, he had clearly distinguished his position from that of de Gaulle by endorsing EMU and clothing it in a federalist language about Europe. In doing so he had sought to mobilize the pro-European element in the French centre-right behind him and also attracted the support of Jean Monnet. Later in February 1968 Mitterrand wrote in *Le Monde*: 'The mission of the French Left is to make our economy a fulcrum for European independence'. This belief in the EC as a factor of independence from the USA underpinned his attitude to EMU and, later, to the EMS: and, particularly with the Vietnam war, informed his advocacy of a European defence system. Later, in 1976 Mitterrand argued for French participation in a reformed 'Snake', in part at least to embarrass the Barre government. In June 1978 he gave his broad backing to the EMS negotiations conducted under President Giscard d'Estaing, though in the context of the June 1979 European Parliament elections he was more critical. This support for the EMS and for EMU can be related to the most consistent underlying theme in his long political career—his attachment to *construction européenne*. Whatever the hesitations and prevarications induced by considerations of domestic political strategy and tactics, notably in relation to the PCF and the unity of the Left, the ERM and EMU fitted readily into the cognitive map provided by Mitterrand's deepest political beliefs.

Despite this underlying conviction, once elected President in May 1981, Mitterrand was slow to put his weight behind the ERM and EMU and to pursue the cause of *construction européenne*. Mitterrand's personal identification with the EMS as the central axis of French international economic diplomacy can be dated to his decision of March 1983 to keep France in the ERM. That decision was the defining moment of his Presidency, measured in two ways: by the policy implications that followed from it (including the opportunity to reopen EMU); and by the way in which, in its wake, Mitterrand 'reinvented' himself as pre-eminently the European statesman. His identification with EMU came later still. It was precipitated by two developments, at the European and international levels: by the IGC negotiations of 1985, culminating in the Single European Act; and, from 1986, by his anxieties about the risk that Germany might be seduced by Gorbachev to cut a deal with the Soviet Union, trading its role in, and commitments to, the West for the prize of German unification. Mitterrand's view of EMU was always shaped, first and foremost, by his historical and ideological view of how the EC should develop as more than a mere trading bloc; and by a strongly developed and historically informed geopolitical sense that led him to seek to 'bind in' Germany to France. Preceding March 1983 the ERM had figured primarily as a tactical issue in Mitterrand's long-term domestic political strategy for uniting the French Left. After 1958 Mitterrand's central political achievement had been to theorize the union of the Left (Lacouture 1998). The ERM was above all perceived as a constraint on, and problem for, that strategy. As an inheritance from the Right in 1981, rather than a part of his manifesto commitment, the ERM—and the purpose of monetary stability behind it—did not interest Mitterrand. He was simply indifferent to the issue, choosing to ignore the issue in May 1981 (and thereby staying in the ERM) whilst he got on with the serious business of implementing the manifesto.

Afterwards the ERM was redefined as an opportunity to realize a refashioned political strategy on two intertwined levels: a strategy of repositioning his Presidency and the Socialist Party towards the centre in domestic politics and of rebalancing monetary power in Europe and internationally. Basic to this strategy was the association of himself with two objectives: the promotion of the larger interests of France as a whole by reinvigorating French leadership in Europe and by exploiting his image as European and world statesman; and the achievement of an image of financial prudence, reliability, and respectability for the Socialist Party. The ERM became the vehicle to pursue and reconcile these twin strategic objectives. Only after some progress had been made towards these objectives could Mitterrand hope to champion EMU credibly. The whole process involved a difficult and complex intellectual adjustment for the President, requiring all his resources as a political craftsman. But, however delayed the process, Mitterrand's personal identification with EMU preceded that of Chancellor Kohl. For Mitterrand, German unification reinforced a personal commitment to EMU that was already long in place. Mitterrand's baptism of fire in relation to the monetary dimension of European leadership came that much earlier than Kohl's—in March 1983.

Strategically, French policy on EMU under Mitterrand had to contend with the fundamental structural reality of German monetary power and French dependency on that power. This basic factor reduced the credibility of two strategic options for making progress towards EMU and thereby gaining greater influence over European economic and monetary policies: the direct threat of French withdrawal from European monetary co-operation to force Germany's hand (the diplomatic and economic costs of exit from the ERM were potentially enormous); and the direct attempt to gain agreement on a design of EMU modelled on France by basing an EMU initiative on French proposals (the cost would be to deter Germany from co-operation). Hence the French strategy that evolved under Mitterrand, with a significant contribution from Roland Dumas and the Quai d'Orsay, was essentially indirect, subtle, and psychological and conducted in strictest secrecy. Its first component was to encourage the Germans to table EMU proposals, identifying the most receptive point in the German governmental system: the German Foreign Minister, Hans-Dietrich Genscher. It relied on tactics of 'divide and rule' between Bonn and Frankfurt, with the focus being on mobilizing the German Foreign Ministry, especially Genscher, and the Federal Chancellor's Office to counter the positions of the Bundesbank. Another element in French strategy was to 'bind in' the Bundesbank by a policy of precommitment to stages with attached dates. This strategy was accompanied by 'salami-slicing': by a gradualist approach to EMU of limited, piecemeal gains, thereby eroding the independence of the Bundesbank. Such a strategic choice informed the proposals for a stage 2 of the EMS, with a European Monetary Fund, and for the Franco-German Economic Council in 1987.

Overall, French strategy favoured the use of sustained indirect pressure for EMU, concentrated on Germany. This strategy bore the strong imprint of the powerful 'Realist' camp in the Quai d'Orsay. Fundamental to the approach of Mitterrand and Dumas after 1984 was a recognition that EMU would not flow from a direct French initiative (or an EC Commission initiative associated with Jacques Delors). It had to come from Bonn, and the most likely candidate for taking the initiative was Hans-Dietrich Genscher, the German Foreign Minister. Hence cultivation of the Dumas–Genscher relationship became basic to French EMU diplomacy.

An additional dimension, from which Mitterrand was more distanced, was provided by the special strategic outlook of the Finance Ministry. Its strategic choices took three forms, essentially complementing the more 'high politics' approach of the Quai d'Orsay and the Elysée. First, Trésor officials used their commitment to a tough and domestically costly *franc fort* policy to 'bind their own hands' in EMU negotiations. They sought concessions from EC partners to match their domestic courage and underpin their domestic political position. This type of strategy involved arguments about equity: that France's disproportionately great efforts at *rigueur* should be properly recognized and rewarded. Secondly, in seeking out concessions Trésor officials and finance minsters made strategic, selective use of economic statistics. French performance was compared to German and others on such dimensions as inflation, balance of trade, and budget deficit. When an advantage in economic statistics was discovered, it was pressed home in negotiations. Finally, Finance Ministry officials saw in broad political support for EMU a means to enforce contentious domestic policy changes to embed a stability culture in France. The constraints of EMU were welcomed as an instrument of domestic modernization. They empowered Finance Ministry technocrats. In short, there was a complex web of strategic choices in relation to EMU amongst which French negotiators manoeuvred. But the most important underlying theme was its indirectness and use of sustained psychological pressure on the Germans.

Intellectually, the commitment to EMU involved a protracted and difficult process of policy reflection for Mitterrand, his ministers, and officials. Part of the problem was to relate EMU to the ideological context of Socialist government and to Mitterrand's own complex personal intellectual history. The ERM and EMU came with a powerful, in-built conservative-liberal ballast that reflected their intellectual origins under Giscard d'Estaing. They had no appeal to those on the Left whose heritage was Marxism and presented difficulties for radicals of the Left like Mitterrand. Hence as long as Mitterrand embraced the unity of the Left, including the French Communist Party (PCF) and CERES, as his basic political strategy, there were no serious prospects for developing policy around the ERM and EMU. For CERES the EMS was the expression of German economic and ideological imperialism. The *Projet Socialiste* of 1979 argued that 'European monetary policy can only be the end of structural transformations destined to surmount the current disequilibrium and not the reverse'. The fault of the EMS was that it involved 'harmonization around German standards' rather than 'concertation'. In this context Mitterrand offered cautious and conditional endorsement of the EMS in the 1981 Presidential election campaign. Once that domestic political strategy lost its primacy, in 1983–4, and the new Prime Minister Laurent Fabius began to seek out the centre ground of French politics, the intellectual challenge was to marry the ERM and EMU to the traditions of social Radicalism and social Catholicism within the Socialist Party. That task was initially taken up by Jacques Delors and his advisers and, from 1984, by Pierre Bérégovoy. An attempt was made to redefine the ERM and EMU in terms of 'modernization' and 'solidarity', of a 'Europe of research' and a 'social Europe'.

The other part of the problem related to the consistency of a negotiable EMU policy with broadly shared Socialist political principles stretching from social democrats like Michel Rocard through social Radicals to Marxists. This problem crystallized around the issue of central bank independence. The intellectual solution—of combining acceptance of the principle of an independent ECB with a new structure of *gouvernement économique* at the EC level—was intellectually elegant. It reconciled the institutional arrangements for EMU with the French republican and socialist traditions in a cognitively coherent manner. But, fatally, *gouvernement économique* proved difficult to negotiate in the face of deep German suspicions and mistrust.

In a series of speeches during his state visit to the Federal Republic of Germany in October 1987 President Mitterrand spelt out in a new form the set of policy beliefs that inspired his European policy and set his ambition for a 'common' European currency and for other projects in that perspective. In particular, in his speech at Aachen's city hall on 20 October he developed the theme of a common Franco-German historical task as 'the motor of Europe'. This metaphor was by no means new, but was to remain the core of Mitterrand's approach to European policy. What was novel was his invocation of the symbolism of Aachen to clothe the Franco-German relationship in a common historical and cultural root: the Empire of Charlemagne. Both countries derived from the same man and his dynasty; were nourished by the same cultural source; and shared the same ambitions. The task for the Franco-German relationship was to reunite their peoples on the Carolingian model, building history together (Bender 1995: 55–7). Mitterrand was in effect providing an historical legitimation for the Franco-German relationship. History was being used to inspire current policies, in defence, technology, culture, and EMU. Following German unification Mitterrand was to return more frequently to the Carolingian model, for instance in his Aachen speech of 9 May 1991. 'Carolingian Europe' was contrasted with 'Germanic Europe'.

In a speech in Germany on 21 October 1987 Mitterrand resorted to more modern historical memories. He held up Robert Schuman, a non-Socialist, as the personification of the intertwined histories of France and Germany: a man who had known what it was like to be French and German. By situating himself in line with Schuman, he was by implication distancing his approach from that of de Gaulle. Mitterrand went on to spell out the deeply personal basis of his commitment to Franco-German relations. He referred to his period as a prisoner of war in Germany and recalled the words of a German woman, spoken to him as he had been arrested after trying to escape. Handing him bread and sausage, she had said to him: 'Sir, I hope that this will make you like Germany' (Bender 1995: 64–5). Mitterrand was intent on setting Franco-German relations in a context of positive human experiences rather than just of overcoming the traumas of war. Above all, he liked to present himself as a 'conviction' European of the first generation, referring to the impact on him of attending the European Congress at The Hague in 1948. He was a man born in 1916 whilst the battle of Verdun raged; who was a soldier and prisoner during the Second World War; who had watched the disintegration of the French army in 1940 and the harsh effects of defeat. EMU was, accordingly, for him a matter of peace or war in Europe.

The commitment to *construction européenne* can claim to be the single most important continuous theme in Mitterrand's long and tortuous political career. He was a federalist 'of the heart', though his head dictated that this position was not to be defended publicly in France. Mitterrand saw himself as a European 'of the first generation', perhaps its last major representative. But Europe did not feature strongly during his Presidential election campaign in 1981 when he refrained from making positive statements about the EMS. On entering office in 1981, the EC was by no means a central focus of his Presidency. Mitterrand was, first and foremost, a consummate political strategist who had learnt to control his political passions and adapt his beliefs to the exigencies of the pursuit, and later tenure, of office. Cast into the political wilderness by the Fifth Republic, his political strategy had been focused on the long haul of attaining the Presidential office. The means was to unite the Left behind his leadership and to adapt to the popularity of the Gaullist notion of national independence (Cole 1996: 72). This strategy forced him to make concessions to the PCF and to the left-wing of the Socialist Party, leading to a more reserved and critical attitude to the EC during the 1970s. Given their hostility to the EC, common ground was achieved by de-emphasizing supranationalism in favour of building a French model constructed around a Keynesian-style economic relaunch, by attacking the subservience of the EC to the multinational corporations, and by prioritizing the issue of solidarity with the Third World and North–South relations. The presence of the PCF and of CERES in the French government, and their appeasement by Mitterrand, inhibited reflection on how the ERM and EMU might serve as opportunities. The role of the ERM as problematic constraint on domestic economic policies and political strategy was more strongly articulated. The appointment of Delors to the Finance Ministry and of Claude Cheysson to the Foreign Ministry in 1981 sent a strongly pro-European signal. But they were harnessed to the political strategy of Mitterrand, as indeed was the President himself. In Mitterrand's words of 1980: '*L'Europe sera socialiste ou ne se sera pas*' (Favier and Martin-Roland 1990: 362).

Mitterrand's Governing Style and EMU

Mitterrand's governing style was deeply marked by his long and complex political past: as a prisoner of war and clandestine resistance fighter and leader; as a politician marked by the complex political wheeling and dealing of Fourth Republic governments; as a talented and ambitious politician who had been exiled in opposition for twenty-three years after 1958; as a man who had worked behind the scenes to put together a reformed Socialist Party since 1971 and taken it into power; and as a 65-year-old man in 1981 who had been politically active for thirty-six years (Nay 1984). The result was an exceedingly complex President whom others found difficult to calculate and labelled 'sphinx-like' and enigmatic. Mitterrand was, above all, a hardened, combative, tenacious, and secretive individualist, inspired by a fundamentally pessimistic conception of human nature (Giesbert 1996). In consequence, as President he was preoccupied with ensuring his freedom of action by multiplying his contacts, hesitant to reveal his hand—even to those closest to him—and happier taking refuge in ambiguity and in biding his time (Favier and Martin-Roland 1990: 529–30). He was at the same time a cultivated man of wide and deep historical and literary reading, an impressive stylist and conversationalist, with a classical education and an intense feeling for the power of language and the political significance of cultural forms. His attitude to politics was complex. On the one hand, Mitterrand was a man of political passion; he cared deeply about peace and social justice, and his political past had reinforced these passions (Cole 1997). Yet he was very much the cool technician of power; personal sentiment did not get in the way of the requirements of gaining and holding power.

Mitterrand was a man hardened by a career of continuing political attacks and setbacks. In consequence, he relied on small circles of those in whom he trusted, but even then only conditionally: a tiny inner circle of those with whom he had a relationship of *complicité*, most notably Roland Dumas; and outer circles where respect played the main role for him, including here Bérégovoy and Elisabeth Guigou. Delors was never in the inner or the outer circles. Mitterrand was a deeply suspicious man. In fact, he practised divide and rule even amongst his closest collaborators and friends, rejecting the idea of a personal cabinet or teamwork (Favier and Martin-Roland 1990: 511; Védrine 1996: chapter 1). Mitterrand's distance was accentuated by a need to be respected as '*un grand homme d'État*'. This need was fed by his fear of not being taken seriously as the first President of the Left in the history of the Fifth Republic and by his sense of living in the shadow of de Gaulle's success in remoulding postwar French politics. The need for respect powerfully conditioned his attitude to the ERM and EMU.

Intellectually too, Mitterrand was complex: '*une formidable macédoine*' in the words of Lacouture (1998). Like Mendès France he had moved to socialism in the 1960s and 1970s, but came originally from a right-wing Catholic milieu and had been both in the employment of the Vichy regime and a member of the Resistance. In the French Saint-Simonian and Comtian traditions he remained fascinated by the modern world of science and technology and its implications. The view of himself as President during a new industrial revolution appealed to his sense of history. Mitterrand enthusiastically embraced the idea that France should lead the world in embracing new technologies. 'Modernization' emerged as a key word of his Presidency from 1982–3 onwards; it involved the choice of opening France to the world. EMU was very much part of this modernization project. And yet he remained deeply uncomfortable with key aspects of modernization, in particular the power and global reach of the financial markets. Mitterrand's past was evident here. He came from a Catholic and provincial background and retained an ambivalent attitude towards money. His discomfort related not just to the dubious morality of speculation but also to the power of those who held money over democratically elected politicians. Global financial markets challenged the republican values to which he was wedded and which he felt that it was his duty to safeguard. EMU offered, above all else, the political counterweight to the power of global financial markets. It offered the choice for modernity whilst providing a new and more effective means of challenging the financial markets. In short, Mitterrand had a very ambivalent conception of EMU.

Mitterrand could charm and persuade with the warmth of his convictions and by his sensibility and charm. He could also confuse and disturb by his sphinx-like quality, by his detachment and isolation, and by his addiction to secretiveness, ambiguity, evasion, and scheming as political instruments. Mitterrand preferred to listen rather than reveal himself, to test others in conversation in a way that could be discomforting (Favier and Martin-Roland 1990: 511). His silence could be deeply unsettling. In relation to EMU these qualities irritated Delors and officials in the German Federal Chancellor's Office. It was often difficult to divine clear positions on EMU. Mitterrand's suspicions focused in particular on the French administration, especially the diplomatic corps and the Finance Inspectorate. He did not expect the Quai d'Orsay and the Trésor to welcome a Socialist government, given their social elitism; he distrusted their long political association with, and enhanced status under, Gaullist governments; and he harboured a distrust of what he saw as their inbred intellectual arrogance and conservatism. Mitterrand's governing style was designed to exploit the expertise of technocrats whilst minimizing their power; to clarify that he would not depend solely on them for information and advice; and to reward those of them who were intellectually honest with him and clearly demonstrated their loyalty. The appointment of Bérégovoy as Secretary-General at the Elysée, of Jacques Attali as special adviser (with responsibility for G7), and of Hubert Védrine as diplomatic adviser bypassed the official administration and signalled Mitterrand's intentions. In distancing himself from the Finance Inspectorate he was symbolically distancing himself from Giscard d'Estaing.

Mitterrand was as much Janus-like as sphinx-like. On the one hand, he was an astute and cunning observer of the balance of political forces and of the strengths and frailties of personalities, testing out weaknesses and biding his time before acting. These qualities of the poker player served him well during the period of *cohabitation* with the more impetuous Jacques Chirac (1986–8). There was a plasticity about his political persona. Steeped in the mores of French politics and of Classical Rome, Mitterrand was the masterful player of symbolic politics, the consummate artist of political language. He sought to reinvent himself, Roman-style, as the embodiment of the historical mission of the French republic (the man of *pietas* and *humanitas*) and, above all, to invest himself with an air of *gravitas* and *severitas*. But, on the other hand, Mitterrand was no mere chameleon when it came to adopting EMU. He was a 'conviction' politician. His convictions were woven into the tapestry of his complex political actions. Foremost amongst these convictions was Mitterrand's belief in *construction européenne* and in Franco-German reconcilation. That belief was tailored to the exigencies of political strategy, but in the process its motivating power was not lost. And, amongst Socialist politicians before and during his

Presidency, very few were more distinctively motivated by *construction européenne* and Franco-German reconciliation than Mitterrand. In the context of Franco-German bilaterals from 1985 onwards Mitterrand emerged as a tireless and persistent advocate of EMU.

The EMS, EMU, and *Construction Européenne*: The Domestic and International Context, 1981–1983

In 1981 Mitterrand's immense personal prestige as the architect of Socialist victory in the Presidential and Assembly elections gave him an enormous authority over policy. But the way in which that authority was exercised in relation to the EMS and EMU was deeply conditioned by the nature of the Left that he took into office; by his personal debts to those who had given him their support; and by his inclination—acquired during the long years of opposition—to balance and play off rival factions and personalities (Bauchard 1986: 11–14). Various domestic political considerations shaped the way in which his pro-Europeanism was expressed and led him to de-emphasize EMU. First, EMU was intimately associated with the policy agenda of the Giscard administration from which he was keen to dissociate himself. Also, EMU was about institutional reform of the EC. Particularly on the Left of the Socialist Party and within the PCF, there was a strongly held view that institutional reforms—like majority voting and the qualifying of the national veto—would threaten the ability of the new French government to build a new model based on an economic relaunch to combat rising unemployment. European policy was the handmaiden of domestic policy. Hence at his first European Council in June 1981 Mitterrand called for a 'European social space' and for a European industrial plan. The nature of the new government's Europeanism was spelt out in the Memorandum on the Revitalization of the Community in October 1981, with its call for EC-wide reflation. In the absence of broad support for this French socialist-style EC policy model—which was not forthcoming—EC institutional reform was looked on with distrust and suspicion. The Genscher–Colombo proposals of 1981 and the Spinelli initiative of 1982 were not welcomed by the government of Pierre Mauroy, which was preoccupied with implementing the programme of 1981 and avoiding impediments to its implementation. The Socialist Party's basic position was anti-federalist.

In addition, the Socialist Party had a strongly Anglophile tradition, seeing Britain as the 'mother of parliaments', as the wartime ally, and as a country with a social democratic legacy. There was a discomfort with the Franco-German 'axis' and a preference for keeping Britain alongside France in European unification, associated with such imposing historical figures as Léon Blum, Pierre Mendès France, and Guy Mollet (Védrine 1996: 120–1, 273–5). The new secretary-general of the Elysée, Pierre Bérégovoy, was a former collaborator of Mendès France: André Chandernagor, the Minister for European Affairs under

Cheysson, a former collaborator of Mollet. Another variant of this attitude, represented by the Culture Minister Jack Lang, emphasized the importance of counterbalancing the Teutonic, North European political world with the Latin, South European. Hence the relationship to Italy, and to post-dictatorship Portugal and Spain, took on significance, particularly with Felipe Gonzales as the first Spanish Socialist Prime Minister since the 1930s and both countries as applicants for EC membership. At their bilateral in Madrid in June 1982 Mitterrand's new support for expediting Spanish entry to the EC was a tangible sign of this viewpoint. From May 1981 to July 1982, whilst Bérégovoy remained at the Elysée, the emphasis was on equality in bilateral relations within the EC. At his bilateral meeting with Chancellor Helmut Schmidt on 7 October 1981 Mitterrand rejected the idea of the Franco-German relationship as an 'axis', characterizing it as a 'privileged friendship'. The political realist in Mitterrand was attracted to the balance of power argument and the cultural argument that underpinned these views in the Socialist Party.

From autumn 1982 onwards Mitterrand's pro-European beliefs were converted into a sustained policy priority to *construction européenne*, focused on the Franco-German relationship. This reprioritization had its fundamental basis in the early policy experiences of the Mitterrand Presidency, not least the desire to offer security to a German political elite worried by stronger neutralist sentiments at home and the failure of early Socialist efforts to reform the international monetary system in the face of US resistance, not least at the G7 summit at Versailles in June 1982 (Védrine 1996: chapter 8). The upward rise of the US dollar was causing severe difficulties to French economic policy. Both developments shifted Mitterrand's attention to the European level as a means of securing French security and economic interests.

Personal chemistry also played an important contextual and catalytic role. In particular, there was a change in the personal climate of Franco-German relations consequent on the replacement of Schmidt by Helmut Kohl in September 1982. Mitterrand's relations with Chancellor Schmidt remained cool and distant, aggravated by Schmidt's hostility to the presence of the PCF in government. With Kohl Mitterrand immediately struck up a warm personal relationship. Kohl stressed his absolute commitment to European unification, setting it in a broad historical context that appealed to Mitterrand. At their first meeting in the Elysée on 2 October 1982 Kohl spoke with emotion of being the last German Chancellor with whom it would be possible to build Europe. His presentation, rooted in his memories of what war had done to his family, deeply impressed Mitterrand and nurtured a sense that these two leaders shared much in common at a personal level. It also struck a strategic chord. Mitterrand was attracted by the sense of historic opportunity offered by Kohl. The change of personal chemistry was assisted by the replacement of Bérégovoy by Jean-Louis Bianco in July 1982 and by Pierre Morel's promotion within the Elysée. A Germanist, Bianco—assisted by Morel—encouraged Mitterrand to develop the theme of Franco-German reconciliation and inject new objectives into that relationship. By 1984 EMU had begun to figure amongst those objectives, albeit in a tentative manner.

For Mitterrand a crucial signal that he could rely on Kohl to protect his flank on economic policy came just before the Copenhagen European Council of 3–4 December 1982. Kohl deterred Stoltenberg from pursuing the issue of a devaluation of the French franc within the ERM, giving an important breathing space to the French President. Mitterrand was encouraged to attach greater importance to his forthcoming speech to the German Bundestag on the twentieth anniversary of the Elysée Treaty and to believe that he could count on Kohl's support in avoiding an exit of the French franc from the ERM in 1983.

The first striking expression of Mitterrand's commitment to *construction européenne* came in the context of the 'Euromissile' crisis of 1982–3. This crisis had been precipitated by the issue of whether US Cruise and Pershing missiles should be stationed in Europe to balance Soviet deployments in Eastern Europe and by worries, not least in Paris, about a strengthening neutralist tendency in German public opinion. By endorsing the logic of the balance of power and deterrence, Mitterrand had already lent his support to a beleagured Chancellor Schmidt at their meeting in the Elysée on 24 May 1981. In return, Schmidt affirmed the full support of Germany for the French franc within the ERM (Védrine 1996: 128–9). Mitterrand was alert to the potential to trade German gains in security policy (by offering his support to Schmidt, and later Kohl) in return for French gains in economic policy (from German support in the ERM). Kohl's backing before the Copenhagen European Council induced not just a greater will to reciprocate but also a desire to give a new impetus to *construction européenne* by proclaiming his commitment to Franco-German reconciliation in the very heart of the German political establishment.

Mitterrand's speech of 20 January 1983 in the Bundestag was the main turning-point (Védrine 1996: 235–7). In it he gave full endorsement to Kohl's strategy on stationing Cruise and Pershing missiles in Germany. But he went further in spelling out his thinking about the Franco-German relationship, drawing in a characteristic Mitterrand manner on Victor Hugo's phrase '*consanguinité franco-allemande*'. Most evident of all was Mitterrand's preoccupation with the security and military aspects of that relationship, which was to prove important in trade-offs with the economic and monetary aspects in 1987–8. He characterized the Elysée Treaty of 1963 as an historical event on the road to a united Europe and set new priorities for its work, especially in developing its military aspects and a joint defence concept. Significantly, the speech—and Kohl's support for the franc in December 1982—formed a major part of the backdrop to his economic decision of March 1983 to keep France in the ERM. But the top priority for Mitterrand at this stage was the defence dimension of the Franco-German relationship. As a consummate strategist, Mitterrand was attuned to the strengths that France could bring to negotiations in this area and the prospects for using concessions here to induce German economic and monetary concessions. He had begun by building up substantial political credit with Kohl.

But the most dramatic event of all as far as EMU was concerned was Mitterrand's personal decision of March 1983 to remain in the ERM. This decision fitted into the larger context of personal chemistry and strategy that had already fallen into place and was the key precondition for putting EMU back on the agenda from 1984 onwards. For Mitterrand the decisive argument was that French withdrawal from the ERM would isolate and marginalize France and reduce his capacity to negotiate other aspects of *construction européenne* on French terms (Védrine 1996: 285–7). In contrast, the economic aspects of that decision left Mitterrand much more troubled. He distrusted Delors and the Finance Ministry and was intent on putting them to the test. Mitterrand's governing style demonstrated a preoccupation with avoiding being a prisoner of 'orthodox' Trésor thinking. Hence he multiplied his sources of ideas and information, inducing uncertainty and suspicion about his real intentions. Within the complex networks of contacts what remained most striking and important was the emergence of a clear Elysée attitude, articulated in memos from the so-called 'club of Five' (see below). Their preoccupations were political, institutional, and strategic: political in seeking to shield the President from the fate that befell the Left in 1924 and 1926, warning that ERM exit would mean dependency on the International Monetary Fund (IMF); institutional in seeking to protect and augment the bargaining resources of the Presidential office in relation to such projects as international monetary reform and 'social' Europe; and strategic in seeking to shift the burden of responsibility onto a German revaluation rather than a third French devaluation (which was seen as politically and economically damaging). These preoccupations counselled a strongly pro-ERM attitude and a stress on activating the Franco-German relationship to deal with the problem, articulated by Attali, Bianco, François-Xavier Stasse, and Guigou in particular.

Mitterrand was unquestionably influenced by what was in effect the institutional view of the Elysée on the ERM and by January 1983 had made up his mind to stay in the ERM. But he was being asked to make economic policy concessions that he resented. The path that he had envisaged for his Presidency was of an influential new France exporting its Socialist policy model to the EC and beyond. Mitterrand was being asked to choose between losing power and influence by exiting the ERM and making radical adjustments to the Socialist model when it was unclear what the programmatic implications would be. The President had to navigate uncharted waters without the clear aid of the Socialist policy model with which he had entered office. In embracing the ERM, and later EMU, Mitterrand had to reinvent himself politically.

Finance Ministry Power under Delors: the '*Tournant*' of 1982, Stage 2 of the EMS, and Defining French Objectives for EMS Reform

In May 1981 the new Socialist government inherited a Finance Ministry with a strong institutional commitment to the EMS and EMU. The director of the

Trésor, Jean-Yves Haberer, had been responsible for international affairs at the time of the Fourcade Plan and then, as director, worked on the EMS negotiations. Like Michel Pebereau, deputy director, he had been close to the thinking of Giscard d'Estaing, with its stress on the Franco-German relationship in building EMU. In a longer-term perspective, since 1962 the Finance Ministry had served under ministers (with the notable exception of Michel Debré 1966–8) who had been committed to EMU. The arrival in power of the Socialists led officials like Haberer and Pebereau to scale down their expectations for EMU. Their conservative-liberal theory of EMU suggested that EMU was no longer a practical proposition.

Their main feeling was a mixture of relief and apprehension when, on 21 May 1981, a meeting involving Mitterrand, Mauroy, Delors, and Bérégovoy decided to maintain the franc's parity within the ERM. Combined with a rise in interest rates and a tightening of exchange controls, this decision curbed speculation in the short term. But the decision of 21 May was taken more on political grounds than based on economic reasoning (Peyrelevade 1985: 128–31). Mitterrand did not want to take risks with European policy by floating the franc. He also sought to protect his Socialist Party in the forthcoming National Assembly elections from political criticisms of an inability to defend the currency. It was not, however, clear to the Finance Ministry and the Banque de France how the situation could be sustained.

It is important to note that Finance Ministry expectations had in any case been lowered after 1979. Policy had been forced to contend with the requirements of ERM membership in the context of the effects of the second oil-price crisis and of the severe pressures under which the Barre government had laboured from within the RPR. The problems of domestic economic stabilization had taken precedence over ERM reform and EMU. By 1981 Finance Ministry officials viewed the ERM as an exercise in crisis management rather than as offering early opportunities for building the European Monetary Fund and developing the ECU's role as a reserve and intervention currency. Hence they were not actively pushing for implementation of stage 2 of the EMS.

The arrival of the Socialists reduced Finance Ministry expectations for EMU even further. In the first place, the new minister, Jacques Delors, was not viewed as a Socialist party heavyweight who was likely to be able to fight the Finance Ministry's corner effectively. He was seen as sharing its preoccupations with respecting the external constraints of the ERM; he was also recognized as a social Catholic on the most pro-European wing of the Socialist Party and therefore unquestionably in favour of the ERM and EMU. Indeed, Delors had referred to the EMS as the 'jewel in the crown' of the EC. But Delors was low in the Socialist hierarchy and lacked influence in the Elysée. After the experience of having the previous Prime Minister, Raymond Barre, as its minister, and hence having a direct line to the Elysée, the shift in the domestic political fortunes of the Finance Ministry seemed radical. Given the new President's deep distrust of technocrats, it appeared all the more vital to have a strong political voice. From the outset Delors had an uphill struggle to persuade his Finance Ministry officials that he was professionally competent at the political level. This political factor altered perceptions of the prospects for EMU. With the Trésor's influence diminished in Paris, its potential influence in giving leadership on EMU in Brussels was judged negligible.

Secondly, the Socialist government was committed to a Keynesian programme of economic expansion based on boosting consumption and investment, expanding the role of the public sector in job creation and social welfare provision, and 'reconquest of the internal market' (by large-scale nationalization). This programme was radically out of line with the inherited Trésor notion of preserving the *grands équilibres*; with the Trésor's reassessment of the importance of stabilization to international competitiveness since the 1970s; and with its interpretation of international economic trends. With the prospects of a widening budget deficit, inflationary pressures, and a deteriorating current account, the outlook for French membership of the ERM looked bleak. France was, in the view of senior Trésor officials, being set on a trajectory that would inevitably expose the contradiction between its external commitment to the ERM and EMU and its new domestic policy priorities. The combination of these political and policy problems with the economic outlook consequent on the second oil crisis induced a deep pessimism about the prospects for ERM reform, let alone EMU.

Thirdly, there was a political conflict at the very heart of the Finance Ministry. In 1981 Delors was very unhappy about losing budgetary matters. The young Budget Minister, Laurent Fabius, was much more closely in touch with the reformist political mood of the new government. Intellectually, he came from a different and more influential tradition within the Socialist Party. Delors was situated within social Catholicism, which was strongly represented in his cabinet by figures like Jean-Baptiste de Foucauld and Jérôme Vignon. Along with his director of cabinet, Philippe Lagayette, they were wedded to prioritizing the ERM as a constraint and to the role of pedagogy and dialogue in the economic policy process. In contrast, Fabius was very much a social Radical in the Mendès France tradition, advocating an activist, reformist policy of 'modernization'. Unlike Delors Fabius had the ear of the President, and his first budget was billed as a 'relaunch for employment' (Favier and Martin-Roland 1990: 405). It involved a 25 per cent increase in the budget deficit, against the background of an expanding current account deficit, and was immediately followed in October 1981 by the first devaluation of the franc within the ERM during the Mitterrand Presidency. A further signal of the political isolation and impotence of Delors came on 7 October when the Council of Ministers firmly rejected his argument that the devaluation must be accompanied by a set of economic policy measures to stabilize the new parity. With the President backing Fabius against Delors's plea for 'realism', he seriously considered resignation. By 29 November Delors was speaking on television about the need for 'a pause in announcing reforms, but in return for better management of those that had already been decided' (Favier and Martin-Roland 1990: 409).

Gradually, during early 1982, Delors and the Trésor emerged from their isolation and began to construct an effective domestic strategy for regaining control over policy. The appointment of Michel Camdessus as director of the Trésor in 1982 in succession to Haberer (rather than the Socialist candidate Henri Baquiast) was an important step in building internal mutual confidence and trust (Mamou 1988: chapter 16). The strategy of the Finance Ministry was to press on the President the inevitability of a second devaluation in 1982, unless there was a shift to budgetary discipline; to activate a network that could educate Mitterrand in economic realities; and to use a battery of Trésor notes to draw attention to the economic and monetary risks of current policies. At the same time, recognizing Mitterrand's deep suspicion of the Trésor, Delors sought to avoid any semblance of Trésor authorship of proposals. The key figures in the emerging network for *rigueur* were Stasse, economic adviser at the Elysée, who from 1982 was supported by Guigou (who was recruited by Bianco from Delors's cabinet as an Elysée adviser); and, at the Matignon, Jean Peyrelevade (whom Mitterrand distrusted) and Henri Guillaume. They were carefully cultivated by Camdessus and Lagayette who sought to mobilize them to press the case for *rigueur*. The decisive argument was political: the danger that the Mitterrand Presidency would succumb to the same fate as the 'cartel of the Left' in 1924 and the Popular Front in 1936—a reputation for financial ineptitude. Stasse pressed this argument on Mitterrand: Peyrelevade on Mauroy. Also of political importance was the role of historical memory: Fabius and Pierre Bérégovoy, Secretary-General in the Elysée, recalled Mendès France's *'courage'* in calling for *rigueur* in 1944–5. As *mendèsistes*, they espoused *rigueur*, though their attitude to the ERM did not alter; they favoured a provisional exit. Mauroy was the most receptive of all to Delors's message.

The first major signal of conversion to *rigueur* came at a meeting of economics ministers with the President and Prime Minister (a *Conseil restreint*) on 2 February 1982. Here a decision of historic significance was made: to limit the budget deficit to 3 per cent of GDP (Mamou 1988: 412). This figure was later to be introduced by French negotiators into the Maastricht Treaty negotiations on EMU. The 3 per cent figure was made public after the Council of Ministers' meeting on 10 March, and endorsed by Mitterrand at his press conference on 9 June 1982. The second major signal was attributable to Peyrelevade and Guillaume. On 28 May 1982 Mauroy endorsed their note advocating a combination of a second devaluation with budget cuts, wage and price controls, and credit restrictions and forwarded it to Mitterrand (Mamou 1988: 415–16). This note—and the influence of Hervé Hannoun in the Elysée—formed the basis for Mitterrand's press conference in which the 'second phase' of his Presidency was announced. Though the word *rigueur* was not mentioned, he spoke of 'mastering' inflation and the *'grands équilibres'*. The discourse of the Trésor was back in usage, if not yet fully in fashion. Mauroy's note also helped shape the package of economic policy measures that followed the second devaluation of the franc in the ERM on 12 June, just three days after Mitterrand's major press conference. In short, in June 1982 the turning-point of the Mitterrand Presidency had been reached.

However, this turning-point came too late, and remained too limited in effect, to rescue the progress of proposals for implementing stage 2 of the EMS as planned in the resolution of the European Council in December 1978. Though French Trésor negotiators had fought for the idea of a stage 2, they did not—for reasons outlined above—play a leading role in enthusiastically backing the EC Commission proposals that were considered by ECOFIN on 15 March 1982. As early as December 1981 ECOFIN had agreed that further development of the EMS must focus on non-institutional reforms. Delors supported Commission proposals for intramarginal intervention, for increasing the acceptance limit for ECU, and, more generally, for strengthening the use of the ECU—all demands consistent with French bargaining positions under Giscard d'Estaing. But there was no serious attempt by Delors and his officials to put the EMF on the agenda. They recognized that, strategically, they were in no position to act as *demandeur*. The priority of the Finance Ministry was, first, to align domestic economic and monetary policies with the requirements of the ERM and then to push for reform of the EMS. In 1981–2 Delors and his officials went throught the motions of supporting the Commission. Haberer and his successor Camdessus were pragmatists on EMS reform. Camdessus's battles were domestic in 1982–3. In relation to the EMS the preoccupation was crisis avoidance and management, not reform; with restoring the Finance Ministry's domestic political status and power. The asymmetry between its domestic political position and that of the German Finance Ministry was not conducive to a strong and influential role on EMS reform and EMU.

But, after the *tournant*, at ECOFIN meetings in September 1982 and February 1983 Delors outlined the core French negotiating positions on EMS reform. Their basic objective was to enhance French room for manoeuvre in the conduct of economic and monetary policy in the new domestic context of a conversion to *rigueur*. In substance they revealed an underlying political consensus both within the Socialist Party—notably about shifting the EMS away from its basis in German standards—and with Barre and Giscard. They also indicated a greater political self-confidence, though one that was to be overshadowed by Mitterrand's complex manoeuvring in early 1983. Delors sought to:

- tackle asymmetry by increasing the obligation on strong currencies to support weaker via intramarginal intervention within the ERM;
- achieve 'balanced' economic convergence around standards agreed by all member states (i.e. not German standards), with states with trade surpluses, notably Germany, reflating to help those under pressure;
- shield EMS countries from US dollar instability by improved policy coordination and developing the ECU as the third international reserve currency;

- widen public and private use of the ECU as a parallel currency in order to decrease the dominance of the D-Mark and, in the long term, to challenge the international role of the dollar;
- develop a single European monetary policy *vis-à-vis* third countries, especially a common position on international monetary reform (Howarth 1998: chapter 2).

For Delors it was a tactical matter of pursuing the line of least resistance in the context of a weak French macroeconomic performance. This approach counselled a greater stress on promoting the use of the ECU than more directly challenging the asymmetric functioning of the ERM. The more direct challenge came later, especially once a Gaullist Finance Minister, Edouard Balladur, interpreted these positions within a more nationalistic frame of reference, and once a more impressive French economic performance strengthened French bargaining positions.

Mitterrand and the Political Management of the March 1983 ERM Crisis

From September 1982 Mitterrand used regular restricted meetings of the Council of Ministers (*Conseils restreints*) to tease out and test contrasting ideas on economic and monetary policy. The domestic context was one of falling public approval for the President and of a sense that Gaullist and UDF criticisms of the incompetence and irresponsibility of the Socialists were proving politically effective. Mitterand's prime test was political: which policy proposals would be most likely to avoid electoral disaster for the Socialists in the May 1986 National Assembly elections? Meanwhile, he deferred a decision on the future shape of economic policy till after the local elections in March 1983.

Within the Finance Ministry Camdessus and Lagayette focused on strengthening Delors's arguments in the restricted Council of Ministers' meetings (Favier and Martin-Roland 1990: 438–9). With Guigou at the Elysée, and Guigou's good relations with Stasse, they had the advantage of improved lines of communication to the heart of the Elysée. The core Finance Ministry argument was that France's continuing internal and external imbalances, and therefore indebtedness, meant that an externally imposed plan of *rigueur* was unavoidable. The basic political choice was between the humiliation of dependency on the IMF, if France exited the ERM, or remaining within the ERM, respecting its disciplines, and seeking its reform. This argument was supported by reference to the disastrous experience of the British Labour government which had been forced into the hands of the IMF in the mid-1970s. It was clear to the Finance Ministry that political arguments and historical parallels would carry more weight with Mitterrand than economic argumentation. Mitterrand was in effect being encouraged to choose the more congenial ground of Europe on which to base his economic policy rather than the less congenial ground of the IMF.

Camdessus and Lagayette made common cause with Peyrelevade and Guillaume at the Matignon. Crucially, they gained the support of the so-called 'club of Five' in the Elysée meetings (Favier and Martin-Roland 1990: 461). This group comprised Attali, Bianco, Guigou, Christian Sautter, and Stasse. It too focused on the choice IMF/ERM but also developed two more political arguments, domestic and European, designed to appeal to Mitterrand: that the Socialist Party's prospects in the Assembly elections of 1986 would be substantially reduced if continuing high indebtedness was to force France into humiliating economic dependency; and that ERM exit meant an end to prospects for French leadership of *construction européenne*. The political key for France was to ensure that the burden of adjustment was born by a substantial D-Mark revaluation (7 per cent) and to avoid another devaluation of the franc. These Trésor and Elysée arguments were reinforced by an economic warning from the Banque de France on 17 December 1982: during 1982 its foreign exchange reserves had diminished by 50 per cent.

By January 1983 Mitterrand had been persuaded that the diplomatic and economic costs of exiting the ERM would be immense. He was looking for ways to avoid an exit from the ERM and being encouraged within the Elysée, in February, to authorize secret, direct dealings with Bonn (Favier and Martin-Roland 1990: 463). But, equally, he was acutely aware of the domestic political difficulties that he faced in unifying his government and party behind a policy consistent with remaining in the ERM. He sought to navigate these difficulties by pursuing a complex double game internally and externally. Externally, Mitterrand's objective was to strengthen his hand in dealing with the Germans. With this objective in mind he encouraged dissent at home, ambiguity about his intentions, and practised brinkmanship right up to the end of the final negotiations in Brussels in March. This aspect of his strategy depended for its effectiveness on convincing the Germans that he was taking the option of exit very seriously. The threat had to be made credible. Hence Mitterrand sought to persuade others that he was keeping his options open. The second aspect was his domestic political interest in getting enough members of his government to come down on his side and in putting ministers and officials under pressure to deliver an economic policy package capable of reconciling European interests with party and electoral interests. In these domestic manoeuvres Fabius was to prove the key. Mitterrand was pursuing a complex 'two-level' game, with very high political stakes on both levels and considerable economic costs in loss of foreign exchange reserves.

Mitterrand's protracted hesitation on the issue of the ERM succeeded in spreading alarm and despondency in the Finance Ministry. At one level his criticisms of the ERM did no more than repeat long-standing and widely shared French concerns about asymmetry. The ERM was unacceptable if it meant adapting French policies to those of its partners. He spoke of the importance of 'mutual disciplines' and 'fair compromises' (*Le Monde*: 26 November 1982). But Mitterrand's deferral of a decision on the ERM until after the local elections on

13 March 1983 fuelled fears that the final decision would be driven by electoral calculation rather than by longer-term calculations of French economic interests. Anxiety was compounded by the way in which the President actively cultivated, behind the backs of Mauroy and his Elysée staff, regular contacts to proponents of '*une autre politique*'. They argued for exiting the ERM in order to gain a new freedom of manoeuvre to pursue a distinctively French policy. Foremost in this camp were Bérégovoy, Minister for Social Security, Fabius, the writer and politician Jean-Jacques Servan-Schreiber, and Mitterrand's long-standing and most intimate friend, the industrialist Jean Riboud. They were christened by Mauroy the '*visiteurs du soir*' (Bauchard 1986: 142). What united these pro-exit supporters was a *mendèsiste* outlook, arguing that *rigueur* had to be learnt and practiced at home rather than imported. But they were also joined by those of a more *dirigiste* persuasion, notably Michel Jobert, Minister for Foreign Trade, and Jean-Pierre Chevènement, Minister for Industry. They favoured more protectionist measures to insulate the French market and increased public investment. Peyrelevade and Stasse were heavily occupied in systematically countering the ideas of what were seen in the French Finance Ministry as Mitterrand's 'cronies'. They were helped by the failure of the '*visiteurs du soir*' to give an agreed definition to the substance of '*une autre politique*'.

Immediately following the losses in the local election results of 13 March, Mitterrand's enigmatic and elusive political persona was at its most visible. In part, this reflected a war within his own political soul. He genuinely hesitated. As Socialist Party leader he remained tempted by the arguments for exit and frustrated by his failed efforts to shift the political agenda in international and EC fora to reflect his party's priorities. Mitterrand was also tempted by the opportunities for European and international statesmanship offered by his office. The local elections brought forth his persona as party leader, frustrated by the constraints of power and tempted by a new policy direction. But by 16 March his persona as European and international statesman, concerned about his place in the history books, had reasserted itself. During this period Mitterrand shifted between being hesitant and using hesitation and ambiguity as tactics to put the Germans under political pressure in the ERM negotiations and to test out his domestic room for political manoeuvre. The effect was to spread alarm and confusion.

Mitterrand focused on one issue with most of his Elysée advisers—the prospect of political renewal by appointing a new Prime Minister and government, whilst raising the issue of ERM exit with Attali and with Mauroy. On 14 March Mitterrand signalled to Mauroy that he wanted to leave the ERM, suggesting victory for '*l'autre politique*' (Favier and Martin-Roland 1990: 466–7). Mauroy made his opposition very plain and defined the ERM to Mitterrand as the test of whether he would remain prime minister. Later that day the President asked Bérégovoy, Fabius, and Riboud to draw up a plan of action to leave the ERM. Intriguingly, Mitterrand did not convey the same clear signal to his advisers in the Elysée, most of whom had been convinced since January that he had resolved to stay in the ERM. They speculated on whether the President was testing Mauroy, and Delors, rather than being serious about ERM exit. But Mauroy spread alarm. In the dramatic events that followed, Mauroy and his advisers played an important role in mobilizing a coalition against '*l'autre politique*', drawing in Attali in the Elysée and Delors and Camdessus.

On 14 March Mauroy, Attali, and Bianco returned to their argument of January–February by pressing on Mitterrand the vital need to mobilize the Franco-German relationship. There was an opportunity to exploit the willingness of the German Chancellor to pay for France remaining in the ERM (and effective future collaboration in *construction européenne*) at the cost of a German revaluation. The political gain would be a tacit admission that the problem was German rather than French. Bianco was immediately dispatched to Bonn.

Faced by the failure of that top-secret mission, Attali, Mauroy, and Delors changed tactics on 15 March. A first tactic was to underline the domestic political costs of an ERM exit. In rejecting Mitterrand's offer of the Prime Minister's office that afternoon, Delors followed Mauroy in spelling out that he would not remain in any government that left the ERM. A second tactic was to disengage a leading member from the 'pro-ERM-exit' coalition. They targeted Fabius as a moderate who was close to the President. Attali gained Mitterrand's backing for the idea that Fabius should seek a briefing from Camdessus on the state of France's foreign exchange reserves and the implications of exit (Favier and Martin-Roland 1990: 469–71). This briefing was justified to Fabius as a means of 'checking' for the President the reliability of the economic statistics being used by Delors. The subsequent briefing on 16 March was crucial in the enfolding story. Camdessus's argument that ERM exit would inflict an even more severe *rigueur* on France and his confirmation of Delors's grim statistics persuaded Fabius to desert the pro-exit camp and inform the President that he would refuse to serve as Prime Minister if the franc left the ERM. Fabius's conversion was an important signal that Mitterrand was likely to opt for remaining in the ERM.

Despite the failure of the Bianco mission, Mitterrand did not relinquish his pressure on Bonn, pointing out what was at stake for European politics. On the same day, 16 March, Camdessus left for Bonn to deliver a private, top-secret message from Mitterrand to Kohl. It was delivered to the German Finance Minister, Stoltenberg, and argued the case for a German revaluation within the ERM. Camdessus stressed German self-interest. German support in this way was crucial to engineering a policy shift in Paris and opening up new opportunities for Franco-German collaboration. This case had already been argued in the German Chancellor's Office by Bianco on 14–15 March, but without success. Bianco had pleaded that the Germans had an unrivalled opportunity to force economic policy change on the Mitterrand Presidency and to pursue a new start in Franco-German reconciliation and *construction européene*. But the experience was humiliating for him, a forceful reminder that the EMS was *de facto* a D-Mark zone. There was little interest in the German Chancellor's Office in what Bianco had to say, and Kohl remained silent at this stage.

Behind the top-secret Bianco and Camdessus visits to Bonn was a strategy agreed between Mauroy and Mitterrand on 14 March, with Delors's support. This strategy reflected the thinking of the 'club of Five' in the Elysée: namely, to identify the problem as German-centred and to test again to the limits the willingness of the Germans to help France by a D-Mark revaluation. On 17 March, following Camdessus's visit, German willingness to consider a 'modest' D-Mark revaluation was communicated to Paris; Stoltenberg visited the Elysée, accompanied by Bianco, to communicate Kohl's position to Mitterrand. This signal, which was tied to an affirmation of German commitment to giving momentum to European unification, convinced Mitterrand that a continued strategy of combining toughness with hesitation could yield further dividends in the negotiations. He remained non-committal in his talks with Stoltenberg.

The centre of gravity with respect to the ERM decision rested not in the Finance Ministry but in the Elysée. By 17 March those closest to Mitterrand had shed any residual doubts that he might exit the ERM (the decision was not publicly confirmed till 21 March). Mitterrand's tactics were becoming clearer: to use hesitation on an ERM exit to exert maximum negotiating pressure on the Germans—what Védrine refers to as 'tactical indecision' (Védrine 1996: 285). He was careful not to reveal his decision to Delors. Delors's negotiating position was spelt out by Mitterrand in stark and conditional terms: if you wish France to remain in the ERM, seek a D-Mark revaluation. This position involved an exercise in bluffing and brinkmanship.

Delors recognized that he faced no major problem in negotiating a devaluation of the franc within the ERM. His greatest negotiating problem was to ensure that the D-Mark took most of the strain. Delors fell back on two strategies in the ensuing protracted and difficult negotiations in ECOFIN on 19–20 March. He dramatized his domestic weakness (not least by returning from Brussels to Paris during the negotiations) in order to induce broad EC, and especially German, support for an outcome that would strengthen his hand at home in putting a stability-oriented policy in place. This strategy was already in evidence when Delors and Camdessus met Stoltenberg and Tietmeyer at St Cloud on 17 March. Delors stressed the tensions in the French government, the uncertainty about Mitterrand's position, and the prospects for his own resignation. A second strand of Delors's negotiating strategy was in evidence in Brussels. He dramatized the 'arrogance' and 'uncomprehending' nature of the Germans as the main obstacle to agreement and the cause of potential French exit from the ERM. The intention of this theatrical behaviour was to corner the Germans into concessions and to accommodate the PCF and CERES at home. During the ECOFIN negotiations Mitterrand sustained heavy pressure on Delors to deliver a good deal for France, whilst keeping Delors in the dark about his real intention. The outcome—a 5.5 per cent revaluation of the D-Mark alongside a 2.5 per cent franc devaluation—went a long way to meeting French aspirations. But it also meant an accompanying tough exercise in budgetary *rigueur* and a need to reflect further on implications for a Socialist economic policy and for domestic political relationships. Mitterrand's great political challenge was to square his external political commitments and ambitions with the realities of domestic politics and with the need to square his Socialist Party. This problem had confounded Pompidou and Giscard. Where they failed, he succeeded.

Reconciling Socialism to Life in the ERM: Delors, Bérégovoy, and the *Franc Stable*, 1983–1986

In 1984, in the aftermath of the March 1983 decision, EMU nudged its way back onto the agenda in Paris, courtesy of Roland Dumas and Guigou rather than of any initiative from the Finance Ministry or the Matignon. The domestic political context was an acute sense of a programmatic vacuum in Paris after March 1983 and that there was a need to put in place ideas that would give a new identity to the Socialist Party in time for its party congress in autumn 1983 and to minimize Socialist losses in the Assembly elections of March 1986. The consequence was a process of political competition to fill that vacuum and invent a new realistic identity for Mitterrand and the Socialist Party. This competition of ideas and personalities was guided by the fact that Mitterrand had provided a fundamental policy decision: that France was to remain within the ERM, adapt to its constraints, and seek out influence within the EC. During 1983 his Presidency's great project was redefined as Europe, and his collaborators were now selected from the point of view of their suitability for the pursuit of this project. Europe was the project around which the Presidential majority was to be refounded, based on a rallying of the centre-left and centred around the Socialist Party.

The challenge was to reconcile this decision with domestic political requirements and align the Socialist Party behind it. The decision to stay in the ERM was justified by Mitterrand in a national broadcast on 23 March in terms of not 'isolating France from the European Community' (Védrine 1996: 484). Lionel Jospin, Secretary-General of the Socialist Party, referred to the decision of March 1983 as a 'parenthesis', reflecting grave reservations within parts of the Socialist party. Nevertheless, the 1983 conference swung reluctantly behind the President. Mitterrand was successful in engineering victory for Fabius's neo-Gaullist conception of the Socialist Party as a rallying (*rassemblement*) behind the President in place of the earlier strategy of the union of the Left and of Jospin's desire to separate it as a party of activists using critical discourse as an instrument to promote socialist values (Philippe and Hubscher 1991: 114–16). This victory hid much internal party unhappiness that socialism was being sacrificed for Europe. The Socialist Party was realigned behind a notion of a presidential majority based on Europe, modernization, and social justice.

Within the French government policy reflection was focused around several institutional venues. In the Finance Ministry the cabinet of Delors, and the Trésor under Camdessus, began to consider the lineaments of economic strategy inside the ERM. At the Social Affairs Ministry Bérégovoy's cabinet sought to contribute ideas, notably on more efficient financing of the budget deficit by financial market reform. Meanwhile, in the Elysée the 'club of Five', guided by Stasse, set to work to map out the precise profile of a strategy of *rigueur* in a European framework. Mitterrand cast about for new unifying ideas, and political figures who could embody them and project a revitalized Socialist Party to the electorate. In the process he unleashed a process of competition between Bérégovoy, Fabius, and Delors for the succession to Mauroy. Mauroy became a more marginal figure. Though the Socialist Party played no significant direct role in this process of policy and political reflection, it was a central object of that reflection.

Delors emerged as a victor of the March 1983 crisis. Mitterrand took what he recognized to be the historic decision to stay within the ERM and, in the context of a third devaluation, to realign economic and monetary policies around the demanding disciplines of the ERM. In national broadcasts on 9 June and 28 June Mitterrand resorted to a newly pedagogic language about the importance of re-establishing the *grands équilibres* (Gélédan 1993: 51–3). The move of Pascal Lamy in April 1983 to be deputy director of cabinet at the Matignon, responsible for EC and for domestic economic issues, symbolized the recolonization of a key post by the Finance Inspectorate. Now two former members of Delors's cabinet, Lamy (his close confidant as deputy director of cabinet) in the Matignon and Guigou in the Elysée, ensured that Delors's concerns were taken seriously in deliberations on economic policy in the wake of the March 1983 decision. Both Lamy and Guigou endorsed the importance that Delors attached to the ERM and to EMU.

Within the Finance Ministry Delors's cabinet, led by Jérôme Vignon and Jean-Baptiste de Foucault, set to work to gather together ideas to fill the policy vacuum. At this stage the key question for Delors and his officials was not how to reform the ERM to accommodate French interests and realize EMU—those ideas were already in place. It was how to find a low-cost way of living with the *franc stable* that was compatible with the social Catholic political perspective of Delors; that would combine a 'new realism' with a social dimension; and that would set the longer-term framework that was necessary to make ERM membership sustainable and EMU viable. Under Delors the lineaments of what was to be christened in 1986 the 'competitive disinflation' strategy were being put in place by de Foucault and Vignon (*Le Monde*: 8 April 1986): the strategy that was later to be taken up by Jean-Claude Trichet as director of the Trésor and Hannoun as director of Bérégovoy's cabinet in 1988–9.

In this exercise economic research within the forecasting division of the Finance Ministry was influential. It produced an economic rationale for the *franc stable* in terms of promoting international competitiveness: in effect returning to the theme developed under Barre. Competitive devaluation was rejected as an inflationary process. Particular stress was placed on giving long-term support to the *franc stable* by measures to restore corporate profitability, to decentralize wage bargaining, to strengthen the role of banks in industrial financing (on the German model), and to restructure public spending by reinforcing its social dimension (for instance, towards vocational training and infrastructural investment). These measures were designed to promote international competitiveness in a socialist framework of solidarity focused on the firm. The *franc stable* policy was being given a specific Delorian content. In the process it was being focused more on the German model. Delors was more comfortable with the Christian-Democratic and Social-Democratic ethos of this model than with Anglo-American capitalism. He was also aware that convergence towards the German model was a *sine qua non* for EMU.

But Mitterrand remained distrustful of the Finance Ministry under Delors, sensing that Delors was insufficiently radical and too much in the hands of the Trésor. This distrust came to a head when Mitterrand used the Council of Ministers' meeting of 23 June 1983 to warn Delors of the political dangers of a one-sided preoccupation with *rigueur*. He accused Delors of being blind to the wider requirements of an active role for the state in modernization and in promoting social justice and cohesion (Favier and Martin-Roland 1990: 498). In reconstructing French economic policies after March 1983 Mitterrand's central *mendèsiste* theme was that *rigueur* was vital but not enough.

Hence, in July 1984, when it came to putting in place the new Socialist government to prepare for the Assembly elections in March 1986, the victors were the *mendèsistes*: Fabius became Prime Minister and Bérégovoy Finance Minister. They were seen by Mitterrand as best able to mount the domestic political counter-offensive at the level of ideas and policy initiatives and to assert strong political control of domestic policy development. Delors was dispatched to the EC Commission as its President. But neither Fabius nor Bérégovoy were disposed to set French policy in a longer-term framework of EMU as Delors had done. They were also less inclined to base domestic policy on the German model, with Fabius more interested in the Japanese model of a 'developmental' state (Fabius 1990: 55–6).

During the period 1984–6 Bérégovoy was to play a crucial role in reinforcing the *franc stable* policy. Advised by André Gauron, the closest to him in his cabinet, and supported by François Monnier, his adviser on macroeconomic policy, Bérégovoy was motivated by domestic political reasons and based his policy on a *mendèsiste* analysis. He saw political advantage in associating the Left with monetary stability and financial rectitude, and he was happy to use the ERM for that purpose. Mendès France's courage as the advocate of *rigueur* in 1944–5 acted as a role model. But, in relation to the ERM, EMU played no serious role for Bérégovoy as it had for Delors or as it came to play for Mitterrand in this period. Monetary stability was for him ultimately a matter of domestic political discipline. At the same time Bérégovoy's *franc stable* policy fitted perfectly into the EMU strategy being put into place by Mitterrand, Dumas, and Guigou. Though Bérégovoy was always absolutely loyal to Mitterrand's will, once it was clearly expressed, he was not intellectually convinced about the strength of the case for giving primacy to EMU.

The main test of Bérégovoy's strength came in July 1985 when the ERM was again in crisis. Caught in the tension between the D-Mark and the Italian lira, Bérégovoy gained the support of Mitterrand for the (unprecedented) decision to revalue the franc with the D-Mark. This decision was opposed by Fabius and by the Banque de France. Mitterrand welcomed it as supportive of his European policy. It sent an important signal about French determination to maintain the *franc stable*. But Bérégovoy was more concerned to be able to claim in the 1986 Assembly elections that he was the first Finance Minister of the Fifth Republic not to have devalued the franc. More questionable, however, was the sustainability of the franc/D-Mark parity in the context of the relaxation of *rigueur* in the run-up to the elections and of higher French than German inflation.

Again based on motives that had nothing to do with *construction européenne*, Bérégovoy chose for his central policy project as Finance Minister a financial-market-reform programme that was to help lay the basis later for a more credible French negotiating position on EMU. The programme, outlined in December 1984, had two main objectives: to reduce the costs of financing the budget deficit by strengthening the financial base and innovativeness of French banks; and to develop Paris as a world financial centre to rival London and eclipse Frankfurt. These objectives were to be achieved by a reform package that liberalized, widened, and deepened French financial markets: by, for instance, creating new negotiable financial instruments and a futures market (Loriaux 1991). Its end result was to be the replacement of an inefficient and ineffective system of credit controls (the *encadrement du crédit*) by a monetary policy based on interest-rate management and open-market operations and, crucially, the ending of exchange controls. In short, the French Socialist government was committed to a programme that would lead to convergence of financial and monetary policies with Germany and Britain. Again, the model of Mendès France as 'heroic' modernizer, pitting himself against the conservatism of French capitalism, was influential.

In developing this financial-market-reform programme Bérégovoy relied on two key figures: Jean-Charles Naouri, his young, intellectually brilliant director of cabinet, and the more controversial Claude Rubinowicz, who was seen by the Trésor as an unreliable outsider in a key cabinet position (Mamou 1988: 244–5). More important than personal animosity to Rubinowicz were differences of view about the pacing and sequencing of reforms and the manner in which they were pursued. Disquiet was even more apparent within the Banque de France, which stressed the dangers of trying to rely on open-market operations before the government bond market was sufficiently developed. Though the financial-market-reform programme was not designed with EMU in mind, it played a key long-term role in inducing an opening of French financial markets, a process of convergence in financial and monetary policies that made EMU a more practical proposition, and a process of cultural and intellectual change within the Banque de France and French financial institutions that facilitated communication and bridge-building with the Germans and others. But, though this linkage to EMU can be traced, it did not form part of Bérégovoy's motives in adopting this programme.

EMU and the *Relance Européenne*: Mitterrand, the Dumas Memorandum, and the IGC of 1985

The process of programmatic reflection and reinvention did not automatically lead Mitterrand to identify EMU as his main project. His first great theme was the pressing need to adapt to the phenomenon of 'globalization' which, as the events of 1981–3 had demonstrated, had left the French state increasingly powerless. The priority of Mitterrand after March 1983 was to pursue the logic of opening France up to the world. Mitterrand adopted the 'big' idea of 'modernization' in order to equip France for the challenge of globalization but of doing so within a framework of social justice. Fabius was identified over Delors as the best collaborator in developing this domestic political theme. For Lionel Jospin as Secretary-General of the Socialist Party modernization under Fabius took on too managerial and technocratic a character. The result was a tension between Fabius and Jospin, with Jospin seeking to preserve the left-wing character of the Socialist Party.

His second great theme, which became more important in 1984, was the importance of building a European counterweight (*contrepoids*) to the other great economic powers of the USA and South-East Asia. By means of active participation in *construction européenne* France could retrieve its influence and achieve an identity in the modern world. But, in Mitterrand's mind, the political, social, and cultural aspects of *construction européenne* figured as strongly as the economic; and, at the economic level, EMU took second place to 'a Europe of research' (especially in aerospace). In relation to this theme he turned to Dumas, Guigou, and Attali to develop ideas. They were more disposed than Fabius or Bérégovoy—or, at this stage, Mitterrand—to prioritize EMU. Mitterrand's initial main interest was in political reform of EC institutions. In May 1984 he declared his support for the Draft Treaty on European Union, adopted by the European Parliament. In June at the Fontainebleau European Council he sponsored the idea of a committee on institutional questions (the Dooge Committee), appointing the veteran politician and Europeanist Maurice Faure to it. A politically reformed EC was seen by Mitterrand as the precondition for building a European counterweight. In taking up this position he was leading the Socialist Party in a new direction.

By the end of 1983 Mitterrand had determined that *construction européenne* would be the organizing theme of his Presidency. A strengthened Europe was the necessary counterweight to the power of the global markets. It was the arena in which policies to promote modernization and a social dimension had to be pursued. His appointment of Roland Dumas, an intimate personal adviser, as Minister for European Affairs in December 1983 was a key signal of this new determination, and was interpreted as such by the German Foreign Ministry. Dumas was a man of great intelligence, charm, wit, grace, and culture: a natural diplomat. He also had the razor-sharp and versatile mind of the trained lawyer and, with a long track record of accomplishing delicate personal missions for Mitterrand, was a master of the arts of concealment. There was no one inside or outside the Elysée in whom Mitterrand deposited more trust. But Dumas could not claim to be a European of the first generation. The murder of his father as a Resistance fighter by the Germans had left a deep mark on his early attitudes. His Europeanism was acquired later: an affair of the head rather than the heart.

Dumas's task, alongside Guigou, Attali, and Védrine, was to help Mitterrand in using the French Presidency of the EC in the first half of 1984 to give a new momentum to what had been a moribund EC. The objectives were to clear away long-standing problems, notably the EC budget issue, in order to open up space for new European initiatives and to establish the President as a European statesman of the first rank These objectives were substantially achieved. The French Presidency was strikingly activist. This involved some thirty bilaterals between Mitterrand and his counterparts and, particularly before the Fontainebleau European Council in June, a newly intensive Franco-German collaboration. Crucially, at Fontainebleau, the solidarity of the Franco-German partnership proved decisive in getting Mrs Thatcher to strike a budget deal, and the principle of linkage between realization of a single European market and institutional reform of the EC was accepted. In getting institutional reform on the agenda the opportunity was open to seize the initiative on EMU.

Before Fontainebleau, on Mitterrand's instruction, Dumas conducted a wide-ranging review of European policy and, in this context, had already put EMU back on the agenda (*Lettre de Matignon* 1984). The French case for the EMS was placed firmly in its international context, reflecting the input of the Quai d'Orsay into the process. The process of arbitration in the SGCI, which was then located under Dumas, also enabled a strong Trésor contribution. In deference to the Trésor reference was made to monetary stability as a condition for sustained economic growth in Europe. But more attention was given to the EMS as a condition of economic independence from the USA, especially as a means of escape from dependency on the US dollar and US interest rates. In this context the Dumas Memorandum of 1 June 1984 referred to the need for a more 'concerted' policy and, eventually, a European currency as a better protection against 'external risks'. This theme was to figure strongly in French positions on EMU from 1988 onwards. In addition, the Dumas Memorandum argued that the EMS enabled a more effective European contribution to the reform of the international monetary system. That reform had, in the French view, to be based on a 'rebalancing' between its three main 'pillars'—the dollar, the yen, and the *'écu'*.[1] Again, this argument picked up on a long-standing theme of French monetary diplomacy, shared by the Quai d'Orsay and the Trésor and appealing to Mitterrand.

More importantly, the Dumas Memorandum outlined French proposals to remedy the weaknesses in the functioning of the EMS and highlighted how within G7, at Versailles and Williamsburg, the French Socialist government had sought to ensure that the EC spoke with one voice on international monetary matters. In the first place, the memorandum sought to reinforce economic policy convergence, but very much phrased in terms of French economic ideas and of reciprocal economic concessions. The idea of medium-term European economic 'programming' was resurrected, with each country's particular needs being taken into account. In addition, the memorandum took up the market success of the public *'écu'* to argue for developing the role of the private *'écu'*. The idea of a stage 2 of the EMS was resurrected. The memorandum looked forward to the eventual creation of a European Monetary Fund with real powers, permitting the defence of European currencies against the US dollar and making the *'écu'* a true European and international currency. The Dumas Memorandum spoke also of consolidation of the EMS, followed by its enlargement: in other words, deepening before widening. Finally, there was a stress on the importance of harmonization of fiscal policies to accompany economic and financial integration.

In the memorandum itself, and in Dumas's discussions with Mitterrand, there was an acknowledgement of the formidable constraints that faced French strategy in trying to press EMU. As unanimity would be required to progress towards EMU, only modest change was to be expected. The most important objective was to overcome German mistrust, which was seen as the single biggest obstacle to EMU. The strategic implications were clear: French negotiators must be able to reassure their German counterparts about the French commitment to monetary stability by securing a *franc stable*; at the same time they had to be tenacious in pressing the case for EMU on the Germans. From this point onwards French strategy on EMU began to fall into place: indirect and essentially psychological pressure; divide and rule between Genscher and Kohl and between Bonn and Frankfurt; a preference for moving by small steps ('salami-slicing' at the independence of the Bundesbank); and seeking to 'bind in' and neutralize the Bundesbank. Dumas emerged as an adept cunning player of French strategy on EMU, happy to work in harness with Guigou as the technical link on EMU at the Elysée.

---

[1] French negotiators preferred to use the term *'écu'* rather than ECU. Because of its historical association with a French coinage under the *ancien régime*, it acquired a symbolic importance in associating France with the new European currency. The ECU (European Currency Unit) was, by contrast, a technical term for a 'basket' currency composed of fixed proportions of different Community currencies. In this book French usage of *'écu'* during the EMU negotiations is respected. Giscard was first to seek to seize political capital from promoting the *'écu'* as the common currency.

The power of Dumas and Guigou, which had been accumulated during the course of the French EC Presidency, was rapidly strengthened (Lequesne 1993: 68–9, 148–55). In December 1984 Dumas became Foreign Minister, combining the functions that had earlier been exercised by the Minister for European Affairs (minus the SGCI which reverted to the Prime Minister, Fabius). In 1985, in time to prepare for the IGC scheduled for the autumn, Guigou was appointed adviser on EC affairs in the Elysée. On her appointment Mitterrand stressed that he wanted her to pursue the EMU dossier as a priority. In relation to EMU, and wider EC matters, an axis of Mitterrand–Dumas–Guigou emerged in 1984–5. The axis was to be retained intact during the *cohabitation* of 1986–8. In preparation for the *cohabitation* Mitterrand appointed Guigou as secretary general of the SGCI in November 1985 (in addition to her Elysée post); and Dumas retained a role as special diplomatic adviser to Mitterrand during the *cohabitation*. In this way a continuity was maintained in handling Franco-German relations and EMU matters.

With the prospect of the first IGC in a generation during his Presidency in the second half of 1985 Mitterrand hesitated between ambition and caution on institutional reform, including EMU. This hesitation was apparent before the Milan European Council in June. On the one hand, Guigou produced a 'memorandum for progress in the construction of Europe'. Its caution on institutional reform, and silence on EMU, reflected a strategic analysis of the formidable difficulties ahead with the British, Danes, and Greeks. But, on the other hand, Attali conducted top-secret negotiations with Teltschik on a more ambitious draft treaty on European union and, in this context, raised EMU (though unsuccessfully). Kohl's enthusiasm for tabling this draft in Milan was not in fact matched by Mitterrand who saw risks in alienating support for the idea of an IGC. For strategic and tactical reasons Mitterrand failed to endorse the Franco-German draft, to the irritation of the German Chancellor's Office.

With respect to the role of EMU in the IGC negotiations Mitterrand shared the analysis of Dumas. In principle EMU was desirable. But, strategically, it was not opportune to press it too hard and publicly on the Germans. They would back away. The key was to induce the German political leadership to seize the initiative on EMU. By making progress on the single European market it would be possible, later, to coax the Germans into active support for EMU. Also, the entry of Spain and Portugal into the EC would provide important new political allies on EMU. In the IGC itself this caution on EMU was further reinforced by the French negotiator, Luc de La Barre de Nanteuil. Marked by the long years of inertia in the EC, this long-serving EC diplomat—who had been brought back to serve as French Permanent Representative in January 1985 by Cheysson—was deeply sceptical. Also, when the IGC began, there were no strong voices calling for EMU within the Foreign Ministry or the Finance Ministry. In fact there were no precise negotiating instructions from Paris. Most important of all in this context, La Barre de Nanteuil's strategic calculation was that any attempt to insert a monetary component (or social component) in the

Treaty would simply be vetoed by Mrs Thatcher; whilst the Germans were interested in political union, not EMU. Hence he saw little prospect for progress in the IGC.

The change in Paris came suddenly in November. Delors took to Mitterrand his case for making substantial progress on inserting a monetary component in the Treaty and creating a legal basis for the EMF. He blamed the lack of progress in the IGC on La Barre de Nanteuil's opposition and complained that the Finance Ministry had not given sufficiently robust support at the ECOFIN on 28 October at which Delors had brought forward his proposals to incorporate the EMS in the Treaty and move to stage 2 of the EMS. More symptomatic of the mood in Paris was a speech by Camdessus as governor of the Banque de France in September 1985. Whilst proposing that the *ECU* should become the EC's intervention currency, Camdessus stressed that 'we should not be in a hurry' and that development should be 'pragmatic'. We should 'develop the practice of joint management between us first'. The Finance Ministry favoured developing the role of the public *ECU* to match the success of the private *ECU*, for instance by increasing EC central banks' acceptance limits on the *ECU* from 50 per cent to 100 per cent. But the director of the Trésor, Daniel Lebègue, was more hesitant on institutional reforms. Delors also enlisted the support of Guigou, who was closest to him in the Elysée, having served in his cabinet, and who shared his views on a supranational EC. Mitterrand's appointment of Guigou as Secretary-General of the SGCI in November was the signal for a new hard push by the French government to give dynamism to the IGC negotiations and to focus on the monetary and social components. When faced by Delors pressing for EMU, Mitterrand's characteristic response was to argue the case for the equal importance of the social dimension to the EC.

Even if hopelessly late in the negotiations, a fresh vigour was imparted by Guigou in the final stages. On 19 November the French delegation to the IGC pressed strongly for the incorporation of monetary policy in the Treaty. But they were faced by stout resistance from the Germans masterminded by Tietmeyer. Other avenues were explored. In contacts to the Federal Chancellor's Office, Elysée officials signalled EMU as of 'priority importance' at the forthcoming Luxembourg European Council on 3–4 December. Dumas took up the issue directly with Genscher, speaking of EMU as a necessary counterpart to the single market and successfully enlisting his support to persuade Kohl. At the Luxembourg Council Mitterrand raised the issue of a chapter on EMU in the Treaty at his first breakfast meeting with Kohl, arguing for a European currency as a necessary complement to the single European market and stressing the vital need for Kohl to persuade Mrs Thatcher to accept this provision. Kohl conceded on these points. But, briefed by Tietmeyer, he insisted that the EMU chapter would have to confirm that progress on EMU would require resort to the full Treaty amendment procedure of Article 236. Because it required institutional reform, it could not be put in place simply by resolutions of the European Council or decisions in ECOFIN. For Mitterrand the result was a disappointment. He had been reminded of the power of the Finance Ministry and of the Bundesbank and of the reluctance of Kohl to assert himself against their corporate views. There was also an underlying irritation with Delors in the Elysée and in the Foreign Ministry: a feeling that Delors had manoeuvred the President into too exposed a position at Luxembourg by an impetuous approach.

The ERM and EMU Under the *Cohabitation*, 1986–1988: The Balladur Memorandum, and the Dumas–Genscher Relationship

In relation to the conduct of EC policy under a prospective *cohabitation* with the political Right, Mitterrand had carefully safeguarded his position before the March 1986 Assembly elections. As Secretary-General of the SGCI and Elysée adviser, Guigou was in a pivotal position to ensure that the President was kept fully briefed on EC issues; whilst the appointment of François Scheer, former director of Cheysson's cabinet, as French Permanent Representative in Brussels in January 1986 ensured a more strongly pro-European vision than that of his predecessor. The President signalled clearly that EC policy would remain within his privileged domain, particularly given the way in which Article 52 of the Constitution gave him the power to negotiate and ratify treaties. The very fact that EMU would ultimately involve Article 52 strengthened his claims in this area. Dumas continued to act as special adviser and to cultivate his close relationship to Genscher.

The Domestic Political Context of the ERM and EMU for Chirac

EC policy in general, and the ERM and EMU in particular, confronted the new Prime Minister and leader of the Gaullist RPR, Jacques Chirac, with a dilemma. On the one hand, the government was responsible for deciding on and conducting national policy under Article 20. It was also clear that the technical expertise to produce concrete initiatives, for instance on reform of the EMS, resided with the Finance Minister, not with the small Elysée staff. More importantly, EC policy offered an enormous opportunity to strike a distinctive profile of political leadership. Chirac pursued a tougher, more nationalistic style on the ERM and EMU, designed to reflect and appease more Eurosceptic elements in the RPR by demanding that Germany meet its obligations and treat the EMS as a symmetrical system of adjustment. Correspondingly, Chirac sought to build up a strong diplomatic team at the Matignon, where Yves-Thibault de Silguy played the key role on EC matters (though less so on the EMS and EMU where the economic team was more important, first under François Heilbronner and then, in 1987–8, under Emmanuel Rodocanachi).

On the other hand, Chirac was constrained from developing a too tough, assertive and independent role in EC policy by his desire not to weaken the prerogatives of the Presidential office to which he aspired. Hence, particularly in relation to the preparation of European Councils, he was careful to respect the President's position. This political context helped to ensure a relatively smooth working relationship between de Silguy and Guigou. At the same time the Matignon resorted to much greater use of informal meetings, chaired by Chirac, de Silguy, or the head of the economic team. On matters like the Franco-German Economic Council, the Basle–Nyborg negotiations, and the Balladur Memorandum they were used to keep Guigou and the Elysée at a distance and to develop political strategies in relation to the EMS and EMU from an RPR/UDF political perspective.

The potential for confrontation on EC issues, and the ERM and EMU in particular, was further exacerbated by other domestic political factors. First, within the centre-right the UDF—and the centrist CDS in particular—was more strongly pro-European. An attempt to distance the government from *construction européenne* would risk damaging splits within the centre-right as the all-important Presidential election approached. Chirac could not afford such a development and set out to bridge differences with the UDF on Europe, mindful of the importance of its voters in the first and second ballots. Of symbolic importance here was the appointment of Bernard Bosson (CDS) in August 1986 as Deputy Minister for European Affairs at the Quai d'Orsay. Bosson took up strongly pro-EC positions, for instance on doubling the Structural Funds in February 1988. He was able to build up room for manoeuvre in the *cohabitation* by exploiting the gap between Mitterrand and Chirac on the pace and objectives of *construction européenne*, situating himself closer to Mitterrand. An additional factor in inducing a measure of solidarity on the EC between the Matignon and the Elysée was the presence of Barre as a continuing critic outside the *cohabitation*. Neither Chirac nor Mitterrand wished Barre, as a potential and threatening Presidential candidate, to be the beneficiary of their disunity. Barre was to emerge as a powerful voice for EMU, and Chirac wished neither to be outflanked by him on Europe nor to lose his support in the second ballot.

Also, the Matignon was quick to notice the high level of public endorsement for *construction européenne*. Though Chirac stressed the difficulties consequent on enlargement to embrace Spain and Portugal, his new government announced on 9 April 1986 that *construction européenne* was one of its major objectives. In a characteristically Gaullist manner the stress was placed on the Franco-German relationship. Seizing the initiative on the Franco-German Economic Council in November 1987 fitted neatly into this strategy. The Matignon's enthusiasm was further fuelled by an opinion poll of November 1986 suggesting that 85 per cent regarded the pursuit of *construction européenne* as 'important' or 'very important'. Such polling formed an important part of the context of the Chirac government's new-found interest in ERM reform and EMU in 1987. On 31 March 1987 the Matignon produced '*Pour Tous Les Francais*' which spoke of 'the deepening of the EMS' and the need for 'progress on the route to monetary union'. On EMU the Elysée, the Matignon, and the Finance Ministry were pulling in the same direction. On this basis Guigou and de Silguy could seek out common ground. Each in dealings with the other claimed to be keen to insulate EMU and EC business in general from partisan politics. But there was an unmistakable climate of mistrust as the Elysée and the Matignon sought to claim credit for new initiatives, like the Franco-German Economic Council and the Elysée looked for ways to trump the Chirac government's initiatives in the area of the EMS and EMU.

The *cohabitation* affected the balance of power between ministries and their behaviour. The main institutional casualty was the Foreign Ministry under Jean-Bernard Raimond, a career diplomat and former adviser to President Pompidou. Raimond was excluded from the European Council because Mitterrand was intent on maintaining balance within the *cohabitation*. With Raimond at his side Chirac threatened to appear the more poweful presence within the European Council. In this context the German Foreign Minister Genscher continued to focus his attentions on the Elysée, where his friend Dumas occupied an advisory role to Mitterrand. During the *cohabitation* Dumas's relationship with Genscher remained a key political axis. From early 1987 onwards it was to be central in laying the ground for the relaunch of EMU.

Finance Ministry officials were quick to identify a corporate interest in seeking out ideas that would encourage consensus within the *cohabitation*. In this way Mitterrand and Chirac would be able to present a united face in EC bargaining, and the Trésor could identify itself with ideas that would be acceptable to whichever candidate won the next Presidential election. For the purpose of engaging the support of Mitterrand, as well as of satisfying key elements within the UDF, it was essential to go beyond a reiteration of traditional French bargaining positions. But, with a Gaullist minister, questions of institutional reform relating to EMU would need to be handled with great caution.

The Finance Ministry under Balladur and EMU

A key victor of the *cohabitation* was the Finance Ministry. Its new minister. Edouard Balladur, occupied the second place in the government hierarchy, just behind Chirac, and was given the title of Secretary of State. Balladur brought a new style to the Finance Ministry. Aristocratic in bearing, aloof and cool in manner, he brought a dignity to the office that pleased many in the Trésor. His caution and subtlety appealed to the ingrained empiricism that was typical of the Trésor. It was also clear from the staffing of the Matignon that Chirac had no real interest in securing a strong grip on economic and monetary issues. Balladur had, in short, the kind of political authority that promised a renaissance in Finance Ministry power. Reflecting the role that Balladur had played in putting RPR economic policy ideas together in opposition, Chirac was content to entrust the new privatization and liberalization programme to him. Balladur was also a man who shared the Trésor's enthusiasm for the '*grands équilibres*'. This domestic political base suggested a strengthened voice for the French Finance Ministry in EC and international economic and monetary diplomacy. A new confidence followed in relation to G7 and to ECOFIN and the EC Monetary Committee.

But, most reassuringly of all, unlike Bérégovoy he displayed complete confidence in the Trésor. Balladur's cabinet appointments ministered to the dignity and status of the Trésor. Trichet was appointed director of his cabinet, with Christian Noyer and Anne Le Lorier emerging as the main figures on EMS and EMU issues. A new atmosphere of trust and intimate collaboration emerged, with Balladur content to delegate to Trichet and to Lebègue, the director of the Trésor till September 1987 (when Trichet replaced him). In relation to the EC Claude Villain (a former Director-General in the EC Commission) was the key adviser. They enjoyed easy relations with Denis Samuel-Lajeunesse and Ariane Obolensky, who were the top Trésor officials for international affairs. A more team-like approach emerged on the EMS and EMU.

Chirac trusted Balladur as the man who could provide the economic policy base for his Presidential election campaign in 1988. Balladur was quick to show that he was a man with acute political antennae. He was a cautious and ambitious man, who was careful to conceal his motives. Secretiveness was married to a careful cultivation of Mitterrand to whom he presented himself as a reliable and competent statesman-like figure, inviting comparison with the erratic Chirac. Balladur was successful at playing the *cohabitation* games to his own advantage, employing a smooth affability and gentle insinuating manner. His sponsorship of EMS reform from 1987 gained the respect of Mitterrand as a useful contribution; whilst this initiative also was rooted in a domestic political strategy that was based on the electoral requirements of Chirac in 1988.

Balladur, International Monetary Reform and EMU

Balladur did not enter office with any new ideas about, or commitment to act on, reform of the EMS and EMU. He was spurred into taking initatives in this area by developments in three areas. First, the USA, under the leadership of James Baker as Treasury Secretary, had been converted to a cause dear to the hearts of the Trésor, a concerted management of the exchange rates of leading currencies. This conversion, first symbolized by the Plaza Agreement of September 1985, was seen as an intellectual victory in Paris, embodying at long last the spirit of the communiqué of the Versailles G7 summit in May 1982 with its reference to 'the necessity of collective action to stabilize currencies'. The Plaza Agreement, with its provision for a managed depreciation of the US dollar, made it once again possible for the Trésor to press the case for reform of the international monetary system. Hence, on coming into office, Balladur was presented with a new opportunity to gain political profile in international monetary diplomacy. Trésor officials set to work to identify ideas, notably that of 'target zones', aimed at influencing the Americans and Germans (Mamou 1988: chapter 4). The Louvre Accord of February 1987 went at least some way to meeting French demands. Crucially, in Trésor minds, this G7 negotiation was linked to the EMS. The Louvre Accord was seen as an important means of taking the pressures off the ERM consequent on the instability of the US dollar (and which had been embarrassingly manifested in December 1986–January 1987). In so doing it opened up new scope for a more active policy on EMS reform.

The linkage between the nature of French demands for international monetary reform and the EMS was also intellectual. On the one hand, the Trésor argued that the EC should demonstrate that it was capable of more effective exchange-rate management than the G7. Hence by 1987 the Trésor was pressing in a new, more intellectually confident way for EMS reform. But, on the other hand, a reformed EMS was also seen as the model for a redesigned international monetary system. In fact, for Balladur the problems of the EMS were secondary to the larger problem of the US dollar and the creation of a wider zone of stability in exchange rates. After the Louvre Accord he was to call for an international monetary system characterized by 'more objectivity' (based on a gold-like standard or an international currency), 'more automaticity' (requiring central banks to intervene to support parities), and 'more symmetry' (with obligations being placed on stronger as well as weaker currencies) (Le Monde: 24 February 1988). These demands paralleled French demands for EMS reform in 1988.

In contrast, developments within the EMS saw the Finance Ministry in a more defensive, embattled, and frustrated position. Along with Trichet and Trésor officials, Balladur went through a baptism of fire in the ERM in 1986–7. The result was a process of policy reflection leading to major new initiatives in 1987–8. The first negative experience involved the initiation and negotiation of an ERM realignment in April 1986, with France requesting a devaluation of the franc at the ECOFIN in Ootmarsum. The request was prompted by heavy, post-election pressures on the franc. It was also timed to pin blame on the financial profligacy of the Socialist period and to give the new centre-right government room for manoeuvre in French economic policy. But it proved an unexpectedly tough and difficult negotiation, in which the Finance Ministry found itself isolated and from which it secured only a small devaluation.

For Trichet this episode was a major learning experience. He, and others in the cabinet, were led to reflect on the costs of this kind of policy move in terms of lost political credibility with EC partners and with the financial markets. Balladur's move had been intellectually supported within his cabinet by the argument that the *franc stable* must reflect economic fundamentals rather than become an objective in its own right; French inflation rates had been exceeding German. But, after April 1986, Balladur and Chirac had no political appetite for further devaluation. Trichet was later to find that this episode had done substantial damage to the credibility of French arguments for EMS reform. For Trichet the lesson of Ootmarsum was long term: that the *franc stable*—and the budgetary and monetary *rigueur* to sustain it—was the precondition of a strong French negotiating position over EMS reform and EMU.

Unfortunately for the Trésor, and for Balladur and Chirac, foreign-exchange-market pressure led in January 1987 to another devaluation of the French franc in the ERM. This episode was far more serious, and was turned by Chirac into a crisis in Franco-German relations. There was something of a division of labour between Chirac and Balladur in managing this ERM crisis. Chirac conducted a war of words on Bonn and Frankfurt, putting the Germans under heavy psychological pressure. In Chirac's view the problems of the French franc had nothing to do with economic fundamentals. They had everything to do with the failure of the German Bundesbank to take appropriate action to defend the ERM from speculation consequent on disequilibrium generated by the falling US dollar. The responsibility to act to defend the franc rested with the Bundesbank, not the French government. As in 1982–3 the French government sought to redefine the crisis: as a D-Mark and not a franc crisis. In doing so Chirac was seeking political damage-limitation within the RPR constituency, conscious of the risks to his Presidential election prospects.

In a calmer, more judicious manner Balladur took up the issue of reforming the EMS on 8 January 1987, four days before the realignment. He spelt out three proposals: to make the ECU a genuine currency which could be used as a reserve currency by central banks and in foreign-exchange-market interventions; for EC central banks to make more use of each other's currencies as reserves (he had in mind the Bundesbank holding francs in its reserves, thereby lending prestige to the French currency and addressing the problem of asymmetry); and for 'harmonization' with the US dollar and the Japanese yen. Balladur worked closely with Delors and with the Belgian Finance Minister and Chair of ECOFIN, Mark Eyskens, to ensure that on 12 January an ERM realignment was accompanied by a request to the EC Monetary Committee and the Committee of EC Central Bank Governors to examine ways of strengthening the EMS. At the ECOFIN meeting Balladur was successful in pressing three areas for consideration: greater use of intramarginal intervention; improved co-ordination of interest-rate policies; and, in the longer term, the possibility of direct intervention by the EMCF.

Balladur was able to exploit the openings created by the sharpness of Chirac's verbal assault to get reform of the EMS firmly on the agenda in 1987. There was a clear continuity with Delors's ideas on EMS reform outlined in 1982–3. But the new elements under Gaullist leadership were a more forceful emphasis on the problem of asymmetry and a stress on interest-rate co-ordination and a position for the French franc in EC central bank reserve holdings. Behind this difference of emphasis and style was a more nationalistic political outlook and constituency in the RPR, to which Chirac was especially sensitive.

Hence Balladur's growing activism on the EMS and EMU was conditioned by consideration of political strategy as the 1988 Presidential election approached. Here the Matignon was an important player, intent on shoring up Chirac's position within the centre-right majority, particularly vis-à-vis Barre and Giscard d'Estaing as alternative contenders from the UDF. By 1987 Barre in particular had emerged as a formidable contender, situated outside the *cohabitation* as an independent and critical voice. What Barre and Giscard shared was a strong commitment to *construction européenne*. Both had spoken out in favour of EMU during 1986–7, with Giscard active alongside Helmut Schmidt in the new Committee for the Monetary Union of Europe and Barre speaking in favour of an independent European Central Bank. Polling evidence suggested a danger of being outflanked on Europe. Hence, consequent on dialogue at the highest political level with Chirac, Balladur set to work to reposition the centre-right government intellectually on EMU and, strategically, to outflank Barre and Giscard. The objective was to create a political opening to the UDF by embracing EMU, whilst at the same time reassuring RPR supporters. The result was only a cautious endorsement of EMU, combined with a more forthright denunciation of the failings of the ERM. For Balladur the domestic political context was the key to the Balladur Memorandum of January 1988 on 'Europe's Monetary Construction'. For Trésor officials it was an opportunity to pursue linkage with the Plaza Agreement and the Louvre Accord.

The Basle–Nyborg Agreement: De Larosière and Empowering the Banque de France

Though the Basle–Nyborg agreement of September 1987 was highly technical in content, and basically conducted by the EC central bankers, Balladur's objective was to use it to demonstrate French political leadership of *construction européenne* and to gain a domestic political profile for the centre-right government and for his own political credentials after May 1988. Hence he sought to impart a strong political leadership to these negotiations, spelling out to the new Governor of the Banque de France, Jacques de Larosière, basic French positions and setting his officials to work to prepare Finance Ministry positions for presentation in the EC Monetary Committee and ECOFIN. At the informal ECOFIN in Knokke on 6 April 1987 Balladur kept up the political pressure, whilst domestically he used his weekly Thursday meeting with de Larosière in his office, accompanied by Trichet, to monitor progress and to seek an informal co-ordination. Work on this project far overshadowed that devoted to the Franco-German Economic Council and even the Balladur Memorandum in the time budget of Trésor officials.

But, respectful though he was towards Balladur, de Larosière was concerned to cultivate an image of independence and strength. Like Balladur, he was a proud and independent figure, attached to the dignity of his office. Moreover, he brought to the Banque de France a formidable reputation. As a former director of the Trésor, he was a seasoned insider who commanded great respect and admiration; and, having just served as managing director of the IMF, he brought a wealth of experience of international negotiations, a grasp of new economic and monetary policy ideas, and a cross-national network of contacts. De Larosière's objective was to lend his own reputation to the process of building up the credibility of the Banque de France as a market-based, technically efficient, and internationally oriented central bank which was aligned alongside the Dutch and German central banks. Hence he was intent on bringing about a process of cultural and intellectual change inside the Banque de France, commensurate with its new role in open-market operations and with a future of free capital movement. For that reason de Larosière was determined to prioritize a close working relationship with Pöhl at the Bundesbank, in effect strengthening a relationship that went back to the time when they acted as sherpas to Giscard and Schmidt and that had been continued at the IMF. De Larosière sought, accordingly, to stress the Basle-based nature of the negotiations; to activate close Banque de France– Bundesbank relations in the negotiations as a means of confidence-building; and to distance himself from impressions of political determination by the Finance Minister. His concern—as later in the Delors Committee—was to take strong personal control of the negotiations and to act very independently.

In the negotiations in Basle de Larosière stressed a pragmatic reform of the EMS designed to restore exchange rate stability by its more flexible operation. This greater flexibility was to be achieved by a more intensive, anticipatory co-ordination of monetary and macroeconomic policies: by intramarginal interventions to stabilize market expectations; and by co-ordinated interest-rate movements to head off market pressures. By contrast, de Larosière distanced himself from Delors's stress on institutional development of the EMS in the form of strengthening the EMCF; this demand implied a politicization of monetary policy by the back door, given the linkage between the EMCF and ECOFIN. In its essentials, the Basle Agreement (at Nyborg ECOFIN endorsed it) was for de Larosière a negotiating triumph. He achieved his objective of reforming the EMS, and his two main negotiating positions, whilst creating a good working basis for improving collaboration with the Bundesbank and re-positioning the Banque de France.

The Balladur Memorandum on Europe's Monetary Construction: Putting an ECB on the Agenda

For Balladur the Basle–Nyborg Agreement constituted an improvement to the credit and intervention mechanisms of the EMS. But it fell short of the fundamental reforms for which the French government had earlier called. In particular, there were two gaps: a failure to correct the basic problem of asymmetry at the heart of the EMS; and the continuing lack of a concerted policy towards the US dollar. The Basle–Nyborg Agreement also faced being outpaced by the speed of change. Within Balladur's cabinet the argument took root that, with full freedom of capital movement under the single European market programme, the EMS would require further adjustment. An effectively functioning single European market required monetary stability. But at political levels the Gaullist calculation was that there were gains in standing up for French national interests in monetary policy.

Though the Trésor's intellectual arguments and the case for plugging the gaps in the September 1987 agreement informed the Balladur Memorandum of 8 January 1988, its catalyst was, as we saw above, in domestic political strategy—to reposition the RPR on EC policy before the Presidential election by moving into new areas, in particular EMU. In short, the stimulus came from Balladur's discussions with Chirac rather than from the Trésor or even Balladur's cabinet. An important part of the political context was the need to offer an alternative to the Giscard–Schmidt proposal for an ECB. Giscard's renewed activism on EMU was unsettling the RPR. Within Balladur's cabinet and the Trésor the key figures in the preparation of the Balladur Memorandum were Anne Le Lorier and Christian Noyer, with contributions also from Ariane Obolensky and from the newly arrived head of the EC section Sylvain de Forges. In giving substance to the proposal they had, interestingly, little to draw on in the form of institutional memory of EMU; for instance, de Forges had nothing on the European Reserve Fund proposal or on the Fourcade Plan, whilst Trichet was actually new to EMU. In drafting the memorandum they sought to reflect the political caution and hesitation of Balladur on EMU. They also tried to link it to the wider debate about the international concertation of exchange rates. De Forges, who had just returned from the IMF in Washington, was especially sensitive to the opportunity to set EMU in this larger context of international monetary reform. Not least, work on the memorandum provided an opportunity to give an overall coherence to Balladur's policy.

The Balladur Memorandum was in one sense nothing new. It returned to the theme of asymmetry (which had inspired the Fourcade Plan of 1974) and went on to argue that, in the absence of 'equal responsibilities' on all members for adjustment, the single market—and freedom of capital movement in particular—would place impossible demands on the EMS. The Memorandum focused on four proposals for reform of the EMS: all EC member states, notably Britain, were to join the ERM and to move to the 'narrow' band of fluctuation, notably in this case Italy; rapid implementation of freedom of capital movement; reduction of asymmetry; and development of a concerted policy towards non-EC currencies, notably the US dollar. But the novelty came in the third part dealing with the 'establishment of a zone with a single currency'. Starting from the premise that by 1992 the EC would be 'a completely integrated economic space', the Balladur Memorandum argued the logic of 'a zone with a single currency . . . that is, a zone in which the one and the same currency would serve as a means of payment in all countries and in which the one common central bank and 'federal' banks in all countries would exist'.

But then, slipping into a more cautious tone, the Balladur Memorandum acknowledged the difficulties raised by proposals for an ECB and confined itself simply to listing the questions that needed to be addressed in ECOFIN and in the EC Monetary Committee. These questions were as follows:

- Are there technical preconditions for achieving a single currency zone?
- Was it possible to envisage a more gradual association of those countries not able to progress as rapidly as others?
- In the case of a single currency, would it be defined in terms of a basket of currencies?
- Would there be one or several monetary units in operation inside the 'European space'?
- Would a 'unitary central bank' need to be set up immediately?
- What would be its powers?
- How would its relations to the EC's political organs and to the national monetary authorities be regulated?

No answers were offered to these questions. They were listed as means of focusing discussion at the EC level. In particular, no commitment was entered into on the question of a single versus a common currency or on the question of central bank independence.

Balladur opted for ambiguous and cautious formulations: in large part for domestic political reasons, seeking to attract UDF support without inflaming Gaullist opinion in an election year. He was also intellectually unsure about the merits of some of the arguments. It was not until May 1990 in *Les Échos* that he finally declared his support for a common currency over a single currency; a thirteenth currency was more compatible with French concerns about loss of sovereignty. In *Le Figaro* he spoke of an ECB by the year 2000 and of the ECB having 'a certain autonomy' (*Le Figaro*: 14 January 1988). However, in *Le Monde* Balladur was more hesitant, stressing that by giving independence to the Banque de France the French government would be in danger of replicating the problems associated with the German Bundesbank: namely, that '. . . the more autonomous a central bank is, the more it is said to resist European co-operation. Would it not, then, be inconsistent to appear to give the Banque de France a more independent status, only to cast doubt on this independence again if it were subordinated to a European institution?' (*Le Monde*: 1 March 1988) Behind Balladur's hesitation was the republican tradition. He was concerned that there should be an 'equilibrium' between finance ministers and central bankers. Given that each had to exercise their own responsibilities, with exchange rate policy falling in the sphere of ministerial responsibility, it was essential to establish a dialogue between the two.

But, most striking of all, the Balladur Memorandum advanced well beyond the Gaullist position on EMU as articulated by Debré in February 1971 and during the Assembly debate about the EMS, and especially its stage 2, in 1979 when Debré had attacked the idea of pooling French reserves in a future EMF. In a manner new for a Gaullist, Balladur was stressing the need to reflect on the *institutional* aspects of the monetary policy construction of Europe. The main thread of intellectual continuity was provided by a characteristically Gaullist focus on 'Europe's monetary construction', with less attention to questions relating to economic policy co-ordination at the EC level. In fact the Balladur

Memorandum was not intellectually adventurous. There was a crucial element of strategic thinking at work: to neutralize the increasingly active role on EMU being developed by Giscard d'Estaing since 1986, and the pro-EMU position of Barre, in the context of the popularity of *construction européenne*. Giscard, in particular, was calling for Balladur to realize his electoral promise of 1986 to make the Banque de France independent. He did so in the context of the requirements of EMU. In short, Balladur was under domestic political pressure to declare his hand on EMU.

Mitterrand, EMS Reform, and EMU during the Cohabitation

During the *cohabitation* Mitterrand's capacity to shape the substance of EMU policy was undermined by the intent of Chirac to reserve economic and monetary policy to the domain of government policy. In fact, he enjoyed very different relations with Chirac and Balladur. Balladur always treated what Mitterrand saw as his prerogatives with respect and handled him with great courtesy. In turn, Mitterrand welcomed 'with interest' Balladur's Memorandum in an interview with *Die Welt* on 18 January 1988. During the same interview the President underlined that he wanted an ECB 'like Giscard', playing off in a characteristically Mitterrand manner different leaders within the centre-right. This reference to Giscard illustrates how Mitterrand's advocacy of EMU was rooted in domestic political strategy. Mitterrand had no intention of being outflanked on EMU by Giscard or by Barre, and by 1988 he saw Barre as the more serious threat as a Presidential candidate: a man with *'un sens d'État'*. He was determined to enter the Presidential election in May 1988 as the 'most European' candidate and to use Europe as a key mobilizing political theme for the Left. More immediately, Mitterrand was preoccupied by the need to demonstrate that he was more adventurous on EMU than Balladur.

EMU and Geopolitical Strategy   Mitterrand was not simply driven by domestic electoral strategy. The urgency with which he pursued EMU was firmly rooted in geopolitical arguments generated by the arrival of Gorbachev as new General Secretary of the Communist Party in the Soviet Union. On his visit to Moscow in July 1986 Mitterrand was deeply impressed by the seriousness with which Gorbachev was pursuing domestic political renewal and a new approach to relations with the West. For Mitterrand Gorbachev opened new opportunities for France to act as a privileged mediator between Moscow and Washington, playing on its role as political leader of the EC. But he also saw potential dangers: of Moscow playing off Bonn against Paris, perhaps by making the Soviet offer of the 1950s—German unification in return for German neutrality. In short, Gorbachev's initiatives were a factor in making Mitterrand wish to speed up Franco-German initiatives designed to strengthen their co-operation and use this as a motor to build European unification (Védrine 1996: chapter 11). EMU was set in this geopolitical framework of analysis from 1986 onwards.

The consequence of this reappraisal of Franco-German relations in the context of Gorbachev was an increase of psychological pressure on Bonn from 1986: by Dumas on Genscher and by Mitterrand on Kohl. But the importance of French pressure alone should not be exaggerated. Crucially, Kohl and Genscher were determined to do all they could to reassure the French that, in talking to Gorbachev, they were not turning their backs on the EC. At the Franco-German meetings in Heidelberg on 26 August 1986 and Frankfurt on 27 October Kohl took up the theme of needing to reinforce Franco-German relations, signalling in Frankfurt that he wished to go beyond the Single European Act to pursue the political unification of Europe. For the first time, in Heidelberg, Kohl responded positively to French pressure for EMU. At their meeting in Chambord on 28 March 1987 Mitterrand was again reassured of Kohl's intention of warding off the risk of a Soviet offer of German unification in return for neutrality. Both forged a deepening personal bond around the idea of sponsoring fresh steps to cement Franco-German relations. In their discussions Mitterrand and Kohl repeatedly returned to the lessons of nineteenth- and twentieth-century history (Védrine 1996: 409–10).

Geopolitical assessment, combined with his intellectual commitment to *construction européenne*, and the reassurance generated by these Franco-German meetings, formed the backdrop to Mitterrand's initiative at the Venice G7 summit on 8–9 June 1987. Here he proposed to Kohl a 'new type of treaty like the Elysée treaty' and called for 'the integration of our armies in precise and significant ways' (Védrine 1996: 412). Mitterrand was carving out a sphere of action that was appropriate to the geopolitical challenge. It also fell firmly within the domain of the Elysée so that he could maximize his freedom of manoeuvre to make an impact on Franco-German relations and European security within the framework of the *cohabitation*. But above all, with the Presidential election less than a year away, Mitterrand was determined to use the celebrations of the twenty-fifth anniversary of the Elysée Treaty to reinforce his image as an international statesman opening new opportunities in Franco-German relations. The key turning-point was Teltschik's visit to the Elysée on 24 July 1987 to pursue the project launched in Venice. Attali used the occasion to establish the idea of a linkage between a Franco-German Defence Council for consultations on defence questions and a Franco-German Economic Council. In effect, Germany's role of *demandeur* in relation to defence issues was being countered by the Elysée acting as *demandeur* on economic and financial co-operation. By this means French negotiators were seeking to bind the Bundesbank into the framework of the Elysée Treaty, exploiting the opportunities opened up by the new negotiations.

The Franco-German Economic Council   Once the Elysée had brought the Franco-German Economic Council into the frame of the negotiations, it was impossible to keep discussions away from *cohabitation* politics. At the second meeting between Elysée and Chancellery staff on 27 August little progress was made. Both sides were reticent: Mitterrand ruled out a sphere of competence of the

Franco-German Defence Council extending to consultations on nuclear weapons; whilst the Federal Chancellor's Office was hesitant about the competence of the Franco-German Economic Council, spelling out the responsibility of the German Finance Ministry in this sphere. By 18 September Chirac was complaining about the failure to press ahead effectively on the monetary side of the Franco-German negotiations. As for Mitterrand, domestic political strategy played a key role: Chirac was determined to claim credit for a key component of the new treaty. By November the issue came to a head, with both the Matignon and Balladur insisting that negotiations of a Franco-German Economic Council were a matter strictly reserved to them.

In addition to sharing Chirac's domestic political perspective on the issue, Balladur was motivated by his own concerns. As a proud minister, he was intent on ensuring that control of these negotiations did not evade him, with consequent loss of face. The Finance Ministry provided him with an attractive argument. In effect, the proposed Franco-German Economic Council was little more than a formalization and development of the existing arrangement by which the director of the Trésor and a Deputy Governor of the Banque de France met with their German counterparts within the framework of the Franco-German summits. But, crucially, the new proposal offered a greater autonomy of action for the Finance Ministry, moving it out of the shadow of the Elysée, in the form of separately timetabled discussions with the Germans. In the context of *cohabitation* politics Balladur was attracted by this argument. He was also encouraged by another Finance Ministry argument: that a Franco-German Economic Council would be a means of binding in the Germans to the defence of the French franc against a third devaluation within the ERM during the *cohabitation*. Such a prospect was seen as politically and economically disastrous for the centre-right. The Franco-German Economic Council was seen in the Trésor as a final nail in the coffin of French devaluations, building on the successful co-ordination of French and German interest rate changes in late 1987 after the Basle–Nyborg Agreement.

The height of domestic tension within the *cohabitation* was reached with the Franco-German summit at Karlsruhe on 12–13 November 1987. On the eve of the summit Chirac signalled that he was unwilling to become involved in the twenty-fifth anniversary celebrations unless he played a fuller part in their preparation. In discussions with Kohl and Mitterrand he spelt out that his condition for being involved was agreement to establish a Franco-German Economic Council. This agreement was achieved, subject to the German condition that the new council had to be a consultative and not decision-making body, in this way protecting the position of the Bundesbank. Following Karlsruhe the Finance Ministry began serious work to flesh out the proposal in a practical form, the key role being played by Trichet as director of the Trésor, assisted by Obolensky, Noyer, and de Forges, with a role for Le Lorier in Balladur's cabinet. In the Elysée there was resentment at the way in which Chirac had 'hijacked' the Franco-German Economic Council and sought to upstage Mitterrand at Karlsruhe.

But, on the other hand, the Elysée and the Matignon—and Balladur—were united in their disappointment that the proposed council was to be relegated to a purely consultative role, a 'co-ordinating committee in the economic and financial area' in the words of the summit communiqué. Their agreed tactical response was to spring a surprise just before the twenty-fifth anniversary celebrations, scheduled to start in Paris on 22 January 1988. They insisted that the the new body be given full formal status within the Elysée Treaty rather than as a separate agreement; and in Article 4 of the new treaty protocol referred to 'co-ordination as closely as possible' of economic and monetary policies. This formalization deeply worried the Bundesbank, which saw once again a 'trick' to bind it into the Franco-German relationship. Following the Paris celebrations, prolonged negotiations followed between Trichet and Tietmeyer to fill in the substance of the new Council but without any new breakthroughs for France. In any case, the scene of action was moving elsewhere—to Germany, where Genscher was taking up EMU with a new political will that took the French Finance Ministry by surprise.

Spain, Germany, and EMU: The Role of Dumas in Activating Genscher The context of the Franco-German Economic Council proposal was not just geostrategic. It was also grounded in the aftermath of the January 1987 ERM crisis. Thereafter, the theme of reinforcing the EMS and of developing the public *ECU* to match its new-found private role found a new place in Mitterrand's speeches and interviews. On 15 January he used a speech at Chatham House in London to declare: 'Either the EMS will succeed—but it is threatened—and Europe can be united or it will collapse and Europe will not unite itself'. This phrase was employed regularly during 1987. Mitterrand's conception of EMU was outlined in an interview with *Corriere Della Sera* on 17 March. He accepted that a European currency would not replace national currencies in the near future. But it was possible to make the *ECU* into a major international currency which, alongside other European currencies, would play a stabilizing role in relation to the US dollar and the yen. The theme was developed further at the Franco-Spanish bilateral with Gonzales in July 1987 where he insisted that, despite German resistance, it was necessary to go towards a common currency. Two key elements of his conception of EMU recur: a reference to a common rather than a single currency; and a stress on its international role.

By 1988 the Spanish Prime Minister Gonzales had emerged as a key figure in Mitterrand's strategic calculations about EMU. They met on 14–15 January in Paris, when Mitterrand was concerned to seize the initiative on EMU after the Balladur Memorandum, and then for a Franco-Spanish summit in Seville on 19 March 1988. The summit closed with a declaration by Mitterrand and Gonzales that they intended to closely co-ordinate their EC policy as the holders of the two successive EC Presidencies in 1989, Spain followed by France. They gave a clear signal that a European currency and an ECB were to feature at the top of the list of matters of joint interest, expressing their 'firm intention of mobilizing our two countries on this subject'. The consequence was an intensification of

Franco-Spanish relations on EMU, involving Dumas co-ordinating with his Spanish counterpart, Fernandez Ordonez and a special role for Guigou in co-ordinating the two Presidencies. Mitterrand saw in Gonzales a figure who commanded greater respect in Bonn than his Italian equivalent, de Mita. Also, he was a fellow Socialist, committed to a political agenda that emphasized the linkage of EMU to a 'social' Europe, and in particular EC harmonization of taxation of savings to accompany financial and monetary integration.

But, though Gonzales emerged as a key ally on EMU, Mitterrand consistently recognized that the Franco-German relationship was the key to relaunching EMU. French strategy was to orchestrate supportive pressures on Bonn, whilst avoiding any impression that the French government was seeking directly to threaten Bonn by building an alliance against it on EMU or prematurely tabling ambitious proposals on EMU. Private psychological pressure was put directly on the Germans, by Mitterrand on Kohl and, most of all, by Dumas on Genscher. It was soon clear to the French that Genscher was the easier target: not because he was more warmly disposed to European unification than Kohl but because he faced fewer problems of consensus-building as head of a relatively small party in the German federal coalition government than Kohl faced as Chancellor and because he occupied a strategic position in the coalition. Hence Dumas came to play a significant part in Elysée efforts to make progress on EMU. By 1987 Dumas and Genscher were reflecting together on how the EMU dossier could be reactivated in the face of Bundesbank and Finance Ministry resistance. In particular, they were agreed that a new initiative on EMU had to come from within the German federal government. Its identification with the French government would serve only to heighten German domestic resistance. In the light of this intelligence, and Dumas's reporting to the Elysée, it was clear by 1987 that French strategy had to be to sustain psychological pressure on Genscher and Kohl to act, not to take independent French initiatives. Throughout Dumas was closely involved in the evolution of Genscher's thinking on EMU, in the critical years 1987–8, and beyond. This transnational political linkage was to prove the most crucial for French policy in getting EMU back on the EC agenda. In fact, Mitterrand and Dumas provided the vital connection between the Balladur Memorandum and the Genscher Memorandum. That connection took the form of Mitterrand's recognition that he must associate himself with a bolder Franco-German move on EMU that would eclipse Balladur; and Dumas was instrumental in coaxing Genscher to act in January–February 1988.

A crucial part of Mitterrand's role in helping to put EMU back on the agenda in 1987 was the provision of historical legitimation to support a reinvigorated Franco-German relationship as the 'motor' of Europe. This favourite and by no means fresh metaphor was complemented by a new stress on the shared historical roots of France and Germany in the Empire of Charlemagne. The historical image of the Franco-German relationship as a refashioning of Carolingian Europe was not original to Mitterrand. It had been employed by de Gaulle in the late 1940s. But its use to underpin the policy of the French state in relation to European unification was distinctive. It represented a cultural image that, within the Socialist Party, was particular to Mitterrand. In no sense did it embody the characteristic image and rationale of Franco-German relations and European unification to be found in the Foreign Ministry, the Finance Ministry, or even the Elysée. There political realism, a sense of the Franco-German relationship as a diplomatic necessity, was more typical. Those more disposed to welcome Mitterrand's historical image were few: Bianco and Guigou at the Elysée; Scheer, the Permanent Representative in Brussels; and the French Ambassador in Bonn, Serge Boidevaix. The image of Carolingian Europe was spelt out during his official visit to Germany in October 1987, notably in Aachen City Hall. His call for a common European currency and for strengthened military co-operation during this visit represented a carefully balanced package that invited a trade-off of interests. But his main interest was in legitimating and inspiring the trade-off by casting it into an historical perspective. In this way he went further than Chirac and eclipsed the more pro-European approach of Barre and Giscard by a more ambitious, less technocratically worded image of EMU.

EMU and the Presidential Election of 8 May 1988 Even before the *cohabitation* began, Mitterrand had determined to make *construction européenne* the mobilizing theme for his re-election. Just as the success of the Fontainebleau European Council had been crucial to the decision to embrace *construction européenne*, so the doubling of the Structural Funds at the Brussels European Council of February 1988, and the dynamic behind the single European market programme evident under the German EC Presidency of early 1988, confirmed to Mitterrand the validity of his choice. During March and early April he worked on his '*Lettre à tous les Français*'. Eight of its seventy-nine pages were devoted to '*Construire l'Europe*', with contributions from Bianco, Hannoun, and Védrine. Mitterrand presented himself as the guarantor of a '*France unie*', dedicated to the pre-eminent objective of building a European power that would surpass the USA and Japan. The advance of the European idea was attributed to his efforts; his re-election would ensure that the process would speed up. EMU was situated in this context. He wrote of 'the transformation of the *écu* into a true reserve currency, able to take its place alongside other international currencies' and 'for a central bank one day or other'. 'The *écu* . . . will provide, with the dollar and the yen, one of the three poles of the new monetary order . . . Yes, Europe will unite by its own efforts—or never.'

During the Presidential election campaign Barre was the most explicit of the other candidates in his support for EMU, arguing in his election programme for 'a European reserve system regrouping the central banks of the member states'. By contrast, Chirac, who emerged as Mitterrand's rival in the second round, avoided references to EMU. He confined himself to praising Balladur's initiative of January 1988 and to broad references to the need for greater economic and monetary solidarity amongst member states. But, in a characteristically Gaullist manner, Chirac kept away from issues of institutional reform. His caution on

Europe was not rewarded. On 8 May Chirac was soundly beaten by Mitterrand (46 per cent to 54 per cent).

Mitterrand, Bérégovoy, and the Delors Committee

The political conditions of the *cohabitation* had not favoured the Elysée in developing a leading role in defining the terms of French negotiating positions on EMU. It had been a matter of seeking out common ground, a search which—as we saw above—was by no means without success. The Elysée lacked the technical resources to do the job and had to cede power to a Finance Ministry in more cautious Gaullist hands. But domestic political circumstances were much less important than external strategic calculations in constraining the Presidential role. Elysée strategy was to rely on the Germans to take the initiative on EMU and then to seek to shape the course of the subsequent negotiations. Hence the Genscher Memorandum was seen as a much more important event by the Elysée than the Balladur Memorandum: not just because it was less tentative in content but, most of all, because it represented the opening on EMU that French diplomacy had been seeking in Bonn.

Nevertheless, the size of his victory in the Presidential election was decisive in strengthening Mitterrand's hand in giving a new political drive to EMU in Paris. He had a clear mandate to pursue *construction européenne*. This had demonstrated its value as a theme around which he could mobilize France behind his Presidency and which could help the Socialist Party retrieve its association with social, economic, and political change and regain governmental power. Above all, Mitterrand felt liberated from the *'dictature de l'instant'*. He could refocus his mind on *'l'avantage de la durée'*, on locating EMU and other EC initiatives in the long-term context of the historic mission and legacy of his Presidency. Mitterrand was writing himself into the history books as a European statesman of the first rank.

In pursuing EMU Mitterrand situated the project in a different conception of democracy and political leadership from that of his new Socialist Prime Minister, Michel Rocard. Under Rocard—whose own ambition was to succeed Mitterrand at the Elysée—the Matignon became newly sensitive to opinion polls and the theme of governing by consensus and a policy of *'réformes tranquilles'*. His objective was to avoid the unpopularity of the previous Socialist governments under Mauroy and Fabius by grounding policy in the support of public opinion. Hence the *Service d'information et de diffusion* attached to the Matignon acquired a new importance in analysing opinion poll data. But this difference of approach between Mitterrand and Rocard did not generate differences of position on *construction européenne* and EMU. In November 1988 78 per cent declared themselves favourable to *construction européenne*; in February 1989 51 per cent ranked it above disarmament and development aid. There appeared to be clear, sustained public support for EMU. In November 1989, for instance,

50 per cent were favourable, and another 15 per cent very favourable, to the replacement of the French franc by a single European currency (Percheron 1991). A poll of January 1989 suggested that 97 per cent of French employers supported EMU.

Furthermore, domestic political strategy underpinned Mitterrand's policy commitment to EMU. Following the National Assembly elections subsequent to the Presidential election, the Socialist Party was dependent on centrist support to sustain a government. By appointing Rocard as Prime Minister, Mitterrand signalled an 'opening' to the centre. Given this political constellation, the President was determined not to be outflanked by Barre and Giscard d'Estaing in his enthusiasm for a common currency and an ECB. At the same time French strategy on EMU condemned Mitterrand to wait on events in Germany, to combine private psychological pressure on Bonn with a low-profile role in the EC. This position was by no means comfortable for the French President. He had to content himself with tolerating an ever-closer working relationship between Delors and Kohl in preparing for the Hanover European Council in June 1988. In the process Mitterrand became increasingly suspicious of Delors's private diplomacy.

The conduct of EMU policy was also affected by the legacy of the *cohabitation*; by Mitterrand's deep distrust of Rocard whom he saw as a rival always waiting his chance to succeed him; and by his ingrained suspicion of technocrats within the administration. Following the *cohabitation* Mitterrand was determined to restore his full control over the substance of EC policy in order to be able to pursue his new mandate to speed up *construction européenne*. Rocard was marginalized in relation to EC policy in general, and EMU in particular, and Guigou's role upgraded. His brief as Prime Minister was to promote education, employment, and 'national solidarity'. Rocard's importance rested in pushing the idea of 'social' Europe. From the outset he stressed the risk that *construction européenne* could prove divisive, privileging the powerful and excluding the weak. He sustained pressure on Mitterrand to pursue the agenda of anchoring and protecting workers' rights in EC law.

Most important of all, Mitterrand was particularly conscious that, having served seven years in office, he possessed '*l'advantage de la durée*': his contacts and knowledge, along with those of his closest advisers, gave him an oppportunity to establish an intellectual ascendancy in relation to EC policy. Dumas functioned simultaneously as Foreign Minister, his personal and most intimate diplomatic adviser, and his closest confidant. He enjoyed a uniquely privileged, private dialogue with the President as the most trusted of Mitterrand loyalists. Guigou too enjoyed a new lease of life as EC adviser in the Elysée, head of the SGCI, and someone who gained status with Mitterrand from her 'insider' knowledge as a former Finance Ministry official. Her particular task was to combat what the Elysée characterized as the 'intellectual terrorism' practised by the Trésor.

Mitterrand's whole approach to EMU was premised on a fundamental distrust of the technocrats in the Trésor. His basic objective was to subordinate technical arguments about EMU to politics. In doing so Mitterrand relied pre-eminently on Dumas and Guigou. Bérégovoy, who was reappointed Finance Minister, was not part of the innermost circle, though he was much closer than Rocard. Mitterrand had confidence in him, but not the complete confidence enjoyed by Dumas. If anything, his position had been weakened by the conduct of the Presidential election campaign. Mitterrand had been sharply critical of Bérégovoy's direction of the campaign in a way that wounded him deeply. It was not a question of doubting the loyalty of Bérégovoy or even his will to control the Finance Ministry. Mitterrand's suspicions were directed at Bérégovoy's officials in the Finance Ministry. With respect to the conduct of EMU policy, Samy Cohen's reference to Mitterrand's second *septennat* as characterized by 'the syndrome of the omniscient presidency' misses the mark (Cohen 1990). Mitterrand was all too aware of the potential for the Trésor to act as an intellectual counterweight and the risk that Bérégovoy would become its captive in EMU negotiations. Crucial to Bérégovoy's influence on Mitterrand was his ability to demonstrate his independence from Trésor orthodoxy and his capacity to master the Finance Ministry on EMU.

Bérégovoy, the ERM, and EMU

Unlike Dumas and Guigou, Bérégovoy entertained reservations about EMU, though not of principle. He was prone to second thoughts, to doubts and hesitations. These diminished during the course of the EMU negotiations but never completely disappeared. These doubts can be linked back to his old political mentor, Mendès France, who in the 1960s and 1970s had not fully and unequivocally declared in favour of EMU. The reservations sprang from his social Radicalism, which embraced *rigueur* in the name of protecting '*les petits gens*' from the erosion of the value of their savings but which also feared to be locked into an economic strategy that inhibited growth and employment. Bérégovoy could not rid himself of a nagging doubt that a policy of sustained high interest rates was crucifying the French economy.

Hence, on returning to the Finance Ministry in May 1988, his priority was to secure a staged cut in interest rates in order to give a psychological boost to the economy (Aeschimann and Riché 1990: 36–45). Somehow that objective had to be rendered compatible with strengthening the franc in the ERM, given Bérégovoy's second commitment—to remain the Finance Minister who had never devalued. The intellectual case that there was a 'margin of manoeuvre' was made by Rubinowicz, who returned to his cabinet as financial adviser. The staged cuts were agreed in May 1988, in the face of passive resistance from de Larosière, and continued into July (a total cut of 0.5 per cent). But by October the cut had been reversed in response to increases in Bundesbank rates, and despite a letter from Bérégovoy to Stoltenberg on 29 June warning of 'grave consequences' from such increases. Bérégovoy's return to office was, in short, a reminder of the constraints that followed from the ERM and that these constraints were German.

Intellectually, Bérégovoy remained a frustrated social radical who suspected that trying to negotiate EMU with Germany would only add to the constraints on French politics. Hence, later, he adopted with enthusiasm the idea of a strong 'political pole' to balance the 'monetary pole' of EMU (later rechristened *gouvernement économique* by the Elysée). Bérégovoy was also preoccupied with the idea of balancing Germany by having as wide a membership as possible in the ERM, including Britain, before contemplating EMU.

Bérégovoy was also the consummate domestic political strategist: continuously calculating his standing in Mitterrand's eyes and his prospects for succeeding to the Prime Ministership (he had again been disappointed in 1988); assessing his reputation within the Socialist Party; and paying attention to his role in contributing to its electoral success. Policy proposals, notably relating to the ERM and EMU, were passed through the filter of these calculations. Hence his preoccupation with getting interest rates down; with making the Left respectable as a financial manager; and with not disappointing Mitterrand who held the key to his political advance. Any potential for inconsistency was ironed out by his basic priority of loyalty to the President. Without Mitterrand he was nothing. Mitterrand's authority of office, combined with his intellectual assurance, social ease, and a certain enigmatic quality, left Bérégovoy ill at ease and intimidated. He compensated with a phenomenal capacity for work and will to display his mastery of the Finance Ministry brief, qualities that he had learnt from Mendès France in the 1960s. Later on in the IGC, compared to Lamont and Waigel, he was to immerse himself in EMU papers, intent on leaving his personal mark.

But Bérégovoy remained acutely sensitive. When it came to political strategy, he lacked the cool indifference of Mitterrand. An autodidact who had for years worked in industry, he remained at heart a simple 'man of the people', bound socially to his city of Nevers, and no player of the sophisticated Parisian social networks. He could never share fully, like Dumas, in Mitterrand's social world, with its ambience of high culture and gracious manners; nor could he feel comfortable with the technocrats of the Finance Ministry, many of whom he found condescending. Bérégovoy remained an isolated figure, plagued by self-doubts and by an intuitive distrust of the rationalizations for EMU offered up by officials.

Bérégovoy's Inner Circle and the Role of Hannoun

Those who worked most closely with Bérégovoy in his cabinet came to value his considerable qualities: his personal warmth and spontaneity; his directness of manner; his prodigious capacity for work; the speed with which he absorbed ideas; his intuitive sense for what constituted sound and sensible argument; his tenacity in argument; his grasp of wider political strategy. But the emergence of an inner circle of loyalists sprang from more than admiration. It was also linked to Bérégovoy's deep need for reassurance. At the very heart of this inner circle of Bérégovoy's cabinet loyalists were Gauron (the closest of all and his *mendèsiste* conscience), Monnier (responsible for macroeconomic policy), and Rubinowicz (responsible for financial policy and Bérégovoy's conscience on low interest rates). It was by no means a stable inner circle: Rubinowicz left in October 1989 and Gauron in October 1991. Both had serious reservations about aspects of ERM policy, especially high interest rates, and about the domestic costs that might be associated with an EMU on German terms. In any case, they had already ceded ground to Hervé Hannoun, who took over as director of the cabinet in January 1989.

Bérégovoy was comfortable with Hannoun: both shared humble origins (though Hannoun was a Finance Inspector); both came from left-wing milieux; and both were workaholics. The arrival of Hannoun was in a certain sense a mixed blessing. The fact that Hannoun had served as economic adviser in the Elysée since 1984 offered an opportunity to strengthen his standing *vis-à-vis* Mitterrand. But his appointment came at a time when the former director of the cabinet, Alain Boublil, had been dismissed because of his embroilment in financial scandal. The political credit of Bérégovoy was damaged. Hannoun was crucially important, with Monnier, in fleshing out long-term economic strategy (they adopted de Foucauld's concept of 'competitive disinflation'); and in giving a new coherence and purpose to the work of the cabinet and the Ministry as a whole. Under Hannoun, Bérégovoy was to be persuaded that EMU was a way of institutionalizing 'competitive disinflation' strategy, of ensuring that *rigueur* was built into economic-policy management and the French economy impelled to modernize. Hannoun was a powerful internal protagonist for the insertion of strict budgetary criteria in the EMU agreement. One beneficiary was Marc Autheman, cabinet member responsible for monetary policy. He had at first been distrusted as too much the eyes and ears of the Trésor and too orthodox on interest rates. But, under Hannoun, Autheman soon established himself as an impressive source of ideas on EMU, particularly related to the development of a 'political pole' to balance the 'monetary pole'. Autheman's power came, however, from the quality of his thinking rather than from achieving the status of an intimate. More important in this latter respect was François Villeroy de Galhau, who after 1990 was to emerge as part of the inner circle (as cabinet member responsible for EC affairs and intimately involved with the EMU dossier). With Hannoun the pro-ERM and pro-EMU ethic of the cabinet was significantly strengthened.

Trichet and EMU

The main beneficiary of the arrival of Hannoun was Trichet. Initially, Bérégovoy had distrusted Trichet because his career (as director of cabinet under Balladur and then director of the Trésor) had flourished under his predecessor as minister. He was too closely associated with the former government. Their relationship did not begin well. On his return in May 1988 Bérégovoy did not disguise from Trichet his criticism of the 1986 devaluation of the franc. Also, Trichet appeared very reserved on the issue of cutting interest rates. After January 1989 the relationship improved. Trichet demonstrated his worth as a crisis manager in relation to the financial scandals that were besetting the Ministry. He also established a good rapport with Hannoun, working with him and Monnier in elaborating the 'competitive disinflation' strategy (Trichet was already familiar with de Foucauld's thinking) and developing a new enthusiasm for EMU (about which he had been cautious in 1987–8). Trichet was important in investing the 'competitive disinflation' strategy and EMU with a wider cultural and historical dimension that was grounded in long-standing Trésor beliefs. His great contribution was to adapt in-house beliefs to the *construction européenne* of the Mitterrand Presidency. In Trichet's mind, EMU took on the quality of an historic mission to modernize France by a precommitment to a process of fundamental reforms that would alter French economic behaviour irreversibly. These reforms would open France up to the world economy and break down traditional social hierarchies.

There was also a more personal theme to Trichet's new endorsement of EMU that stemmed from his literary interests and that brought him closer to Mitterrand's cultural conception of *construction européenne*. Trichet's conception of Europe was essentially cultivated and civilized. EMU was about preserving the specific values of Europe, reinforcing its sense of cultural identity in a global economy dominated by the USA. EMU offered a building block for the long-term development of models of political economy grounded in European values. Trichet's culture was a source of strength in another sense. He was dignified, well-mannered, and a master of personal diplomacy, disarming with his charm and courtesy whilst impressing with his grasp of complex argument. When it came to the arts of negotiation, Trichet was the stylish craftsman, always cool and dignified under pressure. By 1990 he had the complete confidence of Bérégovoy. Bianco, Secretary-General at the Elysée, and Jean-Paul Huchon, Rocard's director of cabinet at the Matignon, were companions of Trichet dating back to their days together at the ENA. They ensured that Trichet's qualities were recognized and respected at the very heart of French government. Mitterrand acquired a deepening trust in Trichet, recognizing a cultivated man who was also the 'perfect' civil servant.

For Trichet the period from 1988 involved a steep learning curve with respect to EMU. He was by no means the originator of ideas or even the agenda-setter. Such roles did not accord with his self-image as the 'perfect' civil servant. His skill was in responding to the shifting political climate: in reading the signals emanating from the highest political levels and adapting Trésor beliefs to those signals. This observation was accurate, for instance, in relation to the proposal for the Franco-German Economic Council and to the Balladur Memorandum during the *cohabitation*. In abandoning his caution on EMU, Trichet was responding to the new enthusiasm emanating from the Elysée and from Hannoun and to the more positive signals from Bérégovoy himself after the seminal Franco-German Economic Council meeting in August 1989. But, reflecting Trésor orthodoxy, he remained conservative on independence for the Banque de France: until, in 1993, the political level required action in this direction. In relation to economic theory, Trichet took on board the credibility theory of inflation. Hence his espousal of the 'hard' ERM after 1987 as a means of locking in low inflation and his growing preoccupation with convergence of long-term interests rates as a measure of market confidence in exchange-rate stability and in the process of EMU. Trichet was, above all, the elegant synthesizer of ideas, matching them to political priorities. Once politically endorsed, he was prepared to work with unremitting enthusiasm for their realization: both as an eloquent spokesman on behalf of EMU and as the well-briefed negotiator, at once tenacious and disarming.

Preparing For Hanover

On being re-elected President, Mitterrand was briefed by Delors on the vital need to seize the opportunity provided by Genscher's Memorandum on an ECB; to ensure that EMU was prioritized by Kohl at the Hanover European Council in June; and to secure a French chair of the proposed committee of wise men on EMU. Mitterrand was quick to seize on the idea of Delors as possible chair, though it was judged premature and possibly counterproductive to lobby for this outcome too directly. Dumas was dispatched to Bonn on 20 May, where he alluded to Mitterrand's fulsome support for the Genscher Memorandum on his recent visit to Lubbers in The Hague. Genscher's proposal for a 'committee of wise men' was endorsed; Dumas confined himself to sketching out the key issues—its composition, its size, its mandate, and its time-scale. Already, Dumas raised with Genscher a deadline of 1992 for EMU. Having already secured the full backing of Gonzales for an ECB and for co-ordinated action with the Spanish government on 19 March, Mitterrand was keen to ensure that the momentum was maintained at the forthcoming Franco-German meeting in Evian. But the key task was to divine how thinking on EMU was developing in the German Federal Chancellor's Office.

In the aftermath of Mitterrand's convincing victory, the meeting of Kohl and Mitterrand at *l'Hôtel Royal* in Evian on 2 June was an occasion for much optimism. Carefully prepared by Attali and Guigou, it was designed to inaugurate a new spirit of co-operation in *construction européenne* on the basis of mutual concession. They signalled in advance that Mitterrand would be pressing the case for an ECB; in turn, the message from the Federal Chancellor's Office was that Kohl was determined to ensure that failure to agree an EC directive on capital liberalization did not disrupt the relaunch of EMU at the Hanover Council. The meeting in Evian was important in two respects. First, and crucially, Mitterrand indicated that he was prepared to agree to liberalization of capital movement in the EC before the Hanover European Council in order to ease the way for Kohl to make progress with EMU. In return, Mitterrand asked that Kohl enter into a commitment to support EC-wide harmonization of taxation on income from savings, emphasizing that this linkage was crucial. But he did not insist on harmonization of this taxation as either a precondition of freedom of movement of capital or a parallel measure. Mitterrand was intent that technical issues like fiscal harmonization should not hold up wider political progress on EMU. This concession came as a shock to the Finance Ministry and Bérégovoy in particular and even met with reservations from Elyseée advisers like Bianco who felt that Mitterrand should have fought harder on taxation of income from savings.

In addition, Mitterrand and Guigou were surprised when Kohl suggested Delors as the chair of the committee to study EMU. At that stage French intelligence, reported by the Finance Ministry, was that Pöhl was likely to take on this task, though he was clearly reluctant to be bound in so tightly to the process. Delors's name was welcomed as a means of ensuring political direction behind the EMU project and as consistent with thinking in the Elysée. Hence an unanticipated outcome of Evian was an informal, top-secret Franco-German understanding on the chairing of the proposed committee.

Shortly after the Evian meeting, before the next ECOFIN meeting on 13 June, Bérégovoy met Mitterrand to stress his reservations based on his concerns about 'fiscal justice' and about the sensitivity of the Socialist majority to the issue of tax avoidance and evasion. He argued that, with zero taxation on income from savings in Britain and Luxembourg, freedom of capital movement would mean an outflow of savings from France, forcing the French government to reduce this form of taxation. The consequence would be a shifting of the taxation burden onto wage income. Hence, without agreement to introduce harmonized taxation on income from savings in parallel, it would be in the French interest to block the capital liberalization directive. Though Bérégovoy had been careful to avoid speaking of harmonized taxation as a precondition, Mitterrand was unreceptive. Bérégovoy was instructed to accept the proposed directive without any conditions for the greater good of making progress with *construction européenne*. In the process Mitterrand signalled to him that this issue was a test of his European commitment.

The meeting was to have a lasting impression on Bérégovoy. He experienced the cool indifference that Mitterrand could exude to those who were not part of the charmed inner circle; and he feared the implications of his isolation from the President on this issue. A gap of ideas and strategy had been revealed: Bérégovoy had shown that he was basically in favour of France spelling out conditions for EMU. He remained deeply uncomfortable about being asked to sacrifice a left-wing principle for Europe and kept on working on this issue. At the ECOFIN on 13 June, where the EC directive on freedom of capital movement was agreed, Bérégovoy succeeded in securing a timetable for consideration of measures of tax harmonization on income from savings. But in 1989 that timetable slipped in the face of opposition from the British and Luxembourg governments and in the aftermath of the tensions generated by

Waigel's withdrawal of the German withholding tax introduced on 1 January 1989.

Before Hanover Mitterrand had further contacts with Delors and with Kohl about the proposed committee to study how EMU might be realized. On 7 June Delors consulted Guigou, spelling out that Kohl wanted a committee comprising the twelve EC central bank governors. Mitterrand's distrust of technicians, who he feared would subvert political objectives, led him to propose to Delors that the central bankers be flanked by an equal number of 'outsiders'. Delors responded by arguing that a committee of twenty-four would be too unwieldy. But an element of Mitterrand's thinking was to be salvaged in the idea— endorsed in Hanover—of appointing a limited number of 'outsiders' to the committee. This discussion was taken up again by Mitterrand and Kohl at the G7 summit in Toronto on 20 June, one week before Hanover. In Ottowa Mitterrand again aired his concerns about EMU being captured by technicians and tried to keep alive the concept of a more independent 'committee of wise men', whilst at the same time recognizing the force of Kohl's strategic argument for making the central bankers assume responsibility. In Ottowa Delors's name was again mentioned to Mitterrand and Elysée officials as possible chair of the committee. On this occasion Trichet first picked up the signal that a major breakthrough was being planned for Hanover and that Delors was being considered as chair for the proposed committee.

In sum, French strategy for the Hanover European Council was to encourage the German government to assume responsibility for relaunching EMU; to avoid the process being captured by technicians; and to ensure its political direction. This approach of relying on the Germans obviated the risk that opposition would be kindled against a plan that was seen as too centred around French interests. Hence Mitterrand opted for a low-profile approach: a strategy of indirection. French strategy was narrowed down to the theme of political direction of EMU: of ensuring that it was not exclusively in the hands of finance ministers (who were kept at a distance) or of central bankers (for whom Kohl made the case). Broadly, Mitterrand was satisfied by the appointment of the Delors Committee, though he remained somewhat sceptical of the will of central bankers to make progress on EMU. On the other hand, he was just as sceptical of the Trésor and the Finance Ministry. The composition of the Committee led to an atmosphere of cautious optimism in the Elysée.

De Larosière, the Finance Ministry, and the Delors Committee: The Meetings of 1 December and 27 April

The appointment of the Delors Committee at Hanover created a shift in power relations in Paris. Having been appointed to the Committee in a 'personal capacity', de Larosière had potentially a freedom of action denied to him in the normal course of monetary policy decision-making. On the issue of propriety de

Larosière was firm. He had been appointed by the European Council; any responsibility he had was directly to the President. Hence, from the outset, de Larosière acted to keep the Finance Ministry at a distance. He did not seek instructions from Bérégovoy; nor did he involve Trichet closely or Autheman in the cabinet. Negotiating positions were drawn up within the Banque de France without co-ordination with the Finance Ministry. At his weekly Thursday meetings with Bérégovoy and Trichet, de Larosière offered no more than very general accounts of progress.

Before Hanover the Finance Ministry had already begun to develop its thinking on EMU, recognizing the need to respond to the very changed situation since the Balladur Memorandum. The Finance Ministry was surprised by the speed of developments, especially in Germany, as well as unsettled by the transition from Balladur to Bérégovoy in May 1988. At this stage an important internal Trésor paper raised two major issues that were later to figure prominently in French negotiating positions on EMU. It argued that the creation of an independent ECB would raise serious issues of democratic accountability. Whilst the paper stressed that the French government should not oppose the principle of an independent ECB, it posed the question of whether the Bundesbank was the appropriate model for securing democratic accountability. The paper compared the British, German, and US models and concluded that a combination of their characteristics was required. But the stress was on the superior features of the US Federal Reserve as a model of how to combine independence with accountability, as well as of how to achieve a better relationship with the financial markets than the Bundesbank. An equivalence to the US Congressional hearings was needed. Another requirement was transparency: the board of an ECB must publish its minutes no later than six weeks after each meeting. In fact, this argument that the French government must focus on the issue of democratic accountability was not to be developed as much as the second argument. It was not really till the debate about setting up the ECB in 1998 that it returned to the fore.

In addition, the Trésor paper introduced the idea of an 'equilibrium' between the political executive and the monetary authority in EMU. An ECB could be independent. But there must also be a body capable of ensuring an appropriate 'policy mix' at the EC level (an idea with which de Forges was familiar from his IMF experience). De Forges and other Trésor officials had in mind a more powerful ECOFIN that could look at the relationship between fiscal, structural, and social policies. An instance of the importance of 'policy mix' was provided, in the Trésor view, by liberalization of capital movement and tax harmonization. Basic to the Trésor paper was that independence on the lines of the Bundesbank had to be supplemented at the EC level by a system of democratic accountability that went beyond the German model. In short, the Trésor paper was an invitation for French bargaining positions on EMU to focus on the theme of democratic accountability. The question that was being posed in the Finance Ministry was whether it was technically feasible to pursue a monetary union without simultaneously strengthening political union. The Trésor's answer was that a context of strengthened political union was indispensable to its effective functioning. In designing that answer the Trésor drew on the French republican tradition.

This technical-level analysis by Trésor officials was supplemented by a more political analysis at the level of Bérégovoy's cabinet. Here the key figure was Autheman, whose brief was to follow Banque de France monetary decision-making. Autheman was spurred into action by the knowledge that the Banque de France was working on its own proposals for the Delors Committee. From Autheman came the idea of a 'political pole' to balance the 'monetary pole' of EMU. Whilst not rejecting the principle of an independent ECB, this proposal was rooted in the republican idea of a *contre-pouvoir*. By November Bérégovoy and Trichet had developed their own agenda for EMU negotiations. At its heart was the idea of a strong 'political pole' (based technically around de Forges's analysis). Its implication was that the institutional design of EMU would strengthen the policy role of the Finance Ministry rather than simply cede power to EC central bankers.

For Bérégovoy in particular an ECB and a single currency were, in any case, too far away in the future to have much relevance to the main economic and monetary problem that France faced in 1988: how to protect the EMS from external shocks deriving from the US dollar and the Japanese yen. It was the external dimension of the EMS that preoccupied him rather than the niceties of the institutional design of EMU. Bérégovoy stressed the importance of developing a joint management of exchange-rate policy. For this purpose the priority was to develop the *ECU* as a European currency in world markets, by entrusting its management to a European Monetary Fund. The *ECU* as a single European currency was not on Bérégovoy's agenda. In an interview with the *International Herald Tribune* on 29 September he preferred not to speak of an ECB as an immediate goal. The emphasis was on a pragmatic, step-by-step development towards a common monetary policy, integrating Britain into the ERM, strengthening the *ECU*, keeping national currencies, and letting market forces work. The first step was to be 'a central bank of central banks': its prime mission to administer the national currency reserves and to manage the parity of the *ECU* with respect to the dollar and the yen. Bérégovoy's preoccupation was EMU as a means of giving Europe weight *vis-à-vis* other states.

In developing these positions on EMU the French Finance Ministry understood itself to be marching in step with the Banque de France, whilst at the same time maintaining an intellectual leadership in developing such ideas as 'policy mix' and a 'political pole' (ideas that went beyond Banque de France thinking). But during the deliberations of the Delors Committee de Larosière was to move beyond the positions taken up by the Finance Ministry, to the annoyance of Bérégovoy and Trichet. From the outset de Larosière took on a much stronger personal leadership role in relation to preparing internal Banque de France positions for the Delors Committee than Pöhl in the Bundesbank or Leigh-

Pemberton in the Bank of England. This high-profile role reflected in part the authority of a Governor of the Banque de France as in effect its '*patron*'. It also stemmed from de Larosière's immense personal experience and authority both as a former director of cabinet and director of Trésor in the Finance Ministry and as a former managing-director of the IMF. He was a rare French official in having a personal memory of EMU that went back to the 1970s. Such an advantage was denied to his Trésor counterparts. De Larosière was a calm, reserved, and immensely dignified and authoritative figure, with his own agenda and sense of what was in the French national interest—which focused on reshaping the Banque de France as a market-oriented institution, part of the Dutch/German 'club' of central banks, and on engineering an appropriate cultural change within the French central bank. The Delors Committee was an important instrument for him to use for that purpose.

In developing strategy and tactics for the Delors Committee de Larosière worked most closely with three Banque de France officials: Lagayette, Second Deputy Governor responsible for international affairs; François Capannera, the Director-General for international affairs; and Jean-Paul Redouin, a more junior official responsible for operational foreign exchange issues. With active direction from the Governor they developed during October 1988 the paper that de Larosière submitted to the Delors Committee. The background to this paper was a strategic reflection which identified two courses of action. One course of action was to specify in advance the precise features of an EMU, and then focus on spelling out the route for arriving at this final destination. It soon emerged that this was the course of action being actively pursued by the Bundesbank. But it would have represented a new point of departure in the French approach to EMU. The alternative course of action was to outline a step-by-step approach, without clearly defining the final goal but focusing on concrete measures for the near future. This approach had been traditionally adopted by French negotiators and was familiar to de Larosière from the Fourcade Plan of 1974. It meant in effect building on the EMS. There was a striking internal consensus on two matters: that de Larosière must seek to seize the intellectual initiative by rapidly tabling proposals (again a traditional feature of French diplomacy); and that, given the uncertainty about how the Delors Committee would progress and expectations of Bundesbank reluctance to make progress, the step-by-step approach offered safer ground.

Driven by these strategic considerations, the Banque de France developed a paper advocating a European Reserve Fund (ERF), with Redouin contributing on its technical aspects. Redouin was careful to consult informally with de Forges in the Trésor in preparing the draft, ensuring no serious dispute. The paper's approach was notably tentative ('possible initial steps that could lead ultimately to economic and monetary union') and self-confessedly pragmatic. Four ideas guided it: initiating 'a training-ground process' aimed at improving co-ordination of monetary policies; strengthening the impact of intervention policies in the foreign exchange markets; creating a permanent 'think tank' on monetary analysis; and increasing the role of the Committee of EC Central Bank Governors by creating the ERF as an 'institutional embryo' of a 'European Reserve Bank'. Of the various functions of the ERF particular stress was placed on intervention in the foreign-exchange markets, consistent with the position embraced by Bérégovoy. Its key role was to be to enable the EC states to pursue a common and coherent policy towards third currencies; and to do so by using currency reserves assigned to it. The de Larosière paper reflected the domestic political climate: notably Mitterrand's references to developing a tripolar structure to the international monetary system (Europe, the USA, and Japan) in the 1988 Presidential election campaign; and Bérégovoy's interest in the external dimension of the EMS. It also drew on traditional French ideas rather than breaking new ground.

The paper's domestic sensitivities were most noticeable in its final paragraph. Here it referred to the important question of the European Reserve Bank's relationship to the political authorities. 'In this respect it would seem that the role of the Council of Ministers would have to be decisive' (i.e. in relation to setting exchange-rate parities and the main lines of EC economic policy). De Larosière was mindful of the comments of Edith Cresson, Minister for European Affairs, in an interview with *Nouvel Économiste* on 5 August 1988. Cresson had rejected the Bundesbank as a model for an ECB; as a body that had been imposed on defeated Germans it was 'inappropriate'. As history the argument was faulty. But it indicated a more widespread aversion to the notion of an independent central bank within the Socialist majority. Rocard and Bérégovoy both shared this sensitivity. Hence de Larosière had to move cautiously if he was not to jeopardize his position (which he saw as exposed). In the same interview Cresson had spoken of the dangers associated with power in the hands of unelected technocrats. By pressing the case for central bank independence prematurely de Larosière risked infuriating the French government and Mitterrand himself. During the Presidential election campaign (in an interview in *L'Expansion* on 17 March) Barre had spoken of an independent Banque de France as a precondition for EMU.

Faced with the ambitious proposals on EMU in Pöhl's paper, and with the strategic realities revealed by participation in the Delors Committee, de Larosière reflected again on strategic options during November. The ERF proposal lost much of its relevance and interest. The Cresson interview in Paris, following Bérégovoy's letter of complaint to Stoltenberg on 29 June about Bundesbank interest-rate policy, had weakened de Larosière's bargaining position at a key moment. He determined that a bold move was required if agreement was to be achieved in the Committee. In order to carry Pöhl along with a final agreement it was essential to avoid confrontation on the issue of central bank independence. But de Larosière required political cover from the highest political level for such a move. Hence, as we noted at the beginning of this chapter, he organized a meeting with Mitterrand on 1 December 1988 just before the main options were due for determination in the Delors Committee. From Mitterrand he got the signal to regard an independent ECB as a precondition for negotiations rather than as a matter for concession. The meeting underlined to de Larosière the seriousness of the President's commitment to *construction européenne*. EMU was, in Mitterrand's eyes, too important and hedged round with political difficulties (especially for the Germans) to allow specific issues of institutional design and policy to stand in its way. The President was behaving consistently with the position that he had taken on the withholding tax at Evian in June 1988.

Mitterrand failed to communicate this understanding with de Larosière to Bérégovoy; and de Larosière did not report to Bérégovoy on his meeting with Mitterrand. The weekly Thursday meetings of de Larosière with Bérégovoy, with Trichet also present, were an occasion for updates on progress in the Delors Committee. But de Larosière stressed throughout that he was acting in an unusual 'personal capacity' as a member of the Committee. By this means he justified his reticence and kept the Finance Ministry at a distance. Symptomatic of this distance was Bérégovoy's interview with *Les Echos* on 16 December. It was clear that for him EMU was still not the immediate priority (compared to harmonization of fiscal policy) and that an ECB and a European currency were not issues for the short term. Bérégovoy stressed the need for European monetary management on two levels: the 'internal' management of the EMS, with national central banks continuing to manage their intra-EC parities; and a joint management of the ECU *vis-à-vis* the dollar and the yen, to be undertaken by the ERF on the terms proposed by de Larosière in his paper for the Delors Committee. This theme of the external dimension of the EMS was still the preoccupation in Bérégovoy's interview with *Les Echos* on 9 March 1989. For de Larosière, it was now very much secondary.

Having determined to work with the Bundesbank model of EMU, de Larosière shifted his attention to the issue of clearly specifying stages to ensure orderly and predictable progress towards EMU and to the issue of the content of the intermediate stage. On stages his preoccupation was not so much fixed dates for transition as the principle of commitment to complete the process. As a central banker de Larosière was disposed to be cautious about timetables and was broadly satisfied with the final outcome. He fought to graft the ERF proposals into the content of the intermediate stage, but more to satisfy domestic strategic requirements than out of firm intellectual conviction. De Larosière's strategic objective was to be seen to have battled for established French positions (hence the issue of the ERF was left unresolved in the final report). But his key objective was to establish himself and the Banque de France as a credible negotiating partner with Pöhl and the Bundesbank and to nudge the Finance Ministry in this direction. As with the Basle–Nyborg negotiations the governor had his own agenda—to reposition the Banque de France as part of the same camp as the Dutch and Germans. In this strategy he judged the Delors Committee negotiations a success.

The publication of the Delors Report in April 1989 met with a frosty response from the Finance Ministry. Trésor officials had multiplied their channels for keeping informed about all the papers considered in the Delors Committee. They recognized that they could not rely on any one channel. In consequence, there werè no serious surprises in April. But there was irritation. At a meeting in the Matignon on 14 April, chaired by Rocard, and in the presence of Dumas, Cresson, and Delors, Bérégovoy stressed his concern about delay in bringing forward proposals for an EC-wide withholding tax. Such delay was an obstacle to moving forward on the basis of the Delors Report. Rocard endorsed his position, stressing his opposition to a Europe without 'rules of the game' to ensure fairness. In *Le Figaro* on 19 April Bérégovoy spoke of the need for a 'European political authority' to define a common monetary policy before EMU was realized. He focused on the risks in leaving EMU too much to officials.

But the most dramatic encounter took place in strict privacy. On 27 April de Larosière was summoned to the Finance Ministry and seated in front of Bérégovoy, members of his cabinet, and Trésor officials led by Trichet. The atmosphere of the meeting was stern. There was a severe introduction by Trichet, who expressed surprise that de Larosière had signed a report that was 'too Germanic' in content and argued that excessive concessions had been made. It was suggested that de Larosière had been systematically in favour of the strongest formulations on central bank independence in the work of the Committee. Bérégovoy, sensitive to the need to demonstrate that he was a 'strong' minister able to stand up for the prerogatives of his ministry, was notably cold towards him. The Finance Ministry was in a distinctly nervous mood. Having lost powers with financial market liberalization and privatization during the *cohabitation*, many of its officials now saw the threat of powers being ceded to central bankers in an ECB.

In reply, de Larosière pointed out that he—along with Pöhl and Wim Duisenberg—had insisted on the principle of central bank independence as the only way to make progress on an ECB and a single currency. He stressed that the question of 'excessive' concessions did not arise. On 1 December 1988 he had cleared with the President the negotiating position that acceptance of central bank independence was a precondition for a successful completion of the work entrusted to the Delors Committee, not an issue for negotiation and concession. The matter had been cleared with the President because he was working in a 'personal capacity' in a Committee that was reporting to the EC heads of state and government. At this point Bérégovoy threw his support behind de Larosière, though privately he was very irritated. At the end of the meeting Trichet was instructed that the priority for the Trésor was to ensure that there would be a strong EC political mechanism to ensure co-ordination of economic policy and to 'balance' the new monetary power. Bérégovoy continued to press the theme of avoiding a technocratic Europe, for instance in *Le Figaro* on 3 May 1989 when he stated his preference for speaking of the 'autonomy' of the ECB and for Europe having a social and fiscal as well as financial dimension. His suspicions were further aggravated by the withdrawal of the recent German withholding tax at the end of April by the new Finance Minister, Theo Waigel. There was a sense in the Finance Ministry, and indeed within the Elysée, that the Germans had reneged on a commitment entered into at Evian. Hence in April–May 1989 the mood within the Finance Ministry on EMU was chilly.

Activating Elysée Leadership of EMU after Madrid: The French Presidency, the Guigou Group, and the Conversion of Bérégovoy

Delors was careful to keep Mitterrand well informed about progress in the Delors Committee and, as early as 3 March, was briefing him on the basic features of the final report. The President was not interested in the technicalities, to the irritation of Delors. His preoccupations were twofold: to ensure that sufficient political momentum was put behind the Delors Report so that the EC did not repeat the history of the Werner Plan; and to complement EMU with decisive action on the creation of a 'social' Europe. Correspondingly, Elysée staff (notably Guigou), Cresson as European Minister, and Dumas were mobilized to ensure full political backing for the Delors Report and for the convening of an IGC on EMU at the forthcoming Madrid Council. Their attentions were focused on the Spanish Presidency and the German government and on ensuring that the imminent French Presidency of the EC was given a clear mandate to make rapid progress on EMU. Diplomatic activity gathered momentum before the Delors Report was published. The Delors Report figured prominently in the Gonzales–Mitterrand meeting in Paris on 31 March; in Dumas's meeting with Genscher in Bonn on the same day; and in the Kohl–Mitterrand meeting on 4 April in Günzburg. The Franco-German summit in Paris on 19–20 April provided the opportunity to agree that progress must be made on the basis of the Delors Report. Dumas and Genscher met again on 2 May in Paris to discuss the Delors Report, as well as the new difficulties over the withdrawal of the German withholding tax, followed by their joint declaration of support for the report on 19 May. Relations intensified as the Madrid Council approached. The Franco-Spanish seminar in Paris on 3–4 June involved three working sessions between Dumas and the Spanish Foreign Minister, Francisco Fernandez Ordonez, on preparations for Madrid. Agreement was reached on two priorities: decisive action on the Delors Report and progress on 'social' Europe to complement EMU. Gonzales's visit to Paris on 8 June was followed by that of Ordonez on 20 June. On 19 June Genscher visited Dumas in Paris, following which there was a joint declaration of support for the Delors Report and 'social' Europe. Finally, on 22 June Kohl met Mitterrand in Paris.

Guigou was the privileged point of contact for Delors and for Pascal Lamy in Paris and was also the key Elysée figure in co-ordinating with the Spanish Presidency and with Bitterlich in the Federal Chancellor's Office. Her importance was also domestic. From early 1989 reports on the work in the Delors Committee were filtered into her bi-weekly meetings in the Elysée with relevant EC cabinet members from the Foreign and Finance Ministries and from the

Prime Minister's and the President's Office. In these meetings the priority issues, notably related to securing a timetable for stages and an early date for an IGC on EMU, were identified and strategy for co-ordination between the current Spanish and impending French EC Presidencies was considered. These meetings drew to the attention of the Finance Ministry the strength of the political commitment to EMU as a key axis of *construction européenne*.

Behind this French diplomatic activism was persistent pressure from Mitterrand to ensure that the forthcoming French EC Presidency was given a clear signal to move ahead rapidly with implementation of EMU. Mitterrand brushed aside reservations from the Finance Ministry and from within the Elysée following the withdrawal of the German withholding tax on 27 April. Bérégovoy and Attali saw Waigel's action as an ominous signal that the Germans were not negotiating in good faith on EMU: that all the main concessions were coming from France without reciprocity. But, despite questioning the timing of Waigel's move, Mitterrand moved quickly to confirm the French position. He impressed on Bérégovoy the vital importance of gaining ECOFIN support for an unreserved implementation of the Delors Report, for a date for stage 1, and for the idea of an early IGC on EMU. French gains from EMU far outweighed the risks attendant on putting full liberalization of EC capital movements in question. At a meeting in the Elysée on 11 May—with Mitterrand, Delors, Dumas, Cresson, and others—Bérégovoy reassured the EC Commissioners present that the French government had no intention of raising difficulties about capital liberalization.

Despite his continuing reservations Bérégovoy presented the French position at the informal ECOFIN in S'Agaro. The reluctance of that meeting to endorse this position, and Delors's manifest irritation after S'Agaro, only increased Mitterrand's determination to bypass the EC finance ministers. Mitterrand also had to contend with Kohl's reluctance to be drawn into setting a date for convening an IGC on EMU. The President sustained the pressure on Kohl right up to, as well as at, the Madrid Council, trying to stiffen his resolve to face up to his domestic political difficulties on EMU. At Madrid Mitterrand got much of what he wanted: agreement to work on the basis of the Delors Report and to start preparations for an IGC; and a date of July 1990 for stage 1 of EMU. What was lacking was a firm date to convene the IGC. After Madrid Mitterrand shared with Delors two fears: that the IGC could be repeatedly deferred unless the French Presidency took action to give new political direction to EMU; and that the Delors Report might be relegated to a 'good basis' for the IGC rather than seen as 'the basis'. The fragility of the Madrid conclusions seemed all the greater in the context of sceptical comments from Pöhl about the prospects for EMU.

Accordingly, the French Presidency was dominated by one key dossier: accelerating the drive to EMU before the succeeding Irish Presidency, which was expected to be less strongly engaged on this issue. In order to give momentum to the Delors Report a division of labour was established.

Bérégovoy was responsible for putting in place the decisions for stage 1; the Elysée was preoccupied with ensuring that a date was set for the IGC, remedying what it saw as the central fault in the Madrid conclusions, and with giving a political drive to EC finance ministers in preparing for the IGC. The other theme was the importance of flanking EMU by progress on 'social' Europe. By 27 July important new signals about EMU were being transmitted. In an interview with *Nouvel Observateur* and other European newspapers Mitterrand spoke of the Delors Report as 'a very fine work' and went on to state that he did not exclude a treaty of less than twelve. In his press conference in Strasbourg on the same day Dumas conceded that not all twelve might want to go forward with EMU at the same speed. He identified two ways forward: amendment of the Treaty of Rome or a new treaty on EMU. The British government was being put under pressure. This theme was taken up again by Mitterrand at the European Parliament on 25 October. He referred to the need for a subtle, adaptable structure for EMU, allowing 'transitions, delays, provisional derogations' to take account of different economic and political situations. Mitterrand argued the dangers in using the metaphor of an army marching in step under a single commander to the same music. The approach to EMU needed to be more flexible. He had in mind in particular Mrs Thatcher. The two Anglo-French summits in February and September 1989 had left Mitterrand with no illusions: the British government had ruled out EMU for the foreseeable future and was wholly at odds with the priorities of the French EC Presidency. Mitterrand was resolved not to be blocked by Mrs Thatcher. This resolution was underlined by both Mitterrand and Dumas in a blitz of visits to EC capitals from 20 August to the end of September 1989. It was done tactfully: the message was that the French government did not want a 'two-speed' Europe but that one or two states could hold up the locomotive. This metaphor of the locomotive was much in evidence in Mitterrand's conversation. The EMU locomotive required an agreed departure time; the British could be expected to climb on board at the last moment.

Mitterrand's activist approach to the EC Presidency was also assisted by a transformed domestic political situation within the RPR/UDF opposition. During the 1989 European Parliament election the RPR and the UDF had, for the first time, agreed to sink their differences in a joint campaign programme—*Pour une Europe unie*. Reflecting a victory for Giscard, the programme called for a 'truly united Europe', 'politically strengthened', and pledged to realize a common European currency. This major concession by the Gaullists left Le Pen's National Front to make the running on the theme of defending national sovereignty; and was later to store up trouble for Chirac within the RPR from those who felt that the Gaullists were abandoning their distinctive message. But, at least in the short run, the Giscard-inspired manifesto provided a secure domestic political base for Mitterrand to press ahead confidently with EMU.

Guigou and the Guigou Group

In July 1989 Dumas responded to the challenge of giving political momentum to the French EC Presidency. He proposed to Mitterrand the idea of a high-level group, to be chaired by the French Presidency, to prepare the questions that would have to be addressed by the IGC on EMU. The Foreign Ministry's purpose was to use this group to sustain political momentum, in particular by keeping up pressure on finance ministries, and to fill the vacuum after Madrid. Hence it proposed that the group should comprise a senior foreign ministry and a senior finance ministry official from each EC state. Guigou was the natural choice for the task of chairing this group, given her Finance Ministry background and senior status within the Elysée and her reputation as a tough, versatile, and well-briefed negotiator there. She decided to maintain continuity with the Delors Committee by appointing one of its two rapporteurs, Tommaso Padoa-Schioppa, as special adviser to the Guigou Group. Guigou identified in him a kindred spirit on EC issues and a man close to Delors on EMU, in effect as a conscience of the Community.

From its outset the Guigou Group had to face the hostility of Mrs Thatcher, expressed at the Anglo-French summit at Chequers in September, and the scepticism of EC finance ministries. This context, plus the aim of conserving the achievements of the Delors Report, gave it a defensive quality. Its work was planned and monitored by a group comprising Guigou, Padoa-Schioppa, de Boissieu, and Trichet. De Boissieu played the key role, acting as an intermediary between Guigou and the Trésor and providing an alternative source of ideas and support for Guigou from the ideas coming from the Trésor. From the outset Guigou and de Boissieu were focused on the requirement of giving momentum to the EMU negotiations. Trichet was more concerned that time should be given for adequate technical preparations in the EC Monetary Committee and ECOFIN in order to protect the Finance Ministry's position. But he was also cautious to avoid challenging Guigou, who was seen as the voice of the President, and de Boissieu, who played a strong role as the French expert on EC affairs. Though defensive, Trichet could not afford to sound obstructive.

Within the Elysée the Guigou Group was seen as no more than a very qualified success. At its first meeting on 5 September 1989, the Dutch representatives were to prove even less conciliatory than the British, making their opposition to the whole exercise abundantly clear. At the fourth meeting on 16 October, for the first time in EMU negotiations, the French pressed the proposal that had been germinating in the Finance Ministry for over a year: the need for a strengthened 'political power' to balance the 'monetary power' and to enable an appropriate 'policy mix' at the EC level. But the idea received only minority support and, to make matters worse, from the 'wrong troops': Greece, Italy, and Portugal. In its final form on 30 October the Guigou Report took the form essentially of a set of questions to be addressed and had not answered the key question of when the IGC might begin. The report agreed that the objective of

EMU was non-inflationary economic growth and that three principles had to be respected: parallelism between economic and monetary union; subsidiarity in the conduct of economic policy; and respect for a diversity of national situations, with no state being compelled to enter a later stage. The key questions were identified as related to the necessary transfer of sovereignty in economic policy (an enlarged EC budget or an EC social policy?); and to the statute and structure of the ECB and its relationship with national central banks. Perhaps the most important success of the Guigou Group was to be found in the consensus that the Delors Report provided the basis for the IGC negotiations. In this respect an important signal was given.

Guigou's involvement on sensitive EMU issues was not dependent on the Guigou Group and even less on her role in the SGCI. As we saw above, from early 1989 these issues found their way on to the agenda of the informal weekly or bi-weekly meetings of cabinet staff organized by Guigou in the Elysée. These meetings institutionalized a system of 'pre-arbitrage', preparing options for consideration by the President with the Finance and Foreign Ministers and the agenda for mini-Council of Ministers' meetings dedicated to EC business. At the Guigou meetings de Boissieu from the Foreign Ministry was always present, along with Guillaume Hannezo from Bérégovoy's cabinet, and Trichet when EMU issues arose. During the French Presidency it took on a new dynamism under Guigou's leadership. It dealt with matters arising in relation to the Guigou Group, to implementation of the Delors Report, especially stage 1, to taxation of savings, to 'social' Europe, and to preparing the Strasbourg European Council. Here again the Guigou/Foreign Ministry axis was vitally important in ensuring a strong political drive on EMU and enduring pressure on the Finance Ministry. In this forum ideas about a strong 'political pole' for EMU were developed and refined. Later, it was to play a role in the French Draft Treaty on EMU, as we shall see in the next chapter. Guigou was very much the watchful eyes and ears of the President, the transmission belt for his ideas, the person whom Trichet had to handle with great care, tact, and respect.

The Conversion of Bérégovoy: The Tegernsee Meeting

Within the Finance Ministry a separate dynamic was at work as Bérégovoy underwent a slow, complex process of personal conversion to the cause of EMU. A first factor was the impact of Mitterrand on him. Intensely loyal to his President, Bérégovoy set about implementing the will of Mitterrand within his ministry and within ECOFIN. As chair of ECOFIN during the French Presidency, Bérégovoy set about his two tasks with vigour: to put in place, by the end of the Presidency, all the measures required for the launch of stage 1 of EMU; and to give momentum to the preparation of the IGC. He also recognized that he held responsibility for France's most important bargaining resource if progress was to be sustained on EMU: the 'good health' of the French franc was the indispensable basis for success in these negotiations. After the ECOFIN on

10 July 1989 Bérégovoy made a point that was to figure prominently in later pronouncements as a signal of French intentions and a symbol of French pedigree for EMU: that if the D-Mark was revalued, the French franc would accompany it. The intellectual connection between the *franc stable* and EMU was the firmest basis of his negotiating position on EMU, both in the EC and at home.

But Mitterrand failed to convince Bérégovoy about the intellectual case for pressing ahead with EMU on the basis set out in the Delors Report. Bérégovoy's deep scepticism had three main sources: his view that an EC-wide withholding tax should be a precondition for complete EC-wide liberalization of capital movements; his view that the independence of the ECB was the core issue, not the single currency, and that it was deeply problematic in the context of the French republican and Socialist traditions; and his unhappiness about the process, about the way in which the Delors Committee bypassed EC finance ministers and failed to take sufficient account of their reservations. Bérégovoy's reservations on EMU were deeply felt and based on a strong argument rooted in his beliefs about French national interest. Above all, Bérégovoy doubted that the Germans were serious about completing the transition to EMU. The political danger lay in making concessions, first giving up on fiscal harmonization as a precondition and then accepting central bank independence, without certainty that the Germans would deliver on a single currency. His Socialist and republican policy beliefs, and his closeness to the Socialist Party, led him to fear the consequences for his party and the country.

The main turning-point for Bérégovoy came with the Franco-German Economic Council meeting at the Tegernsee on 24–5 August 1989, his first with Waigel and the first after the Delors Report. This was important on several levels and in a way that had little to do with its main agenda—agreement of measures for stage 1 of EMU, harmonization of VAT and how to deal with tax fraud in fully liberated capital markets. First, the participants were becoming acutely sensitive to the emerging process of change in Eastern Europe and its potentially profound implications for Franco-German relations and European unification. Coming from Ukrainian stock, and having served as Secretary-General in the Elysée, Bérégovoy took a particular interest in this foreign policy dimension of his work. Tegernsee alerted him to the connection between EMU and these wider international developments. Thereafter, he began to see the need for a stronger political lead on EMU and for a component of political union within EMU. Bérégovoy's conception of EMU was transformed as he reflected on it in the geopolitical framework of the end of the Cold War and German unification. On the importance of this fast-changing East–West context for EMU there was a new meeting of minds with Mitterrand and Dumas and, after Tegernsee, with Waigel. 'Binding' an enlarged Germany into Europe became a key theme in Bérégovoy's policy leadership on EMU within the Finance Ministry. This did not depend on persuasion by Mitterrand or by Dumas. It was the product of his own reflection.

Secondly, an extraordinary personal chemistry developed with Waigel during the Tegernsee meeting. Each identified in the other a warm, affable, and straightforward character. They came to like and trust each other; to share their thoughts and feelings, anxieties and concerns; and to believe that they could do business with each other. In particular, they concluded that Franco-German agreement was the indispensable basis for EMU and that they must retain control of the negotiations in order to ensure a technically satisfactory outcome. Thirdly, and crucially, Pöhl convinced Bérégovoy that the Bundesbank was serious about EMU; that France and Germany could move together rapidly in this area; and that the German problem was not to accept that French economic policy had shown discipline over several years but to be reassured that France was serious about economic stability by accepting the principle of central bank independence as a precondition for EMU negotiations. Bérégovoy responded sceptically to the idea of a 'fast-track' EMU between France and Germany; he continued to fear 'being alone with Germany'. But Pöhl succeeded in undermining a crucial pillar supporting Bérégovoy's strategic analysis of EMU: that Germany was not serious about delivering. Bérégovoy indicated that central bank independence was not an insurmountable obstacle. Indeed, at the subsequent ECOFIN meeting in Antibes he was to endorse the principle.

Despite the personal chemistry and the reassurances at the Tegernsee meeting Bérégovoy continued to reflect with his cabinet on three main concerns: his unhappiness about being in EMU alone with the Germans, without the presence of the British as a balance; his desire to use the EMU negotiations to soften the application of the German model to Europe; and the importance of avoiding the imposition of the Treaty of Rome model on EMU. It was with the greatest reluctance that Bérégovoy concluded that it would not be possible to negotiate EMU with the British on board: and he saw in Nigel Lawson's competing currency proposal a lack of seriousness. But, as we shall see, he later grasped at the British 'hard ECU' plan as an opportunity to negotiate a less Germanic EMU. On this issue he was very isolated. After Madrid Mitterrand, Dumas, Guigou, and many in his cabinet and in the Trésor, were already convinced that the British were not serious negotiating partners; that it might be necessary to agree a Treaty without the British; and that the Franco-German axis was central to EMU.

Reflection on central bank independence led Bérégovoy to embrace the decentralized model of the US federal reserve system as an alternative to the German model. But, fundamentally, he continued to favour the French and Japanese models of monetary policy, in which primacy was accorded to the finance ministry. As late as 6 November 1989 he was confirming his reservations about an independent ECB in a speech to the Frankfurt Chamber of Commerce, with Pöhl sitting in the front row. 'If I had to sum up my ideas, I would say: yes to monetary independence, with economic interdependence, no to technocracy, yes to democracy!' The independence of the ECB was 'an important element in the discussions ahead of us'. But '. . . central bankers cannot be allowed to regard themselves as invested with a superior authority'. As Bérégovoy stressed, only politicians derive their legitimacy from universal suffrage. Hence it was vital 'to define the ECB's democratic legitimation and responsibility'. During 1988–9 Finance Ministry officials also furnished him with an economic argument derived from the economist Michel Aglietta. Aglietta argued that deregulation of financial markets—which had already taken place under Bérégovoy's leadership—was a far more important safeguard against inflation than legal technicalities related to central bank independence (Aglietta 1988).

Bérégovoy was persuaded by two arguments to accept the principle of central bank independence. First, he took on board the argument of Mitterrand, Dumas, and Guigou that it was a strategically necessary concession if the Germans were to be induced to accept the loss of their monetary sovereignty, particularly in the context of the symbolic importance that the D-Mark had assumed in postwar reconstruction. The second argument was developed within his own cabinet: that an independent ECB would complete the policy of competitive disinflation by pursuing the link to the D-Mark as an instrument for credibility to its logical conclusion. Bérégovoy was attracted to the idea of EMU as a means of 'constitutionalizing' and anchoring competitive disinflation so that it had a permanency transcending his own period of office. The external constraint was being internalized. From this process France could only gain. But he never lost the sense that problems of domestic dissent on central bank independence could be used to exert external political leverage on the Germans.

On the design of EMU, Hannezo in Bérégovoy's cabinet had an important influence. In a series of notes, which were passed on to Mitterrand, he argued that EMU involved the very core of sovereignty and in this respect differed from the more technical areas, like the CAP, to which the Treaty of Rome model had been traditionally applied. At the heart of this argument was the proposition that a strong role for the EC Commission in EMU was incompatible with the requirements for democratic accountability and for confidentiality in EMU discussions. Hence EMU had to be designed on an intergovernmental model, strengthening the role of the Council and minimizing that of the Commission. The consequence was tough debate with Guigou, who put the case for the Treaty of Rome model. Her key point—which appealed to Mitterrand—was that there was great danger in entrusting EMU to conservative and reluctant finance ministers: EMU had only been launched by bypassing them and putting the Commission President in the driving seat. Mitterrand opted for a compromise betwen these two positions which was closest to the position of de Boissieu: that EMU was too important to be left to EC finance ministers; but that the European Council rather than the Commission was the appropriate centre for political direction of EMU. During the French Presidency the Treaty of Rome model versus a separate EMU treaty was a live issue, reflected by Dumas at his press conference in Strasbourg as early as 27 July.

German Unification and the Preparations for Strasbourg: Stepping up French Pressure for EMU on Germany

By November 1989 the management of the French EC Presidency had been thrown into what was to prove a long period of self-questioning and difficulty with the arrival of German unification as a political issue. For Mitterrand the issue was not unexpected. Since Gorbachev's arrival in power in 1986 he had been reflecting on the risks of a Soviet offer of German unification in return for a distancing of Germany from Western institutions. Since then he had been using this perception of threat to tease Kohl into making commitments on European unification as a demonstration of German goodwill. But the speed with which events moved in autumn 1989 took Mitterrand, Dumas, and the Foreign Ministry by surprise; and Kohl's behaviour, especially his ten-point plan to the Bundestag on 28 November, was a source of major irritation in Paris. The effect was to stiffen Mitterrand's commitment to EMU as the axis of development of the EC and to sharpen his use of pressure on Kohl before the Strasbourg European Council in December.

Mitterrand's response to events in Germany was complex. At one level, he was keen to emphasize his consistency on the German question and to confirm existing commitments to support German unification, notably in the NATO declaration of 1967. Over many years Mitterrand had spoken of his hope to play a role in ending the 'Europe of Yalta'. He recognized that, logically, the reunification of Europe would involve the unification of Germany (Mitterrand 1996; Védrine 1996: 423 ff.). In an interview in *Nouvel Observateur* on 27 July 1989 the President repeated his view that the aspiration of Germans to be united was legitimate but that it had to be based on genuine dialogue with other states. Hence at the Franco-German summit in Bonn on 3 November—just six days before the fall of the Berlin Wall—Mitterrand emphasized that he had no fear of German unification: 'History is at work, I take it as it comes.' Mitterrand underlined his support for German unification based on free self-determination of the German people. He even praised Kohl as a German patriot. But he also used the opportunity to raise three central French positions: that the faster the pace of change in eastern Europe, the greater the necessity to accelerate European unification as a 'pole of stability and attraction'; that the Oder–Neisse frontier with Poland was not an issue to be reopened in this new context; and that Gorbachev must not be destabilized by rash demands, with potentially disastrous consequences for European security. Hence, Mitterrand focused on the terms of German unification, on the need for prudence and caution. Strategically, he exploited two French advantages: as one of the four wartime Allies with rights over Germany; and as a member of the EC, which was inextricably affected. Mitterrand was particularly sensitive to the fact that the French Presidency of the EC gave him, in this context, a fortunate leverage over Kohl.

But the exercise of this leverage was fraught with difficulties. Mitterrand faced a potentially serious problem in reconciling an accommodation with Kohl and domestic political reactions to the fast-changing situation in Germany. Mitterrand found himself under a great deal of pressure. He felt that he had gone a long way to reassure Kohl that France would respect the principle of free self-determination by the German people. On the other hand, he sensed that Kohl was not taking him fully into his confidence and providing him with the reassurance that he needed on the question of recognition of the Oder–Neisse frontier. He feared being marginalized by direct German–Soviet diplomacy on the German question. Mitterrand's domestic difficulties increased after his return from Bonn. By 10 November, the day after the fall of the Berlin Wall, former President Giscard d'Estaing was taking up a tough position in *Figaro Magazine*: that the realization of a federal Europe must precede German unification if the new German state was not to develop into a factor of instability in a significantly different Europe. The Foreign Ministry position was also very cautious. On 15 November Dumas declared before the National Assembly: 'reunification cannot be a contemporary problem'. Privately, Dumas encouraged Mitterrand to signal French reservations to Kohl more strongly, thereby slowing down progress on German unification and providing new leverage on EMU. The Foreign Ministry was especially concerned about the risk of the Soviet military replacing Gorbachev. It also wanted to make more active use of French concessions on German unification to make faster progress with French objectives, notably on EMU. In the Foreign Ministry analysis, German unification offered an historic window of opportunity to accelerate EMU. Mitterrand too was plagued by inner doubts that stemmed from his historical reasoning: France must not repeat its mistake in 1938–9 in not acting decisively to safeguard Poland. External pressures to take a tougher line with Bonn coincided with personal reservations to induce an attitude of equivocation towards the pace and content of German unification

It was in response to opposition demands that the date of the Strasbourg European Council be brought forward that Mitterrand decided to convene a special informal meeting of EC heads of state and government in the Elysée on 18 November. Its intention was not only to placate domestic criticism of French inactivism but also to subject Kohl to pressure, to soften him up so that he would be more susceptible to French influence. There was no explicit discussion of German unification or of any linkage to EMU. But the atmosphere was, from a French point of view, suitably uncomfortable for Kohl: and linkage was in the minds of Mitterrand and Dumas. It was Dumas who in his meeting with Genscher brought pressure directly to bear by stressing French concerns that new hesitation was creeping into German positions on EMU, especially from the German Finance Ministry but also within the Federal Chancellor's Office. Mitterrand used his visit to The Hague on 20 November to share his anxieties with Ruud Lubbers.

Advised closely by Dumas, Mitterrand focused pressure on Kohl around the issue of the date for the IGC and inaugurated a deterioration of Franco-German relations to their lowest point during their period in power together. The objective was in part to extract concessions from Kohl and in part to be able to demonstrate the setting of a date at Strasbourg as a triumph for Mitterrand's personal diplomacy. In this way Mitterrand's domestic political position could be strengthened at a time when he was vulnerable to domestic criticism for presiding over an eclipse of French power relative to Germany. An issue was problematized that had in fact seemed ready for agreement. On 13 October Bitterlich had indicated to Guigou that Kohl shared Mitterrand's enthusiasm for setting a firm date for an IGC on EMU at the Strasbourg Council and, if necessary, for isolating Mrs Thatcher. The IGC would last from the end of 1990 to the end of 1991, and ratification would be completed by 1993. In early November Mitterrand again confirmed to Kohl his intent to set a firm date at Strasbourg; he wanted the IGC to start in autumn 1990 and the results to be ratified by 1 January 1993. In fact, agreement on this issue seemed so obviously in sight that the date of the IGC did not figure in the Franco-German summit at the beginning of November. It appeared to be a matter of finding a suitable start-date after the German elections of 1990 and before the end of the Italian Presidency. The main uncertainty related to the lack of a firm date for the German elections.

What followed was an attempt to paint Kohl as recalcitrant on Europe and EMU. A contrast was drawn by the Elysée between the positive message of October and Kohl's letter to Mitterrand of 27 November. This letter was seen as a disappointment within the Elysée. It was interpreted as offering a much more cautious approach to EMU, dressed up in a complex package for consideration in Strasbourg. Kohl wanted to schedule an IGC on EMU in 1991, an IGC on institutional reforms, and a third IGC in 1992 tying together EMU and political union in a package ready for ratification in 1993. In his reply on 27 November Mitterrand welcomed Kohl's commitment to agreeing a calendar for European unification. But he also signalled that he intended to use Strasbourg to set a calendar that would enable more rapid progress to be made with EMU. An IGC on political union was desirable but must not slow down EMU. The French President sensed German procrastination on EMU behind this proposal and an opportunity to use this claim as a means of pressurizing Bonn to take a more determined approach to EMU.

The high point of Mitterrand's psychological pressure on Bonn came following Kohl's presentation of his ten-point plan for German unification to the Bundestag on 28 November. Elysée staff were displeased that Kohl had not cleared its contents with Mitterrand. Mitterrand veered between criticism of its content and caution in the face of reassurance from Kohl that the plan did not represent an attempt to accelerate German unification but was rooted in his need to regain some measure of control over political events in Germany. He was motivated less by a sense of personal slight (though his dignity was offended) than by a calculation that Kohl's initiative offered him an opportunity to step up his pressure on Bonn. On 30 November Genscher arrived in Paris to reassure Dumas. Dumas acted as the lightning rod for French complaints: in particular, that no adequate warning had been given about the contents of the ten-point plan: that Teltschik's reliance on merely briefing the Allied ambassadors in Bonn, in the French case Serge Boidevaix, had upset French feelings. He again turned to the theme of mounting French concerns about German hesitation to commit to EMU. Sensing an unwelcome and potentially dangerous change of mood in Paris, Genscher sought an interview later that day with Mitterrand. In their subsequent discussion, which was attended by Guigou, Mitterrand took a robust line with Genscher, pointing to the risk that mismanagement of German unification could lead to a return to the Europe of pre-1914, with its current EC partners—probably led by Britain—seeking security against a larger Germany by creating a counter-balance against it. He went on to suggest that Germany had ceased to be a 'motor' of European unification; it had become a 'brake'. He signalled that he was prepared to challenge Germany at the Strasbourg European Council by proposing a firm, early date for the IGC on EMU, even at the risk of open conflict with Germany and crisis in the EC. Clarity about the relationship between German unification and European unification was essential. On 1 December Mitterrand communicated his intention directly to Kohl, to reinforce the message carried back by Genscher.

The gap between Kohl's and Mitterrand's positions was now apparent. Kohl sought parallel progress between EMU and political union; he also saw that German unification had its own internal dynamic, which it was his challenging task to master. By contrast, Mitterrand viewed EMU as following the single European market and preceding political union. His strategic preoccupation was to establish parallelism between EMU and German unification. In taking up this position Mitterrand was influenced by his fear of being outflanked by Giscard and other opposition politicians who signalled that they wished to see German unification made conditional on concrete measures to create 'a stronger Europe'. Mitterrand hesitated to set conditions, recognizing the danger of being seen to oppose the will of the German people. But he saw in hesitation about the terms of German unification a useful tool with which to extract concessions from Kohl.

Mitterrand took the opportunity to fan the concerns of others, notably the British and Dutch, before and at the Strasbourg European Council, by stressing his criticisms of German behaviour. Right up to the eve of the Strasbourg meeting he kept up the pressure, telling Kohl on the telephone that too great a preoccupation with inner-German relations at the expense of priority to European unification could lead to Germany's isolation. Three days before the meeting Guigou received from Bitterlich the message that Kohl had no problem with fixing a date for the IGC at Strasbourg but that he would press for a delay of one year in order to clear the next German federal elections out of the way first. Though Mitterrand would have preferred an earlier date, he was prepared to respect Kohl's domestic difficulties in order to ensure that the EMU negotiations were not later derailed. He had attained his prime strategic objectives—to bind Germany in to EMU by settting a clear date for the IGC and to prevent any conditionality of EMU on progress with political union. Kohl's reservations at

Madrid had been overcome. Strasbourg could be sold in France as a political triumph for Mitterrand's diplomacy, even though it achieved little different from what had seemed likely to be agreed as early as October.

Conclusions

President Mitterrand's great contribution to the relaunch of EMU was not as a source of ideas about its content or even as a mechanism for transmitting French ideas into the relaunch. Those ideas flowed from the Finance Ministry after it had been re-empowered by the key Presidential decision of March 1983 to remain within the ERM. Above all, Mitterrand was the consummate strategist, blending in a masterful manner vision and cunning and manoeuvring, in a more successful manner than Pompidou and Giscard earlier, to square European and domestic political pressures. As an *animateur* Mitterrand reinvented his Presidency in 1982–3 around a strategic vision of *construction européenne* and a conception of the Franco-German relationship as the 'motor' of European unification. EMU was from 1985 onwards slotted into this evolving symbolism of European statesmanship. This symbolism also accorded with a broad domestic political consensus on the external objective of rebalancing international and European monetary power in the interest of France recapturing influence over economic and monetary policy.

The colder strategic calculation of personal and French interests was always at work, shaping the form that his ideas took and his control of the pace of change. On EMU Mitterrand bided his time, carefully calculating the balance of external and internal political advantage and seizing the favourable opportunity. As we have seen, he was the master in using ambiguity and hesitation as instruments to put psychological pressure on the Germans—as over the ERM in March 1983 and over his response to German unification. What drew together his beliefs and his strategic calculations was a clear sense of French interest in giving priority to EMU. France would gain by retrieving a measure of influence over economic and monetary policy and the potential to reshape international and European economic and monetary relations on its own terms. In order to identify his Presidency with these gains Mitterrand was prepared to take the domestic political lead in getting acceptance of the difficult concessions that were the price of solving the problem of German monetary power and pursuing Franco-German reconciliation, notably on central bank independence. A Gaullist President or a President dependent on the Gaullist RPR for a majority would have found such leadership difficult, if not impossible. Mitterrand overcame the rejection of economic and monetary convergence on German terms that had frustrated Pompidou and Giscard, in his case by politically neutralizing opposition from the Left. The problem of the French Right with EMU would return later in the 1990s.

Mitterrand's strategy on EMU bore a strong domestic political imprint. Once he had adopted *construction européenne* as the axis of his Presidency, he became sensitive to the threat of being outflanked by the UDF, especially Barre and Giscard. Their support for EMU in 1987–8 was a potent factor in stimulating Mitterrand to attend to this issue. On the other hand, his commitment to EMU provided him with a means to highlight differences in the opposition, notably between the UDF and the blend of caution, hesitation, and hostility to be found in the Gaullist RPR. It was Balladur's Memorandum of January 1988 that pushed Mitterrand to conclude that he must regain the initiative on EMU by a bolder approach. In doing so he could not only draw out differences between the UDF and the RPR but also situate himself as a statesmanlike leader of a public opinion that in its large majority endorsed *construction européenne*. His management of EMU in relation to German unification was also strongly influenced by his domestic interest in claiming a political triumph at the Strasbourg European Council and by his efforts to reconcile what he realized could not be prevented at the European level with the containment of domestic criticism of his failure to secure French interests.

As a strategist on EMU Mitterrand relied on two key figures—Dumas and Guigou, the former the trusted confidant, the latter the able technician on EMU. The relationship with Dumas was the key on three major occasions: in retrieving the initiative after the Balladur Memorandum by instructing Dumas to prepare the ground with Genscher; in April–June 1989 after the Delors Report when there were doubts about Kohl's commitment; and from November 1989 over EMU and German unification. Mitterrand worked on and used the Dumas–Genscher relationship to push EMU back onto the EC agenda and to sustain its momentum. In this respect the Mitterrand–Genscher meeting of 30 November 1989 was of particular importance. Dumas and Genscher, who spoke by telephone several times each week, discussed EMU on a continuing basis. By contrast, Bérégovoy and the Finance Ministry were very much on the defensive on EMU. Bérégovoy was overruled in June 1988 and in April 1989. Thereafter, the central issue for Bérégovoy was how he could regain control of EMU negotiations: an issue that is dealt with in the next chapter.

There was no overt conflict within the French government over EMU. But there was a tension beneath the surface. It was in part located in the contending beliefs that were sketched out in an earlier chapter, particularly a social Radical legacy that influenced Bérégovoy and Rocard. But it reflected also a difference of institutional interest and outlook. From his speech in Figeac on 27 September 1982 onwards Mitterrand began the public process of reinventing himself as a statesman, distancing himself from his image as a person of the Left, and emphasizing his role at the service of the general will. He was President of the French rather than the creature of a Socialist majority. The consequence was a latent tension with those for whom the unity and mobilization of the Socialist Party was the prime value, notably Lionel Jospin. Jospin argued that the Socialist Party's role should be kept separate from Presidential strategy, that it should be a party of activists rather than a Presidential 'party of supporters' of the sort advocated by Laurent Fabius. He sought to maintain a more critical discourse about capitalism within the party and a more partisan Left-based approach (Jospin 1991; Philippe and Hubscher 1991). Bérégovoy was acutely sensitive to this tension: always resolving it by reference to his loyalty to the President but persistently uncomfortable with the implications of the concessions implicit in EMU for the Socialist Party. It was not till the Socialist Party conference in Rennes in March 1990 that this tension began to manifest itself strongly and in public, though even then EMU was not an overt dividing issue.

The period 1982–9 was also characterized by an asymmetry within the personal chemistry of the relationship between Mitterrand and Kohl. In 1982 Mitterrand was able to welcome a rather nervous Kohl to the Elysée, noting that the new Chancellor was more keen to please and more deferential than his predecessor. By this time the President had begun a process of reinventing his political persona that was to be given its final stimulus by the March 1983 ERM crisis. In consequence, up till 1990 Mitterrand enjoyed a status and potential for personal influence in his relationship with Kohl that was to serve well his strategy of applying discrete indirect psychological pressure on Bonn to embrace EMU. This pressure reached its high point before and at Strasbourg. Thereafter, as will be clear in the next chapter, the personal chemistry altered, reflecting a shift of power relations between Paris and Bonn.

5
French Strategy for the IGC: Making EMU Irreversible

On 3 December 1991 in Brussels, during a break in the final marathon sitting of EC finance ministers to negotiate the EMU treaty provisions, Pierre Bérégovoy took aside his German counterpart, Theo Waigel, for a private chat. He was making a last-ditch effort to meet the negotiating requirement spelt out to him by President Mitterrand on 27 and 28 November. Bérégovoy was accompanied only by Trichet, Waigel by Wolfgang Rieke from the Bundesbank. The French Finance Minster had just finished presenting the late-tabled French plan for the transition to stage 3 of EMU: its objective to make the transition 'irreversible'. But it was only in this unscheduled tête-à-tête that Bérégovoy revealed the full French position—a fixed final date for stage 3. This position had been spelt out earlier, for instance by Mitterrand to Kohl at the Rome 1 European Council in October 1990, and was repeated at their meeting in Paris on 3 December 1991. But it had not previously been presented in the IGC negotiations or Franco-German bilaterals, even in 'off-the-table' Franco-German discussions.

Bérégovoy appealed to German self-interests in committing to an irreversible EMU. It would 'bind in' future, potentially less responsible, French governments, to a framework of economic discipline and stability and ensure continuity of the policy of 'competitive disinflation' that he had put in place. At the same time he knew Waigel well enough, and his domestic political constraint of keeping the Bundesbank on side, not to be surprised when he received no positive response to the idea of a final date. It was the one and only area of the EMU treaty negotiations where Bérégovoy could not realize his fundamental strategic objective: which was to retain control of the substance of the negotiations whilst realizing the political will of the President. Part of the problem derived from Mitterrand's late specification of the goal of a final date for stage 3, leaving Bérégovoy with too little time to soften up his German counterparts, build up a supportive coalition, and prepare adequately drafted treaty articles. But, for Bérégovoy, the problem also had its roots in an internal doubt that a final date was a realistic proposition in the context of his knowledge of the cognitive and strategic aspects of German negotiating positions on EMU. The proposal fell outside the realm of consensus in the IGC on EMU and in ECOFIN and the EC Monetary Committee. In this respect it was not 'practical' politics. Hence Bérégovoy pushed on the final date, but did not push Waigel over-insistently.

This brief episode illustrates key themes of French strategy for the EMU negotiations after the Strasbourg European Council of December 1989. A first theme was Presidential leadership. Bérégovoy was responding to Mitterrand's central preoccupation—with making EMU and the wider process of European unification 'irreversible'. There remained in Mitterrand's mind, and more so in Bérégovoy's, a lingering doubt about the German commitment to realizing EMU. Mitterrand drew the strategic consequences. It was essential that the French government retain the moral high ground on *construction européenne* and keep up relentless pressure on Bonn. An agreement to make EMU irreversible was a test of German commitment. The question was how irreversibility was to be achieved. Mitterrand and Bérégovoy held different views here, as will become clear later in the chapter. But Presidential leadership was strongly in evidence on this particular issue.

Secondly, once the date for the IGC had been set, bureaucratic politics played an important role. The Finance Ministry set out to seize control of its preparation and conduct. Its task in doing so was made easier by a shift of attention on the part of Mitterrand. By mid-December 1989, with the IGC on EMU secured, he had decided to focus his energy—and that of Dumas, Bianco, Attali, Guigou, and Védrine—on strengthening the political dimension of the EC. Thereafter, there was a slow but discernible shift in the domestic centre of political gravity in EMU negotiations. Bérégovoy was determined to be the master of the EMU brief and to set about the task of persuading the Germans of the limitations of their model for EMU.

A third theme was the tailoring of French negotiating positions to the political requirements of striking an EMU deal with Germany. These positions had to put German negotiators under pressure in order to meet domestic political requirements. Bérégovoy was deeply sensitive to the domestic political context. Within major sections of the Socialist Party there was unhappiness at the prospect of accepting German conditions as the price of EMU. The French model of the 'social' republic was at stake. The external political requirement was to keep the exit option off the German agenda. Bérégovoy was acutely aware of just how much was at stake politically in the conduct of the EMU negotiations: in terms both of German sensibilities on the D-Mark and of the future constraints on French policy. Intellectually, he was less than happy with the negotiating hand that he had to play, even when he had control of it. French concessions, especially on central bank independence and taxation on savings, struck at the core of his Socialist and republican beliefs. On the other hand, given his knowledge of German Finance Ministry and Bundesbank positions on EMU, Bérégovoy did not regard a fixed date for stage 3 as realistic.

Presidential Leadership after Strasbourg: EMU, Political Union, and the Domestic Political Context

During the French EC Presidency of the second half of 1989 Mitterrand's conception of EMU had undergone a transformation. In July the basic aim had been to ensure that the Delors Report did not suffer the fate of the Werner Report. EMU had been conceived in terms of the Community's own history. But by November EMU had been recast in the framework of Mitterrand's historical perspective on unfolding events in Germany and of mounting domestic obsession with German economic and political power. His chief concern was now that France must not repeat the mistakes of the interwar period. It must bind Germany to and within Europe in a set of institutional arrangements that would induce partnership and collaboration and appease political fears within France. EMU was seen as serving two purposes. It was a means to bind Germany in the area where it could most strongly exploit its new freedom of manoeuvre as a unified and sovereign state. It was also a means of recreating a 'hard core' of EC states that could act to head off the threat of a diversion from unifying Europe by pressing on with a big and symbolic project (Cohen 1998: 150–1). Fixing a firm date for the IGC became the symbol, the touchstone, of this historically and politically informed strategy. In short, French strategy for EMU was given fresh direction and legitimation by Mitterrand's historical memories and domestic political concerns.

In January 1990 Roland Dumas conducted a joint assessment, by the Elysée and the Foreign Ministry, of French strategy towards German unification. Its conclusions guided Mitterrand's conduct in the period till late March. Dumas emphasized that, up to the impending elections in the German Democratic Republic on 18 March, French diplomacy had a window of opportunity to extract concessions from Bonn. Thereafter, if a pro-unification majority were elected in the GDR (which materialized), the constraints on French influence would mount. But, in order to prevent a nationalist backlash in Germany, Dumas's review concluded that French pressure on Bonn must be exerted in the strictest privacy and confidentiality. Mitterrand determined to play a game of cat and mouse with Kohl, emphasizing his domestic difficulties over German unification in order to induce Kohl to display his sincerity on Europe by making concessions to satisfy French interests. In fact, such concessions were not so readily forthcoming. After Kohl proposed economic and monetary union between the two German states on 6 February, the Elysée signalled to the Federal Chancellor's Office the need to accelerate the calendar for the IGC on EMU. Mitterrand was concerned about the prospect of domestic criticisms, led by Giscard, of the failure to make German unification conditional on faster and stronger progress in *construction européenne*. But Bitterlich responded by stressing the need to accelerate the general process of European integration, especially political union.

The other conclusion of Dumas's review was that the Germans were *demandeurs* on political union. French strategy should be to take up minimalist positions (in German terms) on political union in order to induce German concessions on EMU. Maximizing French influence within the EMU negotiations was accorded overriding priority. On political union Mitterrand was correspondingly slow to declare his hand to Kohl. His commitment in principle to accelerate progress towards political union was not in fact in doubt. This message was reinforced in discussions with the Italians: at the state dinner for President Cossiga on 29 January; at the meeting between Dumas and De Michelis, the Italian Foreign Minister, on 8 February; and at Mitterrand's meeting with Andreotti on 13 February. Mitterrand deployed hesitation as a tactical weapon for various reasons. First, having committed himself to this objective immediately after Strasbourg, he wanted to give Dumas and his Elysée advisers time to work with him in developing specifically French positions on political union. Such positions had to be developed with care, given political sensitivities in France and the traditional strength of anti-federalist discourse within the Socialist Party (Cole 1996: 78). Mitterrand was particularly conscious of the domestic political risk of providing too easy a political target around which the nationalist elements within the French Right could mobilize public opinion against Europe. This domestic political calculation led him to be very pragmatic about the political-union negotiations.

Additionally, the political-union negotiations offered France an opportunity to develop more robust positions *vis-à-vis* Germany than over EMU. In EMU negotiations the Germans could always point to their superior experience with economic stability. But in political-union negotiations the French could point with pride to their long republican tradition and experience with democratic legitimation. They believed that they had better cards to play in such a negotiation, once they had refined their playing skills.

Finally, at their private meeting in Latché on 4 January 1990 Mitterrand sought to increase his room for manoeuvre. He fended off Kohl's arguments about pressing ahead quickly with political union by focusing on the difficulties surrounding the external management of German unification, especially the importance of guaranteeing the Oder–Neisse frontier as a precondition. Mitterrand made much of the German–Polish frontier issue, pointing out that it was not a matter of trust in Kohl. It involved binding future generations who might be disposed to exploit any uncertainty left over from the process of German unification. Once, by 5 February (when Mitterrand discussed the matter with Kohl by telephone), the idea of a 'four plus two' negotiation had been accepted as the means of regulating this external dimension (the four wartime Allies plus the two German states), Mitterrand dropped his attitude of reserve on European political union. Over dinner on 12 February Mitterrand and Kohl agreed on a second IGC on political union to parallel that on EMU. Guigou and Bitterlich were set to work to prepare a common Franco-German position before the special Dublin European Council on 28 April and in time for the

Franco-German summit of 25–6 April. He used, in private, the language of an ultimate federal goal for the EC, reflecting the distance between his personal position and that of mainstream Socialist party thinking on Europe. In late March Dumas conducted an intensive round of EC diplomacy to build up support for the ideas emerging for the Franco-German initiative, which was finally launched in the Mitterrand–Kohl letter of 19 April.

Discussions in Guigou's 'pre-arbitrage' meetings at the Elysée revealed the important linkage between emerging ideas for French positions on political union and the agenda for the EMU negotiations. The Finance Ministry was sensitized to the important role of EMU itself in forging political union by a strong 'political pole' to balance the ECB. In short, Bérégovoy identified the fact that he had his own role in promoting political union. It also became clear by March that Elysée thinking stressed the theme of strengthening the European Council at the expense of the EC Commission on the basis of the greater democratic legitimacy of the former. This theme suggested to the Finance Ministry the need to accommodate the design of EMU to a more intergovernmentalist model, in which the supranational element was not the EC Commission and the European Parliament but the ECB. Guigou, who was very much a 'Treaty-of-Rome' person and the closest to Delors, was the most uncomfortable with this development. But, backed by de Boissieu, and at the political level by Dumas, the idea gained a political momentum in Paris. The intergovernmentalist model of EMU had its domestic political roots in Dumas's closeness to Mitterrand, in the ideological compatibility of this model of political union with the institutional basis of the French state with its focus of powers in the political executive, and in party and electoral factors. On political union Guigou had to be very discrete, accept Dumas's position, and cede influence to de Boissieu who stressed the domestic sensitivities on sovereignty and national independence. Dumas and de Boissieu were successful in ensuring that the French government proceeded with caution on political union.

As ideas on political union were refined in Paris, and taken up in the Franco-German relationship from early February, so Delors's relationship to Mitterrand became more strained and tenuous. The personal chemistry of this relationship had always been complex and difficult, reflecting in part their differences of educational and career background and in part their experiences of each other. There was mutual respect: on Mitterrand's part for Delors's energy, enthusiasm, and technocratic flair; on Delors's part for Mitterrand's professionalism in the practice of power politics and for his culture. But there was also great tension. Delors was irritated by Mitterrand's governing style, his preference for ambiguity and secretiveness over lucidity and plain speaking, his cultivation of a status gap between himself, as the leader with democratic legitimation, and the President of the EC Commission. This style contrasted with the openness, directness, and ease of his relationship with Kohl, who took the trouble to cultivate Delors. Delors had to rely on Pascal Lamy's close relationship to Guigou to keep himself briefed on Elysée thinking. In turn, Mitterrand distrusted

Delors's careful cultivation of his own independent relationship with Kohl and saw him as too hastily over-accommodative to German unification, to the detriment of French national interests. He saw Delors as lacking the emotional detachment of the statesman, as too prone to mood swings and pessimism, and as having too naive a faith in the power of ideas in politics. By November 1989 there had already been Elysée-inspired criticism of Delors's 'distance' from the French government. Once the Elysée and the Chancellor's Office had started joint work on political union before Dublin, Delors's relationship with Mitterrand became more remote. Mitterrand had little time for Delors's views. He had his own agenda on political union and saw Delors as a poor promoter of French interests.

In defining French positions on political union after Strasbourg, Dumas and Mitterrand were also sensitive to a shift in the domestic political context. By January 1990 there were increasingly strident criticisms, led by Charles Pasqua and Philippe Séguin, of the loss of direction in the RPR since the Presidential election in 1988 and there was pressure on Chirac to establish a clearer Gaullist identity on Europe based on primacy to the nation and the state (Shields 1996: 96–7). The RPR seemed to be eclipsed between the sharply contrasting positions of Giscard and of Le Pen's National Front on Europe. Its mistake had been to align itself too closely with Giscard's UDF in the European Parliament elections of 1989.

Distancing himself from these criticisms, Balladur sought to craft a sustainable Gaullist position between pressure from militants around Pasqua and Séguin and the emerging Franco-German discussions about political union. On the one hand, he attacked Delors's conception of a federal goal for the EC and warned the President to avoid approaching *construction européenne* on a wave of euphoria; whilst, on the other, he began to sketch out a more flexible conception of an EU that would respect national sovereignty and would have monetary, foreign policy, and defence components. Crucially, with respect to EMU, he had by 9 February in *Le Monde* endorsed the idea of a common currency rather than a single currency, as better compatible with respect for national sovereignty and for a more evolutionary approach to European union. On 25 May in *Les Echos* Balladur was even more forceful: a single currency meant the abandonment of sovereignty, which was unacceptable. Trésor officials, especially working on the international side, communicated to Balladur their concerns about the weakening of French negotiating positions that could follow if his arguments were taken seriously in Germany. By 1991 he had ceased to press these views actively.

Under mounting pressure Chirac was less cautious, opportunistically picking his way amidst the complexities and contradictions within the RPR on Europe with an eye to keeping his party behind him. On 3 April 1990 Chirac declared his 'absolute hostility' to the idea of a single currency and stage 3 of the Delors Report. This would mean the end of a national budgetary policy and of an 'independent social policy' (Aeschimann and Riché 1996: 268). But, by the time of the publication of the RPR's carefully worded *Pour l'union des États de l'Europe* in

December 1990, a more accommodating position had emerged. This new manifesto referred to a 'negotiated transfer' of 'elements of sovereignty'. The problems consequent on EMU were played down. Strikingly, during the IGC negotiations in 1991 Bérégovoy had very few problems with the RPR group in the National Assembly's Finance Commission. It accepted the goal of a single currency.

These signs of intensifying factionalism on Europe within the centre-right opposition reduced the domestic political pressure on Mitterrand. The combination of EMU and political union was opening up divides, notably between the UDF and the RPR, and revealing how difficult it would be for a future centre-right Presidential candidate to pull together a credible position on Europe. By contrast, Mitterrand had no comparable problem within his own party. The Socialist Party conference in Rennes in March revealed that Mitterrand had new problems of his own in keeping a grip on his party, with splits between the Rocardians and the Mitterrandist majority and, within the latter, between the two rival tendencies led by Laurent Fabius and Lionel Jospin. These splits centred on party strategy and identity (Bell 1997). But, in contrast to the opposition, the internal party difficulties did not relate to EMU and political union. The Socialist Party's European manifesto of November 1990 endorsed an ECB and a single currency, falling in behind the Presidential leadership. Its key concerns were already reflected in positions taken up by the French government—in particular, the importance of the Social Charter to accompany EMU and of the overall political direction of EMU. It was after the Maastricht Treaty referendum, and its very close result, that the Socialist Party was to return to the theme of a 'Europe of the Left', rooted in popular concerns about growth, employment, and social protection.

Mitterrand sensed that he had considerable domestic room for manoeuvre, so long as he did not overplay his hand on federalism, crafted a distinctively French version of political union, and stood up for the values of the 'social' republic. In response to this challenge he adopted in October 1990 Bérégovoy's conception of a 'political pole' for EMU, labelling it *gouvernement économique* and equating it with strengthening the European Council. This conception provided the overriding political theme underpinning French strategy in the EMU negotiations.

But perhaps the most important direct contribution of Mitterrand on EMU in 1990 came at the Dublin European Council on 25–6 June. Mitterrand's preoccupation was to give a clear and delimited time-frame to both sets of negotiations. At Dublin this objective was achieved. The two IGCs were to open on 13–14 December and to finish their work in time for the ratification of their results before the end of 1992. This outcome was consistent with the way in which Mitterrand conceived the calendar for *construction européenne*: EMU was to begin precisely once the deadline for completion of the European single market had arrived. It was also Mitterrand's way of imposing political will on otherwise cautious, technically minded negotiators by focusing their minds and energies on the requirement to hammer out a deal. It created the context in which he could continue to act as an effective *animateur* of EMU.

Consistent with this same conception, the Elysée then turned to pressing the case for stage 2 of EMU to begin on 1 January 1993. On this issue Guigou was influential, liaising closely with Delors who also argued publicly for this position. Guigou took up this proposal with Bitterlich and gained the backing of Umberto Vattani, Andreotti's diplomatic counsellor; Dumas enlisted the support of Genscher on 17–18 September and 6 October and of De Michelis. The Belgian, Italian, and Spanish governments threw their support behind the French proposal for an early and ambitious date for stage 2. But the critical opposition came once again from within Bonn, with Kohl prevaricating. In this instance, unlike at Strasbourg, direct pressure from the Elysée on Bonn was to be less decisive to the outcome. Mitterrand used the Franco-Italian summit of 8 October to spell out the importance of linking stage 2 to the completion of the European single market. The key determinant of the final fixing of 1 January 1994 for stage 2 was the direct relationship between the Italian government (as the EC Presidency) and the German government, specifically between Vattani and Bitterlich. At Rome 1 on 27–8 October Mitterrand's main independent foray was to impress on Kohl, in privacy, the importance of fixing a final date for stage 3 (Védrine 1996: 459). Based on advice from Guigou, his estimate at this time was that stage 2 should last till 1998 or 2000 but that it was premature to make a formal proposal at such an early and sensitive point in the negotiations. This move was symptomatic of Mitterrand's intent to sustain the pressure on Kohl, putting down a marker for future concentration of French diplomatic energy. But, as will be clear later, from October 1990 onwards there were signs of a weakening of the Elysée's grip on the EMU negotiations.

The Bureaucratic Politics of EMU in Paris: Mitterrand, Bérégovoy, and the Banque de France

Once the date for the IGC had been set at Strasbourg, and the preparatory work for the decisions on stage 1 largely completed under his chairing, Bérégovoy stepped up his involvement in the preparations for the IGC. Domestically, the political stakes were high. He had to persuade Mitterrand to fully entrust him and the Finance Ministry with full responsibility for the EMU negotiations. He had to secure the respect of his officials as a strong minister who could protect the prerogatives of the Finance Ministry. Also, he had to maintain his profile within the Socialist Party. Mitterrand's ingrained distrust of Trésor technocrats and his collusive relationship with Dumas made Bérégovoy's task of gaining control over the negotiations difficult. But Bérégovoy's objectives were clear: to ensure Finance Ministry control over the preparation and conduct of the negotiations in the IGC on EMU; and to inject a Socialist political content into the definition of French positions. In order to accomplish this task Bérégovoy had to make himself irreplaceable to Mitterrand by becoming the symbol of the strength of the French franc. That strength was in turn the precondition for an effective French negotiating position on EMU. On that basis Mitterrand was more likely to cede to his demands.

Bérégovoy's second task was no less demanding: to develop a constructive working relationship with Waigel, based on mutual interests, whilst demonstrating that he was a strong minister able to stand up for French interests. In consequence, strategy wavered between accommodation to the German model and putting the Germans under sustained pressure. Throughout Bérégovoy was driven by one central strategic insight: that credible and effective pressure on the Germans and France's influence in the EMU negotiations depended, fundamentally, on the stability of the French franc within the ERM and the underlying performance of the French economy. By April 1990 he was beginning to gain a new optimism from Trésor forecasts of prospective problems for the D-Mark following German unification. A strong franc was, in Bérégovoy's eyes, the key both to untying French interest rates from the Bundesbank and to maximizing the impact of French pressure in the EMU negotiations. He recognized the changing and complex nature of economic indicators: they could prove erratic. But good performance indicators in 1990 were a resource that he could deploy to his negotiating credit to shift perceptions of French economic attitudes and behaviour, especially in Germany. On balance French economic performance in 1990—notably on inflation, the trade balance, and the budget deficit—encouraged him to toughen up his positions on EMU, especially in the period August to November. The crucial point is that, by 1990, with the date for the IGC set, the *franc stable*'s rationale was, for Bérégovoy, increasingly embedded in the requirements of negotiating EMU effectively and of earning Mitterrand's respect by providing him with an indispensable bargaining resource. In short, it had been transformed into a political instrument in the conduct of EMU strategy.

The Momentum for an Independent ECB

Once the date for the IGC was set, Bérégovoy was faced by a new momentum behind the idea of an independent ECB emanating from intensified Bundesbank lobbying. De Larosière took up this issue with him in January 1990, indicating that Pöhl was determined to use the Committee of EC Central Bank Governors as the forum within which the draft statute of the ECB would be negotiated. This determination, allied to Pöhl's stress on the independence of the ECB as a precondition in a speech in Paris on 16 January, represented a challenge that, if not met by the French, would lead to deadlock over EMU. In effect, de Larosière sought and gained Bérégovoy's approval to pacify Pöhl. Bérégovoy's key sticking points were two: over the role of the ECB in exchange-rate policy; and over a decentralized operation of the ECB. The former was consistent with his emphasis on a strong 'economic pole' to EMU and his continuing primacy to the external dimension of EMU. The latter reflected the importance that he attached to protecting French financial markets in case the ECB should be sited outside France; the more operational functions passed to the ECB, the more the market operators would shift their business to its location. Otherwise, in the negotiations on the draft ECB statute from April to July, de Larosière was able to demonstrate to Pöhl his independence of the French government. He and Lagayette—who as Deputy Governor handled the detailed negotiations in the alternates' committee of the Committee of EC Central Bank Governors—were careful to emphasize their distance from the Finance Ministry. This negotiation was an important opportunity for de Larosière to pursue his prime strategy of aligning the Banque de France alongside the Bundesbank and the Dutch central bank. Hence Lagayette worked most closely with Tietmeyer and André Szasz on the draft. French reservations in the negotiations focused primarily on the role of the ECB in exchange-rate policy, the seat of the ECB, and the capital of the ECB. But on the mandate of the ECB to pursue price stability and to be independent for this purpose the Banque de France and the Bundesbank were in full agreement.

On the issue of central bank independence there remained a latent tension between Bérégovoy and de Larosière. Bérégovoy shared de Larosière's strategic judgement about the value of conceding an independent ECB as a precondition for effective EMU negotiations. But he had greater intellectual reservations. Bérégovoy's nuanced views surfaced at the Franco-German Economic Council on 7 April 1990 in Paris. He clarified the French government's support for the principle of an independent ECB and welcomed the close work between the Banque de France and the Bundesbank in writing it into the draft ECB statute. At the same time he entered two provisos: that exchange-rate policy must be a matter for the political level; and that the independence of the Banque de France would be reserved as an issue for Paris *after* the EMU negotiations had been concluded. Bérégovoy used this meeting (it came in the aftermath of the GDR elections in March) to employ French support for German unification as a means to put pressure on Waigel to accelerate and intensify work on EMU. Also, by affirming the connection between EMU and German unification he sought to persuade Waigel to adopt a more accommodating position on central bank independence. His frustration at his failure to achieve this outcome surfaced with the final agreement of the draft ECB statute by the Committee of EC Central Bank Governors. On 13 November 1990 Bérégovoy stressed in a speech to students in Paris that he would not accept an independent ECB on the Bundesbank model; it had to be balanced by a 'centre of economic power'. In an interview with *Les Echos* on 19 November he opposed the principle of central bank independence in the absence of respect for the views of elected politicians. Though de Larosière and Lagayette were convinced about the importance of strengthening economic policy co-ordination, they regarded direct challenges to the Bundesbank model as counterproductive.

The Organization of the IGC on EMU

The Guigou Group had been a signal of the Elysée's preference for a sharing of power with respect to the EMU negotiations between the Finance Ministry and the Foreign Ministry. Once the date for the IGC was established, Bérégovoy set about the task of ensuring Finance Ministry control of the negotiations. In doing so he was very conscious of heading a powerful and proud ministry which had been losing powers (for instance, as a consequence of privatization and financial-market reforms). Its officials looked to Bérégovoy to show that he could defend their interests with respect to the EMU negotiations.

The problem was to counteract the Foreign Ministry's argument that it had an overall responsibility for EC negotiations for the purpose of ensuring strong political direction and coherence. In order to put the Foreign Ministry on the defensive, the Finance Ministry developed an argument around its impeccable European credentials, contrasting its own willingness to transfer sovereignty over monetary policy in a supranational direction with the reluctance of the Foreign Ministry to do the same with foreign and security policy. In short, the Finance Ministry was giving the better practical demonstration of how to be a good European. This argument was pressed effectively on the Elysée by Hannoun, director of Bérégovoy's cabinet, who had been a colleague of Guigou's at the Elysée. It influenced Guigou, whose advice to Mitterrand on the organization of the IGC was important.

Bérégovoy also resorted to a much more subtle technique, seeking to build a cross-national alliance with Waigel on this issue. He recognized that Waigel had potentially more weight with Kohl than he had with Mitterrand, in part because Waigel was chair of a coalition party, and in part because of the strength of any argument based on keeping the Bundesbank on board in the negotiations. If Waigel could persuade Kohl to give responsibility for the IGC on EMU negotiations to the German Finance Ministry, Kohl could be mobilized by Waigel to persuade Mitterrand of the merits of this approach. In this indirect way the influence of Dumas on Mitterrand could be counteracted. Bérégovoy preferred the role of spectator of the pressures being exerted on the Elysée from Bonn on this issue. At the ECOFIN of 23 July he was content to sit back whilst Waigel and the Danish Finance Minister pressed the argument that EC finance ministers must control the IGC. He focused on the consensual aspects of the French position: the need for stage 2 to begin on 1 January 1993; and the importance of a strong political authority like ECOFIN to balance the ECB.

Guigou was influential in advising Mitterrand to adopt a formal power-sharing arrangement. On the IGC on EMU at the ministerial level Dumas would sit alongside Bérégovoy; at the personal representatives' level, de Boissieu would sit alongside Trichet. The ostensible reasons—pushed by Dumas and acceptable to the Finance Ministry—were to ensure overall coherence between the two sets of negotiations and to enable de Boissieu to make a contribution on legal and institutional issues. But the Finance Ministry was convinced that, within this framework, they could gain and retain the real control of the negotiations. Bérégovoy was also put at ease by his easy personal relationship with Dumas, with whom he found compromise possible. His view on the issue of control of the IGC was simple: 'you don't declare power, you exercise it'. As long as he could deliver the *franc fort* as the basis for French negotiating power, Bérégovoy felt that his position *vis-à-vis* Dumas on EMU was unassailable. He and Dumas were able bilaterally to hammer out a 'Yalta Agreement' for the IGCs, a mutual understanding by which each agreed to recognize the negotiating territory of the other.

But Dumas, Guigou, and Mitterrand still had their own agenda—which was to have in place arrangements that would in the last analysis ensure a political direction of the Finance Ministry. Bérégovoy was trusted, but watched carefully for signs of weaknesss *vis-à-vis* his officials. Dumas's presence sitting beside Bérégovoy at the first ministerial-level IGC meeting in Rome on 15 December symbolized, in somewhat embarrassing terms for the Finance Minister, the different nature of French arrangements for the IGC from those in Germany. On the other hand, only Bérégovoy spoke at that meeting and Dumas did not come to any other IGC ministerial-level meetings on EMU.

German Unification: The Issues of a D-Mark Revaluation and Balancing Germany

As German unification came firmly onto the political agenda, so Bérégovoy became a strong and active supporter of EMU. He situated EMU in his own geopolitical analysis of a changing power structure in Europe and the historical challenge of building new European structures to ensure peace. This analysis reshaped his attitudes towards the *franc stable*, which was now viewed primarily as an instrument for France to secure and influence an agreement on EMU. It also underpinned his improving personal relationship with Waigel since the Tegernsee meeting. They had in common a shared political conception of EMU, as well as a shared political desire to retain control of the EMU negotiations and a collusive relationship on that issue.

But from March 1990 onwards Bérégovoy did not hide his irritation at informal attempts by Bundesbank officials, led by Pöhl, to seek out support for the idea of a D-Mark revaluation within the ERM. Their concern was to offset the inflationary risks consequent on what they saw as mistaken decisions on the terms of German unification. De Larosière reported that, over dinner in Basle at the Committee of EC Central Bank Governors, Pöhl had sought to sound out opinion. The idea surfaced also on the fringes of the EC Monetary Committee and of other international fora. Tietmeyer sought—unsuccessfully—to raise the issue of a general ERM realignment with Trichet. Bérégovoy's position was firm and was put forcibly by de Larosière to Pöhl: if there were to be a D-Mark revaluation, the French franc would be revalued by the same amount. In fact, such a proposal was not officially made by the Germans.[1] The German Finance Ministry drew back in the face of the difficulties that would be caused for the French government by such a proposal. Bérégovoy had signalled clearly that French prestige was on the line and that there was to be no ambiguity about the *franc stable*. By December 1990 Bérégovoy was drawing a different lesson from German unification. This showed the danger of relying on monetary policy rather than budgetary policy to bear the burden of adjustment, with the consequence that the rest of Europe paid in growth and jobs for high German interest rates. What German unification taught was the indivisibility of economic and monetary policy.

The other aspect of Bérégovoy's geopolitical analysis of German unification derived from his traditional position as an Anglophile, a position bound up in his memories of the wartime Resistance. He was preoccupied with the idea of balancing German power in EMU by having as many other states as possible qualify for EMU and, in particular, by seeking to ensure that Britain was on board. In 1990 two developments helped. He got on well with the new Chancellor of the Exchequer, John Major, in whom he recognized a fellow self-made man, less grand and aloof than his predecessor Nigel Lawson. Also, Major's 'hard' ECU plan appeared to Bérégovoy a more serious constructive basis for a British role in the EMU negotiations than Lawson's competitive currency plan of 1989. There were also Trésor officials who saw in the common currency a way forward that was less threatening to their prerogatives. It accorded with ideas that had previously circulated there; and Balladur's adoption of this approach in 1990 reflected thinking within parts of the Trésor. Hence, during 1990, some in the Trésor were disposed to keep options open on a common currency. But it was only with British entry into the ERM in October 1990, and the fall of Thatcher and her replacement by Major in November, that Bérégovoy was offered a window of political opportunity to gain more attention for the potential of the 'hard' ECU plan in Paris.

In addition, Bérégovoy had great respect for the experience and wisdom of the veteran Italian Finance Minister Carli, who chaired ECOFIN in the second half of 1990. Carli's distinction between the 'institutionalist' and 'behaviouralist' approaches to EMU impressed him. It helped to firm up Bérégovoy's view that stage 2 must not be an empty shell; a new institution must be enabled to gain operational experience, notably in exchange-rate policy and foreign-exchange-market operations and in developing the role and usage of the *ECU* as a hard currency. During 1990 he continued to take both Britain and Italy seriously as potential allies on specific issues against Germany. This inclination to conciliate was manifest at the Franco-Italian summit of 8 October 1990. Bérégovoy and Carli agreed on a list of convergence criteria more flexible than those proposed by Germany, and in particular on avoiding a strict public debt–GDP ratio in case of 'unpredictable events'.

[1] Various French studies have claimed, wrongly, that there was an official German proposal. See Riché and Wyplosz (1993) and Fitoussi (1995).

In seeking to balance Germany in this way, Bérégovoy was in an exposed position. De Larosière had turned his back on the idea of a common currency during the Delors Committee negotiations. His preoccupation was to align the Banque de France alongside the Bundesbank as part of his strategy of engineering cultural change towards a more market-oriented central bank and of maximizing his freedom of manoeuvre. But far more serious were the reservations of some in the Finance Ministry, and more in the Elysée and the Foreign Ministry, who saw in a more Germany-centred EMU negotiation better prospects for success. Dumas, Guigou, and Mitterrand suspected that Bérégovoy was too cautious on EMU; and that in flirting with a common currency, and the British 'hard' ECU in particular, he was reflecting reservations within the Finance Ministry. Mitterrand repeatedly clarified to Bérégovoy that the French aim was a single currency and a single monetary policy based on the Delors Report. But Bérégovoy continued to flirt with the idea of a role for a common currency in the transition. This issue came to a head in January 1991.

Stage 1 and Preparations for the IGC

Bérégovoy was otherwise intellectually at home with the negotiations on stage 1 and with the preparations for the IGC in the EC Monetary Committee and ECOFIN. These negotiations were a matter for 'his' institutional fora and hence consistent with the objective of strengthening Finance Ministry control. He was part of a general consensus within these bodies that the more that could be resolved in these fora, away from the eyes and ears of foreign ministries and heads of state and government, the better for the technical quality of the final EMU agreement.

The negotiations on stage 1 had occupied his period as chair of ECOFIN in the second half of 1989. Their emphasis on strengthening economic policy co-ordination by a procedure for mutual surveillance to promote convergence was wholly consistent with Bérégovoy's objective of a stronger 'political pole' to EMU. More importantly, preparation of stage 1 had an important pedagogic value for Finance Ministry officials. It helped to sensitize them to the issues at stake and to reflect on the implications of EMU. During this period Trésor officials experienced a steep learning curve on EMU. It was a case of being introduced to 'practising the scales' of EMU.

But the negotiations in the EC Monetary Committee about excessive deficits produced a more ambivalent response. Bérégovoy and Trichet were by no means uncomfortable with the idea of objective convergence criteria with which to judge excessive deficits. Indeed, during 1990 Trichet introduced the idea of a budget deficit criterion of 3 per cent of GDP, taking the figure from Mitterrand's public commitment in 1982. This proposal was at the time much more specific than German insistence on observance of the 'golden rule' in public finance. Intriguingly in the light of later developments, Hannoun—who was more concerned with budget issues—reacted with concern to the 3 per cent figure; he saw it as an invitation for Socialist MPs to lobby for a relaxation of France's budgetary position, which was then comfortably within 3 per cent (Aeschimann and Riché 1996: 93). On the other hand, Bérégovoy and Trichet were more anxious about German insistence on sanctions against states with excessive deficits. This idea was seen as sensitive in the context of widespread domestic attachment to the values of sovereignty and national independence. On this issue they were slowly persuaded to accept the rationale of the German position.

The French Negotiating Team and the Structure of Core Executive Co-ordination: The Elysée, Dumas, and Guigou

October 1990 represented a turning-point in the location of domestic political power over the EMU negotiations, though one which at the time was barely discernible. It had much to do with a change in the external pressures bearing on the President, notably a growing preoccupation of Mitterrand and Dumas with events in the Gulf and the Middle East, a preoccupation that was to last till March 1991. It was to be replaced by the unfolding events in Yugoslavia which soon overshadowed Franco-German meetings. Against this background EMU lost its central position on the Presidential agenda and Dumas was diverted into other areas. But, as becomes clear later, linkage between concession on the German-inspired proposal to recognize Croatia and Slovenia and the French demand for a final fixed date for stage 3 was to play an important part in the thinking of Dumas and Mitterrand in December 1991.

Two other factors internal to the Elysée help explain the lessening of Presidential engagement on EMU. First, Rome 1 had already revealed a President who was no longer acting as the *animateur* of EMU. He entertained reservations about the wisdom of a special European Council devoted to EMU and about the viability of the ambitious draft communiqué of the Italian EC Presidency. Guigou, by contrast, was more enthusiastic and optimistic. Before and at Rome 1 Mitterrand had contributed unusually little, with the central axis being German-Italian. After Rome 1 the EMU negotiations moved into a more technical idiom which did not interest Mitterrand and for which he had neither skill nor aptitude. In discussions at Council of Minister level he was more engaged on political-union issues, notably foreign and security policy and defence. But, prompted by Guigou, he rallied consistently to the defence of the Rome 1 conclusions against the Germans in 1991.

Secondly, the Elysée underwent important personnel changes that altered the balance of skills and interests that it brought to the overall IGC negotiations. In October 1990 Guigou left the Elysée to become Minister for European Affairs, taking her to the Foreign Ministry. She was replaced by Sophie-Caroline de Margerie, a young diplomat already working in the Elysée. De Margerie had qualities of charm, tact, and subtle diplomatic judgement. But she lacked the insider's knowledge of the Finance Ministry that Guigou had possessed and the skill in getting on top of the detailed technicalities of the EMU brief. Hence, in relation to EMU, the informal 'pre-arbitrage' meetings in the Elysée, now chaired by de Margerie, lost significance. Next, in April 1991, Anne Lauvergeon succeeded Attali as economic 'sherpa' to the President. What was gained in superior organizational skills was lost in terms of the bombarding of Mitterrand with ideas. Overall, there was a loss of impetus behind EMU from within the Elysée, a less secure and confident grip on the issues.

By contrast, Dumas remained a key point of reference on the institutional, procedural, and wider political aspects of the EMU negotiations. Subordinated to Dumas as deputy minister for European affairs, Guigou had difficulties in gaining influence over the two IGCs. Dumas sought to keep IGC matters in his own hands and benefited from his direct, intimate relationship with the President, whom he served as *de facto* chief diplomatic adviser as well as Foreign Minister. In order to tighten his control he appointed de Boissieu as his personal representative in the IGC on political union and to sit alongside Trichet in the IGC on EMU, not—like the British or the Germans—the French Permanent Representative in Brussels (Jean Vidal). De Boissieu was an 'in-house' diplomat who headed the ministry's directorate for economic and financial affairs and whose background on EMU issues stretched back to service in the cabinet of Ortoli in the EC Commission during the EMS negotiations and included the Guigou Group in 1989. He had in effect overall responsibility for the IGC nego-tiations. Michel Casa, Dumas's cabinet member responsible for EC affairs, was very close to de Boissieu and kept in touch with de Margerie in the Elysée.

Confronted by problems of access, Guigou relied on three key relationships to keep her informed: de Boissieu about the IGC negotiations; de Margerie about the Elysée (though she too had difficulty in keeping informed about what went on directly between Dumas and Mitterrand); and Delors about the EC Commission perspective. Her reactions were complex and ambivalent. As a 'con-viction' European, Guigou was uncomfortable with the widespread sensitivity on sovereignty and national independence that she encountered within the Foreign Ministry. Her sympathy was for Delors's supranational positions on EMU and political union rather than the state-centred 'realist' outlook of de Boissieu. Guigou, however, had to proceed with caution, all the more so now that she was deprived of 'in-house' status in the Elysée and was dependent on the resources of the directorate for economic and financial affairs and the goodwill of de Boissieu. On the other hand, Guigou fitted well into an environment of technical dossiers working alongside de Boissieu. Both shared a technocratic mentality. But her biggest problem was that she could not counter the intimate relationship of Dumas to Mitterrand—or the tendency of Dumas and Bérégovoy to treat her as a political junior and keep her at a distance from their bilateral meetings with each other. Nor could she fully understand Dumas, who shared a 'sphinx-like' quality with Mitterrand but whose European convictions—unlike those of Mitterrand—she doubted. Their relationship was by no means easy.

When it came to putting in place a system of co-ordination for the IGCs, Mitterrand was keen to keep the Prime Minister Michel Rocard at a distance. He continued to distrust Rocard as a political rival with ambitions to succeed him. Hence the SGCI was excluded from the process. There were regular reports on the IGCs to the weekly Council of Ministers, but they were confined to Dumas and Bérégovoy. Dumas kept Guigou on the sidelines and was under instructions from Mitterrand to keep a careful watch—with Guigou—on Bérégovoy's commitment to the basic political line. More important were special restricted Council of Minister sessions on the IGCs, which were used with more frequency during the Dutch Presidency and just before Maastricht, for instance on the transition to stage 3. Here again the same people were active, with Guigou more engaged: de Margerie and Lauvergeon from the Elysée were also present. With the appointment of Cresson as Prime Minister in May 1991, Mitterrand was more relaxed about co-ordination. He allowed her a role in two key IGC issues—industrial policy and the fixing of a date for stage 3. Cresson shared Mitterrand's deep distrust of the conservatism of the Trésor; indeed, Mitterrand held her back from a radical restructuring that would have taken the Trésor to the Ministry of Industry. The Matignon became more involved just two to three weeks before Maastricht, though by this stage Cresson was too politically weakened to have a significant impact.

But the key co-ordination took place before Council of Minister sessions and outside the informal Elysée meetings chaired by de Margerie, both of which involved reports on progress rather than policy preparation. Because co-ordination on EMU involved Presidential prerogative, it took on a more informal, complex, face-to-face character than the more formally structured routines of EC co-ordination provided by the SGCI. Mitterrand dealt directly with Dumas and Bérégovoy on a one-to-one basis, receiving written and oral reports from them. He also had regular meetings with them and Guigou. In fact, before these meetings differences had usually been resolved. There were on rare occasions larger meetings, as on 26 January 1991, when others, like Rocard, were involved. Such meetings were arranged for special purposes, in this case to bring Bérégovoy into line behind government policy. Guigou was typically chosen to lead off against Bérégovoy, both in this meeting and in restricted Council of Minister sessions.

Dumas preferred to cultivate an amicable relationship with Bérégovoy. They established between themselves an informal 'Yalta agreement', recognizing a division of labour between themselves and their officials. Guigou and de Boissieu would concern themselves with the legal, institutional, and broader strategic aspects of EMU for European policy. But otherwise the Finance Ministry was to be in the driving seat on EMU. This arrangement suited Dumas because, given his wide-ranging responsibilities, he could never hope to engage himself in the EMU dossier. His first attendance at the IGC ministerial meeting in Rome was his last. But Dumas's confidence rested on his recognition that, with such a heavyweight character as de Boissieu, the Foreign Ministry would punch effectively in the negotiations.

Bureaucratic Politics and the Core Executive in the EMU Negotiations: The Finance Ministry and Interministerial Co-ordination

Bérégovoy's firm determination was to be in the driving seat for the EMU negotiations. Hence, after October 1990, he worked hard and with skill to seize the initiative by demonstrating the prowess of the Finance Ministry in preparing French negotiating positions for the IGC on EMU. The instrument was the agreement of a detailed French Draft Treaty on EMU to be presented as early as possible in order to help steer IGC negotiations around French positions. Such a Draft Treaty also had two domestic uses. It showed that Bérégovoy was countering the EC Commission's Draft Treaty on EMU, a move designed to please the Foreign Ministry and deflect possible criticisms that the Finance Ministry was not sufficiently sensitive to the political component of EMU. In addition, agreement of a French Draft Treaty by the government gave to Bérégovoy and Trichet a clear political framework to guide their negotiations and to counter future criticisms. They sought a mandate to legitimate the arguments that they deployed. By concentrating hard work around the agreement of this text at an early stage, Bérégovoy and Trichet provided themselves with domestic political defensibility.

In autumn 1990 the Finance Ministry negotiating team was put in place. It was headed by Trichet as director of the Trésor, with Denis Samuel-Lajeunesse (director for international affairs) as his deputy, and with an important role for Pierre Duquesne as sub-director in the international affairs division. Duquesne was a relatively young official. Cool, cautious, and reserved in character, and well-briefed on technical details, he was a first-rate economic diplomat. An even younger official, Xavier Musca, was appointed head of the Trésor's bureau for European affairs just before the IGC, working directly to Duquesne. Musca was by temperament more open. But, given the more hierarchical nature of the Trésor, he carried less personal responsibility than his counterpart in Bonn, Grosche, especially in interministerial co-ordination. Musca replaced François Villeroy de Galhau, who moved into Bérégovoy's cabinet with responsibility for EC affairs. A warm, open, and intellectually inquiring man, Villeroy de Galhau instantly gained the confidence of Bérégovoy who relied on him heavily during the negotiations. He was in a pivotal position not just because of his proximity to the minister but also because of his familiarity with the EMU brief after serving as head of the bureau for European affairs. This small group of five, plus Bérégovoy, provided the nucleus of the Finance Ministry's work in the IGC negotiations.

Trichet had one advantage over his counterparts in Bonn, London, and Rome. He was not constrained by an interministerial working group on EMU or by the need to 'bind in' the Banque de France that so shaped Köhler's position *vis-à-vis* the Bundesbank. Interministerial relations were handled at very senior levels. At the ministerial cabinet level Villeroy de Galhau kept in touch with Casa in the Foreign Ministry, with Pierre Vimont in Guigou's cabinet and with de Margerie in the Elysée. They also met regularly in de Margerie's 'pre-arbitrage' meetings in the Elysée. But these meetings were essentially for the purpose of reporting. Only rarely, as with the French Draft Treaty on EMU, did they engage in detailed deliberation on key issues. In addition, Trichet had frequent bilateral meetings with de Boissieu, and—sensitive to the Presidential prerogative at work in EMU—attended relevant meetings of de Margerie's group and gave great attention to cultivating his relations with Guigou and Védrine. Also advantageous for Trichet was the fact that Lagayette, the key figure on EMU in the Banque de France, did not enjoy the power of Tietmeyer, his equivalent in the Bundesbank. But, though Lagayette was more an observer, there were good practical reasons for keeping him involved. Lagayette was a member of the EC Monetary Committee, de Larosière's alternate in the Committee of EC Central Bank Governors, and later part of the Franco-German bilaterals on EMU. Overall, however, Trichet was less preoccupied with guarding his rear than Köhler. The consequence was that he carried an enormous burden of personal responsibility.

Bérégovoy too carried a great burden, aware that he was being closely watched for his reliability in keeping his officials under close control. He liaised closely and directly with the President and with Dumas, on at least a weekly basis. He also reported on a regular basis to the weekly Council of Minister meetings, where other contributions on EMU were also made by Dumas and Guigou. More important were the 'restricted' Council of Minister sessions dedicated to the Maastricht negotiations, especially for the 'end-game' before December. Again, Trichet and de Boissieu were present alongside their ministers at these sessions, which were chaired by the President. But it was clear at these high-level meetings that Trichet did not enjoy the status of intimacy that Köhler enjoyed with Chancellor Kohl. He was not part of Mitterrand's inner or outer circles. Also, Bérégovoy knew better than to let Trichet head up presentations. He could not afford to adopt the relaxed manner of Waigel both because he lacked Waigel's political independence and because Mitterrand was much more suspicious of Finance Ministry officials than was Kohl and was likely to draw negative conclusions about Bérégovoy if Trichet were to be seen as too active. Hence Bérégovoy had to be always on his guard: to ensure that he was fully briefed and displayed his control over the EMU dossier. The EMU negotiations required all of his copious talents for hard work and for absorbing complex and technical issues quickly. Bérégovoy believed that, in order to demonstrate his political strength, he had to show that he was exercising power over the EMU negotiations, not complain about infringements of his jurisdictional territory.

The appointment of Cresson as Prime Minister in May 1991 was a political set-back for Bérégovoy in two senses. His ambition to fill that office was once again frustrated as in 1983 and 1988, suggesting that he did not enjoy

Mitterrand's full confidence. In addition, Cresson was much closer to Mitterrand than Rocard had been. Bérégovoy feared the collusion of Cresson and Mitterrand and that Cresson might try to get more involved in the EMU dossier (which she did in November–December). Relations started badly when Cresson floated the idea of shifting the Trésor to the Industry Ministry. Their weekly meetings were a painful affair (Schemla 1993). Bérégovoy found it difficult to hide his view of her as incompetent, as lacking in judgement and in professionalism, especially in her cavalier remarks about the financial markets which threatened to weaken his negotiating position by raising doubts about the French franc. As her political reputation went into free-fall by August–September, he sought to distance himself from the effects by showing to Mitterrand that he could recapture a margin for manoeuvre in economic and monetary policy.

Bérégovoy identified a window of opportunity provided by the combination of inflationary tendencies in Germany, rising German interest rates, and higher French unemployment to risk a reduction of French interest rates below German levels. This move was made on 17 October, against the advice of Trichet and Hannoun, and especially de Larosière who warned him that France would pay a heavy price in higher interest rates later. It had to be reversed on 18 November as a consequence of the threats posed by the mounting problems of the US dollar. Bérégovoy had at least demonstrated that he was prepared to act boldly in the face of opposition, gaining the approval of Mitterrand. He had also reassured the President by drawing back in the face of the danger that French negotiating positions could be weakened at a crucial pre-Maastricht moment. Bérégovoy was intent on ensuring that France did not regain its image of a country of inflation and devaluation. But he was also immensely frustrated by this demonstration of the limited returns on a policy of virtue and by his continuingly constrained freedom of manoeuvre. He saw long-term political benefits to the Socialist Party from ridding France of the former image. At the same time, the short-term political risks made him very anxious.

Squaring the Council of Ministers: Preparing the Paper 'Progress towards EMU'

From the Rome 1 European Council till the start of the first working session of the IGC on EMU in January the Finance Ministry focused on two tasks—to reflect on the key ideas to guide French bargaining positions; and to use the French Draft Treaty on EMU as a means of gaining control of the process of co-ordination and conflict resolution in Paris. In working on these two tasks the Finance Ministry was working towards one central objective established by the President: that the Rome 1 conclusions were to form the basis of its work. At the political level Bérégovoy was concerned with reconciling this European objective with domestic political concerns in specifying French bargaining positions.

Policy reflection was preoccupied with two areas: the 'political pole' of EMU and central bank independence. Villeroy de Galhau brought to Bérégovoy's attention the speech to the European Movement by Mitterrand in October 1990 in which he had used the term *'gouvernement économique'*. His advice was that Bérégovoy had an opportunity to make this term the central axis of French policy. He was after all the 'father' of the idea, having spoken in July 1989 of the importance of a second 'pillar' to EMU, to be provided by an 'economic power'. Villeroy de Galhau was important in persuading Bérégovoy to make a strong *'gouvernement économique'* a core element in his paper on EMU presented to the Council of Ministers on 5 December 1990.

According to Villeroy de Galhau, the proposal for a *'gouvernement économique'* met two objectives: political and economic. In the IGC France must accord as much importance to the political as to the monetary aspects of the organization of EMU, fighting a rearguard institutional battle against the ambitions of the EC Commission in this field and of the ECB by strengthening the powers of the European Council and of ECOFIN. Given the work already under way on the draft statute of the ECB, it was clear that there was a lack of parallelism between the economic and monetary poles. Hence it was urgent that the Finance Ministry focus its energies on the theme of the democratic legitimation of EMU by putting in place an *'interlocuteur'* alongside the ECB. In this way it would be possible to pre-empt the Foreign Ministry's role on issues of institutional design by building features of the 'intergovernmentalist' model into the design of EMU and maintaining a fundamental coherence in French positions on political union. After all, with economic policy remaining essentially a matter for member states, it was only logical that democratic legitimation in this area should reside with ECOFIN and the European Council. Hence, for reasons of domestic politics as well as of coherent institutional design, Bérégovoy could seize the initiative.

Economically, the case for a *'gouvernement économique'* rested on the idea of a 'policy mix' at the EC level, synthesizing the use of monetary, fiscal, and structural policy instruments. Here Villeroy de Galhau picked up earlier ideas developed in the Trésor by Sylvain de Forges. He identified two risks of 'disequilibrium' against which a *'gouvernement économique'* must insure: lack of coherence between monetary and budget policies, notably by preventing excessive deficits and applying sanctions; and lack of coherence between internal monetary policy and exchange-rate policy. The French government must ensure a 'permanent dialogue' with the monetary authority. Villeroy de Galhau pointed to what he saw as the central deficiency of German ideas on EMU: too little concern about the costs of 'excessive monetary isolationism' to economic growth.

Duquesne and the international division were more important with respect to reflection on central bank independence. They recognized that France had to concede on the principle of an independent ECB at the outset, a point pressed strongly by de Boissieu since 1989. In casting round for a rationale for this concession the Trésor sought for an argument that went beyond that advanced by the Foreign Ministry and the Elysée: namely, that, with monetary independence already lost *de facto* to the Bundesbank, a seat on an independent ECB was a net gain compared with having no seat on the independent Bundesbank. The argument developed in the international division followed two chains of reasoning: that in federal structures member states have an interest in limiting the power of the centre and, hence, central banks in federations tend to be independent (e.g. Germany, Switzerland, and the USA); and that an independent ECB was consistent with France's political determination to prevent a flow of power to the EC Commission. This argument cut little weight with Bérégovoy, who continued to have more problems with central bank independence than many officials in the international division of the Trésor. It also had little appeal to other Trésor officials who argued that a political consensus around monetary stability was far more important than institutional devices like central bank independence. In any case they were disposed to protect a corporate interest in retaining power over monetary policy.

Bérégovoy recognized that his presentation to the Council of Ministers on 5 December was a crucial means for the Finance Ministry to seize control of the IGC negotiations. Hence he and his officials prepared carefully and later (18 January) were to have the paper that had been endorsed by the Council of Ministers circulated within the EC Monetary Committee. Consistent with its purpose, the paper stressed that French economic performance meant that its government was 'in a position to make its voice fully heard in the coming negotiations'. This point was later reinforced: 'France must become the one showing the best results [in the achievement of economic convergence]. It is in this way, within the common institutions of the economic and monetary union, that France will reinforce its influence.' Bérégovoy was establishing his credentials for controlling the IGC negotiations on EMU by tying the definition of French national interests in the negotiations to the policy performance of his ministry.

A notable feature of Bérégovoy's presentation to the Council of Ministers was the strong emphasis on EMU as an element in European political union, on which he was prepared to go further than most French politicians. He had two preoccupations in seeking a strong 'political roof' for EMU. Associating a united Germany in the past with war, he stressed the need to 'bind in' the newly united Germany. In addition, he was concerned by the fact that, with the demise of Communist regimes in eastern Europe, France could no longer act as a balance between two 'superpowers' and was confronted with an overmighty USA. From this analysis he derived the conclusion that it was in France's interest to build a 'strong' Europe to balance the USA. Hence Bérégovoy stressed to his ministerial colleagues the advantage to France from the weight that the *ECU* would give the EC on the world stage, but only if it commanded respect based on the achievement of economic convergence, particularly in inflation and interest rates.

Bérégovoy's focus on the political dimension of EMU did not include providing a rationale for central bank independence. The paper stressed the establishment of a fully democratic *'gouvernement économique'*, stating that: 'the independence of the monetary institution can only be conceived within an inter-dependence with a strong *"gouvernement économique"* '. Guigou and Foreign Ministry officials saw the negotiating difficulties that could follow from this kind of formulation; it sent deeply negative signals to the Germans and could lead them to harden their positions. Trichet too shared this political concern. But it resonated positively with Rocard and other ministers, and even with Mitterrand. Mitterrand was attracted by the idea of using domestic dissension over central bank independence and his own domestic political problems and hesitations as a means of putting extra pressure on the Germans. But, in the end, he was more cautious about using this tactic over central bank independence than he had been earlier over the March 1983 ERM crisis or over German unification. He was too aware of the risk of handing ammunition to German opponents of EMU on a matter of principle for the Germans.

The paper presented on 5 December had one other feature of interest. It finished by endorsing 'the wish of France that the passage to stage 3 of EMU should take place as quickly as possible'. But Bérégovoy drew back from the idea of spelling out the need for a firm date for stage 3. Quite simply, he regarded it as unrealistic and as subordinate to a more central political objec-tive of France—that of ensuring that all twelve member states were able to qualify in order to maintain the cohesion of the Community. Bérégovoy wanted to carve out for France the role of the political champion of Community cohesion against those—notably in the Bundesbank—who were prepared to welcome a relatively quick transition to stage 3 for a select group of states. His paper already included two of the core negotiating principles of the Finance Ministry in 1991: no state may be excluded in advance and no state could be allowed to veto stage 3. These principles were later to be seen as a key contribution by Trichet in the IGC.

Negotiating the French Draft Treaty on EMU: A 'Third Route' to EMU?

The Council of Ministers' meeting on 5 December endorsed for Bérégovoy a set of agreed objectives with reference to which he could set his officials to work on a 'complete' French Draft Treaty on EMU. This Draft Treaty's basic purpose was to provide a coherent, comprehensive, and detailed basis for intellectual leader-ship by French negotiators, based on clearing away internal conflicts especially with the Foreign Ministry. The basic negotiating objectives were:

- to achieve a single currency (the *ECU*) and a single monetary policy with an independent ECB in stage 3;
- to put in place a strong *'gouvernement économique'*;
- to maintain the Community's cohesion as an EMU of twelve, with no exclu-sion and no right of veto.

In Bérégovoy's weekly personal discussions with the President these objectives were given more clarity. EMU was to be achieved as quickly as possible, without threatening the Community's cohesion. Bérégovoy interpreted this instruction as a mandate to negotiate a 'long enough' stage 2 for all to be given the chance to qualify (i.e. no exclusion). It fitted in with his abhorrence of the idea of a 'two-speed' EMU, which had been forcefully promoted by Pöhl. But the process was not to be open-ended; and, in particular, no state should have the power to veto stage 3. By this time Mitterrand and Bérégovoy had in mind 1996–7 as start-date for stage 3. Bérégovoy was also instructed to avoid any concession on independence for the Banque de France at an early point in the transition. He was to play this card 'as appropriate'. Above all, France was to stick to the letter and spirit of the Rome 1 communiqué, which was understood to require the establishment of the ECB as a new institution in stage 2.

Bérégovoy's position was clear. He was intent on ensuring that the President's instructions were followed in detail during the preparation of the French Draft Treaty and the negotiations. He was also determined to remain in firm control, both inside and outside his ministry, and, in order to do so, prepared to throw himself into the technical details. This control had to be established in the process of hammering out key bargaining positions in the French Draft Treaty on EMU. In turn, the Draft Treaty would provide political cover for Bérégovoy and Trichet during the negotiations. But Bérégovoy also never ceased to recognize that his relative power in Paris vis-à-vis Dumas rested on something more fundamental than 'binding in' others to a Draft Treaty. It depended, above all, on France's strengthening economic performance under his leadership (the *franc stable*, a key negotiating resource for EMU, was intimately identified with him) and on Mitterrand's priority to EMU as the chief instrument of *construction européenne*. On these bases he could count on Mitterrand's respect and on his dependence.

How the Draft Treaty was Agreed

The Draft Treaty emerged in a complex and intensive iterative process centred on the Finance Ministry. Bérégovoy had detailed discussions with Trichet on the basis of which Trichet clarified to Musca his instructions for preparing the draft treaty. Trichet also added his own ideas which were influenced by preliminary discussions with de Boissieu on the wider diplomatic aspects of EMU. Both had endorsed the notion of a 'Yalta Agreement', with the technical aspects of EMU to be left to the Finance Ministry. But de Boissieu had pressed the point that EMU must be negotiated within the Treaty of Rome framework, not as a separate intergovernmental arrangement favoured by some in the Trésor. Trésor officials had continued to favour a more flexible institutional arrangement outside the Treaty as a means of avoiding issues relating to the powers of the EC Commission and European Parliament.

De Boissieu stressed that EMU had been put in the Treaty of Rome by the Single European Act and that a French attempt at renegotiation on these lines would alienate the support of the smaller EC states which saw in the Commission a protector of their interests. His message—reinforced by Guigou—was to avoid opening a war with Delors on this issue. This institutional issue was seen in the Trésor as crucial to de Boissieu as part of a background strategic package deal in which the Foreign Ministry and Elysée sought to negotiate common foreign and security policy (CFSP) outside the Treaty of Rome in return for negotiating EMU inside the Treaty. The French Draft Treaty on EMU rested on this underlying institutional deal at the heart of the overall French position on the IGC negotiations.

On this basis a first draft was put together inside the Trésor and was then the subject of discussions between Musca and Villeroy de Galhau, before going to Bérégovoy who worked intensively on its technical details. For Bérégovoy it was essential that the draft should be in good shape before it entered the realm of interministerial negotiation. Villeroy de Galhau was the central player at this key stage, working closely with Musca, liaising between Bérégovoy and Trichet, and ensuring that the the Budget Directorate did not feel excluded by the Trésor on fiscal aspects.

With the first draft it became clear that there would be difficulties with Delors as a consequence of the French view that, though part of the Treaty of Rome, the economic policy aspect of EMU should be entrusted to the Council rather than giving the sole power of initiative to the Commission. This view had the merit of establishing consistency between the intergovernmentalist approach pursued by the French in the political union negotiations and the negotiations about fiscal powers in the EMU negotiations. But it was achieved at the cost of creating an inconsistency within the French negotiating positions on EMU: between the intergovernmentalism being proposed for economic policy and the supranationalism for monetary policy. On this issue there was a clear difference of view with the EC Commission's Draft Treaty on EMU.

The next stage involved interministerial negotiations. It meant drawing in de Boissieu and Guigou, who introduced wider political, legal, and institutional questions (notably compatibility with the Treaty of Rome). It also involved getting the Prime Minister's Office on side and consulting the Banque de France, principally Lagayette and Capannera, on the monetary-policy aspects (chapter 2 of the draft). In this process Trichet played a more important role, particularly with de Boissieu and Guigou, whom he saw as the keys to influence in the Foreign Ministry and the Elysée respectively. Bérégovoy dealt directly with Dumas. Further interministerial work was done on the draft in de Margerie's informal group, involving Villeroy de Galhau, Trichet, and de Boissieu, and in a special meeting at the Elysée chaired by Mitterrand. Mitterrand presided over rather than intervened in the discussions. The Draft Treaty, dated 25 January, was finally approved in a restricted Council of Ministers' meeting involving Mitterrand, Bérégovoy, Rocard, Dumas, and Guigou, with Trichet and de

Boissieu in attendance. To the surprise of officials present, Mitterrand confined himself to only a few remarks on syntax.

During this interministerial stage three essentially institutional issues arose. First, de Boissieu and Guigou raised the institutional issue of who should prepare the decisions of a more powerful ECOFIN. They pressed the case for strengthening the role of COREPER (the Foreign Ministry domain) against the EC Monetary Committee (the Finance Ministry domain), once again to avoid a battle with Delors. Though it meant conflict with Delors on this issue, Bérégovoy was determined to reinforce the EC Monetary Committee. He saw it as a key element of *'gouvernement économique'*, as the main site for negotiating directly with central bankers and thereby avoiding a total split between economic and monetary policies. More generally, Guigou sought to act as a bridge between French proposals and the EC Commission's Draft Treaty. She was keen to press the logic of a French commitment to negotiate EMU as part of the Treaty of Rome. In that case the EC Commission's role must be protected against a more powerful EC Monetary Committee. On this issue Bérégovoy won the day. In addition, as is made clear below, de Boissieu devoted much attention to the provisions for the transition to the final stage. On this matter he succeeded in mobilizing Dumas and Mitterrand behind him at an early stage. Bérégovoy chose not to fight on this ground, knowing the President's deep distrust of the conservatism and caution of finance ministries.

Finally, there was broad endorsement of a long stage 2 to protect Community solidarity and avoid a 'two-speed' Europe. This position opened up a third difference of view with Delors who supported a short stage 2. But it became clear that the preoccupations of the Finance and Foreign Ministries were not the same. The Foreign Ministry was above all concerned with the Latin dimension of EMU and a show of solidarity in this direction; in particular, Spain seemed a viable candidate for stage 3. On this point they were close to Delors. By contrast, Bérégovoy was focused on the importance of keeping Britain on board. Within the Trésor itself there was a stronger compulsion to identify French interests with German attitudes of monetary and budget discipline and to distance France from the Latin countries in this respect. As the negotiations progressed, this Trésor viewpoint was to be reinforced.

Keeping Britain on Board: Bérégovoy and the 'Hard ECU'

During this otherwise relatively smooth process Bérégovoy ran into serious difficulties with Guigou and the Elysée. The cause was coverage of his weekly press conference of 10 January in *La Croix*. Bérégovoy was reported in the 12 January issue as welcoming the British 'hard' ECU proposal as a means of ensuring a 'better counterweight to the monetary power of Germany' by attaching Britain to the EMU process. 'If we produce together a hard *écu* which becomes a common currency for Europe, that's a good thing . . . If, in addition, that should become the single currency of the EC, which is the objective of France, that would be even better.'[2] In the context of what followed it is important to note that Bérégovoy was not challenging the agreed objective of a single currency. But he seemed to be endorsing a more flexible position on the transition. The objective was to avoid a single currency being imposed on restrictive German terms that would narrow the circle of participants to Germany, France, and the Benelux states. Above all, the intention was to keep Britain on board.

His tactics generated alarm in Brussels and from Guigou, combined with suspicion about whether Bérégovoy was on side with respect to basic strategy. Mitterrand was alerted by Delors and Guigou that he was planning a 'third route' to EMU by seeking to reconcile British and German thinking into a new synthesis. These reports, which were influenced by 'spin' from an official close to Bérégovoy, reflected his strong pro-British attitudes and his good relations with the new British Prime Minister, John Major, whom he saw as wanting to play a constructive role. They also revealed a key objective of leading Trésor officials: to keep the door open for Britain to join EMU and to ensure that the powerful City of London was inside the process. Constructive signals from the British negotiator Nigel Wicks suggested a 'window of opportunity' to balance Germany. Bérégovoy was unquestionably open to the idea of a 'hard' ECU: but as an interesting complement to stage 2, not as an alternative to stage 3, and more for the tactical purpose of keeping the British on board. He was sympathetic to an evolutionary approach as 'the best of British', but he was not seeking a 'third way'. Above all, Bérégovoy was a realist, recognizing that the 'hard' ECU plan lacked backing from the Committee of EC Central Bank Governors. His officials were advising him that no one on the British side seemed seriously to believe that the 'hard' ECU was technically feasible; it was a tactical tool to divert progress on EMU. He also found the new British Chancellor of the Exchequer, Norman Lamont, an unsympathetic, cold Thatcherite who lacked engagement on Europe. Bérégovoy was behaving purely tactically in seeking to engage a more positive British role and in signalling that a 'two-speed' EMU, German-style, was off the agenda.

The Finance Ministry was caught off guard by the reaction to Bérégovoy's kite-flying. By 15 January at the first IGC of personal representatives Trichet and de Boissieu were confirming the French commitment to the objective of a single currency, stressing that the Finance Minister was not seeking a 'third way' that would depart from the Rome 1 conclusions. The British proposal coincided with French views that the content of the transition period could be enriched by developing the role of the *écu*. But more serious than this public clarification was the inquisitorial meeting that Bérégovoy faced at the Elysée on 26 January, just

---

[2] French negotiators preferred to use the term '*écu*' rather than ECU. Because of its historical association with a French coinage under the *ancien régime*, it acquired a symbolic importance in associating France with the new European currency. The ECU (European Currency Unit) was, by contrast, a technical term for a 'basket' currency composed of fixed proportions of different Community currencies. In this book French usage of '*écu*' during the EMU negotiations is respected. Giscard was first to seek to seize political capital from promoting the '*écu*' as the common currency.

two days before the French Draft Treaty was presented to the IGC on EMU (Aeschimann and Riché 1996: 90–1). In the presence of Rocard and Dumas, and with Bianco in attendance, Guigou attacked his sponsorship of the British 'hard' ECU as a dangerous distraction from the French objective of a single currency and as supporting a proposal in which even the British government did not believe. She had gained this impression on her visit to London on 9–10 January. Bérégovoy's reply that German policy would lead to a 'two-speed' EMU found no echo from Mitterrand, who feared diversion by Bérégovoy's excessive opportunism to keep the British on board.

At this meeting the President focused on the danger of alienating German support for a project that offered France a great prize—influence within an ECB in place of dependency on the Bundesbank and the D-Mark. He clarified what he saw as the decisive interests of France: if Europe was to be built, that task could only be realized with Germany, not with Britain; and that, in building Europe, France must respect German sensitivities about abandoning the D-Mark for the *écu*. Bérégovoy was made to feel isolated and the object of suspicion. Mitterrand was behaving wholly consistently. At his first meeting with Major at the Elysée on 14 January he had expressed his doubts that the objective of the 'hard' ECU proposal was to achieve a single currency. He saw Major as offering a change of style but not of substance; as lacking in historical vision; and as a dangerous and clever tactician who was alert to opportunities to exploit potential divisions between France and Germany. Major made Mitterrand more cautious and suspicious rather than relaxed about British motives.

French Bargaining Positions

The five chapters of the French Draft Treaty, dated 25 January, were carefully organized around the agenda for the IGC proposed by the Luxembourg EC Presidency so that French negotiators had the authority from the outset to take up clear positions on issues as they arose. Bérégovoy presented it to the IGC on 28 January under three main principles: the creation of an EMU that was viable, democratic, and European. Its viability derived from the strengthening of ECOFIN's policy instruments for ensuring economic convergence, including sanctions designed to avoid excessive deficits, prohibition on bail-outs of debt and monetary financing of deficits, the entrusting of price stability to an independent ECB, and the role of ECOFIN in determining (by qualified majority) the guidelines of exchange-rate policy in the interests of international stability. Its democratic legitimacy depended on a *'gouvernement économique'*, without which it could not hope to be viable. Its European character was based on the responsibility of the European Council for defining the broad economic policy guidelines of the Community and guaranteeing EMU's satisfactory operations (by qualified majority). This French approach was presented as consistent with the Delors Report's stress on parallelism of economic and monetary policies. The independence of the ECB was being complemented by a political structure to ensure dialogue about the relationship of monetary to economic policies.

Of particular interest were chapters 4 and 5 on the transition. During the transition period the rules of the EMS were to be incorporated in an annex of the Treaty and fluctuation margins limited; the instruments of multilateral surveillance were to be improved; and monetary financing of deficits ended. More interesting was the commitment to establish the ESCB at the start of the transitional period. In particular, it would prepare the instruments for stage 3, 'reinforce' the co-ordination of monetary policies, and 'supervise the development' of the *ECU*. It might also manage foreign exchange reserves. These positions were wholly consistent with traditional French preoccupations about EMU and were seen as in the spirit of the Rome 1 communiqué. But they existed in tension with French acceptance of the German view that responsibility for monetary policy should not be shared in stage 2. This tension was to be a source of later difficulties for Trichet and Bérégovoy.

The transition to the final stage was an exercise envisaged for 1996. Then, taking account of progress on market integration and convergence, and developments in the role of the *ECU*, the European Council would verify that the conditions had been met and lay down the period within which the decision to enter the final stage should be taken. There was an attempt to balance the principle of no veto with the principle of Community solidarity in the provision that these decisions would require a qualified majority in favour cast by at least eight states. Provision was also made for derogations, to be adopted unanimously by member states participating in the final stage. The chief influence on the design of these provisions for the transition to the final stage was de Boissieu who stressed the vital need to ensure political direction of EMU by keeping the final decisions distant from the innately cautious finance ministers.

Strategically, the French government sought to position itself in a clever political position, as both reliable to the Germans and a balancer and reconciler in defence of a larger Community interest. On the one hand, it was signalling that it was a serious player to the Dutch and Germans, one of the 'stability-minded' core, firm on convergence, tough on sanctions, and committed to the principle of 'open, competitive markets'. On the other, it stressed its political solidarity with the other states and staked a political position as the champion of European unity against the Dutch and Germans who were seeking a 'hard core' approach. This strategic position was easier to hold onto in the relatively benign economic circumstances of the IGC negotiations than it was to be later. Even so, as the negotiations progressed into April, the French found themselves faced by more difficult choices. The existential problem became how to bridge the gulf that mattered most—between their positions and those of Germany. By April Britain, Italy, and Spain no longer seemed quite so relevant and attractive as allies.

Managing Bilateral Relations During the IGC

Negotiating on the basis of the French Draft Treaty on EMU was complicated by changes in the perceptions of underlying political realities in the Finance Ministry as the IGC progressed. These changes were the consequence of the different nature of the Luxembourg and Dutch Presidencies; of a toughening in German positions; of recognition in the Finance Ministry that the British would play only a secondary role; and of worries about the Italian lira. They led to a reassessment of bilateral relationships. At the same time this political reassessment was not conducted in panic. There remained an underlying confidence that stemmed from the continuing strong position of the franc in the ERM and from the psychological boost that came from realizing that, under the convergence criteria being considered in the EC Monetary Committee and ECOFIN, only France and Luxembourg would currently qualify for stage 3.

The Luxembourg and Dutch Presidencies

French comfort at the beginning of the IGC was secured by the very good relations between Trichet and Yves Mersch and between Bérégovoy and Jean-Claude Juncker, the Luxembourg chairs of the IGC at technical and ministerial levels respectively. They sensed a sympathy for French views, especially on limiting the role of the EC Commission in EMU. But, at the very first IGC meeting of the Dutch Presidency, on 2 July, the French were highly critical of the partisanship of the chair in favour of Dutch positions and of poor preparation on institutional and legal aspects. De Boissieu was especially active here. By the informal ECOFIN at Apeldoorn in September Bérégovoy was expressing his fear that an overcautious Dutch approach meant that the IGC was failing to make progress. He pressed on the Dutch the need to create incentives for ministers to make concessions by forcing them to negotiate over the formulation of proper treaty texts rather than 'issue papers'. In the same spirit of concern that a final agreement might not be achieved, he pleaded in November for a deferment of debate about the linkage between social and economic cohesion and EMU till after the treaty was signed.

Franco-Dutch relations were in fact smoothed by the more accommodative relations between Bérégovoy and Wim Kok, the Dutch Finance Minister. Deadlocks proved easier to overcome at this level than between Trichet and Cees Maas, who chaired the IGC at technical level, or between de Boissieu and Peter Nieman. Kok had a stronger appreciation of the French arguments for a stronger 'economic pole'. He also proved more averse than his officials to the idea of a 'two-speed' EMU and more supportive of a fixed timetable for stage 3. When it came to the sensitive issue (for the French) of the transition to stage 3, he ruled out the Dutch proposal of August for an 'opt-in' for all and for a 'critical mass' as inconsistent with the principles of 'no veto', 'no coercion', and 'no arbitrary lock-out'—principles proposed by the French and agreed in May–June.

Kok was to prove very helpful to Bérégovoy in helping to ensure 'irreversibility' in the final treaty.

Prioritizing Franco-German Relations: The Franco-German Economic Council in March and the Secret Bilaterals

The early IGC meetings in January–February were characterized by mounting tension between Trichet and Köhler as each dug in behind their negotiating positions. These disagreements came to a head at the IGC meeting on 12 March in the aftermath of the German Draft Treaty on EMU. The political alarm bells on EMU first began to sound in Paris with the presentation of the German Draft Treaty on 26 February. Delors reacted angrily, pressing home on Mitterrand, Dumas, and Guigou the argument that the German government had departed from the content of the Rome 1 communiqué. With Mitterrand and Dumas distracted by the Gulf War and the situation in the Middle East, Guigou and de Boissieu became the key figures in developing the political dimension of the French response to this problem. Their reaction was to seek out Mitterrand's support for a constructive, rather than confrontational, response within the framework of the Elysée Treaty and based on respect for all aspects of the Rome 1 communiqué. Bérégovoy was once again reminded that the reconciliation of French and German objectives must have priority over any other considerations. But on this issue he did not need as much persuasion as in January and had in any case learnt the lessons of that episode. He was already disillusioned with Lamont's objection to the 'imposition' of a single currency in stage 3; he could also see that the 'hard' ECU plan was going nowhere and had little to contribute to the substance of the IGC. Bérégovoy's prime objective was to work with Waigel to keep reconciliation of French and German objectives on EMU an 'in-house' matter for the two finance ministries: well away from interference by Delors or the Foreign Ministry.

Hence the Franco-German Economic Council meeting in Paris on 5 March took on an unusual importance. Bérégovoy was determined to use it as an opportunity to take a tough approach on French positions, whilst seeking out a framework of joint effort to reduce Franco-German differences on difficult points, like the content of stage 2. He placed reliance on an open and sincere expression of his convictions as a means of gaining respect and winning support on the German side. Areas of agreement were identified: the final goal of a single currency, a single monetary policy, and an independent ECB; objective criteria for moving to stage 2; stage 2 to begin on 1 January 1994; and stage 2 as having the purpose of reinforcing convergence. Also, and intriguingly in the light of later developments, it was agreed that it was premature to try to fix a date for stage 3. The transition to stage 3 was a matter of ensuring that conditions had been effectively established for a viable single currency. It was in any case the responsibility of the European Council.

But on two issues Bérégovoy focused his persuasive powers. He wanted to strengthen the content of stage 2, pressing the case for establishing the ESCB (European System of Central Banks) in 1994 and giving it significant responsibilities for developing the role of the *écu* and preparing stage 3. He spoke of an 'embryonic' ECB. More eloquently, Bérégovoy pressed the case for a *'gouvernement économique'*. He outlined how central bank independence was seen from a French perspective, stressing the great difficulties that it raised consequent on their historically conditioned conception of the state. The issue of democratic legitimacy was crystallized in his reference to the paradox of his accountability to the National Assembly for unemployment whilst having no influence on monetary policy. This meeting was notable to the French for signs of differences of response within the German side. Köhler seemed more receptive to arguments that EMU could become too remote from the political process than Federal Economics Ministry and Bundesbank officials. Trichet was encouraged to believe that the French could begin to make progress by pressing harder on the more specific issues of economic-policy guidelines and exchange-rate policy. In attempting to do so at the IGC on 12 March, however, he was to run into a wall of German distrust.

Most importantly of all, in Paris Bérégovoy and Waigel agreed to work jointly to iron out differences between French and German positions. Their motives were to help contribute to a wider agreement on EMU which both regarded as a top priority; to ensure that reconciliation of French and German objectives was based on solid technical argument that would ensure EMU's viability; and hence to keep Mitterrand and Kohl, and their respective Foreign Ministries, removed from the problem-solving process. In consequence, the Franco-German bilaterals were internally generated, not imposed by Mitterrand and Kohl. They were also recognized to be highly sensitive and confidential, to be organized in strictest secrecy. Finally, they were not seen as discrete. French and German officials were enjoined to work closely on the fringes of IGC and EC Monetary Committee meetings to expedite agreement.

Though the Foreign Ministry was broadly pleased with this outcome, it was determined to sustain the political pressure and momentum on Germany. This determination was symbolized two days after the Franco-German Economic Council, on 7 March, when Guigou arrived in Bonn. In the morning she had a long, amiable discussion with Waigel; in the afternoon she visited the Foreign Ministry and then Peter Hartmann and Lutz Stavenhagen in the Federal Chancellor's Office. She then went on to visit the Bundesbank in Frankfurt where she encountered more reservations about the idea of being drawn into reconciling treaty texts. Her message was simple: that EMU problems must be set within the joint political commitment to the Franco-German relationship as 'the motor of acceleration of *construction européenne*'. She took up the issue of respect for the engagements entered into at Rome 1 (on which there was agreement in principle rather than detailed implications); she also raised the questions of the content of stage 2 and the need to establish a new institution, the

ESCB, in 1994 (on which there were differences with Waigel and with the Bundesbank). During his visit to Bonn on 11 March Dumas took up the same message, followed on 22 March by a joint communiqué of Dumas and Genscher stressing the importance of rapid progress in reconciling differences on EMU. But this Foreign Ministry pressure was simply underwriting what had been achieved already by Bérégovoy. Its importance was essentially symbolic.

The Franco-German bilaterals (which are covered in detail in Chapter 9) involved Trichet, Lagayette, Duquesne, and Musca. Trichet's negotiating advantage was the unity of his team, which contrasted with the tensions that surfaced regularly between Köhler and Tietmeyer over how far Germany might go in making concessions. In this respect he had a freer hand than Köhler. Trichet was operating with a clear, agreed brief, and he was fluent, precise, and intellectually agile in presenting it. He also had the advantage of experience in dealing with Tietmeyer in negotiations, going back to the 1987 ERM crisis and creation of the Franco-German Economic Council. The abrasiveness that could surface in their exchanges took place within a framework of good personal relations and was eased by Trichet's considerable personal charm. But Trichet also faced negotiating difficulties. First and foremost, he was constrained and put on the defensive by the fact that, with the Delors Report and the ECB Draft Statute, the Germans had already gained many of their key bargaining objectives. Trichet's freedom of manoeuvre in pressing the cases for a stage 2 with substantial content and for a 'gouvernement économique' proved very limited. Tietmeyer enjoyed teasing him on the question of why the French government was so reluctant to grant early independence to the Banque de France if it was seriously committed to an independent ECB. Secondly, Trichet faced a 'two-headed' German team. Köhler played the 'good guy', showing a disposition to work towards agreement; Tietmeyer was the 'bad guy', taking up a hard and often unyielding Bundesbank line. It was difficult in this context for Trichet to assess just how much progress had been made or how far he could go with the Germans. In addition, Trichet sensed that Köhler had a political advantage over him. Köhler was clearly close to Kohl's inner circle, whereas he was not involved in the reflections of Mitterrand and the Elysée.

The first four secret bilaterals were conducted very much 'colloquium-style', with each side explaining the intellectual, cultural, and historical rationale behind its positions and seeking understanding from the other side for its economic policy ideas. The discussions took place against a background of relative satisfaction in the Trésor with the 'even-handed', co-operative and efficient way in which Luxembourg was chairing the IGC on EMU. But the summer and autumn brought about a significant change. First, the French were very disappointed that the Luxembourg European Council in June failed to make substantial progress in agreeing to resolve EMU problems and advancing beyond the positions endorsed at Rome 1. There was a sense in Paris, encouraged by the Elysée, that the Germans were being too accommodating to Major and hence allowing issues to be deferred, complicating the final negotiations and increasing the risk of failure. This French irritation was compounded in late August when the new Dutch Presidency produced Draft Treaty provisions that seemed to be based on an attempt to broker a position to satisfy both the British and the Germans. This took the form of a provision on the transition to stage 3 that envisaged all states retaining a freedom of manoeuvre in the form of a right to 'opt in' by states fulfilling convergence conditions and a requirement of a 'critical mass' of just six out of twelve states to proceed. This provision was seen in Paris as conceding defeat to London and as showing the way to a German-style 'two-speed' EMU. The political alarm bells about EMU problems rang for a second time in Paris, with Delors again lobbying hard for an active French response and engaging Guigou against the Dutch. In consequence, the work of the Franco-German bilaterals intensified and widened. It intensified in the form of more detailed work on writing amendments to the Dutch draft rather than as earlier just focusing on narrowing the differences between the French and German drafts. The bilaterals in Berlin on 13–14 September and Paris on 9 November sought to produce written amendments to the Dutch Draft Treaty proposals. Bilaterals were also conducted in other fora: the Franco-German Economic Council of 5 November; the Franco-German summit of 14–15 November; and on the fringes of the EC Monetary Committee and of the IGC. The Franco-German bilaterals were from September seen by the Trésor as a matter of 'saving the IGC' from the divisive, unpleasant, and less efficient style of the Dutch.

Reappraising the British and the Italians

In fact, the fundamental turning-point for the Finance Ministry was not the presentation of the German Draft Treaty or the initiatives of the Dutch Presidency. It came in April–May as it became increasingly clear that EMU was not likely to be compatible with Community solidarity. France found itself caught between a toughening of German positions on convergence criteria and growing doubts about the Italian fiscal position and the threat to the position of the lira in the ERM. Also during this period the Finance Ministry became finally convinced that the British would settle for an 'opt-out' rather than commit to stage 3. Any residual doubts were removed at the Franco-British summit in Dunkirk on 24 June. Mitterrand's summing up at the end of this summit reflected Bérégovoy's thinking. He contrasted the different theoretical starting-points of the two governments: for the French the single currency was a premise; for the British it was a possible consequence. In fact, Bérégovoy knew that Lamont did not envisage the single currency as even a possible consequence for Britain. Hence Finance Ministry negotiators decided to shift from the position advocated by de Boissieu in favour of clarifying more precisely where France stood on EMU. This decision had two aspects: that France must align itself firmly with those in the first speed to EMU; and that the key negotiating relationship was with Germany. The British, Italians, and Spaniards were secondary.

The biggest Trésor worry was about the Italian lira, reinforced by evidence of lack of financial discipline and by reports from Pierre Achard, economic counsellor in the French Embassy in Rome, that domestic support for the 'hard' lira was falling. Trichet feared that the Italians might seek an ERM realignment during the IGC, derailing the whole negotiations. They were in Trésor eyes the weakest point in the chain holding together the IGC negotiations and in French thinking about stage 3 in 1996–7. Trésor anxiety was further fanned by signs that the Bundesbank favoured a lira devaluation and by concern about a 'domino effect', with the foreign-exchange markets sensing vulnerability of the franc as French exporters faced new difficulties. At the Franco-Italian summit in Viterbo on 17–18 October Bérégovoy raised these concerns directly with Carli and asked for, and received, reassurance. But he and Trichet had come to see the Italians as too unreliable. There was a risk of weakening French negotiating credibility by too close an association with them. Hence, as 1991 progressed, the idea of balancing Germany by building close relations on EMU with other EC states lost its attraction in Paris.

Pursuing French Objectives in the IGC

A particular feature of French strategy in the EMU negotiations was its high profile role on institutional and procedural issues, especially relating to the co-ordination of economic policies, exchange-rate policies, and the transition to stage 3. During February and March French negotiators took the lead in developing the idea of 'balance' between the economic and monetary aspects. At the IGC on 25 February Bérégovoy, supported strongly by Delors, stressed the importance of the role of the European Council in determining the guidelines of economic policy. But by 12 March Trichet was using the IGC to contest the monopoly of initiative by the Commission. He outlined the French conception of *'gouvernement économique'*, arguing that it rested on an 'institutional equilibrium' in which the right of initiative was to be shared between the Presidency, member states, and the Commission. In outlining the role of the European Council in determining the economic-policy guidelines he gave importance to the reports of ECOFIN, not the role of the Commission. In short, the French were pressing an intergovernmental model of economic-policy co-ordination.

These institutional and procedural priorities were rooted in more basic French objectives for the IGC agreed by the Elysée and the Foreign Ministry which involved making the intergovernmental model efficient. De Boissieu was active and influential on these issues, especially at the IGC on 8 October, ensuring a strong political dimension to the French approach to EMU negotiations. Thus French negotiators argued that Council decision-making must be made more efficient by the generalized use of qualified majority voting, including for exchange-rate policy and the transition to stage 3. They also opposed the exclusive right of initiative for the EC Commission over EMU, notably on multilateral surveillance, economic-policy guidelines, the excessive deficit procedure, and exchange rates. Resorting to efficiency arguments, they preferred the right of 'recommendation' rather than 'proposal' for the Commission so as to avoid the risk of *blocage* from the requirement of unanimity to amend Commission proposals. On the same basis, French negotiators rejected co-decision for the European Parliament in EMU and indeed any role for it in the excessive deficit procedure and in exchange-rate policy. But efficiency was not the only basis of French arguments on institutions and procedures. Democratic legitimacy of member-state governments and parliaments was central. Accordingly, French negotiators pressed (unsuccessfully) for accountability of the ECB to national parliaments as well as to the European Parliament.

This French preoccupation with correcting the balance between the economic and the monetary-policy dimensions of EMU was driven by more than just political beliefs. It was also the product of the specific structural context and constraint of the IGC negotiations. French strategy was shaped by the fact that the bulk of the monetary-policy issues had been predetermined in the Delors Report and the ECB Draft Statute. Economic policy issues and issues relating to the transition offered French negotiators the opportunity to stake out a high ground and make a distinctive impact—to realize *'gouvernement économique'*.

Principles of Economic Policy

Though this issue was covered in the French Draft Treaty, French negotiators found themselves from the outset on the defensive as the Germans sought out a high profile role. They opposed the German preference for a detailed listing of economic policy principles. At the second IGC on 29 January Trichet spoke in favour of general references to 'open, competitive markets', 'sound public finance', and 'stable prices' and to a limited range of objectives, stressing in particular disinflation and growth and economic and social cohesion. He rejected the inclusion of privatization and the reference to social partners. But he endorsed the German proposal for a prohibition on indexation of prices and wages. Bérégovoy was particularly sensitive to British and German proposals at Apeldoorn to incorporate supply-side flexibility in the Treaty. Here he saw potentially serious domestic political difficulties. The final Treaty provisions were in all these senses broadly consistent with French positions.

Stage 2: Transition and Content

One of the most potent sources of conflict with the Germans was over the transition to, and content of, stage 2. In staking out French positions Bérégovoy was preoccupied with the objective of ensuring that all were given the opportunity to qualify for stage 3. Hence he preferred somewhat relaxed conditions for entry into stage 2; a lengthy stage 2; and a stage 2 that would be evolutionary and provide a tightening discipline to promote convergence. At the IGC ministerial level on 8 April Bérégovoy pressed the case for an automatic passage to stage 2 on 1 January 1994, in conformity with the Luxembourg 'non-paper' and with the Italian position. He was opposed by the British, Dutch, and Germans who wanted tough entry conditions. The Germans in particular soon put him and Trichet on the defensive by making it clear that there was a trade-off: that automatic entry into stage 2 was at the price of emptying stage 2 of any significant content. The French struggled to give real substance to this transition period.

In pursuit of this idea Trichet returned to the older French idea of getting the ERM anchored in the Treaty of Rome. At the IGC on 19 March he proposed tying entry to stage 2 to annexing the EMS into the Treaty in order to ensure that ERM participation was made irreversible. This step was justified as a guarantee of convergence in stage 2, making tough conditions for this transition less relevant. The position was further developed by Bérégovoy at the IGC on 10 June when, with the Danes, he sought to make the narrow band of 1.5 per cent legally binding in stage 2. In the process he came into sharp conflict with Lamont who saw this proposal as an infringement of national sovereignty. Bérégovoy was concerned with more than the objective of stimulating faster convergence by this means. He wanted to add a new political element to the content of stage 2. And, in particular, he wanted an arrangement that would require all to move in step to stage 3. But by the IGC on 7 October Bérégovoy had shifted his position on a narrow-band ERM imposed by Treaty requirement. His shift reflected the influence of de Larosière, who had spelt out to him the considered view of the Committee of EC Central Bank Governors: that it was risky in market terms to attempt to set a timetable for a narrowing of ERM bands without adequate convergence already in place. Bérégovoy had instead adopted the idea of a two-year period in the narrow band of the ERM as a condition for entry into stage 3.

The Finance Ministry found itself in a more defensive and uncomfortable position on the question of whether independence for national central banks was a condition for stage 2. Bérégovoy was extremely reluctant to concede on this point. Various lines of defence were used: that, for instance, it was not a pressing issue for the Germans if it was agreed that responsibility for monetary policy in stage 2 remained assigned to the national level; and that price stability was fundamentally a matter of political will and consensus, not institutional arrangements. But it was clear that Tietmeyer and others were looking for a clear demonstration of French goodwill on stability. By Apeldoorn Bérégovoy had in private conceded on this point to the Germans, whilst emphasizing his domestic difficulties to Waigel. But in the very final stages of the negotiations in Scheveningen Lamont came unwittingly to Bérégovoy's rescue, taking an uncompromising stand that this proposal was unacceptable. Waigel intervened to signal that the Germans would not continue to press on this issue in the context of agreement on a weak content to stage 2. Bérégovoy's relief and gratitude were palpable to his officials.

A key French objective for stage 2 was to reinforce and extend the use of the *écu*. This objective was already a traditional element of French monetary diplomacy and a long-standing source of difficulty with the Germans. But even by Apeldoorn in September Bérégovoy and Trichet had not clarified the implications of their Draft Treaty's support for the *écu* as a strong and stable currency. They had not declared themselves either for 'freezing' the value of the *écu* in stage 2 (the Commission, Dutch, and Italian view) or for 'hardening' the *écu* (the British, German, and Spanish view). This issue was for the Trésor secondary to the promotion of the *écu* in the transition period as the basis for it becoming the single currency in stage 3. Trichet pursued this objective with vigour in the Franco-German bilaterals, being prepared to make concessions to overcome German reluctance to see the 'basket' *écu* as the basis for the single currency. The main concession made to achieve this objective was on provisions for exchange-rate management of the single currency that favoured a veto role for the ECB and dropped the stronger word 'guidelines' from treaty provisions on the role of the Council in this field.

At the beginning of the IGC negotiations the French government lined up alongside the EC Commission's and the Italian interpretations of the Rome 1 communiqué on the stage 2 institution, arguing for the creation of the ESCB at the start of stage 2 and the allocation to it of some operational tasks. These tasks included 'reinforcing the co-ordination of monetary policies' and 'supervising the development of the *écu*'. But Bérégovoy and Trichet faced an uphill task in the face of German intransigence and German exploitation of the problem of consistency in French positions: between the French government's initial acceptance of the principle that monetary policy was to remain the responsibility of the member states in stage 2 and the objective of trying to ensure that stage 2 was not reduced to an empty shell. The former acted as a constraint on the latter. By the IGC on 9 April it was clear that, though Trichet continued to support the idea of a new institution with substantial tasks, he was distancing himself from the proposal that the ESCB should be given responsibility for co-ordination of monetary policies. For this reason the Belgian proposal for the European Monetary Institute (EMI) to 'prefigure' the ECB was very welcome to the Finance Ministry. This arrangement underlined the point that the stage 2 institution was not a lender of last resort in the classic central bank manner.

From July much French negotiating energy was spent on adding to the tasks of the EMI so that it was clearly distinguished from the Committee of EC Central Bank Governors. In this respect French negotiators felt that they had been effective in gaining ground. They pressed successfully for the EMI to be endowed with its own resources to finance its operations (their proposal was for it to have its own capital); to have an independent legal personality; to have its own seat; to have an externally appointed President (by common accord of the heads of state and government); to have the task of preparing stage 3 (on which they supported the Italian proposal strongly); to promote the development of the *écu*; to be able to give opinion and make recommendations on monetary policy and exchange-rate policy by a two-thirds majority (instead of unanimity); and to be enabled to hold and manage foreign-exchange reserves as an agent of national central banks. By the IGC ministerial level on 11–12 November most of these points had been gained, though Köhler held out for longer on the foreign-exchange reserve issue. At best these gains were a reasonable compromise. De Larosière and many in the Trésor saw a danger in trying to develop the role of the EMI too far. With a stronger EMI the momentum to proceed to stage 3 would slacken. At worst these negotiating gains were to be seen as rearguard actions to cover retreat from the traditional French position which stressed collective exchange-rate management as the basis of the transition to EMU and the idea of co-ordination of monetary policies in stage 2.

Excessive Deficits: Criteria, Procedure, and Sanctions

The criteria, procedure, and sanctions to avoid excessive deficits played a major part in French negotiating objectives. They were, above all, crucial to ensuring that stage 2 was not empty and that 'gouvernement économique' was given some substance. In addition, clear and tough criteria in a binding form with sanctions reflected a traditional Trésor position of favouring firm discipline on domestic policies. There was in fact no reference to criteria in the French Draft Treaty, essentially because work was ongoing in the EC Monetary Committee on deficit and debt levels. But the Finance Ministry had no difficulty with this idea. With the prospect that loss of foreign-exchange reserves would no longer operate as a sanction on governments once stage 3 began, the Finance Ministry saw the need to establish a new basis of credibility for EMU in the financial markets. Hence it

- introduced the concept of a 3 per cent budget-deficit criterion into the negotiations;
- advocated the incorporation of the criteria in the treaty;
- argued for unanimity, not qualified majority, as the basis for amending reference values written into the treaty;
- took the lead in supporting a wide range of sanctions on excessive deficits (in particular, ineligibility for EIB borrowing, suspension of payments from EC institutions and commitments from the Structural Funds, fines, compulsory non-interest-bearing deposits, and suspension of ESCB operations in debt instruments issued by a government);
- sought to restrict the operation of the proposed financial assistance mechanism by pressing for decisions based on unanimity (rather than qualified majority) and a strict definition of shocks qualifying states for support; and
- pressed for ERM membership as the basis for defining one of the key criteria.

De Boissieu was important in two respects in this area. First, he acted as internal advocate of French sponsorship of the convergence criteria and especially the 3 per cent budget-deficit criterion. Mitterrand was prepared to concede on this issue by two arguments coming from the Foreign Ministry: that the President had actually endorsed the 3 per cent figure in 1982; and that tough criteria would be a signal of French seriousness and determination to the Germans. In addition, de Boissieu was active in arguing that the right of initiative in the excessive-deficit procedure must be shared between the EC Commission and the member states. He was once again concerned to situate this procedural issue in the context of the wider French position on the European union. In doing so de Boissieu came into conflict with the Dutch, the Italians, and, not least, with Delors. The French argued that the EC Commission might fail to bring cases of excessive deficit before the Council and that it should be restricted to bringing forward only recommendations, not proposals which would require unanimity to modify. They doubted the Commission's devotion to *rigueur*, and they focused on the issue of designing an efficient procedure. This tough French position was particularly apparent at the IGC meeting on 22 October when Ravasio from the Commission spoke strongly against the French position. It was a position that was also supported by the Germans.

The specification of the convergence criteria was decisive for the French not just as a means to give content to stage 2 but also as the tests for the all-important transition to stage 3. In viewing them the Finance Ministry was concerned about its reputation. Clear and tough criteria were a demonstration of commitment to be alongside the 'stability-oriented' states, to be at least as virtuous on deficits and debt as the Dutch and Germans. From this perspective the idea of weak, imprecise criteria was anathema to the French. But at the same time Bérégovoy was determined to position himself as a proponent of Community solidarity by finding a formula that would not exclude a state like Italy in advance. He worked with Wim Kok, with the Spanish Finance Minister Carlos Solchaga and the Belgian Philippe Maystadt for a compromise, including a French proposal for cyclically adjusted deficits. After Apeldoorn on 22 September the notion of combining tough criteria with provision to take account of a trend in a favourable direction gathered support. The final outcome, with its specific reference values and scope for discretionary judgement, was in this respect a resounding success for the French.

The ECB Draft Statute and External Monetary Policy

With respect to the ECB, by contrast, the French government was more obviously on the defensive, fighting limited rearguard actions against the background of Bundesbank successes in getting its key objectives enshrined in the Delors Report and in the work of the Committee of EC Central Bank Governors on the ECB's draft statute. French negotiators pursued the objective of enshrining the principles of subsidiarity, of Community solidarity, and of democratic legitimacy and accountability in the design of the ECB. A range of French initiatives ran into opposition: notably that the sole subscribers to, and holders of, the capital of the ECB should be member governments; that the President of the Council should be able to suspend ECB decisions for two weeks and to present motions for deliberation to the ECB's governing council; and that council members should be accountable to national parliaments as well as to the European Parliament. These proposals were firmly rejected by the Germans and the Dutch, notably at the IGC on 8 October, with the exception of the Presidency's right to submit motions. On just one of these issues—the capital of the ECB— the French dug in their heels till the very end, entering one of just two French reservations at the end of the IGC, but in vain.

The main French negotiating success was on the question of whether all states should find a place under the roof of the ECB (the position of de Larosière and Bérégovoy) or whether those states with a derogation should be completely excluded (the view of Tietmeyer and André Szasz of the Dutch central bank). Bérégovoy argued, with Christophersen, Carli, and Solchaga, that the EMI 'prefigured' the ECB (he was attracted by Carli's conception of the architecture of EMU outlined in Chapter 12) . Hence the EMI should disappear with the ECB's creation. They supported the Dutch Presidency's proposal for a distinction between the governing council (limited to those who entered stage 3) and the assembly (including all EC central banks and facilitating co-operation between 'ins' and 'outs'). This proposal was seen in Paris as a victory for the principle of Community solidarity.

But the most problematic issue of all affecting the ECB related to the external aspects of monetary policy. The French negotiating position was to ensure Council responsibility for laying down 'guidelines' for the Community's exchange-rate policy; that it should do so by qualified majority; and that it would be required to 'consult' the ECB. At the IGC on 12 March Franco-German conflict on this issue reached its high point. It continued at the IGC ministerial level meeting on 18 March when Bérégovoy used the Plaza and Louvre Agreements of the 1980s as examples of how involvement by political authorities could contribute to greater exchange-rate stability. Within the subsequent Franco-German bilaterals it became clear that this conflict was rooted in sharply contrasting beliefs. French negotiators gave primacy to exchange-rate stability, in particular as a domestic discipline; German negotiators were fixated on domestic stability, seeing the exchange rate as a residual factor. French negotiators also had a more political conception of external monetary policy, seeing it as bound up in issues of political power at the international level that were beyond the proper competence of central bankers. This conflict ran on into the final 'end-game' of the negotiations. The French were able to retain the notion of Council responsibility for agreeing an exchange-rate system and for exchange-rate policy. But unanimity was required for agreement of an exchange-rate system; the term 'general orientations' replaced 'guidelines' in relation to exchange-rate policy; and the French conceded that 'these general orientations shall be without prejudice to the primary objective of the ESCB to maintain price stability'.

The Transition to Stage 3: Making EMU Irreversible

By the time that the IGC got under way the idea of a stage 3 beginning in 1996–7 was already circulating freely within the French government. As part of the Rome 1 communiqué, 1 January 1997 had been identified as the last date for a report on progress, especially on convergence, as the basis for a decision on entry to stage 3 'which will occur within a reasonable time'. On behalf of the Committee for the Monetary Union of Europe, Giscard d'Estaing was active in pressing for a more specific commitment to entry into stage 3 in 1996–7. This proposal had been endorsed at its meeting on 7 December 1990 in Rome. Delors was discussing 1996–7 as the date for stage 3 with Guigou in early 1991; whilst Giscard d'Estaing actively lobbied Mitterrand, Bérégovoy, and Delors. Bérégovoy was more sceptical. He could see the problem of trying to fix a final date when there were significant north–south differences on what was practical and when retaining Community solidarity in the transition was a critical issue. He noted that the Spanish Finance Minister Solchaga was proposing 1999. Hence the French Draft Treaty on EMU confined itself to indicating that by the end of 1996 the Council would verify that the conditions for stage 3 were in place and 'lay down the period within which the decision to enter the final stage shall be taken'. Bérégovoy was more interested in the procedure for defining the conditions than in a final date.

The French took the lead once the issue of transition to stage 3 was taken up at the IGCs on 23 April and 6 June. At the IGC on 2 April Trichet had added a sixth principle to the five presented by Nigel Wicks: the irreversibility of the transition to stage 3, stressing that it was an essential point in the Delors Report. In doing so he revealed the gap between French and British positions and confirmed the Finance Ministry's emerging view that the British were not serious partners in the negotiations. On 23 April Trichet proposed three basic principles to govern the procedure for transition to stage 3: 'no veto, no compulsion, no arbitrary exclusion', designed to avoid British veto and to prepare the way for a British derogation. On the institutional aspect he proposed that the European Council should assume responsibility for this issue, voting by qualified majority. By June it was clear that there was broad endorsement of these principles and of the role of the European Council. But, though they became the common point of reference, the interpretation of these principles proved problematic and divisive right up to the Maastricht Council. What was at least clear in the Luxembourg draft of June was that the process of deciding on the beginning of stage 3 would begin by the end of 1996.

The difficulties of interpretation of the 'no coercion' principle were revealed by the sharp reaction to the Dutch Draft Treaty proposal on the transition to stage 3 submitted at the end of August. This draft was in direct conflict with the French commitment to the 'irreversibility' of stage 3. It provided for an 'opt-in' by states that met the conditions for entry and for a 'critical mass' of six to eight states to be ready and willing. Delors and Guigou mobilized a sense of shock in

Paris that the Dutch had taken a step back from the Luxembourg Draft Treaty provisions. The French view was clear: the 'no coercion' principle was best satisfied by 'opt-outs' for specific countries, not a generalized 'opt-in'. The British problem was being solved at the expense of making EMU irreversible.

The Dutch draft was important in fuelling French diplomatic efforts behind the principle of irreversibility, especially *vis-à-vis* the Germans, with de Margerie lobbying the German Chancellery. Bérégovoy was severely critical of the Dutch proposal at the ECOFIN on 9 September, focusing on the risk that it created of a 'two-speed' EMU. He also brought direct pressure to bear on Wim Kok, who on 29 October produced a new Draft Treaty on EMU. But it still failed to meet French objections. It offered a 'generalized opt-out': within six months of the Council's decision to move to stage 3 any state could exempt itself. This formula was now ameliorated by the proposal for attaching to the treaty a declaration of political commitment to full participation in stage 3.

In the Foreign Ministry and the Elysée the main objection was the lack of a firm legal commitment to make EMU irreversible. A calendar for EMU was seen as absolutely essential. Dumas sought out Genscher's suppport on this issue, pressing in October for 1996; de Margerie focused on Hartmann and Bitterlich; whilst Mitterrand reminded Kohl that the German Chancellor had been recognizing the need for a timetable to complete EMU since May. For Bérégovoy the key issue remained a critical mass as a condition of going forward. In order to reduce the threat of a state being excluded he proposed in the IGC that the European Council should agree to move to stage 3 by a qualified majority of at least eight states. Here he gained the support of the Commission, Italy, Spain, and Belgium. Again in pursuit of the principles of irreversibility and 'no exclusion', Trichet argued at the IGC on 1 October that the procedure for ensuring the appropriateness of entering stage 3 should be repeated more frequently than once every two years as the Dutch Draft had proposed.

Bérégovoy and his officials had identified by November three key issues relating to the passage to stage 3. On the 'no coercion' principle they were fundamentally opposed to the 'generalized opt-out' and favoured dealing with Britain by means of a special derogation in a separate protocol attached to the Treaty. They also saw such an 'opt-out' as involving exclusion from the governing council of the ECB. On this point there was complete agreement with the Elysée and the Foreign Ministry. The second issue of a 'critical mass' was seen as very important and dependent on ensuring that, contrary to the Dutch Draft, the decision on stage 3 was not limited only to those states qualifying under the conditions.

The third main concern was to ensure a balance between respect for clear, tough criteria and political judgement in the decision to move to stage 3. Bérégovoy understood that at Apeldoorn it had been recognized that the decision by the European Council would involve an element of political judgement about how to interpret objective economic criteria. But on the date for stage 3 he was not pursuing a fixed, final date. As he saw it, the European Council would decide on the principle of a transition to stage 3 once it judged that sufficient states had met the convergence criteria. Only then would it fix the date. In short, Bérégovoy expected that the Treaty would leave the European Council with discretion on the final date. What was important—and the subject of discussions with the Germans—was the idea of a protocol on irreversibility. Thierry Walrafen, economic counsellor in the French Embassy in Bonn, was reporting that Bundesbank officials were not happy with an 'open-ended' stage 2, a 'grey zone' in which EMU might lose direction. They wanted some kind of commitment from the French to go to stage 3. Hence agreement with the Germans on such a protocol seemed relatively unproblematic. It was not a matter of putting pressure on the Germans. In this context French officials set to work on drafting a protocol on irreversibility, but—consistent with their reading of Bundesbank thinking—without reflecting on a final date for stage 3.

The 'End-Game': Achieving Irreversibility

French diplomacy during the 'end-game' was motivated by two themes: of 'binding in' domestic parliamentary and party opinion behind the strategy of the French government; and of 'rescuing Maastricht' at the EC level. Domestic political management was eased by the clear opinion-poll evidence of substantial support for a strengthening of European integration, with figures improved on those of 1989. A poll conducted for Le Monde on 29–30 November registered less than 40 per cent as frightened of the process, with 52 per cent feeling that they had more to gain (35 per cent feared that they might lose). On the issue of a single currency 75 per cent were favourable (up from 68 per cent in May 1989) and 21 per cent opposed (1 per cent up). But, despite this favourable domestic context to measures transferring sovereignty, there were new rumblings of anxiety within the political parties. Chirac was critical of an EC Commission that was too amenable to American pressure; Séguin wrote in Le Figaro on 27 November of 'making Europe against the states', 'of a leap into the unknown'. Conversely, Jean Arthuis (CDS), Bosson (CDS), and Alain Lamassoure (UDF) together with thirty-eight other deputies attacked the 'democratic deficit' promoted by the French government in a joint statement; whilst Giscard d'Estaing (UDF) criticized the failure to propose a 'decentralized' federal Europe.

   In part to appease anxious deputies, in part to discipline them in the face of the impending final negotiation, and in part to strengthen their negotiating hand at Maastricht, the government agreed to a special debate on Maastricht in the National Assembly on 27 November. In the previous week Dumas and Guigou, and—as a gesture of symbolic importance—Genscher, had appeared before the Assembly's Foreign Affairs Committee. But, when the same two politicians led up the government's presentation on 27 November, they encountered a more hesitant and qualified support across the political parties—with the exception of the CDS. Dumas's speech on 27 November underlined the priority to EMU in the French negotiating position. He spoke of the economic and monetary 'body' requiring a suitably adapted political 'head'. Guigou brought home the international dimension of EMU, stressing that, by uniting, Europeans would gain more in strength than by taking their chance in isolation from each other. It was Dumas's reference to 'a fundamental change towards a supranational entity' that sparked Gaullist criticism, led by Pierre Mazeaud. Alain Juppé spelt out the Gaullist line as support for a 'Europe of the nations' and rejection of a 'federal construction'. For the Socialist Party, its spokesperson André Bellon emphasized 'the expression of national identities'. Despite the gap between the strong pro-Europeanism of Dumas and Guigou and the reservations that they encountered, the Assembly debate served its purposes. On the other hand, the absence of a vote hid the underlying cleavages that were already beginning to open up before Maastricht.

The theme of 'rescuing Maastricht' served an important mobilizing purpose behind French diplomacy and the activation of the Franco-German relationship from September onwards. It was precipitated by two events and a consequent crisis in Franco-Dutch relations: the Dutch Draft Treaty proposal on the transition to stage 3, with its 'generalized opt-out'; and then, on 30 September, the rejection of the Dutch Draft Treaty on political union, with its federalist ambitions, which was seen as a direct challenge to Paris. Mitterrand was much more interventionist on political union than on EMU, working closely with Dumas. He and Kohl set de Margerie and Bitterlich to work to produce at great speed a Franco-German initiative on security and defence, which was submitted to the Dutch Presidency on 16 October. On EMU Mitterrand's preoccupation was limited to securing irreversibility. This objective was easy to define negatively. It meant getting rid of the 'generalized opt-out' proposal. To secure this objective he had to overcome Kohl's reluctance to see Britain singled out and isolated. But it was more difficult still to give a clear substantive political and legal content to irreversibility. Mitterrand was more interested in irreversibility as a philosophical and historical concept. It proved not easy to engage him in its legal and political difficulties. He was, however, attracted by the idea of a French initiative to attach a special protocol on irreversibility to the Treaty. This idea derived from de Boissieu in the Foreign Ministry. Its first and initial purpose was to address the principle of 'no veto'. All states, whether they met the conditions for stage 3 or not, would 'respect the will of the Community to enter swiftly into the third stage, and therefore no member state shall prevent the entering into the third stage'. The idea of such a protocol was agreed with Kohl during November. But at that stage there was no reference to a final date.

On the idea of a final fixed date Giscard d'Estaing emerged as an influential lobbyist from mid-November. At its meeting on 13 November in Brussels the Committee for the Monetary Union of Europe spoke out strongly against the 'generalized opt-out' formula and proposed a final date for stage 3. Here Giscard was influenced by the pessimism and scepticism of Helmut Schmidt, who expressed his fears of sabotage by the Bundesbank and of German public opinion turning away from EMU by the end of the 1990s. Schmidt's message was clear: an early final date was necessary. Immediately afterwards, Giscard lobbied strongly in Brussels and in Paris, focusing on Mitterrand, Delors, and Bérégovoy. The Committee's proposal was also taken up by Delors with Mitterrand and by Delors's cabinet with Guigou and, in particular, with the Prime Minister, Cresson. Bérégovoy saw the proposal as unrealistic, given the likely divergence between northern and southern states on a 'realistic' date. But a web of support for the idea was beginning to take shape, and Bérégovoy was about to find himself caught up in that web.

The concern to 'rescue Maastricht' was reflected in two developments in Paris. The special restricted Council of Ministers' meetings on Maastricht took on a new importance, initially debating the 'opt-out' problem and moving on only at the very end to the issue of a final date. More specifically, Cresson was given responsibility for overseeing the negotiations on the transition to stage 3 and on industrial policy. On both issues she was active at the Franco-German summit in Bonn on 14–15 November, meeting separately with Kohl and with Waigel, and pressing the vital importance of irreversibility.

On irreversibility a close link emerged between the Matignon and Delors's cabinet in Brussels. The link was provided by François Lamoureux, who had till recently served in Delors's cabinet before moving to Cresson's cabinet. Through this linkage the head of Delors's cabinet, Pascal Lamy, was able to activate attention to the cluster of pressing issues that came under the heading of the transition to stage 3, notably a final date. But, interesting as this Paris–Brussels linkage was, its impact was diluted by two factors. First, Cresson's star as Prime Minister was in rapid descent. She had too little personal authority to assert herself in this area. In fact, she was more comfortable with the other special brief given to her for Maastricht: to write industrial policy into the treaty. Secondly, her relations with Bérégovoy were especially poor. His sensitive political antennae told him that he should cultivate a very close direct relationship with Mitterrand on this key issue rather than allow it to be mediated through the 'erratic', 'unreliable', and 'unprofessional' Cresson who might give birth to a formula that would frighten off the Germans, and the financial markets, at the worst time. The two were locked in conflict as Bérégovoy signalled an emerging and potentially serious budget-deficit problem whilst Cresson's instincts were to rail against financial constraints.

On the transition to stage 3, lines of influence became even more spaghetti-like than usual for the Mitterrand Presidency. Guigou was closer to Delors than was Cresson but less privy than before to the thinking of Mitterrand and what was going on in the Dumas–Mitterrand relationship. She was promoting irreversibility and, by the end of November, a final, fixed date. But she lacked an executive role on the issue and suffered from a poor personal relationship with Cresson. Cresson had the advantage of being given an executive role on stage 3, was close to the ear of the President, and was kept active on a final date by Lamoureux, particularly in pressing Bérégovoy to seize the initiative in this area.

But Bérégovoy was determined to retain control of this negotiation and deal directly with Mitterrand, and Cresson lacked Guigou's familiarity with EMU issues. The Finance Ministry was also intent on keeping Lamoureux at a distance from the drafting of any proposals. Meanwhile, in the background Delors was stressing to Mitterrand, Dumas, and Guigou the vital importance of a precise final date. It was presented as part of the Community method and also as a necessary means of 'binding in' the Germans. Deeper in the background was the figure of Giscard d'Estaing and Mitterrand's desire not to be outclassed by him as a European statesman. At a distance from these complex relationships, Dumas and Mitterrand pursued the issue of a fixed, final date on their own with the Germans, especially during Kohl's visit to Paris on 3 December. But each player had only a very partial view of the larger picture.

During the key part of the 'end-game' Mitterrand had problems in imposing his will. Distracted by illness, he had problems in sustaining a role as *animateur*. Cresson's inability to impose herself on the work of the government increased the sense of a lack of consistent and reliable leadership. The problem was compounded by the fact that Mitterrand had no one within the Elysée who had the confident grasp of EMU issues that had been possessed by Guigou. He retreated into an enigmatic privacy. But, if leadership faltered, it did not amount to a political vacuum. Mitterrand, advised by Dumas and Cresson and cajoled by Delors, felt that Bérégovoy was not being vigorous enough in translating the principle of irreversibility into a timetable written in clear treaty language. As earlier in January, the Finance Minister was boxed into position. There were three key meetings in Paris. On the occasion of the Council of Ministers' meeting on 27 November Mitterrand asked what had to be done to make EMU irreversible. Guigou answered by arguing that the only way was to set an irrevocable final date and that the EC finance ministers had failed to do this. At the end of the subsequent discussion, in which Bérégovoy elaborated his concerns about the practicalities, Mitterrand did not take a decision. He waited till a private meeting afterwards with Bérégovoy at which he made it clear that he expected Bérégovoy to overcome his reluctance and deliver a timetable before Maastricht.

Meanwhile, on 28 November, encouraged by Lamoureux, Cresson convened a special ministerial meeting to prepare the Maastricht summit. It was attended by Bérégovoy, Dumas, Guigou, and twelve other ministers; by Védrine and de Margerie from the Elysée; by Lamoureux from the Matignon; and by de Boissieu and Trichet. On EMU only one issue was discussed—the transition to stage 3—on which Bérégovoy, Dumas, and Guigou spoke. Here Guigou, supported by Dumas, raised the matter of a final fixed date. The meeting gave Bérégovoy two instructions: that the Treaty must contain a reference to a fixed date before 31 December 1998 when the transition to stage 3 would be decided; and that the decision would be taken either by consensus or, in its absence, by qualified majority—without participation by those states with a derogation or exemption.

Hence just two days before the final marathon negotiating sessions in Scheveningen and Brussels, work began in the Trésor and Bérégovoy's cabinet on a text designed to make the transition to stage 3 irreversible whilst respecting the three principles earlier agreed—'no veto, no compulsion, no arbitrary lock-out'. Faced with his knowledge of the views of Waigel and Köhler on the importance of meeting the criteria for the passage to stage 3, Bérégovoy was inclined to caution. He had two options: to propose a fixed date; or to put in place a procedure to ensure that the European Council fixed a final date. He was inclined to the latter. The Bérégovoy plan was presented to the IGC on 2 December and considered as part of the very last business when most delegations were exhausted and concentration was lapsing. By then he had two successes under his belt. At Scheveningen the 'generalized opt-out' was finally removed, to the anger of Lamont. In addition, the French Draft Protocol on irreversibility had been agreed. These successes opened up the opportunity to seize the initiative on the formula for the transition.

The Bérégovoy plan allowed for two procedures (permissive and mandatory) to fix the date by the European Council, which was to adopt the voting rules of the Council of Ministers. It permitted the European Council to agree to fix a date for stage 3 in 1996 on two conditions: that there was unanimity (though a state with a derogation or exemption could not act as an obstacle to that unanimity); and that at least seven states met the criteria. Here Bérégovoy was inserting into the text his concern about a 'critical mass' that had not surfaced in the Matignon Agreement on 28 November. Alternatively, the European Council must agree to set a date for stage 3 in 1998. In this case the conditions applying in 1996 were removed: the decision was to be by simple majority; and there would be no critical mass. The Draft also provided for derogations, and for their abrogation, to be decided by simple majority. Given its late tabling, there was a desultory discussion of its contents. It was decided to refer it (with German reservations about the use of a simple majority in 1998 and the fact that states with a derogation or exemption could take part in that vote) to the EMU technical working party, with an instruction to the Dutch Presidency to work it into acceptable treaty language in time for an extra meeting of EC finance ministers to consider it at Maastricht. The Dutch draft on the transition to stage 3 emerged on 5 December. During this final negotiation, which was the occasion for tensions and arguments between Köhler and the Dutch, Bérégovoy benefited from the strong personal support of Kok for a clear timetable for EMU. But what remained for Maastricht was a procedure for setting a final date but no specification of what that date would be.

What followed at Maastricht surprised both Bérégovoy and Trichet. Early on the morning of 3 December, Bérégovoy tested on Waigel the idea of a final date—1 January 1999– regardless of how many countries qualified—and even if only France and Germany qualified. But he failed to elicit interest, let alone support from Waigel who stressed that what mattered most for the political success of EMU was respect for the convergence criteria. Waigel's reaction was by no means seen as a rebuff. Bérégovoy was broadly happy with the reception of his plan for the transition to stage 3 and confidently expected that the Dutch Presidency could knock it into acceptable treaty language. It was clear that Mitterrand would have liked to have gone further. But, as far as Bérégovoy was concerned, a final date set in 1991 was simply unrealistic.

In fact, unknown to Bérégovoy, Mitterrand and Dumas raised the issue of a final date with Kohl at their final pre-summit meeting in Paris on the evening of 3 December. They did so in the context of discussions about the crisis in Yugoslavia and linkage was made to the issue of recognition of Croatia and Slovenia. This issue was known to be perceived as vital by the Germans. The message was clear: that German agreement to a fixed date for stage 3 could ease a French concession on recognition of Croatia and Slovenia. No deal was struck, but an informal understanding was arrived at.

This discussion with Kohl did not figure in the Council of Ministers' session on 4 December which was dedicated to Maastricht. Bérégovoy reported on the reception of his plan but was not made aware of any other French diplomatic efforts in this area. Dumas limited himself to simply stressing Kohl's commitment to irreversibility and the shared French and German positions on this issue. On the domestic front Mitterrand's central preoccupation at this final stage was to consult and 'bind in' the leaders of the main French political parties; whilst his press spokesman contrasted the unity within the government with the cacophony of discordant voices on Europe within the opposition, inviting the electorate to consider how a centre-right government could possibly achieve sufficient unity to negotiate effectively at Maastricht.

Mitterrand's programme of domestic political consultations was intensive. On 3 December he received Mauroy on behalf of the Socialist Party (who stressed the social dimension of Maastricht); Georges Marchais for the Communist Party (who saw EMU as the subordination of French policy to Germany and the banks); Chirac for the RPR (who gave more attention to the Yugoslav crisis); Barre for the UDF (who concentrated on the need to make EMU irreversible); Pierre Méhaignerie for the CDS (for whom a single currency and a European defence system were the two main prizes); and Gerard Longuet for the Republican Party (who emphasized the need to bring Britain into EMU so that it was not created as a D-Mark zone). The next day the President met Jean Lecanuet (CDS), President of the Foreign Affairs Committee of the Senate, and Jean François-Poncet (UDF), President of the Economic Affairs Committee. More important were his meetings on Friday 6 December, notably with François Périgot, President of the employers' organization the CNPF; with Delors; and with Giscard d'Estaing. Périgot took up the two issues of making EMU irreversible and of a stronger co-ordination of economic policies. In addition to pressing on Mitterrand the need to put the word 'federal' in the Treaty and to strengthen the European Parliament, Giscard focused on fixing as early a date as possible for the transition to stage 3—certainly no later than 1997.

The meeting with Delors on 6 December was made difficult by earlier public criticisms from the Commission President of the lack of French ambition in the political-union negotiations, especially on common foreign and security policy and the issue of extending qualified majority voting. But at their meeting Mitterrand and Delors identified common ground on EMU. They agreed that the British problem was to be dealt with by a special 'opt-out' and that the vital need was to make EMU irreversible and improve on existing drafts. What remained open was the question of how to achieve irreversibility. Delors criticized the Bérégovoy's plan of 2 December as not going far enough. In their analysis and prescriptions Delors and Mitterrand found common ground. They agreed that Kohl could be persuaded to accept a final date written into the treaty; that it was absolutely vital to firm up a date at the Maastricht Council; that to do so was no radical innovation but consistent with the established Community method of expediting business by setting dates; that by being boxed into a separate 'opt-out' the British had lost negotiating power on this issue; and that the best way to minimize the potential for opposition to mount against a final date was to table this at the last moment in Maastricht. Mitterrand confirmed that he would introduce the proposal at the beginning of the Maastricht Council. They also saw political advantage in a proposal that came from outside the Franco-German relationship.

Though the President's energy was dissipated by illness and the stress of preparing for so complex and tough a negotiation, he had been alerted to the prospect of fresh proposals at Maastricht. In an unusual move, he arrived early in Maastricht on 8 December for a quiet dinner at the request of Andreotti. The dinner took place in Mitterrand's small villa with only key officials present—de Margerie and Lauvergeon. Over an entrée of oysters Andreotti outlined an Italian proposal for inserting a final fixed date of 1 January 1999 in the Treaty to ensure irreversibility. Mitterrand remained aloof and seemingly distracted and was not interested in discussing the details of the text. But he made it clear that he was prepared to adopt and sponsor the Italian text. He indicated that he was happy to raise the proposal with Kohl at their breakfast meeting before the first session on 9 December and to introduce the Italian-drafted proposal at that session. At that breakfast meeting Mitterrand was much more engaged. Again, it was not the details that counted, for him or for Kohl. Their agreement was forged around the historical and political significance of making EMU irreversible. Mitterrand's skill was in persuading Kohl to agree for reasons of making history at Maastricht. By this means Europe would be guaranteed a qualitative leap forward.

For Mitterrand making EMU irreversible was the great French success story of the Maastricht negotiations. The British threat to making EMU irreversible had been overcome, first, by eliminating the 'generalized opt-out' and then, at the last moment, by introducing the device of a final fixed date for stage 3. These victories provided him with domestic political capital. They also offset French disappointments over social policy and defence, fields in which Mitterrand would have liked to secure more and where he felt that too much attention had been paid to accommodating the British. Strategically what counted was that he had made his main advances in the area that mattered most for French interests, EMU. But, paradoxically, that advance had been facilitated by the German insistence on writing irreversibility into the Treaty and Kohl's amenability to the idea of a timetable, not as a radical step but as part of the normal Community method of doing business.

Conclusions

In an interview on Antenne 2 on 11 December Mitterrand reflected on Maastricht by claiming: 'We are setting out on a great adventure, but it is a controlled adventure that has not been left to chance'. This claim touched on the very essentials of the French approach to European integration: that here was an opportunity for France to pursue change, but in a controlled manner consistent with better safeguarding French interests. Ultimately, Europe was to be embraced as a superior instrument for fortifying the state's traditional role as protector, shield, and defender of the interests of France. The conception of EMU in Paris stressed its role in making Europe the most powerful economic bloc in the world. By means of EMU Europe could begin to shape the process of global change in its own, and a French, image.

What was much less clear in 1991 was the scale and pace of domestic political, economic, and cultural change that meeting the conditions of EMU would impose on France. The history of France in the 1990s was to be marked by the growing recognition of this reality. In fact, this recognition began to surface with the process of ratifying the Maastricht Treaty, and especially during the referendum campaign in summer 1992. Public disquiet with the Treaty had much to do with a growing sense that its consequences would be not so much 'controlled' as 'sauvage'; that EMU might be not so much a shield and protector against the forces of the global market as a means of institutionalizing its imperatives. In calling a referendum on the Maastricht Treaty Mitterrand was confident that he could mobilize a Euro-friendly French public behind his flagging Presidency. The 'petit oui' of 51 per cent was to be a surprise. Fierce opposition was displayed from the PCF and the National Front on the flanks of the political spectrum and from within the RPR and even parts of the UDF. For Philippe Séguin Maastricht was 'anti-1789', subverting the inalienable principle of national sovereignty (Séguin 1992). On the PCF Left Maastricht was referred to as 'the Europe of economic war, of the law of the richest and the strongest. It is a Europe of domination in total opposition to a Europe of cooperation' (Ainardi 1992: 19). Threatened by this political development, from 1993 there were rising voices in the Socialist Party for a more activist European policy of the Left, focusing on popular issues of growth, employment, and social protection. These voices became louder once the Socialist Party went into opposition following the

Assembly elections of 1993. They were to lead in 1997 to the election of Jospin as a Socialist Prime Minister committed to meet certain conditions before France entered stage 3 of EMU: including a strengthening of the political component of EMU and Italian and Spanish membership.

In 1991–2 France was yet to be confronted with the full implications of just how politically difficult it would be to live with the tough realities of the convergence criteria during a protracted period of economic recession. That shock was to surface with the Presidency of Chirac and the strikes and demonstrations of November–December 1995. What materialized more quickly was the inaccuracy of Mitterrand's statement that nothing had been left to chance. By September 1992 the French franc was in a full-scale ERM crisis, pushed into the firing line after the forced exit of the pound sterling and Italian lira; under protracted attack in early 1993; and its troubles in July 1993 the occasion of an ECOFIN decision to widen the bands dramatically from 2.25 per cent to 15 per cent to save the French government the humiliation of a devaluation. In September 1992 France had been on the brink of exiting the ERM, a step that would have dealt a fatal blow to EMU (Aeschimann and Riché 1996: 155–7). This succession of events befell a France that Mitterrand had presented on 11 December 1991 as one of only two countries (the other was Luxembourg) fully meeting the convergence criteria agreed in Maastricht.

Both the IGC negotiations and their aftermath underlined an essential truth about French interests in EMU: that the gains were long term and involved substantial, and not always fully discerned short- and medium-term costs. Within the French government there was a unity of view about the long-term gains from sharing power over monetary policy at the European level rather than being in a situation of dependency in the 'D-mark' zone or cast adrift and at the mercy of the US-dominated global financial markets. That view had been formed in the aftermath of the March 1983 ERM crisis. On French interest in rebalancing economic and monetary power with the USA and Germany there was an impressive domestic political consensus stretching across parties on which the French government could build in pursuing EMU. The pursuit of this long-term gain in so sustained a manner has the attributes of heroic leadership, the sort of leadership that is seen as a hallmark of the Fifth Republic's strapping of directly elected Presidential power onto the apparatus and ethic of an administrative state that has a sense of operating on behalf of the general interest (Hayward 1983: chapter 1). EMU offered Mitterrand the opportunity to reinvent himself as the European statesman making history: to act as *animateur* and impresario of an impressively united French negotiating effort. His great domestic political achievement was to align the Socialist Party behind him on EMU by his effective use of the resources of the Presidential office combined with his skills as a party manager.

But, as the relationship between Mitterrand and Bérégovoy demonstrated, there were differences of domestic political views about preconditions for, and trade-offs in, the EMU negotiations. These differences related in particular to how far France should go in conceding German conditions for EMU. They crystallized around the issues of central bank independence and taxation on income from savings and around the political issue of 'balancing' Germany and fears of 'being alone' with Germany. The concessions were symptomatic of something more profound. France did not have the postwar economic credibility of Germany and could not aspire to found its strategy on exporting the French economic model as the basis for designing EMU. It was forced to adopt a strategy of indirection, of subtle private psychological pressure, seeking out the weak points in German positions and exploiting German fears of uncertainty about French policy. For the same reason it was tempted to a strategy of 'salami-slicing', of incrementally strengthening Franco-German collaboration or stage 2 so as to undermine the independence of the Bundesbank. What these strategic choices lacked was the confidence that comes from intellectual ascendancy over the terms of the debate about EMU. However much Bérégovoy might try to rebalance the intellectual argument with Germany by improving French economic performance, he failed to endow French negotiators with the confidence of their German counterparts and the sense that negotiators from other member states would readily fall in line behind French positions as the basis for securing a viable agreement. Intellectually and strategically, French negotiators were on the defensive across a wide range of issues.

Nowhere was the reality of France's position better captured than in the debate over 'gouvernement économique'. Here was the major French intellectual contribution to the EMU negotiations, proclaimed with the launch of the French Draft Treaty in January 1991. It crystallized social Catholic and social Radical traditions of economic policy, both influential within the Socialist government. Also behind it stood the edifice of values of the republican state, with the primacy it accorded to the political direction of policy and to volontarisme. In practice, the term was dropped as tactically inopportune in awakening German suspicions that the French motive was to 'hollow out' the meaning of central bank independence. It was a matter of saving elements of the concept in the details of the negotiations: in the reference to the role of the Council in the guidelines of economic policy, in exchange-rate policy, and in the procedure for the transition to stage 3. The convergence criteria and sanctions on excessive deficits—and later the Stability and Growth Pact—were also interpreted as giving substance to 'gouvernement économique'. These details were by no means unimportant. They offered opportunities to develop EMU, possibly in new ways. But they were agreed on German terms so as to restrict the potential for political challenge and damage to a stability-oriented EMU.

Ultimately, French strategy was made defensive and incremental by the underlying structural realities of the EMU negotiations. These structural realities favoured the power of German negotiators, to such an extent that many of the key points were already conceded before the IGC began. French negotiators recognized that German negotiators were being asked to concede the most for EMU: the surrender of the D-Mark, the foremost symbol of Germany's postwar economic achievement and—in Mitterrand's view—the equivalent of France's nuclear *force de frappe*. From the outset they had understood that their strategy on EMU must avoid antagonizing sensitive German public opinion and a delicate domestic political situation for Kohl. Early concessions meant that at least French negotiators stood to lose little in the IGC itself and could point to a reasonable success in incorporating the positions outlined in their Draft Treaty on EMU in the final agreement. And on one issue—the transition to stage 3—they were able to achieve more than the Finance Ministry thought viable in January 1991 and even as late as December. But they did so because German negotiators were united around the principle of making EMU irreversible, not contesting this principle with the French; and because by May 1991 Kohl had begun to speak of the need for a timetable for this purpose. The question was how to make it irreversible. On this vitally important technicality French policy was able to be successful because it was pushing at the open door of Kohl's convictions about the need to make European history at Maastricht. Mitterrand required for his success a political leader in Bonn prepared to act as the bold, heroic European statesman.

6

EMU, the Kohl Chancellorship, and German Political Tradition: The Legacy of Adenauer and Erhard

> I am a German, but I have always been a European . . . Therefore I have always fought for an understanding with France, without which a Europe is not possible.
>
> Konrad Adenauer (1968: 42)

> The only way to do justice to Adenauer's legacy is to treat it as a command to do likewise.
>
> Helmut Kohl (1976: 75)

On 4 October 1982, immediately after his election as German Chancellor, Helmut Kohl flew to Paris with his Foreign Minister Hans-Dietrich Genscher for dinner with President Mitterrand. The symbolic value of the visit lay in the primacy that it signalled to Franco-German reconciliation in the foreign-policy priorities of the new Chancellor. Its substantive content was made plain when Kohl spoke about history and drew on memories of his youth. He presented himself to the French President as the heir to the ideas of Chancellor Konrad Adenauer. At the same time Kohl stressed that he was the first Chancellor to come from the postwar generation, too young in 1945 to be embroiled in German war guilt. The controvery that this latter remark might have sparked was deflected by his central political messsage. Kohl saw himself as representative of a generation that had been touched to the core of its being by the Second World War, as someone who was determined to build a united Europe that would bind later generations, without these painful memories, to a pattern of European politics in which future war would be precluded. He was, in short, a 'European of the heart'.

This short visit left a vivid impression in the Elysée, one that was to be reinforced over time. Kohl was seen as a man with an acute sense of geography and history, firmly centred on his native Palatinate. His geopolitical views and historical outlook were embedded, like those of Adenauer (a Cologner), in the Rhineland in which both shared their roots.[1] From this frontier region they inherited a distinctive outlook which blended provincialism with a sense of a European identity and role. For both of them France was the most proximate

---

[1] On the impact of Adenauer's roots in Cologne see Baring (1969: 48–62); and Schwarz (1980).

power, its history intertwined with their own region, its Catholic and liberal values a source of solidarity and attraction. An historic reconciliation with France was an alternative to the past and tragic seductions of belief in a German 'special path' (*Sonderweg*), the consequence of which had been to leave Germany in physical and moral ruins. After 1945 Adenauer returned to the idea of close Franco-German co-operation that he had pursued in 1919 (Schwarz 1992). Inspiring this priority was a belief that peace in Europe could only be safeguarded if Germany was oriented away from its Prussian basis towards Western roots (Poppinga 1975). Franco-German reconciliation was bound up with his analysis of the historical roots of the German tragedy. As Adenauer wrote to Federal President Theodor Heuss in 1956: the only way to achieve European integration is for 'an ordering of (Germany's) relationship with France' (Adenauer and Heuss 1989: letter of 19 January). Building Europe with France was defined as the number one priority for Kohl, the task against which history would ultimately judge him. Like Adenauer, he was convinced that Europe could only be united on the basis of Franco-German reconciliation, of them acting together as the motor of the process of European integration (Pruys 1995).

Though EMU was not present amongst his political priorities in 1982—like Adenauer he thought rather vaguely in terms of European political union—a set of basic ideas was already in place into which that epic project could later be slotted and that would give it a sense of political direction, meaning, and legitimacy. From Paris Kohl flew directly to Brussels for a meeting of the executive of the European People's Party, which comprised Christian Democratic parties like his own. There his European vision was again in evidence. He remarked: 'If we do not make a decisive advance in Europe in this decade, we shall have missed the opportunity of our generation'.

Kohl as 'Grandson of Adenauer'

'Kohl as Adenauer's grandson' served as a valuable myth behind which Kohl could unite his party and coalition government by identifying himself with the memory of the 'founding father' of the postwar republic. It attached the new Chancellor to a policy legacy—notably European unification and Franco-German reconciliation—that had come to form a crucial part of the political consensus binding together German policies. Hence it helped to situate him 'above' party factionalism at a time when he was insecure in office. It also provided him with a means to mobilize electoral support across traditional class and confessional divides. In addition, the myth was important in offering him an opening for influence in Paris and other European capitals by stressing his preparedness to work for European unification in a context of revitalizing the best in German postwar tradition. Kohl was signalling externally that he was a man to be relied on when it came to using Franco-German relations as a means to transform Europe. This signal had two long-term effects. It created an opportunity for the

Elysée to press on him the case for EMU. It also provided Kohl with an opportunity to line up the reluctant Economics and Finance Ministries and the Bundesbank behind a policy of European unification and Franco-German reconciliation that had become part of the established consensus of the Federal Republic. Kohl had, in fact, one asset denied to Adenauer in his later years. He faced Mitterrand and not the mercurially unpredictable de Gaulle.

But, in other respects, the myth was less convincing. Kohl may have had the rudiments of an historical vision on entering office, but that vision was in substance borrowed from Adenauer rather than original. He also had to inhabit a more structured political system than that with which Adenauer had had to contend after 1949: in particular, the entrenched independence of the Bundesbank and of the Federal Constitutional Court and the more developed roles of the Economics and Finance Ministries at the EC level. In this respect his room for manoeuvre was more limited. Perhaps most seriously of all, Kohl did not cut an historic statesman-like figure, one possessed like Adenauer with a powerful command of rhetoric and an image as patriarch. Kohl's personality was in important respects different: charismatic, but lacking in the quiet dignity of Adenauer; similarly unpretentious and modest in lifestyle and expression, but less self-assured; warmer, more open, and less ascetic, but clumsier in manner and speech. He consciously modelled himself on the average citizen. His image was of a man who incorporated the virtues esteemed by ordinary Germans and with which they could identify: modesty in lifestyle, simple pleasure and pride in his native culture, food, and wine, dogged determination, sincerity, loyalty to friends, a firm sense of values, sentimentality, self-control (Busche 1998).

Yet, despite this attempt to instil public trust in himself, Kohl failed to deliver the kind of 'Chancellor bonus' in federal elections that was achieved by Adenauer in 1953 and 1957. It was not really till 1988 that he showed signs of growing into a statesman-like role and till 1989–90, with German unification, that he fully reinvented himself as the European statesman of historic rank, capable of inviting comparison with Adenauer. That process of political reinvention and growth was to prove timely and decisive in launching and bringing to successful conclusion the EMU negotiations. Kohl at Maastricht was a different figure from Kohl in the Elysée in October 1982. Even then, for instance in his speeches of 1990, he consciously modelled his message on Adenauer.

Adenauer was important for Kohl in another respect. His handling of the great events in European integration in the 1950s and early 1960s—the European Coal and Steel Community (ECSC), the abortive European Defence Community, the European Economic Community (EEC), and the Elysée Treaty—were sources of practical insights into strategy and tactics that, as a historian of the postwar CDU, Kohl had been careful to study. He had learnt from the master manoeuvrer the importance of a flexible and patient approach to unifying Europe, of reacting creatively to opportunities and threats as they presented themselves, and of being a tough, well-prepared negotiator. Above all, he recognized the vital political skills of avoiding dogmatism in European policy and playing the role of broker between rival party factions (Merkl 1962: 634–50; Schwarz 1997: 296). Kohl acquired the skill of 'sitting things out', of excelling others—often cleverer than himself—in the energy and patience that he devoted to finding a solution to a difficult problem (Dreher 1998). His approach to EMU was a matter of waiting for the right moment and then acting decisively. Another lesson that he learnt from Adenauer was about the danger of European unification becoming associated with German hubris. Moderation was vital if Germany was to build Europe on a basis of reassuring Germany's suspicious neighbours (Schwarz 1997: 295). Hence in relation to EMU it was crucial to work with France and to take French susceptibilities as a proud and wounded European power very seriously. In these ways his negotiating style on EMU was deeply indebted to Adenauer.

Kohl's attitudes to EMU owed a great deal to Adenauer. Adenauer had given little thought to EMU in the 1950s and 1960s and, unlike Ludwig Erhard, left no legacy of formed views on this issue. Indeed, more generally he had been uninterested in the technicalities of economic and monetary-policy debates. His attitude to the social-market-economy ideas of Ludwig Erhard had been in part formed by his anti-socialist attitudes and in part by essentially utilitarian considerations.[2] The test was political: did the social market economy offer a credible alternative to Marxism; and did it contribute to the electoral success of his Christian Democratic Union (CDU)? In fact, Kohl had fewer causes for reservation in espousing the social market economy than Adenauer. He did not have to fear Erhard as a political rival. Indeed, Erhard's great contribution was to have established the social market economy as part of the uncontested political consensus of the postwar republic and of the CDU in particular. It was a vital part of Kohl's inheritance, and one that Kohl had no hesitation in endorsing and working within. Moreover, unlike in Adenauer's period, the Economics and Finance Ministries had adapted themselves to the reality of life within the EC, helped by the economic benefits of enlargement in 1973 and 1981 in overcoming the perceived commercial disadvantages of a 'little Europe' of the Six.

But Kohl was no 'grandson of Erhard', a fact that was reflected in his views on EMU. He was no more interested in reflecting on political concepts of economic policy than Adenauer had been. His disposition was to test out economic advice with those close to the practical end of industry, banking and finance, and of political and electoral management. Kohl embraced economic liberalization with caution, measuring its benefits against the risks of short-term political damage, and inclining to slow down the tempo of change and concern himself with its social and political effects. His caution about economic theory was apparent in another respect. Like Adenauer, Kohl was inclined to view the social-market-economy doctrine in the context of the exigencies of European unification. Adenauer's conflicts with Erhard had been about priorities. For Adenauer, better that European unification should act as a brake on the social

[2] On the tensions and conflicts between Adenauer and Erhard, especially on Europe, see Nicholls (1994: 343–9).

market economy than that, following Erhard, the social market economy should constrain and hold back European unification. Fundamentally, like Adenauer, Kohl was driven by considerations of foreign and security policy. This similarity was apparent in the fact that both relied most of all on foreign and European policy advisers: Adenauer on Herbert Blankenhorn, Walter Hallstein, and Felix von Eckhardt; Kohl on Hans Teltschik, Peter Hartmann, and Joachim Bitterlich. When it came to matters of economic policy, they preferred the advice of 'practical' bankers to that of academic economists: Robert Pferdemenges and Hermann Josef Abs in the case of Adenauer, Alfred Herrhausen (like Abs from the Deutsche Bank) in the case of Kohl. A lesson that Kohl drew from Adenauer was that European policy was ultimately a matter for himself in conjunction with the Foreign Minister, not for the Economics and Finance Ministers acting alone. Hence he had little difficulty in inferring how Adenauer would have handled EMU.

EMU: Between European Unification and the Social Market Economy

Throughout his period of office Kohl's approach to EMU was conditioned and complicated by the interplay of two factors. First, he was, as we have seen, the 'grandson' of Adenauer and not of Erhard. He stood intellectually for the primacy of foreign and security policy considerations in designing strategy for EMU. Secondly, he presided over a party, government, and society characterized by a remarkable domestic political consensus embracing European policy and economic policy. As a politician reared in the consensual norms of German politics and ever alert to the electoral interests of his CDU party, Kohl sought to align himself within that consensus. This outlook also shaped his approach to designing strategy for EMU. But Kohl had to deal with the problem that, in reflecting on EMU, divergent strains within the consensus could contradict one another. The line of action that seemed to follow from an approach grounded in the social-market-economy doctrine could be difficult to reconcile with that based on a foreign- and security-policy viewpoint on German interests. Kohl was keenly alert to these potential internal contradictions in relation to EMU, notably between insistence on economic convergence as a basis for monetary union based on stability and a timetable to create irreversibility. Hence, though disposed to follow the commands of Adenauer's intellectual legacy, he was also mindful of Adenauer as the masterful manoeuvrer. On EMU Kohl was constantly keeping tactical alternatives up his sleeve, mastering the arts of keeping a number of balls in the air at once—most notably, ensuring EMU's irreversibility whilst guaranteeing that it would be a 'community of stability'. It fell to Genscher to nail down the pragmatically minded Kohl on EMU.

Before exploring the complex political dynamics of EMU under the Kohl Chancellorship it is important to examine the structural context of inherited policy beliefs and to set them against the backdrop of the German past. Their legacy was to be crucial for the manner in which EMU was debated in Germany, for the broad direction of German strategy on EMU under Kohl and the way in which German interests in EMU were defined, and for the way in which Kohl went about the task of legitimating that policy at home. The cognitive processes and the strategic behaviour of German negotiators, including Kohl, were in an important sense 'prestructured' by historically conditioned ideas. European unification (the legacy of Adenauer) and the social market economy (the legacy of Erhard) were part of a shared consensus within which German negotiators were wrapped. Their saliency as beliefs supported a strikingly high degree of co-operation and mutual learning in formulating agreed negotiating positions on EMU. All were constrained by a recognition that negotiating positions would have to be consistent with *both* sets of normative beliefs: that German interests required an irreversible process of EMU founded on stability and market principles and an independent European central bank. But there were also inconsistencies, tensions, and potential for discontinuity at work in German policy towards EMU, in part institutional in nature and in part related to differences of causal belief about EMU—about what was necessary to make EMU viable and workable.[3] The prime object of domestic discussions during the EMU negotiations was always the question of what were the essential conditions for a sustainably stable EMU and how could they be achieved. They did not involve the question of whether in principle EMU was desirable.

Within this framework of consensus and co-operation Kohl found himself operating with two loose but discernible coalitions of actors in constructing a negotiating strategy for EMU—what can be characterized as the 'security' coalition and the ordo-liberal coalition. Each derived its views on EMU from a different premise and defined German interests in EMU differently. Kohl was, as we have seen, in an ambiguous position. Intellectually, his views were most closely linked to the security coalition—of which Adenauer, Blankenhorn, and Hallstein can be seen as the mentors and Hans-Werner Lautenschlager and Bitterlich prime exponents in Bonn during the EMU negotiations. But politically Kohl had to seek out means of reconciling the two coalitions, of binding the more reluctant ordo-liberal coalition securely into his pro-EMU policy. What united the security coalition was the belief that EMU was centrally about binding Germany into Europe. EMU was perceived as at heart an historic and political issue of making European unification irreversible and securing a viable long-term framework for Germany's peace and prosperity. It legitimated a foreign-policy-driven approach to EMU, in which supranational institution-building was the motor of European integration and an element of political discretion essential to realizing the project. The institutional nucleus of this coalition was provided by the Foreign Ministry and the foreign policy division of the Federal Chancellor's Office. They were seen as having a special joint

---

[3] The degree of inconsistency and discontinuity is exaggerated in Kaltenthaler (1998*b*).

responsibility in the process of defining German interests in EMU, particularly in relation to preparing meetings of the European Council. Hence figures like Bitterlich, Hartmann, and Lautenschlager took on a key significance.

The ordo-liberal coalition was bound together by its belief in the primacy to be given to economic stability. EMU would inflict more damage than benefit to Europe if it were not constructed as a 'stability community'. The central role was accorded not to supranational institution-building but to the functional logic of market forces in ensuring a consistency and co-ordination of economic and monetary-policy behaviour. On this basis alone could a sound, viable, and sustainable European union be built. The ordo-liberal coalition gravitated around the Bundesbank, the Economics and Finance Ministries, and academic economists. As we shall see, Kohl's approach to EMU was conditioned by the fact that he inherited a German position on EMU that, from the 1970s, had come to be dominated by the ordo-liberal coalition.

Historical memory and narrative played an important constitutive role in sustaining the identity of each coalition. They were held together by shared narrative stories that shed particular light on how EMU was to be constructed. For instance, the experience of fixed exchange rates under the Bretton Woods system as negative for domestic monetary policy was deeply fixed in Bundesbank folk memories. The Bundesbank's responsibility for propping up this faltering system had created acute difficulties for its mission to maintain domestic price stability in the 1960s and 1970s. In consequence, its officials harboured a deep-seated caution about entering into, and discharging, external commitments, like the ERM. Even more deep rooted was the Bundesbank's sense of responsibility to avoid anything like the two hyperinflations (1922–3 and 1945–8) that had plagued Germany earlier in the twentieth century. In consequence, the Bundesbank's fixation on 'sound money' policies was deeply rooted in public expectations that it would fight inflation as the top priority. There was a strong pressure on Bundesbank council members and officials to meet these expectations. Both corporate and personal prestige and credibility were at stake in maintaining price stability, even—and especially—in difficult times (Kaltenthaler 1998a: 102–27). The Bundesbank's enormous prestige within Germany derived from its role in exorcizing the ghost of past inflations. In the process it has repeatedly defied pressure from the federal government (Sturm 1998).

The stock of historical memories on which the Foreign Ministry drew was different, relating to the requirements of German security in Europe after the shock and total disaster of two world wars. For its officials the greatest danger was the political isolation of Germany in Europe, consequent on frightening her neighbours into building alliances against her. German interests lay in constructing Europe on a different basis from 'balance of power' politics or the politics of unity around a hegemonic power. From this point of view the path from the EMS to EMU was welcomed as a means of insurance against war. It replaced potentially escalating political tensions directed against Germany as the 'anchor' of an asymmetric system with a balanced, stable structure for sharing of powers in EMU. In short, history—and its uses—penetrated contemporary discourse on EMU. German negotiators had different historical narratives to offer.

History was also important in privileging certain actors in the EMU debate. The best example was provided by Hans Tietmeyer. He was able to carve out a special role as the most articulate, tough, and persuasive exponent of the ordo-liberal approach to EMU. Tietmeyer's intellectual weight and authority within the EMU policy debate did not originate simply from his current posts: first as State Secretary in the Finance Ministry, then as a Bundesbank director and as Vice-President of the Bundesbank. It came from the fact that Tietmeyer could trace his practical experience and involvement with EMU policy to its origins in the Werner Group of 1970. Tietmeyer was in effect a 'founding father' of the ordo-liberal coalition on EMU, the high priest of 'coronation' theory. He embodied his own historical legitimacy.

It would, however, be a mistake to see EMU policy in Germany as the outcome of a war of position between contending coalitions. Policy learning and reflection was not simply confined to the internal world of each coalition but took place, crucially, between the two coalitions. The stimulus was provided, in part, by the Chancellor's ability to use his role in the European Council to present *faits accomplis* to German negotiators wedded to ordo-liberal ideas—as with the Delors Committee and the setting of a date for the IGC on EMU. Deadlines served to focus minds on producing agreed, clear, and therefore effective negotiating positions. There was also the effect of changes in the EC policy context that made EMU seem prima facie a more viable option to members of the ordo-liberal coalition. These changes included the practical experience of managing the ERM since 1979 and its role as a force for economic convergence, especially between France and Germany. The speed with which progress was made with the European single market programme after 1987 also made more credible the construction of a European economy on liberal principles. Finally, and crucially, German unification offered to the Chancellor a sudden opportunity to transform the terms of debate: to upgrade the significance of the foreign and security policy aspects of EMU.

The result of these changes was a rapid learning process in Bonn, involving a restructuring of policy arguments. One outcome was an emerging tension within the ordo-liberal coalition as central tenets of the traditional coronation theory of EMU were abandoned by German negotiators. Academic economists found themselves marginalized, and after Maastricht a large number reacted negatively. Another outcome was that members of the security coalition were made acutely sensitive to the requirement that German positions on EMU be seen to be endorsed by those in the ordo-liberal coalition. In, for instance, binding in the Bundesbank they were accepting that core tenets of ordo-liberalism would define German negotiating positions. But it was not so much a matter of making concessions to the ordo-liberal coalition as willingly endorsing the principles that they advocated. In this respect the inconsistencies and tensions can be exaggerated.

More seriously still, seeing EMU policy in terms of contesting coalitions reifies the source of ideas and tensions underpinning negotiating positions on EMU. Strictly speaking, these coalitions did not contest or provide knowledge. These contributions derived from individuals who were influenced in different, subtle, and complex ways by inherited ideas. Individual negotiators and officials fashioned in different ways the material of ideas and arguments on EMU with which they were provided. In doing so, various motives were at work: sheer intellectual inquisitiveness, institutional loyalty, career ambition, the desire to leave a personal stamp on policy, the search to survive by seeking out a sustainable consensus, and the effects of playing a particular role. This rich store of motivations means that German negotiators cannot be readily squeezed into two simple sets of belief without doing damage to the underlying reality. For instance, to a greater extent than his Foreign Minister Genscher, Chancellor Kohl was determined to avoid being entrapped by being seen as too partisan for a particular belief about how EMU should be constructed. His preoccupation was sounding out the prospects for consensus. Hence Kohl preferred to situate himself more astride the two coalitions as a referee or arbiter.

The contrast between Karl-Otto Pöhl and Helmut Schlesinger within the Bundesbank was instructive in this respect. Pöhl's preference was to manoeuvre between contending ideas on EMU, empathizing with different ideas in the manner of the monetary diplomat. Schlesinger was more the monetary technocrat, pursuing a particular policy belief with conviction. Within the Bundesbank there was a complex, differentiated set of views on EMU: ranging in the directorate from Claus Köhler, who was attracted by the 'binding-in-of-Germany' argument, to the sceptical Schlesinger. Role-play and socialization were also factors. Köhler was a Keynesian by background and worked closer to the practical problems of capital markets and banking. Schlesinger, with his background in the economics division, argued from a stricter ordo-liberal macroeconomic perspective. Wolfgang Rieke, by contrast, as head of the international division, was more sympathetic to the benefits of international and European monetary co-operation.

Tensions about EMU were fuelled by factors of individual personality and of ambition, pride, and vanity. Reputations had to be made and defended; careers were being promoted. Hans Tietmeyer's powerful presence was always a factor to be reckoned with. His immersion in, and familiarity with, EMU negotiations excelled that of all others. To others in the Foreign Ministry, and to his successors in the Finance Ministry, he could be a very uncomfortable, difficult character. Tietmeyer expected to be kept involved after leaving Bonn for the Bundesbank. For Horst Köhler, who succeeded him, the problem was to differentiate himself on EMU so as to make a personal mark whilst keeping Tietmeyer on side. Genscher, as Foreign Minister, and Theo Waigel, as Finance Minister, were always attentive to their personal profile and reputation on EMU matters, each seeking the ear of the Chancellor whilst cultivating media support. Another source of controversy was Bitterlich in the Chancellor's Office:

distrusted by Tietmeyer as 'Genscher's man' and for using his access to Kohl to stitch up agreements on EMU that put the Finance Ministry and Bundesbank in a difficult position, for instance after Rome 1. Another theme running through the EMU negotiations was the mounting personal animosity between Pöhl and Kohl.

The individual views of particular politicians and officials on EMU were shaped by specific idiosyncrasies of birth and of family, educational, career, and generational backgrounds. Key Chancellery officials like Bitterlich and Johannes Ludewig had attended the elite French National School of Administration (ENA), where both had become familiar with Delors. In consequence, better perhaps than anyone else, they were able to put themselves in the shoes of French negotiators. Franco-German relations was the ambience in which they shone. Geography also played a role. The frontier city of Aachen was the birthplace of Hartmann, a key foreign-policy official of Kohl, and of Hans Stercken, chair of the Foreign Affairs Committee of the Bundestag; whilst Bitterlich came from Saarbrücken. Wolfgang Schäuble, head of the Federal Chancellor's Office at the time of the Hanover European Council, and from 1991 chair of the CDU/CSU Parliamentary Party, represented the constituency of Offenburg on the frontier with Alsace. The foreign-policy spokesperson of the CDU, Karl Lammers, was a Rhinelander by birth. Each was influenced, in their individual ways, to give a primacy to Franco-German reconciliation and to the security aspects of those relations. They were all close to Kohl, himself born in the Palatinate. Similarly, on Europe Adenauer had been able to rely on Rhinelanders who shared his basic outlook and priorities: men like Hallstein, who came from Mainz, and Franz Etzel, Finance Minister from 1957 to 1961.

In addition, and further complicating the situation, there was institutional differentiation in the way in which particular sets of beliefs were interpreted. For instance, Economics Ministry, Finance Ministry, and Bundesbank officials and academic economists drew different conclusions about EMU from ordo-liberal ideas. Thus the Bundesbank took a more intransigent position than the Finance Ministry on exchange-rate policy in stage 3 and on the issue of an ERM realignment after German unification. The Foreign Ministry was disposed to take a more unequivocal line on European integration and EMU than the Federal Chancellor's Office which was torn between promoting European integration and playing the role of referee in the contest amongst ministries and arbitrating amongst different parties in the coalition government and amongst different CDU factions. Institutional interests and loyalties proved powerful motives for German negotiators. These help to explain why, though there might be tough internal discussions about EMU within the Bundesbank, once decisions were taken there was a strong premium on discipline in advocating positions. Wolfgang Rieke's international division was looked on with suspicion by Schlesinger, the chief economist, as being too accommodating on EMU. But they were careful to hide such tensions in the interests of Bundesbank loyalty and the credibility and prestige of the institution. More fundamentally, institutional interests were exhibited in the preoccupation of negotiators with control of the negotiating process so that these interests could be protected in defining policy positions. This preoccupation was most evident in the behaviour of Finance Ministry officials.

But the most fundamental danger lies in exaggerating the element of contest and underestimating the potential for communication and learning across these coalitions facilitated by the deeper cultural context of EMU. The approach of German negotiators to EMU was defined in larger terms than contest about *how* EMU should be constructed. Essentially, the security and ordo-liberal coalitions were formed around different 'causal' beliefs: beliefs about how EMU could best be realized. But behind that contest, at a deeper level, was a broader, shared 'normative' belief about the importance of European unification for Germany and about the special role of Franco-German reconciliation within that context.[4]

In this respect Adenauer's legacy had been most decisive. Negotiators and officials within both coalitions shared in the belief that Germany bore a special responsibility for European unification. This notion of German responsibility provided common ground. At the level of public opinion they wished to sustain a permissive consensus on Europe which continued to make it possible for German politicians to play a positive, constructive role in Europe. This deeper, shared normative belief about Germany and Europe eased communication, learning, and consensus-building across institutional boundaries. Brought into stronger focus by German unification, it offered to Kohl a resource to use, to manufacture consent for, to give drive to, and to create coherence in, German negotiating positions. Its presence was to be decisive in the course of the EMU negotiations and took the form of Kohl borrowing Adenauer's historical narrative about Germany and Europe. The two coalitions may have remained visible right through the negotiations and beyond, but what was important to the final agreement was the potential for 'bridge-building' between them offered by history, and in particular by Adenauer's legacy.

Adenauer's Legacy and EMU: The Foreign Ministry and Chancellor Leadership

EMU did not play a central or even marginal role in Adenauer's long Chancellorship from 1949 to 1963 and was far removed from the agenda of the discussions between him and de Gaulle before and during the Elysée Treaty negotiations of 1962–3. Adenauer played the flexible opportunist in European policy and an opportunity to pursue EMU did not seriously present itself, especially once he found himself dealing with de Gaulle from 1958. Their agenda was security, defence, and foreign policy and—to the domestic political embar-

---

[4] This aspect is underplayed in Kaltenthaler (1998*b*).

rassment of Adenauer—de Gaulle's provocative attempt to bind Germany to the pursuit of a reorganization of Europe on intergovernmental terms in the form of a Draft Treaty presented by the French Ambassor to Bonn, Christian Fouchet, in 1962.

But the lines of future cleavage on EMU were intimated in Adenauer's contests over European policy with his Economics Minister Ludwig Erhard: notably over the ECSC in 1950–1 and over the Treaty of Rome negotiations (1955–7). Indeed, a major reason for Adenauer's opposition to Erhard as his successor was his perceived lack of soundness on Europe and on the privileging of the Franco-German relationship (Koerfer 1987). Erhard's position on EMU was most forcefully clarified in his scornful rejection of the EC Commission's 1962 Action Programme for Stage 2, backed by Commission President Hallstein, a protégé of Adenauer. The programme called for monetary union in the form of locked exchange rates in the EEC's third stage after 1970. In the interim there was to be more active and constant consultation on monetary policy, mechanisms for 'mutual assistance' in balance-of-payments crises, and the development of medium-term economic-policy guidelines at the EEC level. Conflict with Adenauer on this issue was muted by the fact that the Gaullist govenment in Paris was quick to distance itself from these proposals. Hence in 1962–3 there was no real EMU debate in Bonn. It was in any case overshadowed by the disagreements between Adenauer and Erhard over the Franco-German Treaty and over Adenauer's support for de Gaulle's veto on British entry to the EEC (Schwarz 1997: 662–75).

The Foreign Ministry and EMU

More important was the long-term impact of Adeanuer's legacy on the way that the Foreign Ministry defined its role in EMU and its negotiating style. This impact was not so much direct as mediated through Blankenhorn, Hallstein (as its first State Secretary), and Eckardt (Blankenhorn 1980; Jansen 1996). They were more unbending in their advocacy of supranationalism than Adenauer—especially Hallstein—and, for instance, critical of Adenauer's preparedness to sacrifice this latter principle in 1962–3 for the sake of accommodation with de Gaulle. Though not in the driving seat on EMU, the Foreign Ministry's influence on the timing and context of these negotiations was to prove of decisive importance. Officials like Lautenschlager and Alois Jelonek had profoundly imbibed the history and culture of their ministry; whilst Hartmann and Bitterlich ensured that this outlook was daily incorporated into Federal Chancellor's Office briefings for Kohl.

A key attribute of Foreign Ministry negotiating style was to push hard in Bonn for strengthening European institutions as an insurance against future risk of a return to 'balance of power' politics. This style surfaced in EMU negotiations. The Foreign Ministry calculated that the stronger it pushed on EMU, the more movement it would get in this direction. In consequence, it ran the gauntlet of being labelled 'Euro-fanatic' and of being drawn into conflict with the Economics and Finance ministries. There was a sense—represented by Lautenschlager as State Secretary—that the Foreign Ministry should not simply live by compromise in Bonn. It must, for instance on EMU, impart a clear sense of political direction deriving from German national interest in strengthening European institutions. This viewpoint drew Lautenschlager into conflicts with Tietmeyer and then Köhler over EMU. It also influenced the outlook of Bitterlich and Hartmann in the Federal Chancellor's Office.

A second aspect of Foreign Ministry style derived from a sense of being a different department, of having a special responsibility for setting specialist arguments rooted in specific departmental interests in the larger framework of international developments and German foreign and security interests. Its task on EMU was not so much to seek out a consensus about what were the overriding German interests as to play a statesman-like role in defining, promoting, and defending those interests. Tietmeyer's arguments on EMU were seen as too narrowly specialist; the intellectual challenge for Lautenschlager was to persuade the Finance Ministry to cede responsibilities to Europe. This task was eased with a Finance Minister like Theo Waigel who was capable of taking a broader political view of EMU.

A further feature of Foreign Ministry negotiating style was a belief that the value of European policy should not derive simply from its domestic popularity. In the case of EMU it was recognized that a bedrock of domestic consensus, even if just permissive, was necessary for progress. But EMU had its own rationale rooted in German foreign and security interests that it was the task of political leaders like Genscher and Kohl to promote. There was, in short, a widely held view that it was the task of political leadership to see ahead of political opinion and set a clear direction for policy.

Finally, the Foreign Ministry had fully identified itself with the Community method, reflecting not least the legacy of Hallstein. For this reason during the EMU negotiations it offered the most sympathetic ear in Bonn to the concerns of the EC Commission. This sympathy surfaced in two key areas: the belief that European integration only works with a clear timetable and with the maintenance of the Commission's right of initiative. In particular, dates (for an IGC, for stage 2, and then for stage 3) were a central and continuing preoccupation of Foreign Ministry officials in the EMU negotiations.

The power of Adenauer's legacy derived from the fact that it stretched well beyond the confines of the Foreign Ministry and the Federal Chancellor's Office. Crucially, it had articulate supporters across the leaderships of all the main political parties. In the CDU of Kohl there was strong support within the federal executive for EMU. In February 1988 Kohl's main internal party rival, Lothar Späth, attached himself to a call for the earliest possible introduction of an ECB. It was to be enormously helpful to Waigel as chair of the Christian Social Union (CSU) that his long-serving predecessor (1961–88) and former Federal Finance Minister, Franz-Josef Strauss, had been an advocate of EMU at the time of the

Werner Report. A key coalition partner, the Free Democratic Party (FDP), could be counted on to back EMU. In 1988 its chair, Martin Bangemann, was Economics Minister and Genscher was a politically popular Foreign Minister of world rank; both were staunchly pro-European. The opposition Social Democratic Party (SPD) had endorsed the essentials of Adenauer's policy on European unification by the early 1960s and by early 1988 was supporting EMU. Former SPD Chancellor Helmut Schmidt was a constant voice in the wings, pressing the case for asserting the primacy of politics in EMU against the doubts and hesitations of the 'monetary technocrats' in the Bundesbank.

Employer, trade-union, and industrial organizations were on the whole much more reticent about relating EMU to foreign and security policy. They were driven by the more utilitarian views of their members about the likely distributional outcomes of EMU (Kalthenthaler 1998b: 29–37). But foreign and security-policy concerns found an echo in the leadership of the big banks, notably the Deutsche Bank. Here a style of economic statesmanship had taken root. Wilfried Guth of the Deutsche Bank was to provide important backing to Schmidt over the EMS in 1978. Herrhausen, chair of the Deutsche Bank, was to play a similar role for Kohl over EMU in 1988–9. He was an exponent of the view that the single European market, EMU, and political union must follow each other in that order. Following the Delors Report Herrhausen argued forcefully that urgent action was required to set up an IGC and that a timetable had to be attached to the stages of EMU. As early as December 1987 Walter Seipp, chair of the Commerzbank, was criticizing the lack of political will to push ahead with EMU. Finally, academic historians and foreign-policy experts were important in sustaining a wider climate of support for a political view of EMU. Here the main role was played by the Bertelsmann Foundation, particularly after the Delors Report, in focusing attention on the issue of a calendar to ensure that EMU was made irreversible. It provided a platform for Genscher and Herrhausen to share their views with other 'influentials'.

EMU as Binding Germany into Europe

The policy arguments of the Foreign Ministry and the wider security coalition on EMU derived from certain basic beliefs about Germany and Europe. These beliefs were in turn inspired by harsh historical memories drawn from a cataclysmic thirty-one-year period (1914–45): of two catastrophic world wars, of a failed Weimar democracy, and of a brutal fascist dictatorship. The core belief was that European security was the most vital of all interests for Germany. From it certain lessons were derived that formed a key part of the framework of policy deliberation on EMU in Bonn. Germany had to tailor its foreign policy to its exposed geopolitical position in the centre of Europe and its multiple borders. It had to be prepared to pay the heavy price of having lost the war. It had to find a means of escape from the isolation and deep mistrust imposed by its own recent traumatic and humiliating history and policy mistakes (Schwarz 1985; Ash

1993). And, less easy to articulate, Germans had good reason to distrust themselves and feel inhibited when it came to discussions about sovereignty and its uses. Where Germany possessed power, as in monetary policy, there was a deep-seated aversion to projecting that power abroad.

The Foreign Ministry's approach to EMU was grounded on certain axioms: to win back respect from others and to earn trust as an equal in the circle of West European democracies; to pursue a strategy of *Westbindung* ('binding into the West') in place of the past failed ambitions of a German *Sonderweg* and of the practice of a *Schaukelpolitik* ('see-saw politics') between East and West; and to find an alternative to traditional 'balance-of-power' politics and politics of 'hegemony' as a means of reconciling German and European security. Crucially, European integration was coterminous with the retrieval of German sovereignty—by sharing it (Baring 1969). It was an historic achievement, identified with sitting down once again with her neighbours as an equal deserving respect and with putting in place institutional arrangements that would underpin Germany's vital interests in security and prosperity (Schwarz 1996: chapter 7). This view of German interest in European integration invested European institutions with a moral authority and not just instrumental significance as agencies for the pursuit of national interest. It prescribed a policy style of restraint and accommodation in European affairs rather than of attempting to lead from the front. It involved a preference for making policy in Europe's name, rather than in the name of national interest, and an assumption of fundamental co-operation between European and German interests. German and European security were to be reconciled by binding Germany into Europe.

This belief system about the primacy of binding Germany into Europe rested on an historically informed analysis that had taken deep root. It could be traced back to Adenauer's Chancellorship; had been taken up by SPD Chancellors Willy Brandt and Helmut Schmidt; and united Kohl, a CDU Chancellor, and Genscher, a FDP Foreign Minister. Seen in terms of traditional international-relations theory, the belief in binding in Germany appears paradoxical. On the one hand, it derived from a soberly realist analysis of Germany's postwar condition and of what was in Germany's vital interest. On the other hand, it produced moral prescriptions for foreign policy that did not fit the accounts of 'national-interest-based' foreign policy characteristic of the Realist theory of international relations. Tough realism went along with a passionate rejection of a German foreign policy infected with any vestiges of nationalism and rhetoric of national interest. European integration was about putting in its place a new, unifying European ideology for Germans. As Blankenhorn had never been tired of repeating: 'There could be nothing more dangerous, indeed, than if the idea developed in Europe that Germany wanted to usurp supremacy via the European idea' (Blankenhorn 1980: letter of 7 September 1953).

Germany would be more secure and more prosperous, the more it bound itself within Europe and the more successful was its policy of reconciliation with France. It would also carve out a new political purpose and vision as orchestrator of European unification. On such a basis Adenauer and later Chancellors were able to discover in the EC an invaluable institutional venue in which their political authority could be nurtured and demonstrated, in which they could invent themselves as statesmen possessed of dignity and vision. The assumption remained that European political leadership would yield domestic political credit to a Chancellor. And, not least, this definition of German vital interests was associated with policy performance. The EC was successful in providing ordinary Germans with a context of enduring security and prosperity that had eluded them for a century and more. Hence challenging a policy of European unification did not prima facie appear to be good domestic politics, even when it involved the surrender of the D-Mark.

The Special European Leadership Responsibility of the Federal Chancellor

This set of policy beliefs about Europe had a strong impact on the role of the Federal Chancellor in European policy in general, and in EMU in particular. Chancellors could make use of their EC role to underpin their domestic political authority. For this purpose, they relied on constitutional provision and on political discourse. Article 65 provided them with the authority to set the 'guidelines' of policy for the government. This provision had, from Adenauer on, a special meaning for European policy, legitimating an active and directive role for the Chancellor (Paterson 1994). In addition, Adenauer used a repertoire of metaphors with which Kohl laced his rhetorical discourse on Europe: 'keeping the caravan on the road', 'laying the foundation stones', 'building the European house'. This language stressed the importance of momentum in European integration, of keeping up the pace of progress. EMU was co-opted into that framework of discourse. An important aspect of Chancellor discourse was the construction of an historical narrative in terms of which Germans could redefine their identity in the postwar world. In this respect EMU could be embedded directly in the theme of German security in Europe. EMU was not a stand alone issue but embedded in the tragic story of Germany's relationship to Europe in the twentieth century. It was about *Westbindung* and the avoidance of a German *Sonderweg*.

From Adenauer onwards, Chancellors developed the strategy of placing specific European projects in the wider context of a panoramic, historic survey of international political developments. In the European domain they could also claim the special expertise that comes from unique access to privileged 'insider' information. Adenauer used events in Hungary and Egypt in 1956 to win round Erhard and others to the Treaty of Rome negotiations. He conjured up memories of the past use of Franco-Russian pincers on Germany to win over the support of his reluctant cabinet for the Franco-German Treaty in 1963. The Treaty's justification was as a means of keeping the unpredictable de Gaulle away from the embrace of the even more unpredictable Soviets, with potentially dangerous consequences for Europe. The alliance with France was, for Adenauer, 'a political dam against the advance of Eastern Communism' and 'an alternative to American hegemony' (Schwarz 1997: 368, 377–8, 667). Willy Brandt was to legitimate his political leadership on EMU at the Hague summit of December 1969 in geopolitical terms. In this case it was necessary to provide a western 'flank' to his initiative in policy towards the East (*Ostpolitik*) so as to reassure EC partners and especially France. Helmut Schmidt used an historically grounded approach to square the Bundesbank council's support for the EMS in November 1978, referring to the onerous historic responsibilities falling on German political leaders in the wake of the Holocaust. Kohl was to follow these precedents in his use of German unification to give new momentum to negotiations on EMU and force the pace on political union.

Also, in selling the need to bring European negotiations to a successful conclusion, German Chancellors appealed less to visions of a united Europe than to the potentially disastrous consequences for Germany of being held responsible for the failure of negotiations. Once the process of negotiating EMU had begun, Kohl was determined above all to avoid any intimation that Germany was sabotaging or undermining agreement. The shadow of the past brought with it a distrust of German motives that must be assuaged. The Federal Chancellor's Office was continually reminding the Bundesbank of its obligations in this respect; there must be no suspicion that specific policy positions on EMU were being set to 'sabotage' prospects of an agreement. Genscher in the Foreign Ministry used similar arguments against the Finance Ministry. It was a message that had to be taken very seriously by German negotiators like Horst Köhler and by Tietmeyer.

Adenauer had also demonstrated how a determined Chancellor could make use of his expanded role in managing relations within the EC to strike out boldly with European projects, in effect engineering rapid domestic *faits accomplis*. From the very outset he had had to contend with scepticism and opposition from within German economic circles: from those who saw the ECSC as a clever French plot to retain control of the commanding heights of German industry and those during the negotiation of the Treaty of Rome who doubted French commitment to realizing an open free-trade area in Europe. This scepticism and opposition had clear parallels over EMU. But, advised by trusted friends in the banking field, notably Pferdemenges and Abs, Adenauer had seized and sustained the initiative. Schmidt adopted a similar approach to the EMS in 1978, seeking out advice and support from bankers like Guth of the Deutsche Bank. In 1988 and 1989, on EMU, Kohl was to turn to Herrhausen of the Deutsche Bank for counter-advice to the scepticism and pessimism of the Bundesbank. A point of continuity between Adenauer and Kohl was the activation of direct discussions with Paris as a means of overcoming resistance to moving ahead with European unification: as in November 1956 over the Treaty of Rome negotiations.

As 'grandson of Adenauer' Kohl had deeply internalized these beliefs, historical memories, and lessons for Chancellor leadership. He made himself into the historic symbol of continuity in European policy and sought to capitalize politically by carefully playing the European card. But, as we shall see, Kohl began as a careful and cautious strategist on EMU—like Adenauer, more the fox than the lion. He sought to be the master tactician, consolidating his domestic power base, especially within the CDU, before striking out to embrace clear positions on EMU and bring its negotiation to a conclusion. His negotiating style was to avoid making any definitive binding commitment to achieve EMU in a specific time-frame. It was German unification that was to endow Kohl with the power to act as the decisive *animateur* of EMU. Yet he never failed to recognize the symbolic value of European policy as a means of cultivating an image of Chancellor leadership and personal authority and of evoking emotional engagement. And there was more at work than simply a borrowing from Adenauer. Kohl had his own strong personal convictions about Europe which derived from his own experiences and those of his family. EMU was slotted into this framework: of Adenauer as a powerful role model and of resonant personal memories.

EMU as Motor of Political Union

Consistent with the 'institution-building' approach to European integration, EMU was perceived as a 'motor' of European political union. It could be incorporated into the 'Community' method of making Europe: by relying on 'spillover' from integration in other related areas, notably the single European market programme and the EMS, to put EMU back on the agenda; by using spillover from EMU to force the pace of political unification in Europe; and by the device of a clear timetable to bind in the process. This type of argument informed Genscher's Memorandum on the creation of an ECB of 26 February 1988 and Kohl's address to the European Parliament of 9 March 1988. In Kohl's view, the launch of EMU would make European political union irreversible. These beliefs also drew together Delors and Kohl on EMU. Their relationship was made intimate by shared normative beliefs about EMU and its relationship to the wider project of European integration. In this sense Delors had more ready access to the ear of Kohl than Pöhl or Tietmeyer, as the latter two discovered to their irritation in 1988. Delors and Kohl recognized each other as 'Europeans of the heart'.

Hallstein was the German mentor of this neo-functionalist conception of the role of economic and monetary policy in European integration. He had stressed that EMU was indispensable to sustain the Common Agricultural Policy (CAP) and to secure the European single market (Hallstein 1969: 140). In the early 1960s, as President of the EC Commission, he was responsible for the Action Programme for Stage 2 with its proposal for Community guidelines of medium-term economic policy. This proposal infuriated Erhard and led to a violent clash between Erhard and Hallstein in the European Parliament on 20 November

1962. Later, when EMU came onto the EC's agenda, the logic of this argument was to support a timetable for EMU with dates (to ensure irreversibility), to accept a new institution for stage 2 with significant tasks, and to build on the ECU as the route to the single currency. Its crowning moment was the Rome 1 communiqué on EMU in October 1990; its retreat apparent in the substance of the German Draft Treaty on EMU of February 1991; and its capacity to strike back evident when Kohl accepted final dates for stage 3 at Maastricht in December 1991. It would be quite wrong to think of a timetable for EMU being forced on Kohl and Genscher or on officials like Bitterlich, Ludewig, and Lautenschlager. Indeed, as early as 1989, both Genscher and Herrhausen of the Deutsche Bank were calling for the setting of a timetable for EMU as a necessary stimulus to decision (Bertelsmann Stiftung 1989: 39–40).

Erhard's Legacy and EMU: The Ordo-liberal Economics Establishment and Stability Culture

The fact that the economic component figured at the centre of postwar European integration meant that, from the outset, the Federal Economics Ministry was forced into a prominent position in EC negotiations. Professor Ludwig Erhard (CDU) and then, in the context of the first EMU negotiations, Professor Karl Schiller (SPD), were crucial to the way in which this ministry defined German interests in economic and monetary integration. Fundamentally, Erhard believed that it was wrong to approve a policy proposal simply because it was 'European'; he was a 'European of the head' rather than 'of the heart' (Laitenberger 1986: 133–4). His commitment to global free trade made him distrustful of the potential for the EEC to develop into a discriminatory trading bloc against other countries. In a letter to Adenauer of 21 November 1958 (which was unsent) Erhard identified what he saw as the central question raised by France's protectionist belief: 'whether and for how long Europe will tolerate being subjected to French dictation, and whether we are doing the right thing in declaring ourselves shoulder-to-shoulder with France in questions of European economic policy (Schwarz 1997: 376–7).

This typically unstated concern was to haunt the approach of Economics Ministry, Finance Ministry, and Bundesbank officials to EMU negotiations, and more clearly the attitudes of German academic economists. As we shall see later in this chapter, it affected key aspects of their negotiating style. In a paper of March 1964 Kurt Schmücker, the Federal Economics Minister, recommended that Chancellor Erhard oppose Giscard d'Estaing's proposal for a common European currency on the grounds that it would lead to the extension of French planning ideas to Europe and the use of Europe to pursue anti-American economic interests. Both would damage Germany. In private, Erhard condemned French pursuit of naked self-interest dressed up as 'Europeanism'; the economic illiteracy of French leaders, especially de Gaulle, with whom he established a very bad working relationship as Chancellor; and German *'Patenteuropäer'* ('patent Europeans') like Hallstein, with whom his working relations were equally bad (Hentschel 1996: chapter 5).

Erhard and European Integration

Erhard developed an approach to European integration different from that of Adenauer and Hallstein and that left a legacy of clearly defined positions on EMU. He distrusted both European integration based on supranational institution-building and the protectionism and *dirigisme* of the French. In essence, his argument was functionalist (Koerfer 1987).[5] The dissolution of national sovereignty required the liberation of market forces and free trade, not new supranational institution-building to drive the process of European integration. Market pressures would force consistent economic behaviour without which a solidly based and durable integration process could not evolve. In turn, the market could only function efficiently and effectively in a framework of economic stability. Hence the process of European integration depended on each state being committed to economic stability. In short, economic stability 'begins at home'. The implication was clear—that EMU was only possible if it was built 'from below' by states like the French putting in place the appropriate domestic preconditions for 'a community of stability'. The greatest danger derived from trying to impose EMU 'from above' by international negotiations.[6]

Three lessons were readily applicable to the later debate about EMU: first, that European integration must avoid setting unrealistic goals that were not grounded in the disciplines of the market; secondly, that sound economic principles must not be sacrificed for the sake of tactical European considerations; and, thirdly, that European integration must not jeopardize domestic economic stability. In the words of Erhard's speech of December 1954 in Paris: 'The precondition of any integration is prior agreement on the principles, systems and goals of action and behaviour'. With this statement Erhard anticipated the rule that economic convergence, based on appropriate domestic policies, must precede monetary union.

In a seventeen-page paper of March 1955, 'Cooperation and Integration', Erhard developed his attack on 'institutional' integration and his advocacy of 'functional' integration (Hentschel 1996: 300–3). He argued that political integration must precede economic integration and that economic integration must proceed cautiously based on convergence of economic-policy principles and not be used to drive political integration. The paper was circulated privately but received no substantial support. Adenauer bluntly rejected this argument in a letter of 13 April 1955 to Erhard. Once Chancellor in 1963, Erhard countered

---

[5] Also, Tietmeyer, 'Geldwertstabilität und Soziale Marktwirtschaft im Zeitalter globaler Märkte', speech to Walter Eucken Institute in Freiburg, 13 January 1997.

[6] Here Erhard was following Wilhlem Röpke's thinking. On Röpke see Sally (1998).

French arguments for closer economic and monetary policy co-ordination—especially at the bilateral with de Gaulle and Pompidou in February 1964—by asking first for French precision about steps to develop an effective political integration. In the absence of the latter he was not prepared to consider the proposal for the co-ordination of fiscal, financial, and social policies by Pompidou at that bilateral (Hentschel 1996: 654–5).

Ordo-liberalism and EMU

As Federal Economics Minister from 1949 to 1963 Erhard was important in imparting a distinctive content to German positions on European economic integration. During this formative period he fought to enshrine the values and arguments of ordo-liberal economists in German economic policy. In this consciously revolutionary approach to German economic policy he was flanked by his State Secretary, Ludger Westrick; the head of the ministry's economic policy division (*Grundsatzabteilung*), Alfred Müller-Armack (later State Secretary); and by the ministry's academic advisory council (*Wissenschaftlicher Beirat*). Ordo-liberal economists shared a common preoccupation: to identify the policy lessons of the failures of the Weimar Republic, notably the economic and political costs of rampant inflation, and of the Great Depression. Their purpose was to put in place an economic order that would be a stronger safeguard against two evils: the collectivist seductions of totalitarian political systems and unbridled *laissez-faire*. This new economic order was to act as a guarantor of freedom in all spheres of life, unrestricted competition forming the indispensable foundation of an open, liberal society. In essence, Erhard and his colleagues saw themselves as battling to put in place a new ethical foundation for the German economy (Ludwig-Erhard Stiftung 1996).

The ordo-liberalism of Walter Eucken and Wilhelm Röpke was paradoxical. It sought to break with the German tradition of state interventionism and cartelized industry, whilst gaining sustenance from certain aspects of German intellectual tradition. The traditional elements were twofold. First, ordo-liberals focused on the importance of an orderly framework of rules for the economy and of institutional arrangements appropriate to an efficiently functioning market, based on sound economic principles. Most notable were rules to promote competition over the longer run and institutional arrangements and financial rules to ensure monetary stability. For Röpke, Günter Schmölders, and others the prime requirement was an independent central bank mandated by law to maintain price stability—a requirement for which Erhard had to fight hard, against Adenauer and the Federal Finance Minister Fritz Schäffer, in the 1950s.[7] In this respect ordo-liberalism was grounded in German traditions: of respect for the expert and for the role of objectivity (*Sachlichkeit*) in public affairs; of

---

[7] The classic formulation of the case for central bank independence was put by Röpke (1958) and Schmölders (1968).

belief in a strong state standing above the economic struggle; and of valuing the clarity and predictability that come from observance of rules in economic policy. Only an independent central bank could guarantee that monetary policy would derive from an expert analysis of the interdependencies and cause–effect relations at work in the economy. The precondition was institutional arrangements to guarantee the depoliticization of monetary policy. This belief formed German attitudes towards EMU negotiations; an independent ECB was a non-negotiable position.

Secondly, ordo-liberalism offered a traditionally German historicist account of how economies functioned. Economic arrangements and economic behaviour were seen as specific to cultural and historical circumstances. Such an account underlined the difficulties of economic convergence within the EC. Germany's culture of economic stability was rooted in, and nourished by, the devastating consequences of two hyperinflations. Without this experience other EC states were unlikely to share German economic priorities and could not be expected to do so. With reference to the Treaty of Rome, Röpke had warned that 'the sick might contaminate the sound'; whilst Erhard had argued that France and other European economies should put their domestic house in order before embracing European integration (Nicholls 1994: 347–8). These arguments became the bedrock on which ordo-liberal views on EMU were later built, disposing German negotiators to erect strict and detailed rules of convergence as tests of the real will and capability of their partners.

Under Erhard there emerged a basic difference of view between the institution-building and functionalist belief systems about the proper ordering of the German interests at stake in Europe. For ordo-liberals the prime interest was defined as economic stability. It was an illusion and source of danger to subordinate pursuit of a 'community of stability', which properly 'begins at home' with sound domestic policies, to the search for German security by imposing EMU 'from above' (Willgerodt et al. 1972). No less importantly, there was a difference of causal belief about how European integration, and EMU in particular, should proceed. For those in the Adenauer/Hallstein tradition viability of EMU depended on specific, detailed objectives, a clear timetable of action, and a central role for the EC Commission. The implications of Erhard's belief in functional integration, articulated in the 1950s, were further clarified by Economic Ministry officials once EMU had surfaced on the EC agenda at the Hague summit of December 1969.

Bargaining Style on EMU

Erhard's and Schiller's legacies were also apparent in the policy style of German negotiators on EMU drawn from the Economics Ministry, the Finance Ministry, and the Bundesbank. This style had its historic roots in the sense of ethical purpose that informed ordo-liberal economics. From it they derived a strongly developed sense of Germany's vital interest in economic stability and in safeguarding its conditions, if necessarily in a robust manner. This interest was represented in the basic German negotiating position on EMU articulated by German ordo-liberals: that a European single currency must be 'at least as stable as the D-Mark'. Tietmeyer and Köhler could be tough, even ruthless, negotiators, prepared to assert German interests and to risk appearing intractable. In this respect their bargaining style, with its rationalist temper and manner of logical exposition, differed from that of Teltschik, Bitterlich, and Lautenschlager. Bilaterals between French and German Finance Ministry officials had, in consequence, a more brittle and strained nature than those conducted between the Elysée and the Federal Chancellor's Office or between the respective Foreign Ministries. German economic and monetary officials were disposed to be didactic, constantly arguing from first principles and warning others of the dangers of being too pragmatic in designing EMU.

At the same time the intransigence that Erhard displayed on matters of European integration was less evident by the 1980s. Even in the 1950s Erhard's intransigent style had only been supported by Westrick, his main ally in opposition to the Treaty of Rome. In contrast, Müller-Armack had worked constructively to build bridges to the Foreign Ministry and to the Federal Chancellor's Office, seeking to build good relations with Hallstein (Hentschel 1996: 303). Tietmeyer and others were closer to Müller-Armack than to Westrick in this respect, sensing that they must not confuse loyalty to their minister with loyalty to the government of the Federal Chancellor.

Membership of the Ordo-liberal Coalition

The domestic reach and grip of the ordo-liberal coalition on EMU was impressive. Its most powerful voices were to be found in the federal ministries of Economics and Finance and, centrally, in the Bundesbank. The symbiotic relationship between knowledge and power was most evident in the Bundesbank. Its power over policy was dependent on strengthening and sustaining a culture of stability. Precisely because the Bundesbank was taking independent decisions on monetary policy, its officials recognized that it had an institutional interest in explaining and legitimating those decisions and in cultivating broad support for the value of stability. Hence its President, directors, and council members were very active in the public arena, promoting the value of economic stability. The fundamental negotiating principle that the European single currency must be 'at least as stable as the D-Mark' was guarded religiously by the Bundesbank.

Beyond the Bundesbank and the Federal Economics and Finance Ministries, the ordo-liberal coalition could count on the support of employers and bankers: the Federation of German Industry (BDI—*Bundesverband der Deutschen Industrie*); the German Industrial and Trade Association (DIHT—*Deutscher Industrie- und Handelstag*); and the banking associations, like the Federation of German Banks (BdB—*Bundesverband Deutscher Banken*) and the savings banks association (*Deutscher Sparkassen- und Giroverband*). It also embraced the influential quality press, notably the *Frankfurter Allgemeine Zeitung* and *Die Welt*. They could be counted on to back the Bundesbank in any contest with the federal government about stability policy and EMU. Hence there were powerful domestic political deterrents to challenging the ordo-liberal coalition, making Kohl see in EMU a delicate and sensitive issue. A critical public opinion could be readily mobilized against a federal government that failed to show proper caution.

Academic Economists and EMU

Academic economists were important in having a long-term impact on the context of EMU policy debate. They shaped the climate of opinion and terms of discourse about EMU and hence the way in which it could be legitimated in Germany on ordo-liberal terms. There were very few enthusiastically pro-EMU academic economists in Germany: Dieter Biehl, Peter Bofinger, and Wolfgang Gebauer were exceptions to the rule. Compared to figures like Herbert Giersch and Horst Siebert (both from the prestigious Kiel Institute of World Economics) they were not important opinion formers.

Ordo-liberal academic economists were, on the whole, even more reserved and sceptical about EMU than ordo-liberal officials in Bonn and Frankfurt. Their ideas were disseminated through a limited number of policy fora. The Council of Economic Experts (*Sachverständigenrat*) was not directly important in relation to EMU, its work focused on its substantial annual report rather than seeking out influence on specific issues. More central was the advisory council of the Federal Economics Ministry, which published its report on EMU on 21 January 1989. The strongest influences on this market-oriented report were Giersch and its author, Olaf Sievert. The advisory council, of which Schlesinger was also a member, sent a letter critical of the Delors Report to the Economics Minister on 5 June 1989. But in practice the centre of gravity in Bonn on EMU was the Finance Ministry, not the Economics Ministry. The Committee for Monetary Theory and Policy of the *Verein für Sozialpolitik* was another forum for access to policy-makers. It met in the Bundesbank and had some Bundesbank officials (like Schlesinger and Otmar Issing) as members. This committee pressed very sceptical arguments on Bundesbank officials. The party foundations—like the CDU's Konrad Adenauer Foundation and the SPD's Friedrich Ebert Foundation—also had discussion groups that drew in academic economists. In addition, individual politicians were on occasion close to particular economists: for instance, Gerhard Stoltenberg to Giersch (Kiel was Stoltenberg's political base). But, overall, academic monetary economists were not closely integrated into the EMU policy process. Indeed, the views of the main German economic research institutes on EMU only really came into the public domain during the hearings of the Bundestag's Finance Committee in September 1991: too late to have any practical influence on policy formation (Krügenau and Wetter 1993).

Over the long term the key policy issue for German academic economists had been imported inflation. During the 1960s, led by Egon Sohmen and

Herbert Giersch, the academic consensus had shifted in favour of flexible exchange rates. The policy argument was that internal stability was to take precedence over external stability. But even that debate shadowed developments inside the domain of official policy-making (Emminger 1975). As early as 1961 Erhard had won the battle in Bonn for a revaluation of the D-Mark in the name of priority to internal stability. Inside the Bundesbank from 1956–7 onwards Otmar Emminger pressed the argument for adjustable parities against rigid adherence to responsibilities under the Bretton Woods system. Later, as President when Schmidt negotiated the EMS in 1978, Emminger sought to limit Bundesbank responsibility to support the ERM by foreign-exchange-market interventions. Such intervention had to be consistent with the Bundesbank's statutory responsibility to 'safeguard the currency'. Hence, buttressed by a German academic consensus, the Bundesbank approached EMU negotiations wedded to the principle of retaining the primacy of internal over external stability. Its implication was the minimization of responsibility for foreign-exchange-market intervention before the final stage of EMU. In short, the crucial policy signal on the primacy of internal stability derived from Bonn (from Erhard). The importance of academic economists stemmed from their role in providing long-term support to this policy idea and argument. Karl Schiller, himself an academic economist, summed up the guiding policy principle established by Erhard as: 'the external economic underpinning of domestic stability policy'.

Deep down, ordo-liberal academic economists were intensely sceptical about the ERM, never mind the prospects for EMU. They were also very suspicious of French motives. Rolf Hasse saw a French strategy of deception; its real aim was to force a looser monetary policy on Europe (Hasse and Schäfer 1990). According to Hans Willgerodt, France lacked, for historical reasons, the stability culture necessary for a viable EMU. Mitterrand viewed money as a political instrument and had no real understanding of, or respect for, central bank independence (Willgerodt 1990). This critique was also forcefully articulated by Roland Vaubel. Two other ordo-liberal themes were articulated by Horst Siebert: that in EMU negotiations there could be no compromise on monetary stability; and that the effective functioning of the single European market depended on the stability of the currencies within the EC, not on the number of the currencies (Siebert 1988: 12).

Unity and Disagreement within the Ordo-liberal Coalition

As with the security coalition on EMU, there were disagreements amongst those who subscribed to ordo-liberalism. On the whole, academic economists were disposed to take a more rigorously theoretical approach to EMU, in the manner of a latter-day Eucken or Röpke. In the Bundesbank Schlesinger and Issing in the directorate, and Helmut Hesse and Reimut Jochimsen in the council, were similarly very orthodox. But, notably in the Federal Economics and

Finance Ministry, officials were closer to the more pragmatic, consensus-seeking approach of Müller-Armack to European economic integration (Müller-Armack 1971). Senior officials like Tietmeyer had been trained in economics at Cologne University under Müller-Armack. They had a clearer understanding of the complexities and subtleties of the political game and had risen to seniority because of their sophistication in taking part in these games. Tietmeyer and Schlesinger could find common ground in their conviction that, as officials, they had a duty of loyalty to the foreign policy of the federal government. That duty involved discretion in making criticisms of EMU negotiating policy and helping and encouraging the government to take an economically responsible approach within that context. In fact, over the period 1988–91, German academic economists had little direct impact on the EMU negotiations. The cognitive learning process about designing an EMU strategy was essentially internal to the negotiating process, very much in the hands of Tietmeyer, Köhler, and other federal and Bundesbank officials.

Another point of difference was that officials in the Federation of German Industry (BDI) and in the Federation of German Banks (BdB), and senior figures in the economics departments of the big commercial banks, were likely to ascribe more importance to the gains from EMU in consolidating and completing the single European market and eliminating exchange-rate risk. These gains were a less important part of Bundesbank calculations which were more focused on avoidance of risk to price stability. As far as the Bundesbank was concerned, the decisive gain from EMU was the export of the German model of economic stability to Europe. Ordo-liberals were, in other words, by no means united in their assessment of the distributional outcomes of EMU, leading to a measure of dynamism in German policy positions.

Nevertheless, despite such differences, there was a widespread disposition to trust in the Bundesbank to articulate and defend German interests in EMU. The ordo-liberal inheritance was a spirit of reverential respect for the preaching of Bundesbank officials on the virtues of sound money and a stability culture. A close, supportive role for the Bundesbank in the EMU negotiations was, for employer, industrial, and banking associations alike, the litmus test for a good outcome that safeguarded their prime interests. For this reason these associations and academic economists were content to stand back and offer little more than minimum comment during the EMU negotiations.

It was only after the Maastricht European Council, and the negative noises in the Bundesbank council statement on Maastricht of 23 January 1992, that German academic economists mobilized opposition. The manifesto of sixty German economists against the Maastricht decisions on EMU in June 1992 was signed by Schiller, Giersch, Hasse, and Vaubel. But its publication was symptomatic of their distance from, and lack of impact on, a negotiating process whose dynamics had eluded them. In attacking these academic economists for being trapped in 'the spirit of the 1970s', the counter-manifesto of the chief economists of the big three commercial banks, organized by Norbert Walter of the Deutsche Bank, reflected growing division within the ordo-liberal belief system, consequent on the differences in response to the pace of external change.[8]

German Negotiating Style: The 'Rule-Based' Approach

For a variety of reasons German negotiators were disposed to a 'rule-based' approach to the EMU negotiations. The Foreign Ministry was concerned to enfold EMU in the traditional Community method. By establishing precommitment to a clear timetable of stages EMU was to be made irreversible. Finance Ministry officials were preoccupied with clear treaty language to rid the treaty of any bugs that might later infect stability policy. They wished to endow the process of transition to EMU and the content of stage 3 with as much certainty and predictability as possible. The consequent 'rule-based' approach found its expression in the detailed elaboration of economic-policy principles; in resistance to dilution of tough convergence criteria; in the preference for rules over financial-market discipline to deal with excessive deficits; and in the preoccupation with the fine details of the exchange-rate system and exchange-rate policy. Later it was to inform the design of the Stability Pact proposal of 1995 with its idea of automatic sanctions on budget deficits in stage 3. This 'rule-based' approach contrasted with a French preference for discretion.

The fact that this German approach rested on a powerful fusion of cultural, cognitive, and strategic elements gave a particular credibility and force to German policy arguments on EMU. The resultant quality of those arguments helped German negotiators to present strong cases and win on key issues. Underpinning the cognitive ordo-liberal and legalistic features that informed German negotiating positions was a deeper cultural background. This element of longer-standing tradition took the form of low tolerance for the uncertainties and risks of the political process.[9] It manifested itself in a respect for ensuring that the appropriate technical experts were left to negotiate a sound, durable EMU; an EMU agreement had to be based on *Sachverstand* (expertise). This attitude privileged the role of the Bundesbank and of the Finance Ministry officials in the negotiating process. Substantively, it sanctified the importance of central bankers in the design and operation of stage 3 and sustained an aversion to political interference in the workings of EMU. It was also related to an enduring distrust of, and anxiety about, how other EC goverments were likely to behave in EMU. Hence EMU had to be about putting in place a strict set of rules that would prescribe their future behaviour.

The cognitive element was provided not just by ordo-liberalism but also by the German idea of the *Rechtsstaat* ('state ruled by law'). Ordo-liberalism encouraged German negotiators to emphasize the importance of a clear institutional framework for EMU based on first principles of economic stability. It

[8] For these manifestos see Hrbek (1992: 225–45).
[9] The classic formulation remains that of Dahrendorf (1968).

gave a strongly deductivist quality to the German negotiating style. It also influenced the German view on how EMU should be designed. EMU negotiations were, first and foremost, a matter of designing stage 3. Then the features of the transition stage could be derived from the requirements of that final stage. This approach was intended to rule out an 'open-ended' route to EMU with its attendant uncertainties and risks. Sitting alongside this ordo-liberalism was the legalistic approach to regulating public life that is so entrenched in German tradition and that was reinforced by the experience of the Third Reich. Built into the German idea of a 'state based on law' is a preoccupation with the certainty and predictability of rules to narrow down the discretion of governments (Dyson 1980). Like ordo-liberalism its concerns had deep roots in modern German history. And its effects ran in the same direction.

But German negotiators were not simply the prisoners of culture and received ideas. There was also an important strategic element in their embrace of a 'rule-based' approach to EMU. Quite simply, they had little trust in the economic and monetary policy credentials of those with whom they were negotiating, not least the French. German negotiators remained unsure, and often unconvinced, that the political cultures and political elites of other member states were willing to carry through the domestic policy reforms required to build EMU on secure foundations of economic stability 'from below'. Hence German negotiators opted to minimize the freedom of manoeuvre of other member states by means of detailed rules. Not least, they hoped that specific precommitments—for instance, to central bank independence, tough convergence criteria, and strong sanctions—would play an educative role for Europe.

Conclusion

By the time that Kohl came to office in 1982, determined to act as 'grandson of Adenauer', German policy positions on EMU were, paradoxically, more clearly defined by those who wished to do justice to Erhard's legacy than those seeking to emulate Adenauer. But this paradox, and the latent conflict that it seemed to conceal, was more apparent than real. In the first place, in relation to European policy, Erhard had been very much on the defensive and isolated. He had proved a weak negotiator, stronger at the level of ideas than at strategy and tactics (Hentschel 1996: chapter 5). With respect to strategy and tactics, Müller-Armack had been the key figure in building support in Bonn, especially before the Treaty of Rome negotiations. Erhard's apparent inconsistency between public commitments to building a federal Europe and private attacks on naive 'patent Europeans' also undermined his credibility. Hallstein, Adenauer, and others were, consequently, inclined to dismiss his paper of 1955 on European policy as both politically unrealistic and incoherent.

Adenauer's legacy was in fact complex. At the height of his powers Adenauer's disposition had been to play the fox rather than the lion, to finesse his positions tactically. He was, in short, inclined to take a more flexible view of European integration than some of his collaborators, like Hallstein. He was also prepared to prevaricate till the balance of political forces at home and abroad moved in his direction, coolly and vigilantly observing changes in the domestic party landscape. As the good student of Adenauer Kohl was no starry-eyed, doctrinaire European. He saw EMU from the beginning through the eyes of the political realist. That view led him to respect the Bundesbank and the Finance Ministry and to note reservations within the CDU/CSU. Kohl was, in private, critical of their conservatism and unwillingness to take the necessary risks to build Europe. But the domestic power of ordo-liberalism was a reality to which he recognized he had to accommodate his approach to EMU.

The latent conflict between a Chancellor whose mentor was Adenauer and the legacy of Erhard was further mitigated by the way in which the Economics and Finance Ministries and the Bundesbank had reconciled themselves to the realities of doing business in the EC. In part, this accommodation had been helped by EC enlargement, notably to include Britain in 1973. This process had blunted the force of Erhard's old argument that the EC was too small and introverted an organization to form the basis of a large, expanding free-trade area in German interests. Hence ordo-liberals were more comfortable with the EC, and their comfort greatly increased by the single European market programme initiated in 1985. The Finance Ministry and the Bundesbank had also taken prime responsibility for what was left of the Werner process, namely the German-centred 'Snake'. There remained very deep reservations about France, compounded by the new Socialist government's expansionary economic relaunch of 1981–2. But, crucially, within the Economics and Finance Ministries and the Bundesbank there was a sense of responsibility for making European unification work. This sense was symbolized in the figure of the Bundesbank President Pöhl, whose qualities as a European monetary diplomat distinguished him from his predecessors.

So, though it was possible to discern two historically conditioned coalitions on EMU, and consequent potential for inconsistencies in German policy, there was a deeper structure of shared belief that represented the long-term primacy of Adenauer's legacy. This legacy was a belief in Germany's historic responsibility for unifying Europe and in doing so through a policy of reconciliation with France. Its effects were decisive for the way in which German negotiators conducted themselves on EMU. It gave them a shared sense of identity and purpose; it smoothed communication and consensus-building across the two coalitions and blurred their edges; and, crucially, it provided Kohl with a resource for Chancellor leadership on EMU. At this deeper level German negotiators were capable of reflecting on their beliefs about EMU and putting them in a context. German negotiators were not trapped within the narrow partisan boundaries defined by contending coalitions.

This overall structuring of policy arguments in Germany lent a stability and predictability to debate on EMU. It meant that German policy on EMU was far removed from being akin to a 'garbage can' of competing ideas. But, equally, German negotiators were far from being simply disinterested recipients of historical givens. The complex texture of German positions was the product of the way in which individuals fashioned views about EMU in their own distinctive ways. This behaviour was apparent within the Bundesbank. Faced with contending pressures, Pöhl was disposed to adopt and drop views, leading to criticism of inconsistency. Other officials of an intellectually inquisitive nature, like Claus Köhler and Rieke, were interested in probing inherited beliefs by confronting them with new evidence, notably about French economic performance. Others in the Bonn Finance Ministry were keen to establish a strong personal profile on EMU in 1989–90 by reflecting on the coronation theory and adjusting German EMU positions to the new reality after the Delors Report.

But the fundamental reality for Kohl in October 1982 was that ordo-liberals had an impressive grip on the way in which EMU was debated in Germany, on the direction of German policy on EMU and on the way in which policy positions were legitimated. Debate focused on the critical importance of economic stability as precondition and goal of EMU. Germany's experiences of the cataclysm of hyperinflation were drawn on to point out the risks that, with EMU, European politicians would take irresponsible risks with people's money. The effect of ordo-liberalism on policy direction was twofold: a stress on the difficult, long-term task of working for convergence of economic policies and performance in Europe; and the vital need for commitment to progress on European political union. These twin German demands were in effect a challenge to other states to get their domestic political acts together before it made sense to start talking seriously about EMU. The responsibility for failure on EMU was being pinned on other states' doors. This policy position was legitimated by reference to the justifiable pride that Germans could have in having achieved the historic prize of a stable currency. The chief beneficiary was the Bundesbank as the architect of that stable currency. It gained an overwhelming authority for its views on EMU.

7

The Political Problem of Reconciling Domestic and International Interests in EMU: The Legacy of Schiller and Schmidt

Helmut Schmidt was always something of a maverick figure in the German debate on EMU. Literate in economics, and a star pupil of Professor Karl Schiller's, he was regarded as a formidable political figure in the world of international and European economic policy. He associated his Chancellorship from 1974 to 1982 with the idea of promoting Germany as a policy model for others (*Modell Deutschland*) and with cultivating the style of an effective 'crisis manager' who was prepared to play a constructive and positive role in economic-policy co-ordination at international and European levels. This outlook made him impatient with what he saw as the parochialism of economic and monetary-policy technocrats who failed to grasp the wider political picture of policy co-ordination. It made him the least deferential of German Chancellors towards the Bundesbank's preoccupation with securing the domestic basis of economic stability.

Schmidt's personal authority had less of a direct moral basis than that of his predecessor Willy Brandt. It was bound up with his image as the efficient, energetic, and decisive manager of government business. He presented himself as Germany's 'executive' (*leitender Angestellter*), as a man who paid great attention to briefing himself fully on policy detail and who represented a guarantee that problems would be tackled in a practical and non-doctrinaire manner (*Die Zeit*: 22 September 1980). In all these respects he was seen as very different from Brandt, who distanced himself from economic-policy debates and whose governing style was to reconcile and to use his authority sparingly (Harpprecht 1974: 213). Schmidt was the 'man of action' or 'fixer' (*Macher*) rather than the visionary (*Seher*), more pragmatic and problem-oriented than his predecessor. He was identified with the belief in giving primacy to safeguarding the economic security and prosperity of Germany as the precondition for tackling social and political problems. In this respect he seemed the ideal Chancellor at a time when Germany faced an increasingly threatening international economic environment during the 1970s. Schmidt's Chancellorship coincided with the oil crisis and with exchange-rate volatility consequent on the collapse of the Bretton Woods system (Glotz 1979: 49–50). He was, not least, the Chancellor who succeeded in retaining the economic discipline of the German trade unions at a critical moment of inflationary threat. Schmidt's political reputation was, in consequence, as a consolidator rather than a social reformer and as an intervener in debates within government rather than as an arbiter.

These qualities put Schmidt in close touch with public opinion. But they also meant that, as Chancellor, his relationship with his own party, the SPD, was one of uneasy coexistence (Carr 1985: 101). He brought it an electoral bonus in the 1976 federal elections, feeding a sense of his political indispensability to the SPD. At the same time, the combination of a small majority for the coalition government with the Chancellor's sometimes abrasive governing style and perceived conservatism threatened to turn intra-party tensions into crisis. Unlike Brandt, Schmidt had no deep reservoir of emotional sympathy and identification on which he could draw in his relations with the SPD. From his defeat as Chancellor in the Bundestag in 1982 to the election of Gerhard Schröder as SPD Chancellor in 1998 he remained an isolated figure. He took a leading role in lobbying for EMU, alongside Giscard d'Estaing. But, unlike Giscard in France, Schmidt had no real influence over German policy on EMU over this period. His contribution took the form of criticisms of the conservatism, technocracy, and parochialism of the Bundesbank and the lack of firm and decisive leadership from Chancellor Kohl. Not until Chancellor Schröder was there a renaissance of Schmidt's belief in the virtues of economic-policy co-ordination at European and international levels.

To the ordo-liberal coalition Schmidt was by no means orthodox. His period as chair of the SPD parliamentary party in the Bundestag and as Defence Minister had given him a wider political perspective on economic policy than, for instance, Erhard and Schiller. Schmidt was in many ways the intellectual heir of Schiller in economics, imparting a neo-Keynesian aspect to his economic-policy judgements. Both were never fully integrated into the ordo-liberal coalition; both had a difficult, strained relationship with the Bundesbank; and both could trace their departures from federal political office, in 1972 and 1982 respectively, to conflicts with the Bundesbank.[1] Schmidt also shared some of Schiller's qualities, notably a sharp analytical mind, an immense intellectual self-confidence, and an impatience with woolly thinking and political 'day-dreaming' and with politicians and officials who failed to properly brief themselves. This impatience made him enemies.

But Schmidt's intellectual horizons were wider than those of the academic economist Schiller. He had cultural interests in literature, history, and philosophy. Allied to the legacy of his long wartime experience as a soldier, these gave him a very different outlook from that of Schiller. Schmidt imbibed a deep stoicism, making him severe on himself and on others and disposed to a pessimism about human nature. This intellectual temperament was reinforced by his reading of Immanuel Kant's categorical imperative. Virtue was vital in public and in

---

[1] For details of the conflicts in 1972 and 1982 see Marsh (1992).

private life and had to be continuously striven for. These virtues included sobriety, steadiness, and predictability; duty, order, and discipline (Rupps 1997: 98 ff., 108 ff.). This outlook led him to take an increasingly critical view of Schiller. Their relationship deteriorated sharply in the period before Schiller's resignation in 1972 (Baring 1983: 790–820). Schiller lacked, in Schmidt's views, both public and private virtues. He was disloyal, quarrelsome, and vain.

More importantly, Schmidt was intellectually very much part of the 'security' coalition. He was deeply reluctant to envisage a Germany throwing its weight around in Europe and the wider world in search of prestige and status. His thinking was governed by a geostrategic sense of German vulnerability as a state with so many external borders and with the dreadful burden of its history (Schmidt 1990). It was situated in a Kantian framework of recognizing an imperative to strive for peace. The result was a politician who situated EMU in a profoundly deep sense of Germany's special responsibility to be a 'calculable' state, using its power modestly but prepared to take risks for the sake of international economic-policy co-ordination and to build Europe. This viewpoint brought Schmidt into conflict with an ordo-liberal style that he saw as too technocratic and arrogant and as endangering Germany's long-term fundamental interests. It also led ordo-liberals to be unhappy with his willingness to commit Germany to reflation at the economic summit meeting in Bonn in July 1978 and to create the EMS.[2]

It was during SPD-led federal governments that German negotiating positions on EMU were first clearly defined. In that process the key political figures were Schiller in 1970–1 and Schmidt in 1978. Both endeavoured to act as policy entrepreneurs on EMU, seizing windows of opportunity opened by political events and policy developments. As this chapter tries to show, they were to have a long-term impact. But that impact was tempered and conditioned by an enduringly powerful, and indeed strengthened, ordo-liberal coalition, led by the Bundesbank. The political problem that confronted Schiller and Schmidt was how to reconcile domestic constraints—represented by the power of the ordo-liberal coalition—with German interests at the European and international levels. As indicated above, Schiller and Schmidt saw these latter German interests rather differently. In consequence, Schmidt was the more challenging figure on EMU. He had more strongly internalized the security coalitions' conception of German interests, even before becoming Chancellor in 1974. But he was also constrained as the broad structural drift at the level of international economic-policy ideas away from Keynesianism empowered the Bundesbank and its allies to resist his initiatives.

---

[2] On the politics of the July 1978 economic summit see Jäger and Link (1987: 286–90).

The Legacy of Schiller: The Werner Group, 'Coronation Theory', and Belief in Parellelism

The work of the Werner Group in 1970 and the subsequent ECOFIN decisions of 22 March 1971 were the key catalysts for developing German negotiating positions on EMU. They were developed under Schiller, who—during the 1950s—had fought a long battle to reform the SPD's economic programme and was the most prominent, brilliant, and energetic economist within the SPD. He opposed the Marxist legacy of commitment to planning and public ownership and advocated a commitment to free trade, a stable currency, and market competition. In aligning the SPD behind the new concept of an 'enlightened market economy with social commitment' he introduced a Keynesian dimension and an emphasis on ethical values into German economic-policy thinking. Schiller favoured modest deficit-spending and demand-stimulation to generate employment and growth and more active state intervention where the market was 'unbalanced'.[3] His beliefs in 'global steering' of the economy by means of a co-ordinated anti-cyclical fiscal policy, in 'concerted action' on macroeconomic policy with both sides of industry, and in 'social symmetry', were met with suspicion within the ordo-liberal establishment. They were seen as threatening a retreat from the disciplines of the market. But these beliefs informed the German approach to the Werner negotiations, especially in the form of the co-ordinated and active fiscal policy provided for in the Law on Stability and Growth of 1967.

Schiller's impact was in part the result of his qualities of character and personality. He was an intellectually robust, self-confident, and argumentative minister, temperamental and capable of being very abrasive in personal dealings. These same qualities were to contribute to his downfall in 1972 and to a difficult and deteriorating personal relationship with Chancellor Brandt and, especially, with Schmidt (Baring 1983). But in 1970 he was at the height of his domestic power, a political star, helping to ensure that the Federal Economics Ministry dominated the Werner negotiations. Schiller's political stature as Economics Minister derived from his high-profile role in the SPD federal election campaign in 1969 and his personal association with its victory. As a political reward, after Alex Möller resigned as Finance Minister in May 1971, he headed a new 'super-ministry' of Economics and Finance. This increased portfolio heightened his political exposure and, in the eyes of others, ministered to his inflated ego and need for self-affirmation. The new 'super-ministry' was also welcomed by Schiller as a means to put him on a footing of greater equality with the French Minister for Economics and Finance, Giscard d'Estaing, in EC negotiations (Baring 1983: 810–20). But the powers that he acquired—when combined with

---

[3] Nicholls (1994: chapter 14). Schiller was intellectually indebted to Alexander Rüstow's stress on the strong state rather than to Eucken.

his personal characteristics—played a part in his acquiring a growing number of ministerial enemies, especially within the SPD.

Schiller's prestige was also associated with his acclaimed success—and that of 'global steering'—in overcoming the economic difficulties that he had inherited as Economics Minister in the Grand Coalition in 1966. During the G10 meeting in Bonn in November 1968, and subsequently in direct talks with the French, Schiller and his State Secretary Johann-Baptist Schöllhorn had demonstrated just how tough and unbending they could be in fending off French calls to ameliorate their economic difficulties by a D-Mark revaluation. Above all, Brandt was not at all interested in becoming involved in economic-policy debates. Once he had launched EMU, he withdrew to leave the negotiations to Schiller. Schiller had, in consequence, much greater political power over the Werner negotiations than Giscard.

Schiller and his Economics Ministry officials were confronted by a political *fait accompli* when Brandt undertook his solo initiative on EMU at the Hague summit of December 1969. That initiative had a clear foreign policy rationale: a 'flanking' measure to reassure the anxious French and thereby limit potential damage to fast progress with *Ostpolitik*. Schiller could not effectively challenge this priority because it was central to the new coalition with the FDP and involved the FDP party chair, Walter Scheel, as Foreign Minister. It also fitted into an underlying domestic political consensus in favour of European unification. Instead, the EMU initiative was seen as an opportunity to educate other European leaders in the requirements of an effective economic and monetary policy at the EC level. In his professorial manner Schiller was determined to set the terms of the EC-level debate on EMU. He was also conscious that it must reflect the new thrust that he was trying to give to German economic policy, whilst also reassuring mainstream domestic ordo-liberal opinion.

With his officials he worked quickly to submit a German proposal to ECOFIN for its meeting on 23–4 February 1970. Its intellectual point of reference was Schiller's own Law on Stability and Growth of June 1967, endowing the German plan with a more Keynesian content than later German proposals in the 1980s. This Keynesian aspect to the German contribution to the Werner negotiations was apparent in the stress on centralizing fiscal-policy competence alongside monetary-policy competence—reflecting the assumption that fiscal policy 'mattered' as an instrument of economic adjustment. It was also demonstrated in the lack of close attention to defining relations between a European central banking system, on the one hand, and ECOFIN and the EC Monetary Committee, on the other. Unlike later, there was no preoccupation with the issue of the independence of the European central bank system.

The major point of continuity with the 1980s was the argument that the move to 'fixed and guaranteed' exchange rates could only safely follow a high degree of convergence in economic performance. This convergence would require a long time, with the final fourth stage beginning perhaps in 1978. But, crucially, the move from one stage to the next should be contingent on the achievement of the essential elements of the prior stage. The ordo-liberal content was represented by the principle that external economic policy must be used to assure domestic economic stability. Hence it was proposed that priority should be given to co-ordination of economic policies for this purpose over any idea of creating a European Reserve Fund. In laying the stress on binding institutional guarantees for economic stability, the Economics Ministry was already putting in place the lineaments of German negotiating positions for Maastricht. It was also seizing the intellectual high ground at an early stage and encouraging others to negotiate around its ideas.

Within the Economics Ministry the key authors of the Schiller plan of 12 February, besides the minister, were his State Secretary Schöllhorn (who was later on the Bundesbank council from 1973 to 1989 as President of the Schleswig-Holstein state central bank); Otto Schlecht in the economic policy division (later State Secretary in the Economics Ministry); a young official from the same division, Tietmeyer, who acted as Schöllhorn's deputy in the Werner Group; and Professor Martin Seidel who worked on the legal aspects of EMU. They were careful to clear these proposals with the Bundesbank and helped provide Schiller with the ideas to act as German policy entrepreneur on EMU in 1970–1. From 1988 onwards, Schlecht, Tietmeyer, and Seidel acted as a force for continuity, using their memories of, and lessons from, the Werner negotiations as a resource for influence in Bonn.

The Werner negotiations, which began formally on 20 March, led to the development of notions of maximalist and minimalist German positions on EMU consistent with ordo-liberalism. The maximalist position was defined as the coronation theory of EMU. According to this theory, monetary union would be the final stage of the European integration process. It would crown a process of economic union in which market principles, notably free capital movement, were enshrined in EC law and practice. It would also be embedded in a framework of European political union that would ensure solidarity, especially in budget policy, by endowing the Council with political responsibility for economic policy. The minimalist position was secured in the Werner Report. This position argued for the principle of parallelism in progress towards economic union and monetary union and that, in the final stage, political union must accompany EMU. EMU was to be a catalyst for political union. The later reservations of Tietmeyer derived from a sense that the Delors Report and the Maastricht Treaty fell short of minimalist German positions defined in terms of ordo-liberalism.

Consistent with ordo-liberal views on EMU, Schiller had concluded by the end of January 1971, three months after the Werner Report, that EMU would make no substantial progress. This conclusion stemmed from the fact that the French Gaullist government had made it clear that it was unwilling to contemplate commitments to institutional reform in the direction of political union by creating a 'centre of decision for economic policy'. In striking contrast to what was to happen in the Maastricht negotiations Schiller endeavoured to safeguard

German strategic interests by negotiating a special precautionary 'time-limit' clause in March 1971. This clause ensured no automaticity in the transition to stage 2 of EMU. Transition to stage 2 was to depend on parallel progress in harmonizing economic policy and in managing intra-EEC exchange rates. In their absence the new monetary-policy provisions and the medium-term credit facilities would cease to be valid. In short, Schiller was successful in ensuring that progress towards EMU was entrusted to incentives rather than to a fixed timetable of stages.

Schöllhorn's unpublished paper on the Werner Report of 23 November 1970 and Schiller's statement on the Werner Report to the Bundestag on 29 January 1971 encapsulated the underlying ordo-liberal attitude to EMU. According to Schöllhorn, EMU would necessitate amendments to the Treaty of Rome; the transition from one stage to the next must represent a 'political turning point'; 'rigid timetables and automatism' were to be avoided; there must be 'effective parallelism' between economic and monetary 'ties'; EMU must act as a catalyst for political union; and the goal was to be a 'stability bloc' within the world economy. The background to Schiller's speech was the difficult Franco-German consultations designed to find a compromise between the proposals in the Werner Report and the position of the French government. It had become clear to Schiller that there was little scope for agreement beyond stage 1 of EMU and that in stage 1 co-ordination of economic policy would be weaker than envis-aged in the Werner Report. Hence he spoke of EMU as a 'daring vision' and 'joint adventure' but stressing the risks involved. 'The belief in European unification could be brought into greater discredit by a mistaken economic con-struction than by anything else.' A monetary union without an accompanying economic and fiscal policy union 'would prove a house of cards that would col-lapse with every gust of wind'. This statement became part of the later folk memory of the ordo-liberal conception of EMU (Nölling 1993: 44–5).

Ordo-liberals were deeply averse to taking risks with economic stability, which was seen as an indispensable pillar of the postwar German state, the con-dition of its liberal democratic order and its continuing prosperity. An important side-effect of the Werner negotiations was the emergence of Tietmeyer as a ris-ing star of the Economics Ministry. He was the main architect of the adaptation of ordo-liberal ideas to the challenge of EMU. Subsequently, as head of the Economic Ministry's economic policy division, and then as State Secretary in the Finance Ministry in the 1980s, Tietmeyer carved out a role for himself as the main embodiment of institutional memory on EMU. From 1988 onwards he was to remain the most articulate and convincing exponent of the traditional ordo-liberal approach to EMU in Bonn and Frankfurt, a role that brought difficulties in his relations with Bitterlich, Lautenschlager, and his successor in the Finance Ministry, Horst Köhler.

The Consolidation of the Power of the Ordo-liberal Coalition on EMU

The room for manoeuvre and potential for influence of German advocates of an institution-building approach to EMU, based on the Community method, was tightly constrained by the events of the early and mid-1970s. Three interwoven sets of external change contributed to the ascendancy of the ordo-liberal coalition on EMU. In the first place, there was the failure to make progress in implementing EMU consequent on the reservations of the French government about the political component of EMU. Though the Paris summit of 19–21 October 1972 set 31 December 1980 as the date to complete EMU, its failure to tackle the political implications provided ammunition to German ordo-liberals. In addition, the development of inflationary pressures and of the balance of payment effects of the oil-price rise from 1973 widened economic disparities. EC enlargement in 1973 to include Denmark, Ireland, and the UK increased disparities further. In the wake of these developments the notion of the EC states developing into a 'community of solidarity' (Solidargemeinschaft) lost credibility. Finally, the experience with the protracted death agonies of the Bretton Woods system up to March 1973 furnished the Bundesbank with powerful arguments. Its officials could point to the dangers of trying to maintain a system of fixed exchange rates against a background of interest-rate differentials and discrepancies in inflation rates and balance of payment positions. Emminger, Vice-President of the Bundesbank, emerged as the intellectual victor of this period. The Keynesian interlude under Schiller proved to be brief.

By 1972 the economic policy division of the Federal Economics Ministry under Schlecht was reflecting on the implications of failure to make progress with 'parallelism'. This principle had been central to the Werner Report and had represented Germany's bottom line in the negotiations. It was faced with the fact that, under the auspices of EMU, little more than an exchange-rate system (the 'Snake') and three intervention support mechanisms had been agreed. Schlecht's and Tietmeyer's basic belief was reinforced: that EMU was fraught with economic and political risks. These risks could only be safely managed in an EMU that was part of a 'state-like' political community, characterized by supranational political structures with their own democratic and parliamentary legitimacy. Such structures would provide the political solidarity that a viable and durable EMU required (a 'community of solidarity' as opposed to a 'community of risk', Risikogemeinschaft). They would provide the framework for binding rules on national budget policies to ensure economic stability and for an EC-wide fiscal transfer system to iron out divergences. In addition, EMU required complete freedom of movement of goods, services, people, and capital. The deferment of the institutional issues of political union till 1975–6 (when stage 2 was supposed to start) was seen as symptomatic of a lack of seriousness about EMU on the part of other negotiators, notably the French and the Commission. In the absence of the required context of political solidarity,

Economics Ministry officials identified three possibilities for consolidating progress on EMU that needed to be probed: a regional fund to strengthen solidarity and help iron out greater economic disparities in an enlarging EC; a strengthened intervention mechanism (the European Monetary Co-operation Fund—EMCF—was established in 1973); and, more problematically, a parallel currency.

Brandt was still eager to seek out opportunities to push ahead with implementation of the Werner Report. Pompidou's encouragement to press on with practical steps towards monetary union was a constant theme in his correspondence with Bonn. But Brandt's convincing personal victory in the federal elections of September 1972, combined with the presence of the more pro-European Schmidt as Finance Minister, opened up new prospects for political leadership on EMU. A window of opportunity was opened on 1 March 1973 when, in the context of a currency crisis centred on the US dollar, the closure of the German foreign-exchange market and speculation about a joint EC float, the British Prime Minister, Edward Heath, visited Bonn. Briefly, faced with Heath's proposal for a common EC response, Brandt flirted with the idea of acting as a policy entrepreneur on EMU. Brandt indicated that he was prepared to consider a European pooling of reserves as part of a managed float of the EC currencies. He saw it as providing a new impetus to EMU and the political construction of Europe and counted on Schmidt's political support in dealing with the Finance Ministry and the Bundesbank (Brandt 1989: 402). But, by the end of the meeting, the British moved to a much more cautious position. The opportunity was lost, and on 19 March the 'Snake' members adopted a joint float—but minus Britain and Italy and without strengthening steps towards monetary union. When Brandt and Pompidou next met four months later, the emerging effects of the oil crisis led both to conclude that further steps towards EMU were impractical in the short term.

Schmidt as Finance Minister: The Changing Domestic Context of EMU

In July 1972 Schiller resigned as Economics and Finance Minister following difficulties within his own SPD about the budget, his increasing isolation within—and alienation from—the party, and culminating in his defeat in the federal cabinet when he opposed the Bundesbank President's proposal for capital controls as a means of protecting the exchange rate before the impending federal elections. He was succeeded by his Hamburg party colleague, Helmut Schmidt, who had been in many respects close to Schiller. Schmidt had supported the latter's battle for economic-policy reform within the SPD and for realism over public expenditure against the SPD's Left. But he brought a new political dimension of priority to Franco-German reconciliation and to European unification. Though a very cerebral figure, and very much the political and economic realist, Schmidt was also a 'European of the heart'. As early as the 1950s he had participated in Jean Monnet's Action Committee for the United States of Europe. Intellectually, he continued to share Schiller's Keynesianism. But his period as Finance Minister and then Chancellor coincided with major structural change in the international political economy that offered new opportunities to the Bundebank and the ordo-liberal coalition to strengthen their grip on policy towards EMU.

Following the 1972 federal elections, in which the SPD achieved their best postwar result, Helmut Schmidt achieved a domestic political victory. In return for ceding the Economics Ministry to the FDP, he succeeded in transferring the division for money and credit (*Abteilung Geld und Kredit*) from the Economics Ministry to his Finance Ministry. This move was deeply resented in the Economics Ministry and resulted in a long-term structural change in domestic control of EMU. It distanced Schlecht and Tietmeyer from financial and monetary policy. Symptomatic of the disempowerment of Erhard's old Economics Ministry was the fact that the State Secretary in the Finance Ministry gained the key role in the EC Monetary Committee and the Finance Minister in ECOFIN. The Finance Minister and his State Secretary assumed responsibility for relations with the Bundesbank. Formally, there was a divorce between the centre of intellectual power of EMU (the economic-policy division of the Economics Ministry) and the operational centre of power (the division for money and credit). Schöllhorn, Schlecht, and Tietmeyer lost their close grip on EMU policy.

Both the Economics Ministry and the Bundesbank regarded this change with deep misgivings. One reason was Helmut Schmidt's political stature compared to the new, relatively unknown FDP Economics Minister, Hans Friderichs. Schmidt was a political heavyweight in the SPD; Friderichs a more marginal figure in the coalition, especially once deprived of monetary and credit policy. More disconcerting still was Schmidt's distrust for ordo-liberal technocrats. Within the Bundesbank there was a suspicion that Schmidt's acquisition of the money and credit division was a prelude to an attempt to politicize the conduct of monetary policy. Schmidt's insistence on the supremacy of politics and his cultivation of a close relationship with his French opposite number, Giscard d'Estaing, promised, in addition, a more politically led, institution-building approach to EMU. His approach to Franco-German relations and to EMU represented a break with what Giscard had experienced under Erhard and Schiller. These concerns of ordo-liberals mounted when, in May 1974, Schmidt succeeded Brandt as Federal Chancellor and one of his loyalists, Hans Apel, followed him in the Finance Ministry.

In practice, there was no immediate major shift in the balance of intellectual power over EMU with Schmidt. With the ending of fixed exchange rates (effectively on 1 March 1973), inflationary financing in many European countries (notably France), and the risk to the stability of the D-Mark from imported inflation, the Bundesbank was able to exploit the consequent uncertainty to strengthen its power over economic policy. In this context Schmidt was deprived of the domestic room for manoeuvre to take a new initiative on EMU. In EMU negotiations Schmidt and then Apel supported the views of their division for money and credit and of the Bundesbank, views which were fixated on the danger from imported inflation. This lack of substantive change on EMU was evident with respect to the foundation of the EMCF in April 1973 and to the Commission's proposals of late 1973 to develop the EMCF's role. The EMCF was little more than an institutional pooling of existing intervention mechanisms. In fact, Schmidt blocked the Commission proposals to pool currency reserves in the EMCF and to develop it into a co-ordination and consultation centre for money and credit policies. In doing so, his officials used classic ordo-liberal arguments: the lack of adequate parallel progress in harmonizing economic policy; and the fact that the EMCF was less independent of ECOFIN than the Committee of EC Central Bank Governors and hence not an appropriate venue around which to construct EMU.

Schmidt's reticence on EMU from 1972–4 was to be understood in terms not just of the Bundesbank's greater strength but also of the mounting domestic political and economic problems of the Brandt coalition, partly consequent on the oil and currency crises but also reflecting Brandt's own weakness as an executive leader of government business. His political stature as an international economic statesman and heir apparent to an enfeebled Brandt would be imperilled by a clash with the Bundesbank. The response of the Pompidou Presidency to the oil crisis had also made the prospects for working with Giscard on progress with EMU non-existent. Intensifying co-operation with a French government pursuing economic expansion in the face of inflationary pressure would destroy domestic political confidence in him. But it was not just a matter of his own domestic credibility. Schmidt saw in irresponsible economic policy responses to the oil crisis elsewhere in Europe a real threat to the stability of the D-Mark and did not wish to become associated politically with such a development. Hence in this period he worked in close co-operation with the Bundesbank, which came to play the leading role at the level of ideas.

Otmar Emminger, the Bundesbank, and EMU

During the Werner negotiations Schöllhorn had been careful to co-ordinate evolving German negotiating positions in detail with the Bundesbank, particularly with Emminger who in 1970 became Vice-President. From 1972–3 the intellectual centre of gravity in developing the ordo-liberal position on EMU shifted towards the Bundesbank. Emminger remained the powerful figure in the further development of Bundesbank thinking on EMU, particularly in relation to the issues for negotiation identified by the Economics Ministry in 1972. In confronting these issues the Bundesbank established policy positions on which it was to draw in the negotiations from 1988 onwards.

Notably, the Bundesbank was not in principle opposed to fiscal transfer mechanisms. They were a necessary part of a 'community of solidarity'. But it was at pains to stress that a European Regional Fund must not distract weaker economies from the imperative of pursuing domestic discipline. On the issue of intervention the Bundesbank was much more active. Its basic position was that any intervention mechanism should not undermine its capacity to discharge its statutory responsibility for domestic monetary stability. Hence it took a strictly minimalist view of the EMCF and sharply rejected the Commission proposals of late 1973. In the same spirit the Bundesbank opposed other proposals to develop the intervention mechanism. These proposals included the Fourcade Plan of September 1974, a French Finance Ministry proposal to spread the responsibility for intervention to support the 'Snake'; and the Duisenberg Plan of July 1976, a Dutch Finance Ministry proposal to strengthen co-ordination of intervention. In particular, the Fourcade Plan was an opportunity for the Bundesbank to assert unequivocal opposition to the idea of symmetry in responsibility for intervention between strong and weak currencies. This theme was to recur in the 1980s.

A more radical idea, already under discussion in the Economics Ministry by 1972, was for a parallel currency as an alternative route to EMU. The most publicized version was the 'All Saints' Day Manifesto for EMU' of November 1975. It proposed a new 'Europa' as a parallel currency of constant purchasing power which would compete with national currencies in all monetary functions. The manifesto was signed by Giersch and gained support amongst other German academic economists. Its appeal was as a market-driven route to EMU that would circumvent the political obstacles to progress that bedevilled implementation of the Werner Report. In this respect the parallel currency seemed to better fit Erhard's functionalist conception of European integration. But, crucially, the parallel currency proposal offended against the Bundesbank's ordo-liberal conception of the need for an effective 'state-like' structure that could guarantee basic economic and monetary rules. Emminger had a residual fear of international financial markets evolving into a 'monetary counter-government' (*monetäre Nebenregierung*), an extraterritorial source of liquidity creation (Emminger 1975: 523). His views on a parallel currency were to dominate German positions in the 1980s.

Hence by 1976, under Emminger's policy leadership, the Bundesbank had refined its thinking on EMU to create an impressive, logically constructed set of policy arguments. Fundamentally, the EC could only proceed to EMU on the basis of seeing itself as a 'stability community' (*Stabilitätsgemeinschaft*). The main development in Bundesbank reflection had followed from its consideration of the events in 1973: the effects of the enlargement of the EC from six to nine member states; the currency crisis precipitated by the crisis of confidence in, and collapse of, the Bretton Woods system; and the oil crisis. By 1975 the Bundesbank was increasingly convinced that the Werner approach of all EC member states moving ahead to EMU as a single convoy was no longer realistic. EMU would require a group of states setting the pace: in short, a 'multi-speed' approach. This viewpoint was to be taken up again by Pöhl in 1990–1. At the same time the Bundesbank directorate was not totally united about EMU. Leonhard Gleske, Bundesbank director for international affairs from 1976, was more pragmatic than Emminger about the relationship between monetary union and economic union (Gleske 1975). For Gleske it was also important that proper caution about monetary integration should not become associated with obstructionism to the wider integration process. Both must proceed in union with each other.

Schmidt and the Birth of the EMS: Challenging the Ordo-liberals

In 1978 Chancellor Schmidt declared his intention to propose 'a major step towards monetary union' that went beyond the 'Snake'. The Bundesbank and officials in the Economics and Finance Ministries were taken by surprise. Despite his reputation as a conservative Chancellor, he had taken a political gamble that involved using the European level to effect changes in the domestic distribution of power over economic and monetary policy. By a combination of tactical manoeuvring, *fait accompli*, and persuasion he aimed to square the ordo-liberal coalition behind his proposal.

Schmidt's tactical manoeuvring involved the discrete use of the privacy of the Franco-German relationship and of the European Council to present potential domestic opponents with a *fait accompli*. Persuasion did not initially take the form of deploying the traditional arguments of the security coalition in support of EMU. That came later in November after he had already been forced into retreat. Instead, he concentrated on offering an economic rationale in terms of German economic interest. Skilfully, he sought to use an exogenous change—the collapsing value of the US dollar—in an attempt to mobilize German banks, industry, and trade unions behind a challenge to the traditional conservatism of the Bundesbank over EMU. Schmidt did so by presenting monetary union as an opportunity to protect German industry from accelerating uncompetitiveness and job losses, consequent on dependency on the irresponsible economic management of the Carter administration and the intra-European exchange-rate instability that followed. This protection was to take the form of co-ordinated action at the EC level in the form of a pooling of reserves and a strengthening of the role of the European unit of account (EUA). Having located EMU in a German-centred economic argument that broadened the agenda beyond economic stability, Schmidt indicated that he was prepared to tackle the problem of asymmetry in the operation of the 'Snake' as a quid pro quo for German gains in trade, growth, and jobs and in improved security within a deteriorating international environment.

In effect, Schmidt was carving out a role as policy entrepreneur, harnessing the EMU project to a 'window of opportunity' created by changing economic circumstances and by political developments within France. This initiative offered him the prospect of developing his image as a European statesman of world rank. Unlike Kohl in 1988, Schmidt was further emboldened to act by a confidence that he could master the technical aspects of EMU. He applied himself to these details in a way very different from that of Kohl. Along with that self-confidence went a profounder distrust of the monetary 'technocrats' of the Bundesbank than in the case of Kohl.

From the outset Schmidt worked closely and in secret with President Giscard d'Estaing on the issue (Ludlow 1982). They had been discussing EMU since early 1977, and Schmidt had been reassured by the new stability-oriented policy under Barre. Though Schmidt finally resolved to take up EMU in February 1978, by the time of the Copenhagen European Council in April he was still determined to keep discussions in private. In Copenhagen Schmidt outlined, outside the formal session, his objectives to create a new exchange-rate system to replace the 'Snake'; a new European Monetary Fund (EMF) in which a proportion of official reserves would be pooled; and intervention obligations for all states. With Giscard he proposed that Horst Schulmann in the Federal Chancellor's Office and Bernard Clappier, Governor of the Banque de France, should be given the task of working out proposals for the Bremen European Council in July. The Bundesbank was being isolated by Schmidt's and Giscard d'Estaing's device of reliance on their economic 'sherpas' for G5.

When the issue broke into the public domain in May, the Bundesbank feared that a *fait accompli* was being prepared. At this point it became politically active. Its approach was to warn Schmidt and the Finance Ministry and to mobilize domestic opinion to defend its independence. On 26 May Emminger, the Bundesbank President, warned the Chancellor not to enter into any binding commitments in Bremen on 6 July. In early June the Bundesbank organized a series of meetings with leaders of the Federation of German Industry, the Federation of German Banks, and the Chambers of Commerce. It also met with Finance Ministry officials. Before Bremen Schmidt was already on the defensive, as became clear when he met on 5 July with industry, banking, and trade-union leaders on the day before the European Council. His attempt at persuading them to support his initiative seemed to be having only qualified success. Warning noises also came from within the CDU and CSU, for instance from Strauss, about not putting the Bundesbank's independence at risk. Even his own Finance Minister was cautious. Though the Bremen communiqué was vague, the essential part of the Clappier–Schulmann paper was retained in the annex. It contained two main challenges to the Bundesbank: that a new European Currency Unit (the ECU) was to be the centre of the new system; and that, within two years of the start of the new system, an EMF was to be established.

After the Bremen European Council Emminger used a cabinet meeting on 12 July to argue successfully that the only way to ensure that the Bundesbank's responsibilities were not infringed and that it co-operated in the new system was to enable it to participate fully in its design. This strategy of brinkmanship was intended to prevent Schmidt hatching a final scheme in private with Giscard. At this point Schmidt agreed that the task of developing the technical proposals must pass to the EC Monetary Committee and the Committee of EC Central Bank Governors, institutional fora in which the Bundesbank had an important voice. Throughout this period Manfred Lahnstein, State Secretary in the Finance Ministry, endeavoured to broker a final deal that would be acceptable to both Schmidt and Emminger and that would be supported by Otto Graf Lambsdorff, the powerful FDP Economics Minister. Lambsdorff was being advised by officials like Tietmeyer, who was very sceptical of becoming involved in an EC exchange-rate system.

Though taken by surprise, the Bundesbank had already developed a coherent and powerful intellectual position on EMU from which Emminger, Gleske, and Claus Köhler were able to derive clear, tough arguments in the technical negotiations. The Bundesbank arguments were that:

- only countries that had clearly demonstrated their commitment to domestic stability should be regarded as suitable candidates for a new exchange-rate system (in effect a 'two-speed' approach);
- flexibility about parity changes should be built into the new system in order to minimize the exposure of central banks to intervention;
- credit facilities should be limited, so that discipline on monetary authorities was maintained;
- limits should be placed on the Bundesbank's obligations to intervene and the possibility of partner countries using D-Marks to intervene (again to safeguard domestic monetary stability);
- the intervention system should be based on the 'parity grid' between existing currencies and not the new ECU 'basket' currency (which as a weighted average of existing currencies could identify the stronger currency as a problem and hence require intervention by its central bank);
- the creation of an EMF was not to affect the Bundesbank's autonomy to determine its own monetary policies.

The domestic constraints on negotiating a symmetric EMS were made forcefully apparent to Schmidt before the key meeting with Giscard in Aachen on 14–15 September. It was clear that the Bundesbank was being effective in pursuing its positions within the EC technical fora. More directly, a meeting between Schmidt and Bundesbank and banking and industry figures on 13 September showed the depth of hostility to an agreement conceding French demands for a symmetric EMS. Pöhl, Vice-President of the Bundesbank, was on hand in Aachen to ensure that Schmidt defended the basic principles of asymmetry.

A key early victory for the Bundesbank was to gain acceptance for its argument that an EMF would require treaty amendment and, given the short timescale for agreement, was better postponed. Hence, in order to maintain political face for the French, provision was left open for a stage 2 of the EMS.

Though it had to concede on the idea of a 'divergence indicator', calculated in terms of the ECU, and creating a presumption to intervene, it was also agreed that the intervention system would be based on the parity grid. The result was an ambiguity that the Bundesbank was able to exploit to its advantage. In the management of the ERM the 'divergence indicator' was politely forgotten. More clearly, the Bundesbank was able to place strict restrictions on the use of ECUs in settlements within the ERM and on the available credit facilities.

The Bundesbank felt some satisfaction in having held the line in the face of a major surprise attack. On this occasion it had seemed in even greater danger of being outflanked than by the Werner exercise. What had finally emerged was much less ambitious. Schmidt's strategy of isolating the Bundesbank had in the end failed as the latter had gathered a formidable domestic coalition behind it (the strategy was not repeated by Kohl in 1988). Schmidt's ambition to act as a policy entrepreneur challenging ordo-liberal orthodoxy had borne only limited fruit in an improved exchange-rate mechanism. Most strikingly, in November 1978, before the Brussels European Council, the Bundesbank secured a special agreement from the federal government on three key points that secured its vital interests:

- a transition into the second, institutional stage of the EMS and an ultimate transfer of currency reserves to the EMF could only be contemplated under Article 236 of the Treaty of Rome (i.e. as a treaty change requiring ratification);
- the federal government would only consent to rules on the EMF consistent with the continued independence of the Bundesbank;
- if confronted with a conflict between internal and external stability, the Bundesbank had the right to solve this dilemma by ceasing to intervene (Emminger 1986: 361 ff.).

This agreement constituted a crucial 'binding of hands' by the federal government in future management of the ERM and in negotiations about the development of the EMS. In attaining this agreement, Emminger had received powerful political support in Bonn from Lambsdorff and assistance from Tietmeyer. The agreement was to be a key focus of reference in ERM crisis management, including after Maastricht in 1992–3.

Schmidt's Legacy

Despite this clear retreat from positions taken up in Copenhagen and Bremen, Schmidt's political leadership on EMU had a lasting legacy in triggering policy change. On 30 November 1978, just before the Brussels European Council, he took the step of visiting the Bundesbank council to lecture it on the limits of the Bundesbank's authority and on the overriding importance of political leadership on EMU as a foreign-policy project. In 1979 Schmidt also explored the possibility of appointing Guth from the Deutsche Bank (a partisan of EMU) as President of the Bundesbank to succeed Emminger (Stoltenberg 1997: 261). When this move failed, Pöhl, the Vice-President, and a former State Secretary in the Finance Ministry and collaborator of Schmidt, replaced Emminger in 1980. Pöhl was more cautious than Emminger when it came to the issue of the limits of the Bundesbank. He recognized that, in addition to Article 4 of the Bundesbank Law of 1957, binding it to 'safeguard the currency', Article 12 pointed out that it had a legal duty to support the general economic policy of the federal government. Article 12 could be interpreted to mean a European responsibility. In sum, the events of 1978 served as a warning to the Bundesbank about the limits of its authority.

Schmidt's legacy was important in a second sense. Courtesy of its new role in managing the ERM, the Bundesbank was drawn into a much more intensive dialogue with EC counterparts: not just in the EC Monetary Committee and the Committee of EC Central Bank Governors but also in bilateral relations. As crises were successfully managed in the 1980s, the sense of collective ownership of the ERM began to displace earlier deep reservations of principle within the Bundesbank. Schmidt succeeded in launching the Bundesbank down a path of development into which it found itself increasingly bound and which led, gradually, to a greater appreciation of the achievements of other EC member states in taking stability seriously. The development of the ERM in the 1980s provided mounting evidence of the way in which Germany's partners were taking economic convergence seriously. That evidence was a stimulus to reflection within the Bundesbank, particularly by those in the international division—like Wolfgang Rieke—and those responsible for capital markets and foreign exchange markets—like Claus Köhler. In capital market and foreign exchange policies an 'informal' institutionalization of Bundesbank–Banque de France relations emerged as bilateral contacts became regularized. For Köhler and Rieke EMU was to become a less distant project that required a greater flexibility of approach.

The Second Stage of the EMS in 1982

In their resolution of 5 December 1978 establishing the EMS, the EC heads of state and government had firmly resolved to create the EMF and to ensure full utilization of the ECU as a reserve currency and a means of settlement no later than two years after the start of the EMS. Hence by 1981 the EC Commission, strongly supported by the new French government, sought to make progress with stage 2 of the EMS. In trying to act as pace-setter on this completion of the EMS Tommaso Padoa-Schioppa, Director-General of DG2 Economic Affairs, came up against the stern and unbending resistance of the Bundesbank and the scepticism of the Economics and Finance Ministry officials, notably of Tietmeyer as head of the economic policy division of the Economics Ministry.

The idea of a stage 2 of the EMS was seen as no more than a statement of political intent. There was no attempt to give it operational form in Bonn.

Three factors combined to sharply reduce the freedom of manoeuvre of Schmidt and prevent him acting as a policy entrepreneur on this issue. The ERM had undergone four realignments by September 1981 and two others were to follow in February and June 1982. The Bundesbank had, in consequence, plenty of evidence from which to argue that the EMS had not established its credentials as a zone of stability. In addition, the new French Socialist government was pursuing an expansionary, Keynesian strategy that invited increased German distrust. Traditional ordo-liberal images of a *dirigiste* France were reinforced, to the detriment of political progress in developing the EMS. In effect, the behaviour of the French government tied the hands of Schmidt. Finally, and crucially, Schmidt's domestic political position weakened considerably in 1981–2. He faced rising unemployment and fiscal-management problems, problems within the SPD, and increasing difficulties with his FDP coalition partner, especially with Economics Minister Lambsdorff.

Hence in December 1981 ECOFIN agreed to consider only 'non-institutional', 'technical', and 'pragmatic' improvements to the EMS. Reflecting the Bundesbank position, Gleske had already ruled out the EMF in the EC Monetary Committee. At the March 1982 ECOFIN, when the Commission's 'technical' proposals were considered, the German Finance Minister, Hans Matthöfer, a Schmidt loyalist, inserted a reservation in the general declaration of support for the development of the EMS. This reservation underlined his pessimism about the prospects for agreement. As chair of the EC Monetary Committee (and Matthöfer's State Secretary), Horst Schulmann pointed out that the safeguarding of the independence of the Bundesbank was the main obstacle to proposals for technical improvements to the EMS.

The Finance Ministry gave full support to the Bundesbank in its opposition to the two key Commission proposals: to remove the acceptance limit on settlements in ECU (currently set at 50 per cent); and to assume responsibility for 'intramarginal' interventions: in effect proactive intervention before currencies reached their limits. The first proposal was opposed because it would force the Bundesbank to hold large reserves of ECUs, thereby weakening its credibility. The second proposal threatened conflict with the Bundesbank's priority of domestic stability. Notably, the March 1982 ECOFIN was overshadowed by the fifth realignment of the EMS in three years. Matthöfer reiterated the position that a 'zone of currency policy stability' required a parallel convergence of economic policies (which was not evident). At the May ECOFIN the new Finance Minister, Lahnstein, was more sympathetic to ideas for promoting the private use of the ECU. But, once again, progress foundered on German insistence that Commission proposals meet the test of demonstrating that they would promote economic convergence and internal stability. The sixth realignment of June 1982, combined with further weakening of Schmidt's domestic political position, finally killed off stage 2 of the EMS.

The discussions of 1981–2 about technical improvements to the EMS were important in clarifying Bundesbank bargaining strategy on EMU. As Bundesbank President Pöhl was keen that the Bundesbank should not be seen as simply negative and an obstacle to EMU. Pöhl signalled clearly to a dismayed Padoa-Schioppa that the Bundesbank was committed to EMU. It had, however, a different approach from the Commission and from the French. The Bundesbank wanted to begin by achieving clear agreement on the institutional arrangements for the final stage of EMU and was happy to enter into such a discussion. From that agreement on principles it would be possible to derive proposals for the intermediate period. The Commission's approach was too open-ended and was likely to lead to an EMU incompatible with stability. It also underestimated the importance and difficulties of economic convergence for a sustainable EMU.

Conclusion

Chancellors Brandt and Schmidt had sought to seize the initiative on EMU, but with different results. EMU was in fact peripheral to Brandt's strategic vision. It was a flanking measure for his *Ostpolitik* rather than a decisive point that had to be won before he could hope to move forward with other issues. He soon became absorbed in negotiating the Eastern treaties at the expense of EMU. Also, Brandt lacked the executive co-ordination skills and substantive economic-policy competence to master the technical aspects of EMU in 1970–1. Instead his politically powerful, 'policy-expert', and intellectually confident Economics and Finance Minister was able to seize the initiative on EMU after the Hague summit. It was Schiller rather than Brandt who was the policy entrepreneur on EMU during the Werner negotiations.

By contrast, Chancellor Schmidt had confidence in his policy expertise, had loyalists in the Finance Ministry, and was prepared to engage himself on EMU. His contribution was very much individual. It was to act as a policy entrepreneur on monetary union. But his chosen strategy—of trying to isolate the Bundesbank before the Bremen European Council—deferred rather than resolved negotiating problems. By July 1978 Schmidt was confronted with a choice: to keep the Bundesbank marginalized, in which case he was inviting a domestic political confrontation with the ordo-liberal coalition; or to ensure its full participation on technical aspects, in which case he would disappoint the French and achieve only minor reform. He had little difficulty in making up his mind. Politically, he stood to lose too much from so direct a confrontation with the Bundesbank. By its participation in the final stages of the EMS negotiations and in subsequent implementation, the Bundesbank was able to carve out a strong role and underline continuity with earlier policy. Post-1979, the Bundesbank sought to divert attention from implementation of the EMS agreement by returning to the policy arguments about EMU established in the

Werner period. The issue was not the EMF, or even just technical improvements to the EMS. It was economic-policy co-ordination to parallel the EMS. That problem definition put the weight of responsibility on other member states to make concessions.

In arguing in this way the Bundesbank was, unwittingly, revealing an inconsistency in Schmidt's approach. Though best known as an effective crisis manager rather than visionary like Brandt, Schmidt sought to mobilize self-respect around the idea of *Modell Deutschland*, of Germany as an economic model. In so far as Schmidt had a strategic vision it was *Modell Deutschland*. But, paradoxically, his 'Model Germany' did not extend to the Bundesbank which he saw as assuming too great a leadership role over policy. Yet, in relation to the EMS and EMU, the Bundesbank was in effect seeking to extend *Modell Deutschland*, in the sense of the German model of currency stability, to a wider Europe.

But, however much he may have been neutralized by the Bundesbank, Helmut Schmidt's legacy was considerable. It was a legacy that Kohl was never likely to acknowledge. Schmidt's legacy was to 'bind in' the Bundesbank to assume a measure of responsibility for European monetary integration. Management of the EMS served to reshape the EC Monetary Committee and the Committee of EC Central Bank Governors as institutional venues for the consideration of European economic and monetary integration. However reluctantly this responsibility was exercised, Bundesbank officials were drawn into reflecting in these fora on how the EMS might be made to operate more effectively. In short, a new dynamic of policy negotiation and learning had been unleashed. Pöhl, Köhler, Rieke, and others were quicker to adapt to this new reality than others, notably Schlesinger. But it was Schlesinger who was on the defensive.

Schmidt's legacy was an alternative to the dominant ordo-liberal approach of returning to the Werner Report, coronation theory, and parallelism. This dominant approach looked backwards; it was essentially pessimistic about prospects for EMU; its strategy was to keep this off the agenda till 'the time is ripe'. With the EMS there was a specific instrument on which to build and the prospect of generating a new optimism about EMU. It was Genscher who was later to attempt to harness that optimism and to argue that the success of the EMS justified moving beyond a strategy of limited steps to improve that mechanism. When it came to getting EMU back on the German and EC agendas, Genscher was to be the decisive policy entrepreneur.

8

Negotiating EMU around the German Model: Agenda-Setting under the Kohl Chancellorship, 1982–1989

Early in the morning of 28 June 1988 Karl-Otto Pöhl, President of the Bundebank, was telephoned by his Belgian counterpart, Jean Godeaux. Godeaux reported on what had been agreed over dinner during the previous evening at the European Council in Hanover under Chancellor Kohl's chairmanship. To his astonishment Pöhl learnt that he, Godeaux, and the other EC central bank governors, alongside some other 'experts', had been chosen to report on how EMU could be realized—with Jacques Delors as chair of the committee. The full extent of Pöhl's horror at Delors's appointment to this key role came out in his subsequent telephone call that day to Wim Duisenberg, Governor of the Dutch central bank, who was on holiday in Portugal and who was seen by Pöhl as a man close to his way of thinking. It took Duisenberg some time to convince Pöhl that he must participate: that there were far greater risks in being on the outside than on the inside; and that the alternative was another, probably less reliable, German on Delors's committee.

This event was a turning-point in Pöhl's relationship to Kohl, beginning a process that terminated with Pöhl's resignation in 1991. It also demonstrated the Chancellor's strategic and tactical subtlety, his adroitness at biding his time and hiding his hand. For Pöhl's ordo-liberal side it showed how, in the hands of Kohl, politics could pollute the proper technical and objective study of how a viable EMU was to be constructed. It also convinced him, at a personal level, that the Chancellor was not a man on whom one could rely. But another side of Pöhl—the monetary diplomat—could also recognize that Kohl had cleverly boxed him into responsibility for what followed. Kohl's strategic acumen told him that the Bundesbank must not be allowed to play the role of critical spectator in the EMU negotiations to follow. He had, in short, outflanked the Bundesbank. Kohl was revealing his consummate artistry in the exercise of power.

Though EMU was to become personally identified with Chancellor Kohl, that identification was to come relatively late—in December 1989—rather than in June 1988. The Strasbourg European Council was in this respect the turning-point and appropriately rounds off this chapter. Thereafter, EMU was 'nested' by Kohl in the management of the complex internal and external political implications of German unification. It served both as a tactical element in the management of that process and as a strategy in its own right for European unification. In short, it was by means of EMU that German and European unification were to be reconciled on terms that reinforced his political authority at home and abroad. In this chapter we examine the role of EMU in the early part of Kohl's Chancellorship. During this period EMU remained an essentially tactical issue, viewed by Kohl through the lenses of domestic party, coalition, and electoral management, of reinforcing his positions in these three related arenas. He did not identify with EMU as a strategy in its own right. Its tactical implications for party, coalition, and electoral management dominated Kohl's conception of EMU. Till December 1989 he was more the Chancellor as 'fox' on EMU than 'lion', cunning rather than brave.

By 1987–8 Genscher had emerged as a more lion-like figure on EMU, intent on nailing down the overly pragmatic Kohl. It was Genscher who was critical to the process of putting EMU back on the German and EC agendas. He was the real 'policy entrepreneur' behind EMU, seeking to coax Kohl into action and box ordo-liberals into acceptance of EMU as politically timely and in German inter-ests. Kohl's contribution was as the master tactician, defining his position in the framework of the complex and shifting balance of forces within his party and coalition and of the need to co-opt ordo-liberals into the process and keep them on board. He was not interested in the intellectual challenges of designing a workable EMU but in designing a process for establishing EMU consistent with his domestic constraints. It took German unification to provide him with the catalyst to redefine his approach to EMU and to sense that he could seize it as an opportunity to make an historic contribution to unifying Europe and to rein-vent himself as an historic Chancellor who had completed Adenauer's work.

But, though 1989–90 was the turning-point, the earlier period was vital. EMU was put on the agenda before German unification. The lineaments of the main strategic choices being pursued by Kohl and Genscher to give momentum to EMU were already discernible. Inherited policy beliefs, especially the 'corona-tion' theory of EMU, were being re-examined. Above all, the balance of domes-tic political forces on EMU had altered, inducing this reflection on EMU policy beliefs and clarification of strategic choices. Intellectually, EMU was 'reframed' before the IGC on EMU was convened.

Kohl's Beliefs about EMU and Governing Style

The keynote speech that Chancellor Kohl delivered on 14 April 1988 to the foreign policy congress of his CDU party was important in three respects as a signal of his views on EMU. It was one of the most comprehensive statements of his beliefs about European policy before German unification; it was delivered in the wake of Genscher's initiative to put EMU back on the agenda in the midst of Kohl's second term as holder of the EC Presidency; and it was part of a cam-paign to restore the fragile authority of the Chancellor within his party. At the core of the speech was a preoccupation with German 'responsibility' for Europe. Kohl's sense of this responsibility was supported by an historical narrative which rejected past notions of a German 'special way' (*Sonderweg*) as the route to isolation and, in the end, disaster. German responsibility for Europe was legitimated by reference to the requirements imposed by the preamble to the German Basic Law—'to serve peace in the world as an equal member of a united Europe'—and by the Paris Treaties of 1955 (Article 7(2))—which spoke of a 'reunified Germany' that 'is integrated in the European community'. Adenauer's message on the day that Germany regained its sovereignty, 5 May 1955, was recalled by Kohl: 'Our goal: a free and united Germany in a free and united Europe'. In the pursuit of this goal Kohl referred to the Franco-German relationship as the 'core community' (*Kerngemeinschaft*), the 'driving force' of European unification. France and Germany shared a 'special European responsibility'. These beliefs framed Kohl's approach to EMU then and later and endowed his approach to Europe and the Franco-German relationship with a greater clarity and continuity than his approach to economic and to social policy.

Despite these clear underlying beliefs Kohl's approach to EMU in this period was complex and ambivalent. He was in principle pro-EMU. EMU was, for Kohl, bound up with his European-centred and Paris-oriented policy and his belief in, and use of, Adenauer as a model. As his speech of April testified, identification of his own positions in European policy with Adenauer was politically very advantageous to Kohl. It mobilized a potentially fractious CDU behind him. Primacy to building Europe also cemented his personal relationship with his FDP coalition partner, Genscher; it gave a common foreign-policy purpose to the new federal coalition government in the wake of the protracted differences between the CDU/CSU in opposition and the FDP over *Ostpolitik*; and it was shared by Franz-Josef Strauss, the CSU's chair, with whom he otherwise had a difficult relationship on foreign-policy issues. For all these reasons he was never tempted to question EMU as a means to restore his domestic political position.

At the same time Kohl's primacy to Europe and to Franco-German reconciliation was not just borrowed from Adenauer. It had even stronger roots in his own personal experience and convictions. Kohl's enthusiasm for uniting Europe was fuelled by deeply felt family memories of the loss of an uncle (Walter) in the First World War and of a brother (Walter) in the Second. As a schoolboy he worked recovering bodies from the rubble left by air-raids. At 16 Kohl joined the new CDU, enthused by the then emerging idea of European union, and was soon joining friends who broke down barriers at the French border (Dreher 1998: 32). The christening of his son as Walter was an act of homage to the past and of symbolism, of faith in a better and different future. His European vision was a generational as well as personal matter. It was bound up with a notion of a special historical responsibility to create a Europe that would never again experience the horrors of 1914–18 and 1933–45. Kohl was aware that later German political leaders were less likely to be motivated by such vivid personal memories in wishing to treat the causes of war by uniting Europe. As he stressed to President Mitterrand in 1982, 'I may be the last Chancellor with whom you can build Europe'. This depth of personal conviction about European unification, and about making it 'irreversible', left a deep impression on others. It served as a resource of persuasion and leadership on which Kohl could draw—and did in relation to EMU after 1989. Kohl's sense of history was crucial to the way in which his Chancellorship unfolded, and his use of historical memory vital to his exercise of power.

On the other hand, Kohl's fundamental caution about EMU was also evident in the speech of 14 April 1988. He spoke of a European central bank and a European currency as a 'delicate' area in which 'particular care' was required. Whilst supportive in principle, the Chancellor was reluctant to act as a bold *animateur* for EMU. Kohl's intensely felt personal commitment to a European vision did not lead him to subsume EMU within his constitutional prerogative to set the 'policy guidelines' of the government (the *Richtlinienkompetenz* of Article 65 of the Basic Law). He drew back from an activist approach of trying to translate his European vision into a specific policy initiative on EMU. The reasons are to be found, in part, in his governing style and, in particular, in the political strength of his successive Finance Ministers, Gerhard Stoltenberg (1982–9) and Theo Waigel (1989–98). Revealingly, Kohl's willingness to lead on EMU was attuned to the domestic political strength of these ministers and their power relative to Genscher. But there was an additional reason for his caution. In his speech on 14 April Kohl promised to work on EMU in 'close co-operation' with the Bundesbank.

The nature of Kohl's strategic and tactical skills as Chancellor were the product of long years spent in scaling the CDU party hierarchy. These years revealed his possession of personal qualities that marked him for leadership: a driving ambition, a sense of optimism, an ability to attract others to work for him and to inspire them, a demanding approach to loyalty from his collaborators, a capacity for ruthlessness, a robust physical and mental constitution, organizational skills, and an ability to present himself as an 'ordinary' German possessing the qualities of that German in an above-average manner (Pruys 1995; Hoffman 1998: 2). Above all, he learnt to excel others in his mastery of the skills of exercising power (Dreher 1998). Before German unification Kohl's governing style was not derived from a strategic vision—even in relation to European unification. It was, above all, rooted in the primacy that he attached to internal party management within his CDU and to use of the discipline of coalition management as a means to enhance his freedom of manoeuvre as Chancellor (Clemens 1998).

The central element in Kohl's governing style was a preoccupation with keeping in check potential rivals within his CDU party. Having risen to power as a party manager and reformer, and served as chair of the CDU since 1973, Kohl understood all too well just what a loose, broad, and factionalized party he led (Huneeus 1996). He was acutely sensitive to the danger of becoming a prisoner of one or more party factions and to the need to retain broad party backing in order to see off challengers. Erhard and (within the SPD) Schmidt had also provided him with lessons about the political risks that followed from immersion in policy detail at the expense of cultivating internal party contacts. Hence his first priority as Chancellor was internal party management so that he remained apart and above party factions, identifying support for himself with party solidarity. In pursuit of this purpose he proved to be a pragmatic Chancellor rather than one concerned with programmatic coherence and resolute implementation. Kohl also relied on carefully cultivating a personal network of party faithful whose careers were bound up with loyalty to him. He took a close personal interest in party officials at all levels, charming them with his warmth and attention. A great deal of time that might have been spent mastering policy, like Schmidt, was devoted to monitoring changes and trends in party opinion and the balance of power between different factions. Only once assured of internal party support was Kohl prepared to push a policy like EMU strongly.

Kohl's preoccupation with internal party management had been reinforced by experience. In summer 1982, just before he became Chancellor, there had been private discussions about replacing him, involving notably Ernst Albrecht and Walther Leisler Kiep. Kohl also attributed the difficulties of Chancellor Schmidt in 1981–2 to his arrogant neglect of the SPD party grassroots and failure to foster emotional bonding with his party. Hence he focused on building up a network of loyalists within the CDU party base, across the various party factions. His small address book became a key tool in the exercise of power. Kohl's aim was to be able to mobilize ordinary CDU officials and voters behind him against any rivals and aspiring challengers. Policy knowledge and management on issues like EMU took second place to party knowledge and management. As we shall see below, the policy expertise and electoral popularity of Stoltenberg as Finance Minister was a major constraint on Kohl's engagement in pushing EMU. But Kohl dominated the internal politics of the CDU.

The second aspect of Kohl's governing style was his reliance on his personal management of the coalition relations with the FDP and the CSU as a discipline to keep the CDU in check. He presented the CDU as a 'governing party', not the government; and his job as to keep the coalition government together by ensuring that its constituent parties retained their own identity. Hence Kohl placed key significance on his role in managing the 'coalition rounds'. Accommodation of the FDP was a key feature of his governing style. He could use the dictates of the coalition with the FDP to force discipline on the CDU. In consequence, Genscher as Foreign Minister occupied a pivotal position in the government, and in private Stoltenberg often complained that Kohl paid closer attention to Genscher than to himself. Intellectually and instinctively, Kohl and Genscher were close on Europe and could fit EMU into their vision of European unification; and Genscher's Europeanism was a useful means of binding more cautious conservative-national elements in the CDU to European priorities. Structurally, this privileging of the relationship to Genscher and its use by

Kohl to keep the CDU in check was reinforced by the logistics of the European Council. As they sat side by side in the European Council, Kohl and Genscher were under pressure to co-ordinate their views closely on European matters.

But Kohl was also acutely aware of the risk of becoming—and being seen to be—Genscher's prisoner. Hence he endeavoured to enhance his freedom of manoeuvre as Chancellor by using the Bavarian CSU to balance the FDP in the coalition government. With respect to his own position within the CDU, and in relation to the management of EMU, Kohl's success in persuading Waigel—the CSU party chair since 1988—to take over the Finance Ministry in April 1989 was crucial. For these reasons Kohl was also deeply indebted to Waigel. Thereafter, Kohl was able to manoeuvre between Genscher and Waigel on EMU, playing them off against each other. He recognized that a politically sustainable consensus on EMU depended on keeping Genscher and Waigel on board. For Kohl the basic test for going ahead with EMU was a politically sustainable consensus behind it (Huneeus 1996). He was prepared to wait, sphinx-like, for clear evidence to emerge about such a consensus before declaring his hand. The prospects of such a consensus were not evident as long as the strictly ordo-liberal Stoltenberg maintained his strong personal position as Finance Minister and potential Chancellor in the wings.

An additional influence on Kohl's governing style was his failure to deliver a 'Chancellor bonus' to the CDU/CSU/FDP coalition in the federal elections of 1983 and 1987. Ominously, his personal popularity dropped further behind that of the coalition vote in 1987, when the CDU/CSU experienced its (then) worst result since the first federal election in 1949. Hence Kohl—unlike Adenauer—lacked a crucial resource for pushing ahead with new policy initiatives like EMU. In consequence, until German unification in 1989–90 his leadership role in EMU expressed itself in deploying his expert skills in the arts of internal party management and of coalition management. It did not take the form of an independent policy leadership founded on exploiting a broad electoral appeal (the 'Chancellor bonus') or on the use of the 'chancellor principle' as embodied in Article 65 of the Basic Law. The 'chancellor principle' rested on the so-called 'guidelines competence' by which the Chancellor sets the basic framework of policy within which ministers work. But Kohl lacked the personal political authority to turn this constitutional provision to his advantage. In this key respect his governing style differed from that of Adenauer. Only Kohl's best electoral result as Chancellor—in 1983—exceeded Adenauer's poorest—in 1961.

Kohl maintained a degree of openness on the substance of EMU and a preference for tactical delay, which could be seen as prevarication by Mitterrand and Elysée officials. In part this openness reflected the lack of a clear grasp of the technical issues involved, an intellectual discomfort with technical economic arguments, and a preference to leave them to others. He lacked command of detail. But it also stemmed from the way in which issues like EMU figured as tactical elements in his political strategy which was to situate himself behind the latent majority. EMU was considered from the strategic perspectives of party, coalition, and electoral trends and objectives—and any possible threats to his personal position in these interrelated arenas. In the period 1982–8 these considerations led him to accept the EMU policy line advocated by Stoltenberg: that monetary union must follow a process of economic and political union. They also induced him to retreat back to a position of caution in 1989, signalling to Mitterrand before the Madrid European Council that he was reluctant to set a clear date for an IGC on EMU and then, before the Strasbourg Council, that he wished to extend the IGC to cover political-union matters.

Kohl's openness on EMU reflected another aspect of his governing style: his preference for informality and improvisation in organizing the policy-making process. He was happy to leave the details of EMU to the Finance Minister, on the basis that this was his responsibility; he was also convinced that it was crucial to bind in the Bundesbank's support on every detail. Hence Kohl's technique was not to immerse himself in EMU files, as Schmidt would have done. But equally he was determined to avoid becoming a prisoner of the Bonn machine, especially on such crucial goals as European unification and Franco-German reconciliation where he recognized that his own responsibilities were engaged. For this reason Kohl relied on managing the decision-making process and controlling the timetable of decision rather than intervening strongly and directly in the policy debate on EMU. His skill was in listening intensely, in absorbing the key points, and in summarizing discussions clearly. But the cabinet played no significant part in this process. It was used as no more than a reporting body, Kohl being most concerned to keep disagreements away from this forum (Dreher 1998: chapter 30). Decisions on EMU were taken in small, flexibly scheduled meetings involving relevant ministers. His technique was to organize co-ordination outside cabinet in informal meetings that set the Foreign Ministry against the Finance Ministry and put them under pressure to reconcile their views to a timetable provided by the EC's calendar. The timetable of decision was a particularly powerful resource that he used to engineer agreement.

Kohl's working method for preparing himself on EMU was to retain his freedom of manoeuvre by relying on close personal contact with a small set of hard-working, highly intelligent collaborators from whom he expected unequivocal loyalty. He placed heavy demands on a very few officials in the Chancellor's Office: notably Horst Teltschik (Kohl's so-called 'third son'), Peter Hartmann, Joachim Bitterlich, Johannes Ludewig, and Edouard Ackermann. During the IGC of 1991 Horst Köhler—unlike his predecessor Tietmeyer—gained a similar status. He preferred to talk with those who wrote and had mastered EMU files rather than to study those files himself. Kohl also liked to work outside official channels, relying on informal contacts for expert advice (especially Alfred Herrhausen at the Deutsche Bank) and sounding out trusted, long-standing friends from his region and locality. Unlike Mitterrand he had no time for 'in-house' intellectuals on EMU, like Jacques Attali. Such 'mavericks' did not impress Kohl. His political instinct led him to trust in those who knew the files in depth, to encourage debate, and to seek out compromises that isolated no significant interest within the party or coalition.

Finally, Kohl was concerned about the 'image-management' aspects of EMU. He sought, in particular, to contain the influence of Genscher and his search for personal political profile on EMU, distrusting especially Genscher's active use of the media. Also, he was preoccupied with ensuring that he was not seen to act on EMU under French or other external pressure. Kohl sought to ground his positions on EMU in a clear statement of German interest and to stake out an independent role for himself (Korte 1998a, 1998b). Hence, as head of the division for communication and publicity in the Chancellor's Office, Ackermann took on a particular importance in designing and getting across his message on EMU as part of a wider political analysis of its implications for Kohl's electoral prospects. Ackermann's staff were crucial to developing an appropriate political language for the Chancellor to use about EMU from 1990. That language was heavily indebted to Adenauer.

Kohl sought to avoid a directive role on the substance of EMU policy in the manner of a Schmidt. He alternated between hiding his preferences and, more frequently from 1990, leading discussion in a certain direction. Above all, Kohl saw the development of EMU policy in highly personalized terms: of who could be trusted to deliver on sound policy substance; of outmanoeuvring opponents; of attending personally to protecting his own position as Chancellor by ensuring a politically sustainable consensus about EMU; and of countering the use of EMU by others as a means of enhancing their public profiles at his expense.

Stoltenberg and Finance Ministry Power over the EMS and EMU

Gerhard Stoltenberg's appointment as Kohl's Finance Minister in 1982 was the political guarantee of a cautious, long-term approach to EMU firmly rooted in the traditional pre-Schiller ordo-liberal tradition. The strength of this guarantee was vouched for by various factors: Stoltenberg's solid grasp of the technical aspects of economic, financial, and tax policies; his interest in the principles of a 'family-centred' social policy reform that went back to his period as a student in Kiel studying under Gerhard Mackenroth; the impressive figure that he cut in negotiations as confident, articulate, lucid, and sophisticated in argument; his appointment of Hans Tietmeyer from the Economics Ministry as his State Secretary, a highly respected policy professional, intellectual heavyweight on EMU, and tough negotiator in Bonn and Brussels; his priority to reversing the approach of the Schmidt government by working closely and in tandem with the Bundesbank to co-ordinate his policy proposals with the objective of persuading the Bundesbank to pursue a strategy of interest-rate reduction; and the fact that he soon emerged in opinion polls as consistently the most popular member of the federal government, well ahead of Kohl. Hence, in relation to EMU, Stoltenberg was able to make maximum use of the constitutional principle of ministerial autonomy over the affairs of their departments (Article 65 of the Basic Law).

The relationship to Kohl was made difficult by Stoltenberg's popularity and comparison with Stoltenberg's reputation as a competent, highly intelligent policy professional. In consequence, though Kohl did not fear him as a conspirator, he viewed Stoltenberg as potentially his most likely replacement. Also, the personal chemistry was not easy. Stoltenberg's formal correctness as a cool 'Northerner' of impeccable good manners and dignified bearing contrasted with the personal ease and 'down-to-earth' manner of the clumsier 'Rhinelander'. At the same time, this same formal correctness inhibited Stoltenberg from engagaging in plotting against Kohl in the manner of other party rivals. Like Tietmeyer, his style was that of the 'lone fighter'. But he was always the loyal and reliable servant of government policy, contributing till 1987 to the strength of the government. He was not seen by Kohl as a man scheming against him.

Intellectually, Stoltenberg's position on EMU was underpinned by Tietmeyer; by Graf Lambsdorff as FDP Economics Minister (till 1984); and, back in Kiel, by Herbert Giersch at the Kiel Institute of World Economics and by Schöllhorn, President of the Schleswig-Holstein state central bank and a former member of the Werner Group. His ministerial office was headed by Horst Köhler, who had served as his economic adviser as Prime Minister in Kiel, had earlier worked under Tietmeyer in the economic policy division of the Economics Ministry, and was later to be Germany's chief negotiator in the IGC of 1991. A smooth relationship to the Bundesbank was also guaranteed by Stoltenberg's concern (and Tietmeyer's) to end the period of critical distance and tension between the federal government and the Bundesbank that had marked the Schmidt years (Stoltenberg 1997: 282). In so far as there was a difference it was one of emphasis. Both Stoltenberg and Tietmeyer had come to regard the EMS as more vital to German economic interests than did some officials in the Bundesbank, like Schlesinger. On the other hand, they felt that they could count on the diplomatic skills of Pöhl as Bundesbank President to keep in check excessive reluctance about the EMS and about the need to respond constructively to possibilities to deepen European economic and monetary integration. Stoltenberg and Tietmeyer shared Pöhl's concern about the degree of parochialism and provincialism that existed within the Bundesbank council. The shared inclination of Stoltenberg, Tietmeyer, and Pöhl was to play a constructive role in G7, IMF, and EC negotiations. But their ordo-liberal roots made them more cautious about international and European economic-policy co-ordination than Schmidt had been.

Saving the EMS: Stoltenberg, Kohl, and the March 1983 ERM Crisis

Stage 2 of the EMS was already off the agenda by October 1982. The issue in winter 1982–3 was crisis management of the EMS, not its institutional development, and the central question was whether the French franc would stay in the ERM. Delors and Stoltenberg had discussed the problems through the winter. Kohl's first major intervention came the day before the Copenhagen European Council on 3–4 December when he instructed Stoltenberg that the French franc was not to be devalued in ECOFIN. They were agreed that the French needed to be given time to clarify their economic policy. Kohl understood that he was acting to help Mitterrand whose commitment to the EMS as a building block for European unification was not in doubt. Genscher's soundings in France confirmed the view that any initial hesitations by Mitterrand were now at an end.

Having been distracted by an exhausting election campaign Kohl was taken by surprise when the ERM crisis broke just over a week later in March 1983. When Bianco visited the Chancellery to argue the case for a D-Mark revaluation as a means of helping to engineer a change in economic policy in France within the ERM, Kohl's instinct was to leave matters to be resolved between Stoltenberg and Delors. Bianco was given no reassurance. But Kohl was not able to sustain this low-profile role as the pressure mounted from the Elysée. On 16 March Michel Camdessus, director of the French Trésor, signalled to Tietmeyer that he wished to personally deliver to Stoltenberg a top-secret letter from President Mitterrand to Kohl (Stoltenberg 1997: 317–19). The contents of this letter, which called for urgent Franco-German consultations, were considered at an evening meeting chaired by Kohl and involving Stoltenberg, Genscher, and Waldemar Schreckenberger as head of the Federal Chancellor's Office. Stoltenberg rejected Mitterrand's call for a large revaluation of the D-Mark, arguing that Germany had still not fully emerged from recession. As chair of ECOFIN during the German Presidency of the EC, Stoltenberg would have to assume responsibility for any realignment decision. Hence Kohl's strategy for managing the crisis was to lock him in to collective German positions and expose him more directly to pressures from Paris. Accordingly, Kohl proposed that Stoltenberg should leave immediately for Paris to meet in strictest secrecy with Mitterrand and deliver the Chancellor's reply verbally and to consult with Delors. For this meeting, and the subsequent ECOFIN negotiations, Stoltenberg was given the following instructions:

- a modest D-Mark revaluation might be possible, but the burden of adjustment must be borne by the French franc;
- any agreement must serve to force domestic policy change in Paris (the Bonn actors were unanimous in seeing Mitterrand's economic policies as disastrous);

- an ERM realignment could not be handled in bilateral Franco-German nego-tiations (they recognized that in the multilateral forum of ECOFIN the voice of states that did not want a D-Mark revaluation, notably Denmark and the Netherlands, would carry a strong weight);
- the final outcome of ERM negotiations must be compatible with the prior-ity of giving a new impetus to European policy—as Genscher stressed, an ERM exit by France would be a major set-back for German ambitions in Europe.

This package of instructions satisfied the different interests at stake in Bonn and crucial to it was the bottom line of ensuring that the ERM was saved—on which Genscher and Kohl were insistent.

Hence an enormous negotiating responsibility was placed on Stoltenberg's shoulders. At his top-secret meeting next day with Mitterrand in the Elysée both recognized the importance of a shared Franco-German interest in a new phase of joint action to build Europe. But no conclusions were arrived at about the nature of an ERM realignment, and there was no clarity about French objectives. At a subsequent meeting with Stoltenberg and Tietmeyer on the same evening, Delors stressed the uncertainty in Paris, the catastrophic consequences for Europe of French exit from the ERM, and the intolerable burden of his weak negotiating position in ERM realignments. At the weekend ECOFIN in Brussels Stoltenberg remained the calm, patient chair, despite the great pressure under which the Germans were placed, accused by Delors of arrogance and indifference. Delors's return to Paris for instructions during the 48-hour negotiating marathon rein-forced to Stoltenberg as chair the lack of clarity in Paris and the urgency of the sit-uation. Faced with potential failure on the Sunday night just before the financial markets opened, Kohl and Stoltenberg consulted by telephone. Kohl's message to him was clear—the EMS must be saved for the sake of Germany's wider interests in building Europe. There was only one condition—a French austerity package. The eventual outcome—involving a 5.5 per cent revaluation of the D-Mark and a 2.5 per cent devaluation of the franc—underlined German willingness to make concessions for the ERM and for European unification. In Bonn's eyes the main victory was to save the ERM. The episode was crucial in revealing the motives that underpinned attitudes to EMU during the Kohl Chancellorship.

Fighting Off Delors's Trojan Horse: EMU and the Single European Act

By 1985 the success in developing use of the private ECU provided a stimulus to Delors as new EC Commission President (in January) and to Helmut Schmidt (in May) to reopen the question of strengthening the EMS (Schmidt 1985). Their proposals took up two themes: developing the official use of the ECU, in paral-lel to its private use, by giving it currency status in all member states; and devel-oping the EMCF into the EMF, able to use the ECU as the EC's intervention currency. Stoltenberg reiterated the German official position that further steps in European monetary integration must be within the general context of the process of economic and political integration. In relation to monetary integration the priority lines of action were liberalization of the European financial markets, especially by France and Italy, and participation of all member states in the ERM (*Handelsblatt*: 31 May 1985). The policy signal was clear: the onus of responsibility for further action on EMU rested outside, not with, Germany. Delors floated his ideas for developing the ECU as a reserve currency at the informal ECOFIN in Palermo in May 1985. But all that emerged were very modest steps to improve incentives for the use of the ECU by central banks.

More important was the determination of Delors to use the IGC convened after the Milan European Council to push ahead with proposals for incorporating EMU in the Treaty of Rome. On this issue he received strong support from Genscher who pressed on Kohl the value of securing a clear commitment in this form. Stoltenberg was determined to resist on the basis that the preconditions for EMU were not in place. His strategy, based on advice from Tietmeyer, was threefold: to argue on the basis of German positions developed for the Werner Report against any attempt to argue for EMU as the development of stage 2 of the EMS; to present a common front with Pöhl so as to borrow the credibility of the Bundesbank; and to work closely with the Luxembourg chair of ECOFIN to contain Delors by ensuring that his proposals went to ECOFIN before the IGC. Hence they would be examined in detail by the EC Monetary Committee. This procedural route gave the Finance Ministry and the Bundesbank more effective means of ensuring that they were not bound by any new Treaty chapter. Faced by hard-line opposition from Tietmeyer in the EC Monetary Committee, Delors attempted to negotiate bilaterally with him to find an acceptable agreement. Tietmeyer used this meeting with Delors to stress that any incorporation of EMU in the Treaty would require full ratification of EMU proposals under Article 236 (involving national parliaments and referendums) rather than decisions by Council under Article 235. He spoke of avoiding an EMU based on secret manoeuvres behind closed doors. In Delors's view, Tietmeyer was raising the hurdles for EMU.

Delors's proposals were brought forward at the 28 October ECOFIN. They involved incorporating the EMS in the Treaty of Rome, giving the EC Commission a role in monetary affairs, and creating an EMF. By couching them in terms of implementing the second stage of the EMS, he incited German opposition. Stoltenberg argued that such proposals were premature and ill-conceived. The first stage of the EMS had still to be implemented, notably British entry and Italian membership of the narrow band. Priority had to be given to abolishing capital controls. But, above all, Stoltenberg phrased his opposition in terms of the Werner Report. A transfer of monetary sovereignty required a prior framework of political union and, in particular, the integration of economic policies. Again the theme was that responsibilty for progress on EMU lay outside Germany.

The incorporation of monetary policy into the Treaty of Rome was not pressed for by the Belgian, French, and Italian delegations to the IGC till 19 November, just two weeks before the Luxembourg Council when the final Treaty details were scheduled for decision. This timing induced a sense in the Finance Ministry and the Bundesbank that EC Commission strategy was to bounce the German Chancellor into an open-ended commitment to EMU in Luxembourg. By this stage they recognized that Kohl was looking for a text to satisfy Genscher, Mitterrand, and Delors and his own inclination to show commitment to EMU, whilst at the same time being acceptable to Stoltenberg and Pöhl. In this context Finance Ministry negotiating objectives were defined in terms of avoiding a monetary chapter in the Treaty that would serve as a Trojan horse. Treaty language had to ensure that the EC Commission was kept out of monetary policy and to to avoid a process of 'creeping' EMU. The response was firm, co-ordinated, and tough reaction, co-ordinated by Tietmeyer. Pöhl spelt out verbally and in writing to Stoltenberg the strength of the Bundesbank's opposition. In relation to the proposal to replace the EMCF by an EMF he stressed two objections: the complications that would follow for the management of monetary policy; and the absence of guarantees for its independence from national governments as long as national central banks were not independent. An ECB was seen as a 'very long way from here'.

Stressing the Bundesbank's opposition, and the inadequate time-scale for incorporating such proposals in Treaty amendment in Luxembourg, Stoltenberg took up a tough position on the EMF with Kohl. The principle of the independence of the Bundesbank was presented as a 'higher interest' of the federal government. There was also no necessary link between realization of the European single market in the new Treaty amendments and incorporation of monetary policy in the Treaty. On a more positive note, Stoltenberg was at pains to stress that in principle the German government was committed to EMU and that his opposition had the support of four other governments—the British, Dutch, Greek, and Irish. In short, he was not alone. Stoltenberg, supported by Tietmeyer and Pöhl, sought to fix Kohl's attention on the single European market as a necessary basis for an EMU that remained premature.

Before the Luxembourg Council on 3–4 December it became clear that Kohl was prepared to sign a monetary chapter, not least to satisfy Mitterrand who was lobbying strongly for commitment to EMU as a necessary complement to the single market. At the same time the strong opposition of the British—underlined during Kohl's visit to London on 27 November—gave him the opportunity to play the role of broker in Luxembourg between the French and British. In doing so he could negotiate a very limited agreement that would command the support of the Finance Ministry and Bundesbank. Kohl's achievement at Luxembourg was to negotiate directly with Thatcher, with Tietmeyer present, a subsection on 'monetary capacity' that she could accept as a commitment to nothing in particular. In framing a suitable subsection Kohl was happy to rely on Tietmeyer's guidance. The Finance Ministry saw it as Tietmeyer's task to shadow Kohl closely in Luxembourg, to ensure that Delors's ideas were kept at bay—not least with help from the British, and to ensure that Kohl did not deviate from the agreed line as proposed by the Finance Ministry and backed by the Bundesbank. In this respect Tietmeyer was more successful than at the Hanover Council in 1988. A useful card for Tietmeyer were the signals from the British Treasury about Nigel Lawson's desire to join the ERM. These signals—communicated by Geoffrey Littler in the Treasury to Tietmeyer and by Anthony Leohnis at the Bank of England to Leonhard Gleske—provided a new incentive to take the British seriously. Kohl was more accommodating to the British in Luxembourg than Mitterrand would have liked him to be.

At Luxembourg Kohl recognized that he needed to play the decisive role on the EMS/EMU component. His strategic interests were in brokering a compromise between Delors and Mitterrand, on the one hand, and Stoltenberg and Pöhl, on the other; and in avoiding discouragement of British entry to the ERM. But the way that Kohl played this role disappointed both Delors and Mitterrand. In the Council session the Chancellor did not respond positively to Mitterrand's argument—made to him earlier in private—that a single currency was a necessary complement to the single market. More importantly, the German Chancellor pressed successfully for a Treaty provision (Article 102a) on 'monetary capacity' that failed to provide the EEC with formal competence in monetary affairs and gave no new role to the EC Commission in this area. Tietmeyer secured defence against 'creeping' EMU in the form of a Treaty provision that future institutional changes to develop economic and monetary policy required use of the Treaty amendment and ratification procedure (Article 236), including consultation with the EC Monetary Committee and the Committee of EC Central Bank Governors. Finance Ministry and Bundesbank officials saw this new provision as a safeguard against attempts by Delors and others to attain EMU by a strategy of stealth that relied on intergovernmental agreements.

For Tietmeyer the key phrase in the new Treaty Article 102a was that, in furthering co-operation in economic and monetary policy, member states 'shall respect existing powers in this field'. This phrase was seen as safeguarding the independence of the Bundesbank, and bore the hallmarks of German drafting. Article 102a had, in his view, been cleared of EMU bugs. Kohl's caution was clear at his press conference at the end of the Luxembourg Council. He stressed his success in ensuring the independence of the Bundesbank. A further sign of the victory of the German ordo-liberal approach came at the next meeting of the General Affairs Council on 16 December. Backed by the Luxembourg Presidency, Genscher resisted renewed attempts to write the EMS into the Treaty as a distinct institution and to insert a stronger reference to the ECU. The cumulative effect of these experiences was to confirm the political ascendancy of the ordo-liberal approach to EMU in Germany, to make Delors very much more cautious about EMU, and to clarify to some actors in Brussels and Paris that progress on meeting key German conditions was a prerequisite for further progress. Stoltenberg and Tietmeyer had been successful in ensuring that German signalling on EMU was clear and unambiguous.

Challenges to Develop the EMS: New Strains and Tensions

Stoltenberg's experience as Finance Minister had done nothing to convince him that French ministers and officials had moved away from their interventionist and centralizing inclinations in economic and monetary policies. Successive Finance Ministers (Delors till 1984; Bérégovoy 1984–6; and Balladur 1986–8) and their senior officials (like Trichet as director of Balladur's cabinet 1986–7) were seen in Bonn as entrapped within traditional French *dirigiste* assumptions. The confidential request for devaluation of the franc that followed the victory of the centre-right in the National Assembly elections of March 1986 sent a very negative signal to the German Finance Ministry and the Bundesbank—which opposed the move—and diminished the political credit of Balladur and Trichet with Stoltenberg and Tietmeyer. Their disinclination to respond more positively to discussions about EMU was, if anything, increased.

Despite these doubts and reservations, and quite independent of any new treaty base for EMU in 1985, new external challenges to the ERM prompted the first real signs of strains and tensions within the ordo-liberal coalition. The question of whether, and how, Germany should respond to the issue of ERM reform no longer elicited so united and harmonious a response. The most striking development was the way in which, in the Basle Agreement of September 1987, German negotiators accepted two of the main EC Commission proposals that they had rejected in March 1982: lifting the acceptance limit on ECU, and intra-marginal intervention. Though presented as 'small steps' by the Bundesbank, they were—from the perspective of 1982—important concessions.

A Turning-Point for the Ordo-liberal Coalition: The January 1987 ERM Crisis

The January 1987 ERM crisis served as a decisive catalyst for policy reflection within Bonn about ERM reform and its relationship to EMU. Bonn politicians were surprised to be caught up in a war of words from Paris that broke out in December 1986–January 1987 during the German federal elections. In December Chirac attacked the Bundesbank for increasing its money-market rates. The subsequent speculative pressures against the French franc were blamed on the Bundesbank by Chirac and Balladur. In response Stoltenberg was critical of Chirac's intemperate words. Chirac returned to the attack, speaking of a crisis of the D-Mark and not of the franc; hence responsibility to act rested with the Bundesbank. On 8 January Balladur excluded a devaluation of the franc. Made nervous by the scale of capital inflows, the Bundesbank pressed for an ERM realignment. Internally, and unusually, Stoltenberg and Tietmeyer were critical of the Bundesbank, arguing that the Bundesbank's rate rise had displayed a lack of sensitivity and that a realignment was not justified by economic fundamentals. But they were outflanked as both the French and the Bundesbank called for a realignment. Stoltenberg sought to regain the initiative. He cleared the German position with Kohl; met with the Bundesbank directorate in Frankfurt on 9 January; and informed Balladur that a realignment would have to involve no more than a 3 per cent change in the franc/D-Mark rate.

In public, Stoltenberg was careful to stand by the German version of events: that the French had unleashed the speculative pressures and must bear the consequences. But at the same time he signalled privately to his officials that the lessons of this crisis needed to be learnt. The EMS must be strengthened to cope with increasing speculative pressures and to avoid future realignments that were not justified by economic fundamentals. Stoltenberg and Tietmeyer also shared the reactions of Kohl and Genscher: that ways must be found to encourage the Bundesbank to be more flexible. Otherwise, the political assaults on the Bundesbank would mount in ferocity. For Stoltenberg and Tietmeyer measures to strengthen the EMS were necessary for two reasons. An exercise in political damage limitation was essential in order to protect the long-term position of the Bundesbank. Also, technically, there was a strong case for improving the functioning of the ERM in order to deal more effectively with speculative pressures.

As Foreign Minister, Genscher drew a different lesson: that, in the long term, the Bundesbank's role as the power centre of the ERM was not compatible with Germany's interest in deepening economic and political union. As these reflections began in the Foreign Ministry, Bitterlich was still serving in Genscher's private office with responsibility for EC and economic affairs. He took with him to the Chancellor's Office in summer 1987 a clear Foreign Ministry view that a bold initiative on EMU was required. Bitterlich and Genscher were very much on the same wavelength about EMU. They agreed in their analysis and in their sense that EMU was fundamentally a matter of political timing.

Containing French Strategy: (1) The Basle and Nyborg Agreements

At the ECOFIN on 12 January 1987 where the ERM realignment was agreed, the EC Monetary Committee and the Committee of EC Central Bank Governors were asked to examine ways of strengthening the operating mechanisms of the EMS. Its chair, the Belgian Mark Eyskens, spoke of 'better economic solidarity'. Three areas were identified: greater use of intramarginal intervention; improved co-ordination of interest-rate decisions; and, in the longer term, the possibility of direct intervention by the EMCF. In addition to stressing the use of EC currencies in EC central bank reserves and greater use of the ECU, Balladur's Memorandum of 12 February 1987 went further. He referred to a 'zone with a common currency and a joint, federally constructed central bank'. But, by the time of the informal ECOFIN in Knokke on 6 April, it was clear that the Bundesbank was determined to narrow the agenda to technical improvements and exclude fundamental reforms. It was reserved on intramarginal intervention. Pöhl was at pains to emphasize that operational aspects of the EMS relating to intervention fell solely within the responsibility of the EC central bank governors and that direct intervention by the EMCF was ruled out.

In these negotiations Pöhl was in a difficult position. On the one hand, Stoltenberg and Tietmeyer were pressing for the Bundesbank to show itself more flexible, particularly by accepting intramarginal intervention. On the other, Pöhl faced strong reservations within the Bundesbank directorate and especially the Bundesbank council. The main suspicion was that considerations of domestic stability would be subordinated to the exigencies of international monetary diplomacy. Objections focused on the issue of intramarginal intervention. Symptomatic of the internal resistance that Pöhl faced was the fact that it was not until 16 June 1987 that the Bundesbank recognized the ECU as a currency, giving it the status of bank money (though not of legal tender). In relation to the negotiations on strengthening the EMS the Bundesbank council agreed a two-point negotiating position: that the principles of stability policy and central bank independence were not to be endangered; and, reflecting Finance Ministry concerns and the views of its international division, that the Bundesbank should not be seen as a brake on European integration.

On one point Stoltenberg and Pöhl were agreed: in rejecting Balladur's proposal that confidence in the ERM could be strengthened if the Bundesbank agreed to hold a certain proportion of its reserves in French francs. In discussions with Balladur Stoltenberg argued that the precondition for the franc developing as an international reserve currency was a continuing and effective pursuit of a stability policy by the French government. For Stoltenberg, as for the Bundesbank, stability began at home. In any case, Stoltenberg was keen to ward off the efforts of Balladur, and of Delors, to give ECOFIN the key role in the forthcoming agreement. Eventually, at the ECOFIN in Nyborg on 12–13 September he was able to ward off the efforts of Delors and Balladur to go beyond the proposals already agreed in Basle by the central bank governors, focusing on developing the role of the EMCF as a 'lender of last resort'. The Nyborg ECOFIN confined itself to approving the Basle Agreement.

Under pressure from the Finance Ministry and from ECOFIN to be more flexible, the Bundesbank's strategy was to ensure that the Committee of EC Central Bank Governors became the institutional venue in which proposals were negotiated. In this way Balladur and other radical reformers could be kept at a distance. This strategy seemed all the more attractive with the appointment of Jacques de Larosière as Governor of the Banque de France. As former managing-director of the IMF he was rated as a highly experienced international monetary diplomat with a firm belief in economic stability. His appointment was seen as a signal that the Banque de France would be more independent- and tough-minded in its dealings with the French Finance Ministry. Moreover, Pöhl and de Larosière had been close colleagues since both acted as 'sherpas' for G5 in the 1970s. Hence during 1987 Pöhl, Gleske, Wolfgang Rieke, and Claus Köhler pursued close bilateral discussions with de Larosière and Lagayette about intervention issues and the balance between intramarginal interventions, interest-rate adjustments, and parity changes. Both sides were agreed in wishing to confine the negotiations within the Committee of EC Central Bank Governors. This underlying agreement about strategy facilitated the 8 September 1987 Basle Agreement. It also made it easier for the Bundesbank to keep the issue of direct intervention by the EMCF away from the agenda. Such a development would enhance the potential influence of ECOFIN over monetary policy.

The Basle Agreement was recognized by the Bundesbank as involving a major German concession about the use of intramarginal intervention and a minor concession on the removal of acceptance limits on settlements in official ECU. But Pöhl was at pains to claim German victories. Intramarginal interventions were to be used sensitively and cautiously and did not impose a new open-ended requirement on the Bundesbank. The Basle Agreement was consistent with the Bundesbank position that exchange rates that lacked credibility could not be supported; whilst the active, co-ordinated use of interest-rate changes as a means of adjustment was seen by the Bundesbank as far more important than intervention. For Pöhl the main German victory was in paragraph 7. Here, recognizing the discipline imposed by liberalization of capital movements, the EC central bank governors committed themselves to pursue policies to stabilize domestic prices and costs, achieve external balance, and ensure exchange-rate stability. In other words, other EC central banks were formally recognizing their commitment to internal as well as external stability. The Bundesbank was succeeding in its strategy of exporting the German model to Europe.

The Basle and Nyborg Agreements underlined the way in which the Bundesbank sought to deal with the French and the EC Commission's strategy of 'salami-slicing' on EMU, of seeking to use institutional developments to achieve EMU by an indirect approach. Bundesbank strategy was to control the institutional venue of negotiations and to articulate a logically coherent conception of the relationship between developing the EMS (which was on the negotiating agenda) and EMU (which was not). The development of the EMS must be consistent with the principles on which EMU should rest: domestic stability and central bank independence. Hence the Bundesbank bargaining style was rigorously deductive and concerned to uncover the hidden code for EMU behind French and Commission proposals for 'reform of the EMS'.

Containing French Strategy: (2) The Franco-German Economic Council

Far more problematic for the Bundesbank was the attempt by the French government to draw the Bundesbank into the political framework of Franco-

German policy coordination provided by the Elysée Treaty of 1963. In June 1987 President Mitterrand proposed to Kohl 'a new treaty of the Elysée type' to commemorate the twenty-fifth anniversary of the Elysée Treaty. Kohl welcomed in particular his willingness to consider a framework of co-ordination to promote Franco-German military integration, desired by the Germans as a means to reduce uncertainty about the implications of French strategy and tactics for German territory. At a meeting in Bonn on 24 July with Hubert Védrine and Attali, Teltschik proposed a Franco-German Defence Council, only to be met with a French counter-proposal for a Franco-German Economic Council. Sensing political difficulties ahead in Germany, Teltschik replied that this French proposal could not be considered without Stoltenberg. But Dumas and Guigou were more successful in gaining the endorsement of Genscher, who pressed the case for a Franco-German Economic Council strongly on Kohl.

Stoltenberg and Tietmeyer were not directly involved until the Franco-German summit in Karlsruhe on 13 November. In Karlsruhe Chirac insisted that he would play no part in the twenty-fifth anniversary celebrations in January 1988 unless Germany agreed to a Franco-German Economic Council. More hesitant than Genscher, Kohl replied that this proposal raised serious difficulties because of different understandings in France and Germany about how economic and monetary policies should be handled. Hence it was necessary to clear the matter with his Finance Minister. That evening Stoltenberg pressed on Kohl the point that, if this concession were necessary, there would have to be one condition—the role of such a body must be strictly consultative, not decision making. Hence the Karlsruhe summit agreed to create two new bodies for the twenty-fifth anniverary: a Security and Defence Council and, in the wording of the Germans, a 'committee for economic and financial co-ordination'. Stoltenberg and Tietmeyer understood that there would be two 'committees' to be set up by intergovernmental agreement, not in binding treaty form.

Substantive negotiations on the new Franco-German body involved Tietmeyer and Trichet during December and January. Tietmeyer was successful in his central objective which was to restrict the new body to a consultative role, involving discussions but not decisions. In so doing, he kept Stoltenberg and the Bundesbank regularly informed about texts as they developed. The Chancellor's Office was kept at bay by the argument that, without Bundesbank approval of the text, there could be an adverse reaction in the Bundestag. After Tietmeyer had secured Bundesbank approval he and Pöhl were taken by surprise. Just a few days before the agreement was to be signed in Paris on 22 January, it emerged that the Federal Chancellor's Office had agreed with the Elysée to incorporate the text in the Elysée Treaty and not in an intergovernmental agreement. The Bundesbank did not receive a copy of the final document till the day before its scheduled signature in Paris. This change of legal status emboldened the Bundesbank council to widen its criticisms. Pöhl argued that the German federal government had succumbed to French 'salami-slicing' tactics. There was unhappiness that the new body was now called the Franco-German Economic 'Council'. More importantly, the Bundesbank council saw a risk that the protocol would bind the Bundesbank to objectives of economic co-ordination established by the new council; and was concerned that Article 4 referred to a co-ordination 'as close as possible'.

What followed was testimony to the mobilizing power of the ordo-liberal coalition. At its meeting on 21 January the Bundesbank council expressed its alarm and irritation at this threat to its authority under the Bundesbank Law of 1957. The Bundesbank's legal staff quickly produced its opinion that the envisaged treaty commitment would infringe the Bundesbank Law under which the Bundesbank was independently responsible for 'safeguarding the currency'. There followed an avalanche of legal, economic, and newspaper opinion that took the Bundesbank's side. Domestically weak, Kohl was sensitive to threats to his personal position. Hence he manoeuvred to establish a sustainable consensus. By 4 February Kohl was conceding before the Bundestag that, if necessary, the Treaty would be amended to confirm the Bundesbank's independence. On 5 February, following the Bundesbank council meeting, Pöhl wrote to Stoltenberg demanding a binding assurance that the new Treaty protocol would not impinge on Bundesbank independence. In a reply of 27 April Pöhl was reassured that the Franco-German Economic Council was to be a consultative and not a decision-making body. But, despite such reassurance, Pöhl continued to vent his irritation at being 'required' to participate in sittings of the Franco-German Economic Council (for instance in an interview for Radio Hesse on 5 June).

For Stoltenberg, Tietmeyer, and Pöhl the lesson of the Franco-German Economic Council was clear. It underlined the need to proceed with the greatest possible caution in negotiations with the French government about institutional questions relating to economic and monetary co-ordination. In Pöhl's reaction there was also an intimation of why he would react with such shock to his appointment to the Delors Committee. He saw it as a breach of convention to require the Bundesbank President to participate in international policy co-ordination that might place him in a position of compromise with respect to discharging his domestic responsibilities.

Containing French Strategy: (3) The Balladur Memorandum

German Finance Ministry and Bundesbank reactions to Balladur's Memorandum on European Monetary Construction of 8 January 1988 were shaped by this background. This memorandum went further than traditional French demands for an end to the asymmetry within the EMS. Balladur argued that a 'zone with one currency' was the logical consequence of the single European market scheduled for 1992. The question of an ECB was finally put on the agenda of ECOFIN. ECOFIN referred consideration of the questions raised by the Balladur Memorandum to the EC Monetary Committee.

Faced by this initiative, and the latest news about the Franco-German Economic Council, there was a difficult discussion at the Bundesbank council meeting on 21 January. In its wake Pöhl stressed that, though the Bundesbank backed an ECB, this was bound to be a long-term matter. There was too much to be done to put in place the single market and bring all EC states into the ERM before an ECB could become a practical matter. Not least, other governments had to begin by making their own central banks independent and by recognizing that an ECB had to be independent of the EC Commission and the Council. Schlesinger, the Vice-President, spoke about EMU discussions as a long way in the future. After the Bundesbank council meeting on 5 May 1988 Pöhl stressed the degree of agreement with the Finance Ministry; the paramount need for action to be focused at the national level in putting in place the conditions for stability; the danger of trying to build on the EMCF rather than the Committee of Central Bank Governors (code for opposing Delors's ideas); and that the time was not ripe for EMU and an ECB.

The Finance Ministry was reassured by its intelligence that the Balladur Memorandum was seen as overambitious within the French Trésor and driven by internal *cohabitation* politics rather than being a considered appraisal of what was possible in EC political terms. Long and toughly worded encounters followed between Tietmeyer and Trichet in the EC Monetary Committee, notably on 29 April. As Chair of the EC Monetary Committee, Geoffrey Littler reported its conclusions to the informal ECOFIN at Travemünde on 16 May. Though these conclusions endorsed the idea of strengthening the EMS, they embodied two of Tietmeyer's main points: that an EMU with an ECB was not a necessary condition for realizing the single market; and that equal weight had to be given to economic and monetary issues. Tietmeyer felt satisfied that his argument that EMU was a very long-term issue had carried the day. In pressing his case that there had been insufficient convergence around stability, he recalled the devaluation of the French franc in April 1986; Chirac's attack on the Bundesbank in December 1986; and the more recent episode of the Franco-German Economic Council. This debate in the EC Monetary Committee showed that, despite their commitment to the EMS and its development, the confidence of Tietmeyer in French readiness to realize a durable EMU with Germany had not noticeably grown.

Genscher as 'Policy Entrepreneur' and Kohl's Political Strategy for the Hanover European Council

Against this background of mounting French pressure, it seemed that German negotiators had been successful in protecting their basic policy positions on EMU. But successful resistance depended on the domestic political authority of Stoltenberg as protector of the power of the ordo-liberal coalition over EMU. Chancellor Kohl's domestic political weakness in 1987–8 appeared to offer a guarantee that little would change. In fact, within a very short time period, the momentum for policy change on EMU was to build up a powerful head of steam. The outcome was a radical transformation of Kohl's approach to EMU at the Hanover European Council in June 1988 compared to the position that he had taken at the Luxembourg Council in December 1985.

In 1987–8 three external catalysts created a new 'window of opportunity' for Genscher to challenge Stoltenberg, Tietmeyer, and Pöhl:

- the political dynamics unleashed by the Single European Act and by progress in implementing the single European market programme;
- emerging prospects for radical change in East–West relations in Europe, consequent on Mikhail Gorbachev's appointment as General-Secretary of the Soviet Communist Party in 1985, and their impact on the way in which Genscher and Kohl viewed Franco-German relations; and
- change in the political balance within the German federal government following the January 1987 election and following Stoltenberg's domestic political problems after September 1987.

These external changes put the ordo-liberal coalition on EMU on the defensive. They provided a 'window of opportunity' for a skilled political strategist like Genscher to emerge as a 'policy entrepreneur' in putting EMU back on the political agenda and for Kohl to reappraise EMU's role within his political strategy.

Genscher as 'Policy Entrepreneur' on EMU: The Genscher Memorandum

Though Genscher's initiative on EMU was to wait for another year, the real turning-point in his reflection on EMU came in early 1987. Genscher's reaction to the January 1987 ERM crisis differed from that of Stoltenberg. During and after that crisis Roland Dumas took up French criticisms directly with Genscher on behalf of the Elysée. Dumas was Genscher's key contact in Paris and a man in whom Genscher had complete confidence, not least as the closest confidant of Mitterrand. Indeed, Dumas's appointment as Minister for European Affairs in December 1983 (and then as Foreign Minister in December 1984) had been interpreted by the German Foreign Ministry as a signal of a more active European policy by Mitterrand. With the *cohabitation* (1986–8) Genscher continued to work most closely with Dumas, even though he lacked ministerial office. There was, in effect, a 'transgovernmental linkage' between the two that brought Genscher closer to Dumas than to Stoltenberg. The fact that Dumas spoke German and that both were lawyers by training added to the personal chemistry. Crucially, Dumas offered Genscher access to the mind of Mitterrand and discussions with him opened up for Genscher the opportunity to act as privileged political interlocutor between Paris and Bonn.

But, though Dumas put him under sustained pressure on EMU, Genscher's conclusions derived from his own independent political analysis. At the heart of this analysis was Genscher's view that continuing asymmetry in the practice of the ERM was not compatible, in the long term, with either the survival of the EMS or the pursuit of the larger project of European political union. For reasons of German vital interests it was necessary to confront those in the Finance Ministry and in the Bundesbank who were content for the EMS to be based on the D-Mark as its anchor. Genscher developed the counter-argument that the EMS was crucial to German interests but that its survival was not compatible with the Bundesbank making monetary policy on a national basis for Europe as a whole. Hence a determined effort was required to draw the Bundesbank, and the 'conservative' Finance Ministry as its spokesperson in Bonn, into a more constructive approach to EMU. Only with EMU could the long-term conditions for a deepening of Franco-German reconciliation be put in place.

The force of this political analysis was strengthened by Genscher's recognition that Gorbachev must be taken seriously as a Soviet reformer. His conclusion was that major changes were possible in relation both to East–West relations in Europe and to German unification. For Genscher the prerequisite of pursuing these changes, which were in Germany's vital interest, was a new political impetus to European unification. This signal from Genscher opened up an opportunity to Dumas to press the EMU issue. But, and this is the key point, with Genscher he was pressing against an open door. To vary the metaphor, Genscher was not a loudspeaker for French interests in Bonn. He was a sensitive antenna.

Wilhelm Schönfelder in the economics division of the Foreign Ministry, and Bitterlich in his private office till summer 1987, provided Genscher with additional arguments. First, the general progress in achieving economic convergence since 1983, consequent on developments within the ERM, diminished the force of Finance Ministry and Bundesbank reservations about EMU. Secondly, German economic interests were bound up with the newly emerging single European market. The logic of completing the single European market was a 'common' currency. As a sign of support within Germany's economic elite, Genscher's attention was drawn to a speech by Edzard Reuter, chair of Daimler Benz, to the CDU's Economic Council (*Wirtschaftsrat*) on 13 March 1987. Reuter had called for 'further development' of the EMS and looked forward to a single currency area in Europe.

This political and economic analysis underpinned Genscher's newly activist approach as 'policy entrepreneur' on EMU in 1987–8. He pressed his case directly on Kohl, skilfully exploiting the Chancellor's relative political weakness after the January federal elections and his own enhanced political strength as the electoral saviour of the coalition. Though he shared the analysis, Kohl hesitated on EMU. He stressed the potential problems with the CSU and within the CDU. Publicly, Genscher tested the political waters for the first time on the issue of the institutional development of the EMS in a speech to EC ambassadors in Bonn on 24 March 1987 (Schönfelder and Thiel 1992: 22). Written by Schönfelder, the reaction to this speech encouraged Genscher to continue returning to the theme in 1987. Later, in the autumn, Genscher was quick to support, as its staunchest advocate in Bonn, the French proposal for a Franco-German Economic Council.

Genscher was driven by his belief in EMU as an essential step in the political unification of Europe. Indeed, EMS reform and EMU had been referred to as early as the Genscher–Colombo initiative of 1981. But the gulf that separated that initiative's contents from the final Solemn Declaration on European Union adopted by the Stuttgart European Council in June 1983 had been a lesson for Genscher in the difficult arts of effectively seizing the initiative in EC affairs. As an experienced strategist Genscher bided his time, waiting for a suitable constellation of political events and policy developments. The appropriate moment was identified in February 1988.

The framework of policy developments was largely in place: the changes in prospect in East–West relations; the momentum of the single market programme; and the success of the ERM in delivering economic convergence. The additional catalyst was the success of the Brussels European Council in clearing away a set of contentious issues and opening up space for new initiatives. Political events were also favourable. In particular, Genscher's domestic political stature had risen as that of Stoltenberg had fallen. The FDP had fought the 1987 federal election on the slogan 'Genscher must remain Foreign Minister' and increased their share of the vote, whilst the share of the CDU/CSU dropped. Thereafter, Stoltenberg was embroiled in complex conflicts within the CDU/CSU about the tax reform package. These conflicts were not resolved till 23 June 1988, they distracted Stoltenberg from other issues, and used up a considerable amount of his political credit. More seriously, from September 1987 onwards, as chair of the Schleswig-Holstein CDU, Stoltenberg was drawn into the Barschel affair which centred on a smear campaign against the opposition SPD candidate organized by the head of the CDU state government, Uwe Barschel, culminating in the latter's suicide. The subsequent crisis of confidence in the CDU in Schleswig-Holstein produced an absolute majority for the SPD in the April 1988 state election, a further political set-back for Stoltenberg.

In addition, the presence of Martin Bangemann, a strong pro-European and FDP chair, as Federal Economics Minister helped to neutralize the traditional scepticism of that ministry towards EMU. An alliance of the Finance and Economics Ministries against Genscher would have created much greater difficulties for an EMU initiative. In this respect the presence of a strict FDP ordo-liberal like Graf Lambsdorff as Economics Minister would have meant much tougher and more searching questions. Genscher was able to count on the passive support of Bangemann who could restrain Economics Ministry reservations in the name of maintaining FDP unity within the coalition. As an FDP leader, he was in any case ideologically sensitive to the importance of building EMU on the economic foundations of market and stability principles.

The crucial new political factor was the German Presidency of the EC, which enabled Genscher to capitalize on these domestic political advantages. The EC

Presidency induced a latent, but real rivalry between Genscher and Kohl about who would be credited with the success of this presidency. Genscher was careful to prepare a strong team in advance (Genscher 1995: 384–5). An experienced Bonn insider and dedicated European, Hans-Werner Lautenschlager, was brought back as State Secretary in 1987. Having handled Germany's difficult EC Presidency in 1983 (when Kohl and Genscher had been distracted by the federal elections), Lautenschlager had the advantage of enjoying the confidence and trust of both political leaders. He was very much a 'European of the heart', but also a cautious and judicious man. The Foreign Ministry division responsible for the German Presidency was headed by Alois Jelonek. Lautenschlager's and Jelonek's political advice, along with that of Schönfelder on economic aspects, was central to the preparation of Genscher's EMU initiative.

The key point about the Genscher Memorandum for the Creation of a European Currency Area and a European Central Bank of 26 February 1988 was that its analysis and timing were German and dictated by Genscher. It was not a case of Genscher acting as a spokesperson for French interests in Bonn or surrendering German interests (as he saw them). Indeed, the Genscher Memorandum was more radical in content than any French initiatives on EMU in unequivocally supporting an ECB. The arguments for taking the initiative were fundamentally political: to use the German Presidency to give a new and decisive impetus to European political unification (an interest that had grown as Gorbachev's serious intent to change East–West relations became clearer); and to gain political credit for Genscher from this initiative. The timing was dictated by a perception that such an initiative would only be possible once, and if, outstanding problems relating to the EC budget and agriculture were resolved. In this respect the success of the European Council meeting in Brussels on 11–12 February in negotiating a complex package deal on these problems was crucial. It cleared the way for Genscher to act, and it also showed how effective co-operation between the Foreign Ministry, the Chancellor's Office, and Delors's officials could be. Genscher's will to act on EMU had already been demonstrated on 20 January 1988 when, in presenting his programme as chair of the EC Council of Ministers to the European Parliament, Genscher had announced that Germany intended to work towards the creation of an EMU. In advance, Genscher discussed his intentions with Delors and with Dumas.

After 12 February work on the EMU initiative began in earnest, with Genscher acting independently of his officials to set the policy direction. The deadline for finalizing the initiative was provided by a meeting on 26 February between Genscher and a group of European journalists to whom the Foreign Minister wished to present his ideas. Written under tight time pressure by Schönfelder, the Genscher Memorandum was an attempt to build the initiative around ideas acceptable to the Finance Ministry and to the Bundesbank, without drawing them into formal consultations. An attempt to consult them in this way would have led to political objections that the Foreign Ministry was stepping outside its legitimate sphere of interest. In order to neutralize such criticisms the memorandum appeared in an unusual form under the name Hans-Dietrich Genscher, not using his title of Foreign Minister. It was a personal memorandum, not a paper as a government minister.

The strategy behind the memorandum was to build in Bundesbank thinking and to be able to claim a basis of consensus for the memorandum. Hence, in content, the memorandum was an exercise in 'bridge-building' with ordo-liberal ideas. Schönfelder consulted Peter-Wilhelm Schlüter, head of the section on EC monetary policy in the Bundesbank. Schlüter was an unusual figure in the Bundesbank: a former EC Commission and Finance Ministry official, and pro-EMU. By strange coincidence, on the same day, 20 January, Genscher and Schlüter had both been delivering speeches in Strasbourg with an EMU content. Genscher had presented the German Presidency's work programme to the European Parliament. Schlüter had addressed the European Parliamentarians' and Industrialists' Council on 'Central Bank Autonomy—A Prerequisite for a European Currency'. In addition to talking to Schlüter, Schönfelder drew on the ideas in Schlüter's address. In effect, Schlüter became Schönfelder's intellectual mentor on EMU questions.

Reflecting Schlüter's influence, the Genscher Memorandum proposed an independent ECB pledged to price stability, on the German model. In so doing Genscher was astutely aligning himself with the Bundesbank's key condition for EMU: despite the fact that Schlüter's address had been followed by criticisms from the Banque de France and the Banca d'Italia directed precisely against this point. The Genscher Memorandum also spoke of parallel progress towards economic and monetary union, stressing their close interrelationship. This position too was not far removed from the views of Pöhl, Gleske, and Rieke in the Bundesbank. But the decisive new element was the procedural proposal for a 'committee of wise men', 'with professional and political authority', to be appointed by the Hanover European Council in June. This committee was to give operational form to EMU, producing its proposals on the design of an ECB and the transitional process within one year.

Given the peculiar nature of its status, the Genscher Memorandum did not go forward for formal consideration in the two-weekly meeting of 'European' State Secretaries (though Tietmeyer robustly questioned Lautenschlager about the procedure being used) or in the cabinet committee for European affairs (though Stoltenberg made known to Kohl his irritation at being bypassed in this way). The Genscher Memorandum was circulated privately and secretly, notably to Kohl, to Pöhl, and to Delors. There was intensive and secret lobbying, bypassing Stoltenberg and Tietmeyer, and helped by the presence of Bitterlich in the Federal Chancellor's Office working for Teltschik on EC matters. Teltschik and Hartmann did not need persuading on the merits of EMU. But in evaluating the Foreign Ministry's analysis of the politics and timing of an EMU initiative, Bitterlich's familiarity with recent Foreign Ministry thinking as a member of Genscher's private office was a bonus.

Genscher made direct contact with Pöhl. The Foreign Ministry view was that it was an enormous advantage to have Pöhl as Bundesbank President, given his sensitive and subtle understanding of economic and monetary diplomacy. Genscher's officials were also quick to see how valuable it would be to have Pöhl as a member of the 'committee of wise men'. Pöhl signalled to Genscher that he was in a very difficult position. On the one hand, in principle he favoured EMU and taking a constructive approach on EMU. But, on the other hand, he had serious difficulties within the Bundesbank directorate, notably with Schlesinger, and within the Bundesbank council, pointing to the 21 January meeting as an illustration. Pöhl stressed that Genscher's proposal would confront him with an impossible conflict of loyalties. He also expressed his reservations about the procedure being used. It was vital to work through the established structures for developing and co-ordinating EC policies.

Genscher was also keen to test and mobilize support at the EC level. The Genscher Memorandum was submitted to the EC's General Affairs Council and considered at its Lake Constance meeting on 5–6 March. More importantly, the German Presidency had been characterized by an unprecedentedly close involvement of Delors by Kohl, with Delors being invited to regular meetings with German ministers and officials in the Chancellor's Office. Their relationship had been further strengthened by the highly successful Brussels European Council. Genscher spotted an opportunity to utilize this close relationship of mutual respect between Delors and Kohl. Delors was encouraged by Genscher to become an important advocate of two key arguments to Kohl: that the committee of wise men proposal was a necessary basis for giving momentum to EMU and preparing treaty change on a sound basis; and that logically the single market required EMU. Kohl had no difficulty in accepting these arguments.

Defending Ordo-liberal Orthodoxy: The Stoltenberg Memorandum and Bundesbank Reactions to Genscher

The Genscher Memorandum caught the Finance Ministry off guard, overburdened by the business of the tax reform, and politically weakened both by consequent conflicts within the CDU/CSU and by the Barschel affair. Also, with its attention focused on challenging the Balladur Memorandum in the EC Monetary Committee, and delimiting the remit of the Franco-German Economic Council, its flank was exposed to challenge. It was, in short, trapped in the crossfire between French initiatives and Genscher's even more ambitious espousal of an ECB.

To add to the Finance Ministry difficulties, by the time of the Bundesbank council meeting on 3 March there were criticisms from Frankfurt of its failure to respond decisively to the weak points of the Genscher Memorandum. These 'technical' weaknesses were identified by Schlesinger and others as: its advocacy of the Europeanization of the employment and growth objectives of the neo-Keynesian Stability and Growth Act of 1967 (which were seen as qualifying the stability objective of the ECB and as a misrepresentation of current German economic thinking and practice); its reference to developing the ECU as a parallel currency (which was firmly rejected by the Bundesbank); its espousal of parallelism between economic and monetary union (many in the Bundesbank held to the coronation theory); and its proposal for a committee of wise men (by means of which EMU could be hijacked by irresponsible people favoured by the EC Commission). Bundesbank officials were alarmed at the unauthorized involvement of Schlüter (not personally approved by his superior Rieke), castigating him for pursuing a personal diplomacy on behalf of EMU, and for going beyond his brief (institutional issues) to speak on economic and monetary issues without bringing in Schlesinger. For the more conciliatory Gleske, the Genscher Memorandum failed to stress the political preconditions of EMU. The priority had to be to develop the EC as a 'community based on solidarity' (*Solidargemeinschaft*), armed with a substantial EC budget on the model of a federal state. Gleske had developed this argument before the European Parliament committee on economic, currency, and industry policy on 22 February. Schlesinger, Gleske and others looked to the Finance Ministry to contain the political and policy damage.

The Finance Ministry turned to the offensive with Stoltenberg's Memorandum on the Further Development of Monetary Co-operation in Europe of 15 March. This memorandum was written by Stoltenberg, by Tietmeyer, and by Günther Winkelmann in the money and credit division and was closely coordinated with the Bundesbank. In contrast to the Genscher Memorandum, the Stoltenberg Memorandum developed its central argument—that the time was not ripe for EMU—from coronation theory. The two memoranda were, in other words, derived from fundamentally different beliefs about EMU. The Stoltenberg Memorandum argued that it was necessary, first, to 'harden' and widen the ERM; then to put political union in place; and, finally, to establish EMU. The focus was on practical steps for 'the strengthening of monetary co-operation'. This strengthening had to be based on a growing consensus on stability-oriented fiscal and monetary policies, the irrevocable liberalization of capital movements, further improvement of convergence, the granting of independence to national central banks, and full participation of member states in the narrow band of the ERM. EMU was seen as a long-term goal and, in contrast to the Genscher Memorandum, set in the framework of the Werner Group's work.

As an enduring community based on solidarity [*Solidargemeinschaft*] . . . it must be founded above all on a far-reaching political and institutional reorganization of the Community towards a more comprehensive union. As was already stated in the Werner Report of 1970, a lasting EMU requires the creation or reshaping of Community bodies and the transfer of extensive powers from national to Community level going beyond mere monetary policy.

In contrast to the personalized nature of the Genscher Memorandum, Stoltenberg's Memorandum appeared under the title of Federal Minister of Finance. Conceived of as a position paper of the federal government, the Stoltenberg Memorandum followed the route of official channels, going to the European State Secretaries' meeting and to the cabinet committee for European affairs. It went also to the EC Monetary Committee as a submission to the discussions launched by the Balladur Memorandum. In these fora the memorandum served as the basis for a rigorous restatement of the traditional EMU policy position and for reclaiming EMU policy territory. But, unlike in December 1985, this time Kohl was less amenable to being tied down by the Finance Ministry.

Kohl, the Chancellor's Office, and Political Strategy for the Hanover Council

Before the Genscher Memorandum there were already signs that Kohl's views on EMU had evolved. He and his officials had already been forced to take up positions. By 1985 French Elysée officials like Attali, Guigou, and Védrine were raising EMU with staff in the Chancellor's Office, notably Teltschik. EMU was also surfacing as a regular issue at Franco-German summits. In June 1985 Attali pressed for EMU in the context of the secret 'commando-style' operation between Chancellery and German Foreign Ministry officials and Elysée officials to prepare a Franco-German Draft Treaty on European union for the Milan European Council. But Teltschik was cautious and disposed to view Attali as an intellectual maverick. He stuck to the German Finance Ministry line that economic union must precede monetary union and underlined the difficulty of progress given the underlying conflict between French and German views of EMU. Officials in the Chancellor's Office resorted to the argument that their hands were tied at the domestic level as a means of warding off French pressure.

The first Franco-German meeting at which Kohl gave a positive signal on EMU was at Heidelberg on 26 August 1986. He spoke of having problems with EMU but of being prepared to make sacrifices for Europe. At the Franco-German meeting in Frankfurt on 27 October 1986 he linked EMU to steps towards European political union. In the light of subsequent developments in 1989–90 the context in which Kohl located these remarks of 1986 was very significant. The Chancellor stressed the changing atmosphere in Moscow and in East Berlin and the need to take further steps to European union before trying to seize the new diplomatic opportunities emerging in Eastern Europe. Already Kohl was beginning to set EMU in the larger framework of East–West relations and German unification. In this respect Kohl's and Genscher's thinking was moving in the same direction.

But following the set-back of the January 1987 federal elections, Kohl was faced with new problems of accommodating the FDP's (and Genscher's) greater political strength with threats to his personal position from within the CDU and sharp criticisms from Strauss in Munich. In November Kohl was re-elected CDU party chair at the federal party meeting in Bonn by only 80.8 per cent. Electoral reverses followed in Schleswig-Holstein and in Bremen (where the CDU fell to 23.4 per cent). Relations deteriorated sharply between Kohl and his combative CDU General-Secretary, Heiner Geissler. The fact that Genscher sought political profile by taking on Strauss and the CSU made Kohl's position even more uncomfortable. Compared with the conciliatory FDP chair Bangemann, Genscher was seen as a force for disharmony, actively using the media for personal political profile.

Hence Kohl distrusted the Genscher Memorandum as an effort to sow dissension and embarrass the Chancellor. His initial reaction was shaped by internal party and coalition management considerations. He was cool and reserved, stressing potential opposition within the CDU/CSU and the greater political difficulties that he faced than Genscher who had the luxury of being part of a much smaller party. In response, Genscher pointed to the positive reaction to EMU within the German political and economic elites and the existence of strong pro-EC lobbies across all the main political parties. On 31 December 1987 in *Handelsblatt* Walter Seipp, chair of the Commerzbank, had called for transformation from the EMS to an EMU with an ECB. More helpfully still, on 8 February 1988 Lothar Späth, Kohl's most dangerous rival in the CDU, and Herrhausen of the Deutsche Bank had jointly called for an ECB 'as soon as possible'. Additionally, Genscher drew attention to the positive climate being generated by the work of the new Giscard–Schmidt Committee for the Monetary Union of Europe. By playing up Schmidt's public profile on EMU he was in effect inviting Kohl to outflank the former Chancellor (with whose strong leadership qualities he was often disparagingly compared). Genscher recognized that it would not be easy to coax Kohl to make a clear and firm decision.

By the time of his next informal talks with Mitterrand at Durbach on 14 March Kohl was taking up positions closer to the contents of the Stoltenberg Memorandum. He justified his reluctance to be drawn on EMU to Mitterrand by citing his preoccupation with the impending state election in Baden-Württemberg (where Späth was head of government). But he also went on to argue that a European central banking system must stand at the end of a process of European unification. First there had to be consensus on economic and financial policies. In effect, Kohl's comments reflected Stoltenberg more than Genscher. Next day, on 15 March in Bonn the Chancellor spoke of an ECB lying 'a good way ahead of us'. It was more important to talk about how we get to EMU than to start discussing the ECB as an institution.

Despite Stoltenberg's tough response, the Genscher Memorandum had not been filed away. Kohl's objective was to play for time. He asked his staff to review the Foreign Ministry analysis of the political rationale and timing of an EMU initiative; tested out for himself reactions from within the CDU and from trusted economic figures (like Herrhausen); sought to explore the implications of Genscher's proposal for a committee of wise men; and attempted to pacify

Stoltenberg, who was incensed by Genscher's course of action. On the question of political rationale and timing the Foreign Ministry analysis was endored by the Federal Chancellor's Office. Domestic and EC conditions for an EMU initiative were seen by Teltschik as much more favourable than ever before. At the EC level the one key open question was who would be French President after the May election. It seemed wise to wait on the outcome. But Teltschik and others were strongly opposed to a committee of wise men. They feared that it would come under too strong a French influence, would raise problems about who should represent Germany, and would be difficult to control and a potential source of political embarrassment to the German government. Kohl rejected this proposal at an early stage.

Domestically, Kohl's calculations were influenced by the change in the relative political fortunes of Genscher and Stoltenberg. Genscher was now by far the most popular German politician, having displaced Stoltenberg who was engulfed by the Barschel affair and the political turmoils of the tax reform. More positively, the Chancellor was in need of an issue on which he could construct an image of European leadership competence. Here the political advice of Wolfgang Schäuble, as head of the Chancellor's Office, was important. Kohl had to act to offset the sense of drift and insubordination in the CDU/CSU parliamentary party and the effects of his strained relations with Heiner Geissler by carving out a strong European role. Always concerned about internal party management, Kohl was encouraged by support for the step-by-step realization of EMU and the creation of an independent ECB contained in the CDU federal executive's paper of 18 February 1988, 'Our Responsibility in the World'. Another factor that played a role in helping Kohl to make up his mind was the figure of Lothar Späth, who was seen as his greatest threat in the CDU. In March, against the federal trend, Späth was to retain the CDU's absolute majority in the Baden-Württemberg state election. Späth was strongly pro-EMU. Hence an EMU initiative seemed to be working with the grain of developments in the CDU and in coalition relations with the FDP. Tactically, Kohl began to warm to the idea.

The first positive public signal of the Chancellor's willingness to support Genscher came on 9 March. Before the European Parliament he spoke of EMU as expediting the attainment of the political unification of Europe: 'only then is the development to European union irreversible'. But, right up until May, Kohl hesitated to finally commit himself to using the Hanover Council to set up a 'committee of wise men'. His first concern was to test the scope for pacifying potential opposition. By March Kohl was accepting the Foreign Ministry view that it was crucial to co-opt Pöhl into a position of responsibility. Hence the proposal emerged for Pöhl to chair one or more committees. Then, in April, building on Bundesbank views that the work could be entrusted to the Committee of EC Central Bank Governors, and Delors's argument to Kohl that the EC central bank governors must be directly involved, the Federal Chancellor's Office identified a way of seizing the initiative from Genscher. The Bundesbank's idea was changed, with the Chancellery advocating in strictest confidence Delors's idea of a new committee composed of EC central bank governors and a few independent figures. The refinement that they should serve 'in a personal capacity' came much later and from a different source, Tietmeyer.

This proposal had several political advantages for Kohl and helped meet his major aims in relation to Hanover. First, and pre-eminently, Kohl was concerned that a route to EMU be defined on a technically viable basis. Hence a role for EC central bankers had much to commend it. He did not want figures like Giscard d'Estaing involved (whom he thoroughly disliked). Secondly, the proposal helped to mitigate domestic and EC opposition. It could be sold to Stoltenberg as reassurance that the exercise would be conducted responsibly, hence buying off his opposition. It would have a similar function in relation to Mrs Thatcher. On these terms the support of Stoltenberg was achieved in April. Later at the G7 summit in Toronto on 19–21 June, Kohl reassured Mrs Thatcher by arguing that such a committee was unlikely to produce anything very radical. Thirdly, in this way Kohl could seize the initative from Genscher, capitalize on Genscher's policy entrepreneurship, and gain the political credit for using the German Presidency to innovate at the EC level. The Chancellor could carve out an independent leadership role on EMU. Finally, by this means the Bundesbank could *de facto* be co-opted into EMU and its potential to act as an external critic neutralized. Kohl's strategy was to bind the Bundesbank into responsibility for EMU, if necessary by presenting it with a *fait accompli* at Hanover.

At the same time Kohl continued to play for time by stressing to Genscher and to Delors his difficulties within the CDU/CSU and the need to await the results of the French Presidential election on 7 May. The Chancellor recognized that it would be politically more difficult to make progress on EMU at Hanover if Chirac were to be elected, not least given such negative perceptions of him within the Finance Ministry and the Bundesbank after the 1987 ERM crisis. The re-election of Mitterrand was the positive signal for which Kohl had been waiting to intensify his personal diplomacy on EMU. By 20 May Dumas, reappointed French Foreign Minister, was in Bonn to discuss an EMU initiative at Hanover with Genscher. But they were now on the sidelines. Kohl was by then intent on occupying the driving seat on EMU. His tactics were to work hand in glove with Delors, exploiting the asset of Delors's popularity which was in the ascendant across the German political spectrum. The success of the German Presidency had convinced Kohl about Delors's technical and tactical skills. Hence Hartmann and Bitterlich in the Chancellery and Pascal Lamy and Gunther Burghardt in Delors's cabinet set to work to prepare the EMU initiative for Hanover. The Chancellor's strategic objectives were clear: to set the seal at Hanover on what was already being seen as a highly successful EC Presidency, and to associate his leadership with the success of that Presidency and with a major new leap forward towards European union.

By the time of the next Franco-German summit, on 2 June at Evian, Kohl was determined to make progress on EMU at Hanover conditional on French concession on an issue that mattered greatly to Stoltenberg but that would be sensitive for a French Socialist government: agreement on complete liberalization of EC capital movement at ECOFIN on 6 June. He was, in short, preparing a political victory for Stoltenberg—just when he needed one—and demonstrating movement on an issue that figured prominently in the Stoltenberg Memorandum of March. Most importantly, it meant for Kohl that the unresolved issue of capital liberalization would not be used to block EMU at the Hanover Council. At Evian Kohl also revealed his hand to Mitterrand on the question of the chairing of the committee to be established at Hanover. He proposed—for the first time—Delors's name, knowing that it would please the French and provide a signal that he was looking for strong political direction of work on EMU. Evian was a considerable personal success for Kohl. The Chancellor played his cards carefully with a newly confident Mitterrand, fresh from a clear electoral victory. Just as in relation to Genscher, he was determined to retain ownership and control of the final proposals at Hanover. As on later occasions in relation to EMU (e.g. before the Strasbourg Council), he did not want to be seen as conceding to French pressure but as making EMU on his own terms.

Very much the power-minded politician and consummate tactician, Kohl was determined to hide his full hand from Stoltenberg, Tietmeyer, and Pöhl, whilst being a good deal more open with Delors and Mitterrand. At the end of May, it was still not clear to Stoltenberg—or even Delors—whether Kohl was in earnest about making progress at Hanover on the lines suggested by Genscher. By the time of Kohl's speech in Frankfurt on 12 June as part of the celebrations for the fortieth anniversary of the German currency reform, Stoltenberg and Pöhl were aware that EMU was on the agenda for Hanover. Kohl was at pains to stress that the German model must be the basis for designing EMU. But what was to be proposed in practical terms remained a mystery. What was clear to them was that Delors and Federal Chancellery officials were much more involved than themselves in strategic and tactical issues relating to the proposed committee. This involvement could be justified by their central role in relation to the European Council and by the exclusion of finance ministers from this forum. At the same time it evoked anxiety and irritation. Most problematic was the marginalization of Tietmeyer who, as Kohl's economic 'sherpa' (as well as State Secretary in the Finance Ministry), was not kept fully informed. Tietmeyer was particularly resentful of the discreet influence of officials in the foreign policy division of the Federal Chancellor's Office and their openness to pressure from the Elysée and from Delors in the secret preparation of the final decisions at Hanover. This degree of secrecy had been urged on Kohl by Delors who feared that leaks could enable opponents of the proposal to mobilize before Hanover. They colluded in a very secretive approach to preparing Hanover.

On 30 May at the second meeting of the Franco-German Economic Council in Paris the committee to study EMU was discussed by Stoltenberg and Bérégovoy. But no attempt was made to work out a joint position in relation to

Hanover. In the first place, the Finance Ministry and the Bundesbank were intent on limiting the new Economic Council to a discussion role. Even though they were under great pressure on EMU, they were not prepared to take the risk that its mobilization on EMU would lead the Franco-German Council to evolve into a decision-making forum. In any case, Stoltenberg and Tietmeyer sensed that power resided with the Elysée and not with Bérégovoy who would only act as a loyal servant of Mitterrand.

One issue did surface in Bonn before Hanover and related to the tactical implications of the agreement of an EC directive on capital liberalization. For the Finance Ministry the rationale for this measure was powerful. It would create a force for economic convergence in the form of market pressures. It was also an alternative to institutional reform of the EMS. What alarmed the Finance Ministry was the argument advanced by Foreign Ministry officials that there was tactical linkage between capital liberalization and EMU. In this view, capital liberalization was a major concession by the French and the Italians. They needed reassurance in the form of German concessions on EMU. This argument was ridiculed by the Finance Ministry. Its view of capital liberalization was framed in the cognitive terms of coronation theory. A tactical approach to capital liberalization threatened to produce a flawed and unsustainable EMU.

Maximizing the Bundesbank's Freedom of Manoeuvre: Pöhl and Hanover

Most irritated of all by the outcome of the Hanover Council was Pöhl. Pöhl had been involved in two sets of discussions with Kohl about how the committee to be established at Hanover might be composed. These discussions conditioned Pöhl's expectations of Hanover. At the first, in March, Kohl had proposed two committees: one to prepare for economic union, and one for monetary union. Both were to be chaired by Pöhl. The intent was to draw the Bundesbank into responsibility. Pöhl rejected this proposal for two reasons. First, it was not sensible to separate discussions of economic and monetary union; and, secondly, acting as chair would put Pöhl in a conflict of interests if he had to defend proposals that ran counter to Bundesbank policy positions. Such a situation would be untenable. Pöhl's strategy was to maximize his freedom of manoeuvre on EMU by distancing himself and the Bundesbank from any such exercise.

Pöhl reiterated this position at a subsequent ministerial-level discussion in Bonn, involving himself, Kohl, Genscher, and Stoltenberg. At this meeting on 26 May two models were considered: the Genscher proposal for five to seven 'wise men'; and/or the proposal for a more limited brief to be given to the Committee of EC Central Bank Governors to work on technical details of monetary union and an ECB. Pöhl indicated that he could live with either proposal. The committee of wise men would leave him free to make his views known when its report emerged. This comment only underlined to Kohl the weakness and danger of the Genscher proposal. Pöhl argued that entrusting work on the ECB to the Committee of EC Central Bank Governors gave the Bundesbank a prospect of realizing its strategy of getting EMU based on the German model. Within the Bundesbank the international division was pressing the idea of central bank governors taking over this responsibility as a means of controlling agenda-setting. From contacts with Thiele in the Federal Chancellery's economics division Rieke concluded that there was support in Bonn for this proposal.

At dinner with Delors in Brussels on 23 June, Pöhl briefed Delors on these discussions in Bonn. He left Delors still convinced that the alternatives were either a committee of wise men or the Committee of EC Central Bank Governors working on monetary union. Indeed, Pöhl had reported on these alternatives to the Committee of EC Central Bank Governors, including the earlier idea of Pöhl as chair of two committees. But what he did not know was that, as early as 11 June, Kohl and Delors had agreed the composition of the proposed committee and who should chair it—Delors.

Torn between the desire to respond constructively to new political pressures from Bonn and steadfast opposition in the Bundesbank council, Pöhl sought in May and June to draw a clear line in the sand. The Stoltenberg Memorandum was explicitly endorsed at the 5 May Bundesbank council meeting, where it was also agreed that the Committee of EC Central Bank Governors was the appropriate forum for EMU discussions. Pöhl castigated the 'illusions' of monetary union in the *Frankfurter Allgemeine Zeitung* on 28 May, stressing how far away were the necessary conditions of co-ordination of economic and financial policies. Then, on radio *Hessischer Rundfunk* on 5 June he expressed his scepticism that the Genscher proposal would make political headway at Hanover. In Pöhl's view, EC politicians were simply not prepared to renounce the necessary sovereignty. An ECB would be the 'crowning of a long process'. Finally, in a note to Stoltenberg just before Hanover the Bundesbank underlined its concerns. The federal government must reinforce its commitment to price stability, to central bank independence, and to a market-led and not an institution-led approach to convergence. By these means Pöhl was trying to close his credibility gap within the Bundebank as a President seen by some as too ready to strike international agreements to be trusted on EMU. His concern was to achieve a better *modus vivendi* with Schlesinger. But the Hanover Council was to reveal again just how exposed was his personal position.

'Betrayal' at Hanover

The outcome at Hanover on 27–8 June was a shock for Pöhl, though Stoltenberg was more relaxed. It had been clear to Kohl, Delors, Bitterlich, and Lamy since the eve-of-Council preparatory meeting in Kohl's house on 11 June—before the Ottowa G7 and before Pöhl's meeting with Delors. There they had agreed a committee composed of Delors as chair, all EC central bank governors (Kohl's proposal), and a few independent members (Delors's proposal). Before, and even at Hanover Pöhl's name remained the most frequently mentioned as possible chair of a committee. But, privately, Kohl had dropped him by early June. Until 11 June Delors had scrupulously avoided pressing his own case for being chair. His cabinet officials had, however, worked to ensure that the idea was put in the minds of Chancellery officials and to establish this idea as part of a trade-off between acceptance of EC central bank governors as the basis for the membership of the committee and giving political direction to work on EMU.

At Hanover Kohl began by taking Mrs Thatcher aside to persuade her that she had nothing to fear from a committee of orthodox central bankers. Then, over dinner, he sprang the proposal agreed on 11 June on his fellow heads of state and government just after they had agreed to renew Delors's mandate as President of the Commission. In the context of a successful meeting others were unprepared to offend Kohl and Delors by objecting. With deletion only of reference to considering an ECB as part of the brief of the committee—to accommodate Mrs Thatcher—the proposal was accepted surprisingly easily. In an unusual step, Kohl gave Bitterlich, Lamy, and Delors the task of writing this aspect of the conclusions to ensure that Delors was able to get the kind of committee that he needed. At this point the draft text was shown to Tietmeyer who approved it, adding one important amendment—in order to ensure the independence of its members, they were to serve in a 'personal capacity'. In this way Tietmeyer was bound into the process by agreeing the final text. Thereafter, the text was incorporated in the normal process of producing the full draft conclusions by agreement between the EC Presidency (in this case the Chancellery and the Foreign Ministry) and the Secretary-Generals of the EC Commission and European Council.

There was a striking difference between the tenor of Kohl's press conference after the Luxembourg Council in 1985 and that after the Hanover Council. At the close of the Hanover Council he spoke of the train having left the station—propelled by an 'enormous thrust' (*Mordsschubkraft*); and of being 90 per cent sure that there would be an ECB by 2000. His speech's tone and content differed radically from his private words with Mrs Thatcher. What he had achieved was to set the EC to work on how an EMU was to be realized, relegating the issue of whether to a given. In a bold stroke, Kohl's strategy of binding in the Bundesbank had been realized.

Finance Ministry officials understood that Tietmeyer's role at Hanover was to 'control' Kohl on behalf of ordo-liberal orthodoxy. In fact, he had been 'bound in' by clever tactics on the part of Kohl and Delors. Within the Finance Ministry there was a general sense of shock that Kohl had favoured Delors so strongly on such a sensitive and delicate issue as EMU. But, on receipt of Tietmeyer's news from Hanover, Stoltenberg was fairly relaxed. He saw the presence of the central bank governors as a guarantee that the committee's work would be professional and reliable. The fact that de Larosière, whom he admired, would present French views was a source of reassurance.

The strongest reaction of all came from Pöhl who spoke by telephone with Tietmeyer and with the government's press spokesman, Friedhelm Ost. His immediate reaction was to try to get Delors's nomination cancelled and to refuse to accept the invitation, arguing that one of his Bundesbank colleagues— like Gleske or Norbert Kloten—should replace him. He saw Delors as too tricky a political animal to chair a group of central bankers, speaking of an 'oil and water problem'; felt that two of the three independents were basically EC Commission appointees who would support Delors and Frans Andriessen, the EC Commissioner on the committee; and noted that there were two Danes, two Spaniards, two Commissioners, and only one German! Given that the Bundesbank's chief concern had always been to keep EC Commission influence away from monetary policy, the composition of the committee horrified Pöhl. The further news from Hanover that Tommaso Padoa-Schioppa, an intimate adviser of Delors, was to serve as rapporteur for the committee further enflamed Bundesbank sentiments. Padoa-Schioppa was remembered as 'unsound': as the originator of the 1982 Commission proposals on stage 2 of the EMS; and as the chair of an independent expert group which in 1987 had advocated a strengthening of ECOFIN.

Above all, Pöhl felt betrayed by Kohl with whom he felt that he had had an understanding. He also felt that he had been kept in the dark by Delors during their meeting on 23 June. Kohl's telephone call to Pöhl failed to calm the situation. There followed angry letters to Kohl, which were not answered. In turn, Kohl was irritated by what he saw as the arrogant and condescending attitude of the Bundesbank towards Delors. With Hanover began the period of tense, difficult relations between Pöhl and Kohl that were to culminate in the sharp disagreement about German economic and monetary union in 1990 and Pöhl's resignation in May 1991. Pöhl's experience and instincts told him that the Delors Committee would put him in a politically impossible position, caught between political expectations and pressures to sign up for EMU and the intransigent opposition of members of the Bundesbank council.

Seizing the Initiative: Pöhl, the Bundesbank, and Strategy for the Delors Committee

The Chancellor's irritation with Pöhl was secondary to his sense of the high stakes involved after Hanover. Given the anger of Pöhl and his reluctance to join the Delors Committee, Kohl and Delors were keen to mend fences as the basis for intensive and productive work in a tight time-frame for the Madrid Council. At the first meeting of the Delors Committee on 12 July 1988 in Basle it was confirmed that the committee would meet in Basle, symbolically identifying it with the central banks and distancing its work from Brussels; and that Gunter Baer from the Bank for International Settlements, and a former colleague of Pöhl's in the Finance Ministry, would act as co-rapporteur alongside Padoa-

Schioppa. In effect, Padoa-Schioppa was being balanced by a known believer in the coronation theory of EMU and critic of the use of EMU for political objectives. These confidence-building measures were accompanied by a visit of the Chancellor to the Bundesbank council on 14 July for discussions on EMU. Unlike on the famous occasion of Schmidt's visit in November 1978, his remarks were conciliatory. But they concealed Kohl's irritation with the 'arrogance' of the Bundesbank and with Pöhl's 'condescending' attitude to Delors.

The Pöhl Paper and Bundesbank Strategy

Pöhl's reluctance to join was soon overcome by colleagues in the Bundesbank, as well as by friends like the Dutch central bank president Wim Duisenberg. They—and not least Schlesinger—persuaded him that only by joining the Delors Committee could he promote the Bundesbank's ideas on EMU effectively. Otherwise, the field would be left open to others. There was early unanimity in the Bundesbank directorate about strategy: that the Bundesbank must actively seize (indeed retrieve) the initiative by tabling comprehensive proposals on EMU at the earliest practical moment. This strategic argument was pressed by Gleske, reflecting views in Rieke's international division. The international division pointed to the danger that the French and Delors (acting as a mouthpiece for the Commission as well as the French) would attempt to gain the intellectual high ground at the start of the negotiations.

But there were other, discrete motives for proceeding in this way. One motive, pressed on Pöhl by the international division, was that in this way sceptics like Schlesinger could be bound into the exercise. They would be less free to snipe from the sidelines, and Pöhl would not be left in 'splendid isolation'. Both Pöhl and Rieke were concerned to head off the prospect of Schlesinger becoming a focus for Bundesbank council opponents of their international outlook. The other motive, which appealed to Schlesinger and others, was that in this way Pöhl himself could be brought under some sort of control. Pöhl was seen by many within the Bundesbank as unreliable in such negotiations, for a variety of reasons: as too happy to make concessions, his first preference being life as an international monetary diplomat; as not sufficiently rigorous and consistent in his economic beliefs; and as not being prepared to brief himself fully on the technicalities, unlike some other central bank governors. For some he remained too much the Bonn 'insider'; for others too much the journalist, overwilling to adjust his views; and for others simply too 'amateur' or indolent. Pöhl was not a 'Bundesbank-first' man or a sufficiently consistent ordo-liberal or a 'workaholic'. In this respect he invited unflattering comparisons with Schlesinger.

Hence, with Schlesinger and the economics division taking responsibility, the Bundesbank directorate set to work to agree a comprehensive draft paper to table at the beginning of the Delors Committee's work. The text went through several drafts, with important contributions from Köhler (on the parallel currency issue) and Gleske, and was ready for the next 13 September meeting of the

Committee. To his great annoyance, Pöhl discovered that the paper had found its way into the hands of other governors on the Committee, notably de Larosière, before its formal presentation. This situation reflected the tension between two elements at work in Bundesbank tactics: on the one hand, Pöhl's desire to remain in control and treat the paper as confidential to himself; on the other, the attempt of Bundesbank officials to actively lobby for support for its ideas from the earliest possible moment.

The Pöhl paper drew heavily on the position paper of April 1988 on further development of the EMS and, importantly, retained that title. Notably, the paper did not subscribe to the coronation theory. In this respect it reflected the thinking of Gleske, Rieke, and Pöhl: that the Bundesbank should avoid taking up too uncompromising and unrealistic a position. The intention was to avoid being seen as unco-operative and engaging in blocking tactics. The paper's key point was that 'monetary integration cannot move ahead of general economic integration, since otherwise the whole process of integration would be burdened with considerable economic and social tensions'. EMU was doomed to failure without 'a minimum of policy-shaping and decision-making in the field of economic and fiscal policy . . . [taking] place at Community level'. But, though complete political union was deemed not necessary for monetary union, the paper hedged its bets. The required loss of sovereignty in economic and monetary policy 'would probably be bearable only in the context of extremely close and irrevocable political integration'. Its conclusion was that EMU 'will still take some time to achieve' and that the economic prerequisites 'will probably not exist for the foreseeable future'. For the foreseeable future there was the prospect of further ERM realignments rather than the locking of currencies required for EMU. Also, in addressing the political problems and risks, the Pöhl paper raised the prospect that a 'rigid timetable' of stages would force two-speed integration and run counter to the objective of unification of Europe as a whole.

The real core of the Pöhl paper focused on outlining the principles of a European monetary order (including an independent ECB, mandated to maintain stability in the value of money). Two existing proposals for the transition were tested against these principles (an EMF and a parallel currency) and robustly rejected. In effect, other members of the Committee were being challenged to desist from pressing such proposals or to contest the German model. The Bundesbank's strategy for the Delors Committee was to seek initial agreement on a long-term global concept of EMU, with clearly formulated basic principles, and to ensure that intermediate steps were geared to those principles. This strategy was designed to avoid serious risks to the efficacy of monetary policy from short-term institutional 'fixes' like an EMF and a parallel currency.

Pöhl's Tactics and Bundesbank Tactics for the Delors Committee

During the work of the Delors Committee there were complex tactical manoeuvres on the German side. Pöhl's preoccupation was to avoid being simply a prisoner of the Bundesbank. In this spirit he sought to appoint an outsider (the pro-EMU economist Peter Bofinger) as his briefer for this work. But this move was blocked by the international division. Hence Pöhl balanced Rieke, head of this division, with Baer—an insider in the committee—as principal briefers. Baer helped to reassure Pöhl about the dedicated, open-minded, and realistic approach of Delors to his task and kept him in close touch with the process of drafting the report.

Also, Pöhl conducted his own personal diplomacy, independently of the international division of the Bundesbank. Here he focused on cultivating his close working relationship with de Larosière, Governor of the Banque de France. The two shared a long-standing friendship and mutual respect. In addition, each could recognize the other's problem: Pöhl stressed his lack of power over 'provincially minded' Bundesbank council members; de Larosière, his problem with the interventionist instincts of the Trésor and of a Socialist government. De Larosière's problems were demonstrated to Pöhl in July–August 1988 when Bérégovoy, the French Finance Minister, followed cuts in interest rates with criticisms of the lack of a supportive response from the Bundesbank. This behaviour sent a very negative signal to the Bundesbank. It was accompanied in August by an interview comment from Edith Cresson, French Minister for European Affairs, that an independent ECB was not desirable. In the context of preparing the Pöhl paper these signals from Paris augured badly for the Delors Committee.

But, crucially, Pöhl sensed that de Larosière was a genuinely independent-minded and brave man, keen to keep Attali in the Elysée and the Trésor at bay. De Larosière's signal to Pöhl before the first major working meeting on 13 December that he had persuaded Mitterrand to accept an independent ECB, mandated to achieve price stability, as a non-negotiable basic principle for EMU, was an unexpected turning-point. Pöhl then sensed, for the first time, that a deal could be done on terms that would meet Bundesbank strategy. He realized that in striking such a deal he was helping de Larosière to accelerate the process by which the Banque de France could be made formally independent of the French government.

Whilst Pöhl attended to his own tactical manoeuvres, the international division of the Bundesbank was taking its own precautionary measures to ensure that Bundesbank positions were effectively presented within the Delors Committee. These measures took the form of working sessions between Bundesbank, Dutch central bank, and Danish central bank officials in Basle before each Delors Committee meeting. The aim was to closely co-ordinate views on drafts; to jointly identify key issues; and to ensure that Duisenberg and Erik Hoffmeyer (Governor of the Danish central bank) were briefed to raise these issues. One reason for this careful preparation was that, unlike with meetings of the Committee of EC Central Bank Governors, no central bank officials were allowed into the Delors Committee meetings. The fact that its members were on their own raised the anxiety of officials that key points—for instance, opposition to a parallel currency—could be overlooked or ineffectively made. In this way Bundesbank officials were seeking reassurance. An additional reason was that they feared that Pöhl lacked the patience, concentration, and technical expertise to brief himself effectively and make a strong and solid contribution.

Pöhl's Negotiating Problems

Pöhl was deeply suspicious about the motives and behaviour of Delors and of some of the independent experts. His capacity to be abrasive was in evidence at an early meeting of the Delors Committee when he clashed sharply with Delors about the status of a paper tabled by Delors, claiming that it had been produced by the EC Commission. Not only did it raise the issues of stages and a timetable (which was opposed by the Bundesbank), more importantly, Pöhl argued that Delors was behaving improperly in using Commission services when he was supposed to be acting in a personal capacity; 'We are not working under the auspices of the Commission'. This issue was as much symbolic as substantive for Pöhl. The paper was withdrawn.

Pöhl continued to be difficult. When Delors spoke in French, he removed his headphones. To appease Pöhl business was from then onwards transacted in English. Another example was his blocking of participation by a Bundesbank official in a proposed informal working group of central bank officials, under Professor Niels Thygesen, one of the independent experts on the Committee, to consider detailed arrangements for stage 2. Again, Pöhl's anger had a substantive and a symbolic aspect. Substantively, he identified collusion involving the French and Italian central banks to give momentum to proposals opposed by the Bundesbank. Symbolically, he was intent on maintaining personal control: 'I am the personal representative of Germany and that role does not extend beyond me'. The working group did not convene.

In fact Pöhl's chief problems were with Schlesinger and with the Bundesbank council. He made sure that Schlesinger saw all papers. Schlesinger's careful and critical reading of Committee papers and his continuing pressure for tight internal co-ordination on the Delors Committee within the Bundesbank was a factor in pushing Pöhl to alternate from more co-operative to confrontational moods. His signals to Pöhl about being firm on particular points were readily heeded. But these abrasive moments were countered by the conciliatory approach of Delors as chair. Pöhl's situation was eased by the fact that, within the Committee, he was pushing at an open door. And much of the actual pushing, at the level of technical argument, was done by Duisenberg and by Hoffmeyer, with Pöhl reinforcing points rather than initiating them.

From the beginning a number of Bundesbank council members, led by Professor Norbert Kloten, President of the Baden-Württemberg state central bank, were the source of considerable difficulties for Pöhl. In particular, Kloten argued in public (the *Wirtschaftswoche* of 15 July 1988) that the composition of the Delors Committee ensured that an ECB would not be constructed on the

Bundesbank model. The game was, in effect, lost before it had begun. Very few of the state central bank presidents—like Kurt Nemitz (Bremen)—shared Kohl's missionary conception of the Delors Committee as part of the political unification of Europe. The rule was acceptance of the principle of EMU—but overriden by deep scepticism about its viability. In part, this scepticism was rooted in ordo-liberal argument. But issues of power and status also played a major role. With an ECB the state central banks stood to lose their large and costly administrative apparatuses. Their power over monetary policy would also be ended. This consideration led them to fear that the President of the Bundesbank had less to lose from EMU, for he would have a seat on the ECB. As the most outspoken critic, Kloten was joined by Hans Wertz (North-Rhine Westphalia) and, from December 1988, by Professor Helmut Hesse (Lower Saxony).

The Bundesbank Contribution to the Delors Report: A Retreat to Critical Distance

By the 14 February 1989 meeting Pöhl was noting a much greater degree of agreement on basic principles in the Delors Committee than he had expected. The high point of his embarrassment came on 19–20 February when the Anglo-German summit met in Frankfurt. Mrs Thatcher took the opportunity to lecture Bundesbank officials on the evils of EMU. This meeting reinforced to Pöhl the difference between his scepticism on EMU and hers, between caution and outright hostility. By 14 March, unmoved by Mrs Thatcher, he was indicating that he was prepared to sign the final draft, leaving the British Governor, Leigh-Pemberton, isolated.

This development in Pöhl's position reflected the fact that by then it was clear that the basic requirements of the Bundesbank had been accepted—notably, on the design of the ECB and on the rejection of a parallel currency. The emerging agreed drafts did not suggest a hard-fought victory for the Bundesbank. In effect, there had been no goalkeeper to block Pöhl's shots. The only area of serious challenge to Pohl's paper had been on an EMF in stage 2. But it was clear to Pöhl that this proposal was a minority position and that de Larosière was seeking its presence in the final report more for symbolic political reasons—to satisfy the Trésor—than out of any technical conviction. Others on the Committee might worry about the lack of detail about the transition between stage 1 and stage 3: stage 2 as an 'empty shell'. But Pöhl's only real concerns were to gain agreement that stage 1 should focus on 'greater convergence of economic performance' through strengthening policy co-ordination 'within the existing institutional framework'; that stage 3 should be the Bundesbank 'writ large'; that a parallel currency and an EMF should be ruled out in the transition; and that there should be no explicit deadlines, other than for the passage to stage 1. Privately, Bundesbank international division officials expressed satisfaction that

80 per cent plus of the Pöhl paper had been accepted. In this respect Pöhl's signature posed no real problem.

The Bundesbank's main direct contribution to the final drafting of the Delors Report was visible in section 2 of chapter 2—'the principal features of monetary union'—and in the part of section 4 entitled 'institutional arrangements' dealing with the mandate and functions of the ESCB. These proposals represented the hard core of the report. In addition, the Bundesbank's emphasis on the problems of the EMS and on the need for 'greater convergence of economic performance' found its way into section 4 of chapter 1 (Pöhl 1996: 185).

But concessions had to be made which provoked internal criticism within the Bundesbank directorate and, even more, from within the Bundesbank council. Bundesbank unhappiness focused on the stress on the role of the ECU in section 2 of chapter 3; on the failure to spell out opposition to a parallel currency more trenchantly in this section; on excessive attention to EC regional and structural policies compared to the role of wage flexibility and labour mobility in section 3 of chapter 2; on the inclusion of de Larosière's proposal for an ERF; and on the failure to make the results of measures to strengthen economic and fiscal coordination in stages 1 and 2 binding on member states.

Faced with these reactions, Pöhl's original sense that his membership of the Delors Committee had been a mistake was reawakened. In commenting on the Delors Report on 18 April he pleaded for realism and a sense of proportion. Privately, he characterized the Report as only a pedestrian description of options, as lacking original and concrete proposals, and as not binding. The crucial area of fiscal policy had been pushed under the carpet so as not to offend political sensitivities about sovereignty. Pöhl was in effect distancing himself from the exercise and began to exercise the prerogatives of the external critic. His concern was to restore confidence and redevelop teamwork in the Bundesbank after the strains of the Delors Committee period. In developing a post-Delors strategy, the Bundesbank directorate returned to traditional themes: warning against 'salami-slicing tactics' designed to erode its independence; stressing the need for caution in seeking to develop the EMS and the risk of promoting tensions within the EC; arguing that the most pressing issue was not the single currency but the stability of existing currencies; and developing the position that EMU must not be at the expense of monetary stability in the 'hard currency' states. Most importantly, the position of political leaders on the Delors Report proposal for binding budget rules in stage 3 was taken as a signal of whether the political will was really there to renounce the necessary sovereignty to enable EMU to work. From discussions at the informal ECOFIN at S'Agaro on 19–21 May 1989 Pöhl concluded that this political will was absent. His reaction was to distance himself further from the Delors Report's idea of a three-stage process.

The Federal Government and the Delors Report

Following Hanover, relations between the Federal Chancellor's Office and the Bundesbank were severely strained. The Chancellery was kept in touch with developments in the Delors Committee by Joly Dixon in Delors's cabinet and, by February, was optimistic that the final report would meet German strategic objectives. As seen by the Chancellery, the twin objectives were to 'bind in' the Bundesbank to a stage-by-stage approach to EMU and, necessary for this first objective, to ensure that EMU was constructed on the German model. The conclusion of Kohl and his officials was that Delors had done an excellent job as chair. Genscher too maintained an interest. He was kept up-to-date on developments by Delors. More importantly, when Delors indicated problems, Genscher arranged to bring together Dumas and Pöhl over dinner to ensure that the political case for EMU was reinforced and to disabuse Pöhl of any reservations about the financial soundness of the French.

A critical voice in the wilderness came from the Economics Ministry. Its State Secretary, Otto Schlecht, was frustrated at being so marginalized and sought out a means by which his ministry's traditional preoccupations about EMU could be ventilated. On 21 January 1989 the Economics Ministry's Scientific Advisory Council delivered a report on 'European Currency Order'. It represented the first substantial involvement by German academic economists in the new EMU debate. The most influential contributions came from Olaf Sievert as chair of the council and from Giersch; whilst, of considerable symbolic importance, Schlesinger from the Bundesbank was also a member.

The report restated the coronation theory of EMU. There was, it argued, no need for intermediate stages to EMU, only a gradual hardening of the ERM based on growing economic convergence. More striking was its rejection of binding budget rules to ensure fiscal discipline in favour of reliance on market forces. Both the coronation theory and the reliance on strengthening financial markets to provide fiscal discipline were rejected in the Delors Report. Hence, unsurprisingly, in a letter of 5 June to the Federal Economics Minister, Helmut Haussmann, the Scientific Advisory Council expressed severe reservations about the three-stage Delors plan and about entering into treaty negotiations on this basis. Though Haussmann endorsed the Council's stress on relying on competition and flexibility in developing EMU, he did not carry sufficient political weight in the federal government to push through these points. Indeed, the arguments about using market forces rather than budget rules found no support in the Bundesbank and little in the Finance Ministry.

During the Delors Committee the Finance Ministry took a background role. There was no full reporting from Pöhl, only occasional letters and oral reports to Stoltenberg and to Tietmeyer. Bundesbank officials ensured that the money and credit division was kept informed. There was also briefing by Baer, who had good contacts in the ministry. Stoltenberg continued to question whether it had been sensible to open up the debate about an ECB and to argue that EMU was not an urgent issue. Indeed, Bérégovoy's letter to Stoltenberg and to other EC finance ministers in July 1988 complaining about the 'go-it-alone' approach of the Bundesbank on interest rates led him to be even more sceptical that the Delors Committee would lead anywhere. By early 1989 Pöhl was telling Tietmeyer that the Delors Report was not to be taken too seriously. In particular, there would be no fixed dates attached to stages 2 and 3, ensuring that the process would take a very long time.

But, though they shared this view, Stoltenberg and Tietmeyer had reservations about the Delors Report. They saw it as in certain respects a departure from the approach of the Werner Report. The Delors Report had not adequately examined the context of political union that they saw as crucial to making EMU viable. The provisions on parallelism between economic and monetary union were seen as weak, with too much stress on monetary union and too little on adequate mechanisms of fiscal discipline in the transition period. In essence the Delors Report was, in their view, cognitively flawed. This flaw would matter less if Pöhl's prognosis proved correct: that Kohl would accept the Delors Report at Madrid but then be content to bury it in the face of the horrendous political difficulties that it created.

The Struggle for Control of German Strategy after the Delors Report: The Timetable Issue and Madrid

The publication of the Delors Report on 17 April 1989 coincided with a major transformation in the balance of political forces in the federal government. This transformation did not bode well for political progress in implementing its recommendations. It made it more difficult for Genscher to return effectively to his role as 'policy entrepreneur'—in this case in relation to the issue of a timetable for EMU. The catalyst for change was provided by the internal party effects of continuing electoral reverses at the state and local level and by scandals and a sense of drift within the federal government. By March 1989, just a month before the publication of the Delors Report, Bitterlich was signalling to Attali and Védrine in the Elysée that Kohl faced severe domestic political difficulties after the Berlin elections of February. The implication was clear: that the German Chancellor should not be pushed too hard by the French at the impending bilateral on 4 April in Günzburg. Bitterlich was not simply behaving tactically. Kohl was confronted with the gravest crisis of his career.

These difficulties were brought to a head by the breakdown of his relationship with Geissler, the CDU's General-Secretary. Kohl was aware that Geissler was plotting against him and that Späth was the favoured candidate to be mobilized for the CDU party congress in September. Advised by Schäuble, Kohl decided to strengthen the government and box in Geissler by a reshuffle in April 1989. The centre point of the reshuffle was the replacement of Stoltenberg at Finance by the CSU's new chair, Theo Waigel. This move had the political advantage of drawing Waigel to his side at a moment when Kohl was very vul-nerable. For Waigel it offered him profile and prestige to build up his vulnerable position as successor to Strauss by following in the footsteps of the first CSU Finance Minister, Fritz Schäffer (1949–57); and it was a logical step after serving as economic policy spokesperson of the CDU/CSU parliamentary party since 1980. Not least, Waigel's appointment gave a new political weight to the Finance Ministry at an important moment for EMU. On EMU Kohl was now man-oeuvring between two heavyweights—Genscher and Waigel. EMU was pro-pelled to the very heart of internal coalition relations within the government, involving directly the FDP and the CSU. As the manager of these relations Kohl's strategic objective was to gain a measure of independence of action, par-ticularly vis-à-vis Genscher. But he remained politically indebted to Waigel for his support at a moment of vulnerability.

In terms of EMU strategy the result was paradoxical. Waigel's responsibility for EMU would 'bind in' his party. This effect was strategically invaluable; the CSU was seen by Kohl as potentially the most volatile and unreliable on EMU. The best way to 'bind in' the CSU was to have its chair as Finance Minister. On the other hand, Waigel's indispensability gave him, and the Finance Ministry, much greater leverage on EMU negotiations after the Delors Report. He was also a self-confident Finance Minister, having begun his career as an official in the Bavarian Finance Ministry and later specialized in budgetary and economic issues.

Much would clearly depend on how Waigel chose to play his cards on EMU. In April–May the signals were not seen as encouraging in the Chancellery and in the Foreign Ministry. Waigel was at pains to emphasize continuity on EMU and, as a long-time admirer of Tietmeyer, readily agreed with his State Secretary's caution and reservations. He was also intent on making a strong individual contribution to rescue the Finance Ministry from the doldrums into which it had been cast by the tax reform. But what was less clear at the time—and was to become clearer later—was Waigel's intellectual identification with the pro-European outlook articulated by Strauss in the 1960s—of a United States of Europe that 'would provide the one framework which would make possible the reunification of Germany and avoid all its latent dangers. Germany needs Europe more than any other country . . .' (Strauss 1965: 9). This outlook was to prove crucial in 1989–90 in binding him together with Genscher and Kohl. He was to prove a loyal and constructive partner of Kohl, retaining the latter's sense of his indispensability.

Waigel and the Withholding Tax

Waigel's first major step was, unwittingly, to send very negative signals to the French government. One of the key conditions that Waigel set for taking on the Finance Ministry was withdrawal of the withholding tax on interest income introduced by Stoltenberg on 1 January 1989. Stoltenberg had introduced this tax solely for domestic reasons of tax equity and to forestall possible legal objections to current tax law: and Waigel withdrew it solely for domestic reasons, namely the negative effects on the German capital market as savings fled Germany. But the French government protested that this step infringed an understanding arrived at between Kohl and Mitterrand at Evian in June 1988: that France had made a concession in supporting the complete liberalization of capital movement in return for an understanding of German support for EC harmonization of taxation on income from savings. The Finance Ministry denied that this move suggested any lessening of German desire to achieve EC-wide tax harmonization of this type. Notably, Kohl signalled to Mitterrand that he could not intervene on this issue—his hands were bound by the domestic political situation—and referred the Elysée directly to Waigel. Whatever the merits of this Franco-German argument, it led the French to paint Waigel, erroneously, as anti-EMU and affected the climate in which both sides discussed the Delors Report and approached Madrid.

Genscher as Policy Entrepreneur for a Timetable

At the political level in Bonn, Genscher was the prime force in seeking to sustain the momentum created by the Delors Report. Crucially, from early April he worked with the French Foreign Minister Dumas to ensure that the Delors Report figured prominently in the Franco-German summit on 19–20 April. At this summit limited progress was made. The Delors Report was accepted as the basis for moving forward on EMU. It was also agreed that both sides should work together to ensure that at Madrid on 26–7 June the European Council acted to ensure continuing momentum. But questions about the substantive issues were left unresolved. Genscher recognized that, on matters of substance, Waigel's support had to be carried. Already, Genscher had been pressing the Spanish Foreign Minister to ensure that EMU was given top priority at the Madrid Council. Indeed, Dumas and Genscher co-ordinated their pressures on the Spanish government. They worked to ensure that the Delors Report was discussed at the informal meeting of EC foreign ministers in Granada on 14 April.

For Genscher the key issues were agreement on the three-stage Delors process; on its basic principle that an agreement to enter stage 1 was a decision to embark on the entire process; and on a procedure to prepare for an early IGC and to fix dates. He used a Bertelsmann Foundation conference on 5 May to outline these views. In fact, at this conference Genscher went further in stressing the need for a final date for EMU—'perhaps 2000'—to ensure a continuing political pressure. Privately, these views were impressed on Kohl and not just by Genscher and some Chancellery officials. The other key influence on Kohl came from Alfred Herrhausen. At the Bertelsmann conference Herrhausen also highlighted the value of a final date for EMU—2001 (Bertelsmann Stiftung 1989). On 31 May, speaking on behalf of his working group of the Action Committee for

Europe, Herrhausen welcomed the Delors Report and supported an immediate start to work on treaty amendments.

These views of Herrhausen, Genscher, and some Chancellery officials—as well as of Delors directly—strengthened Kohl's hand in the meetings of the cabinet committee on European affairs that dealt with the Delors Report in May. The Delors Report was taken as the basis for agreeing a set of principles of economic union and of monetary union. These were agreed with little difficulty. The negotiating objectives for Madrid were also identified: that the Delors Report was an adequate basis for EC negotiations; that the decision to enter into stage 1 must also be a decision to embark on the entire process (i.e. as a single process); and that preparations must begin immediately to start stage 1 in July 1990. But, whereas Genscher and Lautenschlager were pressing for the date for the IGC to be fixed in Madrid, Waigel and Tietmeyer wished to leave the date open pending clarification of a range of technical questions. The Bundesbank strongly supported the Finance Ministry position. On balance, Kohl tended towards the Genscher view. But he was not prepared to overrule Waigel on this issue and was keen to give supportive political signals to a new Finance Minister who had just helped to rescue his position in Bonn.

Waigel as 'Honest Broker' at the S'Agaro ECOFIN

At the informal ECOFIN on 19–21 May Waigel exploited this uncertainty and his strong domestic position. Skilfully, he tried to adopt an 'honest-broker' role: between the French, Italians, Spaniards, and Delors—who wanted unqualified implementation of the Delors Report and an IGC in the near future—and the British—who rejected stages 2 and 3. Waigel began by welcoming the EC's development into a 'community of monetary stability', the federal construction of the ESCB, and the ESCB's independence of governments. But he then qualified his enthusiasm by rejecting Delors's call for an increase of the Structural Funds and, in particular, a timetable for EMU. Monetary integration 'must be learnt by doing'. Delors noted with concern that Waigel failed to give explicit endorsement to the key principle that the decision to enter into stage 1 should be a decision to embark on the entire process. With the focus on preparing for stage 1 the political signal from S'Agaro to the French, to Delors, and to the Spanish Presidency was of caution, of a lack of determined political leadership on EMU from Waigel.

Kohl's Strategy for Madrid

After the disappointment of S'Agaro there was considerable political pressure on Kohl: from Felipe Gonzales, as holder of the EC Presidency, from Delors, and from Mitterrand. At their meeting on 22 June, just four days before the Madrid Council, Kohl pressed on Mitterrand the domestic constraints that he faced on EMU, especially in relation to any decision to convene the IGC. His strategy was to emphasize that his hands were tied by poor results for the CDU in the European Parliament elections of 18 June and by the worryingly good performance of the anti-European Republican Party. Kohl was also distracted as the conflict with Geissler was coming to a head.

The substance of the final Franco-German agreement for Madrid was consistent with the German negotiating objectives agreed in Bonn in May. Kohl and Mitterrand confirmed that the IGC should begin after the start of stage 1 and as soon as the preparations for stages 2 and 3 had sufficiently advanced. This vague formula left open the precise procedure for preparing the IGC as well as the date for its opening.

Genscher and Dumas were content with this outcome. Their main strategic objective was to ensure that the Madrid European Council gave the incoming French Presidency of the EC responsibility for preparing the work of the IGC. In this way strong political leadership in convening the IGC could be guaranteed. Delors and Gonzales were also happy to seek agreement at Madrid on conclusions that incorporated this Franco-German position. The Franco-German agreement had the merit of going further than the disappointing conclusions of the S'Agaro ECOFIN. More importantly, they drew comfort from the prospect that the French Presidency would put Bonn under sustained pressure on preparing the IGC and fixing a date.

But, during and after Madrid, Kohl was more ambivalent than he had been in Hanover. Whilst in principle he supported Genscher's position, the Chancellor was more concerned about being seen to concede under French pressure—especially in the context of the domestic pressures that he faced. He was in no hurry to be rushed into a date for the IGC, and Delors soon concluded that an IGC was some way off—beyond the target date for the completion of the single European market on 31 December 1992. But events outside the control of the French EC Presidency—in Eastern Europe—were to alter views of EMU in Bonn.

Policy Reflection in the Shadows of the Delors Report, Madrid, and the 'German Question'

Endorsement of the Delors Report at Madrid (including the commitment to convene an IGC) was the first big catalyst for officials in Bonn and Frankfurt to reflect on the utility of inherited policy beliefs about EMU. As both Finance Ministry and Economics Ministry officials separately concluded, EMU was going to be realized in politically and institutionally different circumstances from those envisaged in the Werner Report and outlined in the traditional coronation theory. The big question was: in what ways did German policy beliefs about EMU need to be adapted to ensure a viable and durable EMU in these unforeseen circumstances? The second catalyst was the convening of the Guigou Group in September 1989 with the objective of identifying the key questions with which the IGC would have to deal and to reflect on those questions. This innovation of the French Presidency forced the German Finance Ministry to co-ordinate basic bargaining positions on EMU. It gave birth to the working group on EMU co-ordinated by Günter Winkelmann in the Finance Ministry and the paper that it prepared in November 1989.

But ultimately far more important was the reflection on the implications, first, of the emerging developments in Eastern Europe in the late summer and, then, of the fall of the Berlin Wall in November. This development was crucial to the assertion of Kohl's leadership on EMU in a new form from December 1989. At the same time it should be noted that Waigel, Pöhl, and others were also sensitive to the new political significance of EMU. Signals that they were rethinking EMU were first apparent at the Franco-German Economic Council on the Tegernsee on 24–5 August 1989.

The Guigou Group

The establishment of the Guigou Group was indirectly a victory for Genscher. Though the proposal came from Dumas, it reflected the skilful way in which Genscher and Dumas had seized the opportunity opened by the Madrid Council. Their objective was to restore political leadership on EMU and neutralize the inclination of Pöhl to dissociate himself from the Delors Report and pour cold water on further progress. Hence the Group comprised a foreign ministry and a finance ministry representative from each member state. Genscher nominated Jelonek, head of his economics division, and Waigel nominated Horst Köhler, head of the money and credit division.

This initiative came as an unwelcome surprise to the Finance Ministry whose officials had been influenced by Pöhl's reassurances that no significant steps were likely to be taken after the Delors Report. The way in which this institutional forum was designed was disagreeable to Köhler who saw in it a means of subverting Finance Ministry control over EMU. He was determined to retrieve the initiative for the Finance Ministry by seizing the leadership role and, in particular, by prioritizing the sensitive question of budgetary discipline. There was no attempt by Köhler and Jelonek to co-ordinate positions. Each worked to the objectives of his own ministry and had his own agenda. Hence, at the very first meeting of the Guigou Group on 5 September, Jelonek and Köhler clashed over the timetable issue. At the fourth meeting on 16 October Köhler took on the French over the proposal to strengthen the 'political power' vis-à-vis 'monetary power', the first of many such disagreements. What most irritated him was the nature of the qualifications that the French spelt out to the principle of central bank independence: the European Council was to decide 'guidelines' of economic policy, including monetary policy.

Köhler was reasonably satisfied with the content of the Guigou Report of 30 October. It listed the questions for the IGC, but it had made no progress on the date for the IGC. More seriously, it had revealed internal German disputes on this issue. Köhler drew important lessons from this experience. The Finance Ministry must avoid becoming technical adviser on EMU to a Foreign Ministry which handled the negotiations. The Foreign Ministry lacked the technical expertise to undertake this task safely. Most crucially, Köhler identified the importance of strong co-ordination if German interests were to be realized in an EMU agreement. He was reinforced in his determination to ensure that German negotiating strength was not again dissipated through this internal dis-unity. The Finance Ministry must take a stronger lead in Bonn. The Guigou Group had usefully identified the key questions on which preparatory work had to be done in Bonn.

Revising Coronation Theory: The Economics Ministry's Note of 18 July 1989 on EMU

This note was the first public sign of an internal process of inquiry by officials into established departmental beliefs about EMU. It was the product of reflection within the Economics Ministry's economic policy division (*Grundsatzabteilung*), prompted by the report of the Scientific Advisory Council in January, the Delors Report, and the S'Agaro ECOFIN. Two of the three key figures behind this note had beliefs on EMU that went back to Werner: Schlecht, now State Secretary and earlier head of the economic policy division; and Bernhard Molitor, head of the economic policy division and in DG2 of the EC Commission in 1970. Along with Ralf Zeppernick (head of the currency policy and foreign economic policy section in the economic policy division and of a section in the European division), their strategic objective was to regain control of the intellectual high ground on EMU. The note of 18 July signalled the begin-ning of this process, which continued via Zeppernick's presence in the Winkelmann group.

The key feature of the Economics Ministry note was the abandonment of the coronation theory, in effect a parting of the ways with the Scientific Advisory Council. Following S'Agaro, it became clear that member states were not pre-pared to accept either a new economic-policy institution at the EC level (as advo-cated by Werner) or binding budgetary rules (as proposed by Delors). In order to find a way forward in this political context that would be compatible with ordo-liberalism, the Economics Ministry stressed that competition must assume pri-macy as the organizing principle for EMU. The emphasis must be on measures to promote mobility of factors of production, favourable conditions for investment, and increased productivity. In this respect the Delors Report was seen as placing too much trust in interventionist EC regional and structural policies. In relation to budgetary discipline the Economics Ministry note rejected a reliance on simple indicators (e.g. public debt–GDP ratio) in favour of an in-depth and differentiated analysis of the budgetary situation of each member state. This approach to bud-getary discipline was later to be rejected by the Finance Ministry.

The Economics Ministry note of 18 July 1989 was in fact but a stage within a continuing process of reflection on EMU by its economic policy division. The basic and theoretically difficult problem remained how to reconcile ordo-liberalism to an EMU that gave primacy to monetary union. In a series of papers the Economics Ministry argued that the loss of the exchange rate as a mechanism of adjustment with EMU placed extra stress on competition, notably in labour markets and in wage determination. The question was how to promote open markets. The starting-point for the Economics Ministry still carried elements of the traditional ordo-liberal approach to EMU. Emphasis was placed on a regulatory approach at the EC level: on common harmonized economic policies relating to competition, wages, and mobility of factors of production as a precondition for a viable monetary union.

Gradually an intellectual shift occurred. The principle of competition began to be applied to economic policies themselves. The markets would reward those EC states with successful economic policies; other states would adapt; and eventually common economic policies would evolve. Co-ordination by markets, rather than by regulation, seemed the answer to the question of how to achieve a viable monetary union in a context where member states were too jealous of their sovereignty in economic and financial policies to put in place common economic policies by an act of shared political will.

Though the economic policy division went through a significant learning process on EMU, the regulative approach was slow to be displaced. Schlecht was its powerful advocate. At the 23 July 1990 ECOFIN Schlecht stressed parallel progress in co-ordination of economic policy and in realizing monetary union. He pressed for incorporation of the goal of a convergent economic policy in the Treaty, including an effective competition policy, a productivity-oriented wages policy, and an end to wage-indexation mechanisms.

Yet, however hard the Economics Ministry sought to retain intellectual leadership on EMU, it failed to retrieve the visibility and political weight that it had enjoyed in the Werner period. For Schlecht this situation was very frustrating. The Economics Ministry laboured under three handicaps: the loss of the money and credit division to the Finance Ministry in 1972; successive weak FDP ministers (Haussmann 1988–1990 and Jürgen Möllemann 1991–4) who failed to impress their arguments on Kohl; and the intention of Waigel and Tietmeyer (then Köhler) to retain responsibility for EMU, with the result that information was not always fully shared with them. In 1989–91 it had no Karl Schiller. Schlecht was reduced to watching the power play between Genscher and Waigel in the context of a newly visionary leadership by Kohl on EMU.

In relation to the EC level, the Finance Ministry's strategy was to use the EC Monetary Committee to prepare as much as possible of the IGC negotiations. By contrast, the EC's Economic Policy Committee, in which the Economics Ministry was active, lacked the same status and political weight. Whereas the EC Monetary Committee was an arena in which the Finance Ministry's State Secretary could be active, the Economic Policy Committee comprised division heads—in this case Molitor. In 1990—at the 23 July ECOFIN—Schlecht was to make a bid to incorporate the Economic Policy Committee more centrally in preparations for the IGC. But this strategy to upgrade the Economics Ministry's role proved unsuccessful.

A New Personal Chemistry: The Franco-German Economic Council on the Tegernsee, 24–5 August 1989

In examining the development of EMU policy in 1989–91, it is wrong to think of Waigel as someone who was simply dragged along reluctantly by Kohl and Genscher. Politically, he shared in a wider process of reflection about EMU beliefs in the context of the events in Eastern Europe from summer 1989 onwards. As a Bavarian political leader, he was sensitive to these events as an immediate cross-border issue and to the value of situating himself as the political heir of Strauss in his support for European unification.

In this changing context Waigel's first Franco-German Economic Council meeting, organized for symbolic reasons and to capitalize politically in his home state of Bavaria, was to prove a significant catalyst. Here the early negative impressions gained by Bérégovoy were replaced by a new bond of personal warmth and friendship with Waigel that had never existed with the more aloof Stoltenberg. Waigel was a man whose toughness as a negotiator was made all the more effective by his charm and humour. But, though personal chemistry played an important role, it was overshadowed by a sense of sharing in emerging great changes in Europe. The context was the flight of GDR citizens to Hungary, the independent line being taken by Hungary vis-à-vis the GDR, the breaching of the Austrian-Hungarian border by GDR citizens, and the recognition that Gorbachev did not wish to stand in the way of an ending of the division of Europe. This context fed into the discussions outside the formal sessions and changed the whole climate of the two finance ministers' relationship on EMU. Both Waigel and Bérégovoy were excited by the new possibilities to reorder Europe. Both were above all sensitive to the implications of events in Eastern Europe for policies within the EC. A central banker with acute political antennae, Pöhl shared in this sensitivity. As a bon viveur who enjoyed the relaxing surroundings of the lake, he also contributed to the personal chemistry of the Tegernsee meeting.

In a practical sense, Tegernsee was important in two respects. First, Pöhl convinced Bérégovoy that the Bundesbank was in earnest about EMU, particularly when he asserted—outside the official sessions—that he saw no reason why France and Germany should not proceed quickly to EMU. This signal was vital to Bérégovoy. Pöhl was again pressing his view of a 'two-speed' EMU. Secondly, German Finance Ministry officials, notably Köhler and Gert Haller, took the new personal chemistry established at the meeting, and the remarks of Waigel and Pöhl, as clear signals that they must reflect on the established Finance

Ministry approach to EMU. Waigel had emphasized to Bérégovoy how vital he saw Franco-German collaboration within the Guigou Group. From then onwards it was clear to Finance Ministry officials that EMU negotiations were to rest on a shared political drive from Waigel and Bérégovoy for French and German officials to bridge their differences of approach to EMU. In short, Finance Ministry officials had to reflect on established departmental beliefs about EMU.

Köhler's Review of Finance Ministry Strategy on EMU and of EMU Policy Beliefs

Irritated by the way in which the Guigou Group had been foisted on them (and the fact that their first knowledge of it derived from the press), and stimulated by the Tegernsee meeting, Finance Ministry officials began to reconsider EMU strategy and beliefs. In this process the lead role was taken by Köhler, head of the money and credit division and appointed State Secretary in the autumn to replace Tietmeyer on 1 January. Cognitively, the concern was to reflect on how beliefs about EMU needed to be adapted to this new situation. One of the two key objectives of the interministerial co-ordination group under Winkelmann was to work out the theoretical basis of EMU post-Delors.

Köhler was determined to seize the initiative from Tietmeyer as his designated heir. It was clear that Tietmeyer was deeply reserved about the Delors Report, and by background entrapped within his own intellectual 'sunk costs' in the Werner approach to EMU. By contrast, Köhler was more welcoming to the three-stage approach of Delors, seeing the contents of stage 3 and of stage 1 as a substantial negotiating victory for German beliefs. He was, therefore, more open to pushing the process of internal reflection. He also recognized the value of strengthening confidence and trust between the Chancellor's Office and the Finance Ministry. With officials like Teltschik and Bitterlich he worked on establishing a smoother, more collaborative relationship which gave him credibility with the Chancellor. Köhler adusted quickly to changing political realities after Madrid and to the good personal chemistry between Kohl and Waigel and was determined to work within that framework.

Strategically, Waigel and Köhler shared the objective of regaining the initiative on EMU after the Delors Report and the imposition of the Guigou Group. This objective was to be realized in four ways (Köhler and Kees 1996: 146–50). First, the task of Winkelmann's interministerial working group was to develop concrete German negotiating positions on terms led by the Finance Ministry— with Köhler and Haller providing the intellectual input. This work was crucial so that Germany could retain as much impact on negotiations on stage 2 (the weakest part of the Delors Report) as it had on stages 1 and 3. In effect, the interministerial working group was designed to strengthen Finance Ministry control.

Secondly, the Finance Ministry had to manage its relations with the Bundesbank to its advantage. The Bundesbank was an asset to deploy in negotiations within Bonn and within the EC fora. Hence the strategy was to 'bind in' the Bundesbank on every EMU issue. In this respect Tietmeyer's move to the Bundesbank directorate in January 1990 was very helpful, and especially his responsibility there for international affairs. Tietmeyer would sit alongside Köhler in the EC Monetary Committee. The Bundesbank was also to be 'bound in' by its membership of the interministerial EMU group in Bonn. Köhler worked to ensure that co-ordination with the Bundesbank was close and detailed, in the process flattering Tietmeyer.

It was also agreed that there should be a division of labour between the Finance Ministry and the Bundesbank. The Finance Ministry would take the lead in the EC Monetary Committee on excessive budget deficit and economic convergence issues; the Bundesbank would lead on stage 3 issues and the draft ECB statute in the Committee of EC Central Bank Governors. This territorial demarcation made a great deal of strategic sense in the context of both the statutory role of the Bundesbank and the need to concentrate the attention of the Finance Ministry in the negotiations. But it contained a danger that issues might fall between their fields of responsibility. In the IGC negotiations the Finance Ministry was to lose track of two issues: the procedures for entry into stage 3, and the issue of fiscal discipline within stage 3. After the Delors Report, and with the Bundesbank taking the lead on stage 3, the Finance Ministry tended to neglect stage 3 issues in favour of stage 2. Köhler focused his attention on ensuring that the content given to stage 2 did not undermine the stability principles of stage 3.

Thirdly, the Finance Ministry sought to 'bind in' other federal ministries to EMU bargaining positions defined on its own terms. Köhler was intent on ensuring that the Finance Ministry provided the political leadership on EMU in Bonn. In this respect the central problem was the Foreign Ministry: in particular Lautenschlager, with whom as State Secretary he had to contend in the 'European' State Secretaries' twice-monthly meetings; and also Jelonek in the Guigou Group. At the basic working level Winkelmann's interministerial EMU group was an important mechanism in this respect. At another level Köhler relied on using Waigel's strong political weight with the Chancellor against Genscher and his officials.

Finally, Köhler determined to get as much as possible of the preparatory work for the IGC done in the EC Monetary Committee. This choice of institutional venue offered three key negotiating advantages. German views on the prime importance of economic stability were shared by Cees Maas, the Dutch Chair of the EC Monetary Committee, and by its secretary, Andreas Kees. With them Köhler cultivated a close relationship to ensure that the committee was likely to be a sympathetic forum for German Finance Ministry agenda-setting and for promoting its definition of EMU problems. In addition, this forum would bring in Tietmeyer and the Bundesbank, again serving to bind them in. But, perhaps most important of all, here the Finance Ministry could control EMU negotiations away from the Foreign Ministry. That control would be less possible in an IGC setting. Hence Köhler sought to maximize the amount of IGC negotiating conducted in the setting of the EC Monetary Committee.

Winkelmann's Interministerial Co-ordination Group on EMU and Reflection on Inherited Ministry Beliefs about EMU

The interministerial co-ordination group had begun in a loose, unofficial form after the Hanover Council, chaired by Winkelmann who was head of the European monetary section in the money and credit division. Winkelmann was a Bonn civil servant in the classic mould: diligent, courteous, efficient, and inclined to traditional views on EMU. The group's work began in earnest with the preparations for the Guigou Group. Given the Foreign Ministry lead on EMU before Hanover and after Madrid, the Finance Ministry's strategic objective was to move away from the defensive and to establish the clear lead in the Guigou Group and in later developments. In short, the EMU interministerial group was about bringing the Foreign Ministry under control. In relation to the Guigou Group that objective proved hard to achieve. With the Foreign Ministry pushing hard on a timetable for EMU, and the Finance Ministry reluctant, it was difficult to agree bargaining positions for the Guigou Group and avoid a sense of German disunity. The initiative seemed to remain firmly with Guigou and with Jelonek and the Foreign Ministry.

At its first meeting the Winkelmann Group agreed only a very limited paper on procedures. Its work tended to remain reactive to the leadership coming from the Guigou Group in Paris. The main substantive outcome of the Winkelmann Group's work was the November 1989 paper, 'The German Basic Position in Relation to EMU'. It incorporated the positions on EMU agreed within the federal government in May 1989. This paper spelt out the basic ordo-liberal principles for an economic union (where the Economics Ministry contribution was important) and for a monetary union (here the Bundesbank contribution was crucial). In essence these principles did not differ from the content of the Delors Report, except for the addition of more substantial material on the principles of economic union. The four key principles for economic union were: completion of the single market; a common EC competition policy; an effective co-ordination of economic policies, including budgetary discipline; and an effective regional development policy that relied primarily on market mechanisms of adjustment. The five main principles for a monetary union were: a federally organized and completely independent ESCB; a monetary policy mandated to secure price stability; the abolition of the monetary financing of budget deficits; the irrevocable locking of exchange rates in the final stage; and the introduction of a 'common' currency.

The more substantial reflection on the Finance Ministry approach to EMU involved Haller in the economic policy division who then began his close working relationship with Köhler on this issue. When, on 1 January 1990, Köhler succeeded Teitmeyer as State Secretary, Haller was to take up his former post as head of the money and credit division. This reflective work on the theoretical and political basis of EMU was fed into the Winkelmann Group, which was given as one of its tasks clarification of the theoretical and practical basis of EMU in the wake of the Delors Report and the Madrid Council. With the axis focused on Köhler, Haller, and Winkelmann from September onwards, influence on the intellectual shaping of EMU slipped away from Tietmeyer.

Köhler and Haller focused their inquiries on three questions. What is the relationship between EMU and the wider process of European integration? Where lie the main risks? How can they be reduced? The focus was on risk-reduction and management so that a viable and sustainable EMU could be realized. In addressing the first question Köhler and Haller concluded that EMU was to be realized in political and institutional conditions different from those envisaged in the Werner Report. Hence the approach to risk-reduction and management offered by traditional coronation theory was no longer relevant. Monetary union had to be realized without the sustaining political framework of solidarity to ensure that the burden of adjustment would be shared at the EC level. The main risk in these new circumstances was that the costs of adjustment would be imposed on (virtuous) states by states running up excessive budget deficits. In short, the problem was now defined as insuring against the hazard of irresponsible fiscal behaviour at the national level. Haller searched the economic literature on the pros and cons of different solutions to the problem of fiscal discipline, focusing on the use of financial markets as a discipline and of fiscal rules. His recommendation was for the 'regulation of budget deficits'—which later became known as the convergence criteria. In place of the old coronation theory, the Finance Ministry adopted a 'rule-based' approach to EMU. In this respect the reflection process within the Finance Ministry produced a conclusion different from that of the Economics Ministry which was more sceptical about rules.

But the doubts of Köhler and Haller about the viability of EMU were by no means set to rest by the outcome of this theoretical revision of EMU policy. They retained the view that the main danger stemmed from the risk that the political and intellectual consensus underpinning the Franco-German axis on EMU, and the personal chemistry of Waigel and Bérégovoy, might prove fragile. Two open questions worried them. Had the French state the domestic political capability to sustain a 'stability policy'? Far more fundamentally, did the French really share German ideas about the importance of a 'rule-based' and 'market-oriented' approach to economic policy? Short-term tactical concessions by the French to make an EMU deal possible did not amount to a sustainable basis for an EMU. This reservation led them to be continually testing French thinking and resolve—not least, as we shall see, in the secret Franco-German bilaterals of 1991. They did not succeed in ridding themselves of a residual distrust.

Genscher, German Unification, and the Date of the IGC

During and after the deliberations of the Guigou Group Genscher acted as the prime German advocate for using the Strasbourg European Council in December 1989 to set a date for the IGC and to provide the IGC with political guidance. He challenged the argument that the date for the IGC could be set at the end of stage 1. Genscher pointed out that stage 1 could not end until stage 2 was prepared. As stage 2 required institutional changes, it could not begin till the end of the IGC. Hence stage 1 could never end. This contradiction had to be overcome by setting a date in the second half of 1990 for the start of the IGC, that is, just after the beginning of stage 1.

As his critics in Bonn pointed out, Genscher was responding to pressures from Paris and Rome to convene the IGC during the Italian Presidency. Indeed a declaration on precisely this point was made by Genscher and Gianni De Michelis, the Italian Foreign Minister, during the German–Italian summit of 18 October 1989. But Genscher's reason for acting so strongly on this issue was based, above all, on an assessment of German interests in a changing Europe. As the prospects for overcoming the division of Europe, and of Germany itself, became clearer, so Genscher's sense of urgency increased. A window of historical opportunity to promote European unification was opening; EMU was the main embryonic policy instrument available to use for this larger historical objective. In Genscher's calculation, Germany's future security in a fast-changing Europe depended on matching the seizing of emerging opportunities to unify Germany with the creation of new opportunities to deepen EC unification.

The decisive turning-point for EMU occurred as a consequence of the crisis situation in Franco-German relations during the four-week period from the fall of the Berlin Wall on 9 November 1989 to the Strasbourg European Council on 8–9 December. Genscher registered, and responded to, French unease (notably from Dumas). French unease was, in part, triggered by Kohl's manoeuvring to seize the initiative on German unification—in particular with his personal 'ten-points-for-Germany' plan of 28 November and his unwillingness to offer final, definitive recognition of the Oder–Neisse border with Poland. Kohl's actions were prompted by his fear that he would be overrun by events and outflanked by other politicians. This fear was clearly communicated to Paris and was expected to be recognized and understood. Officials in the Federal Chancellor's Office stressed to their Elysée counterparts that recognition of the Oder–Neisse line would not be a problem but that tactically the Chancellor had to move cautiously on this issue to avoid inflaming domestic opinion. There appeared in fact to be no difficulties with Bianco, Guigou, and Védrine. The difficulties were with the President and were attributed by Chancellery officials to the malign influence of Dumas. Mitterrand's unease was seen in the Federal Chancellor's Office as having its main roots in the perceived threat to French interests and power in Europe from a unified Germany. In the Federal Chancellor's Office there was perplexity about the situation in Paris and criticism of the role of Dumas. Kohl had already signalled to Mitterrand that he was in agreement with the idea of convening the IGC on EMU during the Italian Presidency, that is, before the end of 1990, but after the German elections also scheduled for the end of 1990. He and his officials could not understand the problem when Mitterrand began to complain that Bonn was losing interest in pressing ahead with EMU.

At the special European Council meeting in Paris, called by Mitterrand on 18 November, Genscher was struck by the frosty and strained climate between heads of state and government and by the sharp criticisms of Kohl's unwilling-ness to immediately recognize the Oder–Neisse border. He sensed a danger of German isolation, Germany's diplomatic nightmare. But the real impetus for Genscher's engagement on behalf of fixing a date for the IGC at Strasbourg came from his visit to Paris on 30 November (Genscher 1995: 677–81). This visit was part of a set designed as 'damage limitation' in the wake of Kohl's announcement of the 'ten-point' plan without prior notification of, let alone consultation with, EC member states. Viewed as going beyond what Kohl had outlined on 18 November, this plan evoked profound distrust. In his meeting with Mitterrand on 30 November Genscher was subjected to the full force of the President's fears and warnings. He took back to Bonn two messages: that with-out parallel progress on EC unification and German unification a return to the former 'balance-of-power' politics could occur; and that, in the context of preparing the Strasbourg Council, Germany seemed to have emerged as a brake on the European unification process. Genscher spelt out to Mitterrand his per-sonal position: that German and European unification had to advance together. But he recognized that urgent action was needed by the Chancellor.

Genscher took back with him to Kohl what he saw as the crucial, positive message: that Mitterrand accepted German unification as an 'historical neces-sity'. At the same time, he underlined to Kohl what Mitterrand saw as the real issue—how a united Germany would relate to Europe as a whole. Genscher pressed on Kohl the view that it was in Germany's interest not to let slip the opportunity to advance European unification at Strasbourg by agreeing an early date for an IGC on EMU. Otherwise, serious risks would be taken with the future security of Europe and the gains of forty years of European policy poten-tially squandered. Kohl was irritated because nothing that Genscher asked for had not, in his view, been vouchsafed to Paris already.

Kohl's Strategy for the Strasbourg European Council

Kohl had been quick to recognize that the pace of events in Eastern Europe offered him an opportunity to strengthen his domestic political position. By 11 September 1989, at the CDU congress in Bremen, he was exhibiting a more confident, authoritative style, using the efforts of GDR citizens to leave via

Hungary in order to present himself as speaking on behalf of all Germans. He was elected party chair with a comfortable majority and his position further secured by the departure of Geissler as the CDU's General-Secretary and the failure of Späth to secure re-election as a party deputy chair (Dreher 1998: 435–42).

This new confidence was reflected in the context of Chancellery–Elysée consultations about the Strasbourg Council. On 13 October Bitterlich signalled to Guigou that Kohl would press for a firm date for the IGC at Strasbourg. Reference was made to the IGC convening at the end of 1990, without any preconditions, finishing its work at the end of 1991, and Treaty amendments on EMU being ratified in 1992. Meanwhile, Ludewig attended Winkelmann's EMU co-ordinating group to stress the importance of Germany playing a constructive role in the Guigou Group and the particular importance that the Chancellor attached to building EMU around Franco-German reconciliation.

But during November Kohl was totally distracted by the mounting pressure of events in Germany and the opening of the German question as a practical political issue. On the German question, Kohl's strategic objectives were to ensure that he was not outmanoeuvred by forces on the political Right (especially the Republicans exploiting the national issue) or Left in Germany; that he kept ahead of events and shaped them; and that Genscher did not again succeed in eclipsing him as over the events in the Prague embassy in early October when the Foreign Minister had flown to Prague to underline his solidarity with GDR citizens trying to flee via this route. With the accelerating speed of change, Kohl's strategy was severely tested and this absorbed his time and energy. Also, the contrast between the way in which the crowds in Berlin feted Brandt but booed him on 10 November was not lost on Kohl. The 'ten-point' plan of 28 November was an attempt to retrieve the initiative, or at least to pre-empt a leadership role by Genscher or by the SPD. This spelt out a process of increasing co-operation between the Federal Republic and the GDR; spoke of evolving confederal structures; restated the commitment to German unification; but attached no date to its realization. Before Strasbourg Kohl was simply too overwhelmed by the German question and its potential domestic political implications to attend to EMU (Zelikow and Rice 1996).

In relation to preparations for Strasbourg, Kohl had three strategic objectives: to reinforce his commitment to European unification by making a positive German proposal; to avoid being seen as giving in to strong, overt French pressure on the issue of the date for the IGC on EMU; and, in particular, to ensure that this date did not make for domestic political difficulties by clashing with the federal elections scheduled for autumn 1990. Kohl was especially concerned to reduce potential electoral damage from EMU. In this spirit he wrote to Mitterrand on 27 November, two weeks before Strasbourg, on the issue of a calendar for European union. This letter had many of the hallmarks of Waigel's Finance Ministry. It stressed the potentially mounting problems for EMU consequent on the major differences between EC states, noting in particular the scale of budget deficits and the delay in fiscal harmonization. Kohl focused on the importance of evaluating the progress of stage 1 and the need to hand over preparations to ECOFIN and to the Committee of EC Central Bank Governors.

On a more constructive note, Kohl's letter introduced the idea of an IGC on political union as a means of countering the concerns about German unification that were likely to figure at the centre of the Strasbourg Council's deliberations. He suggested that the Strasbourg Council should agree a calendar of work for the IGC, which would complete its work in 1993. The IGC was to have three stages: a first stage on EMU to begin under the Italian Presidency from the end of 1990; a second stage before December 1991 to tackle institutional reforms; and a third stage in 1992 concerned to bring proposals on economic and political union into a coherent whole, depending on the degree of realization of the European single market. The ratification of the IGC would then take place in 1993.

Following Genscher's report of his meeting with Mitterrand, Kohl dispatched a further letter on 30 November. Its objective was to clear up any possible mis-understandings about Kohl's position and to reinforce his European credentials vis-à-vis Genscher. In this letter Kohl admitted to Mitterrand that his desire to defer the IGC beyond 1990 reflected domestic political considerations. The cal-endar proposed on 27 November was an attempt to circumnavigate the threats posed by German federal elections. But the letter also stressed that a deter-mined policy to promote European political union was more necessary than ever in the context of the events in eastern Europe. Genscher had effectively impressed on Kohl the danger of German isolation at Strasbourg. In pressing European political union Kohl was trying to impress on Mitterrand the depth of his commitment to European unification.

In his reply of 1 December, Mitterrand argued that political union was not the top priority, even though desirable. He informed Kohl that he would demand at Strasbourg a fixed date for the IGC. Kohl's response was conditioned by his con-cern to escape isolation at Strasbourg and to ensure that Genscher did not seize the initiative on the European dimension of German unification. Hence—three days before Strasbourg—on 5 December Bitterlich telephoned Guigou to confirm the Chancellor's agreement to fix a date at Strasbourg, convening the IGC during the Italian Presidency.

After Strasbourg: Kohl's Ownership of the EMU Project

As at the special meeting of heads of state and government in Paris on 18 November, the Strasbourg European Council proved to be a very different ex-perience for Genscher and for Kohl. For Genscher and the Foreign Ministry it was a decisive success. They gained clear agreement of support for German unification, tied to the process being embedded in the perspective of European integration. The date for the IGC on EMU was the clearest tangible expression of this new spirit.

But for Kohl the Strasbourg Council was a very unpleasant personal experience (Diekmann and Reuth 1996: 185 ff.). He was subjected to sharp questioning about German policy intentions and made aware of the depths of Mrs Thatcher's distrust of German motives. This experience underlined for Kohl the implications of German isolation if she were to be seen as pursuing a 'go-it-alone' policy. Hence he became determined to reaffirm German ambitions to give a new impulse to European unification. In so doing, as before the Hanover Council in 1988, Kohl was determined to seize the initiative from Genscher—to make European unification his issue.

The main legacy of Strasbourg went beyond the fixing of a time-frame for the start of the IGC. In its wake Kohl determined to make EMU his personal responsibility; to wrap it up in a refashioned vision of Germany and Europe in the context of German unification; and to make it the focus of his European leadership. This change was registered by James Baker, the US Secretary of State, during breakfast with Kohl on 12 December 1989 in Berlin—just three days after Strasbourg. Kohl indicated to Baker that he had made EMU his own project and was intent on forcing its progress (Stoltenberg 1997: 331).

Kohl had by no means ceased to be concerned about the relationship between EMU and the German elections scheduled for autumn 1990. Indeed, the impact of electoral strategy was still visible in his attitude of caution on recognition of the Oder–Neisse border, even though this attitude had negative diplomatic effects. But European unification became an issue about which Kohl became electorally confident. A key reason for this confidence was provided by his success in pushing the date of the IGC beyond the election. The continuing influence of this factor was evident when, after Kohl proposed economic and monetary union between the Federal Republic and the GDR on 6 February 1990, Mitterrand suggested bringing forward the date for the IGC on EMU. In reply, on 13 February, Bitterlich pointed out to the Elysée that such a move was impossible. But the Chancellery used this opportunity to push harder for an IGC on political union. The positive message from Kohl was that it was vital to accelerate the general process of European unification of which EMU was a part. This theme was then taken up by Mitterrand over dinner with Kohl on 15 February. There was a more positive factor at work here. Kohl was able to combine electoral strategy with political principle in assimilating EMU into the larger project of European political unification. He had hinted at this linkage in his letter of 27 November. Now, in February, agreement was reached on a Franco-German proposal for a second IGC on political union, to parallel the IGC on EMU, and on making joint proposals on political union to the next Dublin European Council on 27 April.

Conclusion

An examination of the place of EMU in the Chancellorship of Kohl between 1982 and 1989 highlights the role of Genscher in putting EMU on the agenda and in sustaining momentum behind the issue. His skills as a 'policy entrepreneur' were decisive: his political judgement about timing, his use of his relative political weight, his negotiation of change, his ability to persuade. Genscher was no innovator at the level of ideas. He took what was available. There was no attempt to challenge the German model as the basis of EMU or to raise questions about ordo-liberalism. Indeed, the most telling criticism of Genscher was that he (or more appropriately his officials) did not fully understand the requirements and implications of ordo-liberalism for EMU—though they tried to do so. Genscher's strength derived from his clear and confident sense of where German interests lay, from the security of having a supportive domestic political constituency for his initiatives on Europe, and from having the ear of the Chancellor.

In contrast, Kohl was hesitant on EMU. His clear support for the principle was hedged in practice by a willingness to move on EMU only once a sustainable domestic political consensus had been demonstrated. On that basis Kohl showed that he could act decisively—in May–June 1988, in May–June 1989 and in December 1989. But on each of these three occasions Genscher was the driving force at work. Throughout this period Kohl's motivations were complex: support in principle for what Genscher was trying to do on EMU; a desire to prevent Genscher from seizing the initiative and claiming political credit; and a concern to balance forces and interests within the CDU with the requirements of coalition management. The result was a degree of uncertainty and unpredictability about whether, when, and how far Kohl might lead on EMU—apparent before the Hanover, Madrid, and Strasbourg Councils.

Kohl's decisive contribution took the form of working out a political strategy for EMU. This strategy emerged at Hanover and involved binding in the Bundesbank to the process of designing and negotiating EMU. Its presence within the negotiations could be justified as the safest way to realize Germany's central strategy on EMU which was shared by all the leading players—namely, to gain agreement on the German model as the basis of EMU. This clever political linkage by Kohl proved highly effective in the Delors Committee, yielding gains for the Bundesbank in the substance of the Delors Report and gains for Kohl in reducing the scope for the Bundesbank to act as external critic on EMU. However irritated the Bundesbank was about being bound in this way, Kohl's strategy was less disagreeable than Schmidt's strategy of isolating the Bundesbank from EMS negotiations before the Bremen European Council.

No less important than high-level 'policy entrepreneurship' and games of political strategy was the process of reflection on policy beliefs about EMU. Within the Economics and Finance Ministries this process took the form of the marginalization of the coronation theory of EMU. The result was an emerging divide between the large majority of academic economists, who remained wedded to the coronation theory, and the most influential officials, who—independently of academic economists—worked through revised theoretical positions on EMU. The catalyst for this probing of policy beliefs came from the exposure of officials to a fast-changing political and economic context of EMU and consequent pressures to adapt beliefs. Such pressures were not so directly felt amongst academic economists.

The process of reflection about EMU was also apparent in the Foreign Ministry and the Federal Chancellor's Office in 1989–90. In their case the question was about the implications of changes in Eastern Europe and in relations between the two German states for strategy on EMU. Here, crucially, there was a turning-point in 1989: in November for Genscher and in December for Kohl. Intellectually, it had already formed in their minds: witness Kohl's remarks at the Franco-German meeting in Heidelberg in 1986. But, once German unification was set under way, EMU became endowed with a new significance: as a test of the political resolve of a unified Germany to pursue its course of binding itself into Europe. With this connection the quality of Kohl's leadership on EMU shifted gear. EMU was now at the forefront of Kohl's strategic vision for Europe.

9

German Strategy for the IGC

Nothing better illustrated the personal identification of Chancellor Kohl with EMU, and the transformed nature of his governing style on this issue, than his behaviour at his breakfast meeting with the Dutch Prime Minister, Ruud Lubbers, on 28 November 1991. Lubbers was visiting Kohl to consider a range of issues in preparation for the Maastricht Council which he would be chairing. His preparations had focused on the political-union negotiations, in part because of the fiasco surrounding the collapse of the Dutch Draft Treaty on political union, and in part because he understood that political union was an area in which Germany had certain preconditions to be met before it would sign up for EMU. To Lubbers's surprise Kohl was mainly interested in EMU and, most astonishing of all, spoke of not signing in Maastricht unless EMU was made 'irreversible'. 'Irreversibility' of EMU was made into the *only* German pre-condition, without there being any discernible 'bottom line' on political union.

In fact, Kohl had ceased to make reference to the requirement of parallel progress on EMU and political union after 6 November, just before the Franco-German summit in Bonn on 14–15 November. That summit had already provided a clear political signal that both he and Mitterrand were looking for 'irreversibility'. But Kohl's conception of 'irreversibility' was essentially philosophical and historical and did not extend to an interest in its precise legal implications and forms in EC law. It included a belief in a date for stage 3, though not in a final and fixed date. Dates were after all an established part of the Community method. More importantly, Kohl was aware that a Chancellor's domestic power over EMU was critically dependent on having a timetable in his hands to keep up the pressure on the conservative Finance Ministry and Bundesbank. Hence, for reasons of power, he wanted to be provided with a tool that would enable him to drive forward the decision-making process on EMU. It was, critically, an issue that defined his future power as Chancellor over the process of making European unification a reality. The Chancellor was no more interested in the technical details of EMU than before. He had Waigel and Köhler to attend to the EMU files. Kohl's preoccupation was to put in place the conditions that would ensure that he was able to manage the future process of realizing EMU. In this political ambition he was wholly successful.

What was different for Lubbers, who had been alongside Kohl in European Council meetings since 1982, was the transformation of style. Here was a self-confident, forceful Chancellor, sensing that he was living through a key histori-cal moment for Europeans. Kohl was prepared to set the broad political direction in a newly vigorous manner. In essence, he was signalling to Lubbers that a lot of work had to be done by the Dutch Presidency to ensure that EMU was made 'irreversible'. Kohl had been transformed into a Chancellor whose leadership was driven by a strategic vision of Germany in Europe: a vision that was not new to him and was continuous with that of Adenauer; but a vision that had now become the basic reference point for his behaviour.

But, important as Kohl was, Chancellor leadership was just one of the themes informing German strategy for the IGC negotiations on EMU and the way in which those negotiations were conducted. In order to gain a secure feel for both the content and style of German strategy, and to help make sense of the complex narrative, these various themes have to be clearly identified. In addition, it is vital to delve into more specific features of the way in which the EMU negotiations were handled in Bonn and Frankfurt. These features included the kinds of strategic choices made by German negotiators and the ways in which those choices influenced how they handled the IGC; the process of reflection about EMU and restructuring of argument that took place, particularly consequent on German unification; and the arts of persuasion, including symbolic politics, employed by German negotiators. The EMU negotiations reveal how EMU strategy was born out of a specific German cognitive context and then fed back into that context once it was confronted with changing political and economic realities. The result was a restructuring of policy argument and the construction of German negotiating positions on a different basis from traditional 'coronation' theory. At the same time domestic responses to the outcome of the IGC negotiations illustrated the limitations on that process of elite policy learning. Coronation theory was by no means dead; and a 'D-Mark patriotism' remained a latent and potentially powerful force that constrained German negotiators.

The German Approach to the IGC Negotiations: Key Themes

The approach of German negotiators to the IGC comprised several elements, which served to define its distinctive character, reinforce each other, and provide a powerful coherence. There was, for instance, a symbiosis between Chancellor leadership and the stress on Franco-German reconciliation. The Franco-German relationship upgraded the Chancellor's special role in the EMU negotiations; it provided him with a resource for influencing domestic players, like Waigel and Köhler, notably on 'irreversibility'. Equally, Chancellor leadership did not extend to negotiating the technical details of a viable EMU. That responsibility was left by Kohl to Waigel and the Finance Ministry, with an expert advisory role for the Bundesbank. The potential for conflict was mitigated by the Chancellor's low profile on the technical aspects of the negotiations. Kohl recognized just how politically sensitive EMU was. On the other hand, he and Waigel were united by their recognition of how much was at stake in Europe. This basic political unanimity enabled Kohl to set the pace and take up a firm position on making EMU 'irreversible'. In addition, as we saw in Chapter 1, cultural factors and strategic considerations conspired to lend a 'rule-based' approach by German negotiators. This approach served to reduce future risk and uncertainty about how Germany's EC partners might behave inside EMU. It reflected a deep-seated mistrust that began with the Greeks and ranged through Italy, Spain, and Belgium to include France. This preference to construct EMU on the basis of an edifice of technical rules legitimated the Finance Ministry's lead role and strengthened its ability to see off Foreign Ministry intervention.

Conflict was also mitigated by a basic underlying consensus that German negotiators must achieve an EMU strictly committed to economic stability and an open, competitive market economy on the basis of an independent ECB. Internal discussions were focused on the questions of what were the essential conditions for a sustainably stable EMU and how best to realize these conditions. As an FDP politician Genscher was deeply committed to neo-liberal economic ideas and ensuring that a final EMU agreement was compatible with these principles.

Kohl as Political Strategist

The strategic leadership provided by Chancellor Kohl was decisive in two ways: in setting and monitoring the political direction for these negotiations; and in restructuring the way in which EMU was thought about and debated within Bonn. In this sense his contribution went beyond the simple—though vital—role of acting as *animateur* to the process of negotiation. It extended to the substance: above all, to the theme of German responsibility for Europe and the realization of that responsibility by 'binding' Germany into Europe in the form of making EMU 'irreversible'. But, as we saw in the last chapter, Kohl's strategic leadership could never aspire to a mastery of the technical issues. In this respect he could never get to grips with the substantive details of the EMU negotiations, in the way that Helmut Schmidt would have attempted.

Kohl was an effective political strategist of EMU in two senses. First, once the date had been set for the IGC on EMU at Strasbourg, German strategy for the impending negotiations became bound up in Kohl's vision of European unification. This strategic vision, and its elaboration in vivid metaphor and historical narrative, invested EMU with a new, highly charged symbolic and emotional content. By means of unifying and inspiring symbols, Kohl was intent on more than simply setting a policy direction and evoking emotional engagement from otherwise reluctant and potentially divided German negotiators. His concern was, above all, to legitimate EMU by building a broad societal support. In Kohl's rhetoric EMU was related to an image of the postwar identity of Germans. The IGC negotiations were also shaped by the Chancellor's efforts to construct and dramatize a new image of leadership competence for himself: as the Chancellor of European unity. That image was not just about electoral advantage. It was about Kohl's place in German and European history. A personal ambition that had driven him throughout his long political career was conjoined with a deeply felt belief about European unification rooted in and inspired by his personal experience. What emerged was a vivid, moving political message about EMU. Within the EMU negotiations one of Kohl's chief resources was his effective employment of the arts of symbolic politics. With his advisers, he was important in shaping a rhetorical environment which was conducive to striking an EMU agreement. Kohl's great contribution was as a strategic visionary. It took the form of acting as *animateur* of the EMU negotiations; and, by 'nesting' EMU within German unification, of reshaping how German negotiators perceived the payoffs from an EMU agreement.

Kohl's skills as a political strategist were evident in a second sense. He had the capacity to seize the initiative in relation to decisive points in the EMU negotiations—like the setting of dates for stages 2 and 3. In this respect an important resource of Chancellor leadership was control of the time-scale of the negotiations. By this means Kohl could put German negotiators under sustained pressure to deliver. The result was a continuing pressure on German negotiators to reflect on the policy beliefs underpinning their bargaining positions. Kohl ensured that he remained the one stable point of reference and rest in the EMU negotiations and that others were kept permanently on their toes.

Kohl's influence was further promoted by his skill in drawing Köhler into the framework of his inner circle. There was a trade-off for Köhler. The gains from close access to the Chancellor, his trust and patronage, had an accompanying price—the expectation of unqualified loyalty to Kohl's basic political position on European unification. Kohl was a past master of using close personal relations to his advantage, to ensure that Köhler worked loyally to his agenda. Tietmeyer too had been the loyal civil servant. But he had also always proved more difficult on EMU, a man to be squared and boxed rather than embraced, a man who was immensely respected by Kohl—who recognized in him a formidable asset in EMU negotiations—but who was not tied to Kohl by complicity.

Controlling the Institutional Venue

Strategic leadership in setting and controlling the broad political direction over EMU negotiations was not synonymous with shaping and controlling the substantive contents of the EMU negotiations. The second key theme in the German approach was the way in which Waigel's Finance Ministry sought to control the choice and design of the institutional venues both for preparing German negotiating positions and for negotiating at the EC level. By creating a certain kind of negotiating process it was able to shape how EMU problems were defined and tackled. The Finance Ministry's objective was to be the gatekeeper to the IGC; in pursuit of that objective it engaged in some tough bureaucratic politics in Bonn, notably against the Foreign Ministry.

Its second objective was to 'bind in' and neutralize the Bundesbank at all points of the negotiations. This strategy of 'binding in' the Bundesbank could be readily sold to the Chancellor on political grounds—then the Bundesbank would not be able to act as external critic. By drawing it into responsibility its capacity to argue from a position of principled opposition would be undermined. Also, German economic and industrial opinion could be kept on board in this way. But also important was the argument that this strategy would provide the Finance Ministry with powerful political leverage in Bonn and in Brussels. Finance Ministry negotiators could use to good effect the plea that their hands were tied by the need to carry the support of the Bundesbank. References to the support of the Bundesbank for Finance Ministry positions also endowed them with a major increment of political legitimacy.

Finally, Köhler in the Finance Ministry and Tietmeyer in the Bundesbank were experienced Bonn 'insiders'. They recognized that their power over the EMU negotiations depended on their technical mastery of the negotiating brief. Both were also careful and deliberate in sharing information with others, for instance, the Economics Ministry. By monopolizing access to key institutional venues they were able to maintain privileged information and accumulate expertise about the negotiating process. This privileged information about the state of play and expertise about the process was a crucial source of power in Bonn. Kohl came to depend on Köhler as his best-informed source of technical advice, not hesitating to seek him out directly for briefing.

Managing the 'Core Community': Franco-German Reconciliation

The third theme in the German approach was the pervasive importance attached to Franco-German reconciliation. The Franco-German relationship operated at different levels and involved different transnational linkages. It constituted in effect a complex tissue of contending relations in which negotiators used transnational alliances to maximize their own domestic room for manoeuvre. Franco-German relations were unquestionably ordered in a hierarchy, with Kohl and Mitterrand presiding at the apex, and using their resources of political authority to give a crucial direction to an EMU agreement. At the same time German negotiators made creative use of individual cross-national linkages to bring pressure to bear on their own colleagues and to endow themselves with greater freedom of manoeuvre within the domestic policy process. Genscher–Dumas, Waigel–Bérégovoy, Pöhl–de Larosière—each relationship had its own dynamics and impact on the EMU negotiations. What held them together was a shared belief that negotiation of EMU had to be based fundamentally on reconciling French and German policy beliefs. Finance Ministry and Bundesbank strategy was to impress on the French that a viable and durable EMU could not be achieved if an agreement involved compromise with the basic principles of a stability policy. Hence their bargaining positions took on a strongly didactic quality.

Kohl's Use of Metaphor and Historical Narrative to Reframe EMU

Once the Strasbourg European Council of December 1990 was out of the way, a restructuring of domestic political power over EMU became evident. Genscher moved from centre stage to sidelines in the EMU negotiations. A background factor was personal health. In July 1989 Genscher had suffered a heart attack. By April 1990 a recurrence of heart problems was beginning to cast doubt on his staying power across a wide range of issues. Genscher was less disposed to be combative in relations with both Kohl and Waigel, who did not fully appreciate his health problems. Kohl was also still smarting with irritation after what he saw as Genscher's attempts to outflank him by stealing public publicity for himself on German unification (especially during the Prague embassy episode). A third factor was that, till September 1990, Genscher's time and energy were absorbed by the external dimension of German unification: the 'two-plus-four' negotiations. But he remained important in two senses: as a symbol, particularly to the French, that German unification would contribute to European stability; and as a source of pressure on Kohl to look beyond party political issues to the wider dimensions of European policy. Genscher's two most powerful images were evident in his speech of 23 March 1990 to the Western European Union. The EC was pictured as the 'anchor of stability' for Europe as a whole; whilst German policy was presented in the form of a quote from Thomas Mann in 1952—'We do not want a German Europe, but a European Germany'.

The diversion of Genscher's energies created space for Kohl to stake out a more independent role in European policy. He was intent on making the two issues of German unification and European unification his own and on doing so by sustaining the initiative on them. Arguments from principle and from strategic calculation fused. Kohl believed passionately in both projects and welcomed the historic opportunity to reconcile them. Strategically, he was irritated by the way in which Genscher had achieved political profile on European unification before the Strasbourg Council. By creating a leadership image of mastery of German unification ('Chancellor of German unity') and of European unification ('Chancellor of European unity') Kohl was determined to outflank both Genscher and the opposition SPD in the autumn 1990 federal elections. And, of course, the Chancellor was not immune to the seductions of writing himself into the history books of the future.

From December 1989 onwards Kohl's energies were progressively liberated from the confines of internal party and coalition management. This process was sealed by the first (and only) democratic elections in the GDR on 18 March 1990. The strong performance of the CDU reflected well on Kohl, set the democratic seal on completing the process of German unification rapidly, and suggested the rewards from having been bold on German unification. In this context Kohl redefined his leadership role. He saw the opportunity to win the autumn election and bring the CDU/CSU into line by appealing directly to the German people as a strategist of vision and an *animateur* of historic change. On 22 March Kohl issued his 'declaration of belief in a unified Germany in a unified Europe'. Here the key metaphor was of a united Germany 'nestling' in a united Europe.

The new leadership role of the Chancellor focused on setting EMU in the context of recommitting Germany to the political unification of Europe and reactivating the Franco-German relationship as the key to developing the EC. In articulating this new imagery of the Chancellor of European unity a major role was played by Eduard Ackermann as head of division 5 of the Chancellor's Office—communications and public relations—alongside Michael Mertes and Norbert Prill. They looked back to Adenauer's part in the early years of European integration for inspiration and, not least, in order to stress the theme of continuity with the CDU's venerated first Chancellor. Kohl was readily receptive to their advice that he should focus on persuading Germans to embrace EMU less by reference to material interests and benefits than by using historical memory to justify German responsibility for European unification. Hence Kohl turned to the unity pledge contained in the preamble to the Basic Law and to the founding fathers of the Federal Republic to legitimate his role as Chancellor of European unity.[1]

The first major public signal of the Chancellor's engagement came in a key speech on 'the German Question and European Responsibility' delivered in Paris on 17 January 1990. Here Kohl employed a metaphor that was taken from Adenauer's image of Europe as a house and that was to recur in his speeches and conversations: 'the "German house" must be built under a European roof'. This metaphor was designed to reinforce his core message—that there was no contradiction between German unification and European unification. Realization of European political union was identified by Kohl as the great task for the 1990s; EMU was an instrument for this great and noble purpose. The same metaphor of construction was redeployed in his keynote address to the Hanover Trade Fair on 2 May and again on 10 May in two speeches, one of which was delivered to the Bundestag.

But, following in the wake of the Dublin European Council of April 1990, there was a noticeable development of imagery in the speeches on 10 May. In one speech Kohl elaborated more fully on the image of building a European house. European construction required two main elements: a carefully thought-out architecture which fits harmoniously into the way in which the structure of the European continent has evolved; and a sound structural engineering which guarantees long-term stability. In the second speech on 10 May Kohl employed a new and powerful metaphor. In the Chancellor's words: 'German and European development do not stand in contradiction with each other. Both are sides of one and the same coin.'

---

[1] More generally on the role of historical memory in Kohl's European policy see Berger (1997); and Banchoff (1997).

Hence between January and May 1990 the basic elements of the imagery informing Kohl's strategic vision of European unification were put in place. But with this invocation of history went an acute sense of realism. At his federal press conference in Bonn on 10 January Kohl referred to the fact that: 'the future architecture of Germany must fit itself into the future architecture of the whole of Europe'. At the same time the Chancellor was convinced that completion of German unification could not wait on putting agreements about European unification, including EMU, in place. The reason was simple: German unification was being driven by too urgent a dynamic of its own. It could not wait on the agreement and ratification of EC treaty changes. In any case, Kohl was not prepared to risk losing the initiative in identifying himself with this historic and politically critical process in the teeth of an election campaign. What was crucial was that Germany should precommit herself to European political union—a matter of reaffirming policy belief in a new context—and stake out a strategic position as the initiator of a renewed drive to political unification. In relation to EMU a second element of realism was in evidence during the press conference of 10 January. Kohl stressed the great value that the federal government placed on working as closely as possible and in a relationship of absolute confidence with the Bundesbank in this 'sensibel' (delicate, problematic) area.

Consistent with his positive signal of 17 January 1990, Kohl pursued the theme of the relationship between German unification and European unification in a series of meetings designed to raise his profile on the issue. At their meeting in Paris on 15 February Kohl and Mitterrand initiated joint work between their staffs to prepare Franco-German proposals on political union to accompany EMU. There were important telephone discussions with Mitterrand on 6 March and 14 March, followed by the Franco-German summit in Paris on 25–6 April (just three days before the Dublin European Council). On 17 January and 12 February Kohl had already discussed the direction of his thinking with Delors and was to do so again on his visit to the European Commission to discuss German unification on 23 March. In these discussions Kohl expressed his deep personal debt of gratitude to Delors for his unwavering support for German unification and for a speedy assimilation of the former GDR into the EC. His basic message was that he intended to repay that debt by investing all his political weight and energy behind the project of European political unification. But contacts between Kohl and the British government were limited to two meetings with Douglas Hurd, on 6 February and 12 March, symptomatic of the poor state of relations between Kohl and Thatcher.

In the Kohl–Mitterrand letter of 19 April to the Irish EC President they pressed three ambitious proposals for consideration at the Dublin European Council on 28 April: first, to intensify preparatory work for the IGC on EMU; secondly, to establish a second, parallel IGC on political union to give more unity, coherence, and legitimacy to EC policies and to put in place a common foreign and security policy; and, thirdly, to set 1 January 1993 as the date for ratification of the new, more comprehensive Treaty. Kohl was rewarded at the

Dublin Council by a positive gesture of welcome for German unification and for the idea of a second IGC. Following subsequent preparatory work by foreign ministry officials, at the Dublin Council on 25–6 June 1990 the principle of an IGC on European political union was accepted; the dates for the beginning of the two IGCs agreed for 13–14 December; and the end of 1992 set as the date for the final ratification of the treaty amendments. These dates then became a tool of domestic political leadership for Kohl in relation to EMU. Kohl exploited his duty to ensure that Germany adhered to its commitments as a resource of leadership.

With the Dublin Council in April, the cool, intimidating atmosphere of the Elysée meeting and of the Strasbourg Council had vanished. Strategically, Kohl sensed that he could exploit a unique combination of circumstances to redefine himself as a European statesman of the first rank: the historic opportunity of German unification; his good personal chemistry with Mitterrand, Delors, Gonzales, and others; and the confidence that comes with longevity in office. Seen from this vantage point, his strategic vision of European political unification was by April already proving its value as a political tool. But there was more to Kohl. He genuinely believed in the vision; it was infused with personal meaning and with intense emotional engagement. For that reason Kohl was a genuine *animateur* on EMU. When Kohl spoke of ensuring that German unification did not give birth to a new European problem but rather created an opportunity for Europe to unify, he spoke from conviction and not just strategically.

Finance Ministry Strategy for the IGC

The Finance Ministry's preparations in 1990 for the IGC were dominated by three threats. First, a member state which did not share German economic policy beliefs—Italy—would hold the EC Presidency when the IGC was convened. Italian negotiators could be expected to seek to gain agreement on political guidelines for the IGC on terms unacceptable to the Finance Ministry and the Bundesbank. Secondly, consistent with EC treaty-making tradition, the EC foreign ministers would seek out a leading role in relation to the IGC on EMU. The EC Commission and Italy were likely to favour such a form of IGC organization. Thirdly, the EC Commission's attempts to retrieve the intellectual and political initiative must be contested. These attempts took the form of a Commission working paper of 20 March, a Commission note of 16 May, and a Commission communication to Council of 21 August 1990.

In this context Finance Ministry strategy was twofold: as an insurance to tackle as many sensitive issues as possible in the EC Monetary Committee (and by delegation to the Committee of EC Central Bank Governors); and for Waigel to take a tough political line on organization of the IGCs. To these concerns was added a sense of the accelerating political dynamic behind EMU negotiations, following Strasbourg and the two Dublin European Councils. Köhler recognized that this dynamic created a strategic requirement for the Finance Ministry to retrieve the intellectual and political initiative.

Köhler as State Secretary: The Complex Relationship to Tietmeyer

As new State Secretary in the Finance Ministry from 1 January 1990, Köhler was aware of the strategic parameters in which he had to operate. Because he served simultaneously as international economic 'sherpa' to the Chancellor, he had— uniquely amongst Bonn state secretaries—privileged access to the ear of Kohl. This access gave him—like Tietmeyer earlier—a resource of influence and policy leadership in EMU negotiations. Köhler could directly and authoritatively interpret the aims and concerns of the Chancellor to others. On the debit side, as a new boy in the 'European' State Secretaries' meeting, he was vulnerable to the well-honed skills of a State Secretary like Lautenschlager in the Foreign Ministry. A strategic objective of Köhler was to situate EMU discussions in institutional fora away from Lautenschlager.

The German approach to the EMU negotiations was marked by Köhler's complex and difficult relationship to Tietmeyer. Having served under Tietmeyer in both the Economics Ministry and the Finance Ministry Köhler had enormous respect for his intellectual grasp of EMU issues and his strategic skills as a negotiator. Tietmeyer was in important respects a role model. With Tietmeyer as Bundesbank director responsible for international affairs he had the advantage of being able to continue to draw on his vast store of expertise. Clearing detailed EMU issues with Tietmeyer became an absolute priority for Köhler and governed his approach to the IGC. On issues such as how Germany should respond to the British 'hard' ECU plan Köhler was prepared to defer to Tietmeyer.

On the other hand, Köhler wanted to liberate himself from the overpowering spell of Tietmeyer and was more disposed to reflect on, and be to a degree more flexible, about German negotiating positions. His problem was one of living within the shadow of such a powerful predecessor. This problem—which influenced Köhler's prestige within Bonn—was exacerbated when Tietmeyer was seconded back to Bonn in April 1990 to advise Kohl on German monetary union. The solution lay in justifying doing some things differently from Tietmeyer by reference to the changed geopolitical context of EMU with German unification. In particular, Köhler was prepared to go further in accepting Kohl's priority of 'binding' Germany into Europe; in seeing some truth in the 'institutionalist' approach to EMU—that rules and timetables could help force the pace of structural change in Europe; and in recognizing that French proposals for a strong 'economic policy pole' in EMU made some sense as a means of ensuring a close co-ordination of macroeconomic policy at the European level.[2]

---

[2] Later he even accepted the importance of an intensive dialogue between the Euro-11 Council and the ECB. See Köhler, 'Aufgaben auf dem Weg in die Europäische Währungsunion', speech to the Friedrich-Ebert-Stiftung, Bonn, 11 February 1998.

There were two main differences between them. They differed in style. Köhler stressed the objective of coming to an EMU agreement. His approach was to demonstrate the strength of his convictions and then work to seek out agreement. Tietmeyer was, by contrast, preoccupied with winning on every point. Hence he was much less happy with the secret Franco-German bilaterals in 1991 than Köhler. They differed also in their attitude to risk. Tietmeyer saw the central problem as to reduce risk to economic instability consequent on EMU. He believed that EMU was the most dangerous case to pick to force the pace on European unification. Köhler had more sympathy for Kohl's position that some risk might have to be taken if European unification were ever to be realized.

In another sense Köhler did things differently from Tietmeyer simply because his personal qualities were different. A warm, friendly south German, he was able to strike up a more intimate relationship of close trust with both Kohl and Waigel, who saw him as a man of their type. They responded well to his openness and frankness. Personal chemistry helped to deepen the personal confidence that followed from Köhler's willingness to identify himself more readily than Tietmeyer with the political argument that German unification gave greater urgency and higher priority to EMU. This deepening mutual understanding between Kohl and Köhler was summed up by some Bonn insiders as Köhler becoming the 'adoptive son' of the Chancellor. Like a son, he could get away with speaking his mind. The relationship was by no means one of simple subordination; nor was Köhler driven just by personal career ambition. He wanted to be seen as an influential and effective State Secretary and to be close to the Chancellor for that purpose. He was also prepared to be blunt with Kohl, who appreciated this aspect of Köhler's personality. This close linkage to the thinking of the Chancellor was to prove a source of Köhler's growing strength and confidence by the end of 1990. It rested in turn on the great trust that Waigel had in Köhler as a technician, strategist, and man. He was comfortable with Köhler's direct access to the Chancellor. In consequence, before the IGC Köhler emerged as a forceful and feared State Secretary in the 'European' State Secretaries' meetings.

Despite these skills in playing the Bonn machine under Kohl, Köhler lacked the intellectual self-confidence and articulateness of Tietmeyer. In seeking out the intellectual initiative in the EMU negotiations Köhler relied heavily on Gert Haller, the new head of the money and credit division, to evolve a new, post-coronation-theory theoretical framework for EMU. He also lacked Tietmeyer's cool, determined self-control. Köhler was capable of strongly emotional engagement and tough, attacking behaviour in EMU negotiations: both in Bonn and in Brussels. The EMU negotiations proved a very stressful experience for him, caught as he was between a relaxed minister who relied heavily on him to sort out the technical details, the power and determination of his Chancellor, and the brilliant ego of his predecessor as State Secretary.

In negotiations within the EC Monetary Committee about stage 1 and about preparations for the IGC, Köhler had two advantages: the highly experienced

Tietmeyer, now representing the Bundesbank, sat alongside him; whilst Cees Maas, the chair of the committee from December 1989, and Andreas Kees, its secretary, shared the stability policy beliefs of German negotiators. But he (indeed they) faced a strategic and cognitive challenge. This challenge took the form of evidence that EC member states were not prepared to renounce sovereignty over economic policy in order to make possible a single EC economic policy to complement a single monetary policy. Hence, in relation to stage 1, Köhler focused on maximizing the effectiveness of instruments of EC economic policy co-ordination; and, in relation to the IGC and stages 2 and 3, on solving the problem of excessive deficits.

Preparing Stage 1

German negotiators were basically disappointed with the ECOFIN decision of 12 March 1990 on the stage-by-stage convergence of policies and economic performance in stage 1. In endorsing the principles of price stability and open, competitive markets this decision was judged as an improvement on the more Keynesian Council decision of 1974 which it replaced. Improved co-ordination was to take the form of 'multilateral surveillance' based on 'indicators' and leading to recommendations. In the process the EC Monetary Committee had carved out a new role for itself in preparing ECOFIN deliberations. But these gains were small. For Köhler and Tietmeyer the decision of March 1990 did not go far enough. The provisions on budget discipline remained fundamentally weak. They lacked sufficient legal authority and begged the question of whether member states would actually respect them and prove willing to exercise a genuine responsibilty for ensuring an EC-wide stability policy. To make matters worse, stability policy in stage 1 had not been reinforced by a clear commitment to end monetary financing of budget deficits.

The EC Monetary Committee and EMU after the Completion of Stage 1

The preparatory work for the IGC rapidly gathered momentum after the Guigou Group started work (with the strategic aim of regaining the initiative for EC finance ministers) and was further accelerated by the Strasbourg and Dublin Councils. Its first product was the EC Monetary Committee Report of 10 November 1989 on EMU after the completion of stage 1. Here German negotiators were more successful. They got ordo-liberal principles (notably open markets and price stability) written into the statement of ordering principles for EMU; prioritization to the problem of excessive deficits in the statement of main questions about EMU to be addressed; and support for majority decision-making on matters of budgetary policy.

The Ashford Castle ECOFIN The speed of progress was further manifested when, on 23 March 1990, the EC Monetary Committee produced its report on

EMU beyond stage 1. This report was addressed to the informal ECOFIN at Ashford Castle on 31 March–1 April, the first at which EC finance ministers dealt in depth with EMU issues. Here Waigel was keen to give a positive signal, sharing as he did Kohl's perception that German unification had changed the parameters of the EMU negotiations. He also welcomed Kohl's initiative to push for European political union at Dublin and wished to give a gesture of solidarity. Waigel was helped in doing so because Köhler and Tietmeyer had demonstrably succeeded in making progress in realizing German negotiating objectives. At Ashford Castle the EC Monetary Committee Report was in its basic essentials adopted.

The EC Monetary Committee Report was more concerned with institutional issues relating to EMU: in particular, the design of the ESCB; its democratic legitimation; external currency policy; and ensuring budgetary discipline. In providing for a single monetary policy operated by an ESCB that was independent and pledged to price stability, the report incorporated key German negotiating positions. Additionally, decision-making within the council of the ESCB was to be based on the principles of 'one person, one vote' and normally by simple majority. Here Tietmeyer was representing Bundesbank positions that were being developed for the work on the draft ECB statute to be prepared by the Committee of EC Central Bank Governors. With respect to democratic legitimation, the report took on board German formulations, stressing the duty of the ESCB to implement democratically ratified treaty provisions that expressed its goals and procedures of operation and to explain its policies in public.

Perhaps most gratifying for German negotiators was the sense of progress on the question of excessive deficits. Three principles were established in the March report: no 'monetary financing' of budget deficits; no Community responsibility for the debts of individual member states; and a treaty responsibility to avoid or correct excessive deficits. The report indicated that criteria such as inflation-rate and budget-deficit and public-debt levels were under discussion, including (from German negotiators) pressure for the principle that budget-deficit level should not exceed public-investment level. But there was still a reluctance, shared by some in the Finance Ministry, to embrace the notion of upper limits to deficits and debt in relation to percentage of GNP. Despite Bundesbank pressures for binding rules, the general preference remained to judge deficits excessive in relation to the specific circumstances of each case. Also promising for German negotiators was the acceptance of sanctions for excessive deficits by a majority of states and, by an even larger number, of majority decision-making in Council on the question of whether an excessive deficit existed. But they had more difficulties over external currency policy. Here Tietmeyer was pushing for a right of consultation for the ESCB when the Council was making decisions about an exchange-rate regime. Köhler was less supportive on this issue, recognizing that Finance Ministry powers were at stake. On the division of competences between ESCB and Council on external currency policy it was clear that there were considerable differences of view to be bridged.

Before and at Ashford Castle German negotiators were also able effectively to contest aspects of the EC Commission's informal Working Paper of 20 March on EMU. Their criticisms focused in particular on three aspects: the provision for European Parliamentary 'hearings' for the 'Eurofed' which raised doubts about compatibility with the principle of central bank independence; the reference to an enhanced role for the EC budget in dealing with unexpected economic shocks; and its implications that before the final stage of EMU the ECU could develop into a parallel currency. The strategic objective of Köhler and Tietmeyer was to ensure that the informal ECOFIN deliberated on the basis of the EC Monetary Committee Report—which they had helped shape—and not of the EC Commission Working Paper—which had been written without their participation. In this objective of controlling the flow of ideas they were successful.

From Ashford Castle to the Italian Presidency   The Franco-German Economic Council meeting in Paris on 7 April 1990 was able to capitalize on the success of the informal ECOFIN at Ashford Castle as well as the personal chemistry and understanding generated by the Tegernsee meeting of August 1989. In Paris Waigel demonstrated his commitment to EMU and his unity with Bérégovoy. He was at pains to stress that there was no contradiction between German unification and EMU; instead, German unification would accelerate EMU. There was an urgent need to accelerate preparatory work for the IGC. In making these remarks Waigel was clearly situating himself firmly in the new political leadership behind EMU from Kohl since December 1989. They were wholly consistent with his own fundamental political beliefs about Germany and Europe which were indebted to Strauss.

On 16 May 1990 the EC Commission further shocked the German Finance Ministry and the Bundesbank with its paper on the institutional questions relating to the final phase of EMU. They opposed three key elements of the Commission paper: its recommendation for weighted voting in the council of the 'Eurofed', as encouraging a damaging spirit of compromise amongst national interests; its proposal that the European Council should formulate economic policy 'guidelines', as resurrecting neo-Keynesian ideas of economic 'steering'; and its preference for very general budgetary principles in the new treaty, as a step backwards from the emerging consensus in the EC Monetary Committee about how to tackle excessive deficits. Köhler and Tietmeyer were determined to keep Delors at a distance and neutralize Commission 'salami-slicing' interventions during the preparations for the IGC. A key means to achieve that objective was to mobilize the sense of solidarity and ownership of EMU within the EC Monetary Committee against the Commission. In that task Maas and Kees were reliable allies.

At the ECOFIN on 12 June, anticipating issues under consideration in the EC Monetary Committee, Waigel led the demand that EC finance ministers should be given overall responsibility for the IGC on EMU. Reacting to the EC Commission paper of 16 May, he also spoke strongly against automatic dates for stages 2 and 3. Though these transitions were political decisions, they had to be based on strict fulfilment of certain conditions of convergence. His attitude to stage 2 also revealed the ambivalence about it within his Finance Ministry. Waigel referred to stage 2 having a political rationale, but only a weak economic rationale given that the ESCB would lack any operational responsibility for monetary policy in this stage.

The 23 July 1990 ECOFIN and the British 'Hard' ECU Plan   The final comprehensive EC Monetary Committee Report on EMU beyond stage 1, and dealing with the preparation for the IGC, followed on 23 July 1990. This report went yet further in meeting German negotiating objectives. First, it spoke of using quantitative criteria for budgetary discipline and explicitly ruled out reliance on market mechanisms of discipline alone. Köhler had moved closer to Tietmeyer on the issue of spelling out criteria which were as clear-cut as possible. But the EC Monetary Committee recognized that it must do more analytical work before any general limits on deficits and debt levels could be defined. Secondly, the report accepted the argument for using objective convergence criteria—with a carefully delimited exercise of discretion—in the transition from stage 1 to stage 2. These criteria for entry into stage 2 were spelt out: price stability, respect for budget discipline, membership of the 'narrow band' of the ERM, a positive judgement of the sustainability of convergence by the markets, and the completion of the single European market and its implementation by national laws. On this issue Köhler and Tietmeyer were successful, arguing that, if these conditions were fulfilled before the transition to stage 2, then stage 2 could be relatively short. If they were not met, then the final stage would only be delayed. Finally, and of crucial interest to the German Finance Ministry, the EC Monetary Committee Report stressed that on the substantive economic and monetary issues in the IGC the finance ministers must have the decisive voice.

At the 23 July 1990 ECOFIN, the EC Monetary Committee Report was welcomed. The main issue was the length of stage 2. Bérégovoy proposed that stage 2 should begin on 1 January 1993; Waigel responded by arguing that the sooner stage 2 started, the longer it would last. It was by then clear that the date for stage 2 was to be a particularly contentious issue. Waigel was all too aware of the danger that a high-level Franco-Italian-Commission alliance could take this issue out of his hands.

It was also the first ECOFIN at which John Major made a full presentation of the 'hard' ECU as an alternative route for transition after stage 1. Waigel gave it a polite welcome as a 'useful addition' to the discussions, and it was referred to the EC Monetary Committee for examination on 4 September. But it had only weak support in the German Finance Ministry and no support in the Bundesbank. Köhler was attracted as an economist to the idea of a market-oriented approach to EMU, and politically attracted to the idea of working more closely with the British—with whom he felt closer on economic principles than with the French. But he also identified the key political problem of the 'hard'

ECU plan. His concern was to spell out to Wicks, his British counterpart, that the plan had no hope of eliciting interest unless it spelt out clearly how stage 3 was to be realized.

Tietmeyer was the chief architect of German opposition to the 'hard' ECU plan, focusing on the increased difficulties for monetary policy with this added complication and the consequent dangers to stability. Though he was intellectually more attracted, Köhler sought to minimize conflict with the Bundesbank by taking on Tietmeyer's arguments. As early as the G7 at Houston on 9–11 July German Finance Ministry officials had communicated their severe reservations about the 'hard' ECU plan to their British counterparts. Tietmeyer was able to dispose of it with relative ease at the EC Monetary Committee level. The shared strategic objective of the Finance Ministry and the Bundesbank was that the D-Mark should retain its anchor role in stage 2: in part because the ERM was safer with a known, stable currency as its anchor; and in part because the continuation of the D-Mark's role as anchor was a precondition for maximizing German influence in relation to the transition to stage 3. Tietmeyer and Schlesinger were all too aware of the potential cost to German strategy for the design of stage 3 if the 'hard' ECU worked.

What was also notable about the 23 July ECOFIN was the intervention by Otto Schlecht, State Secretary in the Economics Ministry. Schlecht's strategic objective was to gain a more central place for his ministry in the EMU negotiations. Hence he pressed for incorporation of the EC's Economic Policy Committee in preparing the IGC. This objective related to an intellectual concern that there should be parallel progress on co-ordination of economic policy and realization of monetary union and that market principles of economic adjustment should be written into the final treaty. But the German Finance Ministry had no interest in ceding ground in controlling the IGC negotiations, not even to a ministry so close to its beliefs.

The negotiations within the EC Monetary Committee and ECOFIN in 1990 on preparation of the IGC were, overall, a considerable success for Köhler and Waigel. On such sensitive issues as the ordering principles of EMU, the design of the ESCB, excessive deficits, the transition to stage 2, and the organization of the IGC they had gathered support for German negotiating objectives. But it remained an open question whether this underlying degree of technical agreement on German Finance Ministry and Bundesbank terms could be safeguarded against the strategic manoeuvrings of the Italian EC Presidency and the EC Commission as the European Council geared up to take final decisions about the IGC in late 1990. In this respect the EC Commission Communication of 21 August 1990 on EMU caused some consternation in Bonn and Frankfurt. It spoke of stage 2 beginning on 1 January 1993; of it being of short duration with all states participating; of an ESCB established in stage 2 to co-ordinate monetary policy; of a 'strengthened' use of the ECU in stage 2; and of making entry into stage 3 dependent on a political decision of the European Council, without reference to precisely defined convergence criteria. These proposals ran in the opposite direction from thinking in the German Finance Ministry and the Bundesbank and from the proposals of the EC Monetary Committee.

Bundesbank Strategy for the IGC

Following the Strasbourg Council's decision to name the period when the IGC would be convened, the Bundesbank was spurred to seize the initiative. Given that its strategy had always been focused on establishing agreement on the design of stage 3, and that its statutory responsibility was monetary policy, it was easy to agree a division of labour with the Finance Ministry. Bundesbank strategy was to gain acceptance of the German model of monetary policy as the basis for the ECB. Hence its attention fell on using the Committee of EC Central Bank Governors as the venue within which to control the negotiation of the draft ECB statute for the IGC.

An additional factor in the new sense of urgency was the arrival of Tietmeyer as a member of the Bundesbank directorate on 1 January 1990, with responsibility for the international side of its work. Always sensitive about his authority, Pöhl was concerned to ensure that Tietmeyer did not eclipse him. This concern was motivated, in part, by Tietmeyer's intellectual energy and his grasp of EMU and, in part, by a widespread sense that Tietmeyer was being groomed by Kohl to succeed Pöhl. This sense of Tietmeyer as a Bundesbank President in waiting created distrust from older Bundesbank officials, including Schlesinger, who worried about his degree of independence from a Chancellor on whom his future career prospects depended. Within the Bundesbank attitudes of admiration, fear, and distrust formed around the figure of Tietmeyer. But he was not the sort of person to be deterred from engaging himself fully on EMU.

Pöhl's new activism on EMU was made evident in two ways in January 1990. First, at its January meeting the Committee of EC Central Bank Governors decided on the reorganization of its working arrangements, including a three-year chair (instead of for one year) and strengthening of its research capacity in preparation for stage 1. Pöhl took this opportunity to propose a restructuring of the seating arrangements. Its outcome was that, instead of sitting next to Pöhl, Tietmeyer was moved some yards behind him. The gesture was judged to be symbolic of Pöhl's intent to be independent of Tietmeyer's attempts to control him in negotiations. In practice, Tietmeyer was constantly crawling forward in meetings to brief Pöhl, always concerned that he would make too many concessions.

Secondly, on 16 January, just one day before Kohl's speech in the same city, Pöhl delivered his own keynote speech in Paris: in his case at the invitation of *Le Monde* and on the 'basic features of a European monetary order'. Carefully prepared by the international division, Pöhl's speech was issued simultaneously in English, French, and German and distributed to ensure maximum publicity. In the wake of Strasbourg its objective was to reinforce Bundesbank views on the conditions for an effective negotiation of EMU. These views had been well rehearsed within the Bundesbank directorate in relation to Pöhl's participation in the Delors Committee. They focused on getting agreement on the design of stage 3; and on acceptance (seen then as unlikely) by other member states of the principle of an independent ECB in stage 3 as a test of whether EMU was likely to happen. Pöhl went into detail on the institutional design of an ECB, stressing the principle of its independence from member state governments, and the need for it to be endowed with the authority to pursue a single monetary policy. In particular, Pöhl sought to send clear signals to the French political, economic, and financial establishment about the preconditions for successful negotiation of EMU. His chief concern was that the French might return to their traditional preoccupation with exchange-rate management and intervention. Though the speech had little resonance in Germany, it achieved the front page of *Le Monde*.

Pöhl, the Bundesbank, and the Draft ECB Statute

The speech of 16 January was a prelude to Pöhl seizing the initiative on the issue of the ECB in the institutional arena in which the Bundesbank felt most in control. In the Committee of EC Central Bank Governors it felt that it could make a positive contribution on its own terms. On 10 April 1990 the Committee of EC Central Bank Governors asked Pöhl as its chair to start work on drafting an ECB statute in time for the IGC negotiations. This invitation gave Pöhl a tactical advantage in shaping the course of the negotiations. At this time, having just attended the informal ECOFIN at Ashford Castle, Pöhl was very impressed by the convergence of bargaining positions on EMU and especially acceptance of the German principle of an independent ECB. The work on the draft statute was delegated to the alternates, so that Tietmeyer—assisted by Rieke—took on the main responsibility on behalf of the Bundesbank. It was also clarified to Tietmeyer that Pöhl and de Larosière had agreed that the Bundesbank and the Banque de France should work closely in hammering out agreement. Pöhl had been reassured that the Banque de France would be negotiating in absolute independence of the French Trésor and that de Larosière accepted an independent ECB as the basis of these negotiations. In short, de Larosière had responded positively to Pöhl's signal of 16 January.

The negotiations that followed had three characteristics: a strong co-ordination between Tietmeyer and Lagayette in the Banque de France; a repeat of the co-ordination between Rieke and the Dutch and Danish central bank officials that had shadowed the Delors Committee; and acceptance of Bundesbank drafting as the basis for the negotiations. As with the Delors Committee, the Bundesbank tabled a draft ECB statute at the beginning. This paper was accepted as *the* draft for the negotiation. Its basic principle—that a single currency requires a single monetary policy—was readily accepted. The Bundesbank's approach was to get a detailed and precisely worded agreement on the draft ECB statute, seeing that any ambiguity could later be exploited by the French, Italians, and others. Hence it was not content with merely translating the provisions of the Bundesbank Law of 1957 to the EC level. Instead of a vague reference to 'safeguarding the currency' the Bundesbank insisted on the formulation—'the primary objective of the ESCB shall be to maintain price stability'. Also notable was the provision that 'the ESCB shall act in accordance with the principle of an open market economy with free competition, favouring an efficient allocation of resources'.

In practice, Tietmeyer had difficulties with the group dynamics of the alternates' committee; its ethos of mutual restraint and concession fitted ill with his abrasive and hectoring style. On two issues there were problems. Crockett for the Bank of England and Lagayette for the Banque de France made common cause on the principle of subsidiarity. Their argument—which was designed to salvage some power over monetary policy for national central banks in stage 3—was strenuously opposed by Tietmeyer. This argument was seen as undermining the key and agreed principle that a single currency required a single monetary policy with an ECB endowed with sufficient authority for this purpose. The second issue was the role of the ECB in exchange-rate policy. Here again the Bundesbank saw danger in ambiguity: that the European Council would use political authority over exchange-rate regime to counter the stability policy of the ECB.

Despite these two divisive issues the alternates' committee accepted intellectual leadership from the Bundesbank. In fact, only the exchange-rate-policy issue remained significant—and was not to be finally resolved till December 1991. But even here progress was made in realizing Bundesbank aims. Though empowered to take the decision on the exchange-rate regime, the Council was to engage in prior consultation with the ECB, with the objective of producing a consensus compatible with the goal of price stability. The open question remained the procedure for giving 'orientation' on exchange-rate management. The Bundesbank succeeded in striking out reference to 'guidelines' as too strong and in getting the majority of EC central banks to accept the idea of the same procedure as for decisions about the exchange-rate regime. Hence positive interim reports were delivered to the monthly meetings of the Committee of EC Central Bank Governors. At the informal ECOFIN in Rome on 7–8 September Pöhl outlined progress, drawing attention to the issue of the role of the ECB in exchange-rate policy. After the 11 September meeting of the Committee of Central Bank Governors his satisfaction with progress was evident in his reference to the strong similarities between the ECB and the Bundesbank. The final draft ECB statute was agreed by the Committee of EC Central Bank Governors on 13 November 1990; and on 29 April 1991 Pöhl handed it to the Luxembourg Finance Minister in his capacity as chair of the IGC on EMU, warning against tampering with the internal logic of the statute by attempting to make alterations to it.

The Bundesbank Directorate and EMU beyond Stage 1

But the draft ECB statute was only one of a raft of difficult EMU issues with which Pöhl and the Bundesbank directorate were confronted in 1990. The directorate was forced to reflect on and debate these issues as a consequence of the accelerating pace of work in the EC Monetary Committee (where Tietmeyer was involved) and of the way in which German unification had been managed and its implications for EMU and the ERM. In facing up to these issues the problem of Pöhl's relations with the Bundesbank council and its role in EMU negotiations emerged.

One issue was easier to resolve: the way in which the Bundesbank should define its role in the forthcoming IGC. That role was defined as twofold. First, and pre-eminently, the Bundesbank's role was advisory. It was there to offer expertise (*Sachverstand*), to ensure that EMU negotiations took full and proper account of the complex interdependencies and cause–effect relations that governed the operation of monetary policy. But its brief was delimited by its legal mandate under the Bundesbank Law of 1957 and by the responsibility of the federal government for negotiating international agreements. Bundesbank officials, including Tietmeyer, were at pains to stress that they were not responsible for EMU negotiations. This position had a certain political value; by assigning responsibility to others, the Bundesbank was by implication exposing Köhler and Waigel and enhancing the value of carrying its support. Secondly, consistent with its legal remit, the Bundesbank saw its role as to act as *Advokat*, as lawyer on behalf of the national interest in price stability. The Bundesbank's preoccupation was to defend its postwar achievement in securing a stability culture in Germany. In consequence, its expert advisory role in the negotiations was conducted in a strongly didactic manner. Tietmeyer came to epitomize this manner.

The EC Monetary Committee threw up a far more difficult issue as it debated criteria for measuring excessive deficits and the question emerged of stage 2 and whether these criteria should be used to establish the condition for moving ahead with stage 2. Within the Bundesbank directorate there were major reservations about stage 2. It had no real economic rationale. The Bundesbank's principle of the indivisibility of monetary policy meant that, till the final stage, responsibility for monetary policy must remain solely at the national level. Hence there was no proper scope for institution-building in stage 2. Any attempt to put in place an ECB in stage 2 would undermine its reputation from the start. Consistent with this Bundesbank view, Pöhl distanced himself from the three-stage approach of the Delors Report in the context of his discussions with the Committee for Economic, Currency, and Industrial Policy of the European Parliament on 15 May 1990. An ESCB could not be constructed in stages. In the same spirit, at the ECOFIN on 12 June 1990, Pöhl countered the claim by Mario Sarcinelli that stage 2 could be helpful in providing central bankers with an opportunity to acquire experience of how to operate an EC monetary policy.

Others in the Bundesbank, notably in the international division led by Rieke, feared that stage 2 would prove long in duration and a hostage to fortune. It would provide opportunities for member states to keep using the European Council to reopen the issue of giving real substance to this stage. The result would be political uncertainty and risk that the EC could be diverted from the route to a stage 3 defined on Bundesbank terms. Stage 2 was not only unnecessary; it contained germs that could infect the independence of the ECB.

On 12 June, just following the ECOFIN, Pöhl again raised an issue that had been considered within the Bundesbank—participation in EMU. On this issue the Delors Report and the Pöhl paper annexed to that report had spoken cautiously of a degree of flexibility, whilst stressing the prime importance of full participation by all members in EMU. But discussions in the EC Monetary Committee on criteria for judging deficits excessive and on conditions for entry into stage 2 made it clear that transition to EMU would not be possible without a differentiated approach to integration. Pöhl made public an internal discussion about a 'two-speed' EMU, pointing to France, Germany, and the Benelux states as those likely to move ahead of the rest. The consequence was a chorus of criticism, led by Italy and Spain.

EMU and German Unification

Far overshadowing the impact of work in the EC Monetary Committee was the effect of the Bundesbank's increasingly painful involvement in German unification during the first half of 1990. Pöhl viewed the choice of 1 July for monetary union between the two German states as an act of folly. The fact that Kohl's decision for monetary union on 6 February was taken without consulting the Bundesbank added insult to injury. The subsequent decision of 23 April to convert East Marks into D-Marks on a one-to-one basis for smaller savings deposits overruled Bundesbank advice. As a final shock, the federal government announced on 15 May that it was to create the German Unity Fund to shift borrowing for East Germany outside normal budgetary procedures—again without having consulted the Bundesbank. The result was deeply embittered relations between Pöhl and Kohl and passionate denunciations of the cavalier behaviour of the federal government from members of the Bundesbank council, led by Helmut Hesse and Wilhelm Nölling. At the Bundesbank council meeting of 30 May, in the presence of Waigel and Köhler, Pöhl took the unusual step of reprimanding council members for projecting the wrong image of the Bundesbank.

The effects of the way in which German monetary union was handled in 1990 went beyond personal chemistry and the specifics of competitiveness and unemployment in East Germany and of price stability in Germany as a whole. They fed into attitudes towards the negotiation of EMU. Schlesinger was doubtful that two such huge projects as German unification and EMU could realistically be undertaken at once. Tietmeyer could see the linkage between German unification and European political union. But, still at heart the coronation theorist, he argued in private that to use German unification to accelerate EMU was potentially irresponsible; taking risks with price stability was not in the best interests of integrating Germany into Europe. It involved a misordering of priorities.

Most of all, German monetary union drove home two lessons to Bundesbank officials. First, the way in which the federal government had handled German monetary union demonstrated the ease with which political considerations could override technical considerations, with pernicious effects on inflation and interest rates. Secondly, German monetary union underlined the scale of the difficulties associated with EMU and the urgent priority that had to be given to ensuring that EMU was technically viable. The even greater uncertainties associated with EMU than with German monetary union followed from the fact that EMU involved a new and untried ECB managing a new and unknown currency in a much larger area—and without the huge financial transfers supporting German monetary union. The lesson drawn by Bundesbank officials was that these uncertainties could only be mitigated by a much more rigorous policing of budget deficits and debt than had accompanied German monetary union and by a highly selective approach to membership of stage 3.

More immediately, the Bundesbank was anxious to seek realignment within the ERM to accommodate the effects of German unification. Schlesinger was the first to raise the issue of a D-Mark revaluation, as early as December 1989. For him the issue was not just the logical response to a prospective German unification. It was also important that the Bundesbank should challenge the dangerous notion that the ERM had evolved *de facto* into a monetary union in which exchange-rate adjustment was no longer an issue. Later Tietmeyer began to argue in internal discussions that it would be economically and politically too costly to allow interest rates to bear the burden of adjustment. Following the announcement of the 1:1 conversion rate in April, Pöhl raised the issue of a D-Mark revaluation informally over dinner with fellow EC central bankers on the eve of the next Committee of EC Central Bank Governors' meeting. But it was firmly rejected by de Larosière and never appeared on the agenda of a later meeting or meeting of alternates.

'Binding in' the Bundesbank Council: The Bundesbank Statement of 6 September 1990

The statement of 6 September on EMU, approved unanimously by the Bundesbank council, served two strategic functions for the Bundesbank directorate. First, it bound in and helped reconcile a Bundesbank council that was deeply fractious and mistrustful in the wake of the way in which German monetary union had been handled. Distrust spilled over into attitudes within the council towards the impending IGC negotiations. Members of the Bundesbank council were complaining about being excluded at a time when the directorate was increasingly absorbed by EMU and were concerned to strengthen the directorate's resolve so that similar mistakes to those made with German monetary union would not be repeated. Secondly, the Bundesbank directorate saw an opportunity to turn these internal criticisms to its advantage in the IGC negotiations. A statement on indispensable requirements for an EMU agreement, approved by the Bundesbank council, would be a way of 'binding' their hands. Hence much was made of the fact that the statement was unanimously agreed.

Tietmeyer was particularly sensitive to these strategic arguments, recognizing his exposed position on IGC issues. The value of the exercise was increased by the fact that his responsibility for drafting the statement gave Tietmeyer an opportunity to employ his carefully cultivated arts of manoeuvring between different positions. He could embed within the statement some of his own continuing intellectual reservations about EMU; use the exercise to foster a supportive coalition within the Bundesbank council; and in his relations with Bonn hide behind the council as its servant.

The element of intellectual continuity with the coronation theory of the Werner period and the Stoltenberg Memorandum of 1988 was apparent in the reference to an irrevocable 'community of solidarity' (*nicht mehr kündbare Solidargemeinschaft*)—involving a comprehensive political union—as the prerequisite for a durable EMU. It surfaced also in the sceptical note struck by the reference to continuing pronounced divergences in economic performance, rooted in 'substantial differences in institutional structures, basic economic orientations and the attitudes of management and labour'. Though not listed in the statement, the Bundesbank had identified the problem cases: Greece, Italy, Portugal, Spain, and Britain. Finally, the coronation theory element was evident in the stress on a 'lengthy transitional process', during which time there must be no institutional changes that might impair the freedom of action of national monetary authorities; and on the transition from one stage to another depending on the fulfilment of previously defined economic and economic policy conditions, and not on a timetable.

The heightened sense of caution about EMU was manifested in two aspects of the statement. First, there was the listing of a formidable set of 'indispensable requirements' of an EMU agreement: including economic union as the basis of monetary union; binding rules and sanctions to ensure adequate budgetary discipline; independence for national central banks 'at an early date'; and, most strikingly, inflation 'very largely stamped out in all the countries' and price differences 'virtually eliminated'. With these 'indispensable requirements' the Bundesbank council was adopting a strategic position that suited many presidents of state central banks: of putting the negotiating hurdles so high that EC politicians would refuse to jump them. Many Bundesbank officials, particularly in the international division, were less happy about the kinds of signals being given. For them the statement of September represented too rigid and unrealistic a set of bargaining positions for the IGC. For Rieke in the IGC and for

Schlüter in the EMU working group in Bonn it functioned primarily as a reminder of constraints.

Secondly, the statement drew attention to the implications of the particular transitional problems facing Germany as a consequence of unification. 'There is much to be said for preserving such room for manoeuvre and adjustment as still exists in the field of domestic and external monetary policy and budgetary policy until the economic situation in Germany as a whole and in the EC can be regarded as sufficiently settled'. Only then would it be possible to assess more precisely the risks entailed in EMU. This sentence epitomized the different conclusions about EMU being drawn from German unification in Bonn and in Frankfurt.

Bundesbank–Finance Ministry Relations and Tietmeyer

During 1990 a shared spirit of caution about EMU continued to prevail in both the Finance Ministry and the Bundesbank. Its clearest manifestation was in the shared belief that 'dates do not create convergence': that creating a viable and durable EMU was not a matter of deadlines but of meeting objective criteria. It was this aspect of the Bundesbank statement of 6 September that Waigel most welcomed.

But some discernible differences of emphasis emerged. Within the Finance Ministry officials were more at home with Kohl's metaphor of German and European unification as two sides of the same coin and what this implied for the priority to EMU; more prepared to accept a political rationale for stage 2; more reticent about advocating a 'two-speed' approach to EMU, with its overtones of a German-led 'inner core'; and even more cautious in making soundings about a possible German revaluation for fear of creating negative political waves as the EMU negotiations got under way. These differences reflected the greater degree of exposure of Finance Ministry officials like Köhler to Kohl's political leadership. They were less apparent in the case of Bundesbank officials in the international division precisely because they were more tuned into, and responsive to, external political pressures. By contrast, in a speech to the *Verein für Sozialpolitik* on 3 October 1990 Schlesinger referred to the political unification of Europe as no less important a goal than German unification—but at a different level and of less urgency.

In mediating these differences of emphasis Tietmeyer acquired a special position. Though very much the ordo-liberal, his long experience in international economic and financial diplomacy had endowed him with sensitive political antennae. Above all, Tietmeyer had learnt the arts of adapting strongly held positions to political exigencies: notably from the experience of his exclusion from the creation of the EMS in 1978 and from preparations for the Hanover Council and the Delors Committee in 1988. Now a member of the Bundesbank directorate, he found himself caught between the powerful figure of Schlesinger, proud of his intellectual integrity on EMU, and the new strong political leadership from Kohl. To Kohl he was bound by the loyalty engendered by having served as his personal international economic 'sherpa' whilst State Secretary in the Finance Ministry. He knew all too well how much weight Kohl placed on personal trust. In order to become Bundesbank President Tietmeyer had to cultivate that personal trust. He had a highly developed sense of when and how to adapt. In consequence, Tietmeyer was aware of the limits within which he operated. When he miscalculated, and went too far, he knew how to withdraw gracefully.

At the same time—rather like Delors—Tietmeyer appreciated the political power of ideas and the opportunity provided by his position to seek control of the intellectual high ground of EMU negotiations. That opportunity came from the political requirement for the federal government to carry the support of the Bundesbank: a point conceded by Kohl at his press conference on 10 January 1990. Though formally just an expert adviser on the EMU negotiations, the Bundesbank was in a much better position than the federal government to provide the underlying theoretical rationale for a viable and durable EMU. With the September 1990 Bundesbank statement Tietmeyer was continuing a strategy of seizing the intellectual initiative on how a sustainable EMU was to be realized. Strategically, Tietmeyer sold that statement to Bonn with the argument that it was valuable in strengthening German bargaining positions on EMU. Intellectually, his core message was that it was in Germany's and Europe's interests for an EMU agreement to meet the tests of viability and sustainability. A bargaining position that was grounded in a clear intellectual rationale that fulfilled those tests would be more credible to Germany's partners and more likely to prove effective.

Germany and the Italian EC Presidency: Stage 2, the Organization of the IGC, and Political Union

The coincidence of the launch of the IGC on EMU with the Italian Presidency of the EC was recognized within the Finance Ministry and the Bundesbank as a potent source of danger to their capacity to control the substantive content of the EMU negotiations. Finance Ministry officials had two basic strategies for dealing with this danger. First, to pre-empt the Italian Presidency and the EC Commission they sought to push as much preparatory business as possible into the technical institutional venues—the Committee of EC Central Bank Governors, the EC Monetary Committee, and ECOFIN. These could be expected to be relatively amenable to German ordo-liberal beliefs. Pöhl chaired the first of these; Maas the second; and Guido Carli—a more stability-oriented Italian than most—the third. Secondly, the Finance Ministry relied on Waigel to win key battles against Genscher in the domestic arena. Waigel had three strong cards to play: Kohl's need to bind in the CSU (of which he was chair); his political indebtedness to Waigel for helping him out when most vulnerable in April

1989; and Waigel's importance in binding in the Bundesbank. In short, Waigel offered Kohl the most reliable means to neutralize potentially lethal opposition to EMU. On the two key issues that arose during the Italian Presidency—the problem of stage 2 and the organization of the IGC—the Finance Ministry was to notch up one victory and suffer one set-back.

The Battle over the Content and Date of Stage 2: Rome 1

By general agreement in Bonn and Frankfurt, the provisions on stage 2 represented the weakest part of the Delors Report. Its recommendations on stage 2 rang alarm bells: from the reference in section 4.55 to 'the basic organs and structures of the EMU' being set up in this stage; to them gradually taking over 'operational functions'; to stage 2 as a 'training process'; and in section 4.57 to the establishment of the ESCB. The danger was that the development of such proposals could undermine the key Bundesbank principle, accepted in the Delors Report, of the indivisibility of monetary policy in each stage of EMU.

Against this background, and informed by their experience of the French, the Italians, and the Commission, German Finance Ministry and Bundesbank officials expected an assault on German positions to focus on stage 2. That assault emerged in July–August 1990. On 23 July at ECOFIN Bérégovoy proposed that stage 2 should begin on 1 January 1993 (with the completion of the European single market). This proposal was repeated in the EC Commission's Communication of 21 August. Stage 2 became the major contentious issue at the Franco-German Economic Council in Bonn on 31 August. Here Waigel signalled his difficulties to the French, underlining the Bundesbank's opposition to a timetable for stages 2 and 3. His key points were: that entry into stage 2 should not be a matter of a date but of meeting certain agreed criteria designed to ensure sufficient convergence had taken place; that it was appropriate to use stage 2 to prepare the ESCB but not to give it institutional form; that stage 2 could serve as an opportunity to make national central banks independent with a mandate for price stability; and that the top priority was to put in place binding rules and procedures to avoid excessive deficits. The German Finance Ministry wanted stage 2 to be later and to be of short duration. In theory, it would have preferred to dispense with this stage altogether but recognized the three-stage Delors approach as a *fait accompli*. A long stage 2 was seen as dangerous. This would offer a continuing opportunity and incentive to shift monetary-policy responsibility to the European level.

But Waigel found it difficult to hold the line on this negotiating position. At the informal ECOFIN in Rome on 7–8 September the transition to stage 2 emerged as the most difficult and divisive issue. The German Finance Ministry argued against setting a firm date for stage 2 and proposed objective, clearly specified conditions of convergence for entry into that stage. Though it had allies on this issue, the proposal for a fixed date brought together France, Italy,

Spain, Belgium, Luxembourg, and Denmark with the EC Commission. For strategic reasons, the German Finance Ministry could only welcome the political momentum to seek a compromise on this issue at the level of ECOFIN. The alternative was that the issue would be determined within the European Council by heads of state and government and foreign ministers.

Hence the compromise proposal in Rome from the Spanish Finance Minister Carlos Solchaga was difficult to resist: a fixed date of 1 January 1994 with certain conditions attached (including independence to national central banks, abolition of monetary financing of deficits, and participation in the narrow band of the ERM). It did, however, throw up two other troublesome issues. Solchaga was proposing a long stage 2 till 1999–2000: a proposal rejected by the Finance Ministry because it opened up the scope for 'salami-slicing' strategy against a stability-based design of stage 3. He was also suggesting a parallel currency in stage 2. German fire focused on combating these two aspects of the Spanish plan, whilst suggesting that more detailed work needed to be done on stage 2. In the end, there was no agreement on stage 2 in Rome. But the constraints on Waigel were clear: Kohl's capacity to compromise in the European Council and Genscher's access to that institutional forum.

On the issue of a date for stage 2, Genscher returned to the initiative. In a speech in his own constituency of Wuppertal on 14 October—the day of the elections in the five new federal states—he put his weight behind a date of 1 January 1993. EMU was presented as a 'litmus test' of the will to European union. Hence it was important not to set hurdles for stage 2 too high. Genscher's strong position was influenced by the Foreign Ministry view that the Bundesbank statement on EMU of 6 September had been unnecessarily restrictive and rigid about EMU: a view that was even shared within the Finance Ministry and parts of the Bundesbank. He was keen to send a positive signal, particularly to the French and to an increasingly anxious Italian Presidency, that a newly united Germany was more than ever prepared to speed up European unification. The result of Genscher's intervention was a political row with Waigel, who felt himself under great pressure from an axis involving Genscher, Dumas, Bérégovoy, and Delors.

Kohl was once again irritated by what he saw as Genscher's courting of the media with the objective of putting him under public pressure. Having taken personal ownership of EMU he was, if anything, more irritated than before the Hanover, Madrid, and Strasbourg Councils. Ever politically prudent, and seeking out a sustainable political consensus, Kohl was cautious about naming a date for stage 2 for two reasons. First, the key domestic political event that intervened between the informal ECOFIN and the Rome 1 European Council was the five German state elections on 14 October. They were in effect tests for the impending federal elections in December. Kohl's political instinct was to await their results. Secondly, Chancellery officials were persuaded by Finance Ministry and Bundesbank arguments that the problem was to design a 'sound' EMU. Hence the issue was to identify a 'realistic' date for stage 2. From this vantage point the proposal for 1 January 1993 from Bérégovoy, Delors, and Genscher was seen as unrealistic.

Kohl committed himself on the date for stage 2 once he felt secure in his political command of united Germany. He was also induced to do so by the objective of heading off Genscher's attempt at leadership on the issue. Three days after the German state elections, on 17 October, the Chancellor was telling French television that he supported the Spanish proposal for 1 January 1994 as a reasonable compromise date for stage 2, tied to certain conditions about convergence of economic and budgetary policies. This position on the date for stage 2 was conveyed directly to Andreotti at their pre-summit bilateral on 19 October in Venice.

Propelled by the results of the March GDR elections and now by those of the five new federal states Kohl was riding the crest of a political wave before the IGCs began. In a message to his fellow heads of government on the day of German unity, 3 October, he wrote: 'With the same persistence with which we have striven for our own unity, we shall do our utmost for European unification . . . We are striding with determination towards economic and monetary union. Unified Germany will assist energetically in building political union.' This message was developed in Kohl's government declaration before the Bundestag meeting in Berlin on the next day. German unity was presented as the opportunity to accelerate the work of European unification and Franco-German reconciliation as being of 'existential importance' in this context.

This spirit of political determination to build Europe and a heightened sense of his own personal political strength infected Kohl's approach to the Rome European Council on 27–8 October. At the German–Italian meeting on 19 October he signalled to Andreotti the urgent need to give a decisive boost to EMU at the forthcoming Rome meeting before the German federal election campaign got under way. He also indicated his acceptance of 1 January 1994 for stage 2, subject to certain objective conditions. Conversely, he did not reveal his full hand to the British Foreign Minister Hurd when he visited Kohl in Bonn to discuss Rome 1. At the same time Kohl was not prepared to throw caution to the winds. When, at Rome 1, Mitterrand attempted to press him to go one step further and fix a timetable for the transition to stage 3, Kohl demurred.

No less importantly, Kohl's intensified political signalling about European unification from 3 October onwards opened up new opportunities for a policy entrepreneur like Umberto Vattani to extract concessions from Bonn. As diplomatic adviser to Andreotti, Vattani was charged with preparing a mandate on EMU to be agreed at Rome 1. His two main interlocutors in Bonn were Köhler and Bitterlich, each representing different German beliefs about EMU. Vattani treated Bitterlich as his main interlocutor, briefing him rather than Köhler about the substance of the Italian draft communiqué—which in general terms was implicitly endorsed by Kohl at the German–Italian meeting in Venice. Ninety per cent of the text was agreed between the Venice meeting and Rome 1. During this period Bitterlich brought in Thiele and Ludewig in the Chancellery and endeavoured to ensure that Köhler and Tietmeyer had a view of the texts produced by Vattani. He stressed how hard the Italians were working to get the Germans on board, that German negotiators were being given a privileged position by the Italians, and that the chief problems were with the French. Trichet wanted more reference to the role of the ECU in stage 2 and was expressing deep reservations about any formulation on central bank independence in stage 2.

Bitterlich was to be the privileged German interlocutor not just in preparing for Rome 1 but also at Rome 1 in agreeing the final draft communiqué on EMU. At a key moment in Rome the main German Finance Ministry official was diverted by the Italians to another meeting (on GATT) so that Bitterlich would be left to control German bargaining on the final draft communiqué. Astutely, Vattani had focused on breaking the stalemate on stage 2 in ECOFIN by appealing to Bitterlich in the Federal Chancellor's Office. But Bitterlich was by no means acting independently and on his own initiative and had no sense that he was giving away German positions. He was pursuing the Chancellor's objective that political direction must be given to the IGC on EMU and that its work must be developed on the basis of the Delors Report. The reference to 'the new institution' in stage 2 was seen as a very open formulation, not committing Germany to create an ESCB then, and as perfectly compatible with the EMI that was eventually negotiated. Bitterlich's main concern before and at Rome 1 was to ensure that Kohl remained in command of the process of defining the speed of EMU, consistent with the Chancellor's reading of the domestic political situation. The French were pushing for more speed at Rome 1, with Mitterrand pushing for a date for stage 3. Kohl was at that point more cautious and disposed to act as brake.

The German Finance Ministry had two main objectives for Rome 1: to ensure that stage 2 did not begin on 1 January 1993 to coincide with the date for completion of the single market; and to avoid the establishment of an ECB in stage 2. In relation to the first objective there was a measure of success. The final communiqué referred to 1 January 1994 and specified a set of conditions, including 'sufficient' and 'lasting' progress in real and monetary convergence, especially in price stability and in public finances. But German Finance Ministry officials (and the Bundesbank) were shocked by the reference in the communiqué to the creation of 'the new institution' at the beginning of stage 2, thereby 'opening up the possibility of strengthening co-ordination of monetary policy'. To make matters worse, the communiqué spoke of strengthening and further developing the ECU in the transition stage. Bitterlich, who handled negotiation of the communiqué in Rome, was sharply criticized for conceding the definite article before 'new institution'; it created an opportunity to claim that this institution could only be the ECB.

Waigel and his officials believed that they had been tactically outmanoeuvred before and during Rome 1. In consequence, their negotiating position had been weakened at a key moment. The terms of the mandate for the IGC on EMU provided a negotiating advantage to the French, Italians, and the EC Commission. For the Finance Ministry the key problem was the reference to 'the' new institution in stage 2. For Tietmeyer it was also the use of the name ECU in the Rome communiqué: for how credible could a single currency be if it was associated with a 'basket' ECU whose reputation was of devaluation against the D-Mark?

The 'Battle' over the Organization of the IGC

This set-back at Rome 1 was offset by Waigel's success over the issue of who would control the IGC negotiations on EMU. During the Irish Presidency the question had arisen of whether there should be one or two IGCs. The attraction of one IGC to German Foreign Ministry officials was that it would put Foreign Ministers in charge of the negotiations and ensure a strong political drive to EMU. Foreign ministry responsibility was also an entrenched part of EC practice in negotiating treaty revision. But two arguments led the Foreign Ministry not to actively push this proposal. In the first place, the need to divide the work into two subcommittees of the IGC would still leave Finance Ministry officials in the driving seat on EMU. But, more importantly, the Foreign Ministry had a strategic interest in getting the Finance Ministers to assume responsibility for the final EMU agreement rather than to engage in harsh criticisms from the sidelines. Genscher veered towards a solution that would 'bind in' the Finance Ministers rather than give him an exposed leadership position on EMU. His main strategic interest—and the point on which he pressed Kohl most strongly—was to ensure that there was an opportunity for a trade-off between EMU and political union. By linking EMU to political union there were better prospects of securing progress on political union. Hence Genscher did support the case for close co-ordination between the two IGCs.

The issue of organization and co-ordination of the IGCs was resolved under the Italian Presidency. Köhler's activism on this issue was repaid in the EC Monetary Committee's report to ECOFIN on 23 July 1990. Its proposal that Finance Ministers must be given 'the decisive voice' in the IGC on EMU was advocated by Waigel at the ECOFINs on 12 June and 23 July. Other finance ministers were quick to line up behind Waigel's leadership on this issue, sensing that he was crucial to delivering the support of Kohl. Some, like Bérégovoy, hoped that Kohl could neutralize the efforts of their own heads of state and government to privilege the role of foreign ministers. In fact, Waigel found that he did not have to fight the political battle that he expected in Bonn.

In discussion with Kohl Waigel underlined the political risks of ceding control of EMU negotiations to Foreign Ministers. This would seriously undermine Waigel's own authority as Finance Minister and as chair of the CSU in the run-up to a crucial German federal election in which Kohl and Waigel should be fighting together as chairs of sister parties. The issue was also one of credibility. The result of entrusting economic stability to Foreign Ministers would be a weak treaty in two senses. It would lack a rigorous and rational economic basis. Most seriously of all, it would not gain the support of the Bundesbank. Waigel presented Foreign Ministry control of the EMU negotiations to Kohl as the route to political disaster. Kohl fully endorsed these arguments and had little difficulty with Genscher. For Genscher it was imperative to bind in the Finance Ministry and the Bundesbank and the best instrument for this purpose was to make Waigel responsible for the conduct of the negotiations.

Two factors assisted Waigel in persuading Kohl. First, the role of the Finance Ministry in negotiating the German Treaty on Monetary Union of 18 May set a helpful precedent. It showed that the Finance Ministry could be entrusted with the negotiation of complex issues in international law. Secondly, for the reasons outlined above, Genscher chose not to fight for control of the IGC. The stipulation in the communiqué of Rome 1 that coherence between the work of the two IGCs was to be assured by the Foreign Ministers satisfied Genscher's basic strategic interest. At the same time, in leaving each government to decide on the composition of its own IGC delegations, Rome 1 left the issue of control open. Keen to reinforce political direction, the Italian Presidency, supported by Delors, proposed Padoa-Schioppa as rapporteur for the IGC on EMU and tighter co-ordination of the IGCs. These ideas foundered against the resistance of the Kohl–Waigel axis and the successful mobilization of Jacques Santer, as head of the impending Luxembourg Presidency, to oppose them.

But what was most striking about the situation was that, unlike over the dates of the IGC and of stage 2, Genscher could not be mobilized on behalf of Commission, French, and Italian interests. The reason was very simple. Genscher was not, and never had been, an agent for their views in Bonn. He acted from his own definition of German and European interests. In this case Genscher believed that there was more to be lost than gained by marginalizing the German Finance Minister and, by implication, the Bundesbank. The organization of the IGC on EMU fitted into a recognized strategy of the federal government—to 'bind in' and neutralize potential dissent. On that aspect of the issue of organization of the IGC Genscher and Kohl could readily agree: a lead role for the Finance Ministry would be the most effective means of continuing to 'bind in' the Bundesbank. At the same time the solution arrived at for the launch of the two IGCs at Rome 2 was viewed with some alarm within the German Foreign Ministry: as a rupture with EC tradition and as an opportunity for 'conservative' finance ministries and central banks to impede progress to EMU.

Political Union and EMU

Rome 1 was by no means an unmitigated defeat for the German Finance Ministry and Bundesbank. In fact, one aspect of its final communiqué surprised and reassured their officials: the strength of the language in the area of political union. In the context of the Bundesbank's statement on EMU of September

1990, the reference to the will of the Council to further develop the political dimension of the EC, to transform it into a European Union, to strengthen its effectiveness, and to extend its responsibility into 'complementary areas of economic integration which are essential for convergence and social cohesion' was seen as a very positive signal for the impending IGC negotiations. Waigel and Köhler and Pöhl and Tietmeyer were reassured by evidence of consensus (minus the UK) on extending the rights of the European Parliament in legislation, the definition of European citizenship, and a common foreign and security policy. In his press conference at the end of Rome 1 Kohl referred to two basic principles that would guide German bargaining positions on political union: a federal structure for Europe; and subsidiarity.

In his government declaration of 22 November before Rome 2 Kohl underlined the importance that he attached to European political union as the 'core goal' (*Kernziel*). He legitimated this linkage in two ways. First, Kohl argued that without political union EMU would remain incomplete (a *Stückwerk*); both belonged inseparably together. This rationale derived from long-standing German belief about the importance of a framework of solidarity for an effective and durable EMU. Secondly, the Chancellor used the German Basic Law as the source of a mandate on this issue. He pointed out that its preamble committed German governments to realize a united Europe. That commitment had the same status and authority as the commitment to realize a united Germany. As a united Germany was now in place, German energies must be devoted to a united Europe. In a legalistic culture such an argument carried a particularly persuasive power.

Before Rome 2, which was to fix the mandate for the IGC on political union, Bitterlich was hard at work with Sophie-Caroline de Margerie and Hubert Védrine in the Elysée on a follow-up to the Kohl–Mitterrand message of 18 April. Andreotti's office was kept carefully briefed on progress. The joint message of 6 December to Andreotti had intended to offer a coherent concept of political union. It spelt out joint positions on political union, for instance, on a common foreign and security policy and on European citizenship. But the document glossed over a fundamental difference between German and French conceptions of political union. Though it referred to strengthening the powers of the European Parliament, which Bitterlich insisted was a minimum German position, French negotiators were fixated on the powers of the European Council. This gap in negotiating positions was to surface during Rome 2, where the Dutch Prime Minister Ruud Lubbers provided the strongest criticisms of Mitterrand's lack of support for strengthening the EC Commission and the European Parliament.

Despite this emerging Franco-German problem Kohl continued to give strong leadership on political union. The federal elections of 2 December 1990 had underpinned his political authority and image as the 'Chancellor of German unity'. Kohl's CDU had improved its position (from 34.5 to 36.7 per cent), whilst the share of the vote of the coalition parties (CDU/CSU/FDP) had climbed from 53.4 to 54.8 per cent. For the first time he had provided his coalition with an electoral bonus. Survey results showed 56 per cent support for him as Chancellor (compared to 46 per cent in 1987). Kohl was determined to use this electoral gift as political capital for his European policy. His strategy was twofold: to embed both political union and EMU in an historically legitimated vision; and to exploit the linkage between the two sets of negotiations to gain concessions on political union.

In his press conference of 15 December at the end of Rome 2, Kohl spoke of parallelism between the two IGCs as the indispensable negotiating condition for Germany. Germany was pressing for 'political union on a federal basis of sub-sidiarity', including a common foreign and security policy, new rights for the European Parliament, and—a new emphasis—EC competence in immigration, asylum, and drugs policy and in the war against organized crime. The Chancellor's television address of 31 December 1990 reiterated his message that German unification had given a new impulse to a united Europe and spoke of laying 'the foundation for the United States of Europe'. In a speech of 30 January 1991 Kohl developed his point that the two IGCs were inseparably linked into a statement of Germany's basic negotiating position: Germany could only agree to EMU and to political union as part of a single package.

Putting the German Negotiating Team Together and Preparing German Bargaining Positions: From Rome 2 to the German Draft Treaty on EMU

Despite the political row created by the Rome 1 communiqué provisions on EMU, Waigel was relaxed and confident when he attended the opening cere-mony for the two IGCs in the Montecitorio palace in Rome on 15 December. A number of factors contributed to this mood. First, Waigel sensed victory over Genscher on the issue of organization and control of the IGC on EMU. He could enjoy the symbolism of being joined on the first row of the German delegation at the first working session of the IGC on EMU by Otto Schlecht, State Secretary in the Economics Ministry, who was replacing his departing minister Haussmann. Dumas's presence on the front row of the French delegation con-trasted with Genscher's absence. But the sense of victory was more than sym-bolic. More importantly, the negotiating venue was designed to limit the opportunities for foreign ministers to shape the definition of EMU negotiating problems and the way in which they were solved.

An additional source of satisfaction derived from the fact that the Italian Presidency was at its end. Waigel could look forward to the IGC on EMU being chaired by the finance ministers of two 'stability-oriented' EC states during 1991. He enjoyed good personal relations with Jean-Claude Juncker, the Luxembourg Finance Minister, and with Wim Kok, the Dutch Finance Minister. On matters of economic and monetary policy their underlying beliefs were close to those of Germany. This accident of the calendar of the rotating EC Council Presidency gave Waigel and his officials confidence and trust in the way that the negotiations would be handled. In relation to EMU the opportunities for a policy entrepreneur of the Vattani type or like Padoa-Schioppa and Delors were diminished.

Thirdly, despite the ugly surprise of Rome 1, a great deal of preparatory work had been undertaken in the EC Monetary Committee—especially on the problem of excessive deficits—and in the Committee of EC Central Bank Governors—on the draft ECB statute. By using synergistic linkage with these two technical fora, the finance ministers in the IGC could keep political intervention at bay, clear up the ambiguities left by Rome 1, and pre-empt the European Councils of 1991. The Luxembourg and Dutch Presidencies offered an opportunity to re-establish intellectual continuity after the disruption of Rome 1.

Finally, Waigel welcomed the principle of parallelism between the two IGCs and fully shared Kohl's larger strategic vision of EMU. In this sense Rome 1 and 2 augured well. With respect to political union Waigel's strategic concerns were twofold: first, that states like France, Italy, and Spain might try to outflank Germany by raising specific issues relating to EMU within the other IGC (as was to happen later with social and economic cohesion and with industrial policy); and, secondly, that clear limits should be placed on attempts to use EMU for external political purposes—notably by political discretion over exchange-rate policy and intervention.

The Organization of the German Negotiating Position

German Finance Ministry strategy in relation to the organization of German negotiating positions on EMU focused on turning constraints into opportunity. The constraints took the form of the requirements for political consensus-building generated by the nature of the German governmental system: notably by the federal structure; by the presence of other Bonn ministries with an interest in EMU issues, notably Economics and Foreign Affairs; and by the Bundesbank. Waigel and Köhler were quick to recognize the risks of being politically exposed in the IGC negotiations and the value of taking cover behind well-designed organizational arrangements for co-ordination.

The Federal Dimension   During 1990 the governments of the federal states had expressed their views on the IGCs in two fora: the conference of heads of state governments (*Ministerpräsidentenkonferenz*) on 7 June and on 20–1 December; and the Bundesrat, the second chamber, on 6 April, 13 June, 24 August, 26 October, and 9 November. Substantively, their distinctiveness rested on the emphasis placed on the principle of subsidiarity in economic and financial (but not monetary) policy. The strategic interest of the German states was defined as maintaining their own freedom of manoeuvre in economic policy. Otherwise the Bundesrat and the conference of heads of state governments endorsed the positions developed by the Finance Ministry and the Bundesbank: notably on the top priority to price stability, the independence of the ECB, and the importance of developing economic union to parallel monetary union. But, more importantly, the Bundesrat pressed for participation in the IGCs and in their preparation. On 24 August it demanded representatives from two states. Then, in a Bundesrat decision of 26 October, Bavaria (CSU) and Hamburg (SPD) were designated as the representatives in the IGC on EMU. The symbolic importance of the federal dimension was underlined at the opening meeting of the IGC on 15 December. Alongside Waigel and Schlecht sat two heads of state governments; Köhler was relegated to the second row of the German delegation.

For Waigel this arrangement was politically convenient, not least because much of the political pressure for this participation had come from his own state of Bavaria. Its strategic value was in binding in the Bundesrat and pre-empting potential criticism. Symbolically, this involved an SPD state, Hamburg, and hence could serve a cross-party consensus-building process. Norbert Kraxenberger from the Bavarian Finance Ministry and Hubert Schulte from the Hamburg Finance Ministry joined the German IGC delegation as observers and were invited to take part in the German Finance Ministry's EMU co-ordinating group under Günter Grosche. Waigel reinforced this strategy by regular reports on the progress of EMU negotiations to the conference of state finance ministers (which was also briefed by the two state representatives).

This observer role assisted the Finance Ministry in two other ways. First, it was of symbolic as well as strategic value. It demonstrated that the interests of the federal states—and the positions taken up by the conference of heads of state governments and by the Bundesrat—were being taken seriously. Secondly, the fact that these observers were from state finance ministries helped to strengthen the position of the Finance Ministry in the Grosche Group. But the practical impact of Kraxenberger and Schulte was limited. As state-level civil servants they were not really tuned into issues of international banking and monetary policy.

The Grosche Group in Bonn   In December 1990 Köhler brought back Günter Grosche from Washington to replace Winkelmann as head of the European currency questions section in the Finance Ministry and to head up the detailed co-ordination of German negotiating positions for the IGC on EMU. For Grosche it was a case of being thrown in at the deep end of EMU negotiations. He arrived just in time for Rome 2. But Grosche brought with him three advantages. First, he was very experienced in EC monetary issues, having served as private secretary to Lahnstein and Schulmann as State Secretaries in the Finance Ministry and having worked on the negotiation of the EMS. Secondly, his personal skills complemented those of Köhler. Grosche was a calm, co-operative team player, good at keeping people on side when they might be alienated by Köhler's more robust approach. Thirdly, he shared with Haller, the head of his division, the belief that—desirable though European political union was—EMU must be able to stand on its own two feet. An EMU agreement must stand the test of being validated by a coherent economic theory that would specify the conditions for its effective functioning. Grosche had, in short, an interest in the intellectual basis of EMU negotiating positions.

Köhler's strategy for the IGC was to develop the bargaining positions as much as possible outside the normal co-ordination machinery for EC business in Bonn. Hence he produced a plan for a set of co-ordinating meetings with the objective of retaining control of the IGC negotiations. This plan envisaged regular special meetings at the State Secretary level, chaired by Köhler. The intention was to bypass the 'European' State Secretaries' meeting, which had the disadvantage of meeting in the Foreign Ministry under Foreign Ministry chairmanship. But this initiative floundered in the face of the failure of other State Secretaries to attend. In practice, the 'European' State Secretaries' meeting retained the responsibility for co-ordinating the two IGCs and remained a prime site for gladiatorial encounters between Köhler and Lautenschlager. Köhler tried to keep to a minimum the number of issues that he took to this forum. This objective was achieved by relying on Grosche and Haller to ensure effective co-ordination at a lower level.

Within the Finance Ministry itself there were two levels of interministerial co-ordination. Haller, head of the money and credit division, was to meet with division heads from other ministries on a two-weekly basis to finalize agreement on the details of EMU bargaining positions before they were presented to Köhler. In practice the attendance tended to be by the same people who worked on the Grosche group. This group was important in the sense that Haller and Köhler prepared texts for the ministerial level IGC and were most active within the IGC at permanent representative level.

But the real centre of gravity in co-ordinating the detailed preparation of EMU negotiating positions was the Grosche Interministerial Group which met weekly on Wednesday morning at 9 a.m. The nucleus of this group was the 'gang of five': Grosche, its chair; Rolf Kaiser from the economics division of the Federal Chancellor's Office; Peter Schlüter from the Bundesbank; Wilhelm Schönfelder from the Foreign Ministry (who kept Lautenschlager informed and involved); and Ralf Zeppernick from the Economics Ministry. Professor Martin Seidel, from the Economics Ministry, acted as adviser on EC legal issues and problems of drafting. The meeting was also open to other ministries, an attempt being made to involve the Interior and Justice Ministries. In addition, the two state representatives, Kraxenberger and Schulte, attended as observers to ensure that the proposals of the conference of heads of state governments and of the Bundesrat were respected. This group played the decisive role in developing and co-ordinating EMU negotiating positions.

The working climate of the Grosche Group proved co-operative and positive: in part because of the team-building skills of Grosche as chair; in part due to the good interpersonal skills of its members; and in part because of the underlying consensus about the principle of stability as the basis of EMU negotiating positions and about the strategy of gaining acceptance for the German model as the basis for the design of EMU. There was a shared sense of the powerful constraints underlying German negotiating positions and of the strategic value of emphasizing those constraints. On the other hand, these constraints did not derive from sharp and enduring controversies between federal ministries, between Bonn and Frankfurt, or with the state governments about what German negotiating positions should be. Within the Grosche Group it was relatively easy to operate on the consensus principle rather than the majority principle.

The Grosche Group had four main functions:

- to ensure that German negotiators spoke with one voice by harmonizing positions and agreeing the language in which these would be presented;
- to keep key interests informed in a non-bureaucratic way by reporting on progress of the negotiations and seeking their advice;
- to protect Köhler as personal representative on the IGC from interministerial quarrels, especially from complaints to Waigel from Genscher or from the Federal Chancellor's Office that he was trying to block progress on EMU;
- to act as an advisory group to Köhler: in particular, putting together the German Draft Treaty on EMU; identifying the issues raised by papers and draft treaties from the Luxembourg and Dutch Presidencies, from the Commission and others, notably the French; providing debriefings on IGC meetings; and preparing for subsequent IGCs.

The Bundesbank   Binding in the Bundesbank remained the absolute priority for Finance Ministry strategy on EMU. This binding in took several forms: occasional clearance of negotiating positions between Waigel and the President of the Bundesbank; much more regular discussions between Köhler and Tietmeyer; the role of Schlüter in the Grosche Group in Bonn; the presence of Rieke in the IGC (he was termed the 'watchdog' of the Bundesbank) and at the EC Monetary Committee; and Tietmeyer's involvement in various fora—the EC Monetary Committee (where many issues—notably convergence criteria—were handled), the Committee of EC Central Bank Governors (on the draft statutes of the ECB and of the European Monetary Institute), and the top-secret Franco-German bilaterals (at which Tietmeyer and Rieke were present). Before the six Franco-German bilaterals the key negotiating positions were always agreed between Köhler, Tietmeyer, Haller, and Rieke.

In trying to bind in the Bundesbank, Finance Ministry officials did not always find it easy to read the 'mind' of the Bundesbank. In order to ensure that it made a strong, effective contribution, the Bundesbank endeavoured to construct a highly persuasive, internally coherent, and logically powerful argument about EMU. Under the leadership of the international division a special working group of Bundesbank division heads was established to co-ordinate positions. In this way Rieke and Schlüter were able to draw on advice on economic, credit policy, technical banking, and legal matters. They were also able to bind in their colleagues. What emerged from these internal meetings was a shared underlying approach to the IGC negotiations. It took the form of an insistence on crystal-clear language in treaty provisions for central bank independence, exchange rates, and convergence criteria. This insistence could irritate officials in Bonn, never mind negotiators from other member states

But, despite these internal efforts, it remained clear to Köhler, Haller, and others that Tietmeyer, Rieke, and Schlüter held different views on key EMU issues. For instance, Rieke and Schlüter were more convinced that French politicians and officials were committed to stability. Hence they were more relaxed about the prospects for striking an acceptable EMU agreement. Tietmeyer was much tougher than the other two on convergence criteria. Also, Rieke's and Schlüter's concern about stage 2 led them to be more sympathetic than Tietmeyer (and the Bundesbank council) to the idea of a timetable for stage 3. Yet the scope for flexibility and malleability in the Bundesbank's position was constrained by Tietmeyer's determination to keep a tight grip on the Bundesbank's role in the EMU negotiations. He was concerned by the intellectual inquisitiveness of Rieke and, even more, by his doubts—shared with Rieke—about the reliability of Schlüter. These doubts derived from their memories of Schlüter's private diplomacy in the preparation of the Genscher Memorandum of 1988. Hence Rieke and Schlüter were subjected to close scrutiny by Tietmeyer, and sometimes Rieke rather than Schlüter was sent to the Grosche Group meetings. In turn, Tietmeyer endeavoured to keep Schlesinger on board at all stages, especially when he succeeded Pöhl as President in July 1991.

Overall, the contribution of Rieke and of Schlüter in the IGC and in the Grosche Group was greatly valued by the Finance Ministry. They worked to bridge differences in a constructive manner, both at EC and at domestic levels. Rieke's fund of experience of international monetary negotiations made his advice on negotiating strategy and tactics invaluable. This advice rested on his insight into the negotiating skills of the French, which he encouraged German negotiators to emulate: notably, being first to table proposals and giving them weight by a coherent intellectual rationale. Rieke was also the 'scientific conscience' of the Grosche Group. He was skilful at evaluating its proposals against the Bundesbank's experience and knowledge of financial markets and the operation of monetary policy and intervention in foreign-exchange markets.

The German Draft Treaty on EMU

Before the IGC negotiations got under way properly, the Finance Ministry found itself in a difficult strategic position. It had been forced onto the defensive by the Rome 1 communiqué, notably in its references to 'the' new institution in stage 2 and to developing the ECU. This sense of being under pressure was reinforced by the speed with which the French government and the Commission acted to put their ideas on the negotiating table. The communiqué on EMU from the French Council of Ministers on 5 December was followed on 25 January by the French Draft Treaty on EMU. They underlined Franco-German differences. In part, they reiterated known and worrying proposals, such as support for establishing the ECB at the start of stage 2 and for the ECU as the single currency. But they went further in two key respects: first, in arguing that the independence of the ECB only made sense in the context of a strong, fully democratic 'economic government' based on the right of the Council to issue economic-policy guidelines; and, secondly, in seeking entry of all twelve states into stage 3 as soon as possible. The Commission's Draft Treaty on EMU of 10 December 1990 had earlier alarmed the Finance Ministry. Its contents were not surprising: for instance, multi-annual EC economic-policy guidelines, an ECB at the start of stage 2, and an absence of sanctions in cases of excessive budget deficits. More serious was the speed with which the French had acted to table their Draft Treaty. Köhler identified a risk of strategic failure by the Finance Ministry to seize the intellectual leadership of the IGC negotiations.

Köhler had three immediate objectives: to correct what he saw as the mistakes of Bitterlich at Rome 1; to restore unity and purpose to German bargaining positions in the IGC on the basis of Finance Ministry leadership; and to demonstrate that the Germans were prepared to fight hard for their positions. The attempt to realize the first two of these objectives via the interministerial co-ordinating groups was fraught with difficulty. In the Grosche Group relations were, initially, not smooth. Here Kaiser, for the Federal Chancellor's Office, and Schönfelder, for the Foreign Ministry, were firm in their defence of the Rome 1 conclusions. In their view, the issue of the use of the name ECU could not be reopened; and 'the' new institution in stage 2 referred to the nucleus of the ECB. The Finance Ministry's objections to the former (expressed in the name of the Bundesbank) and its different interpretation of the term 'the new institution' risked putting at stake the reputation of Chancellor Kohl.

At a different level Köhler was confronted by Lautenschlager who emphasized two arguments: the political costs of challenging the Rome 1 communiqué and the political importance of a firm calendar and clear mechanism for transition to stage 3. Even though it was sympathetic, the Economics Ministry was more concerned about its own agenda in relation to the IGC: enshrining the principle of subsidiarity in economic policy (economic policy was to remain with the member states) and getting the principles of the market economy written into the Treaty. Köhler robustly defended the principle of the indivisibility of monetary policy, pointing to the danger of conflict between an ECB and national central banks in stage 2. He also instructed Grosche and Haller to be tougher in ensuring that there was no 'grey area' in stage 2. But, as the IGC began, Köhler found himself exposed and beleaguered.

The means of retrieving the strategic high ground was by using the co-ordination machinery that Köhler had designed to put together a unified position for formal presentation to the IGC. Production of draft papers on individual issues or areas for negotiation by the Winkelmann Group and now by the

Grosche Group would no longer suffice. The authority of the Chancellor was harnessed behind the exercise of producing a German Draft Treaty on EMU in order to strengthen Germany's bargaining position. Kohl could buy the political argument of Waigel and Köhler that in producing such a draft absolute priority must be given to binding in the Bundesbank. He could also subscribe to the strategic objective of using the IGC for gaining acceptance of the German model. In this way an opportunity was opened up for the Finance Ministry to find a way around the Rome 1 communiqué and retrieve the domestic initiative on EMU. But it was clear to Köhler and Grosche that laborious co-ordination with the Bundesbank would slow down progress in tabling a draft treaty.

The first stage in agreeing a unified approach came earlier with the basic position paper of the federal government for the IGC on EMU on 4 January 1991. This paper had two objectives: to give a clear general direction to German bargaining positions and to address the Luxembourg Presidency's priority to the economic-union component of EMU. Given the preparatory work in the Winkelmann Group, especially the position paper of November 1989, the paper was not difficult to agree. Its importance was attested to by the fact that it engaged co-ordination at the division head level, notably involving Haller and Molitor (Economics), with Köhler strongly involved. The imprint of the Economics Ministry was clear in the stress on an economic union based on market principles at home and open markets abroad, governed by effective competition; on the parallelism of economic and monetary integration; on the importance of convergence around low inflation, restricted budget deficits, and small interest-rate differentials before stage 3; and on the responsibility of the partners in collective bargaining for stability, employment, and growth. Otherwise, established positions were reiterated: for instance, that there must be a single monetary policy; that the ESCB was to be independent and to give primacy to the goal of price stability; and that in stage 2 monetary policy was to remain the responsibility of the national authorities. The novelty was the proposal that the ECB should be located in Frankfurt.

This position paper formed the basis for the German submission to the second meeting of the IGC personal representatives on 29 January. Here Köhler proposed that the Treaty should recognize open markets, externally and internally. More strikingly, echoing the Economics Ministry, he spelt out precise objectives—the free setting of prices, the reduction of wage indexation, privatization, and the responsibility of the social partners. Whilst there was general support for the principle of open markets, the attempt to list the objectives of *Ordnungspolitik* in this way exposed Köhler to a chorus of criticisms, notably from Trichet who preferred a more general statement, including cohesion as an objective. By being precise he had stirred up sensitivities, for instance, on privatization. But, at least, Köhler had been able to show how domestic unity and well-timed tabling of proposals had enabled him to help set the agenda of the IGC.

More frustratingly, at the first meeting of the IGC personal representatives on 15 January Köhler had had to state that Germany would limit itself to proposing amendments to precise treaty articles, whilst noting the 'utility' of the EC Commission Draft Treaty and hearing that the French would submit their Draft Treaty to the next meeting. The German Draft Treaty was not to be ready till the fourth meeting. Köhler's key opening points confirmed that German strategy focused on clarification of the content of stage 3 as the basis for designing the transition stage; on the parallelism between the two IGCs, with one not secondary to the other; and on the importance of specifying the basic principles of economic policy in the Treaty.

The German Draft Treaty on EMU became the key tool for Köhler to establish a leadership role in the IGC at home and within the EC. It was kept away from the 'European' State Secretaries' meeting (and Lautenschlager's direct involvement) for as long as possible. The work was co-ordinated by the money and credit division under Haller and by Grosche's interministerial group, with assistance on technical drafting from the legal staff in the Economics Ministry. But the key priority was accorded to the closest possible involvement of Tietmeyer and to binding in the support of the Bundesbank council. Köhler recognized that the 'European' State Secretaries' meeting would in effect be faced by a *fait accompli* once the authority of the Bundesbank council had been secured for the draft. On 14 February Tietmeyer wrote to Köhler, outlining the points on which he had reworked the text and indicating that it had the unanimous support of the Bundesbank council.

The Draft Treaty on EMU was presented for approval to the 'European' State Secretaries' meeting on 23 February, only two days before its submission to the IGC. Here there was strong support from Schlecht in the Economics Ministry, who stressed that it was high time that Germany followed the example of other states. Lautenschlager, who had been kept fully informed by Schönfelder, agreed with the strategy of tabling a general treaty text. But, on behalf of the Foreign Ministry, he expressed his reservations about the risks involved in departing from the Rome 1 communiqué. Strikingly, the Federal Chancellery complained about not being more closely involved.

In response Köhler emphasized that the basic strategic approach underpinning the Draft Treaty (of 'binding in' the Bundesbank and of gaining acceptance of the German model for EMU) had the support of the Chancellor. He gained support for two arguments. First, by providing Köhler with a maximalist position, the Draft Treaty would strengthen his bargaining power, particularly *vis-à-vis* the Commission and the French. It was an advantage to have clear and strong German bargaining positions. Secondly, EMU was a very delicate game for Germany in the context of its history. Against this background it was helpful to put German positions on record as a reference point for later defensibility. But another of Köhler's arguments was less convincing to others. He claimed that clarification of gaps between bargaining positions would aid the process of agreement. It should not be assumed that it would sharpen conflict. This latter point worried the Foreign Ministry which feared that the hurdles for an EMU agreement were being raised too high. Nevertheless, despite irritation with a *fait accompli* and a difference of view about bargaining strategy, Köhler gained the approval of the 'European' State Secretaries' meeting for the German Draft Treaty on EMU. Thereafter, he was able to claim three sources of authority for the draft: the Bundesbank council, the 'European' State Secretaries' meeting, and the Chancellor, whose personal approval was sought by Köhler.

The agreement of the German Draft Treaty on EMU was a turning-point. Köhler was provided with domestic authority for a unified bargaining position; the ghost of Rome 1 was laid to rest as far as domestic-policy positions were concerned; Köhler could credibly signal to his negotiating partners a single German position on key issues, consistent with Finance Ministry and Bundesbank positions hammered out pre-Rome 1; and the Grosche Group settled down to operating in a smooth, consensual manner to brief and defend Köhler.

The German Draft Treaty outlined tough German bargaining positions in seven key areas:

1. *The principles of economic policy*   German *Ordnungspolitik* was spelt out in classic Economics Ministry terms, including a treaty proposal for a European cartel office. Price controls and wage indexation would require the approval of the ECB; prices were to be freely set in a framework of internal competition and externally open markets; and privatization was to be a requirement, as well as freedom of collective bargaining. There was no reference to cohesion or to environment.

2. *Budgetary discipline*   A 'stability-oriented' budget policy required rules to establish an excessive deficit and sanctions within the Treaty, whilst the 'golden rule' that the size of the deficit must not surpass the expenditure on investment—established in the German Basic Law—was advocated. The stress was on precision in the Treaty.

3. *Economic policy co-ordination*   ECOFIN was to be responsible for determining, by qualified majority, the 'orientations' of economic policy. What was striking was the omission of a role for the European Council (seen as too political) and the rejection of 'guidelines' (*Richtlinien*) as, in the German, too strong. There was no reference to an EC financial-support mechanism or to a common economic policy.

4. *The transition to stage 2*   The date of 1 January 1994 was only to apply if certain conditions were fulfilled. Some of these conditions were not controversial: for instance, completion of the European single market, ratification of the treaty, and the largest possible number of member states in the ERM. Others represented a tougher stance: notably, the introduction of domestic legislation to make national central banks independent before their incorporation in the ECSB in stage 3, and satisfactory and lasting progress in convergence (especially on price stability and sound public finance). The 'golden rule' was to be binding from 1 January 1994. These conditions offered bargaining leverage to German negotiators; in return for emptying stage 2 of content, the conditions could be relaxed.

5. *The institution in stage 2*   Here, most starkly, the provisions of the German Draft Treaty departed from the Rome 1 communiqué and from the Commission and French Drafts. There was no provision for the ECB and no function of developing the ECU. With stage 2 the Committee of EC Central Bank Governors would become the 'Council' of EC Central Bank Governors. It was in name and function not a bank. The Council would intensify co-ordination between central banks and promote the co-ordination of domestic monetary policy with the goal of price stability. In this way the principle of the indivisibility of monetary policy was to be safeguarded. This principle was of absolute importance to the Bundesbank. For Köhler it meant no 'grey area' in stage 2. Logically, it meant opposition to the British hard ECU plan.

6. *Exchange-rate policy*   ECOFIN would determine the EC's exchange-rate system on the principle of unanimity after consultation with the council of the ECB, with the aim of achieving a consensus that is compatible with the goal of price stability. These provisions were designed to insulate the ECB from attempts to subordinate internal-stability policy to political aims. 'Close co-operation' with the ECB was seen as inadequate; and ECOFIN's role was restricted to the exchange-rate system and did not embrace wider exchange-rate policies and guidelines on intervention. This aspect of the Draft Treaty was seen as particularly important by the Bundesbank which feared external constraints on internal-stability policy. Here Schlesinger held very firm views.

7. *The transition to stage 3*   The necessary convergence was to be established by reference to three criteria: a high degree of price stability; a lasting reduction of budget deficits; and a close approximation of interest rates. There was no reference to a timetable, even in the loosest sense. Conditionality was to apply to stage 3.

Franco-German Relations after the German Draft Treaty: The Top-Secret Bilaterals

The German Draft Treaty was formally presented to the IGC personal representatives on 26 February by Köhler. Waigel had confined himself to arguing the case for the draft treaty against the doubts and reservations of Genscher. His importance was in enlisting the political support of Kohl for the process rather than in involving himself either in that process or in the technical matters of substance. In this respect his role was very much less than that of Bérégovoy in the French Draft Treaty's preparation. Now that it came to the matter of presenting the German Draft Treaty Waigel was again content to leave this difficult task to Köhler.

The signals at the IGC ministerial-level meeting on the previous day did not point to a good reception. Delors had for the first time spoken strongly on the need to broaden the economic-policy objectives of the EC and to develop a financial-support mechanism. In strong terms he had cautioned against too narrow a definition of the agenda of EMU. Bérégovoy had focused on the importance of economic-policy 'guidelines' and of 'dialogue' between the ECB and other EC institutions. Germany found itself in a minority on two issues: whether criteria for defining excessive deficits should be in the treaty or in secondary legislation; and whether they should be applied flexibly by ECOFIN.

In presenting the German Draft Treaty on 26 February Köhler attempted to give it authority and professional weight by invoking its unanimous approval by the Bundesbank council. But the reaction was not immediate and not always revealed. For instance, the Luxembourg Presidency was disappointed because the German draft was seen as unhelpfully late, short, and poorly constructed. Most strikingly of all, on 27 February Delors took the unusual step of making his reactions public via a press spokesman, attacking the German draft as incompatible with Rome 1. This issue was taken up in a much more discreet manner by the Elysée and by the French Foreign Ministry. They sought respectively to bring Kohl and Genscher into the game to 'save Rome 1' and salvage the diminishing prospects for an EMU agreement.

The strains in Franco-German relations over EMU consequent on the German Draft Treaty were immediately apparent. By the time the Franco-German Economic Council met in Paris on 5 March it was clear to Waigel and Köhler that an exercise in damage-limitation was required. They continued to pursue their objective of showing their determination to fight for German positions. In particular, Waigel spoke of the conditions for transition to stage 2 being more important than any date. Köhler also expressed his extreme disquiet that the French idea of economic-policy guidelines extended to monetary policy, thereby vitiating any meaningful independence for the ECB. But they wanted also to exhibit their objective of working for agreement. The Franco-German Economic Council confirmed that the difficulties were over the details of the route to a final goal that both shared. Privately, the French and German Finance Ministries recognized that the key was to sort out these difficulties within the framework of the Elysée Treaty arrangements. In Paris Waigel and Köhler were happy to endorse the idea of secret Franco-German bilaterals, despite Tietmeyer's reservations. They recognized that, in the absence of a failure to take pre-emptive action, Mitterrand and Kohl and Dumas and Genscher would involve themselves. The visit of Elisabeth Guigou, the French Minister for European Affairs, to Waigel on 7 March—followed by her visit to the Bundesbank—was seen in Bonn as confirmation of this calculation. It was an exercise in showing the political importance that the French government attached to this exercise. It was also used by the Finance Ministry to underline to Guigou the difficulties that they faced with Tietmeyer on this issue and to enlist her in the exercise of persuading the Bundesbank to play a constructive role. But already Waigel and Bérégovoy had resolved to work jointly together to find a way of resolving Franco-German differences.

This agreement in principle did not take the heat out of the differences of detail, as was apparent at the next IGC personal representatives' meeting on 12 March. The atmosphere within the IGC was soured when Köhler and Trichet came into sharp conflict over the issue of the relationship between the French Draft Treaty idea of '*gouvernement économique*' and the principle of the independence of the ECB. This issue crystallized in relation to the question of responsibility for the exchange-rate system and exchange-rate policy. Köhler made clear his doubts that the French, in proposing that the Council could issue 'guidelines' on exchange-rate policy, were serious about the independence of the ECB. In his toughly worded attack on the French he was establishing his credentials with the Bundesbank. On the other hand, negative signals were transmitted to Paris.

In late February and early March Waigel and Köhler were faced with a potentially serious problem. The Foreign Ministry and the Federal Chancellery had an opportunity to make political capital at their expense out of this situation, pointing out that their earlier fears were materializing—that a German Draft Treaty on EMU would sharpen Franco-German conflict. The Finance Ministry's solution was to attempt to transform a problem into an opportunity. This solution took the form of activating direct bilaterals with their French counterparts in an attempt to bridge the gaps between their Draft Treaties on EMU. In so doing they were responding positively to French pressure to handle these difficulties in the framework established by the Elysée Treaty. The strategic value of situating the Franco-German bilaterals within the framework of the Franco-German Economic Council was that it would enable the Finance Ministry to retain control over the EMU negotiations, ward off political intervention, and sustain the momentum achieved with the German Draft Treaty. The risks of such intervention were underlined by the Dumas–Genscher meeting on 21 March, after which they issued a communiqué committing themselves to the Rome 1 conclusions, in particular the establishment of the ECB at the start of stage 2. Hence—with strong support from the Chancellor—it was decided to hold a set of top-secret Franco-German bilaterals on EMU. By 18 March at the next ECOFIN, the French and German Finance ministers were minimizing their differences. Köhler travelled to Paris to discuss the organization of the bilaterals with Trichet. From the outset it was agreed that their composition would be limited to the respective finance ministries and central banks.

In no sense were these bilaterals imposed on the finance ministries by Kohl and Mitterrand, though Köhler was careful to keep his Chancellor briefed about their progress. They were wholly consistent with the established views of Waigel and Köhler, and of Pöhl in the Bundesbank, that EMU could not be realized without French and German participation. Hence an intense bilateral relationship with French counterparts was perceived as a sensible means for ensuring that a treaty agreement was in place for December 1991. Its value had already been demonstrated to the Bundesbank over the negotiation of the draft ECB statute. But, even more importantly, Köhler and Tietmeyer were intent on making use of this new opportunity to press strongly on the French the rationale behind German positions. They saw in the quality of German policy argument the indispensable means to persuade French negotiators to make concessions and gain acceptance for the German model.

Perhaps the most striking feature of the Franco-German bilaterals was the secrecy in which they were held. Altogether, there were six meetings, usually over weekends: 4–5 April in Paris; 18 May in Edinburgh (attached to a meeting of the EC Monetary Committee, which was held at the invitation of the British!); 5 June in Bonn; 25 June in Frankfurt, just three days before the Luxembourg Economic Council; 13–14 September in Berlin, just a week before the informal ECOFIN at Apeldoorn; and 9 November in Paris, just before the Franco-German summit in Bonn on 14–15 November. They were kept out of sight of other IGC negotiators (though the Edinburgh meeting was less successful in this respect). Notably, the meetings were kept confidential in Bonn. They were not even reported to the Grosche Interministerial Group. Their membership was kept very limited. On the German side the Finance Ministry was represented by Köhler, with Haller and Grosche in attendance; the Bundesbank by Tietmeyer, with Rieke in support.

The importance of the Franco-German bilaterals extended beyond their frequency. Preparation for the bilaterals brought Grosche and Haller into closer, more intense contact with their counterparts in the French Trésor, notably Musca and Duquesne. Also, the informality and climate of openness generated by the bilateral meetings contributed to a more general ease in communicating and dealing with negotiating difficulties. And, not least, they fitted into a wider framework of already intensive interaction between both sides and helped smooth those interactions. Köhler and Trichet met in the context of IGC meetings at personal representative and ministerial levels, at least three times a month; the monthly ECOFIN; the EC Monetary Committee; the twice-yearly Franco-German Economic Council; the twice-yearly Franco-German summit; G7; IMF; and OECD. They met some six times a month during 1991, and contacts were almost daily. The bilaterals added an extra dimension of friendliness, conviviality, and personal ease to the negotiating relationship. They operated on a 'first-names', 'coats-off' basis, in English.

The objective of the Franco-German bilaterals was to deal with texts as they evolved over the course of the IGC, to bracket Franco-German differences, and to work on removing them. During the first four meetings the prime concern was to close the gap between the French and German Draft Treaties. The last two meetings in Berlin and Paris took on a new significance. They were preoccupied with 'saving the IGC' in the face of what both sides saw as the failure of the Dutch Presidency. In the process there was a concern not to be seen to be conspiring to dominate the IGC. Hence the meetings did not seek to produce joint Franco-German positions to present to the IGC. To have done so would have offended the Luxembourg and Dutch EC Presidencies, as well as other states. The objective was simply to achieve mutual understanding or, at least, to avoid shouting at each other. But shared understandings could later be difficult to interpret. They were too often accompanied by reservations, making it difficult to speak of agreements being struck.

The discussions were not just technical. They went into background economic philosophy and the lessons of the experience of the 1970s and 1980s. In this respect they partook of the quality of a seminar as well as of a negotiation, the emphasis being on understanding, exploring, and testing each other's assumptions. The deeper cultural 'frames' underpinning EMU negotiating positions came into full view. This philosophical discussion was seen as useful in preparing the ground for compromises. But Tietmeyer, Haller, and others saw it as indispensable if the French were to be persuaded of the superiority of the German model as the basis for an EMU agreement.

There were three key issues in the Franco-German bilaterals: the French idea of *gouvernement économique*; exchange-rate system and policy; and development of the ECU. The first of these issues was soon out of the way in the sense that the French were persuaded that it raised fundamental problems for the Germans, especially for Tietmeyer and for the Economics Ministry. Privately, Köhler was more attracted by the idea of an improved economic-policy coordination, co-ordinated measures to promote structural reforms, and the agreement of minimum standards on taxation, employment, and social policy. But he was cautious to avoid too close an identification with the thinking coming from Delors and from Bérégovoy.[3]

On the development of the ECU brackets were kept around the issue till the final 6 November Franco-German bilateral in Paris, with Tietmeyer especially active on the dangers of associating the future single currency (which must be at least as stable as the D-Mark) with a 'basket' currency which represented an average of European currencies. In Paris Tietmeyer was persuaded to suggest that the brackets might be removed in return for two valuable French concessions on the exchange-rate system and exchange-rate policy in relation to non-Community currencies. The French accepted the principle of unanimity when the Council concluded agreements on the exchange-rate system for the ECU in relation to non-Community currencies (Article 109, para. 1). They also agreed to replace 'guidelines' by 'orientations' when the Council, acting by qualified majority, formulated positions on exchange-rate policy in the absence of an exchange-rate system. Waigel was later delighted when Bérégovoy confirmed these concessions. But, immediately after the Maastricht Council, he was to regret having taken the ECU out of brackets once he was faced with domestic opposition to the new currency, especially within his own CSU. The issue was only finally to be resolved with the adoption of the name 'Euro' in 1995.

Another issue in the Franco-German bilaterals was the linkage between stage 2 and central bank independence. Both sides accepted the principle of an inde-

---

[3] Köhler's position is made more clear in 'Zukunft Europa—Standort Hier', speech to the conference of German savings banks, Leipzig, 30 April 1998.

pendent ECB in stage 3. But the Germans, Tietmeyer in particular, sought to put the French under pressure by suggesting that in making the Banque de France independent at the beginning of stage 2 they would be giving a signal of good intent. Though Trichet insisted that he 'would not let his Banque de France go' without substantial German concessions, the Germans were not prepared to tinker with this linkage. Even so, following the 13–14 September bilateral in Berlin, the French steeled themselves to make this concession—only to be let off the hook by Waigel. This issue was used to tease the French rather than seen as vital for German interests.

The Franco-German bilaterals were taken very seriously by the German side. Köhler took overall responsibility. His key resource, particularly *vis-à-vis* Tietmeyer, was the authority of Kohl. Köhler kept Kohl well-informed and invoked the Chancellor's views to support his positions. In this respect the perspective of Kohl on EMU was transmitted into the preparatory work of the Germans. This preparatory work involved a very close co-ordination between the Finance Ministry and the Bundesbank. Köhler and Tietmeyer liaised tightly together, whilst Haller and Rieke added their own contributions. This involvement gave the Bundesbank direct access to the heart of the EMU negotiations. Indeed, the prior co-ordination with Tietmeyer and Rieke made the Franco-German bilaterals the key forum for hammering out agreement between the Finance Ministry and the Bundesbank.

Tietmeyer's role took on an ambivalent quality. On the one hand, as a loyal and very correct public servant, he emphasized that the IGC negotiations were the responsibility of the federal government. He stressed that he was only there to provide expert advice on behalf of the Bundesbank. On the other, Tietmeyer was clearly the dominant character on the German side, his words carrying a particular authority as both a seasoned negotiator and an EMU specialist. But the glitter of Tietmeyer was tempered by more than self-restraint. Köhler acted to ensure that the ghost of Kohl was ever-present in preparing and managing the Franco-German bilaterals. The invocation of that ghost ministered to the status that Köhler enjoyed and the respect that he had earned.

Kohl, the Chancellor's Office, and the IGC on EMU

As we saw earlier, during 1990 Kohl sought to impart a clear political direction to the EMU negotiations. Once the IGCs had begun, the firmness of this political direction was consolidated and its symbolic content further elaborated. Kohl was determined to use his enhanced personal political authority after the December 1990 federal elections to drive the IGC negotiations, to frame the way in which issues were negotiated, and to legitimate his European policy at home. Politically, the Chancellor was now fully secure in his relations with the CDU/CSU consequent on the electoral bonus that he had delivered them—for the first time—in the federal elections of 1990.

Kohl's first rallying call came in his government declaration to the Bundestag on 30 January 1991: 'Germany is our Fatherland (*Vaterland*), Europe our future'. Invocations of German identity and shared values were framed in an interpretation of German and European history that focused on the destructive power of nationalist politics. As Kohl put it in a speech in Berlin on 10 October: 'the age of the nation-state in Europe is past'. Germany must take the leading role in 'the construction of the United States of Europe'. This sense of mission was above all grounded in historical memory.

The most important development in Kohl's use of historical memory came during the 'end-game' of the negotiations. In a speech to the Bundestag on 27 November 1991 he referred to the political unification of Europe as 'our historic duty'. To the metaphor of Germany unification and European unification as 'two sides of the same coin' he added the historical theme of war and peace in Europe. In Kohl's words: '*Nie wieder Krieg—keine Rückkehr zum Nationalstaat vergangener Zeiten!*'—'Never again war—no return to the nation-state of past times!' But this determination to ensure that there was no reversion to the national rivalries of the past was significantly qualified. In the same speech Kohl stressed how important it was that Germans put themselves in the 'different historical shoes' of their neighbours, referring specifically to the British and the French. This theme of being careful in what one demands of one's neighbours was to prove important in orientating German policy in the final stages of the IGC negotiations.

During 1991 Kohl developed three strategic positions: on the relationship between EMU and political union; on a date for stage 3; and on the importance and means of keeping the British on board. There was also a significant shift in the structure of policy advice in relation to EMU within the Federal Chancellor's Office.

Kohl and Political Union

The Chancellor's central preoccupation was the relationship between EMU and European political union. In another speech on 30 January Kohl spelt out the basic German negotiating position: that he could only agree to EMU as part of a single package with European political union. The two were inseparably connected. During a keynote conference speech in Bonn on 29 April Kohl stressed that 'our core goal remains at the end of the day the political union of Europe . . . I shall only present to the Bundestag and the Bundesrat ratification documents with the results of both IGCs included'. Kohl's energies were devoted to getting the political-union projects off the ground: such as the war on organized crime in Europe, asylum policy, and the rights of the European Parliament. EMU was seen as requiring a different kind of leadership: essentially fine-tuning the progress of EMU, relying on Köhler for reporting on the IGC and Franco-German negotiations, and on Ludewig to offer an independent perspective. The Federal Chancellor's Office confined itself to shadowing the EMU negotiations:

Kaiser in Ludewig's economics division played essentially an intelligence-gathering and monitoring role.

But, once the commitment to detailed negotiating positions on EMU had been enshrined in the German Draft Treaty of February, a new risk surfaced—namely, of asymmetry in the two sets of negotiations. The IGC on political union faced the problem of lack of preparation in depth, with the result that German Foreign Ministry negotiators faced real difficulties in ensuring that it operated effectively in parallel with the IGC on EMU. There was no equivalent to the background work in the Delors Committee, the EC Monetary Committee, and the Committee of EC Central Bankers. In addition, the IGC on political union had a more open-ended agenda and operated in a context of less background consensus about basic organizing principles. There was no equivalent to the phenomenon of fast-growing capital mobility and an emerging neo-liberal economic-policy consensus to bind together the negotiators.

More importantly, the direction in which the two IGCs moved differed, opening up scope for conflict between them. By the time of the Luxembourg European Council in June the IGC negotiations on political union were already signalling danger to Kohl. When measured against the proposals agreed by Kohl with other Christian Democratic heads of government before the Dublin Council in 1990, there was a risk of major disappointment. Most notably, the Luxembourg Presidency was spelling out a 'pillar' conception of the European union. The EC pillar, reinforced by EMU, was to be paralleled by new intergovernmental pillars in which the EC Commission, European Court of Justice, and European Parliament ceded their privileged positions to member states in new areas of co-operation, like common foreign and security policy and interior and justice policy. The prospect was that the work of the IGC on political union would be mainly concerned with refining the new intergovernmental pillars.

By early October Jürgen Trumpf, who was Genscher's personal representative in the IGC on political union, was registering concern in Brussels that the IGC on EMU was moving away from the orthodox EC institutional rules. The source of this concern—that a 'fourth pillar' was being created—derived principally from efforts in the IGC on EMU to restrict the right of initiative of the EC Commission. Köhler had his own agenda here. At the 8 October IGC personal representatives' meeting, backed by Trichet and Wicks, he expressed his determination to keep the Commission out of monetary policy and to ensure that it did not have the sole right of initiative in relation to exchange-rate issues, to multilateral surveillance, and to the excessive deficit procedure. In pressing these points Köhler was exposing himself to direct criticism by Delors to Kohl that he was conspiring with the French to create a new 'fourth pillar'. But in practice Köhler could readily defend and legitimate his position in Bonn. He could argue that it derived from the Finance Ministry's and Bundesbank's belief that the EC Commission would be a force for monetary and fiscal laxity in conflict with the requirements of a 'Community of stability'. Nevertheless, Köhler had to be careful to reassure the Chancellor that he was not challenging the principle that EMU was part of the EC pillar.

Kohl reacted to the negative developments in the political-union negotiations by reaffirming his position at his post-Luxembourg Council press conference on 29 June and at his federal press conference on 1 July. There would only be agreement at Maastricht if 'equal weight' was given to the results of both IGCs. The political-union negotiations must not have less substance than those on EMU. There must be a 'substantial strengthening' of the rights of the European Parliament so that the 1994 elections to the European Parliament took on a more meaningful character; 'decisive steps' in foreign and security policy; and 'urgent progress' in the fight against organized crime (a Europol) and in European asylum law.

But, by the autumn, and—as we shall see—particularly after the Dutch Draft Treaty of September, Kohl was faced by mounting dissonance between his rhetoric on political union and the reality of the negotiations. The French would not give ground on the 'pillar' conception of the European union or on the primacy of strengthening the European Council over the rights of the European Parliament. The turning-point came in November. By 6 November he was admitting to the Bundestag that there were 'unexpected difficulties' in the political-union negotiations; by 12 November he had ceased to suggest any conditionality on political union for an EMU agreement; and by his Bundestag speech of 27 November he was speaking of a 'second-best' solution on political union.

For Kohl the basic strategic objective was to maintain the trust of Germany's neighbours by signing a treaty in December that made European political unification irreversible. That objective was in Germany's vital interest in reassuring her neighbours that a newly united Germany was absolutely intent on preventing a return to the national rivalries of the past. An EMU agreement would powerfully serve that objective. Clearly, failure to make substantial progress in the political-union negotiations was very disappointing to Kohl. But it must not be allowed to undermine the treaty. As he indicated in his Bundestag speech of 27 November, the objective of maintaining trust in Germany depended on the willingness of German negotiators to empathize with the ideas of their counterparts. Hence, despite the strong rhetoric, Kohl refused to identify a bottom line for the political-union negotiations. As he approached the IGC 'end-game', Kohl gave himself maximum flexibility to ensure that there would be no impediment to German agreement at Maastricht.

Kohl and a Date for Stage 3

More centrally in relation to the EMU negotiations, Kohl turned his attention to the issue of a date for stage 3. This issue had been pressed on him by Mitterrand and Delors and had its supporters in the Federal Chancellor's Office and the Foreign Ministry. Being upstaged by Genscher was again a factor. After his meeting with Dumas on 21 March 1991 Genscher had publicly committed himself to

1 January 1997 for the start of stage 3. Genscher at political level and Lautenschlager at official level were persistent advocates of a firm timetable throughout the IGC. There was an additional factor at work in the Chancellor's mind: Kohl's desire to honour the memory of a trusted friend and adviser. Kohl recalled the strong position taken on the issue of a timetable for completion of EMU by Herrhausen before his assassination in 1989.

On 9 April 1991, for the first time, in his speech to the Hanover Trade Fair, Kohl referred to the need to put in place a calendar for EMU. He had in mind as the model the 1992 date for the single European market. Unlike Genscher, however, Kohl did not specify 1 January 1997 or any other date. He confined himself simply to noting that EMU would probably take up most of the 1990s. But the issue of a date for stage 3 was now clearly on Kohl's personal agenda. From April onwards he provided a clear political direction on this issue. At the Franco-German summit in Lille on 29–30 May Kohl signalled to Mitterrand that he was looking for 'clearly fixed progress' on EMU in the form of a timetable to complete the process. By April–May, it was already clear that a timetable for stage 3 was not perceived by Kohl as an issue on which it was a matter of him making concessions in the negotiation. His position was much stronger and more positive. Kohl wanted a date for stage 3 so that the momentum to complete the process was not lost.

His increasing firmness on the issue was apparent during 1991. At his press conference at the end of the Luxembourg Council on 29 June Kohl spoke of a 'clear' timetable: stage 2 on 1 January 1994; and a date to assess progress on convergence and examine candidates for stage 3 before 1 January 1997. In a speech in Berlin on 10 October Kohl expressed his conviction that 'perhaps in 1997 or 1998' the EC would have an independent ECB. Hence, well before the EMU negotiations reached their 'end-game', the German Chancellor had gone a long way to clarify his position on a date for stage 3.

Helping John Major to be at the 'Heart of Europe'

Kohl's other strategic objective was to provide the new British Prime Minister, John Major, with sufficient room for manoeuvre to enable him to reconcile his Conservative Party to a final agreement at Maastricht in December. Major's first working visit to Bonn on 11 February and his 'Heart of Europe' speech to the CDU's Konrad Adenauer Foundation had signalled a new, more engaged style after the mistrust and distance of the Thatcher years. Kohl sensed that he could do business with a new Prime Minister who expressed his intent to work for agreement, even if on points of substance differences remained considerable. In consequence, at the Franco-German summit on 29–30 May, and during his visit on 25 June to Paris, Kohl opposed Mitterrand's argument that their joint objective should be clear progress in the form of preliminary agreements at the Luxembourg Council. Kohl was more concerned than Mitterrand to avoid creating difficulties for Major. In doing so he was backed by Waigel. The Finance

Ministry had its own reason for wanting to keep Britain on board in EMU negotiations. Quite simply, its minister and officials found that with respect to much
of the substance of the EMU negotiations their economic philosophy overlapped more with the British than the French.

But avoiding difficulties for Major did not involve taking an interest in the
'hard' ECU plan or embracing the idea of an 'opt-out' for all in relation to stage
3. Kohl's objective was to put in place a single currency. His strategy for that purpose was to ensure that a clear timetable was designed. Measured against this
objective the British 'hard' ECU plan was unacceptable. Indeed, it could serve as
an alternative monetary future for Europe. On the other hand, for the sake
of securing a larger agreement, Kohl was prepared to help Major with his
domestic political difficulty on signing up to EMU. But his condition for doing
so was that the progress of other states to EMU would not be impeded in the
process.

At the Luxembourg Council Kohl was happy to subscribe to one important
agreement on EMU: on the three principles to govern the transition to stage 3—
no imposition, no arbitrary exclusion, and no veto. This package of principles
was a trade-off satisfying everybody. It enabled Kohl to reassure Major that there
would be no treaty requirement for the UK to move to stage 3. Delors had
already secured Kohl's support for the idea of a British 'opt-out', and in
Luxembourg Kohl signalled informally to Major that support. But, at the same
time, Kohl was adamantly committed to the principle of no veto on the transition to stage 3. Here he found common ground with Mitterrand. But the devil
remained in the treaty details still to be negotiated. As we shall see, when the
Dutch presented a proposal for an opt-out for all in August, the limits of how far
Kohl was prepared to go to accommodate Major were clearly revealed.

The Chancellor's Office and EMU

With the IGC there was a subtle displacement of power over EMU within the
Federal Chancellor's Office. In 1991 Johannes Ludewig was promoted to head
the economic policy division. His growing influence over EMU within the
Federal Chancellor's Office was in part a function of his new authority. But,
more importantly, Ludewig enjoyed much greater personal credibility and professional respect amongst colleagues within the Chancellor's Office than his predecessor. He was less the orthodox ordo-liberal economist on EMU, more
attuned to the political dimensions, and—like Bitterlich—more at home in the
Franco-German relationship. Hence the foreign policy division was more
relaxed about ceding responsibility for EMU to the economic division. Ludewig
became part of Kohl's inner circle, trusted by Kohl to attend to the basic political aspects of the EMU negotiations. In practice, he relied on Kaiser to keep him
abreast of progress in the IGC and was heavily preoccupied with other issues,
not least relating to the new Bundesländer. Ludewig's major engagement came
in the 'end-game' over the issue of dates for stage 3.

Bitterlich was much less involved in the EMU negotiations after Rome 1. The Rome 1 communiqué had exposed him to sharp criticism from the Finance Ministry and the Bundesbank. But his colleagues, including Ludewig, had rallied to his defence, and Bitterlich did not lose his prestige with Kohl. In any case, Köhler was quick to appreciate the value of keeping up good personal relations with Bitterlich as a means of strengthening his own position with the Chancellor. What emerged in 1991 was a division of labour with Bitterlich throwing himself into the political-union negotiations and Ludewig shadowing the IGC on EMU. Both maintained a good relationship based on mutual trust and enjoyed good relations with Köhler. Both saw Köhler as a less difficult man than Tietmeyer. Köhler was seen as someone helping them to deal with Tietmeyer.

Hence, in relation to EMU, Ludewig became Kohl's main adviser during 1991. Though less orthodox than his predecessor, Ludewig was more cautious than Bitterlich. He worked to ensure that the economic policy division 'accompanied' the Finance Ministry during the IGC negotiations in a supportive way. In preparing Kohl on EMU for the Luxembourg Council, Ludewig's briefing coincided with Köhler's. Kohl pressed two main points, both of which were 'orthodox': that there must be no 'grey zone' in relation to monetary-policy responsibility during stage 2 (that responsibility fell solely to the national monetary authorities); and that before the transition to stage 2 there was an urgent need for renewed efforts to achieve a convergence of economic policies. Only on the issue of a date for stage 3 was Ludewig prepared to take a firmer view than Köhler.

Köhler and the IGC

The onus of responsibility placed on Köhler during the IGC negotiations was enormous. Waigel's main contribution was to provide Köhler with solid political support. Otherwise, distracted by his responsibilities as chair of the CSU, and the manoeuvrings for power post-Strauss, he took little interest in the technical aspects of the EMU negotiations. His trust in Köhler's abilities even extended to asking Köhler to represent him at important IGC ministerial-level meetings. This degree of political exposure, alongside the privileged access to Kohl as his economic 'sherpa', meant that Köhler assumed a significance on the German side that was not paralleled by Trichet in Paris or Wicks in London. Köhler became 'the' voice of Germany in the IGC. His ascendancy was underlined by the fact that Jürgen Trumpf, who as German Permanent Representative formally partnered Köhler in the IGC on EMU, restricted his role to following these negotiations and was not often there. In this respect too Köhler was less constrained than Trichet who was partnered by the more forceful Pierre de Boissieu.

Nevertheless, Köhler had a difficult role to play. He found himself caught between powerful figures: Kohl's more demanding political leadership on EMU;

the incessant and critical monitoring role of Lautenschlager and Genscher in the Foreign Ministry; and, above all, the doubts and reservations of Tietmeyer and Schlesinger in the Bundesbank. In playing his role Köhler was determined to avoid being simply a passive, reactive domestic consensus-builder. Though he could not hope to extricate himself from controversies about EMU, Köhler was able to give a direction to domestic consensus-building. This direction was achieved in part by the Grosche Group's work in laying the groundwork for consensus. It was also achieved by gaining general agreement to two principles to guide negotiating positions and the evaluation of outcomes: the principle that the new single currency must be 'at least as stable as the D-Mark'; and the principle that Köhler's prime negotiating task was to design a technically viable and durable EMU. Neither Genscher nor Kohl were prepared to challenge these principles. By reference to these principles a real cohesion was given to the Grosche Group and to the German team in the Franco-German bilaterals. They endowed German negotiating positions with the persuasive power that comes from the effective fusion of cognitive and strategic elements. Beliefs and interests joined in cosy unison, certainly compared to French negotiating positions.

The Content of Stage 3

Köhler's preoccupation in the IGC was with stage 2 and the transition to stage 3. Essentially, the Finance Ministry was happy to leave the content of stage 3 to the Bundesbank. In consequence the substantive content of stage 3 issues in the negotiations was conditioned by the frame of reference of EC central bank governors: which meant the design of an ECB with cast-iron guarantees of its independence and its dedication to price stability, and of an exchange-rate system and policy that would safeguard this design.

The ECB statute was finalized by the Committee of Central Bank Governors on 26 April for presentation to the IGC personal representatives' meeting on 10 May. For Köhler the key issues at IGC level were over the ECB's tasks; the ECB's relations with other institutions; and its structure. With respect to tasks the main issue was prudential supervision. The Bundesbank was resolutely opposed to the idea that the ECB should assume this task as potentially incompatible with its monetary-policy responsibility. On prudential supervision Article 105(6) and Article 25 of the draft ESCB statute closed the door on prudential supervision, but not firmly. Acting unanimously, and after consulting the ECB, the Council might confer specific tasks relating to prudential supervision on the ECB. On the second issue of relations with other institutions the main battle was fought and won by Köhler at the IGC personal representatives' meeting on 8 October. He successfully opposed two proposals: a French proposal that the President of the Council should have the power to suspend for two weeks a decision of the ECB (as political interference); and a British proposal that national central bank governors should be accountable before their national parliaments as well as the European Parliament (as undermining its supranationality).

The most sensitive issue related to the structure of the ECB and came to a head at the IGC ministerial-level meeting on 25 November. In even sharper terms than the Dutch Draft Treaty provisions, Köhler supported a clear institutional divide inside the ECB against those wanting 'out' member states to be associated as much as possible in the work of the governing council. By creating a 'chamber of governors' comprising all EC governors, the 'out' states could be involved in certain non-monetary decisions. But they would be excluded from monetary-policy decision-making in the governing council and the executive board. Though there was some support from Bérégovoy, it was decided to defer decision on this issue pending discussions between Lubbers and Kohl. To the satisfaction of Köhler, the final IGC ministerial-level meeting on 2–3 December resolved to create a separate 'general council' to incorporate the 'outs'. At this meeting Köhler announced that the German government would be seeking to have the ECB located in Frankfurt.

Otherwise, Köhler was content to score negative victories on stage 3 in the IGC: to concentrate on warding off the implications of the French 'gouvernement économique' and the idea of a common economic policy contained in the Commission and French Draft Treaties. At the first IGC personal representatives' meeting on 15 January Köhler—backed by Maas and Wicks—attacked the Commission's Draft Article 3g on a common economic policy in the name of the principle of subsidiarity. But, with respect to a common economic policy, the Germans were unable to replace the word 'guidelines' with 'orientations' to soften the formulation. The German fear was that a common economic policy could be used to 'bail out' member states in economic difficulties when they should be encouraged to take individual responsibility for tackling those difficulties. For the same reason Köhler saw the Commission's proposed financial-assistance mechanism as a dangerous 'bail-out' scheme. At the IGC personal representatives' meeting on 10 September he sought a compromise based on a narrow definition of the objects of such a mechanism and a requirement of unanimity for Council action. In the final formulation of Article 103a qualified majority voting applied to financial assistance for natural disasters; otherwise unanimity was the rule. With respect to Article 103 (economic policy) and Article 105(1) (monetary policy), Köhler was satisfied that he had achieved his objective of blocking a common economic policy by the use of the plural. Article 103 referred to 'the broad guidelines of the economic policies of the member states'; Article 105(1) to the ESCB supporting 'the general economic policies in the Community'. In this context the term 'guidelines' was less threatening.

The other stage 3 issue on which Köhler was very active was the most contentious for the Bundesbank—how the exchange-rate system and exchange-rate policy were to be managed in stage 3 (Article 109). This issue was showing its symbolic as well as practical importance by the IGC personal representatives' meeting on 12 March and the IGC ministerial-level meeting on 18 March. Köhler stressed that the principle of unanimity must apply to Council decisions on the exchange-rate system (subject also to requirements to respect price stability and to seek the consent of the ESCB). As we saw above, he achieved acceptance of the principle of unanimity at the end of the negotiations as part of a trade-off in the Franco-German bilaterals.

With regard to exchange-rate policy Köhler argued that it was better for the ESCB to be responsible. He presented the exchange-rate issue as the litmus test of the real seriousness of other governments in expressing their support for the principle of an independent central bank dedicated to price stability. On this issue Köhler was under great pressure, caught between a 'tough-as-iron' Bundesbank position and the threat of isolation in the IGC. The Bundesbank insisted on the 'cleanliness' of the treaty language, arguing from its own history that the exchange rate was the exposed flank of a central bank. Köhler demonstrated a measure of willingness to compromise: for instance, on the need for a link between the Council and the ESCB on exchange rate policy. But he continued to insist on very strict treaty conditions. This issue ran on into the 'end-game' of the IGC negotiations. At the final IGC ministerial meeting on 2–3 December Waigel achieved what he regarded as a notable victory on exchange-rate policy. 'General orientations' replaced 'guidelines' in relation to Council action in this area. More important still was the final sentence in Article 109(2): 'These general orientations shall be without prejudice to the primary objective of the ESCB to maintain price stability'. That sentence enabled Waigel to carry the agreement of Schlesinger.

In warding off these efforts, of the Commission and of the French particularly, to politicize economic and monetary policy in stage 3, Köhler achieved substantial victories that were recognized by the Bundesbank. But it is possible to identify a strategic failure here. In part because of the delegation of stage 3 issues to the Bundesbank, and in part because the initiative on stage 3 was being seized by others, the Finance Ministry did not succeed in fully developing its own agenda for stage 3. This failure was most significant in relation to fiscal discipline within stage 3. The strategic focus was on establishing fiscal discipline as a condition for entry into stage 3. This gap was later recognized and plugged by the German Stability Pact proposal of 1995.

Another gap involved the failure to press more strongly for the incorporation of indicators of flexibility in the treaty relating to economic structure. As economists Köhler and Haller were quick to appreciate that the economic logic of abandoning exchange-rate changes as a mechanism of adjustment was greater flexibility in labour markets and in wages policy. On these key points, however, they made no real progress. They assumed that this economic logic was understood by all and would require political action. But they failed to precommit other governments to act in this critical area for a viable stage 3.

The Transition to Stage 3

The issue of the transition to stage 3 was taken up early in the IGC negotiations but not pushed strongly by the Luxembourg Presidency which recognized it as too contentious and difficult to admit of quick resolution. Here is another issue in which, to an extent, Köhler can be accused of strategic failure.

The first main discussion of the transition to stage 3 took place in the IGC personal representatives' meeting on 23 April. But already the difference of views had been mapped out. At the 2 April meeting Trichet talked of 'irreversibility' for stage 3; whilst earlier still, at the Franco-German Economic Council on 5 March, Bérégovoy had spoken of 1 January 1996 or 1997 for the transition to stage 3. At the 8 April IGC ministerial-level meeting Köhler stressed that 'stage 3 requires a Community of stability'. This *Stabilitätsgemeinschaft* had to be realized in stage 1 (because stage 2 would be so short). The IGC meeting on the 23 April suggested progress in the direction sought by Köhler. In particular, there was consensus that a high degree of convergence was necessary for stage 3; and some agreement with the conditions for stage 3 spelt out in the German Draft Treaty (price stability, budget deficit reduction, and alignment of interest rates—though with more questioning of the latter condition). These three conditions were taken up in the Luxembourg Presidency 'non-paper' of 12 June, which otherwise confined itself to stating that the European Council, after receiving reports, should set a date for stage 3.

Köhler's basic position was clear. Convergence was the key to stage 3. Dates for review of progress and examination of likely qualifiers for stage 3 might be useful in creating a pressure to put measures for convergence in place and sustain them. But a fixed, final date for stage 3 was another matter. Given this position, Köhler was happy with the Dutch draft article of August on the transition to stage 3, with its provision for an 'opt-in' for all. As we shall see, he was less content with the Bérégovoy plan presented at the final IGC ministerial level meeting on 2 December (on which a German reservation was entered). Köhler's preference was for the maintenance of discretion for member states to decide whether they wished to 'opt in' and for a minimum number of states qualifying before agreeing to proceed with stage 3. Hence the 'end-game' at Maastricht on final dates was not wanted or sought by Köhler or by Waigel.

The IGC personal representatives' meeting on 23 April was important in producing broad agreement on the principles that should govern the transition to stage 3: no compulsion, no veto, no arbitrary exclusion. These principles were endored at the informal ECOFIN on 11 May and then at the Luxembourg Council. Köhler's main contribution was not so much to the elaboration of these principles, with which he was happy, as to putting in place guarantees that responsible decisions would be taken about stage 3. At the IGC personal representatives' meeting on 4 June he argued that, in taking decisions on the transition to stage 3, the European Council should be assisted by the ministers of finance. This provision was eventually incorporated in Article 109j(2).

In so far as Köhler committed a strategic error, it lay in his failure to get the three principles agreed in May–June to be delegated to the EC Monetary Committee.[4] This shift of institutional venue would have taken the issue out of the political limelight, enabled finance ministry and central bank officials to give

---

[4] Köhler admits this error in Köhler and Kees (1996: 161–2).

more precision to the principles, and permitted a more technical assessment of the long-term effects of alternative ways of giving these principles practical expression. In that way, the European Council might have been offered a *fait accompli* on the transition to stage 3. In practice the outcome at Maastricht was to prove an unpleasant *fait accompli* for Köhler.

Principles of Economic Policy

As we saw earlier, the principles underpinning an economic union were regarded by the Germans as a fundamental issue. Köhler singled out for attack the reformulation of Article 2 in the EC Commission's Draft Treaty at the first meeting of the IGC personal representatives on 15 January. It failed to mention either price stability (let alone prioritize it) or convergence. Whilst German negotiators would have preferred a narrower formulation of the objectives of the EC, they were successful in incorporating German priorities. In the final Treaty formulation of Article 2 references were inserted to 'sustainable and non-inflationary growth' and to 'a high degree of convergence of economic performance'. On this issue Köhler had the support of Wicks and Maas.

More problematic was the attempt to incorporate the positions on the goals of economic policy in Article 102 outlined in the German Draft Treaty. The goals of privatization, no wage indexation, and no state control of prices were opposed within the IGC on two grounds: as contrary to the principle of subsidiarity on which German negotiators themselves insisted; and on the argument that the EC must acknowledge that there was room for a variety of models of economic success. On the principle of subsidiarity the Bundesbank had taken a strong stand, reflecting its concern that EC responsibility for economic policy could prove a Trojan horse for governments to gain influence over monetary policy. This principle could then be used by other negotiators to impede Köhler in pressing German demands on the content of economic policy. More surprising still was the way in which Köhler's demand that freedom of collective bargaining should be anchored in the Treaty was countered. Other negotiators pointed to Germany's high labour costs as evidence that the German model was in decline. This proposal made no headway in the IGC.

Despite these reverses, Waigel and Köhler kept trying to reopen the issue of flexibility. For instance, at the informal ECOFIN at Apeldoorn on 21–2 September Waigel made common cause with Lamont on the need for greater supply-side flexibility. The main success of Köhler was in inserting in Treaty Articles 3*a*, 102*a* (economic policy), and 105 (monetary policy) reference to the principle of 'an open market economy with free competition'. But, as we saw above, there was a failure to develop indicators of labour-market and wage flexibility for the Treaty.

Schlecht, Molitor, and Zeppernick in the Federal Economics Ministry were disappointed that the principles to underpin economic union outlined in the German Draft Treaty were not more influential within the negotiations. In a series of papers the Economics Ministry had been arguing that the loss of the exchange rate as an instrument of economic adjustment would make other instruments, notably labour-market and wage adjustment, more significant. But the new Economics Minister Jürgen Möllemann did not prove effective in giving a strong political profile to this argument in Bonn; and Köhler, faced with widespread opposition, did not press it as strongly in the IGC as Economics Ministry officials would have liked.

In the face of this situation Economics Ministry officials began to reflect on whether the regulative approach to economic policy contained in the German Draft Treaty was sustainable and what might replace it. This reflection led the Economics Ministry to become converted to the principle of competition of economic policies amongst member states. According to this principle, the markets would reward those states with higher non-inflationary output growth and employment. Those states penalized by the markets would adapt their economic policies till, eventually, common economic policies would emerge from a process of market-led co-ordination. The assumption on which this revised approach to making an economic union was based was that, with a monetary union in place, EC politicians were capable of learning what was required to live with an open market.

One source of strategic problems for Köhler was the recourse of other member states to the IGC on political union as a venue for a more sympathetic hearing on economic-policy issues. The main examples were provided by social and economic cohesion and by industrial policy. Alongside the details of the transition to stage 3, the relationship between EMU and social and economic cohesion was an issue area in which the EC Monetary Committee failed to seize and retain the initiative. From Köhler's point of view, it would have offered the opportunity to establish principles to constrain the proliferation of transfer payments. Instead, social and economic cohesion was initially raised and pressed within the IGC on political union. Köhler took up a strong position and pressed Trumpf, the German personal representative in the IGC on political union, to be firm. When social and economic cohesion came up at the IGC on EMU personal representatives' meeting on 4 June, Köhler argued that EMU was not to the disadvantage of 'less-developed' states. He gained support from Belgium, Britain, Denmark, and the Netherlands. The issue came to a head following the intervention of the Spanish Finance Minister at the IGC ministerial-level meeting on 7 October. Frustrated by slow progress on the issue, he demanded that social and economic cohesion be given priority in the next IGC ministerial meeting in November. At the IGC personal representatives' meeting on 4–5 November Köhler tried to kick the issue into touch by proposing that social and economic cohesion was more appropriately taken up in the negotiations about the Community's own resources and the Structural Funds scheduled for 1992. In representing Waigel at the IGC ministerial level on 11–12 November, Köhler gave added force to this argument. He pointed out that, if EMU led to a vast process of resource redistribution, there would be serious domestic problems of gaining acceptance for EMU in Germany. At the final IGC ministerial level on 2 December Köhler reiterated this danger and spoke of the danger that a new 'convergence fund', as proposed by Spain, would dilute the force and credibility of the convergence criteria. On this issue Köhler received strong support from the British, French, and Luxembourg ministers. The Spanish final reserve on this issue led to its resolution at Maastricht—the creation of the Cohesion Fund (Article 130d) as essentially a symbolic side-payment for the Spanish, Portuguese, Greeks, and Irish.

A second example of the difficulty that Köhler could have in controlling the content of negotiations came over the issue of industrial policy. Here the pace was set by the French government, which pressed this issue in the IGC on political union where the Foreign Ministry was leading. To add to the difficulties, industrial policy was the responsibility of the Economics Ministry. There was a succession of memos from the Finance Ministry to the Economics Ministry on the need to take a tough line on this issue. But the Economics Minister, Möllemann, was seen as not pulling his weight. For these reasons Köhler did not get a grip on the issue of industrial policy. There was consolation. Article 130 (industry) referred to action 'in accordance with a system of open and competitive markets' (a key Economics Ministry concern); and, at Maastricht, the French demand for qualified majority voting for specific measures of industrial policy was rejected. But the Finance Ministry remained concerned that an infrastructure for intervention was being created.

The two issues of social and economic cohesion and of industrial policy became matters of domestic controversy during the IGC 'end-game' of October–December. Köhler and Lautenschlager clashed over them in the ministerial 'mini-cabinet' charged with co-ordinating German positions at Maastricht. For Köhler industrial policy and social and economic cohesion were substantively important; they had to be subordinated to the ordo-liberal principles of economic policy and not to undermine the discipline of convergence. They were also symbolic of his success in controlling the terms of the negotiations so that a viable and sustainable EMU designed around German principles was guaranteed.

Convergence, Excessive Deficits, and Stage 3

For Köhler convergence, in the form of legally binding rules and tough sanctions to enforce them, was the key to a viable and sustainable EMU. With respect to convergence, his strategy of gaining agreement on German terms was relatively successful. As we saw earlier, this was helped by delegating this issue to the technical world of the EC Monetary Committee. Here, outside the more political realm of the IGC, the main substantive negotiations took place on the excessive-deficit procedure and on the convergence criteria for entry into stage 3. By means of locating as much as possible of the convergence negotiations in this institutional venue Tietmeyer was 'bound in'—though not perfectly.

The German negotiating position was to have clear, quantitatively defined reference values for convergence written into the Treaty. They would be modifiable only by unanimity, and their breach would automatically constitute infringement of the ban on excessive deficits. These criteria were not to be incorporated in secondary legislation, subject to change by qualified majority, and not to be treated as just prima-facie evidence of infringement. Three main objectives underpinned this tough negotiating position:

- to create urgent, sustained pressure on member states to adjust economic policies to the support of stability;
- to use clear rules to introduce as much certainty and predictability as possible into decisions about who qualifies for stage 3;
- to reassure a sceptical public opinion at home that the single currency would be at least as strong as the D-Mark.

A further objective was in the minds of German negotiators but less clearly expressed: to create a mechanism for distinguishing between the 'sheep' and the 'goats'—in other words, a 'multi-speed' EMU. Köhler spelt out the basic German position at the IGC ministerial-level meeting on 25 November. Here he sharply attacked Lamont for opposing the application of the excessive-deficit procedure in stage 2. Köhler emphasized that budget discipline was a precondition for a 'Community of stability' which must be put in place before the transition to stage 3. Köhler had come to see Lamont as lax and unreliable as an ally.

The first major discussion on convergence in the IGC took place at the ministerial-level meeting on 8 April. Here Köhler was able to make substantial progress. He began by repeating the argument that 'real' and 'monetary' convergence conditions must have priority over a date for stage 2. On this point he gained the support of the British, Danes, and Dutch but again, predictably, found himself pitted against the French. More reassuringly, there was widespread agreement on the need for multi-annual convergence programmes in stage 2, with the objective of securing progress on price stability and sound public finances. But the real breakthrough came in relation to stage 1. Taking up an idea from the Luxembourg Presidency, Köhler pressed on the EC Commission the urgent requirement to introduce convergence programmes in stage 1 because, he argued, stage 2 would be short. Again representing Waigel, at the IGC ministerial level on 10 June, Köhler stirred controversy by referring to the need for 'crash programmes, not cash programmes'. Then, at the informal ECOFIN in Apeldoorn in September, Waigel announced that Germany would submit a convergence programme based on its medium-term financial planning. This announcement was designed to underline German commitment to this process and to encourage others to prioritize it.

In the EC Monetary Committee the Germans were the toughest of the tough on the convergence criteria for stage 3. Here Tietmeyer pressed, in vain, two main points: that there should be an absolute criterion for inflation (rather than as measured in terms of the three best-performing states); and that the deficit criterion should be under 3 per cent (1.5 per cent), with no exceptions. His other major demand was that member states must demonstrate that convergence was 'sustainable'. The EC Monetary Committee report of 5 June, which was considered at its meeting of 17 June, summed up discussion as 'near consensus' on a 60 per cent public debt–GDP ratio and on a 3–4 per cent budget debt–GDP ratio. The risk of dilution emerged once the issue of convergence criteria reached the level of the informal ECOFIN at Apeldoorn on 21–2 September. There the 60 per cent debt–GDP ratio found broad acceptance. But in discussion the idea of a 'judgemental' aspect in assessing progress towards this ratio gained ground.

When the final report on convergence criteria from the chair of the EC Monetary Committee to the IGC ministerial level was made on 7 October, its broad thrust was acceptable to Köhler. The report spoke of 'near consensus' on the 60 per cent debt–GDP ratio; majority support for a 3 per cent deficit–GDP ratio; and agreement that they were not to be incorporated in secondary legislation. Reference was also made to the principle of the 'golden rule' and to the need for effective sanctions in order to give 'proper seriousness' to economic-policy co-operation. Köhler's energies were dedicated to preventing dilution of the debt criterion. In the hope that he could ward off this danger, at the IGC personal representatives' meeting on 4–5 November he accepted the demotion of the 'golden rule' to the status of an auxiliary criterion. It soon disappeared from the treaty text. The informal ECOFIN at Apeldoorn in September had demonstrated the strength of the lobby for a 'judgemental' element. By means of the Bundesbank council statement of 7 November Tietmeyer tried to strengthen Köhler's will to resist any softening of the criteria. At the next IGC meeting on 13 November Köhler delivered by actively opposing a 'judgemental' element as a dilution of the Monetary Committee text. But, in the interests of securing agreement before Maastricht, and preventing further softening by putting the criteria in the hands of the heads of state and government, Köhler was forced to concede ground. In Article 104c exceptions to the strict application of the debt and deficit criteria were incorporated in the final Treaty. These exceptions with respect to compliance with budgetary discipline, plus the failure to gain acceptance for an absolute criterion for inflation in the EC Monetary Committee, were seen by Tietmeyer as serious flaws in the final agreement. Köhler had not, in his view, done enough to ensure that convergence was 'sustainable'.

The Transition to, and Content of, Stage 2

At the outset of the IGC negotiations the transition to, and content of, stage 2 were the two decisive, interrelated issues for Waigel and Köhler. Their initial position was to get tough on the date and the entry conditions for stage 2. In that way they could best guard against the danger that, at the end of the negotiations, stage 2 might have some substantial content, as the French and Italians and the

Commission wanted. Waigel and Köhler were agreed that stage 2 must be short and clear, with no 'grey zone' in the form of an ECB with monetary-policy responsibilities. At the Franco-German Economic Council on 5 March, at the first Franco-German bilateral on 4–5 April, and then at the IGC ministerial-level meeting on 8 April Köhler pressed for tough entry conditions for stage 2.

The 8 April IGC was the first real signal that a change of negotiating position might be possible. It began to emerge that the content of stage 2 was likely to be not so great a problem. Two aspects of the discussion there played a role. First, there was a clear consensus that in stage 2 monetary policy was to remain the responsibility of the member states. Secondly, there was support for Köhler's demand that immediate action was needed by member states in stage 1 to make substantial and urgent progress on convergence. In making this demand Köhler was not primarily motivated by an intention of making 1 January 1994 an acceptable date for stage 2. His concern was to find a means of making rapid progress on convergence in the face of the insistence of member states on the principle of subsidiarity in economic policy. Member states were to adopt convergence programmes as a matter of their own responsibility. Notably, Köhler was still pressing for the priority of tough entry conditions over automaticity for stage 2.

But, once—at this relatively early stage—it became clear that convergence programmes were to begin in stage 1, and that the principle of the indivisibility of monetary policy was generally accepted, Waigel and Köhler could be more relaxed about the date for stage 2. With a weak stage 2 and an instrument to promote convergence in place for stage 1, it was possible for them to envisage that all could qualify for stage 2. By the time that 1 January 1994 was confirmed at the Luxembourg Council in June they had no serious problem with this issue. When the date for stage 2 was raised at the IGC ministerial-level meeting on 9 September, only the British maintained their general reservation about 1 January 1994. On the other hand, there was still much negotiation to be done to clean out stage 2. Two main issues needed resolution: the 'new institution' in stage 2; and the 'hardening' of the ECU.

The issue of the new institution and its powers was handled within the IGC. At the 8 April IGC meeting the general view was that the German Draft Treaty proposal for a 'Council' of EC Central Bank Governors was incompatible with Rome 1. Improved co-ordination was not enough for stage 2. By the time of the informal ECOFIN in Apeldoorn there was a clear emerging consensus around the Belgian idea of a European Monetary Institute. But Waigel and Köhler accepted this with reluctance. It was not by name a bank. But important and difficult issues remained about the EMI's status and responsibilities. At the IGC ministerial meeting on 11–12 November, mindful of the requirements spelt out in the Bundesbank council statement on EMU of 7 November, Köhler rejected the proposals for an externally appointed President and Vice-President and for the EMI to be given its own capital. They gave too 'supranational' a character to the stage 2 institution. His strongest words were reserved for Bérégovoy's proposal that, voluntarily, member state central banks could delegate the holding and management of their currency reserves to the EMI. Despite continuing German and British reservations on the latter proposal, it was clear at the 11–12 November IGC meeting that Germany was under great pressure to concede on these issues.

The issue of 'hardening' the ECU in stage 2 was initially dealt with in the EC Monetary Committee before going to the IGC. Köhler and Tietmeyer welcomed the idea of 'hardening' the ECU. They were attracted to the Spanish proposal to harden the ECU as a 'basket currency', though Tietmeyer was firm in rejecting the British 'hard' ECU as a parallel currency which offended against the principle of the indivisibility of monetary policy in stage 2. But their support did not extend to the Spanish and British ideas of a new stage 2 institution to manage this currency. At the IGC ministerial-level meeting on 11–12 November the Dutch Presidency proposed a 'freezing' rather than 'hardening' of the ECU in stage 2. Köhler finally declared that he was prepared to accept the Dutch proposal provided that the EMI was not charged with 'promoting' the ECU. In the protocol on the statute of the EMI its task was restricted to 'facilitate the use of the ECU and oversee its development'. Hence Köhler traded a 'hardening' of the ECU for a delimitation of the EMI's role with respect to the ECU.

The Bundesbank and the IGC

During the IGC the relations between the Bundesbank and the federal government were clouded by the aftermath of German unification. The distrust engendered by the way in which German monetary union was handled poisoned the atmosphere in EMU negotiations. As we saw earlier, this poisoning was most apparent within the Bundesbank council and found expression in its 'tougher-than-tough' statement of 6 September 1990 on EMU.

Once the IGC on EMU had got under way, the relationship between Pöhl and Kohl deteriorated sharply. The relationship was stretched to its limits by incautious remarks made by Pöhl at an appearance before the European Parliament's economic committee session on EMU in Brussels on 19 March. Pöhl attributed the 'disaster' in East Germany to an ill-prepared monetary union. His intention was to underline the risks attendant on EMU. But his choice of words was seen as sensational within the media and produced a public reprimand from the Chancellor who felt that he was being undermined. The effect was to underline to Pöhl his dangerously exposed position. Worn down by the burdens of mediating between the Bundesbank council and the federal government over German monetary union and EMU, he resigned on 16 May.

The effect on Kohl was to increase his preference for a Bundesbank President who was a 'known quantity' to him and, in his view, was possessed of the qualities of reliability and loyalty. The long-serving Schlesinger was appointed as President from July also with other objectives in mind: to 'bind into' the negotiations the individual credited as being the sharpest critic of EMU; to make fuller use of his personal authority within the directorate and council to effectively sell an EMU agreement; and to provide German negotiators with an alibi for being tough on EMU in the form of a 'stability-policy' guru as Bundesbank President.

Before his resignation Pöhl had already articulated thinking within the Bundesbank directorate on an issue that Finance Ministry officials regarded as too politically sensitive. In March he distanced himself from the three-stage approach of the Delors Report by advocating a flexible model of a 'multi-speed' EMU. Pöhl identified Germany, France, the Netherlands, Belgium, and Luxembourg as the states that could establish straight away a joint ECB and a single monetary policy. This proposal was built on an idea that Pöhl had floated to Bérégovoy as early as the Franco-German Economic Council in August 1989. But it created problems for the Finance Ministry: in part because of the avoidable damage to the sensitivities of states like Italy and Spain; and in part because the idea of a 'fast track' to EMU was regarded as heretical. Though Finance Ministry officials saw a 'multi-speed' EMU as the inexorable consequence of tough convergence criteria, they were committed to the idea that all states should be given an equal chance to prepare for stage 3. On the 'fast track' Pöhl was expressing a personal and not corporate Bundesbank position.

As the responsible Bundesbank director, Tietmeyer was concerned to ensure that the Bundesbank council was 'bound in' during the course of the negotiations. At the same time he sought to locate the responsibility for the negotiations with the Finance Ministry. In both these ways he protected his career interest as the potential Bundesbank President after Schlesinger. There was in any case a degree of intellectual unity on EMU between Tietmeyer and the majority of the Bundesbank council. This unity was provided by adherence to the coronation theory of EMU. Strategically, Tietmeyer recognized the need to adapt to new political and economic realities. But, intellectually, he retained doubts about the adequacy of the Finance Ministry's revised conception of EMU under Köhler and Haller. Within the Bundesbank, at a greater distance from Bonn, he could afford to indulge those doubts.

Tietmeyer made skilful use of the Bundesbank council to put pressure on Köhler to deliver on key points in the IGC. In this respect, as the 'end-game' approached, the Bundesbank council statement of 7 November was important. Köhler's record in meeting the requirements on the responsibilities of the EMI spelt out in that statement was mixed, with the balance on the plus side. He failed to deliver for the Bundesbank on two issues: the EMI was to have its own capital; and its president was to be externally appointed. On another issue Köhler delivered in good part: there was no requirement for a general transfer of reserves so that the EMI could intervene in currency markets. On the plus side, Köhler had three successes: the EMI was not to 'promote' the basket ECU; it was not to undertake other banking activities; and all decisions of major importance in the council of the EMI were to be unanimous. Tietmeyer's concerns about the way in which the IGC was negotiating the convergence criteria after the informal ECOFIN at Apeldoorn surfaced in the requirement in the Bundesbank statement of 7 November that the criteria should be defined 'in more detail' and were 'in no circumstances' to be softened. Here Köhler was judged notably not to have delivered. But during the final IGC Köhler did deliver on two key issues in the the Bundesbank statement: exchange-rate policy; and a clear institutional divide between 'ins' and 'outs' within the structure of the ECB.

In so far as there was a divide inside the Bundesbank, it was between members of the international division like Rieke and Schlüter and the exponents of the coronation theory. Rieke and Schlüter were loyal Bundesbank officials who were careful to keep Tietmeyer carefully informed, and Tietmeyer endeavoured to keep them on a tight rein. But communication was far from perfect. One reason was a difference of position, focus, and interest. Tietmeyer was concerned first and foremost to keep the Bundesbank council on board. Rieke and Schlüter found themselves more directly caught up in the accelerating dynamics of the IGC negotiations and sympathetic to the mounting pressures under which Köhler was negotiating as the 'end-game' approached. For this reason they were less purist about tough convergence criteria.

Also, there was a difference of intellectual position. Tietmeyer was still disposed to frame EMU issues in terms of coronation theory. Rieke and Schlüter were well aware of the clear rejection of a timetable for EMU in the September 1990 Bundesbank council statement on EMU. However, unlike Tietmeyer, Rieke and others in the Bundesbank were not averse to a timetable. In Rieke's view, a date for stage 3 had virtues. A timetable would create sustained pressure on the French and others to shift towards the German model. This would, most importantly, avoid the danger of a long, open-ended stage 2, which would give continuing opportunities to the French and others to remake EMU in their own image. Hence, as much for strategic as cognitive reasons, Rieke favoured a date for stage 3. He was, in consequence, less alert to this issue during the final 'end-game' in the IGC and at Maastricht than Tietmeyer would have liked him to be. Tietmeyer continued to understand that the proposals for a timetable for stage 3 involved no more than a review of progress every two years.

In practice, however restrictively Tietmeyer defined his role in the IGC negotiations on EMU (as an external expert adviser), he was intimately involved: both courtesy of Köhler's regular, detailed consultation and by means of the secret Franco-German bilaterals. The situation was different with respect to the IGC on political union. Here the Bundesbank had no right to claim that it could act as an expert adviser. It could not, and did not, expect to be involved. On the other hand, the Bundesbank council statement on EMU of September 1990 had firmly underlined the traditional coronation-theory requirement that EMU's durability depended on a 'far-reaching' and 'comprehensive' political union. With reference to this demand the Bundesbank was no more than a distant spectator. Those involved with the political-union negotiations in the Federal Chancellor's Office and in the Foreign Ministry did not, in any case, subscribe to the coronation theory of EMU. Even the officials dealing with the IGC on EMU—Köhler, Haller, Grosche, and Rieke—were more concerned to ensure that EMU was a free-standing, self-sufficient project. In short, there was a substantial cognitive gap on the relationship between EMU and political union between Tietmeyer and the IGC negotiators. To this factor was added the failure of the Bundesbank to make precise its own view on what were the minimum requirements for political union to make EMU viable. In a speech in Rotterdam on 11 November Schlesinger spoke of the need for an accompanying political commitment to iron out economic and fiscal discrepancies within the monetary union. But he was short on detailed prescriptions.

Indeed, a case can be made out for accusing the Bundesbank of strategic failure with respect to political union. If it believed that certain minimum requirements for political union had to be in place for EMU to be viable, the appropriate strategy would have been to get the EC Monetary Committee to identify these requirements and spell out in technical terms the effects of their absence. Köhler was not keen on such a move because he did not want to pursue a collision course with his Chancellor. It remains, nevertheless, a striking omission that the EC Monetary Committee did not consider this central issue when examining the viability of EMU. Alternatively, the Bundesbank could have tried to spell out on its own the minimum 'technical' requirements on the political-union side. It conspicuously failed to do so. In doing so the Bundesbank would have opened itself to the accusation of interfering in the responsibilities of the Federal Chancellery and of the Foreign Ministry. The Bundesbank was faced with a dilemma: either do the intellectually honest thing and spell out the minimum requirements consistent with coronation theory or avoid political exposure to protect itself. Bruised by the humiliations of German monetary union and of the 19 March fiasco, it opted for the latter approach. As a technocratically minded President, less comfortable with the political world than his predecessor, Schlesinger was not inclined to support a 'high-profile' approach on political union before Maastricht. So, by default, the Bundesbank's position on political union was interpreted externally as requiring tough fiscal discipline mechanisms. Such a requirement was shared by the Finance Ministry and seen as adequate by many Bundesbank officials. But it remained unclear whether, and in what ways, Schlesinger, Tietmeyer, and the Bundesbank council were looking for much more.

The EMU 'End-Game': Saving the Treaty

The 'end-game' was characterized by the search by German negotiators to put in place a strategy to save the Treaty after what was perceived in Bonn as errors and confusion in the Dutch Presidency. This phase involved a shift in the negotiating climate in Bonn, notably a sense of mounting urgency and of the high stakes involved for Germany. It meant that the high degree of self-containment that Köhler had been able to achieve as a negotiator was more difficult to sustain. The domestic co-ordination and briefing mechanism took on a more political character. There was a higher-profile role for the Chancellor; for a new intensive bilateral diplomacy by him and his most trusted officials; and for the ministerial 'mini-cabinet' charged with co-ordinating strategy and tactics for the Maastricht Council and with briefing the Chancellor in detail. With the Maastricht Council looming, the Federal Chancellor's Office and the Foreign Ministry took on an added importance in preparing strategy and tactics. Not least, the Chancellor was engaged in mobilizing and securing domestic political support and preparing the ground for German concessions.

The Dutch Presidency

The 'end-game' began in September. Its first trigger was the Dutch Presidency's issue paper of August on the transition to stage 3. This paper caused a storm and led both Delors and the French to draw Kohl's attention to the danger posed by Dutch mishandling of the negotiations. Their fire was directed at the paper's intergovernmentalist and voluntarist approach to the transition to stage 3. Essentially, the paper sought to embody the principles of no veto and no arbitrary exclusion. It provided an 'opt-out for all'; and proposed that, if a certain group of states (a 'critical mass' of six) had met the proposed conditions and taken separate individual decisions to go ahead to stage 3, they had the right to do so. The sympathy of Köhler for this approach was apparent at the IGC personal representatives' meeting on 3 September and the ministerial-level meeting on 9 September. His personal preference was for ensuring flexibility in the final treaty provisions with respect to the procedure for transition to stage 3. But Wim Kok found himself confronted with hefty resistance; partly to the 'two-speed' conception of EMU underpinning the paper; but, above all, to the intergovernmentalist approach. He withdrew the offending text in favour of the formula that the decision on stage 3 would be taken in the European Council on the basis of unanimity.

This episode, reinforced by messages from the Commission and from the Elysée, sent a very negative signal to the Federal Chancellor's Office where officials were displeased with the Dutch Draft. The Dutch Presidency was seen as failing to deliver on a fundamental requirement of an EMU agreement: irreversibility of the process. With its intergovernmentalism, the Dutch paper was transforming EMU into a 'fourth pillar' of the EU. More generally, the Dutch Presidency was criticized for failing to bring forward well-formulated texts in good time to ensure an EMU agreement at Maastricht. The Federal Chancellor's Office joined Köhler in pressing the Dutch for an early Draft Treaty on EMU. This Draft eventually appeared on 28 October and tried to mitigate German and other criticisms by proposing a declaration of intent to complete EMU and to be attached to the main Treaty. But Chancellery officials did not share Köhler's attachment to flexibility. They were keen to embed EMU firmly within the Community method, which meant using dates as a force for change. In this context Kohl signalled to Köhler the importance of 'saving the treaty' by making rapid progress in the Franco-German bilaterals. Hence at the two final Franco-German meetings in Berlin (13–14 September) and Paris (9 November) there was a strong political momentum to be prepared to make concessions.

More dramatically, on 'Black Monday', 30 September, the EC foreign ministers rejected the Dutch Draft Treaty on political union, plunging the negotiations into crisis. In principle, Genscher was sympathetic to the Dutch Presidency's rejection of the 'pillar' conception of the Luxembourg Presidency in favour of a return to the traditional Community approach. But he recognized that the new Draft Treaty was completely unacceptable to the French and that the 'federal' wording of the treaty would make it impossible for the British to sign. Hence Genscher did not come to the defence of the Dutch. His concern was to find common ground with Dumas and use the Franco-German axis to help save the Treaty. In this spirit, on 14 October, Kohl and Mitterrand launched joint proposals on European security and defence, with Bitterlich playing the key role in the Federal Chancellery.

Upgrading Franco-German Relations

The sense of error and confusion in the Dutch Presidency and fears about Maastricht prompted a high-profile role for the Chancellor and the Federal Chancellor's Office. This involvement took the form of further upgrading of the importance of Franco-German relations. The effects on the EMU negotiations were apparent in the atmosphere surrounding the three key Franco-German meetings involving Waigel and Köhler outside the IGC during November: the Franco-German Economic Council (5 November) in Bonn; the final Franco-German bilateral (9 November) in Paris; and the Franco-German summit (14–15 November) in Bonn. During the period 4–15 November Köhler and Trichet were also together at three IGC meetings and one ECOFIN. In total, they were together on EMU business for eight out of eleven days. But even more important than the intensity of the meetings was the pressure to cut down on the number of treaty issues still 'bracketed': notably on the role of the ECU, the exchange-rate system and policy, and the transition to stage 3.

Between 6 and 12 November Kohl shifted away from his stress on progress on European political union as a condition for agreement in Maastricht. He was intent on ensuring that the forthcoming Franco-German summit transmitted positive signals and contributed to narrowing down the agenda of outstanding issues for negotiation to manageable proportions. On 15 November, at the Franco-German summit, a breakfast meeting of Waigel and Bérégovoy, and their officials, with the French Prime Minister, Edith Cresson, was an occasion for the Germans to press their case on two outstanding issues: some remaining reservations about exchange-rate policy following the approximation of positions at the bilateral on 9 November; and industrial policy, which was being strongly promoted by Cresson to Kohl. Notably, at the subsequent press conference, Waigel and Bérégovoy pronounced themselves to be committed to realizing the principle of irreversibility in the treaty provisions on EMU. But, by this stage, it was not at all clear to either how this political commitment could be enshrined in the Treaty in a realistic and practical manner. Waigel continued to hope that Köhler could resolve this at a technical level; Köhler was torn between loyalty to the Chancellor and his personal reservations about the practical problems of realizing this principle.

The Ministerial 'Mini-Cabinet'

Following the Franco-German summit Kohl began to finalize his negotiating positions on EMU and on political union. This process involved a combination of top-level bilaterals (for instance, with Andreotti on 28 November and Mitterrand on 3 December) and meetings with his European ministers and key officials. There was an important interaction between the two, with Kohl using the information from bilaterals to structure debate and shape outcomes in the ministerial 'mini-cabinet' and in his other flexibly organized meetings with Waigel, Genscher, and key officials.

These 'mini-cabinets' were at the heart of Kohl's preparations for Maastricht. This approach to Maastricht fitted into the Chancellor's governing style which was to seek out agreements between responsible ministers before matters went to cabinet. So the real detailed debate about priorities, strategy, and tactics was confined to the 'mini-cabinet' level. This group brought together Kohl with Genscher, Waigel, Möllemann, and other relevant ministers, with key officials present and often active in discussion: in particular, Lautenschlager, Köhler, and Trumpf. Here the final strategy for the 'end-game' was elaborated, Kohl briefed on the details of the treaty texts, and Genscher and Waigel 'bound in'.

In relation to EMU there were gladiatorial contests within the 'mini-cabinet' between Lautenschlager and Köhler. These involved four main issues:

- how detailed the convergence criteria should be and how strictly interpreted, with Lautenschlager pushing for more recognition for a 'judgemental' element so that Germany was not seen to be working to exclude certain states from stage 3;
- social and economic cohesion, with Köhler arguing that funding cross-national networks would have undesirable budgetary implications and send out the wrong signals about the importance of domestic discipline for convergence;
- industrial policy, where—as with cohesion—Köhler stressed the threat to the principles of an ordo-liberal economic policy; and
- the institutional and procedural issues relating to the transition to stage 3, with Lautenschlager opposing the principle of unanimity in the European Council as in conflict with the principle of no veto.

It soon became clear that the most difficult issue was the transition to stage 3. There was broad agreement within the 'mini-cabinet' that stage 2 should not be too long; hence some provision on dates for review and examination was necessary. Agreement also emerged on the need to avoid a blocking minority on stage 3. But what remained open was the kind of dates to be inserted in the Treaty and the kind of majority to apply when taking the decision about transition to stage 3. Agreement on these terms was made possible by Kohl's firm commitment to the principle of 'irreversibility' of EMU, a principle that had taken stronger form in his mind by mid-November. Kohl led from the position that Germany must demonstrate at Maastricht its will to bind itself to Europe.

The gladiatorial contests waged in the ministerial 'mini-cabinet' reflected a legacy of infighting between Lautenschlager and Köhler. The main venue for that infighting had been the regular meetings of the 'European' State Secretaries. Here Köhler had been concerned to resist efforts by the Foreign Ministry to co-ordinate in a detailed way work in the two IGCs. His strategy for doing so was to put Lautenschlager under continuing pressure by being very tough, sometimes abrasive, on the issue of the relationship between EMU and political union. He cleverly contrasted the statements of Kohl and Genscher on the importance of parallel progress and linkage between these two sets of negotiations with the respective performances of the Finance and Foreign Ministries. Köhler's argument took the form of comparing the hard work being done on the details of EMU with the absence even of an agreed concept for the political-union negotiations. In a provocative manner he questioned why the Foreign Ministry was failing to make linkages to EMU to force concessions on political union. Köhler also complained in this venue about the failure of the Foreign Ministry to see off the issues of industrial policy and social and economic cohesion in the IGC on political union.

At one level, Köhler was not being serious about the linkage between the two sets of negotiations. His strategic objective as an IGC negotiator was to divert discussion from what was going on in the EMU negotiations and fend off criticisms of Finance Ministry positions. But, at another level, Köhler was being serious. He believed that the unbalanced approach of Germany to the IGC negotiations constituted a major problem. In strategic terms, Köhler had been negotiating on the basis of a theory of the self-containment of the EMU negotiations. Like Haller and Grosche, he wanted them to stand alone. But, from a mixture of residual intellectual reasons and of bureaucratic politics in Bonn, he took pleasure in trying to embarrass a Foreign Ministry that had in the past been such a difficult partner for him. The coronation theory of EMU was a useful tool to resurrect and deploy for this purpose. This kind of robust argument also prudently anticipated the reservations of the Bundesbank and protected Köhler's negotiating credit with Frankfurt.

The relationship between political union and EMU was a continuing theme between Köhler and Lautenschlager. Lautenschlager protested about the arbitrary selection of a list of high barriers on political union as putting at risk an agreement on EMU. He also pointed out the difficulties under which Germany laboured in the political union negotiations. Solutions involving 'two-speeds' and 'opt-out' clauses were less favoured than in the EMU negotiations. By the 'end-game' he could point to two German achievements in the political-union negotiations: in extending the right of co-decision of the European Parliament; and in keeping alive the notion of parallel progress in EMU and in political union by the idea of a treaty commitment to a review conference in 1996. In effect, Germany would get 'two bites of the political-union cherry' before stage 3 of EMU.

Chancellor Kohl and 'Irreversibility' of EMU

The German approach to the 'end-game' was structured by three clear commitments of the Chancellor, which put his negotiators under pressure to deliver:

- the transition to stage 3 of EMU must be made 'irreversible', or he would not sign the Treaty;
- the EMU package must stand up to the test that the single currency would be at least as stable as the D-Mark; and
- Germany would not identify a 'bottom line' in the same way for the political-union negotiations.

Kohl articulated these principles in a new, forceful, but astutely selective way on 27–8 November, just under two weeks before the Maastricht Council. In his speech to the Bundestag on Wednesday 27 November the Chancellor prepared the ground for a 'second-best' solution on political union, with the prospect of a second phase of reform to follow; and stressed his determination to ensure that a final decision on stage 3 was not deferred till 1996. That same evening he was visited by John Major, for the second time in two weeks. Here Kohl was conciliatory, picking out common ground and fostering a climate of principled support for signing an agreement. He reiterated his concern that Britain should not be isolated. But it remained unclear how Kohl's expression of willingness to help Major to avoid a special derogation for Britain could be squared with his commitment to irreversibility. That commitment was less in evidence when talking to Major.

On Thursday 28 November in Bonn, at his breakfast meeting with Lubbers, and then on the same day with Andreotti as part of the German–Italian summit, Kohl was much more forthright. With Köhler in attendance, the Chancellor stressed to Lubbers how difficult it would be to get agreement at Maastricht. The basic message was that 'Black Monday' had revealed the pitfalls ahead and that Kohl was 'risk-averse' on political union. Kohl's own position remained faithful to the Community approach to political union agreed by the Christian Democratic heads of government in 1990. But he had to recognize that the French would not move beyond intergovernmentalism in key new areas of development. Kohl's flexibility on political union—which was a disappointment to Lubbers—contrasted with his tough stand on EMU. He told Lubbers that the treaty provisions on the transition to stage 3 must be unambiguously clear and very specific. Kohl was talking about 'binding' dates, rejecting the 'opt-in' approach proposed by the Dutch in August. He stressed that, whatever happened in the political-union negotiations, there must be no watering down of the EMU treaty provisions. 'There has to be irreversibility in the treaty, or I shall not sign it.'

This unequivocal signalling from Kohl was the key to the way in which the transition to stage 3 was finally negotiated. It was signalled selectively: to Lubbers and to Wim Kok; to Andreotti; to Mitterrand, whom he visited on 3 December, and to Cresson; and to Delors. Each in his or her way responded to that signal by considering with their closest officials and advisers how irreversibility might be embodied in the treaty. Within the Federal Chancellor's Office Bitterlich and Ludewig were most active on the timetable issue. But, though Kohl's political direction was crucial, he remained ambiguous on the content of irreversibility and uninterested in its legal implications and form. He thought of irreversibility in the political and philosophical terms of the historian. Köhler and Waigel did not think that a 'final' date for stage 3 was being sought by the Chancellor. Also, the Federal Chancellor's Office signalled to the Dutch, French, and Italians and to Delors's cabinet that, for domestic reasons, the Germans could not develop substantive proposals on irreversibility. That work had to be done elsewhere—as it was, in Paris, Rome, The Hague, and Brussels. Hence, voluntarily, the Federal Chancellor's Office was delegating to other national capitals the final substantive work on treaty proposals on the transition to stage 3.

Having endorsed irreversibility at the end of the Franco-German summit Kohl and Mitterrand continued to discuss the form that this might take. After 28 November Mitterrand began to raise the issue of a final fixed date with Kohl, not least at their meeting in Paris on 3 December. It was also being taken up with Genscher. Dumas sought to establish a linkage between finding a procedure to satisfy the German interest in recognition of Croatia and Slovenia (a French concession) and a final date for stage 3 of EMU (a German concession). Kohl was reluctant on both counts. He had difficulties with the idea of a final fixed date, his political antennae sensitively attuned to future domestic electoral difficulties that might ensue; and he saw EMU as too delicate an issue to be decided on terms other than his conception of Germany's best interests. Hence Kohl did not arrive at Maastricht with his mind made up to sign up Germany for a fixed, final date for stage 3.

Mobilizing Parliamentary Support

A key part of the EMU 'end-game' was mobilizing parliamentary support for the federal government's final negotiating positions at Maastricht. The strategy of 'binding in' the federal states bore fruit in the language of the Bundesrat's declaration on the IGCs which was approved following a long debate on 8

November. This declaration spoke of the Bundesrat's strong support for EMU, for the objectives pursued by the government in the EMU negotiations, for the way in which state representatives had been integrated into the negotiations, and for the need for 'balanced' progress in the political-union negotiations. In political terms the most striking feature was the unanimous adoption of the resolution by CDU, CSU, and SPD state governments. There was no attempt to use the Bundesrat as a platform to cast doubt on the wisdom of EMU. The main reservations attached to the failure to anchor the principle of subsidiarity firmly enough in the Treaty and to the lack of progress on political union.

Again, in the Bundestag debates on 17 October, 6 November, and, most importantly, on 5 December, there was an absence of fighting spirit. Indeed, if one examines Kohl's general policy speeches to the Bundestag during 1991 a notable feature is the lack of dissent from those parts of the speech dealing with Europe. What was important from 27 November onwards was the focus on war and peace in the legitimation of European policy. The broad acceptance of this historical narrative was important in deterring opposition to EMU. In opposing EMU one was risking being branded as an old-fashioned and dangerous nationalist. Crucially, the narrative of war and peace had a strong resonance within the SPD. Hence Kohl succeeded in sharpening the rhetorical force with which German belief in EMU was articulated and further shifting the ground away from an economic cost–benefit debate about EMU. That debate focused on the principle that the single currency 'must be at least as stable as the D-Mark'. But that principle was seen as something that could be safely entrusted to German negotiators and to Bundesbank approval of the terms negotiated. It was a matter of ensuring that the final EMU agreement was based on expertise.

On 5 December the chair of the SPD parliamentary party, Hans-Ulrich Klose, argued in the Bundestag that 'the process of European unity must be irreversible'. In so doing Klose made it possible for Kohl to frame his strategy and tactics for Maastricht in cross-party support. At no time during the IGCs, or whilst they had been prepared, had the SPD federal executive seriously considered making an issue of EMU by raising doubts about its wisdom. The reasons for this lack of opposition were, in part, cognitive and, in part, strategic. The SPD leadership shared the historical narrative of Kohl and, as the traditional party of the German left, saw itself as the least nationalist of German parties. To associate itself with EMU as a nationalist issue would do damage to its sense of identity and basic political credibility. Strategically, its reading of German electoral history was that opposition to the foreign and European policy of the incumbent government was dangerous. It had cost the SPD dearly in the 1950s over European policy and the CDU/CSU dearly in the 1970s over Eastern policy. Hence the SPD rallied to the support of the government. There was just one notable point of hesitation on 5 December. Despite general endorsement of the principle of irreversibility, the political parties also agreed that it would be necessary for the Bundestag to discuss the issues of EMU again prior to the commencement of stage 3.

Finishing the IGC on EMU: From Scheveningen to Brussels

The 'end-game' within the IGC involved Köhler and Waigel in a marathon session of meetings between Saturday 30 November and Tuesday 3 December. Following a preparatory meeting of the IGC personal representatives on 30 November, Waigel arrived for the informal ECOFIN in Scheveningen on 1 December and the subsequent IGC ministerial meeting in Brussels on 2–3 December. But Köhler remained an active player beside him.

The Finance Ministry was negotiating in a context of positions agreed within the ministerial 'sub-cabinet': in particular, to make the transition to stage 3 irreversible; and to ensure that the German model of economic stability was safeguarded. It also had its own agenda: most importantly, to ensure that a draft treaty was finalized in detail so that the heads of state and government meeting on 9–10 December would be presented with a *fait accompli*. Waigel was deeply concerned by the prospect that finance ministers would prove to be marginal figures at the Maastricht Council and keen to tie Kohl's hands so that concessions on EMU could not be made at the expense of softening the convergence criteria. He too saw potential domestic political difficulties. This strategic objective imposed a constraint on Waigel and Köhler in Scheveningen and Brussels. They had to operate on the basis of the principle—'better concessions made by us here than leaving Kohl to make concessions in Maastricht'. The Finance Ministry approached this final negotiating round in an ambivalent mood: pleased that so many key German bargaining positions had been satisfied; but anxious that embarrassing and politically costly last-minute concessions might have to be made.

After over three days of detailed and exhausting negotiations the final Draft Treaty had only one German reservation attached to it, compared to seven British and two French reservations. Fundamentally, Waigel and Köhler were satisfied with the final Draft. There was no reference to social and economic cohesion in the Draft Treaty: only majority support for a political declaration attached to the main Treaty. The reference to 'social protection' was removed from Article 2. Unanimity was retained as the basis of Council decision-making in the case of the financial-support mechanism when dealing with 'other exceptional circumstances' (i.e. not catastrophes). Less satisfying were the provisions for a 'dynamic' element in examining compliance with budgetary discipline (Article 104c(2)).

The main German victory in this final stage was over the exchange-rate system and exchange-rate policy. At Rieke's prompting Waigel telephoned Schlesinger at home from the German delegation office in Brussels before this issue came up in the final meeting. In the conversation they confirmed that the formulation 'guidelines' was unacceptable but that they could both live with 'general orientations'. After this proposal was accepted in the IGC, Waigel instructed Rieke to give Schlesinger the good news immediately. Rieke's proposal that Waigel should call Schlesinger was motivated by his fear that, if this issue was not resolved straightaway, it would be decided at Maastricht by the heads of state and government. In that case Kohl might well concede on 'guidelines'. It was imperative that Waigel should agree only to something that Schlesinger would be able to live with and be willing and able to defend in the Bundesbank council. By bringing together Waigel and Schlesinger on the final text on exchange rates Rieke was encouraging Waigel to find a solution to a problem that was more vital for the Bundesbank than for the Finance Ministry. The Finance Ministry was attracted by the prospect of being in a stronger position when dealing with exchange-rate issues, for instance in the G7, without the Bundesbank breathing down its neck. Hence on this issue Rieke played a key role in securing a text amenable to the Bundesbank.

The German reservation was confined to the procedure for the transition to stage 3. Here Waigel and Köhler were taken by surprise. At the informal ECOFIN in Scheveningen a clear majority supported the principle of irreversibility, including Waigel and Köhler, who endorsed a draft protocol on irreversibility attached to the Treaty. The general 'opt-out-for-all' clause in the Dutch Draft Treaty was deleted (which, privately, disappointed them); and it was agreed that the 'no compulsion' principle was to be satisfied by a separate British 'opt-out' protocol. Then, next day, in the final stage of the discussions, Bérégovoy produced a plan designed to make stage 3 irreversible and embody the principle of no veto. This plan specified two procedures for fixing a final date for stage 3: the first, in 1996, required unanimity in Council on whether to go forward and on setting the final date (and also that a majority meet the criteria); and the second, in 1998, required only a simple majority to decide on who had met the conditions and to fix the final date (with no critical mass required to qualify and no question of deciding whether it was appropriate to go forward).

The Bérégovoy plan caught Waigel and Köhler off guard. By this late stage in the proceedings Köhler, like others, was too exhausted to focus on discussion of the plan. In consequence, and also as a result of Wim Kok's refusal from the chair to return to issues that Köhler wanted to raise, the German objections were not fully clarified—and a row ensued between Köhler and Kok. Köhler was in a difficult position because he was simply unsure whether the Bérégovoy plan met the aspirations of the Chancellor. Hence he was keen to enter a reservation. What was clearer to Köhler was the difficulties that it posed for the Finance Ministry. The Finance Ministry's main interest was that the treaty provision on the transition to stage 3 should allow a very small number to move ahead reasonably quickly. Hence Köhler objected to the procedure for 1996 on two grounds: that he preferred a qualified majority in Council so that a small group of states could not veto progress; and that the requirement that a majority qualify could again serve to halt the progress of the few. More broadly, there was concern in the German delegation about unclear wording in the text.

In the immediate aftermath of the German reservation, in the early hours of 3 December, Bérégovoy lobbied Waigel briefly in private. Waigel, who was accompanied only by Rieke, was sounded out for the first time on the idea of a final date (which had not been included in the French plan), with 1999 being mentioned. But the idea did not properly register in Waigel's mind, and he did not brief his officials and consider with them how they might pre-empt such a last-minute initiative. By next day Köhler was in touch with Maas to spell out his reservations and stress the need for urgent work to be done to clarify and to agree the text on transition to stage 3 before the heads of state and government convened on Monday 9 December. By Thursday 5 December, following further intensive discussions with the Germans, Wim Kok had produced a more precisely worded text for discussion at a special meeting of the IGC on the evening of Sunday 8 December in Maastricht. This text was not, however, destined to be the last word.

Making EMU Irreversible: The Maastricht Council

As far as German interests in the EMU 'end-game' in Maastricht were concerned, the only open issue was the transition to stage 3. In Bonn the ministerial 'mini-cabinet' had agreed just two negotiating instructions for Kohl in relation to EMU:

- to fight off any attempt to reopen issues already decided in the IGC;
- to achieve irreversibility in the transition to stage 3.

In effect, this negotiating mandate fused together the interests of the Finance Ministry (in keeping intact the agreement that it had negotiated) and of the Federal Chancellor's Office and the Foreign Ministry (in securing irreversibility).

Despite the attempt by Bérégovoy to raise the issue of a final date with Waigel, both Waigel and Köhler were surprised by the content of the Italian text on the transition to stage 3 tabled at Maastricht. They had not expected a final date. The actual changes in the Italian text were minor, but nevertheless very important. Crucially, the route that the text took shaped the outcome. Andreotti brought the text on 8 December; agreed it over dinner with Mitterrand; both then cleared it with Kohl; and the text was presented on 9 December to the European Council, before being forwarded to the finance ministers for detailed scrutiny. There were two main textual changes (Article 109j(3 and 4)). In 1996 the procedure was to involve a qualified majority vote, not unanimity: something that was acceptable to the Finance Ministry. But the key sentence for the Germans was that: 'If by the end of 1997 the date for the beginning of the third stage has not been set, the third stage shall start on 1 January 1999'. In other words, a final date was inserted.

Neither Waigel nor Köhler were happy with this outcome. Their preference was for a clear procedure for the transition to stage 3 that would have required the Council to review and examine progress on regular basis but that would have allowed flexibility about precisely when to proceed. In this respect the Dutch Draft Treaty was satisfactory. But the sequence of Bérégovoy plan, Dutch clarification, and Italian amendment between 2 and 9 December had a different preoccupation behind it—a more single-minded dedication to the principle of irreversibility that had the hallmarks of the French and the EC Commission. They knew that Kohl was bound up with this process; that Kohl wanted and welcomed a timetable for EMU; but that he had difficulties with the idea of a final date. Waigel was persuaded to go along with the Italian text on the basis that it had the merit of more fully securing irreversibility, whilst holding on to the requirement that 'member states fulfil the necessary conditions for the adoption of a single currency'. At least it secured a substantial time span in which economic convergence could take place. And, in the context of the performance of EC economies in 1990–1, there was no reason for serious reservations about their capacity to achieve the necessary convergence.

Kohl did not go to Maastricht determined to sign up for a final date for stage 3. What impelled him to agree to such a date was the objective of demonstrating German commitment to irreversibility and his determination to show that no other EC state exceeded Germany in this commitment. Underpinning this determination was Kohl's deeply felt personal belief in an historical narrative about Germany and Europe that gave deep significance to the treaty being negotiated at Maastricht. That narrative was not just unchallenged in the German delegation at Maastricht; it was shared. Officials like Köhler could understand what Kohl was doing and applaud his motives, whilst having deep reservations on technical grounds.

But, within the German delegation, never mind back home in Bonn and Frankfurt, privately held doubts remained about whether the transition to stage 3 was grounded in strong policy analysis and represented an effective German negotiating strategy. The Treaty's commitment to a final date, in the name of irreversibility, raised a key difficulty: that this commitment—when combined with a 'judgemental' element in assessing budgetary discipline—would drive out the principle of economic stability as the bedrock of a sound, durable EMU. German negotiators could find themselves forced to accept a 'second-best' solution, or worse, in 1999. In the last analysis, excellent as had been its negotiating performance, the German Finance Ministry had failed to close a major gap in the Treaty. It had not delivered a complete negotiating *fait accompli*.

Conclusion: 'D-Mark Patriotism', 'Coronation' Theory, and Trusting the French

Right up to the 'end-game' at Maastricht an underlying continuity in the German negotiating position had been provided by Kohl's clear recognition that EMU was a sensitive (*sensibel*) area of policy requiring particular caution. This insight was continuously replenished by the Chancellor's intimate cultivation of his party's grassroots; by his awareness of the sturdy and proud independence of the Bundesbank; and by his acceptance that the source of the Bundesbank's power was less statute law than the strength of support in German public opin-

ion for the goal of price stability. Kohl had been tutored in the basics of the classic 'coronation' theory of EMU and its implications for EMU policy priorities.
He was also alert to the political risk of 'D-Mark patriotism' being mobilized and
diverted in a more nationalistic, anti-European direction.

The risk of 'D-Mark patriotism' and the threat of 'coronation' theory as a critical benchmark were the two major domestic difficulties and constraints with
which Kohl's strategy for EMU had to contend. He sought to deal with them on
two levels—strategic and cognitive. In order to gain an acceptable EMU agreement Kohl pursued a double strategy: of binding in the Bundesbank and the
CSU and thereby neutralizing their opposition; and of getting agreement for
EMU based on the German model. In effect, the two parts of the overall strategy hung inseparably together. Kohl could seek to maximize his negotiating
power by stressing his domestic weakness *vis-à-vis* German public opinion and
resistance within the governing coalition and from the Bundesbank. In other
words, he could claim that his hands were 'tied'.

The other key part of Kohl's approach was more cognitive than strategic. It
involved deterring those who would appeal to 'D-Mark patriotism' and those
who would insist rigorously on 'coronation' theory by cultivating the 'permissive' domestic political consensus on Europe. This cultivation took the form of
deploying vivid metaphor and historical narrative to offer a vision of Germany
in Europe and a basis for German identity that would associate opposition to
EMU with an old, discredited nationalist politics. It was the practice of the arts
of persuasive discourse and symbolic politics that provided the Chancellor with
the opportunity to transform the terms of debate and escape from some of the
restrictions that he faced. It was in this respect that Kohl was able to be bold.

During the course of the EMU negotiations these cognitive and strategic
components of Kohl's approach were very successful. A potentially critical public opinion was kept at bay. This success owed much to a sophisticated and
timely political strategy, which was able to transform the dangers of domestic
opposition into a powerful external negotiating position on EMU. German
negotiators could inhibit their opposite numbers by pointing out the risks to an
EMU agreement if German opinion was alienated. There was an additional factor that eased the position of German negotiators. Unlike in so many other areas
of EC policy, there was no lobby at work. The prospective material effects of
EMU within Germany were too complex and diffuse to enable major sectional
interests, like the Federation of German Industry (BDI), to take up clear positions. Hence EMU negotiators were freed from the problems of working out
strategy for dealing with specific sectoral interests. In so far as they had such a
strategy it was to bind in the Bundesbank. The Bundesbank took on something
of a surrogate role for organized interests and for public opinion. The maxim
was to keep the Bundesbank on board and stop worrying about domestic opposition.

But, even before the Maastricht Treaty was signed on 7 February 1992, Kohl's
approach was being challenged. The permissive consensus behind building

Europe was still in place, and parliamentary ratification of the Treaty on European Union was not threatened. However, once the terms of the final EMU agreement became clear, D-Mark patriotism was sparked into life and the continuing influence of 'coronation' theory reaffirmed.

D-Mark patriotism surfaced in two main locations—the popular press and Waigel's CSU. On 11 December 1991 the headline of Germany's most popular daily newspaper *Bild Zeitung* spoke in ominous terms of 'Das Ende der Mark' ('The End of the Mark'); to be followed by Rudolf Augstein's column in the weekly *Der Spiegel* which spoke of Maastricht as a French plan to seize power and success from Germany. Peter Gauweiler in Waigel's CSU began to attack the ECU as 'esperanto money'. A bitter and personalized battle was joined within the CSU. So shocked was Waigel that the question was raised in the Finance Ministry of whether the ECU issue should be reopened before the signature of the Treaty on 7 February. But that option was ruled out in favour of a fight to win within the CSU. Waigel resorted to the tactic of uniting the CSU around EMU by using pro-EMU quotes from its former long-serving and populist party chair, Franz-Josef Strauss, to silence populist internal critics. At this point the real value to Kohl of having bound in the CSU chair into the EMU agreement was apparent.

The other main strand of domestic criticism adopted a very different point of reference and mode of discourse—the 'coronation' theory of EMU. Here the criticism was less populist and more academic in style. Its centre of gravity was the respectable world of German academic economics, the Bundesbank, and the quality press. Professor Karl Schiller used the pages of *Der Spiegel* immediately after the Maastricht Council to question the haste in which EMU was to be realized. Most potently of all, on 23 January the critical 'head of steam' within the Bundesbank council was released by its statement on the Maastricht decisions on EMU. This statement, drafted by Tietmeyer, and agreed unanimously, returned to the theme of 'a comprehensive political union' as a requirement of a durable EMU (outlined in the Bundesbank council statement of September 1990). 'The Maastricht decisions do not yet reveal an agreement on the future structure of the envisaged political union and on the required parallelism with monetary union. Future developments in the field of political union will be of key importance for the permanent success of the monetary union.' Again, in line with 'coronation' theory, the Bundesbank statement argued that 'the fulfilment of the entry criteria or the convergence conditions must not be impaired by any dates set.' In agreeing this text the strongest voices in the Bundesbank council—like Reimut Jochimsen—were speaking in tune with Tietmeyer. The quality press, led by the *Frankfurter Allgemeine Zeitung*, was quick to fall in line behind the Bundesbank. On 11 June 1992 sixty German economists published their manifesto against Maastricht in its pages.

Though always aware of the risks involved with EMU, Kohl was taken by surprise by the speed with which criticism mounted. As early as his late-night press conference in Maastricht on 9 December the Chancellor was disputing that the single currency would be called the ECU, arguing that this issue remained open. His concern to contain the force of criticisms from 'coronation' theory was apparent as early as his press conference of 11 December on Maastricht. Here he spoke of political union as a 'first step compromise' and 'complete fulfilment' of the entry preconditions as the 'decisive criterion'. In his report to the Bundestag on 13 December Kohl admitted that he had hoped for more on political union but stressed that EMU, along with the single European market, had unleashed a dynamic process that would reap dividends on political union in 1996.

But it would be wrong to think that the concerns in the Federal Chancellor's Office, Foreign Ministry, and Finance Ministry were simply about domestic political support. Particularly within the Finance Ministry there were residual doubts about whether, when the chips were down, French politicians would be willing to make the internal adjustments necessary to enter stage 3. This doubt mattered simply because, if EMU was to be realized, it had to involve France alongside Germany. The convictions of de Larosière and, to a lesser extent, Trichet were not in question. On the other hand, French Socialist and Gaullist politicians continued to be seen as unreliable on central bank independence and economic stability. Quite simply, however prepared they were to strike an EMU agreement for strategic reasons, French politicians were seen as acting from different philosophies of economic and monetary policy. There was a sense that French politicians were being opportunistic in striking an EMU deal on largely German terms. Thereafter, they would be alert to opportunities to escape from the constraints of budgetary discipline and to soften the single currency. Though the treaty negotiations were at an end, German officials were sensitive to the need to identify and close down those opportunities. Ultimately, only one 'end-game' mattered—negotiating the transition to stage 3. And, in the view of the Bundesbank council, though not of the Foreign Ministry, that 'end-game' had been imperfectly regulated in 1991.

10

Italian Policy Beliefs about EMU: External Discipline versus Internal Protection

> Our agenda at the table of the Intergovernmental Conference on European Union represented an alternative solution to problems which we were not able to tackle via the normal channels of government and parliament.
>
> Carli 1993: 435.[1]

Nobody personified the main thrust of Italian policy on EMU as much as Guido Carli. As Treasury Minister from 1989 until 1992, he headed the Italian delegation for the meetings of ECOFIN and the IGC on EMU. Indeed, Carli opened the IGC on EMU in December 1990 in the impressive surroundings of the Palazzo Montecitorio in Rome. He was the only person present who had been involved in the Bretton Woods negotiations in 1944. For Carli was the international monetary diplomat on the grand scale: after Bretton Woods, he became the first President of the European Payments Union (1950–2) and, as Governor of the Banca d'Italia from 1960 to 1975, a long-term participant in international and European monetary fora. As a banker and as a minister, Carli also symbolized the technocratic dilemma at the heart of the Italian system: how to reconcile the profligacy of politicians with professional credibility.

To Carli (and key technocrats), solutions to pressing economic-policy problems were not available via the normal institutional channels because of the diffuseness of power within the state administration, and the consequent *immobilismo*. A greater fiscal and monetary discipline was necessary for two reasons: to contain the 'party-state' (*partitocrazia*); and to secure Italy's chief foreign-policy interest, its European role.[2] EMU provided the means to achieve both objectives: it would be a new *'vincolo esterno'* (external tie) to encourage domestic discipline and at the same time tie Italy to a deepening European integration process (Grande 1995, on the notion of being bound).

Throughout the postwar period, successive Italian governments have given priority to placing the nation firmly within the evolving European integration

---

[1] This and later texts have been translated from the original.

[2] *'Partitocrazia'*: literally, 'rule-by-party'. Other expressions are 'party government' and the 'party-state'. The latter is preferred here. See Bufacchi and Burgess (1998: 4) for a brief discussion of terms. Calise (1994) advances the notion of 'particracy'. Guzzini (1995) has extended this to suggest a fully-fledged theory of the state. Here, the parties are an integral part of the state, legitimizing it but dependent on systemic clientelism.

process (Ferraris 1992).[3] After 1945, European unity was seen as offering the means to rehabilitate Italy in the international community and, equally importantly, as serving as a bulwark against a combined domestic and external Communist threat. Both aspects became a defining feature of the ideology of the Christian Democrats (Democrazia Cristiana, DC), a party which dominated every Italian government from 1945 to 1992. The European vocation was upheld by successive Christian Democrat leaders from Alcide de Gasperi to Giulio Andreotti, and it became the prevailing ethos of Italian diplomacy.[4] Whilst the emphasis given to 'Europe' by DC politicians varied, none challenged the core assumption.[5] Moreover, this vocation formed part of the psyche of the wider nation. To most Italians, it was unthinkable that 'Europe' could be built without Italy.

In recent years, both the EMS and EMU have confronted deeply entrenched traditions at home. But, when forced to choose between upholding the domestic status quo, on the one hand, and instituting radical reform to comply with new European demands, on the other, Italian governments and public have opted for 'Europe'. The commitment to remaining in Europe's inner circle has been absolute. The commitment has also served the interests of a domestic coalition seeking policy reform in favour of greater monetary and fiscal discipline. This coalition has been able to utilize the pervasive support for 'Europe' to advance more radical domestic policy shifts.

This case study argues that long-term institutional weaknesses and perceptions of policy failure at home provided a motivation for Italian reformers to seek external help in instituting domestic changes. The Italian state structure was perceived as akin to an archipelago: it exhibited a dispersal of power and authority. The partitocrazia fed on this structure and utilized the spoils of office to serve its own political interests. This internal structure had external consequences; it undermined Italy's contribution to EC decision-making. At home, the leadership of the Treasury (Tesoro) and of the central bank (Banca d'Italia) had to accommodate themselves to this institutional and political weakness. A process of reform was under way in the 1980s: the central bank, in particular, sought to assert its preferred policy agenda. But, more generally, the

[3] There is, of course, a wide-ranging debate on the depth of the Italian commitment to European integration and on the priorities that ought to be pursued. See the publications of the prestigious Istituto Affari Internazionali, Rome (including International Spectator) and articles in the journal, Politica Internazionale. See Merlini (1993a, 1993b); Aliboni and Greco (1996).

[4] McCarthy (1997: 50) makes the same, widely acknowledged point: 'To the DC-led governments being European meant supporting federalism'. He adds that the Italian willingness to surrender national sovereignty might be explained by the fact that 'the weak state had less sovereignty to lose'. He also argues that Italy's Europeanism 'contains a healthy dose of national self-interest'. He cites the bargaining stance adopted on the ECSC and the EDC. European integration has, in addition, provided a legitimacy, domestic and international, for the postwar state.

[5] For example, Emilio Colombo gained a higher domestic profile on Europe than did Giulio Andreotti. As noted in Chapter 11, Andreotti and Gianni De Michelis were pro-European more by calculation than by emotion, and both showed an interest in a wider geographical orientation in Italian foreign policy.

re-emergence of EMU onto the EC's agenda brought the contradictions between important elements of the Italian state tradition and the imperatives of Italy's European (and international) obligations into sharper relief.

However, the specific response to EMU has to be placed in a longer-term context in which there were both indigenous and exogenous pressures for shifts in economic policy. Italy's membership of the EC had not, until the 1980s, penetrated so deeply into domestic state–economy relations. The *partitocrazia* was sustained, and an 'internal protectionism' (*protezionismo interno*) along with it; those advocating liberal, market-based reform were in a clear minority. But the problems experienced in the 1970s started to change attitudes: notably inflation, currency instability, rising budget deficits, and monetary indebtedness. A different policy environment emerged in the 1980s, following the acceptance of the EMS, the shift to currency stability and to disinflation, the increasing independence of the central bank, and the pressure for financial-market liberalization. A momentum had been created which favoured a depoliticized, technocratic management in Italy: the power of the state was being 'hollowed out' by these and other policy shifts, encouraged by the demands of EC membership (Della Sala 1997).

Globalization and liberalization, and the transition to a single European market, were ushering in a new era. The course and momentum of these changes was beyond the control of any single set of domestic or international actors. By the time EMU reappeared, those clinging to the traditions of 'internal protection' had been greatly weakened. All major forces accepted an overriding foreign policy commitment to Italy's place in the developing European integration process. Policy leadership was exercised by a monetary elite able to determine Italy's EMU mandate. This monetary-policy establishment accepted the rationale for, and Italy's obligation to enter, EMU.

Amongst Italian technocrats there was by no means a full recognition of the implications of EMU membership. This technocratic elite saw EMU as part of an ongoing series of policy reforms that emphasized the need for discipline in a stronger international market. But the new policy environment of which EMU was a part could not—by its very nature—be seen as being readily controllable. Much more obvious was the foreign-policy imperative: Italy had to remain a full core member of the EC. The EMU negotiations appeared unstoppable and often uncontrollable by Italy. Thus the government in Rome had to accommodate itself to them. In short, the Italian monetary-policy establishment was not master of its own destiny.

This chapter forms a necessary background to the analysis of the specific Italian response to EMU after 1988. It examines the policy dilemma consequent upon institutional weakness at home, which established the motivation for EMU to be seen as a *vincolo esterno*. In addition, Italian attitudes to EMU were pre-structured by the set of inherited policy beliefs about the Italian economy and its relationship to the rest of the EC. Major shifts in these beliefs were already apparent before the relaunch of EMU in 1988. A series of policy reforms over the previous decade help to explain how a system previously noted for its political manipulation of monetary policy, its fiscal profligacy, and its currency instability came to embrace an EMU based on the iron discipline of the Bundesbank.

The following chapters examine the Italian response to EMU more directly: focusing on strategy, cognitive beliefs, and the negotiation process. Chapter 11 considers the Italian preparation for the IGC on EMU: how the negotiating mandate was determined and the early policy response to EMU between 1988–90. Chapter 12 analyses Italian negotiating priorities, the extent to which these were accommodated in the IGC, and Italian strategy for the negotiations. This detail has more foundation if the background context is fully outlined first.

The Need for a *Vincolo Esterno*: Institutional Weakness at Home

The motivation to seek an externally imposed economic discipline stems from the traditional weakness of the state institutions at home. Since the *risorgimento* ('rebirth') of the Italian state in the 1860s, a distinctive vocabulary has developed to describe key features of its political system: *trasformismo* (co-option); *partitocrazia* (the party-state); *clientelismo* (clientelism), *parentela-clientela* (patron-client); *lottizzazione* (the allocation of the spoils of office according to party strength); and now *tangentopoli* ('kickback city'; corruption), amongst others.[6] This terminology indicates the lack of autonomy of both the state institutions and civil society, and their interwoven nature. The state has exhibited a complex diffusion of power—within an idiosyncratic version of pluralism—to the extent that the scope for substantive policy innovation is limited. Indeed, the state is said to suffer from an *immobilismo*.

At the end of the 1980s—and thus in parallel to the EMU discussions—the postwar Italian party system practically collapsed. Writers talked of a regime crisis or of the end of the 'First Republic', and of the 'de-legimitization' of the political class (Della Porta 1997; McCarthy 1997). Political turbulence was evident in the so-called *tangentopoli* bribery scandals, which further undermined the system. These scandals reported an extreme manipulation of clientelist traditions. The revelations originated in Milan under the investigative magistrate Antonio Di Pietro and initially involved the Socialists (PSI). But they came also to engulf Italy's largest party, the DC (see Waters 1994). Scores of leading politicians and public figures were implicated in fraud and bribery cases—including Giulio Andreotti (DC), seven times prime minister, and Bettino Craxi (PSI), head of the longest postwar government. The consequence was the disbandment of the DC party and upheaval in the Socialist and Social Democratic Parties (PSI and PSDI). As Giovanni Goria, a former Prime Minister, commented, the entire

[6] There is, of course, an extensive literature in English on the modern and contemporary development of the Italian political system. See, in particular: Bufacchi and Burgess (1998); Furlong (1994); Ginsborg (1990); Gundle and Parker (1996); Hine (1993); La Palombara (1987); McCarthy (1997); Sassoon (1986); and earlier: Kogan (1966), Woolf (1972). See also the bibliographical guide of Bull (1993).

system was being placed under arrest (cited by Waters 1994: 171; see also Della Porta 1997). The *lottizzazione* system was more than 'much-maligned' (La Palombara 1987: 77). It involved the heads of public agencies acting as conduits for illegal payments to political parties. Waters (1994: 172) highlights some of the worst cases: the head of a major construction company confessing to large payments to the DC and PSI in order to obtain contracts from the National Roadways Agency (ANAS); the ex-finance director of ENI (National Hydrocarbons Agency) revealing Swiss bank accounts for the parties to which ENI deposited funds throughout the 1970s; whilst a whole array of public-agency chiefs were accused in other cases. Later allegations focused on the link between senior DC politicians, including Andreotti, and the mafia.

Administrative Culture

Such clientelistic habits have occurred in the context of a diffusion of power within government. The administrative culture has displayed many contradictions: a Napoleonic hierarchy, mixed with poor co-ordination and efficiency. Cassese (1993: 318–21, 1998) has detailed these contradictions:

1. A very high degree of legalism is mixed with a low level of *étatisme*. Parliament has too much control over the executive. Laws not only prescribe rules, they also regulate every detail of the administrative machinery. Traditionally, very little room was left to delegated legislation or to statutory instruments, though this situation has changed somewhat in relation to the EU.[7] Paradoxically, state power has weak social and constitutional 'roots'.

2. The organization of the state apparatus is both centralized and fragmented. The civil service is, following the Napoleonic code, centralized. Yet, the organization of ministries can be split into a multi-tier, territorial structure or by sectoral branches. In addition, there is a vast 'para-state' sector—which is difficult to 'control'—of regulatory bodies, and assistance and entrepreneurial bodies. ENI and IRI are two well-known examples of public corporations; whilst INPS deals with social security matters.[8]

Similarly, financial control exhibits both centralization in revenue collection and decentralization in the authorization of expenditure.

3. In personnel matters, recruitment is not based on tasks and merit. Rather it tends to be dictated by the needs of society and political groups.

The civil service is characterized by the disproportionately high number of lawyers and the large number recruited from the south. There is gross over-staffing in southern offices and a lack of personnel in the north. Those recruited from the south have distinct values, such as 'possessive' attitudes towards the office. There is a long-term geographical imbalance in the bureaucracy in terms of both territorial distribution and composition of personnel.

---

[7] The use of delegated legislation for EC matters was extended by two notable laws: Law 183/1987 and Law 86/1989). See below and Giuliani (1996: 122).

[8] On the history of the state-holding sector, see Allen and Stevenson (1974).

4. Administrative procedure displays too much control *ex ante*, but hardly any control *ex post*. Prior to any decision being reached, the distribution of power 'maximises the number of interventions and the veto right of each office on the others, and transforms the decision process into an uphill struggle to implement any decision' (Cassese 1993: 321). By contrast, efficiency and results seem not to carry any weight. Attention is on procedure, rather than outcome.

These long-term features of the Italian state system have, in more recent times, as has already been noted, been subjected to a number of challenges, as a result of increased public dissatisfaction. Nevertheless, the historic features largely remained intact in the 1988–91 period of EMU negotiation.

The state structure is marked by a log-jam: pluralism, with many potential veto points. Guiliano Amato, whilst Minister at the Tesoro (1987–9), commented that:

I have the sensation of moving in an archipelago . . . Single ministries are much less responsive to the collegial will of the government and much more to that of 'the triangle' which each forms with the corresponding parliamentary commission and the interest groups of the sector . . . All in all, the system is centrifugal, everything has to be negotiated, everyone negotiates with everyone else, every procedural step is a negotiation, and at each negotiation either one stops or one loses a part of what one is proposing. (Quoted in Ginsborg 1990: 423)

Ginsborg refers to the Italian system as being 'blocked', reminiscent of the writings of Crozier and of Hoffman on France in the 1950s.[9] Well-entrenched cultures inside the state bureaucracy reinforce this *immobilismo*: the picture is of a near-Kafkaesque bureaucracy: archaic, internally centralized, overstaffed, slow-moving, and suffering from a suffocating legalism (Allum 1973: 246).

Abiding by EC rules

The administrative consequences of this state tradition for European relations is indicated by the well-known problems Italy has experienced in applying and maintaining European Community law. Official EC data indicate the poor Italian record in transposing European law into national law and in complying with the decisions of the EC Court of Justice. In 1989, Italy was the worst offender in terms of the number of suspected infringements of EC law reported by the European Commission. Since then, the pattern has fluctuated, though the Italian performance appears to have improved.[10] In any event, the quality of such data is limited and the figures hide much. Giuliani (1996) has delved deeper and argued that the Italian problem has been one of successive governments adopting a reactive policy style in relation to new EC measures, whilst other EC states have been more effective in anticipating them. Moreover, he argues that

---

[9] Ginsborg (1990: 420); Crozier (1964); Hoffman (1963).

[10] Italy has not been the worst offender since, whilst it was only the second worst offender in 1990 and 1993. See Commission (1994).

domestic actors have found it expedient to accept a sub-Pareto optimality in relation to EC implementation, rather than to risk wider and potentially damaging domestic reforms. (This latter point is taken up below in the context of the forces seeking 'internal protection'.)

Legislative reform in the late 1980s sought to incorporate a number of devices to clear the backlog of EC directives. Law 183/1987 introduced a new form of administrative delegation enabling departments to issue decrees giving force to a specific list of EC directives (Hine 1993: 296; Giuliani 1996: 122). The ineffectiveness of this measure led, however, to a new draft proposal, Law 86/1989, dubbed the 'Legge La Pergola'. This proposal sought to further extend the use of delegated legislation and of direct administrative implementation. One of its most notable provisions was the so-called 'legge comunitaria'. This law was designed to introduce a fixed parliamentary timetable for the annual passage of all outstanding EC law requiring transposition into national law. The government would be required to submit to Parliament in February each year a package containing timetables for implementation and authority to implement by decree. The basic principle was not new—twice before there had been approval of packages of EC measures—but the 1989 Law sought to routinize the practice (Giuliani 1996: 122–3). In the event, the law was not approved: after the watershed elections of April 1992, the Amato government opted for a quick approval of a reduced version (the 'mini comunitaria'). Under the Prodi government in April 1998 a single package was approved, almost unanimously, which combined the annual laws of 1995, 1996, and 1997. Beyond such measures, however, there is a more basic problem of the poor application of existing national laws (Seidentopf and Ziller 1988: 141).

The archipelago nature of the state structure affects individual actors within the institutions and the role played by the institutions themselves. The established departments of state differ in their technical efficiency and reputation. As in other systems, the Foreign Ministry (*Ministero degli Affari Esteri*) enjoys a prestige owing, in large part, to the nature of its work. It is one ministry that displays a self-confidence and a relatively clear sense of mission (Hine 1993: 291). Perhaps closer to the norm are the ministries of the Treasury (Tesoro, dealing with monetary policy and the authorization of public expenditure), of Finance (tax revenue), and of the Budget and Economic Planning (preparation of public-expenditure planning).[11] For many years—including the period covered by this study—these ministries and others were often seen as having an internal misallocation of staff; poor quality personnel; low morale; poor training and career-development systems; and high unionization disrupting personnel management (Hine 1993: 236). The existence of three separate ministries in the

---

[11] This differentiation affects international representation also. The Tesoro sends representatives to the EC Monetary Committee; under Mario Sarcinelli this function was upgraded. The Finance and Budget Ministries have a largely domestic focus; though the Budget Ministry sends a representative to OECD meetings, and Finance was involved in Italy's EMU convergence programme in 1991. More generally, on the Ministry of Finance, see Radaelli (1997).

same field represented something of an anomaly, making the co-ordination of economic policy problematic.[12]

The Tesoro and Sarcinelli

The Tesoro (Treasury) was, by the 1970s, a ministry captured by the *partitocrazia*, but also one condoning the profligate economic policies of populist party leaders. It lacked institutional credibility as an independent economic-policy actor. Increasingly, public opinion came to associate it with the economic ills of the 1970s: the accumulation of public debt and successive monetary crises. Indeed, the public debt it had stored up in this period came to haunt Italian monetary policy in the following two decades and imperilled the nation's position within the EC: its position in EMU most notably (see below; Scobie *et al.* 1996).

In the 1980s, the Tesoro became enveloped in the wider processes of reform (the shift to price and exchange-rate stability, central bank independence, financial-market liberalization) which would significantly alter its institutional role and authority. Internally, however, it was slow to adapt. The appointment of Mario Sarcinelli as *Direttore-Generale* in 1982 brought to its helm a forceful new figure. Sarcinelli was an ex-Deputy Director-General of the Banca d'Italia, and one who had survived the most reprehensible attacks from the *partitocrazia*.[13] The *Direttore-Generale* of the Tesoro has traditionally benefited from the power and status of a Napoleon, and Sarcinelli was a dominant leader.

Sarcinelli typified the technocratic dilemma at the heart of the financial and monetary-policy process: how to reconcile professional credibility with the varying pressures for compromise exerted by the *partitocrazia*. No doubt in response to the earlier attacks on him at the Banca d'Italia, Sarcinelli was rather more resolute than most of his peers in this regard, though he also was helped by serving alongside a sequence of ministers of sound reputation and some personal expertise. His relations with the final minister under whom he served, Guido Carli, brought the dilemma to a head.

Sarcinelli respected Carli, who was himself a leading technocratic figure (see below). But, as minister, Sarcinelli found Carli too weak in the face of the financial profligacy of a government led by Andreotti and comprising Gianni De

---

[12] A new 'super-ministry' was created in 1996 by the Prodi government to address this problem. Carlo Ciampi headed a merger of the Treasury and Budget Ministries, and was responsible for 'Economic Affairs'.

[13] Sarcinelli had entered the Banca d'Italia in 1957. In 1976, he rose to become a Deputy Director-General. Later, he became embroiled in the so-called 'Banca d'Italia affair', the target of trumped-up charges in March 1979 (Cornwell 1983). This was the result, *inter alia*, of the investigation launched by the Banca d'Italia into the affairs of the Banco Ambrosiano, headed by Roberto Calvi. Sarcinelli was imprisoned for a brief period before all charges were dropped against him, but their effect was to undermine his chances of becoming Governor of the central bank, for which he had been the heir apparent (Cornwell 1983: 103). Sarcinelli returned to the bank, but moved to the Tesoro in 1982.

Michelis (Foreign Minister). Both these politicians would later face serious charges of corruption. Sarcinelli resigned his post in February 1991 in frustration at the weakness of Carli in standing up to the demands of De Michelis for credit facilities to be extended to the USSR and to Algeria.[14] He publicly accused Carli of being entrapped in a fiscal process dominated by lax politicians. Sarcinelli exhibited a disdain for most of the leaders of the *partitocrazia*. There may also have been a suspicion of corruption in his mind about this particular deal. In any event, the case illustrates Sarcinelli's sense of authority, and his fear that feebleness at home would imperil Italy's role in Europe. But it also indicates a basic difference of interpretation of the requirements of office. Carli believed in the necessity for compromise. Ministers were constrained by the peculiarities of the Italian legal and governmental system; in any event, in Carli's view, precedence must ultimately be ceded to elected politicians. Carli had been Central Bank Governor at the time of the infamous 1975 agreement on the monetization of the deficit. Other officials close to the relevant ministers found Carli 'totally Andreotti-dependent' by 1990. Carli gave to the Andreotti government the legitimacy of his personal reputation as a respected central banker. His espousal of the *vincolo esterno* thesis is somewhat paradoxical. Inherent in the notion is a desire *not* to compromise with elected politicians who behave irresponsibly.

In Carli's defence, it can be noted that the status of the Ministro del Tesoro within government was lower whilst he was there than subsequently—later budget discipline occurred under a strong Prime Ministerial lead (notably under Amato in 1992)—and that the option of resignation appeared to have little purpose. Carli's immediate successor, Piero Barucci (1992–4), claimed in his memoirs that the traditional conception of the Tesoro as an island in a turbulent world marked by populist politics is misconstrued (1995: 319). It is a mistake to believe that political decisions can be taken in a neutral, technocratic manner: nor should they for reasons of democracy. Indirectly, Barucci provided a defence of Carli's own role. But the central dilemma is acknowledged.

At the Tesoro, Sarcinelli was undoubtedly a powerful figure: he was one of the longest serving officials to hold the post, and he served four ministers (Andreatta; Goria; Amato; and Carli). Whilst at the Tesoro, Sarcinelli instituted a number of internal reforms—he established a new council of external economic advisers, for example—and some of these were left to his successor, Mario Draghi, to implement.[15] Yet the Tesoro as an institution remained much as before. In his resignation letter, Sarcinelli noted that, although there had been some improvement in the quality of senior Tesoro staff, progress remained very

---

[14] See his resignation letter published in *Il Mondo*, 18 Mar. 1991.

[15] Later, Draghi would implement a number of internal reforms affecting the structure and quality of personnel in the Tesoro. A new structure was based on five functional departments: (1) public-debt management and privatization; (2) accounting and the budget; (3) international policy; (4) banking and stock-market policy; (5) supervision and surveillance. The heads of these departments now had international experience; some were drawn from outside the Tesoro.

fragile.[16] Sarcinelli was, in effect, operating in the last period of the *ancien régime* of the old-style *partitocrazia*: the pace of reform was constrained by the political environment of the period. It meant, however, in EC and EMU affairs, that the only two Tesoro actors that mattered were Sarcinelli (later Draghi) and Carli. Moreover, in such policies, they were obliged to be *individual entrepreneurs* acting to overcome the *immobilismo* (the inertia, diffuseness, and laxity) of the governmental process.

In their desire to marry a European commitment with domestic reform, the leaders of the Tesoro could find crucial support in the *Ministero degli Affari Esteri* (Foreign Ministry). The institutional ethos of the latter was to ensure that Italy remained in Europe's inner circle. Whilst Italian Foreign Ministers, such as De Michelis, have eschewed the precepts of economic and monetary discipline, whilst professing support for Italy's position in Europe, senior ministry officials have been more consistent. Both for the EMS and EMU, officials have prioritized the European commitment and urged that the consequent domestic costs be borne. The *vincolo esterno* thesis was readily linked to Italy's European vocation.

The Banca d'Italia

By contrast to the Tesoro, and standing out as something of a beacon in the archipelago state, the Banca d'Italia had since the 1960s achieved a uniquely high domestic and international prestige *as an institution* (Goodman 1992). The central bank has developed a reputation for political independence amongst the internecine domestic party squabbles. Almost alone it has resisted penetration by the *partitocrazia* and its practices. Moreover, the Banca d'Italia attained a near monopoly status in Italy as a provider of economic expertise. The establishment of a strong research department in the 1960s under Governor Guido Carli— with a staff complement in the 1980s of about 200—gave the bank a high status in its technical analysis. Its political independence and economic expertise was widely recognized amongst its international partners, not least within the discussions of the BIS (Bank for International Settlements) in Basle and the Committee of Central Bank Governors of the EC. The respect was for both the institution and its individual personnel.

As an institution, like most central banks, the Banca d'Italia sustained a cohesiveness to the outside world. Its traditional political independence was until the 1980s due mainly to its own reputation and stature, rather than its legal foundation (Goodman 1992; Eizenga 1993). The practice of senior appointments helped to reinforce this independence. The Governor, the Director-General, and the two Deputy Directors were each appointed by the Banca d'Italia's sixteen-member Board of Directors, with ratification by the President of the Republic

[16] In his resignation letter (published in *Il Mondo*, 18 Mar. 1991), Sarcinelli suggested that it would take the departure of just one or two senior figures to precipitate the breakdown of the Tesoro. A general improvement had occurred, however: he cited a number of cases where staff, for example, had obtained work experience abroad helped by the British Council.

and the government traditionally automatic. There was no time limit on their appointments. Moreover, since 1948 all Governors have been appointed from 'within', usually on the basis of the promotion of the Director-General in the central bank.[17] Thus, successive governments have had a highly constrained choice of Governor. A partial exception to this detachment by government concerned the appointment of a new Director-General in 1994.[18] This isolated episode has not, however, disrupted the traditional respect for the Banca d'Italia's independence.

The relationship between the Banca d'Italia and the Tesoro in monetary-policy management, and the power of state institutions in the financial markets, were fundamentally transformed during the course of the 1980s. This transformation had important implications for the structure of the domestic-policy process and for Italy's position with respect to EMU. It was the result of a set of major policy shifts undertaken by Italian governments during the course of the 1980s. These shifts were part of a collective policy-learning process, a reaction to the financial mismanagement of the 1970s, and they altered both the power of state institutions at home and the hold of EC policy constraints over them. These will be discussed later; first, in order to set them in context, it is necessary to consider the longer-term conflicts in the economic-policy debate in Italy.

External Discipline versus Internal Protection: The Two Souls of Faust

The Italian response to the relaunch of EMU in the 1980s can be set in the context of domestic debates on European and economic policy. The Italian response to EMU was 'prestructured' in the sense that both strategy and cognitive beliefs were placed in the context of historically conditioned ideas about the economy and its relationship to the rest of the EC. In the event, the Italian negotiating stance on EMU represented a victory for those who accepted the domestic imperatives consequent upon Italian participation in the integration process. This victory had been prepared by a series of policy shifts made during the previous decade: and these will be briefly outlined later. But this victory cannot be

---

[17] From 'within' here refers to the Banca d'Italia itself and the *Ufficio Italiano dei Cambi*, UIC (the Italian Exchange Office). The UIC is 'responsible for the technical side of Italy's foreign exchange management. Although legally a separate body from the central bank, the UIC is nonetheless directly dependent upon the Banca d'Italia, whose governor serves as its president' (Goodman 1992: 56).

[18] Displeased at some of the Governor's policy pronouncements and the bank's decision to raise interest rates in August, the new Berlusconi government sought to impose an outsider as Director-General. This pressure failed, but instead of the promotion going to the senior deputy—Tommaso Padoa-Schioppa—he was bypassed in favour of Vincenzo Desario, the junior deputy and former head of the bank's supervision arm (*Financial Times*, 21 Oct. 1994; *The Economist*, 25 June 1994, 29 Oct. 1994). The widely respected Padoa-Schioppa may have lost out because of his close association with former governor Carlo Ciampi, who as Prime Minister was opposed by Berlusconi (*The Economist*, 25 June 1994).

fully understood without reference first to the conflicts and ambiguities that underlay policy on a longer-term basis.

Leaders across the political spectrum have long accepted the imperative of supporting Italy's role as a core member of the EC. But they have differed in their domestic response to the implications of membership, and indeed of Italy's international role. This domestic response is also linked to more general differences over economic policy. The debate might be conceived as being loosely structured around two competing 'advocacy coalitions' on Europe and economic policy.[19] But, in doing so, it is important to emphasise *the openness, range, and differentiation* of such 'coalitions'. The policy debates should be seen as revolving around different sets of beliefs and interests, to which actors have attached themselves, to varying degrees and not always consistently. In the general policy debate, it was not a case of technocrats in opposition to party politicians, as individuals wore different hats. The debate should not be understood as being between two insular, exclusive 'camps' in conflict. With this qualification in mind, some analytical clarity can be offered. The policy conflicts can be seen as being ranged between those who have sought to bind Italy by external ties and obligations—a *vincolo esterno*—in order to secure domestic reforms of an essentially liberal character; and those who have opted for a kind of 'internal protectionism' (*protezionismo interno*), bound up with clientelistic favours and serving anti-competitive interests.[20] Carli (1993: 3–7) describes this dichotomy of forces in the postwar economy as a struggle between the 'two souls of Faust', the new and the old, good and evil.[21]

The cleavage connects both domestic and EC policies. Giuliani (1992, 1996) has offered a somewhat different, though complementary, perspective. He argued that Italian policy and strategy in relation to the EC has been 'nested' in a complex domestic bargaining game. Italian domestic actors have accepted an apparently sub-optimal equilibrium in which contending forces battle for 'political resources to be spent reactively in the national arena or in future EC/EU bargaining on single policy issues' (1996: 128).[22] The 'established institutional

---

[19] Sabatier (1998: 99), for example, relates the notion of 'advocacy coalitions' to 'belief systems'. He comments that one of the premises of his advocacy coalition framework is the 'ability to map beliefs and policies on the same "canvas" [and this] provides a vehicle for assessing the influence of various actors over time, including the role of technical information'. It is in this basic sense of a 'map' of beliefs that the concept is relevant here.

[20] The notion of there being two advocacy coalitions in relation to EC policy was suggested by Radaelli and Martini (1998).

[21] In the opera of that name, Faust makes a pact with the Devil, Mephistopheles, to gain youth and love on earth, whilst accepting the Devil as his master in the afterlife. An equation of the Italian economy with the Devil may be appropriate, but Carli clearly sees liberalism as virtue and its opponents as the devil. In reality, as noted elsewhere, Carli had to make his own personal accommodation with the devil, in the form of the *partitocrazia*.

[22] Giuliani (1996: 128–30) argues, for example, that the poor performance of Italian governments in implementing EC measures is to be explained by a number of (rational-choice-type) factors. First, the strategy of Italian ministers not opposing EC initiatives in the Council of Ministers accumulates goodwill which might be called upon in other instances of greater domestic concern. Secondly, 'the lack of EC investigating and sanctioning powers makes the option of national (rather than EC-level)

setting' is both the 'effect and the shaper' of official preferences (1996: 128). These organizational characteristics have spread from the Italy–EC relationship to the internal arena. Actors

> preferred to maintain the realized equilibrium as stable as possible rather than to risk potentially damaging reforms. Synthetically, it worked because the establishment of a 'protected political and policy market' satisfied the most crucial participants, quite independently from the widespread social costs. Probably, the continuous growth of these same costs is already representing the most powerful challenge to the outlined framework . . . (1996: 131–2)

Such a portrayal is surely correct in emphasizing the conflicting interests underpinning much of the inertia and *immobilismo* of the Italian system, alongside a strong public consensus in support of European integration. The approach followed here seeks to widen the focus, however, to take account of cognitive beliefs and understandings. The consequences of the domestic policy shifts in Italy in the 1980s formed an essential prelude to the Italian perspective on EMU (see below). For these reasons, a contrast between two general sets of belief is preferred here. The notion of *'protezionismo interno'* is a more inclusive formulation than that suggested by Giuliani, and that of a *vincolo esterno* seems perculiarly relevant to the EMU area.

The two notions also help to place matters in an appropriate historical context. In the immediate postwar period, external ties were used to safeguard liberal democracy and a market economy. The most prominent figures to adhere to this equation were Alcide De Gasperi (Christian Democrat Prime Minister 1945–53); Luigi Einaudi (economist and Liberal Party politician); and Angelo Costa (President of Confindustria, the employers' organization). De Gasperi prioritized Italy's Western links, Einaudi engineered liberal reforms at home, and Costa pressed for businesses to be allowed flexibility. Later leaders, such as Andreotti, saw themselves as the inheritors of De Gasperi's foreign-policy imperative. Andreotti, who had worked with De Gasperi, dismissed doubts at home to take the lira into the EMS in 1979. In addition, by the late 1980s the financial orthodoxy of Einaudi was somewhat back in vogue: in large part as a means of securing a continued European role. By then, Einaudi was a point of reference for both the Banca d'Italia and the Tesoro. Einaudi had been an early mentor of Carli who was now Minister at the Tesoro.

---

obstructionism a worthwhile strategy, especially if, as frequently happens in Italy, the prevailing reactive style discounts future implementation costs at a very high rate'. The Italian failure to meet EC obligations can also be excused as being the result of factors outside the government's control and Italy's EC partners have shown a common defensive interest in not seeking to investigate domestic problems too deeply. Domestically, actors can ascribe costs and responsibility for unpopular decisions to Italy's EC partners. 'Europe', notes Giuliani, can be a 'political anaesthetic' easing the path of fiscal or monetary reform. The Italian failure to spend most of the funds assigned to it from the EC budget can also be attributed to the fact, he argues, that domestic actors see a relative advantage in rejecting the more stringent conditions and procedures of the EC funds in favour of the greater laxity of alternative domestic sources of finance.

The policies advocated by Einaudi after the Second World War represented a distinct and controversial paradigm. In August 1947 he shifted from being Governor of the Banca d'Italia to be Budget Minister and Deputy Prime Minister. His impact is generally acknowledged to have been monumental (Kogan 1966: 44). Indeed, the 'Einaudi line had a more direct influence on the operation of the economy than did the Constitution on postwar politics' (Allum 1973: 246).[23] Einaudi was the foremost Italian economist of his day, a near-religious adherent to classical liberalism (with roots in the Manchester School) (De Cecco 1972: 160–1). The Christian Democrat administration of Alcide De Gasperi found it politically convenient to have Einaudi, a member of the small Liberal Party, charged with tackling the severe and multiple problems of the economy. As minister, Einaudi pursued classic deflationary policies: government spending was curtailed, the money supply was reduced, and credit restrictions introduced. The tough liberal measures produced gains: inflation fell and the lira stabilized. The Christian Democrats collected the political gain with a major election victory in April 1948: the middle classes were pleased inflation was being taken in hand and the agricultural subsistence peasantry were left relatively unscathed by a credit sqeeze. For a period, Italy 'seemed to have become the bastion of *laissez-faire* ideology' (Sassoon 1986: 22). But the Einaudi medicine had distorting and disruptive effects: investment fell, unemployment rose (De Cecco 1972). Einaudi sought renewal by favouring exports, and the stagnation of the economy in 1947–50 only improved with the new international export opportunities associated with the Korean War.

There are parallels here between the Einaudi period and that of EMU in the 1990s: both in terms of the perceived needs of Italian foreign policy and of the prevailing intellectual consensus behind monetary policy. In Einaudi's period, the control of inflation was seen as essential to safeguard the lira, and currency stability had been set as a condition of participation in the new Western order, with the Bretton Woods negotiations (Sassoon 1986: 26). The emphasis given to disinflation and currency stability, in part as a means of securing an international voice for Italy, would later find resonance in the EMU debate of the early 1990s and in the notion of a *vincolo esterno*. The collapse of the Bretton Woods system led to a de-emphasis on currency stability and a belief in the advantages of competitive devaluation. The EMS, to a limited degree, and the new EMU project, much more clearly, reaffirmed the salience of discipline via a *vincolo esterno*. Moreover, in the late 1940s, Einaudi and his followers were able to impose a straitjacket on policy at home because of the assumption that this was necessary to gain American favour. The influence of the economic liberals was also due to the fact there was a paucity of economists in Italy at that time advocating opposing philosophies (De Cecco 1972: 160). Again, a parallel with the orthodoxy attached to the Maastricht criteria is evident. The Italian consensus in the 1990s was that there was no acceptable alternative to participation in EMU.

[23] Einaudi had earlier been a Liberal minister in the pre-Mussolini era.

But whilst the Einaudi legacy stressed neo-liberalism in monetary policy, it existed in an uneasy tension and compromise with those seeking state intervention to satisfy infrastructure requirements. Following the Einaudi line meant rejecting the new-style planning and intervention pursued in Britain and France; and, ironically, less aid was obtained from the US-instigated Marshall Plan as a result (Sassoon 1986: 22). American advisers sought New Deal, Keynesian-style intervention to create jobs; Einaudi sought currency stability and exports. But the Einaudi approach was never adopted as pure *laissez-faire*. The effect was to bequeath 'a conception of the public sector as a subordinate' (Sassoon 1986: 23). Whilst it grew obese and served clientelistic political interests, the public sector never assumed a central planning role in the economy. Public intervention has been extensive, but also full of contradictions and inadequacies (Padoa-Schioppa Kostoris 1996: 279).

By contrast, the 'statist' coalition was concerned to ensure protection from competition. As Carli argued, external protectionism was not possible given the commitment to Italy's integration into the new Western order (1993: 3–7). Instead, such forces opted for a kind of *protezionismo interno*. This involved easy credit facilities, tax rebates, public subsidies, relaxed fiscal controls, and so on. More particularly, in the 1970s, it meant a de-emphasis on the control of inflation and of currency stability. Instead, a belief in the advantages of competitive devaluation fostered greater fiscal and monetary indiscipline. In addition, at all levels, state regulations have given 'rights and duties, obligations or prohibitions, barriers to entry or inhibitions from exit', sustaining anti-competitive attitudes (Padoa-Schioppa Kostoris 1996: 277). This internal protectionism survived in those areas not covered by the liberalizing content of EC and other international policies, and it encouraged illegal and corrupt practices to serve the interests of some of its proponents. Redistributive financial transfers from the EC budget fitted easily with the desire for internal protectionism: they cushioned the impact of competition from abroad and indirectly served the political supremacy of the *partitocrazia*. The largesse of the Common Agricultural Policy went to the natural supporters of the hegemonic political party, the Christian Democrats, and at times it was administered corruptly. In short, the domestic interests of the *partitocrazia* were against the intrusion of EC policies and discipline into the established mores of the internal protectionism on which its power rested.

The desire for internal protection stemmed from a distinct political culture, but also from economic inequalities at home. The cultural roots have already been alluded to in an earlier section: the weakness of civil society; the tradition of clientelism; feelings of vulnerability and insecurity, and so on. Both the Catholic and Communist cultures have undermined the scope for liberalism. In addition, the Italian economy has long been riven by structural weaknesses: between modern, productive sectors and firms and traditional, inefficient sectors and firms; between the internationally competitive and those dependent on the protection of the home market; and most glaringly, the large inequalities between the north and the south. The Italian economy, and indeed society, can be seen as being beset by a series of contrasts: Locke (1995), for example, argues that Italy is a constellation of local economic orders.

The problems of the south traditionally exemplified the demand for state support. It was also from here that the Christian Democrats had a traditional bedrock of voters. The Mezzogiorno remains one of the least industrialized regions of Europe; it demanded and received large-scale public investment.[24] The policy, however, caused both external and internal problems for Italy. The EC Commission repeatedly attacked state aids to the south. Moreover, at home, criticism by the 'productive' north of the 'parasitic' south increased in the late 1980s, undermining national unity and encouraging the growth of the Lega Nord (Northern League).[25] The Cassa per il Mezzogiorno (fund for the south) was disbanded, as was the preferential resource allocation to the south. Such policies no longer synchronized with the prevailing economic orthodoxy, nor with Italy's external role. Moreover, a similar momentum provoked a debate on fiscal federalism, seeking to overcome the disjunction between centralized taxation and local decision-making on expenditure.

In contrast to the south, the level of industrialization in the centre-north is higher than that of the UK or France and comparable to that of the USA and Japan (Cangliozzi 1991). Northern industrialization was predominantly focused on its integration into international markets, rather than on serving the needs of the variegated domestic economy. Having the advantage of being located closer to the large European markets, it has a natural European vocation.[26] It has also had a history of entrepreneurship, and industrial activity in the north has managed to maintain a high level of technological innovation and competitiveness. Not suprisingly, the demands for increased market openness and for economic liberalization have their spiritual home in the north.

Yet, the economic elites of the north have traditionally formed a symbiotic, even incestuous, relationship with politicians in Rome. Business attitudes towards the role of the state have been variously ambiguous, confused, inviting, and hostile.[27] Such attitudes have existed amongst firms of all sizes: large,

[24] The Cassa per il Mezzogiorno (fund for the south) was created in 1950 to help redirect public resources to boost economic and social development in the area. More generally, the state undertook to allocate at least 40% of its investment expenditure (investimenti a pioggia) to the south (Allen and Stevenson 1974: 203). The Cassa was seen as an important policy innovation: inspired by a similar philosophy to that of the French Plan, but one bedevilled by inefficiencies and allegations of corruption (Ginsborg 1990: 331; Allen and Stevenson 1974: 207, 210).

[25] A separatist-inclined political movement led by Umberto Bossi. Bufacchi and Burgess (1998: 109) note that 'Of all the anti-system phenomena, the Northern League had, by the Autumn of 1992, done most in consolidating its hold on the minds of voters'.

[26] After 1945, Italy's customers had to be predominantly Europe and North America: the USA dominated Latin America; Britain and France Africa and Asia; and all three the Middle East (Sassoon 1986: 16).

[27] Carli commented that, 'The Italian entrepreneurs have never considered the state as a social organization for which they were responsible, even together with the other groups in society. This was probably a defect that goes back to our origins. It is of the utmost gravity, and is responsible for more than one of the evils and structural weaknesses from which we suffer today' (G. Carli, Intervista sul capitalismo italiano; ed. Scalfari; Bari 1977: 71; cited by Ginsborg 1990: 470). More recently Dente has made

medium, and small. Moreover, some of the major companies have been led by single families (Agnelli at FIAT, Berlusconi's Fininvest)—and the heads of others have enjoyed high public profile (Pirelli; De Benedetti; Benetton)—whilst company operations have often eschewed transparency. Companies have also developed complex structures: most notably, Mediobanca the Milan-based merchant bank controlled 'a spider's web of cross-shareholdings in nearly every large financial and industrial company in the private sector'; it could make or break company operations (Friedman 1996: 264–5). To its critics, Mediobanca (led by Enrico Cuccia) represented the old status quo that stifled competition, restricted access to equity capital, and maintained a credo of oligopoly (Friedman 1996: 264–5).

Business leaders, and their organization *Confindustria*, have not pursued a clear or consistent liberal path. The constituency for market liberalization has traditionally been small. Ginsborg (1990: 73) refers to a division that gradually emerged after 1945 'between a conservative majority and progressive minority in Italian industry'. The majority were often safely esconced in monopoly conditions of production, whilst the minority, concentrated in engineering (FIAT, RIV, Olivetti), rubber (Pirelli), and in steel (Finsider), were more conscious of the strictures of market competition. Much more recently, *Confindustria* was slow to advocate privatization, whilst major business leaders obfuscated on liberalization in the 1980s.

Nor was economic liberalism to be found in the *partitocrazia*, of course. As Furlong notes, 'Until the mid-1970s there were very few within the DC willing to support radical free market policies' and thereafter they remained a minority (1994: 162). This situation continued until the late 1980s. Einaudi's party, the Liberal Party (PLI), for example, which was in government between 1947–62, was only in government in 1972–3 (under Andreotti) during the whole period until 1979 (Hine 1993: 100–2). In the 1970s and 1980s, its vote was between 1 and 4 per cent. Against the backdrop of the recent upheavals in the Italian party system, writers have again highlighted the chronic long-term lack of a liberal culture in Italy.[28]

Much more distinct was the neo-liberal input of academics and technocrats. Most notable in this regard have been the distinct contributions of Beniamino (Nino) Andreatta (an economics professor who served as Tesoro Minister, 1980–2); Mario Monti (an economics professor at Bocconi who became an EC Commissioner in 1995); and Guido Carli himself.[29] The indigenous 'liberal' movement was thus isolated and relatively weak until the 1980s.

a similar claim, to the effect that small and medium-sized firms in the north have never developed a strong sense of identification with the Italian state (Dente 1997).

[28] Berlusconi's Fininvest was owned 100% by his family and kept its accounts and operations secret. Mediaset was subsequently quoted on the Italian stock exchange. On FIAT, see Romiti (1988).

[29] See Bufacchi and Burgess (1998: 249–53) for a brief discussion. They cite Alexander Passerin d'Entreves writing in 1974 of 'a cynical view of the State, based on the assumption that politics is a matter of getting the upper hand and that all men, if not potential criminals, are at any rate would-be profiteers or tax-evaders' (1998: 250).

The culture of internal protection has been subject to increasing challenge since the late 1970s, as a result of the changing external position of Italy. Two major international developments were to prompt this challenge: the emergence of global financial markets and liberal economic policies across the Western world in the early 1980s; followed by the intensification of the European integration process (the Single European Act; capital liberalization; the Maastricht Treaty) which served to reinforce these external pressures on Italy. These pressures strengthened those political and technocratic figures in Italy urging reform, enabling them to argue that a liberal shift was essential to maintain Italy's international position.

A new discourse on economic policy emerged, which accepted the need for a radical shift. This discourse served to disenfranchise economists from political parties, with senior advisers across the spectrum converging in their assessment of the implications of the Maastricht Treaty (Radaelli and Martini 1998). Radaelli and Martini (1998) have outlined how the Treaty greatly reinforced a 'fiscal adjustment coalition', favouring a greater discipline, relative to a 'public expenditure coalition'.

The Radaelli and Martini portrayal of the types of actors involved in each coalition is instructive, as it relates to the EMU debate also. They identify the fiscal reform coalition as comprising a technocratic elite in government, employers organizations, the *Partito Repubblicano Italiano* (PRI, Italian Republican Party),[30] a few top socialists such as Giuliano Amato and Giorgio Ruffolo, and the 'technocratic rump' of the DC led by Andreatta. In addition, a number of think-tanks provided supporting arguments, data, and a climate of opinion. Individuals within think-tanks such as the *Istituto per la Ricerca Sociale* (IRS), *Centro Europa Ricerche* (CER), Nomisma, and Prometeia, themselves formed part of this reform coalition.

In short, the climate of opinion looked very different by the 1990s. The domestic antecedents to this change are to be found in the reaction to the financial crises of the 1970s and the impact of a series of major domestic-policy changes.

Policy Learning: Defer to the Market, Stay in *Serie A*

Over the course of the 1980s, three major policy shifts were to be made in Italy. These were:

- the shift to price and exchange-rate stability, overcoming the competitive devaluations of the past (involving the entry of the lira into the EMS);
- the gradual 'divorce' of the Banca d'Italia from the Tesoro after 1981; and,
- the pursuit of financial liberalization.

The combined effect of these policy shifts can be summarized as:

[30] But on Carli's liberal commitment, see Chapter 11.

- a major strengthening of the institutional (structural) power of the Banca d'Italia in the domestic management of monetary policy;
- a contrasting impact on the autonomy of the Tesoro in this same area: on the one hand, a weakening as a result of central bank independence and the increased power of the financial markets; on the other, a much enlarged room for manoeuvre in managing the public debt;
- the heightened role of technocratic expertise in managing monetary policy, given the reduced scope for political manipulation;
- an intensification of the domestic constraints on Italian policy-making consequent on EC-level commitments; and
- an increasing acceptance of the utility of these same EC-level policy obligations to engineer and sustain the domestic reforms seen as being both necessary and desirable by technocratic elites at home.

By the end of the 1980s, monetary discipline at home was a *sine qua non* of a continuing European role for Italy.

The policy shifts can be explained by reference to two financial crises in the 1970s: the first occurred in response to the oil price shock of 1973, the second after the oil crisis of 1979. The economic recession prompted by the first oil crisis led to demands for fiscal expansion at home. These demands were at a time when the *external monetary discipline* of the Bretton Woods system had already collapsed. Monetary policy became subordinated to fiscal needs: currency depreciation followed inflation. In 1974 the Banca d'Italia persuaded Ugo La Malfa, the Tesoro Minister, to request an IMF loan. However, the tight monetary policy adopted by the Banca d'Italia after the loan could not be maintained as a result of the political pressures on the coalition government. In 1975, Emilio Colombo as Minister of the Tesoro sought fiscal expansion: he pressed the Banca d'Italia (under Guido Carli) to accept an obligation for it to 'monetize' the fiscal deficit. By acting as the residual buyer of Treasury bills at auction, the Banca d'Italia would cover the cost of government profligacy. The price paid by the bank was huge in terms of the loss of monetary control. In 1975, the fiscal deficit reached 12 per cent of GDP, and half of it was financed by money creation. Moreover, a 1975 agreement between the employers (*Confindustria*) and the trade unions (CISL, CGIL, and UIL) resulted in a higher degree of wage indexation and an extension of its coverage; all in the name of buying industrial peace in a turbulent climate (Salvati 1985). The balance of payments crisis that occurred in 1975 forced the Banca d'Italia to stop defending the currency and allow it to float.

The lessons were clear. The 1975 obligation on the Banca d'Italia critically weakened its ability to promote monetary stability. Moreover, monetary instability was the result of a profligate *partitocrazia* unrestrained by an externally imposed discipline. The experience of Italy after the 1979 oil shock vindicated such an interpretation. Italy was experiencing fast economic growth, but the inflationary impact of the oil shock was great. The response of the Italian authorities was quite different in this case. Priority was given to monetary stability, not full employment. The Banca d'Italia tightened its monetary policy and endeavoured to stabilize the lira. The policy lessons that had been learned from these experiences eased the path for the entry of the lira into the EMS in 1979.

A turning-point had been reached at the start of the 1980s, though not all accepted it. Some still sought 'internal protection'. The demand by industry for devaluation to restore competitiveness was resisted. The popular mood had shifted: a march of 40,000 in Turin in 1980 opposed the demands of the trade unions.[31] The degree of monetization of the fiscal deficit was substantially reduced. Monetary policy increasingly shifted to price and exchange-rate stability after the lira entered the EMS in 1979, and the domestic authority of the Banca d'Italia was restored with the initiation of its divorce from the Tesoro in 1981. Again, the lesson was that monetary discipline is achieved via an external constraint: the EMS itself had reinforced the shift to further reform. At the same time, those clinging to the tradition of 'internal protection' were placed very much on the defensive. The EMS, and the emergence of global liberalization, unleashed a new momentum in the 1980s.

Before considering the further reforms of the 'divorce' of the Banca d'Italia and of financial liberalization, it is instructive to consider briefly Italian attitudes towards European monetary co-operation in the 1970s. The shift of emphasis brought about by the reforms of the 1980s will thus be made more apparent, by looking at what went before them.

From Werner to the EMS

From an Italian point of view, the case of EMU at the time of the Werner Plan (1970) is no more than a partial guide to the situation Italy faced in the later instances of the birth of the EMS and the relaunch of EMU. There are certain points of consistency in the stance adopted in all three cases by successive Italian governments. In 1970, as again later, the Italians stressed that:

- before taking the first steps towards closer monetary co-operation there should be an agreement on the long-term objectives;
- monetary co-operation should be accepted as being part of a wider package, involving further political integration;
- to be effective, agreement on EMU should involve the operation of new EC-level institutions to manage the transitional stages (on this latter point, see Carli 1993: 233).

Italian governments have seen their stance as an expression of the *communautaire* tradition: involving timetabled stages and institutionalization, whilst moving

[31] The small, centrist PRI is one of the oldest parties in Italy. Anti-monarchist and secular, it has been a long-term advocate of 'rigour' in public spending. Whilst its electoral support has been very limited, it has been a frequent participant in government coalitions and has had disproportionate political influence. Indeed, it was almost continuously in government between January 1979 and April 1991. It returned to government, briefly, under Ciampi in 1993–4.

towards grander political objectives. From Werner onwards, Italian governments have sought political union, enhancing the European Parliament, and increasing citizenship rights.[32]

One major point of differentiation between the cases of Werner and the EMS, on the one hand, and the relaunch of EMU, on the other, is that only in the first two instances did the respective Italian governments seek to tie progress on monetary co-operation to the adoption of 'parallel measures' involving economic aid from EC funds to states experiencing difficulties. After the EC summit in Paris in October 1972, Giulio Andreotti, in his second term as Italian Prime Minister, declared:

I am happy to note agreement on the necessity for a close parallel between progress in the field of economic union and development towards a monetary union. This is a necessity which is strongly felt by Italy, whose economic and social structures—characterized by deep regional imbalances—could not cope with a homogeneous monetary system without risking further tensions. (*Keesing's Record of World Events*, 25539, 1972)

When Andreotti was Prime Minister for the fourth time, his government in 1978 advanced a similar argument and feared the consequences of EMS entry for Italy. By contrast, by 1988 and afterwards, the relevant Italian governments believed that it would be politically damaging to identify themselves with a weaker economic periphery (seeking a new 'Cohesion Fund') and also that the climate in the EC had shifted so as to make such demands unrealistic.

But the major dimension of differentiation between these cases of monetary co-operation is not one of policy, so much as of the shift in coalition possibilities at the EC level. From the Italian point of view, the scope for alliance-building differed substantially across all three instances. In both 1970 and 1988–90, the Italians faced a polarized debate between France, on the one hand, and Germany and The Netherlands, on the other. In addition, in both instances, the Italians were somewhat marginal to this core divide and to determining progress to overcome it. Italian distance from the Franco-German axis was even more pronounced, and consequential, in the case of the EMS in 1978. But the differences between 1970 and 1988–90 were of crucial importance. The Pompidou administration had been minimalist in 1970, eschewing ambitious objectives and supranational institution-building. The potential for an alliance between Paris and Rome was therefore negligible. By contrast, the Dutch and the Germans in 1970–2 stressed the importance of a firm political commitment being made and to the development of the appropriate EC institutions. In these respects, they were natural bedfellows for the Italians. By 1988–90, however, the position of Mitterrand was to seek a firm political commitment to full EMU and, at least initially, to plan for the transition towards it to be managed by strong new EC institutions. By contrast, the Germans now appeared more cautious: EMU was to involve monetary, but not economic, integration; no

---

[32]   The Turin march of October 1989 represents a sea change in attitudes. The march was connected to the threat of redundancies at FIAT: the company laid off 20,000 workers.

significant powers in monetary policy should be granted to EC institutions until the very end of the transition towards EMU; and a long-term commitment to the goal of EMU should be conditional on the degree of economic convergence achieved at different stages of the transition. Thus, from the Italian perspective, France had moved closer to Rome whilst Germany and The Netherlands had shifted away from it. The coalition possibilities had been transformed.

In reality, the Italian position had also changed between 1970 and 1988–90. Policy beliefs had undergone a major readjustment, in response to new economic pressures. As already noted, EMU was now placed in the frame of price and exchange-rate stability; central bank independence; and financial liberalization. The domestic context was very different by 1988.

The discussions following the Werner Plan also took place in a contrasting international environment, marked by the collapse of the Bretton Woods system. The response of Italian governments to this development was reactive and shifting. They were also marginal to the progress of events at the international and EC levels. The governments of Emilio Colombo and of Andreotti had wanted to delay the introduction of an autonomous EC exchange-rate system till the time when economic integration had advanced sufficiently. The Italians had opposed the early introduction of the European 'Snake' system and the European Monetary Co-operation Fund. Indeed, when Colombo was Tesoro Minister (July 1973–March 1974) he proposed the adoption of a crawling-peg system as an alternative (i.e. a system of progressive but limited adjustments in exchange-rate parities) (Tsoukalis 1977: 88). But, once it had been 'faced with a run on the lira and with pressure from its EEC partners to remain in the snake, Italy began to favour a Community responsibility for interventions in the exchange markets and an extension of the credit system' (Tsoukalis 1977: 144). The Italians were now 'maximalists': favouring a progressive pooling of reserves, a large extension of credit facilities, and an active role for the Fund in the exchange markets (Tsoukalis 1977: 144). The Italian stance had moved towards 'Europeanized' solutions.

Italy and the 'Snake'

But the Italian authorities had an unhappy experience with the 'Snake'. The government of Mariano Rumor (with Colombo in charge of the Tesoro) was forced to take the lira out of the system after less than a year (in February 1973). The lira could not live with the new constraint, and it did not re-enter. In this respect, it followed the pattern set by the pound sterling, which had quit even sooner. By 1976, Italy was on the outside of a D-Mark bloc of Germany, Benelux, and Denmark. A two-tier structure had emerged, though this was far from stable. Indeed, at times the situation appeared somewhat chaotic.

Outside the 'Snake', the exchange rate of the lira was at the mercy of fiscal profligacy at home. The value of the currency fell, alongside high inflation. Between 1970 and 1978 the effective exchange rate of the lira fell by 45 per cent

(OECD 1979: 136). Monetary discipline was lacking, in the absence of a *vincolo esterno*. By 1979, however, a shift in attitudes at home together with the onset of the EMS created a more disciplined policy environment.

Italy and the Birth of the EMS

The discipline that the EMS entailed came as something as a shock for the Italian monetary authorities. Neither the Andreotti government nor the Banca d'Italia had envisaged such an arrangement. They sought flexibility and looseness in any new European system. Instead, a Franco-German axis effectively presented them with a stark choice: either to accept a tough monetary discipline as a condition for staying as a full EC member, or to be consigned to an undisciplined periphery outside a new EC core. After much hesitation, the Italians accepted the new *vincolo esterno* of the EMS. Doing so represented a decisive turning-point for Italy's monetary policy and for its commitment to 'Europe'. The same choice would be made a decade later in relation to EMU.

The negotiations on the EMS in 1978 proved something of a nightmare for the Italians. The Italian position suffered from both policy and strategic weaknesses. These were the result of inconsistency, confusion, and poor judgement. As Spaventa writes, 'the targets of our action were not very clear at the beginning and, as they became clear, were subsequently discarded or modified as a result of the opposition of our partners' (1980: 71). Spaventa cites the example of whether the government sought a wider band of fluctuation in the EMS or not. The Tesoro Minister, Filippo Pandolfi, in July 1978 firmly stated that it did not, whilst Paolo Baffi, Governor of the Banca d'Italia, claimed it did, and subsequent policy was to seek such a band (1980: 71–2).

The domestic debate on whether Italy should join the EMS, and if so on what basis, exposed the divisions on the position of Italy in Europe. The clash was between those who saw EMS participation as essential if Italy was to remain a full player in the EC, and those who doubted whether Italy could live with the domestic costs of joining the new European discipline.[33] In this case, the divide between the adherents to the *vincolo esterno* and *protezionismo interno* positions differed somewhat. Here, some otherwise ardent Europeanists doubted whether the lira was ready for the new discipline of the EMS, and they were thus closer to their 'opposite' camp.

The sceptics on EMS entry stressed the various economic costs that Italy might have to bear. At first, Guido Carli, then head of *Confindustria*, was one of them. He saw the EMS design as faulty. It was tilted against deficit countries (an early recognition of the problem of asymmetry), and it lacked an adequate

---

[33] After the EC summit in Paris in October 1972, Giulio Andreotti, Prime Minister, made clear his support for both the European Parliament and an extension of citizenship rights. The Parliament, he said, must become 'fully representative and with wider powers at its disposal' (*Keesing's Record of World Events*, 25539, 1972).

policy towards the US dollar (Ludlow 1982: 209). Two ministers also expressed their misgivings about the likely impact of EMS entry. The severist critic was Rinaldo Ossola, Minister for External Trade and a leading expert on monetary matters. He stressed the theme of homogeneity: the 'Snake' had this to some degree but was still problematic; the new EMS would be less cohesive and was thus doomed from the start (Ludlow 1982: 210). Giovanni Marcora, Minister for Agriculture, foresaw an intolerable burden on Italian agriculture, unless special provision was made (Ludlow 1982: 211). He urged that the lira should not enter for at least six months. His concerns found expression in the Italian demands for 'parallel measures': reform of the EC budget, to give more aid to Italy, and of the CAP, in order to offer greater help to Mediterranean producers.

The Banca d'Italia, a natural constituency for the *vincolo esterno* stance, found itself in this case closer to the sceptics. It feared that the new EMS would prove unworkable, or at least that the Italians would not be able to live with it. Between the two European Council meetings of Copenhagen (April 1978) and of Bremen (July 1978) the Bank supported a loose arrangement. Such an arrangement would involve 'reference rates expressed in terms of effective exchange rates without compulsory interventions' (Spaventa 1980: 69). A repeat of the 'Snake', rigid as it was, but now including the currencies previously left to float, was not seen as sustainable: a view which paralleled that of Ossola. The Bank was also concerned about asymmetries in the new system: like others, it saw this as too biased towards German interests. Thus, the strategy should be to seek a wider margin of currency fluctuation. Paolo Baffi, the Governor, felt Italy was not ready to join: disinflation and currency stability required more sensitive management. In the Italian case, reduced inflation might force a revaluation of the lira, rather than vice versa (Spaventa 1980: 69).

Those keen to keep Italy a full player in the EC, stressed the need to make domestic reforms to accomplish this task. The Andreotti government announced its intention to introduce an ambitious stabilization programme to its EC partners in July 1978. The plan, named after Filippo Pandolfi, the Tesoro Minister, highlighted the need to reduce the PSBR and to lower labour costs. As such it had provoked much controversy within the governing coalition and with the unions.[34] Now, implementation of the plan was being justified in terms of the demands of EC membership, in order to win more support for it. Later domestic pressures would undermine the implementation of the plan and delay the policy of disinflation (McCarthy 1997: 53). In 1978, however, the *vincolo esterno*' argument had an effect: Carli, for example, changed his position. 'If Italy is too weak to participate in the EMS', he commented, 'it is also true that she is

---

[34] Spaventa (1980: 69) describes the debate as one between two positions: 'those who believed that the external and/or political aspects of the EMS were far more important than the balance between economic costs and benefits and those, instead, who gave greater emphasis to the economic side of the question. The former were in favour of joining even without Britain . . . the latter thought that Britain's refusal would remove the major political reason for joining, so that the decision should depend on whether certain minimal conditions were satisfied.'

too weak not to participate' (Ludlow 1982: 210). The argument had thus shifted to one of a *'vincolo esterno'*: Europe demanded what had hitherto been blocked. This shift was a clear precursor to the Maastricht case a decade later.

The Andreotti government had shown that it had special policy concerns as to the potential effects of the EMS on the domestic economy. The fact that these were effectively brushed aside suggests a lack of bargaining power and/or a failure of strategy in the negotiations. Spaventa suggests the latter. He writes of a 'rather velvety hand [being] shown during the negotiations with our partners' (1980: 70). The Italian concerns were regarded as unique, to be dealt with by special measures. At the decisive Brussels European Council of December 1978, Andreotti was offended by the brutal dismissal of all of his pleas (Spaventa 1980: 84). Strategically, the Italians were also effectively excluded from the Giscard–Schmidt alliance which was the driving-force behind the EMS launch. There was resentment in Rome at not being included in the Schulmann–Clappier–Couzens (German–French–British) working group designing the EMS (Ludlow 1982: 114–15). At their most extreme, the French and German governments appeared to regard their Italian counterpart as a dispensable ally. A potential alternative ally, the British government, proved uninterested in siding with Rome, and was at times equally offensive as the French and the Germans. Denis Healey and the Treasury in London adopted a very dismissive attitude to their Italian suitors (Ludlow 1982: 238).

The narrowness of the EMS debate—relative to the more ambitious notion of EMU—excluded other dimensions from being taken into account. The general differences between the 'economist' (behaviouralist) and 'monetarist' (institutionalist) positions evident in the debate over the Werner Plan were not fully exposed in 1978–9. The effect was to prevent Italian 'gains' in other areas (e.g. the parallel measures) and to limit the scope of possible coalitions for the Italians to join.

Central to strategic thinking in Italy was a division over the importance of ensuring that Britain was a participant in the EMS. Great effort was exerted to persuade the Callaghan government in London to join, and Italian strategy appears to have relied much too heavily on the prospect that it might succeed. Italian leaders felt they had shared interests with the British on the EMS. Baffi, and the Banca d'Italia, regarded British entry as being of 'decisive importance', and he and his staff continuously pressed London to join (Ludlow 1982: 216). Pandolfi, Tesoro Minister, appeared to share this view. By contrast, British entry was not seen as crucial by Andreotti, the then Prime Minister and never an Anglophile. He complained that Callaghan had given him no help at the Brussels European Council in December 1978 (Ludlow 1982: 259). Similarly, the Foreign Ministry believed Italy should join the EMS with or without Britain: 'one could even say that they did not care much whether Britain was in or out' (Spaventa 1980: 69).

The case for allying with Britain was to help press the case for wider margins of currency fluctuation. When such overtures failed, the Italians 'wanted a wider band for their own country at all costs' (Ludlow 1982: 238). By 14 November 1978 it had been agreed in the Committee of Central Bank Governors that the lira could operate within a 6 per cent band. The final arrangements had a cosmetic aspect: technically any member state could avail itself of this facility, though in reality only the Italians sought it. It eased Italian embarrassment.

Despite the concerns noted earlier, the political climate in Italy allowed its negotiators much latitude on the question of EMS entry. The initial negotiating brief had been determined by a small group of technocratic officials (see Chapter 11). Subsequently, Andreotti as Prime Minister was determinant. There was 'nothing in the domestic political situation' which 'required him to revise his initial assessment of the Franco-German initiative at Bremen, which was essentially that, whatever the economic disadvantages that might arise from membership, the political costs of non-participation would be still greater' (Ludlow 1982: 215). Andreotti consulted, but kept his own counsel. He did not guide, 'he merely decided' (Ludlow 1982: 271).

The decision to place the lira in the EMS from the start was delayed, however. The decision was Andreotti's alone. It was his response to the brush-off he had experienced at the decisive European Council in Brussels in December 1978. The choice in Brussels had been posed too starkly. Andreotti sought to use the delay to advantage. Attempts were made to extract concessions from the Germans and the French. Giscard agreed to a greater latitude for the Italians in the event of a realignment. But no other concessions were obtained.

Instead, Giscard and Schmidt piled on the political pressure. They told Andreotti that EMS participation was the ultimate European test (Ludlow 1982: 216). Such symbolism would have struck a strong chord with the Italian premier: for all his opportunism, he did display a consistent belief in Italy's European vocation, in keeping with his early mentor, De Gasperi (Ludlow 1982: 206). In addition, Giscard and Schmidt warned that non-entry would be seen abroad as Andreotti being too soft on the Communists, the latter professing severe misgivings on the domestic costs of EMS participation.

Andreotti finally announced the decision to enter to the Camera dei Deputati on 12 December. The week-long delay had added to the political discomfort of his partners in the government majority. The previously embattled Prime Minister was now 'obliged to almost nobody and in command of almost everybody' (Ludlow 1982: 273). The decision to enter the EMS served Andreotti's interests within his coalition, and encouraged those in his party who wanted to ditch the Communists (McCarthy 1997: 53). The period of the so-called 'historic compromise' was drawing to a close. The irony was that the break with the Communists undermined the implementation of the Pandolfi Plan, which had been touted as a *sine qua non* of full EC membership. The struggle for disinflation was to be a prolonged one.

Domestic misgivings about the EMS remained. Both unions and business sought to keep the option of devaluation open: it had become part of an Italian tradition. The divide soon came to parallel the *vincolo esterno–protezionismo interno* contrast outlined above. It was not until the EMS had operated for several years that *Confindustria* declared its support for Italian participation in it. The EMS constraint gradually tightened and it was to prove crucial in the struggle for monetary stability in Italy (see below, and Farina in Francioni 1992).

Italian concerns over the design of the EMS were not eased by the failure of the EC to institute a 'second phase' of the system by establishing a European Monetary Fund in 1981. This institutional development had been foreseen in the Bremen European Council communiqué of July 1978 (Dyson 1994: 103–11, *passim*). The EMF would have been a reserve pool and a system of credit facilities for participating states. Both were seen as being in the Italian interest. The EC's Committee of Central Bank Governors in effect blocked these initiatives, pushed by the strong resistance of the Bundesbank. Tommaso Padoa-Schioppa, of the Banca d'Italia but at the time on secondment to the EC Commission as Director-General for Economic and Monetary Affairs, pressed the case for the EMF. In doing so, he incurred the animosity of the Bundesbank: a factor that would later reappear when he was nominated as rapporteur to the Delors Committee on EMU in 1988.

The case of EMS entry highlights several themes of longer-term importance. As at the time of the birth of the 'Snake', Italian negotiators had pressed for a more flexible system. Both at the time of the Werner and of the EMS negotiations, they had sought greater economic help for Italy: in the early 1970s they sought parallelism; at the end of the decade they tried to link the establishment of the EMS to EC budget reform. Given Italy's bad experience with the 'Snake', Italian negotiators stressed the problem of asymmetry in the EMS: a consistent theme repeated most notably in 1987–8. A relatively new aspect was the identification of the EC with a *'vincolo esterno'* discipline: the EMS required the previously unpopular Pandolfi Plan; Maastricht required its own set of domestic reforms. Finally, all three cases—Werner, the EMS, Maastricht—showed the high priority Italy attached to remaining a full EC member in the inner circle. No one exemplified this commitment more than the otherwise wily and seemingly 'unprincipled' Andreotti.

In terms of alliance-building, Italy was clearly closer to Germany at the time of Werner than it was at the time of the EMS and the EMU negotiations. It endeavoured to build a bridge with Britain on the EMS, but was rebuffed: later, on EMU, it saw such an option as a lost cause. For the EMS, Italy failed to secure an effective and consistent alliance with France. Some years later, on EMU, Italy would again rue the shifts in the French negotiating position.

Whatever the misgivings of the Banca d'Italia on the EMS regime, it used the lira's entry as a further boost to the case for greater monetary stability. Indeed, in the second year of EMS membership, the Banca d'Italia stressed that participation had already made a very substantial contribution to the policy of disinflation, both directly (through exchange-rate stability) and indirectly (in obliging firms to change their behaviour and lower their costs).[35] For its part, industry gradually came to recognize the benefits of currency stability: particularly in the case of exporters. The EMS had promoted the stabilization of the price of imported materials and reduced the risk from export price instability. It also helped to increase domestic wage flexibility. Carlo Ciampi, as Governor of the Banca d'Italia, pressed for reforms to the wage indexation system (*scala mobile*). 'The protection of wages', he argued, 'should be sought by respecting the rules that produce monetary stability and not by means of practices that trigger a wage-price spiral' (Banca d'Italia 1982: 184). The reforms to wage indexation made in 1983 and, more significantly, in 1985 greatly reduced the effects of the system, before it was finally abolished in 1992 (OECD, July 1986; Banca d'Italia, Feb. 1986; 1992: 53). The *vincolo esterno* of the EMS had worked: leading Italian economists saw it as a fundamental factor underlying the shift to disinflation. The Italian case showed that the EMS was 'an effective disciplinary device for inflation-prone countries', bringing large credibility gains, penalizing inflation, and making the public aware of the EMS penalty on inflation (Giavazzi and Pagano 1988: 1055). Again, the accumulated legacy of 'internal protection' was being dismantled.

Divorce, Italian Style

The ability of the Banca d'Italia to promote the shift of policy was, of course, helped by its increasing independence from the Tesoro. The initiation of the divorce came, in effect, from Carlo Ciampi, the new Governor of the Banca d'Italia, after 1979. The Minister of the Tesoro, Professor Beniamino Andreatta, had set down various alternative means for securing more independence in a confidential letter to Ciampi. Andreatta tended towards grandiose schemes and radical change. Ciampi replied by opting for the quickest and simplest solution—setting down a new understanding in an exchange of letters, without the need for parliamentary legislation—and the Tesoro published the result. The Tesoro took the credit for making the change: perhaps not unreasonably, given that its support for the divorce contrasts with the stance adopted by finance ministries in many other EC countries which jealously guarded their control over their central banks.

The shift of policy had been prompted by a set of factors. First, it was again part of the reaction to the failures of the 1970s: a reaction evident amongst public, as well as technocratic, opinion. Epstein and Schor argue that the Banca d'Italia sought independence precisely 'to curb the power of labor and other social groups' (1989: 162). Yet, trade union pressure for expansionary policies was already less than it had been, given increasing union weakness. This

---

[35] The attitudes of the PCI and trade union leaderships were somewhat enigmatic, however. To their critics they were seen as engaged in posturing and not so prepared to provoke a political crisis over the issue.

weakness facilitated the shift to the monetary stability associated with the Banca d'Italia. Secondly, the Banca d'Italia's success in managing the exchange rate after the 1976 stabilization programme increased its credibility, and the EMS constraint later strengthened this role. But at the heart of the shift towards independence was the relationship between Andreatta and Ciampi. Ciampi sought monetary stability; Andreatta accepted that the Tesoro's hands needed to be tied to obtain this shared goal. The Tesoro was entrapped in the *partitocrazia*: it needed to be bound.

The decision on the divorce did not bring a dramatic change in the degree of monetary independence, though actual practice gradually did so.[36] But it was the re-emergence of the EMU debate that represented a golden opportunity to complete the process on a formal basis. The Banca d'Italia supported the principle of the independence of national and European monetary institutions throughout the EMU discussions of 1988–91. Later, the Maastricht Treaty's provisions on stage 2 gave the Banca d'Italia the excuse to speed up the completion of its independence.

Two final steps were taken. The first, and more significant, involved a new law which gave the Banca d'Italia's Governor the exclusive right to set the discount rate (Ciampi 1992: 66).[37] The fact that this law was passed early in 1992 shows the impact of the IGC negotiations. The second step was taken with a law in 1993 under which the Tesoro's current account with the Banca d'Italia was reformed in accordance with the Maastricht Treaty's provisions on the abolition of the automatic financing of the public sector.

At least in legal terms, the Banca d'Italia after 1992–3 enjoyed considerable autonomy from the Tesoro. In practice, a mutual dependence remained. The Banca d'Italia's ability to implement an autonomous monetary policy is put under great pressure by the poor state of the public finances. High levels of public debt increase the chances of conflict between monetary and fiscal-policy targets (Scobie *et al.* 1996). High interest rates to abate inflation also raise public-debt interest payments and lead to fiscal targets being overshot. In the summer of 1994 the Berlusconi government exerted great pressure on the Banca d'Italia to reduce interest rates for this reason. The pressure failed, but it is indicative of the threat stemming from fiscal weakness. For its part, independence has given the Tesoro much greater scope for manoeuvre in managing the public debt. The Tesoro benefited from being able to concentrate on 'normal' finance ministry tasks, and in the early 1990s it acquired enhanced responsibilities, not least in relation to the privatization programme. Later, in 1996 it would form the core of a new 'super' economics ministry.

---

[36] See the Governor's remarks to shareholders, 30 May 1981 (in Banca d'Italia 1981).

[37] The Tesoro was still able to finance part of the deficit through a more restricted overdraft facility, and it was still responsible (officially, at least) for the policy on the discount rate. Moreover, on some occasions the bank voluntarily acted as a residual buyer of government debt in order to prevent a crisis in the securities market or to moderate the 'crowding-out' effects on credit to the corporate sector.

Financial Market Liberalization

The final case of a policy shift to be highlighted here—that of financial-market liberalization—also affected the relations between the Tesoro and the Banca d'Italia, as well as the relations of both with the markets. Again, EC obligations acted as an important *vincolo esterno*: EC pressures for full capital liberalization gave added strength and speed to the domestic process of reform. The result was to enhance further the role of technocratic state management in the markets, and to discipline the traditions of the *partitocrazia*. The EMS constraint had greatly affected the private sector in Italy. But with the shield of capital controls the Tesoro was protected from reducing its deficit, and the public sector generally was cosseted. Liberalization strengthened the power of the market over the state.

Prior to the reforms, Italy's financial markets had been heavily regulated and closed. They lagged far behind other major economies. From 1958 onwards, external financial transactions had been subject to a control system which prohibited unauthorized transactions abroad. Moreover, within the EMS in the 1980s, exchange controls had remained a key instrument of policy. They helped, in fact, to slow the rate of lira depreciation, despite Italy's high inflation rate (Artis and Taylor 1988; Giavazzi and Spaventa 1994). By limiting the depreciation, capital controls had contributed to Italy's disinflation.

In the main, the liberalization measures were introduced between 1981 and 1988, and implementation was complete in 1990, as required by the EC directive of 1988 on capital liberalization. The most important step was taken in 1987–8, with the abolition of all capital controls except those concerning short-term movements. In 1990, all remaining controls on short-term capital movements were removed; and reforms of the banking sector and of the stock exchange followed the year after.

Domestically, the initiation of financial liberalization owed much to the lead given by the heads of the Tesoro, aided by the Banca d'Italia and Ciampi in particular, and supported by an external policy community of liberal economists. Sarcinelli, as Direttore-Generale of the Tesoro, was a key figure throughout. A report in 1982 by a committee headed by Mario Monti had urged liberalization and had been rejected by the Tesoro which had initiated it. The committee was composed of academics outside the governmental system; those inside were not ready to change. Sarcinelli wrote the foreword to the report, distancing the Tesoro from its conclusions. The climate of opinion amongst the financial establishment at this time was strongly opposed to change. The Banca d'Italia— a self-confident institution—believed in its own ability to use the existing discretionary mechanisms.

Reform required the policy entrepreneurship of those at the top of the financial establishment. Giovanni Goria, as Tesoro Minister, set up a new committee in 1986, this time chaired by Sarcinelli. It included Monti and Luigi Spaventa; the latter associated with the Left. The Sarcinelli Report was timely: it argued that Italy had no alternative but to get in step with the wider international momentum behind financial-market liberalization.[38] The subsequent law which realized the definitive liberalization of capital movements in 1988 was in fact drafted by Sarcinelli himself, as Minister for Foreign Trade, and guided through Parliament by his successor, Renato Ruggiero in the government of Goria. Ruggiero, like Sarcinelli, was a civil servant; a former Secretary-General in the Ministry of Foreign Affairs.[39] Reform had thus been dependent on the policy entrepreneurship of two technocrats strongly committed to Italy's international vocation in general, and to retaining the place of Italy in the inner circle of the EC, in particular.[40]

The reforms of the banking and financial sector represented the first instance of economic liberalization in Italy; only later, in the 1990s, did deregulation affect state–industry relations. The Italian pattern thus contrasts with that of Britain, though it parallels that of France after 1984. Historically, business has displayed ambivalent attitudes towards market competition.[41] Regonini and Giuliani have explained why reform was so late in Italy, and why it was so little affected by the experience of the USA and Britain (1994: 124–5). They cite: the lateness of Italian industrialization, with its backward character and the fragility of its entrepreneurial class; a political culture of alienation hostile to the values of liberal individualism; and a political-institutional system which hinders economic and administrative reform in the general interest (1994: 135–6). Privatization began only when governments were 'pressed by the need to meet the challenge of the single EC market, the urgency of fiscal consolidation and the financial crisis of public enterprises' (OECD 1993: 53). Only then did the loss of political control over enterprises appear as an acceptable cost. It is also true that a determined start to privatization came only in 1992: immediately after the agreement at Maastricht.

External pressure was crucial to effecting change in the Italian state tradition. For their part, the Banca d'Italia and the Tesoro had not initially believed in the disciplinary effects of openness to the international financial markets. With lib-

---

[38] In his resignation letter (see Il Mondo: 18 Mar. 1991), Sarcinelli highlights a set of measures that are needed to secure the full independence of the Banca d'Italia. The most important of these concerns the discount rate, and this was subsequently achieved. The other two measures that he highlighted concerned the ability of a Tesoro inspector to temporarily nullify decisions of a Banca d'Italia board, and the right of the Tesoro minister to suspend Banca d'Italia decisions, under certain conditions. Sarcinelli reports that Carli's attitude on these matters was that there was plenty of time to implement them: stage 2 of EMU would not begin until 1994 and it might last for more than three years.

[39] The report was entitled, 'Financial Wealth, the Public Debt and Monetary Policy in the Perspective of International Integration' (Sarcinelli 1986).

[40] Ruggiero later became the first Secretary-General of the World Trade Organization.

[41] The notion of policy entrepreneurship, developed by Kingdon (1984), stresses the role of agency in the policy process. The advocacy-coalition framework is a more structural model. Yet Sabatier (1998: 115) recognizes the 'dubiousness' of assuming that shared beliefs alone will prompt actors to act in concert. We recognize that agents must seize opportunities for policy influence and find the notion of 'entrepreneur' helpful.

eralization, the power of the market has increased. Both institutions then came to see the market as the judge of policy performance. In the words of one senior observer,

Today, the Banca d'Italia and the Tesoro are the import agents and the authorized interpreters of the austere market sentiment. The relative power of both institutions [vis-à-vis the markets] has declined, but the relative power of their technocratic heads has increased compared to that of the ministers. (Personal interview)

This situation is the outcome not only of financial-market liberalization, but also of the other two policy reforms cited here: central bank independence, and price and currency stability. The three sets of reform are part of an integral whole emphasizing a new environment marked by the power of the market over government, and the power of technocratic heads in relation to ministers. The boundaries of state–economy relations have been redrawn, with the effect that outside pressures have been made much stronger. As Della Sala has described it, the Italian state has undergone a process of 'hollowing out' (1997).

The *vincolo esterno* was highly significant in promoting the policy changes in the first place. The pressure exerted by EC policy commitments on capital liberalization, competition policy, the single market in general, and EMU was an essential factor reinforcing and speeding up the domestic momentum for reform.

But the process of reform was not under co-ordinated control. Given that it was the result of both domestic and external pressures, and also that its very nature was to take power away from state institutions, the momentum was not readily controllable. As a result, there is no suggestion here of a conscious, direct conspiracy by a power-hungry technocratic elite. The purpose of reform was, in part, to limit the power of politicians by accepting the demands of the market. The indirect effect was to increase the relevance of technocratic judgement of such market pressure. But the market constrained technocrats also; the policy agenda was limited and the options narrowed. The Tesoro had more power for its Minister and Director-General to exercise before liberalization than afterwards. Key actors had the will to reform and they had to overcome many internal obstacles, but structural constraints squeezed them until they did so.

It remains unclear how conscious such individuals were of the long-term effects of their actions. Theoretically, it would be wrong to seek too deterministic an explanation: information was limited and had to be interpreted, and there was a significant element of uncertainty about their actions, in the face of unforeseen contingencies. A rational-choice model would be too limiting here. The apparent acceptance of the logic of the *vincolo esterno* is not the same as an awareness of the impact on domestic power relations of market liberalization. Carli claims that ministers had little appreciation of the latter. Specifically in relation to EMU, he concluded that 'The Italian *classe politica* did not realize that by agreeing to the Treaty, it put itself in the position of already accepting a change of such magnitude that it would hardly leave it unscathed' (1993: 437). This may be a *post-hoc* defence of his own compromised position as a minister.

But the more fundamental point is that both ministers and their officials had little option but to go with the momentum of change. All were constrained by the increasing contradictions between the Italian state tradition, on the one hand, and sustaining the EC commitment and international competitiveness, on the other. The traditional pattern, and boundary, of state–economy relations was changing. Both before and after Maastricht, external discipline and the primacy of market principles and forces was 'hollowing out' the Italian state, as Della Sala has argued (1997: 27). At the same time, the established party system was moving towards crisis point. Already, by the time of the re-emergence of the EMU debate in 1988, the dog could no longer bark as loudly: internal protection was no longer as feasible in the old form. This change of environment was crucial to how Italian policy on the EMS and EMU developed.

11

Framing EMU as a New *Vincolo Esterno*: Policy Entrepreneurs, Co-ordination, and Reflection in Italy, 1988–1990

The general tendency within the Italian state apparatus for diffuseness and *immobilismo* was in stark contrast to the negotiating demands of EMU after 1988. The latter required firm direction in the domestic-policy co-ordination process. EMU also challenged the tradition of *protezionismo interno*: it would require the government to accept a rather severe external discipline on both monetary and fiscal policy, indirectly challenging the mores of the *partitocrazia*. Yet, both public and political elites were deeply committed to Italy's place in 'Europe': the prevailing consensus placed top priority on keeping Italy in the 'inner circle' of the EC. A 'window of opportunity' thus existed for those seeking greater discipline and able to mobilize the official policy process: they could secure the coveted European prize.

Following Kingdon's (1984) well-known model, it can be argued that a 'policy window' had opened, as a result of three separate process streams—problems, politics, and policy ideas—coming together. The co-ordination problem was overcome by a relatively small technocratic elite operating within the 'core executive'. Political conditions facilitated their lead: key ministers in the *partitocrazia* tradition were distracted and ceded position, seemingly content that what was negotiated today could be reinterpreted tomorrow. Yet, a wider momentum surrounded the EMU process in Italy. As already outlined in the previous chapter, the tide of policy ideas was already favouring the capacity of a technocratic elite to seize the opportunity and provide a lead for Italy on EMU. The state was being 'hollowed out' by the effects of policy reforms which gave primacy to market principles and forces and which accepted the obligations of earlier externally imposed discipline. The stimulus of such changes was towards a depoliticized, technocratic management of monetary policy. Consistent with this momentum, a small nucleus of technocrats acted as 'policy entrepreneurs' on EMU, seizing the window of opportunity to strengthen the shift towards discipline and the market. They were able to act in relative isolation from other government actors and outside pressure groups.

The policy style was predominantly reactive (Richardson 1982), responding to the EMU lead emanating from the EC level, and from France and Germany in particular. This followed a pattern: in general, few Italian leaders have made a significant impact at the European level, most have 'punched below their weight'. More particularly, the instigation and direction of the EMS had displayed Italy's somewhat marginal role in EC monetary affairs. Not suprisingly, the relaunch of EMU onto the EC's agenda in 1988 owed relatively little to Italian actions.

But, in their reaction, Italian actors quickly became cheer-leaders for the new project. Whilst Italian politicians made little input at the EC level into the setting of the EMU agenda, senior officials and academics provided support and intellectual justification during its early gestation. In part, this input was because the early path taken by the EMU project—from Basle-Nyborg, Hanover, and the Delors Committee—privileged technocrats rather than ministers. But it was also consistent with the predominant passivity on the part of ministers in policy-making, be it domestic or European. Again, technocracy filled the void.

The response to the EMU debate was relatively clear, coherent, and consistent. Before the IGC on EMU began, the Italian stance had been fully elaborated. Paradoxically, a 'weak' state sustained 'strong' co-ordination on the basis of a common set of values and priorities amongst the key technocratic actors.

This chapter is in two parts. The first section examines how and why a small technocratic group was able to exert domestic policy leadership over EMU. It analyses the policy co-ordination process and the relative roles of the key actors, both ministerial and official. The second section then considers the early response to the relaunch of EMU, highlighting the core negotiating concerns for the Italians and analysing the input of Italian actors into the EC policy process. Such a discussion forms an essential prelude to the analysis in the following chapter of Italian negotiating priorities and strategies in the context of the IGC in 1990–1.

Policy Entrepreneurs and the Core Executive: The Technocratic Opportunity

The co-ordination attained in the case of the EMU negotiations was amongst the best of its genre. It is not easily attained. Executive monopoly over major EC negotiations and the non-interference of other parts of the bureaucracy helped. The passivity of ministers, in particular the distraction of Andreotti as Prime Minister and Gianni De Michelis as Foreign Minister, in turn ceded the initiative to a technocratic elite.[1] The rarefied nature of monetary policy isolated the process. Mobilization by sectoral interests was difficult. Public opinion could be relied upon to support almost any new project that advanced the European integration process and Italy's place within it. But, ultimately, a 'hard shell' surrounded the co-ordination process (Della Sala 1997).

[1] The term 'Prime Minister' is preferred here, though the official title is 'President of the Council of Ministers'.

The EMU case was thus exceptional: a weak state, which by tradition exhibits a dispersal of power, gave rise to a well-defined network for policy co-ordination. The paradox emphasizes the importance of gauging bureaucratic action within distinct policy sectors, rather than on the basis of simple strong state/weak state generalizations (Atkinson and Coleman 1989). The techno-cratic elite—or 'task force'—that operated on EMU had a relatively clear con-ception of its role, and its members shared a set of values, concerned with Italy's role in Europe, that supported that performance. Bureaucrats and politicians co-operated relatively easily: in part because one of the politicians (Carli) was an ex-technocrat himself, and because two others (Andreotti and De Michelis) dis-played little interest in the actual content of EMU policy.

EC Policy Co-ordination Across the Archipelago

The normal pattern is strikingly different. The governmental machine has struggled to co-ordinate policy on EC matters.[2] As one senior official com-mented,

It is difficult to say that we have a 'co-ordination mechanism' as such for EC policies. It is all ad hoc. Each ministry has its own responsibility and domain; coordination is prompted when a problem becomes of major political interest. It is not like the French system; we feel the lack of a co-ordinating body. Various initiatives have come and gone, but the problem still remains. (Personal interview)

In short, EC co-ordination has suffered from the archipelago nature of the gov-ernmental process.

Historically, the *Ministero degli Affari Esteri* (Ministry of Foreign Affairs) has had the prime lead in co-ordinating Italian policy on EC matters. Its role is but-tressed by its link with the Italian Permanent Delegation in Brussels. Within the Ministry, the Directorates-General for Economic Affairs and for Political Affairs have been the two co-ordinating agencies, with the emphasis on the former at least until Maastricht. During the EMU period, Vanni d'Archirafi served as Director-General for Economic Affairs until July 1991, when he was succeeeded by Giovanni Jannuzzi. Under Jannuzzi, a co-ordinator specifically for EC affairs was established (Roberto Nigido, previously Jannuzzi's deputy).[3]

The expansion of the EC Council of Ministers led to the close involvement of a number of 'functional' departments in Rome. There was no 'gatekeeper' within government. Most ministries had a 'diplomatic counsellor' to help with international liaison. They formed a network co-ordinated by the Foreign Ministry and were drawn from its own junior staff. But their status and existence

[2] On EC co-ordination, see Hine (1993: 290–7). At the time he was writing a number of reforms had been touted, but few, if any, appear to have affected EMU policy, or perhaps wider EC policy co-ordination.

[3] When Italy held the EC Presidency in 1996 interdepartmental co-ordination was placed under the ministry's EC co-ordinator (at the time Rocco Cangelosi; previously the ministry's representative in the IGC on EMU).

varied. For example, not all Tesoro ministers felt the need for a diplomatic coun-sellor. Carli did not have such a counsellor, though his successor Barucci did. Counsellors normally had little input into policy. Indeed, this network was not able to address the basic problem of policy co-ordination.

Nor had organizational reform succeeded in establishing a stable and effective structure to initiate and co-ordinate EC policy. In most recent governments there has been no interministerial committee to supervise EC policy *per se*.[4] Each minister attending a meeting of the Council of Ministers was expected to report to the Prime Minister. And ministers were obliged to report to the Tesoro on any financial aspects of EC policy. In 1980, a department for EC co-ordina-tion was established in the Prime Minister's office (Hine 1993: 294). But, for most of its existence, it had a purely domestic function of managing the receipt of EC funds, not of co-ordinating external policy. In any event, it quickly suf-fered from a lack of resources, and a separation from the Permanent Delegation in Brussels, which was seen as very much part of the Foreign Ministry's fiefdom. In 1987, legislation envisaged the minister heading the EC co-ordination depart-ment leading a grand committee to oversee the implementation of EC law. A 1988 reform of the Prime Minister's Office signalled new resources for the department. Yet, the new arrangements were slow to be enacted: and Hine (1993) reported that the grand committee had never met.[5] To compensate for this problem, Umberto Vattani, Diplomatic Counsellor under Andreotti (1988–92), sought to take a more active role in EC co-ordination, though his activism upset a number of his peers. Thus, the policy co-ordination function was exercised by different governmental actors within the core executive, with little consistent or routine pattern.

Co-ordination for the Delors Committee: The Banca d'Italia to the fore

During the early period of the EMU debate the establishment of the Delors Committee gave a primacy to the role of the Banca d'Italia. EMU was discussed at Basle, well away from the ECOFIN and Tesoro orbit. Domestically, however, the Banca d'Italia was on safe ground: for both it and the Tesoro shared a basic consensus of views on EMU, and the bank had already established its institu-tional strength over the course of the last decade. Thus, the Banca d'Italia orga-nized its own system of co-ordination, as an island apart. Its co-ordination emphasized the role of the Governor (Carlo Azeglio Ciampi), Italy's represen-tative on the Delors Committee. Ciampi reported progress to Giuliano Amato, Tesoro Minister throughout the period. But there was no regular framework of

---

[4] Ciampi when PM (1993–4) did have a small interministerial committee, focusing mainly on priva-tization issues and negotiations with the EC Commission.

[5] In October 1996 the government of Romano Prodi announced the creation of a 'strategic com-mission' charged with preparing for Italy's participation in stage 3 of EMU from the outset. The com-mission was to be made up of thirty members and was to be chaired by the Under-Secretary at the Tesoro, Roberto Pinza (*Agence Europe*, 17 Oct. 1996).

bilateral meetings between Governor and Minister. For his part, Mario Sarcinelli, as *Direttore-Generale* at the Tesoro, was not directly briefed by the Banca d'Italia. Amato and Sarcinelli served in other fora—ECOFIN and the EC Monetary Committee—distant from the Basle process, and they were not yet required to take up a negotiating position. The Delors Committee was for Ciampi alone. Later, when EMU was considered by the Committee of Central Bank Governors, other Banca d'Italia officials would be drawn in, notably Lamberto Dini, Ciampi's Deputy.

Within the Banca d'Italia, there was no special system of regular briefings established for Ciampi before each session of the Delors Committee. Instead, the briefing process was informal and ad hoc. Francesco Papadia, of the bank's research department, co-ordinated the briefings for Ciampi. EMU entered the agenda of the Banca d'Italia's board, which was made up of departmental heads. But these meetings were large, formal occasions not suited to a briefing role. By contrast, Ciampi gave extensive debriefings to his staff after the sessions of the Delors Committee. The fact that Tommaso Padoa-Schioppa, Deputy Director-General of the bank, served as co-rapporteur to the Delors Committee, gave bank staff an additional and unique focal point at home. He could brief and seek briefings, and he frequently did so. Padoa-Schioppa already had an established reputation at the EC level, and he would continue to be closely involved in the EMU process.

The EMU Steering Group Emerges

After the Delors Report was published, EMU entered the sphere of the ECOFIN and the European Council: the Tesoro, the Prime Minister's Office, and the Foreign Ministry became involved. The establishment of the Guigou Group brought Sarcinelli (Tesoro) into the process. He led the Italian delegation, with Rocco Cangelosi (Foreign Ministry) alongside him, and a representative of the Banca d'Italia behind them. Sarcinelli was much the more prominent participant of the two. He was already Chair of the EC Monetary Committee (1989–90) and an experienced monetary diplomat.

Whilst the Guigou Group brought in the Tesoro, the prospect of the Italian EC Presidency in the second half of 1990 provided the Foreign Ministry with the opportunity for a leadership role. De Michelis, as Foreign Minister, convened a small steering group of officials early in 1990 to handle EMU for the EC presidency. This informal, ad hoc mechanism survived until the end of the EMU negotiating process in 1991. The Foreign Ministry instigated, but did not seek, nor would it have been able, to dominate or lead the group. The policy content of EMU ensured that the Tesoro had the lead from now on, supported by the Banca d'Italia.

The steering group was at the level of officials, with personnel from the Prime Minister's Office, the Foreign Ministry, the Tesoro, and the Banca d'Italia. This composition was somewhat different from that established prior to the

EMS negotiations in 1978. Then the group had been composed of only one representative from the Tesoro (Filippo Pandolfi, the minister at the time) and had not included the Director-General. The group had also not included anyone from the Prime Minister's Office. Instead, a five-member group had comprised: Pandolfi; Baffi (as Governor of the Banca d'Italia); Ciampi (Deputy-Governor); Rainer Masera (from the bank's research department); and Renato Ruggiero (an official of ministerial rank at the Foreign Ministry following his return from the EC Commission) (Ludlow 1982: 147). Of the EMS group, only Ciampi would play a direct role in the EMU discussions (via the CCBG), though not as part of the domestic co-ordinating group.

In 1990, the EMU steering group comprised: Umberto Vattani (diplomatic counsellor to the Prime Minister); Vanni d'Archirafi (Director-General for Economic Affairs in the Foreign Ministry); Sarcinelli (Director-General of the Tesoro); and Padoa-Schioppa (Deputy Director-General, Banca d'Italia).[6] These officials were to play a key role in the EMU negotiations during the Italian Presidency, including the Rome I European Council meeting. In 1991, a revised group continued to co-ordinate the Italian negotiating position for the IGC on EMU. Sarcinelli was replaced by Mario Draghi at the Tesoro at the end of February 1991, and Giovanni Jannuzzi took over from Vanni d'Archirafi at the Foreign Ministry in the following July. This group was complemented by Rocco Cangelosi, who served as the Foreign Minister's personal representative in both the IGC on EMU and that on political union.[7]

This list of dramatis personae indicates the relatively small number of core executive personnel involved in co-ordinating Italian negotiating positions. Even allowing for those officials in the Tesoro, Banca d'Italia, and Foreign Ministry closely involved in a supporting capacity, the total cast of personnel remains small.[8] The key figures were Draghi, Padoa-Schioppa, and Vattani.

These key officials were able to play a policy leadership role owing, in part, to the passivity of the relevant ministers. This passivity was the result of distrac-

---

[6] A number of the officials most closely involved in EMU have published contributions to the European debate. For a brief selection, see: Bini-Smaghi et al. (1994); Cangelossi and Grassi (1996); Papadia (1991); Padoa-Schioppa (1994); Padoa-Schioppa and Saccomanni (1992); Sarcinelli (1987, 1996). Likewise, Draghi had written extensively on international monetary economics before entering the Tesoro.

[7] Carli, as Minister, led the Italian delegation to the IGC on EMU. He was joined on occasions by the Italian Permanent Representative to the EC. The latter, however, had little involvement. This contrasts with the case of some of the other national delegations. In 1990, De Michelis had sacked the then Permanent Representative, Pietro Calamier, rather suddenly and replaced him by Frederico Di Roberto. Di Roberto attended the IGC on political union, but very rarely that on EMU. Instead, Rocco Cangelosi, Di Roberto's junior, was the 'Foreign Minister's Personal Representative' on both IGCs.

When the IGC met at the level of officials (typically every other week), Draghi led the Italian team, with Cangelosi alongside him and Augusto Zodda, Draghi's deputy, behind him with Francesco Papadia (of the Banca d'Italia).

[8] In addition to Zodda for Draghi, there were Fabrizio Saccomanni, Francesco Papadia, and Lorenzo Bini-Smaghi for Ciampi and Padoa-Schioppa, and Roberto Nigido for Vanni d'Archirafi. If Andreotti, De Michelis, and Ciampi are added, then the total list numbers no more than sixteen, including two staff replacements.

tion, in the case of Andreotti and De Michelis, and physical weakness, on the part of Carli. The role of these three ministers requires brief explanation.

Andreotti and EMU: Guile Displaced by Technical Realities

Ministerial intervention in policy matters has traditionally been limited in Italy. The archipelago nature of the state, in general, serves to inhibit such a lead. As Hine and Finocchi have noted, this limitation is particularly relevant to the role of the Prime Minister (1991: 81). Few occupants of this office have had a high leadership profile, articulating core values, and imposing policy on fellow ministers. Instead, Prime Ministers have had to 'spend their time resolving tensions between coalition partners, and between departments, by negotiation and consent'.

Andreotti exemplified such a role in abundance. Vilified for his clever machiavellian cunning, he was seen as cold and cynical, dwelling on tactics rather than pursuing principle. Andreotti was a product of the Italian postwar system. He had first entered Parliament in 1946, and he was to serve as Prime Minister on seven occasions (for a total of over six years). From 1983–9 Andreotti was Foreign Minister, and then Prime Minister until June 1992. Prior to the EMU negotiations, he had survived some twenty-five attempts at his impeachment, and he had been tainted by a succession of scandals.[9] His long-term political reputation came to rest on the outcome of a trial begun in September 1995 in which he was accused of being linked to the Mafia.

Almost a decade earlier Italian policy on the EMS had been set down by a small group of technocrats. Ludlow (1982: 147) explains that in the early period of the EMS debate, 'Both the objectives and the tone of Italy's approach to the negotiations were set by a small group of technocrats to whom Mr. Andreotti entrusted almost entire responsibility'. The group was able to exercise considerable latitude until the final stage when the political climate remained divided over whether Italy should accept what was on offer and enter. The turning-point came at the start of October 1978. Thereafter, the group remained responsible for the technical negotiations. But Andreotti as Prime Minister was 'determinant' at the political level both at home and abroad (Ludlow 1982: 206). Andreotti had to manage inter-party relations. Political leadership—and guile— was needed on the issue.

In the case of EMU after 1988, Andreotti was operating in a different political context. He again allowed the formation of a technocratic group to define the negotiating brief. But in this case, crucially, the technocratic assessment was much more positive and united than it had been on the EMS. The policy momentum behind disinflation, stable exchange rates, central bank independence, and

---

[9] Indeed, 'There has virtually been no scandal or affair in Italy's post-war history in which Andreotti has had no role: at the very least, even if he was not directly implicated, he happened to be in charge of the ministry in whose area of responsibility a given scandal occurred' (Chubb and Vannicelli 1988: 128).

financial market liberalization was very much supportive of EMU. The domestic debate on EMU was, indeed, muted and limited. As argued in the last chapter, those who favoured 'internal protection' were on the defensive by the time EMU reappeared on the agenda. Thus, Andreotti and the *partitocrazia* were obliged to follow the technocratic lead on EMU.

Andreotti accepted the importance of Europe to Italy. Yet this acceptance was primarily a matter of calculation: of the costs and benefits to Italy's foreign policy position. Andreotti had worked alongside De Gasperi in the early years of European construction, an experience that left its mark on him. Yet Andreotti lacked the same normative and emotional commitment to European unity that had been evident in De Gasperi, or more latterly with DC counterparts like Emilio Colombo. Andreotti's judgement was a matter of *realpolitik*, of judging the balance of interests. His political guile masked his core political values; critics saw him as amoral.

Andreotti showed a commitment to keeping Italy in Europe's first division. This commitment was a key anchor affecting how he approached European policy and strategy, including EMU. It gave him a basic frame of reference.

It also exposed his prime sensitivity and vulnerability. He had been offended by Italian exclusion from the technical group working on the EMS proposals in 1978 and by the brutal dismissal of his national concerns at the December European Council. In the end-game, however, he was influenced by the private comments of Giscard and Schmidt to the effect that entry into the EMS was the ultimate European test and that exclusion would be seen as a break with the Western alliance. Andreotti took Italy into the EMS having obtained few concessions. During the course of the 1991 IGC on EMU, Andreotti again faced Franco-German pressure. This time the message was that the test of Italy's credibility as a partner would be her acceptance of clear and tough convergence criteria. If Italy wanted to be part of Europe's first division, it had to accept high standards. The message was unmistakable: there was no point in Italy continuing with its earlier demands on this issue. Again, Andreotti accepted the need to shift position.[10] The balance in the poker game was clear. Both episodes indicate Andreotti's readiness to compromise to safeguard Italy's European position.

Tying Germany down in a strong, wide-ranging treaty also appealed to Andreotti. He feared the power of an independent, united Germany. Andreotti's foreign policy instincts were heavily tied to the Cold War, where German power was divided. Yet, at the extraordinary European Council meeting in Paris in late November 1989, Andreotti (aided by De Michelis) proved more accommodating to Kohl on a declaration of support for German unity than did either Mrs Thatcher or Mitterrand. Again, strategic judgement rather than principle was relevant here. Similarly, the design of EMU owed much to the monetary power of Germany. But EMU placed this power within a European architecture and gave Italy some check on how it was wielded.

---

[10] See discussion above on Andreotti's European stance.

Andreotti and Kohl had a long-term political relationship, not least via chris-tian-democratic networks. Their respective parties shared a strong European commitment. But the leadership styles of Andreotti and Kohl were diverging by the time of the EMU negotiations. Kohl was taking an increasingly principled stance behind European unity, stressing personal values and historical duties. Andreotti was much less comfortable with such a political discourse.

Andreotti's approach to the EMU negotiations was couched in these terms. It stressed strategic calculation, rather than an interest in substantive policy con-tent. Andreotti's perspective was fixed on the question of whether a deal was likely and whether Italy would be a core partner. On most other aspects, his style and instinct was to cede position to others: in this case, to Carli and the 'Gang of Three'. Andreotti crossed the stage when tactical judgements and guile were needed. He helped to steer the crucial European Council meeting in Rome in October 1990 towards an ambitious communiqué. To the extent that he out-manoeuvred the British at the summit—this interpretation is only partially cor-rect—then this result was symptomatic of his more general strategic fixation. Later, at the Maastricht European Council, he was formally responsible for tabling the provisions on 'automaticity' for stage 3 of EMU. This move was con-sistent with his judgement on Italian interests: it would ensure the establish-ment of a club from which, he hoped, the rest would find it difficult to exclude Italy.

Yet, away from tactics and guile, Andreotti was more the recipient of policy messages than a proactive leader. The Franco-German pressure on Andreotti in 1991 to accept tough convergence criteria was a policy lesson he needed to learn more than most. The essential point was that the traditional fiscal laxity of the *partitocrazia* was not acceptable if Italy was to remain at Europe's top table. Andreotti had to digest a radical new message. It must have pierced his soul. To that extent, Andreotti personified the tension between old habits and a deeper European tie. Andreotti symbolized a regime struggling to overcome a fault-line and the public backlash against its failings finished his political career in the elections of April 1992.

De Michelis and EMU: No Time for Accountancy

Andreotti formed a relatively easy working relationship with his foreign minis-ter, Gianni De Michelis. The two were very different social beings, but in polit-ics both saw themselves as pragmatists. Critics would see them both as also being calculating and manipulative. Like Andreotti, De Michelis's political standing was later tarnished by allegations of corruption.[11] They were different

---

[11] In July 1995 De Michelis was sentenced to a four-year prison sentence in connection with bribery by businessmen lobbying for lucrative motorway-construction contracts near Venice. De Michelis had been the leader of the Socialist Party (PSI) machine in Venice. De Michelis had also been a close asso-ciate of his former party leader, Bettino Craxi, who fled to Tunisia after the corruption revelations

personalities, though. For his part, De Michelis, who served as Foreign Minister from August 1989 to June 1992, was an intelligent, loquacious, bon vivant, liable to pursue grand policy gestures.

De Michelis was an unusually assertive Foreign Minister by the standards of his predecessors. His position on European integration was somewhat flexible and pragmatic. He did not seek a federal Europe. He expressed sympathy for the ideas of Ralf Dahrendorf. Unlike Andreotti, De Michelis was an Anglophile. He formed a warm working relationship with his British counterpart, Douglas Hurd, for example. The two launched a bilateral initiative on EC foreign-policy co-operation in 1991: a rare counter-example to British isolation in the evolving EC negotiations. De Michelis was closer to Andreotti in another respect. Both gave priority to Italy's interests in other contexts: between 'North' and 'South', and between Europe and the Mediterranean. Andreotti was never as strong an advocate of European unity as, for example, Emilio Colombo, and neither was De Michelis. Both displayed a wider orientation. This wider concern was seen as a matter of counter-balancing Italy's interests and of carving out a distinctive role for her. In the same vein, De Michelis launched a much-vaunted initiative for co-operation in Central Europe (the 'quadrangle' initiative), after the collapse of the Berlin Wall in 1989. This quadrangle was to form a network of relations around Italy's European borders. But, whilst De Michelis could lay claim to a greater innovation than many of his predecessors, he was not a diligent policy manager. His record of actual success is open to question. An Italian Foreign Minister does not have much international clout. But De Michelis often lacked the commitment to see matters through to completion.

On the other hand, his agenda became crowded by European and international events, which were moving at an exceptionally rapid pace. The surrounding tumult of the collapse of Communism in Europe and the IGC on political union dominated his portfolio. His more general preparations for the Italian EC Presidency in the second half of 1990 were overtaken by other events: accommodating the new united Germany in the EU, responding to the Gulf Crisis, and dealing with Yugoslavia.

De Michelis was diverted from EMU, but willingly so. He was not a politician to show interest in the design of EMU; it would not have enthused him. It is difficult to discern any distinctive impact on EMU by him. He was content to leave responsibility for EMU to Carli and the Tesoro.

For De Michelis, as for Andreotti, the issue was essentially a strategic one. The momentum behind EMU at the EC level was a substantive one and it was supported by the monetary-policy establishment at home. The prime concern was thus to secure Italy's place in it. The foreign-policy interest was to ensure that Italy remained part of Europe's first division. The rest could be left to the monetary policy elite of the Tesoro and the Banca d'Italia. In any event, De

amidst the *tangentopoli* affair. De Michelis's flamboyancy was reflected in his authorship of a guide to night-spots in Rome in 1988. See *The Times*, 8 July 1995.

Michelis's ministerial position militated against substantive policy intervention in this area.

Carli and EMU: Breaking Free of Andreotti?

By contrast, Carli, as Tesoro Minister between August 1989 and June 1992, carried the chief responsibility for EMU. His position by this time had become somewhat enigmatic. Carli's technical knowledge and experience was far greater than that of other EC finance ministers. On EMU, Carli had seen it all before: Bretton Woods, the European Payments Union, and the Werner Plan.[12] Yet, when he became Ministro del Tesoro in 1989 he was already 75 years old. Carli was tired and ill when the IGC began: he was physically unable to endure the long negotiations.

Moreover, Carli's policy stance was somewhat compromised. His laxity on fiscal discipline led to the resignation of Sarcinelli. Carli, in his memoirs, refers to the 'two souls of Faust' to describe the tension in postwar Italian economic policy between those favouring state intervention and those on the side of the market (1993: 3–7). In reality, a similar tension existed within in his own soul: how to reconcile personal credibility on economic discipline with political accommodation to Andreotti and De Michelis. Yet, given the distance of the latter from the EMU process, Carli was probably not 'Andreotti-dependent' in this area. Indeed, Andreotti was disposed to accept Carli's guidance on EMU matters. Carli appears to have played a strong role on the issue of the convergence criteria in the autumn of 1991, for example. Moreover, in his memoirs, he offered the thesis of the *vincolo esterno* as a defence of his own actions whilst minister: he was consciously tying the hands of the politicians via the EMU agreement.

In any event, the EMU negotiations were long and arduous and the IGC personal representatives met much more frequently than did their ministers. Carli could set the general priorities and the parameters, but a void remained. This void was filled most directly by his senior official, Mario Draghi.

EMU Co-ordination and the 'Gang of Three'

In the absence of a strong ministerial input on EMU, Italian participation in the EMU negotiations emphasized the key role played by three senior officials. Mario Draghi, Umberto Vattani, and Tommaso Padoa-Schioppa formed the nucleus of the ad hoc group co-ordinating Italian policy and strategy on EMU.[13] Each of the three had a distinct contribution to make.

[12] See section on his career at start of Chapter 10.
[13] Until February 1991 Sarcinelli was Director-General at the Tesoro and a key participant in the ad hoc group; Draghi succeeded him.

As the Prime Minister's Diplomatic Counsellor, Vattani's role was concerned with diplomacy and strategy.[14] His instincts were close to those of Andreotti. The Prime Minister found him a useful 'fixer', a man to help him wheel and deal. Vattani was calculating, less concerned with the substance of policy than with the guile needed in its negotiation. He shared the Prime Minister's core obsession with avoiding Italian relegation to Europe's second division. In that sense, Vattani was an exponent of the most basic policy belief of the foreign-policy establishment in Italy.

As Andreotti's 'sherpa' for the G7 international meetings, Vattani had established relations with many of the leading monetary-policy figures in the EC, including Köhler in Germany and Trichet in France. Vattani was also a participant in a wider foreign-affairs network, with long-term links. He toured the EC capitals in 1990 when Italy held the Presidency, participated in other bilateral meetings in 1991 (notably with the French and the Germans), and attended all the European Council meetings. Vattani was a key official on the political stage of EMU, which he entered keenly when tactics and guile were required.

Padoa-Schioppa was a very different personality. As a former Director-General for Economic and Financial Affairs in the EC Commission (1979–83), he had an insider's knowledge of the EC and was a strong advocate of European unity. He was very close to Delors; indeed, he was closer to him than was any other Italian figure. His domestic influence belied his post as Deputy Director-General at the Banca d'Italia. He had been directly involved in the genesis of EMU, given his role as co-rapporteur for the Delors Committee and as Special Adviser to the Guigou Committee. Prior to the start of the IGC, Andreotti had suggested that Padoa-Schioppa might again serve as a rapporteur for the negotiations, but this was rejected by the incoming Luxembourg Presidency. Nevertheless, Padoa-Schioppa's advice on the progress of the IGC was listened to closely by Andreotti. Padoa-Schioppa also knew Carli from the latter's period as Governor of the Banca d'Italia. Padoa-Schioppa participated in many of the top-level bilateral meetings surrounding the IGC negotiations. He was also a regular member of the Italian delegation at European Council meetings throughout the negotiation of EMU (1988–91). Padoa-Schioppa was a technician helping to set Italian policy.

But Draghi was in the driving seat for the IGC: as Director-General of the Tesoro he had the chief negotiating responsibility. Prior to taking up his Tesoro post, he had acquired substantial international expertise, not least as executive director of the World Bank (1984–90).[15] He also had an established academic reputation. Yet Draghi faced constraints. He had been thrown into the IGC after

[14] Vattani served as Diplomatic Counsellor from 1988 to 1992, when he moved to be ambassador in Bonn. Vattani was born outside Italy in Skopje in Yugoslav Macedonia. Before entering the diplomatic service in 1962, he served briefly as a junior officer in the Banca d'Italia (1961–2).

[15] Draghi was Professor of Economics at the University of Florence from 1981–91, having gained a Ph.D. at the Massachusetts Institute of Technology in 1976. From 1984 to 1990 he served in Washington. After moving to the Tesoro, he gained additional responsibilities, not least as chairman of the committee on privatization. In 1994 he became Chairman of the G10 Deputies.

it was already well under way, and the growing domestic problems of the public debt vied for his attention. Whilst EMU demanded a considerable portion of his time on a weekly basis, his attendance at the IGC had to be reduced to accommodate other domestic concerns.

The co-ordination on EMU clearly differed from the normal EC management processes. Though informal and ad hoc, it was tight and efficient. The core group usually met on a weekly basis in 1991, in different offices. Domestic 'turf-fighting' over policy responsibilities was not a major problem. More generally, the traditional supremacy of the Foreign Ministry had to cede position to the maligned Tesoro, supported by the Banca d'Italia. The world of diplomacy was obliged to accommodate to that of international monetary networks, as the IGC process brokered new domestic practice.

Italy and the Emerging EMU Agenda

The 'relaunch' of EMU onto the EC's agenda in 1988 was not the result of Italian actions. Indeed, few Italian figures would have a significant impact on the design of EMU prior to the Italian Presidency of 1990. A notable, technocratic exception was Padoa-Schioppa, who straddled the milieu of the Commission with that of central bankers. Padoa-Schioppa sustained a rapport with Delors and served as rapporteur for the Delors Committee and the Guigou Group.

For other Italian actors, instead of being passive bystanders they became cheer-leaders for the new policy goal. Academic economists, for example, provided intellectual justification for EMS reform. More generally, Italian officials placed EMU within what they saw as a traditional *communautaire* framework, a vocation to which they fully subscribed. The political acceptability of EMU was never seriously questioned. Moreover, as shown above, economic-policy shifts at home were already making the implications of EMU part of a new consensus on reform. Conditions which would have proved highly controversial in an earlier period were now a price the Italian authorities were prepared to pay.

The route followed by the EMU initiative in 1988–90 privileged the role of officials, rather than ministers. The technocratic policy frame was fully consistent with the logic of a *vincolo esterno*. Italian representatives pressed for an EMU design which: (1) involved a binding commitment by all to realize its objectives; and (2) had strong institutions to lead market behaviour. Such beliefs not only reflected policy lessons learned in the 1970s, they were also shaped by the domestic Napoleonic state culture. These beliefs placed the Italians in a distinct, loosely francophone, bloc in the early EMU debate.

The EMS had offered Italy only 'half a cake'; she sought more. Support for EMU had remained a residual concern since the 1970s. The so-called Genscher–Colombo initiative of 1981 had attempted to revive the European integration process. It called for a new Act leading to 'European Union' and it concentrated on various institutional reforms. In a brief supporting statement, it also endorsed EMU as part of a wider process of economic integration which would strengthen Community solidarity.[16] The political climate across the EC meant that the initiative as a whole had little impact. Subsequently, the Craxi government (with Andreotti as Foreign Minister) supported Delors's attempts (backed by the French and the Belgians) to revive EMU by inserting references to it in the Single European Act in 1985. The Italians found the very modest reference to EMU in the Act much less than they had wanted; successive governments in Rome retained latent support for EMU throughout the period.

Public Opinion and Europe

The domestic political climate was highly conducive to further European integration. As Hine noted in 1993, support for Europe is 'shared by virtually all Italian parties, social movements, and interest groups' (1993: 287). Since the 1970s, the Communists had backed Italy's EC membership. Both Left and Right accepted European unification as the main foreign-policy priority. European integration gave Italy a voice and status. The EC also prevented any single nation exercising hegemony over Europe. After 1990 it received additional legitimation as a framework for containing the power of the united Germany.

Public opinion polls regularly showed strong support for further European integration. As Hine notes, 'At the level of mass opinion, Italy is as near to the model *federateur* state as it has been possible to get' (1993: 287). Any Italian government is under pressure from public opinion to work for closer integration. For example, in June 1989, on the same day as the elections for the European Parliament were held, a referendum on Europe took place in Italy, initiated by senators and deputies in the European Federalist Movement. Some 88 per cent of Italians voted in favour of a transformation of the EC into an effective Union, with a government, a parliament, and a European constitution.[17] Moreover, as Daniels notes, 'The strong party backing for the referendum again demonstrated Italy's "maximalist" stance on the question of institutional reform' (Daniels 1990: 169).

On EMU, there was little active public debate on its content or its implications for Italy in the years before the Maastricht Treaty was actually signed. Those determining Italian policy could do so in relative isolation, confident that the public backed them.

---

[16] See 'Draft European Act'; *Bulletin of the EC*, 11, 1981: 87–91. The references to EMU are contained in 'Draft Statement on Questions of Economic Integration'. Here, most stress is on economic integration, with only a passing reference to EMU.

[17] The referendum, held on 18 June 1989, asked, 'Do you think that the European Communities should be transformed into an effective Union, with a government responsible to the Parliament, entrusting to the same European Parliament a mandate to draw up a draft European constitution for ratification directly by the competent organs of the member states of the Community?' (quoted in Daniels 1990: 168–9).

Italian Economists and EMU: A Rationale for Reform

The EMS and EMU had attracted the attention of many of Italy's leading economists. A number of them achieved international influence. Domestically, many
crossed over between 'insiders' and 'outsiders' in relation to the government.[18]
Most had long favoured moves towards EMU (Monti 1992), though their work
had different emphases.[19] Mario Monti (Bocconi University, Milan), as already
noted, was a long-term advocate of economic liberalism and of Italy's European
role: he was dubbed the 'heir to Einaudi'.[20] Within government by the late
1980s, Carli and Sarcinelli shared similar views, as did many Banca d'Italia
officials. Many of the most prominent Italian economists were part of the CEPR
network and contributed to the pan-European debate on EMU. Their work provided a justification for a strengthening of the EMS. Francesco Giavazzi (Venezia
University) and Alberto Giovannini (Rome and later Columbia University), considered the EMS as a D-Mark zone (1987*a*) and the link between the EMS and
capital controls (1987*b*). Giavazzi and Marco Pagano (Napoli) wrote of 'The
advantage of tying one's hands', for inflation-prone countries participating in
the EMS (1988). Giorgio Basevi (Bologna) had been a signatory to the 'All Saints
Day Manifesto' of 1975 advocating the establishment of a parallel currency.
Later, in the post-1992 uncertainty, he urged a rapid shift to full EMU, with a
strong ECB but no convergence conditions. By contrast, Luigi Spaventa (Rome)
was more of a maverick: he had been a long-term sceptic on the EMS and he
would later attack the contradictions and inadequacies of the Maastricht
design.[21] The predominant view was, nevertheless, to support a stronger and
more complete form of European monetary co-operation: such external discipline would help Italy. In short, Italian policy-makers found a supportive academic climate for EMU.

[18] For example, Alberto Giovannini became an economics professor at Columbia University in New
York and special adviser at the Ministero del Tesoro, Rome.

[19] The cases cited are by no means exhaustive, but they do illustrate something of the nature of the
debate. Other prominent academics to become involved in the debate on EMU, before and after
Maastricht, included Giuliano Amato and Romano Prodi (each subsequently served as Prime Minister);
Vincenzo Visco (subsequently Finance Minister in the Prodi government); as well as Alberto Alesina;
Filippo Cavazzutti (subsequently a Member of Parliament); Marco De Cecco; Giampaolo Galli (Head
of Research, Confindustria); Vittorio Grilli; Rainer Masera; and Tiziano Treu. The writings of economists employed in the Banca d'Italia (e.g. Padoa-Schioppa; Papadia; Saccomanni; Stefano Micossi) and
in the Tesoro (Sarcinelli, Draghi) should also be noted.

[20] See review of his work by the left-wing economist Michele Salvati in *Corriere della Sera*, 11 Dec.
1992. Salvati uses this term.

[21] Spaventa, associated with the Left, did, however, sign the pro-EMU manifesto co-ordinated by
Daniel Gros and Alfred Steinherr in response to the critical statement issued by sixty German economists in June 1992 (Steinherr 1994). Later he argued that the Maastricht provisions were undermining
the existing EMS (*Il Mundo*, 2–9 Oct. 1995).

From Basle–Nyborg to Hanover: Policy in the Shadow of the D-Mark

More specifically, the return of EMU onto the EC's agenda is to be explained, in large part, by the reactions to the 1987 crisis in the ERM and to the proposed abolition of capital controls within the EC (Dyson 1994: 129). Both elements affected early Italian thinking on EMU. Both were tied to a concern over German dominance of European monetary policies. The ERM after 1983 was used as a disciplinary device on domestic policy, with Germany increasingly setting the terms of the arrangement (Dyson 1994: 227).

The Basle–Nyborg Agreement of September 1987 was a response to the enforced ERM realignment earlier in the year. The Italian authorities had joined their French and Belgian counterparts in pressing for an automatic financing mechanism for interventions within the ERM bands and for a more equitable sharing of the burden in such interventions (Dyson 1994: 122). They were opposed by the Germans, the Dutch, and the Danes. This cleavage paralleled a number of the divisions that emerged later in the EMU negotiations. The Basle–Nyborg Agreement was a compromise, but one that actually gave a lower priority to currency intervention than to domestic adjustment of interest rates and to a shared monetary-policy discipline. German leadership remained unscathed; the problem of asymmetry still rankled.

After the Balladur Memorandum of January 1988 had returned to the problem of asymmetry in the ERM, the Italian Tesoro took up the same theme. An Italian memorandum was prepared, by Sarcinelli and Zodda, his deputy, in collaboration with the Banca d'Italia. It was circulated by Giuliano Amato, as Tesoro Minister, to his ECOFIN colleagues on 23 February.[22] Amato referred to the initiative from the Commission under Delors to press ahead with the complete liberalization of capital movements within the EC in accordance with Article 13 of the Single European Act. Amato placed this initiative alongside the problem of ERM intervention: the central theme was that capital mobility would increase the burden of macroeconomic adjustment for Italy and would make the defence of the lira more difficult. Thus, Italy sought a greater symmetry in burden-sharing within the EMS (Padoa-Schioppa 1988; Dini 1988). A central problem of the EMS was the 'structural fault' of Germany's large external surplus, yet Germany had persistently failed to tackle this difficulty for its partners. German economic and monetary policies were seen as being driven by self-interest, whilst the EC public good was neglected. As a consequence, Amato argued that the EMS lacked an engine of growth. Certainly, price stability should be respected by all. But growth was also a shared objective. The criticisms of asymmetry and of a lack of a motor for growth would be revived when Amato, as Prime Minister, was forced to bring the lira out of the ERM in the currency crisis of September 1992.

[22] See reprint in *Il Sole 24 Ore*, 25 February 1988. Amato served as Treasury Minister from July 1987 to August 1989.

The Amato paper thus contributed to the debate in early 1988 on the need to reform the ERM. Whilst there was a confluence of French and Italian interests, there was no direct co-ordination between Amato and Balladur to launch their separate initiatives. Amato and Balladur were not particularly close in their personal relations; there was no co-ordinated strategy. Given their similar currency problems, both converged in finding the current ERM 'too German-centric'.

The Italian authorities thus took no leadership role in the relaunch of EMU. At the time, the Amato paper was not seen as presaging a shift to a single currency or to a European central bank. Even within the monetary establishment in Rome it was not regarded as a major contribution or a radical turn of policy. The Amato paper was placed in a context of seeking reform of the existing ERM, not of promoting EMU. The lead given on EMU by Hans-Dietrich Genscher was thus much more significant. Genscher circulated a memorandum to his fellow foreign ministers just three days after the Amato Paper had been distributed. Yet, the two papers were 'worlds apart'. The Genscher Memorandum, and the paper of his colleague, Gerhard Stoltenberg, on 15 March, represented a critical shift in the debate and the leadership of Germany prior to the European Council in Hanover.

Padoa-Schioppa had some personal influence over the attitude of the Commission President. He and Delors had been close friends since 1979 (Grant 1994: 116). In the spring of 1986 Padoa-Schioppa had warned Delors about the implications of free movement of capital—a provision in the single market programme—for the operation of the ERM. The later Padoa-Schioppa Report made the same point in substantial technical detail. Now, in March 1988 Padoa-Schioppa visited Delors to stiffen his resolve. A single market, with capital liberalization, required a single currency. Moreover, Genscher's new initiative provided an opportunity which the Commission must exploit.

Back home, the prospect of moving ahead on EMU emboldened the Italians to agree to the EC Directive on capital liberalization in June 1988, on the eve of the Hanover summit.[23] It was no coincidence that Italy took its own decisive domestic step on capital liberalization at this same stage. The emerging EC obligations affected domestic reform; both Amato and Sarcinelli felt Italy had to get fully in step. With the French and Italian agreement on capital liberalization, Chancellor Kohl was freed to move ahead on EMU.

The government of Ciriaco De Mita appears to have played no significant role prior to the Hanover European Council in the design of what came to be known as the 'Delors Committee' on EMU. Both Sarcinelli and Padoa-Schioppa attended the summit with De Mita and Andreotti (then Foreign Minister). At a press conference following the summit, De Mita incautiously referred to Padoa-Schioppa being appointed as the sole rapporteur to the new committee. This remark quickly elicited a German backlash against Padoa-Schioppa.

---

[23] Other factors clearly influenced the Italians: for example, German and British pressure; the prospect of further ERM reform after Basle–Nyborg.

The Devout Courtier: Padoa-Schioppa and the Delors Committee

Padoa-Schioppa had provoked German irritation whilst he was at the EC Commission between 1979 and 1983. As Director-General, his support for the second phase of the EMS had clashed with the stance adopted by the Bundesbank. The Padoa-Schioppa Report of 1987 further raised the sensitivities of the Bundesbank. The report had argued that the combination of capital liberalization and the commitment to stable exchange rates under the ERM left no room for independent monetary policies. A review of the institutional arrangements for monetary-policy co-ordination was, therefore, necessary if stability and an effective single market were to be ensured. The Bundesbank feared the 'institutionalist' (or 'monetarist') leanings of Padoa-Schioppa. The report was seen as suggesting enhanced authority for ECOFIN at the expense of national central banks (Dyson 1994: 118, 130). Moreover, the Bundesbank questioned the strength of Padoa-Schioppa's commitment to price stability as the key policy objective. By the first July meeting of the new Delors Committee, opposition to Padoa-Schioppa as the sole rapporteur led to the appointment of Gunter Baer, of the BIS in Basle, alongside him.[24]

Nevertheless, Padoa-Schioppa was a very prominent figure in the committee. Padoa-Schioppa joined Joly Dixon of Delors's cabinet in regular private meetings to brief Delors as chair. Such briefings were very extensive and gruelling for Delors. Later, both Padoa-Schioppa and Baer drafted the final report.

To the Banca d'Italia (and the Italian government), the establishment of the Delors Committee represented a significant turning-point. A clear mandate had been given at Hanover for the realization of EMU, not just the reform of the EMS. Ciampi and his staff were pleased to be in the driving seat: as adherents of the utility of external discipline, they looked forward to the design. Their thinking focused on the final goal ahead and how to achieve it. In doing so, a number of accumulated beliefs came into play.

The Genial Architect: Ciampi, Institutionalism, and the Delors Committee

The 'institutionalist' approach of the Italian monetary establishment was fully evident in the discussions of the Delors Committee. Ciampi submitted a paper (in several instalments) entitled, 'An Operational Framework for an Integrated Monetary Policy in Europe'. It was prepared within the Banca d'Italia by Fabrizio Saccomanni and Francesco Papadia and followed on from a submission by the Banque de France. Ciampi's paper began by noting that there was a limit to what could be achieved in monetary-policy co-ordination by 'non-

---

[24] On the Delors Committee see Chapter 16.

institutional, pragmatic arrangements' (Ciampi 1989). In the same vein, it noted that the 'parallel currency approach' had already been rejected within the Committee.

Thus, full monetary co-ordination required an institutional mechanism. In supporting the creation of a 'central monetary institution' (never named) the paper expressed a commitment which would be consistently adhered to by the Italian authorities throughout the EMU discussions of 1989–91. The importance of institutional mechanisms was emphasized in a critique of the Werner Report jointly authored by Padoa-Schioppa and Baer and submitted to the Delors Committee in September 1988. In this submission, the Werner Report was criticized for leaving unclear 'who should make the decisions and how responsibilities were to be distributed' in the EMU process (Baer and Padoa-Schioppa 1988). It is indicative that leading Italian figures identified the debate as one between 'institutionalists' and 'behaviourists' (rather than the more common terms 'economists' and 'monetarists') (e.g. Bini-Smaghi *et al.* 1994). In the same vein, Padoa-Schioppa, as co-rapporteur to the Delors Committee, had pressed strongly, and successfully, for the Committee's report to commit itself to a treaty to sanction EMU, rather than an intergovernmental agreement.

This institutionalist emphasis stems from long-established and deep social roots. It is part of the cultural inheritance—of Napoleonic order and of legalism, to shape and guide human behaviour. Institutionalism overcomes human fallibility, and discretion; it provides for rule-based behaviour, predictability, and discipline. In the post-1988 Italian debate on EMU, institutionalism was consistently accorded a higher priority than was a reliance on market discipline, a feature of much of the domestic reform in the 1980s.

This emphasis was part of a long-established pattern. Over the course of the history of European integration, successive Italian governments have adopted a strongly institutionalist position. Integration, in both the economic and the political spheres, was seen as requiring strong, supranational institutions able to direct and reshape behaviour. In the more overtly political spheres, such institutions should be clearly democratic and accountable. This point was, for example, pressed by Alcide De Gasperi, as Italian Prime Minister, in the negotiations for a European Political Community in 1952. Subsequently, it was a recurring theme of Italian speeches on political union and the reform of the EC's institutions.

In Ciampi's 1989 paper, an 'institutional scheme for a common monetary policy based on the official ECU' was outlined, alongside a market-led scheme for the private ECU. Whether such a scheme was to be activated at the end of stage 2 or at the start of stage 3, it would require the creation of a central monetary body. This body would control the liquidity creation of the national central banks via the control of the supply of ECUs to them. The governing body of the ESCB—of which the central institution would be a part—would decide each year 'how much money and credit should be created overall in the Community' (Ciampi 1989). The central institution would have the power to ask member central banks to hold compulsory reserves in ECUs. 'Through this link', it argued, 'the stance decided in common would be transmitted to all members of the system'. The support for supranational institution-building was clear.

The rationale was set out in an unabashed manner. It was argued that 'capital mobility and the exchange rate constraint already drastically reduce the room for autonomous monetary policies' (Ciampi 1989). Moreover, national rescue was provided for: very much an Italian interest. If a currency came under what was considered to be unjustified attack, the central institution would provide ECU credit and thereby help restore balanced conditions in the market. At the heart of Italian thinking on EMU were the loss of effective sovereignty, the need to overcome asymmetry in the ERM, and the vital importance of supranational control.

These attitudes became clearly identified with a francophone camp on the Delors Committee. The rejection of (the illusion of) monetary sovereignty placed Ciampi alongside colleagues such as Jacques de Larosière (France) and Mariano Rubio (Spain). But the institution-building envisaged for stage 2 placed Ciampi poles apart from Karl-Otto Pöhl (Germany), Wim Duisenberg (The Netherlands), and Erik Hoffmeyer (Denmark). Ciampi pressed his argument that monetary sovereignty was an illusion on John Major when he first visited Rome as Chancellor of the Exchequer in 1989. As Ciampi put it, it was not a question of sovereignty, but of having a finger on a button; when the Germans pressed the button, he had to follow suit, Ciampi commented. The distance between the Italians and the British, the Danes, the Dutch, and the Germans would be evident later in the IGC of 1991. To Pöhl, Ciampi was dwelling on grandiose designs, rather than ensuring their stability via effective convergence.

Yet, in another sense, the Italians entered the EMU debate with a foot in both camps. Ciampi and his staff could agree with the Bundesbank on the end result for EMU: monetary stability supported by central bank independence. But they shared the French view on how to arrive at this destination (by firm institutional leadership and by progress on the basis of linked steps). In contrast to the French, central bank independence at home or at the European level caused no anxiety to the Italians.

Ciampi's input into the deliberations of the Delors Committee involved one significant break with the past. At the time of the EMS negotiations in 1978, he had been involved in the discussions on the possible incorporation of 'parallel measures' to support the weaker economies. Domestic political pressure obliged him (as Deputy Governor) to pursue such a line. But by 1988–9, policy at home had shifted some considerable distance, as already noted, and Ciampi was free to vent his scepticism on the utility of incorporating compensating fiscal measures. Moreover, by 1988 the position of Italy relative to the rest of the EC, as measured by GNP per capita, had also been transformed. An emphasis on 'cohesion' measures might now mean that Italy would be required to contribute, rather than to receive, financial aid.

From the Delors Report to Rome I: Sustaining EMU

The Italian response to the Delors Report was not to dwell on its semantics, but to endeavour to maintain the pressure for EMU. At the Madrid European Council in June 1989, Mitterrand pressed for a start-date for an IGC on EMU: he wanted it to begin during the Italian EC Presidency in the second half of 1990. Mitterrand received very little support. Mrs Thatcher had recommitted Britain to ERM entry and her partners did not wish to push her too far, too soon. Yet, as Padoa-Schioppa commented to Andreotti at the Madrid European Council, it is dangerous to leave an ice-cream out of the fridge for too long. The momentum was all important: the Italians looked forward to an IGC.

The Guigou Committee set up by the Madrid European Council of June 1989 was another forum for the inclusion of Padoa-Schioppa as an actor in the EMU process. He was appointed as Special Adviser to the committee, in addition to the rapporteurs supplied by the Commission. Padoa-Schioppa's ill-defined role was as a 'sweeper', helping to maintain the coherence of the deliberations as they progressed. But the work of the committee was relatively light: shadow-boxing rather than real negotiation.

Between the Guigou Report of October 1989 and the start of the IGC in Rome at the end of 1990, the European landscape was transformed, with the collapse of the Communist regimes of Eastern Europe. The Italians were quick to recognize a link between German unification and control of German power via schemes such as EMU. They sustained this position from the Paris meeting, to a meeting of the CSCE (Conference on Security and Co-operation in Europe) in Ottawa the following February, and to the Dublin European Council in April. In this respect they were at one with Delors, and they supported the establishment of two IGCs: one for EMU and the other on political union.

With the onset of the Italian Presidency in the second half of 1990, the EMU negotiations grew near. To the Italians, the Delors Report remained the guiding document for the pending negotiations. They gave little credence to the British alternatives of competing currencies and a parallel currency (Carli 1989). Carli told the press that he had no desire to see currencies 'at war with each other' (Agence Europe, 16 December 1990). Instead, he referred such a discussion back to the Ciampi paper submitted to the Delors Committee. The ECU might play a role in the transition, but it could not be left to market forces: he was a self-avowed 'institutionalist', not a 'behaviourist'.

British intransigence was one major constraint on the prospects for the Italian Presidency; another was the increasing caution on EMU shown by the Bundesbank in response to the process of German monetary unification in July. The whole process of German unification took place during the Italian Presidency. The wider ramifications for European security were focused on the CSCE, and its summit in Paris in November. In addition, further political distraction was caused by the Gulf Crisis, with its demands on the EC's unity and resources. The Italian Presidency's agenda was crowded.

But progress on EMU continued. Sarcinelli as Chair of the EC Monetary Committee submitted a report in July to ECOFIN, and Carli presented a report on behalf of ECOFIN (27 October) to the Rome European Council. These covered the difficult issues of identifying objective principles for convergence (Sarcinelli), and the transition to stage 2 (Sarcinelli and Carli). The Sarcinelli Report went a considerable distance in assuaging German fears—in accepting the need for quantitative criteria for convergence; objective tests for the start of stage 2; and for finance ministers to have the lead on EMU—testimony to the concern to convince Bonn and Frankfurt that the will to accept the discipline of EMU existed. During the same period there was a flurry of position papers: these included a paper from the Banca d'Italia setting out a blueprint for stage 2 (Banca d'Italia 1990a).

Italian attitudes were already relatively well known at this stage. Ciampi's contributions to the Delors Committee had shown the consensus in Rome on there being firm institutional foundations for EMU. With this 'institutionalist' approach came a preference for clear dates to be set for the transition. Ciampi, and his colleagues in Rome, firmly believed in the irreversibility stipulations of the Delors Report. In consequence, waiting for a requisite convergence was not part of Italian thinking.

The battle lines were drawn. Along with these attitudes went a pattern of loose alliances: in general, the Italians were much closer to the French, the Belgians, the Greeks, the Portugese, and the Irish, than they were to the Germans, the Dutch, the Danes, or the British. Moreover, the Italian position at the start of the IGC was very close to that of the Delors Commission. The Italians saw themselves as being firmly within the *communautaire* tradition. The proximity of the Italians to their partners on EMU contrasted, nevertheless, with their alliances on political union. Here, the Italians were closest to the Germans (on institutional reform), but could also accommodate the British (on defence).[25]

Conclusion

It is clear from the foregoing that, prior to the opening of the IGC negotiations, much of the Italian preparation had already been made. A normally weak state apparatus had, paradoxically, established a very strong form of policy co-ordination. A small technocratic group within the 'core executive' had exploited a window of opportunity for policy influence. The co-ordinating task force had a clear conception of its role; it had shared values relating to maintaining Italy's European commitment and apparently also to EMU serving as a new 'vincolo

[25] This was evident in the joint declarations on EPU of Genscher and De Michelis in April 1991 and of Hurd and De Michelis in October 1991.

esterno'; and it believed in a depoliticized, technocratic policy frame for monetary management. A 'hard shell' existed around the coordination process: the definition of the negotiating mandate was not subject to outside intervention in the manner of pluralistic politics (Della Sala 1997).

The core negotiating priorities on EMU were also clear in the 1988–90 period. The Italian position was institutionalist (or 'monetarist') to the core: the transition to a single currency should be managed from stage 2 onwards by a central monetary institution possessing supranational powers; the transition should follow a linked, stage-by-stage process; and the transition should be irreversible and according to a set timetable. The final stage would be modelled on the Bundesbank system; which was, in turn, not so distant from the self-image of the Banca d'Italia. The Italian stance was clear, coherent, and would prove to be consistent. It could be readily identified with particular camps or alliances.

Italian actors approached the IGC in a very positive spirit: maximalist in their objectives and seeking to be bound by the commitments entered into. Moreover, domestic co-ordination was relatively unproblematic: the archipelago was co-ordinated without any major inter-institutional battles. But accommodating Italy to the IGC meant devising a mandate and a strategy with realizable objectives. The need for a *vincolo esterno* exposed the critical problem at the heart of the Italian position: economic weakness at home might prevent Italy from joining the EMU discipline the technocrats craved. The extent to which the Italian negotiators were successful in this regard will be examined in the final chapter of this case study.

12

Italy and the IGC: Negotiating External Discipline, Avoiding Exclusion, 1990–1991

> Since it is now certain that EMU cannot take place without Italy, we must take care to ensure that the state of our finances cannot be used as a pretext to delay the process of integration.
>
> Giulio Andreotti, 18 April 1991

The onset of the IGC negotiations in 1991 witnessed a weakening Italian influence over the content of the EMU agreement. Before the IGC began, the Italian position had been maximalist, even grandiose. An EMU was sought which involved a binding timetable, strong institutions, and weak conditions for entry. During 1991, however, the Italians were often in retreat. They were abandoned by the French on many issues of crucial concern. The French shift towards the German–Dutch policy coalition represented a threat as far as Rome was concerned. The Italians were increasingly seen as a liability, too weak to participate in EMU. Indeed, the Dutch and the Germans were setting entry tests for EMU in a manner which seemed designed to exclude Italy.

During the course of the IGC there was the psychological shock for Italy that the unthinkable might happen: EMU might go ahead without her. The Italian negotiators faced an uphill struggle. The negotiating team underwent some changes in this period (see Chapter 11). Sarcinelli, a strong figure in the Tesoro, resigned and was replaced by Draghi, who had little time to settle in before being flown off to the IGC. Also, Carli grew weaker, the result of failing health. The nature of the IGC meant that the Banca d'Italia, like many other central banks, was more distant from the EMU negotiations than it had been previously. Each of these factors meant the task of ensuring that Italy remained part of the EC's 'inner circle' had rarely been so difficult.

The stakes were high for Italy, and reconciling competing national interests was no easy task. The domestic reforms of the previous decade would either be reinforced by participation in EMU or exclusion would likely blow them off course. EMU was a 'policy window' for reformers to exploit, to secure recent gains. But EMU also posed dilemmas. Most notably, the momentum in the IGC, particularly after the French shift towards Germany, was to set tough entry conditions for EMU. The convergence criteria might be too difficult for Italy to satisfy. The *vincolo esterno* thesis implied a tight policy straitjacket, but it presupposed a generous initial fitting. If Italy was claiming membership of the 'first division', how could it insist on the standards of the lower leagues? Moreover, in one sense, defining the Italian interest on this issue pitted the fiscal management interests of the Tesoro against the monetary credibility of the Banca d'Italia. Yet the technocratic heads of the Tesoro shared the belief in fiscal rectitude. They could not reject it in principle, only how it might be set down in the Treaty.

The support of the political parties and the public for full Italian participation in the EC also shaped the negotiating context. It made entry into EMU imperative; anything else would be punished domestically as failure. Moreover, it provided a legitimacy for accepting a tough EMU deal. Indeed, the domestic scope for ratification seemed to be widely set. It was unclear what likely EMU package would *not* be ratifiable. Italian negotiators thus had much leeway, but by the same logic they were denied the bargaining power of insisting on a particular deal in case anything else would not be accepted at home. The *vincolo esterno* thesis recognized the legitimacy of the EU in Italy. It sought to apply this legitimacy to the need for fiscal and monetary discipline.

In parallel to the progress of the IGC, political developments at home meant that the Andreotti government grew weaker. Public disaffection with the established political system was increasing. This was exacerbated by the revelations of the *tangentopoli* corruption scandals. Andreotti and the *partitocrazia* were the *'ancien régime'* in decline. This weakness followed the economic impact of the 'hollowing out' of the state by the shift towards market reforms and discipline over the previous decade. The old regime had less hold over the new technocratic thrust of macroeconomic policy. The consequence was that, on several fronts, the Andreotti government was on the defensive in 1991. It needed the benefit of a deal at Maastricht to show that it could deliver what the Italian public wanted.

The present chapter addresses two main dimensions of the IGC process in relation to Italy. First, the policy content of the negotiations is analysed and the successes and failures of the Italian actors assessed. The chapter portrays a process of Italian retreat from their earlier maximalist ambitions. Some victories were scored. on the EMU timetable ('automaticity') and on flexibility in the fiscal convergence criteria. But these successes were somewhat shallow: on 'automaticity' the Italians were brokers for wider and stronger political forces; similarly on fiscal flexibility, the Italian negotiators achieved a limited success by acting alongside others. Overall, the distinctively Italian impact on the IGC was modest. The deal was largely determined by others, and not to an Italian design. The instances of Italian failure were more evident: on the design of the institutions to manage EMU, and the establishment of strict and numeric convergence criteria for entry into stage 3, for example.

The second dimension addressed by the chapter is that of Italian strategy in the IGC. It is argued that there was little prospect of the Italians achieving greater success in 1991, given the constraints of their position. Italian influence was limited by the interests and priorities set in Rome; by the shift of position by the French away from the Italians towards the Germans; by Italian exclusion from the Franco-German axis; and by the absence of any alternative alliance, such as with the British.

Yet, Maastricht represented something of a residual success for the Italians. The Andreotti government endeavoured to bask in the glow of a new ambitious European venture. More particularly, a new *'vincolo esterno'* was established. The course of subsequent Italian policy was set; profligacy was limited; the old practices of the *partitocrazia* constrained. From 1992 to 1998, there was pain to endure and uncertainty to overcome to reach stage 3. Serious doubts arose as to whether Italy would be able to participate in stage 3 from the outset. But, the Prodi government secured the European prize in 1998: it was in Serie A, and that was the overriding national priority.

Avoiding Relegation from Europe's First Division

During the course of 1991, the high ambitions set for EMU by the Italians were to contrast increasingly with a deterioration of their bargaining power and strategy in the IGC. The deterioration, whilst by no means a simple linear progression, was very evident by comparison to the pre-IGC period. It had both a political and an economic dimension. It led to heightened fears in Rome by the middle of 1991 that Italy might be excluded from EMU and thereby from Europe's first division.

Politically, the Andreotti government was becoming weaker. There was a minor government crisis (in a *'coup de théâtre'*) in April when the Republican Party (PRI) withdrew from Andreotti's five-party coalition, protesting that government posts had not been reallocated as promised. Andreotti survived, but speculation about an election—one year early—increased. The governing parties were defensive: neither the DC nor the Socialists wanted to face the polls. They feared the increasing popularity of the *Lega Nord*, amidst evidence of increasing public disaffection with the existing regime.

Added to this political weakness was rising concern, both at home and abroad, about the performance of the Italian economy. Slow economic growth was pushing up the government's budget deficit. In addition, fiscal policy became more lax in the run-up to the impending elections in April 1992. The lira came under increased pressure: already it was heading towards a large devaluation. The wait for the elections induced a sense of frustration, even paralysis. Such feelings were evident in Ciampi, at the Banca d'Italia, and in Carli, at the Tesoro. But Carli was also growing weaker, physically and politically.

These developments took their toll at the EC level. Fears rose that Italy's major partners might try to shut her out of EMU, just as Rome had been sidelined in the elaboration of the EMS proposals and had struggled to gain entry into the Group of Seven. Most notably, the French increasingly distanced themselves during the course of 1991 from their Italian counterparts. In Paris, the Italians were seen as the weakest part of the chain holding the EMS together. A devaluation of the lira might derail the EMU negotiations and result in no deal. Jean-Claude Trichet, of the Trésor in Paris, became especially concerned on this account and he communicated such fears to his minister, Pierre Bérégovoy.

The Dutch, predictably, were more puritanical. At an informal ECOFIN meeting in Luxembourg on 11 May, the Dutch presented, in rather dramatic terms, the case for a 'crash programme' of budget austerity by the weaker EC states. The proposal was clearly targeted at the worsening situation in Italy. The Dutch feared that the Germans might back out of an EMU deal because of such divergences (Connolly 1995: 262). Carli was enraged, citing the damaging effects that the use of such language might have on market behaviour.

Yet the Italians were obliged to respond. The government accepted that the EC momentum was behind such measures. The Tesoro and the Banca d'Italia were themselves anxious about the deteriorating economic position. Carli announced to his fellow IGC ministers on 10 June that the Italians would be submitting a convergence programme to them soon. As his Spanish and Portuguese colleagues intended to make the same commitment, it was important not to be outflanked. Indeed, the Italians submitted their programme first—to the ECOFIN meeting on 11 November 1991.

The strategic implications of the deteriorating Italian position stretched wider. Two rounds of bilateral meetings in October 1991—one with the French, the other with the Germans—highlighted the Italian plight. At Viterbo, on 17–18 October, Bérégovoy met Carli and his officials. Bérégovoy made clear his anxiety as to the implications of a weakening lira. He also stressed the need for the Italians to accept clear convergence rules in order to secure an EMU deal with the Germans. A similar signal was given when Mitterrand saw Andreotti in Perugia. The Italians, particularly Vattani, had tried to press for flexibility in the convergence criteria, to give Italy maximum scope for entry. Parallel talks with the Germans reinforced the French message. Vattani, Draghi, and Padoa-Schioppa met Horst Köhler and Gert Halle in Milan. The Italians were left in no doubt that their desire to avoid precise reference values in the convergence criteria for stage 3 was a non-starter. Precise figures were a condition for a deal on EMU. Moreover, they would be the test of entry for the Italians.

The Andreotti government had to reconcile itself to the inevitable. By the end of October, a critical month, the IGC on EMU had agreed on the two figures of debt levels being less than 60 per cent of GDP and deficits no more than 3 per cent. The Italians had conceded, though the figures were qualified with some built-in flexibility (see below).

Andreotti and Vattani became animated about the need to ensure that Italy remained in the EC's inner core, and an equal member of the transition to EMU. This concern was the number one priority: Italy's foreign-policy interest demanded that she should not be relegated to a second-class status. Andreotti and Vattani focused on the end, leaving Carli, Draghi, and Padoa-Schioppa to sort out the means. The domestic press focused on whether Italy was still in Europe's first division. The fears raised complemented the sense of public disenchantment with the existing political leadership. Italian negotiators were left in no doubt that they were expected to secure a deal which kept Italy firmly at the centre of the EC. It is in this sense that the scope for domestic ratification of an EMU agreement was widely set. During the course of the IGC it gradually became clearer that the high ambitions Italy had set for EMU would have to be scaled down significantly. The Italian voice was not being listened to as much as before.

Maximalist Ambitions: The Italian Negotiating Positions

Yet, the IGC negotiations began with the Italian government setting relatively ambitious priorities on EMU. It is instructive to identify them and to assess the record of success or failure for the Italians in the negotiations. On 15 December 1990, when the IGC opened, with Guido Carli in the chair, the Italian government's priorities on EMU were clear. Italian negotiators had three key concerns:

1. *Irreversibility and automaticity*   The government sought a firm commitment to proceed to the final goal of an EMU. Given an agreement to proceed to EMU, the transition process should be irreversible. Irreversibility would remove uncertainty over policy implementation, not only at the EC level, but also domestically. All governments could thus expect to gain from the mutually binding agreement in that it would send a clear signal to the international financial markets.

For most members of the Italian co-ordinating group on EMU, this commitment meant that stage 2 should be as short as possible. EMU could be secured in this way against the risk of an infinitely prolonged transition period, which might arise from insufficient economic convergence or the reluctance of some states to proceed to the final objective. Instead of any further conditionality to the commitment to proceed, progress to the final stage should be automatic on the basis of a clear timetable.

Moreover, this commitment required that no country should be able to block the progress of the majority to EMU. This concern was clearly influenced by the perception of Mrs Thatcher's opposition to EMU: it was necessary to prevent a right of veto. Progress should be made on the basis of majority decision-making.

At the same time, the Italian government was extremely concerned to avoid being left outside any transition to EMU by a so-called 'inner group' of EC states. The notion of the '*vincolo esterno*' required Italy to be bound by the discipline of participation; exclusion from any part of EMU would threaten Italy's economic progress and isolate her in the international markets. The decision on which states would be allowed to participate in stage 3 should therefore be made by a simple majority vote. Italy could assume that its chances of securing the necessary support for its own participation would be greater on this basis. The discussion on these aspects was closely linked to that of the convergence conditions for progress to EMU.

2. *A strong institution for stage 2*   The government's approach to the institution-building required for EMU was dominated by the beliefs of the Banca d'Italia on EC monetary co-operation. Governor Ciampi argued that the issue of the EMU architecture should be kept separate from that of which states might participate. EMU should be seen as a condominium, shared by all, and states should enter the building when able to do so. Such a formulation justified the Italian input into these discussions. The Italian view of the foundations and design of the architecture was that drawn up by the Banca d'Italia.

As part of the EMU architecture, a strong central monetary authority should be created for stage 2 which, together with the national central banks, would have extensive monetary competence. This arrangement was necessary for the gradual integration of monetary policies and for a smooth transition to currency unification. As a matter of practicality, in order to prepare for the formulation of a single monetary policy in stage 3, the embryonic European central bank 'must have a strong consultative role on the quantitative aspects of monetary policy during the second phase' (Banca d'Italia 1990*b*: 5). In particular, the stage 2 institution should be able to lay down monetary policy guidelines for the Community. A new '*vincolo esterno*' should be sustained throughout the transition.

3. *The convergence criteria*   A major determinant of when Italy might be able to join in a full EMU was the specification of any conditions concerning the convergence of national economies prior to entry to stage 3. Although the Delors Report had not adopted any explicit conditions, such a notion was promoted later within the EC Monetary Committee and the IGC. Italian negotiators had to react to such proposals.

The major area of contention for the Italians was the proposals on fiscal conditions. The Italian position, largely inspired by the Tesoro, was that the setting of quantitative fiscal conditions was without economic rationale. Setting explicit reference values for public debt and deficits ignored the contrasting circumstances of individual states. Moreover, setting strict quantitative conditions would make the Treaty vulnerable to future unforeseen developments (such as adverse economic shocks or downturn in the business cycle), threatening a delay in progress towards EMU. Once it realized that it was no longer possible to avoid some fiscal stipulations, the Italian government supported the view that such conditions should not be given treaty status; they should be established in secondary legislation, open to subsequent modification by the Council. This procedure would help to keep the EMU project on course, whilst avoiding the danger of Italian exclusion by an overly rigid entry test.

In addition to these three key negotiating objectives, the Italians were obliged to set out their position on other matters of lesser concern to them. These issues will be considered later.

Within the Italian co-ordinating group, there were some differences of policy emphasis at certain stages. Two examples are notable. First, for the Banca d'Italia, a top priority was to obtain an agreement on a strong European monetary institution for stage 2, not least to ease the transition to stage 3. The Tesoro was expected to advocate this case in the appropriate fora. However, in 1990 Sarcinelli remained unconvinced of the necessity for such a strong institution in stage 2. By 1991, when Draghi succeeded him and made the case, the momentum within the IGC was moving away from such a notion. Draghi recognized that the battle was already lost. Secondly, the Tesoro believed by 1991 that the most important issue was flexible terms for the convergence criteria: these would be critical for Italian participation. By contrast, the Banca d'Italia did not oppose tough convergence criteria. As a central bank, it saw such a constraint as part of a new set of controls on lax politicians. It also recognized that the momentum in the negotiations was in this direction. Yet, in public they supported the position of the Tesoro when required to do so. Thus, Italian attitudes were not uniform or without differentiation. Yet the degree of consensus that did exist was striking.

Negotiating Successes: Andreotti, Vattani, and Rome I: Padoa-Schioppa's Formula for 'Automaticity'

In sum, the progress of the negotiations in 1990–1 indicated only limited success for the Italian objectives. There were two notable instances of victory: first, on the timetable and 'automaticity' formula to proceed with EMU; and, secondly, on the introduction of a less rigid perspective on the fiscal element in the convergence conditions. The former achievement came at the last stage of the negotiations in Maastricht; the latter involved a rearguard action to fend off the pressure for a tough stance by the Germans and the Dutch. Apart from these items, the Italian 'success' was the general one of having helped to establish an agreement to proceed with EMU: a policy seen as, in its overall effects, beneficial at home. In other words, relatively few successes could be ascribed primarily to the Italian negotiators. They were side-players to the dominant Franco-German axis.

The Roman Road to EMU: Andreotti and Rome 1

The balance sheet of the EMU negotiations can be differentiated according to the three priority goals that the Italian negotiators set themselves. With respect to the commitment to go ahead with EMU, the Italian government can claim two notable successes. First, at the Rome European Council of 27–8 October 1990, Andreotti, as Prime Minister and Chair, engineered an agreement that stage 2 of EMU should begin on 1 January 1994. This agreement overcame the differences of view within Germany on the matter, and it circumvented the entrenched opposition of Britain and Denmark to such a commitment. Andreotti's contacts with other EC leaders prior to the Rome meeting, and the heavy spadework of Vattani, had established that EMU would be the main item on the agenda. At a meeting of the European Peoples' Party a few days before the Rome Council, Chancellor Helmut Kohl told Andreotti that he was ready to set a date for stage 2 at this first Rome Council, but that he might not be able to do so if the issue was deferred to the second Rome European Council in December—which coincided with the German federal elections (*The Economist*, 3 November 1990). Kohl favoured 1 January 1994 for the start of stage 2. In giving this signal, Kohl was prepared to override a domestic dispute between Hans-Dietrich Genscher (as Foreign Minister) who favoured a start-date of 1 January 1993 (the single market launch), on the one hand, and Theo Waigel (as Finance Minister) and the Bundesbank, on the other, who opposed setting any fixed date. In responding to Kohl's signal, the Italians were moving well ahead of the discussions that had taken place in an ECOFIN meeting in Rome just six weeks earlier, where there had been major differences of view on stage 2.

The UK government sought to block this agenda. In the week prior to the Rome Council, on 21 October at Chequers, Andreotti attempted to persuade Mrs Thatcher of the merits of such an approach. He had little prospect of doing so: Mrs Thatcher often displayed a scarcely veiled contempt for Italian politicians, and Andreotti was one of the lowest in her estimation. Their two characters were diametrically opposed: he was a master tactician; she prided herself on her resolution. To the British, Andreotti at Chequers was typically oblique; to the Italians, Andreotti's overtures had been brushed aside.

President Cossiga was the next to try to move Mrs Thatcher. He paid a visit to Number Ten with De Michelis (24 October).[1] Mrs Thatcher liked Cossiga's charm, but it was De Michelis who engaged her in a substantive discussion over lunch. To Mrs Thatcher, De Michelis was barely any better than Andreotti. Yet, De Michelis tried hard. He stressed that he was prepared to be very flexible in the drafting of the relevant text for Rome: no reference to a 'single' currency would be made, for example. This approach was intended to be accommodating to the British government's separate initiative on an alternative 'hard ECU' plan. Mrs Thatcher rejected his attempt at conciliation: she told him she did not wish to compromise. She thought the European Council should focus on the GATT negotiations, rather than on EMU.

Mrs Thatcher misread the signals from the Italian Presidency. She records in her memoirs that 'As always with the Italians, it was difficult throughout to distinguish confusion from guile' (1995: 765). Moreover, 'What I did not know was that behind the scenes the Italians had agreed with a proposal emanating from Germany and endorsed by Christian Democrat leaders from several European

---

[1] In her memoirs, Mrs Thatcher describes Francesco Cossiga as 'highly competent', 'a man of principle', 'in negotiations he always played a straight hand; he could be relied upon to keep his word', 'and he was an undoubted Anglophile' (1995: 83). Cossiga served as Prime Minister from 1979–80 and as President from 1985 to 1992.

countries at an earlier caucus meeting that the GATT should not be discussed at the Council' (Thatcher 1995: 765). Yet, Mrs Thatcher created her own misunderstanding. She records that Andreotti's pre-Council letter made no mention of GATT as an agenda item (1995: 765). Moreover, the meeting of Christian Democrat leaders was not *secret*: the signals were there to be read. Mrs Thatcher thought she had the backing of Kohl. Douglas Hurd had reported to her that in his own meeting with the Chancellor, the German leader had taken a soft line (Thatcher 1995: 765). But Kohl was on record as backing a date for stage 2 and for deadlines for the IGC.

For his part, Andreotti was too astute not to move ahead without Kohl's backing. At the opening of the European Council meeting, Mrs Thatcher immediately intervened to tell Andreotti as Chair that the discussion should focus on the difficult GATT negotiations, and not on EMU. Andreotti replied that the Council was not able to be briefed on GATT. Delors supported him: this task was one for the Commission and it had not been asked to give such a briefing.

That same evening, the first working session began with EMU. Vattani and Padoa-Schioppa had advised Andreotti to limit the discussion: he should ask all heads of government, in turn, to state their positions briefly. He should then summarize these contributions by reference to the text already prepared by Vattani and Padoa-Schioppa. The text would maximize the agreement. Andreotti followed this advice and read the prepared statement. Mrs Thatcher immediately objected: the text did not take account of Britain's position. Andreotti told her not to insist as she was in a minority of one. Andreotti moved onto the next item, whilst private discussions sought to resolve matters.

Careful and delicate diplomatic efforts had weaved agreement on a Council text before the Rome summit had opened. Vattani had been the main interlocutor. The text favoured by the Italians was prepared by Padoa-Schioppa and Vattani; it involved painstaking negotiations with each EC government. But Vattani had insisted on not showing the text to anyone: he wanted to keep his cards close to his chest. Such secrecy was unprecedented: Vattani later prided himself on the effectiveness of his method. At Rome, Vattani had told Niels Ersboll, the Council secretary, that he would submit the text on EMU at a late stage, indicating the desire to keep control of the wording.

By the British, Andreotti would later be accused of not respecting established practice: the objection of a major government should be accommodated; it should not be left isolated. In the event, however, such was the outcome. Nevertheless, private contacts did take place overnight. Vattani and Padoa-Schioppa discussed matters with Ersboll, Williamson, and Lamy. Williamson said he thought Mrs Thatcher was willing to compromise. Vattani was sceptical, but at 1.35 a.m. he phoned Nigel Wicks to check. Wicks said he would discuss the text in the morning. Vattani told the others Wicks would not come and that he was not interested. The Italian text was circulated to each of the other delegations at 5 a.m. At a breakfast meeting, the Italians went over the text with Andreotti and De Michelis. Wicks interrupted to report that Thatcher asked to have an insertion made into the text. This dissociated the British from the EMU conclusions. The text did not specifically refer to Britain: Vattani said to Wicks that it was unrealistic not to cite the dissenting country. An angry Wicks conceded that the text could specifically refer to Britain by name. Such a national reference was unprecedented in EC practice and it isolated Mrs Thatcher. Her subsequent cavalier interpretation of the Rome outcome was to provoke Sir Geoffrey Howe and instigate her own downfall.

Italian strategy in relation to Britain rested on a two-pronged approach. Whilst Andreotti and De Michelis were seeking to persuade Mrs Thatcher to compromise in advance of Rome 1, Vattani was secretly drafting a communiqué which would seek to gain support for the Italians' maximalist position on EMU. Yet, the overtures to Mrs Thatcher appear to have been genuine. Vattani's original draft sought to accommodate the hard ECU initiative. The British Prime Minister, however, misread and misjudged the political signals.

By 'hiving off' and isolating the British opposition, the Italians had made more progress than Jacques Delors or De Michelis had thought possible. The success was reflected in several key points. First, it established the goal of a 'single currency'. The draft Italian text on the final day had referred to the goal of the EC establishing its 'own currency' rather than a 'single currency', a stipulation designed to appease the British. At the breakfast meeting of the Italian delegation—involving Andreotti, De Michelis, Vattani, Padoa-Schioppa, and Vanni—Andreotti said that the phrase 'own currency' could now be replaced as the British were making their own separate statement. Andreotti proceeded to check the revision with Kohl, who agreed; the Italian text was thus strengthened. Secondly, the Rome meeting could boast that a date had been set for stage 2 with few conditions attached, in line with Italian preferences. This date would be challenged in the IGC subsequently—by the Germans, the Dutch, the Danes, and the British on 8 April—on the grounds that adequate convergence was also a prerequisite.[2] Yet, the commitment to the date survived. By the informal ECOFIN meeting at Apeldoorn in September, all except the British accepted the start-date, albeit with certain minimal conditions.[3] The Italians were to prove less successful, though, with respect to the Rome 1 text on a strong monetary institution in stage 2, something which they very much desired (see discussion below).

'Automaticity' and Padoa-Schioppa's Formula

More substantially, another related Italian success on the issue of the EMU timetable would come at the Maastricht European Council of December 1991.

[2] In the discussion in the IGC ministerial meeting of 8 April 1991, the Danes, the Dutch, and the Germans said that an automatic transition to stage 2 was not possible alongside the necessary reference to objective convergence criteria. The risk was of a bad start to stage 2. Lamont for the UK argued that the content of stage 2 was more important than making an early start: the British wanted to finalize the content first. France, Belgium, Portugal, and Delors argued with the Italians that Rome 1 had settled the start-date; as did the Luxembourger IGC Presidency (Juncker).

[3] See DG2 Briefing Note for the Apeldoorn meeting, 9 Sept. 1991.

The Italian negotiators were successful in having their own formula on 'automaticity' accepted in a last-minute settlement.

At the last IGC before Maastricht, Pierre Bérégovoy, the French Finance Minister, raised the idea of inserting dates into the timetable for stage 3. Ministers and their officials discussed the notion informally over lunch. Both the French and the Italians had long favoured such a commitment. In the last days prior to Maastricht much attention was focused on this matter in different capitals, involving close liaison between Brussels, Paris, and Bonn. There was strong support in the IGC for 'automaticity', but the problem was how to formulate such a provision in the Treaty.

Padoa-Schioppa became a key conduit. He had strong EC ties to use here. He was very close to Delors and had easy access to his entourage (Pascal Lamy, Joly Dixon, and Giovanni Ravasio, head of DG2 in the Commission).[4] On the plane to Maastricht, Padoa-Schioppa advised Andreotti that success was now possible on setting an 'automatic' date for stage 3. Since mid-November, the French and the German governments had been referring to the need to make EMU 'irreversible'. Padoa-Schioppa passed Andreotti a note as to how 'automaticity' might be formulated, and the latter pursued the matter on arrival in Maastricht.

Andreotti had a private dinner with Mitterrand on the first night, joined by Vattani and Caroline de Marjorie. The Italian premier put the general notion to Mitterrand, who accepted it. He then suggested that he and Mitterrand should have a meeting with Kohl the next day before the negotiations resumed. They did so and found Kohl in agreement on the insertion of the formula. Vattani liaised about the text with other delegations. At Andreotti's initiative, the European Council then approved the proposal, and the ECOFIN ministers were instructed to put it into precise treaty language.

The final agreement combined dates with a complex procedure: a qualified majority in the European Council before the end of 1996 could set a date for stage 3; if no date has been set by the end of 1997, Stage 3 would begin on 1 January 1999 (Article 109j of the Treaty on European Union (TEU)). Thus, though they were by no means operating in a vacuum, the final formula on 'automaticity' was originated by the Italians. This initiative was possibly the most significant, lasting single success for the Italian negotiators during the whole EMU process.

Negotiating Failures: Maximalist Dreams Scuppered

The Institutional Design: Linking Stages 2 and 3

Perhaps the greatest area of failure for the Italians was the design of the institutions for the transition to EMU. Here the Banca d'Italia had staked out its most prominent position. It preferred to specify as much as possible the detailed

---

[4] Ravasio became head of the Directorate-General for Economic Affairs in February 1990.

arrangements for Stage 2 and believed in a strong ECB to govern this key transitional phase. In the event, the Maastricht Agreement fell well short of these objectives. The progress of the EMU negotiations left this Italian position increasingly isolated.

The Italians felt that they had scored a notable victory with their writing of the conclusions of the European Council in Rome in October 1990. They referred to: 'the creation of a new institution comprising Member States' central banks and a central organ, exercising full responsibility for monetary policy . . . At the start of the second phase, the new Community institution will be established.'

The Italian Presidency (Padoa-Schioppa, in particular) attached great significance to the use of the definite article to refer to *the* new EC institution at the start of stage 2. It meant, in their view, that the institution created in 1994 would be *the* ECB. This stipulation, and other references in the Rome communiqué, suggested that a strong institution would be established at the start of stage 2. Certainly, much discussion had taken place at Rome on this phrasing. The Dutch and the German delegations insisted on the use of the indefinite article in the communiqué, precisely because they wanted to have an institution in stage 2 which possessed only limited powers. During the Rome gathering, Vattani pressed the Germans to agree to the Italian wording. Joachim Bitterlich, from the German Federal Chancellor's Office and representing Kohl, accepted this wording, despite being aware that neither the Bundesbank nor the Finance Ministry would want it. The Italians reportedly diverted the less pliable German Finance Ministry official present to a meeting on GATT, in order to concentrate on winning over Bitterlich. This outcome left the Dutch isolated at Rome. As the Dutch were the only ones to raise any objection later in the full meeting of the Council, Andreotti was able to override their opposition. Later, in the subsequent IGC on EMU, the Dutch would enrage the Italians with some of their proposals. But, at Rome, to the surprise of many (including Delors and De Michelis), the Italian Presidency had scored a notable victory for their position.

But the success of the Rome European Council proved to be short-lived. In the early IGC meetings, the divergences on this matter were soon clear: in effect, most implicitly accepted that 'the' in the Rome communiqué actually meant 'a' central monetary institution. The stage 2 institution would be different from that of stage 3. The Italians, the French, and the Commission sought to defend the Rome 1 position. At the IGC personal representatives' meeting of 9 April, both the French and the Italian representatives argued in favour of a strong body to guide the transition and they noted that adequate time had to be given to establish the ECB before stage 3 began. A note from Draghi to his IGC colleagues (8 April) stressed the need to give the 'ECB' a 'crucial role' in stage 2. Draghi wrote that, 'I do not see the alleged inconsistency between the letter of the Rome Conclusions, which unambiguously asks for the establishment of the ECB at the start of the second phase, and their substance, i.e. the functions attributed to the ECB in the second phase'. Failure to allow the ECB to prepare the way adequately risked delay or placing the transition on 'shaky ground'.

The adequacy of the institutional arrangements for the transition to stage 3 had long been a key Italian concern. The previous December, the Banca d'Italia had circulated a report to the Committee of Central Bank Governors entitled, 'The Functions of the European Central Bank in the Second Phase of EMU'. It addressed fears that the responsibilities of national central banks and of the Stage 2 institution might be confused and chaotic. The report distinguished between the 'qualitative' and the 'quantitative' aspects of monetary policy. It recommended that the ECB should take the lead on the former aspect, leaving national central banks to retain responsibility for the latter. The 'qualitative' aspect concerned the structural characteristics of policy instruments (the nature of the instruments), whilst the 'quantitative' concerned the effective size or level of a given instrument (e.g. interest rates or liquidity) (Bini-Smaghi et al. 1994: 35–6). The Banca d'Italia was convinced that national and European competences could, and should, be clearly delineated during the transition. The effect would be to give the stage 2 body a significant role.

More or less at the time of Draghi's IGC letter, however, the French were shifting their position and accommodating the Germans. This shift must be placed in the context of the series of secret Franco-German bilateral meetings on EMU which was instigated at this time. By the end of April 1991, only the Italians were now willing to support 'ECB' as the title for the stage 2 body; whilst the Dutch and the Germans vigorously opposed this formulation. At the Luxembourg IGC ministerial meeting on 10 June, the Italians still argued that an ECB should be created at the start of stage 2. But the momentum was against them. Away from the gaze of Chancellor Kohl, the Germans had consistently sought a minimalist institution for stage 2, as had the Dutch. The British sought to avoid any significant institution-building at all. In April 1991, Baron Snoy for Belgium proposed the modest title of 'European Monetary Institute' for the new body. But the negotiations on this issue proved inconclusive: the IGC returned to this problem in the autumn, under the 'hawkish' Dutch Presidency.

Castles in the Sand: the Stage 2 Institution

The Italian negotiators continued to press for a strong stage 2 institution. An informal ECOFIN meeting at Apeldoorn in September represented a turning-point. The meeting agreed that an 'EMI' would be created at the start of stage 2: the institution was to be modestly defined. The agreement on the EMI was seen by the Italians as a defeat. It meant the rejection of the assumptions of the Delors Report, the conclusions of the Rome Council, and the traditional 'Community method' of creating an institutional 'engine' to oversee the full period from transition to completion (Bini-Smaghi et al. 1994: 35).

The 'war' continued in another guise. After the Apeldoorn meeting, the IGC negotiated the structure, presidency, legal powers, and reserve capital of the EMI. On these matters, the Italian position enjoyed some limited success. The Italians argued at the IGC ministerial meeting on 9 September that, if a distinct body (the EMI) was to be created, then it should be abolished when the ECB began in stage 3. This notion had support: from the French, the Belgians, the Spanish, the Irish, the Greeks, the Portuguese, and the Commission. Carli pressed the point at Apeldoorn, where it was accepted (Bini-Smaghi *et al.* 1994: 37). The intention was to avoid the danger of some states, such as Italy, being excluded from the management of the ECB, if they were 'outside' stage 3, after they had participated in the EMI. Such a move was consistent with Ciampi's notion of how to build the EMU architecture. But the Germans and the Dutch continued to oppose this formulation through November until the last IGC before Maastricht.

A clear cleavage on this matter was apparent at the IGC meeting of ministers and officials on 25–6 November. The Italians (supported by the Spanish, the Irish, the Portuguese, and the Greeks) sought to integrate as much as possible the governors of the central banks of 'out' countries into the structure of the ECB, albeit on the basis of them having limited voting rights on monetary matters. By contrast, the Germans, the French, the Dutch, and the British wished to create a separate body in which the 'outs' would be involved in certain non-monetary decisions. The protocol on the ECB and the ESCB attached to the Maastricht Treaty makes clear that all central bank governors are to be members of the 'Governing Council' of the ECB (Art.10).

On the other remaining EMI issues, the Italians again found themselves opposed most vigorously by the Germans, the Dutch, and the British. Indeed, 'In the face of strong German opposition, any idea of giving the EMI substantial responsibilities in the coordination of monetary policies was, *de facto*, withdrawn (Bini-Smaghi *et al.* 1994: 38). The CCBG drafted a statute for the EMI in little more than a month; the Dutch Presidency endeavoured to insert further restrictions into that text. But during November the will to compromise was clear (Bini-Smaghi *et al.* 1994: 39). Wim Kok, the IGC Chair, supported the idea that the EMI should have a president drawn from outside the central bank governors themselves and that it should have a limited amount of capital of its own. The Germans opposed these ideas very vigorously at the IGC ministerial meeting of 11–12 November, but Horst Köhler was willing to concede on the question of the EMI managing some reserves (Bini-Smaghi *et al.* 1994: 39).[5] With the Maastricht summit deadline looming, the remaining issues were settled in the IGC meetings of late November and early December. The Italians were least satisfied with the agreement reached on the EMI's legal powers. They had wanted the EMI to have full legal authority. But the EMI's decisions were not to have the status of Community law and were to be subject to the approval of the ECB upon its creation.

[5] On the question of the EMI's management of reserves, Pierre Bérégovoy had proposed an arrangement whereby states could voluntarily delegate exchange-reserve management to it and this notion was supported by the Italians, the Spanish, the Belgians, the Luxembourgers, the Greeks, and the Portuguese (IGC ministerial meeting, 11–12 November). This was opposed by the Germans, the Dutch, the British, the Danes, and the Irish.

The Italian delegation was satisfied that some provision for preparing for stage 3 was made in the EMI's statute (albeit less than the Banca d'Italia thought technically necessary). The Commission was itself very sympathetic to the technical case made by the Italians on this issue. The Banca d'Italia and the Tesoro had authored a joint paper detailing the responsibilities that the stage 2 institution should have and the transitional arrangements that it might make. However, its partners had regarded such detailed preparation as premature. Cees Maas, as IGC Chair, was reluctant even to discuss the paper. In the final phase of these negotiations, though, the Italian approach received some support from the German delegation. In particular, after a bilateral Italian–German meeting of officials in Milan in October 1991, Horst Köhler—the senior German Finance Ministry negotiator—seemed to recognize that the proposals of the Banca d'Italia on this matter did not represent a threat to the Bundesbank's authority in stage 2. An IGC personal representatives' meeting of 4–5 November displayed little support for an Italian attempt to expand the preparatory tasks of the EMI. But the next month Carli was successful in establishing that the EMI should prepare by the end of 1996 the 'regulatory, organizational and logistical framework' for stage 3 (Art. 4.2 of Protocol on EMI). Papadia had drafted the text, which Draghi and Carli had presented.

Yet the final design of the stage 2 institution was much weaker than that originally sought, especially by Padoa-Schioppa and the Banca d'Italia in 1990. The logical conclusion was that the final construction of the EMI was much closer to the model promoted by the Germans, and the British, than that originally advanced by the French and the Italians (Kenen 1992). The Italian stance had been weakened by the shift of position by the French early in 1991: an example of a wider pattern in which the French effectively eschewed coalitions with the Italians in this period in favour of hammering out common positions within the Franco-German axis (see below).

The Convergence Criteria: Opportunity or Block?

The Italian objective of seeking to avoid strict and numeric convergence criteria for entry to stage 3 was also a battle lost in most respects.

In one sense, there was a clash of interests for the Italian government on this issue. Tough conditions would establish a more credible 'vincolo esterno'. But, the tougher they were, the more difficult it would be for Italy to participate in the 'first division'. Carli believed in the utility of a 'vincolo esterno'. But the Italian delegation's reservations focused on the practical definition and status of these conditions. Carli and Draghi were in the driving seat on these issues. Ultimately, they had the responsibility to evaluate the deal that was available. They were placed in an awkward position: to be perceived as seeking more flexible conditions might be interpreted as defending the interests of Italy's weak fiscal position. Such a move would send out a negative signal about Italian ambitions to be in 'division one'. It would alienate the Germans and the Dutch (and increasingly the French) and weaken the impact of the *'vincolo esterno'* (Giavazzi and Spaventa 1988).

In any event, compared to the Italian stance of 1990, the final package at Maastricht was very different in content. Tough convergence criteria were adopted, with strict and numeric reference values. Indeed, the criteria were so tough that the prospect of Italy being able to participate in stage 3 by 1999 was soon seriously in question.

By the second half of 1991 the main issue of contention for the Italian delegation was the nature of any fiscal conditions for entry: involving references to national debts and deficits, as well as the legal status of any such commitment. The Italians pressed for the fiscal criteria to be specified in secondary EC legislation. As they argued at the IGC personal representatives' meeting of 10 September and of 22 October, it would be easier to alter the criteria in the light of subsequent events. Whilst they were also resigned to the imposition of EC financial sanctions against recalcitrant states, they had reservations about an excessive deficit constituting a breach of a state's legal obligations (IGC ministerial meeting of 10 June 1991). By late November, however, the Italians accepted a Dutch text on this issue: it was time for compromise.

The Italians were soon fighting a rearguard battle. They were worried about a threshold value being set for an excessive deficit. Any such reference had to be credible and saleable; yet, some of the conditions being floated might not even be met by Germany. The informal ECOFIN meeting at Apeldoorn on 21 September had shown that there was majority support for clear, objective criteria on excessive deficits; for the procedure by which the Commission would report on such a deficit; and for a decision by the Council of Ministers on the measures required to correct it.[6] Yet, even after Apeldoorn, the Italians continued to argue—as at the IGC ministerial meeting on 7 October—against specific reference values on excessive deficits. In their view, the trend was the important point; and, in any event, the values might have to be changed in the light of unforeseen events.

As already noted, the Andreotti government came under intense political pressure from both the French and the Germans to accept a degree of toughness and its own bargaining power was weakening with its economic troubles at home. Agreement on a 60 per cent debt-to-GDP ratio was soon reached, leaving the debate to focus on the proposal of the EC Monetary Committee for a 3 per cent deficit-to-GDP ratio. The Italians argued that the criteria needed to be applied in a dynamic, not a static, manner to take account of diverse trends across countries. They were joined in this argument by the representatives of Belgium, Britain, Denmark, Greece, Ireland, Portugal, and Spain. Carli argued

---

[6] Reported in Commission Note on IGC ministerial meeting of 7 Oct. 1991; Apeldoorn meeting was on 21 Sept. 1991.

at the IGC of 7 October that price stability was not the only policy objective to be sought; therefore there was a need for flexibility in interpretation in other matters. Draghi liaised with his French counterpart, Jean-Claude Trichet, on the need for greater flexibility. The French proposed a new form of words, and were supported by both the Italians and the British (Nigel Wicks) in doing so.

The eventual agreement showed some recognition of the Italian concerns; and Draghi could claim some modest success. Article 104c(2) incorporated a dynamic element in the assessment of a member state's budgetary situation: a deficit may not be judged excessive if it is declining substantially and continuously towards the 3 per cent level or if the problem is judged to be temporary; likewise, if the debt level is diminishing to a sufficient extent and approaching 60 per cent of GDP then it may also not be judged to be excessive. It was also agreed to state the reference values in a protocol to the Treaty, making them amenable to subsequent amendment by the Council of Ministers, acting unanimously. In addition, the Italians joined others in pressing, successfully, for the EC Commission to have the task of evaluating the degree of convergence achieved by member states, albeit supported by an advisory committee of national appointees (Articles 104c, 109c). The Commission could be expected to favour as wide a membership of stage 3 as possible. The success in establishing a more dynamic interpretation of fiscal rectitude was, then, a shared one: the Italians managed to persuade the more powerful French delegation to draw a line on the degree of toughness being sought.

Of their Own Free Will?

The question arises of why the Italian IGC delegation agreed to what were still very tough fiscal conditions. The objective conditions suggested that Italy would have severe difficulties in meeting these tests. Various explanations can be offered. First, as noted earlier, the Andreotti government was forced to recognize by October 1991 that no other deal was available. The French had moved to back the German position: the Treaty must have clear numeric criteria. The Italians had to accept that such a concession was necessary to secure a deal. There was no point in repeating the 1978 ploy of delaying acceptance of the EMS. The Italian government was thus left with a stark choice: between self-imposed exclusion from the start or the chance to show that Italy could perform as a first division EC member. It opted for the latter.

A second explanation is that leaders such as Andreotti and De Michelis may well have believed that the convergence rules could be renegotiated later or could be interpreted more flexibly when the crunch came. In other words, the battle was to be fought later. What was being negotiated was a matter to be considered some years in the future. Moreover, by reputation, they were not disposed to feel bound by the letter of such a law. In addition, both may have felt too weak to block acceptance of these conditions, even if they had wished to do so. As noted earlier, their governmental strength (and that of the *partitocrazia*) had dissipated by the end of 1991, for a combination of political and economic reasons. In any event, they ceded position to their technocratic colleagues: Carli and the 'Gang of Three'.

Thirdly, as already noted also, attitudes towards the convergence criteria varied amongst the technocratic negotiators themselves. The Banca d'Italia, and Padoa-Schioppa in particular, gave a much lower priority to this issue. For its part, the Tesoro was left to grapple with Italy's conflicting interests in this respect. The domestic policy momentum in recent years had favoured monetary and fiscal discipline. The support for a *'vincolo esterno'* implied a certain degree of toughness and Carli was a major advocate of this thesis. The convergence criteria represented a domestic weapon, as well as a test of external rectitude. Without them, Carli and Draghi believed, the politicians could not be relied upon to accept long-term budget discipline.

Finally, the insertion of the 'trend' notion into the criteria could be sold as a point of reassurance. Whilst some of Italy's partners proclaimed the austere constraint of the Maastricht text, as Calvinist puritans, in truth the text was open to conflicting interpretations. This flexibility would be evident in May 1998 when the EU accepted Belgium and Italy as participants in stage 3, despite the fact that their respective debt levels far outstripped the 60 per cent Maastricht stipulation. In 1991 the convergence criteria could be seen as targets: a form of 'side-payment' to give Italy an incentive to meet the tests of membership.

Let the British Take It or Leave It

Its firm commitment to ensuring progress to EMU meant that the Italian government took a clear stance on Britain's reluctance to commit itself to a single currency. Andreotti had isolated Mrs Thatcher at the Rome European Council in October 1990, as had his predecessor Bettino Craxi at the Milan summit of June 1985 on the decision to hold an IGC that culminated in the Single European Act. In 1991 the Italian negotiators were sceptical that any single treaty could be accepted by all twelve governments. Thus, if it persisted in opposition, Britain must be isolated. The Italians seemed unaware of the terms of a private understanding reached between Kohl, Lubbers, and Major at the Luxembourg European Council (Hogg and Hill 1995: 81–2). This understanding was that the British would negotiate in good faith, but that it would be offered an opt-out, if at the end of the process, it felt unable to sign up for EMU. The IGC negotiations were thus left to run their natural course.

The issue of opt-in/opt-out was raised most prominently during the Dutch Presidency. At the end of August 1991, the Dutch chair of the IGC officials, Cees Maas, produced a proposal which would have granted all governments the right to decide whether they wished to join stage 3 at the date when a future Council agreed the final phase should start. This proposal involved little prior commitment to EMU by any government. At the IGC ministerial meeting of 9 September, the Italians were quick to reject the Dutch approach and its implied multi-speed process. A revised text circulated by Wim Kok, the ECOFIN President, a month later and the full Draft Treaty circulated by the Dutch on 28 October were barely more acceptable to the Italians. Roberto Nigido emphasized the hidden dangers in a less than lucid Dutch text. The Italians lobbied hard on this issue: notably in two bilateral meetings (of officials) with the Dutch in The Hague; a separate meeting (of officials) with the Germans in Milan; and in a formal bilateral meeting of Andreotti and President François Mitterrand in Perugia (Italy). Draghi, Vattani, Padoa-Schioppa, and Nigido pressed the Dutch on the terms of any opt-out. On 8 November, Draghi sent an official memorandum to the Dutch, French, and German governments and to Delors setting out the Italian opposition to the Dutch text of 28 October. The Italian government was the only one to reject a general opt-out in any guise, notably at the IGC personal representatives' meeting of 13 November. It was totally united in doing so. The Italians opposed a later compromise offered by Belgium and Luxembourg which would have given an opt-out to all in the expectation that the majority would immediately renounce it. The Italian officials believed that this issue could not be settled within the IGC, but that it must be placed on the agenda at Maastricht. This background helps explain the attention that the Italians gave to the 'automaticity' formula at Maastricht.

Framing the Wider Package

In addition to the three key policy priorities already considered, the Italian contribution to the IGC negotiations can also be examined in relation to three other areas of lesser importance to Rome. These concerned: (1) the general policy objectives set by the EC in the context of EMU; (2) the establishment of a new 'cohesion' fund; and (3) the involvement of the existing EC institutions in the management of EMU.

On the general policy objectives for EMU, the Italians found themselves in close agreement with the texts presented by the Commission and by the Luxembourg Presidency. The Italians made clear at the first IGC meeting of personal representatives on 15 January 1991 that it would not be presenting a full draft treaty of its own. At the second IGC personal representatives' meeting of 29 January, the Germans proposed that the economic policy-objectives to be respected by member governments should include reference, *inter alia*, to open markets, free prices, and to privatization. The Italians were quickly in conflict with them on these matters. At these first two IGC meetings, the Italians objected to the inclusion of privatization; they had reservations about the free circulation of capital with respect to third countries; and they found reference to the reduction of wage indexation delicate. On the privatization issue, at least five other EC states agreed with the Italian stance, whilst Belgium also found indexation and free circulation problematic. A clear policy—indeed, ideological—cleavage was apparent. In fact, the final text of Article 2*a* makes no direct reference to privatization or price regimes.

The demand for new financial aid by Italy's Mediterranean partners—the so-called 'cohesion monies'—placed her in an awkward position. Rome could sympathize with the motives and philosophy behind the demands; it had made similar requests itself before. But it did not wish to identify itself as part of a soft, periphery alliance. It was doing all it could to be accepted as a member of any inner core of EMU. Some, such as Ciampi in the Committee of Central Bank Governors, took a much more sceptical stance. Whilst at the time of the EMS negotiations he had pressed for similar monies to be made available, in the EMU discussions he displayed scepticism about the value of such measures and refused to back them, despite overtures from the Irish and others to do so. A deeper contrast also existed. At the time of the EMS negotiations, Italy would have expected to be a recipient of such monies. By the EMU negotiations, however, any judgement based on relative GDP-per-capita measures might have led Italy to be a paymaster. At no stage did Italy place itself in the position of seeking such cohesion money for itself. Instead, its IGC negotiators adopted a mid-position on the issue: between its Mediterranean and Irish partners and the 'hawkish' Germans, Dutch, and British. At the IGC ministerial meeting of 25–6 February, the Italians argued that the case for the new facility was stronger given the rigorous provisions likely to be made on national fiscal discipline. In the event, given the sharply opposed views of its partners, the issue was effectively postponed until after the Maastricht summit.

In the IGC discussions on the involvement of the existing EC institutions in EMU policy matters, the Italians were relatively more *communautaire* than most of their counterparts. They supported the inclusion of the European Parliament (EP) in the EMU policy process. The final Treaty assigns certain rights of accountability to the EP, and these had been fully supported by the Italians. The Italians had also supported the use of the new co-operation procedure for legislative acts on EMU: such a procedure would have made the Parliament an effective co-partner. But only the Belgian and Greek delegations supported this position and it was lost. On other matters, the Italians endeavoured to have institutional issues resolved in collaboration with the other IGC on EPU (European political union): as had been their motivation in 1990 when suggesting close co-ordination between the two conferences. More suprisingly, the Italians went along with the overwhelming majority of their colleagues in supporting the limitation of the Commission's rights on EMU policy, notably at the IGC personal representatives' meeting of 12 March. The specific issue in this instance was the management of exchange-rate policy; the Italians agreed with the French, Germans, and British. This position was, however, consistent with their emphasis on the primary role of an ECB, tempered by accountability to the European Parliament.

Strategy and Coalitions

French Perfidy and German Intransigence?

Italian negotiators sought to strengthen their EMU bargaining position by attempting to build coalitions with their partners. In the course of the EMU debate between 1988 and 1991 it was evident that certain policy cleavages existed; these cleavages took on a dynamism of their own during the course of the IGC negotiations. At the start of the IGC, the Italian position was generally closest to that of the French. Both shared a set of policy beliefs about:

- the utility of setting a clear timetable for progress towards a single currency;
- the irreversibility of the EMU process;
- progress not being dependent primarily on the degree of convergence achieved between the economies of the participating member states;
- a limitation in the specification of any convergence criteria; and,
- the transition to be guided by a strong monetary institution in stage 2: a European Central Bank.

Until at least the spring of 1991, the Italians regularly found themselves in sympathy with their colleagues from Paris in the EMU negotiations. This proximity was not replicated, however, in the IGC on political union.[7] Paris and Bonn disagreed over defence policy and the role of the European Parliament.

The reverse pattern applied in relation to Italy and Germany. There was a wide gulf on EMU between the Italian and German positions; the Italians were 'monetarist' and institutionalist to the core, whilst the Germans preached the 'economist' and behaviouralist position. The Italians found German intransigence exasperating at times. They also feared that the Germans wished to exclude them from EMU. Such fears were sustained throughout 1992–8, with what were regarded as unhelpful comments from Waigel and from the Bundesbank. By contrast, in 1991 Italian–German proximity on political union was much greater. De Michelis and Genscher, for example, agreed two joint declarations in this period: one on the early convening of the IGC (in October 1989) and the other on institutional reform (April 1991). Italian and German political visions of the future of the EC were close. The April declaration set out a six-point plan to enhance democratic legitimacy and the role of the European Parliament in EC law-making and the appointment of the Commission.

This pattern of positions gave some scope for the Italians to build coalitions. Yet, in the event, the Italians became more, rather than less, isolated as the IGC wore on. In large part, this isolation was because the French shifted away from them, whilst the Germans remained distant. The Italians were marginalized,

[7] The French and Italian attitudes on political union were much more divergent. See, for example, reports of Franco-Italian summit of 17–18 October 1991 in Viterbo, near Rome, and De Michelis's attempts to bridge differences with the French on European defence policy. This move followed an Anglo-Italian declaration and a separate Franco-German initiative, to which Spain adhered.

never able to break into the Franco-German nexus. To Paris, compromise with Germany seemed the indispensable prerequisite for an EMU agreement, and both parties sought to reduce their differences in the regular and secretive bilateral meetings they held from April 1991 onwards. The French *rapprochement* with the Germans had notable effects. As Bini-Smaghi *et al.* note for the later stages of the IGC, 'The pro-EMU influence that France and Italy tried to exert was weakened by their failure to act convincingly on two points that were crucial for the German block: respectively central bank independence and fiscal adjustment' (1994). On both points, the Italian position had maintained a strong consistency; the French stance shifted towards Germany. Likewise, both France and Italy initially opposed any reference to long-term interest rates in the EMU convergence conditions. In the end, Germany won on this point. France and Italy opposed setting the entry conditions for Stage 3 in the main body of the Treaty. But France moved closer to the German position on this point also (Bini-Smaghi *et al.* 1994: 23).

The Italians were also obliged to recognize the need to compromise with Germany. Failure to do so might lead to no agreement on EMU or, even worse, a deal going ahead without Italy. The French were first to show a willingness to compromise, but the Italians were also obliged to recognize the same reality. As one senior Italian official put it, 'the Germans set a high price, and then they were suprised when we indicated we were prepared to pay it'. In any event, Kohl and Genscher were probably as accommodating as any German leaders could be.

Miles away from London

The Italian and the British positions on EMU were, with rare exceptions, very far apart. Mrs Thatcher had felt ambushed at the Rome European Council meeting of September 1990. The effect was to sour relations with Whitehall, which was clearly wary of the Italians. A letter from Draghi to Cees Maas on 22 October 1991, suggesting that states with a derogation or 'opt-out' from EMU should not be eligible for financial assistance designed to foster convergence, received a sharp rebuke from Nigel Wicks on 25 October. The Italian position was seen as 'unhelpful' and as challenging the positive spirit of the British negotiators. Moreover, a later letter from Draghi to Maas of 8 November opposing a general opt-out was not circulated to London, a clear recognition of the divide between the two camps. Later, in the ERM crisis of September 1992, the British and the Italians would pursue divergent strategies. At the Bath ECOFIN meeting, Lamont felt let down by the failure of Piero Barucci to support his demand that the Bundesbank lower their interest rates. In turn, London summarily dismissed all requests from the Amato government for a multilateral realignment of the ERM. The British were prepared to leave the Italians isolated in the face of the speculators; ironically, the British stance led directly to their own currency crisis on 'Black Wednesday'. On EMU (and the EMS) there seemed little scope for the two governments to build alliances, though they had managed to do so on European defence policy.[8]

No 'Club Med'

Other coalitions were more clearly discernible. Away from their 'Big Three' partners, the Italian stance was often close to that of the Belgians, the Greeks, and the Portuguese. Less often, the Italian position was shared by the Spanish and the Luxembourgers. Each coalition related to distinct sets of issues: voting blocs were not often consistent or uniform. By contrast, the Italian philosophy on EMU was most divergent from that of the Dutch and the Danes, as well as from that of the Germans. Moreover, rarely would the Italians have found themselves in unison with any of these three or with Britain against the French or the rest.

It would be misleading to refer to a consistent Latin 'bloc' in the IGC negotiations.[9] The southern states did not often act in unison; their positions varied. The Spanish appear to have resisted such a group identity and the Italians sought to avoid being assigned to a weaker, slower set of states. More fundamentally, the Latin bloc lacked a clear and consistent leader: the French shifted away from their 'Latin' allies at the start to accommodate Germany.

Any Deal is Better than No Deal?

From a bargaining perspective, the Italian 'win-set' on EMU seems to have been broadly cast, with a large degree of permissiveness. It would have been difficult for other governments to calculate what deal would not be accepted by the Italians. Hence it was not possible for the Italian negotiators to make much use of the bargaining strategy of 'binding themselves' by stressing domestic constraints on an EMU agreement. The Italian team lost on the issue of institution-building for EMU in stage 2: but this matter was clearly not a sticking-point for an agreement. Moreover, the deal struck on 'automaticity' at Maastricht was regarded as the 'cherry on the cake': desirable, but not an essential condition. The related issue of a possible general opt-out was fought vigorously by the Italians. On this one issue there was a greater likelihood that they might not have signed at Maastricht. With respect to the convergence criteria, it is unclear whether the Italians might have rejected a deal which was significantly more

---

[8] By contrast, they managed to do so for the IGC on political union: both governments issued a joint declaration on security and defence matters in October 1991. This declaration was then followed by a Franco-German initiative: the two declarations appeared to expose, rather than heal, differences. The Anglo-Italian declaration had been agreed in June 1991, but at British insistence its publication was delayed until October. The timing of its release was clearly tactical.

[9] Such references tend to overlook the cultural and historical problems of including Greece in a 'Latin' bloc.

restrictive. Most of all, Andreotti, and his team, clearly accepted that a deal had to be signed at Maastricht in December 1991. During the negotiations they were prepared to show a reasonable degree of flexibility in order to secure that deal. An additional factor in closing a deal at Maastricht was the calculation that it would sustain the political capital of a government (and a system) increasingly tarnished by scandal and undermined by an *immobilismo*. The Italian government faced impending parliamentary elections which were expected to be difficult.

The Italians were limited in the threats or inducements that they could utilize. The scope for participation in package deals, side-payments, and threats of rejection—the normal fare of successful bargaining—was restricted. In addition, once Italian negotiators had accepted the value of using EMU as a device for more effective domestic discipline, it became less easy to introduce into bargaining arguments about the consequent degree of 'pain'.

Italian participants in the EMU negotiations recognized their two-level nature and the dynamic interactivity of EC and domestic factors. As one senior official commented:

We always had a sense of a double-level strategy. You had to be rather restrictive in Brussels—or, rather, seek to slow a liberalizing momentum—in order to have more room for manouevre at home. In Rome, we transmitted the sense of urgency of reform, and also emphasized that we had fought a strong battle in Brussels. We were caught in between.

The '*vincolo esterno*' involved a particular version of a two-level game: here the domestic 'reverberation effects' were of prime importance. But seeking external discipline meant the Italians carried less bargaining clout at the EC table. Straddling the two levels involved very different Italian performances.

Conclusions

The Italian position on EMU was full of contrasts. The Italian government was one of the most enthusiastic advocates for EMU. But the design for EMU was, in the main, not one of its choosing. It sought a maximalist agreement, but its negotiating hand was weak. It appears to have been willing to ratify a varied range of possible EMU agreements, but it was unable to form any lasting and significant coalition on EMU. Perhaps most consequentially, it saw EMU as a new '*vincolo esterno*' to impose discipline and reform. However, during and after the negotiations there arose serious doubts about whether Italy would be able to join stage 3 in the first 'wave' and thus remain a full EC player.

The prospects for a distinctive Italian impact on the EMU negotiations—outside the special circumstances of the 1990 EC Presidency—were always going to be slim. Rome 1 had seemed a major diplomatic success, but the Italians did not have the muscle to maintain the triumph. Its domestic position was too weak.

At times, others seemed to want to set the stage 3 entry rules in a way that would exclude the Italians. The Italian strategy for the IGC was unable to sustain any major or consistent alliance with another government. Italy was purposely excluded from the Franco-German coalition, and the British seemed to play a separate game.

Ultimately, the Italian position in relation to EMU appeared to be one of dependency amidst hegemony. Italy needed EMU, but EMU was defined by others. After the ink was dry on the Maastricht Agreement, the worries increased as to whether Italy would be able to survive in the EMS and to be in a position to join stage 3 of EMU. The problems evident in 1991 became more acute. Amidst tremendous speculative pressure against the lira, the Amato government was obliged to leave the ERM in September 1992. The Germans had offered limited help, but British and French opposition to an ERM realignment left Italy to act unilaterally. The shock of exit was as much psychological as it was economic. Italian opinion saw the nation as irrevocably linked to the EC, but Italy had been forced to leave the club. The foreign-policy imperative meant that Italy's chief priority was to seek re-entry as soon as possible, to recoup lost ground. Successive governments sought to prepare re-entry. They soon called upon the ground swell of pro-European sentiment amongst public opinion at home to buttress the policies intended to help Italy enter stage 3. These included controversial reforms to pension provision and a supplement on income tax.[10] Eventually, in November 1996 the lira was able to re-enter the ERM.

Italy was faced with two alternatives. Either it would be allowed to squeeze into the first group of states to begin stage 3 in 1999 or it might be asked to wait until a second wave entered in 2001. The Prodi government stressed its commitment to joining as soon as possible. It was helped by the election of the Socialist government in France in May 1997. Lionel Jospin, the new Prime Minister, said that Italian entry (along with that of the Spanish) was an essential condition for France. Old hopes of a Franco-Italian coalition resurfaced.

But comments from Germany revived earlier divisions. In 1995–6 Theo Waigel repeatedly poured scorn on Italian prospects for EMU.[11] The Italians

[10] The pension reform in 1995 eased the fiscal pressure. Then, a 'one-year Euro-tax on incomes as part of [the] drive to be among the founding members of the planned single European currency' was adopted by the government of Romano Prodi in November 1996 (see report in *Financial Times*, 20 Nov. 1996). Prodi headed a coalition (the Olive Tree alliance) elected in April 1996. A former economics professor, Prodi had also been head of IRI, the state industrial-holding company.

[11] There were repeated reports of German doubts concerning Italy's prospects. After the Valencia meeting of ECOFIN on 30 September, the *Financial Times* reported that 'Germany has all but eliminated Italy from the first wave of EMU countries' (FT, 2 Oct. 1995). In the same period, Waigel had been quoted as saying that it was 'unlikely' that Italy would be in the first wave on a single currency, which provoked uproar in Rome (FT, 15 Nov. 1995). Waigel forecast Italy's exclusion when he appeared before the Bundestag's Finance Committee in September 1995 (see *Agence Europe*, 25 Sept. 1995). See also Theo Waigel's speech of 19 September 1996 at the Ludwig Erhard Foundation. At the end of a German–Italian bilateral summit on 7 February 1997, Chancellor Kohl was obliged to deny that his government had any plans to exclude Italy (see *Agence Europe*, 8 Feb. 1997).

Further controversy had been raised by the EU Commission's April 1997 forecast that Italy would faced the additional challenge of Waigel's demands for a 'Stability Pact' with automatic penalties on those stage 3 participants which broke the rules on fiscal discipline. The Bundesbank's own report in 1998 on the degree of convergence achieved amongst the EU states was severe in its judgements on the Italian (and Belgian) preparedness. Efforts by both governments to cut their 'extremely high' debt burdens were 'insufficient' (*Independent*, 28 March 1998). There remained 'grave doubts about the sustainability of the governments' financial position', requiring them to 'undertake additional, firm and substantive commitments' in this area. Chancellor Kohl's cabinet endorsed the Bundesbank's assessment, fearing that anything else would make EMU not saleable in Germany.

But compromise came on the basis of political interests overriding economic judgements. By the point of decision, in May 1998, EU governments were determined to press ahead and to avoid damaging splits. The impetus within the EU was for inclusiveness, rather than exclusion. A flexible interpretation of the Maastricht criteria served the interests of several governments. The Italian stress in the IGC on flexibility was now in vogue, and Italy herself was a chief beneficiary. At the special Brussels European Council on 2 May, Italy was accepted as a participant in stage 3 from 1 January 1999 onwards. Prodi, who had earlier said that he would resign if Italy was not accepted for stage 3, had secured his major European prize.

EMU had also been secured as a continuing and far-reaching *vincolo esterno* for the Italian economy. The need for fiscal and monetary discipline at home had been met by applying the legitimacy of the EU. But, far-reaching as it seemed, the domestic impact of the EMU constraint was likely to be uneven. It intruded into some policy sectors more obviously than in others.[12] Other sectors of the Italian economy were more vulnerable to the mercies of the domestic system. Similarly, the onset of stage 3 raised the possibility that it might exacerbate subnational inequalities and the 'dualism' of a society built on contrasts. In these respects, the partial nature of EMU was consistent with other forms of 'modernization' brought about by external shocks. EMU might create fault-lines in the domestic economy and society, raising doubts about the stability of the regime and also Italy's ability to sustain the obligations of membership.

In aspiring to join the EMU club, Italy carried risks at home. The contradiction was a familiar one: this was the starting-point for Italy when first faced with EMU. As such, the agreement on EMU signed in 1991 was a defining moment affecting the future course of Italian development.

not meet the Maastricht criteria on the budget deficit. The French Foreign Minister, Herve de Charette, made a notable public move to back Italy's position (see *FT*, 30 Apr. 1997).

[12] We are grateful to Claudio Radaelli for having raised these points with us. See Radaelli and Bruni (1998).

13

The British Political Tradition and EMU: Policy Legacies, Beliefs, and Co-ordination

The decision on a single currency is 'not for our generation to take'.
Margaret Thatcher, 18 June 1990

I hope my fellow heads of government will resist the temptation to recite the mantra of full economic and monetary union as if nothing had changed. If they do recite it, it will have all the quaintness of a rain dance and about the same potency.
John Major, *The Economist*, 25 September 1993

The Trouble with Europe

It has become an accepted truism in British politics that few issues have caused as much turbulence over the last three decades or more as 'Europe'. Ostensibly an issue of foreign policy, 'Europe' has penetrated deep into the domestic political arena. 'Europe' has identified factions in both the Conservative and the Labour Parties, and brought down ministers and prime ministers. Within official policy circles, 'Europe' has created major strategic dilemmas and cognitive challenges. For the public at large, 'Europe' has often seemed an intrusion, destabilizing accepted conditions. Much less frequently has 'Europe' been seen as an opportunity, an arena for political leadership and coalition-building.

At the same time, successive governments have accepted that Britain is tied to the European Union by economic interest, if not by emotional commitment. Policy has been led by 'Europeans' of the head rather than of the heart. The initiative in 1985 for a single European market was unusual: Britain had been, in part, responsible for its launch and its content meshed very strongly with British values and interests. The Thatcher government believed that this initiative might be a turning-point in Britain's relations with the rest of the EC. The horizon soon darkened again, however, with the debate over European monetary co-operation from 1988 onwards. Membership of the ERM opened up a divide within the government between those who had come to see exchange-rate discipline as a useful monetary constraint and those who eschewed such external commitment for reasons of free-market ideology and/or because they wished to maintain their freedom of political manoeuvre. The question of ERM entry cut deep into the unity of the Thatcher government. This issue was nowhere near resolved, when it became enlarged by the agenda of EMU. 'Europe' was forcing the pace much too fast for London.

EMU also represented a frontal assault on many of the traditional ideological concerns of the Conservative Party. It threatened core concerns about nationhood, sovereignty, and gradualism. It also raised questions about the sensitivity of monetary policy to market conditions. The Thatcher government was, in consequence, ill prepared to meet the challenges of the new debate on EMU. Mrs Thatcher was becoming increasingly strident on Europe, and her position was in fundamental conflict with the principles on which EMU was based. Her management of the Conservative Party, and the wider political debate, weakened. The issue of 'Europe' was recognized to be part of the reason for her downfall as party leader and Prime Minister. As such, it established a fault-line within the Tory Party which continued, and at times deepened, throughout the period in office of her successor, John Major.

When Major took over as Prime Minister in November 1990, he gave top priority to restoring the unity of his party and improving its prospects for re-election. This concern sustained a severe constraint on the scope for adapting policy and strategy in the IGC on EMU. Despite the contrasting situations of the Thatcher and Major leaderships, British policy and strategy on EMU were always couched in the internal politics of the Conservative Party. On this basis, Major scored a notable victory for himself and his party at Maastricht.

But the Maastricht outcome was one of semi-detachment on EMU for Britain. Britain's major continental partners placed EMU in a vision of Europe which only a minority in Britain shared. There was a greater emphasis in Britain on the political risks attached to this ambitious new project and a questioning of its economic viability. The Major government deferred the point of decision for Britain until these concerns could be lessened. The choice was avoided in a manner which provoked comparisons with the 1950s. Time will tell whether the choice made served Britain's foreign-policy interest.

The next three chapters provide a study of how the governments of Margaret Thatcher and John Major responded to an agenda not of their choosing and how they negotiated their way through it. This first chapter considers the way in which the response to EMU was 'prestructured' by the legacies of the debates on European monetary cooperation in the 1970s and 1980s. The most potent legacy was the disruptive impact of the issue of ERM entry in the 1985–90 period of the Thatcher government. But the chapter also examines how the response to EMU was prestructured by a set of wider policy beliefs about Britain's place in Europe. The chapter identifies the key policy actors on EMU and the perspectives they placed on EMU. Finally, the way in which policy and strategy on EMU were co-ordinated at home is analysed. This emphasizes the importance of the culture and practices of the Whitehall machine to the choices made on EMU.

These elements form the backdrop to the analysis of how the British government engaged in the EMU debate with its EC partners. Chapter 14 considers the early reaction in London to the reappearance of EMU on the Community's agenda. It considers the two alternative schemes—for a competing currency and a parallel currency—put forward by the British government. It analyses their birth and their demise; in other words the failure of a strategy to reformulate EMU in terms acceptable to Britain. After this failure, the British were obliged to negotiate on a terrain they found objectionable. Chapter 15 analyses how the British negotiated EMU between 1990–1. It highlights the key priorities and the strategy pursued. It places these in the context of the party constraint surrounding John Major's choices. The chapter closes by noting that the aftermath of the Maastricht negotiations affected how Britain managed the ERM crisis of September 1992. Policy was dictated by short-term domestic political pressures, and strategy was left out of kilter with the demands of successful negotiation in Europe. The final act of the drama appeared to parallel many of its opening features.

Lessons from History? Policy Beliefs and Strategy on European Monetary Co-operation, 1970–1990

The difficulties of the Thatcher and Major governments on EMU were foreshadowed by the position adopted by Britain in the context of earlier moves towards European monetary co-operation. A divergence was already evident between Britain and her major EC partners in these respects. What was not apparent in these earlier episodes, however, was the intensity and bitterness displayed in the dispute within the Thatcher government after 1985 as to whether sterling should enter the ERM. The acrimony of the personal dispute tended to hide the fact that this was a battle of principle fought across several terrains. The conflict was over foreign policy (Britain's place in Europe), party ideology (the application of Thatcherite values to monetary policy), and the management of government policy (the degree of consultation accepted by Mrs Thatcher). These principles, whilst evident in the earlier phases, had rarely been so keenly contested as in the ERM dispute. The fact that this dispute continued into the early stages of the new debate on EMU meant that it was a powerful legacy for those involved in determining Britain's response.

The divergence found between Britain and her EC partners across each of the different phases of the debate on European monetary co-operation, from the 1970s to the 1990s, suggests the importance of conflicting economic interests, political beliefs, and the institutional norms of Whitehall. Each of these long-term features affected the manner in which EMU was handled by the Thatcher and Major governments. More specifically, this troublesome issue began with a snake.

Britain, the Werner Plan, and the 'Snake'

The original moves to consider EMU, of which the Werner Plan of 1970 was the key step, were, in some respects, born out of a concern to protect the EC from the impact of British entry (Tsoukalis 1977: 169). The six EC states wished to prevent the Community descending into little more than a free trade area: an 'EFTA' writ large. More specifically, the position of sterling and its role as an international reserve currency was a point of major concern, not least to the French. Geoffrey Rippon, the minister charged with handling Britain's EC entry, reassured his prospective partners on 7 June 1971 that:

the British government were prepared to envisage an orderly and gradual run-down of official sterling balances after our accession . . . We shall be ready to discuss after our entry into the Communities what measures might be appropriate . . . in relation to sterling with those of the other currencies in the Community in the context of progress towards economic and monetary union in the enlarged Community. (Quoted in Heath 1998: 375)

Edward Heath as Prime Minister was keen to display Britain's 'European' credentials. He told the Commons, on 10 June 1971, that he had promised President Pompidou that 'we would play our full part in the progress towards economic and monetary union' (quoted in Heath 1998: 375). The Six had reaffirmed their commitment to EMU a couple of months earlier (22 March 1971), but the British response to the Smithsonian Agreement the following December left doubts as to London's commitment to fixed exchange rates. In the event, British entry was not the main problem for the EC in this regard. EMU quickly became embroiled in a wider external pressure, amidst the maelstrom of the collapse of the Bretton Woods system.

Whilst Heath was personally committed to EMU, circumstances meant that Britain barely affected the development of the new project. The Werner Plan led to the so-called 'Snake in the Tunnel' arrangement, seen as stage 1 en route to EMU (Dyson 1994: 83–8).[1] By this, the Nine sought to keep their currencies within a separate grid to promote exchange-rate stability. The 'Snake' began in April 1972, but Britain managed to stay within it for only six weeks, much to Heath's personal disappointment.[2] Heath reiterated his government's commitment to EMU at the October 1972 EC summit in Paris (Heath 1998: 387, 391), but it was to be 1990 before Britain returned to a fixed-exchange-rate system. A

[1] The chronology should be set against wider international developments. In August 1971, President Nixon announced that the US dollar would no longer be convertible into gold, as established by the Bretton Woods system of 1944. The Smithsonian Agreement of the following December introduced new rules to allow greater fluctuation of currencies against the dollar. The 'Snake' of April 1972 was an attempt to enhance these arrangements and give greater stability for the Europeans. It can be properly understood as 'the snake in the (dollar) tunnel'.

[2] Other participants soon had problems staying in the 'Snake'—notably France (which withdrew in January 1974, rejoined July 1975, left again March 1976)—but Britain was the first to exit in June 1972. Denmark left at the same time, but rejoined in the October, and Italy left in February 1973, not to return. See Johnson (1996: 211).

visit by Heath to see Willy Brandt, on 1 March 1973, illustrated the contrast between his aspirations and the practical outcome. Heath expressed his concerns to the West German Chancellor about the impact of the weakening US dollar on sterling and the other EC currencies and suggested that the EC should act together. Brandt was highly receptive to such sentiments. Indeed, Brandt proposed a joint float of the EC currencies and a pooling of their reserves. This was an ambitious plan, given the air of monetary crisis. However, the plan was not realized. According to Brandt, his ideas were soon scuppered by Whitehall and they came to nought (Brandt 1989: 402). By contrast, in his memoirs, Heath attributes the failure to opposition within Brandt's Cabinet (1998: 694). In any event, it was evident that Heath's European ambitions were ahead of Britain's ability to deliver. Britain followed the USA, rather than its new European partners, and allowed its currency to float. It did so upon its exit from the 'Snake' on 23 June 1972. In 1973 alone, sterling fell by 20 per cent against the strongest European currencies (Stephens 1996: 3). Anthony Barber, as Chancellor of the Exchequer, used the freedom for devaluation as a stimulus to Britain's trading position. The bubble of the 'Barber boom' was the result.

British detachment from the 'Snake' reflected its wider problems of EC participation. Her difficulties stemmed from the distinctiveness of her international (economic) interests. Sterling was still the world's second reserve currency until the late 1970s. The sterling balances held by foreign banks exposed the pound to any deterioration in Britain's balance-of-payments position and to short-term swings of mood on the foreign-exchange markets. In the new post-Bretton Woods era, maintaining a stable exchange rate would be difficult for Britain, and market pressure on the pound played havoc with her monetary policy. Moreover, there was a natural tendency for Britain's economic cycle (of growth and recession) to be more in keeping with that of the USA than with that of her EC partners. This asymmetry was probably the result of Britain's pattern of wider international trade relations and also of a similarity in the structures of the British and US capital markets.[3] In any event, the basic constraint was that Britain's economic convergence with her EC partners was very difficult to manage.

Britain and the Birth of the EMS

These considerations formed the backdrop to the British response to the initiative of Chancellor Schmidt and President Giscard d'Estaing for the creation of the EMS in 1978. The Labour government of James Callaghan was wary of such proposals (Ludlow 1982). In part, this wariness was because of the political legacy of Britain's renegotiation of EC entry and the referendum held on continued EC membership in June 1975. But it was also buttressed by an economic rationale. This combination of a strong domestic party constraint and of a per-

---

[3] This point is made by Alex Brummer in *The Guardian*, 21 Oct. 1997.

ception of distinct economic interests presaged the later debate on EMU in the 1980s and 1990s. Moreover, not for the first time, Britain sought an international solution, rather than engagement in a regional bloc.[4] Any move against the US dollar would hit British trading interests far more than it would the rest of the EC. Hence, Britain attempted to pursue a global approach via the IMF (where the US was guaranteed to be involved and where British influence was higher at that time, given that her Chancellor, Dennis Healey, was Chair of the IMF's Interim Committee). The stabilization plan presented to the IMF by the British implicitly called for German revaluation as a key means to its objective. Despite the plan making little headway—consistent with the historical pattern of such matters, the USA was uninterested in the British alternative and not especially fearful of the European initiative—the British were still wary of the putative EMS. Treasury officials advised that a fixed sterling–D-Mark rate would damage the British economy. The effects would be a worsening de-industrialization, the need for restrictive fiscal measures, lower growth, and rising unemployment. Such advice must have weighed heavily on a Labour government, especially one facing an election shortly.

From start to finish British involvement in the launch of the EMS veered between the distant and the conflictual. The fact that it was a former colleague, Roy Jenkins (as Commission President), who sparked off the new EMU debate in October 1977 was of little consequence to the Labour government. Jenkins's reputation was divisive within the party, and anchored firmly on its right-wing. He lent the notion of EMU minimal extra weight in the party. Indeed, Jenkins's move made little impact on domestic debate in Britain. Britain was unprepared: Callaghan was surprised by Schmidt's announcement of his EMS initiative at the Copenhagen European Council in April 1978. And, although Kenneth Couzens of the British Treasury was appointed along with Bernard Clappier (France) and Horst Schulmann (Germany) to prepare a paper for the Bremen European Council, it was the latter two that seized the initiative, with Couzens sidelined and even humiliated, owing to British obfuscation over the issue. London was left resentful and suspicious over such Franco-German co-ordination. The Bremen Council in July 1978 reinforced the momentum behind the initiative and increased the dilemma for Britain. British fears were exacerbated when the Aachen Franco-German summit in September seemed to stitch up the EMS deal.

Callaghan was sensitive to the political advantage consequent on British participation. But Healey and the Treasury emphasized the negatives. As Healey recalls in his memoirs,

Edmund Dell was strongly against the EMS in principle from the beginning, as was the Treasury, while Harold Lever was strongly in favour. The Bank of England was mildly in favour, since they thought it would exert a useful discipline on British governments. The Foreign Office was strongly in favour; it is in favour of anything which includes the

---

[4] Discussion here draws upon that of Ludlow (1982); also Dyson (1994).

word 'European'. I was fairly agnostic until I realised . . . how it was likely to work in practice; then I turned against it. (Healey 1989: 439)

In reality, Healey's influence on Britain's EMS negotiations was marked by characteristic bombast and aggression (Ludlow 1982: 186). The wider domestic political climate was also not conducive to a positive response: though much of the press supported entry, pressure from within the Labour Party was largely hostile, the government was in a minority position in the Commons, the Tory opposition generally never seemed more than lukewarm, and an election was close.

Hence, Callaghan went to the Brussels European Council in December 1978 resolved not to enter and expecting to be seen as the awkward partner. In reality, some of Britain's partners were prepared to see her exclusion for fear that sterling would not sit well in the new EMS. In any event, the conflicts and sourness that arose amongst Britain's partners deflected attention from Callaghan's own position. Such wrangling delayed the launch of the EMS until March 1979. Prior to the Brussels summit, Sir Michael Butler, the UK Permanent Representative to the EC, had already brokered a deal, backed by Giscard, to tackle the problem of British exclusion. This deal involved a distinction between the EMS and the ERM: Britain would be a member of the former but the only EC state not to belong to the latter. Butler had distinguished himself as someone able to 'square the circle' between the opposing interests of Britain and of her partners. He would attempt to play a similar role, with his 'hard' ECU initiative, a decade later.

Indeed, a number of other parallels exist between Britain's response to the EMS launch and to the new EMU debate after 1988. British reactions to the EMS initiative revealed a series of strategic choices, which had far-reaching consequences, and some of which would recur a decade later.

First, for both the EMS initiative and the relaunch of EMU, the relevant British governments seriously underestimated the determination to proceed on the part of their French and German counterparts. They underestimated their sense of urgency. The Clappier–Schulmann decision in 1978 to brush aside Couzens left the latter 'dramatically and publicly wrong-footed and humiliated' (Ludlow 1982: 112). But Couzens's own failings were symptomatic of those of Whitehall and its ministers.

Secondly, Callaghan was surprised by the willingness of the rest of the EC to fall into line behind what had become the Giscard–Schmidt initiative at Bremen in July 1978. This surprise parallels Mrs Thatcher's own miscalculations on EMU a decade later at the Hanover, Madrid, and Rome European Council meetings. Callaghan had expected to lead a rebellion at Bremen; instead he was in danger of being left isolated. Similarly, Mrs Thatcher would later believe that the opposition forces were much stronger than they actually were.

Thirdly, in both the EMS and EMU cases, the British proved unable to build adequate coalitions with other EC governments. A British attempt to sabotage the Clappier–Schulmann proposals in 1978, playing on fears of a Franco-

German carve-up, effectively came to nought. A more sensitive approach on the EMS might have elicited a better response, particularly from the Dutch. Britain's ability to form coalitions with her partners was already becoming undermined, however, by a dispute over the level of her payments into the EC budget. Differences of economic interest were evident. Italian overtures for an alliance with London on the EMS were met, according to Ludlow, with a brusque, even arrogant, dismissal by Healey and his officials (Ludlow 1982: 146, 238). Healey rejected Italian proposals for wider fluctuation margins in the EMS for 'non-Snake' countries. The British eschewed identification with the problems of the Italians. But they had no other coalition to put in its place. Similarly, on EMU, Britain had few allies: the result, in the main, of its refusal to show sufficient flexibility so as to broker a coalition on economic policy with ideological soul-mates such as the Dutch and the Germans (see Chapter 15).

Fourthly, the unwillingness to entertain a long-term, binding commitment undermined other, more piecemeal, objectives. The British support for 'parallel measures' (more EC expenditure) in 1978 advocated by the Italians was ineffective precisely because it was unclear whether London would sign up for the EMS anyway (Ludlow 1982: 179). On EMU, a similar unwillingness to sign up for a single currency in the long-term crucially undermined the British advocacy of an alternative 'hard' ECU scheme. British rigidity on both the EMS and EMU left her manoeuvred into a corner: the British outcome was by default rather than by design. For EMU, the Major government in the end simply went for a double negative: an opt-out from both EMU and the Social Chapter. This strategy left it unable to exercise much clout in other areas.

Fifthly, for both the EMS and EMU, London underplayed the political case for participation. This underestimate was, in part, the result of the pre-eminent role played by the Treasury in the calculation of the costs and benefits associated with each. For its part, the Foreign Office did not encroach very far on this terrain. It failed to press the political arguments for entry—for example, that UK interests in other areas would be enhanced—with sufficient vigour. David Owen, Foreign Secretary at the time, lacked interest in the issue, paralleling the relative disinterest of Douglas Hurd on EMU later.

Sixthly, government decision-making emphasized the role of a relatively small number of actors: the core executive (Rhodes and Dunleavy 1995). This restrictiveness was by no means unique to the EMS and to EMU. The EMS initiative was not discussed by the Cabinet until almost the eleventh hour, on 2 November 1978 (Ludlow 1982: 219). Similarly, Mrs Thatcher kept the issue of Britain's subsequent entry confined to a few ministers and officials as a means of blocking any such proposal. On EMU, in the early period Mrs Thatcher again refrained from using the Cabinet as an effective policy-making forum. Such a practice enabled her to control matters: she determined strategy. Later, Major was rather more inclusive. By then, of course, Major was concerned with the strategy of binding in his rivals rather than with considering the political arguments behind alternative policy positions.

Seventhly, the primacy of the Treasury on both the EMS launch and on EMU gave the British response in both cases a distinctive imprint. On both the EMS and on EMU, officials in the Bank of England appear to have been more favourably disposed to such policies and, indeed, perhaps better informed as to the nature of the EC-wide debate. Ludlow, perhaps reflecting the 'Brussels' view, is scathing of what he sees as the Treasury's myopia on the EMS. The opposition of its senior officials had its roots, he argues, 'in a want of imagination and a surfeit of prejudice' (Ludlow 1982: 295). Their scepticism and political miscalculation proved costly. The pre-eminence of the Treasury was the result of the way in which Callaghan handled the issue. Whilst Schmidt had presented the established bureaucracy with a *fait accompli* on the EMS, the British Prime Minister let a department make the running which was known to be profoundly sceptical on the issue, as indeed were their counterparts in Paris and Bonn (Ludlow 1982: 108). The Treasury was allowed to dominate the EMS issue. According to *The Guardian*, the Treasury view of the EMS was, 'Here is a nutty and possibly damaging idea which the PM is embarassingly keen on. Why doesn't somebody generate a public outcry against it before it is too late?' (Ludlow 1982: 186). Treasury scepticism on EMU also resulted in political miscalculations and a weakness of response.

A final parallel exists at the head of the Treasury. For both the negotiations on the EMS and on EMU, the respective Chancellors were, by reputation, poor EC negotiators. Denis Healey's bombast and aggression in EC negotiations and in bilateral negotiations lost Britain friends and respect. The same applies even more strongly to Norman Lamont, whose conduct in the IGC, including at Maastricht itself, and in ECOFIN (at Bath) was widely criticized. In both cases, the ministerial lead undermined the effectiveness of British strategy.

Of course, the comparisons to be drawn between the launch of the EMS and of EMU are not so easy to make. The political contexts were quite different. EMS was too big an issue for the lame-duck Callaghan government. Callaghan became a prisoner of his party in the autumn of 1978, exacerbating his indecision. For the early period of EMU, the reverse might be said: the Tory Party was a prisoner of the Prime Minister. In addition, the pattern of coalitions across the EC was quite different. At the birth of the EMS, there was much more scope for a London–Paris co-ordination, and Italy was much more keen to ally with Britain. After 1988, neither partner saw Britain as a suitable ally.

Yet, parallels do exist and may even be part of a longer-term pattern in Britain's relations with Europe. In this respect, there are questions about both the strategy and the cognition underlining the policy process in London. However, it is also clear that the actors leading the policy process have given it a strong imprint. In that sense, the choices were not predetermined: they owed much to agency, as well as to structure. On both the EMS and EMU, alternative policy options and strategies were available at particular points of the process.

On EMU, the immediate legacy was the conflicts within the Thatcher government in the second half of the 1980s over Britain's relationship to the operation of the EMS. If the birth of the EMS was the 'First Act' of this drama, then the relaunch of EMU was only the 'Third Act'. The intervening events are crucial to an understanding of the position in which the British government found itself when confronted by EMU. It is these events, intense and conflictual as they were, which formed so central a part of the mind-sets of the British negotiators at Hanover in 1988 and beyond.

The ERM Débâcle: Policy Entrepreneurs and Mrs Thatcher's Court

Just two months after the ERM began, the Conservatives entered government. Their intentions on the ERM were far from clear. The general election manifesto included a commitment to join when the conditions were 'ripe'. The party's manifesto for the European Parliament elections, a month after they had taken office, went much further and stated that:

We regret the Labour government's decision—alone amongst the Nine—not to become a full member of the European Monetary System. We support the objectives of the new system, which are currency stability in Europe and closer coordination of national economic policies, and we shall look for ways in which Britain can take her rightful place within it. (Quoted in Howe 1994: 111)

Yet this commitment stood in contrast to the lukewarm response shown by the Shadow Cabinet when in opposition. Neither Howe nor Mrs Thatcher had displayed much enthusiasm for entry, and nor did they do so once they were in Downing Street.

The extent of Tory interest in the ERM in this early period became the source of later dispute. It became important in relation to the claims of consistency made by the protagonists in the conflict over ERM entry in the late 1980s. The credibility of such claims affected the interpretation of the effectiveness of European strategy under Mrs Thatcher and the degree of consultation on policy she permitted in this area. Most notably, Howe claims that he was not lukewarm on the ERM in the late 1970s and early 1980s. Rather, he was biding his time waiting for the right moment to press the case for entry. He may well have held this position, but it was not made clear in public. Moreover, if this was his position, then it no doubt compounded his later problems when he did come to advocate entry, as he failed to take the opportunity to prepare the ground with Mrs Thatcher (Howe 1994: 690–2).

The new government's official position did indeed display a lack of enthusiasm. An initial meeting on 17 October 1979 to discuss possible ERM entry concluded that this might occur in the medium term (Howe 1994: 274). It was not regarded as a priority or as a pressing issue. In fact, under Sir Geoffrey Howe as Chancellor of the Exchequer, the Thatcher government stayed out of the ERM. It stuck to the mantra that Britain would join 'when the time is right', though no indication was given as to the conditions which might signify that entry was justified.[5] British detachment from the new mechanism came to be seen as a stable position. Yet, by the second half of the 1980s the situation proved anything but stable.

What changed stemmed from the decision of Nigel Lawson to urge entry, after he became Chancellor of the Exchequer in 1983. He succeeded Howe who had moved to be Foreign Secretary. Lawson operated as the chief policy entrepreneur on the issue, persuading his officials, allying with Howe (who had become a more assertive ERM supporter), and trying to bend Mrs Thatcher to his will. The initiative thus came from the top, not from the Treasury or the Bank.

This entrepreneurship is in itself a telling point. The Treasury, in particular, continued to detach itself from the evolving European debate. The ERM was hardening, and French and Italian attitudes had shifted. But Treasury officials failed to move. They saw Number Ten as unreceptive: but Mrs Thatcher in 1985–7 was nowhere near as antagonistic to the Community as she would be later. The distraction of the Treasury was the result of a complex mix of factors. As in 1978–9, a fixed exchange rate with Europe seemed to fit uncomfortably with the conditions of the British economy. Moreover, the Thatcherite revolution had placed policy on a terrain which gave a lesser priority to stable exchange rates. The Treasury was concentrating on other policy tools and indicators, essentially domestic ones. Moreover, the legacy of Britain's disputes over her EC budget contribution had inhibited a more positive approach to European policy. There were also strategic and cultural elements at play here. As in 1978–9, left alone, the Treasury eschewed a longer-term perspective or wider calculations of political interest. It lacked any strong pro-European lead. The Treasury existed within a different intellectual and cultural milieu from that of its major continental partners. In short, to move the Treasury would take a firm ministerial initiative.

A Turning-Point

The ebullient Lawson provided such a lead, and he gradually won the backing of his officials. Yet, in the grander picture, the Treasury was no longer the problem. Lawson's chief opponent was the Prime Minister herself, with Howe in Lawson's support. The top three ministers in the Cabinet became embroiled in the most significant dispute of Mrs Thatcher's final years in office. The policy disagreement was fundamental and far-reaching, whilst it also became a bitter personal conflict between the Prime Minister and her two leading ministers. Hereafter, 'Europe' would be an increasing source of conflict within the government. Disputes connected to European monetary policy led Mrs Thatcher to demote Howe, formed the background to Lawson's resignation, and contributed to Mrs Thatcher's own downfall. The new debate on the ERM and

---

[5] In reality, as Lawson notes, the position had originally been that the pound would enter 'when the time is ripe'; 'right' was adopted later without apparent reflection. See Lawson (1992: 485).

EMU was a turning-point. It created a conflict within the Tory Party which was sustained through to the leadership of William Hague in 1997.

Given the newspaper accounts which appeared over these years it is all too easy to dismiss this ministerial dispute as something of a soap opera. The drama meant that the policy question often appeared to be overshadowed by feelings of injured pride, threatened status, and oversized egos. The picture was of a psychological drama of intrigue and vengeance. Mrs Thatcher came to suspect Howe of plotting against her leadership; whilst Howe and Lawson issued an ultimatum to her. The opposition and the media fed on these clashes: it was too tempting to personalize the substance of the dispute.

But, beneath this tabloid portrayal was a much more serious contest over the direction of Britain's European policy. This contest took place against the background of the long-term division in British policy, already noted, between those who sought constructive engagement with Europe and those who were more resistant. As such, the Thatcher versus Howe / Lawson debate on the ERM was one of principle, concerned with the substance of monetary policy and Britain's role in Europe. This early dispute evolved and became enlarged as EMU made further progress in the EC. But the personality clashes involved in the dispute cannot be explained without reference to the investment each of the three leading ministers was prepared to make on behalf of their respective philosophies on monetary management and on Britain's place in Europe. Contesting principles led to the personal rancour, rather than the reverse.

Howe and Lawson were also promoting their cause within the constraints of Mrs Thatcher's governing style. Her personal stance on the ERM hardened progressively over the course of her premiership. This evolution contrasted sharply with that of Howe and Lawson. As a result, a deepening cleavage confused and disrupted British policy-making on Europe. This cleavage undermined the effectiveness of government strategy towards its European partners. In terms of the internal reflection on policy content, it inhibited a wider discussion of alternatives and adaptation to changing conditions. Institutionally, a pall hung over Whitehall intimidating both ministers and officials entering the European debate. The atmospheric pressure was heavy indeed. More specifically, the ERM dispute undermined the Cabinet. It led to an increasing detachment on the part of Mrs. Thatcher and her trusted aides. She conducted European policy on a more exclusive basis, avoiding full Cabinet discussions and minimizing consultation with her Foreign Secretary and Chancellor. This style entrenched the dispute yet further. The normal structures of government were seen to be irrelevant. By default, Howe and Lawson had little alternative other than cabals and plotting.

The positions of the two ministers were quite different, however. The fact that they came to coalesce is itself evidence of Mrs Thatcher's tactical failure. A less intransigent position on her part might have seen the success of a 'divide and rule' approach. For Lawson's shift to support ERM entry did not mean that he countenanced participation in EMU. The latter was a step much too far: to him it was an inescapable component of a federal Europe, which he rejected. On EMU itself, there was much compatibility between Lawson and Thatcher. The Thatcher–Lawson split was ironic. Lawson had previously been seen as Mrs Thatcher's soul-mate. She had been his mentor at a time when she was still battling against those she dismissed as 'wets'.

On the ERM, Lawson took a distinct, even maverick, stance. His support for the ERM appeared to envisage a 'hard' mechanism, eschewing realignments in most instances. The ERM would impose a necessary discipline on British monetary policy. Some thought this position illogical.[6] The effect of both the ERM and EMU on monetary discipline would be similar. Yet Lawson stuck to his position consistently.

If Lawson was the policy entrepreneur, Howe was his crucial ally. Opposition from Howe would have isolated Lawson and stopped ERM entry in its tracks. Howe's position was more advanced than Lawson's. In fact, he came to support not only ERM entry, but also a softer, more constructive line on EMU. Lawson's liaison with Howe was more a matter of tactics.

The timing of the ERM dispute followed Lawson's career path. Lawson claims in his memoirs to have become 'convinced of the desirability of British membership of the ERM as Financial Secretary before [he] left the Treasury in September 1981' (Lawson 1992: 484). Yet there is no independent corroboration available of his interest. Indeed, some of those with responsibility in this area at the time have no recollection of him expressing such a view. Certainly, his post as Financial Secretary precluded him from being closely involved in such matters. If his support existed, it was probably kept internal to the Treasury. In any event, in September 1981 Lawson entered the Cabinet as Energy Secretary, and so he was further away from such policy decisions. Even after he returned to the Treasury as Chancellor in June 1983, it was to be another eighteen months before Lawson took up the issue.

Lawson as the Policy Entrepreneur

Lawson felt he had to wait. He drew lessons from recent British experience. UK policy in 1984–5, when the pound had gone through various crises, was akin to an implicit exchange-rate policy. Yet Britain had not gained the benefits of an explicit policy: a signal to the market, international co-ordination. His view of the latter would be greatly enhanced in the following period with the G7 co-ordination of the Plaza (September 1985) and Louvre (February 1987) Accords. Both Accords stemmed from the desire to manage the US dollar, after it had risen considerably. EC co-ordination within the G7 had been particularly useful. The dollar's rise disrupted Britain's monetary policy, as it did that of its partners. Now the Reagan administration shifted away from free-floating, and Lawson thought Mrs Thatcher should follow suit. Lawson was keen to adopt the mon-

---

[6] See review of Lawson's memoirs by Peter Jay in the *Financial Times*, 6 Nov. 1992.

etary discipline of the ERM—which was now embarking on a period of greater success—rather than to continue to rely on domestic monetary targets, which were now in a mess.[7]

Lawson's initiative on the ERM was not at first welcomed with much enthusiasm by his colleagues or his officials. Lawson records Peter Middleton, the Permanent Secretary, and Terry Burns, Chief Economic Adviser, as being opposed, as was Ian Stewart, the Economic Secretary (1992: 486). Middleton, a mercurial figure, moved quickly to sit on the fence. He was wary of the political climate at Mrs Thatcher's Number Ten court. He also regarded Lawson as somewhat unpredictable. Like Middleton, Burns remained cautious and pragmatic. Both came to accept ERM entry as a means of discipline, not because of any gain in Europe. Floating exchange rates were not working and the ERM was the only option available. The economy needed an anti-inflation anchor and the ERM provided this. Both Lawson and Howe pressed Middleton and Burns to support ERM entry. Gradually, the latter came to see their objections as less valid, given the policy alternatives available, and less tenable politically, given the lead by Lawson (and Howe). In short, it is important to note that the lead on the ERM was taken by Lawson, as Chancellor, and not by his officials.[8]

Lawson's activism began with him raising the issue with Mrs Thatcher on 28 January 1985; she asked him to produce a paper on whether it was now right to join the ERM. The drama became intense over the course of 1985. In February, September, and November meetings were held, attended by Mrs Thatcher, Lawson, Howe, Robin Leigh-Pemberton (Governor of the Bank of England), and senior officials, to discuss ERM entry. A clear division emerged in these meetings: Mrs Thatcher was the only senior minister to remain resolutely opposed to entry. The November meeting (which also included Leon Brittan, the Trade and Industry Secretary, Norman Tebbit, as Party Chairman, and William Whitelaw as Deputy Prime Minister) proved to be a particularly rancorous event. As the penultimate speaker, Whitelaw commented that, 'If the Chancellor, the Governor and the Foreign Secretary are all agreed that we should join . . . then that should be decisive' (Lawson 1992: 499). However, Mrs Thatcher now dug her heels in: 'If you join the EMS, you will have to do so without me'. An awkward silence followed and the meeting broke up with no decision having been taken.

Mrs Thatcher's opposition had been bolstered by the briefings that she received from Sir Alan Walters, her independent economic adviser.[9] Walters was a loyal, reassuring confidant during Mrs Thatcher's repeated battles on the ERM and other issues. He was her soul-mate and one able to supply her with

[7] The money-supply indicator (M3) was rising too quickly, but inflation was falling and Britain was in a recession.

[8] Other Treasury officials, like Geoff Littler, the British representative on the EC Monetary Committee, were more enthusiastic ERM supporters.

[9] Walters was the PM's official adviser between 1981 and 1984 and in 1989, but he also served on an informal and irregular basis at other times.

the intellectual weapons to carry her through internal debates. As early as January 1982, Walters had sent the Prime Minister a memorandum arguing against ERM entry and this note had influenced her greatly. Mrs Thatcher's natural ideological constituency—the monetarists—adopted different positions on systems like the ERM. All believed in sound money and policy being based on a clear rule: but for some that rule was a domestic money-supply target, whilst for others it was an external exchange-rate target (Dyson 1994: 235). The latter position, which Lawson came to adopt, favoured international co-ordination. Walters did not: he opposed what the ERM offered, in favour of basing sound international co-ordination on domestic action to put the economic house in order. The technical argument went as follows: in such a system capital moblity will equalize nominal interest rates so that, in a high inflation country, real interest rates will be lower than they would be otherwise, prompting an unwanted expansion. This expansion will in turn raise inflation differentials and prompt a divergence of real exchange rates. In short, rather than being a means to tackle inflation, the ERM was doomed to fail (Walters 1986; Dyson 1994: 191). Walters's critique of the ERM as being 'half-baked' was an ideal complement to Mrs Thatcher's own instincts to protect British sovereignty against European encroachment. Mrs Thatcher was strengthened in her resolve to pursue a 'go-it-alone' strategy.

The battle between Chancellor and Prime Minister continued. Whilst Mrs Thatcher became resolute, Lawson persisted with the ERM issue, upset at not getting his way. In December 1985, he sent senior Treasury (Peter Middleton, Geoff Littler) and Bank of England (Anthony Loehnis) officials on a confidential visit to Bonn to discuss contingency planning in the event of entry. But little came of the meeting. Instead, the pound was left to fall in 1986. But by the following year Lawson shifted policy significantly. He followed an implicit policy of 'shadowing' the D-Mark's exchange-rate fluctuation; if the pound could not enter the ERM, he could still peg it to the D-Mark. Pressure built up on the pound, but Lawson kept its rate 'capped'. Then, and even more so later, Lawson's decision would be attacked as being inflationary. By the spring of 1988 a public rift between Chancellor and Prime Minister on exchange-rate policy was apparent. The policy of shadowing the D-Mark was abandoned. Very soon, however, the issue of exchange-rate management became enveloped in the wider policy debate on EMU. In June 1988, the European Council meeting in Hanover agreed to establish the Delors Committee to study EMU. By the time the Committee reported to the next summit of heads of government in Madrid in June 1989, the British government was being ripped asunder by the ERM issue and by tactics on EMU (Thompson 1995).

Prior to Madrid, the Foreign Secretary and the Chancellor had three private bilateral meetings on the ERM and EMU (Howe 1994: 577). Their objective was to give the government a more credible strategy, as they saw it, by breaking the link between stage 1 of EMU and proceeding to the final stage. This stance was their response to the 'irreversibility' clause in the Delors Report (paragraph 39):

the one that rankled the most with the British government. Both feared that Mrs Thatcher would stick to an untenable strategy: implacable opposition. To Howe and Lawson such a strategy was futile. Moreover, Howe feared for the loss of British standing in Washington if Britain was relegated to the second rank of the EC. In reality, the disagreement between her and her two senior ministers had as much to do with tactics as with principle. All three could accept stage 1, but only Howe was open to persuasion to go further. Howe and Lawson wanted a more positive tone to be struck: to accept early ERM entry so as to slow down progress on an IGC. Without ERM entry, both feared the 'irreversibility' commitment of the Delors Report might be activated and that Britain would be in too weak a negotiating position to stop it. Mrs Thatcher, by contrast, was isolating herself in an increasingly strident anti-European approach.

Howe and Lawson agreed to try to overcome Mrs Thatcher's rigid stance by means of a coalition with the Dutch. They engineered an Anglo-Dutch summit at Chequers on 29 April 1989, with Mrs Thatcher exposed to the charms of Ruud Lubbers, her opposite number, just after the publication of the Delors Report on EMU. Lubbers began by expressing his shared concern over the 'irreversibility' commitment in the Delors Report. He too preferred a more cautious approach, though he accepted that EMU should be the long-term goal. He pointedly commented that the effectiveness of Britain's opposition to the Delors Report would be greatly enhanced by its membership of the ERM (Lawson 1992: 915). Mrs Thatcher was infuriated: 'laying into the Dutch with ferocious gusto' (Howe 1994: 578). The attempt at coalition-building had failed. As Howe puts it, 'The experiment in cross-frontier Cabinet government had been in vain' (Howe 1994: 578).

The ministerial confrontation was becoming ever more intense. A few days after the Dutch meeting, at their weekly bilateral, Lawson again pressed the Prime Minister to accept ERM entry. Mrs Thatcher replied that: 'I do not want you to raise the subject ever again; I must prevail' (Lawson 1992: 918). The words seemed to reflect her increasingly aloof manner.

Once again, in the heat of the fray, Sir Alan Walters tried to bolster Mrs Thatcher's intellectual case. He sent the Prime Minister a paper (11 May) setting out conditions to be met before ERM entry could take place. At the Madrid summit Mrs Thatcher would call up this briefing and request Charles Powell to draft a statement based on it. This statement would be the basis of her 'concession' on the ERM. To Walters, Madrid offered an opportunity to strike a deal between Britain and her partners. Sterling would enter the ERM, if *inter alia* the single market was completed; capital liberalization implemented; and the financial sector opened up. In short, ERM entry was being traded for the establishment of a truly free-trade area. Walters was reversing the logic of Britain's partners: rather than the single market requiring the ERM, the completion of the single market made it possible to consider ERM entry. Yet even Walters was implicitly accepting that Mrs Thatcher would have to concede to the increasing political momentum behind UK entry. His was a last-ditch attempt to gain time and, if possible, other policy benefits. The reasoning was soon overcome, however, by the short-term political intrigue between the three leading members of the government. Howe and Lawson did not recognize the validity of Walters's justification of Mrs Thatcher's tactics at Madrid. In the longer term, Walters's logic was also ignored: when Britain did finally enter in 1990, his 'Madrid conditions' were in effect abandoned.

In the weeks prior to the Madrid summit, the intrigue deepened. Sir Leon Brittan from the European Commision tried to help Howe and Lawson by pressing Mrs Thatcher to join the ERM as a means of entering the EMU debate more effectively.[10] Again, Mrs Thatcher would have none of it (Thatcher 1995: 710). Lawson felt the game was still to be won. In evidence to the Commons Treasury Select Committee on 12 June, Lawson sought to make the case for ERM entry and to rebuff Sir Alan Walters's well-known criticisms of it.

The Howe–Lawson axis became more assertive. Lawson initiated a draft internal Treasury paper on the ERM issue that might be presented, jointly with Howe, to Mrs Thatcher prior to Madrid. The paper was entitled, 'EC Issues and Madrid', and was some twelve pages long. It was drafted by Tim Lankester at the Treasury, who then liaised with John Kerr at the Foreign Office. Successive drafts shifted the emphasis from the economic to the political case for entry. No date for ERM entry was specified: though entry by the end of 1992 was envisaged (Howe 1994: 578). Three conditions for entry were stipulated: the full implementation of capital liberalization; entry into the 6 per cent band of the ERM; and the reduction of inflation (Lawson 1992: 929–30). The paper was forwarded to the Prime Minister on 14 June. On 20 June, Mrs Thatcher met Howe and Lawson to tell them of her implacable opposition. The next day she forwarded to them an alternative paper drawn up by Charles Powell and based on Walters's text of 11 May. This paper removed any reference to a date for entry and it added new conditions: the final completion of the single market and the establishment of a 'level playing field' on the monetary front (Lawson 1992: 932).

Both Howe and Lawson recognized that the new conditions were designed to delay sterling's entry into the ERM beyond 1992. In response, a second Howe–Lawson paper three days later reiterated their position. According to Mrs Thatcher's account they insisted that conditions for entry into the ERM were not enough: there must be a date (1995: 711). Significantly, the Howe and Lawson memoirs do not claim to have insisted on a clear date. Neither refers to the content of this second minute (Lawson 1992: 932; Howe, 1994: 579). Howe

---

[10] Leon Brittan was close to Howe. Both had been editors of *Crossbow* magazine, and the two were personal friends. Although not uncritical of Brittan's actions, Howe had much sympathy for him after his resignation over the Westland affair. As Howe notes in his memoirs, 'it was poor Leon who emerged as the Minister with the smoking gun in his hand' (1994: 469). When Mrs Thatcher moved Howe from the FCO shortly after Madrid, he contemplated resignation. Significantly, Howe confided in two figures: Lawson and Brittan, the latter by phone to Brussels (1994: 587). Brittan advised Howe to resign, but he decided not to do so. The extent to which Leon Brittan was involved in the ERM drama is not clear, but he had privileged access to Howe.

indicated to Lawson that he would be prepared to resign if he was not satisfied with the line taken at Madrid; Lawson agreed to resign with him should he do so.

A final pre-summit meeting of the three protagonists was held at Number Ten hours before Mrs Thatcher was due to leave for Madrid. Howe and Lawson threatened to resign. Mrs Thatcher later wrote that it was a 'nasty little meeting' at which she was being 'blackmailed', primarily by Howe (1994: 712). Mrs Thatcher refused to set a date, but said she had agreed a set of conditions. Mrs Thatcher refused to speak to Howe on the journey to the summit; and Howe had little idea what she intended to say when she got there (Howe 1994: 581–2).

In fact, Mrs Thatcher did respond at Madrid by adopting a new tone and outlining a set of conditions which would govern sterling's entry. She reaffirmed the commitment to join the ERM. Charles Powell had produced a statement for her based on the Walters paper of 11 May and the Howe–Lawson papers. Both sides claimed victory. Mrs Thatcher had set no date for entry, but Howe and Lawson detected that the conditions were less stringent than those set out in the earlier Walters paper (Lawson 1992: 934). The conditions would indeed prove malleable when Britain did finally announce its decision to join the ERM on 5 October 1990.

Howe and Lawson saw her move as having helped to avoid a stronger commitment at Madrid on an IGC on EMU (Howe 1994: 583). Mrs Thatcher seemed very ill at ease at the subsequent press conference: hardly the manner of a victor. There was an immediate response to Mrs Thatcher's new tone. Her European partners, and most of the British press, saw her statement as a significant concession. EC leaders believed Geoffrey Howe had won a domestic battle over the Prime Minister. A series of EC leaders congratulated him during a break in the Madrid meeting: Genscher, van den Broek, Ellemann-Jensen, and Tindemans were among the first. Delors said, 'Congratulations, Geoffrey, on having won the intellectual argument within the British government' (Howe 1994: 583).

Back home, however, Mrs Thatcher behaved as if Howe had transmitted some disease to her whilst they were both away in Spain. Mrs Thatcher sought revenge. Howe and Lawson were unsure how to handle her: Mrs Thatcher's entourage saw them as entering the next Cabinet meeting 'very sheepishly', not at all with the confidence of victors. The outcome of the Madrid summit quickly became embroiled in sharply conflicting interpretations. Howe and Lawson thought it diplomatic to whisper their victory; Mrs Thatcher and her aides tried to rewrite history. Mrs Thatcher could not afford to sack both her Chancellor and her Foreign Secretary together, so she targetted Howe. On 24 July, Howe was demoted: to be Leader of the House of Commons, but with the title of 'Deputy Prime Minister'—a misnomer and a sop after much wrangling. Mrs Thatcher's account in her memoirs indicates her vengeful and dismissive intent (1995: 757). John Major was given a sudden step up to be Foreign Secretary.

Mrs Thatcher found Lawson little better on the rebound. The Chancellor remained committed to ERM entry. He also became increasingly resentful of the anti-ERM influence of Sir Alan Walters, portrayed in the media as a Rasputin figure behind Mrs Thatcher's throne. On 18 October, the *Financial Times* reported Walters as saying that the ERM was 'half-baked'. The differences of opinion over the ERM between Lawson and Number Ten were being trailed across the nation's media. The tension was not sustainable. Lawson was being baited by the press over Walters's role. Finally, on 26 October Lawson delivered another ultimatum to the Prime Minister: either she sacked Walters or he would resign. Mrs Thatcher refused to comply, so he resigned, plunging the government into renewed crisis. Lawson had been due to fly to Germany to press Britain's common currency plan as an alternative to a single currency. His resignation before he was due to leave merely reflected how far Britain's European policy was enmeshed in bitter personal disputes between ministers. Mrs Thatcher had wanted to have Nicholas Ridley fill Lawson's shoes as Chancellor (Thatcher 1995: 717). Like her, he was ardently anti-European. But he displayed, as Mrs Thatcher has put it, a 'scorn for presentational niceties' which made him an unsafe pair of hands. Mrs Thatcher did not dare to appoint Ridley, so she again turned to John Major. He was switched to the Treasury, after just three months at the FCO (Foreign and Commonwealth Office).

By the following spring (1990) Mrs Thatcher found Major becoming 'worked up about both ERM membership and EMU' (1995: 721). In reality, Major was being made aware of the determination of Britain's partners to press ahead for full EMU and of the lack of interest in Britain's alternative plans. Britain had to be more thoroughly engaged in the negotiations. Yet Major denies that he was attracted to ERM entry principally because of the increased bargaining clout this move might give on EMU. Rather, he was persuaded on economic grounds. Market opinion was overwhelmingly in favour of entry; Britain was paying a price for being outside. The new Chancellor had long conversations with Terry Burns about the ERM. Yet when Burns set out the policy alternatives in a memorandum for Major shortly after the Chancellor's arrival, Burns's tone remained cautious and broadly neutral. Major recognized that ERM entry was the best option left for the government. The targeting of a domestic inflation rate had been discredited by the performance of the UK economy. The ERM would give government policy a necessary anchor. Major sought to convince the Prime Minister that there was no alternative to entry. His approach was revealing for what it indicated about his style when confronting difficult negotiations. Major was pragmatic, free of emotion and dogma. He was also persistent in the pursuit of the objective. With all the difficult history of the ERM behind him, Major chose gentle persuasion for his discussions with Mrs Thatcher (Stephens 1996: 146). He knew that Mrs Thatcher could not afford to lose another Chancellor on the issue, but he eschewed confrontation. Instead, he targeted his arguments on the prospect of political and economic gains from lower interest rates after membership. Interest-rate levels were a matter very close to the Prime Minister's own heart: she believed low mortgage rates were crucial to her electoral position. Major had judged the psychology correctly.

Mrs Thatcher's own account of this episode is somewhat anodyne, dismissive of Major's role, and seeking to limit any damage to herself. She does admit, however, that at a meeting with Major on 13 June: 'I eventually [said] that I would not resist sterling joining the ERM. But the timing was for debate. Although the terms I had laid down had not been fully met, I had too few allies to continue to resist and win the day' (1995: 722). In reality, Major was manoeuvring her further into a corner. The *Financial Times* had run a story the day before reporting that sterling would enter in September or October. A few weeks later, Major talked of the 'Rubicon' having been crossed: British entry was going to happen (*Financial Times*, 11 July 1990). Market expectations rose: they posed their own constraint on the Prime Minister's options. Major was ensuring that Mrs Thatcher would be forced to accept that there was no alternative to entry. At the same time Major launched the initiative for a hard ECU, to extend Britain's European strategy (see Chapter 14).

Both Mrs Thatcher and Major agreed that sterling should enter the wider ERM band of plus or minus 6 per cent. Mrs Thatcher had difficulty accepting that there was a 'correct' exchange rate, however, and apparently envisaged easy realignments in a flexible arrangement. 'I never envisaged', she pointedly claimed later, 'that a Conservative government would talk itself into the trap of regarding a particular parity for sterling as the touchstone of its economic policy and indeed its political credibility' (1995: 723). When she finally agreed to ERM entry, she reportedly chose the rate herself: a central parity of D-Mark 2.95. This level was the close of market rate that day. Yet some officials believed that the Bank had been urged by ministers to boost the rate to this level in order to justify the predetermined rate.

The government was to stumble into the ERM. Political factors determined the principle, the timing, and the method. Mrs Thatcher could not agree with the economic case for it. She was ambushed by the politics. She blocked Major's desire to enter the ERM in July 1990. In her memoirs she gives an economic rationale for the further delay: she did not accept that inflation was yet fully under control. But by the autumn the signals on inflation looked better: interest rates could now be cut. Thus, Mrs Thatcher insisted that ERM entry be accompanied by a simultaneous interest-rate cut (Thatcher 1995: 724). Such a move had already been advocated by John Smith, then Labour's Shadow Chancellor. In any event, the cut gave Mrs. Thatcher a fig-leaf with which to cover her own U-turn.[11] Both the Bank of England and the Treasury had opposed such a reduction. The Governor of the Bank of England, Robin Leigh-Pemberton, sent a letter to the Prime Minister trying to block the cut. Officials felt that using the ERM to reduce interest rates rather than as a means for monetary discipline was wrong. It certainly inverted the logic of the argument that had been deployed for entry since 1985. To the Bank it smacked of a short-termism: wanting jam today, instead of planning for the long term. Mrs Thatcher

[11] As Stephens notes, 'The interest rate cut had been the essential concession she had extracted in this moment of defeat' (1996: 169).

finally granted Major's wish to join the ERM on the last day of the Labour Party Conference on Friday 5 October 1990.

The timing seemed highly political. The Conservatives needed a political gain, and ironically ERM entry gave it to them. They were suffering an 8–10 per cent deficit in the polls against a resurgent Labour Party. Tory support had been dented by the Poll Tax and by high mortgage rates. The opposition argued that entry at this time represented a clear breach with the conditions that Mrs Thatcher had enunciated at Madrid in 1989. These conditions had included a stipulation that UK inflation rates should converge with those of her partners: yet Neil Kinnock pointed out that inflation in Britain was currently 10.6 per cent, whilst in the ERM countries it was much lower at 3.9 per cent (*Independent*, 6 October 1990). Kinnock said entry was the 'action of a cornered government', and this was difficult to deny.

Entry had come about because the political climate demanded it, and because Major felt that he had no other strategy available. Major had 'raised expectations of membership this autumn to such a pitch that to have dashed them by further postponement could have triggered a confidence run on the pound', noted Peter Jenkins in the *Independent* (6 October 1990). The move was widely greeted with approval in the press, in the City, in industry, and by the CBI. Shares rose, as did the pound. There was palpable relief that the entry issue had now been settled.

The proposed rate provoked some domestic controversy. Brian Reading in the *Sunday Times* (14 October 1990) was one of the first to argue that entry was occurring at the wrong time, at the wrong rate, and for the wrong reason. Some in the Bank of England, such as Andrew Crockett, had sought a lower rate (as low as D-Mark 2.85) and argued that the current market rate was not necessarily the best guide. By contrast, Eddie George wanted a higher rate to impose greater discipline. Robin Leigh-Pemberton, as Governor, accepted the D-Mark 2.95 rate—though criticizing the interest-rate cut—as the key prize was entry. The problem was how it would go down with Britain's partners and what illfeeling it might build up for the future.

The manner of Britain's decision to enter upset some of the other EC members. Whilst the decision to join was for the British, the rate at which sterling should join was a decision requiring unanimity in the EC Monetary Committee. John Major phoned Karl-Otto Pöhl, President of the Bundesbank, to tell him personally of the decision. When he told Pöhl of the rate (D-Mark 2.95), the latter said, 'But this is a matter for negotiation'. The Bundesbank and the other central banks would have to defend the rate, and EC protocol required a collective agreement on the matter. According to Pöhl, Major replied, 'No, the rate has been decided by the Prime Minister'. Major denies making such a comment, arguing that the rate chosen was that prevailing in the market. A lower rate—in effect, a competitive devaluation—was not a realistic option. The effect, however, was more or less the same. Whitehall had announced both the decision to enter and the D-Mark 2.95 rate to the public on the Friday. Announcing the rate in advance of any negotiations effectively bound Britain's partners.

Delors suggested to Major that sterling's entry should be discussed by a special ECOFIN meeting. London brushed the idea aside. Instead, Nigel Wicks (Treasury) was sent to the weekend meeting of the EC Monetary Committee with the tightest of negotiating briefs. He was to accept D-Mark 2.95 or 2.96, nothing more (Stephens 1996: 169). Britain's partners fell into line, but not without protest at the British way of handling the matter. Mario Sarcinelli, the Italian chair of the committee, reportedly 'argued for change, any change, in the UK's proposed central rate of DM2.95—simply to teach the British that they could not dictate to their new ERM partners' (*Financial Times*, 8 October 1990). Sarcinelli, like Delors and others, was especially irritated that the British had announced the rate in relation to the D-Mark alone and not in relation to the ECU. On the substantive issue, Hans Tietmeyer, for the Bundesbank, indicated that he would prefer sterling to enter at a lower rate, as such a rate would be more sustainable over the long term. However, whilst D-Mark 2.95 was at the upper limit of what he envisaged, it was acceptable. French officials, and some others, argued for a higher rate for fear that the pound would leap to the top of its band (where in fact it did go initially). But, again, the differences were small. The French would have preferred D-Mark 3.00, but they felt D-Mark 2.95 was reasonable. The range of disagreement over the central parity rate was thus not very great: especially when set against the wide fluctuation of sterling in previous years. What rankled, however, was the manner of Britain's announcement. Wicks and Andrew Crockett (the Bank of England) were left in no doubt as to their partners' distaste. The Committee accepted the UK's proposed rate, but Sarcinelli was instructed to raise a complaint about procedure in his report to the ECOFIN meeting on the Monday. This outcome boded ill for the future.

Mrs Thatcher had been forced into the ERM against her better judgement. Less than seven weeks later she would be forced out of office. Subsequently she would use her reluctance to join the ERM as testimony to her own anti-federalist stance. Out of power she magnified her opposition to Europe. 'Europe' was the immediate cause of her downfall. Her negative attitude to the 'hard' ECU proposals and to 'constructive engagement' led to Howe's resignation and a successful leadership challenge.

The history of Britain's protracted disputes over ERM entry has a rich mix of different aspects. At the level of personalities, all three of the chief protagonists were slain by the issue or by associated issues. Mrs Thatcher survived but was too weakened to prevent Major taking sterling into the ERM. Major was no Fortinbras, but rather someone able to manipulate and manoeuvre Mrs Thatcher to concede. His ability to do so was almost completely the result of the battle that had gone before. The missing element was that Mrs Thatcher apparently believed that conceding to Major was better than losing to Lawson. Lawson had become too difficult for her to handle. By contrast she saw Major as a protégé, and accepted that an ERM victory would help his profile in the country.

In terms of the governmental process, the ERM issue showed both the strength and the weakness of Mrs Thatcher's power as Prime Minister. The

Whitehall machine, often portrayed as being of Rolls Royce quality, was circumscribed in its operation by the atmospherics of the Prime Minister's leadership. Mrs Thatcher was able to block entry, despite repeated initiatives by her most senior ministers between 1985–90. Her intransigent manner pushed Howe and Lawson to act outside normal Cabinet processes and this style greatly intensified the nature of the dispute. They were left with few tactical options. Mrs Thatcher herself encouraged the conspiratorial atmosphere by her increasingly exclusive, isolating manner. Her behaviour brought Howe and Lawson together, when in reality more flexibility on her part could have kept them divided. For their part, Howe and Lawson displayed tactical failures in their attempts to shift the Prime Minister. A wider conspiracy, including other ministers, could have proved more effective. Yet, eventually, the Prime Minister lost on the ERM issue. The irony of this drama was that none of the three main protagonists survived in office long enough to affect the policy of ERM membership in operation. Mrs Thatcher was pushed into a corner, forced at the end to act against her own judgement. Entry foreshadowed the end of her premiership.

The entrenched nature of Mrs Thatcher's dispute with Howe and Lawson undermined both strategy and policy planning in relation to the evolving EC debate on monetary co-operation. Britain's partners received signals of intransigence tempered by periodic confusion. The ERM dispute inhibited adaptation to the new conditions of the EMU debate. Bargaining strength on EMU was sacrificed by the complex manoeuvres surrounding ERM entry. History is likely to endorse the calculation of Howe and Lawson at the time that ERM entry in 1989 would have strengthened Britain's influence over the course of the EMU debate. It is also likely to concur that it was the strident opposition of Mrs Thatcher which prevented this move. Policy reflection was heavily circumscribed by the Prime Ministerial lead, as options were foreclosed.

Despite the bigger issues which underpinned it, the entry of sterling into the ERM was almost entirely governed by short-term domestic conditions. The timing of ERM entry was party political and the rate was chosen by the Prime Minister, somewhat distant from normal specialist advice. The combination of entry with an interest-rate cut emphasized the short-term, personal perspective affecting the decision. The full economic implications of the decision to enter were left somewhat obscured by the delicate political factors at work. These features gave a vulnerability to sterling's ERM membership.

The dispute between Thatcher, Lawson, and Howe existed in the short term: a crucial, intense chapter of history but one which obscured longer-term choices. For the importance of the ERM case lies in how it reflects a longer pattern of debate about Britain's place in Europe and how it foreshadowed consideration of EMU. The split between Mrs Thatcher, on the one hand, and Howe and Lawson, on the other, represented at a more substantive level a divergence of policy philosophies and principles. Each was pursuing a different conception of Britain's role in Europe. Each was prepared to go to the stake in the belief that they were acting in the national interest, rather than from personal pride (Howe

1994: 692; Thatcher 1995: 690). Domestically, the divisions opened up by entry would remain evident in the later debates. As already noted, the ERM case was a turning-point, signalling a longer-term cleavage on Europe. Those who cheered entry—such as the CBI, the leaders of certain major industrial firms, the TUC—and those who bemoaned it—the Institute of Directors, backbench Tory Eurosceptics—would remain largely the same when the issue moved on with the progress of EMU.

Paradoxically, if there was palpable relief on Britain's entry into the ERM, there was also something similar when sterling was forced out of it (see Chapter 15). 'Black Wednesday'—16 September 1992—was also dubbed 'White Wednesday' by Eurosceptics to indicate the sense of liberation. Membership now appeared to have been an abberration: Britain's natural inclination seemed one of standing aside. Once again, it was not only the course of the economic cycle which differed on either side of the channel, but also the 'political cycle' as well. The divisions in the British debate were at variance with those of its major partners. This divergence had deep historical roots.

Policy Beliefs and the Structure of the Debate on Europe

To understand the course of the British debate on EMU, it is useful to consider the long-term features of British policy discussions on Europe. Britain has been dubbed an 'awkward partner' for the repeated disputes it became embroiled in with the rest of the EC (George 1990). The list of disputes is, indeed, impressive: renegotiation of the terms of entry in 1974–5; rejection of ERM membership; the demands for more money from the EC budget in the early 1980s, and again later; opposition to the IGC in 1985; and hostility to the Social Charter. With the exception of the latter, each of these disputes occurred before EMU re-emerged as a serious proposition. In many of these instances, the British government was isolated within the EC. Yet the term an 'awkward partner' is an ambiguous one: it could suggest a malevolent approach or a maladroit one. By itself, the notion does not account for the origins of the disputes; few would argue that the British deliberately set out to be awkward, merely to upset their partners. Instead, the focus should be on the recurrence of disputes, and the discordant values and interests (Buller 1995; George 1995). British semi-detachment, when it has occurred, has stemmed from deep roots. Mrs Thatcher's bombast and aggression in the 1980s was an appeal to a set of attitudes which were well established before she became Prime Minister.

A full explanation of the roots of such 'semi-detachment' would have to take account of the sense of nationhood, of the interpretation of sovereignty, and of wider cultural distinctions. They would be placed alongside a detailed analysis of Britain's economic interests—its divergent trade pattern and economic cycle—as well as its differences of economic philosophy. Indeed, the perspective might also be extended almost boundlessly back in time.

The Price of Victory

A key turning-point was the differential impact of the Second World War on Europe's constituent nations. In the absence of invasion or defeat, Britain 'felt no need to exorcise history' (Monnet 1978: 450). The 'Dunkirk Spirit' and the struggle of the 'Battle of Britain' shaped later attitudes (Hennessy 1992). They strengthened the feeling of nationhood and reinforced the commitment to national sovereignty. Indeed, the maintenance of national sovereignty continued as a core assumption in policy-making. The symbolism of 'Crown in Parliament' was a potent one. Nothing was to disturb the principle of parliamentary sovereignty, a defining feature of the uncodified British constitution.

For domestic policy, such beliefs were placed alongside an assumption of the efficacy of the British state. Governmental office—in effect synonymous with controlling the 'state'—meant, 'we are the masters now', in Lord Shawcross's famous phrase. The confidence with which the Attlee government pursued its radical domestic programme stemmed from a faith in a 'go-it-alone' strategy. Indeed, the title of its 1945 manifesto—'Put the Nation First'—symbolized this self-belief (Featherstone 1988).

Externally, victory in 1945 further enhanced a sense of specialness in relation to Britain's place in Europe and the rest of the world. The wartime alliance with the USA, which had been so crucial to the victory over Hitler, bequeathed a strategic belief in the primacy of Atlanticism for British foreign policy. The Anglo-American relationship was 'special' precisely because no other European nation possessed anything similar in relation to Washington. For its own part, 'Europe' was of lesser importance to Britain than either the Atlantic connection or the Commonwealth.

Such attitudes not only induced a sense of separation from the rest of Europe but also an overestimation of Britain's international standing. As Jean Monnet, one of the leading draftsmen of the integration process, told the British: 'It was the price of victory—the illusion that you could maintain what you had, without change' (quoted in Charlton 1983: 307). Successive governments assumed a weight for Britain in the world that became increasingly out of step with economic realities. This exaggerated belief ran the risk that London would overplay the strategic resources it had to persuade others to accept its own policy conceptions and agenda. If there was the recognition that Britain lacked the resources to see through an international policy, then the instinct was to make up the shortfall by coming to an agreement with the USA, rather than with the rest of Europe. The outcome of the Suez Crisis in 1956 could be seen as reinforcing such an attitude.

British membership of the European integration process was delayed, in part, by a sense of Britain's global reach. 'Europe' was, for several reasons, too small to satisfy Britain's perceived national interests. Britain chose the 'open seas', to protect the economic and security investments it had around the world. Membership, when it came, was largely on the basis of a reassessment of

Britain's economic interests in the relative importance of gaining access to the growing Continental market. It was not couched in a wider or deeper foreign-policy vision. Few British leaders could, or would wish to, claim, to be Europeans of the 'heart'. Entry into the EC was much more a matter of prag-matic, technical calculation. In the same vein, doubts about membership were soon reinforced by the calculation that Britain was not reaping the expected eco-nomic rewards. Entry had occurred amidst deepening economic problems prompted by the oil crisis, and at a time of growing divergence within the Community. On many accounts, the British looked for the *'juste retour'* from EC membership.

Nor did entry fundamentally disturb deep-rooted assumptions in Britain about Atlanticism and globalism. After Britain became a member of the EC, 'Europe' was again seen as being too small. Changes in the international econ-omy—notably interdependent, open markets—were now interpreted as requir-ing Britain to think 'global' rather than merely 'European'. Globalization demanded open markets, but was consistent with a world of formally indepen-dent nation-states. 'Thatcherism' in the 1980s found this combination appeal-ing. Indeed, 'Thatcherism' suggested that 'Europeanism' was outdated, slow to adjust to the demands of globalization. Thus EMU tended to be seen by Mrs Thatcher and her supporters as stemming from an ill-conceived notion of build-ing regional blocs against the competitive, liberal logic of globalization.

The contrast between Britain and her partners is revealing. Leaders like Kohl, Genscher, Mitterrand, Delors, and Andreotti drew very different conclusions from the experience of war. For France, Germany, and Italy, the symbolic reson-ance of European integration—the ideas, concepts, values associated with the project—has been much more positive than negative. Indeed for these states, 'The symbolic dimension forms a cradle in which other factors are nested and conditions other kinds of judgement about the pros and cons of integration' (Wallace 1997: 685). For Britain, however, the situation has been quite different. As Wallace has noted, 'The symbolic dimension to integration is either absent or negative for large sections of British opinion' (1997: 686).

At a general level, British attitudes towards, and understandings of, the European integration process are thus to be explained by a complex mix of fac-tors. Added to a sense of detachment has been a tendency to calculate gains and losses case by case in the short term, and an absence of an overarching long-term vision of Britain's place in Europe. These features have had a pervasive influence. British domestic debate has often been out of kilter with that of many of its partners.

At the same time, the constraints posed on British governments by the struc-ture of beliefs evident in wider society should not be exaggerated. Young goes so far as to argue that 'European policy remains largely in the hands of a Westminster and Whitehall elite' (1993: 183). Certainly, at times, public opinion has proved malleable on Europe, able to be led in somewhat different directions (Nugent 1992: 198). Even Mrs Thatcher led in different directions: for example, on the single market and on EMU. Earlier, Harold Wilson engineered a substantial 'yes' vote in the 1975 referendum on continued EC membership after a prolonged period of polls showing public opposition.

At other stages, government leaders have perceived as a constraint a latent scepticism in public opinion and have hesitated to move ahead of it. This assessment of public opinion formed a backdrop to the policy of the Callaghan government in the late 1970s and it inhibited some of the Tory 'wets' on Europe in the 1980s. By the end of the 1980s, the government, and the Treasury in particular, felt that public opinion wished it to be generally cautious on EMU. But this assessment was not so different from elsewhere in the EC. Moreover, British opinion had not yet been formed; the dispute at this stage had not crystallized. It was ready to be led.

Within the confines of government, the policy debate was affected by the particular traits of the Thatcher and Major governments. Both presented very different leadership styles. They also served in different political contexts: Mrs. Thatcher had an enviable record of electoral success and length of service; John Major had to save his party from disunity and the prospect of electoral defeat. Each leadership style affected the climate in which ministers and officials felt able to engage in debate on policy and strategy. The workings of government were affected by the personal imprint of the two Prime Ministers.

As will become clear, the debate on EMU was handled firmly within the 'core executive'. The history of the ERM issue and of EMU (up to Maastricht) suggests the primacy of battles at court, rather than a more significant and wider domestic engagement. One of the chief protagonists at the time, Sir Geoffrey Howe, describes the Thatcher policy process on Europe as being 'cocooned' (Howe 1994: 691). The relative autonomy of official policy-making was indicated by the distance of the City, the CBI, and professional economists from the process.

The City and the EMU Debate

It was difficult to discern a common or consistent view on EMU in the City of London. The proposal for a hard ECU (see Chapter 14) was an exceptional case: Whitehall was in the market for an alternative scheme to EMU and the existence of a relevant City committee (the European Committee of the British Invisible Exports Council)—led by Sir Michael Butler of Hambros—lent the proposal an independent legitimacy. Members of this committee—such as Sir Jeremy Morse of Lloyds—identified themselves as having a personal interest in European matters. Yet, whilst the committee monitored progress on EMU, it could not represent City opinion more generally. The committee was made relevant by Butler's own advocacy of the 'hard' ECU plan. Beyond its advocacy of this scheme its representational role and influence were limited.

Apart from this particular episode, however, the City neither had a platform on which to express a view nor was a consensus likely to form around one. Little else could have been expected. The City had diverse, even conflicting, interests on EMU, given the spread of its institutions and the City's international role. Moreover, the tendency in the City is to focus on the short term, on issues having an immediate impact. The City was more focused on other issues, such as the liberalization of financial services. EMU remained a possibility for the future, but it was by no means certain to happen. Some, like those on Butler's top-level City committee, formed a private pro-EC network, but they eschewed a strong lead on EMU. Professional economists in the City were obliged to consider EMU for the medium to long term, and several such as Graham Bishop (Salomon Brothers), Roger Bootle (Lloyds, then Greenwell Montagu, HSBC), Tim Congdon (Lombard St Research), David Kern (NatWest), and Malcolm Levitt (Barclays) gained a particular profile on the matter. But, there was no 'City view' as such. Individual bank economists took more pro-EMU (e.g. Kern, Levitt) or more sceptical stances (e.g. Bootle).

Nor did the banks attempt to enter the EMU debate in the manner of their counterparts in Germany. There is little tradition of them acting in such a manner, and it is by no means clear that they would have been able to agree on EMU. For its part, the British Banking Association remained distant from Whitehall on EMU matters: it was reactive and slow to focus on the technical implications. Whilst it discussed the 'hard' ECU and the location of an ECB, it established no common view on either.

After 1991, and especially following the start of stage 2 of EMU in 1994, attention in the City gradually shifted to consider the practical implications of EMU for different financial activities—primarily, what the City needed to do in order to have EMU business conducted in London—and this focus involved a more varied range of personnel and organizations.

Academic Economists and the EMU Debate

Both the Treasury and the Bank of England remained alert to the progress of the technical debate amongst academic economists. But there is no evidence that the latter had a direct impact on the course of official thinking. The network of economists represented by the Centre for Economic Policy Research, co-ordinated by Richard Portes in London, made notable indirect contributions to the European debate. But there is no sign that they affected official UK attitudes to any significant degree. In the British context, neither were they prominent opinion-shapers nor was their endorsement especially sought.

The more prominent debate involved applied economists in the City together with financial journalists. Amongst these economists, politicians of all persuasions could find the support that they sought. Some, such as Tim Congdon and Anatole Kaletsky (*The Times*) established strong Eurosceptic profiles. Alan Walters, who served as Mrs Thatcher's economic policy adviser, was of course strongly opposed to Britain's membership of the ERM. Others, like Sam Brittan (*Financial Times*) and Gavyn Davies (Goldman Sachs, *Independent*) were much more sympathetic to the ERM and to EMU.

British economists tended to favour market-based policy solutions, rather than placing them in an institutionally led frame. This orientation complemented the government's emphasis on the role of markets and on gradualism in new EC policy ventures such as EMU. This outlook had deep roots in British classicial and neo-classical economics. The influence of Adam Smith, David Hume, and later Friedrich Hayek pointed to the imperative of building a liberal political economy from 'below' by unilateral national action rather than by international negotiation and agreement. Within Whitehall, this formed the background to the Odling-Smee draft for competing currencies in 1989 and the proposal for a 'hard' ECU (parallel currency) thereafter (see Chapter 14). In the context of the IGC negotiations, economists in Whitehall, the Bank, and beyond were attracted to issues concerned with market flexibility, notably of labour, and (real) economic convergence (with real exchange-rate stability) prior to the adoption of a single currency. Nominal criteria were more open to manipulation, whilst real convergence was a matter determined by the markets. A specific proposal for the use of financial markets to achieve fiscal discipline was made by Graham Bishop (Salomon Brothers), but made little political headway (see Chapter 15).

British Business and EMU

The relationship between the Conservative Party, under Mrs Thatcher, and organized business interests had undergone a major revision. The Thatcherite philosophy rejected corporatist ties with the CBI and others, preferring more individual consultations. This policy style changed the context of CBI influence on Europe. From 1985 onwards—when Lawson as Chancellor was making his first moves on the ERM—the CBI gave entry clear backing. But it was to be another five years before Mrs Thatcher agreed to entry.

Later, the CBI's Economic and Financial Committee, chaired by Sir David Lees of GKN, established a working group on EMU. It comprised several industry economists: Andrew Sentance (CBI); Richard Freeman (ICI); Christopher Johnson (Lloyds); and Gottfried Bruder (Commerzbank, London). By 1990, the CBI supported EMU and Britain's participation within it, but this support failed to sway the Tory government.

A clear divergence on Europe opened up between the Conservative Party in Parliament and the heads of many leading British firms. This divergence became more noticeable as the Major government turned more Eurosceptic after 1992 and Blair's New Labour conducted a charm offensive amongst the captains of industry. Several leading firms publicly backed EMU, including British Aerospace; British Airways; BP; Shell; Glaxo; Guinness; Northern Foods; Unigate; ICI; and Barclays.

The pro-EMU stance of the CBI—supported by successive internal surveys of its members—contrasted with the staunchly Eurosceptic position of the Institute of Directors (IoD). The IoD represented a different clientele, dominated by smaller firms. It enjoyed growing political influence given its generally Thatcherite orientation. But, again, on EMU the IoD took a reactive role. It was politically useful to ministers to cite the IoD as a counterpoint to the CBI to show the disparate range of opinions within British business.

Policy-making on EMU in Britain was thus confined. Whitehall and the Bank of England remained relatively more insulated on this matter than in many other policy areas. Those affecting the content of policy operated within the confines of the 'core executive' (see below). In order to more properly discern the nature of the debate on EMU within the Thatcher and Major governments it is thus necessary to disaggregate the leading players. A starting-point is to distinguish between those who sought 'constructive engagement' by Britain on EMU and those who were more strongly opposed to participation of any kind. The following analysis begins with the debate at the ministerial level and then moves to the contributions of senior officials.

The 'Europhiles'

The pattern of the political debate on EMU was tied to that on EMS entry. In this respect Lawson occupied a peculiar position. Whilst he advocated EMS entry, he proclaimed himself to be vehemently opposed to EMU, because of its threat to British sovereignty. Few others at the centre of the policy process followed his line.

Instead, those accepting the tenets of constructive engagement supported ERM entry and saw the possibility of negotiating an accommodation with EMU.[12] Chief amongst this group was Sir Geoffrey Howe, in government until 1 November 1990 (Howe 1994: 691). He had been at pains to press the case for Britain not ruling out EMU. His later successor at the Foreign Office, Douglas Hurd, and Hurd's junior, Tristan Garel-Jones, were broadly in the same mould. Hurd had been an official in the FCO himself and in the 1970s was seen as an acolyte of Edward Heath. He had remained consistently in favour of accommodating Britain to an evolving EC. Whilst not having the same passion for 'Europe' as Heath, Hurd's commitment was stronger and deeper than that of Major. Indeed, in private he became frustrated, on occasions, at Major's unwillingness or inability to break out of the European-policy constraints imposed by the Tory Party. For his part, Tristan Garel-Jones had not taken any noticeable interest in the Community prior to becoming Minister of State in 1990, when he was Deputy Chief Whip. Press reports saw him as Mrs Thatcher's place-man to keep a check on Hurd. In reality, Garel-Jones—who had spent part of his childhood in Spain—became more 'Europhile', and ultra-loyal to both Hurd and Major.

[12] A further identification of Tory Europhiles was provided much later at the start of the UK Presidency of the EU in 1998. A pro-EU (and pro-EMU) letter in the *Independent* was signed by Lord Howe; Sir Leon Brittan; Lord Carrington; Kenneth Clarke; David Curry; John Gummer; Sir Edward Heath; Michael Heseltine; Chris Patten; Ian Taylor; Lord Tugendhat; and Lord Younger (5 January 1998).

Beyond the FCO, other ministers championed the European cause. Michael Heseltine, who had resigned in January 1986 as a result of the 'Westland affair', had long been identified with a pro-European stance. He campaigned from the backbenches on this issue; and he was an early champion of Britain's ERM entry. He pressed the case for entry before the Hanover European Council, when Lawson was fighting the same cause (*Financial Times*, 24 February 1988). After Howe's pointed attack on Mrs Thatcher's betrayal of Britain's European interests, Heseltine challenged Mrs Thatcher as Tory Party leader in November 1990. Though losing out to Major, the latter brought him back into the Cabinet as a means of healing the rifts. In government, Heseltine was one of the few ministers to take a close interest in the IGC negotiations: regularly asking questions of Hurd and Lamont when they reported on the progress made. On one occasion he commented to Norman Lamont, the Chancellor, that the IGC on EMU must be an exciting experience and one that imbued participants with the sense of creating history. Whether he was being ironic or not, such a sentiment could hardly be ascribed to the then Chancellor. Lamont was ill at ease in the IGC negotiations (see later) and was identified with the Eurosceptic Right of the party.

Chris Patten, who became Party Chairman under Major, was perhaps the British Tory most sympathetic to Continental Christian Democracy. He had a genuine philosophical interest in such beliefs: he is himself a Catholic. But he was also concerned with the strategic question of bridging the divisions between the Tories and the Christian Democrats in the European Parliament. Patten was close to Major and a key pro-European influence on him. Major's famous 'Heart of Europe' speech, delivered in Bonn in March 1991, had been partially drafted by Patten. Indeed, the term 'heart of Europe' only occurred in the speech in the context of Major's adoption of Patten's idea of forging closer relations between the Tories and the Christian Democrat parties in Strasbourg.

There were, then, a number of ministers in the Thatcher and Major governments supporting 'constructive engagement'.[13] Under Mrs Thatcher, their role was largely confined, though she had to tolerate Howe and Hurd at the FCO. Mrs Thatcher herself was, of course, more disposed to the European cause at some points (such as the single market) than at others. Under Major, the pro-Europeans had more opportunity to air their views: the climate was more tolerant to them. But, even under Major the actual policy input of the rest of the Cabinet on Europe was minimal. Policy and strategy were determined by a small group led by Major, Lamont, Hurd, and Garel-Jones (see below).

The 'Eurosceptics'

Overall, taking into account both ministers and senior officials, those favouring 'constructive engagement' in EC matters probably formed a majority in the

---

[13] Others, such as David Hunt, John Gummer, Malcolm Rifkind (at least in this period), and Peter Walker, might also be cited. But they were not prominent on EMU.

1988–91 period. Yet, of course, Mrs Thatcher's lead in her last years imposed a strongly Eurosceptic frame on policy and strategy. This frame defined the limits of the options to be considered and created a unique environment in which alternatives might be advanced.

Over the course of her career, Mrs Thatcher's stance on European matters had shifted somewhat. Under Heath, she had supported British entry into the EC. Indeed, at the time she was a member of the Conservative Group for Europe, becoming its patron in 1976 (Heath 1998: 379, 695). In the early 1980s she drew a sharp contrast between her party's support for the EC and the shift of the Labour Party to advocate withdrawal. In 1985, she signed the Single European Act, arguably a stronger retreat from national veto rights than was the Maastricht Treaty. Despite her later self-portrayal as a 'Boadicea' figure, Mrs Thatcher had proved to be flexible on Europe until the late 1980s. Indeed, rather than being 'Boadicea' she could equally be seen as a 'Canute'-like figure, given her inability to stop the tide of integration.

In any event, in her later years as Prime Minister, Mrs Thatcher's stance on Europe hardened considerably. In parallel to this, her leadership style and her attitude towards dealing with the rest of the EC underwent a significant shift. In her later years, Mrs Thatcher became more detached from her Cabinet, less consultative, more reliant on her own instincts. She retreated into her inner circle of advisers and trusted confidants. She was also suspicious of plots against her, not least by the ERM advocates, Howe and Lawson. By 1988, Mrs Thatcher was less open to contrary advice and this style was most evident in European policy. Whilst she had shown flexibility on the Single Act, she now became more resistant to compromise on new EC developments. She knew best, because 'her interests were axiomatically those of Britain' (Howe 1994: 691). But, as Howe puts it tersely, 'The insistence on the undivided sovereignty of her own opinion dressed up as the nation's sovereignty was her own undoing' (Howe 1994: 691). Mrs Thatcher set herself a course of action in which she invested her much-vaunted stridency and resolution. Style and policy thus came to build a wall around her, which inhibited the reflection and adaptation that might have been prompted by the wider government machine.

Mrs Thatcher consistently sought to block or divert the path of EMU. She:

- tried to block the full realization of EMU by opposing any reference to the creation of a European Central Bank in the communiqué of the European Council at Hanover in June 1988;
- wanted Robin Leigh-Pemberton and Karl-Otto Pöhl (Germany) to stop the Delors Committee backing EMU in 1988–9;
- supported Britain's two alternative schemes—competing currencies and a 'hard' ECU—with the intention of stopping or diverting the momentum behind EMU. In the end, her dismissal of the potential of the 'hard' ECU after the Rome 1 summit in October 1990 led to her own downfall;
- was the spiritual head of plans for Britain to 'opt out' of EMU: plans hatched from early 1990 onwards. When told in a note from John Major in May 1990

of the dangers of Britain being left behind in a second tier of the EC, she wrote back, 'What's wrong with that if the other tier is going in the wrong direction?' (Thatcher 1995: 724).

Yet, of course, Mrs Thatcher failed to block EMU and her diversionary tactics became all too transparent to her EC partners. If she had remained Prime Minister in 1990–1 there is no doubt that she would have been obliged to have Britain negotiate a deal in the IGC. She had rejected exclusion from an IGC in 1985 and would surely have done so again. That being the case, she would have had to oversee an appropriate negotiating strategy. Indeed, if she had not been so unguarded at the Rome summit and had thus not provoked Howe to resign, the likelihood is that she would have attended the Maastricht European Council herself. If she had, then it is not at all clear that she would have obtained a different deal than did her successor, John Major. After all, the opt-out did appease all sides in the Tory Party. On the other hand, by mid-1991 Mrs Thatcher was telling journalists that Major should just say 'No' to EMU and force the rest to go outside the Treaty of Rome (Stephens 1996: 201). The implication is that she would have endeavoured to have made the transition to stage 3 more difficult. Yet, she might have had less bargaining clout than had Major: by 1990 she had become deeply unpopular with the other EC governments.

Mrs Thatcher's European stance combined elements old and new. At times she was inclined to accept the need for gradualism as espoused by Whitehall, though by 1990 she had convinced herself that small steps carried long-term dangers. Her strong sense of British patriotism led her to cling to national sovereignty as an abiding principle of foreign policy. And her economic principles strengthened her scepticism. Her mind-set placed EMU in the context of a tradition that drew upon Hayek and Friedman and which emphasized competition and markets. The starting-point for Mrs Thatcher—though not for Lawson— was that the exchange rate was comparable to any other market price and should be determined freely. Proposals for EMU inherently conflicted with such a disposition, as Sir Alan Walters repeatedly reminded the Prime Minister. Thus, her economic views served to strengthen her political opposition to EMU. EMU was neither desirable, on political grounds, nor viable, on economic grounds. This general disposition was communicated to all those close to her. All knew the type of discourse that was preferred at court.

Mrs Thatcher and German Unity

The prospect of German unification stiffened Mrs Thatcher in her opposition to deeper European integration. To her, a united Germany would be 'simply too big and powerful to be just another player within Europe . . . Germany is . . . by its very nature a destabilizing rather than a stabilizing force in Europe' (Thatcher 1995: 791). The French response—to 'rush to European federalism as a way of tying down Gulliver' (Thatcher 1995: 814)—was rejected. A federal

Europe would be both unstable (given German power) and an obstacle to harmony with the USA. It made little difference that US attitudes displayed much less fear of such developments. In 1989–90, Mrs Thatcher insisted on the prerogative of the four Second World War allies to determine the course of German unification. She also urged a new treaty to guarantee Poland's borders. She tried, and failed, to make common cause with a nervous Mitterrand to control the resurgent Germany. The enigmatic Mitterrand had initially given support to Mrs Thatcher's concerns in private. But he came to place German unification in a very different context, of which EMU played a large part. Each of Mrs Thatcher's moves reflected a thinking shaped by the conditions of the 1940s. Germany could not be trusted; Britain needed to stand with the USA; and French resolve to defend itself against its neighbour had to be stiffened.

Each of these moves angered Kohl. Indeed, he appears to have felt personally hurt by them. German unification reconfigured the Chancellor's pattern of political friendships: Delors and Mitterrand gained; Mrs Thatcher was ostracized. In 1990 Hurd acted as the prime intermediary between London and the Federal Chancellor's Office. The Thatcher–Kohl relationship had never been warm, as Craddock recalls: 'Mrs. Thatcher underestimated Herr Kohl and there was no natural sympathy. She responded coolly to his genuine attempts to establish a rapport. She did not take to the food on her visit to his home village of Deidesheim [30 April 1989]' (Craddock 1997: 135).[14] The perspectives each had on the future of Europe could hardly have been further apart. The prospect of German unification traumatized the relationship between the two, and it never recovered.

Mrs Thatcher's response to the imminence of German unity was shared by her entourage, but not by others in the government or in Whitehall. Hurd as Foreign Secretary and Major as Chancellor rejected her interpretation. Hurd, in particular, was very annoyed by her approach and manner.[15] Both Hurd and Major saw the task after Mrs Thatcher's departure as mending bridges to Bonn.[16]

Some indication of the thinking of Mrs Thatcher's entourage is given by the reports of a seminar held by the Prime Minister at Chequers in March 1990. The seminar was attended by six leading academics and other experts and addressed the implications of German unity. A confidential memorandum written by

[14] Mrs Thatcher recalls that at Deidesheim Kohl had said, privately, to Charles Powell that he hoped the setting would convince the British Prime Minister that he 'was as much European as German'. In response, Mrs Thatcher 'had to doubt his reasoning' (Thatcher 1995: 748). This was a telling clash of cultural perspectives.

[15] In his memoirs, Heath notes that he was 'appalled by the rabid, bigoted, xenophobic attacks on Germany within the UK during this momentous period' (1998: 713). Moreover, by abandoning Britain's earlier support for German unity, 'Mrs Thatcher undermined at a stroke the trust which a whole generation of German politicians had reposed in us'.

[16] Sir Percy Craddock, the PM's Foreign Policy Adviser from 1984 to 1992, indicates that he also sharply disagreed with Mrs Thatcher's approach to Germany, both before and after the collapse of the Berlin Wall (Craddock 1997: 135).

Charles Powell, the Prime Minister's Private Secretary, was leaked to the *Independent on Sunday* (15 July 1990). The seminar discussion appears to have been well balanced in its judgements, with many of the guests emphasizing the positive contribution the Federal Republic had made (Urban 1996: 124–6). However, the Powell Memorandum revealed deep-rooted fears and prejudices concerning the German condition. Powell recorded 'less flattering attributes' of the German character: 'angst, aggressivenes, assertiveness, bullying, egotism, inferiority complex, sentimentality'. He also noted 'a capacity for excess' and 'a tendency to over-estimate their own strengths and capabilities'. As Neal Ascherson commented in the same issue of the *Independent on Sunday*: 'few member states of the European Community can ever have discussed one of their partners in terms like these'. But the evidence points not to the prejudice of the guests; rather, it is a telling illustration of the discourse prevalent in the Thatcher entourage.[17] Powell, a former diplomat in Bonn, was writing his minutes with the intended reader—Mrs Thatcher—very much in mind. The Powell mind-set was fixed in the world before 1945.[18] Mrs Thatcher's own response to German unity seemed to display a similar perspective. At the end of the seminar, she accepted that she was isolated in her instinctive anti-Germanism (Urban 1996: 128).

The furore caused by this episode had been stirred as a result of comments attributed to Nicholas Ridley, a Cabinet minister, in an interview with the *Spectator* just before the publication of the Powell Memorandum (14 July 1990). If the memorandum could be excused as a crisp stimulant to further reflection, the comments of Ridley took on the character of bile. The Secretary of State for Trade and Industry talked of a 'German racket to take over the whole of Europe', with the prospect of Kohl trying to take over everything, and Britons objecting to being dictated to by Pöhl in the Bundesbank. EMU meant a loss of sovereignty to Germany and 'You might as well give it to Adolf Hitler, frankly'. The Germans were buying the support of their neighbours, whilst the French were merely their 'poodles'. He dismissed his Cabinet colleagues, Hurd and Major, as 'doormats' for Britain's partners to walk over. As *The Times* commented, few could doubt that Ridley meant what he was reported as saying (13 July 1990). There was also the widespread suspicion that Mrs Thatcher's own private thoughts on Germany were close to those of Ridley's. Indeed, Mrs Thatcher struggled to try to keep Ridley in the Cabinet, despite the furore over his interview.

---

[17] Writing of the characteristics of the Germans, Powell wrote in his report that 'It was easier—and more pertinent to the present discussion—to think of the less happy ones' (*Independent on Sunday*, 15 July 1990).

[18] Horst Teltschik, in Kohl's Kanzleramt, wrote an amusing reply to the Powell Memorandum in *The Economist* (21 July 1990). He also made the serious point that British thinking was locked into the pre-1945 world.

Mrs Thatcher's 'soul-mates'

Ridley had supported Mrs Thatcher consistently on the ERM and on EMU. Whilst he was in the Cabinet, Ridley bombarded Mrs Thatcher with notes urging her to oppose totally the ERM and EMU. Mrs Thatcher received similar notes from Alan Walters, her erstwhile Economic Adviser, albeit of a more technical kind. Walters continued to pass Mrs Thatcher anti-ERM/EMU notes after he was forced to resign as a result of the Prime Minister's battle with Lawson. Both Ridley and Walters were key allies of Mrs Thatcher, reinforcing her anti-European inclinations.

The loyalty to Mrs Thatcher of Charles Powell, her Private Secretary from 1984, was unquestioned. Powell had served in Bonn before 1979 and later in Brussels until he entered Number Ten. Few FCO officials appear to have been left so disenchanted by their European experience.[19] Powell came to admire Mrs Thatcher's tenacity over the EC budget and his sympathies grew in her direction. But Powell's role was somewhat difficult to define. His post was not that of chief foreign policy adviser; that role belonged to the more Euro-friendly Sir Percy Craddock (Craddock 1997: 142). Powell's task was not that of a Kissinger, advising on European policy. Yet, the trust and intimacy he established with Mrs Thatcher placed him in a more influential position than was normal. His record suggests that he followed the Prime Minister's instincts, rather than attempting to correct them. Howe, most notably, regarded his appointment to Number Ten as a serious mistake (Howe 1994: 396). In opting for a more politicized role at Number Ten, Powell's antennae appear to have malfunctioned. He compounded Mrs Thatcher's miscalculation of the momentum behind EMU and failed to prevent her from making a series of tactical mistakes at EC summits (Hanover and Rome most notably).

Over the course of her premiership, Mrs Thatcher developed an intimate trust with her personal court. Members of the court developed a privileged knowledge of, and a sympathy for, her personal thoughts (Thatcher 1995: 20). Powell was one such intimate, but another was Bernard Ingham, Chief Press Secretary from 1979 to 1990. Ingham redefined the role of the press secretary and developed an intense personal loyalty to the Prime Minister. Through Cabinet splits, battles with the 'wets', the Westland affair, the poll tax, and countless other controversies, 'He never let me down', as Mrs Thatcher noted in her memoirs (1995: 20). Ingham had only limited policy influence, but in attending every European Council session and a host of bilateral meetings with Mrs Thatcher, he fed on and reinforced her increasing antipathy to the EC and its ambitions. His indirect influence on Mrs Thatcher was much greater than was normal for the job he held. Leaving his post with his premier, he moved effortlessly across to be a 'John Bull' Eurosceptic newspaper columnist.

[19] Sir John Coles, Private Secretary to Mrs Thatcher as Prime Minister between 1981–4 was reportedly another.

After Mrs Thatcher left office, a number of 'Eurosceptics' remained. The most directly involved in EMU was Norman Lamont, who replaced John Major as Chancellor of the Exchequer. Lamont's policy stance in 1990–1 is somewhat difficult to define, given his ministerial style and loyalty to Major. His appointment as Chancellor caused some political suprise. It was interpreted as an act of gratitude by Major for Lamont's support in the leadership election. It was also the least disruptive option, as Lamont stepped up from being Chief Secretary to the Treasury. By reputation, Lamont was on the Right of the party and sympathetic to the Eurosceptic position. Indeed, immediately before ceasing to be Chief Secretary to the Treasury, Lamont spoke on 15 November 1990 to the Bruges Group (a rallying point for Tory Eurosceptics). In his speech he clearly restated his opposition to a single currency (quoted in Blair 1998: n. 57). His appointment offered some reassurance to the Right of the party, when Major was desperate to heal wounds.

Lamont was intellectually unconvinced by ERM entry, both on political and economic grounds, but he remained quiescent as a result of the realities of government office. As Chancellor, he was bound to the obligation that he could say and do nothing that might undermine the credibility of British policy. Lamont kept his doubts buried. Indeed, Lamont appears not to have raised any substantive policy dispute on EMU with Major during the entire course of the IGC. The one exception was telling in this respect. It arose after a Treaty Draft from the Dutch, who were holding the EC Presidency in the second half of 1991. This Draft proposed that membership of the ERM should become an integral treaty obligation on all signatories in stage 2. Lamont insisted that this proposal should be rejected as part of the government's opposition to any legal obligations during stage 2 of EMU. Neither Hurd nor Major regarded the issue as being as objectionable as did Lamont. Britain was comfortable with ERM membership at the time. But the Chancellor threatened to resign over the issue. Apart from this exception, Lamont appears to have been part of the Major consensus on EMU and to have kept any other disagreements very much to himself.

Later, after leaving office, Lamont became a more strident Eurosceptic, backing John Redwood's leadership challenge against John Major.[20] Lamont's assertiveness at this stage may have had an opportunistic element to it. It helped to protect his political position after the débâcle of the ERM exit in 1992. Euroscepticism was also increasingly in favour amongst Tory MPs after the election of that year.

Others in the Cabinet were closely associated with the Eurosceptic line. As Employment Secretary, from January 1990 onwards, Michael Howard served under both Mrs Thatcher and John Major. His post meant he was not directly involved in EMU policy, but in 1991 he joined the Cabinet committee discussions on Maastricht, where he underscored his firm opposition to the Social

---

[20] Lamont's dismissal from the Major government on 27 May 1993 was the source of much personal bitterness on his part. On the back benches, Lamont attacked the government's European policy. See Lamont (1995).

Charter. Chris Patten urged Major to adopt a softer line on the Social Chapter at Maastricht. But Howard apparently threatened to resign if he did so (Blair 1998). Major knew that Howard and his supporters had to be accommodated, and he accepted that there was little scope for compromise on the issue. Another sceptic to be placated was Peter Lilley, who had replaced Ridley at the DTI in July 1990. But Lilley was less involved than Howard, given the focus of his post.

Beyond the Cabinet, the instincts of an important figure at the Bank of England, Eddie George (Deputy Governor, 1990–3; Governor, 1993–), were close to those of the Eurosceptics. His personal political profile with Mrs Thatcher, and with Lawson, was much stronger than tradition suggested. George's experience (and certainly his chief interest) was predominantly on the domestic, rather than the international, side.[21] A forceful, domineering character, George's promotion served as a check on the more Europhile tendencies of Leigh-Pemberton and the Bank's international staff. George showed a sensitivity to tactics. He accommodated himself to the prevailing political wind: he gave strong backing to the 'hard' ECU proposal, overshadowing the scepticism of his colleagues, as a way out for the Thatcher government. After Maastricht, he portrayed himself as being pragmatic on a single currency. But his utterances were typically sceptical of the prospects for, and the viability of, establishing a single currency. He repeatedly emphasized the dangers to EMU from incorporating states with high unemployment or with large public debts. Few who knew him saw him as Europhile in the domestic debate.[22]

Though the Eurosceptics may have been outnumbered in government, they held some of the key positions. Mrs Thatcher's premiership was a courtly affair: she granted access and influence according to political sympathies. It was also a reign which created and maintained a threatening, ultimately stultifying, political climate, prohibiting a more open, consensual policy discourse on Europe. This climate distorted policy debate, inhibited the flow of intelligence and expertise, and constrained strategic planning. In the end, this Eurosceptic pall was to prove her undoing. There was palpable relief at her departure amongst those most closely involved in shaping Britain's European policy.

The Tory Divide on Europe

The political climate when Major took over as Prime Minister in November 1990 was more supportive of constructive engagement on Europe. In effect, Howe's resignation speech, with its criticisms of the dogmatism and missed opportunities of the past, was closer to the national mood than was Mrs

[21] Since he joined the Bank in 1962, Eddie George had worked at the BIS in 1966–9 and at the IMF in 1972–4.

[22] George's first term as Governor expired in June 1998. The delay in announcing his reappointment for a second term was attributed to George's hostile views on EMU, which contrasted with those of the Chancellor, Gordon Brown.

Thatcher's position. Within the Conservative Party in Parliament, the balance had changed, but the divisions remained strong. Indeed, the cleavage within the party was to be of growing importance from this point onwards. Mrs Thatcher's natural allies on the Right sought reassurance that her European stance would be protected, whilst those who had backed Michael Heseltine in his leadership bid against her looked for the very break the Right feared. A raw nerve had been exposed and it required sensitive treatment by the new party leader. This sensitivity prohibited any radical shift of policy. Indeed, it seemed as if peace could only be achieved through delicate balance and compromise.

The parliamentary party had a stronger proportion of pro-Europeans in this period than it did after the new intake following the May 1992 General Election.[23] Moreover, the backbench Eurosceptics lacked unity in 1990–1. The different nuances between their positions were evident in their speeches and writings.[24] The new Major team also acted to thwart Eurosceptic influence at Westminster. Bill Cash was removed from the chairmanship of the backbench committee on European affairs, to be replaced by the arch-loyalist Sir Norman Fowler. Similarly, Sir George Gardiner was replaced as Chairman of the rightist '92 Group by Cyril Townsend (Blair 1998).

Nevertheless, the threat to party unity was still clear. It was evident in the various parliamentary debates held on the IGC negotiations in December 1990, and June, November, and December 1991.[25] More particularly, in September 1991, a group of fourteen junior ministers, from the No Turning Back Group went to see Major at Number Ten to make clear their Eurosceptic concerns (Blair 1998). Just days after the Maastricht summit, in the House of Commons on 18–19 December 1991, twenty-four Tory MPs either abstained or were absent from supporting the government position on the Treaty. Amongst those abstaining was Mrs Thatcher. In addition, seven Conservative MPs actually voted against the Government, including former ministers John Biffen and Norman Tebbit. Major still had a majority of almost 100 at the start of the IGC negotiations, but the party often seemed on the verge of internal warfare on Europe. Moreover, the main threat to Major's position seemed to stem from the Eurosceptic Right. Many in this group had felt that their fears were being confirmed by Major's 'Heart of Europe' speech in March 1991. Beyond Westminster, the Eurosceptic influence of the newspapers owned by Rupert Murdoch and Conrad Black were

[23] Garry (1995: 175) reports a postal survey of Conservative MPs conducted in November and December 1991, which had a response rate of 45.7%. Of these, 42% were classified as 'pro-EC' and 39% as 'anti-EC'. Garry also notes that a good proportion of Major's supporters in the November 1990 leadership election were anti-EC.

[24] See, for example, Teresa Gorman (1993), Michael Spicer (1992), Teddy Taylor in *The Times*, 13 Dec. 1991. Also, see speech of Jonathan Aitken, a Eurosceptic, in the Commons on 31 October 1991. In this he said 'we would be wise to trust our negotiators . . . I do not share the fears of some of my Eurosceptic friends that a giant sell-out is being secretly prepared' (quoted in Blair 1998). Aitken was leader of the largest Eurosceptic group, the European Reform Group. Major subsequently rewarded Aitken with a ministerial post.

[25] The relevant Commons and Lords select committees also held their own deliberations on the IGC agenda.

an additional, and significant, threat. Such pressures were especially potent given that an election was on the horizon.

These tensions came more clearly to the surface in the 1992–7 Parliament. Major had a much smaller majority of twenty-one, with fifty-four new MPs. The turnover meant an exchange of 'Major's friends' for 'Thatcher's children', as Seldon has put it (1997: 285). The party had shifted further towards Euroscepticism. A survey of opinions on EMU held by Tory MPs in 1994 found: 'Backbench attitudes to a single currency were uncompromisingly hostile, by large majorities' (Baker *et al*. 1994: 228). The parliamentary siege on the ratification of the Maastricht Treaty was intense.

The tensions and divisions in the Conservative Party in 1990–1 created a highly charged and unstable political climate. Mrs Thatcher had not had to face anything comparable on Europe during her reign as leader. John Major had to deal with this unprecedented situation and avoid the party tearing itself apart. By giving priority to healing the divisions within his party, Major was 'nesting' his strategy for the IGCs within the internal demands of the Conservative Party. His strategy at the negotiating table cannot be explained without reference to his attempts to maintain domestic party unity at Westminster. The rationale behind his actions can only be understood in relation to the combination of the two contexts (Tsebelis 1990).

The Major Dilemma

> Emotionally I am an agnostic on the subject of a united Europe. I've no longer-term vision of a federal Europe and I don't wish to diminish the languages and cultures of the Member States. [I am] a European by logic, not emotion.
>
> John Major, *Spectator*, 25 October 1997

Mrs Thatcher's successor, John Major, displayed very different leadership characteristics on Europe. His own temperament, the wider political mood, and the lessons he drew from Mrs Thatcher's fall impelled him towards a more inclusive and tolerant style. This style fitted his own rather unformed European attitudes.

To those working closely with him in 1990–1, Major appeared to have few ideological predilections on Europe. In general, Major was not a dogmatic figure. He approached EMU more pragmatically, in the manner of the banker of his younger days, calculating costs and benefits. Mrs Thatcher, in her memoirs, reports that early in April 1990 Major argued that UK 'strategy must be to slow-down' the advance towards the second and third stages of the Delors Plan, but to 'ensure all the while that the UK was not excluded from the negotiating process' (Thatcher 1995: 720). Major was clearly open-minded, but his tactical instinct was to think of an effective defence rather than an advance plan.

Major appealed easily to both wings of his party. He was not completely attached to either engagement with or detachment from Europe. He had barely focused on Europe before becoming Foreign Secretary in 1989. As Seldon confirms, 'The two dominant factors shaping his thinking on Europe were always the balance of opinion in his Party, and the balance of the arguments on the particular issue under review' (1997: 163). His instinct was to find consensus. Michael Portillo later recalled that, 'As a brilliant handler of people, it must have appeared to [Major] that pursuing the middle way, and being affable to both sides, offered the best prospect of holding the party together' (*Spectator*, 25 October 1997). During the course of 1990–1, Major acted consistently to placate the different factions of his divided party.

This consensualism had consequences. What Major's European stance lacked was a stable, coherent vision: a sense of long-term purpose and direction, a frame in which to place Britain's European policy. In the absence of such a strategic vision, he tended to become absorbed by tactics, an area in which he excelled. This lack of vision was shared by a number of modern British leaders. But it offered a sharp contrast to the dogmatic position of his predecessor. Unlike Mrs Thatcher, Major did not display much sensitivity on the thorny issue of sovereignty *per se*. He lacked an emotional commitment on Europe, positive or negative. His was a pragmatic stance. At times, he must almost have wondered what the fuss was about.

But Major did have clear positions on the specifics of the IGC negotiations. When he entered Number Ten, senior Whitehall officials, led by Nigel Wicks at the Treasury, pressed the case for shifting position on EMU. This shift was to accept a single currency in the long term but to adopt the 'hard' ECU in the transition towards it. Though he was more receptive to such a discussion, Major rejected the move. He was not prepared to give a prior commitment to stage 3. Similarly, in other areas to be covered by the looming negotiations such as the Social Chapter, Major clearly accepted that existing government policy was correct and should be upheld.

Against this background of pragmatism and the need to placate his party, Major focused on his IGC strategy. Major believed that significant gains could be made for Britain in the negotiations if the tactics and style were altered. He judged that many of Britain's problems on Europe stemmed from Mrs Thatcher's confrontational and strident manner. Many advised him to this effect, notably Chris Patten and Sarah Hogg. Major believed that the mood in the Cabinet, and to a lesser extent in the Tory Party, was for policy to be more pro-European. The new Prime Minister was determined to turn his back on the rancour of the Thatcher period.

In keeping with the greater tactical emphasis, Major gave new priority to forming understandings with the key EC leaders. His relations on EMU with President Mitterrand were always going to be distant, given their very different views of the 'hard' ECU (see Chapter 14). They also failed to establish a personal rapport. Major thus focused on Chancellor Kohl. On EMU, there was more reason to do so: Germany was the crucial player and Anglo-German economic philosophies overlapped more closely. Moreover, Major indicated that he was not bothered 'about the baggage of history' (Seldon 1997: 165). Such a statement from Mrs Thatcher would have been unthinkable. The two were of different political generations.[26] Major conducted a charm offensive. In his Bonn speech of March 1991, he talked of placing Britain at 'the heart of Europe', and of negotiating in good faith in the IGC. He would endeavour to maximize the extent to which Britain could agree on a new Treaty. Britain would not block an EMU agreement, but it might not be able to sign up for it. Major had no special affinity with European politics, but he was a much more sensitive tactician than Mrs Thatcher bothered to be.

The European stance of both Mrs Thatcher and John Major owed much to the circumstances of their periods as party leader. But the priority Major gave to party unity indicates the greater importance of seeing his actions on EMU as being nested in the parliamentary politics of Westminster (see also Chapter 15). Major focused on the boundaries of what his parliamentary party would accept. He then had to apply this constraint to the IGC negotiating table. He moved between the two arenas of the IGC table and of the corridors of the Commons. In the event, Major achieved more success in both arenas than many thought possible. At Maastricht, he satisfied his immediate objectives on both EMU and the Social Chapter. He was widely recognized to be a persistent, well-briefed, and effective negotiator. At home, Major managed to keep his party together most of the time. It is not clear that anyone could have done this better than he did.

But the shallowness of Major's views on Europe left him vulnerable to changes in the political wind. Indeed, before his electoral humiliation in 1997, Major was attacked for being too much of a weather-vane on the subject. Major was obliged to ride the storm of the parliamentary debates on the ratification of the Maastricht Treaty. He accommodated Kenneth Clarke, as Chancellor of the Exchequer, who insisted on a 'wait-and-see' policy on EMU entry. This policy was, after all, his own original instinct. But Major faced trauma after trauma on Europe from those Eurosceptics in his own ranks whom he reportedly labelled 'bastards'. Major shifted his own position: out of office in 1997 he argued that the Tories should oppose EMU entry. He had responded to the party's mood again.

Within the frame: Ministers and Officials

The policy-making process on EMU within the government had two interlocking dimensions: the ministerial and the official. The ministerial lead in the debate on EMU set the frame in which policy options were evaluated and strategy was determined. This lead defined a remit for officials in Whitehall and in the Bank of England. As for the senior officials, identifying their attitudes and priorities is difficult, given the political parameters within which they operated. On Europe, as seen above, they worked within a very prickly groove.

[26] Margaret Thatcher was born in 1925; John Major in 1943.

Yet, senior officials were not mere foot-soldiers following the ministerial lead. The British civil service had distinct inherited traditions affecting the relationship between ministers and officials. The Northcote–Trevelyan Report of 1853 had wished to see senior Whitehall officials 'possessing sufficient independence, character, ability, and experience to be able to advise, assist, and to some extent, influence, those who are from time to time set over them' (Hennessy 1989: 511). It was but a short extension to argue that the tenured official had to speak the truth, fearlessly unto power (Hennessy 1989: 494). Moreover, officials, as 'servants of the Crown' rather than of ministers, could be seen as guardians of the national interest. This poses a controversial yardstick by which the actions of senior officials might be judged in relation to British policy on EMU. If there were failings of understanding, of strategy, and of tactics, then how far can these be atributed to the 'advice' of Whitehall officials? To suggest that it was ministers alone 'who got it wrong' ignores this conception of the role of Whitehall officials.

An alternative interpretation of the civil servants' role was that they should act as chameleons, deferring at all times to the political will of the government. The convention has been of the political neutrality of a civil service that is permanent, serving governments of different persuasions. Such a conception was shared by Lord Bridges, a former Cabinet Secretary and Permanent Secretary to the Treasury who served two strident political figures, Churchill and Attlee. On this basis, ministers alone are responsible for the actions taken by the government. On EMU, it still leaves the question open of the quality of the information given to ministers by their 'servants'.

In reality, neither of these conceptions comes close enough to the nature of the policy process. The civil servant's role has to be placed in a wider institutional perspective. Senior officials convey and interpret messages, and in doing so they help to shape policy and strategy. On EMU, ministers were operating within the accumulated cognitive understandings and strategic resources of Whitehall and the Bank. Ministers were, to a degree, operating within the Whitehall 'village', to use Heclo and Wildavsky's phrase (1974). The policy process on EMU was relatively confined, more distant from outside domestic intervention than in other policy areas. And the Whitehall village had developed a much longer-established institutional frame on Europe.

For the Thatcher and Major periods, Wallace has noted the compartmentalization of policy on Europe in Whitehall. A general pattern emerged, she argues, in which ministers and officials 'tended to approach European issues case by case, addressing each on its merits, rather than through the lens of general integration policy' (Wallace 1997: 686). Though generalization is hazardous, this tendency appears to reflect a longer-term pattern.

Whitehall has typically viewed European policy as a matter of calculation, rather than of conviction. Britain's entry into the EC was the result of a pragmatic judgement of the relative benefits to be expected. Moreover, such calculations have traditionally been couched in the short term. Milward, for example, is scathing in his criticism of the short-termism of both the Foreign Office and the Treasury on Europe at the start of the 1950s (1984: 500–1). On the rare occasions when they looked to the longer term, 'the level of their comment dropped from penetrating and well-ordered expertise to rambling and alarmingly ignorant self-indulgence'. He contrasts this practice with that of the French: the latter placed European unity in a longer-term political calculation; Whitehall resisted such grand perspectives. The consensus was to maintain a long-term flexibility of choice and was sensitive to an encroachment on the prerogatives of Whitehall and of Parliament. Britain's involvement in the EC was to be carefully measured, step by step.

On European monetary questions, this general tendency was reinforced by the primary role given to the Treasury. The operation of the Bretton Woods system, and of managing sterling's international role, had bequeathed a legacy of Atlanticism in the Treasury. The intellectual influences felt in the Treasury also tended to be much more Atlanticist than European. Moreover, the Treasury has been the quintessential exponent of calculations being made on the basis of short- to medium-term gains and losses.[27] The FCO's distance from the Treasury meant that longer-term political strategy was even less likely to be taken into account. In addition, the Treasury has endeavoured to maintain primacy over the Bank of England on such policy matters: the latter has had a more favourable European disposition. Thus, to the Treasury, the question of entering the ERM was seen in this light: an issue to be judged on its economic merits, in facilitating a greater monetary discipline, and with little reference to wider political considerations. The view extended only as far as that which was readily calculable. It emphasized economics, not politics.

In the cases of the birth of the ERM and the relaunch of EMU there was a failure in Whitehall to fully appreciate the political momentum on the Continent behind these new initiatives. Parallels are evident here with the situation in the 1950s (Camps 1964: 47, 64; Denman 1996). In some cases, signals appear not to have been picked up in London. That they were not adequately picked up can be attributed to two factors. First, for both the ERM and EMU, ministers were not receptive to such messages. Politically, the instinct was to keep 'Europe' at bay. This defensiveness affected the will and the ability of senior civil servants to communicate the appropriate messages to ministers. If officials did recognize the strength of the momentum, disbelief could be replaced by a sense of impotence.

But if there were problems in the response of British governments to the EMS and to EMU, it seems too shallow to attribute such difficulties only to ministers. Beneath the political level, a second problem may have existed in how Whitehall officials themselves interpreted and responded to European signals. Like

---

[27] Camps (1964) makes only brief reference to the role and thinking of civil servants. At the time of the Macmillan government's switch to seek EEC entry, she notes, however, the lead given to entry by the Economic Steering Committee of senior civil servants, chaired by Sir Frank Lee of the Treasury, in 1960 (1964: 280–1, 293). The Committee had, indeed, looked at options over the short and long terms.

Milward before him, Ludlow (1982) was scathing in his criticism of how Treasury officials responded to the EMS initiative. Similarly, officials in Delors's entourage were highly critical of how the Treasury as an institution handled EMU after 1988. To them, the failures of British policy and strategy on EMU stemmed to a significant extent from the poor accommodation of the Treasury to the demands of EC politics.

Establishing generalizations about Whitehall or the Treasury is difficult, given their complexity and relative insularity. But, at root, the way in which Whitehall responded to EMU may be attributed to a wider feature: the collective *Weltanschauung* on 'Europe'. The administrative culture, norms, and values affect the calculation of 'intelligent choice' (Feldman and March 1981: 177). Sufficient information was probably available on EMU at the right time and of an appropriate quality (Wilensky 1967, p. ix). But that information had to be interpreted. The 'new institutionalist' perspective is relevant here: institutional settings matter. The behaviour, objectives, and values of those operating in Whitehall are shaped by the type of institution it is. This setting affects the frame in which choices are considered at the level of officials and, by extension, at the ministerial level also. To put it more formally, problems of strategic calculation stem from the cognitive understanding of actors in their institutional settings.[28] And the setting of the Treasury gave a particular focus to the domestic consideration of policy and strategy. This focus was grounded in a culture, a worldview, a *modus operandi*, and a set of interests that diverged substantially from that of Britain's EC partners.

The way in which policy on EMU was managed domestically will be discussed later. First, it is necessary to identify the key officials and their involvement in the internal debate.

The Key Officials

The overwhelming priority of the senior civil servants involved in EMU was with strategy. The struggle was to reconcile the political direction and tactics of ministers with a desire to minimize British isolation in the EC. Implicit in this struggle was an advocacy of 'constructive engagement'. But strategic calculations tended to be seen in the practical context of the short to medium term and placed in their appropriate compartments. More general policy and strategic reflection went by default.

Two of the lead officials on EMU were the successive Permanent Representatives in Brussels, Sir David Hannay (1985–90) and then Sir John Kerr (1990–5). Both played a key role in channelling information and advice to ministers, tailored to the political line set by their political masters.

---

[28] Following a 'new institutionalist' approach, Bulmer (1992), for example, has suggested that British semi-detachment in the EC stems from a strong institutional logic permeating, *inter alia*, public administration. Bulmer and Burch (forthcoming) take a more sympathetic view of the adaptation of Whitehall to the demands of EU membership.

Hannay pushed the idea of Whitehall preparing an opt-out on EMU in early 1990. He alerted Delors to an opt-out as an option. Such thinking paralleled that of John Major himself. In April 1990, Major was pressing Mrs Thatcher to accept the Delors Plan on condition that all states would have a general 'opt-in' when it came to the point of decision (Stephens 1996: 162–3). Hannay was in the same mould as his predecessor, Sir Michael Butler. Both sought means of building bridges, of reconciling distinct British interests with those of the rest of Europe. Hannay advocated decoupling the three stages of the Delors Plan, whilst in 1978 Butler had distinguished between membership of the EMS and of the ERM.

Kerr sailed closer to the wind. He had already taken political risks. He helped Lawson and Howe to draft their dramatic ultimatum on the ERM to Mrs Thatcher prior to the Madrid summit in 1989; he opposed Lawson's competing-currency alternative in the same year; he concurred with the EMU agenda set by the Guigou Group; he tried to overturn Mrs Thatcher's strategy at the Rome 1 summit in October 1990; and he repeatedly made clear his unhappiness with the 'indolent' Lamont during the IGC period. Indeed, at Maastricht he joined Nigel Wicks, of the Treasury, in blocking Lamont from entering a Major–Lubbers meeting arranged to patch up Britain's EMU opt-out. Later, in the UK Presidency of late 1992, Kerr's clashes with Lamont grew in their intensity. A rare error of strategic judgement by Kerr was to occur later in 1994 when he advised Major to adopt a rigid and narrow stance on Council voting weights (qualified majority voting) in the context of enlargement to include former EFTA states.

Kerr enjoyed an access and an influence on EMU, in significant part, owing to his own career expertise. Exceptionally, Kerr was an FCO official who had served in the key Treasury post of Principal Private Secretary to the Chancellor of the Exchequer. In this post he had served Howe and then Lawson, between 1981 and 1984. This experience gave him a familiarity with the EMU brief and with Treasury thinking denied to many others. It also meant that Kerr had worked alongside, and gained the respect of, Nigel Wicks. The two—almost as different as chalk and cheese—would lead for Britain on the IGC on EMU in 1990–1. Kerr's influence was also enhanced by the close rapport he developed with Delors. This rapport was much closer than that established previously by Hannay.

Kerr and Hannay had each been the senior FCO specialist on the EC (Assistant Under Secretary) prior to going to Brussels. Kerr's successor in this FCO post, Michael Jay, was a very different personality: a rather more cautious figure in his dealings with ministers. Jay was the lead official for the FCO at home on EMU, but he faced a more difficult task in entering the Treasury's priv-ileged terrain than did Kerr, given the latter's background. Yet, he too was obliged to focus on strategy and the prospects of exclusion. Thus, in November 1990 he supported an attempt to soften the government's stance on the hard ECU in order to secure more clout in the forthcoming IGC negotiations.

Beyond the FCO, 'constructive engagement' found favour at the Bank of England. This support was most clearly expressed by Robin Leigh-Pemberton, the Governor, and his lead international officials (first Anthony Loehnis and then Andrew Crockett). Leigh-Pemberton was to display his willingness to accommodate EMU when, as a member of the Delors Committee, he signed its report in 1989. A number of other Bank officials were 'fellow-travellers' on EMU, accepting the Delors path as technically valid. The exceptions were Eddie George and Christopher Taylor (Economics Division, then European Division). Both were more attracted to the 'hard' ECU than their colleagues and both were more 'gradualist' on EMU. These apart, attitudes were somewhat more positive. Loehnis had formed a basic pro-EC orientation whilst being a junior FCO official in the 1960s, well before he became the Bank's Executive Director for International Affairs (serving from 1981 until February 1989). Loehnis accepted the utility of a single currency in a single market, though he saw this goal as being for the long term (Loehnis 1988). He was an old Etonian and a loyal official of the Bank, in whose employment he had been since 1977. He was followed as Executive Director by Andrew Crockett, who was a natural supporter of Britain being at the heart of Europe. An enthusiast for the ERM, he was exasperated at Mrs Thatcher's general intransigence on Europe, and he never saw Britain's alternatives to the Delors plan as viable (though see Crockett 1991).

As already suggested, the perspective of the Treasury was somewhat different. The disposition of its leading personnel was much more varied and, in general, less favourable. Lamont's officials were no doubt obliged to be at least as enigmatic as he was. Earlier, in Lawson's period, Geoffrey Littler, Second Permanent Secretary (Finance) and Britain's representative on the EC Monetary Committee (he was its Chair, 1987–8), was something of an exception. He came to be identified with ERM entry and 'constructive engagement'. Littler was culturally more at home in Europe than were a number of his Treasury colleagues.

Littler's senior colleagues had much less contact with European matters. At the head of the Treasury, Sir Peter Middleton (Permanent Secretary 1983–91) was a pragmatist on the ERM, as was Sir Terry Burns (Chief Economic Adviser).[29] 'Europe' was incidental to their thinking in this respect. Indeed, Middleton had identified himself with the prevailing monetary orthodoxy of the early Thatcher period, when he had formed an informal nexus with Sir Alan Walters and Eddie George (Bank of England) to steer policy in the Prime Minister's preferred direction. The philosophy and long-term planning of EMU were thus quite alien to his own instincts. Burns had moved to support a stable exchange rate and with it ERM entry, whilst also backing the 'hard' ECU alternative. Neither Middleton nor Burns were natural Europhiles.

Littler's successor, Nigel Wicks, was to be the chief enigma in relation to EMU. He endeavoured to keep his own instincts private, whilst accommodating himself to different political masters and to the exigencies of EC negotiations (in the Monetary Committee, in the IGC, and in bilateral meetings). In the process,

[29] Formerly of the London Business School, Burns was Chief Economic Adviser to the Treasury and Head of the Government Economic Service from 1980 to 1991. In 1991 he was promoted to the rank of Permanent Secretary. He was still in this post when the Conservatives lost office in May 1997.

Wicks emitted complex and by no means consistent signals: sometimes for 'constructive engagement', sometimes being more reserved. Wicks is commonly seen as the 'archetypical civil servant' (Stephens 1996: 233). In his memoirs, Howe described him as 'talented', but 'diffident' (1994: 474). Seen as straightforward, but cautious, Wicks was trusted and respected by all. By the time EMU came along, he had had a broad and varied experience.[30] As Second Permanent Secretary he served as the British representative on the EC Monetary Committee and as deputy to the Chancellor for the Group of Seven finance ministers' meetings. He was to be a long-term player on this scene. After Maastricht he was to be a two-term Chair of the EC Monetary Committee: a distinction granted by his EC colleagues in recognition no doubt of how he handled his very difficult brief and how he contributed to the discussion.

Wicks's post drew him into repeated controversy. He was seen as endeavouring to protect his own back.[31] In his post, he needed to. In 1989–90, Wicks was one of the Whitehall figures who were instrumental in bringing forward the 'hard' ECU plan hatched by Paul Richards in the City: at a time when it was dangerous for a civil servant to put his head above the parapet on Europe. At the Rome 1 summit in October 1990 his own instincts and his political instructions appeared to be in acute conflict. In any event, Wicks seemed resigned to Britain's EC partners signing a separate declaration in favour of a single currency (see Chapter 14). Whether she was conscious of the implications or not, this move increased the political pressure on Mrs Thatcher when she returned home. Howe resigned shortly afterwards, precipitating Mrs Thatcher's fall. At Maastricht, Wicks barred Lamont from entering the Major–Lubbers meeting patching up Britain's opt-out from EMU. At an informal ECOFIN in Bath in September 1992, Wicks failed to stop Lamont going right out on a limb to so attack the Bundesbank President, Helmut Schlesinger, that almost all Britain's partners were outraged.

Wicks clearly had a difficult line to follow. He was obliged to defend a position which veered between atheism and agnosticism in the 'Jesuit Order' of the EC. His own instincts were probably to be more constructive on Europe, but he accepted the role of the archetypal civil servant, serving his political masters, even if like Mrs Thatcher and Lamont they were Eurosceptic. The dilemmas faced by Wicks were, to some extent, those of the government machine as a whole.

---

[30] Wicks began his career with BP (1958–68), before entering the Treasury (1968–75). He became Private Secretary to the PM (James Callaghan) between 1975–8, and then returned to the Treasury (1978–83). Internationally, Wicks has worked at both the IMF and the World Bank (1983–5). He moved back to London to be Principal Private Secretary to Mrs Thatcher (1985–9), before moving to the Treasury as Second Permanent Secretary (Finance). He was still in this post when the Conservatives lost office in May 1997.

[31] With his role at Number Ten and at the Treasury, Wicks had already been close to controversy: with Mrs Thatcher over the Westland affair in 1986; and with Lawson at the time of his increasing tension with Mrs Thatcher and Sir Alan Walters over the ERM.

The Domestic Policy Process on EMU

The Whitehall Machine

The actors determining EMU policy and strategy operated within a distinct institutional setting. How Whitehall managed policy on EMU displayed many traditional features of its institutional inheritance (on the latter see Hennesey 1989). As Heclo and Wildavsky noted many years earlier, the British civil service is 'the tightest club there is' (1974: 375). It has 'a compactness, coherence, in short, a community united by ties of kinship and culture' (1974: 36). Moreover, as Bulmer and Burch have noted, 'What is remarkable about British central government's adaptation to the EU . . . is the extent to which, while change has been substantial, it has been more or less wholly in keeping with British traditions' (Bulmer and Burch forthcoming).

Within the Whitehall 'village', EMU was a policy subject to tight co-ordination under Treasury leadership. No single politician or official in Whitehall led the policy, but no one sang out of tune. Lateral co-ordination was maintained. No significant turf-fighting occurred over departmental responsibilities. Such features are typical of how Whitehall has handled EC business (Bulmer and Burch forthcoming). Whilst only a few ministers were directly involved, beneath them a few senior officials dominated the co-ordination process. Again, this pattern is consistent with the notion of the 'core executive'. What was distinctive, however, was that the lateral co-ordination was firmly under the control of the Treasury, rather than the Cabinet Office. After the Delors Committee period, the Treasury was even more the master of its turf in this respect. Another peculiarity was that the establishment of the Delors Committee meant that, from the start, the co-ordination had to include officials from the Bank of England. More generally, the hallmark of the co-ordination was its relative domestic insularity. As already noted, few outsiders penetrated the policy-making process. This no doubt strengthened the internal co-ordination, but it also left it vulnerable to a narrowness of vision.

Lateral Co-ordination: the Bank and the Treasury

Prior to the creation of the Delors Committee at Hanover in June 1988, there was little planning in Whitehall on EMU. Mrs Thatcher had underestimated the momentum behind EMU and her dispute with Lawson over the ERM effectively blocked out discussion of it. The Delors Committee was the spur to action, however, and the response of Whitehall was a tried and tested one: to create an interdepartmental committee to monitor progress. The committee was chaired initially by Sir Geoff Littler, Second Permanent Secretary (Overseas Finance) at the Treasury, and then by his long-term successor, Nigel Wicks. This committee was in effect the first of a sequence under Wicks. Yet, the fact that the Delors

Committee comprised the Governor of the Bank of England as the sole British representative created difficulties in how the committee could monitor, let alone control, his work.

Robin Leigh-Pemberton (Governor from 1983–93) was determined to maintain propriety and not to be seen as a stooge of Whitehall. Whitehall knew relatively little of Leigh-Pemberton's initial views on EMU, and it had no more idea of how he might interpret his committee role. During the course of the Delors Committee's deliberations (September 1988 to April 1989) ministers did not assert themselves strongly, particularly in the key period before Christmas. The subject arose in the regular three-weekly meetings between the Governor and the Chancellor. But the Governor rarely met the Chancellor and the Prime Minister together. Indeed, it was not until 14 December 1988 that Leigh-Pemberton saw Mrs Thatcher, Lawson, and Howe together about the Delors Committee: one of only two such meetings the four appear to have had (the second was on 15 February 1989) (Thatcher 1995: 708). Such encounters placed the Governor in an embarrassing position: he was ill at ease as a committee member who had been appointed in a 'personal capacity' taking direction from his political masters. In the second of his meetings at Number Ten, Leigh-Pemberton was pressed to produce his own document and/or to submit a dissenting report. The ministers soon gave up on him as a lost cause, however. Additional meetings took place at Number Ten with Mrs Thatcher, Lawson, Howe, and officials present, to discuss the government's response (Lawson 1992: 907–9). Mrs Thatcher was told that the Delors Committee was going in a 'thoroughly unsatisfactory' direction (Thatcher 1995: 708). The first draft of the Delors Report was available to Whitehall in February 1989: the speed at which the report had been drafted suggested that the earlier meeting with Leigh-Pemberton in December 1988 had already been called too late to significantly alter the course of the Committee's work.

Beneath this level, Whitehall officials soon complained of being kept distant from the Governor's work. The flow of papers and information from the Bank was timed to prevent them from establishing negotiating positions for the Governor before his next Committee meeting. In this respect, the Bank's representatives were loyal lieutenants, protecting the Governor, reflecting the traditional deference of the staff at Threadneedle Street. They were acutely conscious of the political sensitivities involved, but there was also an element of them wishing to protect the Bank's own turf against incursions from the Treasury and the FCO. Moreover, central banks appreciate the power of information and they thrive on secrecy. It must also have seemed sweet revenge to Bank officials to be able to keep the Treasury at arm's length: the boot was usually on the other foot. In reality, however, the Treasury was able to obtain an early draft of the Delors Report from another source: the UK Permanent Representative's Office in Brussels, thereby circumventing the stonewalling of the Bank at home. The source was a member of Delors's cabinet. There was an element of farce at work: the Treasury played along with the Bank's secrecy, not revealing that it already had a draft of its own. In any event, there were delicate balances to be struck. Some in the Bank feared that the tensions created with the Treasury over the Delors Committee might threaten the Bank's interests in other policy areas, such as the modernization of the financial markets and of monetary controls. Nor would Leigh-Pemberton have wished to provoke Whitehall unnecessarily: the tensions on the Wicks Committee did little to ease the position of the Governor as he sought to cross this political minefield.

Wicks was to play the lead role in Whitehall on EMU throughout the relevant period: from the Delors Committee to the Maastricht European Council. But it was not a case of dominant personal leadership. The system tends to resist domination by any single minister or official. At the Treasury's behest Wicks drove the policy, but in tandem with others who travelled with him.

The Wicks Committee played a key role in 'binding-in' officials from the Foreign Office and officials from the Bank of England. The FCO was directly represented by Michael Jay. But the prime FCO input was via the UK's Permanent Representative in Brussels: Sir David Hannay and then Sir John Kerr. This office, which carries ambassadorial rank, was seen as one of the FCO's key postings. The office was a vital source of intelligence, given its liaison with the EU institutions. The Permanent Representative, and his Deputy, represent the UK in the Committee of Permanent Representatives (COREPER), which prepares meetings of the Council of Ministers. The established routine is that the Permanent Representative returns to London regularly, normally each Friday, for consultations. Both Hannay and Kerr did so throughout their periods, and they were consequently able to participate in the Wicks Committee.

The Brussels office—known as 'UKRep' (UK Permanent Representation, Brussels)—has always been an FCO agency, but a majority of its forty or more staff are now drawn from the rest of Whitehall, as is the Deputy Permanent Representative (Bulmer and Burch forthcoming). This practice gives other departments their own point of contact and source of information.[32] Amongst the staff of the UK Permanent Representation are several officials seconded from the Treasury in London. On occasions the Deputy Permanent Representative has been drawn from the Treasury, as with David Bostock (1995–), but between 1982 and 1991 this post was held by David Elliott from the Cabinet Office (1978–82). Bostock served as the Financial and Economic Counsellor in the Brussels office from 1985–9, before returning home to the Treasury. Following Bostock as the Treasury's man in UKRep was Robert Bonney. Both Bostock and Bonney were key points of EC intelligence for the Treasury.

---

[32] Heath (1998: 394), who set up the UKRep office, records that he 'insisted on putting officials from Whitehall home departments into the staff of UKREP Brussels . . . This was a very effective way of propagating a European outlook within departmental culture . . .' In addition, civil servants can be seconded as short-term 'Detached National Experts' to the EC Commission. This arrangement has increased the level of EC experience in Whitehall.

Kerr and Wicks represented Britain on the Guigou Group and on the IGC on EMU. They knew each other already, having worked together in Washington in 1984–5. Kerr's sharpness was widely recognized: colleagues described him as an excellent negotiator, 'a brilliant player of complicated games at several levels'.[33] In his Brussels role, Kerr was in close contact with many senior ministers, including Major whilst Chancellor. Major followed the established practice of staying the night as the guest of the Permanent Representative prior to ECOFIN meetings. The two established a close working relationship, based on mutual confidence and personal warmth. This grew when Major became Prime Minister. Kerr acted as an unofficial sherpa to Major at Maastricht, staying on bended knee beside him inside the Council chamber well beyond what protocol allows (Hogg and Hill 1995: 145). Moreover, whilst Wicks was the lead official on EMU, Kerr was the only British official to sit in both the IGC on EMU and that on political union. This gave him a privileged overview; amongst ministers only the Prime Minister could match this perspective.

The Wicks Committee also drew on the expertise of the Bank of England. The first representatives were Anthony Loehnis and John Arrowsmith (European Adviser to the Governor).[34] Andrew Crockett then replaced Loehnis as Executive Director for International Affairs in February 1989. Each had their own specialist international experience from the world of central bankers. Loehnis had also worked in the FCO in the 1960s. Crockett arrived after a seventeen-year stint at the IMF; four years later he left London again to be head of the BIS in Basle. Loehnis, then Crockett, chaired the Bank's own internal committee on EMU, which met throughout the period. Crockett was a very active member of the EC Monetary Committee, alongside Wicks (involved, for example, in their discussions on setting numeric reference values for the convergence criteria, and on the issue of 'real' convergence) and in the Committee of Central Bank Governors' Alternates Group (working on the draft statutes for the ECB). Apart from Kerr, Crockett was the non-Treasury official most involved in setting EMU policy. As the IGC wore on, however, the Bank officials felt more and more distant from the domestic-policy co-ordination mechanism. This detachment was not just a matter of the Treasury maintaining its supremacy. It was also a consequence of the speed and intensity of progress in the IGC itself.

The normal process of Whitehall co-ordination on EC matters gives a primary role to the European Secretariat of the Cabinet Office. The chief support to the Secretariat has come from the Foreign Office and the UK Permanent Representation to the EC in Brussels (UKRep). The Secretariat is a relatively small unit—just eight officials were assigned to it in 1992—and it was created in 1970 to handle Britain's entry negotiations into the EC. After accession, it

---

[33] In February 1997 when it was announced that Kerr was to return home from being Ambassador in Washington to become Permanent Under-Secretary of State—the head of the FCO (replacing Sir John Coles)—the *Independent* noted that Kerr's reputation was of one who could dominate 'his mission with his sheer intellectual brilliance'. It also saw him as having 'a finely-tuned wit' (8 Feb. 1997).

[34] Arrowsmith was thus the only Bank official to serve on the Wicks Committees throughout.

became a permanent addition to the Cabinet Office.[35] One of half a dozen sec-retariats within the Cabinet Office, the Deputy Secretary in charge of it has a privileged view of official information on EC matters; and he or she participates in weekly forward-planning meetings with the Cabinet Secretary (Hennesey 1990: 391). The convention has been that the Deputy Secretary attends and briefs the Prime Minister personally for every European Council, and attends virtually every meeting of the Cabinet when it discusses EC affairs (Seldon 1995: 132). The task of the Secretariat is to provide a focus, beyond the FCO, on EC matters, and its two leading officials by convention are not drawn from the Foreign Office (Seldon 1995: 132). The task of co-ordination has obliged the Secretariat to be 'proactive', one of a new type of entity within the Cabinet Office in more recent years.

The Secretariat is charged with ensuring that ministers and senior officials are apprised of looming EC questions; reconciling any conflicts that appear between Whitehall departments; and monitoring the implementation of agreed policy. The Secretariat was involved in work on the Single Act and the internal market, and on enlargement. It has routinely been engaged in discussions of negotiating tactics to be employed with EC partners (Seldon 1995: 133). In the mid-1980s, David Williamson, in charge of the European Secretariat, had been highly regarded by both Howe and Mrs Thatcher. The Foreign Secretary believed that Williamson was able to temper Mrs Thatcher's worst instincts on the EC. She appears to have listened to him more closely than she did to his successors.

But monetary policy was a difficult terrain for the European Secretariat to enter. It has always been dominated by the Treasury and the Bank. This tradi-tion was maintained on EMU, and the Secretariat was not the lead agency. Indeed, the European Secretariat played little role at any stage. Instead, David Hadley, its head (July 1989–February 1993), served as Britain's second represen-tative on the IGC on political union, alongside Kerr. Hadley was deeply involved in co-ordinating policy on political union; by contrast, he never attended any of the IGC meetings on EMU. In a more limited manner, officials from the Secretariat provided support in more specialized tasks (such as legal drafting) for the Wicks committees, for Britain's representatives on the IGC, and for the team at Maastricht.

Rather more involved from the centre was Sarah Hogg, the head of the Policy Unit in the Prime Minister's Office under Major from 1990 to 1995. The Unit was created in 1984, to be a body more focused on serving the immediate needs of the Prime Minister than its predecessor, the CPRS, had been (Hennesey 1990: 657–8). Hennesey notes that under Mrs Thatcher the 'Policy Unit was hers to its last paperclip' (1990: 658). During the Thatcher period, its head, Brian Griffiths (1985–90), had given little attention to European matters. Griffiths had felt shut out on Europe by Charles Powell, Mrs Thatcher's key aide. If there was a failure

---

[35] On the Cabinet Office, see Bender (1991); Lee (1995: 152); Hennessy (1990: 390); Civil Service Yearbook (Aug. 1992); Dowding (1995: 140–4); Bulmer and Burch (forthcoming).

to prepare and plan positions on EMU in 1988–9, then an obvious target of such criticism would be the Policy Unit under Griffiths. The Unit is dependent, though, on the lead it is given. In any event, the Major government had to confront the reality of the IGC on EMU. As an ex-financial journalist, Hogg monitored the progress of the Wicks Committee for the Prime Minister by attending its meetings. Indeed, she saw her role as reporting back, rather than as actively intervening in the Whitehall committee. This role was no doubt convenient to all: as a result she did not threaten the Treasury's turf neither did her activities conflict with Wicks's responsibility as the lead official on EMU. Hogg acted as Major's intellectual bodyguard and political adviser, focusing on the short term. But she was in no position to challenge the Treasury's political supremacy or its technical expertise.

Whilst Wicks was the lead official for the Treasury, his senior colleagues remained somewhat distant from the EMU negotiations. Terry Burns, for example, as Chief Economic Adviser, was involved in policy discussions on EMU with the Chancellor, but was much less involved in matters of strategy in relation to the negotiations. By contrast, several officials beneath Wicks played a key supporting role. Paul Gray, like Wicks, had also served at Number Ten. He was Economic Affairs Private Secretary under Mrs Thatcher and, briefly, under Major, from 1988 to 1990. He then moved to the Treasury as Under-Secretary in charge of the Monetary Group, a post from which he served on the Wicks Committee covering the IGC and, indeed, headed a subcommittee dealing with the more specific, technical items. Following the return of David Bostock from UKRep in 1989, he became Under-Secretary and Head of the EC Group in the Treasury (1990–4). In 1991, the draft of the UK opt-out on EMU was supervised by a Treasury lawyer, Mark Blythe, who is said to have produced such a complicated and detailed text that it would inevitably be seen as being 'over the top' by Britain's EC partners. Yet, such work was fully in line with the meticulous, tightly controlled operation of the Treasury on EMU. For command over detail, Major looked to Wicks and his colleagues who fed him numerous long briefings.

The Wicks Committee played a key role in London. Its functions were typical of such committees: to allow the lead department to test wider Whitehall opinion so as to gauge the bounds of acceptability, and to keep the rest of Whitehall informed of the progress being made. The committee helped to validate the Treasury's policy position: an important need given the highly charged political atmosphere. But a common criticism of such committees—especially those led by the Treasury—is that they are designed to keep rival departments at bay.

On a range of technical issues, however, like convergence and, more obviously, the ECB statutes and banking supervision, the Treasury needed to coordinate with the Bank. The Gray Subcommittee of 1990–1 was specifically designed to allow close co-operation between the Treasury and the Bank. Its membership was drawn exclusively from these two bodies. The consultation mechanism of both sets of committees was not intended to—and nor did they—undermine the Treasury's hold over the EMU portfolio. Moreover, with the developing momentum of the IGC, both the Wicks and the Gray Committees became more distant from the action. By the second half of 1991 their role was less important. So much of the action was taking place in Brussels, at such speed, that the Whitehall committees could not keep pace with the growing portfolio.

In sum, the character of the co-ordination in London, and its particular nature, emphasized the degree of tight control exercised by a relatively few senior officials. Moreover, such exclusivity on EMU could be found in other national capitals, such as Rome. Amongst the departments of Whitehall, the Treasury was, with minor exceptions, able to maintain its lead position on EMU and to defend its 'turf'. There was little challenge to its position: the FCO, the Cabinet Office, and the Prime Minister's Policy Unit were all kept at bay. Only Kerr, as UK Permanent Representative in Brussels and, to a lesser extent, Crockett as the Bank's International Director, encroached upon the supremacy of the Treasury. But Kerr's input was largely one of tactics: advising on what would 'fly', what was the most effective defence. Wicks and the Treasury played the central role throughout. The institutional norms and traditions of the Treasury thus infected how EMU was handled.

The Treasury and EMU

The Treasury is 'a quintessentially British institution' (Stephens 1996: 233). Its contemporary strengths and weaknesses are symptomatic of the general predicament of the British government. As a policy-making department, rather than a policy implementer, it has a relatively small staff, though by tradition this staff is drawn from amongst Whitehall's best (Hennesey 1990: 395). Its internal structures are based on 'a flexible, adaptable, and highly responsive command structure; small, well-integrated central divisions' which recognize the importance of good and fast communication (Thain and Wright 1995: 179–80). Overall, it has a strong collective identity and exhibits an overwhelming self-confidence (Hennesey 1990: 396; Pliatzky 1989). Such traits serve as an important bulwark against the rest of Whitehall: the Treasury must claim a special expertise to maintain its dominance (Heclo and Wildavsky 1974: 42). Its power rests on the importance of money to government and the extensive intelligence network it has by virtue of its systems of financial control, reaching into every other department.

Yet the unchallenged hegemon in Whitehall has had to adapt to the different policy styles and bargaining politics of the EC. Philip Stephens, an informed journalist with *The Financial Times*, has made some trenchant criticisms in this regard. Despite the Treasury's involvement in European monetary co-operation, he argues that its culture has 'remained stubbornly British' (1996: 233). Indeed, whilst it is 'true that small groups of officials travelled regularly to meetings in Brussels, Washington, Paris and Bonn . . . The contacts with other finance ministries and central banks . . . rarely went beyond these formal meetings'. In consequence, 'There was no real intelligence, no network of personal relationships to inform the government of the private thinking elsewhere in Europe' (1996: 233). Dowding (1995: 129) also notes that Treasury officials have traditionally been the least enthusiastic supporters of the EC in Whitehall.

Yet it is difficult and hazardous to generalize about the European adaptability of the Treasury. On the face of it, there are the institutional mechanisms available to allow the Treasury to develop a strong EC awareness. These mechanisms include the secondment of its own officials to UKRep in Brussels; the negotiations on the annual EC budget; the importance of ECOFIN and the EC Monetary Committee; and the strength of domestic lateral co-ordination in Whitehall. Yet, there are important contrasts to be drawn in the internal workings of the Treasury. These contrasts give rise to differing images of the department on Europe. Indeed, it is more difficult to refer to a 'Treasury' view on Europe than it is to speak of an 'FCO' view. For the period covered here, at least, European policy was 'ghetto-ized' within the Treasury. A relatively small number of Treasury officials had meaningful contact with their European counterparts. As one Treasury official put it, the people right at the top of the Treasury were not 'Brussels focused', unlike their counterparts in Bonn, Paris, and Rome. 'Europe' was not central to the department's business and was often seen as an unwelcome intrusion. The history of Britain's wrangles over its EC budget payments had taken its toll, and the Treasury's system of requiring compensatory cuts in domestic spending for extra EC funding (termed 'EUROPES') offered some encouragement to a Eurosceptic perspective amongst its officials.[36]

Wicks was an exception: EC monetary co-ordination was at the top of his agenda. Moreover, as already noted, Wicks was much respected in EC monetary circles, not least as the man who coped with an impossible ministerial neckbrace on Europe. But beyond him and his immediate officials, there was little depth of expertise on European matters. Those less involved in European policy tended to be criticized as 'insular, preoccupied with domestic problems and displaying deep scepticism about Europe', as one senior insider put it. Whilst Littler was the British representative on the EC Monetary Committee, his colleagues back home were apt to distance themselves from European matters by referring to the EC as 'Littler-land'. This contrast between the rather more pro-European attitudes of staff involved in international, rather than domestic, matters, has been paralleled in the Bank of England.

EC participation produced institutional frustrations for the Treasury. It could intervene strongly in discussions in Whitehall on EC policy. But ministers from other departments were able to attend Council of Ministers' meetings beyond its 'control', and with a limited scope for accountability later. To the Treasury's dismay, ECOFIN proved slow to develop the sort of control over other areas of

[36] On EUROPES (pronounced 'Euro-pez'), see Bulmer and Burch (forthcoming); Dowding (1995: 138–9).

EC policy that the Treasury thought necessary on the basis of its own domestic experience. The Treasury also contrasted its own domestic control over Whitehall departments with what seemed to be the weaker reach of finance ministries elsewhere in the EC. Thus, whilst EC participation had given a significant institutional boost to the FCO, the same could not be said for the Treasury. The one tended to see it as an opportunity, the other as something of a headache. Such frustrations could encourage Eurosceptic-type instincts and signals.

The Old Lady, the Treasury, and the Europeans

The Bank as an institution is marked by three characteristics which affected its input into the EMU process. First, the Bank's role has meant that it has been a rather more internationalized body than the Treasury, on the whole, has been. Bank staff were thus by instinct more likely to favour constructive engagement in European matters, though again a crucial contrast appeared between its international and domestic divisions. Secondly, in its internal structure, the Bank is dominated by its Governor: he sets the climate of opinion in which others must operate. Leigh-Pemberton's stance on EMU thus had to be supported and protected; later, George's innate scepticism held greater sway. Finally, by tradition, the Bank and the Treasury are highly defensive in their working relations with each other. This detachment was reflected in their co-ordination on EMU.

The Bank's role has always perforce been locked into an international network of central bankers, based on the Bank for International Settlements (BIS) in Basle, established in 1930. In the postwar period, these contacts grew with the Intra-European Payments Agreement, the European Payments Union, and the Group of Ten, though the BIS remained the chief institutional anchor (Dyson 1994: 48–9). In 1964 the EEC created the Committee of Central Bank Governors, again based in Basle (Dyson 1994: 70). The Bank has a long tradition of positive engagement in such international fora, helping to design viable international policies and building up credibility with its foreign peers. Notably, it could define its role on the Delors Committee in these same terms. Whilst the Chancellor of the Exchequer and the international finance officials in the Treasury were also very much involved in some of these same networks (the IMF, World Bank, Group of Ten, OECD), the 'club' of international and European central bankers has proved stronger (Dyson et al. 1995). Bank of England officials tend to know their international counterparts rather better than do those of the Treasury. Moreover, within this European 'club' Bank officials would rarely feel as isolated on EMU matters as did the men from the Treasury. The Treasury's knowledge of the thinking in other central banks was also very much dependent on the indirect channels of the Bank of England (led by Leigh-Pemberton, Loehnis, and then Crockett) (Stephens 1996: 233). Given the importance of the Bundesbank, and even the Banque de France, to the EMU process in general, to the launch of the hard ECU and to the operation of the ERM, this distance from other central banks was a significant constraint on the Treasury's intelligence resources.

During the period of the EMU debate, the Bank of England took a number of organizational initiatives to deal with the issues that it raised. An informal committee was created to shadow the Delors Committee. This committee was an expanded version of the group that briefed the Governor for the monthly BIS/Committee of Central Bank Governors' meetings. It comprised Anthony Loehnis, Lionel Price, Christopher Taylor, John Arrowsmith, Robert Lindley, Michael Lewis, and occasionally Eddie George (then Home Finance Director). Its briefings for Leigh-Pemberton on EMU began in the summer of 1988 with a history of European monetary co-operation. In doing so, it eschewed the larger political issues and focused on the practical issues of how EMU might be built. This approach was fully in keeping with the Governor's own pragmatism. Later, in March 1990, a European Division was created, headed by Lionel Price and then by Michael Foot. This division was to co-ordinate all policy relevant to Europe. It fed the European Steering Committee, which was chaired by the Governor himself and comprised all the Bank's directors. An EMU subcommittee was also created, chaired first by Loehnis and then by Crockett, and composed of some dozen or more officials. A foreign exchange subcommittee dealt with ERM issues. The flow of information and decision clearly went via the Governor. This flow was testimony, in part, to Leigh-Pemberton's own pro-European stance. It also involved a desire to keep his more sceptic Deputy, Eddie George, from taking the lead in this area. In any event, each of these reforms reflected the higher priority that the Bank now accorded to European co-operation.

Many of the reforms did not survive into the Eddie George period. The European Division proved to be short-lived. Whilst George Blunden (Deputy Governor, 1986–90) had pressed for its creation, one of his successors, Rupert Pennant-Rhea (1993–5) sought its disbandment. In July 1994 it was restructured out of existence, just months after the start of stage 2 of EMU. This move was fully in line with the philosophy of the new Governor, Eddie George (1993), an innate Eurosceptic. The restructuring was justified on the grounds that specialist EC analysis should not be left in an isolated compartment, but be integrated into operational work. The change of climate within the Bank—from the period of Leigh-Pemberton to that of George—was also reflected in the Bank's loss of most of the senior personnel previously involved in the European Division.

The Bank has traditionally been a very hierarchical institution, a feature that affected its relations with the Treasury. In the 1950s all communication from the Bank to the Treasury would pass via the Governor. This control protected the Governor's autonomy. As one senior insider put it, 'The Bank is by tradition a very authoritarian regime: it works through the Governor . . . There is reason for such paranoid behaviour: the Bank in reality has more status than power, it is the Treasury's preacher, so its only safeguard is to intervene at the highest level'. Stephens also notes that the Bank had influence, rather than authority, over British monetary policy (1996: 276). Power was lopsided: 'The Treasury owns the foreign currency reserves, has responsibility for any decisions on interest rates, and has the final say over operations in the government securities, or gilt-edged, market'.[37] In short, 'The Bank essentially is its [the Treasury's] agent' (1996: 83). Tensions between officials in both institutions have been a long-term feature of their relationship. As one Whitehall observer put it, 'The Bank has a certain paranoia about being pushed around . . . The Treasury sees the Bank as being underworked and overpaid; the Bank certainly has a more sedate working climate'. On EMU, these features were certainly evident in the way that Bank staff dealt with their Whitehall colleagues during the period of the Delors Committee. Moreover, the willingness of Leigh-Pemberton to go out on a limb and sign the Delors Report was a shock to the established norm of Treasury supremacy on monetary policy.

Beneath Leigh-Pemberton was Eddie George (promoted to be Deputy in 1990; Governor from 1993 onwards). He developed a much stronger personal political profile with Mrs Thatcher and Lawson than was the case with his predecessors (Stephens 1996: 69). His profile was enhanced by his own knowledge of economics. As noted above, George had established an axis with Sir Alan Walters and Sir Peter Middleton (Treasury) in the early 1980s, which determined much of monetary policy. Leigh-Pemberton as the 'gentleman-chairman' tolerated such contact as well as any likely clandestine intrigue. In part, no doubt, Leigh-Pemberton's own passivity had encouraged such activity. George had thus accommodated himself to the prevailing political climate. He would do so again when he quickly shifted to champion the 'hard' ECU proposal.

The FCO: Talking European

As is already clear, EMU brought both the Bank and the Treasury into a close working relationship with the Foreign Office (FCO). The FCO, not surprisingly, has a relatively small economics team. A chief economic adviser headed a team of less than a dozen economists. But their work had shifted to focus on Europe more and more. The FCO in the 1980s believed that a European issue like the ERM was legitimate territory for it to encroach upon, though the Treasury always resisted such moves. A paper setting out the economic arguments for ERM entry was prepared by the FCO's economic advisers and sent from Howe to Lawson in August 1985. This engagement was mostly a consequence of Howe shifting from the Treasury to be Foreign Secretary in 1983. Howe brought with him an increasing interest in the ERM, thereby enhancing the internal role of the economic team in the FCO (Simon Broadbent and Jim Rollo, both advocates of constructive engagement). Howe had separate bilateral meetings with Lawson during the period of the Delors Committee in which both agreed that

[37] The respective roles of the Bank and the Treasury were subsequently revised under the chancellorships of Kenneth Clarke and Gordon Brown.

the strategy should be for the UK to enter the ERM as a means of slowing down progress on EMU (Howe 1994: 577; and see above). This manoeuvring culminated in the Madrid 1989 ultimatum presented by Howe and Lawson to Mrs Thatcher and Howe's own resignation from government in 1990. Howe's immediate successor, Major, was in post too briefly to establish such priorities, and Hurd as Foreign Secretary (1989–95) was never really interested in economics. The ERM issue never properly engaged the FCO in conventional channels of policy co-ordination. It was far too highly charged an issue for that. Instead, it was a matter of ministers and officials being engaged in cabals and cliques to counteract Mrs Thatcher on both principles and tactics. The prevailing atmosphere at this time cowed officials across Whitehall from being too assertive on the issue.

The FCO had learned to tread warily with Mrs Thatcher. It had lost its nerve in the context of the outbreak of the Falklands War, and it had lost credibility at Number Ten (in contrast to the Treasury) in the bitter disputes on the EC budget. Mrs Thatcher derided the FCO, mouthing clichés to the effect that it represented 'foreigners' rather than the British. In 1987, just prior to the relaunch of the EMU debate, relations between Mrs. Thatcher and the FCO were at one of their lowest ebbs and the Prime Minister considered hiving off EC policy to another department, such as the Cabinet Office (Hennessy 1989: 405; Dowding 1995: 138). For a generation the FCO had advocated 'constructive engagement' for Britain in Europe, whilst EC membership has also boosted its institutional reach in Whitehall (Hennessy 1989: 404–5; Dowding 1995: 129).

By the time of the IGC negotiations, the ERM issue had been settled and the debate had shifted. The FCO's first priority was the political union portfolio. In this regard it was obliged to work closely with the European Secretariat in the Cabinet Office. The head of the Secretariat, David Hadley, chaired a regular series of meetings on political union which involved a wide range of Whitehall departments. Given that 'political union' was a broad and varied portfolio, the FCO could not lead on this in anything like the way that the Treasury led on EMU. The FCO's absorption in political union had consequences. A greater FCO input on EMU would have given greater priority to Britain's overall strategic interest and to 'constructive engagement'.

The FCO's contribution to the Wicks Committees on EMU involved both its own senior official on the EC (Kerr, then Michael Jay) together with the UK Permanent Representative in Brussels (Hannay, then Kerr).[38] The number was thus very limited. The FCO's relations with the Treasury over EMU were very much focused on the working relationship between Kerr and Wicks on the IGC, not least because of Kerr's own career experience at the Treasury. Jay had more of a watching brief on the Wicks Committee for the IGC. He was fully involved in planning meetings with Hurd, Lamont, and Major. He later co-ordinated the general briefing document for Major to take to Maastricht, though Wicks

---

[38] Jay served as the lead FCO official on the EC from 1990–5; in 1996 he became Ambassador in Paris.

prepared the EMU section. Unlike Kerr, however, Jay had little or no experience of monetary matters and his attention was primarily focused in other directions. The FCO's relations with the Bank never had any reason to be subject to the 'turf-fighting' disputes that the latter had with the Treasury. Certainly, Hannay and Kerr were frustrated at the tactics of the Bank during the Delors Committee, but there was to be no repeat clash of that kind.

EMU Cocooned

The foregoing analysis has outlined how EMU as a policy responsibility was managed at the level of officials within the core executive. It has been argued that it was kept enclosed within a cocoon of senior officials. Traditional norms and practices were evident throughout: only a few senior officials were involved; the lateral co-ordination was kept on a very tight rein; and the Treasury maintained its dominance in monetary matters. Indeed, the supremacy of the Treasury was maintained over the normal processes of EC policy co-ordination that have developed in other sectors. Central Whitehall departments—the Cabinet Secretariat, the Policy Unit—were kept at bay. The main novelty in the process of domestic co-ordination was that Kerr (as Head of UKRep in Brussels) was parachuted into it, and he played a key role as an individual.

It is somewhat misleading, however, to stress the role of the 'Treasury' *per se* in this process. It was the Overseas Finance section that handled the matter under Wicks. The involvement of other senior Treasury personnel (Middleton as Permanent Secretary and Burns as Chief Economic Adviser) was limited. This partial involvement at the top of the Treasury contrasts with the situation found in Bonn, Paris, and Rome.

Moreover, whilst the Whitehall cocoon involved relatively few, it was also cut off from outside intervention. There was, perhaps, little scope for external intervention, given the nature of the IGC process, and few appear to have sought it. But the vital aspect of this process was that Whitehall did not invite such intervention. Little consideration appears to have been given by those 'inside' the process to the potential costs of such isolation.

The final element of the core executive—and of the 'Whitehall cocoon'—is that of the ministerial lead and Cabinet discussion. It is already clear that ministers were operating in a relatively narrow, tightly defined, and enclosed world of officialdom when it came to EMU. Ministerial action did not disturb this pattern. Indeed, it had largely set the narrow bounds itself.

Only a few are called: Ministers and EMU

The background to co-ordination on EMU was the turmoil within government over the possible entry of the pound into the ERM, discussed earlier. Mrs Thatcher had sought to 'control' the dispute, which became more a matter of cabals and cliques than the normal fare of Whitehall coordination. The ERM

issue not only distracted Whitehall's attention; it also meant that early preparations on EMU in 1988–9 were handled in a somewhat oppressive and perplexing
atmosphere. As one senior official put it, 'With policy so disorganized, officials
were unclear what they were expected to deliver: they remained very inhibited'.
Mrs Thatcher, and her adviser Charles Powell, became more defensive, even distant, from the Whitehall system. Like the officials, ministers also recognized the
highly charged atmosphere and the dangers in dissension.

By 1990, a pattern of Cabinet involvement had already been set. The Cabinet
received reports on the progress of the early and tentative discussions on EMU
and EPU (European political union). It did not, however, function as a delibera-
tive body with papers circulated prior to an informed discussion. It had rarely
done so on EC matters under Mrs Thatcher. Cabinet discussion tended not to
focus on the grand picture, but rather on short-term tactical considerations.
Neither the full Cabinet nor the relevant Cabinet committees were very important in shaping policy. The real discussion took place between the Prime
Minister and the Chancellor and/or the Foreign Secretary, with a few select
officials present. Howe in his memoirs notes how meetings of small groups of
ministers were a growing feature of the Thatcher governments. Mrs Thatcher
'liked them . . . because membership of each group could be chosen to suit her
own thinking' (Howe 1994: 458). On occasions, Mrs Thatcher also liked to
involve outsiders as a stimulus to new policy-thinking that broke free of
Whitehall (Urban 1996: 90). In short, under Mrs Thatcher, the Cabinet as a body
was not in a position to exercise leadership on policy and strategy in relation to
Europe.[39] Yet, in so far as the Cabinet remained distant from the process, this
pattern parallels that found in the cases of France, Germany, and Italy.

This centralization of the policy process stemmed from the setting of foreign
policy-making in Mrs Thatcher's later period. Craddock, Mrs Thatcher's
Foreign Policy Adviser, noted that this was one of 'a highly centralized administration, increasingly concentrated about one figure; a Prime Minister repeatedly
re-elected, growing in authority and, as it seemed, in success; an atmosphere at
No. 10 of hyperactivity and close loyalty; a view of the world that was simple,
clear and dogmatic' (1997: 30). Howe also observed her increasingly imperial
style. To her 'there was no distinction to be drawn between person, government, party and nation' (Howe 1994: 691).

Despite differences in self-perception and style, Major essentially sustained this
modus operandi for the Cabinet when he became Prime Minister. Once the IGC
negotiations were under way, Norman Lamont as Chancellor of the Exchequer
would make regular monthly reports to Cabinet on the progress of the EMU
negotiations, whilst Douglas Hurd did the same on EPU. Such reports were
largely pro forma: Lamont tended to say relatively little and there was not much
debate. Similarly, the pre-IGC draft treaty provisions on the 'hard' ECU were

[39] The operation of the Cabinet system, in general, varies greatly across different policy sectors
(Burch and Holliday 1996: 259). The role of the Cabinet may also vary according to other factors, such
as the party in power and style of leadership (Burch and Holliday 1996: 150–1).

reported to Cabinet, but they were not subject to much debate. The essential decisions on this document had already been taken by Major, Lamont, and Hurd.

The institutional route followed by EMU was steered by the Treasury. The Cabinet committee system was adapted to deal with the demands of the IGCs. The senior committee in this area was the Ministerial Committee on Defence and Overseas Policy, or OPD, which was small and chaired by the Prime Minister himself. Several meetings of the committee were held to cover the business of the two IGCs. The composition of the committee was, however, enlarged, for these purposes. Thus, when EMU was discussed, it was in the context of the enlarged version of OPD, chaired by Major. The enlargement of the committee made its composition close to that of its own subcommittee on European Questions, known as OPD(E). The latter was always chaired by Hurd, as Foreign Secretary. The Treasury and Lamont were keen, however, not to have EMU discussed by a committee chaired by Hurd and the FCO. The Treasury garnered Cabinet Office support to have OPD meetings on the IGC on EMU. Thus, OPD dealt with EMU, though it looked rather like OPD(E), given its extended composition, with the novelty of the PM in the chair. In reality, OPD(E), chaired by Hurd, only considered political union, which was also discussed at times in the enlarged OPD format.

The inclusion of officials in the OPD and OPD(E) meetings was limited. Kerr, as Permanent Representative in Brussels, had privileged access to both types of meetings, though he was not always free from his Brussels commitments to attend. When he did, he was 'in attendance' at OPD(E) meetings and allowed to speak. He also attended the special OPD meetings on the two IGCs and answered questions put to him by Major. Kerr's role here, as Permanent Representative, was exceptional and it gave him an overview of ministers' views. It is rare for non-Cabinet Office officials to attend meetings of Cabinet committees. Thus, Wicks did not attend the OPD or OPD(E) meetings. But it was unlikely that he incurred any significant disadvantage by not doing so; the crucial meetings were elsewhere and he was often involved in these.

In any event, there were not many Cabinet committee meetings. Some of those involved are dismissive of their importance, for reasons similar to those already noted for the Cabinet itself. The more important discussions were those between Major and Lamont, sometimes with officials such as Wicks and Kerr present, sometimes with Hurd included. Sarah Hogg was involved in many of these meetings, particularly when the Prime Minister met Lamont alone. At times, Lamont would also meet Hurd alone on EMU. Small group meetings of these different types were much more frequent than Cabinet committee meetings. Indeed, they became more so in the last weeks before Maastricht. Such meetings were broadened when the discussion involved the subject matter of the other IGC (e.g. including Michael Howard at Employment or Kenneth Baker as Home Secretary).

Officials found that some of these meetings lacked sufficient focus on the specifics of the IGC agenda. They would complain of a lack of direction being given to them as negotiators. The broad parameters of government policy were clear, but an IGC requires a mass of technical issues to be addressed. In IGC meetings Wicks had to extemporize on occasions, to fill in the gaps in his brief from London. This practice further enhanced his key role in the negotiations.

Major sustained a close interest on EMU throughout. In committee meetings he would often indicate that EMU was his chief concern. Major sought to be well briefed, from various sources: by the meetings he had with small groups of ministers and officials; by his own direct briefings from Kerr and Wicks; and from the messages he was given by Sarah Hogg on the progress of the Wicks Committee. Hogg helped him understand some of the technicalities. Major knew Wicks well from his days as Chancellor, and he placed great trust in him.

Major's close involvement in EMU matters was a result not only of the intrinsic importance of the subject and his own career background in banking and finance. That background shaped his attitude of caution and risk aversion on EMU. But another factor encouraging Major to take a 'hands-on' role was Lamont. It was not only Lamont's views on EMU in the 1990–1 period which became the subject of much subsequent dispute, but also the firmness of his ministerial grip. Lamont had an intellectual air about him, a reflective style which seemed opposed to the diligence required by his office. Lamont appeared disorganized and distracted. In reality, his reputation was often lower outside the Treasury than inside. His closest officials were loyal, but they also had a better appreciation of his style. Nevertheless, beyond the Treasury, fellow ministers and senior officials complained of his negligence: of him not being prepared to absorb his briefs on EMU.[40] The result, they alleged, was that the Chancellor had insufficient grasp of the subject and gave too weak or too distant a direction to negotiators. A common complaint was that he was too dependent on his young Private Secretary, Jeremy Heywood. Heywood was seen as having to cover up for Lamont's inattention.[41] Lamont also relied on him for advice. Away in Brussels, Lamont was reportedly inclined to phone back to London to ask Heywood his opinion on advice given to him by senior officials, such as Kerr and Wicks, who were on the spot. Kerr and Wicks found it somewhat galling to be told by Lamont that 'Jeremy' did not think theirs was a good idea!

Lamont was, by general consent, a poor negotiator: ill at ease in large setpiece negotiations and lacking the skills to gain allies, such as Bérégovoy and Waigel, in private conversation. At a crucial moment in the Maastricht European Council, Lamont walked out of a meeting of finance ministers when it proceeded to discuss Britain's opt-out. Some critics charge that the walk-out was more to do with the fact that he had not mastered his brief and that he was having difficulty answering the questions being raised, rather than any British

---

[40] Seldon (1997: 375) reports a similar view from the 'inside'. Lamont, he writes, 'was never industrious or very able, and was carried by his civil servants'.

[41] In 1998 Heywood moved from the Treasury to the Prime Minister's Private Office under Tony Blair. The *Financial Times* described him as a 'high-flyer', 'impossibly young and extraordinarily bright'(*FT*, 13 Feb. 1998).

'bulldog' defence. Certainly, such histrionics failed to impress his fellow European ministers. The British opt-out was part of the deal that the other governments would be asked to ratify and their ministers thus had a right to review all aspects of the Treaty. Hardly anyone doubted Lamont's intellectual competence: he would have understood the technicalities better than many finance ministers. According to his critics, the problem was his lack of concentration.

Lamont was loyal to Major's policy line on EMU and he did not appear to feel outflanked by the Prime Minister on EMU. He was, however, in a difficult position and one which undermined his ability to control policy planning. After all, the Prime Minister had started with the EMU brief whilst Chancellor (October 1989–November 1990); he knew it well. He knew and trusted the lead officials, Wicks and Kerr, from his Treasury and FCO days. They briefed him directly, as well as in joint meetings. In addition, Sarah Hogg gave him separate briefings. Major practically had as much access to the developing EMU brief as did Lamont. The Chancellor was surrounded by a network that he did not control. The network had not been created to 'conspire' against Lamont—it stemmed from the peculiarities of an IGC. But the activism of the Prime Minister was facilated by the IGC, and he used it to maximum effect.

By contrast, Hurd at the FCO appears to have been given much more space to handle the other IGC. Both Tristan Garel-Jones, his Minister of State, and Kerr were much more respectful of Hurd's qualities and role than either were of Lamont. They were both close to Major: the difference in what they communicated to him about Hurd's and Lamont's negotiating performance would have been telling. Also relevant to Major's handling of the two IGCs was his own high respect for, even deference to, Hurd on foreign affairs. Major had been at the Foreign Office much too briefly to get a proper grip on it; by contrast, Hurd was an FCO man to the core. Major's forte was within the domain of the Treasury. Hurd's commitment to constructive engagement helped him to limit Britain's isolation on political union. Weeks after the collapse of the Berlin Wall, the British were negotiating with the French (Jean-Pierre Chevènement) on new forms of defence collaboration in Europe. Later, in October 1991, Hurd managed to secure a joint declaration on CFSP (Common Foreign and Security Policy) and defence with the Italians (October 1991). The British stance on political union was never as isolated as it was on EMU. But, in addition, Hurd's diplomacy reinforced Britain's engagement in the central debate. The situation contrasted sharply with Britain's strategy and mandate on EMU.

Ministerial co-ordination on EMU has thus become a matter of some controversy. The character of the rest of the co-ordination process is less open to dispute. It was tightly controlled, involved few, and maintained a clear and consistent voice in the negotiations. The narrowness of the domestic co-ordination process was matched by a rigidity at the EC negotiating table. What Britain's negotiators had to sell was not what many, if any, wished to buy. EMU may have been a case in which 'crack troops have been put at the disposal of confused strategic objectives' (Wallace 1997: 687). But the foregoing suggests that the

Whitehall machine was itself culpable in the elaboration of those objectives. In process and policy-thinking, Britain maintained a semi-detachment from the EMU debate.

Conclusions

This chapter has provided a prologue to the drama of Britain's handling of EMU policy. It is a deep and substantial prologue, as the approach to the main acts—including ERM entry—proved so tortured. Rarely have so many major figures been slain before the main action begins; the drama of the response to EMU opens with blood across the stage. Yet the themes presaged in the overture came to haunt the subsequent drama.

More definitively, the priorities and strategies noted on the ERM find expression in the subsequent acts on EMU. This chapter has noted the common problems of cognition and strategy exhibited at the time of the launch of the EMS and of EMU. The inner turmoil of the Thatcher government on these matters was amply illustrated by the analysis of how it considered entry between 1985–90. This record established certain foundations on which the subsequent EMU response would be based. Ministers and officials could be identified with contrasting priorities and strategies. The division between Europhiles and Eurosceptics was, in the main, a consistent one between the ERM and EMU debates of the Conservative government.

Yet, historical fortune also played its part in determining Britain's response to EMU. Mrs Thatcher survived as Prime Minister the crises of the Falklands War in 1982 and of the Westland affair in 1986 when either might have brought her down and led to a softer British stance on Europe. Similarly, in November 1990, if Michael Heseltine had won the Tory leadership contest, he would probably have adopted a more positive stance on EMU than that pursued by John Major. Contingent domestic factors served to determine the outcome in each case, but with far-reaching consequences. This feature emphasizes the impact of Mrs Thatcher's and John Major's leadership on the course of British policy on EMU, testifying to the importance of agency in this account. A change of leader in any of these instances would probably not have led to a dramatic shift of policy—the British debate was too circumscribed for that—but even lesser changes could have had significant consequences.

The forces shaping the debate on EMU had deep cultural roots. The emphasis on national sovereignty, globalism, gradualism, and following the market were part of the British political tradition and they framed the response to EMU. Political leaders—Europhile or Eurosceptic—and the key officials were embraced by this tradition. As a result, support for Europe was more a matter of calculation—often isolated and short term—rather than emotion and idealism. Policy on EMU was confined in another sense: it was made within the Whitehall 'village', more isolated from domestic intervention than is often the case in other areas. Administratively, policy was co-ordinated by an efficient machine. The way the machine processed the policy and gauged strategy was structured by a complex combination of a narrowly set ministerial lead and the inherited beliefs and practices of Whitehall officials.

By the time EMU reappeared in 1988, the contours of the British response were already largely set.

14

Resisting EMU: Political Strategy, Policy Entrepreneurship, and Policy Reflection before the IGC

The setting of the new agenda for EMU in 1988 caught Whitehall off guard. It was still in the throes of a bitter internal dispute over whether sterling should join the ERM; it was ill prepared for the new debate; it underestimated the momentum of support for EMU elsewhere in the Community; it misjudged its own strategy for blocking progress; and it was left to react to an agenda increasingly out of its control. Such problems can be seen as the latest manifestation of a long-term problem for Britain in Europe. As Young has noted, Britain has suffered because she has 'not been able to take control of developments in the Community; instead at the best, she has simply been able to delay and dilute initiatives' (1993: 181).

On EMU, Britain did, however, come forward with its own alternative proposals: first for a competing currency, then for a common currency. The problem was that different motives lay behind their promotion. Most of Britain's partners rightly detected that Mrs Thatcher was advancing them for *tactical* reasons—to *delay or dilute* EMU—rather than to engage in a debate about contrasting designs for a viable route to EMU. Other ministers, such as Howe and Major, did seek a more constructive negotiating position, which tended to replace stridency with confusion. This ambiguity of purpose was compounded by the timing of their launch. The first scheme was launched too late, whilst the second was advanced both too late and in too rigid a fashion to win sufficient backing from Britain's partners.

The failure to restructure the EMU debate in Britain's direction can be attributed to many of the factors discussed in the previous chapter. These factors covered the cognitive dimension (e.g. differences of cultural understandings, the sense of Britain's position in the world, and the narrowness of policy calculations), the problems of party management (the political straitjacket imposed on European policy by ministers), and the institutional setting (the norms and practices of Whitehall).

But the specific failure of Britain's two alternative schemes was also the result of a strategic weakness. This weakness derived, first, from overestimating the British ability to steer the EC agenda. In reality, Britain alone did not possess the necessary monetary power or intellectual influence. Secondly, there was a failure to understand the strength and structure of the EMU debate amongst

Britain's EC partners. The Thatcher government misjudged the balance of political forces on EMU in other member states and its effectiveness at the EC level suffered as a result. This was most notable in relation to Germany. In 1988 it misinterpreted the caution of the Bundesbank and the reservations of its President (Pöhl) as offering reassurance that nothing much was likely to happen on EMU. It failed to understand the weakness of Kohl's domestic position and the consequent scope for Genscher to be assertive at the EC level. This miscalculation was crucial. It meant that London was ill prepared to respond to the new momentum on EMU. The failure of Britain's two alternatives has to be seen first, therefore, in this earlier context.

Caught off Guard: Hanover and the Delors Committee

Before 1988, there was perhaps little reason for Britain to fear the emergence of a new agenda on EMU. Indeed, the Thatcher government had felt that in the previous three years the EC tide was going in its direction (see Charles Powell, quoted in Grant 1994: 89). The thorny problem of Britain's budget payments had been resolved (at Fontainebleau, June 1984). The Thatcher–Delors relationship was relatively more amicable then than later (Grant 1994: 88). London supported South European enlargement. More notably, the government believed that the EC agenda was moving its way: the philosophy of the single European market seemed Thatcherite in its essentials. The Conservatives were to look back on this period as the 'high point' of their European influence. Indeed, there was much reason for them to feel comfortable with 'Europe' in this period: unusually, it seemed more of an opportunity than a threat. No clouds appeared on the horizon.

On the whole, ministers paid little attention to the reference in the Single European Act confirming that EMU was a Community goal. This reference was judged to be no more than the relatively meaningless declaratory politics in which the EC often indulged. Lawson has claimed that he sent a minute to Mrs Thatcher at the time of the Single Act arguing against EMU being included in the text. If so, his warning was ignored. At the time, the Belgians, Italians, and the French had pushed for a strong commitment to EMU to be included in the new Act, but Delors thought that the final outcome was derisory. The Kohl government had been successful in establishing that any move to EMU would require the adoption of a new EC treaty. Both the Germans and the British appear to have regarded this stipulation as a major wall of defence against any precipitous step being taken. The British felt they had common cause with the Germans on future moves towards EMU.

In short, in 1988 London either gave scant attention to the new debate on EMU or was sceptical that it would lead to anything serious. The government was in any case distracted by its deep internecine internal struggle over exchange rates and Britain's membership of the ERM (Thompson 1995, 1996).

Ministers failed to pick up the signals. Mrs Thatcher did not give EMU much attention. More suprisingly, given their interest in the ERM, neither did Lawson or Howe. Nor did most of the senior civil servants in the Foreign Office, the Prime Minister's Office, and the Treasury. Within the Bank of England no meaningful examination was made of the emerging EC debate in the first part of 1988. As a result, London underestimated the significance of the papers circulated by Edouard Balladur and Giuliano Amato, the French and Italian Finance Ministers, in the first weeks of 1988 on the strengthening of the EMS and also the later papers from Hans-Dietrich Genscher (Foreign Minister) and Gerhard Stoltenberg (Finance Minister) of Germany. The examination of their content appears to have been considered as a technical exercise for officials, rather than as meriting the political attention of the top echelons in Whitehall or the Bank.

Moreover, none of these early moves passed through the normal EC channels (Monetary Committee, COREPER). Article 102a of the Single Act had indicated that any moves to EMU would have to pass through the Council of Ministers (ECOFIN) and the EC Monetary Committee. This route would involve the hard-nosed sceptics of the finance ministeries, rather than the 'unpredictable' world of EC diplomats.[1] In the event, the omens were there to read; though not necessarily where London might have expected to find them, and they were not able to be communicated down a single, clear institutional channel.

The failure to recognize the momentum behind EMU in 1988 was a major instance of how the British 'machine' could get it wrong on Europe. This episode was a key turning-point in the development of the EC and the cost of being out of step was high. An opportunity existed to revise or divert the EMU initiative before it progressed further. But London was ill prepared to seize this opportunity. As noted in the previous chapter, the lack of preparedness had deep roots. It stemmed from the attitudes adopted towards 'Europe' and the way in which Whitehall approached it. More specifically, the 'intelligence' failure combined misinterpreting the signals and the inadequate communication of them. No doubt official messengers feared what might happen to them if they delivered an unpopular message. The oppressive political climate in which senior officials were operating on anything remotely connected to the ERM was not conducive to effective communication. But Whitehall officials themselves underestimated the political momentum on EMU amongst Britain's partners. To some extent there were domestic factors leading the Treasury to be distracted: in particular, the increasing concern over inflation at home. For various reasons, the main point is that London had its eyes off the EMU ball before Hanover.

The Thatcher government had rejected any necessary link between the establishment of the single European market and a single currency. Indeed, London was not convinced by the so-called 'inconsistent triangle' of policy objectives outlined in the Padoa-Schioppa Report of April 1987. This report gave a gentle

---

[1] Indeed, the EC Monetary Committee had blocked Delors in his attempt to have a more ambitious provision on EMU in the Single Act.

nudge in the direction of a fresh look at EMU. 'Monetary policy coordination and the mechanisms of the EMS will have to be significantly strengthened if freedom of capital movements and exchange rate discipline are to survive and coexist', it argued (Padoa-Schioppa *et al.* 1987; also Dyson 1994: 118). But London disagreed. Indeed, its rejection of a necessary linkage was shared at this time by many other EC finance ministries and central banks. The EC Monetary Committee had rejected such a link in a paper to an informal ECOFIN meeting in May 1988 at Travemünde prepared by its Chair, Geoff Littler, from the Treasury.

Side-Stepped at Hanover

Against this background, the European Council meeting at Hanover in June 1988 saw the Thatcher government ill prepared for any new EMU initiative. This lack of understanding was reflected in the Prime Minister's own comments afterwards to the effect that she did not expect to see EMU occur in her lifetime (Grant 1994: 120).

Mrs Thatcher's unreadiness was compounded by the less than intimate political relationship she had with Chancellor Kohl at this time (see also Chapter 13). Just over a week before Hanover, Mrs Thatcher met Kohl at the G7 economic summit in Toronto. She had an hour's private meeting with him. She understood that he would propose a committee of central bankers to study EMU, rather than another formulation. Mrs Thatcher felt the prospect of her being able to stop a committee being established was 'ebbing away' (1995: 740). But Kohl had reassured her with the emphasis on the inclusion of central bankers: they would bring realism, even scepticism, to the discussion. Kohl did not, however, discuss with her the more contentious notion of Jacques Delors chairing the committee. This proposal would arise only at Hanover. For her part, Mrs Thatcher restated to Kohl her 'unbending' opposition to an ECB being set as an objective. This issue was, she thought, the critical one, as it would make EMU a more tangible goal.[2] In the event, she succeeded in avoiding any such reference in the final communiqué. She also managed to have deleted any reference to the creation of a single currency (Grant 1994: 120). Mrs Thatcher felt she had scored a victory. But, in truth, she had misjudged the game.

The Hanover meeting established what became known as the Delors Committee on EMU. Whitehall had had no advance notice of Delors—an EMU devotee—being chosen to head it. Nor was it involved at all in determining the composition of the rest of the committee.[3] Mrs Thatcher had felt it difficult to say no to Delors as Chair: she did not yet regard him as a demon; and she had just backed his reappointment as Commission President. Nevertheless, the deci-

[2] Officials, such as Sir David Hannay, the UK Permanent Representative in Brussels, appear to have reinforced the assessment of the ECB issue as the key one at Hanover.

[3] Kohl proposed Delors as Chair in a discussion at dinner on the first night (Grant 1994: 120). No one rejected the proposal, so Kohl asked Delors to set about drawing up the conclusions on this point.

sion to have Delors chairing the EMU committee and the remit given to it unleashed a powerful momentum behind EMU and a single currency: precisely the outcome Mrs Thatcher was trying to avoid. The committee was given 'the task of studying and proposing concrete steps leading towards this union'. In other words, the committee was not to consider *whether* EMU should occur: there was a recognition that it had already been agreed in the Single Act that it should. Instead, the committee was to work out a path to that goal. Mrs Thatcher misinterpreted the signals. She judged the central bankers to be a blocking device, rather than a legitimating mechanism.

The Treasury was surprised by the decisions reached at Hanover. It soon felt that the Delors Committee gave too much power to the Governor of the Bank of England, who was acting in a personal capacity. The Treasury's turf was threatened: progress on EMU was being made beyond the confines of ECOFIN. Moreover, Lawson as Chancellor had not been consulted by the Prime Minister about possible moves on EMU prior to Hanover. His relations with Mrs Thatcher had already become tense because of their dispute over ERM entry. Thus, Lawson notes that 'she did not even seek my advice, choosing to rely almost exclusively on Charles Powell' (the PM's Private Secretary) (Lawson 1992: 902). Moreover, Mrs Thatcher barely had a better opinion at this stage of Geoff Littler, the Treasury's lead official on EC monetary matters and then Chair of the EC Monetary Committee. He was already seen as an ERM sup-porter. Number Ten's relations with the Treasury—ministerial and official—on Europe were strained and detached. This distance only served to heighten the anxieties in the Treasury over what might develop.

To Lawson and the Treasury, Hanover was badly mishandled by Number Ten. 'The others, when they discovered where she stood at Hanover, must have been amazed at her innocence', he writes in a somewhat self-justificatory man-ner (Lawson 1992: 903). The responsibility for the strategy pursued at Hanover does seem, though, to lie with Mrs Thatcher and Powell. Powell has since com-mented that, 'we thought the Delors Committee was a good way of sidelining the idea. Kohl told us it was just a committee. We underestimated the other side' (Grant 1994: 120). Moreover, Mrs Thatcher's insistence on avoiding any ref-erence to the creation of a European Central Bank seemed to be contradicted by the remit of the Delors Committee. When challenged about this in the Commons, by Neil Kinnock, she replied that, 'Monetary union would be the first step, but progress towards it would not necessarily involve a single currency or a European Central Bank' (*House of Commons Debates*, 30 June 1988). The idea that a monetary union would not involve these features was cited by her critics as suggesting that the Prime Minister had not properly understood the subject. Lawson dismisses Mrs Thatcher's statement as 'positively mind-boggling' (1992: 904). For his part, Howe makes no substantive reference to this turning-point in his memoirs. He too, as Foreign Secretary, appears not to have appreciated the full significance of the creation of the Delors Committee. To Mrs Thatcher, Powell, and Howe the proposal to have the committee composed, in the main, of central bank governors actually seemed to offer reassurance. The hard-headed central bankers were unlikely to be carried away by EC euphoria; in particular, Mrs Thatcher expected Karl-Otto Pöhl of the Bundesbank and Robin Leigh-Pemberton of the Bank of England to form common cause to put the brakes on any move to EMU. In any event, the matter would come back to the heads of government the following year at Madrid.

The Delors Committee

Mrs Thatcher had placed great store by the likelihood that Pöhl and Leigh-Pemberton would scupper the EMU initiative (Thatcher 1995: 708), and Howe had followed her lead (1994: 576). Mrs Thatcher had a good personal relationship with Pöhl. She had invited him to be a guest whilst she was on holiday in Switzerland; and she admired the Bundesbank's anti-inflation record. For the Delors Committee, however, she misjudged the basic attitude of this somewhat mercurial figure. On the Delors Committee, he indicated that he was in favour of EMU as an objective, but he was a hard-headed realist on how it might be reached. Pöhl had his own difficulties on the Committee: colleagues saw him as indolent and distracted. Moreover, his subsequent statements seemed inconsistent.[4] In any event, Mrs Thatcher's roadblock for the Delors Committee had been misconstrued.

As part of an Anglo-German summit in Frankfurt on 19–20 February 1989, Mrs Thatcher visited the Bundesbank President. Her aim was to strengthen his resolve in opposing EMU. But her style undermined her purpose. She gave Pöhl a stern lecture and her didactic manner stunned her Bundesbank hosts. The lecture appears to have produced little benefit for the British. When the Delors Report was published, Mrs Thatcher was angered that 'his known opposition to the Delors approach simply was not expressed' (Thatcher 1995: 708). She had considered him 'strongly hostile to any serious loss of monetary autonomy for the Bundesbank' (1995: 708). Yet, the Delors Report envisaged a European monetary institution that had a stronger status even than the Bundesbank, offering reassurance to Pöhl.

There was a lesson here which went unheeded: a strategy that placed great emphasis on German support was not buttressed by any rigorous check by Whitehall on whether the Germans would actually fall into line. No check was made on Pöhl. Similarly, in 1989–90 insufficient attempts were undertaken to ally fully with the Bundesbank on the 'hard' ECU alternative advanced by London. The Thatcher government was not adept at EC coalition politics. Mrs Thatcher too readily assumed that the president of a central bank with such an

---

[4] After the Madrid European Council the following year, which had considered the Delors Report signed by Pöhl, Mrs Thatcher quoted a speech made by Pöhl on 22 June 1989 which struck a negative note. Pöhl was quoted as saying that the requisite renunciation of sovereignty was premature, and that neither an ECB nor a single currency were necessary for an EMU to function (House of Commons Debates, vol. 155, col. 1112, 29 June 1989).

enviable record for monetary discipline would be 'one of us'. She misunderstood not only Pöhl, but also the politics of the Bundesbank. The Bundesbank President was much less his own master than she assumed. Lamont would make a similar mistake when chairing an informal ECOFIN meeting at Bath in September 1992.

Nor could Mrs Thatcher rely on Robin Leigh-Pemberton. A consensual, clubbable personality, he was not a natural rebel to stand out against his immediate peers. His personal relations with Mrs Thatcher were not good: before finishing his term he would have at least one spectacular row with the Prime Minister. Thatcherite 'bloody-mindedness' was not his style, nor did he wish to be seen as Mrs Thatcher's poodle. He jealously guarded the status of the Bank of England against Whitehall pressures. For him, professional reputation and credibility amongst his fellow governors were at stake. European central bank governors form a tight-knit club, focused on the Bank for International Settlements (BIS) in Basle and the EC's Committee of Central Bank Governors (CCBG) (Dyson et al. 1995).

More to the point, before Hanover, Mrs Thatcher had never had a serious discussion with him on EMU; she had no direct knowledge of his true views. She suspected Leigh-Pemberton of being in consort with Lawson on the ERM and on tying the pound to the D-Mark. But she was probably unaware of his generally pro-European views. He had shown his sympathy for the ERM with his close involvement in the discussions of the CCBG which led to the Basle–Nyborg Agreement of September 1987 (on this, see Dyson 1994: 121–3). Whilst he certainly brought to the committee a pragmatic attitude that disavowed idealistic rhetoric, the question before the committee was couched in deceptive, technical terms: how could EMU be established? He could sign up for this technician's report. Indeed, he signalled this very interpretation of the pending Delors Report in a speech in London in February 1989. The eventual report, he said, should not be seen as advocating EMU, but as answering the technical questions that underlay it.

The Delors Committee met eight times at the BIS headquarters in Basle, between September 1988 and April 1989 (Grant 1994: 121). It is clear that Leigh-Pemberton proved himself to be no 'push-over' either in his dealings with Whitehall or in the deliberations of the committee. He had just been reappointed as governor for a second term and, smarting under some press criticism, he was determined to demonstrate that he was his own man.

The impact of Leigh-Pemberton on the committee can be noted in three ways. First, he failed to build any effective alliance with Pöhl. He attempted to do so from the beginning, mainly on the fringes of the Basle meetings.[5] Each time he felt that Pöhl was in line, Pöhl either failed to deliver or did so only weakly. Both did, however, successfully block the first draft of chapter 1 of the Delors Report, which listed reasons as to why a single currency was a desirable

---

[5] In parallel to these moves, Anthony Loehnis sought to build an alliance via Wolfgang Rieke of the Bundesbank.

goal. Both were appalled by this draft: it compromised the stance that the committee was dealing with a technical design for an objective set by the politicians. With this exception, though, Leigh-Pemberton soon realized that Pöhl could not be relied upon. Thus, his first negotiating strategy had collapsed.

Secondly, Leigh-Pemberton decided not to submit a full paper to the committee, setting out an intellectual case for a different way forward. Such a course was urged on him by Mrs Thatcher (Thatcher 1995: 708) and by Lawson (1992: 909). Leigh-Pemberton was the only major member not to have a paper in the annex to the report: a fact that caused some embarrassment to staff at Threadneedle Street subsequently. But Leigh-Pemberton's style was not as a counter-intellectual, setting out an alternative technical blueprint. He lacked the training. In any event, he was in an exceedingly difficult political position in this respect. A draft paper had been prepared within the Bank, mainly by Robert Lindley. Some, like John Fleming and John Arrowsmith, supported the idea of the Governor submitting such a paper. The arguments against doing so, however, were too powerful. Politically, it would overexpose the Governor at home on such a highly charged issue. Procedurally, it would be difficult for the Bank not to show any such paper first to the Treasury. If the latter objected to any part of its content the Bank would be in a quandary as to how to react and Leigh-Pemberton's position on the committee would be compromised. Nevertheless, the Bank's decision not to submit its own draft paper meant that it had missed an early window of opportunity for Britain to be more fully engaged in the intellectual debate on EMU and to help steer its course. This decision was critical for Britain's position in relation to EMU. It also meant that British economists were less fully involved than they might have been. The preparatory work was very much in the hands of the international staff of the Bank.

Instead, the third aspect of Leigh-Pemberton's work was that Bank staff supplied him with a whole series of partial amendments to the draft report of the committee. As a lawyer, he was well suited to dissecting the detail, and he had been well briefed by his staff. But, at its last meeting, he was not able to press for the adoption of each of the amendments: he sensed that Pöhl and others were becoming bored and losing patience with the British position. Pöhl had already indicated his intention of signing the committee's report. Leigh-Pemberton sought to have the committee make some concessions to him to ease his own domestic political position. He played on their sympathy for his plight.

The main thrust of the amendments that he did press was to introduce a much greater conditionality into the recommended route for EMU, and to help block any strong commitment to a system of fiscal transfers. A 'francophone' bloc led by Jacques de Larosière had managed to have the report endorse the irreversibility of a decision to embark on a transition to EMU (paragraph 39).[6] Yet, Leigh-Pemberton was able to hedge this commitment in a later clause

---

[6] The clause states that the 'decision to enter upon the first stage should be a decision to embark on the entire process'. It thus suggested an automatic link between stage 1 (and ERM membership) and full EMU.

(paragraph 43). This paragraph noted that the conditions for moving from one stage to another cannot be defined precisely in advance. Indeed, the report argued against any commitment to a timetable (paragraph 15). Such conditionality was close to the Whitehall preference for gradualism and flexibility. Moreover, Leigh-Pemberton helped to block Maurice Doyle of Ireland obtaining a strong commitment on a system of fiscal transfers. Instead, the fiscal transfers were to deal with stability matters—differential shocks to member states—and not to differential income levels. Both sets of contribution—inserting a greater conditionality into the way forward and opposing new fiscal commitments—were designed to signal Leigh-Pemberton's determined defence of British positions.

But Leigh-Pemberton knew the domestic political pressures. By the last stages of the Committee's work, he felt isolated. At home, Leigh-Pemberton discussed whether he should resign as Governor: the counter-pressures were so great. He was already in his second and final term as Governor. Yet, faced with the intense pressures emanating from the Thatcher camp—not a group to pull their punches—his decision to go ahead and sign the report, even in a personal capacity, took great courage. His fellow members of the committee certainly recognized this and there was much regard for his fortitude. At home, however, the response from the Thatcher government was coldness and silence. To his severist critics, Leigh-Pemberton was guilty of treachery. Others simply felt he had rushed ahead of what was feasible for the UK. In any event, Mrs Thatcher failed to reply to a letter from the Governor and the two did not see each other for most of the next year.

The government had been forewarned of the report, and ministers had already given up on Leigh-Pemberton as a defender of their position. In her memoirs, Mrs Thatcher records that she had two main meetings with Lawson and the Governor about the work of the Delors Committee on 14 December and 15 February. She concluded that Delors had made all the running (Thatcher 1995: 708).[7] Lawson (1992: 909) reports that the February meeting discussed the draft report, that is, shortly before it was to be agreed and signed the following month. At this very late stage, Mrs Thatcher and Lawson urged Leigh-Pemberton to submit a dissenting statement to be included in the report. He declined to do so. Lawson also recalls that 'it was decided that we ought to prepare a contingency paper mentioning distinctively British proposals for improved monetary cooperation in Europe which would not involve any amendment of the treaty, [but] it should for the time being be kept in reserve and not tabled' (1992: 908). Thus, Leigh-Pemberton had decided against presenting a 'minority report' and Number Ten and the Treasury opted not to act on any 'contingency paper'.

---

[7] Lawson (1992: 907–9), however, refers to there having been a series of meetings, involving Mrs Thatcher, Leigh-Pemberton, himself, Howe, Charles Powell, and 'usually' Brian Griffiths (of the PM's Policy Unit).

The Treasury was furious with the Governor. The anger stemmed from the lack of reference he was making to the Treasury (and the committee headed by Nigel Wicks) between the Delors meetings (discussed in Chapter 13). The Treasury wanted to have greater 'control' over him. Lawson had managed to circumvent the Bank's stonewalling attitude and obtain an early draft of the Delors Report from the Brussels office of the UK Permanent Representative. But Treasury staff continued to berate their Bank counterparts for their unforthcoming approach at home.[8] This clash was the source of a lingering animosity for some time afterwards. To the Treasury, Leigh-Pemberton again exercised too much freedom of initiative when the CCBG later discussed the Draft Statutes for the European Central Bank.

At the FCO, Howe was also disappointed by the content of the Delors Report and Leigh-Pemberton's role in it (Howe 1994: 576–7). Howe 'certainly did not exclude the eventual possibility of EMU', but he did not wish to be bound to any notion of irreversibility (Howe 1994: 576). The UK's Ambassador in Brussels, David Hannay, appears to have shared Howe's sentiments and to have acted on this basis in the Wicks Committee shadowing the work of the Delors Group. For the FCO, the prime objective was to decouple the different stages of EMU, to avoid automaticity. But the immediate task of both Howe and Lawson, prior to the European Council in Madrid in June 1989, was to gain Mrs Thatcher's approval for sterling's entry into the ERM, as discussed in Chapter 13. Entry, they believed, would give Britain more influence over the steps to be taken after the Delors Report (Howe 1994: 577).

Before then, Lawson had already launched a pre-emptive strike against the Delors Committee's expected conclusions. His arguments would underpin much of the British government's position on EMU for the next year or so. On 25 January 1989, he made a speech at Chatham House in London in which he stressed the dangers of EMU to national sovereignty. It was clear, he said, that EMU 'implies nothing less than European Government—albeit a federal one— and political union: the United States of Europe'. That was 'simply not on the agenda now, nor will it be for the foreseeable future'. Any attempt to move towards EMU would be 'deeply divisive and damaging' to the EC. The push to EMU was either a result of 'carelessness' or of a 'smokescreen to obscure the lack of sufficient progress towards the Single Market'. Indeed, 'neither the British Government nor the British Parliament is prepared to accept the further Treaty amendment which the President of the Commission evidently envisages'.[9]

---

[8] Though Lawson had obtained an early draft of the Delors Report at a time when the Bank was refusing to supply the same, Treasury staff seem to have continued to hide their prized possession by haranguing Threadneedle Street for a copy!

[9] Lawson's reference here is to the speech by Jacques Delors in presenting the Commission's new annual programme to the European Parliament. Delors had spoken of the prospect of another IGC to amend the institutional provisions of the Treaty of Rome (for EP debates, see *Official Journal of the EC*, Annex 2-373, speech of 17 January 1989).

After the Horse had Bolted: Britain's Response to the Delors Report

The publication of the Delors Report in April met with immediate opposition from the British government. Lawson fired off a series of political salvoes: mus-ket-fire to scatter the enemy. After an ECOFIN meeting in Luxembourg on 17 April, Lawson repeated his warnings against EMU. EMU implied a United States of Europe; this was not on the agenda; the government could not agree to a treaty amendment (*Independent*, 18 April 1989). The ECOFIN meeting failed to give a ringing endorsement of the report. Whilst Lawson had attacked it, Bérégovoy (France) had defended it, though Waigel (West Germany) and the rest had said little. It was clear that a battle was looming at the forthcoming meeting of the heads of government in Madrid.

But the British went to Madrid embroiled in another domestic bargaining game. If a year earlier, at Hanover, Mrs Thatcher had taken her eye off the ball in relation to EMU, at Madrid she was very much on the touchline. As noted in Chapter 13, the three senior Cabinet ministers—Mrs Thatcher, Howe, and Lawson—were collectively involved in a bitter dispute over whether sterling should be placed in the ERM. Howe and Lawson both felt that ERM entry would place Britain in a stronger position to ward off EMU. Indeed, at their encouragement, Sir Leon Brittan, now an EC Commissioner in Brussels, arranged to see the Prime Minister to reinforce that same argument. Each of them failed, though, to move Mrs Thatcher from her opposition to both the ERM and EMU. There may have been an opportunity for the UK to exercise more clout. An informal ECOFIN meeting in S'Agaro on 20 May gave a less than full endorsement of the Delors Report (Lawson 1992: 920). Lawson had again attacked the report and Delors appeared deeply disappointed by the reac-tion of the EC ministers. However, Mrs Thatcher's intransigence cut Britain off from any such spoiling tactics. Her own approach yielded few gains. At Madrid, she agreed to clarify the conditions on which Britain would enter the ERM.

Moreover, she adopted an unusually 'calm, quiet, measured' tone in the sum-mit meeting when it discussed EMU (Howe 1994: 582). Mrs Thatcher herself was: 'of course, opposed root and branch to the whole approach of the Delors Report. But I was not in a position to prevent some kind of action being taken upon it' (Thatcher 1995: 750). The admission that she was unable to prevent progress on EMU is telling. The Prime Minister was constrained by the Howe–Lawson ultimatum on ERM entry, but she failed to deploy ERM entry as a bargaining lever with her Community partners. Thus, she had the worst of both worlds. On the one hand she was forced to shift on the ERM—in response to the Howe–Lawson ultimatum—though not to the point of actual entry. On the other, the shift came too late and was not utilized as a means of gaining more bargaining strength with the rest of the EC. Howe and Lawson had wished to extricate British policy from what they saw as the overly rigid stance adopted since 1985 on the ERM. But policy was not properly extricated. The shift was too little, too late. Instead of bargaining gains, there came a perception of vulnerability. Her EC colleagues saw Mrs Thatcher as being on the defensive, ceding ground.

In the same vein, when Mrs Thatcher reported back to the Commons on the Madrid outcome, she was surprisingly effusive in her praise for stage 1 of the Delors Report. Her comments came despite the fact that it was based on a requirement of ERM entry. No matter, Mrs Thatcher declared that it was 'very much in the interests of British industry and the City of London, while fully protecting the powers of this House' (*House of Common Debates*: vol. 155, col. 1110, 29 June 1989). She found the Madrid conclusions 'sensible and practical'. She believed progress on using the ECU might be speeded up.

Whilst it is also true that Mrs Thatcher indicated her line of opposition on EMU at Madrid, she was left floundering somewhat on the sidelines. She indicated that Britain had serious difficulties with stages 2 and 3; it could not accept a single currency; and it intended to bring forward its own alternative proposals. But the Madrid summit did move ahead on EMU, though not in a dramatic manner. The commitment to EMU was reaffirmed and a date for stage 1 agreed. Despite British objections, it was accepted that there was to be an IGC after stage 1 had begun. Yet its precise start-date (and, not suprisingly, its conclusion) were left open. The UK appended a separate declaration asserting that there was 'no automaticity' about stage 2. Later, Mrs Thatcher told the Commons that, 'We have ensured that there is nothing automatic about the move to the subsequent stages' (*House of Commons Debates*: vol. 155, col. 1109, 29 June 1989). Yet, rather like her victory the previous year at Hanover—avoiding any reference to EMU involving a European Central Bank—this triumph proved to be hollow. Then, as now, the central issue was the agreement to move ahead: then it was the establishment of the Delors Committee, now it was the commitment to an IGC.

Indeed, the decisions made on EMU at Madrid signified that an agenda had now been set. From here on, the British government was obliged to react to the path mapped out in the Delors Report. Its first response was to bring forward alternative proposals to those of the report. The problems that these alternatives encountered were to do with their timing and with the perception that the British motive was not to help build EMU but rather to bury it. The alternatives merit careful attention for these reasons, for what they indicate about the path chosen on EMU by the other eleven states, and for the light that they shed on Britain's relations with her partners.

Britain's Belated Alternatives: The Competing Currency and the Hard ECU Plans

The Madrid European Council had placed Mrs Thatcher on the defensive over EMU. Her response was to claim, somewhat cavalierly, that Britain had her own ideas on EMU separate from those of the Delors Report. The government would bring these forward to broaden the terms of the EC debate. This reaction showed Whitehall to be waking up too late. The Delors Report had already been accepted and set a very different agenda.

The weakness and confusion in British strategy also became evident in the launch of two consecutive proposals. The first was for a system of competing currencies (published in October 1989); the second was for the creation of a parallel currency, or a 'hard' ECU (published in June 1990). The second alternative was sustained until the final stages of the IGC on EMU, in the autumn of 1991. But neither elicited much support in the Community.

The likely failure of both schemes left the British to start thinking of a fall-back strategy on EMU. From the middle of 1990 onwards—just after the actual launch of the 'hard' ECU proposals and well ahead of the commencement of the IGC—Whitehall began to consider pressing for a separate 'opt-out' on EMU. The British strategy thus became a dual one. If it could not set the negotiations on a different track, then Britain would give itself the option of jumping off the train. Whitehall's deliberations on the opt-out strategy will be discussed in Chapter 15. First, it is necessary to examine the fate of Britain's bid to alter the EMU agenda.

Both sets of proposals—the competing-currency plan and the notion of a parallel currency—failed because of a similar set of factors:

1. Both were originated by the Thatcher government, an administration that had a history of being isolated as the 'awkward partner' (George 1990). Its reputation was of not wishing to see 'Europe' built. Its proposals on monetary cooperation thus met with an instinctive suspicion.

2. Within the Thatcher and Major governments there were such divergent views on Europe in general, and EMU in particular, that they would inevitably find it difficult to sustain a clear and consistent consensus behind the alternative proposals. The purpose of the proposals was thus always liable to conflicting interpretations, both at home and abroad.

Indeed, the conflicting attitudes towards the 'hard' ECU plan held by Sir Geoffrey Howe and Margaret Thatcher would lead the former to resign and provoke a leadership challenge, the result of which would be the Prime Minister's downfall in November 1990. In short, the attempt to establish an alternative European policy would have far-reaching domestic political consequences: the end of the Thatcher era.

3. At the Community level, the Delors Committee had already rejected the principles on which the British alternatives were based. Indeed, it had established a momentum—sustained by the Madrid summit—behind a different conception: specifically, that of a *single* currency—not a system of competing or parallel currencies. In Pöhl's paper to the Delors Committee, the Bundesbank's hostility to such notions was clear for all to read. There was a problem of timing here: the proposals may have made more headway if they had been launched much earlier. The period before, or even during, the deliberations of the Delors Committee would have been more opportune, given that this stage was the one

when ideas were beginning to be set. But to put forward alternatives in the autumn of 1989, and then to try to have another bite at the cherry the following summer, suggested that London was underestimating the momentum that had already been established behind EMU. It struggled to adapt to this momentum; its proposals always seemed to refer to yesterday's debate. Launching the proposals when it did simply seemed to magnify the distance between Britain and the other eleven and increased the perception that a wrecking strategy was at work here.

4. It was unclear how the two British alternatives met the diverse interests of other EC governments. Some governments—especially the French and the Italians—sought a *single* currency in order to overcome the power of the D-Mark. A system of competing currencies or a parallel currency would be liable to leave the Bundesbank and the D-Mark dominant. Their concerns about dependency on Germany were thus not addressed by the British proposals. On the other hand, German critics feared the lack of monetary discipline that they identified in the British alternatives. The Bundesbank found the British proposals technically flawed. Concerns were expressed about the possible effects on inflation, the control of the money supply, and the co-ordination of monetary policy generally that might result from the adoption of such proposals.

5. The British failed to exploit the opportunities that did exist for the promotion of their alternatives. There was an area of uncertainty in the developing plans for EMU—about stage 2 and how to make it viable—which provided scope for competing technical arguments. For most of Britain's partners, however, the decisive point was that schemes adopted for stage 2 should be clearly seen to lead directly to the objective set for stage 3: a single currency. To Britain's partners, this question seemed to elicit obfuscation from London. As a result, the opportunity to create new, countervailing alliances was lost.

Some of Britain's partners did find merit in the hard ECU proposal; albeit, to a limited and temporary extent. French officials had thought in terms of a parallel currency since the 1960s. The original Genscher Memorandum of February 1988 had talked of the ECU as a possible parallel currency, but this notion was set aside by the Delors Committee. Later, the Spanish government sought to build on the 'hard' ECU notion and advanced its own version, in the clear recognition that it was part of a transitional process to a *single* currency. Pierre Bérégovoy and the French Trésor were for a time attracted by the fact that the British plan did not require the independence of the Banque de France. Hans Tietmeyer reported to his EC colleagues that the Bundesbank was considering proposals for hardening the ECU, though not for a parallel currency, whilst Horst Köhler in the German Finance Ministry was interested in the substance of the proposal. Yet the French and German interest was not sustained, and the British were not able to build a bridge with the Spanish—all because the British disagreed with the single-currency objective. In consequence, the British were not adept at building alliances, and their case remained an isolated one.

In sum, critics of the British alternatives charge that they failed because they were put forward by the wrong government, at the wrong time, in the wrong manner, and for the wrong reasons.[10]

The 'hard' ECU scheme became enwrapped in the different leadership styles of Mrs Thatcher and John Major. Under Major, the 'hard' ECU became the means by which the British could become more closely engaged with its partners in the EMU debate. A new vigour was brought to the scheme, and officials were sent to sell it to the rest of Europe. But the scheme had been launched whilst Mrs Thatcher was Prime Minister and her approach to it emitted very different signals to Britain's partners. Across both governments, the 'hard' ECU was a distraction: one of modest impact across the Community, but of much greater force domestically. The British debate on EMU and the planning and preparation of the government and the Bank of England were each led off course by it, as Sir Leon Brittan in Brussels repeatedly warned the government. The 'hard' ECU became a mirage, blurring domestic perceptions of the European scene.

The 'hard' ECU highlighted the problems of officials negotiating on Britain's behalf. Its adoption filled a glaring vacuum in Britain's negotiating position. Without it, Britain had nothing else to say other than 'no'. But, by the time Mrs Thatcher stepped down as Prime Minister, it was clear that the plan was dead in EC circles: it had won insufficient support. From this point onwards, key officials in Whitehall and the Bank realized that Britain's stance had to adapt and move closer to that of its major partners. Not to do so would leave Britain isolated and without influence. Instead, senior officials pressed for greater flexibility: in particular, for an accommodation with the long-term goal of a single currency. But their political masters were adamantly opposed. The dilemmas of officials negotiating on this brief were ignored.

For his part, John Major was to be intimately associated with both of Britain's alternatives. The first, the competing-currency plan, was passed to him at a time of crisis: when he succeeded Lawson. The plan's launch had been botched, whilst the second alternative—the hard ECU—was all but sunk by Mrs Thatcher herself. Major was dealt an almost impossible hand. He was already faced with the problem of reconciling a priority to maintaining party unity with a commitment to 'constructive engagement' for Britain in the new EC debates. But this problem was exacerbated by the confusions and contradictions that underpinned Britain's two alternatives. Such confusion was, perhaps, an inevitable result of the disunity in the party and government on almost anything to do with Europe. Confusion hid, or appeased, the irreconcilable. Yet, if Britain's alternatives were going to have any mileage in them, then clarity and commitment were needed. The Thatcher government was unwilling to give such leadership and this heavily circumscribed Major's strategic effectiveness.

---

[10] This interpretation was advanced by Tristan Garel-Jones (Minister of State for European Affairs at the FCO shortly after the scheme had been launched) in *The Times*, 21 June 1993.

What to bring back from Spain? A Competing Currency

The history of the first alternative scheme—for a system of competing currencies—was relatively short. It began at the Madrid summit, at a time when the rest of the Community had more or less endorsed the path to a *single* currency outlined in the Delors Report. To much surprise, Mrs Thatcher announced to the press after the summit that the British Treasury was already working on alternative plans. Lawson in his memoirs recalls that:

The first I and my senior officials knew of this proposal was a report on the radio from Madrid which stated that the Treasury was already working on alternatives to Delors. Peter Middleton subsequently told me that he heard the news when driving his car, and was so astonished that he nearly crashed into a tree. (Lawson 1992: 939)

Mrs Thatcher repeated the commitment later in the Commons (29 June 1989).

In truth, Treasury officials had been thinking of various ideas, but they were far from ready to go public with them. Nevertheless, Lawson pursued an alternative scheme, inviting staff to submit their ideas. He soon took up the notion of a 'competing currency'. This need to come up with a new idea appealed to Lawson. According to one insider, he enjoyed 'sprouting ideas'; he was 'always interested in doing dramatic things'. Some of his officials found this tendency difficult to fathom, uncertain of his commitment. His position of support for (a hard) ERM but opposition to EMU was seen by some as illogical: the effect on monetary discipline was quite similar.[11] Nevertheless, following Lawson's lead after Madrid, John Odling-Smee (Under-Secretary, then Deputy Chief Economic Adviser, at the Treasury) prepared a draft, much of the work on it being done during August 1989, the close season. Odling-Smee chaired a group working on this idea which also involved, from the Bank of England, John Flemming, Michael Foot, and Christopher Taylor. For the first time in the EMU debate, and somewhat belatedly, close working relations were established between the economics sections of both the Bank and the Treasury. In any event, Lawson so disliked this draft that he decided to present the idea orally to the ECOFIN meeting in Antibes in September 1989; giving his personal imprint on the proposal. The formal paper was not circulated until some weeks later (2 November 1989).[12] The impression was of a hurried and uncertain gestation.

Even worse, from the start, the plan's purpose was unclear. If it was to build bridges with Britain's partners, then even Lawson found the Odling-Smee paper to be so purely Hayekian in its philosophy that it would not be credible to the rest of the EC. Not surprisingly, it was the intellectual inspiration from Hayek in the plan that appealed to Mrs Thatcher. In her memoirs she recalls it as 'an in-

[11] See article by Peter Jay in the *Financial Times*, 6 Nov. 1992.

[12] See: 'An Evolutionary Approach to Economic and Monetary Union', HM Treasury, London; 2 November 1989.

genious alternative' (1995: 716). The proposal was approved at a meeting of Mrs Thatcher, Lawson, Major (Foreign Secretary), and Ridley (Trade and Industry) on 25 October 1989. Treasury officials were astonished that Mrs Thatcher went along with the idea as it assumed sterling's entry into the ERM at a time when the issue still split the Prime Minister and Chancellor. Yet in reality, British motives were different. According to Mrs Thatcher, the meeting accepted 'that [the plan's] purpose was mainly tactical in order to slow down discussion of EMU within the Community' (1995: 716). Mrs Thatcher was looking for a diversion, not a technical alternative. Treasury officials quickly realized that 'it was all a game to pull Mrs Thatcher out of a problem'.

The plan was based on the notion that the existing national currencies in the EC might compete for usage by consumers, firms, and institutions. Despite the political machinations surrounding it, the plan had a respectable intellectual pedigree. The single market in financial services and capital liberalization would enable an effective competition among currencies and drive down the transaction costs of switching currencies. Consumers and firms would opt for low-inflation currencies. Because of this ease of exchange, national monetary policies would also be obliged to compete to establish their anti-inflationary credentials. Moreover, the country with the most credible anti-inflation stance would derive the greatest benefit in terms of the lowest interest rates. Critics were quick to identify the shortcomings of the scheme. Inherent in the system of competition would also be a sense of confusion. The circulation of multiple currencies in each country could create a sense of chaos, even monetary crisis, to the ordinary consumer. On the other hand, if differences of national rates of inflation remained low, the usage of foreign currencies at home might remain low. This would defeat part of the purpose of the scheme.

It was the scheme's modesty which appealed to the British. It only involved the implementation of stage 1 of the Delors Report, and no treaty changes were envisaged. In other words, the plan represented no further advance than what had already been agreed at Madrid: another example of Britain reconciling itself to yesterday's agenda and underestimating the momentum of its partners to move further ahead. The competing-currency plan combined a stress on evolution, competition, and co-operation: traditional principles of British policy on Europe in recent decades (Dyson 1994: 136).

The competing-currency plan made little headway in winning the support of Britain's EC partners. Most crucially, it was rejected by the Germans. Though Pöhl indicated in private his agreement with Lawson's analysis of the weaknesses of the Delors Report at Antibes, in September 1989, this agreement did not translate into support for Lawson's alternative plan. The fundamental concern of the Bundesbank was that increased currency substitution would undermine the effectiveness of national monetary policies; and Germany had to be free from any threat to stability-oriented policies. At a CCBG meeting in December, Pöhl floated the notion of a mechanism by which market forces might reward monetary-policy virtue. But this idea was very different and seen as part of a transitional programme.[13] Increasingly, the consensus was for EMU to mean the adoption of a single currency; and it was not clear how or whether the British plan would achieve that goal. A commitment to a single currency was particularly important for the French and the Italians: a competing-currency system (or the later proposal for a parallel currency) was likely to leave the D-Mark dominant. In Paris and Rome the attraction of EMU was precisely to rescue their states from dependency on German monetary policy. The British plan was thus badly framed to win allies to its cause.

Though the competing-currency plan was conceived under Lawson's tutelage, it was to be his successor, John Major, who would be responsible for its launch, after Lawson resigned on 26 October 1989. Indeed, Lawson had resigned the day before he was due to attend an ECOFIN meeting on EMU, where he expected to be promoting his alternative plan (Thatcher 1995: 716). Lawson had been attracted to the intellectual principles of the competing-currency plan, discussing them with his Treasury officials. Major never engaged in this kind of discussion; his instinct was to discern the likely political implications. Treasury officials saw him as having very acute antennae in this regard. Major saw the plan as a means of enabling Britain to be more engaged in the European debate: an instinct he would develop much more strongly later.

Policy Entrepreneurs from the City: A Hard ECU?

Within a few weeks it was already clear to the outside world that the competing-currency plan was dead. However, the government's desire to have an alternative plan to that of the Delors Report was to be rescued by separate initiatives from a young City banker, Paul Richards at Samuel Montagu, and by a former senior FCO official, Sir Michael Butler, now also in the City at Hambros Bank. Butler and Richards were the key policy entrepreneurs at the start. Their initiative emerged in November 1989—in the light of the impending failure of the competing currency scheme—and led to the 'hard' ECU scheme launched by the Thatcher government the following June. Within a few months of the 'hard' ECU being launched, however, it became clear that this second British initiative was also going to founder. It failed to win the active support of any of Britain's partners, though some of them did see potential in developing certain components of it.

The details of the 'hard' ECU only interested the *cognoscenti*. But its adoption by the British also serves to clarify a number of important aspects of the government's perception of the national interest and its conception of strategy in the EC. The 'hard' ECU showed:

- the near-desperation of Whitehall for a proposal to fill the negotiating vacuum on EMU and offer negotiating leverage;

[13] The idea was that central banks would make their monetary growth targets explicit, specific, and comparable. Market judgement would then penalize the wicked and reward the virtuous. See Dyson (1994: 137).

- the ability of outside individual policy entrepreneurs to rescue Whitehall from their strategic impasse;
- the choices opened up for coalition-building as the IGC loomed ahead;
- the disjunction of views between senior officials and ministers on the potential for a strategy based on such a scheme or a revision of it; and
- the limited adjustment to policy countenanced by ministers once it had become clear that the scheme was winning little support.

In effect, the short history of the hard ECU initiative encapsulates so many of the features typical of the British government's stance on EMU as a whole, if not also in other areas.

Genesis

The hard ECU was later said to have emanated from the 'City'. But such an interpretation was not the full story. It passed through the hands of several senior Whitehall and Bank of England officials at a very early stage and was nurtured by them. The sensitivity with which they handled the scheme—maintaining a cautious distance at first, but advising on its best route to the top—was testimony to the pall over official circles on anything to do with 'Europe' at this time. The 'hard' ECU might rescue their position, but they thought it best that they did not make the running with it. A figure who cut across 'insider'/'outsider' boundaries would be an ideal exponent for the scheme.

Sir Michael Butler fitted the bill admirably: he had a foot in both worlds. He was a former UK Permanent Representative in Brussels, but he now chaired the European Committee of the British Invisible Exports Council (BIEC). The committee's purpose was to identify key EC issues of relevance to invisibles exporters and to promote an awareness of their implications.[14] The Committee was not an independent City body, but Butler could use it to help launch the 'hard' ECU idea. This status was strategically important, both to the authors of the 'hard' ECU and to Whitehall.

The committee was more of a privileged insider than an independent outside body. It had been set up in May 1988 by the Bank of England, which asked Butler to chair it and help to select its membership. The committee was to liaise with the Bank of England, the Foreign Office, the Treasury, and the Department of Trade and Industry, each of which were directly represented on the committee, on matters of common concern. The committee normally met in the Bank of England. Overall, the committee cut across 'insider'/'outsider' boundaries, not least in that its composition included current and retired Whitehall mandarins. It was an elite club. The committee had a membership of the 'great and the good'. Sir Michael Franklin, formerly head of the European Secretariat in the Cabinet Office and a man of diverse Whitehall experience, was the Deputy

[14] See 'British Invisible Exports Council—European Committee: Terms of Reference', November 1988.

Chair. Others included John Kerr, then the lead official in the FCO on the EC; the heads of major clearing banks (Sir Jeremy Morse of Lloyds Bank was particularly prominent); the heads of insurance companies; and the Stock Exchange. The involvement of Kerr was especially relevant. He would later be the 'personal representative' for Britain on both IGCs leading up to Maastricht.

Butler led the committee to take a close interest in the Delors Report. With his past experience and connections, he had access at the top. He became active on the issue in various ways. The main thrust of his argument was to urge Whitehall to show greater flexibility and a will to engage in debate as a means of increasing British influence. Butler made representations to both Mrs Thatcher and Lawson on EMU prior to the Madrid European Council. He warned both that the rest of the EC might move ahead without Britain. Indeed, he argued that some of Britain's partners doubted that Mrs Thatcher would actually remain opposed to progress. He noted that they cited her willingness to compromise on the Single European Act in 1985 and on the agricultural budget in 1987 as relevant precedents for this view. In addition, he pointed out that the Single Act had involved a commitment to EMU. Butler criticized Lawson's argument against EMU on grounds of sovereignty. The sharing of sovereignty is a question of degree, he said, and Britain had already agreed to much sharing. Different forms of EMU involved greater or lesser sacrifices of sovereignty. On behalf of his committee, Butler urged the government to negotiate constructively. British exclusion would severely damage the interests of the City. But the government could play it long: urging that progress be slow and measured, and that it should involve a consideration of alternative paths to those outlined in the Delors Report. Less than two weeks before the Madrid summit, Butler met Mrs Thatcher and urged her to accept stage I of EMU, but to seek to slow down progress in other respects. His advice may have had an effect: as already noted, at Madrid, Mrs Thatcher did do most of what he was recommending.

That autumn Butler focused on the preparations for the Strasbourg European Council in December. He argued that the competing-currency plan was inadequate: it was unlikely to be seen by the rest of the EC as a sufficient alternative to stages 2 and 3 of the Delors Report. The government must accept the long-term goal of fixed exchange rates or of a single currency. Such a commitment would be seen as the test of whether Britain was entering the debate constructively. At this crucial juncture, Butler's strategic judgement would be proved to be correct as EMU made further progress in 1990–1. Butler was saying directly what some Whitehall officials were saying or thinking privately. But ministers took little heed of such warnings.

With hindsight, there was a window of opportunity to exploit at this time. But it would not exist for very long, it was not to occur again, and Whitehall was ill prepared to exploit it whilst it was available. London had woken up to the EMU debate too late. In 1988–9 a window existed for discussion on how to create a viable stage 2. But most of Britain's partners looked for a stage 2 scheme that would lead directly to a single currency in stage 3. The British alternatives failed to adapt to this fundamental concern.

The endorsement of the Delors Report had set the EC on a particular course for EMU: one which led to a single currency. An acceptance of a long-term goal of a single currency or of locked exchange rates might have allowed the British to present proposals which could be cast as a pragmatic response to the thorny problem, neglected by Delors, of how to manage the transition. The Achilles' heel of British strategy on EMU was its unwillingness to countenance a single currency as a long-term goal, even though they would later seek to maintain the possibility of 'opting in' at a subsequent period. More flexibility on the definition of the end result would have made the British much more persuasive and effective exponents on the means. Yet ministers seemed impervious to such strategic reflection. Instead, the mistiming of the 'hard' ECU plan, the unwillingness to accept any commitment to go further, and a general negative manner towards the whole EMU debate meant that Britain missed any opportunity that might have existed in the autumn of 1989.

The consequence was that the EMU train continued to move ahead. Mrs Thatcher conceded a start-date for an IGC at the Strasbourg summit in December 1989. Despite her talk of alternatives, Britain was failing to refocus or restructure the EMU debate. As Mrs Thatcher recalls, she 'had little hope of blocking' the establishment of an IGC (Thatcher 1995: 759). She had hoped that Kohl would accept a delay to the IGC, but 'in a classic demonstration of the way in which the Franco-German axis always seemed to re-form in time to dominate the proceedings, Chancellor Kohl went along with President Mitterrand's wishes' (1995: 760).[15] Her comments are an important testimony to the isolation of British strategy. Strasbourg presaged the dilemma for Britain: on EMU, Thatcher could not stop the momentum; and whilst she sternly resisted signing the Social Charter at the same summit, the rest still went ahead anyway. What was apparent also was the cognitive gap between Mrs Thatcher, on the one hand, and Kohl and Mitterrand, on the other, in their approach towards Europe. The latter placed Europe in an historical perspective of which Mrs Thatcher had little appreciation.

Prior to Strasbourg, Butler had outlined his views on the need for constructive engagement in a paper for his committee on 3 November (the day after the formal publication by the Treasury of the competing-currency plan). In the paper, he raised the possibility of a revised British alternative focusing on the further development of the ECU. This had been very briefly mentioned in the Treasury's own paper. Butler highlighted the notion of a *parallel currency* as being the basis for a different kind of stage 2 from that envisaged by Delors. Butler forwarded his paper to a number of key figures: Sir Geoffrey Howe;

[15] Mrs Thatcher recalls that she decided to be 'sweetly reasonable' throughout the summit. It was clear to her before her arrival that Germany had shifted position and bowed to French pressure on this (in return for Mitterrand's endorsement of German unification). See Thatcher (1995: 760); Grant (1994: 134).

David Howell (Chair of the Commons Select Committee on Foreign Affairs); and to John Major as Chancellor of the Exchequer. Butler also gave evidence to the House of Commons Select Committee on Foreign Affairs in the context of its discussion of the prospects for the Strasbourg summit.

In parallel to Butler's moves, Paul Richards sketched out an actual proposal for a parallel currency. He set down his ideas in a paper that he prepared for a meeting with Nigel Wicks at the Treasury on 24 November 1989.[16] This paper was far more explicit and detailed than Butler's own earlier speculative comments about a parallel currency. Richards mapped out a scheme whereby a European Monetary Fund would set a 'European Standard' for national exchange rates based on the 'best' performers in the EC, rather than the average of the existing exchange rates. The EMF would issue ECUs, which would be fixed in terms of the new standard, in exchange for national currencies on demand. Firms and individuals could choose whether to use the new, stronger ECU which would operate alongside national currencies. Richards's scheme would replace the stage 2 provisions of the Delors Report. The impending IGC would need to consider the appropriate institutional arrangements; a further IGC would be necessary if and when the EC wished to move to a single currency. The entire scheme was designed to satisfy Whitehall's preference for an evolutionary process based on a market-oriented mechanism (and to fill the negotiating vacuum for the IGC). Richards was thus giving substance to Butler's own kite-flying about a parallel currency.

It is intriguing that both figures were following separate paths in the autumn of 1989; neither was in touch with the other. Their initiative entered an elite network, however, in which several hidden hands helped its progress. Members of this network had moved from senior Whitehall positions to jobs in the City. Butler was part of this network, and from November onwards he was floating the notion of a parallel currency. Richards's contacts were more limited. He met Wicks and Joe Grice from the Treasury. Wicks encouraged Richards to develop his proposal on a 'hard' ECU further. Moreover, another hand at work was that of Sir Michael Palliser, who had been Britain's first Permanent Representative to the EC and subsequently Permanent Secretary back at the FCO. He was now the chairman of Richards's own bank, Samuel Montagu. Richards kept Palliser informed of developments. Palliser contacted John Kerr at the FCO about Richards's ideas. Kerr, as a member of the Butler Committee, was thus made aware of both Richards's and Butler's initiatives at a very early stage. Kerr was also in touch with Wicks about these matters: they had both recently been the two UK members on the Guigou Committee preparing the material for the IGC on EMU. The 'hard' ECU initiatives of both Butler and Richards thus had the blessing of several important mentors.

As the lead Treasury official for EC monetary matters, Wicks was very conscious that, with the failure of the Lawson scheme, the Whitehall cupboard was

[16] The Richards paper was dated 22 November 1989 and was addressed directly to Wicks. It was entitled, 'An Evolutionary Approach to an Inter-Governmental Conference on EMU'.

bare. A former Principal Private Secretary to Mrs Thatcher, Wicks's political antennae led him to tread carefully. Given the extreme sensitivities in Whitehall on these matters, a proposal seen to be originating from the City would have a legitimacy and an attraction all of its own.

It was some time later, however, before Richards and Butler had direct contact. At the suggestion of his colleague at Samuel Montagu, Nicolas Wolfers, Richards sent Butler a copy of a revised proposal drawn up on 4 January 1990. The two met at Hambros on 22 January. They were joined by Wolfers and Sir David Hancock, formerly the Treasury representative in Britain's EC delegation and head of the European Secretariat in the Cabinet Office. Like Butler, Hancock was now at Hambros. Wolfers and Hancock were thus two further hands behind the initiative. From here on, Butler and Richards would work in tandem on what was regarded as a joint proposal.

Butler brought to the initiative his contacts with, and experience of, Whitehall. In the later stages, when the proposal had reached ministers, Butler would take the lead; Richards never met the ministers about the proposal at that time. Richards had extensive technical discussions, though, with senior officials in the Treasury and the Bank of England, especially the latter. Richards circulated several further revised drafts of the proposal prepared in the period to late March.[17]

Significantly, Richards attended a meeting at the Bank on 23 March 1990, with some fifteen to twenty officials present, including the new Deputy Governor, Eddie George. George saw much promise in the proposal and urged that it be advanced further. George's sponsorship of the proposal within the Bank was of critical importance to its advancement. A few days later, Richards presented a paper to a BIEC meeting at the Bank, involving senior officials from the Bank and Whitehall. Kerr from the FCO attended that meeting.[18]

After a slow start, the Bank came to give very close attention to the 'hard' ECU scheme. In response to an enquiry from Butler, a paper on the 'hard' ECU by Richards was found languishing in an in-tray, still to be acted upon. The middle to senior echelons of the Bank's staff appeared not to be taking the paper seriously or giving it sufficient urgency. Yet officials in both the Bank and the Treasury were themselves already thinking of schemes based on 'hardening' the ECU before they were approached by Butler and Richards. In this respect, Butler and Richards were filling a vacuum that others had identified.[19]

What stirred the Bank's staff into action was the credibility that Butler brought to the initiative, and then the support that Eddie George gave to it. Whatever reservations might have existed below his level, the backing of the

[17] Altogether, Richards produced three main drafts (22 November 1989; 4 January 1990; and 28 March 1990) and three interim drafts (on 22 February; 4 March; and 14 March).
[18] Richards attended an 'academic panel' meeting chaired by John Flemming at the Bank in early July.
[19] Indeed, the All Saints' Day manifesto on EMU in 1975, signed by economists across Europe, had supported the idea of proceeding on the basis of creating a parallel currency.

Deputy Governor was decisive. George recognized the political mileage to be gained from this scheme in Whitehall. The Bank now came to play the key role. Its input in refining the scheme's technical details was much stronger than that of the Treasury. The Bank's early work on the proposal was undertaken within its economics division, by John Flemming (Director), Tony Coleby, and Christopher Taylor. But with Taylor soon shifting to the newly created European Division, subsequent work was done by Taylor and Andrew Crockett. Both Flemming and Eddie George stayed closely involved, however, as did John Arrowsmith, the Chief European Adviser.[20]

The impact of the Bank on the design of the proposal was to develop it into a more 'active' version. Richards had been tentative, floating different ideas, and suggesting in his paper of 4 January that the 'hard' ECU might even be kept for larger transactions by firms and institutions. Use by individuals would develop over the long term. Several Bank officials saw his approach as too passive. It was essentially an accounting-unit approach, envisaging a minimal currency in the form of an inter-central bank mechanism for locking members of the ERM onto a very tough standard. By the time that the proposal was being hammered out in the Bank, there was more stress on the ECU as a managed currency, with a European institution issuing it to the general public. Moreover, central banks would operate in the money markets in the 'hard' ECU and set interest rates in it. A further revision was the inclusion of repurchase provisions to ensure that the EMF did not validate excessive liquidity creation by individual national central banks. This addition was a particular concern to the Bank of England (and Eddie George in particular). It strongly believed that the EMF must have this power to control liquidity creation by national central banks, both on grounds of stability policy and also to meet the objectives of the Bundesbank.

By contrast, the Treasury sought to curtail the putative EMF. It did not want the EMF to develop into a central bank able to run European monetary policy. The Treasury, and Wicks in particular, favoured the more passive version. The Treasury's instinct was against a managed currency with a central bank determining interest rates. Instead it wanted a currency board preserving a fixed exchange rate and accepting the interest-rate commitments that implied. To the Treasury, the EMF would be there to ensure that the new currency would be as good as the D-Mark. To the Bank, however, the appeal of the new currency was precisely that it might at times be supported by an even tougher stance than that of the Bundesbank on the D-Mark. Though these differences of interpretation on the 'hard' ECU divided the Bank and the Treasury, both endeavoured to blur these distinctions to outsiders.

Officials in both the Bank and the Treasury harboured reservations about the 'hard' ECU. Few were outright enthusiasts for it. Most accepted that it was the

[20] Christopher Taylor sent Richards a detailed critique of his early proposals on 25 January 1990 as part of a continuing dialogue about the design of the scheme. This focused on the weaknesses of the existing ECU; the definition of the ECU; the conversion of contracts into the hard ECU; and the re-denomination of national currencies.

best option left to the government given the progress of the EMU debate. The Treasury was prone to see it as a useful tactic. Within the Treasury, work on the 'hard' ECU plan was undertaken mostly by Paul Gray (Under-Secretary beneath Wicks) and Joe Grice (of the Exchange Rate Policy Analysis Division). The work was not co-ordinated by the Wicks interdepartmental committee on EMU (discussed in the previous chapter). Its progress depended much more on individual entrepreneurship. But the Treasury had been well disposed to such an initiative. As already noted, the idea of a parallel currency scheme had been discussed within the Treasury prior to the Butler and Richards initiatives. Such consideration was only tentative: arising in one of the brain-storming sessions in which Sir Terry Burns, Chief Economic Adviser, liked to indulge. The Treasury was fully aware of Butler's representations, and Richards had met Wicks about the scheme as early as late November 1989. In any event, Burns became convinced that the 'hard' ECU plan had potential. Burns had positioned himself firmly behind the UK's entry into the ERM; the constraints of the 'hard' ECU were a modest next step, and the scheme had much political value. Significantly, Burns was a major influence on John Major, Chancellor during the gestation of the scheme. Major would also focus on the politics, rather than the economics, of the plan. The other key Treasury figure—Wicks—had himself encouraged Richards to develop his plan further. Like some of his counterparts at the Bank, Wicks had a number of reservations about the scheme, but at least it gave him a basis for developing a strategy. It was an advance on just having to say 'no'. John Odling-Smee, Burns's deputy, was more sceptical about this British alternative than he had been of the competing-currency plan that he had himself drafted for Lawson. To him, it was half-baked and too complicated. Yet, he played his part in advocating the scheme in London and the rest of Europe.

Thus, before the scheme reached the ministerial level, it had received crucial support from several key figures. Eddie George had instructed Taylor to tell Wicks that the Bank believed the 'hard' ECU was a good idea. Such backing was highly significant. George was a more acceptable figure to ministers than the Governor, Leigh-Pemberton. The Governor remained sceptical about the 'hard' ECU's merits and prospects. But he was in effect sidelined in the desperate search for a British alternative. George was making the running. He had regretted that the Bank had not been more involved in working out the competing-currency plan after Madrid. For their part, the political instincts of Wicks and Burns at the Treasury led them to realize that it was the best option available and worth pursuing.

Butler and Richards knew little of the internal discussions between the Bank and the Treasury on the 'hard' ECU. At the same time, with the refinement of its technical details, Butler could now help to sell the scheme to ministers and their key aides. First, he sent the outline on 6 March 1990 to Charles Powell, Mrs Thatcher's aide at Number Ten. Powell passed it to Sir Alan Walters, Mrs Thatcher's economics guru, and encouraged Butler to meet him. Walters thought the 'hard' ECU plan was absurd: it was not based on sound economics and Europe did not need the complications of an extra currency. To him, the main attraction of the scheme was that it would give the government more room for manoeuvre in the negotiations on EMU. Though he was no longer her adviser, Walters believed that Mrs Thatcher subsequently also shared this assessment: the prime benefit of the 'hard' ECU proposal (as with the earlier competing-currency plan) would be as a force to derail the EMU momentum.

Butler used various access points within the government. One senior minister replied to a paper from Butler by stressing the need for delicate handling of the proposal.[21] The minister recognized the potential of the scheme in helping to advance Britain's negotiating position, but to be effective it had to be presented with contrasting emphases at home and abroad In London, it would be necessary to stress that any transition to stage 3 would depend on market forces; in Brussels, however, this point should be downplayed. Similarly, the emphasis on a new institution being created would have to be treated lightly in Whitehall. The less the EMF looked like a Community institution, and the more like a revision of the CCBG and/or like the BIS, the better. The proponents of the 'hard' ECU within government were thus deeply conscious of the problem of persuading Mrs Thatcher to accept it.

On 28 March 1990, Butler sent the proposal to Mrs Thatcher, with copies to Major and Hurd.[22] According to Butler's proposal 'the ecu would . . . become a dual European currency alongside each national currency, and be at least as strong as the D-Mark; the preferences of users would determine whether it gradually came to predominate in cross-border transactions and thus a candidate to become the E.C.'s main (*or even one day single*) currency' (emphasis added). The carefully crafted statement sought a balance between whether the 'hard' ECU was itself the end result or whether it was part of a transition to a single currency. This balancing-act would be crucial when it was eventually launched.

A Less than Immaculate Conception

Butler met Major to discuss the proposal. Major was already minuting Mrs Thatcher on 9 April 1990 that his partners in ECOFIN seemed intent on a full EMU and that he was finding that the tentative 'hard' ECU notion was meeting with 'little support' (Thatcher 1995: 720). He had recently attended the informal ECOFIN meeting at Ashford Castle in Ireland. The meeting had received a paper from the EC Monetary Committee which had given unequivocal support to a single currency managed by a European central bank. Major's comment to Mrs Thatcher was a reflection of the support given to a single currency at Ashford. He had confined himself to discussing the actual notion of a 'hard'

[21] Evidence from private correspondence.

[22] The submission comprised a four-page statement by Butler outlining the essential points of the scheme and indicating the endorsement of it by his BIEC Committee, together with a nineteen-page exposition on the 'hard' ECU by Richards.

ECU on the fringes of the meeting. Major was clearly sensitive to the signals from his EC counterparts. By contrast his premier was resolved to resist or ignore them. Mrs Thatcher was impatient with what she felt was Major's 'india-rubber' response to his EC partners (1995: 720).

Butler first met Mrs Thatcher about the 'hard' ECU plan on Friday 17 April, when a brief from the Treasury to the Prime Minister endorsed his plan. Butler was said to have 'performed a magnificent selling job' in this meeting (S. Brittan in *FT*, 21 June 1990). Mrs Thatcher asked Butler whether he was suggesting that she 'give up the pound'. He replied that even if the plan was successful, it would be 'unlikely that we would be asked to give up the pound in your career'. In case there was any doubt, Mrs Thatcher insisted that 'I'll never give up the pound'. A few days later, on 23 April, Butler returned to the fray in a note that he wrote to Mrs Thatcher. He stressed the significance of the issue for the City, British influence in Europe, and the outcome of the next election. Britain had the chance to get its way, he wrote, 'But I'm afraid you are not there yet'. Indeed, 'you cannot hope to sell [the rest of the EC] a definition of monetary union which does not include as its *aim* either permanently fixed parities or a single currency' (emphasis in original). This comment was a repeat of his admonition of six months earlier. But it made no more impact now than it had then.

Butler reassured Mrs Thatcher that any move beyond the 'hard' ECU could be made subject to a unanimous vote in the European Council, but such reassurance appears to have made little impact on her.[23] The day after Mrs Thatcher met Butler she saw Major to discuss the plan. Major made a similar argument to that of Butler. The Chancellor repeated his earlier minute, arguing that the best option was to seek an 'opt-in' for all before stage 3. This approach was to remain his strategy in 1990–1. Mrs Thatcher, however, was 'extremely disturbed to find that the Chancellor had swallowed so quickly the slogans of the European lobby' (Thatcher 1995: 721). Major, she thought, 'was drifting with the tide' (1995: 721).

The discussions within government continued into June. The concept of the 'hard' ECU was now much more in the public domain. Further press coverage had been given to it, and Butler had circulated the proposals more widely.[24] Butler also took the opportunity to raise the 'hard' ECU plan with key figures in Europe.

Notably, on 21 May he sent a copy of the proposals to Pöhl, President of the Bundesbank. This correspondence took place at a time when Butler remained uncertain as to whether the British government would take up the plan. Pöhl replied on 19 June by citing the rationale offered in the Delors Report against a parallel currency. To him, it was hard to see how adding another currency to those already in circulation would pave the way to monetary stability in Europe.

---

[23] A week later, Butler sent Mrs Thatcher a further paper outlining how the 'hard' ECU could resist speculative attacks.

[24] In May Butler sent a copy of the proposals to Lord Cromer, former Governor of the Bank of England and member of the House of Lords Subcommittee on EC matters.

Pöhl, in short, rejected the 'hard' ECU scheme even *before* the British government adopted it. Yet, the government remained uncertain of Pöhl's attitude for some time later.

There is a thesis to be written on how and why London repeatedly 'misinterpreted' Pöhl's stance on EMU. From the Delors Committee to the 'hard' ECU, London misunderstood him, unsurprisingly since Pöhl emitted a series of contradictory signals. The aura of the Bundesbank is of stability and consistency. By contrast, its President appears to have behaved in anything but this fashion. For at least some weeks after Butler received Pöhl's reply on the 'hard' ECU, senior officials at Number Ten remained uncertain about Pöhl's attitude. Likewise, on 25 July, Major as Chancellor gave evidence on the 'hard' ECU proposal to the House of Commons Treasury Select Committee. When asked to respond to comments attributed to Pöhl in the press which were critical of the scheme, Major replied that Pöhl had merely given an immediate off-the-cuff reaction. Having recently met him over lunch in London, Major felt that Pöhl was being won over to the scheme. Brian Sedgemore MP replied that 'I think we all know that Karl Otto Pöhl is a politician and is capable of saying one thing to you and one thing to us over a cup of coffee!' (Minutes of Evidence taken before the Treasury and Civil Service Committee, 25 July 1990). Much later, Pöhl made public his rejection of the plan at a conference at the London School of Economics on 9 November 1990. In a sharply worded condemnation, he said that the 'hard' ECU provided 'the worst possible recipe for monetary policy' in Europe (*FT*, 10 November 1990). The timing of his comments came just days after the resignation of Sir Geoffrey Howe as Deputy Prime Minister and prior to the leadership contest which ousted Mrs Thatcher. Howe had resigned in response to Mrs Thatcher having broken the 'bat' of the 'hard' ECU plan, by undermining its attractiveness to Britain's partners. Pöhl's earlier inconsistency had been a poor guide to the true feelings of the Bundesbank on the matter.

To return to the genesis of the 'hard' ECU plan, on 7 June Butler attended a luncheon meeting of the Association for the Monetary Union of Europe (AUME), attended by Giscard d'Estaing, Helmut Schmidt, and Lord Callaghan, amongst others. A few days later, Butler reported on the meeting to Charles Powell, urging him to stress to Mrs Thatcher that time and influence were slipping away. The forthcoming Italian EC Presidency was preparing for the IGC. His proposals had met with interest from other EC figures, and they might serve to divide the French and the Germans. The Italians might also side with the 'hard' ECU for stage 2. In the event, Butler's calculation on this score was to prove to be overoptimistic by far.

Despite the differences between Major and Mrs Thatcher on the EMU debate, the government came to adopt the 'hard' ECU plan with some speed, if not alacrity. The support of Wicks, Burns, and George was critical in this regard. But, most of all, there was a vacuum to be filled with respect to Britain's negotiating position. Butler met Major again to pursue the matter. The FCO became more involved. A crucial ministerial meeting was held at Number Ten on 19

June at 8 a.m., attended by Mrs Thatcher, Major, Hurd, and Ridley (Stephens 1996: 164). A compromise was reached on the presentation of the plan. It was to be launched as a common currency, which might one day become a single currency. Major, the Chancellor, launched it in a speech to the German Industry Forum at the Institute of Directors in London the next day. In a crucial paragraph, he stressed that: 'In time the ECU would be more widely used: it would become a common currency for Europe. In the very long term, if peoples and governments so choose, it could develop into a single currency' (*FT*, 21 June 1990). This formulation hid different nuances. Specifically, it was not clear how and when the 'hard' ECU might lead to a single currency. Some of Britain's partners looked for a binding commitment, but London saw the process as voluntarist. Critics elsewhere in the EC alleged that an ambiguity underpinned the British conception.

In many instances disagreements within EC governments on EMU can be detected. The problem in this case was that the political leadership on the 'hard' ECU was unclear, and that this lack of clarity affected the central plank of Britain's overall approach to the EMU negotiations. This lack of clarity soon started to become apparent. First, when Robin Leigh-Pemberton, Governor of the Bank of England, welcomed the proposal on the following day, the gloss he put on it proved politically embarrassing to the government. The 'hard' ECU, he said, would 'be a very useful intermediate step between the . . . existing EC currencies and a single EC currency'.[25] It could lead down the path set by the Delors Report. Such an interpretation was an anathema to Mrs Thatcher, and he must have known it. The Prime Minister's interpretation was quite different. In an interview two days before Major's speech, she had said that the decision on a single currency was 'not for our generation to take' (Keesing's Archives). In the House of Commons, responding to Leigh-Pemberton's comments, Mrs Thatcher said that the 'hard' ECU plan 'does not mean that we approve of a single European currency; it says specifically that we do not'. Major's carefully crafted formula that the 'hard' ECU might lead to a single currency had been scuppered by the Prime Minister.

Mrs Thatcher's rejection of the single-currency goal meant that Britain's partners were almost certain to oppose the 'hard' ECU scheme. The ECOFIN ministers had committed themselves to a single currency at Ashford Castle some three months earlier. Both the Treasury and the FCO had recognized that the way in which the plan was presented was all-important; Mrs Thatcher had wrecked their hopes. She was never a convert to the principles of the 'hard' ECU. She was attracted by its role as a diversionary tactic. Yet, her refusal to maintain the formula that the 'hard' ECU *might, one day*, lead to a single currency undermined this very tactical purpose. To those believing in 'constructive engagement' with Britain's EC partners, such an approach represented inept strategic management. The 'hard' ECU would not survive as a credible distraction in the

[25] The statement by Leigh-Pemberton was made to the House of Lords and was quoted by Neil Kinnock in the House of Commons on 21 June 1990 (*House of Commons Debates*, vol. 174, col. 1108).

rest of Europe for very long. Mrs Thatcher implicitly accepted that she could no longer block the momentum that had built up behind EMU. She was reduced to spoiling tactics, at home and abroad.

The 'hard' ECU was a major domestic distraction. The Thatcher and Major governments trumpeted the scheme as evidence that the British were not being obstructionist, that they had something positive to contribute to the debate. Such a claim served to head off attacks by those believing in constructive engagement. Moreover, officials in the Treasury and the Bank devoted much time and effort to refining the plan's technical details. They had not seen it as a mere diversionary tactic. Some of them became engulfed by its technical artistry and sustained an interest in its development well beyond the signing of the Maastricht Treaty and the ERM crises of 1992–3. Yet the scheme only had polit-ical relevance to the EMU negotiations in so far as Britain's partners might be persuaded to take it up. On this criterion, it was already clear in 1990 that the plan was dead in the water.

Rigidity at Home Kills Initiative in Europe

Despite the problematic launch, the government sent forth its emissaries to try to rally support for the 'hard' ECU in the rest of Europe. On 23 July 1990 Major presented the 'hard' ECU plan to his colleagues in ECOFIN. It was referred to the meeting of the EC Monetary Committee scheduled for 4 September. The response in ECOFIN was polite, but little substantive interest was evident. The Germans had already indicated their severe reservations about the plan some two weeks earlier at the G7 summit at Houston. The politeness shown at the ECOFIN meeting was on political grounds. The Germans and others wanted to tilt the policy balance in London. They 'wanted to boost Mr Hurd and Mr Major inside Britain as *Europa-freundlich* politicians who deserved to be encouraged at the expense of Mrs Thatcher' (*The Economist*, 21 July 1990). But politeness 'did not mean they were taking [the 'hard' ECU] seriously'.

Officials in London showed varying degrees of enthusiasm for the plan. Kerr was won round to it, but he was never as attached to it as were Wicks and Burns. Kerr's office helped to co-ordinate the sales drive in Europe. The visits to other EC cities involved both senior Treasury and Bank staff during the summer and autumn of 1990. Visits were made to most EC capitals.[26] With the exception of Madrid (see below), the rejection of the British plan was plain and often blunt on each of these bilateral visits.[27]

The hard ECU plan was duly discussed in the EC Monetary Committee on 4 September 1990, with Wicks and Crockett presenting the scheme. By contrast,

[26] The delegation to Bonn and Frankfurt included Eddie George and Andrew Crockett; Crockett and Odling-Smee went to Rome; Odling-Smee travelled to The Hague; Crockett and John Flemming trav-elled to Spain and Portugal; Burns (Treasury) went to Athens and Dublin.

[27] In addition, Butler and Odling-Smee saw Yves Mersch in London during the summer: he was to chair the first period of the IGC in 1991 on behalf of the Luxembourg EC Presidency.

it was discussed in much more cursory terms in the CCBG. Leigh-Pemberton had distributed the relevant papers to his central bank colleagues, with a covering letter presaging the series of bilateral visits by the British. But by September 1990, the CCBG agenda was already full with the drafting of the ECB statute and the 'hard' ECU proposal suffered as a result. It was discussed only briefly at the September meeting; Crockett was left to lobby on it over lunch. He also presented it to the CCBG Alternates Group. Leigh-Pemberton felt ill at ease in discussing the plan, given his own endorsement of the Delors path and his private scepticism on the 'hard' ECU. He sensed that few of his counterparts wished to reopen a discussion already settled in the Delors Committee. But he was not alone: one of those closely involved now recalls that the plan 'was heard and commented upon out of politeness: to ease the discomfort of the British representatives in having to present it. It was impossible for our EC partners to side with it: that was the legacy of Mrs Thatcher's attitude towards the rest of the EC. The 'hard' ECU was never a serious proposition.'

The EC Monetary Committee discussed the plan in some detail, and a series of objections were raised. The reactions were not uniform. The French Trésor showed some limited and temporary interest in the scheme until early in 1991. This interest gave British Treasury officials a glimmer of hope that they might be able to make some headway. Pierre Bérégovoy was well disposed to accommodating the UK in EMU, as a counterbalance to Germany. The Trésor was also cautious about central bank independence and found some attraction in the British scheme precisely because it did not involve such a change. French interest did not extend beyond the Trésor. Political imperatives led the Elysée to reject it. For the Elysée, the inclusion of Germany was far more important than that of the British. They saw the British scheme as taking too long and the outcome as too uncertain; the French wanted a government-driven approach to a single currency with clear deadlines. The British government's refusal to countenance the single-currency goal meant that the opportunity for an alliance with Paris was lost. If Treasury officials in London sought constructive engagement in Europe, this refusal must have been deeply frustrating. The German response, led by Tietmeyer, was firmly negative, though for varying reasons. Some believed it would not work—the EMF would not be able to fulfil its function—others could not accept that Europe needed an additional currency. It was safer to rely on the anchor currency—the D-Mark—in the transitional phase, as Wolfgang Rieke (Head of the Bundesbank's International Department) stated at a seminar held at Hambros Bank in London on 11 October. Indeed, the Bundesbank considered a hardening of the ECU in stage 2 based on this notion. A paper by Hans Tietmeyer, which took account of the EC Monetary Committee's discussion of 4 September, argued for a 'hardening of the basket-type ecu' by one of several means.[28] This issue would be discussed further in the IGC in the context of an eventual agreement to freeze the ECU during the

---

[28] See his paper, 'Thoughts on the "hardening of the ecu" ', 12 October 1990.

transition. For their part, the Commission staff feared that the British 'hard' ECU plan ran the risk of creating uncertainty and instability. The need for a thirteenth monetary policy, when the aim was to have a single one, was questioned by Joly Dixon, a member of Delors's cabinet, at the same Hambros seminar of 11 October. Elsewhere, the general European reaction to the 'hard' ECU was consistent with the label attached to it within the Bank of England: it was crazy, but elegantly crafted.

British strategy was encountering increasing problems. The opportunity to present a more positive stance was provided by sterling's entry into the ERM on 5 October 1990. Yet even this was badly mishandled with the rest of the EC (see Chapter 15). The decision had been treated as if it were a unilateral act, not one to be negotiated with those already in the club. This seeming arrogance disturbed many of Britain's partners. The failure of senior officials in the Bank and in the Treasury to avoid such embarrassment was costly to wider British strategy based on the 'hard' ECU.

The Rome 1 débâcle

The British position veered further off course. Mrs Thatcher went to the Rome European Council meeting (27–8 October 1990) with an untenable position. She wanted to discuss the GATT negotiations; the rest did not. The other eleven agreed a set of provisions on political union; she refused to go along with it. The rest wanted to set a date for the start of stage 2 of EMU—1 January 1994 was eventually agreed—she refused to do so. British strategy was at an impasse. Mrs Thatcher later recalled that, 'My objections were heard in stony silence. I now had no support. I just had to say no' (Thatcher 1995: 767). Instead, Britain derogated from the final communiqué with the statement that, 'The United Kingdom, while ready to move beyond Stage I through the creation of a new monetary institution and a common Community currency, believes that decisions on the substance of that move should precede decisions on its timing'. The text, drafted by Wicks and agreed with Prime Minister Giulio Andreotti's aide, Umberto Vattani, was a classic example of the British reluctance on Europe. A similar statement might have been made to Jean Monnet in 1950 or after Messina in 1955.

The British were appalled at the manoeuvrings of the Italian Presidency (see also Chapter 12). Vattani had discussed his impending draft with British officials, including Kerr, Wicks, and Hadley (Cabinet Office) beforehand. But they had little notion of what might come later. At Rome, an initiative from Vattani to Wicks on the telephone in the early hours of the morning met with what Vattani felt to be a rebuff. Taking this rebuff as evidence of a refusal to compromise, the Italians went ahead and drafted a communiqué which isolated the British. Yet the Italians had sought compromise well ahead of the summit. Two successive visits to London, first by Giovanni De Michelis, the Foreign Minister, and then by Andreotti, had both involved the Italians stressing their intention to make EMU the top priority at Rome. Mrs Thatcher was insistent that GATT should be the priority, which left an unbridgeable gap. The Italians were seeking a compromise on the substance of EMU. References would be made to a 'single or a common' currency in the final communiqué, to recognize Britain's 'hard' ECU plan. Mrs Thatcher refused to listen to such overtures; she wanted to block progress. Thus, on arrival Mrs Thatcher was already isolating herself. It was a case of Thatcher *contra mundum*.[29]

Mrs Thatcher and her entourage had not prepared the ground properly for victory, nor had they read the signals correctly. The Prime Minister, as noted in the last chapter, had lost credit with the Germans as a result of her attitude to the impending unification of Germany. Mrs Thatcher and Hurd had expected Kohl to be more pliable on the date for stage 2 (Thatcher 1995: 765–6). But Kohl had advised Andreotti that the summit now seemed the best chance to set a date. A prior meeting of Christian Democrat leaders had agreed that GATT would not be discussed at Rome. Mrs Thatcher went into battle ignoring both signals.

Mrs Thatcher later attacked the Italian presidency as 'incompetent' and her entourage spoke of an ambush. An article in *The Economist* expressing similar thoughts was mistakenly interpreted in Rome as having official British sanction (*The Economist*, 3 November 1990). But the problems at Rome stemmed as much from unpreparedness and poor strategy and tactics on the part of the British, as from Italian guile. Mrs Thatcher had not heeded the warnings of the FCO or of Kerr, the UK Permanent Representative in Brussels. Her immediate entourage—notably, Charles Powell—had seemingly sustained her isolation and misjudgement.

Mrs Thatcher's Resignation

The Rome summit proved to be the immediate cause of her domestic downfall. That downfall was related to her handling of the 'hard' ECU plan and her response to the growing momentum of EMU. At first it might seem puzzling that the 'hard' ECU—a seemingly obscure, modern-day, 'Schleswig-Holstein' question[30]—could cause such damage. But it was enwrapped in the bigger issue of how Britain should negotiate with its European partners. Mrs Thatcher was seen to be undermining all attempts at a constructive engagement on EMU. Speaking in the House of Commons on 30 October 1990, immediately after the Rome summit, Mrs Thatcher argued that she would not hand over sterling or

[29] The phrase is used in Craddock (1997: 205).

[30] The analogy of the Schleswig-Holstein question is used to suggest obscurity. In the context of the disputes of the 1850s and 1860s, Lord Palmerston said that only three people understood the Schleswig-Holstein question: the Prince Consort, who was dead; a German professor, who had gone mad; and himself, who had forgotten all about it. Critics suggested that some adopted the 'hard' ECU plan without fully understanding it.

the powers of the House to Europe. Moreover, in her view, there was little chance of the 'hard' ECU being used in preference to the existing national currencies of the EC. This comment was a clear roadblock on EMU and a scuttling of the 'hard' ECU.

It is ironic, perhaps, that this particular reference to the 'hard' ECU should have been seen as so consequential when Mrs Thatcher had undermined it at the start and when Britain's partners had already shown little interest in it. But this new comment proved to be the straw that broke the camel's back. Mrs Thatcher's handling of both EMU and the 'hard' ECU led Sir Geoffrey Howe to resign as Deputy Prime Minister on 1 November 1990. In his Commons resignation speech, he noted that the effect was that batsmen sent to the crease would realize that the captain had already broken their bats (the 'hard' ECU) (13 November 1990; text reproduced in Howe 1994: 697–703). Howe's resignation led to the challenge to Mrs Thatcher's leadership. Within a few weeks of her incautious remarks, she would no longer be Prime Minister.[31]

Her successor as Prime Minister, John Major, declared his intent to enable Britain to be more fully engaged in the debate in the EC. The following spring he formulated this commitment as placing Britain at 'the heart of Europe'.[32] The style was very different. Yet, little changed in substance. The 'hard' ECU plan continued to be pushed in the same manner. Mrs Thatcher's remarks at Rome were ignored: Major stuck to the original formula that the 'hard' ECU might one day lead to a single currency. The credibility of doing so was open to question: Mrs Thatcher's indiscretion had fanned the flames of suspicion and distrust of British motives. To persist, without further policy adjustment, led to a failure in Europe which was all too predictable.

As a Window at Home Opens, That in Europe Closes

Immediately, after the Rome débâcle, senior officials in Whitehall and in the Bank—led by Wicks—endeavoured to revise British strategy. In their view further adaptation of the 'hard' ECU proposal was necessary. The visits to Britain's partners had gone badly; the discussions in the CCBG and the Monetary Committee were no more promising. It was becoming clear that the 'hard' ECU, as it stood, would not win allies to its cause. That being so, the prospect was of a failure to restructure the EMU debate and an inability to slow it down. After the turmoil of Howe's resignation, the climate in the Tory Party seemed to favour a shift to a more positive approach. Wicks and the Treasury responded by considering how the 'hard' ECU plan might be further adapted.

---

[31] The leadership election was held on 20 November. She was persuaded that her vote was too low to continue, so she announced two days later she would not continue to contest the leadership. She formally resigned as PM on 28 November 1990.

[32] Speech in Bonn, 11 March 1991.

Just days before the first ballot for the Tory leadership, on 16 November 1990, Wicks circulated a key paper. This paper discussed how the 'hard' ECU plan might be linked to the adoption, by at least some countries, of a single currency. Wicks was flying a kite amongst his fellow officials to test their reaction. But, to mix the metaphor, he was also stepping out across the Rubicon that ministers had forbidden. It is worth considering the content of, and the reactions to, Wicks's paper in some detail as it provides a very useful picture of official thinking at this time: on the very eve of the IGC.

Wicks's ideas went beyond the then current government formula. His three-page paper sought to elaborate a clear interpretation of Major's original proposal of 20 June, in the context of Rome 1. The proposal was placed in the context of what seemed likely to be agreed for stage 2 of EMU. The notion was to permit member states wanting to move to a single currency to do so, whilst allowing those that did not to retain their control over national monetary policy. Wicks sought to distinguish a stage 2 based on the 'hard' ECU and a stage 3 based on a single currency. At the start of stage 3, the EMF already proposed for stage 2 would effectively become a central bank for the single currency states. Both stages would appear in the Treaty, but the commitment would only be to stage 2. Stage 2 would be designed to create the conditions in which a single currency might be introduced. But the adoption of stage 3 would depend on a future decision by each state's parliament. Wicks called his approach a staged or a voluntarist one. It did not represent a radical shift in policy, but a partial adaptation of it. Yet it signalled a more positive stance towards the goal of EMU, representing a break with the negativity of Mrs Thatcher. Indeed, the advantage of the proposal, he argued, was that a split between the UK and its partners could be delayed further into the future.

There were some positive reasons for believing that Britain's partners might give serious attention to such a revised scheme. The Giscard–Schmidt Committee on Monetary Union was understood to be thinking along similar lines. Other EC governments were already thinking of how a 'hard' ECU scheme might be tied to the goal of a single currency: Spain, in particular, had circulated a paper on this theme a little earlier (September 1990). In addition, Wicks had received encouraging signals from Horst Köhler (in the German Finance Ministry), and he was aware that Bérégovoy in Paris was endeavouring to keep Britain on board. In short, Wicks believed that flexibility would bring strategic gains for Britain.

Wicks remained tentative, however, conscious that what would be seen domestically as a dramatic shift might prove too little, too late for Britain's partners. The problems of gaining support from Britain's EC partners suggested to Wicks himself that the scheme might be sidelined straightaway. At home, he noted the difficulty of winning over ministers. Their likely stubbornness was self-defeating. The Wicks revision would remove a block on the rest going ahead, whilst allowing Britain to learn to live with the 'hard' ECU. True, Britain might lose clout over the latter, but British influence would wane, in any event, at the point when the rest went ahead with a single currency. In reality, the choice was between the rest moving ahead (and Britain opting out) and all being tied to the 'hard' ECU, to a greater or lesser extent. The rigidity of British strategy led to the first option by default; the British undermined the 'hard' ECU themselves.

In any event, negotiating such a scheme with Britain's partners would have been difficult. The problems related to the timing of the proposal and to the momentum of the negotiations. Different interpretations can be given of the chances of success for the Wicks proposal. On the one hand, if Wicks's revised scheme had been taken up, it would have given Bérégovoy more clout in Paris in his desire to bring Britain on board and to resist central bank independence. Similarly, Wicks's scheme would have tempted Köhler, in the German Finance Ministry, to have taken a stronger lead on this issue against Tietmeyer and the Bundesbank. Köhler was looking for a clear political signal that the 'hard' ECU was designed to lead to a single currency. He never detected one and, in consequence, he felt unable to mount a domestic challenge. In short, officials in both the French and German Finance Ministries were prepared to pay a price for British participation. On the other hand, by this stage, ideas on the design of EMU had progressed some considerable distance. A year earlier, there would have been a clearer 'window of opportunity' at the EC level, though the domestic scope had been heavily constrained at that time. Now, the reverse was probably true. The British debate was yet again out of synchronization with that of the Continent. The Germans and the Dutch—two key allies for any British initiative—wanted to avoid any confusion of monetary responsibilities: in effect, they preferred an 'empty' stage 2. The putative British scheme would involve complex institutional arrangements: an EMF running a common currency and an ESCB managing a single currency. Moreover, states using the 'hard' ECU as a single currency would be able to claim greater power over its management than that possessed by states merely using it as an additional, common currency. In other words, if Britain stayed out of a single currency, she could have lost influence over the 'hard' ECU. Such a prospect could have antagonized others, like Spain, who might have feared that the scheme facilitated a two-tier Europe (a 'monetary Schengen', as Wicks called it). This latter prospect was one Britain itself had already opposed.

Wicks's colleagues were even more cautious on the question of whether the new scheme could 'fly' in the EC. In his reply to Wicks on 20 November, David Hadley in the Cabinet Office regarded Wicks's ideas as an advance. But Hadley questioned how far the other eleven were willing to go to accommodate Britain and its peculiar sensitivities on the single-currency goal. He judged that they must be expecting Britain to be left outside a treaty on EMU. They might find Wicks's proposal attractive, if they wished to reduce British isolation, but it was not clear that they did so. Moreover, he doubted whether the scheme would be acceptable to ministers at home. He found their position illogical. On the one hand, the 'hard' ECU was based on the notion that it could become a single currency if governments and people so chose. Yet, on the other, British ministers were refusing to sign a treaty which would provide for that choice to be exercised, even if that decision was subject to stringent conditions such as unanimity. The real risk was that the government's present position would leave it marginalized in the IGC. Thus, Hadley believed that any change should be made as soon as possible.

Michael Jay at the FCO had a similar reaction. In his reply to Wicks on 23 November, he accepted that the government would want to persist with the 'hard' ECU; therefore, the more credible the proposals the better. Jay recognized the twin negotiating problems: first, winning over ministers at home; secondly, promoting the scheme in Europe. He concurred with Hadley's comments on both aspects. There was also a shared scepticism about whether Britain's partners would accept the new formulation. But, like Hadley, Jay believed that, if ministers were willing to approve it, then it should be launched as soon as possible.

Officials at the Bank of England were very sceptical that the scheme's technical problems could be overcome and whether the rest of the EC would be willing to go along with it. In his reply to Wicks on 27 November, Crockett repeated the Bank's support for a more active version of the 'hard' ECU plan. It saw this development as essential to gain support from Britain's EC partners. With this in mind, Crockett argued that the EMF should from the beginning be able to exercise discretion over monetary policy in a countercyclical direction. The EMF must also have the capacity to develop itself into a full ECB. But the problem of the loss of influence for Britain over the hard ECU, if it decided not to adopt it as a single currency, was a serious one. Crockett questioned whether what Wicks proposed was much better than the option of a relatively 'empty' stage 2, with an institution with limited functions, to which all could belong. The latter might be less threatening. But the key test was a tactical one: to overcome the suspicions of Britain's partners. They would need reassurrance that Britain did not intend to veto progress to a single currency.

In the event, the British government did not adopt this new, amended 'hard' ECU scheme. The new Prime Minister rejected the principle of any commitment to a single currency. Major ruled out any radical break in policy on EMU. The Wicks initiative was seen as typical Whitehall sophistry: principle and party interest were both against it. Party unity—which he was so keen to restore—necessitated a return to the previous status quo. The new government stuck to the original 'hard' ECU formulation. Major simply sought to erase the memory of Mrs Thatcher's contradictory statements on it.

This episode is significant in that it indicates the extent of the unease felt at the level of senior officials and the underlying continuity between Mrs Thatcher and Major on points of principle. Officials had realized that the prospects for the original 'hard' ECU plan being adopted by the rest of the EC were extremely dim. Wicks was by no means alone in believing that Britain needed a new negotiating stance: that it should move closer to the positions of others to avoid the isolation, if not ignominy, it had suffered at the Rome European Council in October 1990. But it is not clear how hard Wicks and others pressed the case for change on ministers. A shift of policy in a delicate area such as this would have required a sensitive, but forceful, lead. Ministers had to be prised from their established mind-set. It is difficult to judge whether senior officials were ready and able to set about the task. The substance of the correspondence between officials indicates support for 'constructive engagement' on EMU. Perhaps Wicks's proposed revision was already too late. It might have made little difference in Europe. But it revealed a very clear gap in policy priorities and strategic thinking between ministers and officials. This point was a defining one, coming as it did on the very eve of the IGC. Senior officials would be sent into a battle which they themselves knew that they would lose. The battle was advanced for the domestic imperatives of protecting national sovereignty and of maintaining the unity of the Conservative Party.

The Hard ECU and the IGC

Before the IGC on EMU began, the 'hard' ECU scheme was formalized in a Bank of England paper in December 1990, and the Treasury published a text of the necessary treaty changes in January 1991.[33] The Treasury text represented Britain's opening contribution to the IGC. France and Germany submitted full Draft Treaties for the IGC to consider. Britain did not. Given its agnosticism or opposition to a single currency, it could not go beyond offering a much more limited alternative.

There was also a cultural constraint. As one senior insider put it, 'We don't normally write papers about grand concepts: we were uncomfortable with the style of debate that had begun with the Delors Report'. In truth, this inhibition seems more relevant to European strategy, than to domestic policy. The difference is telling. The French approach to Europe is seen to be different. Paris tends to begin negotiations by tabling a clear position paper. This move obliges others to respond to their lead. By contrast, Whitehall has felt more inhibited in striking out with a long-term blueprint. More generally, to the British, 'everything depended on the detailed mechanical questions of how EMU might be made to work: and at that point we calculated that our concerns would win the day'. Some in Whitehall were thus prepared to let Britain's partners take the initiative. The British would react to their text. The effect, however, was clear. Despite the attempt to sell it as a practical, 'nuts and bolts' proposal, the 'hard' ECU had already received little support and much criticism.

Yet, on the hard ECU, the British found an unexpected ally in the Spanish. The bilateral visits of the summer and autumn showed that it was the Madrid

---

[33] See *The Hard ECU in Stage 2: Operational Requirements*, published by the Bank of England, December 1990; and *Economic and Monetary Union Beyond Stage I: Possible Treaty Provisions and Statute for a European Monetary Fund: Proposals by the UK Government*, HM Treasury, January 1991.

government that took the 'hard' ECU the most seriously. Once again, a strategic question loomed. Did an opportunity exist for Britain to build an alliance with Spain and restructure the pre-IGC debate? In the event, the British effectively ignored the Spanish and continued playing their own domestic game. For to form a partnership would have required London to accept a firm commitment to an eventual single currency: precisely what ministers had set their face against.

At the start of September 1990 Spain circulated a document with the pertinent title, 'Staying the Course'. It highlighted the key line of division: the Spanish wanted to use a version of the 'hard' ECU as the basis for stage 2 before the transition to a single currency. A single currency would thus not have to await the 'crowding-out of existing national currencies by the 'hard' ECU'. It also sought an independent monetary institution to be created at the start of stage 2, which could 'be transformed easily into the final ECB'. A further Spanish paper to the IGC on 24 January 1991 set out the concept of a 'hard-basket' ECU. The paper envisaged 'not the creation of an "abstract" ECU' independent from national currencies. Instead, it would involve a basket ECU modified at each realignment to ensure no diminution of its value against any of the currencies in the system. The current 'basket' ECU would be transformed into a 'hard-basket' ECU.[34]

To others, including the Commission, there were problems with the Spanish concept, as well as with that of the British. The composition of the ECU would become uncertain: tensions in the EMS would encourage speculation, thus increasing the variability of ECU interest rates and the risks associated with its use.[35] More fundamentally, most current market operators were opposed to all 'hard' ECU proposals and, instead, favoured the Commission's own proposal to freeze the ECU as part of the transition to EMU. The Commission noted that different voices in the City of London were arguing precisely this during the same period.[36] A scheme based on the Commission's alternative was eventually adopted in late 1991.

---

[34] The January paper also sought to counter fears that their proposal might put at risk the huge private ECU market. In addition, it called for the immediate issuance of fully backed ECU notes: a subject which it noted had already been discussed in the Monetary Committee as early as 1982.

[35] See, for example, internal Commission Note (DG 2/02189; G. Ravasio) of 17 April 1991 which makes the following additional arguments. First, each realignment would provoke a revision of the basket and would force market operators to change their strategy and their cover operations. Moreover, because of the exchange guarantee given to the ECU, its interest rate would be a market rate, different from its theoretical rate based on the average of the interest rates of the component currencies. As a result, the entire yield curve associated with it would be structurally inverted. In addition, acceptance of the scheme would require the revision of all the EMS rules and agreements and of the CAP price policy.

[36] See paper by Graham Bishop (Salomon Brothers) of 11 April 1991, 'Eculand—The 13th Member of the EC?'. There he argues that 'the solution to the problem of the uncertainty about the ecu's composition is simple and obvious: freeze it'. Earlier, a paper from Shearson Lehman Brothers on 7 December 1990 had said that the parallel currency notion was dead, economically and politically. Both statements are reported in the EC Commission Note of 17 April 1991, referred to above.

The European debate on the 'hard' ECU was most intense in April 1991. The Commission lobbied against it as the EC Monetary Committee held a wider debate on making the ECU a harder currency in stage 2 of the transition to a single currency. Cees Maas, as Chair of the Monetary Committee, concluded in his report of the meeting that the majority opposed both the British and the Spanish schemes. Monetary policy must remain with member states in stage 2, and both of these schemes involved a new institution with powers to issue notes and intervene in the markets. He noted, in particular, that the French and German representatives believed that the 'basket' ECU could be hardened—given a 'no devaluation' guarantee, with the basket being adjusted at realignments—without giving monetary powers to the stage 2 institution. By now the French had retreated from the Rome 1 position of a meaningful role for the stage 2 body. The shift accommodated a crucial priority for the Germans, and the rest of the EC was too weak to block them. It was too late to be suggesting a strong stage 2 institution. There probably had been a majority for this six months earlier, but not now. By failing to secure a position on this issue with the French in the earlier phase, the British lost the battle in April 1991.

Yet even a few months later an opportunity to salvage the situation may have existed. As late as June there seemed to be potential for a bloc of member states to press forward successfully with the Spanish variant of the 'hard' ECU. Participation in such a coalition would have required London to back the commitment to a single-currency goal. Press reports suggested that the British government was, indeed, softening its stance and getting ready to link its proposal to a single currency (*Financial Times*, 16 May 1991). In an internal note, the EC Commission noted that Norman Lamont at an AUME conference in London in June had adopted a more conciliatory stance.[37] If Britain made the shift, it estimated that there might be five member states behind the Spanish proposal: including Germany, Belgium, and perhaps Luxembourg. But the Major government failed to make the shift, and the cause was lost. It is, of course, all too easy to overestimate the chances of forming a coalition behind something like the Spanish proposal. Lamont may have been misunderstood; alternatively, he might have been muddying the water to stall matters.

In mid-1991 Butler also continued to press the 'hard' ECU case, with vigour. He recognized that a sketch of the required institution-building would be essential to win over Britain's EC partners. He urged such a task on Number Ten, but its response appeared laggardly. In default, he worked on this endeavour himself. In his mind, an EMF would exist alongside an ESCB from the start of stage 2: a juxtaposition that came to be queried both at home and abroad. Butler also took up the theme of the fear of a loss of sovereignty, writing directly to Hurd on the subject. Butler claimed support and interest amongst Britain's partners throughout the autumn. But he never doubted that an effective coalition required Britain to sign up to a single currency as the eventual goal.

[37] The conference, organized by the Association for the Monetary Union of Europe (AUME) was entitled, 'EMU in a Turbulent World'. The Commission note was written in DG 2 (2/03157).

Ministers also persisted with the 'hard' ECU into the autumn of 1991. This was well beyond the time when most of the key officials in Whitehall and the Bank believed that the concept had any real negotiating potential. For a year or so key officials had been considering whether and how Britain might 'jump ship' and support one of the other dominant European conceptions of EMU. To them, the hard ECU had failed where it mattered: in Europe. Ministers, however, persisted with the notion. Their persistence was surely not owing to any illusions that the rest of the EC might be won over at the last minute; but rather, because the scheme had another strategic use at home. At the informal ECOFIN meeting in Apeldoorn at the end of September 1991, Lamont still pressed the British case. Indeed, he claimed that his officials were working on a further revision of the concept. His comment must have produced yawns from Britain's partners. But the signal it gave was also directed at the party back home, which was where it was felt to matter most.

Conclusions

The early response to the EMU debate (1988–90) was a classic example of Britain's divergence from the rest of her EC partners. This divergence found expression in Mrs Thatcher's strident opposition. At first, she was still the successful party leader. Her self-confidence was high after her third successive election victory. She dominated the domestic political landscape. To a considerable degree she also possessed an hegemony in the political argument on Europe. Apart from a few isolated exceptions, there was little outside challenge to the basic principles of policy she was pursuing on Europe. But, as with the ERM, EMU had a 'wheel of fortune' quality about it. Mrs Thatcher's management of her party fell apart in November 1990.

But the domestic debate was out of kilter with that of its major partners and this divergence affected Britain's influence over the momentum of EMU. Caught off guard at the outset, Whitehall was sceptical that EMU would come to much. When it engaged in the debate it was almost too late: what London proposed as alternatives was out of step with the perceived interests of its partners. Ministers persisted, however, and in a very rigid manner. Officials warned them, perhaps much too late, about the consequences of their strategy. From there on, the British were set on a path that seemed increasingly to involve separation. The possibility of an 'opt-out' being extended to all EC states required a more flexible British strategy, in order to win allies to the cause. Crucial in this respect was an acceptance of a single currency as a long-term goal. This move was not one that ministers were prepared to contemplate. In short, when the EMU agenda was being set, Britain failed either to widen it—to have alternative paths considered seriously—or to stall progress towards its realization. Bargaining power was weakening as EMU progressed. This weakening of position would become more obvious as the IGC proceeded in 1991.

Might these European questions have been handled differently and with more success in 1988–90? If the question of Britain's ERM entry had been settled earlier, the atmosphere in Whitehall would have been transformed. Entry could have been deployed as a bargaining lever on EMU, as Lawson and Howe urged. The fact that it was not, and that entry when it came in October 1990 was mishandled, weakened Britain's influence on EMU. The ERM episode constituted an awful hangover for everyone in Whitehall. It inhibited policy reflection and kept strategy ambiguous. Ministers and officials were intimidated by the constraints imposed by Mrs Thatcher's court. Major, as her successor, was left to grapple with her legacy.

The government miscalculated on the timing and content of its alternative proposals. Such miscalculation is part of a wider and longer pattern: official British policy on Europe has typically focused on yesterday's debate (Stephens 1996: 165). The first British alternative—for a system of competing currencies—was a non-starter in 1989, after Madrid. It might have had more potential before, or just after, Hanover in June 1988 when ideas were more fluid and some minds (though not, perhaps, those in the Bundesbank) more open. The second alternative—for a 'hard' ECU—also came too late: just months before an IGC was to be held to negotiate a single currency. It might have had more influence if it had been launched in the previous September for the Delors Committee in place of Lawson's scheme. It could then have been presented as a practical design for stage 2. To be effective, however, the British would have had to accept the scheme only as part of a transition to a single currency, as did the Spanish with their variant which also came too late. Immediately after Madrid, many recognized the Delors Report had left a gaping hole on the transition to EMU. Hence, despite the Committee's rejection of a parallel currency scheme, a British initiative of this sort might have won a good number of adherents. Such a move would have been consistent with the views of the Europhile members of the Cabinet, but Mrs Thatcher was increasingly ostracizing them. After the Rome summit in October 1990, divisions on the form and content of stage 2 had become more set and the limited British proposals were out of synchronization with what Germany and France wanted.

What is also striking about the British debate in this period is its separation from its major partners. British policy was hatched in a cosseted, distinctive setting with little real attempt to engage its partners in substantive debate about the means and ends of EMU. British understandings of these matters were often at variance with those of other EC actors. Mrs Thatcher contemplated an EMU without a single currency or a central institution. Lawson accepted a fixed-exchange-rate constraint (a 'hard' ERM) as good for domestic policy but found a single currency a political intrusion. Howe did not wish to rule EMU out, but resisted telling anyone how Britain should judge when to actually say 'yes' and on what terms. Major seemed genuinely to desire to place Britain at 'the heart of Europe', but was hemmed in by the past, by the balance of opinion within the Tory Party, and by his own lack of emotional commitment to Europe. Thus, he persisted with the 'hard' ECU scheme after it had been effectively sunk by Mrs Thatcher on its launch. He was unable to countenance a more flexible stance. Yet Britain could not win allies without accepting the goal of a single currency.

Windows of opportunity did exist for the British to reshape the EMU debate in this early period. The problem was that the domestic and the European 'windows' did not open at the same time. Nor were there many such opportunities. Moreover, the Thatcher government, in particular, neglected the arts of coalition-building in the EC. When she left the European stage in Rome in October 1990, Mrs Thatcher was dismissive. The EC, she said, was 'on the way to cloud cuckoo land' (quoted in Denman 1996: 268). Later, the Major government sought to improve its tactics and give its strategy a different gloss. But the decision to stick with the existing policy principles precluded British participation in effective coalition-building. Indeed, the fundamental reality was that most of her partners were moving ahead, towards a single currency, and Britain was failing to alter their course or speed. By the time the IGC on EMU opened in December 1990, British bargaining power was already severely weakened.

15

John Major: Between the Party and the IGC

With the Thatcher government failing to block the convening of the two IGCs, John Major was left to bridge the irreconciliable.[1] He was caught between the demands of his party and the constraints of successful EC negotiation. The divisions within the Conservative Party militated against any radical shift of policy on Europe. After the turmoil of Mrs Thatcher's last months as leader, the mood of the party also favoured a less strident stance on Europe. Finding himself suddenly cast as leader, Major gave priority to the unity of his party, accepting the European policy constraints this imposed upon him. To his critics, this unwillingness to break free and set his own course more definitively was evidence of a lack of statesmanship. Yet in the name of 'statesmanship' Major found critics seeking to pull him in different directions on 'Europe'. Faced with the choice of living within the constraints of his party or of displaying flexibility on European matters in order to be a more effective negotiator, Major accepted his party role. He had chosen his course and invited judgement on that basis. A keen party tactician, he focused on creating a more positive style of negotiation at the EC level. The problem was that without a shift of policy, 'style' alone could not turn the EMU negotiations towards the government's agenda. No effective bargaining coalitions could be forged on the basis of style, rather than substance.

Given the divergence between party opinion and the IGC agenda on EMU, Major's government was fighting a rearguard action. Its deepest wish was that the EC would not agree on any binding commitment to a single currency. On that basis, British options for the future would be left open. The Major government, like that of Mrs Thatcher's before it, approached the EMU issue with a distinctive philosophy. Its approach was voluntarist and market-oriented. The philosophy defended national sovereignty, whilst having the perceived virtues of pragmatism and liberalism. As noted in Chapter 13, these values had deep roots in British political culture and in the sense of Britain's place in the world.

The constraint, however, was of Britain's strategic weakness in the EMU negotiations. At one level this weakness was a matter of failing to form effective coalitions around key British policy objectives. But at a deeper level, this weakness stemmed from Britain's lack of structural power to persuade or cajole its

---

[1] Under the then existing Treaty, the convening of an intergovernmental conference (IGC) required only a simple majority of member states. This article (236) was repealed by the TEU. Both IGCs—that on EMU and that on political union—began in December 1990 in Rome and were concluded at the Maastricht European Council a year later.

EC partners. Germany had the monetary power to oblige the rest to accept many of its core beliefs on EMU. Britain did not. As a result, Britain's core beliefs were marginalized and seen as being out of step. But the fundamental disjunction was between the Major government's choice of strategy in the EMU negotiations and the structural power it could back it with.

In 1990–1, the Major government repeatedly emphasized that it would negotiate constructively in the IGCs and in good faith.[2] But as the negotiations wore on, it became more and more clear that British policy and strategy were set on a separate path from that of most of the EC states. Keeping faith with the policy principles laid down under the Thatcher government, and with the demands of party unity, John Major negotiated an 'opt-out' for Britain from stage 3 of EMU. At Maastricht, his officials proclaimed that he had won 'game, set, and match' for Britain. The outcome certainly represented an adroit handling of his brief and was consistent with all that he had said beforehand.

At this important stage of EC history, the British government eschewed, like others before it, the political vision of 'Europe' in which EMU was placed by many of its partners. It backed off from the political risks, cautious about the economic viability of the project. Britain deferred its decision, facing a stark choice later. Parallels could be drawn with British policy in the 1950s. Major's choice was consistent with the short-term interests of his party. Whether it met the long-term interests of Britain awaits judgement in the light of future events.

Major's choices met the short-term conditions in his party. But the balance of opinion within the Tory Party was unstable and Major soon came unstuck. After his surprising, and very personal, victory in the May 1992 election, the parliamentary party contained many more Eurosceptic MPs. But the pivotal event was the exit of sterling from the ERM in September 1992. Major had invested much political capital in the ERM and his government sought to maintain its obligations. The irony is that what was proclaimed as a testament to Britain's European commitment collapsed, and the Conservative Party became more sceptical about EMU than ever. The ratification of the Maastricht Treaty at Westminster became something of a nightmare for Major's leadership. From start to finish, appeasing the different factions in his party on EMU satisfied short-term interests, but left Major exposed as events unfolded.

Major, the Party Leader

On EMU, Major abided by the constraint of maximizing party unity at all times. His choice of policy and strategy was always 'nested' in the interests of his

---

[2] The British negotiators were at pains to stress on a number of occasions their willingness to participate actively and constructively in the IGC (e.g. personal representatives' meetings of 15 January 1991; 25–6 February 1991). Moreover, this was a key theme of a letter on 25 October 1991 from Wicks to the IGC Chair, Cees Maas, in which he attacked the proposals of Prof. Mario Draghi (Tesoro, Italy) concerning the status of states outside EMU.

party.[3] The comments he made, off the record, to a journalist about his problems with the ratification of the Maastricht Treaty in July 1993 are also applicable to the conditions of 1991: 'Don't overlook that I could have done all these clever decisive things which people wanted me to do—but I would have split the Conservative Party into smithereens. And you would have said I acted like a ham-fisted leader' (23 July 1993).[4] With his concern for party unity, Major had to be sensitive to the signals he gave to his party. These seemed to vary according to the party mood. In 1991, the 'development of a federal Europe' was rejected, to reassure his party of an essential continuity with the past.[5] But at the same time, this language was softened by rhetoric such as Britain should be 'at the heart of Europe', to indicate a change of approach. The phrase took on much political significance. It was first used in the keynote speech he made to the Konrad Adenauer Stiftung (a Christian Democrat think-tank) in Bonn on 11 March 1991. The location was highly significant: it indicated Major's desire to build bridges with Kohl. Yet, the 'heart of Europe' phrase was used on this occasion only in relation to the relatively minor issue of inter-party co-operation between the Conservatives and their Continental allies in the European Parliament.

Immediately, however, the image became more important than the actual context. At home, the press compared Major's Bonn speech with the Bruges speech of Mrs Thatcher in October 1988 (*The Times*, 12 March 1991). The contrast of ideas was a stark one. Mrs Thatcher had sought to ring-fence the scope of EC integration and to clarify the limits that her government set for it. Major was talking the language of 'constructive engagement', and was praised for doing so by the pro-European wing of his party. Much later, when the balance within the Tory Party had changed again, Major sought to qualify the pro-integrationist implications of the 'heart of Europe' phrase. He had meant, he said, that Britain should engage in vigorous debate with its EC partners, rather than vacate the stage (*Daily Telegraph*, 22 November 1995: quoted in Seldon 1997: 761). His Bonn speech certainly contrasted with that he gave at the University of Leiden on 7 September 1994. The stress in Leiden was on achieving 'the right sort of Europe', of preventing it from going 'off the road' by 'frank' argument. The difference of domestic political context between the two speeches was all-important.

In consequence, many observers dismissed Major's leadership as being weak. Labour's Shadow Foreign Secretary, Gerald Kaufman, dismissed Major's IGC tactics. Major, he said, was 'the man who came to dither' (quoted in Seldon 1997: 168). Yet, such a judgement underestimates Major's skills. He managed his party with an adroitness that few of his peers could have matched. The will to engage in negotiation more constructively with Britain's partners indicated his confidence in handling the complexities of the bargaining process. Whilst he held to no dogmatic position on Europe, he did seek to uphold some basic principles, as noted in Chapter 13. His strategy might be attacked as shallow or

---

3 See Tsebelis (1990).   4 Quoted in Baker *et al.* (1994).

5 The quote is from the motion put to the House of Commons by the government in November 1991 before the Maastricht European Council.

doomed to fail without more substantial policy adjustment. But Major set party unity as a top priority and his options were circumscribed as a result.

Major's achievements as party leader, at least in the period November 1990 to May 1992, were considerable. His party performance can be assessed along several dimensions: effective party management; a winning electoral strategy; achieving predominance in domestic debate (hegemony of political argument); governing competence (for example, rejecting options having implementation problems); and winning another election.[6] By most estimates, Major would score highly on many, if not each, of these benchmarks (Lynch 1998). He had to steer between not only his internal party factions, but also between the siren calls of their supporters in the press. Yet, he kept his party together and he scored a notable triumph in the May 1992 General Election.

In addition, his stance on EMU received relatively broad support in 1990–1. There was more support for his 'wait-and-see' approach than any distinct alternative. If she had been able to pursue her increasingly strident approach as Prime Minister after November 1990, it is very doubtful whether Mrs Thatcher would have achieved as much.

The most contentious criterion is related to governing competence, where different interpretations exist.[7] Gamble's (1994) notion of the 'politics of power' suggests the importance of the maintenance of executive autonomy. The opt-out obtained on stage 3 of EMU can be seen as the most effective means available of maintaining the autonomy of the government, free from a binding commitment to participate. A second notion advanced by Gamble—that of effective management of foreign affairs—is subject to a more controversial assessment. Major's 'triumph' at Maastricht combined with his role in the Gulf War , enhanced his reputation on the international stage. Yet, effective foreign-policy management can also be defined as the pursuit of a vision, of policy coherence for the short and long term. To his critics, Major's EMU policy lacked clear principles and foresight. Placing himself within the straitjacket of internal party politics left Major exposed to charges of weakness and of failing to rise above his party in the name of statesmanship. Major was criticized for following his party, rather than leading it. To some extent, Major was damned if he did, damned if he did not. Major had a difficult hand to play. Moreover, not only did Major face conflicting demands at the time, judgement of his strategy also came to shift with the passage of time.

Major and the Negotiating Strategy in the IGC

John Major's choices on EMU were constrained not only by his party and by the structure of EMU bargaining positions in the rest of the EC, but also by the legacy of Mrs Thatcher's strategy.

---

[6] This follows the concept of statecraft elaborated by Bulpitt (1986).
[7] For an insightful discussion of these aspects, see Lynch (1998).

The scope for a direct threat to veto a treaty on EMU had largely evaporated. At home, such a strident position would have been likely to have caused ructions in the party at almost any time, but certainly in November 1990. At the EC level, Mrs Thatcher might have deployed a veto at the start of the EMU debate, but the momentum behind it was now too strong for that. Her early comments to the effect that EMU would not occur in her lifetime could be seen as a veto threat. Yet, even Mrs Thatcher had soon recognized that she was not able to block progress. Her recollection of the Madrid European Council to the effect that 'I was not in a position to prevent some kind of action being taken' on EMU could be applied more generally (Thatcher 1995: 750). It explains her position at the Hanover, Strasbourg, and Rome European Councils. Indeed, by the time the IGC began, not only was a British veto unlikely to block EMU, but the danger was of the rest going ahead in a maximalist fashion on several fronts and excluding Britain. Mitterrand had already floated the idea of excluding a 'problem state' from the treaty-making process in 1989. By the spring of 1991, the IGC had effectively agreed two key principles affecting EMU participation: no veto and no exclusion.

Whilst the Major government was not in a position to stop the rest from agreeing to an EMU deal, it was able to use the need for ratification of a treaty in all member states as its own lifeboat. It was the basis on which it was to secure its own opt-out from stage 3 of EMU. The rest accepted that Major would not be able to ratify an all-inclusive treaty involving a clear commitment to a single currency. In the language of 'two-level games', the strategic use of uncertainty was deployed to strike a deal. Major's partners allowed him to extricate himself from any commitment to a single currency. The Major government had planned an opt-out as its fall-back position, and this option was to be activated when it could no longer affect the agreement amongst the rest.

Moreover, the scope for sustained, indirect pressure against a binding commitment to a single currency was also narrowing as the IGC opened. Mrs Thatcher had been left isolated at the Rome European Council. The rest had backed a communiqué setting the goal as a single currency, whilst Britain had inserted a note to the effect that it was 'not able to accept the approach set out'. The Major government knew the destination the rest wanted to reach. There was little prospect of being able to redefine it.

Earlier British pressure had failed. As noted in Chapter 14, both Mrs Thatcher and Nigel Lawson had stressed that EMU was too big a step for the EC to take. It contained political dangers (the threat to identity, democracy, and sovereignty) and economic risks (the design of EMU was too speculative and not sufficiently tied to market conditions; or, more fundamentally, EMU would not work). The intellectual case was reinforced by Alan Walters's critique of the fundamental fault in the ERM. Such arguments had failed to stop the progress of the EMU debate. They might have had more effect if they had been deployed earlier and with a keener tactical sense. Lawson's main assault, for example, came as the Delors Committee was already coming to a conclusion. The British case was also put in a blunderbuss style: it was largely insensitive to the nuances of position adopted by the rest.

The Major government reiterated similar arguments about the political and economic risks of EMU. But, with the onset of the IGC, such arguments had to be more closely targeted to the specific issues being negotiated. In the debate on the convergence tests to be applied before stage 3 might begin, the British stressed how strong was the degree of convergence that would be needed. The emphasis was on 'real' convergence criteria, like unemployment and flexible labour markets, rather than nominal indicators alone, such as inflation rates (see below). The political aspect was also pursued: stages 2 and 3 should be de-coupled to allow a clear new point of decision for all. Such decoupling sought to 'salami-slice' the EMU debate and expose the most vulnerable period: that of the transition.

Indeed, the main issue for the Major government had become one of how it might 'divide and rule' in the EMU debate. Paradoxically, given the criticisms of its own imperial history, the British have found it very difficult to deploy such a strategy within the EC. The judgement of Bini-Smaghi *et al.* on this aspect in relation to EMU seems exaggerated. They record that the 'UK negotiators mas-terfully forced a dilution of solutions, weakened in exchange for the mere hope that Britain would sign in the end' (1994: 42). In reality, the British impact was more often to reinforce tendencies that existed already. The impact was rarely decisive. The agreement woven by the rest was not, in its essentials, disrupted by the Major government. This conclusion is clear from an analysis of the nego-tiations and Britain's contributions to them. The potential for coalition-building by Britain will later be discussed further.

This Far and No Further: The Negotiating Mandate

The approach of the British government to EMU had, to a large extent, already been set prior to John Major becoming Prime Minister on 28 November 1990. It rested on two fundamental policy beliefs:

- that progress in European integration should be gradual and should main-tain a flexibility of choice at each new stage; and,
- that increased monetary co-operation should be led by evidence of market sentiment and performance.

The stance of the British negotiators in the IGC combined a strategy of seeking to resist binding commitments on EMU, with an emphasis on a market-led approach to monetary policy. As Lamont expressed it, 'Our approach is . . . evo-lutionary and market-driven' (Chatham House speech: *FT*, 31 May 1991). The British fell back on their traditional preference for *gradualism* in building European co-operation. The emphasis was on pragmatism, testing what was feasible and making progress accordingly. 'Time' was an ally, not a constraint.

This stress was evident in the motion put before the House of Commons by the government in November 1991, just before the European Council at Maastricht. The motion expressed support for the government's stance to date, urged an agreement at Maastricht, but rejected federalism. The only reference to EMU is on the basis of seeking an agreement which: 'Enables this country to exert the greatest influence on the economic evolution of the Community while preserving the right of Parliament to decide at a future date whether to adopt a single currency' (*Independent*, 16 November 1991).From start to finish, the government's position was to 'wait and see'.

But the emphasis on gradualism masked an inner tension within the British camp. As already noted in Chapter 13, there were two distinct tendencies in official thinking on Europe in general, and EMU in particular. The first, following the lead of figures such as Sir Geoffrey Howe and Douglas Hurd, was to favour 'constructive engagement' with Britain's partners. Adherents to this view wished to avoid outright rejection of new long-term goals, but wished to have the transition towards these placed on a gradual, conditional basis. The second tendency was for detachment: involving an acceptance of the single market, but a suspicion of any additional commitments. This latter position was associated with Margaret Thatcher, Nicholas Ridley, and, less evidently, Norman Lamont. 'Gradualism' was a prescription of useful ambiguity; it enabled different shades of opinion to be reconciled.

Gradualism was reinforced by the stress on a market-led approach. This stress was essentially an input from Thatcherism, though it could claim deeper historical roots in the Anglo-Saxon tradition of market liberalism. Thatcherism was by instinct *'behaviouralist'*: the EC should be built 'through the convergence of the economies and policies of member countries; the passage to a more advanced stage of unification must be the natural outcome of a process in which the behaviour of economic agents and policymakers has converged' (Bini-Smaghi *et al*. 1994: 11). Neither traditional British policy on Europe, nor Thatcherite philosophy, could countenance the alternative 'institutionalist' approach to EMU: the building of institutions and legal frameworks to reshape market conditions and behaviour.

The British stance was to try to ensure that the conditions attached to any transitional arrangements remained weak. 'Subsidiarity' meant a severe limitation on the transfer of economic or monetary policy responsibilities to the EC level during the transition to what others defined as a single currency. To the British, 'subsidiarity' also meant progress being cautious and slow; putting off the day when anything serious might happen.

The difference between the Thatcher and Major governments was largely one of tone and style. Mrs Thatcher sought to resist all progress towards a single currency; though with the Rome 1 summit she had been brought to the very eve of the IGC negotiations. There was no doubt that Britain would join in those negotiations, just as it had done in 1985 for the Single European Act. John Major took over as Prime Minister little more than two weeks before the IGC opened.

What changed was a greater will to engage in the debate—to advance British ideas—but what remained was a resolute commitment to the same general principles. Mrs Thatcher left office seeing herself as Boadicea, battling against foreign incursions onto British sovereignty. For all the rhetoric of placing Britain at the 'heart of Europe' and trying to persuade others, Major had an equally clear sense of the line that could not be transgressed.

From a 'Fire-Break' to an 'Opt-out': Decoupling Stages 2 and 3

From the Hanover summit in 1988 onwards, the British sought to prevent a binding commitment being made to a single currency: either on its own behalf or on behalf of the EC as a whole. During the IGC it still seemed possible that such an objective might be achieved. The rest remained divided on the terms of the transition to stage 3. The British proposal for a 'hard ECU' recognized a single currency as a possible long-term outcome, but it was not seen as an inevitable or a binding one. This position was not so far apart from that of the Dutch or of some of the key actors in Germany, but the British were not prepared to move closer to them in order to form a more effective alliance behind slowing EMU down. With this refusal, and the increasing determination of its partners to move ahead, it was inevitable that Britain would have to be dealt with separately in an 'opt-out'.

This case stands in stark contrast to that of Britain and the Single European Act. Mrs Thatcher was strongly in favour of the single market and she conceded that it should be placed in a new treaty-type arrangement. She sought to avoid any form of exclusion from the process (Moravcsik 1991). Yet by 1991 the Major government positively sought an opt-out from EMU.

There was also something of a contrast here with the case of the Social Chapter in 1991. For the latter, it was assumed that there would have to be some kind of accommodation between Britain and its partners, involving a compromise text. Prior to Maastricht, there was little indication that an opt-out on this for Britain might be available. Such an arrangement was negotiated in the final hours at Maastricht. Formally, the other eleven states signed a protocol in effect 'opting in' to the Social Charter of 1989. The calculations involved were different. On social policy, the UK aimed at securing 'positive externalities' of lower costs for its exporters (Moravcsik 1993: 504). An asymmetric pay-off matrix meant that 'defection' from this bargaining game was judged by the Major government to be more beneficial for the UK. But, on EMU, the Major government simply wanted to wait and see whether a single currency was adopted and to leave open whether it might join in the process. Hence its negotiating strategy was necessarily reactive and highly dependent on what its EC partners might do.

On one interpretation, British exclusion from EMU was predictable from the time of the Delors Committee. In its 1989 report, it endorsed the irreversibility of a decision to embark on a transition to EMU (paragraph 39). This provision was the result of pressure from Jacques de Larosière, Governor of the Banque de

France, and his 'francophone' allies. The stipulation greatly upset Whitehall. It reinforced the support for a binding commitment to EMU and placed Britain in an awkward position.

Yet, British isolation was not a foregone conclusion after the Delors Report. A window of opportunity for forging an alternative alliance existed at this stage. Despite all the subsequent recriminations levelled at Robin Leigh-Pemberton for his role in the Delors Committee, he had managed to qualify the provision on irreversibility in the report with others that pointed in an opposite direction. Notably, paragraph 43 stated that the conditions for moving from one stage to another could not be defined precisely in advance. Indeed, the report argued against any commitment to a timetable. A further provision in paragraph 15 also introduced conditionality into the process. Such conditionality was close to those in Whitehall who believed in a gradualist path. It was also close to the initial negotiating stance of the Germans and the Dutch. The Delors Report thus contained an ambiguity that might have been exploited.

In any event, with the prospect of the Madrid European Council endorsing the Delors Report, the Thatcher government was left to reconsider its strategy. Whilst the initial response *after* Madrid was to present alternative plans for monetary co-operation, some within government had already started to contemplate the UK opting out of a move to EMU made by its EC partners. Though for the first three decades of its existence, such differential participation in the EC club had been unthinkable, the climate had begun to change.[8] This shift was, in significant part, owing to what was seen as the intransigence and isolation of the British position. The most relevant precedent occurred at the Strasbourg European Council, in December 1989, which had ended with the UK not signing up for the Social Charter, agreed by the other eleven. Now there arose the idea of establishing a 'fire-break' between the putative second stage of EMU and the transition to the final goal of a single currency. The UK and the other states would not then be obliged to participate in stage 3. Much later, private references to a 'fire-break' were presented to the public as an 'opt-out' or even an 'opt-in'. In substance, the terms meant the same.

Developing the 'Fire-Break' at Home

A 'fire-break' was discussed at one of the first meetings of the Whitehall co-ordinating committee chaired by Nigel Wicks. The committee was established

---

[8] Two cases can be cited, in addition to Strasbourg in 1989. First, at Milan in June 1985 Bettino Craxi, the Italian Prime Minister and the then EC President, had called for a straight majority vote on the convening of an IGC (which subsequently led to the Single European Act). Secondly, at Brussels in June 1987 Wilfried Martens similarly called for a vote on a proposal related to the so-called green currency system underpinning the CAP. In the 1985 case Britain was joined by Denmark and Greece; in the 1987 vote it was alone. The will to move ahead on the basis of a majority vote was widely recognized to stem from an exasperation with the obstinacy and divergence of the British stance on a number of European issues during this period. These traits were closely identified with Mrs Thatcher's leadership (Howe 1994: 531; Thatcher 1995: 549–50, 730).

early in 1990, after the Strasbourg European Council had reached a final agreement to hold an IGC on EMU. Sir David Hannay, then the UK's Permanent Representative in Brussels, was one of the first to refer to a 'fire-break'. The 'fire-break' discussion began from a recognition that the UK would not be able to block some or all of its EC partners from committing themselves to EMU. Moreover, it was also based on the assumption that the UK would not be able to insist on a further point of decision between stages 2 and 3. The logical alternative was for the UK to think of a 'fire-break' separating itself, and perhaps others, from those moving ahead to a single currency.

The discussion of a 'fire-break' formula was kept to a small circle within government. When raised with them, Hurd and Major accepted the logic of seeking this solution. But Mrs Thatcher refused, seeing it as allowing progress to an objective that she could not countenance. Whether she would, or could, have blocked all progress towards a single currency had she remained Prime Minister is, of course, very much open to question. She had certainly failed to stop the momentum up to and including the Rome summit of October 1990.

By the spring of 1990 there was some confusion about the UK's position. This confusion was evident in the way in which the 'hard' ECU plan was launched. But by then, Whitehall had already started to discuss seriously the possibility of Britain having an opt-out on EMU. Given the scepticism as to whether the 'hard' ECU had any prospect of being adopted, Whitehall recognized that an opt-out was the fall-back position.

Moreover, Britain's partners were beginning to contemplate separate arrangements for her. Karl-Otto Pöhl suggested in June 1990 that a 'two-speed' monetary union might be the only way forward (*FT*, 19 June 1990). The immediate reaction of Delors was to reject the notion as weakening the path of EMU. Delors made such comments at a General Affairs Council in Luxembourg in June 1990 (*FT*, 19 June 1990). But he appears soon to have taken a different attitude to a specific opt-out for the UK. Sir David Hannay floated the idea of an opt-out to Delors in July 1990. Both agreed that it was a possible solution if progress proved difficult. Delors was to openly support the idea by the following spring.

The need for a possible opt-out became enveloped in EC-level discussions about the nature of stages 2 and 3. This linkage would remain the case throughout the IGC. In the summer of 1990 discussion centred on the duration of, and conditions for, the second stage. In July, an EC Monetary Committee Report recommended that stage 2 should be as short as possible. This idea was not to be adopted. By the October European Council in Rome, it had been agreed that stage 2 should begin in 1994. Six months later it looked increasingly as if stage 2 would offend no one. In spring 1991 it was accepted that the conditions for participation in stage 2 would not be very restrictive. The Major government could live with them.

But there was still the debate about the transition to stage 3. An initial German paper to the IGC had argued that there must be unanimous agreement in the Council before stage 3 could begin. This view was shared by the Dutch. On this basis, London could thus feel that it would be able to avoid a binding commitment. This was certainly Major's belief. In his 'heart of Europe' speech in Bonn in March 1991 he said 'we are confident that the IGC will be able to work out arrangements which protect the right of a future British Parliament to make a decision later' (*The Times*, 11 March 1991). Soon afterwards, Jean-Claude Trichet argued in a French paper to the IGC in April 1991 that the transition to stage 3 should be based on the twin principles of 'no coercion and no veto': no member state could be forced to enter into it, nor could any government stop the rest from going ahead (Bini-Smaghi *et al.* 1994). Such principles seemed to underscore the notion of an opt-out.

Yet, for tactical reasons, the British negotiators were keen not to accept sep-aration too soon. At an informal ECOFIN meeting in Luxembourg, on 11 May 1991, the Trichet principles were accepted. An opt-out for the UK was raised in the discussion by Jean-Claude Juncker, the chair of the meeting and the Finance Minister of Luxembourg. As he later commented to the press, 'The prospect of a two-speed monetary union was raised—and no one was shocked' (*FT*, 13 May 1991). In the meeting, Norman Lamont accepted that such an arrangement might have to be the conclusion. But he preferred that it should not be adopted yet and that it should not be made public. Delors, a participant in the discussion, was, however, unguarded before the press. He mentioned the idea of an opt-out immediately afterwards, claiming paternity of it. Delors referred to the possi-bility of a clause in the Treaty which would allow a future British parliament to make a decision on participation in stage 3 (*Keesing's Archives*, 11 May 1991). Later, faced by British criticism, Delors regretted his mistake and was more cir-cumspect. As the *Financial Times* reported, 'After Saturday's meeting, the Commission President refused to elaborate on his idea, hinting indeed that he might have been precipitate in raising it so long before the expected wrap-up of EMU negotiations in the autumn' (*FT*, 13 May 1991). Lamont tried to play down the idea: he commented that the suggestion was 'constructive but not a dra-matic breakthrough' (*FT*, 13 May 1991). In reality, though, a special protocol for Britain (or an 'opt-out') was now a serious proposition.

Avoiding Commitments in Luxembourg

A further intriguing twist occurred during the Luxembourg European Council in June. At a private meeting—attended by John Major, Helmut Kohl, Jacques Santer (Council President), Ruud Lubbers (Council President-to-be), and Jacques Delors—the British Prime Minister raised the possibility of the UK hav-ing an opt-out on EMU. He stressed that his government genuinely sought con-structive engagement in the debate—it would negotiate in good faith—but the final agreement might prove unacceptable to the UK. Those listening to him accepted that an opt-out might have to be the solution. Indeed, John Major might have been able to secure the deal at Luxembourg. There was intense lobbying on Major, though, by his EC partners to agree a certain set of principles on which a final EMU deal might be established. John Kerr, the UK Permanent Representative in Brussels, pressed Major to clinch such a deal. Delors also wanted him to do so. Kerr's fellow IGC member, Nigel Wicks, urged equally strongly that Major wait. In the end, Major preferred to leave as much open as possible.

Major had good reasons to back off. As Sarah Hogg and Jonathan Hill—two key aides in the Major team—recalled, while Major 'had agreement in principle to some kind of opt-out from monetary union for Britain, he was reluctant to try to clinch a deal on that too soon' (Hogg and Hill 1995: 81). The UK first wanted to ensure that stage 2 would be in an acceptable form, before accepting that it would be part of it. As one close aide put it, 'We didn't want to buy a pig in a poke'. Stage 2 had to be made 'bug-free'; thorough work still needed to be done on it. Later, the British team would recall their own thoroughness in this period and contrast it with what they saw as the haste and lack of caution on the part of the Danes on their own provisions.

There were also tactical reasons not to close the deal at Luxembourg. Major had recently stressed that he wanted Britain to be 'at the heart of Europe'; an opt-out secured so soon would contradict that notion. Moreover, Britain wanted to be fully involved in the negotiations, in case it did at some point in the future opt to enter stage 3. Not least, it wished to participate in the setting of the convergence criteria that would govern membership in stage 3. John Major emphasized to all around him that 'Nothing is agreed, until everything is agreed'. He wished to keep open, and not close down, influence over the final outcome. Indeed, an illustration of the lost influence for Britain arising from a deal on an opt-out came at the Maastricht European Council itself. The Franco-Italian initiative on 'automaticity' was constructed entirely without British input.

Excluded from the private meeting at Luxembourg on the 'opt-out', many of Britain's other partners were left unaware or unsure about the understanding that had been reached. Later, some in the IGC spoke seemingly in ignorance of it. Back in London, Treasury staff began drafting a protocol for a UK opt-out. It would be examined within Whitehall with a fine-tooth comb to ensure it was 'risk-free' for Britain. On the opt-out, the Major government played its cards close to its chest. It wanted to avoid Britain's EC partners dissecting in detail a draft protocol in advance of Maastricht, for fear that it might be undermined.

Away from the informal ECOFIN meeting of April and the June European Council, the issue of an opt-out for Britain had received relatively little attention within the formal IGC negotiations during the first half of 1991. But it hung over the discussions of the IGC in the second half as a result, not only of British concerns, but also of the actions of the Dutch EC Presidency. The Dutch were themselves very cautious about the transitional arrangements for EMU. They were at least as adamant as the Germans that economic convergence was a prerequisite to begin stage 3. A deferred decision on whether and how to begin stage 3 would allow a review as to whether this convergence had been achieved. The Dutch stance was thus highly accommodating to the British. Paradoxically, however, whilst the Dutch Presidency was proposing a novel structure of opt-outs and postponed decisions on EMU, in the other IGC on Political Union its draft treaty text was based squarely on a traditional '*communautaire*' philosophy.

A Near-Rescue by the Dutch

In any event, the Dutch Presidency began by circulating a text in August, authored by the Dutch Chair of the IGC Personal Representatives, Cees Maas. Maas had an abrasive style, and the substance of his text was no less provocative. The August text proposed leaving the question of whether to proceed to stage 3, and the selection of participants, to a meeting of the European Council some time in the future. This formulation gave little prior commitment to EMU by any government. But there was little support for the Maas Draft.

Under intense political pressure, Wim Kok, the Dutch Finance Minister, was obliged to distance himself from the paper prepared by his chief official. Yet a text circulated under his own name the following month also failed to win majority support. The issue came to a head at the informal ECOFIN meeting at Apeldoorn (21–2 September). The meeting closed with general agreement on three basic principles: no member state should have a veto on the progress of the rest to a single currency; no member state should be coerced into joining a single currency; and no member state should be excluded from joining a single currency if it met the appropriate conditions for doing so. The consensus was for the UK 'problem' to be dealt with by Britain being granted a derogation.

Lamont and Wicks were increasingly isolated. The British government opposed the notion of a derogation, as it implied a commitment to join later. There should be no obligation to do so. At the same time, in its desire to keep its options open, it argued that states should have the right to join later under the same conditions as the initial participants. British reservation was also apparent in its opposition to a fixed date for stage 2, until its content had been decided. But the main sensitivity related to stage 3. Previously, the British would not accept the 'no veto' principle on stage 3: the decision to proceed should be made on the basis of unanimity. But, at Apeldoorn, Lamont caused some surprise when he accepted the notion of a two-speed/two-tier process, as supported by the Dutch and the Germans. Both the British and Dutch agreed: stage 3 should only begin when a sufficient number of member states had taken separate, individual decisions to participate.

British opposition to being offered a derogation or a separate declaration on EMU brought them into immediate conflict with Delors. Delors's intervention on this theme at Apeldoorn increased British anxieties. Indeed, a few weeks later, Kerr wrote to the Commission outlining why neither a declaration nor a derogation would assuage British fears about being forced into EMU at a later date.[9] He listed three main objections. First, a declaration outside the Treaty would not confer the necessary legal certainty. Secondly, the right of a member state to take a separate decision must be contained within the Treaty. Finally, there was no rule of EC law that Community obligations should necessarily be binding on all states if there were good reasons for not making them so.

Wicks also found himself in conflict with the Italians. He wrote to Maas, as IGC Chair, to complain about a letter circulated by his Italian counterpart, Mario Draghi.[10] Draghi's letter had indicated Italian unease about an opt-out. It had suggested, *inter alia*, that states with some kind of derogation ought not to be able to qualify for any EC financial assistance intended to help member states to converge. A later letter from Draghi on 8 November, stressing vehement Italian opposition to any general opt-out, was not circulated to London. But it was clearly intended to rally others to the cause.

The British pinned their hopes on the Dutch, who produced a revised Draft Treaty on 28 October 1991. The relevant provision stated that:

The Council shall not oblige a member state to participate in the third stage if a member state has notified to the Council that the national parliament of the member state does not feel able to approve the irrevocable fixing of its currency at the provisional date. Such a member state will be called 'Member state with an exemption'. (Article 109g(2))

The Dutch attached a 'Declaration on the transition to Stage 3 of EMU', to buttress the commitment to a single currency. This stated that:

The Governments of the Member states express their strong preference for a swift transition to the third stage of EMU with the full participation of all member states;

. . . [they] declare that it is their strongest intention to participate in stage 3 of EMU from the proposed date without exemption.

Not suprisingly, the British government liked the main treaty provision (Article 109g). But it rejected the notion that it might sign the attached declaration. The Danish representatives took a similar line. Both liked the assumption of a 'general opt-out' that did not single out any member state by name. All national parliaments should retain a free choice.

But there was little prospect that a majority of the EC states would accept the Dutch formulation. This prospect was reduced by the fact that the British refused to accept the declaration. Most opposed to any general opt-out or any deferred decision on stage 3 were the Italians. The Germans, the French, the Spanish, the Belgians, and the Luxembourgers also had serious reservations about the Dutch text. For its part, the Commission feared that the credibility of the commitment to EMU would be undermined; confused signals would be given to the markets; the will to converge might be undermined. The

---

[9] Letter of 25 October 1991, from John Kerr to David Williamson, Commission Secretary-General.
[10] The Draghi letter is dated 22 October 1991; that from Wicks, 25 October 1991. Wicks referred to the draft texts on Article 109e bis and 109g, paragraph 7.

Commission's own legal service believed that a separate provision could be made for the UK, and contrasting provisions might apply to other member states that wished to refer back to their national parliaments before embarking on stage 3. The provisions for the latter might involve a longer lapse of time or a two-stage vote during the period in which the European Council and ECOFIN would make the relevant decisions to proceed with stage 3.[11]

A compromise draft was presented by Belgium (Grégoire Brouhs) and Luxembourg (Yves Mersch). This draft sought to allow only those member states to make use of the opt-out that had formally reserved this possibility during the ratification of the Treaty. In other words, all member states would have an opt-out, but some might revoke this right at the outset. This compromise received little support.

The pressure to limit the opt-out to the UK, and perhaps Denmark, was growing. There was some frustration amongst the British over how the Danish delegation was pursuing the opt-out goal. It was seen as 'deserting' the cause during the difficult period of November (Hogg and Hill 1995: 140–1). As noted earlier, the British felt the Danes were being too lax in the drafting of an opt-out. The Danes were more ready to accept an individual solution. By contrast, 'all the remarkable skills of British diplomacy were deployed' to blur the distinction between a general and a specific opt-out (Bini-Smaghi et al. 1994: 19). But the British were going against the tide.

At home, Whitehall began work on the draft of a British opt-out on EMU. It had not been possible to define the details at an earlier stage, as Whitehall needed to await the elaboration of the putative EC treaty before it could define what exactly it wished to opt out from. Moreover, from August onwards the Dutch Presidency had raised British hopes that a separate opt-out would not be necessary: all states might have one. Mark Blythe of the Treasury's legal staff supervised the drafting of the British text, working primarily with the Cabinet Office and with the UK office in Brussels. The full opt-out draft was not widely distributed in Whitehall. It was not even discussed in the interdepartmental Wicks Committee shadowing the IGC. For their part, both the Cabinet Office and the UK office in Brussels found Blythe's text overelaborate. It had painstakingly cut Britain off from stage 3, unless Westminster voted to join in. Indeed, to John Kerr (Brussels) and David Hadley (Cabinet Office) the draft was so obsessed with ensuring that the UK did not have to join stage 3, that it had lost sight of the objective of making it possible for her to join later. At Maastricht, Major would refer to the provision as being for an 'opt-in', rather than for an 'opt-out'. This formulation was closer to the preference of key officials in London for 'constructive engagement' on EMU. In the meantime, however, the British fought on two fronts. They tested their ideas on a separate protocol with selected EC partners, whilst at the same time trying to pursue the idea of some

[11] See Legal Service Note on differentiated arrangements for moving to stage 3, dated 4 November 1991.

kind of general opt-out. A specific UK opt-out provision was entering the assumptions of the IGC negotiators more and more during November.

By later that month, the Commission had worked out its own texts. The Commission sought to shift the discussion away from the Dutch general opt-out, to much more specific provisions on Britain and Denmark. Two alternative solutions to the problem were considered by the Commission. First, a unilateral declaration might be made by the UK, which would reserve the right of its Parliament to decide on an irrevocable fixing of its currency. This alternative was seen as least damaging to the EC cause, but it would not provide the legal certainty sought by London and stressed by Kerr. The second alternative was for an exemption protocol for Britain alone annexed to the Treaty, stating that: 'the Council shall not oblige the UK to participate in stage 3 if, within (n) months, it has notified the Council that its Parliament is not able to approve the irrevocable fixing of its currency at the provisional date'. This latter provision gave legal certainty to the UK, without questioning the binding commitment of others.

The End-Game

The final negotiations before the Maastricht summit pursued the idea of separate protocols for Britain and Denmark. An informal ECOFIN meeting at Scheveningen, an IGC of personal representatives, and a final IGC at ministerial level in Brussels were held within a four-day period at the start of December. It was decided to delete the general opt-out clause (now Article 109g(3)) and all references to a member state 'with an exemption' were also removed from the text. Instead, it was envisaged that a protocol would be attached to the Treaty to deal with any state not able to commit itself to stage 3. This procedure was designed to ensure that the state concerned would be exempt from the relevant rights and obligations under the Treaty until it requested abrogation of the exemptions. The aim was to underline the irreversibility of the process towards a single currency and to prevent any veto by a member state. The provisions were intended to cover the position of the UK and Denmark. But both states expressed their opposition to the abolition of the general opt-out and expressed their reservations on the new provisions. Lamont, in particular, was incensed by the course being taken in these meetings.

More radically, a provision was added for two new procedures that would trigger stage 3: decisions would be made at the end of 1996 and at the end of 1998. The dual-date formula was originated by Bérégovoy, the French Finance Minister, and it moved the IGC towards the 'automaticity' clause agreed at Maastricht. The Germans were concerned about the 'laxity' of these provisions and sought to tighten them up.[12] But, once the British and Danish were 'hived off', they forfeited the prospect of affecting this new, much stronger

---

[12] Specifically, Köhler argued that the French formulation would allow states that did not qualify for entry into stage 3 to vote on whether it should begin. Moreover, the envisaged derogation for some states might be abrogated all too easily, thus further affecting the process.

commitment to proceed. London and Copenhagen were being sidelined. Ostensibly, they were more on the defensive in this area than earlier in the Dutch Presidency.

At the Maastricht European Council, the Major government proceeded slowly with its opt-out request. Major had given Wicks clear instructions not to show the opt-out protocol, drafted by the UK Treasury, to any of his EC partners until half-way through the second day's session (Hogg and Hill 1995: 153). The British camp was still concerned not to raise the issue too soon. Such caution created the risk of tension with the rest of the EC. The delay could be seen as a further instance of British high-handedness, following on from the criticism of how Britain arranged its ERM entry the year before. References by the British to 'our' protocol ignored the fact that everyone else would have to agree to it.

Into this delicate situation walked Lamont. He was already annoyed by the course taken in the pre-Maastricht meetings. The Chancellor had not bothered to brief himself fully on the content of the protocol. His attitude was 'take it or leave it'. The British released their draft when Lamont was to negotiate with his ECOFIN partners. The Chancellor was soon unable to answer detailed questions about it from his fellow ministers. Brusqueness followed indolence. Lamont was in difficulty and tempers rose. The Chancellor's volatility led him to walk out of the negotiating session, leaving his partners perplexed. Lamont later recalled that:

At the last meeting I simply produced a piece of paper which deleted everything and said it didn't apply to Britain. And, although I said it was not acceptable, and to my intense irritation, they proceeded to go through it line by line and alter it. I said this was simply not acceptable: none of this can be altered. Take it or leave it. (BBC TV, *The Poisoned Chalice*, 9 May 1996)

Lamont told Major that his ECOFIN colleagues were 'messing about' with 'our' protocol. The implication was that such negotiation was an unexpected intrusion into British affairs. Yet the protocol would be part of a treaty binding on all: twelve EC states which would have to ratify the British protocol. To senior British officials, Lamont's walk-out was plain silly, served no purpose, and was potentially seriously counterproductive.

Suddenly, the opt-out deal seemed to slipping away from the hands of the British. Wicks, Kerr, Hogg, and Major seem to have been genuinely anxious that the deal might be lost. Others felt they had to join in.[13] As Tristan Garel-Jones, Minister of State for European Affairs at the time and closely involved at the Maastricht session, later recalled:

A very, very senior Treasury official [the reference appears to be to Wicks] who was there on the team came to me and said, 'Minister, the Chancellor has left the meeting: he's walked out and he's taken all of us with him and our opt-out is actually now being discussed by the others and we're not there'. That was really quite a major crisis because

---

[13] Cf. Lamont's more recent claim that *he* negotiated the opt-out, and that Major's input was minimal: *The Times*, 23 June 1995.

by then everything else was falling into place. (BBC TV, *The Poisoned Chalice*, 9 May 1996)

Nor were Britain's partners too pleased with the opt-out discussion. Wim Kok, the Dutch Finance Minister chairing the ECOFIN session, complained about Lamont's behaviour to Ruud Lubbers, his Prime Minister. With Kok's approval, Lubbers asked to see Major separately when the European Council took a break at about 6.45 p.m. (Hogg and Hill 1995: 154). Hurd, Jay, Kerr, and Stephen Wall (Charles Powell's successor as Major's foreign affairs Private Secretary) went with their Prime Minister. Only when the meeting was in session did Lamont discover that it was taking place. Again, Tristan Garel-Jones has recalled that Lamont had to be shut out: 'Norman Lamont arrived and wanted to go into the meeting. Of course, it's embarrassing—John Kerr's an official and I'm a minister of state—but we had to say, "Chancellor, you can't go into the meeting". We had to be quite firm about that.' Later, the respective finance ministers (Lamont and Kok) were called in to the meeting. As Hogg and Hill record: 'The Prime Minister nailed the protocol into place. The mood lightened. The Finance Ministers left. Then Ruud Lubbers and John Major moved onto the big outstanding issue: the Social Chapter' (1995: 154).[14] Thus, according to the Major camp, Lamont almost lost the opt-out, but it was secured by Major in his meeting with Lubbers. When asked to comment on Lamont's claim that he negotiated the opt-out and not Major, the Prime Minister was dismissive. 'I'm very surprised to hear Norman say that and so will everyone present at the negotiations', he said (BBC TV, *The Poisoned Chalice*, 9 May 1996).

When the heads of government reassembled just before 9 p.m., the EMU protocol was formalized. Kok presented the text for a British opt-out, and it was accepted with no opposition and with little or no discusion.

The ease with which it was accepted reflects several factors. First, the basic principles of the opt-out for Britain were no great surprise to the rest of the EC at Maastricht. They had formed part of the working assumptions of the negotiations for at least the previous month. The FCO, at least, had not expected any great battle over the EMU opt-out at Maastricht. Secondly, after Lamont's walkout at lunch, time was slipping away before the summit was due to close. The time constraint, and an increasing frustration with British pedantry, limited the scope for a discussion of its content. The ease of acceptance might also suggest how unnecessary Lamont's walk-out actually was. He had faced no determined challenge or opposition to the opt-out and had simply overreacted. If the latter is true, then Major had 'rescued' the situation after Lamont had behaved as the 'party-pooper'. But, in reality, the British opt-out on EMU was not in any fundamental danger at Maastricht. The rest were already resigned to it. Lamont's walk-out had simply created an unhelpful diversion, a distraction of energy from other business, and, above all, unnecessary embarrassment.

---

[14] Helmut Kohl joined them for their discussion on the Social Protocol. Kohl was not present, though, for the discussion on the EMU opt-out.

Whatever the explanation, the Major government had achieved its key EMU objective of 1991: it had avoided making an irrevocable commitment to a single currency. Britain could wait and see. It had reconstructed the scenario of the 1950s, when Britain stood aside from the establishment of the ECSC and the EEC. Dispute has arisen since Maastricht, however, over how long the opt-out was to be exercised. Lamont has written that, 'I always supposed [the government] would announce its decision at the general election preceding any move towards a single currency. It never occurred to me that we would try to keep our options open until 1999' (*The Times*, 23 June 1995). Such a formulation questions the purpose of having an opt-out in the first place. By contrast, both Major and Kenneth Clarke, Lamont's successor, maintained that the government would decide on stage 3 when it could judge the prevailing economic circumstances in which it was to be established. The Tory government struggled to maintain party unity on this issue.

The opt-out gave freedom. But it also imposed constraints. The eleven paragraphs of the Protocol giving the UK an opt-out left a future British government under no obligation to move to stage 3. So long as a decision to enter was not made, UK monetary policy would remain subject to national law, and the Bank of England need not be made independent. But, outside stage 3, the UK would have no rights to participate in setting the rules for the club (e.g. management of single currency; the counter-inflation policy of the ECB; the decision on which states should be allowed to participate in stage 3; the selection of heads of ECB). The Protocol provides that the European Council was to decide on a possible later UK entry bid by qualified majority voting (QMV). Such a decision would follow a recommendation from the Commission, following consultation with the European Parliament. The Protocol recognizes that the UK 'shall have the right to move to the third stage provided only that it satisfies the necessary conditions'. The Council would decide on whether the conditions laid down in the Treaty (paragraph 10; Article 109k(2)) were met. No doubt a British decision to end its exclusion would be welcomed. But in the deferred, subjective, and political judgement by the Council there were inherent risks that the bargaining between the UK and the rest might involve other conditions being asked of the latecomer.

The Major government sanctified its own conditional status. But it failed to prevent the rest from making their commitment to EMU irrevocable. There was disappointment at the deal on 'automaticity' made by the rest. But having gone for an opt-out, Britain could exert no influence over this wider deal. London had played a narrower game. The key officials (Hogg, Jay, Kerr, and Wicks) now drafted a summary of the Treaty for ministers back in London. It was time to proclaim victory.

The Major government could champion its success in not being obliged to participate in the final transition to EMU. But the opposition on this was difficult to identify; the 'no coercion' principle had been accepted by all. Moreover, the boundaries of an acceptable EMU agreement (the 'win-set') for the UK were so narrow and in many respects distinct from those of its EC partners that, in retrospect, its path to isolation was largely predetermined before the IGC began. Against this background, it is perhaps surprising how far the British government was able to engage itself in the IGC negotiations on the core content of the EMU package.

Sovereignty and Subsidiarity in Stage 2

Within the IGC negotiations, the British took every opportunity to try to limit the loss of sovereignty involved in the transition to a single currency. If, following the Delors Report, a stage 3 was defined as the adoption of a single currency, then Britain would not be able to commit itself to this in advance. However, it might be able to join in stage 2, if this was defined in relatively modest terms. The task was thus to minimize the constraints and commitments entailed in stage 2. This minimization could be done in the name of 'subsidiarity': the effect would be to limit the loss of sovereignty until the point at which some went ahead with a single currency.

Its own advocacy of a parallel currency ('hard' ECU) managed by a European Monetary Fund was said by critics to be a contradiction of this philosphy. Since the autumn of 1990, London had sought to give increased emphasis to the significance of the EMF's role. It allowed the EMF to be seen as a stage 2 institution. Yet, when the 'hard' ECU was not under discussion, the British sided with the Dutch and the Germans in rejecting the creation of a European Central Bank in stage 2. It followed their lead in arguing that the stage 2 institutions should be limited in design and modest in their powers. True, an EMF could not be mistaken for an ECB. But to argue for the first and to oppose the latter seemed a significant shift of tone, and perhaps logic, as some senior Whitehall officials themselves accepted.[15] The official defence was that the two positions were compatible. The EMF proposal left responsibility for national monetary policies at the level of the member states, whilst the Franco-Italian proposals for an ECB in stage 2 passed much of this responsibility to the new European body.

The Dutch and the Germans sought a modest stage 2 for their own reasons. A key reason was that monetary-policy responsibility could not be shared between national and European authorities in the transition. Such a sharing would sow confusion and disturb market confidence. Moreover, market confidence could not be conjured up by grandiose institutions and long-term deadlines. It had to be nurtured by the behaviour of the appropriate institutions. When, by March 1991 onwards, it could not successfully advocate its own 'hard' ECU scheme, the British fell back on this line of argument. Both arguments put off the prospect of a loss of sovereignty.

The 'hard' ECU notwithstanding, British negotiators endeavoured to secure a weak stage 2 of EMU. This objective covered a number of major items. First,

---

[15] See discussion below on proximity of British, German, and Dutch views on EMU.

since Hanover, Britain had opposed any commitment to the creation of an ECB. At the Rome summit of October 1990, Britain had dissented from a commitment to a new monetary institution from stage 2 onwards. The general communiqué referred to *the* monetary institution being established from the start of stage 2: to the Italians, and less certainly the French, this reference implied a strong institution to govern *both* stages 2 and 3. Later, Britain readily joined the Germans and the Dutch in their interpretation of the clause; the stage 2 body should be separate from that of the stage 3 one. There was a symmetry of interests between the three governments. The Germans and the Dutch did not wish to contemplate 'even a partial transfer of [monetary] sovereignty before the final stage' (Bini-Smaghi *et al.* 1994: 35). The British wanted to be able to sign up for stage 2 and thus did not want this to threaten sovereignty in any conceivable manner. The three governments, together with the Danes, insisted that an 'ECB' should only be created towards the end of stage 2. From spring to autumn, the defenders of the Rome 1 position were becoming fewer and fewer: the Italians and the Commission were increasingly isolated. By September 1991, the IGC had agreed that the stage 2 institution should have the modest title of 'European Monetary Institute'. Its responsibilities were defined accordingly.[16]

The second point of resistance for the British concerned the status of ERM participation. They opposed the idea that participation in the ERM should be fixed by law (Hogg and Hill 1995: 140). Norman Lamont felt particularly strongly about this issue. His feelings about it appear to have been stronger than were those of Major and Hurd. Indeed, according to Lamont, he threatened to resign over it. Differences on the meaning of the Treaty in relation to participation in the ERM were sustained after the Treaty had been signed. Some governments, such as the French, believed participation in the ERM in stage 2 was an essential precondition for entry into stage 3. The British, by contrast, believed that it was more a matter of a currency observing the discipline of the ERM, rather than actually belonging to it (see TEU: Article 109j(1)).[17] Neither the British nor the French managed to have the issue resolved at Maastricht.

Thirdly, the British government sought to uphold its general rights of national sovereignty in relation to both economic and monetary policy. It rejected any 'parallelism' between a commitment to proceed with monetary integration and an acceptance of new fiscal co-ordination at the EC level. The Delors Report had referred to the importance of parallelism, though it had not made clear provision for it. The British opposed calls for more 'Cohesion' aid from an expanded EC budget to the peripheral member states (see below). To the Major government, fiscal policy was subject to the principle of 'subsidiarity': it should prop-

---

[16] The EMI was to prepare for the creation of the European System of Central Banks (ESCB) and the European Central Bank (ECB) to operate in stage 3.

[17] The English text of Article 109j (1) states that the assessment of whether a member state has achieved the appropriate convergence will be based, *inter alia*, on 'the observance of the normal fluctuation margins provided for by the Exchange Rate Mechanism of the European Monetary System, for at least two years, without devaluing against the currency of any other Member State'.

erly be left to national parliaments and governments to determine. In part, this position stemmed from the belief in 'no taxation without representation'. The British were joined in this stance by the Dutch and the Danish delegations. On this issue, the Germans were isolated from their normal camp. The Germans may have been willing to countenance increased fiscal powers at the EC level—as, of course, were the states that were likely to receive more aid from a bigger EC budget—but only as part of a wider and more ambitious political union. The UK government rejected any new EC powers in this regard. Nor was it attracted to the idea of a *'gouvernement économique'* in the French Draft Treaty of February 1991. The Major government opposed even this intergovernmental arrangement.

Fortunately for the British, these ideas gained little support in the IGC. The final Treaty merely states that member states will regard their economic policies as a matter of common concern and that they will conduct them with a view to contributing to the objectives of the EC (TEU: Articles 102*a*, 103). Member states are to participate in a multilateral surveillance procedure to help promote co-ordination and convergence of their policies (TEU: Article103). These provisions are not covered by the British opt-out and so apply to the UK also. In the IGC negotiations on multilateral surveillance, the Major government had joined the Dutch and the Germans in emphasizing the responsibility of member states for economic policy, in line with the notion of subsidiarity, whilst accepting the need for strengthened co-operation in this regard (IGC ministerial meeting of 26 February 1991).

The economic provisions of the Treaty refer to the avoidance of 'excessive government deficits' (TEU: Article 104*c*). Whilst Britain was covered by some of these provisions, including being subject to monitoring by the Commission and the EC Monetary Committee, it was not governed by the procedure attached to them, which can involve fines on a member state (see Protocol, para. 5). Reports and recommendations are to be made concerning British policy, but here the opt-out avoids any significant incursions into UK sovereignty (TEU: Article 109*e*).

In the IGC negotiations, British negotiators opposed limiting national autonomy on excessive deficits. First, they argued against any regulations constraining member states in the extent and management of their budget deficits. The Major government favoured virtue in this area, but not when it was imposed by EC law. It had made plain its view at the IGC personal representatives' meeting of 29 January 1991 and at the Third Inter-Institutional Meeting on EMU in Strasbourg on 11 June 1991. Secondly, the British government believed that there should be no financial sanctions imposed on those governments that failed to follow the convergence obligations. Its representatives queried the application of sanctions and the action that might be taken if these were not followed (IGC personal representatives' meeting of 21 May 1991). Later, they also argued against financial sanctions on the ground that the action of market forces would be a sufficient discipline on member states (IGC personal representatives' meeting of 10 September 1991). Thirdly, the British government believed that any policy recommendations as to how governments ought to act to achieve convergence should remain secret. The IGC discussed whether member states might be 'shamed' into appropriate behaviour by the Council agreeing to publish such recommendations. This proposal was vigorously opposed by the British (IGC personal representatives' meeting of 10 September 1991).

With respect to monetary policy, the British also secured clear exemptions. The opt-out Protocol specifies that British monetary policy is to be determined by its own national law (para. 4). Most of the articles of the Protocol on the statute of the ESCB and the ECB do not apply to Britain. The conduct of monetary policy by the ESCB, the ECB's right to issue currency, the rules on national central banks, the decisions of the ESCB, decisions on the board members of the ECB, and the fixing of currency rates do not apply to Britain or the Bank of England.

Lamont took particular pride in the maintenance of the 'Ways and Means facility with the Bank of England if and so long as the United Kingdom does not move to the third stage' (paragraph 11). This met a specific interest of the Treasury and much attention had been paid in London to this issue. Whilst the Major government agreed that in the transition to a single currency there should be no monetary financing of government deficits by central banks, it was concerned not to have to abandon its practice of short-term financing. The right to maintain 'Ways and Means' allowed Whitehall to continue to draw heavily on its short-term lending facility with the Bank.

The provisions of the protocol followed Whitehall's concern that its positions on monetary policy were not being upheld within the IGC. The British argued that each member state should be allowed to decide for itself whether and when to make its central banks independent (IGC ministerial meeting of 10 June 1991). But the tide was against them, so an exemption was sought. Whilst the final Treaty stated that the process of independence should begin in stage 2 (TEU: Article 109e(5)) and be completed by the time the ESCB is established (TEU: Article 108), it was qualified by the phrase 'as appropriate'. This qualification allowed Britain not to grant independence to the Bank of England unless and until Britain agreed to participate in stage 3. Paradoxically, after the IGC was over, when Lamont asserted his Euroscepticism, he shifted ground to back the idea of making the Bank of England independent. This appeared to be another case of the idea being good, but not if it was 'imposed' by the EC.

The government also argued that member states should be able to continue to possess foreign-exchange reserves. It raised a number of objections to the transfer of management or ownership of foreign-exchange reserves to a new Community institution. A 'Non-Paper' circulated by the British in March 1991 asked: 'How can ECB responsibility for implementing a Community exchange rate policy in Stage 2 be reconciled with continuing national responsibility for domestic monetary policies?'.[18] There were sound financial reasons for sub-

[18] 'Foreign Exchange Reserves: A Non-Paper by the UK', distributed to EC Monetary Committee members in March 1991.

sidiarity and for member states to hold reserves for their own benefit. Similarly, in the context of the design of the ESCB statute, Britain insisted that official foreign-exchange reserves should continue to be held, if a member state so wished, outside the ESCB by its 'Treasury' (4 July 1991 Note by Commission to CCBG on current 'state of play' of negotiations). The final Treaty stated that the tasks of the ESCB include 'to hold and manage the official foreign reserves of the Member States' , though governments can continue to hold 'working balances' (TEU: Article 105(2, 3)). More generally, the ESCB has the responsibility to define and implement the monetary policy of the EC.

Finally, the government was concerned to protect national sovereignty against any increased power for the existing EC institutions. It argued that decisions on EMU made by the Council of Ministers should be on the basis of *unanimity*. This issue was related to that of economic-policy co-ordination, as noted above. More fundamentally, it also arose in the context of defining the decision-making process on the transition to the third stage. The final Treaty states that the decisions of the European Council on the transition to stage 3 are to be taken on the basis of a qualified majority (TEU: Article 109j). The provision prevents any individual state from exercising a veto on the commencement of stage 3. A separate protocol on the transition to stage 3 refers to the 'irreversible character' of the process and states that 'no Member State shall prevent the entering into the third stage'. The debate on the transitional arrangements underlined the anxiety of almost all of Britain's partners that London might seek to block progress, adopting the intransigence associated with the Thatcher style.

The IGC negotiations on this issue became complicated by the contradiction between the British desire not to be bound—which was to lead to its opt-out—and the will of the majority to make the commitment to a single currency irreversible. Until the autumn of 1991 there was still reason for the British to hope that they could remain part of the pack but not tied to the final destination. If unanimity in the Council were required before stage 3 could begin, the British position would be safeguarded. But, if the decision were to be taken only by a qualified majority, then the Major government was in trouble without some further means of protection. The debate in the IGC swung backwards and forwards between these two alternative modes of decision-making (Bini-Smaghi *et al.* 1994: 16–17). The initial Commission Draft Treaty had provided that the decision to move to the final stage was to be taken by the European Council and enacted by the Council of Ministers by qualified majority. The French Draft Treaty followed the Commission line. But the German Draft Treaty stipulated that unanimity by the European Council on the matter was required. The UK could rally to this position: an opening had appeared. The Spanish 'took an intermediate position, requiring unanimity until a certain date and a majority thereafter' (Bini-Smaghi *et al.* 1994: 16). By April, most governments could support the proposal of Jean-Claude Trichet that there should be three basic principles governing the passage to stage 3: no right of veto; no coercion to join; and no arbitrary exclusion (Bini-Smaghi *et al.* 1994: 17). These principles seemed to please most of the delegations. Yet their subsequent interpretation became the source of further dispute.

If Britain was going to be successful in its insistence on unanimity before stage 3 could begin, then it needed to be able to rely on the Germans and the Dutch maintaining a similar stance. The Dutch began their Presidency by staking out a clear position that was favourable to British concerns. But their Draft Treaty of August stirred up the debate close to boiling-point. It foresaw a general opt-out for all, adopting what it saw as the no-coercion principle. Whilst this was immediately supported by a grateful British team and, significantly, endorsed from within the German camp, it created a major backlash on the part of most of the others. But whilst the Dutch remained faithful to the British almost until the end, the Germans appeared more ambiguous. Under the strong lead of Kohl, they shifted from the Dutch position and firmly endorsed a formula on 'irreversibility', which eschewed a unanimity rule. As a result, the British had lost the big prize—the Council could act without there being unanimity—and they had to settle for an isolated solution.

The British were more successful in their position on the role of the existing EC institutions. They believed that in EMU matters the role of both the Commission and the European Parliament should be severely circumscribed. In the event, the Treaty keeps the Parliament at arm's length from EMU decision-making. In the discussion on the Commission's powers, the British indicated their 'dread' of the Commission using its traditional powers in EMU matters (IGC personal representatives' meeting of 21 May 1991). In the event, few governments sought to promote the cause of the Commission. The Treaty obliges the Commission to share its normal powers of initiation with the ECB in specified areas, and the Council is given much wider scope to amend Commission recommendations. The club of EC finance ministries displayed a common interest in defending their collective powers.

Follow the Market

Whilst the Thatcher and the Major governments believed in a strong nation-state, they also believed in free markets (Gamble 1988). Since its own EC Presidency of 1981, the Thatcher government had trumpeted the theme of liberalization and deregulation in the EC market. Indeed, it was the most prominent of the larger member states to press for the liberalization of the service sectors as part of the single-market programme (Bulmer 1992: 24). More particularly, Thatcherism promoted the liberalization of the British financial-services industry: from the abolition of exchange controls in 1979, to the 'big bang' and beyond in the City in 1986.

In the UK, the financial-services sector has had a global, rather than a merely European, orientation. The British interest was defined in terms of seeking an inflow of capital from across the world (the USA, Japan, and the Far East), not just from within Europe (Gamble 1988: 113). Moreover, the importance of the financial-services sector to the British economy is much greater than for most of its competitors. The City of London remains one of the top three financial centres in the world, and is easily the leader in Europe. The position of the City in the event of a single currency being adopted was thus of major concern to any government in London. As noted in Chapter 13, the City as such made little direct intervention in government policy-making on EMU in 1989–91. Some individual actors did so: most notably Butler and Richards on the 'hard' ECU plan, and Graham Bishop on financial-market discipline (see below). But, more generally, the interests of the financial-services sector as a whole helped to define the British agenda as the negotiations loomed. The City had an implicit power and it formed a vital part of the context and understandings of Britain's negotiators.

'Thatcherism' approached EMU armed with a basic ideological belief in the power and utility of markets. Government policy should remain in step with the will of the markets. Markets had the power to break the grandiose institutional designs of European idealists. As Mrs Thatcher used to say so often—and as she commented in her memoirs specifically in relation to the EMS and EMU— 'there is no way in which one can buck the market' (1995: 726). Moreover, Thatcherism tended to see EMU as being based on a notion of building insular regional blocs which contradicted the imperatives of globalized markets. 'Europe' was too small; EMU was not in step with the new priorities. Consistent with its past traditions, Britain had to think globally to secure its international interests. EMU was a distraction from the bigger issue of economic adjustment by *unilateral* national action: putting one's own house in order before building new international designs. Such a view had its roots in classical liberal political economy, which had held such sway in the tradition of British economists. In the modern period, globalized markets required economic restructuring to ensure competitiveness. Thus, Mrs Thatcher's apparent 'stubbornness' at her last European Council in Rome, in October 1990, came with her attempting to prioritize the GATT negotiations rather than EMU. Her tactic had a deeper ideological rationale. Her antipathy to EMU cannot be explained without reference it. Moreover, the stress on the need for Europe to restructure in order to compete globally was one which was taken up by the Blair Government in its EU Presidency of 1988. 'Globalism' was seen as meeting the long-term national interest.

These clashes of culture and cognitive outlooks between Britain and her EC partners were displayed in the IGC on EMU. The IGC had embarked on a learning exercise in seeking to design a technically viable and politically acceptable EMU specification. To this learning exercise, the British brought their intellectual commitment to a 'behaviouralist' or market-oriented approach. They expressed their belief in:

- strict and tough convergence criteria to govern the transition and entry to stage 3;
- labour-market flexibility as a measure of convergence;

- opposition to formal financial sanctions on errant member states: market discipline would be sufficient;
- judging market trends correctly: recognizing the relevance of cyclical factors when determining if an excessive government deficit existed or not;
- no need for new 'Cohesion' monies to the periphery to help these member states achieve convergence; and,
- no need for a new financial-assistance mechanism to help member states suffering exceptional difficulties in endeavouring to achieve convergence.

Within the IGC negotiations, on 2 April, Wicks enunciated a set of five principles that London believed should underpin stage 2. The very first principle was that the movement towards monetary union should be undertaken in such a manner as to allow both markets and the public to become familiarized with it on a progressive, gradual basis. Whilst this principle was an oblique reference to the 'hard' ECU scheme, it made a point of more general concern to the British. This was a concern espoused by both the Treasury and the Bank of England. Both had a strong attachment to allowing market forces to determine the pace of change. The role of the authorities was to assist the functioning of the market, not to move ahead of them. Even pro-European ministers like Howe (earlier) and Hurd shared this outlook. All shied away from the kind of prescriptions set down in the Delors Report.

The eventual content of the Treaty would only partially reflect the precepts of a market-based approach in general. Moreover, the arguments of the Major government in this regard placed it in various 'coalitions'. Its stress on the need for convergence generally placed it alongside the Germans, the Dutch, and the Danes. Yet, when it came to the definition and treatment of national budget deficits, the Major government shifted from the 'hawks' to the 'doves'. Its arguments coincided with the cause of the Italians, the Belgians, and other likely errant states. The British argued in favour of more flexibility of interpretation to take cyclical factors into account. Similarly, when the stress on markets came into conflict with subsidiarity, the British opted for the latter. As much policy discretion as possible should be left with governments themselves. The British advocacy of the importance of markets appeared a little maverick to its partners, not least to the German ordo-liberals.

In general, the British government supported strict and tough convergence criteria to govern entry to stage 3. In part, this position stemmed from a desire to slow down progress towards a single currency. But it was also a testament of faith in market economics. At an IGC ministerial meeting on 8 April, Norman Lamont gave his backing to the Danes', the Dutch, and the Germans' emphasis on securing such convergence. Substance, as he put it, was more important than dates. Such a comment was a classic statement of the 'behaviouralist' approach: monetary union could only be viable on the basis of a convergence demonstrated by market performance. The British Treasury believed that the discipline set down in the Treaty was good in its own terms.

By September 1991, the IGC had come close to finalizing the definition of the convergence criteria. The British now argued that the criteria should include an explicit reference to the flexibility of labour markets (Bini-Smaghi *et al.* 1994: 25; IGC ministerial of 9 September 1991). Economists in the Bank of England had become excited by the relevance of market flexibility and the levels of production costs as measures of 'real' convergence. As early as October 1990, British negotiators had suggested the use of 'real economic' criteria in assessing the readiness to join a monetary union. Wicks and Crockett raised this issue at the informal EC Monetary Committee meeting in Siena that month. Ideas of this kind had been pushed by economists in the Bank of England, such as Roger Clews. At that stage the Germans had rejected the notion as impractical; moreover, they believed other measures were more important. The French had not taken up the matter. Now, in 1991, the notion of the levels of production costs was raised in the Wicks Committee in London, which discussed the possible inclusion of rates of unemployment, regional wage differentials, and unit labour costs. But Treasury officials displayed much less enthusiasm for their inclusion. There, officials recognized the economic logic but were concerned about the political implications of being judged by such criteria. Nominal criteria were more readily 'controllable' by governments; real convergence meant market behaviour would be decisive. Institutional self-interest made finance ministries, in general, hesitant. There were other, technical reasons, for coolness. The Dutch and the Germans thought it too difficult to include a measurement of labour-market flexibility. Others seemed to fear an attempted derailment of the process by the British. The final text of Article 109j (1) made a limp reference to the Commission taking account of other indicators, including the integration of markets and unit labour costs.

Perhaps somewhat surprisingly, in the debate on budget discipline the Major government lined up with those opposed to the inclusion of the so-called 'golden rule' as advocated by Germany. The 'rule' advocated that a government's deficit should only be designed to serve the financing of investments, not consumption. The British sought greater flexibility for national governments. They joined the French and the Irish in opposing the Germans, the Dutch, and others. The British did not believe such a binding commitment was necessary. Subsidiarity was a higher concern than fiscal rectitude.

Similarly, the British repeatedly opposed the imposition of financial sanctions on member states for errant behaviour in running up excessive budget deficits. The Major government believed in good housekeeping but not by EC diktat. In the autumn of 1991, it argued that market mechanisms could be a sufficient discipline without the need for the legal incursions proposed in the drafts of Article 104a, b (IGC personal representatives' meeting of 10 September 1991; Bini-Smaghi *et al.* 1994: 27). In the flow of policy ideas, the deployment of such an argument was made too late.

Market Discipline and the Ideas of Graham Bishop

The complex attitudes of the Bank of England and the Treasury to the scope for market discipline in EMU had been displayed earlier in their response to a set of proposals advanced by Graham Bishop of Salomon Brothers in the City of London. The response to Bishop indicates a concern with institutional prerogatives and interests, rather than an acceptance of a market model for discipline on excessive budget deficits. Bishop's ideas confronted established assumptions about the role of central banks in setting prudential rules and in managing banking supervision in their domestic financial markets. Across the EC, the central bankers' club regarded his ideas as a direct threat to their role and authority. Bishop's ideas met with some intellectual sympathy in the EC Commission and in national finance ministries. In particular, some in the British Treasury liked the market philosophy on which his approach was based. But neither the Treasury, not its counterparts elsewhere, were prepared to back his ideas strongly enough to overcome the fears and misgivings of the central banks.

Bishop responded to the provisions of the Delors Report. The report had concluded that fiscal discipline on the part of national governments required binding budgetary rules. Whilst market forces might have a disciplinary influence, they would either be too slow and weak or too sudden and disruptive. Instead, rules had to be established to ensure fiscal discipline on the part of national governments. It had been agreed early on that EMU required that there be no monetary financing of government debt by a central bank and no 'bail-out' of government debt by other central banks.

Bishop disagreed with the dismissal of market forces in the Delors Report. By November 1989, he noted that the 'no monetary financing' and 'no bail-out' rules raised complex issues of the relationship between public finance management and the prudential supervision of financial markets (Bishop *et al.* 1989; Dyson 1994: 156). With these (desirable) rules the onus for fiscal discipline was diverted onto the shoulders of the financial institutions. The solvency of national governments became an issue for the financial markets, as central banks could no longer guarantee repayment loans to governments. In consequence, there was a need to re-examine the system of prudential rules (capital-adequacy ratios) set for the institutions operating in the financial markets. The efficacy of capital markets needed strengthening and such reform would mean a tightening of the rules for banking supervision.

The Bank of England was committed to the modernization of the UK financial-market system, with a view to increasing its efficiency. The Bank's overall view of EMU was closely linked to its focus on the functioning of the financial markets. Moreover, economic thinking in Britain had displayed a deep and long-term attachment to the idea that the role of the authorities was to assist the functioning of the market. In principle, Bishop's philosophy went with the groove of official thinking.

When Bishop's proposals entered the sphere of officials in the British Treasury, the response was divided. Some, most notably David Peretz (who worked with Wicks on the international side), were attracted to Bishop's ideas. Most officials, however, were much more cautious. Institutional proprieties suggested that the Treasury should not encroach onto the Bank of England's territory in this area. The Bank had statutory responsibilities for market supervision. Moreover, the Treasury had its own institutional interests to defend. Like other finance ministries, the Treasury had an interest in an easy servicing of government debt. Some of the Treasury officials most directly involved in this area, such as Michael Scholar and Rachel Lomax, opposed Bishop's ideas.

For its part, the Bank of England firmly rejected the proposals. The Bank—primarily Brian Quinn (responsible for banking supervision and Chair of the CCBG supervisory subcommittee), but also Ian Prenderleith (concerned with markets) and Andrew Crockett—stressed the difficulties involved for banking supervision and prudential rules. Moreover, there was a strong sense in the Bank, and in parts of the Treasury, that it was wrong in principle to alter supervisory frameworks in the interests of monetary policy. The use of disciplinary measures could come into conflict with supervisory requirements. Bishop's ideas would radically change the relationship between the Bank, the Treasury, and the markets. Politically, the Bank shied away from being placed in a position where it was being asked to make judgements about the wisdom of different EC government's fiscal policies.

In advancing his ideas, Bishop made a key presentational error. He presented the notion of using financial-market discipline as a sword to attack errant governments, rather than as a shield to protect the financial system. Bishop's language was too threatening; he had raised too many political sensitivities.

Bishop lacked a champion. From the beginning he had decided to stay clear of the British government, feeling that its embrace would be the kiss of death to his proposal in Europe. Learning lessons from the 'hard' ECU proposal, Bishop did not seek out Nigel Wicks nor did he route his ideas via Butler's BIEC City committee. Bishop circulated his paper to the Treasury and to the Bank essentially to help refine his ideas but not to solicit official support.

But Bishop's main focus was the Commission, whilst he also endeavoured to get the Dutch, the French, the Germans, and the Italians on side. Bishop had repeated contact with Brussels officials. The critical phase came in autumn 1991. At a meeting in Brussels, Bishop pressed Giovanni Ravasio, Joly Dixon, and Geoffrey Fitchew to advocate the incorporation of his ideas into draft treaty language for the IGC. Attitudes in the Commission were divided, a feature which prevented it from being an effective champion. Notably, DG15, responsible for financial services, was opposed.

Earlier, a paper by Bishop had been circulated by Wicks to the rest of the EC Monetary Committee. The Committee had considered Bishop's proposals on 17 June 1990 in the context of its discussions on excessive deficits. Padoa-Schioppa, as Chair of the EC's Banking Advisory Committee, prepared a report for the EC Monetary Committee opposing Bishop's ideas. A report from the Monetary Committee the following month reiterated that markets could not be relied on by themselves to induce the necessary corrections to unsound budgetary policies in sufficient time. A little later a distinction emerged between those who sought legally binding 'rules' (where a breach of the budget criteria to be specified in the Treaty would automatically constitute an infringement of the ban on excessive deficits) and those who wished to settle for a lesser binding 'procedure' (where a more detailed examination of a state's deficit might be triggered). The Germans and the Dutch, and sometimes the French, insisted on binding rules, whilst the British (in the form of the Treasury), along with several other delegations, were only prepared to accept a binding procedure.

The issue was linked to the question of possible sanctions that might be imposed on states with an excessive deficit. The British were highly sensitive on the imposition of sanctions given their commitment to national sovereignty. Other states backing a binding procedure were prepared to accept sanctions that would bite. Wicks and Gray (for the Treasury) were placed in a quandary: government policy was opposed to sanctions, but it did not wish to oppose discipline. They therefore pressed for further study of reinforcing market discipline. Crockett and Arrowsmith, the Bank of England's representatives on the Monetary Committee, privately sought to discourage the Treasury from too great an emphasis on market mechanisms. Such market mechanisms should not undermine prudential requirements nor politicize the supervisory process.

From mid-1990 onwards, Bishop engaged in direct discussions with finance ministries across the EC. He found some support, but even his supporters judged the prospects for the adoption of his ideas slim. Individual officials showed intellectual sympathy. These included Günter Grosche (Finance Ministry), Rolf Kaiser (Chancellor's Office), and Wolfgang Riecke (Bundesbank) in Germany; Villeroy de Galhau (Bérégovoy's cabinet), Xavier Musca (Trésor), and Sylvan de Forges (Trésor) in France; and Guido Carli in Italy. But there was wider resistance, especially from the central banks. Given the dominance of the CCBG over the territory of banking rules, their opposition was crucial.

Nevertheless, the Commission, along with Britain and Greece, did support an emphasis on financial-market discipline in two IGC meetings during this period (IGC ministerial meeting of 7–8 October 1991; and personal representatives' meeting of 22 October 1991). But the case made little headway. The majority favoured discipline by the threat of sanctions. The British moved to accept that payments from the EC's structural funds might be made conditional on the maintenance of sound budgetary policies. This was not enough, however, to satisfy most of the IGC delegations. The final Treaty included financial sanctions where excessive deficits persisted (TEU: Article 104c(11)).

The episode illustrated the conflicts of philosophy and institutional self-interest that arose in the IGC. The Major government was caught between favouring market mechanisms and resisting incursions on its sovereignty. The Treasury was sympathetic to market mechanisms, whilst the Bank of England was highly concerned about prudential rules and banking supervision. The Bank lined up with other EC central banks in resisting Bishop's market-based process on the grounds that it was too destabilizing. The Treasury never overcame the awkward link between this issue and that of sanctions on excessive deficits.

Avoiding Obligations

When it came to the specification and treatment of excessive budget deficits, the British were again on the side of flexibility. The British stressed the need for market sensitivity in the interpretation of what constituted an excessive deficit. A numeric reference value of 3 per cent had been agreed by September, but the British supported the demand of a number of member states for a greater flexibility of interpretation. Lamont argued that cyclical factors had to be taken into account when assessing government deficits: states might be in different positions in the economic cycle. Reference should be made to the trend. Such a concern reflected the reality of the UK's economic divergence. The criterion of 3 per cent should apply only over a multi-annual period; the 3 per cent threshold could be exceeded in a single year without triggering a penalty procedure (IGC ministerial meeting of 7 October 1991). Under the final Treaty, temporary and limited deviations were to be allowed if there was evidence of adjustment measures to bring the deficit back within the limit. The argument for a 'dynamic' interpretation of the 3 per cent criterion had been pressed by France, Italy, and Belgium, but also included, rather suprisingly perhaps, Denmark (IGC ministerial meeting of 7 October 1991). It was thus not a simple case of the 'disciplined' versus the 'undisciplined'.

At the beginning of the IGC, discussion focused on the possible definition of economic-policy aims in the Treaty. These aims were to be followed by all member states. The Germans proposed the inclusion of references to 'open markets'; to 'privatization'; and to abolition of both state control of prices and wage indexation (IGC personal representatives' meeting of 29 January 1991). Normally, the British Conservatives would have applauded these policy aims, as they were close to the precepts of Thatcherism. Yet, their inclusion clashed with the desire to defend sovereignty and to uphold the principle of subsidiarity. The British expressed their strongest opposition against any legal constraints on the power of member states to control prices and wages (16th IGC personal representatives' meeting, 3 September 1991). Their arguments complemented those of Belgium, Luxembourg, and Portugal. In the final Treaty, Article 102a lists a number of economic-policy aims—including 'an open market economy with free competition'—but the other German references were not adopted.

The commitment to market economics led the Major government to seek to limit any expansion of the Community budget. In the IGC the issue took several forms. The Spanish government led a group of weaker member states (Greece, Ireland, and Portugal) in stressing 'economic and social cohesion' as a policy guideline for EMU and, on occasions, in urging it as a technical prerequisite for stage 3 (IGC personal representatives' meeting of 1 October 1991). The British, along with the Germans, the French, and the Dutch, opposed such an emphasis. The fear was of bigger EC payments to the periphery adding greater burdens to the donors. Moreover, Britain joined the others (and DG2 in the Commission) in arguing that EMU would not be to the disadvantage of the peripheral states (IGC personal representatives' meeting of 4 June 1991). The weaker states had pressed for an emphasis on cohesion in the Treaty, but the final outcome fell short of their demands. Articles 2 and 3 include economic and social cohesion in the list of the aims of the EC, but the most substantial reference was separated from the main text in a separate protocol on the issue.

The Spanish and the Portuguese also led their allies in pressing for the creation of a new 'Cohesion Fund'. At the IGC on 28 October, Delors feared that this issue could prevent EMU being agreed. The Spanish threatened to block the entire Treaty at the final IGC before Maastricht unless it was satisfied on this matter. The Spanish complained that this issue was not being given adequate attention in the IGC. When it had been given top billing in the IGC of 11–12 November, the divisions had been very clear. The Germans argued that EMU should not lead to a vast redistribution of resources: otherwise, there would be ratification problems at home. For Britain, Lamont argued that financial transfers should not be a substitute for convergence, nor should there be any disincentive to tackle budgetary problems. There was a danger of opening Pandora's box by accepting the demands of the weaker states. Wicks pressed hard until the end for as tough a language as possible on this matter (Hogg and Hill 1995: 150). The Spanish believed that they had scored a modest victory. By contrast, the British believed that the Spanish had won too much. The Treaty provided for a cohesion fund to be established by the end of 1993 (Article 130d) and a protocol defined its basic scope. The review of the EC's structural funds and the establishment of the new fund became a thorny issue for the British Presidency in 1992. The British contented themselves that, at least, the Maastricht commitment was less open-ended than had been the provisions on the Integrated Mediterranean Programmes established by the Single European Act.

The Major government also opposed EC financial assistance to member states experiencing difficulty in achieving convergence. The Commission proposed a 'financial assistance mechanism' to states in difficulties or seriously threatened by such difficulties in the transition (Article 104 of its Draft Treaty). It saw this as a stabilization instrument and as a means to help in the painful convergence process. Both the British and the Dutch opposed this proposal from the outset. The Germans opposed it less strongly at the start, and the French only swung to oppose it later. The final IGC before Maastricht agreed a compromise package. The package was weaker than that originally sought by the Commission, but the latter had rallied its allies. The initial opposition of states such as Britain had been worn down.

British Strategy and Coalition-Building in the IGC

As already noted, the strategy of the Major government in the IGC cannot be understood on its own. It was nested in the difficult parliamentary politics of the Conservative Party at Westminster. John Major's prime strategic objective was to maximize the unity of his party during the IGC, with a view to winning the subsequent general election. On both tests of leadership he was successful.

The specific negotiating objectives in the IGC followed from the imperatives accepted at Westminster. The essential aim was to avoid a binding commitment to the adoption of a single European currency. This aim was met by the special terms of the UK 'opt-out' on stage 3. This solution was seen as second best. The Major government would have preferred something like a generalized 'opt-out': that is, stage 3 not being binding on any government. Other formulations may have satisfied the same aim: for example, a decision on stage 3 being made by unanimity. The purpose was to defer the point of decision and to avoid commitments in the meantime. The strategy was defensive, just as it had been since the Delors Committee had given EMU a serious momentum. It was also cautious: EMU held many risks and unforeseen events might make it not viable. Major, the banker, was protecting his assets. The positive element behind the search for a general opt-out was a desire to avoid British isolation or exclusion. The Major government did not wish to limit the options for the future. But, as the IGC wore on, it became increasingly clear that a generalized opt-out was not going to be agreed. An isolated opt-out was the only alternative. The government persisted with the 'hard' ECU in 1991 in the hope that this scheme might define an acceptable, and in some ways more substantial, stage 2 and weaken the desire to make binding commitments on stage 3. The prospects for avoiding such commitments were already minimal when John Major took over as Prime Minister.

A focus on the strategy deployed in the IGC raises questions about the choices made. Given the Major government's objectives, was the outcome on EMU the best result available? Might a modified strategy have produced bigger gains? Such questions pose many problems of interpretation. First, it is impossible to resolve a counter-factual question in history. The necessary evidence cannot be available. Secondly, the form of a 'nested' bargaining game makes any such calculation very complex. It requires a judgement in two different contexts: in this case, Westminster and the IGC table. Thirdly, the situation that the government faced was a dynamic one and calculations had to take account of this instability.

It is clear, nevertheless, that the Major government had few allies around the IGC table. Its strategy had not secured very effective coalitions. Narrowing the question in these terms allows some further reflection on the choices that were made. What modifications were necessary to British strategy in order to secure more effective coalitions around the IGC table? Leaving aside the actual strategy pursued, John Major had three other options available to him when he took over as Prime Minister in November 1990. These were:

- to back *the Spanish variant of a 'hard' ECU*. This would have involved accepting a single currency as a long-term goal, using this commitment as the basis for coalition-building, whilst urging a greater conditionality before the final stage was reached;
- to support *the Germans and the Dutch* in pressing for an empty stage 2, for uncompromisingly tough convergence criteria for stage 3, and for unanimity in the Council on stage 3. Each stipulation would have ensured that the hurdles were raised for stage 3;
- to accept the design of *the Commission and of the French* on stage 3. This design was less rigorous in form than that envisaged by the Germans and the Dutch and thus less threatening to national sovereignty in both fiscal and monetary policy.

The last option represented the most radical shift. It would have involved a major 'U-turn' of policy to accept the single-currency goal and to have backed those who were the most keen to make transition to it certain and irreversible. This option was clearly not acceptable given parliamentary opinion at home. Major had no choice but to reject it.

The other two strategic options were more feasible. Both involved an acceptance of a single-currency goal. But British pressure might have put it far away in time and weighed it down with prohibitively heavy conditionality. It is arguable that either would have represented a better deal than a stark opt-out.

The Spanish advocacy of a hard ECU made them potentially the closest allies, although they were less attractive because of their lack of power at the negotiating table. Yet the Commission (as late as June 1991) feared that with a shift by Britain there might be five states lined up behind the Spanish proposal. At one stage, the proposal might have also tempted the French, especially Bérégovoy, as a means of establishing an alliance with the UK as a counterbalance to the power of Germany. However, the Spanish scheme, like its British forerunner, was probably tabled too late to secure maximum support. Soon after Rome 1, the major players sought to ensure that any stage 2 central institution had no more than a weak role. The progress of the IGC weakened the effectiveness of this Spanish-centred coalition.

The German and Dutch position had the greatest potential. As some officials in London recognized, a coalition with them might have had the greatest potential to secure Britain's long-term interests. Both governments maintained a rigour in monetary policy and both championed free markets. Neither would give any quarter on their financial rectitude. In short, they were natural soulmates for the Conservatives. Dutch officials consistently eschewed any automatic transition to a single currency (though Wim Kok was prepared to accept an automatic transition). As already noted, their Draft Treaty sought to provide an 'opt-in' for all: a provision very close to what the British sought. Moreover, some negotiators, notably the Italians, saw the Dutch Presidency in the final stage of the negotiations as ready 'to pursue the chimera of a British–German accord at the cost of deviating from' the objective of a united Europe (Bini-Smaghi *et al.* 1994: 43).

The picture in Germany was not wholly clear. But London could have made common cause with those, like Waigel and Köhler in Bonn and Tietmeyer in the Bundesbank, who sought tough conditions before stage 3 was countenanced. In effect, there was scope here for a transnational coalition, and one which might just have been enough to entice Kohl. The German position was not uniform between the key domestic actors, and it evolved over time. Kohl had a domestic battle to win on the transition to stage 3. Compromise with the Germans would have been much more likely earlier—such as before the end of 1989—than later. But, even as the IGC opened, there might have been scope for a deal. This scope is further borne out by the fact that, once the IGC did get down to discuss the specific details of the EMU design, the British found themselves in agreement with both the Germans and the Dutch much more often than they did with any of the other EC states (see Chapter 17). Setting aside the British refusal to enter-tain any kind of commitment to a single currency, all three had much in com-mon on the technical design of EMU. Moreover, the proximity of the British to these other two states has to be set alongside the major points of disagreement that existed between Germany and France in the first months of 1991. The lat-ter two compromised in order to obtain at least part of what each sought; the British rejected such possibilities. But if they had managed to form an alliance with at least some of the German actors, then the course of the negotiations might have been significantly revised. As Joly Dixon, a senior member of Delors's cabinet, observed, 'The British under Major could be a lot more mis-chievious than ever they could be under Thatcher' (quoted in Ross 1995: 88). In short, the EMU outcome could well have been different with a more flexible British stance. This episode may be another instance of the missed opportuni-ties identified by Denman (1996).

Instead, the Major government opted for 'safety first' on party unity and took the least radical option. The existing mandate was polished and more effort given to a charm offensive. But, without modification of the stance on a single currency, the strategy remained out of synchronization with the requirements of successful coalition-building in the IGC. By March–April 1991, Whitehall officials were well aware of the limitations of the approach. An amicable sepa-ration looked the most likely result. Major firmly believed that there was no alternative. No other negotiating brief in the IGC would have produced bigger gains where it mattered most: in Westminster. Given this parameter, Major maximized his victory. It was, in these terms, 'game, set and match' for John Major.[19]

[19] Hogg and Hill (1995: 157) report that Major always disliked this formulation given in briefings by his officials.

The absence of effective alternative coalitions involving the British proved to be very consequential to the terms of the agreement amongst the rest. The Dutch and the German governments were wooed away. Britain faced a Treaty largely written by its partners, and the terms of its opt-out meant the rest would determine many of the early arrangements for the transition.

The obstacles in the way of John Major adopting a more radical shift of policy and strategy were, of course, very substantial. The Thatcher style in EC summits had antagonized Britain's partners and made them suspicious of London's motives. By 1990, Britain was a much less central player than it had been in the IGC of 1985 for the Single European Act. More fundamentally, Britain had not broken into the Franco-German coalition for many years. To have done so now would have been difficult. Bonn and Paris had shown a long-term willingness to compromise with each other. Both showed mutual respect and enjoyed increasing credibility with each other. Neither felt the same towards London. London had shown itself to be rigid and uncompromising. It did not have the will to offer either Bonn or Paris enough to be able to break into their bilateral relationship.

By 1991, Kohl showed warmth towards Major. But in the absence of compromise by Britain the rapport was shallow and temporary. Whitehall had often misread German positions on EC policy in general (e.g. the budget) or EMU in particular (e.g. the Delors Committee). Kohl spoke the language of federalism, which the British found an anathema. Moreover, with the end of the Cold War the Thatcher government viewed German power in Europe with renewed suspicion, and the Germans reacted against this hostility (Wallace 1997: 680). German unification had had a powerful negative effect on relations between Mrs Thatcher and Kohl, and this legacy overshadowed the Major years. It formed part of the reason for Major choosing to make his 'heart of Europe' speech in Bonn, on 11 March 1991. Christopher Mallaby, Britain's Ambassador in Bonn, had been 'concerned by how low Britain's standing in Germany had sunk [and] had been pressing for just such a statement' (Seldon 1997: 166). The effect of Major's more constructive style was limited. His path to an opt-out was eased.

On the other hand, Major and Mitterrand were further apart in their policy goals on EMU. They were also very different political personalities. An early visit by Major to Mitterrand in Paris in January 1991 went disastrously. The French President suspected that Major was using 'divide and rule' tactics between Paris and Bonn. Mitterrand asked Major whether the 'hard' ECU plan that he was promoting was intended to lead to a single currency. He found Major's reply to be obfuscation and never took the 'hard' ECU seriously thereafter. The Elysée overruled Bérégovoy's (an Anglophile) and the Trésor's interest in the British 'hard' ECU. It was ruled off the agenda. A further visit to Paris by Major to see Mitterrand on 11 September failed to have much impact on the terms of the EMU negotiations. French suggestions that the British might cave in at the last minute and sign up for the EMU Treaty simply infuriated London. On other aspects, like CFSP, the British and the French could find common cause, but primarily because the latter also sought to protect national sovereignty (cf. Wallace 1997).

The attitudes of the IGC participants to the British negotiating tactics varied. Criticism that the British pursued 'divide-and-rule' tactics seems to be misplaced. British tactics would have proved more effective if they had shown some adaptation in the IGC. Some regarded the British government as being 'consistently negative' in the IGC (Bini-Smaghi *et al.* 1994: 42). Such attacks were directed at the political line laid down by the Major government. Other participants identified a more positive element in the British approach. They identified a willingness on the part of the British officials—Wicks and Kerr—to act as 'honest brokers' in the IGC discussions.

Honest Brokers in Europe?

The willingness to act as an 'honest broker' was related to the unease of the British negotiators at being regarded as wholly negative, with nothing to contribute. Ultimately, the disposition of Wicks and Kerr to favour 'constructive engagement' tempered their commitment to a strategy which accepted the prospect of isolation. Acting as an 'honest broker' was a limited palliative. It did not involve a shift of negotiating mandate. Rather it expressed a willingness to help the rest make progress. It also reflected a concern at the cumulative cost that might be borne from a history of being isolated in EC negotiations. The motive was to build up credibility in the longer term. Such a motivation recognized the importance of reputation in EC bargaining. The IGC negotiators were used to participating in established networks. Many also had experience of the EC Monetary Committee, ECOFIN, and/or COREPER. Such bodies involve a regular pattern of meetings, and they display a sense of common purpose. These features inculcate a sensitivity to credibility and reputation amongst peers.

The will to be an 'honest broker' was not shared by all those negotiating for Britain. Lamont, as a Eurosceptic, accorded it low value. Certainly, Major's instinct was to be conciliatory. At the Luxembourg European Council in June 1991 he indicated in private that he did not seek to wreck the prospects of an EMU agreement, though Britain might have to opt out from it. Yet, there is little evidence of Major himself acting as an honest broker. He did not seek to engineer compromises amongst the rest. Number Ten staff were also encouraged to be sceptical about the objectivity of the FCO on the prospects for EC negotiations. Major feared that the FCO had been seduced by Europe.

A disposition to help engineer compromises does not mean, however, that it necessarily had significant effects. There is little hard evidence of Wicks and Kerr forging solutions amongst their peers from a stance of British detachment. Kerr claims to have brokered a compromise on granting 'co-decision' powers to the European Parliament in the passage of EC legislation. The deal involved limiting the new procedure to single market legislation. This reconciled French and German positions in terms consistent with what could be sold politically to London. The British contributions on issues such as setting the convergence criteria and on respecting market economics can be best seen as serving distinct British interests. Kerr and Wicks were clearly concerned to limit the extent of Britain's isolation on EMU. But such a priority belongs under another heading. The engagement of British negotiators as honest brokers appears to have been more at the margin: for example, helping to clarify linguistic nuances when English was being used. Even such marginal effects, however, could bolster the image of Wicks and Kerr as 'playing with a straight bat'. Small instances could help to erase fears and suspicions and to create goodwill. A stronger indication of Wicks's reputation as an honest broker came after the IGC was over. Wicks served two successive terms as Chair of the EC Monetary Committee, despite the fact that sterling left the ERM. He was placed in the position of helping to keep the other member states on the EMU path, whilst Britain seemed to be veering further away from it.

On the Margins, but Tied to the Core: Britain's Exit from the ERM

Just months after the Maastricht negotiations were complete, but before the Treaty was anywhere near being ratified, the Major government found itself in a deep and bitter EC crisis. Britain had just begun its term of office holding the EC council Presidency. In the summer of 1992, the UK government acted to defend the pound sterling. In doing so, it served to safeguard the ERM and protect the EMU project. But the policy ended in ignominious defeat. The supreme irony is that the Major government, which had prided itself on its cherished EMU 'opt-out' from the Maastricht Treaty, had behaved as if it was resolutely committed to EMU (Stephens 1996: 258). The immediate cause of the defeat was massive speculation against sterling by powerful actors on the international exchange markets. George Soros, for example, was reputed to have made $1 billion in profit from his speculation. But the full explanation for sterling's humiliating exit would have to take account of government failures of strategy, of co-operation with partners, and of information and intelligence. Whilst the context was, of course, distinct, some of these failures were an extension of what had gone before.

Britain's European strategy was, in fact, to experience one of its biggest failures in decades. Confidence in EMU had been undermined by the rejection of the Maastricht Treaty in the Danish referendum on 2 June 1992. But there were also more fundamental destabilizing economic factors at play. A combination of a severe tightening of German monetary policy with a relaxation in US policy in the first half of 1992 created special problems for sterling. From the summer onwards, Britain had joined with others in urging the Bundesbank to reduce German interest rates. German rates had risen to cope with the exceptional circumstances of unification. Kohl's policy of a 1:1 exchange between the D-Mark and the Ostmark, and of paying for reconstruction in the East not by higher taxes but by a large increase in the budget deficit, built up an inflationary pressure. High interest rates strengthened the D-Mark and put pressure on the monetary policy of its partners. Britain could find common cause with the French, the Italians, and others in urging a reduction in German rates. The UK economic cycle was out of line with that of its major EC partners and, in its recession, it desperately needed lower interest rates. The German response was to refuse any significant cut, without an ERM realignment involving devaluation of the currencies under greatest pressure. The French were adamant that no such change could take place in advance of its referendum on Maastricht on 20 September. The British refused to move without the French; they paid little heed to the fate of the Italians. The tangled web presaged a major crisis for the EMS.

British tactics exacerbated a bad situation. With the UK holding the EC Presidency, Norman Lamont chaired an important informal ECOFIN meeting in Bath on the weekend of 5 September. On the eve of the session, Lamont and Wicks decided to scrap plans for a review of the world economy (ahead of the IMF's annual meeting a few weeks later) and instead opted to use the meeting to attack Bundesbank policy and gain a binding commitment to the reduction of German interest rates (Stephens 1996: 228). In doing so, they made a major tactical error. In the ECOFIN meeting, Lamont pressed the Bundesbank President, Helmut Schlesinger, four times to pledge a reduction in interest rates. To do so broke an important informal rule: no one should be asked to deliver what they do not have the domestic power to commit themselves to. Whilst many of Lamont's fellow ministers, including his French and the Italian counterparts, sympathized with his objectives and encouraged his endeavour, no one dared back his tactics. Lamont's weaknesses as a negotiator had been exposed again. For his part, Lamont felt he had been used as the fall guy.

Schlesinger was incensed at the challenge to the Bundesbank's independence: he was only stopped from walking out by Theo Waigel, the German Finance Minister. A short communiqué, anodyne in tone, was finally agreed. Lamont then caused still further upset by interpreting the statement as a major concession by Schlesinger. The Bundesbank President was enraged. His remarks then and later would serve to undermine the stability of currencies such as the pound. Notably, Wicks—an experienced EC monetary diplomat—had failed to restrain the irascible Lamont. Stephens even suggests that Wicks may have encouraged Lamont in his endeavour (1996: 233).

Lamont had failed, and ECOFIN had missed an opportunity to agree an orderly realignment. He had caused great offence, but had not gained any advantage. As Stephens records, 'The criticism of Lamont's chairmanship . . . was near unanimous' (1996: 231). Lamont had resisted a discussion of an ERM realignment for fear that sterling would end up being categorized alongside the lira and the peseta, instead of the franc or the D-Mark. If Britain, Italy, and Spain had countenanced a co-ordinated devaluation, Schlesinger might well have been willing to extract a reduction in interest rates from his Bundesbank Council (Stephens 1996: 232). But nothing was tabled. Lamont would not move without the French.

Further opportunities were missed, to the detriment of the Major government. On the weekend prior to 'Black Wednesday', with the lira under extreme speculative pressure, the Italians sought a meeting of the EC Monetary Committee to consider a realignment (*Guardian*, 1 December 1992). The Belgians and the Dutch supported the move, whilst the German reservation was all too clear. The Italian request 'was obstructed in London, Paris and Madrid; although it is not clear whether the request was ever clearly communicated' (*Guardian*, 1 December 1992). The possibility was not properly explored. Jean-Claude Trichet of the French Trésor and Chair of the Monetary Committee made no move to call a meeting (see Stephens 1996: 237). The Secretary of the EC Monetary Committee, Andreas Kees, was away on holiday. Instead, two German officials—Horst Köhler (Finance Ministry) and Hans Tietmeyer (Bundesbank)—travelled to Paris and then to Rome on Saturday 12 September to broker a unilateral devaluation of the lira.

When Wicks was phoned that night by Trichet, the latter did not mention the possibility of a committee meeting or of the German interest in a realignment. In any event, the British had set their face against such possibilities. The British wanted to survive the remaining days beyond the French referendum. Thereafter the options would depend on the French vote. Publicly, London argued that the problem lay with high German and low US interest rates; not with the sterling–D-Mark rate. Officials at the Bank of England had become much more sceptical as to the prospects of defending the pound. But the Treasury remained committed. John Major made an impassioned 'no devaluation' speech to the Scottish CBI; earlier that summer he had even talked of sterling replacing the D-Mark as Europe's strongest currency. British policy had become rigid and narrow.

By leaving the Italians isolated the British were exposing the pound to increased attack. The problems deepened when, on the following Tuesday night, Schlesinger unguardedly told a journalist that the weekend moves would have been more effective if they had involved a broader realignment. The clear implication was that sterling should have been devalued along with the lira. The effect on the markets the next day was electric. On the Tuesday and the Wednesday, the Bank of England spent something between $30 and 38 billion from its reserves trying to keep the pound within its ERM margin (Stephens 1996: 254). Never before had the Bank been forced to intervene so heavily in a crisis.

Wednesday 16 September 1992 was horrific for British ministers and officials. The mood was one of a 'disbelieving impotence' in the face of the mounting speculative pressure (Stephens 1996: 245). Major bound his senior Cabinet colleagues to the decisions taken. Douglas Hurd, Kenneth Clarke, and Michael

Heseltine all became involved in making decisions on monetary policy, much to the chagrin of the Treasury (Stephens 1996: 250). Frenetic contacts between EC partners proved too late. EC central bank governors held two telephone conferences that day. John Major spoke to both Helmut Kohl and Pierre Bérégovoy (*Guardian*, 1 December 1992). Any hopes of the Bundesbank making further cuts to its interest rates were illusory. A hastily convened EC Monetary Committee meeting that evening accepted Britain's request to take the pound out of the ERM, but rejected London's request to suspend the ERM in its entirety. Instead, the ERM limped along to its next crisis in July 1993.

The September crisis had been the result of intransigence, inadequate co-ordination, misjudgements, and poor strategy. Responsibility for the crisis extended across the EC. The EC was hamstrung by the intransigence of the Bundesbank and of the French, both preoccupied with domestic difficulties. The problem for sterling had been set, many argued, by entry in 1990 at the wrong rate and in a manner which upset its partners. Both factors stored up difficulties for the future. Tactical errors had exacerbated the situation. Lamont mishandled relations with the Bundesbank, most infamously at Bath. He misinterpreted the Bundesbank's position. The Major government refused to recognize market signals and initiate a joint realignment. It failed to win support. It was to experience the disadvantages of being outside the Franco-German axis. In the next weeks the Germans were to extend to the franc support of the type denied to the pound sterling. Britain left Italy isolated, only to deflect market pressure back on itself. And, ironically, given its EMU stance, its actions served to protect France, support the ERM, and defend the Maastricht project. Major and Lamont hemmed themselves into an overly rigid and narrow policy, and one that neglected the imperatives of ensuring EC support for its external policy. Some of these features seemed to be part of an all too familiar pattern.

These failures stemmed from the conception of the ERM held in London. Entry in 1990 had been prompted for the domestic motive of seeking economic discipline. There was no sense of playing a role in building Europe and of British interests benefiting from this larger process. With strategy so strongly driven by isolated domestic considerations, the British were ill prepared to play EC monetary politics. Any strength given to the EMS system by British actions in September 1992 was coincidental, a by-product of a domestic-inspired policy.

The humiliation of sterling's exit from the ERM led Major to veer away from his original Maastricht stance. The Eurosceptics on his backbenches grew in strength—not least as they sensed evidence of the misuse of German power in Europe. Major moved to assuage their sensitivities. The government shifted further and further away from 'constructive engagement' and towards isolation. Had it not been for the subsequent insistence of Kenneth Clarke, as Chancellor of the Exchequer, that the policy of 'wait and see' on EMU should be adhered to, doubtless Major would have readily dropped the stance that he himself had earlier invented. Black Wednesday was a watershed for Tory policy on Europe.

Afterwards, Britain seemed more distant from EMU than ever. The negotiating objectives set in 1990–1 seemed a distant memory. Major no longer dared to talk of Britain being 'at the heart of Europe', as he had in March 1991. Detachment was the prevalent mood, not 'constructive engagement'. Once again Britain's European policy was marked by a fundamental short-termism. Its shifts were prompted by the internal demands of the Tory Party. It was also anchored, however, in an inability to think 'European'. The belief was that the European project involved too many risks and was cut off from wider global conditions. Again, there were echoes of the past.

Conclusion: Inevitable Heartache or Avoidable Failure?

It was predictable that the EMU initiative would cause severe political difficulties in Britain. The continuing drama of the ERM dispute within the government cast a pall over attitudes towards the new initiative. More generally, the notion of establishing a single currency confronted fundamental values and beliefs within British political culture. It challenged assumptions about nationhood and sovereignty, as well as the need for gradualism in developing European co-operation. These assumptions had a special resonance with the Conservative Party. They were core elements of the party's ideology (see Lynch 1998). EMU thus came to have a deep and continuing impact on the unity, purpose, and sense of identity of the party. It established a fault-line within the party which was a major contributory factor to its subsequent electoral defeat in May 1997, its largest in 150 years. Parallels were drawn with Tory divisions over the repeal of the Corn Laws.

From the start, the EMU debate was one that both the Thatcher and Major governments would have preferred not to have arisen. There was little scope for reconciling EMU to traditional concerns. But the response to EMU was also affected by the specific institutional contexts of the Thatcher and Major governments and of the Whitehall administrative machine. Mrs Thatcher and John Major had different styles, priorities, and perceptions as leaders, born out of contrasting political conditions and generational backgrounds. These differences had consequences.

In the late 1980s, Mrs Thatcher's premiership sustained a climate in Whitehall on Europe that was variously stultifying and intimidating. Mrs Thatcher was increasingly staking out a stance on Europe which was trenchant and intolerant of dissenting opinions. The climate was prohibitive in terms of a wider debate, reflecting on policy and strategy. In 1988–90, Mrs Thatcher had more leeway with her party than had Major subsequently, but she was losing her hold over it as time went on. Her stridency became more controversial and she proved unable to maintain party support. Her previous record had displayed tremendous success in all of the conventional measures of party leadership (Bulpitt 1986). But by 1990 she was veering off the road, ignoring the normal rules and signs. The effect of her policy and strategy was to isolate Britain and to cede influence at the European level, sacrificing opportunities to make a more measured impact. The legacy was constraining and disruptive to her successor.

Against this background, John Major was more consensual. Whitehall had a more tolerant atmosphere in which to reflect on policy and strategy. Yet a narrow road was still chosen. This narrowness was the result of Major giving prime emphasis to restoring the unity and electability of the Conservative Party. Major's reputation soon came to be divided between the period prior to the 1992 election and the period afterwards. For the first period, he received widespread praise for his skills as a party manager and as a 'fixer' at Maastricht. By these measures he achieved considerable success. In his own terms, Major scored 'game, set, and match' in both IGCs. Major's difficulties in maintaining party unity after 1992, however, soon led him to be seen as vacillating. Michael Portillo has written that Major's 'apparent oscillation between Euro-enthusiasm and scepticism was highly destabilizing' (*Independent*, 3 October 1998). By contrast, Edward Heath saw him as being 'held to ransom' by the Right (1998: 715). The skills for which Major was praised in the earlier period now became the focus of brickbats. But it is not clear that any of his colleagues could have done a better job in managing a party that increasingly developed a 'kamikaze' instinct. In any event, Major's historical reputation ought not to be judged at the level of internal party management alone. Rather, it is to be seen in the context of the lead he gave on policy and strategy and how well these served Britain's long-term interests. In these respects, it is evident that Major set both policy and strategy within narrow confines and that he made minimal adaptation to the progress of the EMU negotiations. Too often Major, like his critics, made judgements in the context of short-term conditions. EMU, however, was of profound long-term significance.

With the ministerial priorities, the hands of Whitehall were tied to a certain structure and pace of debate. Yet, the ministerial drive does not account for the full policy process. Historically, the British civil service has had different understandings of the relationship that ought to exist between senior officials and ministers. As noted in Chapter 13, civil servants were to be seen as either chameleons, following the political line of ministers, or as guardians of the national interest, acting on behalf of the Crown. In practice, the conceptions are not so sharply differentiated. Whitehall officials are intimately involved in providing and interpreting information, advising on the road-map. The 'new institutionalist' approach suggests that the policy impact of Whitehall should be seen in a wide perspective. It sees the inherited mind-set—the cultural norms, values, and identities of Whitehall—as being relevant in governing the cognition and strategic calculation underpinning ministerial choices. Indeed, the consistency of British policy and strategy on Europe over the last half a century suggests that ministerial choices have been, at least partially, embedded in the kind of Whitehall practice and understanding outlined in Chapter 13. The scope for altering the course of ministers will be more constrained at some points, rather than others. Mrs Thatcher's leadership was an extreme case. But even in this period it would seem unrealistic to see the political direction of policy as being autonomous.

Errors were made. The momentum behind EMU in 1988–90 was not properly recognized. Early initiatives received an inadequate response. The significance of the establishment of the Delors Committee was underestimated. The potential for alternatives to EMU was exaggerated and identified too late. It seems barely credible to suggest that Whitehall had no part to play in these failures of cognition and strategy. Part of the problem may be the incompatibility of policy styles between Whitehall and the EU. Wright (1996: 149), for example, has argued that 'a first class integrated national machine—such as that of the British—may suffer from inflexibility and . . . aversion to accommodation and coalition-building'. Those officials that were disposed to accommodation may have resigned themselves to British exclusion from the transition to EMU, as a result of the domestic political priorities. But to resign oneself in this manner sustains the political errors that come from a failure to adapt.

The approach of the Thatcher and Major governments to EMU was undermined by a strategic weakness. They lacked the structural power to persuade the rest of the EC to negotiate around their own voluntarist, market-based model of EMU. The British remained isolated. The strategy deployed by the British was never likely to forge effective coalitions to reshape the EMU agenda. Successive British governments have found it difficult to adapt to EC politics. It has not only been at home that the British mind-set has been out of kilter with coalition politics. No doubt the one helps to explain the other. In any event, the Thatcher and Major governments ceded influence over EMU to the Franco-German axis. Indeed, EMU gave a major boost to their bilateral ties. A parallel exists here with the late 1940s, when the French, Jean Monnet included, sought to have the British join them in a bilateral leadership of the emergent integration process. The British failure to participate in the European Coal and Steel Community negotiations in 1950 strengthened Franco-German *rapprochement*. Since then British governments have struggled both to understand and adapt to the coalescent impulses of the Franco-German relationship.

Ultimately, in the IGC on EMU, the Major government had little bargaining power. The rest went ahead despite British reservations, and the course followed was one they themselves largely determined. The prospect of ratification difficulties at home was used in order to win an 'opt-out' for Britain on stage 3. Her partners accepted that she could be 'hived off'. Few other concessions were made to Britain. At an early stage, a shift by Britain to accept a commitment to the adoption of a single currency in the long term might have been used to secure an alternative arrangement for all on the transition to stage 3. As noted, Wicks and other British officials were urging a shift of strategy in November 1990. But even in terms of the EC negotiations alone such a move was already probably too late. British negotiators could not deliver it. In any event the party political interests of the Prime Minister precluded any such move. Because of the domestic constraints, British negotiators remained isolated from effective cross-national coalitions.

The immediate outcome of the EMU negotiations for Britain was the opt-out, an expression of the desire to avoid long-term commitments and to favour gradualism. France and Germany led their partners by placing EMU in a political vision of Europe. Political risks were accepted on its behalf. The British had no such vision or the corresponding willingness to take risks. The attachment to gradualism was, in part, a reflection of the sense of economic risk involved in this ambitious and complex new project. In a parallel to the situation in the 1950s, the Major government preferred to hold back and see if the venture succeeded.

The effectiveness of this strategy was confronted by the reality of the momentum that EMU gained in 1997–8. Eleven of Britain's partners were set to move ahead towards a single currency as from 1 January 1999. The stark choice of 'if' and 'when' to enter loomed. Set against this background, the contours of the domestic political debate had been revised, but the issues remained highly contentious.

The political mood had changed. The election of the Blair Government in May 1997 represented a significant, though still uncertain, shift towards a more positive European stance. Major's legacy was now seen as something of a constraint: given the lack of preparation, the new government announced that Britain was not ready to join in the first wave of EMU. Gordon Brown, as Chancellor of the Exchequer, announced a set of conditions on 27 October 1997 that would have to be met before entry was feasible. The impression was of a government that wanted to say 'yes', but that felt hamstrung by Major's legacy. By contrast, the defeated Conservative Party cast aside Major's 'wait and see' approach. William Hague, the new party leader, advocated ruling out EMU entry for at least ten years.

A new divide was apparent in the domestic debate. That which could not be delivered by parliamentary leadership in 1991 (or in 1997), became the objective of an awakened business leadership in 1997–8. Political indecision was judged by the heads of many of Britain's largest firms to carry significant economic costs. By late 1998 the Blair government was attacked for its timidity on the single currency. The charge was of cowardice in the face of the Eurosceptic pressure emanating from the newspapers of Rupert Murdoch and Conrad Black. Yet Blair, somewhat like Major before him, felt constrained by political pressures. Public opinion still seemed hostile to EMU, and Blair was intent on winning a second term of office. Political leadership on 'Europe' was as fraught with political risks as ever.

How these conflicting pressures would be settled was unclear. Whether they would be resolved in the manner of a fundamental reassessment of Britain's place in Europe or whether such a choice would again be fudged was difficult to predict. Certainly, the history of Britain's troubled relationship with Europe—and with EMU in particular—weighed heavily against a radical break. Britain had faced defining moments on Europe in the past and had still managed to shy away from a fulsome re-examination of its own place in the integration process. EMU was set to be one of the biggest challenges faced by Blair and the spectre of how, in its different ways, it had helped to defeat both Thatcher and Major must already have been haunting him.

16

Jacques Delors as Policy Entrepreneur and *Ingénieur* of the EMU Negotiations: Agenda-Setting and Oiling the Wheels

Just how important was Jacques Delors's leadership on EMU? The fact that Delors became personally identified with the relaunch of EMU before either Chancellor Kohl or President Mitterrand has encouraged the view that his leadership as Commission President was a crucial variable in explaining why, so quickly after he assumed office, EMU was revived and successfully negotiated. This view of Delors's significance appears to be further supported by his chairing of the Delors Committee in 1988–9. He was deeply and continuously active on EMU from his appointment as Commission President in January 1985; he worked unceasingly to put it back on the EC's agenda, overcoming the firm resistance of Mrs Thatcher especially at the Luxembourg European Council in December 1985; he created the necessary basis for 'spillover' with the '1992' target for the single European market, the insertion of EMU as a commitment in principle into the treaty framework with the Single European Act, and the Delors package of 1988; and he laboured to keep the EMU negotiations on track through periods of difficulty and threat to progress. Delors's two great triumphs were in procuring the chair of the Delors Committee and in steering it to produce a unanimous report. The Delors report provided a vital basis of technical legitimacy for EMU and set the key parameters for the subsequent treaty negotiations. He can also be seen as having got his way over a fixed timetable for EMU and over dealing with the British problem by a separate 'opt-out'.

Indeed, Delors's most important long-term contribution can be seen as predating his period as Commission President. His achievements in the latter role would have been impossible, and any EMU treaty negotiations abortive, in the absence of the conversion of the French government to a policy of *rigueur* in the framework of a commitment to the ERM in 1982–3. Delors had fought to get the French Left to prioritize the fight against inflation since his period in the French Planning Commission in the 1960s when he had become interested in incomes policy. As Finance Minister in the Socialist government he had waged a lonely struggle on this issue till the Prime Minister Mauroy joined his side. Without his success in laying the domestic political and economic basis in France to support the EMS it would have proved impossible to coax others, notably the Germans, into EMU negotiations. Failure in that domestic struggle would in any case have led Delors to remove himself from the field of contenders for the post of European Commission President.

The argument that Delors's leadership was decisive gains additional credence from his personal authority in this area. After working for seventeen years in the Banque de France (1945–62), he had strengthened his reputation as an economic expert in various posts: as an official in the French Planning Commission (1962–9), as a key reformer in the cabinet of the French Prime Minister Jacques Chaban-Delmas, as Chair of the European Parliament's Committee on Monetary Affairs during the early period of the ERM, and as French Finance Minister from 1981 to 1984. From 1973 to 1979 Delors had served as one of the two members of the General Council of the Banque de France chosen by the Finance Minister. In the light of later developments on EMU it was striking that Giscard d'Estaing's admiration for Delors's qualities as a technician led him to select him, alongside Raymond Barre, to fill one of these two posts. A *complicité* on EMU between these three figures dates back to this pre-EMS period. There was a measure of intellectual sympathy between Delors and Barre both on Europe (they were 'Europeans of the heart') and on the primacy to fighting inflation, whilst Giscard's admiration went back to his contact with Delors during the Chaban government. At that time in restricted meetings at the Matignon Chaban, Giscard and Delors had joined in welcoming the Werner report. Delors continued to want to work on the basis of the Werner approach to EMU. His personal authority in the area of international economic relations was further underlined when Mitterrand asked him to brief the executive committee of the French Socialist Party on the EMS in 1978. He used the opportunity to caution the Socialist Party against taking too tough a position of opposition against the EMS and to argue that this should be seen as an opportunity to go much further. In short, EMU engaged Delors's intellectual interest and was bound up with his career experience, to a far greater extent than in the cases of Kohl and Mitterrand. His expertise was a source of his credibility to the French President and the German Chancellor. He offered an alternative source of advice on EMU-related matters to political leaders who did not like to feel that they were prisoners of their domestic administrative systems.

The problem with this attribution of causal significance to Delors's leadership on EMU is that it fails to attend to the very much weaker resources for leadership available to him compared to a German Chancellor or French President. Though Delors came to view Directorate-General 2 (Economic and Financial Affairs) as a valuable think-tank, the Commission did not possess the depth of financial and monetary expertise comparable to that to be found in the national central banks and finance ministries. Hence he sought to compensate in two ways: by relying on cultivation of an informal cross-national network on EMU to provide him with ideas; and by working himself and his cabinet extremely hard to ensure that he had mastered the EMU brief. Delors also lacked the direct democratic legitimacy of national political leaders. It was, accordingly, essential for him to work to sustain the interest of national political leaders: to ensure that Kohl made EMU a priority, to sustain French pressure on the Germans, and to work to ensure reconciliation of Franco-German objectives. It was also vital to build external support for EMU in other arenas through which pressure could be brought on national political leaders: like the Committee for the Monetary Union of Europe, the Association for the Monetary Union of Europe, and the European Round Table of Industrialists. The Treaty of Rome did not provide him with the legal basis for Commission initiative on economic and monetary policies to be found in other EC policy sectors. Delors was forced to seek out a stronger legal basis, which he sought by bringing EMU into the treaty frame-work through the Single European Act in 1985. But, under the rules of the game established in 1985, EMU would require formal treaty amendment devised by an IGC. That process inexorably handed power to the national governments as controllers of the IGC.

Given these relative weaknesses Delors was constrained in his options as a strategist for EMU. He could not seriously hope to negotiate EMU around an EC Commission model of what EMU might look like or how to get there. Delors endeavoured to ensure that EC Commission and European Parliamentary competences were strengthened, for instance, in relation to the Commission's right of initiative in the excessive deficit procedure, in exchange-rate policy, and in the economic-policy guidelines. But this behaviour was essen-tially defensive rather than proactive, an attempt to save the 'Community method' in EMU from the spread of an 'intergovernmental' model from the political-union negotiations. Delors found himself constrained in a similar way to the French government. Faced with the structural reality of the ERM as a D-Mark zone and of the intellectual ascendancy of the German model, he opted for more subtle strategies of indirection in order to achieve EMU. These strat-egies included 'salami-slicing' at the independence of the Bundesbank by reform of the ERM so that the power of the Bundesbank was emasculated; seeking to 'bind in' the EC central bankers and especially the Bundesbank to the process so that they would be encouraged to assume constructive responsibility; main-taining sustained 'behind-the scenes' psychological pressure on the German Chancellor to face down domestic opposition to EMU; and exploiting 'spillover' effects from the European single market programme. In employing these strat-egies of indirection, however, he lacked the authority and political weight of the French President.

As a consequence of these structural problems facing his leadership on EMU, Delors's importance lay less in the definition of the content of EMU than in sus-taining political momentum behind the negotiating process. His top priority in 1985 was to restore credibility to the Commission by putting it at the centre of the negotiating process. He did so by focusing his attention and energy on cul-tivating the European Council as the key arena of political discretion where political leaders could escape the detailed control of their officials. Here 'Europeans of the heart', like Kohl and Mitterrand, could be induced to make concessions for the sake of building Europe. Delors saw his task as being to provide the technical arguments that would embolden 'Europeans of the heart' to enter into EMU negotiations and that would attract the support of 'Europeans of the head'. In this way Delors tried very hard to carve out an intellectual contribution. He was to be more successful on EMU than on political union, and by 1991 his approach was in difficulties.

But ultimately Delors's contribution was strategic and tactical rather than cognitive—as *ingénieur* and as *animateur* of the process, working closely with Kohl and Mitterrand and successive EC Presidencies; as a craftsman of the strategy of indirection; and as a manipulator of EC institutional venues for negotiation to help shape outcomes. Delors oiled the wheels of a negotiating process whose principal spokes radiated from national capitals. Though alert to cognitive gaps in the EMU negotiations, notably the transition stage and aspects of the social dimension, he was able to have very little impact in closing them. The economic and political realist in Delors was quick to accept that EMU would have to be negotiated around German ideas; and the part of Delors's idealism that welcomed the benefits of economic stability saw positive gains from taking the best of the German model to drive down inflation. On the other hand, the other aspect of Delors's idealism was unhappy with the lack of attention to building dialogue and social partnership into EMU, to the failure to attend to its social dimension. As a social Catholic Delors maintained intellectual reservations about the adequacy of what had been negotiated at Maastricht as the basis for a viable EMU. Yet, in his capacity as Commission President, he was prepared to subordinate his ideological views on the appropriate content of an EMU agreement to the requirement of acting as broker of an agreement commanding general political support in national capitals.

In comparison with other EC policy sectors, Delors's role in the EMU negotiations had some distinctive as well as typical characteristics. Unusually, it involved the support of only a very small group of Commission officials, with little in the way of broad input from Commission directorates and many even within DG2 feeling uninvolved. Delors was interested in building up a brains trust to provide expert advice, in part relying on his own officials—notably Joly Dixon—but also on an informal cross-national network—involving people like Tommaso Padoa-Schioppa in Rome. In this respect he worked outside normal Commission channels. More typical was the attempt to mobilize sectoral interests on behalf of EMU, such as the European Round Table of Industrialists. Delors kept in touch with Giscard and Schmidt's Committee for the Monetary Union of Europe and was especially grateful for its support, notably in rejecting a parallel for the single currency and over a fixed date for stage 3. But contacts were very sporadic. He recognized that the monetary dimension and the role of central bankers in this area gave exceptional characteristics to EMU. Influence and power was a matter of breaking into and being accepted by a narrow, exclusive, and proud group of 'expert' actors who were jealous of the arcane secrets of the monetary profession. Hence Delors's role in EMU was different from that in other policy domains. It involved subordinating the role of sectoral mobilizer to that of the discrete, expert interlocutor.

Delors's role varied over time. It was more important in the agenda-setting stage and in organizing the process than in defining the actual content of the negotiations. Most crucially, it took the form of setting the context in which Kohl could move forward in 1988. Delors played a vital part in a change of mood from scepticism and pessimism to euphoria between 1985 and 1988. The EMU negotiations would not have been a practical possibility without this mood change—and without the 1992 target for the single European market.

The Informal Presidentialization of EMU: Delors's Beliefs and Strategy

Delors's approach to EMU was inspired partly by his profoundly moral conception of politics and partly by the parallels that he drew between his experience in the French Planning Commission and the nature of the European Commission as an institution. These two strands of influence induced a paradox and strain into his handling of EMU. He could veer between being pedagogic and didactic, the impatient and sometimes maximalist intellectual politician, and playing a more background role of seeking out influence in a strategically and tactically astute manner. This tension was never finally resolved. It helped explain his reputation for mood-swings on EMU.

Delors's moral conception was deeply rooted in his social Catholicism and the fact that he was a Catholic of the Left long before becoming a member of Mitterrand's Socialist Party in 1974. This social Catholicism took a Jansenist form, which led him to be severely demanding on himself and a hard taskmaster for his collaborators (Milési 1985; Rollan 1993). Delors was a rather private, solitary figure, immersing himself deeply in dossiers, seeking intellectual mastery of his brief, and intent on winning by the quality of his argument. These qualities led to his irritation with Mitterrand's failure to master the technical aspects of the EMU brief. They were associated with an inclination to play the pedagogue in economic policy and a somewhat didactic style in argument. A passionate believer in the power of ideas, he was above all a critical realist. This philosophic position—again very Jansenist—made him an often uncomfortable companion. Delors's realism led him to condemn the illusions on the Left about money and economics, notably as Finance Minister under Mitterrand (Favier and Martin-Roland 1990: 406). Equally, his commitment to political change and insistent questioning of the status quo led EC central bankers and many EC finance ministers to remain suspicious of him. Jansenism endowed Delors with an individualistic sense of moral responsibility, a quality that found expression in a pedagogic style of alerting people to the historical significance and, not least, the practical logic of policy choices like EMU. But, if social Catholicism was important in shaping *Delorisme*'s character, giving it a particular quality of intellectual and moral seriousness, it also influenced its outlook on EMU. Delors's advocacy of *rigueur* was in part inspired by the virtue attached to frugality (Maris 1992: 294–7).

He was, in consequence, far too independent-minded either to be a team player on EMU within the Commission or to play courtier at the Elysée and act at the bidding of Mitterrand. Delors saw his role as to clarify to French policy-makers what the conditions were for realizing EMU from an EC perspective. He was no mere agent of the French government; indeed, during the IGCs of 1991, he enjoyed better relations with John Kerr than with Pierre de Boissieu. On German unification, for instance, Delors backed Kohl unequivocally whilst Mitterrand prevaricated. These didactic and independent-minded attitudes could lead to an impatience with the inability of others to see the larger picture and the significance of what was at stake. The result was occasional volatile mood-swings. On EMU Delors could alternate rapidly between optimism and pessimism. These attributes were to characterize his chairing of the Delors Committee. Delors's variant of social Catholicism was closer to Calvinism than to the moral flexibility, and as he saw it casuistry, of the world of Andreotti. In consequence, he was ill at ease with the way in which the Italian government prepared for the Rome 1 European Council on EMU in October 1990.

In addition, social Catholicism gave Delors an acute sensitivity to the importance of promoting solidarity as an indispensable requirement for a viable EMU. Though he accepted the market as an institution for allocating resources, and the vital importance of economic stability, he had a profound attachment to the concept of economic justice and the social basis of capitalism (De Bodman and Richard 1976). This concept found expression not in an *étatiste* and *dirigiste* outlook but in a profound belief in the value of dialogue by means of 'social partnership' as a means of achieving economic efficiency, monetary stability, and redistribution of wealth (Maris 1992). Dedication to these goals of efficiency, stability, and equity provided, not least, a point of ideological overlap with European Christian Democratic parties. His belief in solidarity formed a basis for the mutual sympathy and empathy that he enjoyed with Kohl and left him somewhat critically distant from what he saw as the French tradition of individualism, which he sought to correct. But Delors's thinking was wider-ranging and more abstract than that of Kohl. EMU was about reinforcing 'the European model of society', an issue of guaranteeing civilized values in the global marketplace. Hence he looked to creating collective bargaining at the European level; to an EC industrial policy; to the development of fiscal transfer mechanisms; and to 'economic government' via the European Council and ECOFIN to ensure a co-ordinated approach to growth, employment, and stability.

The influence of his years in the French Planning Commission (1962–9) was felt in three ways. Delors had learnt there the value of using an indirect, 'behind-the-scenes' approach to seeking out influence. He was acutely sensitive to the risks involved in direct political initiative by the EC Commission. It was far more effective to encourage governments and central banks to do what you wanted and to rely on exerting influence through personal networks for this purpose. On EMU he was to work with and through such figures as Guigou in the Elysée in Paris (she had formerly served in his cabinet at the Finance Ministry), Padoa-Schioppa in the Italian central bank in Rome (former Director-General of DG2), the Dutch Central Bank Governor Wim Duisenberg and the Belgian Jean Godeaux, the Belgian Finance Minister Philippe Maystadt and the Dutch Finance Minister Wim Kok.

Delors also brought from the French Planning Commission a belief in the mobilizing power of ideas. There was in this respect an important parallel with Jean Monnet, who had served as the first head of the Planning Commission and from there developed his thinking about how to unify Europe. Delors drew the conclusion that strategic and tactical skills were never enough. They had to be married to proposals whose influence derived from their intellectual quality. Presidential leadership in and beyond the EC Commission depended on this symbiosis. Hence Delors was constantly in search of ideas that could serve his purpose as an *animateur*. As Commission President he sought to situate economic and monetary problems in a European frame of reference. Examples were provided by his sponsorship of the idea of a 'co-operative growth initiative' in 1986 and his initiative in setting up a group under Padoa-Schioppa to explore the implications of freedom of capital movement in the EC for economic and monetary policies. Delors delighted in flying intellectual kites and challenging others to rethink their positions. He preferred to leave the 'small' politics of the Commission to others, notably Pascal Lamy, his tough-minded, workaholic head of cabinet.

A final influence from his years in the French Planning Commission was his fascination with structural policy and his neo-Keynesianism. Delors was always unhappy with a narrow conception of EMU that was preoccupied with monetary and budgetary policies. He had a much wider conception of an EMU based on strong economic-policy co-ordination that incorporated ideas of structural adjustment as well as of fiscal policy. For him neither the binding budget rules of the Delors Report nor the peer review of excessive deficits and the tough convergence criteria of the Maastricht Treaty were enough. Even a system of EC-wide fiscal transfers only made sense in a context of policies aimed at promoting structural adjustment. Hence Delors's conception of EMU embraced an EC-wide industrial policy, reform of collective bargaining, social dialogue, and promotion of a more flexible economic structure. He did not share the monetarist view that monetary policy is neutral, that it can be pursued in a self-contained way because it does not affect employment and growth, at least in the long run. In Delors's view, monetary policy has real effects, altering the distribution of benefits and costs in society, and hence is political. Correspondingly, though respectful of the principle of central bank independence, monetary policy needed to operate in a framework of economic-policy guidelines that were concerned with growth and employment and with structural adjustment. A viable EMU depended on a flexible 'policy mix' at the EC level, in particular on a broadening of the competence of the EC in economic policy.

This neo-Keynesianism seemed old-fashioned to many involved in the EMU debates of the 1980s, symptomatic of an intellectual locked in to the debates of the 1960s. Delors could be dismissed as the champion of an outdated economic-policy model that had been discredited by the experience of the 1970s. He was at the same time sufficiently economically literate to recognize that the monetarist paradigm of the 1980s was even more old-fashioned, with its intellectual roots in nineteenth-century neo-classical economics. But it was the case that Delors faced an inbuilt difficulty in leading on EMU by the power of ideas when the dominant ideas in EC institutional fora like the Committee of EC Central Bank Governors and the EC Monetary Committee (and even parts of the EC Commission) represented a different paradigm from that with which he was operating. In order to be listened to in the EMU debate, and to be taken seriously in the above fora, Delors had to alter his discourse and reflect more deeply on causal policy beliefs like central bank independence in 1988–9. At the same time he never lost his critical distance from the monetarist paradigm.

Delors was no typical product of the Parisian intellectual and administrative establishment. Like Bérégovoy he was an autodidact, lacked the polished verbal skills of the French elite, and unashamedly enjoyed simple tastes, notably sport and family life. But in other respects he differed from Bérégovoy. Delors was more comfortable with *énarques* (the graduates of the ENA) and had himself achieved the status of an intellectual. He was active within a progressive Catholic milieu and had taught in the University of Paris and at the ENA (where Lamy, Bitterlich, and Ludewig got to know him). Yet Delors retained an ambiguous position: on the 'inside' of the Mitterrand government as Finance Minister and of the French Socialist Party; yet always the 'outsider', someone with whom those outside his milieu often felt uncomfortable. This discomfort was related to Delors's austere temperament, the tough Jansenist moralism at the centre of his politics, and his didactic style.

Delors's own sense of being the 'outsider' was apparent not just in his strained relations with Mitterrand, whose enigmatic character he found extremely frustrating, but also in his relations with the EC central bank governors. He was preoccupied with being accepted and respected by these central bankers, a preoccupation with personal roots in the fact that his father had worked for the Banque de France and that he himself had worked and met his wife there. Hence, over EMU, Delors's relations with Pöhl took on a particular sensitivity for him. He sought to gain Pöhl's respect, not least by cultivating closer relations to Duisenberg, Godeaux, and Ciampi in order to help persuade Pöhl of his *bona fides* on EMU.

Though an intensely private man, Delors was alert to the value of performance in political life. He was adept at employing charm, warmth, and his 'down-to-earth' interests, not least in sport, to forge relations of *complicité*, most notably with Kohl. His mood-swings and volatility were in part performances used to put colleagues under pressure. The cinema-loving, jazz-loving, and sport-loving Delors was a man fascinated by the performer. Hence he was no mere austere intellectual. Delors valued communication as an instrument of politics and was deeply attuned to its nuances. His skills in handling discourse were apparent in his use of television, where he excelled in making complex issues accessible (Drake 1995). They also emerged in the debate about EMU. For instance, in 1986–7 he was very careful to avoid the words 'EMU', 'ECB', and 'single currency'. Instead Delors employed code words like 'strengthening monetary co-operation' and 'reform of the EMS'. Later, once EMU was back on the agenda, he kept away from the term *'gouvernement économique'* used by the French government. Though he agreed with its content, Delors recognized the need to tailor political language to the exigencies of a successful EMU negotiation. Delors's bleakly pessimistic moods were also used to energize Kohl and Mitterrand. Examples of this tactical use of mood-swings include the period after the Delors Report ran into difficulties at the S'Agaro ECOFIN in May 1989; after the German Draft Treaty on EMU was presented in February 1991; and during the 'end-game' just before Maastricht when he lobbied actively for a final fixed date for stage 3.

Delors's belief in the importance of strategic vision led him to feel ill at ease with the 'small' politics of the EC Commission and its internal problems of consensus-building in the face of influence from different national policy styles and administrative cultures (Cini 1996). He saw the need to energize the Commission as an instrument of political leadership in Europe. In order to tackle this problem of fit between his conception of the Presidential office and the reality of fragmentation and poor co-ordination in the EC Commission Delors relied heavily on an immensly talented cabinet, led by Pascal Lamy who had earlier worked with him in the French Finance Ministry. The cabinet's functions were to act as his brains trust, to relieve him from the burdens of day-to-day conflict-management within the Commission, and to mobilize the Commission behind his vision (Grant 1994; Ross 1995: chapter 2). Above all, Delors looked to them to create for him the time to put in the hard intellectual work needed for Commission leadership, not least on EMU. Some two hours per day were devoted by Delors to background intellectual reading. In addition, and to the irritation of some Commissioners, Delors met three to four times a year with the Director-Generals of the Commission. This venue gave him an opportunity to explain strategy and to diffuse his message. It was used to activate support for EMU.

Delors continued to be frustrated by problems of internal fragmentation and bureaucratic politics within Brussels. With reference to EMU these problems were best exemplified by the independence and power of the EC Monetary Committee in preparing the business of ECOFIN. They reflected a competition for power and status between Council and Commission and the EC Monetary Committee's self-conception as adviser to both ECOFIN and the Commission. Delors was impatient with the degree of independence enjoyed by Andreas Kees as Secretary of the EC Monetary Committee, and wanted to strengthen the Commission's influence over its work. Kees maintained a distance from the

Commission and clashed with Delors, working to ensure that the EC Monetary Committee remained a closed, secretive world with its own rules. These rules precluded a monopoly of the right of initiative for the Commission on ERM and EMU business and led to the Chair of the EC Monetary Committee claiming equal status with the Commissioner in ECOFIN (Kees 1994). Hence Delors sought to bypass the EC Monetary Committee and ECOFIN by looking to the EC foreign ministers (like Dumas and Genscher) and the heads of state and government. Delors needed an internal working structure and method on EMU appropriate for the confidential, high-level relations and trust that he sought to cultivate with the European Council as the principal means to activate and sustain progress on EMU.

Delors was especially sensitive to the risks of exposing a politically sensitive and technically complex and difficult area like EMU to normal Commission decision-making processes. He feared it would fall victim to internal conflicts and persistent leaks when what was needed was a unified position and confidentiality for success in the negotiations. This proneness to conflicts and leaks was the product of the Commission's openness towards, and penetration by, outside interests (Drake 1995; Cini 1996). The Commission's cohesiveness was further undermined by its own multinational and multicultural character. In endeavouring to take united action it is required to synthesize, or at least placate, distinct administrative traditions and policy styles (Cassese and Della Cananea 1992; Cram 1994). Not least, in Germany DG2 was seen as having closer national ties to France and Italy than to the more stability-minded Germans, Dutch, and Danes. It was, accordingly, little trusted in Bonn and Frankfurt, where trust mattered to Delors. This suspicion was not fully deserved; many DG2 officials were strongly influenced by the German economic model. But it was a suspicion that made for sensitive relations over EMU. Other DGs, notably those operating the Structural Funds, were viewed as inclined by interest and ideology to favour large-scale financial-transfer mechanisms. Their role in EMU was likely to excite counterproductive reactions in key national capitals. A further problem was Delors's lack of trust in the professional competence of some Commission officials and in their loyalty to his political line. These attitudes were manifested in unusually strong terms in his relations with Ravasio's predecessor as Director-General of DG2. Against Commission tradition, Delors acted to have him removed and replaced by Ravasio. Delors and his team were expert at channelling EMU work in the Commission to avoid these problems. The result was a high degree of centralization of internal power on EMU. EMU was an extreme case of the informal 'presidentialization' of the Commission under Delors.[1] Delors was in effect the Commission for much of the EMU negotiations, at least before the complex, detailed work began in the IGC.

This exceptionally strong personal position on EMU was embedded in Delors's wider success in transforming the office of Commission President into

[1] More generally on informal presidentialization see Ross (1995).

the base for asserting a strength of EC Commission leadership not seen since the years of Walter Hallstein, the first Commission President (1958–67). Between Hallstein and Delors, only Roy Jenkins (1977–81) could lay claim to a high profile—though his achievements in office were much more modest than either of the other two. The fact that other EC Commission Presidents faded into obscurity relatively quickly proves the rule: that the office of Commission President provides a weak base for the exercise of leadership in the EC. To become influential the Commission President needs the 'window of opportunity' offered by a favourable conjunction of policy developments and political events combined with a bold, well-tuned strategy and personal and political credibility. Even then the constraints are formidable. As Delors came to recognize during the British Presidency of the EC in 1986, signs of too overt and dynamic a Commission leadership threaten to unleash countervailing forces at the national level. By 1991, well before the ratification problems of the Maastricht Treaty, Delors was again alert to this threat. It made him more subdued during the IGC negotiations on EMU (Dinan 1994: 206; Ross 1995: 78–9).

Delors's dominance of the EMU brief rested on a series of factors, some specific to EMU, others related to wider political and policy developments.

1. Circumstances were favourable for a relaunch of the EC following the success of the Fontainebleau European Council in June 1984 in resolving a range of outstanding issues, including the EC budget and the CAP. Effective EC problem-solving by the French government, of which Delors had been part, opened new opportunities for EC Commission leadership to the incoming President in January 1985. His visits to EC capitals in 1984 had taught him that priority must be given to the single market. But EMU was seen as an opportunity waiting in the wings.

2. His position benefited from the combination of the effective launch of the single European market programme, consequent on the Single European Act, with the 'Delors package' to strengthen the EC's financial position and secured at the Brussels European Council in February 1988. By these means Delors conspired to create his own opportunities. He could establish linkage between the single market, exchange-rate management, monetary policy, and redistributive action at the EC level.

3. Under Delors as French Finance Minister the Mitterrand Presidency had converted to budgetary *rigueur* in June 1982 and confirmed its European vocation in March 1983. This convergence of economic policies between France and Germany made EMU in principle a more credible option. Delors had played a key role in making that convergence possible.

4. Delors enjoyed political support from the Franco-German axis, and not just from Mitterrand. More importantly, he had a close and good working relationship with Kohl. His relations with Kohl were to improve further with the German EC Presidency of the first half of 1988 and the help that he offered over German unification in 1989–90. Delors's social Catholicism placed him at the centre of gravity of Franco-German politics and indeed EC politics, though well

away from the position of the Thatcher government. Also, he was deeply attuned to the theme, shared by Kohl and Mitterrand, that European unification was about preventing future war in Europe. The Hague Conference of 1948 was a formative influence on his political consciousness.

5. Delors was a politician with a future as well as a past. He came to Brussels to make a future career in Paris, not to finish his career. Kohl was quick to identify in him the ideal successor to Mitterrand in the Elysée and hence took him very seriously. By contrast, most of Delors's predecessors had effectively finished their political careers in Brussels.

6. During his career in the Banque de France and the French Planning Commission, and during his trade-union work from 1953, Delors had become involved at a very early stage with European issues and interested in policy-learning from the social dimension of the Dutch, German, and Swedish economic models. This familiarity with comparative economic policy was followed in the 1970s by a growing consciousness of the historical decline of Europe, geostrategically as well as economically. European unification was seen by Delors as a process of reversing that decline. His subsequent period as Minister of Finance (1981–3) and Minister for Economic and Financial Affairs and the Budget (1983–4) meant that he came to Brussels with a good reputation in European economic and financial affairs and familiar with the politics and fora of EC economic and monetary policies. The fact that his expertise in this area matched, or overshadowed, that of most national leaders in 1988–91 gave him an advantage in EMU negotiations. This expertise was important in his bilateral relations with Mitterrand and Kohl. It also biased him towards prioritizing the EMU portfolio. In 1985 he centralized the monetary portfolio by taking it on himself and by becoming a regular attender at the monthly meetings of the Committee of EC Central Bank Governors. He was marking time and gaining relevant contacts and expertise to facilitate the launch of EMU.

7. In sponsoring the single market programme and getting agreement on the 'Delors package', Delors was quick to demonstrate that he was an effective strategist. Though in 1985–7 EMU proved much more difficult for him, and he suffered reverses, he had shown that he could 'engineer' a set of circumstances which were conducive to important agreements at the EC level. In this role as *ingénieur*, Delors had also shown that he was not just master of his own Commission but also capable of exploiting linkages and 'spillover' to move European integration forward. Hence his appointment as Chair of the Delors Committee added more than just weight and significance to what might otherwise have proved a more mundane exercise. It offered to Kohl and Mitterrand a safeguard that the European interest would be promoted to engineer an agreed report on EMU.

Delors's entire approach as Commission President emphasized strategic planning. In this respect he acted in keeping with the French administrative tradition, which values strategy highly (Grant 1994: 105). Rather like the Commission itself, Delors had a bias in favour of policy drafting, testing, and experimentation, notably in the areas of structural policy and economic and social cohesion. The Commission has from the beginning interpreted its role to be that of an *animateur*, producing ideas, policy papers, and programmes (Ludlow 1991: 97). Delors recognized the parallel between the EC Commission and his work at the French Planning Commission and between his own background and that of Monnet. Under Jérôme Vignon (recruited from his cabinet in the French Finance Ministry), he expanded the 'Forward Studies Unit' (*cellule de prospective*) to provide him with an internal 'think-tank' on 'horizontal' issues that crossed various directorates-general. This worked to embed projects like the single market and EMU in the concept of the 'European model of society'. This model accepted the market and competition. But it also argued that a civilized society depended on a co-operative approach to industrial relations, negotiated fiscal transfers, and an extensive welfare state. Especially after 1989 Vignon worked to draw intellectuals into the task of 'thinking Europe'.

By 1988 an informal 'presidentialization' of Commission power had made Delors master of his ship and had become associated with improved organizational and policy effectiveness. Lamy had worked to ensure that a strongly centralized and hierarchical power structure was established, consistent with the French tradition. What had been a horizontal power structure now took on a steeper pyramidal form, with Delors and his cabinet at the apex and weaker commissioners relegated to the base (Grant 1994: 105). Lamy emerged as, arguably, the most powerful person in the Commission after Delors (Ross 1995: 26). He managed a complex, informal network, turning the top of the Commission into a more flexible and innovative 'task-force' type of organization in place of a traditional 'top–down' management hierarchy. In this context some were privileged and some excluded, with consequent resentments and tensions (Edwards and Spence 1994). Membership of the network required extremely hard work, dedication, and great talent.

A distinct Delors network on EMU took shape between 1988 and 1991. He took a hands-on approach to managing it, leaving less than usual to Lamy. This approach reflected his decision to retain the monetary portfolio for himself in 1985. The network comprised:

1. Delors's cabinet. The most important attribute of Delors's cabinet was its French ethic of *militantisme*, of dedication to his strategic line and its energetic implementation. Whilst Lamy had a general input, and was important in managing political relations with Paris on EMU, especially on the date for stage 3, Joly Dixon had specific responsibility for EMU after his arrival from the EC delegation in Washington in 1987. Within the cabinet EMU involved relatively few, Dixon dealing directly with Delors. François Lamoureux, deputy head of cabinet from 1989 to July 1991, had some input, particularly—reflecting his legal skills—on writing texts for the Delors Committee and on institutional matters. But he was more concerned with political-union questions. Lamoureux was to be especially important as a channel for Lamy to Paris over the date for stage 3 after he had left for the French Prime Minister's Office. In 1991 Michel Petite took on the role of adviser on legal and institutional matters.

2. Leading officials from DG2 (Economic and Financial Affairs). Both Delors and Christophersen placed great trust in Giovanni Ravasio, its Director-General from February 1990. He attended the IGC personal representative meetings on behalf of the Commission, alongside Lamoureux, was a member of the EC Monetary Committee, provided regular briefings to Delors during the IGC, and had good relations with Padoa-Schioppa. Other key figures came from the monetary affairs directorate, notably Jean-Paul Mingasson, its director until 1989; his successor, Jean-François Pons; and Hervé Carré. Like Ravasio, Mingasson was trusted by Delors and Lamy, and he and Ravasio worked closely with Dixon. In the Economic Service Alexander Italiener and Horst Reichenbach were important, for instance on regional stabilization and budgetary aspects of EMU. But some officials in DG2 felt marginalized on EMU, forced to react to initiatives from Delors with which they had little or no sympathy.

3. The head of the Commission's Legal Services, Jean-Louis Dewost, who consistent with established practice reported to the Commission President. He had been appointed in 1989 by Delors and was a known loyalist to the President, intervening in internal disputes on a range of EC matters to protect Delors. Dewost was important on the legal issues surrounding the transition to stage 3, but tended to be overshadowed on EMU by Lamoureux.

4. Henning Christopherson, the Commissioner for Economic and Financial Affairs from 1989, and his deputy head of cabinet, Jan Schmidt. Christopherson participated in the IGC ministerial meetings and worked relatively amicably with Delors who saw him as competent and reliable. But they were never very close. In so far as there was a problem it did not stem from ideological incompatibility with a Danish Liberal politician. There was a considerable overlap of viewpoints on EMU. Christophersen was not viewed as intellectually creative enough to satisfy Delors's appetite for new ideas and proposals. The combination of their overlapping portfolios (leading Delors to draw directly on DG2 staff) with the informal 'presidentialization' of EMU made for some tensions, though no overt conflict.

5. David Williamson, Secretary-General of the Commission since 1987. He co-ordinated a group of senior staff during the period of the two IGCs of 1991, endeavouring to maintain coherence on institutional questions between both sets of negotiations. Williamson was regarded as a close ally of Delors, for whom—to the irritation of his cabinet—he worked directly. His contribution on EMU was limited to institutional issues, on which he liaised closely with Ravasio, and to the European Council meetings.

Participation in the Delors-centred Commission network was restricted to a very few carefully selected, able, and trustworthy people, in all about ten. Communication with officials in DG2 was limited and closely controlled, leading to criticism of lack of co-ordination between officials and the College. The Delors cabinet sought tight control of Commission work on EMU throughout. Dixon and Lamy were the key figures alongside Delors. With the combative Lamoureux, who specialized in text drafting, they acted to maintain Presidential discipline. DG2 was kept distant from the Delors Committee, but inclusion in the later stages also remained controlled. Ravasio was the great exception to this generalization.

Before 1988 Delors worked most closely with Mingasson on the monetary aspects of EMU and, some five to six times a year, arranged a working lunch with Mingasson and Padoa-Schioppa at which ERM and EMU-related issues were discussed. But the real catalyst to build a team working for Delors on EMU came with the Delors Committee. Delors prepared his work as Chair of the Delors Committee with a group of four: Dixon and Mingasson from the Commission, and the two rapporteurs Padoa-Schioppa and Gunter Baer (from the Bank for International Settlements in Basle). As the negotiations progressed, these five met weekly, assisted by Dewost and Lamoureux on the drafting of texts. The Madrid European Council, which set the date for stage 1, acted as the catalyst for a small, flexibly composed working group on EMU to prepare for the IGC. This included Dixon, Schmidt, Ravasio, Pons, and Carré (on monetary aspects), Michael Emerson (on economic-policy aspects), as well as the legal service. This group was made responsible for, and was especially active in producing, the Commission Communication on EMU of August 1990 and the Commission Draft Treaty on EMU of December 1990. Delors and Christophersen would sometimes attend.

In addition, Delors sought carefully to manage the involvement of the College of Commissioners in EMU, keeping it at a distance. This behaviour was part of a pattern which caused irritation in the College. During the 1985 IGC on the Single Act, Delors had not consulted colleagues about the various Commission submissions to the negotiations. Instead, he had worked with the then Secretary-General, Emile Noel, and his aide Lamoureux to draft the texts (Grant 1994: 72). Similarly, the drafting of the Commission's submission to the IGC on EMU in December 1990 was limited to Dixon, Schmidt, Dewost, Ravasio, Emerson, and Carré. The College was in effect presented with a *fait accompli*, provoking criticism from Leon Brittan about the lack of College involvement. The Delors Report on EMU in April 1989 was discussed by the College in only the most limited manner and endorsed (though Delors was not seeking its endorsement). Delors argued that he was acting in a personal capacity for the European Council, not as President of the Commission, and that the work was merely 'technical' and preparatory rather than political. In this way he kept reporting and discussion to a bare minimum, assuming an underlying consensus on the principle of EMU and minimizing the risk of leaks by Commissioners and their officials. There was more regular reporting to the College on the IGC negotiations on EMU from Delors and from Christophersen, and on 23–4 November 1991 a Commission seminar on the state of play in the negotiations was held. But these reports and the seminar had no real practical impact. In short, Delors and his network were in control throughout. His strategic vision dominated. Nobody in the College seriously sought to disturb his grip on EMU.

This organization of EMU policy formation was incredibly demanding on Delors. He had to work immensely hard to keep up with the technical aspects of the negotiations, especially during the phase of the Delors Committee. Commission sources were in fact only part of the network that he built and used on EMU. Delors sought to enrich his information and develop new perspectives by keeping in regular contact with Padoa-Schioppa, former Director-General of DG2 and a contact to the world of EC central bankers. He was briefed about the state of play in the Elysée through Guigou and in the Matignon through Lamy's contacts. In relation to the German Federal Chancellor's Office Delors relied on Bitterlich, who was constantly in touch. He also had direct contact with Kohl of a more regular, relaxed, and informal nature than with Mitterrand. Not least, he attended to a great deal of pre-European Council manoeuvring himself, particularly before Hanover and before Maastricht when he was in touch with Mitterrand and Kohl on 'irreversibility'. Much of what Delors did was hidden even from those closest to him.

This pattern of policy formation was particular to the EMU process. In other policy sectors the norm is for the Commission President to face a much more substantial challenge when seeking to exercise leadership. Even within the Commission, the policy arena is typically much more crowded, with different DGs vying for position and influence on the basis of ill-defined and overlapping responsibilities for multidimensional policies. By contrast, EMU was placed in a different and isolated milieu: composed of central bankers (in the Committee of EC Central Bank Governors); finance ministers and their officials (in ECOFIN); and finance ministry officials and their central bank equivalents (in the EC Monetary Committee). The institutional venues were thus very distinct and required carefully crafted strategy and tactics in dealing with them. Crucially, the ability of the Commission to provide a cognitive lead was constrained by the in-depth technical expertise, reputation and mystique, and norm of exclusivity, that characterized the monetary-policy milieu.

Delors as *Animateur, Ingénieur*, and Entrepreneur: Securing the Chair of the Delors Committee

In assessing Delors's contribution to the EMU negotiations it is analytically useful to distinguish between three roles. He acted as:

- *animateur*, inspiring by his intellectual passion and rigorous argument and galvanizing action;
- *ingénieur*, conspiring to put in place the appropriate infrastructure to support EMU negotiations and oiling the wheels of those negotiations once in place;
- entrepreneur, setting the EC policy agenda by bringing forward timely proposals for EMU.

As *animateur* he was important: both in galvanizing the Commission behind EMU and in building and sustaining a cross-national network of EMU enthusiasts who could operate in their domestic contexts to achieve his objectives—for instance, Philippe Maystadt in Belgium, Guigou in France, Padoa-Schioppa in Italy, Jean-Claude Juncker and Jacques Santer in Luxembourg, and Kok in the Netherlands. Benelux was disproportionately represented in this network. More distant was Giscard d'Estaing, who was neverthless useful and respected because of his expertise on EMU and because of his influence within the French Right. But this animating of a network gave him no more than background and indirect influence: useful to sustaining momentum, especially at critical junctures such as before the Madrid European Council in 1989, though—as the French and German chapters show—ultimately not decisive. Delors lacked the direct political legitimacy necessary to be an effective *animateur* at the European level. More important was his role as *ingénieur*, especially in relation to the Delors Committee. Delors was vital, first in engineering the infrastructure of policy developments that made it possible to get EMU back onto the agenda, and then in keeping the EMU negotiations on track.

His role as policy entrepreneur on EMU was crucial. This role was more indirect than direct. It involved creating the political circumstances and the policy context that would induce 'spillover' effects, which in turn would favour Franco-German initiatives on EMU. Delors succeeded in writing a commitment in principle to EMU into treaty form with the Single European Act. He also gained important reforms to the EMS, notably intramarginal interventions, with the Basle–Nyborg negotiations. The '1992' target for the single European market enabled him to prioritize freedom of capital movement in the EC. The Delors package of 1988 gave the EC a much enhanced role in structural adjustment and economic and social cohesion. In addition, he made some progress on the pillar of economic policy co-ordination in the Delors Report. It was precisely when he departed from the strategy of indirection to produce his own proposals that he found himself confronted with opposition, as in 1985. As we shall see, there was an inbuilt and enduring tension between his recognition of the need to seek out 'behind-the-scenes' influence—which originated in the French Planning Commission and the ideas of Jean Monnet—and the pedagogic and didactic style that followed from his Jansenist background. Delors's role as policy entrepreneur on EMU was circumscribed by the constraints, noted above, under which the Commission operates in general and the particular realities both of the operation of the EMS as a German-centred system and of the pivotal position of the EC central bankers on EMU.

Delors was the first of the three key *animateurs* on EMU—the others being Kohl and Mitterrand—to recognize the potential for progress and to take action to try to realize it. He had long harboured thoughts of realizing EMU and viewed the EMS as the 'jewel in the crown' of the EC. It was only natural that he should take up 'strengthening monetary co-operation' when in late 1984, with Lamy, he toured all the then ten national capitals to discuss the basis on which the EC might be 'relaunched'. Like Jenkins earlier, he looked for the 'big idea' to inspire his Presidency: and, like Jenkins, he was also attracted by the notion of pursuing monetary integration. But the support was not forthcoming: Thatcher and Lawson were adamantly opposed, whilst in Germany Stoltenberg signalled serious reservations. Delors raised other options—the single market; institutional reform; and defence policy. He found support immediately for the first, and later for the second.

Despite this inauspicious beginning Delors attempted to set the scene for future initiatives on EMU by taking over the monetary portfolio in the Commission. This gave him the opportunity to attend the Basle meetings—and, crucially, dinners—of the Committee of EC Central Bank Governors. These meetings and dinners provided him with an important source of intelligence and policy-learning that were to prove indispensable in helping him later to master the task of chairing the Delors Committee. To prepare himself he relied in particular on Mingasson and on Padoa-Schioppa as an insider in the world of central banking, instituting regular lunches with them. Delors made it his practice to attend its meetings every month, in contrast to his predecessor. His approach was not to carve out a leading role, in the form of pushing the EC central bank governors to frame monetary policies in an EC context. He saw his attendance as an investment in gaining their acceptance. The initial coolness of their reaction to him as such a high-profile 'outsider' in their club proved a painful experience for Delors. This experience confirmed his views about their excessive conservatism. It also led him to work even harder to be accepted and to adopt a modest, 'clubbable' style. The fact that for over three years Delors had put in this investment was vital in making his chairing of the Delors Committee in some way credible. In the absence of this investment Delors's task would have been very much harder in 1988–9. He had acquired a degree of familiarity with this enclosed world of central banking.

At the same time Delors did not hesitate to push his agenda on EMU in other venues. In the first month of his Presidency, in January 1985, he raised the question of strengthening the EMS in the European Parliament. His approach took up the arguments that he had used as French Finance Minister. In particular, he seized on the success in developing the private ECU as an argument for a parallel development of the public ECU, setting his eyes on its future role as a reserve currency alongside the US dollar. Delors presented these ideas at the subsequent informal ECOFIN in Palermo in May. But he was confronted by the same suspicious Pöhl who had rejected his proposals for EMS reform in 1981 and who Delors had then characterized as lacking commitment to 'European solidarity' (*L'Expansion*, 4–7 September 1981: 57). After Palermo's very modest technical changes to the ERM Delors's view that progress on EMU in ECOFIN, as well as in the Committee of EC Central Bank Governors, would be slow and require great patience was reinforced. If, in private, he criticized the central bankers as too conservative on EMU, he saw the EC finance ministers as unable to see the wood for the trees. Delors remained impatient to educate others in the larger historical and international realities. Part of that reality was that Britain, France, Germany, and Italy as well as the others were too small to exert influence on a global scale. Only a Europe united politically and economically could act to promote and defend its own values (Delors and Alexandre 1985).

Delors saw in the IGC established in Milan in June 1985 a venue in which more progress might be made than within ECOFIN. Though the focus of the IGC was on the single market and institutional reforms, Delors saw an opportunity to find a way round this institutional constraint by securing a treaty commitment to EMU that would force change on ECOFIN. The result was conflict with the EC Monetary Committee and ECOFIN about their institutional prerogatives and especially with the Germans about any reference to EMU in the Treaty. Delors tried to counter these procedural difficulties by promising to bring proposals to these fora before they went to the IGC. Tietmeyer led the German resistance in the EC Monetary Committee by making it clear to Delors that two ideas were completely unacceptable: the EC Commission must acquire no authority over or in relation to monetary policy; and any transition to EMU would require the full process of treaty amendment under article 236 of the Treaty of Rome because it involved institutional reform. Furthermore, that treaty amendment must involve the EC Monetary Committee and ECOFIN. It could not be left as a matter for intergovernmental agreement via Article 235 or circumvent or exclude EC finance ministries and central banks.

Delors brought his proposals to ECOFIN on 28 October 1985, but ran into great difficulties over his attempt to get a seat on the EMCF for the Commission and to provide for the EMCF to evolve into the European Monetary Fund consistent with the envisaged stage 2 of EMU. It was an object lesson for Delors about the dangers of behaving in too *volontariste* a manner. He decided against a direct appeal to the IGC, leaving it to the Belgian government and others to raise the issue of EMU there on 19 November. Instead, Delors concentrated on mobilizing support in Bonn, by talking directly with Genscher and with Kohl, and in Paris, where Mitterrand took up the issue. It became clear that Kohl was prepared to envisage a small reference to EMU in the treaty, but that specific references to an EMF or to an EMU outside the bounds of normal treaty revision and ratification was not on the agenda and that much greater progress on economic convergence was a prerequisite for taking monetary union seriously. By the time of the Luxembourg Council in December, when he again spoke to Kohl on this issue, Delors had narrowed down his objective to a treaty reference to EMU. In his more optimistic mood he saw the outcome as a small but significant step forward; in his bleaker mood as a very minimalist result. What did emerge was a pattern of working with the Belgians (especially Maystadt), the French, and the Italians, prefiguring later alliance-building that was to characterize the IGC in 1991 when Delors was closest to the positions of these countries.

The lesson learnt by Delors was that a more patient strategy of indirection was likely to yield a better return on EMU. He had tried to act as policy entrepreneur on EMU and failed. In future he was more guarded in his language, preferring to use code words for EMU. This prudence was reinforced by his experience of the British Presidency of the EC in the second half of 1986. He saw political risks in the Commission being seen to be too prominent. Hence he shied away from new projects like EMU to focus on what the Council had already decided and to demonstrate that the Commission could deliver, notably on the single market and financial reform. In this way Delors's credibility—especially with Kohl—would be enhanced. He was acutely aware of the reluctance of Pöhl and Stoltenberg on a single currency and of the need to enlist Kohl to face them down.

Delors also shifted direction away from measures to strengthen monetary co-operation, sensing that these touched too directly on the prerogatives of the Bundesbank. By February 1986 Delors was launching the 'co-operative growth strategy', developed in DG2. The idea was that the EC needed an economic policy mechanism to ensure that the achievements of the single market were not undermined by 'non-co-operative' policies. In particular, the objective was to promote a more co-operative German economic policy by offering an alternative to the 'locomotive' theory that had earlier been pressed on Germany in international fora like G10. Responsibility was no longer placed on Germany to pull others out of recession but on all states to use their discretion to vary fiscal and monetary policies in the interests of growth and employment. This idea made no headway in the face of fears, especially in Germany, that it would undermine domestic economic stability.

Delors's other priority from 1986 onwards was to push liberalization of EC capital movements under the single market programme. He pressed for this despite opposition within France and the reservations of Bérégovoy in 1988. In this way Delors hoped both to ensure that Europe was not left behind in the accelerating process of globalization of financial markets and to address an obstacle that some states saw to moving ahead with EMU. Intellectually, Delors recognized that EMU's logic was an integrated European capital market and that its social counterpart was harmonized taxation of income from savings. But, in contrast to Bérégovoy, this social perspective took second place to his global perspective and to his strategic assessment. Strategically, he saw in freedom of EC capital movement a lever to shift the intellectual parameters of the debate about economic and monetary policies in Europe and put EMU firmly on the agenda. In an effort to map out the policy implications of the combination of a single market and of the EMS, Delors took the initiative to establish the Padoa-Schioppa Group.

Padoa-Schioppa's Report refrained from directly pushing for EMU (its British and German members objected) (Padoa-Schioppa et al. 1987). Its main contribution was the thesis of the 'inconsistent triangle'. According to this thesis, only two of the three legs of the triangle of freedom of capital movement, stable exchange rates and autonomy of domestic monetary policies, were consistent. In short, with the single market (i.e. no exchange controls), and with stabilized exchange rates under the ERM, it would prove impossible to sustain effective national monetary policies. Alternatively, with the single market in place, and monetary policies still conducted at the national level, the ERM would collapse. The message was that hard choices were necessary. Delors saw this exercise as helpful in giving intellectual ballast to his efforts to exploit spillover effects from the single market programme and put EMU back on the agenda. The Padoa-Schioppa Report's 'inconsistent triangle' served a useful pedagogic purpose, but its detailed analysis was not so influential amongst EC central bankers and finance ministries. They picked up the negative signal that Padoa-Schioppa was trying to give a monetary policy role to ECOFIN. But the main criticism was that the report underestimated the importance of building stability 'at home' as a basis for economic and monetary co-operation.

The Padoa-Schioppa Report was, in any case, overshadowed by two other preoccupations of Delors in 1986–7: the EC's financial reform, culminating in the 'Delors package' agreed at the Brussels European Council in February 1988; and the Basle–Nyborg negotiations. These were far more important in preparing the ground for EMU. The negotiation of the Delors package pitched him into conflicts and, at the Copenhagen European Council in December 1987, failure when a furious Kohl rejected the first draft communiqué. Its passage was, however, vital in creating a new opening for reform. It coincided with Genscher's Memorandum on an ECB. Meanwhile, Delors put all his efforts into using the Basle–Nyborg negotiations to 'deepen' the EMS. For Delors this 'deepening' had two aspects: reinforcement of monetary co-operation to demonstrate the capacity of the EC to act together; and strengthening the EMS's role in forcing economic convergence, especially in the fight against inflation. By tabling a paper at the ECOFIN in Nyborg in September 1987 Delors attempted to strengthen the agreement hammered out in Basle by the central bank governors. But he made no direct reference to EMU, an ECB, or a single currency. The paper made a link between the single market and 'going forward' (code for EMU) by strengthening the EMS. In taking this line at Nyborg he succeeded in angering the EC central bankers, who felt that their responsibility was being undermined, without any gain.

Despite such slow and frustrating progress Delors noticed a change of mood on EMU in 1987. Balladur and Genscher began to talk about an ECB, and other EC politicians, bankers, and industrialists were starting to talk in increasing numbers about what would follow the single market. Giscard d'Estaing, who was also lobbying Balladur, met Delors regularly in 1987 to keep him in touch with the evolving work of the new Committee for the Monetary Union of Europe. The Giscard–Schmidt Committee wanted to go further than the Padoa-Schioppa Report (with which it was disappointed) in developing proposals on EMU and was lobbying across EC capitals. There was a sense of dynamism and opportunity in EC affairs which Delors and the Commission had helped to create. The Giscard–Schmidt lobbying in particular fed a climate of optimism at the top level of the Commission in which debate about EMU could prosper.

In fact, despite these positive signals, Delors held back from participating in this emerging debate, sensing that he might provoke negative reactions. During early 1988, in parallel with the discussions on the Balladur Memorandum in the EC Monetary Committee, Delors's cabinet reflected on the relationship between the single market and strengthening the EMS. They concluded that there was a logical and a political link but that the former did not make the latter necessary. This distinction meant that Delors was not formally in conflict with the conclusions of the EC Monetary Committee. But Delors and his cabinet were clear that the EC Monetary Committee would never be the source of progress on EMU. They identified the political requirement as being to build bipartisan support in Paris, particularly by encouraging the cautious Gaullists like Balladur, and to support Genscher to press on EMU and to persuade Kohl to take it up.

In any case, till February 1988, Delors was too preoccupied with the Delors package and what it showed about the difficulties of change in the EC. It suggested that the EC was not yet ready for a repeated Werner-type exercise in unification. A failed effort at relaunching EMU would be a serious set-back to his Presidency. Hence, after the Brussels European Council had—thanks largely to Kohl—cleared away the EC financial-reform issue, Delors was very cautious about aligning the Commission behind the Genscher Memorandum. He preferred a 'wait-and-see' approach in relation to Bonn. Before producing his memorandum Genscher had discussed his ideas with Delors, who was surprised by his boldness on EMU.

By mid-March Delors determined to push for EMU, after consulting Padoa-Schioppa and others in Brussels on the implications of the Genscher Memorandum and of the emerging work of the Giscard–Schmidt Committee. Delors was persuaded that he must seize the opportunity opened up by the Brussels European Council to forge a close working relationship with Kohl on EMU during the German EC Presidency. In several meetings, in which they discussed the Genscher Memorandum, he sought to persuade Kohl that EMU was ripe for action; that the lesson of EC history was that clear proposals from a group of recognized experts were essential as the basis for progress; and that in agreeing this way forward Kohl was committing himself to no more than a technical exercise and buying time before the later need for a political decision by the European Council to go ahead. Most importantly, they agreed that any action must be secretly prepared. Between March and June Delors and Kohl colluded on EMU, preoccupied by the risk of leaks especially to Pöhl and the Committee of EC Central Bank Governors and keeping Mrs Thatcher, Stoltenberg, and Tietmeyer at arm's length.

At the basis of the preparations for the Hanover European Council was a private deal between Delors and Kohl. Delors proposed to Kohl that the EC central bank governors should form the main element in the committee to report on EMU. Since he took over as EC Commission President he had recognized that the political key to EMU was to convince the EC central bank governors that the project was credible. The proposal was, in short, consistent with this view. This device would provide the legitimacy of their expertise and 'bind' them into the final report, enhancing its authority. It would provide the foundation of expert preparation that a future successful IGC on EMU would require. In short, it appealed to the technocrat in Delors, his conception of the task as essentially technical, and his tactical approach of reassuring the German Chancellor that he had nothing to fear politically from this exercise. He also argued the case for a strong political direction of the committee to ensure that it arrived at worthwhile results. In arguing this case Delors was appealing to the other aspect of Kohl's political nature—as a fellow 'European of the heart'.

Delors's technique was not to ask directly to be Chair. The idea was in his mind but evoked an ambivalent response. He was attracted to it as a means of ensuring political momentum in the face of formidable obstacles and as a means of helping to write history. Equally, Delors was aware of the existing burden of work, meetings, and trips that he carried without adding this enormous extra task. He confined himself to arguing to Kohl against Pöhl—the EC central bankers' favoured candidate—as too conservative and obstructive to do the job. His cabinet used contacts to the Federal Chancellery to canvass more boldly on Delors's behalf. By 2 June Kohl was talking in strictest privacy of Delors as Chair, raising his name at Evian with Mitterrand. At the pre-Council meeting on 11 June at Kohl's home in Oggersheim Delors was sufficiently confident to respond positively to Kohl's suggestion that he take on this role. But, in a subsequent meeting in Brussels on 23 June with Pöhl, he hid this understanding—a tactic that was to leave a permanent mark on Pöhl's relations with him.

When Kohl succeeded at Hanover in gaining acceptance of Delors as Chair, following the renewal of his mandate as EC Commission President, Delors sensed that he had won a major personal victory. The membership of the Delors Committee had been carefully worked out in detail between himself and Kohl, taking others completely by surprise. Against the odds the EC central bankers had been 'boxed' into assuming responsibility for EMU. To them were added EC Commissioner Frans Andriessen because of his expertise on institutional issues, Alexandre Lamfalussy to add the prestige of the Bank for International Settlements, Miguel Boyer to represent a new EC member (Spain) and the Southern dimension, and Niels Thygesen as a long-standing expert on EC economic and monetary issues.

Achieving a Unanimous Report: Delors as *Ingénieur* of Agreement in the Delors Committee

Delors's talent at 'behind-the-scenes' manoeuvring had been displayed to perfection in the preparations for Hanover and in gaining the Chair of the Delors Committee. But he now found himself in a more exposed position than ever before. The task of welding together the EC central bankers into an effective working group was made all the more difficult by a combination of factors. In the view of Pöhl and others, Delors had not played the role of 'honest broker' in preparing Hanover. He had conspired with Kohl to pursue his own agenda. There were also memories of Delors breaking cover to act out a more didactic role on EMU, as before Luxembourg in 1985 and at Nyborg in 1987. These memories were associated with attitudes of distrust towards a 'crafty' politician who had insinuated himself into a position of power.

For Delors, exercising power over EMU as Chair of the Delors Committee was much more problematic. He had succeeded in getting the kind of committee that he wanted: EC central bank governors flanked by a set of three 'outsiders' sympathetic to EMU, and an EC Commissioner. He had also lined up Padoa-Schioppa, his intellectual intimus on EMU, as rapporteur, and was proposing Mingasson as co-rapporteur. But he was confronted with some severe strategic, tactical, and cognitive problems that had to be addressed urgently, given that the report had to be ready before the Madrid European Council in June 1989. After the joy of Hanover, the sense spread in Delors's entourage that there would be a price to pay and that the task ahead was fraught with difficulty and danger and could end in failure. Pöhl's anger was a serious problem in its own right, and it took the good offices of Wim Duisenberg, the Governor of the Dutch Central Bank, to persuade him to soften his initial position. Not for the last time, Duisenberg was to prove very important in helping to make agreement possible in the Delors Committee. Without his mediation Delors would have been in much greater difficulties.

Chairing the Committee was to prove a particularly tense, difficult, and at times depressing experience for Delors, not least as he sought to keep his temper under control in the face of Pöhl's provocations and a sense on occasion that progress was being blocked. From the outset Delors recognized that he would have to be a cautious and discreet Chair, avoiding any hint that he was trying to foist a particular vision of EMU on the Committee. If he was to be tolerated by the central banking 'club' (he could never aspire to be accepted as a member), his approach had to be sensitive and responsive rather than assertive and interventionist. Delors sought to act as the 'broker', open and receptive, patiently seeking out consensus and avoiding any semblance of 'divide-and-rule' tactics. He focused on playing the role of the good listener, seeking to steer the committee towards unanimous agreement. This role was evident when the Belgian, French, and Italian Governors (Jean Godeaux, Jacques de Larosière, and Carlo Ciampi) produced early on ideas for a European Monetary Fund. Though they were in closest intellectual sympathy with Delors (or, more correctly, precisely because of this fact), he distanced himself, expressing his reservations in terms of the difficulties that this proposal would produce for his efforts to build group cohesion.

The pre-eminent strategic and tactical problems revolved around the question of rebuilding fences with the EC central bank governors and creating parameters within which a spirit of co-operative problem-solving could flourish. To achieve these objectives Delors took a series of confidence-building steps. In July he dropped Mingasson in favour of Baer, responding to a telephone conversation with Pöhl who proposed Baer. Though this move could be seen as a defeat for Delors, it had the advantage of making a positive gesture to Basle and appeasing German critics by putting in place a more balanced team. Delors also proposed that the Committee should meet in Basle at the end of the regular meetings of the Committee of EC Central Bank Governors. These two moves emphasized a degree of distance from Brussels. Later, once the work had seriously begun, Delors made the concession of ceasing to speak in French and holding the Committee's work in English, without interpreters, in order to regain the interest of Pöhl and others who—to Delors's concern—were ceasing to use their ear-phones. These gestures were designed to prevent impatience, create a climate of confidence (especially in Delors), and foster group cohesiveness. In addition, Delors wanted to show that he would take whatever time was necessary to reassure and convince committee members. He sought out individual EC central bank governors both before and after committee meetings, spoke to them on the fringes of ECOFIN meetings, and briefed them over dinner at the monthly G10 meetings in Basle. Delors's fundamental objective was to achieve a report whose persuasiveness and power would derive from the unanimity of an expert and highly respected committee. Later, when Pöhl's initial anger had subsided, Delors held a series of bilaterals with him to try to resolve outstanding problems. In these meetings Delors was very accommodating, seeking to disarm the Bundesbank President and give him what he needed to deal with his internal problems with the Bundesbank council.

Most important of all, Delors determined to achieve this objective by narrowing the focus of discussion. From the outset he stressed that the Committee was not concerned with the question of *whether* EMU should be pursued. It was being asked to report to the European Council on *how* EMU could be realized. By this means Delors sought to minimize the scope for differences of normative belief about EMU to disrupt progress. The Delors Committee was to occupy itself with causal beliefs about the role of, and relationship between, monetary and economic factors in making EMU possible. 'Optimal currency area' literature was the one theoretical tool that might have been used to raise the question of whether EMU was appropriate for the EC. But Delors ensured that it was confined to the question of the nature of the steps to achieve EMU, not employed to open up debate about the pros and cons of EMU. At the same time he pressed on the central bank governors the point that the heads of state and government had placed great personal trust in them to accomplish a major mission as part of constructing European political union and that they were working to a deadline of April 1989 so that ECOFIN could give its advice in time for the Madrid European Council in June.[2]

Delors's style was to depoliticize discussions by focusing on very precise technical points, to define the exercise as technocratic. He had to circumvent the problem that EC central bank governors had a range of views on whether EMU

---

[2] See Delors's interview in *Le Monde*, 20 July 1988, in which he also sketched out the key questions with which the Committee would be concerned.

should be pursued. This delimited focus was the vital secret to the relative success of the Delors Committee and to helping Padoa-Schioppa and Baer, the enthusiast and the sceptic, to work easily in tandem. Also, by stressing this mandate, Delors was able to insist that EC finance ministers were kept at arm's length. They were working for the European Council, which did not include finance ministers (though it did include foreign ministers), and the Hanover conclusions required them to act in a 'personal capacity'. This opportunity to demonstrate their independence appealed to proud EC central bankers. It also helped to build team loyalty. The context of working to the European Council also gave Delors the justification for keeping foreign ministers more fully informed than finance ministers. Dumas and Genscher were particular beneficiaries. Delors recognized that they would be decisive in giving political momentum to the report before the Madrid Council.

Again, to tackle his credibility problem and build confidence, Delors worked immensely hard during the summer and autumn of 1988 to read up on the economics and history of EMU. By July he had identified six key questions: a parallel or a single currency; who was to manage the currency; what was to be the definition of the ECU; what concrete steps were needed in the transitional stage; what was the appropriate relationship between the economic and monetary pillars; how it was to be translated into institutional terms (*Le Monde*, 20 July 1988). He consulted Werner for his experience, asked for and devoured huge amounts of reading matter, and relied in particular on Padoa-Schioppa and Dixon as sources of ideas and synthesis. For Delors there were two vital requirements. First, he wanted to ensure that no stone was left unturned in his effort to ensure that EMU was put on an adequate theoretical basis. Secondly, he intended to be up to scratch on EMU, to outdo all others in his personal preparation and mastery of the issues. To support him Dixon and Mingasson drew very selectively on expertise in DG2, notably Emerson and Daniel Gros; whilst the Danish economist Niels Thygesen, a member of the Delors Committee, retained close contacts to Gros. From September, in addition to his regular, soon-to-be weekly meetings with his 'gang of four', Delors spent two full working days a month immersed in EMU issues with Baer, Padoa-Schioppa, and Dixon. Though a member of the Committee, Andriessen was not involved in these briefings and, to his irritation as a Commissioner, was kept on the sidelines. In all, during the period of the Delors Committee, this work accounted for some one-third of Delors's working time. In this respect there was no comparison between his tenacious commitment and concentrated hard work and that put in by Pöhl either in the Delors Committee or for the Committee of EC Central Bank Governors.

These intense meetings briefed Delors on both the relevant technical issues for the next meeting and the likely attitudes and reactions of individual committee members. The most problematic were seen to be Pöhl, Erik Hoffmeyer of the Danish central bank, and—to a lesser extent—Duisenberg. In contrast, support was expected from Ciampi, Godeaux, and de Larosière—with

Duisenberg as a calming influence on Pöhl. Andriessen, Alexandre Lamfalussy, and Thygesen were viewed as 'reliable'. The main concern of Delors and his briefers was to avoid a division into opposed camps or coalitions. In this respect Duisenberg was to prove an invaluable 'go-between', especially to Pöhl and Robin Leigh-Pemberton. Leigh-Pemberton was seen as courteous, constructive, and, given his difficult domestic position, as in need of support. Even Pöhl, despite the difficulties that he made, was viewed as too weak on the technicalities of monetary policy to offer a serious threat of blocking the exercise. That threat came more from Hoffmeyer, who was most withering in his criticisms of the 'pedestrian' nature of the work being done in the Committee and was regarded as the most difficult to handle.

The first question was to identify and assess approaches to EMU. Padoa-Schioppa sketched out two—the 'domestic' and the 'international'. The 'domestic' approach sought to create a central-bank type of institution, like an ECB with a single monetary policy and single currency. This approach was associated with the Bundesbank. It rested on the principle that monetary policy was not divisible. Hence no powers could be given to a European monetary institution till the final stage. An EMF was not on the agenda. More favoured by Padoa-Schioppa and Delors at the outset was the 'international' approach. This approach involved the creation of an IMF-like institution for the EC, on the lines of the earlier French proposal for an EMF. There seemed an obvious political attraction in maintaining national monetary systems and putting them under a common constraint. This seemed to offer a line of least resistance. Also, by some sharing of power, it would be possible to avoid an 'empty shell' during the transition stage and to establish early on an international role for the ECU. Padoa-Schioppa was pointing to the difference between a maximalist German approach (an ECB) and a minimalist French approach (an EMF). Delors was careful to avoid taking up a clear public position on this issue. Instead, he invited the members of the Committee to address this issue by submitting proposals. In doing so he was inducing the Bundesbank to declare its hand at an early stage on the appropriate approach and outcome. Delors was also seeking to ensure that the Banque de France presented an alternative paper so that there was a genuine intellectual debate.

In order to smooth the path to a unanimous report Delors and his advisers determined at an early stage not to table a general draft, which would alienate others, but to provide specific analytical support papers for each meeting and to encourage others to submit their own papers. But Delors ran into difficulties even with these more focused papers, for instance, that on the lessons of history ('Werner Revisited'). These problems came to a head in November 1988. Pöhl was intent on identifying anything Delors produced with the Commission's agenda and attacking any notion that the Commission could have anything useful to say about monetary policy. The tactical problems of managing the Committee in the face of such an irritable Pöhl led Delors to encourage Pöhl to be more constructive by outlining German views. By November he had come round to the view that progress could only be made on the basis of accepting certain German conditions, not, for instance, by pressing on matters like a European Monetary Fund and a parallel currency.

Delors had two intellectual difficulties at the beginning with the Pöhl paper presented to the Committee. Though in principle not averse to central bank independence, he did not want an ECB modelled too strictly on the Bundesbank. He was also not happy with the reliance on the simple principle of a single currency being 'at least as strong as the D-Mark'. These reservations were concealed. But they reflected two preoccupations. Delors envisaged some happy mean between a fully operational ECB and no EC-wide responsibility in monetary policy, reflecting traditional French thinking on EMU. In addition, he was concerned about a 'political counterweight' to the ECB. He argued that EMU could not be reduced to just one policy objective—stability—and two instruments—money and budget rules. Though stability was a vital, even para-mount objective, maintaining the conditions for growth and employment depended on a larger repertoire of instruments. He had in mind developing an EC-level countercyclical policy to promote growth and employment (*Westdeutsche Allgemeine Zeitung*, 6–7 May 1988). For Delors, EMU would only be viable with strong co-ordination of both fiscal and structural-policy instruments and the retention of some fiscal flexibility. In short, his main priority was to give much more prominence to the economic-policy pillar of EMU than envisaged in the Pöhl paper which focused on the monetary-policy pillar.

Though Delors was not deflected from these beliefs about EMU, the Delors Committee was a rapid learning experience about what was politically realistic as the basis for unanimity. He was not convinced by the arguments in the Pöhl paper, but he was quick to learn that an independent ECB pledged to price sta-bility was a price to be paid for agreement on EMU to anchor the most impor-tant principle for the Germans—that the single currency must be 'at least as stable as the D-Mark'. In his role as Chair the politically astute realist took prece-dence over the idealist. His starting-point was to identify what was non-negotiable. Once Delors recognized that the main principles in the Bundesbank model of EMU as spelt out in the Pöhl paper were non-negotiable, he deter-mined to lead the Committee in this direction. Hence he was cautious about pushing his views on a 'political counterweight' or an EMF in stage 2.

In his efforts to secure agreement he steered the Committee away from three controversial but crucial areas: challenging national fiscal sovereignty by argu-ing for strong fiscal-policy co-ordination and a strengthened EC budget; consid-ering how an appropriate mix between the use of monetary, fiscal, and stuctural-policy instruments was to achieved; and going into detail about the practical steps to arrive at the final stage, including the nature of institutional arrangements in the transition stage. Reference to a 'transfer of decision power' in an early draft from Baer was deleted by Delors as 'inopportune'. Delors pointed out that the Committee was working in different structural circum-stances from those of the Werner Committee of 1970. Not only had economic theory evolved to give a greater role to monetary-policy instruments. More importantly, EC structural policies were now a significant factor, and the single European market meant that competitive forces were much more important in securing economic adjustment. Hence there was less need to be so ambitious on the fiscal side. Similarly, to secure the signature of Leigh-Pemberton at the final meeting numerous linguistic changes were made to the text, introducing a stronger element of conditionality in the final text that Delors much regretted. This steering was tactically very shrewd. But for some, like Lamfalussy, it was intellectually unsatisfying; and for others, like Hoffmeyer, a sign that the Delors Report was a less serious piece of work than the Werner Report had been.

Delors was far more satisfied with the content of the Report than he was to be with later developments, notably the Stability Pact proposal from Theo Waigel in 1985. These later developments strengthened the monetary pillar rather than protected the idea of a balance between the economic and monetary pillars that he saw as integral to the Delors Report.[3] He was pleased that he had succeeded in getting a unanimous report, against all the odds. There was also a new clarity about what the final stage should look like. But, above all, Delors was also satisfied with the provisions dealing with the economic-policy pillar, feeling that these went well beyond Bundesbank proposals and represented his own distinctive contribution. The key for him was paragraph 27:

In order to create an economic and monetary union the single market would have to be complemented with *action in three interrelated areas*: competition policy and other measures aimed at strengthening market mechanisms; common policies to enhance the process of resource allocation in those economic sectors and geographical areas where the working of market forces needed to be reinforced or complemented; macroeconomic coordination, including binding rules in the budgetary field; and other arrangements both to limit the scope for divergences between member countries and to design an overall economic policy framework for the Community as a whole.

These three complementary areas of action, especially regional and structural policies and macroeconomic policy, were detailed in paragraphs 28–30.

At the same time Delors was also left with feelings of reservation and pessimism about the cognitive gaps in the final product. What emerged differed from Delors's causal beliefs about the conditions for a viable EMU. The weaknesses of the final Report were evident to him: the emptiness and vagueness of the transition stage; the weak formulation on the irreversibility of the process once it had begun; and the failure to focus more on the wider global impact of a united Europe (a theme close to his heart since the 1970s). Some progress seemed to have been made on irreversibility in paragraph 39: '. . . the decision to enter upon the first stage should be a decision to embark on the entire process'. This reference to the importance of a clear political commitment was, however, qualified in paragraph 43: 'The conditions for moving from stage to

---

[3] For Delors's criticisms of the Stability Pact see his proposal 'Pacte pour la Coordination des Politiques Économiques', Paris: Groupement d'études et de recherches Notre Europe, 6 August 1997.

stage cannot be defined precisely in advance; nor is it possible to foresee today when these conditions will be realized. The setting of explicit deadlines is therefore not advisable.' Delors contented himself with the belief that these cognitive gaps could be closed by patient preparatory work before and during the IGC on EMU; and, later, by adopting the view that the emptier stage 2, the shorter it should be in order to sustain momentum.

Delors had cleverly presided over an exercise in group dynamics and learning that had, at the very least, produced a new consensus about the nature of the final stage to which EMU was heading. That consensus—on a single currency rather than just locked exchange rates—replaced initial adverse reactions to a Delors paper that had contained this reference. The final stage might be too preoccupied with monetary union (that was to some extent inevitable given the Committee's composition) and too unclear on the transition, but it represented an important beginning. It had been made possible, in part, by the way in which the exercise was defined as technocratic. Once that definition was accepted, those sceptical about EMU found it difficult to be obstructive. They began to understand the issues better (central bankers were, for instance, by no means experts on institutional issues) and to take some pride in their work. They could also hide behind the Committee for protection, arguing that they had fought their hardest and could not be held responsible for individual items in the Report which were embedded in elaborate compromises. There was an additional factor of image and reputation. All were united in wishing to be seen as having done a constructive job on behalf of the European Council. Above all, the Delors Committee borrowed something of the working culture of Basle central bankers: its essential 'clubbability', founded on intensive interaction, their delimited and highly specialized agenda, and their sense of protecting their territory from predatory finance ministers. For Delors it was quite unlike the much more conflictual College of Commissioners. There was an underpinning of shared beliefs, a mutual respect, and an absence of personalized attacks. His greatest challenge was to prevent them attacking him as the 'outsider'. Once Delors had succeeded in calming Pöhl, he benefited from the role of peer pressure in containing Hoffmeyer and encouraging Leigh-Pemberton to sign. In relation to persuading Pöhl to sign, Duisenberg was to play a vital 'go-between' role in the final meetings of the Committee.

Preparing for the IGC on EMU: Delors in Retreat

With the Delors Report the high point of the Commission President's involvement in EMU had been reached. Work now moved to ECOFIN, the EC Monetary Committee, and the Committee of EC Central Bank Governors, whose task, after the Madrid European Council had endorsed the Report, was to prepare the ground for a future IGC. The sense of urgency had gone once the Madrid Council had failed to set a date for the IGC. Delors was disappointed; he sensed that British obstruction had enabled Kohl to keep his powder dry on EMU. His assessment was that, if by 1993, the target for the single-market programme had been fully met, then an IGC was possible. In other words, Delors's expectations were modest. Stage 1 was to begin in July 1990, but the IGC could be some five years ahead. Ominously, some EC central bank governors had distanced themselves from the report soon after its publication as an incomplete, essentially academic exercise. There was a widespread view that it would be consigned to the political filing cabinet. The Madrid Council had to some extent overcome the reservations expressed in the informal ECOFIN at S'Agaro in May. But it remained unclear whether the Delors Report would be the basis, or only one basis, for the work of preparing the IGC.

After Madrid, the centre of gravity on EMU shifted to the French Presidency. Delors and Mitterrand agreed that priority should be given to three aspects of EMU. First, during the French Presidency all the necessary legislation was to be prepared for stage 1. This work gave a new importance to the role of Christophersen and DG2 in fleshing out the details for strengthening mutual surveillance for the purpose of reinforcing economic convergence. An embryonic form of non-monetary-policy co-ordination began to be put in place. DG2 also started work on the costs and benefits of EMU, designed to co-opt academic economists and to bestow a technical legitimacy on the project. This work culminated in the 'One Market, One Money' study of October 1990, and its preliminary results—that EMU would bring net benefits—were endorsed by the informal ECOFIN at Ashford Castle in March 1990.

Secondly, having failed to set a date for the IGC in Madrid, Mitterrand was determined to succeed in Strasbourg in December. But this process offered no real opportunity to Delors. Mitterrand proved less willing to work closely and in confidence with him in preparing this issue than Kohl had done before Hanover. Thirdly, Paris proposed establishing a group under Guigou to prepare the detailed questions for the IGC and in this way maintain political momentum. Delors welcomed this as a clever move, but had two concerns. His first fear was that the result of drawing in national finance-ministry and foreign-ministry officials could be a diversion away from the agenda of the Delors Report. On this point Delors was reassured when his proposal that Padoa-Schioppa should be appointed special adviser was accepted. This appointment provided continuity with the Delors Committee and, along with feedback from Carré, a direct line to what was going on in the Guigou Group. His second fear was that Guigou, though trusted as a former member of Delors's cabinet in the French Finance Ministry, was not of sufficient intellectual and political weight to make significant progress.

Far overshadowing the importance of the Madrid European Council was the effect of the fall of the Berlin Wall and German unification in marginalizing Delors's role in EMU negotiations. As long as EMU was 'nested' in the economic spillover effects of the single market, Delors could occupy a central role in the debate. But, once Mitterrand and Kohl 'nested' EMU in German unification, the negotiating parameters were redefined in a way that disadvantaged Delors and shifted the centre of gravity to the Franco-German relationship. From November 1989 onwards the economic spillover argument for EMU ceased to occupy central stage. As long as this argument had been central, Delors had been able to seek out intellectual leadership by organizing policy expertise behind EMU, exploiting the power of 'quality' ideas and building policy networks. But now Delors found himself responding to events outside his control.

On German unification Delors did not see eye to eye with Mitterrand. Delors was quick to endorse German unification in November 1989 and later made it clear that he would do all in his power to ease and speed the assimilation of the five new *Bundesländer* into the EC. In doing so he counted on gaining political credit with, and leverage over, Kohl, who contrasted Delors's behaviour with that of Mitterrand. But Delors had some difficulties in cashing in that credit. He too sought to convince Kohl to accelerate the timetable for EMU and make a firm commitment at Strasbourg to a date for the IGC. His influence here was, however, marginal, even non-existent.

Delors had two more serious set-backs. At the Dublin 1 European Council in April 1990 he sought privately to persuade Kohl to agree to a new EC fund to help with the reconstruction of the new *Bundesländer*. Delors's objective was to help reduce the suspicions engendered by German unification by drawing EC states into the process of managing the process. Kohl was firm in his rejection of this proposal, arguing that to table it would be to further aggravate those states. More importantly from the viewpoint of EMU, Delors could foresee the crippling effects that the burden of managing German unification would have on the ERM as Germany's difficulties were exported to other member states through its anchor role in the system. Delors's proposal to Kohl was designed to help Germany by sharing its burden. It was a bold and imaginative proposal at the time and all the more so in the light of the ERM crises of 1992–3 and the accompanying bitter criticisms of German monetary policy.

Also, in a series of bilaterals before Dublin 1 Delors tried to convince Kohl, Mitterrand, and others that a hurried, ill-prepared IGC on political union contained major risks of failure. He argued the case for setting up a committee of experts on political union to prepare the work for such an IGC. Without a clear intellectual frame of reference the negotiations would drift into diplomatic improvisations. This argument was supported by comparison with the Delors Committee on EMU, the Community method of seeking to build on intellectual leadership, and the history of successes and failures in European integration. Again, Delors failed. Mitterrand and Kohl were desperate to move ahead quickly. Intellectually, Delors preferred moving ahead with the IGC on EMU separately from that on political union because the latter was too poorly prepared. But, politically, he accepted that Germany was looking for balance between EMU and gains in the form of political union. From April onwards, having lost this initial battle, Delors became increasingly absorbed in dealing with the consequent problems. His time and energy was diverted towards political union.

Delors's other major defeat was over the organization of the IGCs in the autumn of 1990. On this issue he faced problems. IGCs were by definition a matter for governments which would decide just how much right of initiative was to be given to the EC Commission in making proposals. On EMU Delors felt that he—and indirectly the Commission—had made a mark on the agenda of the negotiations. But his attempt to find an equivalent to the Delors Committee in political union had failed. It was clear that the Commission was to be an outsider in political-union negotiations, fighting to get its ideas heard rather than having a privileged role in organizing ideas. Delors identified distrust of the Commission as a political problem. Hence he sought a less exposed position and carved out a more prudent approach designed to avert charges of arrogance. At the same time the structure of the IGC mattered. For Delors that structure had to fulfil two purposes: to ensure intellectual coherence and rationality, particularly in dealing effectively with the institutional aspects of treaty revision; and to prevent the EC finance ministers from gaining control over EMU. Control by EC finance ministers would have potentially malign effects on EMU negotiations. They would become overly obsessed with technical details and with the monetary and budgetary rather than the wider economic and political aspects of EMU. They would also seek to create EMU as a separate pillar of the Treaty. Hence it was vital to Delors that both EMU and political union should be negotiated under a common umbrella, with a lead role for the General Affairs Council. Delors lobbied for measures to strengthen co-ordination between the two IGCs: for instance, supporting the Italian government's proposal that Padoa-Schioppa should be the rapporteur for the IGC on EMU; arguing that institutional experts should be appointed in both IGCs; and stressing the importance of regular meetings of the two IGCs. But, again, he was unsuccessful and was left with what he regarded as a bad choice for the organization of the IGCs, inferior to that of the IGC that prepared the Single European Act, much of the text of which had been prepared in Delors's office.

The effects of these set-backs were not just to confirm Delors's sense that he was more marginal, even on EMU, but also to generate an underlying shift of attitude. The optimism of Kohl and Mitterrand in 1991 contrasted with the warnings of Delors that they were failing to think through their ideas properly. Delors deplored a lack of intellectual coherence and rigour in preparing the IGCs. Though these problems were particularly acute in the political-union negotiations, they were by no means absent in the EMU negotiations. Delors was well aware of the gaps in the Delors Report. He had serious doubts about whether ECOFIN and the EC Monetary Committee would address the need to think beyond monetary and budgetary to wider economic and political issues, to give some real substance to the transition stage, and to strengthen the institutional and procedural arrangements for EMU, especially to ensure a smooth transition to the final stage. On these questions the Commission needed to be active. It was, however, not in a position to secure a role of intellectual leadership. Delors had slipped into a background role. He was now more the *animateur* on the smaller stage of the Commission. On the larger scale the initative as strategic leaders on EMU had passed to Kohl and Mitterrand.

After the Strasbourg European Council had fixed the date for the IGC, DG2 shifted its attention from preparing stage 1 to reflecting on stages 2 and 3. It was agreed early in 1990 that work would begin on a Draft Treaty that would clarify Commission positions. The main substantive work on macroeconomic policy aspects, especially on co-ordination of fiscal policy and budgetary rules, was done in Emerson's directorate; the main work on monetary policy was undertaken under Carré in the monetary affairs directorate. There were some tensions, consequent on scepticism within DG2 about some of Delors's ideas and discomfort with being asked to lend this intellectual support. This discomfort was associated with Delors's attempt, assisted by Vignon, to ground EMU in 'the European model of society'. Delors's talk of avoiding 'social dumping', of industrial policy, and of labour-market regulation caused problems for many economists in DG2. This early work also sensitized Delors to the debate about the risks of a long stage 2. Emerson's directorate argued for a short stage 2; the monetary directorate for no transition stage. Along with Jean Pisani-Ferry, economic adviser in DG2, they stressed the vulnerability of the ERM in any transitional period and the risks of complacency on the problems of exchange-rate stability. Others, like Ravasio and like Reichenbach in the Economic Service, were closer to the EC Monetary Committee view that exchange-rate stability was an important condition of moving ahead to EMU and that stage 2 must be long enough to demonstrate that this condition had been fulfilled. This debate was resolved in favour of a shorter stage 2.

DG2's exercise in co-opting academic economists into evaluating the costs and benefits of EMU—the 'One Market, One Money' study of 1990—was noteworthy in two respects. First, it sought to shift the intellectual background of the debate about EMU away from the problematic ground of 'optimum currency area' theory to a more institution-centred theoretical approach. 'Optimum currency area' literature induced scepticism about whether the EC as a whole was ready for EMU. It pointed to problems of economic adjustment consequent on lack of symmetry in business cycles, on inflexibility of wages and prices, on low labour mobility, and on the absence of a developed and large-scale fiscal-transfer mechanism. These problems would be highlighted in the form of rising unemployment and subsequent political pressures once adjustment by means of interest-rate and exchange-rate decisions had been abandoned by national governments. The theoretical approach in 'One Market, One Money' stressed, by contrast, the importance of reputation and credibility for EMU and hence the role of institutional arrangements like central bank independence. By this means the costs of disinflation could be lowered.

Secondly, the 'One Market, One Money' study was noteworthy for its stress on fiscal flexibility (*European Economy*, 1990 introduction). A necessary condition for a viable EMU was seen to be safeguards against the risk of it being welfare-reducing in the context of country-specific shocks and the absence of exchange-rate adjustment. These safeguards would have to take the form of a fiscal-transfer system, approximating the functioning of automatic stabilizers in federal states, or of flexible forms of fiscal co-ordination in which national fiscal policies should have room for manoeuvre to look after their own economies. These academic contributions, to which Pisani-Ferry and Emerson were sympathetic, helped to steer DG2 away from the preoccupation with detailed and quantitative budgetary constraints characteristic of the EC Monetary Committee. It also accorded with Delors's political view that in certain circumstances budget deficits and public debt were socially desirable. The 'One Market, One Money' study was important in persuading the Commission to develop the idea of a financial assistance mechanism, This mechanism fell short of being an automatic stabilizer but was designed to offer a safeguard in the face of country-specific shocks that could have destabilizing effects within EMU.

The Commission Communication of 21 August 1990 on EMU incorporated these arguments in favour of a short stage 2, of avoiding too tight and rigid a definition of excessive deficits, and of having a fiscal mechanism for stabilization. Though criteria for excessive deficits were under consideration in the Commission, and advocated by Christophersen at the ECOFIN on 23 July 1990, they were not seen as so important in the context of a short stage 2 whose central purpose was defined by the Commission as to prepare for stage 3 (rather than to organize convergence). In any case, far more important than specifying detailed criteria as mechanisms to promote convergence were proposals to give substance to stage 2 in the form of responsibilities for the new Eurofed. In particular, Eurofed was to have roles in reinforcing the co-ordination of monetary policies, supervising the development of the ECU, and being enabled to hold and manage foreign reserves (the latter idea taken from Lamfalussy's paper to the Delors Committee). Here Delors and Christophersen were influenced by the traditional 'monetarist' approach to EMU of the Commission. Measures to promote monetary union would produce convergence by means of the financial discipline of increasingly co-ordinated monetary policies.

This 'monetarist' aspect was qualified by a stress on parallelism. Co-ordination was also to be strengthened by a framework of multi-annual guidelines and a financial-assistance mechanism, both to be determined by qualified majority in Council. Consistent with this line of thinking, at the informal ECOFIN in Rome on 6 September 1990 Christophersen put forward two proposals: to establish Eurofed at the beginning of stage 2; and to strengthen multilateral surveillance by extending it beyond budgetary policy to cover the whole range of structural policies. This package was designed to achieve parallelism in monetary and economic-policy co-ordination and shift the agenda beyond money and budgets. Whilst sharing these concerns, Delors's special interest was in ensuring that the European Council played the key role in the transition to stage 3. Here his main fear—shared by Christophersen—was that EC finance ministers would stand between the Commission President and the European Council, predetermining decisions and reducing the flexibility of the European Council.

The Role and Impact of Delors and the Commission in the IGC

At the opening of the IGC Delors had several clearly defined positions on EMU, notably:

- Priority was to be given to institution-building as the motor for integration and for changing of patterns of behaviour.
- EMU was, ultimately, a *political* project—its objective being to advance the cause of European unification on the basis of the 'European model of society'. It was not merely a question of economics. EMU required a firm political lead from the European Council and commitment in the form of a clearly defined timetable for completing EMU.
- The establishment of EMU should complement the existing EC framework, maintaining its central institutional features, and respecting the traditional domain of the Commission, especially its right of initiative.
- A single currency could be 'sold' as being in the rational self-interest of firms and consumers operating in the new single market. EMU was a logical next step, an economic spillover from the single market and the EMS, rather than a revolutionary advance.
- Recalcitrant states, like Britain, should not be allowed to block the progress of integration in this sector, preferably being given a special 'opt-out'. By summer 1990 Delors was articulating to the British Permanent Representative in Brussels his conviction that a British 'opt-out' was the only way forward.

These positions were very much anchored in the tradition of the Community method associated with Jean Monnet and Walter Hallstein, a tradition that stressed the leading role of institutions, of stage-by-stage advance with a timetable, and of the appeal to rational self-interest.

The first difficult question was whether the EC Commission should go further than the Communication of August and submit a Draft Treaty on EMU at the opening of the IGC in December. This idea was encouraged by the Italian EC Presidency, and pushed strongly by Padoa-Schioppa. It was also backed by the impending Luxembourg Presidency. Following an assessment of the arguments in Lamy's regular meeting with heads of cabinets of Commissioners, Delors threw his support behind the proposal. The counter-argument was that a Commission Draft Treaty would put the Commission in an exposed position and invite reaction, not least from the Bundesbank. By 1990 Delors was appreciating the value of a more cautious, low-profile role for the Commission, with hints—not least from the French government—that there was a dangerous level of distrust towards its activities. But, on the bonus side, this approach would serve to open up the debate and help to retrieve an intellectual leadership for the Commission within the IGC negotiations. The College of Commissioners agreed the principle of a Draft Treaty being prepared but did not see, let alone approve, the actual text. The Draft Treaty on EMU was drawn up very hurriedly; being written in less than a week. It was, however, destined to be only one of the texts guiding the negotiations. The Luxembourg EC Presidency wished to avoid having the Commission text as the sole, or even main, text for negotiation. It could at least lay claim to be the only serious Draft Treaty other than the French and German versions. But it was the content of the latter two drafts that set the main parameters for the IGC and the context within which the Commission had to seek out a role as broker in 1991.

The second question was what sort of role Delors and the Commission would play in the IGC negotiations. They alternated between playing two roles: that of spelling out their own ideas for a viable EMU and seeking out influence for these ideas and their corporate interests; and that of acting to broker agreement between contrasting national positions. In the first role they played the partisan advocate, driven in part by the economic-policy beliefs of Delors and senior Commission officials, in part by considerations of intellectual consistency with the wider institutional patterns of the EC (no separare EMU pillar) and in part by the corporate self-interests of the Commission in retaining its monopoly of initiative on economic-policy guidelines, exchange-rate guidelines and the excessive-deficit procedure. The second role involved playing the political realist, assessing the potential and scope of possible agreement between member-state governments, for instance, on assessment of excessive deficits (criteria and trends). Optimal outcomes for the Commission involved agreements that coincided both with its partisan beliefs and interests and the requirements of a ratifiable solution for member-state governments. Such agreements included the final, fixed date for stage 3 and the combination of criteria with trend in assessing excessive deficits. But in other areas optimal agreements were not forthcoming, notably on the financial-assistance mechanism and the powers of the European Parliament in EMU. In such cases Delors opted for agreement over influence, though not without reservations. In doing so he was deeply influenced by his sense of a new political climate of distrust towards the Commission by 1990–1.

The third question was the nature of the division of labour within the Commission for the IGCs. The internal arrangements suggested that, after the preparations for the IGC on EMU had been made, Delors retreated to a background role. He took over prime responsibility for ministerial-level meetings of the IGC on political union (accompanied by Andriessen), where the difficulties were most acute in the absence of proper preparation. During 1991 the Gulf Crisis, followed by the mounting crisis in Yugoslavia, diverted his attention to the issues surrounding a common foreign and security policy. The Uruguay Round of GATT negotiations was another source of distraction. Christophersen took on the ministerial-level meetings of the IGC on EMU, with Ravasio attending the IGC meetings at the level of personal representatives. Delors remained the alert observer and listener, especially by means of the EMU working group. In this role he was part of a wider learning process in the Commission during early 1991 about the implications of a longer stage 2 than had been anticipated in the Commission Draft Treaty.

But, given the logistical problem that the two IGCs met simultaneously, Delors only occasionally attended sessions on EMU: for instance, ministerial-level meetings on 25 February, 8 April, and 12 November. He used these sessions to argue for a broader conception of economic policy; to talk about economic and social cohesion; and to suggest that two extra convergence criteria be added, on youth unemployment and long-term unemployment. At the informal ECOFIN in Apeldorn on 21 September Delors offended the British by pressing the case for a specific derogation for them from entry into stage 3. These inter-ventions were, however, exceptional. Delors acted as *animateur* on just three EMU issues—institutional structures, social and economic cohesion and the financial-assistance mechanism, and the transition to stage 3.

A Longer Stage 2

The tabling of the German Draft Treaty on EMU at the end of February 1991 was a turning-point for Commission views of stage 2. Delors objected to what he saw as a departure from the Rome 1 communiqué, with which he judged the Commission Draft Treaty to be consistent. The contrasts with the Commission Draft Treaty were stark: no reference to economic and social cohesion; the lack of a social counterpart to the principles of the market economy; no role for the Commission or the European Parliament in economic-policy co-ordination; no provision for retaining the Commission's monopoly of initiative or for qualified majority voting in exchange-rate policy; and no ECB in stage 2, leaving stage 2 empty of any significant content. The Commission had supported a strong stage 2 institution for three reasons. An ECB in stage 2 would give a clear political sig-nal of intent to proceed and lend credibility to the process; it would be the appropriate venue for more effective co-ordination of monetary policies; and it would be necessary for the detailed technical preparations required for stage 3.

In briefing Delors and Christophersen Ravasio pointed to the implications of one particular aspect of the German Draft. It sought to make the transition to stage 3 dependent on fulfilling specific criteria on deficits, interest rates, and price stability, consistent with the work being undertaken in the EC Monetary Committee. This approach had implications for the length and functions of stage 2. In the Commission's view stage 2 was to be short and concerned essen-tially with preparing stage 3. But work in the EC Monetary Committee and the German Draft suggested a stage 2 whose prime function was to organize con-vergence. In that case stage 2 would be longer than envisaged; the argument for a strong stage 2 institution was weakened; and the Commission needed to devote more attention to establishing the nature of the criteria by which adequate convergence could be measured. In March–April the EMU working group in the Commission reflected on these implications of a longer stage 2 dedicated to promoting convergence. Christophersen was converted to the logic of a longer stage 2 before Delors. He saw in specific criteria a possibility of building automaticity into the transition to stage 3. In Christophersen's view, vague criteria opened the way for continuing deferment of stage 3. Hence, as early as March–April 1991 a key aspect of the Commission's negotiating position was altered.

The Institutional Structure of EMU

During the IGC, Williamson's working group on strengthening the political and institutional dimension of the IGCs reported directly to Delors, with Ravasio and Williamson co-ordinating closely on institutional issues in the negotiations on EMU. For Delors these issues were vital in order to ensure the coherence of EMU with the overall Community structure and working method and to provide effective direction to policy. As President he was determined to maintain the Commission's two main traditional roles in EMU: as the representative of the Community interest, not least on the world stage (for instance, in negotiations on international exchange-rate regimes); and as the motor of integration. Institutional issues were, in particular, a source of great problems for Delors with Paris. He had to protect EMU from an intergovernmental model propagated by the French government. Delors's great fear—that the IGC on EMU might create a new 'fourth pillar'—was shared by the Belgians, the Dutch, and the Italians.

The Commission's Draft Treaty paid close attention to institutional issues because their importance to its future powers was recognized. Its salient features were: a strong role for the European Council in the transition to stage 3 (to keep the EC finance ministers and central bankers in check); the generalized use of qualified majority voting in Council; the importance attached to the Commission's monopoly of the right of initiative in multi-annual economic-policy guidelines, exchange-rate policy negotiations, the financial-assistance mechanism, and the excessive-deficit procedure; a consultative role for the European Parliament in multilateral surveillance, the excessive-deficit procedure, and the transition to stage 3; and the restriction of the new Monetary Committee in stage 3 (later to be called the Economic and Financial Committee) to a strictly advisory status. It was later in the IGC negotiations, on issues related to the transition to stage 3, notably the idea of a 'critical mass' and the arguments about derogations and a generalized 'opt-out', that the Commission found it had little guidance from its Draft Treaty and the Communication of August 1990.

On EMU Delors avoided his worst fears of a 'fourth pillar'. He was disappointed with the failure to establish the ECB in stage 2. Taking a position close to the Italian, Delors could only judge the EMI to be very much a second-best outcome. But it proved possible to enhance its tasks in the final IGC negotiations: including an externally appointed president, its own capital, a role in promoting the ECU, and the possibility of holding and managing foreign-exchange reserves. Otherwise, broadly speaking, the Maastricht Treaty offered him and the Commission a reasonable result. The Treaty provided a satisfactory outcome on the role of the European Council; tolerated a substantial amount of qualified majority voting, notably in exchange-rate policy and economic-policy guidelines (though not on financial assistance); and retained the Commission's traditional monopoly of the right of initiative in economic-policy guidelines, the financial-assistance mechanism, multilateral surveillance, and the excessive-deficit procedure (but usually defining this right in the softer form of recommendations that could be amended in Council). On the other hand, the Treaty gave the Commission virtually no role in international negotiations on exchange-rate regimes; produced a weak result on the powers of the European Parliament over EMU, notably in multilateral surveillance and the excessive-deficit procedure and in the limited support for use of the co-operation procedure for legislative acts under EMU; and gave the Economic and Financial Committee more powers in preparing the work of the Council and carrying out tasks for the Council than Delors and the Commission would have preferred. The outcome was mixed but, on balance, by no means negative.

This outcome cannot be credited solely to the lobbying and influence of Delors, Christophersen, and Ravasio. If it was a victory, it was a case of shooting into an open goal presented by de Boissieu's package deal in Paris. There were undoubtedly major worries in the Commission about a 'fourth pillar', expressed by Ravasio at the IGC on 8 October. On 26 November Ravasio raised the issue of the weak role of the EC Commission in international exchange-rate negotiations, reflecting Delors's view of the importance of a unified external Community position. Delors lobbied hard on the issue in Paris, approaching notably Dumas, Guigou, and Mitterrand, as well as in other national capitals—where, in particular, he lobbied Wim Kok. He also concentrated on finding allies in the Belgian, Dutch, German, and Italian delegations in the IGC on political union. But de Boissieu was in many respects the key. He was influential in Paris in dissuading the French government from pursuing the logic of the intergovernmental model in both IGCs in favour of an institutional package deal. This deal involved trading acceptance of EMU as part of the Treaty of Rome model (something that was not wanted in the French Finance Ministry) as a counterpart to negotiating CFSP and interior and justice policy outside this model. This approach had the advantage of limiting the war with Delors on institutional reform and ensuring that it was conducted mainly outside the IGC on EMU. The Commission was also helped by the greater sympathy of the Dutch Presidency for its concerns on institutional issues. In particular, Kok was very close to Delors.

Overall, however, Delors was deeply disappointed with the institutional arrangements put in place by the Maastricht Treaty. The turning-point for him was the informal meeting of EC foreign ministers in Dresden at the end of the Luxembourg Presidency. There Delors proposed that the concept of 'three pillars' should be dropped in favour of the idea of a 'common tree with different branches'. This proposal was designed to reinforce the notion of a shared institutional basis for the different parts of the Community, a notion designed to safeguard the prerogatives of the EC Commission in the new fields of common foreign and security policy and interior and justice policy. Despite the support of a clear majority of EC states, the abstention by Dumas—and the unwillingness of Genscher to break ranks with France—torpedoed Delors's proposal. Delors continued to struggle in vain against the 'three-pillar' concept.

Economic and Social Cohesion and the Financial Assistance Mechanism

At the IGC ministerial-level meeting on 25 February Delors addressed the need for a broader and more ambitious conception of economic policy. His theme was that EMU should be armed with policy instruments to promote both stabilization and structural adjustment. He referred in particular to research and development policy, industrial policy, cohesion policy, and a financial-assistance mechanism. Delors was returning to one of his key arguments—that EMU must be about more than a single monetary policy and the abolition of excessive deficits. He warned that the EMU negotiations threatened to produce a dangerous disequilibrium between the economic (undeveloped) and monetary (developed) pillars.

Economists in DG2, notably Pisani-Ferry, Italianer, and Reichenbach, were concerned to flesh out Delors's conception of an EMU that was focused around improving not just economic efficiency and financial stability but also equity. This definition of political purpose by Delors drew their attention back to the issue of fiscal transfers from richer to poorer regions and member states. The question for them was whether a large federal budget, American or German style, was necessary to ensure that the participating countries benefited from monetary union in terms both of stabilization and of political sustainability. They looked back to the MacDougall Report of 1977 on The Role of Public Finances in European Integration. This report had envisaged EMU in the context of an EC budget representing some 8–10 per cent of the Community's GDP, an enormous increase on the currently very limited size of the EC budget. The studies by Pisani-Ferry, Italiener, and Reichenbach were important in scaling down the MacDougall approach. They argued that, in order to make monetary union viable, only a relatively small EC budget for regional stabilization and equity purposes was needed (0.1 to 0.2 per cent of Community GDP). The most important economic stabilizers were contained within national budgets in policy areas that member states were not likely to cede to the EC. Most vital of all was that those stabilizers were able to operate (an argument that later could be applied against the Stability Pact).[4] More important at the EC level was inter-regional transfers. Hence the EC Commission adopted much more modest views on the budgetary implications of EMU than had been conventional in the 1970s.

The Commission's most ambitious proposal was for a financial-assistance mechanism. This was envisaged as a discretionary mechanism for states in difficulties or seriously threatened with difficulties. But, in order to minimize opposition, the proposal was presented in guarded language. The financial-assistance mechanism was to be an instrument for the purpose of stabilization, not of redistribution. In the Commission's view, it would help countries dealing with asymmetric shocks and in overcoming the painful effects of rapid convergence. It was seen as an instrument for maintaining political consensus in hard times. The proposal fell short of an automatic stabilizer, which was strongly supported only by Spain. On this issue the Commission was forced onto the defensive by the concerted opposition of the British, Dutch, and—to a lesser extent—the Germans. They pressed for unanimity in Council voting; strictly circumscribing the shocks that would qualify for assistance; and for limiting assistance to stage 3. The main set-backs for the Commission were the provisions in the final agreement that unanimity was required except in the case of natural disasters, where qualified majority voting applies, and that such assistance was only to be given in the case of 'difficulties caused by exceptional circumstances'.

Delors had a more differentiated approach to economic and social cohesion. He saw stronger economic and social cohesion as vital to the viability of EMU and shared the views of Manuel Marin, the Spanish Commissioner, on this issue at the Commission seminar on the two IGCs on 24 November. But, as the careful strategist, Delors also spotted danger in raising new funding issues in the context of the IGC. As early as 8 April at the IGC on EMU he proposed that there should be a reference to economic and social cohesion in the Treaty article on economic policy (especially Article 102*b* of the Commission Draft Treaty) but that the finances for any new initiative should be looked at as part of the review of EC finances and Structural Funds scheduled for 1992. At the Luxembourg Council in June, in the IGC on political union on 28 October, and in the IGC on EMU on 12 November, Delors spoke of the danger that the IGC could be blocked by the attempt to make EMU conditional on new spending programmes. Delors recognized that the main work on economic and social cohesion was being undertaken in the more sympathetic venue, the IGC on political union. But even here the majority was not prepared to go beyond a declaration attached to the Treaty. More importantly, he had his own reservations of principle about adding a new funding mechanism when three Structural Funds were already in existence. Delors saw this initiative as inconsistent with increased transparency by means of simplifying structures and mechanisms in the Treaty, rather than making them more complex.

[4] On the importance of fiscal freedom for adjustment once national governments cede use of interest-rate and exchange-rate policies see Goodhart (1990).

Politically, the strongest pressure on economic and social cohesion came from the Spanish government, led by Gonzales himself, and was echoed by Marin within the Commission. The Spanish Finance Minister Carlos Solchaga was sharp in his criticism of the Dutch Presidency for neglecting this issue, demanding at the IGC on EMU of 14 October that it be made a priority for the next ministerial-level IGC in November. At the final meeting of the IGC in Brussels on 2–3 December Solchaga entered a reservation. He pointed out that a declaration of political intention attached to the Treaty would not satisfy his government and meant that unanimity could not be guaranteed at Maastricht. Intellectually, the idea for a new 'Convergence Fund' had derived from the Portuguese government and was quickly sponsored by the Spanish, Greek, and Irish governments. Delors and Christophersen were sympathetic. Given their disappointment with the financial-assistance mechanism, the Cohesion Fund offered an alternative means of lending support to those faced with the most severe difficulties in meeting the conditions for stage 3.

The question for the Commission was how to prevent the proposal from wrecking the Maastricht European Council. The Commission latched on to two key arguments to reconcile the French, Dutch, and Germans at Maastricht. The first argument was that the Cohesion Fund would serve as a compensation to the Spaniards for what had proved to be a miscalculation of their net EC budgetary contribution after entry in 1986. By 1990–1 they were not getting the net budgetary gain that had been anticipated. In addition, the Cohesion Fund could be presented as an alternative to a general increase of Structural Fund spending in 1992, easing the problems of the impending review. At Maastricht economic and social cohesion gained the status of a protocol to the Treaty, in which it was agreed to establish the Cohesion Fund. The Cohesion Fund was also regulated by Articles 129c and 130d, notably referring to financing trans-European networks in the field of transport.

Though the Commission was successful in brokering a deal on economic and social cohesion, and though the financial-assistance mechanism found its way into the Treaty, the overall outcome fell well short of realizing Delors's conception of an EMU based on a wide mix of policy instruments and balanced between its economic and monetary aspects. The arguments in 'One Market, One Money' about the need for fiscal measures of stabilization to counter asymmetric shocks found only weak reflection in the debates of the IGC and in the Treaty.

The Transition to Stage 3: Seeking a Final Date

Going back to the Delors Committee, the idea of a clear timetable for the stages of EMU had been uppermost in Delors's mind. He and his advisers saw it as simply an extension of the well-tried-and-tested Community method by which setting dates works to concentrate minds on the requirements of agreement to meet a deadline. The unwillingness of the Delors Committee to consider the

idea of setting dates for the transitional and final stages had been a disappointment and also a signal. Dates were only likely to be set by the European Council.
Hence on this issue he would have to work in the strictest confidence with heads
of state and government and then highly selectively. This area of the IGC negotiations was shrouded in secrecy, even from those working closely with Delors,
like Christophersen.

The dates 1996–7 were established in Commission minds before the IGC
began. Consistent with the Rome 1 communiqué, the Commission Draft Treaty
referred to an appraisal by the European Council within three years of the start
of stage 2 in January 1994. This appraisal was envisaged as broad and political,
sensitive to the differing conditions in member states, not as involving the use of
specific and detailed convergence criteria. Commission thinking was reinforced
by the conclusions of the meeting of the Giscard–Schmidt Committee for the
Monetary Union of Europe, held in Rome on 7 December 1990. In a subsequent
letter to Delors on 12 January 1991 Giscard pressed for stage 3 to begin in
1996–7. Giscard was to be an important background figure in reinforcing
Delors's resolve on this issue, especially in November 1991.

From May through to November Commission reflections on the transition to
stage 3 were overshadowed by two issues: the 'opt-out' and the convergence criteria. At first the 'opt-out' was simply an answer to the question of what was to
be done about the British problem. It had been in Delors's mind since summer
1990 when it had been raised with him by the British Permanent Representative
in Brussels, David Hannay. Hence he was very content with the proposal in the
Luxembourg non-paper of 12 June for specific derogations for those not wanting to precommit to stage 3. It seemed to satisfy the principle of 'no compulsion'
in the transition to stage 3. Though Delors would have liked to see Major
pressed harder at the Luxembourg Council to concede an 'opt-out' at this stage,
he regarded this as a foregone conclusion. At the same time it did not resolve the
wider questions relating to the transition to stage 3: namely, how to secure the
two other principles proposed by the French and agreed by ECOFIN in May—
'no arbitrary lock-out' and 'no veto'.

The shock came with the Dutch text of late August. In the view of the EMU
working group in the Commission it was too accommodating to the British in
dropping the idea of specific derogations in favour of an 'opt-in' for all those
states which met the criteria. The resulting uncertainty would, in its view, be too
disruptive. There was also a risk of arbitrary lock-out from the suggestion that
only those states which were in stage 3 could determine which states were later
able to enter. At the informal ECOFIN in Apeldoorn in September it became
clear that opposition to this aspect of the Dutch Draft was overwhelming. Kok
responded to criticisms from Delors by amending the text and proposing that a
political declaration be attached to the Treaty committing states to full participation in stage 3. The EMU working group in the Commission saw this as still
too weak to ensure a smooth transition to stage 3. It was opposed to the 'generalized opt-out' and continued to seek specific derogations for individual states.

At Sheveningen on 1 December the Commission's view was victorious. It was agreed to solve the British and Danish problems by derogations. This outcome cannot be attributed solely, or mainly, to Delors and the Commission. The crucial factor was Franco-German rejection of the 'generalized opt-out'.

The second issue that dominated Commission thinking on the transition to stage 3 during the summer and autumn was the nature and role of the convergence criteria. Here Dixon and Ravasio were very active. It is, however, important to remember that they were reacting to a debate on criteria that had been initiated by EC finance ministries, which saw in them a means to strengthen their control domestically. Convergence criteria were not pushed by the Commission. But, once it became clear that stage 2 would be long and be essentially about establishing convergence, the Commission concluded that specification of criteria was more important to the process of transition than had been envisaged in the Communication of August 1990 and the Commission Draft Treaty. Hence, after the IGC had begun, the Commission had to reappraise its view of criteria. A DG2 working paper of 16 May for the EMU working group summed up the position. The Commission was accepting the proposed 60 per cent debt/GDP ratio as consistent with the EC average at that time and therefore not unrealistic for member states. The big issue was the budget-deficit criterion. Working with an estimated growth of nominal GDP in the range 4–8 per cent implied a deficit criterion of between 2.3 per cent and 4.4 per cent. The Commission opted to support a budget-deficit criterion at the top of the range: in other words, of 4 per cent or more. This position reflected beliefs in greater budget flexibility, the social and political value of public spending, and in avoiding creating hurdles that would divide the EC. In taking this position the Commission had the support of Britain, Italy, Ireland, Greece, and Portugal. For similar reasons, at the IGC on 13 November, Ravasio advocated an exchange-rate criterion that referred to respecting the normal margins of fluctuation in the ERM 'without significant tension', rather than 'without devaluation'. The EMU working group also wanted the criteria to be incorporated in secondary legislation so that they could be modified by qualified majority vote. This position (which was close to the Italian) reflected its view that the criteria had little economic rationale and that it was better to toughen them as stage 2 progressed.

By the time of the Dutch Presidency Delors was taking a greater interest in the convergence criteria. His particular concerns were to break the grip of EC central bankers on their definition and to show that the EC was concerned with developments in the 'real' economy when assessing states' readiness to proceed to stage 3. With these concerns in mind he proposed to the IGC that two criteria relating to unemployment should be added: youth unemployment and long-term unemployment. Delors sought to establish them in principle rather than to suggest specific numeric values. But the proposal quickly foundered. The Spanish Finance Minister led the opposition, pointing out that a different way of measuring unemployment in Spain would seriously disadvantage his state compared to others. The general reaction was one of surprise. Delors seemed to be raising the hurdles to stage 3 and cementing a 'two-speed' EMU. But the proposal was part of his wider objective of strengthening the economic-policy pillar of EMU by putting unemployment more at the centre of the IGC's agenda.

Additionally, the Commission preferred the use of inducements rather than sanctions as means to eliminate excessive deficits. At the IGC on 14 October it outlined its opposition to the suspension of EC budget payments. On withdrawal of EC Structural Fund aid and of access to the European Investment Bank it equivocated, seeing this as a possibility on 14 October but rejecting it at the IGC on 24 November. Above all, Delors and the EMU working group feared jeopardizing other EC objectives, like economic and social cohesion. By the autumn Dixon and Ravasio were intellectually sympathetic to Graham Bishop's idea of relying on a strengthening of market mechanisms as an alternative means to curb excessive deficits. It offered a means of diverting the focus of the IGC away from a preoccupation with 'over-rigid' criteria. But they were inhibited from putting specific proposals to the IGC by the negative report from the EC Monetary Committee on 17 June and by opposition within the Commission from DG15 (financial institutions) on grounds of creating risks for prudential supervision.

Though recognizing the force of the argument that specific criteria could facilitate rather than impede the transition to stage 3, the Commission was cautious about setting hurdles so high that the transition could be made too difficult and became a factor dividing the EC into 'ins' and 'outs'. Hence it welcomed the consensus that emerged in the informal ECOFIN at Apeldoorn in September. There was support for objective criteria, but they were not to be used mechanically. The Commission sought a balance between application of the criteria and political judgement in the transition to stage 3. As early as June it was clear that the EC Monetary Committee was recommending a 60 per cent debt–GDP ratio, with the proviso that ratios above that figure would be judged to infringe the criterion if effective action was not being taken to reduce them. On balance, the final choice of criteria—notably on deficits and exchange rates—was tougher than the Commission wanted and thought economically justified. On the other hand, the emphasis on discretionary judgement taking account of 'trend' in the debt and deficit levels reflected Commission thinking. The key to this outcome was, however, the consensus promoted by the Belgian and French governments in favour of a 'criteria plus trend' formula that would not threaten the cohesion of the EC in the transition to stage 3.

But, with time and energy devoted to the 'opt-out' and convergence criteria issues, the larger and crucial problem of how to secure the principle of no veto remained unresolved. On this problem Delors and his cabinet became active in November. In their minds, the issues of convergence criteria and a final date for stage 3 were linked. Delors's defensiveness on criteria and an offensive position on a final date were, in effect, two sides of the same coin. In particular, Delors had been reluctant about convergence criteria. Christophersen and Ravasio convinced him that criteria were the only way forward, seeking to persuade him with the argument that they would help ensure that stage 2 did not remain open-ended. Delors was, however, adamant that the criteria would have to be accompanied by 'quasi-automaticity' in the transition to stage 3.

For Delors two developments were influential. First, on 14 November Giscard wrote to him to outline the conclusions of the meeting of the Giscard–Schmidt Committee in Brussels on the previous day. In addition to condemning the 'generalized opt-out' the Committee was seeking a final fixed date for stage 3. This message was also conveyed by Christophersen, Pons, and Padoa-Schioppa who had all been present on 13 November. Pons assessed the idea of a final date as unrealistic given the differences between northern and southern states on the transition period that they required. At a meeting of Delors with the board of the Association for the Monetary Union of Europe on 28 November, the case for a fixed date was made again. More importantly still, Kohl was signalling by this time that he was seeking irreversibility of EMU as the precondition for signing the Treaty at Maastricht and would not accept the Dutch 'generalized opt-out'. The messages from the Federal Chancellor's Office to Delors's cabinet (DG2 was not involved here) suggested an opportunity to promote new proposals to incorporate the principle of irreversibility into the transition to stage 3. It was clear to Delors, however, that any such proposal could not come from the Commission, a route that would invite rejection as the Commission seeking to 'impose' its view; that, for domestic reasons, Kohl could not be expected to deliver on a final date and was likely to be very reluctant to sign up to such a detailed commitment at Maastricht; and that tactically any proposal would have to be tabled at Maastricht if it was to avoid running into political difficulties.

Hence in the days before Maastricht Delors and his cabinet shifted their attention to encouraging key contacts at the member–state government level to generate proposals for fixing a final date for stage 3. The key relations on this issue were with the French government. In particular, on behalf of Delors Lamy contacted Lamoureux who had moved in summer 1991 to Cresson's cabinet in Paris. Lamoureux, who possessed a sharp political mind, was himself convinced that it was necessary to activate the French Prime Minister. On 28 November she took the initiative and organized a meeting in the Matignon at which Bérégovoy was instructed to present proposals for fixing a final date at the last IGC in Brussels. This move was seen within Delors's cabinet as crucial. Meanwhile, Delors dealt directly with Mitterrand and with Lubbers. At a meeting on 6 December he and Mitterrand were agreed on the primacy to be given at Maastricht to fixing a final date more precisely than had been achieved by the Bérégovoy plan of 2 December. With the 'generalized opt-out' dead, and in the light of the widespread reservations about the adequacy of Bérégovoy's formula, both sensed that Maastricht offered an opportunity to go further. Delors's meeting with Lubbers on 7 December was an opportunity to plant the idea of a final date in the mind of the EC Presidency.

But, though Delors worked hard on the issue with the French, he was by no means the hidden author of all that followed, in particular the 1999 deadline. First of all, he was very distracted by his much greater anxieties about the political-union negotiations. Here he identified the most acute problems that could derail Maastricht. With reference to the political-union negotiations he was referring to 'organized schizophrenia' and 'institutional odd-jobbing' and clashing in public with Dumas. The date for stage 3 was by no means his only preoccupation. Delors was preoccupied in the week before Maastricht with agreeing a three-page Commission warning to the heads of state and government about the risks associated with the new 'pillar' concept for the future of European integration. This initiative brought him into conflict with the senior British Commissioner, Sir Leon Brittan.

Secondly, Delors's entrepreneurship on behalf of a fixed date was paralleled by similar activity in national capitals: notably, Guigou in Paris and Padoa-Schioppa in Rome. There is, however, no evidence that either of these figures was liaising directly with Delors or with each other. Certainly they knew Delors's mind well. But what they did was more closely linked to their conception of the Community method and the role that fixed dates had played in the history of the EC. More importantly, they were responding not to Delors but to the signals about irreversibility emanating from Kohl and Mitterrand since 14–15 November. Their assessment of strategic opportunity to press on a fixed date was also influenced by the loss of British bargaining power once an 'opt-out' was finally settled on 1 December. The main opponent of a final date had been marginalized. Hence, though Delors activated his cabinet on this issue, the final outcome of a fixed date was not the product of a single, co-ordinated conspiratorial exercise conducted by him and his senior cabinet staff. It was grounded in a change of political atmosphere centred on Kohl. Delors, Mitterrand, Guigou, and Padoa-Schioppa were reacting to that change. But, whilst Delors and his cabinet were facilitating these reactions, they were not structuring them independently.

An Overall Assessment of the IGC Negotiations

In the IGC negotiations the Commission had to manage a built-in tension. On the one hand, in its role of intellectual leadership it was attracted to its traditional 'monetarist' (or 'institutionalist') approach to EMU, which went back to the 1960s and was consistent with the Community method and its own corporate interests. This approach shaped the positions taken by the Commission in the IGC. On the other, in its role as broker of agreements between member states, it had to find means of wedding together some (crucially Germany) which were attached to the 'economist' (or 'behaviouralist') approach and others (like Italy) which were attached to the 'monetarist' approach. In practice, this tension was somewhat defused by the fact that an IGC negotiation did not lend itself to the traditional role of intellectual leadership based on the

Commission's monopoly of the right of initiative to Council. Hence it was obliged to seek out influence by a strategy of indirection.

The Commission's 'monetarist' approach was kept alive, for instance, in the Communication on EMU of August 1990 and the importance it attached to a clear timetable of stages. But as early as the Delors Committee it had been apparent that, in the interests of brokering agreement and getting the prize of a unanimous report, the Commission President was prepared to defer to the 'economist' approach (notably in the Report's rejection of a firm timetable for EMU). Such a concession was vital if the Bundesbank was to be kept 'on board'. Consistent with this approach, by March–April 1991 Christophersen and DG2 were beginning to accept the logic of a long stage 2 with specified convergence criteria. However, despite this conversion—which was strategic and tactical in motivation—they looked at convergence criteria through the lens of the 'monetarist' approach, like the Belgians and the Italians. And they continued to stress the virtues of a clear timetable for stage 3. The Commission can, accordingly, be seen as a member of the 'monetarist' coalition, alongside Belgium, which was most consistently *communautaire* on institutional matters in the IGC. Others who were traditionally part of the 'monetarist' coalition proved less reliable than Belgium on institutional matters. The French opposed the involvement, to any significant degree, of both the Commission and the European Parliament in EMU. The Italians supported the inclusion of the Parliament, but not the Commission.

A survey of positions adopted in the IGC on EMU on thirty-seven issues shows the proximity of the Commission to the French and the Italians.[5] On this qualified data, the position adopted by the Commission was closest to that of France (with whom it was allied 71 per cent of the time) and of Italy (with whom it was allied on 64 per cent of occasions). By contrast, the Commission was rarely on the side of Britain (7 per cent) and was less often allied with Germany (21 per cent). The Commission's fortunes on the issues surveyed were mixed. It favoured automaticity for stage 3 (a victory), but on relatively soft convergence terms (a defeat). It supported a strong monetary institution for stage 2 (an ECB), on which it lost. It also advocated a strong role for the European Council (victory), the Commission (mixed outcome), and the European Parliament (only limited victory). The identification of the Commission with the 'monetarist' approach threatened conflict with the British, Dutch, and Germans, exposing its position and diminishing its credibility and influence as a broker. Delors's instinct was to avoid such exposure.

[5] Whilst this survey is invaluable, given the rare availability of such information, it has a number of important limitations. The data are based on confidential EC Commission minutes on, and reports of, the IGC meetings. The issues included in the calculations are those where the positions of several delegations were given and where a clear division existed between them. The list of issues cannot be representative of the whole subject-matter considered by the IGC; nor is it weighted according to their significance. The validity and reliability of the data are dependent on the individual authors of the minutes and reports obtained.

Despite the close collusion between Delors and Kohl in launching EMU in 1988, and the fact that this remained vitally important across the general political terrain of the Maastricht Treaty, the actual positions adopted by the Delors camp in the IGC negotiations were much closer to those of Paris than Bonn. This paradox is partly to be explained by the conditioning influence of Delors's French background and the French ethos of his cabinet under Lamy. It also suggests Delors's negotiating skill as a broker of agreement. He managed to persuade both Mitterrand and Kohl that he was 'on side'. Crucial to that skill was his identification of the 'bottom line' of acceptability for each side and skill in communicating to each side the requirements of a deal on EMU. The practice of this skill depended on Delors's ability to stand aside from his own intellectual convictions about EMU. Delors played the role of cautious and discreet partisan advocacy, trimming his didacticism by reference to the requirements of agreement and to the need not to squander the invaluable resource of the Commission's role as broker.

Delors's Historical Contribution

Delors's great contribution to the negotiation of EMU was the consummate skill with which he identified the appropriate strategic choices for the Commission and pursued the logic of those choices. He recognized that the legal and technical limitations of the Commission compared to member-state central banks and finance ministries—and the critical role of the Franco-German relationship for EMU—made strategies of indirection more suitable than any attempt to engineer agreement around an EC Commission model of EMU. In this context the personal dimension of his role was crucial, in particular his use of his friendship and relationship of trust with Kohl and Mitterrand to help modulate and steer the pace of Franco-German collaboration on EMU. As 'Europeans of the heart' they were bound together by sentiment and style: a personal acceptance that concessions were necessary in order to unite Europe and secure its peoples against future war. They were united in their view that, after the single European market, EMU was the appropriate tool to pursue this purpose. Delors was important in pressing this argument on Kohl and in sustaining a spirit of preparedness to make concessions on EMU for the larger sake of a united Europe.

Specific characteristics of EMU as a policy sector shaped Delors's leadership style. The acute sensitivities that EMU raised about fiscal and monetary sovereignty, and the secrecy and mystique that surrounded monetary policy and central bankers, disposed him to work in privacy, relying on a combination of persuasion and psychological pressure. For the same reasons, Delors's preference for the informal 'presidentialization' of power in the Commission was carried to extreme lengths over EMU. It seemed the appropriate internal working method in a strategic context in which he and his cabinet were forced to work in confidence behind the scenes. In consequence, Delors's impact was on oiling the wheels of the negotiating process, on making a treaty agreement on EMU possible at the important micro-political level.

This impact took two main forms: securing the Chair of the Delors Committee; and ensuring that the Delors Committee delivered a unanimous report. The unanimity that underpinned the Delors Report was his single greatest achievement. Without it progress would have been close to impossible. The Delors Report played a key role in setting the later agenda. At the same time, this achievement has to be seen in perspective. He 'delivered' what the European Council—led by Kohl and Delors—wanted at Hanover: a study that answered the question of *how* EMU could be realized, not *whether* it was desirable. Delors had, in short, the valuable resource of the authority of the European Council at his disposal in the Delors Committee; he did not define the mandate (though he did influence it). Also, in facilitating the formation of a consensus about how EMU was to be realized, he embedded the approach of the Bundesbank in the content of the report. Delors's approach was designed to facilitate Pöhl's signature of the report. But there was a price to pay for 'binding in' Pöhl. Delors's ability to define the content of the EMU agreement was tightly constrained.

At the same time Delors's role as a policy entrepreneur for EMU was also crucial. As Commission President he put in place in just three years the '1992' target for the single European market, succeeded in writing a commitment in principle to EMU into the Treaty, and reformed the EC budget to give it an invigorated role in structural adjustment and economic and social cohesion. These policy developments were vital in creating a momentum of spillover into EMU. They also created a new political context of euphoria at the EC level that opened up a window of opportunity for EMU by 1988.

Delors's great disappointment was not so much with the Maastricht Treaty provisions on EMU as with what followed. He was, above all, a partisan of balance between the economic and monetary pillars. With Waigel's Stability Pact the importance of economic-policy co-ordination (which Delors saw as being recognized in the Delors Report and in the Treaty) ceded place to a one-sided preoccupation with the monetary pillar. As a political realist, Delors could live with the content of the Maastricht Treaty provisions on EMU as a reasonable preliminary working basis. As an economic expert, he had some reservations. Most of all, he would have liked to see in the Treaty a broader and more ambitious conception of economic policy. He had in mind a conception that embraced the fiscal and structural requirements of a viable EMU able to deal with asymmetric shocks and to promote growth and employment. He consoled himself with the thought that the economic-policy guidelines (Article 103), and the practical problems thrown up by the transition to stage 3, would give the Commission another 'bite at the cherry' in strengthening economic-policy co-ordination (though he was later disappointed). He also took up some of these concerns in the White Paper on Competitiveness, Growth, and Employment of

1993. In Delors's mind an independent ECB was not so great a problem as for Bérégovoy and Mitterrand. But it needed to be set alongside the requirement for an appropriate 'policy mix' at the EC level. In addition, Delors would still have preferred a short stage 2 and more flexible convergence criteria: here he differed from Bérégovoy. More generally, he saw the Treaty provisions on EMU as too detailed and complex. His preference was for a short text with a lot of secondary legislation. This outcome was for him the result of the poor design of the IGCs, entrusting excessive power to EC finance ministry officials and central bankers who sought to incorporate too much technical detail in the Treaty.

The influence of Delors on oiling the wheels of the EMU negotiations was dependent on his skills in cultivating two relationships: with the French President and the German Chancellor in their self-designated roles as the motor of European unification; and with the Council Presidency. These two relationships could coincide, as in the German Presidency of early 1988 and the French of late 1989. Interestingly, Delors's relations with Kohl before the Brussels Council and before Hanover in 1988 were far more intimate than with Mitterrand before Strasbourg.

The experience of Roy Jenkins in the launch of the EMS underlined to Delors the overriding political importance of Kohl in the context of German economic and monetary power and the basic fact that EMU required a greater concession from Germany than from others. Delors was more successful in gaining the trust and respect of Kohl than Jenkins had been with Schmidt. By contrast, Delors and Mitterrand shared a coolness towards each other. The Commission President would complain that he could never work out what the French government actually wanted on EMU. But with Kohl Delors established a rapport: both came into politics from a Catholic background, had similar 'down-to-earth' tastes and common underlying policy attitudes. They met much more frequently and in privacy for long discussions in contrast to the more formal sessions Delors had with Mitterrand in the Elysée. In contrast, Kohl would not hesitate to visit Delors in Brussels. They had some six private dinner meetings each year. The relationship did not always deliver what Delors wanted, for instance on the organization of the IGCs or on his idea for a Community fund for the new *Bundesländer*. But the relationship was crucial before the Hanover Council and in securing for Delors the Chair of the Delors Committee. This genuine friendship and *complicité* with Kohl helped Delors to oil the wheels of the EMU negotiating process.

Delors's influence in oiling the wheels was further dependent on working closely and in confidence with the Council Presidency. The best opportunity for Delors arose with the German Presidency in 1988. At that time the Council Presidency coincided with the most powerful player in EMU. In this context Delors could focus his energies and talents as a negotiator before Hanover. Otherwise, he had to cultivate the relationship between the Council Presidency and Kohl on EMU to secure the necessary German support for progress. Here experience varied. During the Spanish Presidency of 1989 there was a good relationship with Gonzales who in turn worked closely with Kohl and Mitterrand to ensure progress on the Delors Report at Madrid. In contrast, before the Strasbourg Council Mitterrand preferred to work directly on the Germans, keeping Delors at a distance. The Italian Presidency kept Delors informed before Rome 1 but in fact negotiated much of the preliminary draft of the communiqué in advance with Bitterlich in Bonn. Hence Delors could not determine his relations with successive Council Presidencies. Each had its own conception of how it wanted to work, and that either opened up or closed down opportunities for Delors to have influence on EMU. On EMU his worst relations were with the Dutch Presidency of 1991. He was critical of its inefficiency in handling the EMU negotiations and in particular of the 'generalized opt-out' as too accommodating to Britain and as in breach of the Community method.

But throughout the EMU negotiations Delors never wavered in his judgement that progress was dependent on his relationship to Kohl. The vital strategic requirement was to carry Kohl's support and use him to 'bind in' the Bundesbank and the German Finance Ministry. Hence, Bitterlich and Ludewig in the Federal Chancellor's Office became the major addressees for complaints and worries about Finance Ministry and Bundesbank positions, notably before Rome I and after the presentation of the German Draft Treaty in late February 1991. Delors was encouraging Kohl and Mitterrand to find ways of bridging their differences on EMU and was aware of the Franco-German bilaterals that began in April. The major failure was over the organization of the IGC on EMU. The consequences of Delors's failure to strengthen the General Affairs Council's role as co-ordinator of the IGCs were that finance ministers in ECOFIN seized full control of the IGC on EMU and that the co-ordination between this and the other IGC on political union was weak. Through this failure to oil the wheels of the EMU negotiations the outcome was seriously affected.

The nature of the IGC in 1991 made sustained co-ordination between the Commission President, Council Presidency, and German government difficult, if not impossible. The leadership role of the Commission waned with the onset of the twelve-dimensional 'chess' of this intergovernmental process. In addition, the direct, secret Franco-German bilaterals excluded a role for the Commission. On a more positive note, the Luxembourg Presidency had to rely heavily on the resources of the Commission during the first half of 1991. Its successor—the Dutch—was, by contrast, much more independent in this respect. The Dutch felt that their predecessor had been too close to the Commission. They had their own substantial experience and expertise. More to the point, the Dutch Finance Ministry had strong opinions on almost every part of the EMU project. The Commission became highly critical of the way in which the Dutch managed the IGC negotiations; by August Delors was complaining to Kok. Their abrasive style appeared ill suited to brokering compromise. The Dutch Presidency then caused the crisis of so-called 'Black Monday' in September when it published its first full Draft Treaty. The Commission feared that the Dutch approach would undermine consensus and lessen the prospects for an overall agreement, with EMU as the prime casualty.

Overall, Delors's role in EMU varied with the phase and time period of the negotiations. It was more prominent in the agenda-setting phase. Pollack has concluded that the EC Commission can act as an effective policy entrepreneur: 'when member governments have imperfect information and are uncertain of their own policy preferences and when [the] supranational institutions possess more information and clear preferences; in these circumstances, entrepreneurial institutions may provide focal points around which the uncertain preferences of the member governments can converge' (Pollack 1997: 130). Imperfect information and unclear national preferences did offer scope for Commission entrepreneurship on EMU in 1988–9. The Commission also helped to open up opportunities for an entrepreneurial role on EMU by the priority it gave to freedom of EC capital movement. EMU was being introduced through the back door of economic spillover effects from the single European market programme. Delors had new scope to act as a 'purposeful opportunist' on EMU and unquestionably took advantage of the situation that he had helped to create and the uncertainty facing national governments (Cram 1994: 199).

But this point was secondary to another factor that inhibited Delors's emergence as a policy entrepreneur. EMU seemed to involve an obvious loser— Germany. The winner–loser aspect of EMU reduced its attraction as an issue for Commission initiative (Peters 1996: 73). In this context it took a German actor, Genscher, to play the key entrepreneurial role in bringing the idea forward. Delors's contribution to agenda-setting was to encourage Kohl to assume the role of sponsor, the role of ensuring that the idea of EMU was put back on the EC table and the most suitable means found for taking it forward and giving it momentum. In playing this role, Delors's contribution was to stress the case for political direction, symbolized by his own role as Chair of the Delors Committee. It was also to find a way forward that would evoke least resistance from powerful national interests, especially in central banking (Cram 1994). There was, however, an important difference between succeeding in encouraging Kohl to put the issue back on the agenda and the particular form that EMU took once on the agenda. That form was shaped by the Bundesbank's influence in the Delors Committee, with Delors's imprint clearer on the economic-policy pillar of the report.

In the aftermath of agenda-setting, Delors's role was weaker and more distant. EMU was then located in a technical negotiating milieu dominated by national actors who were concerned to limit, or even exclude, the role of the Commission. EC finance ministries and central banks had accumulated vast experience and reputation and had their own closeted networks with a complex infrastructure of meetings, lunches, and telephone calls. The legal and technical resources of Delors and the Commission, and their networks, were no match at this level of negotiation. With the IGC Delors and the Commission risked being seen as partisan advocates, as cheer-leaders for certain positions. The cost of over-zealous pursuit of intellectual leadership in such a context was potentially to undermine the Commission's role in helping to broker agreement. Hence it tended to distance itself rather than throw itself actively into the negotiating process. The outcome of the IGC was always in the hands of the twelve governments.

In the final analysis, Delors's historical contribution to EMU needs to be seen in a longer time-frame than the Commission Presidency alone. There he was endeavouring to make EMU 'from above', by exploiting and seeking to create opportunities for the Commission to speed progress on EMU in the context of intergovernmental bargaining. This chapter has focused on his real achievements here, but also on the enormous constraints that he faced. More important in the long run was Delors's contribution to making EMU 'from below'. Ultimately, EMU was only possible if France—as the central partner alongside Germany in European unification—put in place appropriate domestic conditions. What happened at Maastricht can be seen as, first and foremost, a by-product of unilateral national action taken by the French Socialist government in 1982–3. Delors succeeded, with Mauroy, in putting in place the economic and political conditions in France that made it possible for him to take up EMU as Commission President. Without a stability-oriented French policy dedicated to the ERM the developments at the EC level on EMU after 1985 would have been outside the realm of the politically possible. Delors's greatest contribution to EMU was arguably before he became Commission President. He was the domestic architect of his own good fortune in that role.

17
Conclusions and Reflections

In the preface it was noted that this account of the EMU negotiations is essentially history written from below, not above. It explores the important detailed questions of how and why particular negotiating positions emerged in different countries and compares the nature and styles of their negotiating processes. The corresponding weakness in handling the international and macroeconomic aspects was, to some extent, offset by the emphasis given to the 'prestructuring' of the EMU negotiations in Chapter 1. There, the important point was made that the EMU negotiations had a degree of autonomy from the moves and conceptions of individual players. But in this book we have concentrated on how EMU negotiators managed strategic and cognitive uncertainty in their specific, and relatively isolated, institutional milieux. This approach was chosen because it was clear that the skills of negotiators as craftsmen in handling the materials that they were given were a vital factor in making agreement possible. In the literature on European integration there is precious little literature on the nature of these skills and how they are used in treaty negotiations. This book is designed to help close that gap by offering insights into the cognitive, strategic, and institutional dynamics of the EMU negotiations.

This final chapter reflects on five questions. What have we learnt about the nature of the EMU negotiations? Why was it possible to come to an EMU agreement so quickly? What have we learnt about the nature of coalition-building within EC treaty negotiations? What are the theoretical implications of the study? How successful was the EMU agreement at Maastricht in reconciling objectives and putting in place the conditions for a viable EMU? In answering the last question attention is given to cognitive gaps, institutional innovation, legitimacy, and external stability. The chapter concludes with some reflections on the risks of 'lock-in' to a politics of deflation.

Much of what follows picks up on themes and arguments developed in Chapter 1. One such theme—signalled by the question of how successful was the agreement—is the neglect of the relationship between EMU and political union, a major asymmetry in the Maastricht negotiations. In Chapter 1 this neglect was attributed to the contrast between an underlying expert consensus on monetary policy and the 'garbage can' of ideas on political union: the former was much more amenable to successful negotiation. Here we give more attention to the conditioning influence of two interrelated aspects of the EMU negotiations. In the first place, the process was politically isolated as a 'core-executive' activity. This feature conditioned the motives that informed the negotiations, for instance, the emphasis on using EMU as a discipline to 'bind' domestic politics rather than on building an infrastructure of transnational democracy to support EMU. Secondly, linked to this executive elite dominance, a bureaucratic politics of competition to control the territory of the EMU negotiations played a key role in shaping outcomes. The more that EMU negotiators had insisted on the linkage to political union, the more they would have been inviting EC foreign ministers and heads of state and government to take up EMU in their own institutional venues.

The result was a paradox. By isolating the negotiating process in their own venues, EC finance ministries and central banks were able both to pursue a technically rational outcome on EMU and successfully negotiate an agreement free from the complexities of political-union negotiations. On the other hand, the factoring out of political-union issues left some critical gaps in the treaty negotiations on EMU. The negotiations had not focused on the risks that were associated with a politically exposed ECB lacking an overall democratic institutional framework to establish legitimacy and with a potentially highly problematic relationship between rulers and ruled.

Legitimacy is a second major theme of this chapter. The EMU negotiations were both facilitated and bound by a 'sound' money paradigm. This paradigm had, as we saw in Chapter 1, deep roots in changes in the international political economy associated with the collapse of the Bretton Woods system, changes that had challenged the sustainability of the Keynesian paradigm of demand management and the welfare state (Cox 1994: 45–59). It was transferred at the European level by the role of Germany as an economic model emulated by others, by the enhanced political role of central bankers, and by the informal rules established in managing the ERM and institutionalized in fora like the EC Monetary Committee and the Committee of EC Central Bank Governors (Marcussen 1998). At the same time, the presence of other powerful political traditions in Europe set limits on the willingness of negotiators to put in place all the main neo-liberal conditions for an effective EMU agreement (for instance, encompassing labour-market and wage and price flexibility). Hence for neo-liberals it was an imperfect EMU. Equally, the EMU agreement failed to address traditional and deeply entrenched Social Democratic and Christian Democratic concerns about solidarity. It seemed to narrow rather than open up the range of political choice in Europe.

What have we Learnt About The EMU Negotiations?

Much of the character both of the EMU negotiating process and of its outcomes derives from its location in the 'core executive'. It has served to strengthen elite dominance and to transfer power within elites, especially in favour of central bankers, by entrenching monetary and fiscal-policy rules. This restricted territory of debate privileged a newly ascendant 'sound' money paradigm which, not least, advocated central bank independence as a central precondition for non-inflationary growth. Actors were disposed to promote the interests of the institutional milieu in which they operated. Hence the motives that inspired EMU had more to do with empowering executives and 'binding' the political process than with democratic issues of accountability, transparency, participation, and identity. What was missing from treaty debate was a model of a European transnational democratic polity as an essential basis for system stability (Chryssochoou 1994: 1–14). EMU remained a matter of inter-elite communications and elite management. There was no sense of the individual citizen-voter as the major determinant of EMU politics and policies. In this respect EMU was a pronounced case of democratic elitism. It also shared fundamental characteristics of the wider process of European integration, with its spirit of technocratic trust in the politics of expertise to deliver public benefit rather than of embodying democratic characteristics in the process of arriving at collective binding decisions (Featherstone 1994: 149–70). The political risk derived from the increasing incongruity between the deficiently democratic nature of the EU decision-making system and the more direct and popular impact of its policies. The role of EMU in sharpening this political risk and as a pronounced case of democratic elitism owed a considerable amount to the ascendancy of a 'sound' money economic paradigm and its prestige and status within European core executives. Its underlying ethic was deeply distrustful of politicians and of the political process as giving an inevitable inflationary bias to policy (Hoffmeyer 1992: 36).

The 'core-executive' nature of the EMU negotiations affected the nature of debate in another way. An effort was made to manage debate—notably economic—so that it would not complicate or undermine negotiating positions agreed at elite levels. The motives did not involve collusion against the public interest or derive from anti-democratic sentiments. What inspired officials to limit and shape debate was considerations of the credibility of their negotiating positions. Their remit was to negotiate effectively, and they evaluated debate with that lens. The outcome was a sense, especially amongst economists, that debate had been forbidden and that the casualty had been a public starved of informed assessment of different options attached to EMU (Fitoussi 1995). This consideration also affected access to the policy process: those who were too critical were constrained by the prospect of future exclusion.

Even key actors at elite level could feel themselves to be prisoners of conventional wisdom. In his last speech as Danish Central Bank Governor, Erik Hoffmeyer (who had served from 1965 to 1995) stated:

It would be wonderful if I could break free by yelling like the boy, Oskar, in Günter Grass's Tin Drum or write like one of the favourite authors of my youth, Voltaire, who so effectively demolished the hypocrisy and stupidity of the conventional wisdom of his age in the four days that it took him to write Candide. But I can do neither. (Hoffmeyer 1994: 3)

Hoffmeyer's central message was that influence depended on following the reigning consensus (Hoffmeyer 1993: 83).

Another theme that has emerged has been the combination of a technocratic ethos, giving a transnational community of experts—principally central bankers—a powerful role in defining the contents of the EMU negotiations, and strong and resolute political leadership, especially in driving forward the process by imposing deadlines. The role of political leadership manifested itself in three main interrelated ways. First, political leaders were vital as *animateurs* and as *ingénieurs* of the EMU negotiations. Their role was in inspiring negotiators, not least in giving symbolic content to the negotiations, and in oiling the wheels of the negotiations, whether by identifying and designing appropriate institutional venues or by cultivating personal trust and confidence. Here Andreotti, Delors, Kohl, and Mitterrand excelled in finding political formulas and methods for integrating domestic and EC interests. It was, above all, vital that they recognized each other as 'Europeans of the heart', politicians who believed that it was necessary to make concessions to sustain momentum towards European political unification and make it irreversible. In this context Mrs Thatcher and Major found themselves marginalized over EMU. The agenda was set by others whose motives they did not share. In fighting a rearguard action they failed to emerge as effective *animateurs* or *ingénieurs* of agreement on EMU at the EC level.

Political leadership was also demonstrated in a capacity to reconcile political interests on two levels, domestic and European, and to reconcile those interests with wider international interests. For this reason a central theme underpinning EMU was the effort to rebalance international political power over monetary policy. This motive was a vital unifying factor behind French policy on EMU, from Pompidou to Mitterrand. But in the French case it proved difficult to reconcile domestic Gaullist sensitivities on national sovereignty, which were especially powerful during the Pompidou and Giscard Presidencies, with ambitions for EMU as a means of countering US and German monetary power. It was Mitterrand's personal political triumph to reconcile his Socialist Party and a centre-right threatened by splits on this issue to EMU. British Prime Ministers had much greater difficulties, in part because neither Thatcher nor Major were 'Europeans of the heart', and in any case because of domestic political constraints within the governing Conservative Party. Their challenge was how to reconcile a disagreeable agenda on EMU being successfully promoted by other EC leaders with domestic political constraints, when EMU was itself a factor in increasing these constraints. By contrast, in Germany and Italy a pervasive domestic political consensus on European unification and an underlying willingness to surrender sovereignty for that purpose made EMU less politically problematic. Even so, domestic sensitivities about monetary stability and the powerful symbolism of the D-Mark meant that Kohl had to move with caution. But in the end he chose to act boldly, putting his trust in Germans having learnt the lessons of history and having learnt to identify Europe with peace and prosperity.

This 'two-level' gamesmanship can be seen as a particular facet of political leadership: the 'nesting' of a problematic game like EMU in related or 'higher-order' games that alter the assessment of payoffs. Here Delors was important in relating EMU to the single European market programme and to the Delors financial package of 1987. It could be situated in a new context of freedom of capital movement and of economic and social cohesion and EC support for structural adjustment. Kohl and Mitterrand provided the next decisive linkage by situating EMU within German unification, thereby giving EMU a new political symbolism and meaning and a new urgency. Thatcher's attempts to avert German unification and to give centrality to GATT free-trade negotiations over EMU were, in contrast, ineffective. EMU had already established a political momentum; its advocates had already 'nested' it in specifically European projects and issues.

The most potent venue for political leadership on EMU proved to be the Franco-German relationship. Transgovernmental linkages between finance ministers and foreign ministers were generally important. But those between Bérégovoy and Waigel and between Dumas and Genscher took on a special quality of intensity. They had a degree of autonomy from the dynamics of intragovernmental relations in each state, based on shared corporate interests and bureaucratic politics. At the same time Kohl and Mitterrand were vital in animating and 'engineering' the EMU negotiations, determining their shape and pace. Delors's importance resided in cultivating both, drawing out their enthusiasm, and honing their strategic and tactical judgements. It was in this nexus that the institutional venues for EMU negotiations were designed; the key signals of preparedness to act and of capacity to be trusted transmitted; and the stimulus given to officials to reflect upon conventional wisdom about how to realize EMU.

Much of the fascination of the EMU negotiations stems from the complex blend of cognitive and strategic, of inquiry and learning, and of pursuit of interest, that epitomized the process. They existed in a complex dialectical relationship. But what was most striking was the interplay between the pursuit of strategy to achieve a *politically acceptable* outcome across two levels of interest and the process of reflection about how a *viable* EMU was to be realized. As is stressed later in the chapter, that process of reflection involved an emulation of the German model (though not necessarily a model that accurately mirrored German reality). This development helped German negotiators achieve an outcome that was based around their own definition of the basic conditions for an effective EMU.

But, in the final analysis, no amount of expert consensus and of policy reflection and learning could put EMU on the agenda. Agenda-setting depended on policy entrepreneurs like Delors, Genscher, and—to a lesser extent—Balladur. They identified the opportunity to be creative on EMU and seized that opportunity. In this particular sense the individual proved an enormously important factor in the EMU negotiations.

Why Was An EMU Agreement Possible?

In 1987 there was no debate within the EC Monetary Committee or the Committee of EC Central Bank Governors about EMU. In May 1988 the Chair of the EC Monetary Committee, Geoff Littler, reported to the informal ECOFIN at Travemünde that an EMU with an ECB was not a necessary condition for realization of the European single market. The view of the EC Monetary Committee was that a study of how EMU was to be realized was not necessary. The focus should remain on strengthening the EMS. Just over three-and-a-half years later a complex EMU agreement had been negotiated. In answering the question of why such a rapid agreement was possible it is also worth recalling Delors's expectations after the Madrid European Council had accepted his report in June 1989. He believed that an IGC was likely only after the single market programme had been completed, and that the argument that more needed to be done to give it effect could run on well into the next decade. Hence an IGC was perhaps four or five years away. This aspect underlines the importance of the diplomatic theme of binding a unified Germany more closely into Europe for the speeding up of the process of agreement.

Perhaps the most impressive feature of the EMU negotiating process was its degree of structure. The process was not a 'garbage can' of competing proposals, of contesting beliefs about how to devise a viable EMU, and of flexible, issue-specific participation (Cohen *et al.* 1972: 1–25). It was not a fluid, indeterminate negotiation like that on political union. The agenda was relatively clearly structured at an early stage thanks to the work of the Delors Committee and the Guigou Group. This structuring was by no means pre-ordained. Actors within the negotiations, especially Delors and de Larosière, chose to embrace policy proposals that were consistent with the requirements of achieving unanimity and especially making it possible for Pöhl and the Bundesbank to stay on board. This choice reflected both a normative belief in the value of EMU as an indispensable element of European unification and a belief that its long-term gains far exceeded its costs. But it meant that a range of alternative models were either suppressed in negotiations or not pressed with maximum vigour.

The speed and relative ease with which EMU was negotiated was not attributable to one single factor but to the combination of a range of economic, diplomatic, and political factors. Throughout the negotiations political factors were consistently important in endowing EMU negotiators with a degree of freedom of domestic politics and in inducing them to define national economic and monetary interests in a European framework. In the early stages the economic rationale was dominant. EMU was principally defined as an economic spillover from the single market programme and from measures to strengthen the EMS in the face of speculative pressures associated with mounting capital mobility. Later, from 1989, the diplomatic rationale of binding enhanced German power into a European framework became decisive for the French, and economic arguments were transformed into the instruments for this purpose. Hence the precise importance of particular factors varied over time. They also varied across countries. The arguments in the 'peripheral' states, like Greece and Portugal, remained much more about importing external discipline and being at the European top table.

The Economic Basis

The economic basis for an EMU agreement was provided by three factors. These were crucial in reshaping definitions of national economic-policy interest and persuading national policy-makers that those interests could, at least in principle, be advanced jointly. The conclusion was not inevitably that EMU was the logical or necessary choice. That jump required supportive diplomatic and political beliefs. But economic developments provided additional evidence and persuasive arguments in favour of EMU that facilitated the process of negotiation.

First and foremost, the EMU negotiations were structured around, and informed and legitimated by, a new set of shared economic-policy beliefs. Their emergence was to be explained by the discrediting of Keynesian orthodoxy with the economic shocks of the 1970s and the subsequent opportunity for ideas that were more relevant to the problems of inflation and competitiveness. After the first oil crisis of 1973 and the collapse of the Bretton Woods system, EC states had been through a long and painful period in which economic divergence drove out prospects for EMU. In most EC states politicians showed themselves prepared to pay a high price in inflation to avoid or contain recession. Slowly, from the mid-1970s onwards, interrupted in the French case between 1981 and 1983, a new consensus about the primacy of 'sound' money and public finances began to emerge across the EC (McNamara 1998). It was on the whole pragmatic (rather than derived from monetarist orthodoxy), imitative of the perceived superior performance of the German economy over this period in containing inflation, influenced by the problems of managing the ERM in the context of the second oil crisis after 1979, and shaped by the emerging role of EC central bankers as policy leaders. This consensus took the form of a new primacy to monetary-policy instruments and saw monetary policy as, in the long run, neutral with respect to growth and employment. Price stability was judged to be the priority objective that could be pursued without ultimately jeopardizing other economic objectives. What followed in the EMU negotiations was imitation of the EC economy judged to have been most successful in managing monetary policy—Germany. The EMS provided a transfer mechanism for ideas of 'sound money' (Marcussen 1998). But this convergence was not simply to be understood in terms of the power of monetarism (Forsyth and Notermans 1997: 17–68).

This new shared economic belief was further reinforced by the growth of capital mobility. Proponents of 'sound' money ideas greeted freedom of movement of capital for two reasons: the disciplinary effects of financial markets on national budgets; and as a source of allocational efficiency. A shared learning process about these effects was facilitated in ECOFIN and the EC Monetary Committee by the experience of managing ERM crises in the 1980s. This experience drew attention to the power of the markets in structuring and disciplining fiscal and monetary-policy behaviour. Capital controls had promised a means to regain power over public spending. But once they vanished with freedom of movement of capital, new pressures were placed on public spending. In short, the ascendancy of 'sound' money ideas in Europe owed a great deal to the political power of the financial-services sector in driving policy decisions about deregulation.

This shared learning experience also highlighted the structural power of the D-Mark in the ERM. The consequence was an EC-wide 'epistemic community' in monetary policy by the late 1980s. It involved shared normative and causal beliefs amongst central bankers about the vital importance of policies that were credible to the financial markets. These beliefs helped the process of forging unanimous agreement in the Delors Committee and afterwards in the IGC around a shared normative basis. It also meant that the monetary-union component acquired primacy in the EMU negotiations. Fiscal policy was seen as essentially an epiphenomenon of monetary union.

The Maastricht Treaty empowered this consensus about 'sound' money and public finances and gave its advocates—principally EC central bankers—authority over the process of domestic reform. What followed was a long period of both monetary and fiscal contraction in the 1990s as member-state governments sought to fulfil the strict convergence criteria (De Grauwe 1998: 73–93). In this context growth rates declined. This deflationary policy stance rested on the nature of the EMU agreement negotiated at Maastricht. It had its economic foundations in 'sound' money ideas and generated pressures to restructure budgets and reform welfare states. Hence the consensus about 'sound' money was not only important in facilitating agreement. It also affected its content. The EMU negotiations were not concerned with fixing responsibility for stabilizing aggregate demand and avoiding the risk of negative demand shocks. That agenda was associated with a Keynesianism that was perceived as discredited.

A second powerful economic factor facilitating speedy agreement was the context of macroeconomic expansion in the late 1980s. In the three years 1988–90 GDP growth averaged 3.4 per cent, well above the average of 2.3 per cent for the decade 1981–90. Unemployment fell from a high of 10.8 per cent in 1985 to 8.3 per cent in 1990, its lowest level since 1981. The effect was to induce a climate of optimism about the EC economy and to reduce the saliency of distributional issues in the negotiations. Strict numeric convergence criteria, like the 3 per cent budget deficit–GDP ratio, did not seem overambitious. The budget deficit–GDP ratio averaged 4.4 per cent for the decade 1981–90. It fell continuously from 5.2 per cent in 1982 to 2.7 per cent in 1989 (rallying to 4 per cent in 1990 and 4.4 per cent in 1991). In the case of the French the ratio was well within 3 per cent for the decade (2.2 per cent), with a low of 1.1 per cent in 1989. Hence it was fairly unproblematic for French negotiators to propose the 3 per cent deficit criterion. Tough as some of the conditions might be, for instance for Italy, there was a sense that they were in principle achievable. By late 1991 this climate of optimism was already beginning to fray. As growth slowed, unemployment rose and budget deficits began to climb in 1992–3 the ratification and the implementation of EMU took on a different, more conflictual character. Hence the political character of the EMU negotiations was decisively influenced by their macroeconomic environment. There was a 'feel-good' factor at work amongst negotiators in 1988–91 that was quickly to vanish in 1992.

The third economic factor at work was economic 'spillover' effects from other EC programmes. The climate of optimism within the EMU negotiations was generated not just by general economic expansion but also by the success of the EC in realizing its other commitments. Of foremost importance here was progress in implementing the single market programme. This progress created a 'halo-effect' for the EC institutions and raised questions about what the EC could do next to secure and develop its recent success. EMU seemed to be a logical next step. Like the single market programme it would serve to reduce the transaction costs in doing business in Europe and ensure a 'level playing-field' without competitive distortions produced by volatile exchange rates. Also, by 1988 the EMS was seen as a success story in creating a zone of monetary stability in the EC. Economic performance was converging around low inflation and low budget deficits. There was greater exchange-rate stability than in the early 1980s. These performances induced reflection on what might be done to go beyond the EMS in its present form. As this debate gathered momentum in 1987–8, there was a new incentive for the Bundesbank to channel monetary developments down a track to an end-state (EMU) which reflected Bundesbank thinking rather than being the outcome of a series of incremental moves to build on the EMS. Seen from this perspective, the EMU negotiations were not possible without the establishment of the EMS and its consolidation (especially in March 1983) and without the Single European Act. These created essential economic preconditions that did not exist when the Werner exercise took place in 1970.

The Political Basis

Vital as they were in providing a common basis and a new set of incentives and constraints for negotiators, economic factors alone could not guarantee a speedy EMU agreement. Underlying political factors were also crucial in giving a particular shape to the process and contents of the EMU negotiations. These included its 'core-executive' character, which endowed EMU negotiators with considerable discretion; and the impact of the specific institutional structure of the negotiations in channelling agreement in particular directions and influencing the agenda. At the same time the enduring importance and diversity of state traditions across the EC was revealed in the difficulty that member states had in reconciling certain basic political beliefs in an EMU agreement. The agreement was as interesting for what it overlooked as for what it contained.

As we saw in Chapter 1, the 'core-executive' character of the EMU negotiations had its basis in the high degree of uncertainty attached to the costs and benefits of EMU. Hence it was difficult for sectoral interests to mobilize, and there were few pressures to participate in the negotiations. The one interest that was directly involved was EC central bankers. Correspondingly, the negotiations were organized in order to 'bind in' this interest. Domestic and EC-wide ratification difficulties were mainly defined in terms of ensuring that the EC central bankers endorsed the final agreement. Though there were some detailed points of difference, the EMU negotiating teams in different national capitals were broadly similar. They comprised finance ministry, foreign ministry, chancellery, and central bank officials. Ministries that acted as sponsors for sectoral interests were kept at a distance, especially those for industry, employment, and social policy. In this way it proved possible to control, by narrowing, the agenda of the negotiations. The policy process only began to change as budgetary and social-policy decisions were taken in the 1990s in order to implement the requirements imposed by the EMU agreement. At that point, as in France in November–December 1995, mobilization and polarization became evident. But they did not bother the EMU negotiations before Maastricht. In this context the beliefs and strategies of a tiny network of negotiators took on an enormous importance.

At the same time EMU negotiators were operating in a highly structured institutional context. The basic substantive content of the EMU negotiations was resolved in and around two intimate and relatively isolated institutional venues—the EC Monetary Committee and the Committee of EC Central Bank Governors, each with its own character. These bodies, dedicated to safeguarding the independent status of their members from the EC Commission, the Council Secretariat, and the Committee of Permanent Representatives (COREPER), provided the epicentres of the negotiations. The Commission was diplaced from its normal, traditional role, based on its sole right of initiative for EC business. This institutional structuring privileged a tiny set of finance ministry and central bank officials. Most importantly, it helped define the agenda and the kinds of proposals brought forward, making the negotiations less indeterminate and random (Mucciaroni 1992: 459–82). It also facilitated an efficient negotiating process by providing venues in which instant communication was made possible by close and strictly confidential personal contacts. There was also sufficient trust for negotiators to be more prepared to put all their cards on the table and explain the real reasons behind their positions in the EC Monetary Committee and the Committee of EC Central Bank Governors than in other venues.

ECOFIN acted to locate as many of the negotiations venues in these as possible. One of the key informal rules guiding the EMU negotiations was that an agreement hammered out in these venues and ECOFIN was infinitely better than an agreement left to the European Council and the rest of the Council of Ministers structure. Heads of state and government and foreign ministers would produce outcomes that were less than adequate from a technical point of view. This rule played a vital role in expediting an EMU agreement. As the negotiations progressed, these venues took on an increasingly 'club-like' character. Particularly amongst EC finance ministers and central bankers there was an intensified sensitivity and pride about institutional prerogatives. EMU was about reinforcing those prerogatives and establishing the right to do so by showing that they could exercise them effectively. Hence, for ECOFIN, the EMU negotiations were both an opportunity and a constraint. This factor served to facilitate and expedite agreement.

These institutional characteristics of the EMU negotiations were important in narrowing down the agenda and helping, via the EC Monetary Committee to prepare a consensus on macroeconomic policy in the somewhat rarefied atmosphere of the independent expert (Kees 1994: 127–8). This consensus took the form of borrowing from the best performing national model, Germany. In the EC Monetary Committee and the Committee of EC Central Bank Governors officials did not seek to create a new model for EMU. Their inclination was to diffuse existing best practice, to imitate. In this way they provided the EMU negotiations with a technocratic legitimacy, justified by functional arguments about best performance.[1]

The EMU negotiations were concluded successfully precisely because certain highly contentious issues, which were rooted in conflicts of basic political belief, were factored out of the bargaining. Three such issues were most notable: the appropriate kind of political union to make EMU viable; the economic and structural-policy aspects of EMU, notably fiscal policy co-ordination in stage 3; and the proper scope for the political direction of EMU and for making the ECB's operations open and accountable. The more central that these issues had become in the EMU negotiations, the less credible would it have been to contain their negotiation within the EC Monetary Committee/Committee of EC Central Bank Governors nexus or even in the IGC on EMU. Hence institutional self-interest in controlling the negotiations had costs in terms of the agenda. Success in negotiating an agreement was bought at the price of an agreement that was less than adequate in treating the basic requirements of a viable EMU.

The Diplomatic Basis

Ultimately, what made a speedy EMU agreement possible was the harnessing of these economic and political factors to the diplomatic objective of creating the conditions for a stable peace order in Western Europe. A stable peace order can be defined for this purpose as one in which war is not considered as an option in

---

[1]   On isomorphism and legitimacy see Radaelli (forthcoming).

the relations between states. The role and impact of devastating wars in Europe since 1870 made the attempt to find a new basis for inter-state relations the top diplomatic priority in Western Europe. This took the form of European unification as a means of containing German power and Franco-German reconciliation as a means of unifying Europe and eliminating the conditions under which war could ever again be seen as an option.

EMU had always been nested in this larger framework. But it was the shock of German unification and the consequent threat of imbalance within the Franco-German relationship that gave urgency to the EMU negotiations. Otherwise, various reasons could have been found to postpone the exercise. German unification represented a radical change in underlying political conditions. For the French, the Italians, and others, EMU became a litmus test for continuing German resolve to pursue European unification. Dumas and De Michelis sought to nest German unification inside EMU. In their efforts to make EMU a condition for German unification they were unsuccessful. Instead, Kohl ensured that EMU was nested inside German unification, which was for him the most urgent project in late 1989 and early 1990. But, equally, German unification gave a new meaning and centrality to EMU and altered perceptions of the associated benefits and costs for Germany. EMU was vital to giving a new impetus to Franco-German reconciliation in the context of the anxieties and alarms in Paris consequent on German unification. Hence the Franco-German relationship took on a central role in the EMU negotiations. Bilateral meetings of Kohl and Mitterrand, the Franco-German Economic Council, and the secret Franco-German bilaterals during the IGC operated as an inner link within the wider EMU negotiations. They gave purpose and direction to the overall negotiations, based on the shared and sustained momentum from Kohl and Mitterrand.

Political leadership from Kohl and Mitterrand acted as the vital animating and organizing force behind the EMU negotiations, assisted by Delors in oiling the wheels of the process. Their great contribution was as *animateurs* and *ingénieurs*, organizing, monitoring, and evaluating progress. Above all, they set deadlines as means of focusing the minds of EMU negotiators on the political imperative to agree. In doing so they were motivated both by their personal beliefs, rooted in their own historical memories, and by long-term calculations of diplomatic benefits for their states. Kohl and Mitterrand sought to escape the confines of EMU as negotiated by bureaucracies and constrained by bureaucratic politics and to focus on the big issues of creating a viable European structure to ensure a stable peace order in the wake of German unification. Without this political leadership, agreement would have proved protracted and quite possibly elusive.

An additional background factor was the rebalancing of international monetary power that was seen as a central consequence of EMU. EMU offered a geopolitical benefit in the form of a strengthening of the political and monetary role of the EC in the global economy. This strengthening would follow as the

European single currency displaced the US dollar as a world reserve currency and a trading currency. As we saw, this motive was particularly potent within the French government. But it represented a long-term factor rather than an important variable in explaining why a speedy EMU agreement was possible between 1987 and 1991.

The Nature and Patterns of Coalition-Building

A central theme of this study has been the centrality of the Franco-German relationship as the motor of the EMU negotiations. Reconciliation of their objectives was seen by their negotiators, and not least by others, as a necessary precondition for a successful negotiation. There was, in effect, an inner negotiation within the larger negotiation: its purpose to clarify the vital interests of both sides and their different background intellectual assumptions, and to seek means to bridge differences. The institutional venues within which this inner EMU negotiation took place were provided by the Elysée Treaty of 1963 as modified in 1988. Most notable were the Franco-German summits (especially those held in May 1989 and November 1991); informal meetings of Kohl and Mitterrand (as in June 1988 at Evian); and the Franco-German Economic Councils (in particular of August 1989 and March 1991). These were paralleled by regular meetings of opposite numbers from both sides' finance ministries and central banks. In addition, from April to November 1991 French and German IGC negotiators held six top-secret bilaterals on EMU, designed to narrow differences and thereby speed progress in the larger negotiation. For neither French nor German EMU negotiators was there another bilateral relationship that, in diplomatic and political terms, came anywhere close to the significance attached to this relationship. It was driven by the Elysée, the Chancellor's Office, and both foreign ministries and based on the absolute primacy attached to Franco-German reconciliation. Other EMU negotiators were prepared to tolerate Franco-German collusion because they recognized that the negotiations could founder in the face of the traditional differences of conception of EMU in France (the 'monetarist' and institution-building conception) and in Germany (the 'economist' and behavioural conception).

The pre-eminence of the Franco-German relationship has to be understood in the context of a much more complex pattern of coalition politics on EMU. Most notably, there was no effective countervailing coalition to their bilateral partnership. Indeed, both Paris and Bonn were also led to compromise with each other because neither could lead an alternative winning coalition. They needed each other if there was to be a successful EMU deal. Yet both came to the EMU negotiations with policy positions much closer to several other partners than with each other. Covering as they did a wide-ranging agenda, the EMU negotiations displayed a varied pattern of coalitions on distinct sets of issues. The Franco-German relationship had to overcome the contrasting siren calls of their natural partners in order to bridge the gaps evident in the negotiations. A further complication was that, as the EMU initiative progressed, it became subject to the contrasting approaches of the successive EC governments holding the six-month, rotating EC Council Presidency.[2] In the Council meetings and in the IGC, it is the Presidency which assumes the role of business manager amongst the EC governments: initiating; brokering deals; and co-ordinating.

The Council Presidency and Coalition-Building: The Impact of the Luxembourg and Dutch Presidencies in 1991

French and German EMU negotiators were very careful not to challenge the role of the Council Presidency in managing the EMU agenda and in running meetings. Successive Presidencies affected the progress of the EMU initiative by their different leadership styles, bargaining positions, and working relationships with the EC institutions (in particular the Commission and the Council Secretariat). There was, at the same time, much variation in the significance of individual Presidencies on EMU, as a result of the legacy of previous commitments agreed under earlier Presidencies, the particular priority and urgency accorded to it by the Presidency in question, and the resources available to the Presidency. Decisive turning-points came with the European Council meetings in Hanover (June 1988), Madrid (June 1989), Strasbourg (December 1989), Rome (October 1990), and Maastricht (December 1991). A European Council meeting could be a turning-point without the host Presidency itself playing the key role—as with Madrid. Some Presidencies occurred when progress on EMU was slower or sidelined—as with the Greek Presidency of late 1988 and the Irish Presidency of early 1990. Moreover, a Presidency could play a major role on EMU without the European Council meeting that it hosted being decisive—as with Luxembourg in the first half of 1991. Despite this variation, the pattern of bargaining coalitions on EMU cannot be fully appreciated without reference to the role of successive Council Presidencies. Some of these Presidencies have already been referred to in the national case studies. But few studies exist of the role of the Council Presidency in an IGC setting, and the impact of the Luxembourg and Dutch Presidencies on the EMU negotiations in 1991 was distinctive and significant (Kirchner and Tsagkari 1993).

The Luxembourg strategy in the first half of 1991 was to create a solid base and a clear momentum for the IGC. In contrast to the IGC in 1985, when the Commission and the Luxembourg Presidency had worked hand in glove to prepare the Luxembourg European Council of December and the Single European Act, the two became more distant in 1991, causing some acrimony between

---

[2] The six-monthly Presidency involves chairing all the meetings of the Council of Ministers and the European Council. On the Council Presidency, see Hayes-Renshaw and Wallace (1997); Johnston (1994); Kirchner (1992); Westlake (1995).

them. Instead, the Luxembourg Presidency oriented itself to building a consensus in the milieu of the IGC, which was that of finance ministries and central banks. But a consensual approach was combined with considerable ambition. In the event, the Luxembourg Presidency produced a first Draft Treaty at the end of April, just three months after the initial working session of the IGC. This Draft was subsequently revised, with a concluding Draft Treaty on 18 June prior to the European Council meeting in Luxembourg. Both texts on EMU were well received by a majority of EC governments. Indeed, the texts represented the majority view on all points. The Luxembourg Presidency had achieved the substantial progress that they had sought and had fostered a consensus behind it. Their Permanent Representative at the time—Joseph Weyland—estimated that, by the first Luxembourg Draft Treaty, some 80 per cent of the final outcome was already on the table (Kirchner and Tsagkari 1993: 17). In that respect, Jean-Claude Juncker as Chair at the ministerial level and Yves Mersch as Chair at the level of Permanent Representatives had, by common consent, managed the IGC business well.

The Dutch approach was somewhat different. At first it was akin to a bull in a Delft china shop. As one of the Dutch officials closely involved in the IGC put it, 'the big difference was that the Dutch had strong views on everything': attributing Dutch attitudes to a strong Calvinist streak. This remark applied to both the IGC on EMU and that on political union. Part of the problem was that the Dutch conception of the two spheres was quite distinct, if not contradictory. On political union, Piet Dankert, Minister for European Affairs, pursued a traditional *communautaire*, quasi-federal model, which alienated the British and the French. By contrast, Wim Kok, Minister of Finance, and Cees Maas, his personal representative (and Chair of the EC Monetary Committee since December 1989), seemed to envisage a very different structure for EMU. The transition to EMU was to be conditional on intergovernmental agreement, and stage 3 was seen as an inevitable harbinger of a 'multi-speed' integration process, splitting the EC between the 'ins' and the 'outs'. EMU was anything but a *communautaire* design. Both ministers were Socialist members of a coalition government, led by Ruud Lubbers (a Christian Democrat), and both had impeccable European credentials. The difference of conception appears to have been rooted in the distinct cultures of their two departments: foreign affairs and finance.

The initial Dutch approach managed, overall, to upset just about everybody and please no one. In the IGC on political union a 'three-pillar' approach had been suggested by the French and backed by the British. The effect was to place foreign policy and home affairs and justice matters firmly in separate intergovernmental pillars, leaving the rest, including EMU, under the traditional Community pillar. The Luxembourg Presidency had adopted this notion, much to the irritation of the Commission. At a meeting of foreign ministers in Dresden in June Delors and others pressed for the pillar approach to be overturned. The Commission President counted a majority in his support, as did the

Dutch which judged seven or eight states to be with them.[3] Both claimed that Pierre de Boissieu, the French IGC representative, was seeking to revive the anti-*communautaire* Fouchet Plan of his grandfather. Determined to overturn the three-pillar idea, they left Dresden in upbeat mood. Other participants were not so sure that they had a majority behind them, or that opposition to the pillar approach was very firm. Nevertheless, the Luxembourg Presidency sought compromise. They invited Delors to provide a text to insert in the preamble of the Treaty to assuage the feelings of their critics. The new insertion referred to 'a process leading gradually to a union with a federal goal'. But the Dutch and the Belgians were not satisfied.

Once in the Presidency the Dutch now took a bold, assertive stance. They decided to strike out the pillar approach from the Draft tabled by the Luxembourg government. In essence, they upheld and returned to the Community model. A number of IGC participants suspected close collusion between Delors and the Dutch: that he had visited The Hague in August to help write the new text, or that he had extensive telephone discussions about it (Grant 1994: 195). The Dutch do appear to have been encouraged by Delors and his staff to pursue this course. Certainly Delors was delighted with the move. It reflected what he had urged, and thus the Commission was obliged to back the proposal when it was placed on the table. Prior to their initiative, the Dutch toured EC capitals at the end of August and early September. They judged that their approach would find support from four governments, four would be neutral, and four would be against. This assessment led Dankert to conclude that all was to play for and that they must press ahead with their case. They did so in the face of contrary advice from Peter Nieman, the Dutch Permanent Representative in Brussels and member of the IGC on political union, and from Maas, both of whom stressed that Dankert had gravely misunderstood the French position.

Publication of the first Dutch Draft provoked a storm of protest. As one key figure recalled, 'On Monday 13 September we learned that the only state supporting the draft was the Dutch' (Kirchner and Tsagkari 1993: 28). The launch date became known as 'Black Monday'. A major strategic error had occurred as a result of both diplomatic miscalculation and a domestic political struggle for power over EC policy between Ruud Lubbers as Prime Minister, Hans van den Broek as Foreign Minister, and Dankert. Subsequent to this humiliating defeat, the Dutch revived the three-pillar notion, and the battle on political union moved on.

There was barely more support for the Dutch proposals on the transition to stage 3. The Dutch backed strict convergence criteria of sound monetary policy and budget discipline. Their own reputation in these areas was second only to that of the Germans. They were strongly committed to the 'economist'

[3] Grant, C. (1994: 188–91). He records the following as supporting Delors's position: the Netherlands, Belgium, Greece, Spain, Italy, Portugal, and Germany. Britain, Denmark, France, and Luxembourg opposed them.

approach to EMU. This tough stance led the Dutch to believe that only a core set of countries would be ready to enter stage 3—those with the strongest economies—whilst the weaker states would have to be held back. A split Community was seen as being inevitable with EMU. But few dared to speak of a 'two-tier' Europe because of the political sensitivities involved. The Dutch were prepared to be bolder and speak the truth. In fact, after an informal ECOFIN in May, Juncker, for Luxembourg, told the press that a 'two-speed' EMU had been raised in their discussions and 'no-one was shocked'. The Dutch may well have believed that they had more support on their side: they expected Germany, France, and Luxembourg to back them. Moreover, the Dutch concern that stage 3 should only begin when the right conditions existed led them to sympathize with the desire of the British to decouple stages 2 and 3 of the process. A greater conditionality would safeguard the transition.

Against this background Maas produced his ill-fated text at the end of August 1991. It had three aims: to establish that a 'two-speed' EMU was inevitable; to prepare for this inevitable outcome in the transitional arrangements for stage 3; and to use these arrangements as a means of keeping the British on board. The text stated that the Council of Ministers, or the European Council, should:

- discuss which member states fulfil the conditions for participation in stage 3 and the date of the beginning of this stage;
- in the light of this discussion, member states which fulfil the conditions shall decide whether they will participate in stage 3 at the proposed date.

A provision of this kind would eschew any notion of irreversibility or 'automaticity', as sought by some, and would have involved very little advance commitment. The Dutch text was widely criticized, not least by Delors himself, who saw it as anti-*communautaire*. It found support only from within the German camp and from the British. To the Dutch, the opposition seemed to be more a result of their advocacy of a non-*communautaire* procedure, rather than a rejection of the principle that they were seeking to have recognized. In any event, the episode illustrated the potential for a coalition between the British, the Dutch, and the Germans, but one that London did not pursue. Instead, the political attack against the Dutch proposal led Wim Kok, as Minister of Finance, to withdraw the text that had been prepared by Maas.

A later Dutch text circulated at the end of September 1991 also provoked much opposition. This text entailed what became dubbed as a generalized 'opt-out' clause: that is, within six months of the Council's decision to move to stage 3, any state could exempt itself from the decision. Again, the Dutch were determined to ensure a safe passage to a single currency: if its own government were not completely satisfied that the new currency would have a secure base, it could extricate itself from the venture. Opposition to this latest Dutch proposal grew, but it remained on the table until the final phase. It was not removed from the Draft Treaty until the last IGC, before the Maastricht summit. That it lingered for so long was the cause of much animosity.

It is evident that the Dutch were ploughing a lonely furrow in the IGC. No other government, save for some in Germany, sought the kind of model that they espoused: *communautaire* for political union, but intergovernmental, heavily conditional, and divisive on EMU. The partnership with the Commission could only be partial and inconsistent. The Dutch were much more entrepreneurial and adventurous than was the Luxembourg government. But they had a prospectus that isolated them and that inevitably irked their partners. The Dutch were obliged to prepare several revised texts during their Presidency: a partial Draft on EMU on 29 August; a Draft Treaty on 24 September; a new Draft on EMU on 28 October; and a 'working document' on 8 November. These revisions reflected not only the intensification of the negotiations, but also the distance of the Dutch from the, admittedly shifting, majorities in the IGC. Two months of the IGC had been 'wasted' whilst the Dutch wrote and defended their initial Treaty (Grant 1994: 194).

The Dutch were eschewing the traditional mediating role of the Presidency. Others saw them as charging ahead and seeking to split the opposition ranks. This approach did not endear them to the Commission, the other EC body interested in mediation. A briefing paper from DG2 was highly critical of the Dutch approach at their first IGC on 2 July. It commented that the paper tabled by the Dutch 'contained several futile or unrealistic elements', reflecting their isolated views. There was 'hardly any attempt to stimulate negotiation': a damming indictment of a Council Presidency. Later, another Commission paper lamented the Dutch failure at the informal ECOFIN in Apeldoorn 'to find negotiating formulas' that would make progress possible. Moreover, in July the Presidency appeared ill prepared on some important legal aspects and to answer questions on major problems. Prime amongst the latter was what arrangements might be made for those states excluded from stage 3. This question was inevitable, given Dutch promotion of a 'two-speed' EMU. But their inadequate response said much for their neglect of the position of their weaker brethren.

The explanation for this major strategic error appears to lie, in large part, in the conflicts emanating from Dutch domestic politics, within which its Council Presidency was 'nested'. In this respect, it illustrates the constraints of a 'two-level' bargaining game. The balance of opinion within the Dutch Parliament was to press its government to pursue a *communautaire* structure and to reject the 'three-pillar' approach. The promotion of the Draft Treaty owed much to the relative autonomy of departmental ministers in the Dutch government and to the individual role of Dankert as Minister for European Affairs. Dankert assured his colleagues that the *communautaire* text that he was proposing would gain support from the French: he cited the backing of Guigou for such a claim. He, and others, believed that the Germans would endorse the plan: it was close to their federalist orientation. The Dutch had collaborated closely with the Commission on the preparation of their Draft. Yet, other ministers and officials in The Hague still thought his strategy dangerous: Maas and Nieman argued as much on the very eve of its launch. Lubbers was uncertain, but he suffered from a lack of influence over EC policy in his coalition government. Moreover, his fellow leaders in the European People's Party had previously publicly backed a Community-based political union. For his part, van den Broek as Foreign Minister had very poor relations and a constant battle over policy responsibilities with Dankert. In any event, he was occupied with the deepening Yugoslav crisis.

Dankert's ability to persuade the government to back him stemmed from the assessments that he gave of EC support. But any such support soon evaporated. The Franco-German axis was again crucial. The two foreign ministers—Genscher and Dumas—agreed to reject the Dutch Draft. The Dutch believed Kohl to be sympathetic to them. In the end, however, Kohl was not prepared to have a row with the French about it. Kohl and Genscher, as well as De Michelis, feared that insistence on the Dutch text would endanger the prospects for agreement at Maastricht. Even Delors distanced himself from the Dutch text at the IGC on political union, saying that he would go along with the majority position (Grant 1994: 194). Van den Broek said that he would correct the error of his domestic foe and submit a revised text.

The Dutch had sought to engineer a new EC coalition around a federal ambition and a Community-based approach to political union. On EMU they had pursued a different approach. The result was comprehensive failure. They alienated the French and British on political union, and the French, Germans, Italians, and others on EMU. In particular, by adopting a formula on the transition to stage 3 that seemed to go too far to accommodate the marginalized British they irritated the Germans and angered the French, the two main players. The combination of this formula for a 'two-speed' EMU with a style of negotiation that sometimes appeared unduly abrasive and brusque, even arrogant and divisive, constituted a potent mixture.

By contrast, the Luxembourg Presidency had been much more concerned to go with the consensus and positioned itself accordingly. Whilst it was also of the 'economist' school on EMU, it took up a less trenchant stance than the Dutch. For example, it sought tough convergence criteria to govern the start of stage 3, but opposed a requirement of unanimity in the Council or a generalized opt-out. In the detailed negotiations of the IGC, the Luxembourg government positioned itself close to both their German and French counterparts. They also sought to accommodate the British, and at the same time, satisfy the French and Germans, by hiving off their particular opt-out. Overall, the Luxembourg Presidency could claim to be as central to the evolving consensus as any state represented in the IGC on EMU. Yet, of course, they were not strong enough to deliver bargaining deals. The IGC was managed by two contrasting Presidencies: one lacking resources but an effective mediator by seeking out consensus; the other too conflictual to be an effective mediator.

Bargaining Coalitions in the IGC

The progress of the EMU negotiations between 1988 and 1991 exhibited a number of cleavages between national governments. At the same time, over the course of the negotiations, issues were reformulated and cleavages reformed. The EMU negotiations had an important dynamic quality, a quality that helped to facilitate the final agreement. The identification of particular coalitions below should not, therefore, be taken as offering a static picture. Rather, it is a basis on which to locate shifts that helped to secure the final agreement.

The most prominent divisions were as outlined below.

1. First, there was the division between two blocs: the Netherlands, Germany, and Britain, on the one hand; and, France, Italy, and the Commission, on the other. The final Treaty entailed compromises on the basis of crucial shifts of position made by: Germany on automaticity; France on convergence; and France again on the stage 2 institution.

The division between the two blocs was consistent with that on the basic philosophy towards EMU between the 'economist' (behaviouralist) and the 'monetarist' (institutionalist) approaches. In other words, the positions on the other issues were largely predictable from this dimension. But by 1991 France had shifted on certain issues towards the 'economist' bloc. Also, some variation of positions taken on ideological and institutional issues was discernible. For instance, Luxembourg was generally identified with the 'economist' bloc. But it took a somewhat softer position on the transition to stages 2 and 3, accepting automaticity. Both the Dutch and Luxembourg governments—reflecting the Socialist Parties in their coalition governments—opposed German moves to insert an ideological support for free markets and privatization into the list of general policy objectives in the Treaty.

2. The 'monetarist' coalition was not consistently *communautaire*. France opposed the involvement, to any significant degree, of both the Commission and the European Parliament. Italy supported the involvement of the European Parliament, but not the Commission. The Commission appeared most consistently 'monetarist'. By contrast, the Dutch, in the 'economist' bloc, were more favourable to the role of the Commission and of the European Parliament than were the French.

3. The only other significant issue-based bloc was that supporting the creation of a new 'Cohesion Fund' to help the 'peripheral' states meet the convergence targets. This bloc united Greece, Ireland, Portugal, and Spain, with Italy taking an intermediate position. Away from this issue, however, the bloc of 'periphery' states did not maintain a cohesive position. Spain shifted its stance away from these same partners on the related issue of the establishment of a new financial-assistance mechanism. Greece supported the *communautaire* institutionalist position; Portugal and Spain did not; whilst Italy took an inconsistent stance. Moreover, not all the periphery states shared the same basic EMU philosophy. Whilst Italy was firmly 'monetarist', Greece, Portugal, and Spain

supported the German proposal for inclusion of the 'golden rule' in the convergence criteria. This support was no doubt motivated, in part, by a perceived need to establish their own credentials on EMU.

4. The key issue for the UK—sovereignty—was a cleavage on which it had few sympathizers. As already noted, the Netherlands offered support, which Germany opposed, given its stance on irreversibility. Denmark sought a general opt-out. But its position was distinctive in other respects. The Danes accepted an unconditional start to stage 2 (unlike Britain); did not seek unanimity before stage 3 could begin (again unlike the British); and endorsed an important role for the ECB in banking supervision (once again unlike the British). They were also 'softer' on the convergence criteria than the Germans or the Dutch; took a more compromising stance on the stage 2 institution than the other two; and were more prepared to have the Council of Ministers play a role.

Analysis of the positions adopted in the IGC across the range of issues by the four major states and the EC Commission yields some interesting coalition patterns.[4]

1. Britain was notable for having the least convergence of position with other states. Yet, in two notable cases there was a high degree of proximity: with Germany, followed by the Netherlands. On many aspects of the technical design of the transition to EMU all three shared an 'economist', market-oriented philosophy. It was the resistance to a prior commitment to a single currency and the sensitivity on national sovereignty which prevented the British from participating in an effective coalition with the Germans and the Dutch. Lubbers's inventory of outstanding problems prior to Maastricht highlighted the fact that the British were involved in about half of them. He took this list as his guide and sought to accommodate London. Lubbers and Major at Maastricht rescued the British opt-out and produced a deal on the Social Chapter. Both of these outcomes were crucial to the completion of the Maastricht agreement. In this particular respect, the Dutch Presidency proved to be an effective mediator. The British were, of course, far from accepting the *communautaire* conception. Indeed, British positions on EMU were much further away from those of the EC Commission than those of any other member state. Particularly striking was the gap between British and Italian positions, the largest between any of the major EC states.

2. French positions were more convergent with a larger number of member states than were the British or the Germans. France was most convergent with Italy and the EC Commission. But, to a lesser extent, it was also close to Belgium, Ireland, Luxembourg, Portugal, and Spain. The 'francophone' bloc was a loose one, with significant disagreements: for example, on attitudes towards the role of the Commission and the European Parliament, the general

---

[4] These findings are based on an analysis of minutes of the IGC on EMU meetings in 1991. The issues selected are those where the positions of several delegations were clearly given and where a division existed between them. A major limitation is that issues are not weighed according to their significance. Also, no account is taken of positions in the EC Monetary Committee meetings earlier. Note that the validity and reliability of the data are dependent on the individual authors of the minutes.

policy principles set for EMU in the Treaty, and the establishment of a Cohesion Fund. The attraction of seeking influence through leadership of its own coalition on EMU was also undermined by French recognition that the key compromises would have to be struck with Germany and that, by contrast, its own coalition partners were weak and, in the case of Belgium and Italy, weakening. Yet, it is significant that France and Germany began the IGC negotiations with positions that were substantially apart. Indeed, six other member states and the Commission were closer to the French than were the Germans. The distance that France and Germany had to bridge to broker a deal was considerable. But the greatest divergence for the French was with the Dutch. The French initiated the three-pillars notion, and they championed the monetarist approach to EMU. The Dutch rejected both. Mitterrand was deeply irritated at the end of the Maastricht Council by what he saw as the excessive willingness of the Dutch to appease the British, which he saw as futile. Lubbers's later candidature for the post of Commission President was to suffer from this memory.

3. German positions were most convergent with the Netherlands, followed by Luxembourg and Britain. They were least convergent with Belgium, Greece, Ireland, Italy (least convergent of all), Portugal, Spain, and the EC Commission. Despite the shared policy visions of the Germans and the Dutch, there were significant points of distinction. These disagreements created difficulties for their coalition. The Dutch political leadership, especially Lubbers, did not attach the same importance as the Germans to the independence of national central banks. They believed that what mattered was a stability culture and that such a culture was better promoted by responsible social partnership than by legal devices like central bank independence. Indeed, the Dutch central bank was formally dependent on the Ministry of Finance and remained so for some time after the Maastricht agreement. In Dutch politics there was a greater emphasis on fighting inflation on the basis of a consensual society, and the Dutch showed themselves to be irritated by the tight monetary policies pursued in Germany. Thirdly, the Dutch Finance Ministry did not link EMU to political union, as did Kohl. To the Dutch, EMU was a 'stand-alone' technocratic project. It was useful in so far as it supported the single European market and promoted economic convergence. There were political reasons for supporting EMU—to create a greater awareness of the need for stability policies—but they were not dependent on building a political union. At the same time, most Dutch politicians were fervent advocates of political union, for wider reasons. This support for political union whilst denying that EMU required political union left the Dutch with a basic dichotomous position. The rationale for EMU and political union was different, and hence the design of each could diverge sharply, as evidenced in their first Draft Treaty. It also meant that the Dutch had to be persuaded to accept the principle of irreversibility for EMU. At a crucial meeting between Lubbers and Kohl on 28 November, the German Chancellor made this a condition of German acceptance, to Lubbers's surprise. In short, the Dutch and the Germans could see each other as unreliable partners in the fray of the battle.

4. Italy's closest and most important partners were France and the EC Commission. In consequence, her stance was also convergent with that of a number of other states, in particular Belgium, Luxembourg, and Portugal. The Italian position was closer to that of Greece than was the French stance. The problem for the Italians in the IGC was that the French believed that they were an increasingly weak and ineffective partner and that, after 1990, the French ditched them in order to compromise with Germany. An additional difficulty was the divergence between the Italian and Dutch positions. Indeed, by their pronouncements on the need for convergence and for immediate corrective measures by errant states in mid-1991, the Dutch incensed their colleagues in Rome. The Italians also found the Dutch provisions on the opt-out and a 'two-speed' process to be the polar opposite to their own thinking. Dutch negotiators like Maas were seen by the Italians, and others, as unnecessarily aggressive.

5. The positions taken up by the EC Commission were closest to those of France and Italy. By contrast, the gap was greatest with Britain, followed by Germany and the Netherlands. This contrast was a reflection of the 'econo-mist'/'monetarist' divide, with the Commission advocating the institutionalist approach associated with the latter. Effective leadership in the IGC by the Council Presidency did not depend on the support of the Commission. The Luxembourg Presidency proved to be an effective business manager on the basis of its sensitive mediation between governments, rather than its collusion with the Commission. The Dutch were encouraged by the Commission to remove the three-pillar structure in the Draft Treaty. But this step led to failure and humiliation. The IGC context emphasizes the intergovernmental mode of deci-sion-making, and the Commission can be left on the fringe. In this respect, the effectiveness of a Council Presidency can differ from that required by the nor-mal EC legislative process.

Leadership in the Negotiations and the Franco-German Relationship

Putting this pattern of coalitions together, some important features emerge. First, despite the early significance of the economist/monetarist cleavage, the progress of the negotiations displayed few stable winning coalitions. Those that did exist tended to be issue-specific and transitory. Such coalition activity expressed itself in a vast tapestry of informal relationships that were estab-lished during coffee and lunch breaks in IGC and EC Monetary Committee meeting sessions, during scheduled and requested breaks in proceedings, as well as in meetings outside conference sessions. Coalitions were often partial, with insufficient internal strength and momentum to sustain them. Coalition members lacked consistency in the policy positions taken up. Members moved between alternative formations on different issues. The 'peripheral' states lacked unity vis-à-vis the core. The Commission, supported mostly by the Belgians and the Italians, lacked the authority to press its institutional demands.

As a result, leadership in the IGC was not possessed by any single actor for very long or on many issues. Leadership required a willingness to compromise with negotiating partners, to bridge the gaps apparent in the IGC. Despite heading the largest bloc, the French recognized that their allies were too weak to form a credible winning coalition. The Germans found that they had fewer followers and disavowed many of the wider positions taken up by the Dutch and the Danes. In other words, neither France nor Germany had effective alternatives to compromising with each other. The Franco-German relationship was thus crucial to the IGC outcome, and on this basis each partner shifted to accommodate the other.

In displaying a will to engage in bilateral compromise, the French and the Germans were drawing upon resources built up over a generation. *Realpolitik* led them to prioritize each other in their foreign-policy calculations. But the experience of bilateral co-operation had led to cognitive and affective responses on both sides. Both sought to accommodate each other. Over the course of the EMU initiative, there was a consistent preoccupation in Bonn and Paris to ensure that the other did not feel isolated on a key issue by actions taken by the Council Presidency. Thus, there was a sense in Paris in late 1990 that the Italians were pushing the Germans too hard on EMU. A similar sense was apparent in Bonn in late 1991 after the Dutch tabled their 'opt-in for all' plan for stage 3. Together with the federal ambitions in the Dutch Draft Treaty of September, the Germans recognized that the French were being placed in too exposed a position. There was, in short, a mutual concern that the course taken by the negotiations, and the initiatives pursued by the Council Presidency, should not serve to isolate the other over an issue of vital interest.

Ultimately, in analysing the nature and pattern of coalitions across the numerous complex issues in the EMU negotiations, it is vital not to forget the shaping influence of two sets of factors. First, as we indicated above, definitions of vital political and diplomatic interest created an inducement to reconsider differences of economic-policy belief. Mutual perception of a vital national interest in Franco-German reconciliation, sharpened and focused by German unification, provided the impetus to bridge and overcome major gaps in negotiating positions. Secondly, the working style and ethos of the EC Monetary Committee conditioned the IGC on EMU. It did so through overlapping membership and through the delegation of key issues to the EC Monetary Committee. The EC Monetary Committee was highly experienced in policy preparation and advice and in seeking out consensus. Those skills had been refined in operating the EMS since 1979. Its working style was dedicated to getting beyond the lowest common denominator of agreement. It did so by focusing on best performance and was assisted in this task by the consensus that had already emerged on price stability as the measure of best performance before the IGC began. Best performance was the lodestar of its activities (Kees 1994: 140). This style and ethos spilled over into the IGC, making it easier to conduct negotiations as a learning process. It militated against the formation of contending coalitions.

Theorizing about Maastricht

Recognizing the historic importance of the Maastricht agreement on EMU, several studies have offered different kinds of theoretical explanation of its negotiation. To cite just some of the more prominent examples: McNamara (1998) emphasized the role of ideas in shaping the Maastricht agenda, in particular of a neo-liberal economic policy consensus; Verdun (1996) focused on the Delors Committee as an 'epistemic community' and EMU as a product of policy learning and a consensus amongst monetary policy experts; Kaltenthaler's (1998b) study of Germany and EMU gave primacy to the role of domestic institutional factors in constraining policy choice; whilst Sandholtz (1993) stressed the significance of supranational leadership and Cameron (1995) the importance of transnational actors. A number of conference papers adopt Putnam's (1988) notion of 'two-level' bargaining to explain the politics of the EMU bargaining process. Our own approach has built on the work of Dyson (1994), which placed EMU in a longer historical context and which examined the complex structural factors facilitating the EMU agreement.

Moravcsik (1998) offers the most challenging interpretation of the EMU negotiations, in an impressive and wide-ranging study that examines five key instances of history-making decisions on European integration. His approach highlights the motives and interests underlying national preferences in the Maastricht negotiations, seeing them as subsumed in the general nature of international co-operation rather than representing something that was *sui generis*. In essence, Moravcsik argues that the Maastricht negotiations are to be explained as a series of rational choices by national leaders. National preference formation is explained by relatively stable structural economic interests rather than by geopolitical interests and ideology; inter-state bargaining by asymmetrical interdependence (structurally empowering Germany), not by supranational leadership; whilst the institutional choices were the product of the desire for more credible commitment rather than of federalist ideology or of efficiency gains from centralized technocratic management.

In a notable concession, Moravcsik concludes that the relative importance of 'European ideology' and 'economic interests' in the EMU negotiations is more closely balanced than in other instances of EC negotiations and is more difficult to disentangle. In assessing German preference formation, the most important case given his stress on German power over outcomes, he is more circumspect: 'economic interests were at least as important as European federal ideology and probably more so. Nonetheless both may have been necessary for significant forward movement' (1998: 389). But Moravcsik remains committed to asserting the primacy of structural economic interests.[5]

---

[5] In some instances, Moravcsik makes a lot of relatively little: 'economic interests' are found to explain the British position on the Social Chapter, for example, whilst 'geopolitical interests' are more relevant to foreign policy (CFSP) issues (1998: 426–7).

There are many problems with Moravcsik's interpretation. For instance, he neglects a key contrast between the British and the German positions on EMU. As already noted, on so much of the technical design of EMU, the economic philosophy of the Germans, the British, and the Dutch was exceptionally close. An effective alternative coalition was available on this basis. But the reason why it was not activated owed much to what Moravcsik terms 'European ideology'. The Thatcher and Major governments had an ideological commitment to the protection of national sovereignty, whilst the German government sought to place EMU in the context of building Europe and overcoming painful historical legacies. The different ideological frames were crucial in preventing the realization of an otherwise natural coalition founded on economic interest. Secondly, the implications of EMU for economic interests were much more complex, multifaceted, and uncertain than Moravcsik allows, for instance in the German case. He himself concedes that in such a context geopolitical interests and ideology matter more. Thirdly, the erosion of the German menace and the collapse of the Soviet threat are viewed by Moravcsik as reducing the importance of geopolitical interests and arguments as factors in European integration, in favour of deepening economic interdependence (1998: 479). This interpretation ignores the perceived threat of increased strain from German unification and from potential economic and political turmoil in eastern Europe and the former Soviet Union. The threat of new strains acts as an inducement to seek to strengthen the system. Moravcsik seriously underestimates the geopolitical interests at stake in creating a 'stable peace order' in Europe (Boulding 1978). Fourthly, negotiators like Bérégovoy and Waigel were not simply motivated by arguments from economic interest. They internalized geopolitical arguments, especially in the context of the end of the Cold War. The crucial Franco-German Economic Council meeting in August 1989 was important precisely because their officials became aware of the role of geopolitical concerns in reframing their views on EMU.

Moravcsik notes that 'European federal ideas played a secondary, but significant role in shaping national positions' (1998: 429) and goes on to concede that they 'appear to have been responsible for general national tendencies for and against integration' (1998: 430). Strikingly, he argues that, in their absence, 'it is possible that the economic arguments for EMU could not have triumphed' (1998: 430). At the same time he stresses that the utility of such ideational explanations are limited, not least because they 'tell us little about the timing of the movement toward EMU' (1998: 429). Yet the timing was decisively influenced by Genscher's judgement in 1988, a judgement that was geopolitical and ideological in inspiration. Structural factors may have made his move possible. But it was his presence, political strength, and ideological resolution that were critical to timing. German unification was also far more important than Moravcsik allows. It brought forward the time-scale of negotiations and added the political-union dimension.

The cognitive dimension of the EMU negotiations also appears to be much more important than Moravcsik recognizes. The shifts in normative and causal beliefs affecting monetary policy seem crucial to an understanding of why EMU could enter the agenda in 1987–8. A shared learning process about the value of 'sound money' ideas, stable exchange rates, and central bank independence helped to account for the re-emergence of EMU in this period and not some years earlier. Moreover, the cognitive dimension is important in relation to the search in the IGC for viable technical solutions, when much of the discussion was at the frontier of the existing economics literature. The clash of ideas and cultures was, of course, important in this forum and a learning process was evident with respect to what plans were technically feasible as well as politically acceptable.

Apart from the impact of geopolitical interests, 'European ideology', and policy learning, other points of difference between the approach of Moravcsik and that presented here relate to the role of agency, the relevance of domestic sectoral interests, and the importance of the institutional setting. Whilst Moravcsik places much emphasis on the calculations of leaders such as Kohl, Mitterrand, Genscher, Waigel, Schlesinger et al., their distinctive input is not pursued. It is buried under structural explanations. Yet, without the enthusiastic support of French and German political leaders and a permissive public consensus in both countries, Moravcsik concedes—as seen above—that 'it is possible that economic arguments for EMU could not have triumphed' (1998: 430). The role of agency is unduly neglected. We prefer to see the role of agency and structure as one of mutual constitution, rather than to view structure as 'ontologically primitive' (Checkel 1998: 326).

With respect to the relevance of domestic sectoral interests, Moravcsik gives much attention to the views on EMU of domestic business organizations. Yet no evidence is presented that such views were anything other than a background contextual factor to the formation of government policies and strategies. They are assumed to be important. Our research found little evidence that outside domestic groups had a significant direct input into government policy-making on EMU: largely for the reasons cited in Chapter 1.

Our account also places more emphasis on the relevance of the institutional setting to the IGC negotiations. One major example will suffice to indicate the implications: that of the creation and role of the Delors Committee in 1988. We offer a different historical account of how the decision on the format of the Delors Committee was made. Moravcsik claims, incorrectly, that: 'Delors backed Genscher's proposal to create a committee of five independent experts— but Kohl and Stoltenberg, backed by Thatcher, insisted that the committee involve central bank governors acting in their personal capacity' (1998: 434). He continues: 'Kohl suggested Delors chair the committee; Delors and the French, seeing this as biasing the committee toward German preferences, were able to secure only the participation of three private experts'. This account is misleading. More generally, we stress the private collusion of Delors and Kohl on EMU before the Hanover European Council of June 1988. They were motivated by the fear of leaks to Pöhl and the Committee of Central Bank Governors, and determined to keep Thatcher, Stoltenberg, and Tietmeyer at arm's length. We note that it was Delors who proposed that EC central bank governors should form the main element in the committee and that he persuaded Kohl that Pöhl should not chair it. Instead, Delors's cabinet canvassed on behalf of the Commission President, Kohl took up the idea and offered him the post (11 June 1988 at Oggersheim), and Delors hid this deal from Pöhl when the two met subsequently (23 June), a tactic that soured their personal relations thereafter. The confirmation of Delors's appointment at Hanover took other governments by surprise, and Delors believed that he had scored a major personal victory and got the committee that he wanted.

This history is important for what it indicates about the strategic calculations being made at the time. Kohl and Delors clearly saw the committee as a means of binding-in the respective central bank governors, obliging them to take responsibility for EMU, and linking their credibility to the initiative. As Delors stressed, the committee was asked to supply an answer to the question of 'how' EMU might be established, not 'whether' it should be. The agenda was thus confined and depoliticized. Some of the most important central bank governors opposed Delors's appointment as chair. Pöhl recognized that the format of the Delors Committee was intended to trap him, compromising his domestic position. Delors's success was in gradually overcoming the personal opposition to his appointment and steering the committee to a unanimous report, when this outcome had seemed very unlikely until the last meetings (rather than structurally determined). Such unanimity contradicted the expectations in London, based not least on Pöhl's declared intention not to sign and the perceived interests of the Bundesbank. The Delors Report of 1989 represented a hard-fought compromise between the different positions advanced on EMU. A 'francophone' bloc, led by de Larosière, managed to have the report endorse the principle of irreversibility (paragraph 39): but the report eschewed any commitment to a timetable (paragraph 15). A further notable example is that the report's provisions on the economic-policy pillar (paragraphs 27, 28–30, dealing with regional and structural policies and macroeconomic policy) went well beyond the proposals submitted by the Bundesbank, and Delors believed that they owed much to his distinct contribution.

The content of the report displayed the prevailing norms and priorities of the central bankers, tempered by Delors's steer (Dyson et al. 1995). The design of the Committee had also served to bolster the distinct identity of the Committee of Central Bank Governors. By stressing that members were serving in a personal capacity on behalf of the European Council, Delors was able to keep EC finance ministers at arm's length, but to keep foreign ministers (like Dumas and Genscher) more fully informed. This institutional expedient helped to maintain the lead of the European Council over the early EMU initiative, self-consciously avoiding the project being ensnared within the more cautious ECOFIN domain. It is a matter of speculation whether a committee with a different composition and/or remit would have had the same impact or produced the same report. But the motivations and interests that lay behind its creation and management suggest a delicacy borne out of a belief in a distinct institutional cause and effect. The Delors Report set the terms of much of the subsequent debate on EMU. Governments found it difficult to withdraw what had already been conceded.

Moravcsik's dismissal of institutional politics leads him to some erroneous conclusions on the path taken by the EMU negotiations. He asserts that: 'In mid-1990 governments had begun to transfer authority from ECOFIN and the Monetary and Central Bank Committee to foreign ministers and heads of state' (1998: 441). The opposite is closer to the truth. Prior to the Rome 1 European Council in October 1990, ECOFIN and the Monetary Committee were successful in establishing their control over the impending IGC on EMU, thwarting an Italian attempt to integrate the two IGCs more strongly precisely to give foreign ministers a primary leadership role. During the course of the IGC on EMU, foreign ministers made only a modest input into the negotiations and, in almost all cases, the lead official (*de facto* and *de jure*) in the IGC was the finance minister's representative, not that of the foreign minister. The one group that did not enjoy an increase in influence on EMU in 1990–1 was that of the foreign ministers. It is true that the heads of state and government maintained an overall strategic lead. But the Luxembourg European Council in June 1991 was not especially significant for what it decided on EMU, allowing the IGC to run its course. Even at Maastricht the finance ministers played a key role.

Moravcsik's study is of major importance in setting out a conceptual model, and sustaining parsimony across distinct historical cases. There are a number of aspects to his study with which we agree: most notably, his stress on the utility of bargaining models. Yet, as this brief critique makes clear, his parsimony is too limiting and his approach too inflexible. An adequate explanation of the EMU process requires recognition of the cognitive and institutional dimensions of the shaping of policy and strategy, and of the role of 'agency' as well as 'structure' in the process. It is now appropriate to reflect on our own conceptual framework.

Theoretical Implications of the Study

At one level, this book can be seen as being predominantly a study of contemporary history. It has presented an extensive historical narrative of how and why the EMU agreement was reached in 1991. It has delved into national policy-making more deeply than has hitherto been the case, yielding some important empirical conclusions. At the same time the historical narrative has been guided throughout by the conceptual framework elaborated in Chapter 1. This framework was developed in the context of recent theoretical debates in Political Science and International Relations. It is important to return to that discussion and consider what theoretical implications can be drawn from the empirical case studies. Given that the task set for the study was not primarily one of 'theory-building', the conclusions drawn here are limited and can be elaborated briefly.

In the empirical case studies, a multi-causal explanation has been presented of how and why the EC re-entered into negotiations on establishing EMU. No single causal factor dominated the process. Indeed, the relevance of the factors that have been highlighted varied between national settings and at different stages of the process. The explanation has thus been broadly set, incorporating factors which were exogenous to the specific policy process and factors which were endogenous components of it. The exogenous factors were discussed more extensively in Dyson (1994) than they have been here. The current study was conceived of as building on that earlier work by focusing on the importance of endogenous factors within the negotiation process. In that sense the theoretical approach is 'constructivist', highlighting the role of process and of cognitive and institutional factors in particular in shaping how interests are defined (Checkel 1998; Wendt 1992).

The exogenous factors affecting the re-emergence of EMU in 1988 included structural developments in the realms of knowledge, finance, the wider economy, and geostrategy:

- a consensus of policy belief around the importance of 'sound' money and finance and of policy credibility, facilitating agreement about priority to central bank independence and numeric convergence criteria (McNamara 1998);
- developments in the wider international political economy, notably the increasing power of global financial markets and dollar-induced instability in Europe;
- the optimism deriving from the EC being in the upswing of the economic cycle and from the increased 'nominal' convergence of the major EC economies;
- the policy leadership position of Germany, given the anchor currency role of the D-Mark in the EMS;
- the geopolitical uncertainties unleashed by Gorbachev's reforms and the consequent search to strengthen a stable peace order in Europe.

The endogenous factors contributing to the re-emergence of the EMU debate included:

- the personal beliefs and experiences of political leaders and key negotiators, especially as they conditioned valuations placed on European unification and strengthening Europe's voice and power in the world;
- their use of historical memories and narratives to give political meaning, direction, and legitimacy to negotiations. In the conditions of uncertainty and complexity represented by EMU these factors were more important than Moravcsik (1998) allows;
- the evolving operating norms and rules of a 'hardening' ERM, including an increasing concern about the asymmetry of the EMS;

- the easing of negotiation by linkage of progress on EMU with agreement on EC capital liberalization;
- the design and use of European institutional venues to give momentum to the process and to control its direction;
- the political insulation of the EMU policy process, separating monetary-policy actors from wider interest-group conflicts and privileging the technical expertise of central bankers;
- the capacity of the Franco-German relationship to provide initiative and momentum, with its unique inner channel of co-operation.

A conjunction of factors provided the opportunity for a renewed debate on EMU. Some of the factors represented long-term conditions and were to continue throughout the 1988–91 period; others were more temporary in nature. The range covered by these exogenous and endogenous factors indicates the complex epistemology involved in developing a valid explanation of how and why EMU came about.

Further theoretical reflections can be expressed as a set of propositions.

> *Proposition 1: Whilst exogenous changes provided the necessary conditions for the re-emergence of EMU, they alone were not sufficient to explain when and how the project moved forward. Ultimately, the process of policy change was dependent on endogenous variables.*

Examining the endogenous nature of change can be better understood in terms of the three key dimensions of the EMU negotiating process discussed in Chapter 1. These dimensions refer to the *strategic behaviour* and the *cognitive processes* of actors within the distinct and evolving *institutional settings* of the EC. Given the richness of each of these dimensions, some further reflection is appropriate on how they shaped the EMU process.

Theories of bargaining typically take national preferences as exogenously given. By contrast, in this study of EMU their formation has been seen as having an important endogenous element. They cannot be fully understood without reference to the strategic, cognitive, and institutional dimensions affecting the individual actors involved in the negotiations. Choices were framed, or partially structured, but decisions were taken amongst real options (see also Sandholtz 1993: 5). This point will be discussed further below. At this stage, it can simply be noted that what negotiators did was not just 'structured' but also 'structuring', contributing to how the process as a whole evolved. They were craftsmen dealing with the materials available to them.

The literature on bargaining highlights key factors within the process. Transgovernmental linkages were important—between Kohl and Mitterrand, Dumas and Genscher, Bérégovoy and Waigel, plus Delors's own complex networks—in oiling the wheels and sustaining direction. Negotiators were concerned to strengthen their hand in the IGC. By stressing that their hands were tied domestically, Kohl and Waigel sought to transform domestic vulnerability into negotiating strength. Binding-in the Bundesbank had a dual effect: it limited the scope for negotiators, but it also extended collective responsibility from Bonn to Frankfurt. Conversely, in Italy, negotiators used widespread public support for the EU to strengthen their hand over domestic reform. EMU was also 'nested' in other games, with the effect that it transformed the perception of payoffs. For Kohl and Mitterrand, EMU was nested in German unification; whilst for Delors it was 'nested' in the spillover effects of the single market and the EMS. For Major, whether he chose it or not, EMU was 'nested' in the domestic game within the Conservative Party about Europe. This constrained his actions throughout.

The complexity and intensity of the bargaining process had the character of multidimensional chess. Participating in the bargaining game meant a constraint on the actions of individual negotiators, so that the course of the game influenced their perceptions and moves and the game as a whole gained a measure of autonomy in relation to these perceptions and moves. In the words of Kilminster: 'Only the progressive interweaving of moves during the game process, and its results—the figuration of the game prior to the twelfth move— can be of service in explaining the twelfth move' (Kilminster 1979: 97; also Bauman 1989: 34–5). To be understood properly, the motives and actions of EMU negotiators had to be seen within the framework of the negotiations as a whole.

With respect to the cognitive dimension, the case studies noted that knowledge was not simply a given and was highly imperfect. There was a lack of knowledge and control by individual negotiators in relation to what was going on in key areas of the game. This point applied to a powerful actor like the Bundesbank at key points in the game. There was also an important learning process at work: notably in France about the price to be paid for securing EMU, by meeting German conditions, and within Germany as negotiators redefined their positions in the light of new information about the French commitment to stability-oriented policies. The learning process was by no means smooth and uniform at national levels and was itself a source of disagreement and potential conflict.

Within the negotiating process, institutions changed over time, both in terms of their capabilities and their identities. This change was notable in the upgrading of the importance of ECOFIN, the EC Monetary Committee, and the Committee of Central Bank Governors. This institutional setting helped to define the agenda as actors there jealously guarded their prerogatives. Much of their behaviour was to be understood in terms of turf-fighting to ward off the intrusion of the EC Commission, the heads of state and government, and the foreign ministers.

The institutional setting mattered.[6] The EC Monetary Committee and the Committee of EC Central Bank Governors provided the consensus around certain ideas that proved crucial in framing the negotiations, in particular a belief in

---

[6] For a 'new institutionalist' perspective on the EU, see Bulmer (1994: 351–80).

capital liberalization and a belief in stability-oriented economic and monetary policies. These venues gave a structure to the process and a measure of predictability to the outcomes. They also endowed negotiators with a sense of an EC monetary identity (Kees 1994: 130). At the same time the institutional milieu was not a static determinant of the process and outcome of the EMU negotiations. The economic-policy consensus and sense of monetary identity had been constructed over time, and with difficulty, within these venues and informed by national experiences with handling the ERM. Out of this process had also emerged a sense of institutional capability that was to be important during the EMU negotiations. But this consensus, identity, and capability were the product of institutional dynamics and learning within the EMU process. They were not a given.

At the heart of the EMU negotiations was the interplay between these cognitive, strategic, and institutional dimensions: between EMU as knowledge and ideas, EMU as power and interest, and EMU as rule-based behaviour. The connectedness at work in the negotiations between these three dimensions and the richness of cognitive, strategic, and institutional dynamics were important. Actors modified their meanings in the face of new developments (like German unification) and new evidence (such as about the costs of devaluation within the ERM). They were also caught up in the strategic and tactical dynamics of the negotiating game, revising their meanings in the face of the sequence of moves and the requirements of retaining their freedom of manoeuvre to shape later moves and clinch an agreement on their own terms.

The interaction between cognitive and strategic dimensions was brought out most clearly in the politics about the choice and design of institutional venues that was bound up with every stage of the EMU negotiations. Strategic arguments about the need to maximize power over outcomes by acting as 'gatekeeper' to the negotiations were connected to cognitive arguments about shaping how EMU problems were defined and negotiated by controlling who participated in the process. This theme recurred in the Delors Committee, the Guigou Group, the preparations for the IGC, and the organization of the IGC.

This interaction between the cognitive and strategic dimensions was complex so that beliefs had the quality of both an intervening and an independent variable. In one sense, cognitive dynamics were responsive to the progress of moves in the negotiations and to a process of learning about the requirements for a politically acceptable EMU agreement ratifiable in all member states. There was a process of learning about what was negotiable and what was not in terms of accommodating national interests, particularly in Paris, Brussels, and Rome in 1988–9. But in another sense beliefs acted as signposts, directing as yet unclearly specified interests in particular directions. Beliefs acted as the roadmaps for EMU strategy. Kohl's and Mitterrand's beliefs about European unification and Franco-German reconciliation were of enormous importance in this respect. Mrs Thatcher's beliefs about the primacy of the sovereign state were significant in pushing definitions of British interest in the opposite direction. Beliefs could also act as constraints on the operation of the intelligence function in negotiations. The activity of preparing strategy and tactics, for instance by the British government before Hanover, Madrid, and Rome 1, could be impaired by a lack of appreciation of the seriousness and determination of the Germans and others to move ahead with EMU.

> *Proposition 2: The endogenous factors displayed the interactivity of structure and agency.*

In ontological terms, the account offered here on EMU has followed the basic assumptions of the 'critical realist' approach in the social sciences, as developed by Roy Bhaskar (1979).[7] The part played by 'structure' and 'agency' is to be seen as being mutually dependent; indeed, the two are inherently relational concepts.[8]

Agency in the EMU process occurred and had meaning only in relation to already deeply structured settings. These settings had different kinds of structure, which interacted in complex ways. But structures did not determine the outcomes directly; rather they defined the range of options and strategies pursued by actors within the process. The opportunities and constraints imposed on action in the structured setting of EMU were both physical (time, space) and social (intended and unintended consequences of previous action or inaction). In formal terms, as Hay has outlined, the critical realist sees strategic action as:

the dialectical interplay of intentional and knowledgeable, yet structurally-embedded actors and the preconstituted (structured) contexts they inhabit. Actions occur within structured settings, yet actors have the potential (at least partially) to transform those structures through their actions. This impact of agents upon structures may be either deliberate or unintended. (1995: 200–1)

This stress on the consequences of agency and the impact of strategic action on the structured setting is consistent with the explanation of the EMU process offered here. The interactivity of structure and agency underpinned the progress of EMU. Actors engaged in a learning process within a distinct institutional context, and the institutional setting itself evolved both in terms of collective identities and capabilities.

> *Proposition 3: Whilst structuralist explanations can explain why an EMU agreement was possible—by stressing the interests and constraints deriving from domestic politics, the bargaining interaction across the domestic and European levels, the structure of policy ideas, and the changing impact of the institutional setting—there remains a crucial sphere which can only be attributed to the role of agency, acting beyond the dictates of structural constraints. Structure did not determine agency in any simple or monocausal*

---

[7] In seeing 'structure' and 'agency' as being interactive the approach pursued here is also in line with Giddens's (1984) notion of the duality of the two aspects, though his conception of 'structure' has been seen as problematic (Hay 1995: 197–9).

[8] The discussion here follows Hay (1995).

manner. In choosing EMU, key actors were exercising some discretion, and personal beliefs and interests affected their intentions.

Would any German Chancellor have behaved like Kohl over EMU? Any Commission President like Delors? Or any French President like Mitterrand? To pose such questions is to recognize the part played by historical contingencies. Others around Kohl—Stoltenberg, for example—were much more cautious. What if Stoltenberg had replaced Kohl, or if his domestic political weight had not declined so sharply in 1987–8? What if Claude Cheysson had become Commission President in 1985 instead of Delors, as seemed likely at one stage? What if the French elections had been scheduled earlier? If Chirac had become President in 1988, would he have given the same commitment to EMU? What if Thatcher had been forced to resign over the Westland affair in 1985–6? Imagine how different the Hanover Council might have been with a President Chirac confronting a Chancellor Stoltenberg. How French economic interests in EMU were conceived might have been very different.

These questions highlight the importance of the attributes of the key actors: their *cognitive beliefs* (personal experiences, understandings, and interpretations); their *strategic views*; and their *capabilities* as party and national leaders. The role of agency was apparent in how key actors framed EMU within a set of personal beliefs and commitments and were prepared to act as *animateurs* of the negotiating process, giving purpose, direction, and meaning to that process. Three examples stand out:

1. The personal memories, beliefs, and instincts of Kohl deeply affected his understanding and use of EMU. The family history of the loss of his brother in the Second World War, and his sense that he was the last Chancellor of the war generation, made Kohl inclined to place EMU in a geopolitical frame of Germany tied to 'Europe'. Against this background, Kohl also sought to emulate Adenauer's European policy leadership and style, a feature that emboldened his own leadership on EMU. There was an ingrained sense of German responsibility for Europe.

2. The decision of Mitterrand to locate EMU in an historical vision and to pursue irreversibility derived from his personal experience. Mitterrand clothed EMU in historical symbols and myths stressing the Carolingian roots of Franco-German reconciliation, and identifying EMU as a matter of war and peace in Europe. In office, Mitterrand 'reinvented' himself as a life-long European, highlighting his attendance at the Hague Congress of 1948. This commitment strengthened Mitterrand's willingness to overcome domestic opposition to the requirements of EMU and eased the path of compromise.

3. The personal commitment of Delors to EMU as a project vital to the building of 'Europe' had roots in his own personal background and expertise. EMU remained Delors's top priority throughout the 1988–91 period. His commitment was evident in his emotional rhetoric about EMU being a question of survival for Europe.

Moreover, key actors exercised an autonomy in making strategic judgements on EMU, displaying a discretion in their choices, beyond the dictates of the immediate structural conditions. How innovative actors could be was evident in the case of Bérégovoy and Waigel at the Franco-German Economic Council in August 1989. Another example was provided when Kohl and Delors opted for central bankers (rather than 'wise men') as the major component of the committee to study EMU in 1988. Kohl, Mitterrand, and Delors maintained an overall strategic view of the progress of EMU throughout 1988–91, at the level of the European Council, in order to secure their personal leadership of the process. The part played by Kohl and Mitterrand as *animateurs* and strategists was vital to the sponsorship of the project, and they worked with Delors as *ingénieurs* to oil the wheels of the negotiations.

The role of policy entrepreneurs in advancing new ideas and initiatives had significant strategic effects. Notable in this regard were: Genscher on the relaunch of EMU in 1988; Kohl and Delors in the design of the Delors Committee; Butler in the launch of the British 'hard' ECU plan in 1990; Vattani and Padoa-Schioppa in getting an ambitious mandate for the IGC on EMU agreed at the Rome 1 European Council in October 1990; and Padoa-Schioppa in the final formula on dates for stage 3. Political developments may throw open windows of opportunity. But it does not follow that these opportunities will be seized. Effectively seizing opportunities requires fine-tuned strategic and tactical skills by actors within the policy process.

The importance of leadership skills was evident in various ways:

- Delors's informal 'presidentialization' of authority within the EC Commission, reinforced by his successful stewardship of the single market initiative and of the EC budget reform package. By 1988 Delors had the highest profile of any Commission President since Hallstein;
- Mrs Thatcher's personal command of Britain's EC policy, downgrading the contributions of senior colleagues and limiting the scope of cabinet discussion;
- the increasing political authority of Kohl within his coalition government, relative to Stoltenberg in 1988 and to Genscher in 1990;
- Mitterrand's leadership of the French Socialist Party from 1983 to accept the constraints of the ERM and embrace EMU; and
- the successful manipulation of the politics of *cohabitation* in 1986–8 by Mitterrand, leading to his subsequent election victory and his personal leadership of EMU.

The combination of these different elements—cognitive, strategic, and leadership capacity—highlights how key actors affected the course taken by EMU in a manner which might not have been evident if other leaders had taken their place.

What has been presented in the case studies is a 'micro-history' of the EMU negotiations, with a focus on its internal dynamics. This focus stemmed from the judgement that exogenous factors were a necessary, but insufficient element in the explanation of how and why the EMU agreement was negotiated. The critical shortfall is made up by factors endogenous to the EMU policy process, understood along the three dimensions of cognition, strategy, and institutions. What emerges is the imperviousness of the EMU negotiations to explanation in terms of a single causal model. The picture is of the negotiations as multi-causal, subject to quite strong random influences and to discontinuities at key points. The enduringly complex interplay of exogenous and endogenous elements, of structure and agency, and of the common and the specific, precludes a single causal model, even in relation to a specific stage (say agenda-setting) or a particular event or decision.

The conceptualization of how and why the EMU agreement was reached must combine each of these different elements. Structuralist accounts help to address the questions of how the EMU negotiations were possible and what range of outcomes was possible. But, as Dyson has stressed, structural accounts are themselves complex and multidimensional and leave considerable scope for indeterminacy in the negotiating process (Dyson 1994: 15–18). Outcomes are narrowed, nevertheless, by the structured setting. What is missing in such an account is what is happening *within* the negotiating process, the endogenous nature of change. In focusing on this sphere, both structure and 'agency' must be factored into the analysis, in a manner that recognizes that in practice both structure and agency are interwoven. Agency must itself be contextualized within its structural setting, but must be seen as structuring and not just structured.

Conceptualizing the EMU process is not easy; nor can it be seen as typical of other policy sectors covered by the EU. The EMU negotiations were unusual in being both 'history-making' and 'policy-shaping': concerned with designing a future architecture for Europe, as well as with narrower questions of technical design (Peterson 1995: 69–94). They were also more confined than is often the case. Above all, the negotiations were ensconced in 'core-executive' territory. This isolation reflected, as noted in Chapter 1, both the 'high-politics' nature of decisions about national currencies and the lack of sectoral mobilization when distributional effects were unclear and uncertain. More often, EU negotiations are on 'low-politics' issues, processed in wider and more diffuse policy networks, comprising state and non-state actors (Richardson 1996: chapter 1). The EMU negotiations took place in a *sui generis* environment: they were both isolated and ad hoc. This distinctiveness affects the tailoring of the conceptual framework for the analysis of the EMU process. It makes it especially important to get 'inside' the EMU negotiations, confined as they were, and to recognize the interplay of both structure and agency.

How Successful Was The EMU Agreement?

In one vital sense the EMU agreement was successful. It reconciled objectives of EC member states across a range of issues, from the design of the ECB, through the requirements of the excessive-deficit procedure, to ensuring irreversibility and no imposition of stage 3 on Britain and Denmark. An enormous amount was achieved in a short period of concentrated and exhausting negotiation. Crucially, the EMU agreement probably represented the maximum sacrifice of national political autonomy that could be reached voluntarily. But three questions arise. Was it minimally adequate from a technical point of view? An obvious gap here was in relation to the external dimension of a stable EMU. Was it adequately legitimated and politically sustainable? Questions arise about the European model of society, as well as about transparency, democracy, and the uniqueness of the institutional design. Was the German model transferable to the EC level? This question again touches on problems of legitimacy. The answers to these questions clearly depend on views about the underlying beliefs on which the EMU agreement was negotiated. As we have seen, those beliefs were essentially about the virtues of 'sound' money and public finances.

Cognitive Gaps in the EMU Agreement

An important aspect of the legitimacy of the agreement was the ability to provide a functional justification for it as putting in place the minimum requirements for a viable and sustainable EMU. The core question was whether the attainment of these technical requirements was compatible with the maximum sacrifice of political autonomy that member-state governments were prepared to make. Did the agreement incorporate 'saddle-point' solutions that met this condition? (Scharpf 1994: 232).

Seen from the perspective of the 'sound' money consensus that the EMU agreement embodied, considerable progress was made in finding such 'saddle-point' solutions. Most notably, the principle of central bank independence was accepted, the ECB was dedicated strictly to price stability, the 'no bail-out' rule was enshrined in treaty form, and rules were put in place to ensure that fiscal policy served the purpose of economic stabilization. But there were important cognitive gaps. Despite pressure from British and German negotiators the principle of supply-side flexibility—and labour-market and wage flexibility in particular—was not written into the Treaty. This gap was significant. Neoliberal theory pointed to the need to ensure economic efficiency by providing for new mechanisms of economic adjustment once exchange-rate flexibility had been renounced. The neglect of this logic of neo-liberalism raised serious questions about the viability of EMU, even in the minds of some who had negotiated the Treaty, for instance on the German side. Some measure of comfort was found in a neo-liberal belief in the power of market forces to harmonize economic policies. Markets would reward virtuous states and penalize the wicked, as defined in neo-liberal terms, and force a learning process towards supply-side flexibility. Other member states would have to learn to accept the logic of regional, sectoral, and firm-level flexibility in labour markets and wage bargaining. But what was clear over this issue—and over that of incorporating privatization in the Treaty—was that there were pronounced limits to the ideological acceptability of neo-liberal logic in a number of EC states, even when their negotiators endorsed 'sound' money policies. These limits defined their political willingness to sacrifice political autonomy. They also made the EMU agreement an imperfect neo-liberal statement, an asymmetrical design which placed confidence in monetary policy and market forces as Trojan horses for supply-side flexibility.

The cognitive gaps seemed even wider from a neo-Keynesian perspective. Seen from this angle, a viable EMU had to provide against the risk of negative demand shock and locking in deflation. This risk manifested itself as the high price paid by member states to qualify for stage 3 during the period 1991–6. It took the form of severe recession and the huge economic and social costs of a rising underlying level of unemployment (De Grauwe 1998: 91). Consequent falls in tax revenues and increases in public spending exacerbated the problems of meeting the deficit-reduction strategy required to qualify for entry into stage 3. The weakness of the EMU agreement stemmed from a failure to identify a responsibility for stabilizing aggregate demand.[9] In the negotiations and later there was a striking silence on the role of demand in sustaining high levels of employment, whilst the agreement provided the EC with no instruments to control demand. In neo-Keynesian analysis monetary policy has 'real' effects on growth and employment and cannot be considered as an economic strategy to be pursued on its own terms. Hence interest-rate decisions are of general importance for government economic policy and should not simply be left to an independent central bank. It is also important that automatic stabilizers are allowed to operate rather than put in too rigid a straitjacket of convergence criteria.

In this respect Keynesians were disposed to see the Werner Report of 1970 as intellectually superior to the Delors Report and the EMU agreement at Maastricht. The Werner Report had attached prime importance to a new 'centre of decision for economic policy' endowed with powers to co-ordinate fiscal policy, whilst ignoring the issue of the independence of the system of central banks. It sought a general harmonization of budgetary policies, both their revenue and their expenditure elements and the distribution between consumption and investment expenditure. Seen from this perspective, a viable EMU needed a system of fiscal and infrastructural policy co-ordination to address the objectives of growth and employment. It could take the form of a fiscal-transfer system to provide 'automatic stabilizers' or of a co-ordinated

---

[9] La Malfa and Modigliani (1998: 16).

investment programme financed out of public debt and separated out from convergence criteria which would apply only to current expenditure. The basic fault of the EMU negotiations derived from the neglect of aggregate-demand management and the assumption that monetary policy did not have 'real' effects. This fault had its basis in a consensus about 'sound' money and the way in which causal beliefs about the conditions for a viable EMU had been framed by this consensus. A comparison of the Werner and Delors Reports, and the dilution of the EC Commission's proposed financial-assistance mechanism, showed how the basic economic policy consensus had changed in eighteen years.

This outcome reflected more than just a shift of economic-policy paradigm. There was also an important factor of continuity that linked together the failure to implement the Werner Report's provisions on fiscal policy and the failure to address fiscal-policy issues more clearly in the Maastricht negotiations. That common factor was an unwillingness to cede political autonomy over fiscal policy to the EC level to the extent necessary to meet the minimum technical conditions for a viable EMU defined in Keynesian terms. Hence Keynesians had most to complain about, and to fear from, the EMU agreement hammered out at Maastricht. There had been a failure to insure adequately against deflation and demand shocks.

There was an additional reason to doubt the validity of the particular form that 'sound' money ideas took in the EMU agreement. At its core was the argument that price stability depended on acceptance of the principle of central bank independence. There were two main objections to this argument which surfaced in the French Trésor. The first objection, which was put by Bérégovoy in the negotiations, was that price stability was fundamentally a matter of political will and consensus-building, not of institutional arrangements. Hence it was unwise to place too much trust in this principle as an independent variable. In the hands of neo-Keynesians, this argument took the form of the correlation between certain kinds of wage-bargaining arrangements (either strongly centralized and neo-corporatist, or strongly decentralized at the firm level) and price stability (Calmfors and Driffill 1988: 13–61). These institutional arrangements could be seen as at least as important as an independent variable. But this argument for a convergence of wage-bargaining arrangements did not find its way into the EMU negotiations.

The second objection was more behavioural. It took the form of the argument that a central bank cannot in practice behave independently. In the first place, an ECB will inevitably be exposed to political pressures. The question is whether these pressures will be focused on, and contained within, some institutional framework (a *gouvernement économique*) or left unstructured to play directly and behind the scenes on the ECB. But the argument for a clearly defined framework for communication and defining reponsibilities made little headway in the face of German mistrust and power. In consequence, the issue of transparency in the relationship between the ECB and governments was not tackled. The casualty was the accountability of both sides to the public.

Secondly, an ECB has to attend to building and retaining a constituency of political support. In order to meet this requirement, arrangements for democratic accountability of the ECB take on a special importance. This point was grasped in the French Trésor as early as 1988, but played a very secondary role in the negotiations. On the ECB others found themselves negotiating around the Bundesbank version of 'sound' money and public finances rather than an Anglo-Saxon version. The treaty negotiations were far more preoccupied with criteria of central bank independence than with criteria of transparency and accountability and clear procedural rules in the operation of the ECB: for instance, whether minutes of meetings should be published, and the nature of reporting to explain how the ECB is setting policy to meet its objectives. On such matters the Maastricht Treaty was unclear and undemanding.

Institutional Innovation and the System of EMU Governance

The Maastricht Treaty agreement created an unprecedented institutional structure at the European level to manage EMU. It could not be fully equated with any of the traditional models that had been followed during the course of the European integration process. It broke with the 'Community method' by keeping the Commission at bay, whilst remaining firmly based on the principle of technocratic leadership. The ECB for stage 3 was at the apex of a federalist structure, above the various national central banks whose governors continued to have significant power relative to that of the executive board in Frankfurt. Despite this weak centre in the ECB, it was largely independent of elected political leaders. The powers of the ESCB were substantial and its governing bodies (Governing Council and Executive Board) were to act on the basis of simple and qualified majority-voting (Articles 10 and 11 of the ESCB/ECB Protocol). It was clearly not intergovernmental, being more than a forum of inter-central bank co-ordination. This characteristic was signified by the absence of a formal veto power for any of its members. But the scope for strong national interests in the governing council—where the balance of voting power rested with the national central bank governors—created dangers of inertia in policy formation; weak development of a European-wide outlook; and scope for conflict on national lines (Centre for Economic Policy Research 1998).

The key institutional relationship was that created between the ESCB/ECB and ECOFIN. The Executive Board of the ECB was comprised of members serving an eight-year term of office and who were appointed by the heads of state and government (Article 11 of the Protocol). They were to enjoy political independence from all outside bodies (Article 7). The Treaty gave the ESCB/ECB operational independence in the conduct of monetary policy, and it was strengthened by the commitment to maintain price stability and to the 'no bail-out' of national finances from EC funds. Decision-making in monetary policy was heavily centralized under the terms of the Treaty, though much of the implementation process was left decentralized in the hands of national central banks, which were themselves required to be independent. The ESCB was thus designed as a structure ring-fenced from outside political interference.

But the separation was by no means absolute. The dividing line was most blurred in relation to the setting of the exchange rate of the single currency. Here the final word appeared to rest with the Council of Ministers—in practice, ECOFIN (Article 109). In this respect the Treaty placed ECOFIN in a position that was broadly in line with the traditional Community model. For formal exchange rate agreements with non-EU countries, ECOFIN was to act, on the basis of unanimity, on a recommendation from the Commission *or from* the ECB and after consulting the European Parliament (Article 109).

The procedure for establishing informal accords—likely to be more important given the absence of legally binding agreements with the USA and Japan over the last quarter of a century—was somewhat less clear (Henning 1997: 36–8). Indeed, the various types of informal understandings were left unspecified. Article 109 (paragraph 2) states that the Council may formulate 'general orientations for exchange rate policies' in relation to non-EU currencies. German objections in the IGC had led to the removal of the term 'guidelines' in this context. For informal exchange-rate policies, the Council was to act on the basis of qualified majority voting (QMV). Its autonomy was subject, however, to the stipulation that: 'These general orientations shall be without prejudice to the primary objective of the ESCB to maintain price stability'. It was not clear whether the ECB would be able to reject 'orientations' not consistent with this objective (Henning 1997: 37). Alternatively, such orientations might be thought to be binding on the ECB if they were consistent with domestic price stability. The basic question was left unanswered: who is to determine whether an external rate is consistent or not with the inflation objective? German practice suggested that ultimately such a responsibility was to lie with the Council itself, an assumption that was widely shared in the IGC. But the Treaty sustained an ambiguity which still had to be resolved if the EU was to assume its proper responsibilities in the international system.

Away from this particular sphere, the strength of the ESCB/ECB was primarily the result of the weakness of the surrounding institutional setting. The Maastricht Treaty kept both the European Parliament and the Commission some distance away from the management of EMU. The Treaty gave the Parliament the right to be consulted on the appointment of the President and Executive Board of the ECB. The President of the ECB was to report to the Parliament annually in a plenary session (Article 109b(3)). In addition, the President and his colleagues on the Executive Board of the ECB were to attend Parliamentary committee meetings upon invitation in order to account for the policies of the ECB and to answer questions put to them. Whatever the utility of these provisions in making the ECB accountable, they did not constitute a significant brake on its power over monetary policy.

The EMU agreement placed the Commission in a position somewhat at variance with its normal role. Its traditional right of initiative was qualified (Italianer

1993: 96). First, as already noted, for decisions on exchange-rate agreements, but also for secondary legislation in the monetary field, the Commission *shares* the right of initiative with the ECB. Secondly, in a number of cases (e.g. when decisions are taken in relation to a particular member state, such as sanctions or balance of payments support), the Council decides on a recommendation rather than on a proposal from the Commission. The effect is that *unanimity* is not required for the Council to amend the recommendation from the Commission. Thirdly, in other cases (e.g. economic-policy guidelines, or the appointment of the ECB board), the Commission makes a recommendation to the Council which *then* makes recommendations to the heads of state or government. Finally, the right of the Council, in certain instances, to request a proposal from the Commission (the existing Article 152) is extended in a number of EMU areas to *individual* member states (Article 109d).

The Maastricht Treaty made a number of innovations to the role and work of the Council of Ministers. The Treaty was the first such agreement to differentiate between different formations of the Council of Ministers. A declaration affirms the existing practice of ECOFIN, rather than that of other councils dealing with EMU matters. Moreover, it was also specified that ECOFIN ministers were to be invited to European Council meetings when matters concerning EMU were to be discussed. ECOFIN ministers had previously been left out of European Council meetings. In 1988–90, Mitterrand, Kohl, Delors, and others were convinced that progress on EMU was more likely on the basis of the European Council exerting a political lead over and above that of ECOFIN. These provisions strengthen the leadership role of ECOFIN within the Council of Ministers structure. Other parts of the Treaty introduced qualified majority voting in the Council (e.g. on the excessive-deficit procedure, exchange-rate matters, and monetary policy) as well as a requirement that the Council consult the ECB on any of its own proposed Acts or draft national laws within the ECB's field of competence (Article 105(4)).

More substantively, the role of ECOFIN in EMU had been the source of greatest dispute in the negotiations. The provisions included in the Treaty left much unresolved. Indeed, its role was to be significantly affected by subsequent agreements. The area of dispute concerned the role of the EU in co-ordinating economic policy. The final Treaty sustained a major contrast between the two poles of EMU: whilst monetary policy was centralized at the EU level, economic policy was not. This contrast was a consequence of the failure to establish a *gouvernement économique*, as Delors and the French had sought, and a break with the more balanced design of the Werner Plan. As a result, the economic pole was weak. Under Articles 102a and 103 of the Maastricht Treaty, member states accepted a 'multilateral surveillance procedure' of their economic policies and agreed to establish 'broad guidelines' for them. But the scope and content of the EU's economic policy was barely defined (Articles 2, 3, 3a). Moreover, the co-ordination in economic policy was to be non-binding on member states. Article 103 detailed the procedure by which the 'broad guidelines' might be adopted (the Commission proposes, the Council recommends, and the European Council may adopt). However, where a member state's policy is found to be inconsistent with these guidelines, or a risk to EMU, then the Council (by QMV) merely *recommends* remedial action to the state concerned. A provision was inserted to allow the Council to make such a recommendation public (Article 103(4)). In other words, the Treaty settled for the threat of a state being 'named and shamed' to the world. It was felt that such action could prove very powerful. Yet, this procedure also ran the risk of an open political conflict between a state and its EU partners. The provision was, at the same time, symptomatic of a desire to reject fiscal federalism and to maintain national responsibility for budgetary management.

After Maastricht, the concern over how EMU stability might be ensured on the basis of an appropriate mix of (European) monetary and (national) fiscal policies intensified. In 1995 Theo Waigel, the German Finance Minister, pressed for an agreement to maintain budget discipline after the start of stage 3. With the prospect of a generous interpretation of the convergence criteria allowing the maximum number of EU states to begin stage 3 in 1999, German anxieties on the stability of EMU after its launch intensified. Fears were expressed that an individual state—perhaps from amongst those with poor records of fiscal discipline—might attempt to be a 'free-rider'. That is, as any single country's unilateral fiscal action might have little impact on the EMU area as a whole, such a state—especially a small state—would have an incentive to run the highest permissible budget deficit (*Financial Times*, 13 January 1998).

Much acrimony ensued, especially between France and Germany, and this overshadowed the Dublin European Council of December 1996. The new French government of Lionel Jospin, elected in May 1997, feared the deflationary effects of a tight fiscal straitjacket. For its part, the Kohl government suspected a weakening of the French commitment to stability policies. Finally, at the Amsterdam European Council in June 1997 a Stability and Growth Pact was agreed in the form of two resolutions, followed by two Council regulations (Breuss 1998). The pact was intended to enforce budget discipline after the launch of stage 3. National budget deficits were to remain within the 3 per cent of GDP ceiling set at Maastricht, consistent with the objective of sound budgetary positions close to balance or surplus. The two Council regulations dealt with strengthening the surveillance mechanism, with defining normal and exceptional situations for fiscal policy, and with determining the form that sanctions should take. German leverage had proved very effective in shaping the agreement, though in practical terms its deterrent effect was more important than the possibility of making sanctions stick.[10] Jospin had to settle for vague assurances about the importance of maintaining growth and employment. Just as EMU stressed 'monetary' rather than 'economic' union, the Pact emphasized 'stability' rather than 'growth'. Both represented a German attachment to the

[10] Köhler, 'Deutschland und Europa vor der Währungsunion', speech in Cologne, 18 March 1998: 9.

notion that states should 'put their own house in order' before new sound European structures could be built.

The consequence of the pact was to reinforce the role of ECOFIN in ensuring that states complied with the strictures on budget stability. All EMU states had a tough, clear benchmark by which their domestic policies were to be judged. The light touch of the 'broad guidelines' had been revised. *Gouvernement économique* was always a poorly defined term, and Waigel's pact did not seek to realize it. Nevertheless, ECOFIN had been placed centre-stage. Rather than being a redistributive authority under a fiscal federalism, ECOFIN was to be a policeman acting alongside the ECB.

The new system of governance for EMU had been clarified. It remained heavily skewed to the advantage of the ECB. It had no parallel at the EU or national level. EMU had adopted the Bundesbank model, but without the other parts of a conventional government structure. In monetary policy, ECOFIN, the European Parliament, and the Commission remained weak appendages. The ECB had more authority in its domain than the Commission normally has across its different fields of responsibility, and more than the old High Authority of the ECSC possessed.

The institutional design of EMU bequeathed important concerns about legitimacy. To its critics, the ECB was portrayed as the apotheosis of technocracy, created in the belief that monetary stability was too important to be left to politicians concerned about their re-election prospects. The institutional design of EMU left the citizen distant from those possessing power over monetary policy. Within the member states, monetary policy had largely remained opaque, but EMU lifted monetary management further away. The EMU structure was even more complex and confusing than the rest of the EU system: a system beset by its own intricate and distracting institutional designs (Featherstone 1994: 149–70). The ECB was likely to have to struggle to gain public understanding. Legitimacy benefits from a simplicity of institutional structure: a feature lacking in EMU. Simplicity requires a clear and united vision. By contrast, the IGC on EMU sustained competing visions of how EMU should be managed. As with the three-pillar structure of the Maastricht Treaty as a whole, complexity on EMU was the price of compromise.

There were political risks inherent in the authority of the ECB, especially in the combination of wide discretion in operating monetary policy with negligible transparency and accountability. Without a high degree of transparency and accountability of the ECB it would prove difficult to secure the support of a more sceptical European public than that faced by the Bundesbank in Germany. A situation could arise in which national governments blamed economic problems on a rigid and secretive ECB and resorted to policies that produced an unbalanced fiscal and monetary policy mix. In such a case, the new institution would find itself deprived of public support, undermining EMU as designed at Maastricht. The EMU structure emphasized a grey-faced technocracy, when legitimacy appeared to require accountability and transparency in the exercise of power, as with elected politicians. By October 1998 it was clear that the ECB intended to make its decisions in secret, using forecasts that it would not reveal, to achieve objectives that it did not need to justify. Issues of accountability and transparency had not figured strongly in the EMU negotiations of 1988–91. By 1999 political realities suggested the need for an urgent rethinking in this area.

Even more than for the rest of the EU's institutional structure, the design of EMU created such problems in terms of public understanding that its legitimacy was likely to rest on its policy outputs rather than its rules and architectural design. The Maastricht Treaty left fundamental questions unresolved about the transparency of the ECB's operation. These questions became the focus of much press attention as the ECB began its work in 1998. The Treaty stressed the political independence of the ECB and assumed that such independence stood in inverse relationship to the principle of accountability. The provisions on the accountability of the ECB—mainly before the European Parliament—were weak, and other forms of accountability were left unexplored (Eijffinger 1998). In short, the institutional design of EMU added significantly to the risks of the project as a whole.

Imperfect Legitimation: 'Binding Leviathan' and the 'European Model of Society'

Underpinning the EMU negotiations was a clear political theory in terms of which the agreement was legitimated. That theory was provided by neo-liberalism as a rationale for 'sound' money policies. The EMU agreement can be seen as a substantial, even if incomplete, victory for neo-liberalism and a Trojan horse for an economic-policy revolution in Europe based on supply-side economics and an agenda of deregulation and privatization. It empowered both finance ministries and central banks to push through what they judged to be overdue reforms in EC member states, extending beyond the specific terms of the Treaty to include reform of social policies as well as of labour markets. The political theory underpinning the EMU agreement legitimated a process of 'binding Leviathan'. This process took the form of central bank independence and rules constraining the conduct of fiscal policy. The aim was to protect Europe's citizens, consumers, and savers against two risks: inflation, generated by politicians seeking short-term popularity, and public-debt accumulation crowding out the availability of private financial assets. To this was added the argument that expanding public indebtedness narrows the scope for later budgetary choices as debt-servicing charges rise, in effect penalizing future generations.

But, however justified in these terms, a fundamental question remained about the justifiability of the EMU agreement in terms of Europe's wider and more complex political traditions. Neo-liberalism was only one such tradition, and certainly less dominant politically than Christian Democracy and Social

Democracy and—in France—Gaullism. These latter traditions supported a notion of a 'European model of society', which gave a high priority to social solidarity and responsibility for tackling poverty, unemployment, and inequality. This model supported a comprehensive welfare-state provision and a regulated labour market.[11] But the combination of budgetary constraints and the increased stress on supply-side reforms rather than demand management with EMU raises doubts about the viability of this model and of the political traditions that support it. Elements of the 'European model of society' were discernible in the Maastricht Treaty, notably in reference to 'a high level of employment and social protection' and to 'economic and social cohesion and solidarity among member states' in the principles listed in Article 2. They were also important in narrowing down the agenda of neo-liberalism, with supply-side reform issues kept out of the Treaty.

But the impact of the 'European social model' was defensive rather than shaping the overall design of the EMU agreement. Far more important than the role of the 'European social model' as an independent variable affecting the EMU agreement was the role of that agreement as an independent variable in shaping social, labour-market, and industrial-relations reforms as the 1990s progressed. EMU extended what Rhodes has termed a 'subversive liberalism' in which governmental choices are increasingly constrained by electoral demands for fiscal prudence and by financial-market liberalization (Rhodes 1994). EMU threatened the survival of deviant social policy cultures at the national level (Liebfried 1992). Social security reforms generated huge national strikes in France in 1995 and undermined the credibility of the government of Alain Juppé, who lost the Assembly elections in 1997. In the same year there were national strikes against pensions reforms in Italy. By 1998 the need for, and blockage of, social-policy reforms in Germany had become a central issue in the Bundestag elections. In Belgium budget cuts were eventually made by resorting to decree. EMU seemed to be calling into question the whole basis of the 'European social model'. Crucially, that process required legitimation in the form of express consent in national elections.

More generally, EMU confronted the established state traditions of member states. Following on from the liberalization measures of the single European market programme, EMU challenged the strongly regulative and statist instincts of Southern Europe, most notably (Featherstone 1999). In Italy and Greece, EMU strengthened a reform process which weakened the capabilities of the state in relation to the domestic economy and market. The deregulatory agenda of the EC complemented, in this respect, the external effects of globalization and financial-market liberalization (Rhodes 1996: 305–27; 1997). At the same time, states on the southern periphery of the EU remained dependent on fiscal transfers from the Community's structural funds. To some significant degree, 'core–periphery' relations were being recast by the deregulatory agenda

---

[11] See the research project on EMU and the European model of society being co-ordinated by Andrew Martin and George Ross at Harvard University's Center for European Studies.

of which EMU formed a part. This recasting of 'core–periphery' relations assumed increased salience in the context of the evolving debate about new forms of flexible integration in the EU. In short, EMU served both to redefine relations between member states and the rest of the EU and to reinforce the momentum behind a recasting of the domestic role of the state. Both consequences further complicated the basis of legitimation for EMU.

It is clear that the EMU negotiations and agreement raised more questions about legitimacy than they solved. They were bound to do so when they rested on a narrow basis of accepted political beliefs in Europe about the proper ends of government. Negotiators did not attend carefully to the normative justifiability of the EMU agreement in terms of Christian Democratic, Social Democratic, and Gaullist beliefs. That issue existed in the background: for instance, in the reservations of Delors and of Bérégovoy about the weak 'social' dimension of the agreement. There was a serious risk of the withdrawal of consent in one or more national elections to the 'sound'-money value system on which the EMU agreement was based. The EMU agreement had narrowed the parameters of choice and thereby seemed to put democracy at risk in the eyes of non-neoliberals. Extremism was then offered an opportunity to present itself as a rational alternative offering the only real choice, as in the mobilization of opposition to EMU by the French National Front (Schmidt 1997: 37–48).

The political challenge for the 1990s (and beyond) was to develop a discourse to explain and justify EMU that was credible in terms of Christian Democracy, Social Democracy, and Gaullism. But, by 1998, it still remained unclear what that discourse would look like. One possible beginning was the unity of the French Socialist government under Jospin and the French Gaullist President, Chirac, behind the notion of trading a loss of sovereignty for a gain in anchoring the principle of subsidiarity in the EU's institutional arrangements. That formula did not, however, address directly the question of whether, and in what ways, the 'European social model' should shape the further construction of EMU. What was clear was that with EMU the process of European integration had ceased to be supportive to that model of society and that the direction of change was very much from EMU to the 'European social model' rather than in the reverse direction.

These legitimacy problems threatened the viability of the EMU agreement. Given the abiding influence of traditional Christian Democratic, Social Democratic, and Gaullist beliefs it remained difficult, if not impossible, to meet the full technical requirements of the 'sound'-money model of EMU. Equally, the continuing grip of a 'sound'-money consensus in EC finance ministries and central banks ensured that neo-Keynesian proposals for fiscal federalism and co-ordinated investment programmes aiming at stabilizing aggregate demand were also kept off the EMU agenda. The consequence was to lock EMU in a dangerous technical 'double bind', in which neither neo-liberals nor, still less, neo-Keynesians were confident that EMU possessed the instruments to ensure its own efficient functioning and survival.

The limitations of the EMU agreement were also indicative of a deeper problem of reconciling certain basic political beliefs that were deeply embedded in different state traditions within the EC (Dyson 1980). For the British government, for instance, an absolutist interpretation of parliamentary sovereignty caused fundamental difficulties with both EMU as an issue of constitutional principle and the principle of central bank independence. The French republican tradition and German ordo-liberalism yielded radically different prescriptions for the institutional design of EMU. In short, European state traditions constrained the scope for agreement. Their continuing vitality left question marks over the overall adequacy of the EMU agreement, especially in ensuring an institutional balance that would facilitate the co-ordination of economic and monetary policies and that would subject EMU to clear democratic accountability.[12]

The Transferability of the German Model

A key feature of the EMU negotiations was the assumption that Germany offered the most appropriate policy model on which to base the design and operation of EMU. French Trésor negotiators would have liked to introduce the US Federal Reserve model as a basis for seeking to ensure more effective arrangements for democratic accountability, but they bowed to the political realities created by the need to 'bind in' Germany to the negotiations. Broadly speaking, most—if not all—EMU negotiators saw that the superior performance of the German economy offered an argument for imitating it as a model. Some—especially central bankers—went further and identified with the Germany economy as a normative model. Whatever the basis of this policy-transfer process—utilitarian and strategic or normative—there was a widespread view that the German model was the basis around which to negotiate (Radaelli 1997).

But questions arise of whether the German model was transferred to the EC level and whether it could ever be transferred there. The EMU agreement in fact shifted the ideology of the German model to the EC level (notably in the stress on open and free markets and price stability) and an isolated institutional aspect of that model (central bank independence) to the EC level. However, the deeper institutional underpinnings were not, and could not be, transferred. Central to the German model had been a complex system of 'organized capitalism' (Dyson 1983). Its organized character had come from a legal framework of regulation for industrial relations; a structure of corporate governance involving banks and employees in decision-making; a collective-bargaining system based on the idea of social partnership; the dual system in vocational education and training; and the role of house banks in providing industrial financing for the corporate giants. These elements reflected a commitment, and institutional capability, to

[12] Interestingly, these criticisms were taken up by Erik Hoffmeyer, former Governor of the Danish central bank (1992: 37). He refers to the ECB having an accountability problem and a counterpart problem in the absence of a clear, stable relationship between the monetary and economic policy pillars.

support social solidarity and an attitude of 'long-termism' in industry. At the heart of the German model was a complex, interwoven set of institutional arrangements for safeguarding consensus around the market model by managing and ameliorating the effects of its functioning. It was a framework of 'burden-sharing' for the Bundesbank in its pursuit of price stability, not least in respect of the system of collective bargaining and its success in containing and reducing labour unit costs. Such a framework for the EC was not put in place by the EMU agreement, and it would be unreasonable to expect that such a transfer could take place either in the time-scale of the agreement and its implementation or even at all given the degree of 'exceptionalism' of the German model. Hence an isolated aspect of the German model—an ECB modelled on the Bundesbank—could not be expected to operate in the same way.

Also, as the 1990s progressed, new questions arose about the adequacy of Germany as a policy model for EMU (Dyson 1996: 194–211; 1998). German GDP growth rates were below average; structural unemployment rose; budget-deficit and public-debt problems mounted; whilst by 1997–8 a 'reform blockage' on tackling these problems was apparent in Bonn. German unification was more than just a crippling economic burden. The East showed no signs of importing the traditional West German model. It evolved loose and flexible institutional arrangements quite different from those of 'organized capitalism' and more akin to a 'post-modernist' model of society in which group interests and identities remain flexible, pragmatic, and weak (Padgett 1996). The question now was whether these arrangements would spread to the West of Germany. This question was given a new urgency as German companies and banks recast their strategies and identities in the context of new global and European challenges. By 1995–6 they began to refocus on equity-based strategies which gave a new priority to maximizing shareholder value, led by such traditional bulwarks of the German model as Daimler-Benz and Deutsche Bank. As they moved investments offshore, and redefined themselves as global players, German policy-makers were forced to reflect on how to reform domestic business conditions in Germany to maintain their presence. These reflections pointed in the direction of deregulation and taxation reforms, designed to ease the costs of doing business in Germany. In addition, rising structural unemployment and a poor job-creation record in Germany raised further questions about the adequacy of the German model. There was new political pressure not just for tax cuts and reduced social obligations on business but also for flexible labour markets.

Paradoxically, German negotiators of EMU had unleashed forces pushing for the radical reform of the German model at the same time as they sought to ensure that EMU was built around that model. They had transferred their ideological principles to the EC level but they had not transferred the institutional supports that made the market compatible with German Christian Democratic and Social Democratic values emphasizing social solidarity. The effects of EMU conspired with those from globalization and from the single European market to set in train processes of development that cast doubt on the very model on which they had sought to base the design of EMU. As the wider model came into question, two things changed in EMU negotiations: deeper reservations crept in about taking the principle of central bank independence too far; and the credibility of the German model for developing the working of stage 3 lost ground. The French in particular were able to return with new vigour and credibility to the theme of *gouvernement économique* and to shift attention to the new Euro-11 Council (not provided for in the Maastricht Treaty) as the centre of gravity for institutional development in stage 3. As the German model was beset by questions, new space was opened to negotiate about strengthening fiscal policy and structural-policy co-ordination that had not been available in 1991. These negotiations were facilitated once social democratic parties were simultaneously in government in London, Paris, Rome, and, in September 1998, in Bonn. Subject to important historically conditioned differences amongst them, there was potentially a new opportunity to reflect on the design and operation of EMU.

A Politically Sustainable EMU?

The fundamental point remained that the German model failed to offer an adequate basis for a sustainable EMU. One solution to the problem of sustainability was a role for Germany as a hegemonic state capable of policing EMU. That solution lost credibility as the 1990s progressed. In the absence of a hegemon the question arose of whether there was an alternative solution. That solution would take the form of a new sense of solidarity that would support 'burden-sharing' within EMU, whether in the form of higher taxes or budget and welfare cuts to help adjustment in other regions and countries (Cohen 1994: 149–65; Mackay forthcoming). The EU's political structures did not facilitate the emergence of such a solidarity. In particular, the role of political parties as shapers of political will and mobilizers of opinion remained focused on the national level and the exigencies of winning elections at that level. Hence a political vacuum existed at the heart of EMU, one that could readily be filled by populist appeals to xenophobic attitudes, especially from the political Right. There was a strong incentive under the existing political structures of the EU for national political parties to seek to protect the public from the erosion of welfare benefits or from higher taxation consequent on EMU. EMU's political Achilles' heel was the prospect of people being asked to make sacrifices for others with whom there was a weak sense of identity. This vulnerability was sharpened by the close inherited ties of citizenship and identity with the solidarity provided by national welfare policies. In cutting back those policies, EMU threatened to become associated with weakening solidarity and attacking citizenship and identity. EMU's 'sound'-money policy agenda confronted political cultures in Continental Europe that placed a high valuation on full employment policies and solidarity, compared to Britain and the USA (Borre and Scarborough 1995: table 7.2; Lipset 1996).

EMU, Stability, and the International Monetary System

The political risks associated with EMU were not matters of purely internal concern within the EU. The launch of EMU represented the most significant change in the international monetary system since the collapse of the Bretton Woods regime in the early 1970s. How the single currency is managed and how it is accommodated within the international system will affect monetary stability both at home and abroad. An important political gain that motivated key EMU negotiators, especially the French, was an improvement in Europe's power position in relation to the international monetary system and a reduced exposure to the constraints of dependence on the US dollar.

The arrival of the new single currency will challenge the international position of the US dollar and raises the prospect not just of a second global currency but also of the creation of a new international monetary architecture (Bénassy et al. 1994: 9–22). The dollar has been dominant for at least half a century, as a store of value, a medium of exchange, and a unit of account. At the end of 1995, the US dollar comprised 61.5 per cent of official foreign-exchange reserves held by the world's central banks, and in 1992 the dollar served as the invoicing currency for almost 48 per cent of world trade (Henning 1997: 9). Such dominance is not easily disturbed. Yet, at the time of the EMU negotiations, the EC Commission was estimating that the new single currency would substantially replace the dollar (EC Commission 1990). Similar estimates were made by Gros and Thygesen (1992: 295). Henning (1997) offered a more balanced view. He noted the importance of how the US and European capital markets develop and integrate for the evolution of the dollar and the euro. The European capital market will require further efforts at deregulation and harmonization before it can rival the US market in breadth and depth. In addition, how the EMU authorities manage the euro in relation to the rest of the world will be crucial. The Bundesbank traditionally eschewed an international role for the D-Mark, but the sheer economic size of the EU could force such a development. Henning concluded that the potential for the euro to grow was substantial, but that its development was likely to be gradual. In the long term the euro might match the dollar.

Even this more modest scenario would, however, represent a major shift in the international system. The discharge of the EU's international responsibilities under EMU was left unclear by the Maastricht Treaty. The famous question posed by Henry Kissinger when the EC introduced a tentative system of foreign-policy co-ordination (European Political Co-operation) in the early 1970s was left unanswered in relation to EMU. Kissinger asked: when I want to discuss foreign policy, who do I call in Europe? Whom the USA, or the rest of the world, might call to discuss the position of the euro was equally uncertain. As noted above, the responsibility for determining the international exchange rate of the euro was seemingly shared between ECOFIN and the ECB. This ambiguity was compounded in relation to international representation. Article 109(4) merely states that the Council shall act 'on the position of the Community at international level' as regards issues of relevance to EMU. A similar provision was made in relation to the negotiation of external agreements with outside states or within international organizations (Article 109(3)). The IGC was intent on avoiding a lead role for the Commission on EMU akin to that it possessed in relation to world-trade negotiations. But the vacuum was not filled. In this instance, when the Council acts, it will be in response to a Commission *proposal*, with the requirement that it can only be amended by unanimity. By contrast to the curtailment of the Commission's powers of initiation in other areas, this provision strengthens the role of the Brussels body.

But it was left unclear who would represent the EMU regime in the IMF or in Group of Seven talks. Claims could be made by the ECOFIN chair, the relevant Commissioner, and the Presidency of the ECB. In the case of the ECOFIN chair, however, account would have to be taken of the position of EU governments outside the single currency. Difficulties also arose in relation to the membership rules and structure of the IMF, which assumed political representation by states possessing their own currency. Should EU states continue to be represented in the IMF or should there be a collective representation on behalf of the EMU regime as a whole? Further questions in relation to EMU were raised about how the IMF might calculate the balances of payments of the EU and/or its member states and to whom the IMF might lend in the event of payments crises (Henning 1997: 51). The arrangements for quotas at the IMF also seemed in need of adjustment. In relation to the G7, some saw EMU as strengthening the prospects for a reformulated G3, at least for monetary policy.[13] Such a development—placing the EU alongside the USA and Japan—had long been speculated about in the past, in the context of the emergence of new regional international blocs.

It is clear that the transition to a single currency will require issues to be resolved, not only within the EU, but also at the level of the international monetary system. Moreover, the transition to EMU was being undertaken at a time of a wider uncertainty and fluidity in the international system. The evidence of financial crises amongst the so-called Asian tiger economies, Japan, the former Soviet Union, and Latin America created an exceptional instability. In September 1998 President Clinton talked of such crises as representing the biggest economic threat in the postwar period. The G7 appeared to have been overtaken by wider economic developments, and the IMF seemed to be losing the power to manage crises. Governments had become smaller in the new global economy. Tony Blair noted in September 1998 that 40 of the top 100 economies in the world were companies, not countries. Even long-standing advocates of globalization accepted the need for a new architecture for international financial regulation, with George Soros attacking 'market fundamentalists'. New attention was being paid to problems of transparency (such as

[13] Köhler, 'Aufgaben auf dem Weg in die Europäische Währungsunion', speech to the Friedrich-Ebert-Stiftung, Bonn, 11 February 1998.

between international accounting standards), poor risk assessment, and the inadequate supervision of financial markets. The transition to EMU was set to take place against this backdrop. The issue of how to handle the 'excess reserves' of the EMU states—consequent upon the elimination of exchange-rate risk amongst the EU currencies—loomed over future policy discussions (Henning 1997: 16). Some 25 to 50 per cent of EU reserves might be superfluous: equivalent to $50–100 billion.

EMU would also disturb the EU's pattern of external relations. It was set to weigh heavily on the future agenda of EU–US relations, straining their bilateral mechanisms of co-ordination (Featherstone and Ginsberg 1996). Such strains were likely to arise if each sought to promote the competitiveness of its own currency and build up its own currency area. As a relatively self-contained economy, with a trade–GDP ratio lower than those of the USA and Japan, the euro area might be tempted to adopt a policy of 'benign neglect' of the external exchange rate. It had, on the other hand, to face up to the problem for successful implementation of EMU posed by the US dollar's competitive advantage inside Europe. A familiar currency like the dollar was likely to prove more attractive to market agents than a new and untested one. Moreover, EMU was now part of the 'acquis communautaire', the conditions that new entrants to the EU would have to accept. EMU intensified the problems of assimilation faced by the candidate countries of East Central Europe. Indeed, EMU represented a strong reinforcement of pressures towards flexible forms of integration, with the prospect of new states adopting the single currency at different dates after their formal entry into the EU.

With so many imponderables, it was unclear whether EMU would itself contribute to international stability or not. The Maastricht Agreement had left a number of gaps that needed to be filled before EMU could be accommodated within the international system, and international institutions like the IMF needed to adapt themselves to the onset of the single currency. The EMU project was thus set to have manifold international consequences. These consequences underlined the risks to the viability of the initiative. It was not only the EU that was set on a journey to an unknown destination.

Some Final Comments: 'Locked' Into A Politics Of Deflation?

The EMU agreement that was negotiated at Maastricht was clearly an historic event and was understood in such terms by its participants (though the British notably regarded it as misguided). In solemn treaty terms it laid out the structure for what was to follow: strenuous domestic efforts to meet the strict numeric convergence criteria and stay within ERM fluctuation bands without devaluation; framed within the challenge of meeting the final fixed date of 1 January 1999 in order to qualify for the final stage and to remain in Europe's 'first division'. The Maastricht Treaty created obligations to be honoured in word and deed, in letter and in spirit. The consequence was a 'lock-in' to a politics of deflation in the first half of 1990s, which caused output loss and contributed to escalating unemployment and rising budget deficits as tax revenues fell and public spending rose in a context of recession. The EU-11 government debt grew from some 55 per cent in 1990 to nearly 75 per cent of GDP in 1997. In 1991 EMU negotiators recognized that major policy adjustments would be necessary. But they had not appreciated how difficult the exercise would prove. That underestimation had much to do with failure to appreciate just how costly German unification would prove, as unprecedentedly high German interest rates were generalized via the ERM. From the outset EMU was faced with an economic shock. This also had to do with the adequacy of the economic-policy beliefs on which the Treaty had been constructed. There had been no requirement on policy-makers to stabilize aggregate demand and attend to the costs of negative demand shock. What was lacking was an appreciation that durable budgetary consolidation is an appropriate task for periods of growth, not of recession, to which such exercises can only contribute. Paradoxically, by hindering the prospects for economic recovery, the pursuit of convergence criteria 'to the letter' imposed a heavy burden of unemployment and debt at the start of stage 3. The origins of that problem lay in the linkage between the terms of the EMU agreement at Maastricht and the 'sound'-money economic consensus in which that agreement was framed and later interpreted.

At the same time the EMU negotiations were not finally closed at Maastricht. Crucial issues had been deferred for later resolution—notably, the politically controversial question of how large a grouping should go ahead to stage 3. Other gaps emerged with time—for instance, on fiscal policy in stage 3 and on the precise relationship between 'ins' and 'outs'. And, led by the French, opportunities were taken to reopen issues like *gouvernement économique*. Most problematic of all was the failure to address the conditions for the political viability of EMU. The biggest gap of all was caused by the lack of attention to the requirements of political union for a sustainable EMU. The EC's institutional structures—before and after EMU—had not served to generate a genuinely European party system and European consciousness and solidarity that could buttress and legitimize the effects of monetary discipline and fiscal retrenchment or of a growth of centralized fiscal power. Instead, the political apparatus of legitimation remained firmly entrenched in national elections and domestic party competition, the efficacy and meaning of which was devalued by the form that EMU took. It was predictable that the effects of EMU, especially if negative for unemployment levels and welfare-state provision and accompanied by calls for fiscal transfers, would polarize domestic party political opinion. Unless EMU could deliver clear, substantial, and early economic benefits, the political advantage would lie with its more xenophobic opponents in member states, notably from a Right that was increasingly divided on Europe by the 1990s.

EMU represented and reflected the EU's comparative advantage in producing regulation rather than engaging in large-scale distributive and redistributive politics (Majone 1996: 263–77). It was about rules to curb excessive deficits, prevent 'bail-outs', and secure price stability, not about large-scale EC fiscal transfers and the ceding of sovereignty over taxation and social policies. Designing and operating such rules was very much an activity for technical experts—EMU as 'government by experts'—and very much preoccupied with efficiency, not equity. But EMU could never hope to sustain this degree of technocratic insulation. Interest-rate decisions, exchange-rate policies, and budgetary consolidation raise deeply problematic and controversial issues of equity as well as efficiency. EMU's operation will be immersed in political questions about who should bear what burden and how, questions that involve the clash of interests and different conceptions of fairness. It will have to handle these immensely difficult questions in the absence of European-level political structures designed for this purpose.

The most questionable element in the EMU negotiations was not so much the quality of the economic analysis as the quality of the underlying political analysis. This lacked a viable political theory for sustaining EMU and for achieving the changes associated with its introduction, establishment, and consolidation. What was lacking was a model of a transnational democratic polity to underpin a venture that directly affected all Europeans. The open political question was whether the political conditions for a sustainable EMU could be put in place in time to support the ECB in stage 3. In their absence EMU was fragile, and the ECB politically exposed. Rather than providing the glide path to European unification, EMU threatened to unleash the political storm that could wreck 'ever closer union'. What Europe needed by the 1990s was not a technocratic project in the traditional Monnet style but a project to put in place a democratic structure and style, one engaging political action at the European level and encouraging identity-building at that level. EMU was not that political vision and, more seriously, could not thrive in the absence of such a vision. It represented the triumph of an ideal of technical elitism over the idea of political democracy. In this context EMU's political asking-price was dangerously high, unless it could deliver a major economic revival in Europe—and was blessed with the absence of an early external economic shock.

Appendix: List of Interviewees

Personal interviews (one or more) were conducted with those listed below.

Belgium

Jan Michelsen, Banque Nationale de Belgique
Baron Snoy, former Chef de Cabinet in Ministry of Finance, Personal Representative on IGC on EMU
Pierre van der Haegen, Banque Nationale de Belgique
Alfons Verplaetze, President of the Banque Nationale de Belgique

Britain

John Arrowsmith, Senior Adviser on EC Affairs, Bank of England 1985–94
Graham Bishop, Salomon Brothers, London
David Bostock, UK Permanent Representation, Brussels, and HM Treasury
Sir Samuel Brittan, *Financial Times*
Simon Broadbent, former Chief Economic Adviser, FCO
Roger Brown, British Bankers' Association
Sir Terence Burns, Chief Economic Adviser, HM Treasury, 1980–91, then Permanent Secretary
Sir Michael Butler, formerly UK Permanent Representative, Brussels, later Chair, European Committee of British Invisible Exports Council
Andrew Crockett, former Director for International Affairs, Bank of England, 1989–94
John Footman, Private Secretary to the Governor, 1986–9, Bank of England
Tristan Garel-Jones MP, former Minister of State for European Affairs in FCO
Eddie George, Deputy Governor, then Governor of the Bank of England
David Hadley, former Head of the European Secretariat, Cabinet Office
Sir David Hannay, UK Permanent Representative to EC, 1985–90
Baroness Hogg, Head of Number Ten Policy Unit, 1990–4
Lord Howe, former Chancellor of the Exchequer, Foreign Secretary, and Deputy Prime Minister
David Howell MP, Chair of House of Commons Select Committee on Foreign Affairs
Douglas Hurd MP, Foreign Secretary, 1990–5
Sir Bernard Ingham, Press Secretary to Mrs Thatcher 1979–90
Christopher Johnston, Association for Monetary Union of Europe
David Kern, Economic Adviser, National Westminster Bank
Sir John Kerr, UK Permanent Representative to the EC 1990–4, UK member of Guigou Group and of IGC on EMU
Mervyn King, Chief Economist, Bank of England
Lord Kingsdown, Governor of the Bank of England 1983–94
Norman Lamont, Chancellor of Exchequer, 1990–4 and member of IGC on EMU
Lord Lawson, former Chancellor of the Exchequer

Malcolm Levitt, Barclays Bank's European Adviser
Sir Geoffrey Littler, formerly Second Permanent Secretary in HM Treasury and Chair of EC Monetary Committee 1987–8
Sir Anthony Loehnis, former Director for International Affairs, Bank of England
Sir Kit McMahon, former Deputy Governor of the Bank of England
John Major, Prime Minister, 1990–7
Sir Peter Middleton, Permanent Secretary, HM Treasury, 1983–91
Gus O'Donnell, HM Treasury and Press Secretary to John Major as PM, 1990–4
Rupert Pennant-Rae, former Deputy Governor of the Bank of England
Richard Portes, Centre for Economic Policy Research
Sir Charles Powell, Foreign Policy Adviser to Mrs Thatcher, 1983–90
Richard Pratt, member of EC group, Treasury
Lionel Price, former Head of Economics Division and of European and International Divisions, Bank of England
Brian Quinn, former Director responsible for banking supervision, Bank of England
John Redwood, Head of the Policy Unit in the PM's Office 1983–6; Minister in DTI, 1989–90
Paul Richards, Samuel Montagu, author of UK's 'hard' ECU plan
Jim Rollo, Chief Economic Adviser, FCO
Christopher Taylor, formerly Economics Division and 1990–4 European Division of Bank of England
Sir Alan Walters, Personal Economic Adviser to Mrs Thatcher, 1981–4 and 1989
Neil Williams, formerly CBI

France

Pierre Achard, former Head of SGCI, adviser to Barre, and Economic Counsellor in the French Embassy in Bonn
Edouard Balladur, Minister of Finance, 1986–8; Prime Minister, 1993–5
Jean-Paul Betbeze, Chief Economist, Crédit Lyonnais
Jacques le Cacheux, OFCE
Jean-Michel Charpin, Chief Economist, Banque Nationale de Paris
Dr Stefan Collignon, Chief Economist, Association for the Monetary Union of Europe, Paris
Jean Cordier, Economics and Research Department, Banque de France
Christopher Crabbie, British Embassy, Paris
Prof. Christian de Boissieu, University of Paris
Sylvain de Forges, Trésor
Jean-Baptiste de Foucauld, Head of Commissariat Général du Plan and former member of Delors cabinet as Finance Minister, 1981–4
Luc de La Barre de Nanteuil, former French Permanent Representative in Brussels
Jacques de Larosière, President of European Bank for Reconstruction and Development, Governor of Banque de France, 1987–94, and member of Delors Committee
Roland Dumas, former Foreign Minister
Pierre Duquesne, Head of International Affairs, Trésor
Elisabeth Guigou, former technical adviser to Mitterrand on EC, former Head of SGCI, former European Minister and Chair of Guigou Committee

Guillaume Hannezo, adviser on EC in cabinet of Pierre Bérégovoy, Finance Ministry, 1989–91

Hervé Hannoun, director of Bérégovoy's cabinet 1989–92; earlier economic adviser in Elysée

André Icard, Chief Economist, Banque de France

Erik Izraelewicz, Economics Editor, *Le Monde*

Pierre Joly, Commisariat Général du Plan

Philippe Lagayette, Deputy Governor of Banque de France, 1984–92, and director of Delors cabinet 1981–4

Anne Le Lorier, EC adviser in cabinet of Balladur as Prime Minister

Corinne Lhaik, Economics Editor, *L'Express*

Bertrand Maigret, Association for the Monetary Union of Europe, Paris

Jacques Melitz, INSEE

Pierre Menat, Ministry of Foreign Affairs, cabinet of Raymond, 1986–8, cabinet of Juppé 1993–5, Elysée 1995

Xavier Musca, Head of EC section, Trésor, Finance Ministry, 1990–3

Prof. Jean-Luc Parodi, Institut d'Études Politiques, Paris

Christian Pfister, Economics and Research Department, Banque de France

Georges Pineau, European Monetary Institute, former economist in Banque de France

Jean Pisani-Ferry, DG2 of Commission, 1987–90, then economist in CERII

Jacques Regniez, economic adviser in cabinet of Balladur, 1986–8

Prof. Jean-Jacques Rosa, Institut d'Études Politiques de Paris

Claude Rubinowicz, member of cabinet of Bérégovoy, 1984–6 and 1988–92

Michel Sapin, Finance Minister, 1992–3

François Scheer, General Secretary in Foreign Ministry during IGCs, Ambassador in Bonn

Jean-Claude Trichet, Governor of the Banque de France, director of Bérégovoy's cabinet, 1986–7, Director of Trésor 1987–94, and French negotiator in IGC on EMU

Francois Villeroy de Galhau, Technical Counsellor on EC affairs in cabinet of Pierre Bérégovoy, 1990–3

Charles Wyplosz, INSEAD, Professor of Economics

Germany

Dr Joachim Bitterlich, active in Foreign Policy Division, Federal Chancellor's Office, since 1987 and later its head

Prof. Dr Peter Bofinger, University of Würzburg

Dr Johann-Wilhelm Gaddum, Vice-President, Bundesbank

Dr Hans-Dietrich Genscher, Foreign Minister

Günter Grosche, Head of EC section, Finance Ministry, 1990–3, chairing EMU group in Bonn, later Secretary to EC Monetary Committee

Dr Wilfried Guth, former Chairman of Deutsche Bank and member of Giscard–Schmidt Committee for EMU

Dr Gert Haller, former Head of Money and Credit Division and former State Secretary, Finance Ministry

Dr Peter Hartmann, former Head of the Foreign Policy Division in Federal Chancellor's Office, then State Secretary in Foreign Ministry

Erwin Huber, Bavarian Finance Minister and former European Minister in Bavaria

Prof. Dr Otmar Issing, Chief Economist, Bundesbank

Prof. Dr Reimut Jochimsen, President of State Central Bank, North-Rhine Westphalia and member of Bundesbank council

Rolf Kaiser, Head of EC section, Economics Division, Federal Chancellor's Office

Dr Karl Knappe, Bundesverband Deutscher Banken

Prof. Dr Claus Köhler, Credit Division, Bundesbank, 1974–90

Dr Horst Köhler, former State Secretary, Finance Ministry and the lead German negotiator in the IGC

Helga Kohnen, EC adviser, SPD Parliamentary Party

Dr Norbert Kraxenberger, Bavarian Finance Ministry and member of IGC on EMU

Dr Reinhard Kudiss, Bundesverband der Deutschen Industrie

Dr Hans-Werner Lautenschlager, State Secretary, Foreign Ministry, 1987–94

Theodor Martens, German Permanent Representation, Brussels

Prof. Dr Mannfred Neumann, University of Bonn

Herr Niemann, EC adviser, FDP Parliamentary Party

Dr Wilhelm Nölling, former President of State Central Bank, Hamburg, and member of Bundesbank council

Karl-Otto Pöhl, former President of Bundesbank

Dr Wolfgang Rieke, Head of International Division, Bundesbank, 1978–94

Dr Hans-Eckart Scharrer, HWWA Institute for Economic Research, Hamburg

Dr Wolfgang Schäuble, Chairman CDU/CSU Parliamentary Party, formerly Head of Federal Chancellor's Office

Prof. Dr Helmut Schlesinger, former President of Bundesbank

Dr Peter-Wilhelm Schlüter, former Head of EC section, Bundesbank and member of EMU group in Bonn, European Monetary Institute

Dr Werner Schönfelder, Foreign Ministry, a former member of EMU group in Bonn

Harry Schröder, Economic Adviser, Commerzbank

Ludwig Schuster, Economics Ministry

Prof. Dr Martin Seidel, Senior Legal Adviser, Economics Ministry, and former member of EMU group in Bonn

Dr Gerhard Stoltenberg, former German Finance Minister

Dr Horst Teltschik, formerly Head of Foreign Policy Division, Federal Chancellor's Office

Dr Hans Tietmeyer, President of Bundesbank and former State Secretary in Finance Ministry

Jürgen Trumpf, German Permanent Representative during IGC and now Secretary-General of Council of Members

Dr Theo Waigel, Finance Minister, 1989–98

Prof. Dr Norbert Walter, Chief Economist, Deutsche Bank

Klaus Weber, Head of EC section, Bundesbank

Prof. Dr Wolfgang Wessels, University of Cologne

Günter Winkelmann, former Head of EC section, Finance Ministry 1984–90

Dr Ralf Zeppernick, Head of Grundsatzabteilung, Economics Ministry and former member of EMU group in Bonn

Italy

Andrea Bonanni, *Corriere della Sera*

Carlo A. Ciampi, former Governor of the Banca d'Italia and member of Delors Committee, and Finance Minister

Rocco Cangelosi, Foreign Ministry

Gianni De Michelis, former Foreign Minister

Sergio de Nardis, Confindustria

Tana de Zulueta, former correspondent of *The Economist*

Prof. Mario Draghi, Head of Treasury Ministry since 1991 and Personal Representative on IGC

Prof. Domenico da Empoli, University of Rome

Simon Goss, British Embassy, Rome

Robert Graham, former *Financial Times* correspondent in Rome

Giovanni Jannuzzi, former Director-General for Economic Affairs, Foreign Ministry

Prof. Cesare Merlini, Institute of International Affairs, Rome

Stefano Micossi, formerly of the Banca d'Italia, then EC Commission

Prof. Mario Monti, EC Commissioner

Roberto Nigido, Foreign Ministry

Tomaso Padoa-Schioppa, Banca d'Italia, former Director-General of DG2, co-rapporteur to Delors Committee and Special Adviser to Guigou Committee

Francesco Papadia, Banca d'Italia

Riccardo Rettaroli, Associazione Bancaria Italiana

Massimo Riva, *La Republicca* columnist

Fabrizio Saccomanni, Banca d'Italia

Prof. Mario Sarcinelli, Banca Nazionale del Lavoro, former Head of Treasury Ministry and Chair of EC Monetary Committee

Paolo Scamacci, Associazione Bancaria Italiana

Prof. Luigi Spaventa, University La Sapienza

Umberto Vattani, formerly Diplomatic Counsellor to Andreotti, then Italian Ambassador to Bonn

Augusto Zodda, Ministero del Tesoro

Luxembourg

Yves Mersch, Director-General Trésor in Finance Ministry, Personal Representative on IGC on EMU and its Chair in first half of 1991, member of EC Monetary Committee

Netherlands

Wim Duisenberg, Governor of the Dutch Central Bank, member of Delors Committee, President of the EMI and then of the ECB

Ruud Lubbers, Prime Minister, 1982–94 and President of EC Council at Maastricht

Cees Maas, Treasurer General in Finance Ministry, 1986–92, Personal Representative on IGC on EMU and its Chair in second half of 1991, member of EC Monetary Committee

Brussels

Alan Ashworth, formerly Banking Federation of the EC
Rudiger Bandilla, Head of Legal Secretariat, Council of Ministers
Lionel Barber, *Financial Times* correspondent in Brussels
Sir Leon Brittan, EC Commissioner
David Buchan, former *Financial Times* correspondent in Brussels
Hervé Carré, director of monetary policy in DG2 and co-rapporteur for Guigou Group
     on EMU
Bernard Connolly, formerly of DG2, EC Commission
Georges Caravelis, European Parliament Committee on Economic, Monetary, and
     Industrial Policy
Henning Christophersen, EC Commissioner for Economic and Financial Affairs,
     1989–94, member of IGC on EMU
Joly Dixon, ex-Delors cabinet, advising Delors on EMU
Martin Donnelly, cabinet of Sir Leon Brittan
Dick Eberlie, CBI, Brussels
Michael Emerson, formerly Director for Economic Policy, DG2, EC Commission
Elena Flores, DG2, EC Commission
Charles Grant, formerly *The Economist*'s correspondent in Brussels
Peter Greiff, Journalist
Daniel Gros, Centre for European Policy Studies, Brussels and adviser to DG2 on EMU
Günter Grosche, Secretary to the EC Monetary Committee, 1994–
Rainer Hellmann, journalist
Alexander Italianer, DG2, EC Commission
Andreas Kees, Secretary to the EC Monetary Committee, 1978–93
Philippe Lemaitre, *Le Monde* correspondent
Alisdair McIntosh, UK Permanent Representation to EC
Georgios Markopouliotis, EC Commission
Theodor Martens, German Permanent Representation to EC, former Bundesbank
     official till 1991
Jean-Paul Mingasson, Director for Monetary Affairs, 1982–9, DG2, EC Commission
Michael Nielson, DGI2, EC Commission, and formerly in Office of UK Permanent
     Representative
John Palmer, correspondent, *The Guardian*
Marco Piconi, Italian Permanent Representation
Wolfgang Pini, Secretary to ECOFIN and to the IGC on EMU, Council of Ministers
Giovanni Ravasio, Director-General of DG2
Edmond Roussel, Economic Analyst, Bloomberg
Jan Schmidt, Chef de Cabinet to Christophersen, EC Commission
Amicar Theias, Council Secretariat
Michel Therond, Financial Adviser, French Permanent Representation
Dominique van der Wee, DG16, EC Commission
Thierry Vissol, DG2, EC Commission
David Williamson, Secretary-General, EC Commission
Helmut Wittelsberger, DG2, EC Commission

Miscellaneous

Dr Gunter Baer, formerly Secretary-General of Committee of EC Central Bank Governors and now Secretary-General of the Bank for International Settlements, Basle, co-rapporteur to Delors Committee

Jacques Delors, formerly President of the EC Commission and Chair of Delors Committee

Dr Eric Hoffmeyer, Governor of the Danish Central Bank and member of the Delors Committee

Alexandre Lamfalussy, Bank for International Settlements, Basle, then President of European Monetary Institute, member of Delors Committee

Pascal Lamy, Director of Delors cabinet, 1985–94

Dr Hans-Peter Scheller, former Secretary to the Committee of EC Central Bank Governors, later Secretary-General of European Monetary Institute

Prof. Niels Thygesen, member of Delors Committee and adviser on EMU to DG2

References

Abadie, F., and Corcolette, J. P. (1994). *Georges Pompidou 1911–1974*. Paris: Ballard.
—— —— (1997). *Valéry Giscard d'Estaing*. Paris: Ballard.
Adenauer, K. (1968). *Erinnerungen 1959–1963*. Stuttgart: Deutsche Verlags-Anstalt.
—— and Heuss, T. (1989). *Unserem Vaterland zugute: Der Briefwechsel*. Berlin: Siedler.
Aeschimann, E., and Riché, P. (1996). *La Guerre de Sept Ans: Histoire Secrète du Franc Fort 1989–1996*. Paris: Calmann-Lévy.
Aglietta, M. (1988). 'L'Evolution du SME vue par un expert français', *Documents*. 4, October.
Ainardi, S. (1992). 'Maastricht: c'est trop sérieux: la parole au peuple!', *Cahiers du Communisme*. 5.
Albert, M. (1985). *Le Pari français*. Paris: Éditions du Seuil.
—— (1991). *Capitalisme contre capitalisme*. Paris: Éditions du Seuil.
Aliboni, R., and Greco, E. (1996). 'Foreign Policy re-Nationalization and Internationalism in the Italian Debate', *International Affairs*. 72, 1, January: 43–51.
Allen, K., and Stevenson, A. (1974). *An Introduction to the Italian Economy*. London: M. Robertson.
Allison, G. (1971). *The Essence of Decision*. Boston: Little Brown.
Allum, P. A. (1973). *Italy—Republic without Government?*. London: Weidenfeld & Nicolson.
Amato, G. (1976). *Economica, politica e istituzioni in Italia*. Bologna: Il Mulino.
—— (1990). *Due anni al Tesoro*. Bologna: Il Mulino.
Amouroux, H. (1986). *Monsieur Barre*. Paris: Robert Laffont.
Andersen, S. (1994). *Hoffmeyer*, Copenhagen: Borsen.
Andreotti, G. (1991). *Governare con la crisi*. Milano: Rizzoli.
Artis, M. J., and Taylor, M. P. (1988). 'Exchange Rates, Interest Rates, Capital Controls and the European Monetary System: Assessing the Track Record', in Giavazzi *et al.* (1988: 185–206).
Ash, T. G. (1993). *In Europe's Name: Germany and the Divided Continent*. London: Jonathan Cape.
Atkinson, M. M., and Coleman, W. D. (1989). 'Strong States and Weak States: Sectoral Policy Networks in Advanced Capitalist Economies', *British Journal of Political Science*. 19, 1, January.
Axelrod, R. (1984). *The Evolution of Cooperation*. New York: Basic Books.
Baer, G. D., and Padoa-Schioppa, T. (1988). 'The Werner Report Revisited', paper submitted to the Committee for the Study of Economic and Monetary Union (the Delors Committee).
Baker, D., Fountain, I., Gamble, A., and Ludlam, S. (1995). 'Backbench Conservative Attitudes to Europe', *The Political Quarterly*, 66, 2, April–June.
—— Gamble, A., and Ludlam, S. (1994). 'The Parliamentary Siege of Maastricht 1993: Conservative Divisions and British Ratification', *Parliamentary Affairs*, 1: 38–60.
Banca d'Italia (1990*a*). 'A Blueprint for Stage II of Economic and Monetary Union' (in Italian), 25 July; reprinted in *Bollettino Economico*. Banca d'Italia, 15, October 1990.

Banca d'Italia (1990*b*). *The Functions of the ECB in the Second Phase of Economic and Monetary Union*. Rome, 24 December.

—— *Annual Report*. Rome, various issues.

—— *Economic Bulletin*. Rome, various issues.

Banchoff, T. (1997). 'German Policy Towards the European Union: The Effects of Historical Memory', *German Politics*. 6, 1, April: 60–76.

Banks, J. (1991). *Signaling Games in Political Science*. Chur, Switzerland: Harwood.

Baring, A. (1969). *Aussenpolitik in Adenauers Kanzlerdemokratie*. Munich: Oldenbourg Verlag.

—— (1983). *Machtwechsel: Die Ara Brandt-Scheel*. Stuttgart: Deutsche Verlags-Anstalt.

Barucci, P. (1995). *L'Isola italiana del Tesoro*. Milan: Rizzoli.

Bauchard, P. (1986). *La Guerre des deux roses: du rêve à la réalité 1981–1985*. Paris: Grasset.

Bauman, Z. (1989). 'Hermeneutics and Modern Social Theory', in D. Held and J. Thompson (eds.), *Social Theory of Modern Societies: Anthony Giddens and His Critics*. Cambridge: Cambridge University Press.

Baumgartner F., and Jones, B. (1991). 'Agenda Dynamics and Policy Sub-systems', *Journal of Politics*. 53, 4: 1044–74.

—— (1993). *Agendas and Instability in American Politics*. Chicago: University of Chicago Press.

Bell, L. (1997). 'Democratic Socialism', in C. Flood and L. Bell (eds.), *Political Ideologies in Contemporary France*. London: Pinter: 16–51.

Beloff, Lord (1996). *Britain and the European Union: Dialogue of the Deaf*. London: Macmillan.

Bénassy, A., Italianer A., and Pisani-Ferry, J. (1994). 'The External Implications of the Single Currency', *Économie et Statistique*: 9–22.

Bender, B. (1991). 'Whitehall, Central Government and 1992', *Public Policy and Administration*. 6, 1, spring: 13–40.

Bender, K. H. (1995). *Mitterrand und die Deutschen: Die Wiedervereinigung der Karolinger*. Bonn: Bouvier.

Berger, T. (1997). 'The Past in the Present: Historical Memory and German National Security Policy', *German Politics*. 6, 1, April: 39–59.

Bertelsmann Stiftung (1989). *Die Vollendung des Europäischen Währungssystems: Ergebnisse einer Fachtagung*. Gütersloh: Verlag Bertelsmann Stiftung.

Bhaskar, R. (1979). *The Possibility of Naturalism*. Brighton: Harvester.

Bini-Smaghi, L., Padoa-Schioppa, T., and Papadia, F. (1994). 'The Transition to EMU in the Maastricht Treaty', *Essays in International Finance*. Princeton: Princeton University Press, No. 194, November.

Biron, D., and Faire, A. (1978). 'Le Marc souverain', *Le Monde Diplomatique*. November: 18.

Bishop, G. *et al.* (1989). *Market Discipline CAN Work in the EC Monetary Union*. London: Salomon Brothers, November.

Blair, A. (1998). 'A Very British Affair: The Major Government and Maastricht', Political Studies Association Annual Conference. University of Nottingham, 7 April.

Blankenhorn, H. (1980). *Verständnis und Verständigung. Blätter eines politischen Tagebuchs 1949–79*. Berlin: Propyläen.

Borre, O., and Scarborough, E. (1995). *Beliefs in Government. iii: The Scope of Government*. Oxford: Oxford University Press.

Boulding, K. (1978). *Stable Peace*. Austin, Tex.: University of Texas Press.

Brandt, W. (1989). *Erinnerungen*. Berlin: Ullstein.

Breuss, F. (1998). 'Flexibility, Fiscal Policy and the Stability and Growth Pact', *Fourth ECSA World Conference*. Brussels, 17–18 September.

Bufacchi, V., and Burgess, S. (1998). *Italy since 1989: Events and Interpretations*. London: Macmillan.

Bull, M. J. (1993). 'Italy', in J. Loughlin, *Southern European Studies Guide*. London: Bowker/Saur.

Buller, J. (1995). 'Britain as an Awkward Partner: Reassessing Britain's Relations with the EU', *Politics*. 15, 1, February.

Bulletin of the European Communities, various issues; Luxembourg: Office for the Official Publications of the EC.

Bulmer, S. (1992). 'Britain and European Integration: Of Sovereignty, Slow Adaptation, and Semi-Detachment', in George (1992).

—— (1994). 'The Governance of the European Union: A New Institutionalist Approach', *Journal of Public Policy*. 13, 4: 351–80.

—— and Burch, M. (forthcoming). 'Organizing for Europe: Whitehall, the British State and European Union', *Public Administration*.

Bulpitt, J. (1986). 'The Discipline of the New Democracy: Mrs. Thatcher's Domestic Statecraft', *Political Studies*. 34: 19–39.

Burch, M., and Holliday, I. (1996). *The British Cabinet System*. Englewood Cliffs, NJ: Prentice-Hall.

Busche, J. (1998). *Helmut Kohl—Anatomie eines Erfolges*. Berlin: Berlin Verlag.

Calise, M. (1994). 'The Italian Particracy: Beyond President and Parliament', *The Political Science Quarterly*. 109, 3.

Calmfors, L., and Driffill, J. (1988). 'Bargaining Structure, Corporatism and Macroeconomic Performance', *Economic Policy*. 6, 1988: 13–61.

Cameron, D. (1995). 'Transnational Relations and the Development of European Economic and Monetary Union', in T. Risse-Kappen (ed.), *Bringing Transnational Relations Back In: Non-State Actors, Domestic Structures and International Relations*. Cambridge: Cambridge University Press.

—— (1997). 'Economic and Monetary Union: Transitional Issues and Third-Stage Dilemmas', University of Pittsburgh, Center for West European Studies, Policy Paper No. 4, May.

Camps, M. (1964). *Britain and the Economic Community, 1955–1963*. Oxford: Oxford University Press.

Cangelosi, R. A., and Grassi, V. (1996). *Dalle Communita All'Unione: Il Trattato di Maastricht e la Conferenza intergovernativa del 1996*. Milan: FrancoAngeli.

Cangliozzi, R. (1991). 'Italy's Dualistic Integration into Europe and Industrial Development in the Italian South', *Review of Economic Conditions in Italy*. 3: 345–400.

Carli, G. (1989). 'The Evolution towards Economic and Monetary Union: A Response to the H.M. Treasury Paper', *Il Tesoro*. Rome, December (in Italian).

—— (1993). *Cinquant'anni di vita Italiana*. Rome: Editori Laterza.

Carr, J. (1985). *Helmut Schmidt, Helmsman of Germany*. London: Weidenfeld & Nicolson.

Cassese, S. (1993). 'Hypotheses on the Italian Administrative System', *West European Politics*. 16, 3, July.

—— (1998). *Lo Stato Introvabile*. Rome: Donzelli editore.

—— and Della Cananea, G. (1992). 'The Commission of the European Economic Community: The Administrative Ramifications of its Political Development

(1957–1967)', in E. V. Heyen, *Yearbook of European Administrative History*. Baden-Baden: Nomos.

Centre for Economic Policy Research (1998). 'The ECB: Safe at any Speed?' *Monitoring the European Central Bank*, 1.

Charlton, M. (1983). *The Price of Victory*. London: BBC.

Checkel, J. (1998). 'The Constructivist Turn in International Relations Theory', *World Politics*. 50, 2: 324–48.

Chryssochoou, D. (1994). 'Democracy and Symbiosis in the European Union: Towards a Confederal Consociation?' *West European Politics*. 17, 4: 1–14.

Chubb, J., and Vannicelli,M. (1988). 'Italy: A Web of Scandals in a Flawed Democracy', in A Markovits and M. Silverstein (eds.), *The Politics of Scandal: Power and Process in Liberal Democracies*. New York: Holmes & Meier.

Ciampi, C. A. (1989). 'An Operational Framework for an Integrated Monetary Policy in Europe', in the Collection of Papers Submitted to the Committee for the Study of Economic and Monetary Union, April.

—— (1992). 'Lending of Last Resort', *Banca d'Italia Bollettino Economica*. 14: 63–70.

Cini, M. (1996). *The European Commission: Leadership, Organization and Culture in the EU Administration*. Manchester: Manchester University Press.

Civil Service Yearbook (1992); London: HMSO, August.

Clemens, C. (1998). 'Party Management as a Leadership Resource: Kohl and the CDU/CSU', *German Politics*. 7, 1: 91–119.

Cohen, B. (1994). 'Beyond EMU: The Problem of Sustainability', in B. Eichengreen and J. Frieden (eds.), *The Political Economy of European Monetary Unification*. Boulder, Colo.: Westview: 149–65.

—— (1998). *The Geography of Money*. Ithaca, NY: Cornell University Press.

Cohen, M., March, J., and Olsen, J. (1972). 'A Garbage Can Model of Organizational Choice', *Administrative Science Quarterly*. 17, 1: 1–25.

Cohen, S. (1990). 'Diplomatie: Le Syndrome de la Présidence Omnisciente', *Esprit*. September.

—— (1998) (ed.). *Mitterrand et la sortie de la Guerre Froide*. Paris: PUF.

Cole, A. (1996). 'The French Socialists', in J. Gaffney (ed.), *Political Parties and the European Union*. London: Routledge: 71–85.

—— (1997). *François Mitterrand: A Study in Political Leadership*, 2nd edn. London: Routledge.

Commission of the EC (1993). *The Economic and Financial Situation in Italy*, Report for DG2. Luxembourg: Office for Official Publications of the European Communities.

—— (1994). 'Eleventh Annual Report to the European Parliament on Monitoring the Application of Community Law—1993', *Official Journal of the European Communities*. C154/37, June.

Committee for the Study of EMU (1989). *Report on Economic and Monetary Union in the European Community* (the Delors Report). Luxembourg: Office for Official Publications of the European Communities.

Connolly, B. (1995). *The Rotten Heart of Europe: The Dirty War for Europe's Money*. London: Faber and Faber.

Cornwell, R. (1983). *God's Banker: An Account of the Life and Death of Roberto Calvi*. London: V. Gollancz.

Cox, R. (1987). *Production, Power and the World Order*. New York: Columbia University Press.

—— (1994). 'Global Restructuring: Making Sense of the Changing International Political Economy', in R. Stubbs and G. Underhill (eds.), *Political Economy and the Changing Global Order*. London: Macmillan: 45–59.

Craddock, P. (1997). *In Pursuit of British Interests: Reflections on Foreign Policy under Margaret Thatcher and John Major*. London: J. Murray.

Cram, L. (1994). 'The European Commission as a Multi-Organization: Social Policy and IT Policy in the EU', *Journal of European Public Policy*. 1: 195–217.

—— (1997). *Policymaking in the European Union: Conceptual Lenses and the Integration Process*. London: Routledge.

Crockett, A. (1991). 'Monetary Integration in Europe', speech to a conference in Washington, 13–15 January.

Crozier, B. (1964). *The Bureaucratic Phenomenon*. London: Tavistock.

Czarniawska, B., and Joerges, B. (1996). 'Travels of Ideas', in B. Czarniawska and G. Sevon (eds.), *Translating Organizational Change*. Berlin: Walter de Gruyter.

Dahrendorf, R. (1968). *Society and Democracy in Germany*. London: Weidenfeld and Nicolson.

Daniels, P. (1990). 'Italy', in J. Lodge (ed.), *The 1989 Election of the European Parliament*. London: Macmillan.

D'Auria, G., and Bellucci, P. (1995). *Politici e burocrati al governo dell'amministrazione*. Bologna: Il Mulino.

De Bodman, E., and Richard, B. (1976). *Changer les relations sociales: la politique de Jacques Delors*. Paris: Les Éditions d'Organisation.

Debré, M. (1972). *Une certaine idée de la France*. Paris: Fayard.

De Cecco, M. (1972). 'Economic Policy in the Reconstruction Period, 1945–1951', in Woolf (1972).

de Gaulle, C. (1970). *Mémoires d'Espoir, i, Le Renouveau, 1958–62*. Paris: Plon.

De Grauwe, P. (1998). 'The Risk of Deflation in the Future EMU: Lessons of the 1990s', in J. Arrowsmith (ed.), *Thinking the Unthinkable about EMU*. London: National Institute of Economic and Social Research: 73–93.

Della Porta, D. (1997). 'The Vicious Circles of Corruption in Italy', in D. Della Porta and Y. Meny (eds.), *Democracy and Corruption in Europe*. London: Pinter.

Della Sala, V. (1997). 'Hollowing out and Hardening the State: European Integration and the Italian Economy', *West European Politics*. 20, 1, January.

Delors, J., and Alexandre, P. (1985). *En sortir ou pas*. Paris: Grasset.

Denman, R. (1996). *Missed Chances: Britain and Europe in the Twentieth Century*. London: Cassell.

Dente, B. (1997). 'Sub-National Governments in the Long Italian Transition', *West European Politics*. 20, 1.

Develle, M. (1988). *Vive le Franc*. Paris: Olivier Orban.

Diekmann, K., and Reuth, R. (1996). *Helmut Kohl, Ich wollte Deutschlands Einheit*. Berlin: Propyläen.

Dinan, D. (1994). *Ever Closer Union? An Introduction to the European Community*. London: Macmillan.

Dini, L. (1988) 'Introductory Statement to Panel Discussion', in Giavazzi *et al.* 1988.

Dowding, K. (1995). *The Civil Service*. London: Routledge.

Drake, H. (1995). 'Political Leadership and European Integration: The Case of Jacques Delors', *West European Politics*. 18, 1.

Dreher, K. (1998). *Helmut Kohl: Leben mit Macht*. Stuttgart: Deutsche Verlags-Anstalt.

Du Franc Poincaré à l'Ecu. (1993). Paris: CHEFF.

Dyson, K. (1980). *The State Tradition in Western Europe.* Oxford: Martin Robertson.

—— (1983). 'The Cultural, Ideological and Structural Context', in Dyson and Wilks (1983).

—— (1994). *Elusive Union: The Process of Economic and Monetary Union in Europe.* London: Longman.

—— (1996). 'The Economic Order—Still Modell Deutschland?' in G. Smith, W. Paterson, and S. Padgett (eds.), *Developments in German Politics.* London: Macmillan: 194–211.

—— (1998). 'German Economic Policy after 50 Years', in P. Merkl (ed.), *The Federal Republic of Germany at 50.* London: Macmillan.

—— Featherstone, K., and Michalopoulos, G. (1995). 'Strapped to the Mast: EC Central Bankers between Global Financial Markets and the Maastricht Treaty', *Journal of European Public Policy.* 2, 3, September.

—— and Wilks, S. (1983) (eds.), *Industrial Crisis.* Oxford: Blackwell.

EC Commission (1990). 'One Market, One Money', *European Economy.* 44, October.

Edelmann, M. (1964). *The Symbolic Uses of Politics.* Urbana, Ill.: University of Illinois.

Edwards, G., and Spence, D. (1994). *The European Commission.* London: Longman.

Eijffinger, S. (1998). 'Accountability of Central Banks: Aspects and Quantification', paper delivered to Fourth ECSA—World Conference. Brussels.

Eizenga, W. (1993). 'The Banca d'Italia and Monetary Policy', *SUERF Papers on Monetary Policy and Financial Systems*, 15, Tilburg.

Elias, N. (1978). *What is Sociology?* London: Hutchinson.

Emminger, O. (1975). 'Deutsche Geld- und Währungspolitik im Spannungsfeld zwischen innerem und äusserem Gleichgewicht (1948–1975)', in Deutsche Bundesbank (ed.), *Währung und Wirtschaft in Deutschland 1876–1975.* Frankfurt am Main: Fritz Knapp.

—— (1986). *D-Mark, Dollar, Währungskrisen. Erinnerungen eines ehemaligen Bundesbankpräsidenten.* Stuttgart: Deutsche Verlags-Anstalt.

Epstein, G. A., and Schor, J. B. (1989). 'The Divorce of the Banca d'Italia and the Italian Treasury: a Case Study of Central Bank Independence', in P. Lange and M. Regini (eds.), *State, Market and Social Regulation: New Perspectives on Italy.* Cambridge: Cambridge University Press.

European Economy (1990). 'One Market, One Money', 44. Brussels: Commission of the European Communities, October.

—— (1991). 'The Economics of EMU', special edition 1. Brussels: Commission of the European Communities.

Evans, P., Jacobson, H. K., and Putnam, R. D. (1993) (eds.). *Double-Edged Diplomacy: International Bargaining and Domestic Politics.* Berkeley: University of California Press.

Fabius, L. (1990) *C'est en allant à la mer.* Paris: Seuil.

Favier, P., and Martin-Roland, M. (1990). *La Décennie Mitterrand, 1: Les Ruptures (1981–1984).* Paris: Éditions du Seuil.

Featherstone, K. (1988). *Socialist Parties and European Integration: A Comparative History.* Manchester: Manchester University Press.

—— (1994). 'Jean Monnet and the Democratic Deficit in the European Union', *Journal of Common Market Studies.* 32, 2: 149–70.

—— (1998). ' "Europeanization" and the Centre-Periphery: The Case of Greece in the 1990s', *South European Society and Politics.* 3, 1.

—— and Ginsberg, R. (1996). *The United States and the European Union in the 1990s: Partners in Transition*, 2nd edn. London: Macmillan.

Feldman, M., and March, J. (1981). 'Information in Organizations as Signal and Symbol', *Administrative Science Quarterly*. 26.

Ferraris, L. V. (1992). 'Italian-European Foreign Policy', in Francioni (1992).

Finnemore, M., and Sikkink, K. (forthcoming). 'Norms and International Relations Theory', *International Organization*.

Fitoussi, J. P. (1995). *Le Débat interdit*. Paris: Arléa.

—— et al. (1992). *La Désinflation compétitive, le mark et les politiques budgétaires en Europe*. Paris: OFCE and Éditions du Seuil.

Forsyth, D., and Notermans, T. (1997). 'Macroeconomic Policy Regimes and Financial Regulation in Europe, 1931–1994', in D. Forsyth and T. Notermans (eds.), *Regime Changes—Macroeconomic Policy and Financial Regulation in Europe from the 1930s to the 1990s*. Oxford: Berghahn: 17–68.

Francioni, F. (1992) (ed.). *Italy and EC Membership Evaluated*. London: Pinter.

Freudenberg, M., and Unal-Kesenci, D. (1994). 'France–Allemagne: Prix et Productivité dans le Secteur Manufacturier', *Économie Internationale*. 60.

Friedman, A. (1996). 'The Economic Elites and the Political System', in Gundle and Parker (1996).

Furlong, P. (1994). *Modern Italy: Representation and Reform*. London: Routledge.

Gamble, A. (1994). *The Free Economy and the Strong State: The Politics of Thatcherism*. London: Macmillan.

Garry, J. (1995). 'The British Conservative Party: Divisions over European Policy', *West European Politics*. 18, 4, October.

Gélédan, A. (1993). *Le Bilan Économique des Années Mitterrand 1981–1994*. Paris: Le Monde-Éditions.

Genscher, H.-D. (1995). *Erinnerungen*. Berlin: Siedler.

George, S. (1990). *An Awkward Partner*. Oxford: Oxford University Press.

—— (1992) (ed.). *Britain and the European Community: The Politics of Semi-Detachment*. Oxford: Clarendon.

—— (1995). 'A Reply to Buller', *Politics*. 15, 1, February.

Giavazzi, F., and Giovannini, A. (1987a). 'Models of the EMS: Is Europe a Greater Deutschmark Area?' in M. Bryant and R. Portes (eds.), *Global Macroeconomics: Policy Conflicts and Cooperation*. London: Macmillan: 237–76.

—— —— (1987b). 'Capital Controls in the European Monetary System', *Euromobiliere Occasional Paper*. 1, May.

—— Micossi, S., and Miller, M. (1988) (eds.). *The European Monetary System*. Cambridge: Cambridge University Press.

—— and Pagano, M. (1988). 'The Advantage of Tying One's Hand: EMS Discipline and Central Bank Credibility', *European Economic Review*. 24: 1055–82.

—— and Spaventa, L. (1988) (eds.). *High Public Debt: The Italian Experience*. Cambridge: Cambridge University Press.

Giddens, A. (1984). *The Constitution of Society*. Cambridge: Polity Press.

Giesbert, F. (1993). *La Fin d'une Époque*. Paris: Fayard.

—— (1996). *François Mitterrand, une vie*. Paris: Seuil.

Gill, S., and Law, D. (1989). *The Global Political Economy: Perspectives, Problems and Policies*. Baltimore: Johns Hopkins University Press.

Ginsborg, P. (1990). *A History of Contemporary Italy*. London: Penguin.

Giscard d'Estaing, V. (1977). *French Democracy*. New York: Doubleday.

—— (1981). *L'État de la France*. Paris: Fayard.

—— (1988). *Le Pouvoir et la Vie*: 1: *La Rencontre*. Paris: Compagnie Douze.

Giuliani, M. (1992). 'Il processso decisionale Italiano e le Politiche Comunitarie', *Polis*. 6, 2, August: 307–42.

—— (1996). 'Italy', in D. Rometsch and W. Wessels (eds.), *The European Union and Member States: Towards Institutional Fusion?* Manchester: Manchester University Press.

Gleske, L. (1975). 'Nationale Geldpolitik auf dem Wege zur europäischen Währungsunion', in Deutsche Bundesbank (ed.), *Währung und Wirtschaft in Deutschland 1876–1975*.

Glotz, P. (1979). *Innenausstattung der Macht*. Munich: Steinhausen.

Goldstein, J. (1993). *Ideas, Interests and American Trade Policy*. Ithaca, NY: Cornell University Press.

—— and Keohane, R. (1993) (eds.). *Ideas and Foreign Policy: Beliefs, Institutions and Political Change*. Ithaca, NY: Cornell University Press.

Goodhart, C. (1990). *Fiscal Policy and EMU*. London: LSE Financial Markets Group, Paper 31. London: Centre for Economic Performance and the Financial Markets Group.

Goodman, J. (1992). *Monetary Sovereignty: The Politics of Central Banking in Western Europe*. Ithaca, NY: Cornell University Press.

Gorman, T. (1993). *The Bastards: Dirty Tricks and the Challenge to Europe*. London: Pan.

Grande, E. (1995). 'Forschungspolitik und die Einflusslogik Europäischer Politikverflechtung', in M. Jachtenfuchs and B. Köhler-Koch (eds.), *Europäische Integration*. Opladen: Leske and Budrich.

Grant, C. (1994). *Inside the House that Jacques Built*. London: Nicolas Brearley.

Gros, D., and Thygesen, N. (1992). *European Monetary Integration: From the European Monetary System to the European Monetary Union*. London: Longman.

Guillaume, S. (1984). *Antoine Pinay ou la Confiance en Politique*. Paris: Presses de la FNSP.

Gundle, S., and Parker, S. (1996). *The New Italian Republic: From the Fall of the Berlin Wall to Berlusconi*. London: Routledge.

Guzzini, S. (1995). 'The "Long Night of the First Republic": Years of Clientelistic Implosion in Italy', *Review of International Political Economy*. 2, 1, Winter.

Haas, P. (1992). 'Introduction: Knowledge, Power and International Policy Coordination', *International Organization*. 46, 1: 1–35.

Haberer, J. Y. (1973). *La Monnaie et la Politique Monétaire*. Paris: Institut d'Études Politiques.

—— (1990). 'Le Ministère de l'Économie et des Finances et la Politique Monétaire', *Pouvoirs*. 53: 27–36.

Hallstein, W. (1969). *Der Unvollendete Bundesstaat*. Düsseldorf: Econ Verlag.

Harpprecht, K. (1974). *Willy Brandt: Portrait and Self Portrait*. Los Angeles: Nash.

Hasse, R., and Schäfer, W. (1990) (eds.). *Europäische Zentralbank*. Gütersloh: Bertelsmann Stiftung.

Hay, C. (1995). 'Structure and Agency', in Marsh, D. and Stoker, G. (eds.) *Theory and Methods in Political Science*. London: Macmillan.

Hayes-Renshaw, F., and Wallace, H. (1997). *The Council of Ministers*. London: Macmillan.

Hayward, J. (1983). *Governing France: The One and Indivisible Republic*, 2nd edn. London: Weidenfeld & Nicolson.

Hazareesingh, S. (1994). *Political Traditions in Modern France*. Oxford: Oxford University Press.

Healey, D. (1989). *The Time of My Life*. London: M. Joseph.

Heath, E. (1998). *The Course of My Life*. London: Hodder and Stoughton.

Heclo, H., and Wildavsky, A. (1974). *The Private Government of Public Money: Community and Policy inside British Politics*. London: Macmillan.

Hennessy, P. (1989). *Whitehall*. London: Secker and Warburg.

—— (1990). *Whitehall*. London: Fontana.

—— (1992). *Never Again: Britain, 1945–51*. London: Cape.

Henning, C. (1997). *Cooperating with Europe's Monetary Union*. Washington: Institute for International Economics.

Hentschel, V. (1996). *Ludwig Erhard: Ein Politikerleben*. Berlin: Ullstein.

Hine, D. (1993). *Governing Italy: The Politics of Bargained Pluralism*. Oxford: Clarendon Press.

—— and Finocchi, R. (1991). 'The Italian Prime Minister', *West European Politics*. 14, 2, April.

Hirsch, F. (1969). *Money International*. Harmondsworth: Penguin.

Hoffman, G. (1998). 'Meine Jahre mit Kohl', *Die Zeit*. 24 September.

Hoffman, S. (1963). *In Search of France*. New York: Harper and Row.

Hoffmeyer, E. (1992). *The International Monetary System—An Essay in Interpretation*. Amsterdam: North-Holland.

—— (1993). *Pengepolitiske Problemstillinger 1965–1990*. Copenhagen: Danmarks National-bank.

—— (1994). 'Thirty Years in Central Banking', *Occasional Papers*, No. 48. Washington: Group of Thirty.

Hogg, S., and Hill, J. (1995). *Too Close to Call*. London: Little, Brown and Co.

House of Commons Debates (Hansard); various volumes as listed.

Howarth, D. (1998). 'French Policy on European Monetary Cooperation and Integration, 1968 to 1994'. D.Phil. thesis, University of Oxford.

Howe, G. (1994). *Conflict of Loyalty*. London: Macmillan.

Hrbek, R. (1992). 'Kontroversen und Manifeste zum Vertrag von Maastricht', *Integration*. 15, 4: 225–45.

Huneeus, C. (1996). 'How to Build a Modern Party: Helmut Kohl's Transformation of the CDU', *German Politics*. 5, 3: 432–59.

Iida, K. (1993). 'Analytic Uncertainty and International Cooperation: Theory and Application to International Economic Policy Cooperation', *International Studies Quarterly*. 37: 431–57.

Ikenberry, G. (1993). 'Creating Yesterday's New World Order: Keynesian "New Thinking" and the Anglo-American Postwar Settlement', in J. Goldstein and R. Keohane (eds.), *Ideas and Foreign Policy: Beliefs, Institutions and Political Change*. Ithaca, NY: Cornell University Press.

Italianer, A. (1993). 'Mastering Maastricht: EMU Issues and How They Were Settled', in K. Gretschmann (ed.), *Economic and Monetary Union: Implications for National Policy Makers*, Maastricht : European Institute of Public Administration: 51–113.

Jacobsen, J. (1995). 'Much Ado about Ideas—The Cognitive Factor in Economic Policy', *World Politics*. 47, 1, 1995: 283–310.

Jäger, W., and Link, W. (1987). *Republik im Wandel 1974–1982: Die Ära Schmidt, Geschichte der Bundesrepublik Deutschland*, v, Stuttgart: Deutsche Verlags-Anstalt.

James, H. (1996). *International Monetary Cooperation since Bretton Woods*. Washington: IMF.

Jansen, T. (1996). *Konrad Adenauer and Walter Hallstein—The Basis of Trust*. London: The Greycoat Press.

Jeanneney, J. M. (1994). 'De Bretton Woods à la Jamaique: Contestations Françaises', *Économie Internationale*. 59, July.

Jervis, R. (1976). *Perception and Misperception in International Politics*. Princeton: Princeton University Press.

Johnson, C. (1996). *In with the Euro, Out with the Pound*. London: Penguin.

Johnston, M. (1994). *The European Council: Gatekeeper of the European Community*. Boulder, Colo.: Westview.

Jospin, L. (1991). *L'Invention du Possible*. Paris: Flammarion.

Kaelberer, M. (1996). 'Germany's Incentives for European Monetary Integration', *German Politics and Society*. 14, 3.

Kaltenthaler, K. (1998a). 'Central Bank Independence and the Commitment to Monetary Stability: The Case of the German Bundesbank', *German Politics*. 7, 2, August: 102–27.

—— (1998b). *Germany and the Politics of Europe's Money*. Durham: Duke University Press.

Kees, A. (1994). 'The Monetary Committee as a Promoter of European Integration', in A. Bakker, H. Boot, O. Sleijpen, and W. Vanthoor (eds.), *Monetary Stability through International Cooperation: Essays in Honour of André Szasz*. Dordrecht: Kluwer.

Keesing's Record of World Events. London: Longman. Various annual volumes.

Kenen, P. (1992). *EMU after Maastricht*. Washington: Group of Thirty.

Kilminster, R. (1979). *Praxis and Method*. London: Routledge & Kegan Paul.

Kindleberger, C. (1970). *Power and Money*. London: Macmillan.

—— (1984). *A Financial History of Europe*. London: George Allen and Unwin.

Kingdon, J. (1984). *Agendas, Alternatives and Public Policy*. Boston: Little, Brown.

Kirchner, E. (1992). *Decision-Making in the European Community: The Council Presidency and European Integration*. Manchester: Manchester University Press.

—— and Tsagkari, A. (1993) (eds.). *The EC Council Presidency: The Dutch and Luxembourg Presidencies*. London: University Association for Contemporary European Studies.

Koerfer, D. (1987). *Kampf ums Kanzleramt: Erhard und Adenauer*. Stuttgart: Deutsche Verlags-Anstalt.

Kogan, N. (1966). *A Political History of Postwar Italy*. London: Pall Mall Press.

Kohl, H. (1976). 'Konrad Adenauer. Erbe und Auftrag', in H. Kohl (ed.), *Konrad Adenauer 1876–1976*. Stuttgart: Belser Verlag.

Köhler, H., and Kees, A. (1996). 'Die Verhandlungen zur Europäischen Wirtschafts- und Währungsunion', in T. Waigel (ed.), *Unsere Zukunft heisst Europa. Der Weg zur Wirtschafts- und Währungsunion*. Düsseldorf: Econ.

Korte, K. R. (1998a). 'The Art of Power: The "Kohl System", Leadership and Deutschlandpolitik', *German Politics*. 7, 1: 64–90.

—— (1998b). *Deutschlandpolitik in Helmut Kohls Kanzlerschaft*. Stuttgart: Deutsche Verlags-Anstalt.

Krügenau, H., and Wetter, W. (1993). *Europäische Wirtschafts- und Währungsunion: Vom Werner-Plan zum Vertrag von Maastricht. Analyse und Dokumentation*. Baden-Baden: Nomos.

Kuisel, R. (1981). *Capitalism and the State in Modern France*. Cambridge: Cambridge University Press.

Lacouture, J. (1984). *Pierre Mendès France*. New York: Holmes and Meier.
—— (1998). *Mitterrand, une Histoire de Français*, i, ii. Paris: Éditions du Seuil.
Laitenberger, V. (1986). *Ludwig Erhard: Der Nationalökonom als Politiker*. Göttingen: Muster-Schmidt.
La Malfa, G., and Modigliani, F. (1998). 'Attention! L'Eurochômage Pourrait Tuer l'Euro', *Le Monde*. 7 March.
La Palombara, J. (1987). *Democracy Italian Style*. New Haven: Yale University Press.
Lauber, V. (1983). *The Political Economy of France*. New York: Praeger.
Lawson, N. (1992). *The View from No. 11: Memoirs of a Tory Radical*. London: Bantam.
Lee, M. (1995). 'The Ethos of the Cabinet Office: A Comment on the Testimony of Officials', in Rhodes and Dunleavy (1995).
Lequesne, C. (1993). *Paris-Bruxelles*. Paris: Presses de la Fondation Nationale des Sciences Politiques.
Lettre de Matignon (1984). 'La Communauté Européenne', 109, 1 June.
Liddell Hart, B. (1968). *Strategy: The Indirect Approach*. London: Faber.
Liebfried, S. (1992). 'Towards a European Welfare State? On Integrating Poverty Regimes into the European Community', in Z. Ferge and J. Kolberg (eds.), *Social Policies in a Changing Europe*. Boulder, Colo.: Westview.
Lindblom, C. (1990). *Inquiry and Change*. New Haven: Yale University Press.
Lipset, S. M. (1996). *American Exceptionalism: A Double-Edged Sword*. New York: Norton.
Locke, R. M. (1995). *Remaking the Italian Economy*. Ithaca, NY: Cornell University Press.
Loehnis, A. (1998). Speech to the Inter-Group 'European Currency' of the European Parliament, Strasbourg, 15 June.
Loriaux, M. (1991). *France after Hegemony*. Ithaca, NY: Cornell University Press.
Ludlow, P. (1982). *The Making of the European Monetary System*. London: Butterworth.
—— (1991). 'The European Commission', in R. O. Keohane and S. Hoffman, *The New European Community: Decisionmaking and Institutional Change*. Boulder, Colo.: Westview Press.
Ludwig-Erhard Stiftung (1996). *Soziale Marktwirtschaft als Historische Weichenstellung: Zum Hundertsten Geburtstag von Ludwig Erhard*. Düsseldorf: ST-Verlag.
Lynch, P. (1998). 'Conservative Statecraft, European Integration and the Politics of Nationhood', *Political Studies Association Annual Conference*. University of Nottingham, 7 April.
McCarthy, P. (1997). *The Crisis of the Italian State: From the Origins of the Cold War to the Fall of Berlusconi and Beyond*. New York: St Martin's.
Mackay, D. (forthcoming). 'The Political Sustainability of European Monetary Union', *British Journal of Political Science*.
McNamara, K. (1998). *The Currency of Ideas: Monetary Politics in the European Union*. Ithaca, NY: Cornell University Press.
Majone, G. (1989). *Evidence, Argument and Persuasion in the Policy Process*. New Haven: Yale University Press.
—— (1993). 'The European Community between Social Policy and Social Regulation', *Journal of Common Market Studies*. 31, 2: 79–106.
—— (1996). 'A European Regulatory State?' in J. Richardson (ed.), *The European Union: Power and Policy-Making*. London: Routledge, London: 263–77.
Mamou, Y. (1988). *Une Machine de Pouvoir: La Direction du Trésor*. Paris: Éditions La Découverte.

March, J. (1996). 'Institutional Perspectives on Political Institutions', *Governance*. 9, 3: 247–64.

Marcussen, M. (1998). 'Ideas and Elites: Danish Macro-Economic Policy Discourse in the EMU Process', Ph.D. thesis, University of Aalborg, September.

Margairaz, M. (1983). 'Le Mendèsisme', *Pouvoirs*. 27.

—— (1989) (ed.). *Pierre Mendès France et l'Économie*. Paris: Éditions Odile Jacob.

—— (1990). 'Ministres des Finances: Personnalités, Structures, Conjonctores', *Pouvoirs*. 53: 101–8.

Maris, B. (1992). *Jacques Delors: Artiste ou Martyr*. Paris: Albin Michel.

Markovits, A., and Reich, S. (1997). *The German Predicament—Memory and Power in the New Europe*. Ithaca, NY: Cornell University Press.

Marsh, D. (1992). *The Bundesbank: The Bank That Rules Europe*. London: Heinemann.

Mendès France, P. (1989). *Oeuvres Complètes*, v: *Préparer L'Avenir 1963–73*. Paris: Gallimard.

Merkl, P. (1962). 'The Structure of Interests and Adenauer's Survival as Chancellor', *American Political Science Review*. 56, 3.

Merlini, C. (1993a). 'Italy and Europe', in J. Storey (ed.), *The New Europe: Politics, Government and Economy since 1945*. Oxford: Blackwell.

—— (1993b). 'Six Proposals for Italian Foreign Policy', *International Spectator*. 28, 33, July–September: 5–21.

Micossi, S., and Rossi, S. (1986). 'Controlli sui movimento di capitale: il caso Italiano', *Giornale degli Economisti e Annali di Economica*. 45, January–February.

Milési, G. (1985). *Jacques Delors*. Paris: Pierre Belfond.

Milward, A. (1984). *The Reconstruction of Western Europe 1945–51*. London: Routledge.

Mintz, N. (1970). *Monetary Union and Economic Integration*. New York: New York University Press.

Mitterrand, F. (1980). *Ici et Maintenant*. Paris: Fayard.

—— (1996). *De L'Allemagne, De La France*. Paris: Odile Jacob.

Monnet, J. (1978). *Memoirs*. London: Collins.

Monti, M. (1992). *Il Governo dell'Economia e della Moneta*. Milan: Longanesi and Co.

Moravcsik, A. (1991). 'Negotiating the Single European Act: National Interests and Conventional Statecraft in the European Community', *International Organization*. 45, 1: 19–56.

—— (1993). 'Preferences and Power in the European Community: A Liberal Intergovernmentalist Approach', *Journal of Common Market Studies*. 31, 4: 473–524.

—— (1994). 'Why the European Community Strengthens the State: Domestic Politics and International Cooperation', *Working Paper No. 52*. Harvard University: Centre for European Studies.

—— (1998). *The Choice for Europe: Social Purpose and State Power from Messina to Maastricht*. London: UCL Press.

Mucciaroni, G. (1992). 'The Garbage Can Model and the Study of Policy Making: A Critique', *Polity*. 24, 3: 459–82.

Müller-Armack, A. (1971). *Auf dem Weg nach Europa: Erinnerungen und Ausblicke*. Tübingen: Wunderlich.

Muron, L. (1994). *Pompidou*. Paris: Flammarion.

Nay, C. (1984). *Le Noir and Le Rouge ou l'Histoire d'une Ambition*. Paris: Grasset.

Nicholls, A. J. (1994). *Freedom With Responsibility: The Social Market Economy in Germany 1918–1963*. Oxford: Clarendon Press.

Nölling, W. (1993). *Monetary Policy in Europe after Maastricht*. London: Macmillan.

Nugent, N. (1992). 'British Public Opinion and the European Community', in George (1992).

Odell, J. (1982). *US International Monetary Policy*. Princeton: Princeton University Press.

OECD (1979), *International Financial Statistics Yearbook*. Paris.

—— *Economic Surveys: Italy*. Paris: OECD, various issues.

Padgett, S. (1996). 'Interest Groups in the Five New Länder', in G. Smith, W. Paterson, and S. Padgett (eds.). *Developments in German Politics*. London: Macmillan: 233–47.

Padoa-Schioppa, T. (1994). *The Road to Monetary Union: The Emperor, the Kings, and the Genies*. Oxford: Clarendon.

—— (1988). 'The EMS: A Long-term View', in Giavazzi *et al*. (1988).

—— *et al*. (1987). *Efficiency, Stability and Equity*. Oxford: Oxford University Press.

—— and Saccomanni, F. (1992). 'Agenda for Stage Two: Preparing the Monetary Platform', *CEPR Occasional Paper*. 7, London.

Padoa-Schioppa Kostoris, F. (1996). 'Excesses and Limits of the Public Sector in the Italian Economy: The Ongoing Reform', in Gundle and Parker (1996).

Papadia, F. (1991). 'L'Unione economica e monetaria', *Affari Esteri*. 22, 89, winter.

Paret, P. (1986) (ed.). *Makers of Modern Strategy*. Princeton: Princeton University Press.

Paterson, W. (1994). 'The Chancellor and Foreign Policy', in S. Padgett (ed.), *Adenauer to Kohl: The Development of the German Chancellorship*. London: Hurst: 127–56.

Percheron, A. (1991). 'Les Français et l'Europe: Acquiescement de Façade ou Adhésion Véritable?' *Revue Française de Science Politique*. 41.

Peters, G. (1996). 'Agenda Setting', in Richardson (1996: 61–76).

Peterson, J. (1995). 'Decision-Making in the European Union: Towards a Framework for Analysis', *Journal of European Public Policy*. 2, 1: 69–94.

Peyrefitte, A. (1994). *C'était de Gaulle*. Paris: Fayard.

Peyrelevade, A. (1985). 'Témoignage: Fallait-il Dévaluer en Mai 1981?' *Revue Politique et Parliamentaire*. 87.

Philippe A., and Hubscher, D. (1991). *Enquête à l'intérieur du Parti Socialiste*. Paris: Albin Michel.

Pliatzky, L. (1989). *The Treasury under Mrs. Thatcher*. Oxford: Blackwell.

Pöhl, K. O. (1996). 'Der Delors-Bericht und das Statut einer Europäischen Zentralbank', in T. Waigel (ed.), *Unsere Zukunft heisst Europa. Der Weg zur Wirtschafts- und Währungsunion*. Düsseldorf: Econ.

Pollack, M. A. (1997). 'Delegation, Agency and Agenda-Setting in the European Community', *International Organization*. 51, 1: 99–134.

Pompidou, G. (1974). *Le Noeud Gordien*. Paris: Plon.

Poppinga, A. (1975). *Konrad Adenauer: Geschichtsverständnis, Weltanschaung und Politische Praxis*. Stuttgart: Deutsche Verlags-Anstalt.

Prate, A. (1978). *Les Batailles Économiques du Général de Gaulle*. Paris: Plon.

—— (1987). *La France et sa Monnaie: Essai sur les Relations entre la Banque de France et les Gouvernements*. Paris: Julliard.

Pruys, K.H. (1995). *Helmut Kohl—Die Biographie*. Berlin: Edition q.

Putnam, R. (1988). 'Diplomacy and Domestic Politics: The Logic of Two-Level Games', *International Organization*. 42: 427–460.

Radaelli, C. (1995). 'The Role of Knowledge in the Policy Process', *Journal of European Public Policy*, 2, 2: 160–83.

Radaelli, C. (1997). 'How Does Europeanization Produce Domestic Policy Change? The Case of Corporate Taxation in Italy and the UK', *Comparative Political Studies*. October.

—— (forthcoming). *Technocracy in the European Union*. London: Addison-Wesley Longman.

—— C. M., and Bruni, M. G. (1998). 'Beyond Charlemagne's Europe: A Sub-National Examination of Italy within the EMU', *Regional and Federal Studies*. 8, 2: 34–51.

—— and Martini, A. (1998). 'Think Tanks, Advocacy Coalitions and Policy Change: A First Look at the Italian Case', in D. Stone, M. Garnett, and A. Denham (eds.), *Think Tanks in Comparative Perspective*. Manchester: Manchester University Press.

Régniez, J. (1995). 'L'Esprit et la Lettre. Les Origines de la Stratégie du Franc Fort', *Commentaire*. 71: 603–10.

Regonini, G., and Giuliani, M. (1994). 'Italie: au-delà d'une democratie consensuelle?' in B. Jobert (ed.), *Le Tournant neo-liberal en Europe: idées et recettes dans les pratiques gouvernementales*. Paris: Éditions L'Harmattan.

Rhodes, M. (1994). ' "Subversive Liberalism": Market Integration, Globalization and the European Welfare State', *European Consortium for Political Research Workshops*, Madrid.

—— (1996). 'Globalization and the West European Welfare States', *Journal of European Social Policy*. 6, 4: 305–27.

—— (1997). 'The Welfare State: Internal Challenges, External Constraints', in M. Rhodes, P. Heywood, and V. Wright (eds.), *Developments in West European Politics*. London: Macmillan.

Rhodes, R. A. W., and Dunleavy, P. (1995) (eds.). *Prime Minister, Cabinet and Core Executive*. London: Macmillan.

Richardson, J. (1982). *Policy Styles in Western Europe*. London: Allen & Unwin.

—— (1996) (ed.). *European Union: Power and Policy-Making*. London: Routledge.

Riché, P., and Wyplosz, C. (1993). *L'Union monétaire de l'Europe*. Paris: Seuil.

Risse, T., Ropp, S., and Sikkink, K. (forthcoming) (eds.). *The Power of Principles: International Human Rights Norms and Domestic Change*. Cambridge: Cambridge University Press.

Rollan, A. (1993). *Delors*. Paris: Flammarion.

Romiti, C. (1988). *Questi anni alla Fiat (*an autobiography*)*. Milan: Rizzoli.

Röpke, W. (1958). *Jenseits von Angebot und Nachfrage*. Zürich: Erlenbach.

Ross, G. (1995). *Jacques Delors and European Integration*. Cambridge: Polity Press.

Roussel, E. (1994). *Georges Pompidou 1911–1974*. Paris: J.-C. Lattès.

Rueff, J. (1963). *L'Age de l'Inflation*. Paris: Payot.

—— (1972). *Combats pour l'Ordre Financier*. Paris: Plon.

Rupps, M. (1997). *Helmut Schmidt: Politikverständnis und geistige Grundlagen*. Bonn: Bouvier.

Sabatier, P. A. (1998). 'The Advocacy Coalition Framework: Revisions and Relevance for Europe', *Journal of European Public Policy*. 5, 1: 98–130.

—— and Jenkins-Smith, H. (1993) (eds.). *Policy Change and Learning. An Advocacy Coalition Approach*. Boulder, Colo.: Westview Press.

Saint-Geours, J. (1979). *Pouvoir et Finance*. Paris: Fayard.

Sally, R. (1998). *Classical Liberalism and International Economic Order: Studies in Theory and Intellectual History*. London: Routledge.

Salvati, M. (1985). 'The Italian Inflation', in L. Lindberg and C. S. Maier (eds.), *The Politics of Inflation and Economic Stagnation*. Washington: Brookings Institution.

Sandholtz, W. (1993). 'Choosing Union: Monetary Politics and Maastricht', *International Organization*, 47: 1–39.

Sarcinelli, M. (1986). *Financial Wealth, the Public Debt and Monetary Policy in the Perspective of International Integration*. Rome: Ministero del Tesoro (in Italian).

—— (1987). 'Towards Financial Integration in a European and International Context: Exchange Liberalisation in Italy', *Review of Economic Conditions in Italy*. 2: 125–46.

—— (1996). ' "Insiders" and "Outsiders": What Kind of Cohabitation?', *Banca Nazionale del Lavoro Quarterly Review*. Special Issue: European Monetary Union: The Problems of the Transition to a Single Currency, Rome, March.

Sassoon, D. (1986). *Contemporary Italy: Politics, Economy and Society since 1945*. London: Longman.

Scharpf, F. (1994). 'Community and Autonomy. Multi-Level Policy-Making in the European Union', *Journal of European Public Policy*. 1, 2: 219–42.

Schemla, E. (1993). *Édith Cresson, la femme piégée*. Paris: Flammarion.

Schmidt, H. (1980). 'Der Kanzler ist kein Volkserzieher', *Die Zeit*, 22 August.

—— (1985). 'The EMS: Proposals for Further Progress', *The World Today*. May.

—— (1990). *Die Deutschen und ihre Nachbarn*, 2nd edn. Berlin: Siedler.

Schmidt, V. (1997). 'Economic Policy, Political Discourse and Democracy in France', *French Politics and Society*. 15, 2: 37–48.

Schmölders, G. (1968). *Geldpolitik*, 2nd edn. Tübingen: Mohr.

Schoen D., and Rein, M. (1994). *Frame Reflection: Towards the Resolution of Intractable Policy Controversies*. New York: Basic Books.

Schönfelder, W., and Thiel, E. (1992). *Ein Markt—Eine Währung. Die Verhandlungen zur Wirtschafts- und Währungsunion*, 2nd edn. Baden-Baden: Nomos.

Schwarz, H. P. (1980). *Vom Reich zur Bundesrepublik*. Stuttgart: Deutsche Verlags-Anstalt.

—— (1985). *Die gezähmten Deutschen. Von der Machtbesessenheit zur Machtvergessenheit*. Stuttgart: Deutsche Verlags-Anstalt.

—— (1992). *Erbfreundschaft Adenauer und Frankreich*. Bonn: Bouvier.

—— (1996). *Konrad Adenauer*, i: *1876–1952*. Oxford: Berghahn Book.

—— (1997). *Konrad Adenauer*, ii: *1952–1967*. Oxford: Berghahn Books.

Scobie, H. M., Mortali, S., Persaud, S., and Docile, P. (1996). *The Italian Economy in the 1990s*. London: Routledge.

Sedillot, R. (1979). *Histoire du Franc*. Paris: Éditions Sirey.

—— (1989). *Histoire Morale et Immorale de la Monnaie*. Paris: Bordas.

Séguin, P. (1992). *Discours pour la France*. Paris: Grasset.

Seidentopf, H., and Ziller, J. (1988). *Making European Policies Work: The Implementation of Community Policies in the Member States*. London: Sage / EIPA.

Seldon, A. (1995). 'The Cabinet Office and Coordination, 1979–87', in Rhodes and Dunleavy (1995).

Seldon, A. (1997). *Major: A Political Life*. London: Weidenfeld & Nicolson.

Shields, J. (1996). 'The French Gaullists', in J. Gaffney (ed.), *Political Parties and the European Union*. London: Routledge.

Siebert, H. (1988). 'Europa braucht Regeln der Stabilität', *Frankfurter Allgemeine Zeitung*. 29 July.

Spaventa, L. (1980). 'Italy Joins the EMS: A Political History', *The Johns Hopkins University Resarch Institute, Occasional Paper*. No. 32, June.

Spicer, M. (1992). *A Treaty Too Far: A New Policy for Europe*. London: Fourth Estate.

Stasse, F. (1994). *La Morale de l'Histoire: Mitterrand et Mendès France 1943–82*. Paris: Seuil.

Steinherr, A. (1994) (ed.). *30 Years of European Monetary Integration from the Werner Plan to EMU*. London: Longman.

Stephens, P. (1996). *Politics and the Pound: The Conservatives' Struggle with Sterling*. London: Macmillan.

Stoltenberg, G. (1985). 'Die ECU geht am Kern vorbei', *Handelsblatt*. 31 May.

—— (1988). 'The Further Development of Monetary Cooperation in Europe', Memorandum to ECOFIN Council, Ministry of Finance, Bonn, 15 March.

—— (1997). *Wendepunkte: Stationen deutscher Politik 1947 bis 1990*. Berlin: Siedler.

Stone, D. (1989). 'Causal Stories and the Formation of Policy Agendas', *Political Science Quarterly*. 104, 2: 281–300.

Strauss, F. J. (1965). *The Grand Design*. London: Weidenfeld & Nicolson.

Sturm, R. (1989). 'The Role of the Bundesbank in German Politics', *West European Politics*. 12: 1–11.

Susskind, L., and Cruikshank, J. (1987). *Breaking the Impasse*. New York: Basic Books.

Thatcher, M. (1995). *The Downing Street Years*. London: Harper Collins. First published 1993.

Thain, C., and Wright, M. (1995). *The Treasury and Whitehall: The Planning and Control of Public Expenditure, 1976–1993*. Oxford: Oxford University Press.

Thompson, H. (1993). 'The UK and the Exchange Rate Mechanism 1978–90', in B. Brivati and H. Jones (eds.), *From Reconstruction to Integration: Britain and Europe since 1945*. Leicester: Leicester University Press.

—— (1995). 'Joining the ERM: Analysing a Core Executive Policy Disaster', in Rhodes and Dunleavy (1995).

—— (1996). *The British Conservative Government and the European Exchange Rate Mechanism, 1979–1994*. London: Pinter.

Touchard, J. (1978). *Le Gaullisme 1940–1969*. Paris: Seuil.

Treaty on European Union (TEU), signed at Maastricht, December 1991.

Triffin, R. (1960). *Gold and the Dollar Crisis*. New Haven: Yale University Press.

Tsebelis, G. (1990). *Nested Games: Rational Choice in Comparative Politics*. Berkeley: University of California Press.

Tsoukalis, L. (1977). *The Politics and Economics of European Monetary Integration*. London: Allen and Unwin.

Ungerer, H. (1997). *A Concise History of European Monetary Integration*. Connecticut: Quorum.

Urban, G. R. (1996). *Diplomacy and Disillusion at the Court of Margaret Thatcher: An Insider's View*. London: I. B. Taurus.

Védrine, H. (1996). *Les Mondes de François Mitterrand: A l'Elysée 1981–1995*. Paris: Fayard.

Verdun, A. (Forthcoming), 'The Delors Committee, an Epistemic Community?', *Journal of European Public Policy*, 6, 2.

Wallace, H. (1997). 'At Odds with Europe', *Political Studies*. 45: 677–88.

Walsh, J. I. (1994). 'International Constraints and Domestic Choices: Economic Convergence and Exchange Rate Policy in France and Italy', *Political Studies*. 42, 2, June.

Walters, A. (1986). *Britain's Economic Renaissance*. Oxford: Oxford University Press.

Waters, S. (1994). ' "Tangentopoli" and the Emergence of a New Political Order in Italy', *West European Politics*. 17, 1, January.

Wendt, A. (1987). 'The Agent-Structure Problem in International Relations Theory', *International Organization*. 41, 3: 335–70.

—— (1992). 'Anarchy is What States Make of It: The Social Construction of Power Politics', *International Organization*. 46, 2: 384–98.

Werner, P. (1991). *Itinéraires Luxembourgeois et Européens*. Luxembourg: Éditions de l'Imprimerie Saint Paul.

Werner Report (1970). *Report to the Council and the Commission on the Realization by Stages of Economic and Monetary Union in the Community*. Luxembourg: Office for Official Publications of the European Communities, Supplement to Bulletin 11.

Westlake, M. (1995). *The Council of the European Union*. London: Cartermill.

Wilensky, H. (1967). *Organizational Intelligence*. New York and London: Basic Books.

Willetts, D. (1987). 'The Role of the Prime Minister's Policy Unit', *Public Administration*. 65, winter: 443–54.

Willgerodt, H. (1990). 'Das Problem des Politischen Geldes', *Hamburger Jahrbuch für Wirtschafts- und Gesellschaftspolitik*. 35.

—— Domsch, R., Hasse, R., and Merx, V. (1972). *Wege und Irrwege zur europäischen Wirtschafts- und Währungsunion*. Freiburg: Haupt.

Woolf, S. J. (1972) (ed). *The Rebirth of Italy 1943–50*. London: Longman.

Wright, V. (1996). 'The National Coordination of European Policy-Making: Negotiating the Quagmire', in J. Richardson (1996: 148–69).

Young, J. W. (1993). *Britain and European Unity, 1945–1992*. London: Macmillan.

Zelikow, P., and Rice, C. (1996). *Germany Unified and Europe Transformed: A Study in Statecraft*. Cambridge, Mass.: Harvard University Press.

Name index

Index